To the Student

Law and Business: The Regulatory Environment, Fourth Edition was created to provide you with a high-quality educational resource. As a publisher specializing in college texts, we strive to provide you with learning materials that will serve you well in your college studies and throughout your career.

The educational process involves learning, retention, and the application of concepts and principles. You can accelerate your learning efforts utilizing the Study Guide accompanying this text:

- Study Guide to Accompany Clark/Aalberts/Kinder *Law and Business: The Regulatory Environment,* Fourth Edition.

This learning aid is designed to improve your performance in the course by highlighting key points in the text and providing you with assistance in mastering basic concepts.

Get your copy at your local bookstore, or ask the manager to place an order for you today.

We at McGraw-Hill sincerely hope this text package will assist you in reaching your goals, both now and in the future.

LAW AND BUSINESS

The Regulatory Environment

LAW AND BUSINESS

The Regulatory Environment

Fourth Edition

Lawrence S. Clark

Robert J. Aalberts

Peter D. Kinder

McGraw-Hill, Inc.

New York St. Louis San Francisco Auckland Bogotá Caracas
Lisbon London Madrid Mexico City Milan Montreal
New Delhi San Juan Singapore Sydney Tokyo Toronto

LAW AND BUSINESS
The Regulatory Environment

This book is printed on acid-free paper.

1 2 3 4 5 6 7 8 9 0 DOC DOC 9 0 9 8 7 6 5 4 3

ISBN 0-07-035162-7

This book was set in Times Roman by Better Graphics, Inc.
The editors were Kenneth A. MacLeod, Peitr Bohen, and
Bernadette Boylan;
the text and cover designer was Keithley and Associates;
the production supervisor was Leroy A. Young.
New drawings were done by Keithley and Associates.
R. R. Donnelley & Sons Company was printer and binder.

Library of Congress Cataloging-in-Publication Data

Clark, Lawrence S.
    Law and business: the regulatory environment. —4th ed. /
Lawrence S. Clark, Robert J. Aalberts, Peter D. Kinder.
        p.   cm.
    Includes index.
    ISBN 0-07-035162-7
    1. Commercial law—United States.   I. Aalberts, Robert J.
II. Kinder, Peter D.   III. Title.
KF889.C55   1994
346.73'07—dc20
[347.3067]   93-24356

About the Authors

Lawrence S. Clark is a professor of business law and dean of the College of Business Administration at Louisiana State University in Shreveport. Mr. Clark received his J.D. from the John Marshall Law School and his L.LM. in Taxation from DePaul University. As dean, Mr. Clark serves as an accreditation advisor with the AACSB and was president of the Southwestern Business Deans's Association for the 1993–1994 academic year. As a business law professor, Mr. Clark continues to be active in CPA education, the Academy of Legal Studies in Business, and other scholarly activities. Mr. Clark lives in Shreveport, Louisiana, where he pursues personal interests in antique cars, sailing, and community service.

Robert J. Aalberts is the Ernst Lied Professor of Legal Studies at the University of Nevada, Las Vegas. He received his J.D. from Loyola University, an M.A. from the University of Missouri, Columbia, and a B.A. from Bemidji State University of Minnesota. Prior to his academic career, Professor Aalberts was an attorney with the Gulf Oil Company. He is the author of numerous law review and business journal articles and is currently the editor-in-chief of the *Real Estate Law Journal* as well as being a staff editor of the *Journal of Legal Studies Education*. In his over 9 years as a legal studies professor, he has received four universitywide teaching and research awards. Professor Aalberts is an active member of the Academy of Legal Studies in Business and the American Real Estate Society.

Peter D. Kinder is a lawyer and a professional writer. An honors graduate of both Princeton University and the Ohio State University College of Law, he was of counsel to the Boston law firm of Fitch, Miller & Tourse and served as an Assistant Attorney General for the state of Ohio. He has written primarily in the areas of government regulation, business, and finance. He is coauthor of *Ethical Investing* (1984) and is currently president of Kinder, Lydenberg, Domini & Co., an investment advisory firm specializing in corporate accountability research. He lives and works in Cambridge, Massachusetts.

To Our Wives

Georgia A. Clark,
Barbara E. Aalberts,
and
Amy D. Kinder

CONTENTS

The fourth edition marks an important milestone for our book. After serving as a coauthor for our first three editions, Peter D. Kinder has left work on our book to be able to devote greater management time to Kinder, Lydenberg, Domini & Co., Inc., an investment advisory firm specializing in social investment research. Mr. Kinder provided important leadership in regard to the philosophy, style, and approach of our book. His keen wit and artful writing style remain in every chapter.

Robert J. Aalberts has succeeded Mr. Kinder and has brought a valuable new perspective to *Law and Business*. Mr. Aalberts is the Ernst Lied Professor of Legal Studies at the University of Nevada, Las Vegas. He has gained national stature as a result of his research, publications, and editorial work in the areas of business, employment, and real estate law. He is currently the editor-in-chief of the *Real Estate Law Journal* as well as a staff editor of the *Journal of Legal Studies Education*. Mr. Aalberts's love of and skill in teaching is shown by the fact that he has received four universitywide teaching and research awards.

THE BOOK'S PHILOSOPHY

The fourth edition builds on the philosophy of earlier editions: we have attempted to offer a book which effectively motivates students to learn, fosters genuine interest in the law, and, where possible, presents the law in social, economic, and business contexts. We want students to come away from *Law and Business* with, first, knowledge of how things work, and, second, an understanding of how better to make things work.

WHAT'S NEW IN THIS EDITION

We have made many revisions in this edition. We continue to add coverage where events and trends in the law dictate. The collapse of most of the Communist world has radically changed the world as we've known it since 1945, altering international business practices. Domestically, the end of the 1980s and the beginning of the 1990s has witnessed a discernible shift in social, political, and economic attitudes and a repudiation of the "greed decade." With the recent election of the first Democratic president in 12 years, advocates for the environment, employee rights, and universal health care, as well as those calling for more government intervention in such important business sectors as banking and the trading of securities, have gained considerable strength. We have attempted to integrate these developments throughout this edition.

We have also made some major additions which we feel will contribute significantly to the overall understanding of business law. At the end of each chapter, we have introduced a section called "A Note to Future CPA Candidates." This addition represents nearly two decades of study and accumulated knowledge of the CPA exam by Lawrence S. Clark—the first author of this text. Moreover, the section not only gives future CPAs a head start in understanding and preparing for the CPA exam, but for all students it offers a concise and effective review of the chapter.

We have also added a notable amount of "classic" cases. These include such venerable cases as *Hadley* v. *Baxendale, McPherson* v. *Buick, Lefkowitz* v. *Great Minneapolis Surplus Store, Marvin* v. *Marvin, Hirabayashi* v. *United States*, and a number of others.

The chapters have all been updated with the newest statutory and regulatory changes, as well as proposed model acts. Some of the more significant revisions, and where they appear, include:

- Model Employment Termination Act: Chapter 15
- Revised Uniform Partnership Act (RUPA): Chapter 17
- Limited Liability Companies (LLC): Chapter 22
- Securites Act of 1933, Regulation A: Chapter 23
- SEC rules 144 and 144A: Chapter 23
- Americans with Disabilities Act: Chapters 23, 30, and 46
- The Family Leave Act of 1993: Chapter 46
- The Older Workers Benefit Protection Act: Chapter 46
- The Civil Rights Act of 1991: Chapter 46
- The Clean Air Act of 1990: Chapter 47
- Updates on Superfund Acts (CERCLA and SARA): Chapter 47

We have added a total of seventy new cases. Many of these cases are followed by an analysis of what really happened to those involved in the case, as well as the ethical, social, economic, and political implications. Moreover, many of the new cases included are likely to become "landmark" cases. These include:

- *Cippollone* v. *Liggett Group, Inc.*: Chapter 3
- *Quill* v. *North Dakota*: Chapter 3
- *Simon and Schuster* v. *New York State Crime Victims Board* ("Son of Sam" case): Chapter 5
- *Jacobson* v. *United States*: Chapter 5
- *Bily* v. *Arthur Young*: Chapter 24
- *Lucas* v. *South Carolina Coastal Commission*: Chapter 25
- *Mexicali Rose* v. *Superior Court of Alameda County*: Chapter 34
- *Cruzan* v. *Director, Missouri Department of Health*: Chapter 29
- *Toibb* v. *Radloff*: Chapter 43

- *Arkansas* v. *Oklahoma*: Chapter 47
- *Saudi Arabia* v. *Nelson*: Chapter 48

Finally, we have greatly expanded our previous discussions or have introduced the following noteworthy legal and ethical issues:

- Employee drug testing: Chapter 15
- New developments in the employment at will doctrine: Chapter 15
- Employee whistleblowing: Chapter 15
- Misappropriation theory: Chapter 23
- *Ultramares* theory: Chapter 24
- Right of publicity and its descendibility: Chapter 25
- Application of the fair use doctrine to "reverse engineering" of software and home videos: Chapter 25
- Patentability of gene fragments: Chapter 25
- Regulatory "takings" and property rights: Chapter 27
- Sexual harassment in housing: Chapter 28
- Living wills and durable powers of attorney: Chapter 29
- AIDS and health insurance: Chapter 30
- U.S. government as a holder in due course: Chapter 37
- "Equity skimming" and FHA and VA mortgages: Chapter 42
- Mortgage foreclosure, deficiency judgments, and "workouts" in the 1980s: Chapter 42
- "Keiretsu," "dango," and Japan bashing: Chapter 44
- "Testers" for employment discrimination: Chapter 46
- Hiring "quotas," "race norming," and the Civil Rights Act of 1991: Chapter 46
- "Glass ceiling initiative": Chapter 46
- Sexual orientation and workplace rights: Chapter 46
- Sexual harassment by coworkers and customers: Chapter 46
- New developments regarding smoking in the workplace: Chapter 46
- *Electromation* case and "quality circles": Chapter 46

- Developments in worker replacements and strikes: Chapter 46
- Developments in the protection of "wetlands": Chapter 47
- Environmental audits: Chapter 47
- New developments in the environmental liability of lenders: Chapter 47

We have made many other changes in addition to the foregoing, including correcting errors pointed out by vigilant readers. Our goal, as in earlier editions, is to clarify and to explain. Therefore, we welcome your reactions.

APPROPRIATE COURSES FOR THIS BOOK

Our book has been written as a comprehensive presentation of the law appropriate primarily to undergraduate business students. It has been successfully used by adopters of both one-semester and two-semester courses.

There are many different types of law courses found in a division or college of business. We know our book is being successfully utilized in the following types of courses:

- A legal or regulatory environment of business course
- A traditional business law course
- A business law course tailored to the specific needs of students preparing to take the CPA exam

In addition, we believe our book is an appropriate resource for a course devoted to small-business management.

THE STRUCTURE OF THIS BOOK

We have written and structured *Law and Business* with these two needs in mind. Each part begins with an introduction which places its chapters in context. The book itself begins with an extensive introduction to law's place in soci-

ety. And many chapters—including those on administrative, environmental, and antitrust law—place their subjects in historical and social contexts.

The same impetus impelled a close attention to definitions and to the origins of words. Words which baffled generations of law students—like "liquidated"—are explained in legal and etymological terms to help students understand their current use.

Of course, merely placing a concept in context benefits the student little if the concept itself is not clearly explained. In this regard, verbal description alone sometimes is not adequate, and a picture may be worth far more than a thousand words. Sample pleadings, financing statements, wills, deeds, and the like can save hours of classroom time. So, too, can diagrams and flowcharts. Where we have felt that such devices would illuminate concepts for the student and save teaching hours, we have used them.

COVERAGE AND ORDER IN THIS BOOK

One of the most challenging problems in writing a business law text is determining where to cover material which relates to two subject areas, such as contracts and sales. In addition, we know that legal environment and business law instructors enjoy developing their own order of chapters and parts. For example, many adopters of *Law and Business* choose to cover Part VI, Sales, after Part II, Contracts, and/or Chapter 42, Security Interests in Real Property with Part V, Property. (As a historical note to our book, Sales followed Contracts in our first edition, but many adopters indicated a strong preference for Sales to be grouped later in the book with the other Uniform Commercial Code parts and chapters.) We have attempted to respond to these challenges by providing maximum instructor flexibility and learning assistance.

Law and Business has been written to limit repetition and promote chapter coverage flexibility by adopting a cross-accessing system. It features:

- Part openers which relate the part's subject matter to other areas of law
- Introductory chapter outlines
- Cross-reference within chapters
- A glossary with references to chapters in which each term is discussed
- An expanded index

These tools lead readers quickly and surely to amplified coverage.

END-OF-CHAPTER MATERIALS

Each chapter ends with the same sequence of materials:

- A conclusion
- A Note to Future CPA Candidates
- Discussion Questions
- Case Problems

The conclusion, in most cases, refocuses the student's perspective from the detail of legal tenets to the larger issues posed by the chapter. It is, therefore, not a summary but a synthesis. We have found that students who prepare their own summaries are considerably better off for the exercise.

Our new feature "A Note to Future CPA Candidates," provides a summary of the major points of law for each chapter which can be expected to be tested on the business law portion of the CPA. Non-CPA candidates may also find this a useful learning tool, since the CPA exam tends to test key chapter concepts.

The list of key words and the discussion questions are consciously designed to facilitate learning. The key words highlight the most important terms introduced or used in the chapter. The discussion questions, usually numbering ten, follow the sequence of the chapter and ask the student to define concepts. In some instances, the discussion questions ask for analysis of issues presented in the case briefs.

END-OF-PART PROBLEMS

The end-of-part problems are unique to *Law and Business*. Each set is made up of four questions, which together require students to apply, review, integrate, and appraise what they have learned.

The problems appear under three headings:

- Practical problems
- Summative problems
- Ethical problems

Practical problems require that the students draft a legal document of some sort—a contract, a will, a financing statement, and others. These problems are designed to reveal the analysis behind a document's contents. Summative problems bring together in one hypothetical fact pattern many disparate strands from the immediately preceding chapters. Each set of end-of-part problems contains two summative problems which foster critical thinking.

The end-of-part problems always conclude with a problem of ethics. We have purposely constructed these problems so that their answers are not obvious—if, in fact, answers exist. Many ethical problems are not clear-cut, and students need to appreciate the kinds of dilemmas the real world can force upon them.

The ethical problems in these parts of the book are far from being the only material in it which raises moral questions. Such questions are implicit throughout the book, and the instructor's manual notes many of these.

COURSE DIRECTED TOWARD THE CPA EXAM

Law and Business is an ideal choice for a course directed toward helping accounting students prepare for the business portion of the CPA exam, for the following reasons:

- *Law and Business* covers every business law topical area.
- Chapter 24 specifically covers accountants' legal liability.

- Our chapters feature "A Note to Future CPA Candidates," which provides a summary of the major points of law which can be expected to be tested on the exam.
- Chapter problems present similar concepts found on the CPA exam.
- End-of-part Summative Problems help develop a student's cognitive learning relating to business law.

In addition, for almost 20 years, author Lawrence S. Clark has been part of a national CPA review team which "takes" and evaluates each exam immediately after the exam is completed. As a result, Mr. Clark has gained valuable insights which have been incorporated into *Law and Business*.

SUPPLEMENTARY MATERIALS

This text is accompanied by the full range of teaching aids which teachers of business law have come to expect. These include:

- An Instructor's Manual prepared by the authors
- A Study Guide prepared by Wayne R. Wells and Janell M. Kurtz (St. Cloud State University)
- A Test Bank prepared by Wayne R. Wells and Janell M. Kurtz (St. Cloud State University)
- A set of two-color overhead transparencies featuring all the charts and illustrations in the text

Each of these aids is fully integrated, chapter by chapter, with the text.

The Instructor's Manual contains—for each chapter of *Law and Business*—suggested solutions to the questions and problems in the text.

The Study Guide contains an essay on studying business law. It also provides an introduction to each part and chapter and self-test study questions of the types normally used in undergraduate business law courses: multiple choice, true or false, and short essay. The answers to these questions appear in the guide.

The Test Bank holds approximately 2000 test items. It is also available from the publisher in RHTest format for use with IBM microcomputers with 3.5 and 5.25 disk configurations.

ACKNOWLEDGMENTS

While we remain solely responsible for this book's faults, many individuals made valuable contributions.

As we stated earlier in the preface, we are deeply indebted to Peter D. Kinder for his important leadership role in the development and creation of *Law and Business*. Peter remains a good friend and strong supporter of this book. We wish him continued success with his innovative firm, Kinder, Lydenberg, Domini & Co., Inc., and their Domini 400 Social Index. We also wish to acknowledge the splendid past work of another colleague, Carolyn Hotchkiss, of Babson College. Carolyn provided a contributed chapter for both the Second and Third Editions: Chapter 48, International Transactions.

Throughout our work, the business law students at Louisiana State University in Shreveport have made invaluable criticisms of the materials and pedagogy used in this book. LSU-S business law instructors have been of great help on this and earlier editions: Amy Oakes, Rowena Comegys Denhollem, and Martha Lavardsen. In addition, the counsel of Professor Cecil Ramey and his students at Centenary College, also in Shreveport, is recognized and appreciated.

The authors also wish to thank the following colleagues and professionals for their suggestions and help. Professors Lorne Seidman, Michael Clauretie, and Donald Hardigree, all of UNLV's finance and business law department, and Professor David Hames of UNLV's management department, were always close by and ready to offer highly useful and insightful recommendations on a number of points of law and business. Kenneth C. Fonte, of the law firm of Golden & Fonte, New Orleans, was also very supportive, as he has always been.

The reviewers of the fourth edition are due special thanks. Their thoughtful, perceptive analyses contributed significantly to its strengths. The reviewers included: William Halm, Ferris State University; J. Scott Kirkwood, Wingate College; Wayne Klein, Boise State University; and Michael Litka, University of Akron.

We also wish to acknowledge once again the invaluable assistance of the reviewers of our earlier editions (shown at their institution when the review was completed):

First Edition
Michael Bixby, Boise State University
Donald Cantwell, University of Texas at Arlington
Larry Curtin, Iowa State University
Arthur Davis, Long Island University
Philip DiMarzio, Northern Illinois University
Jeffrey Figler, San Diego City College
Frank Forbes, University of Nebraska
Glen Grothaus, St. Louis Community College
William Harwood, Dutchess Community College
Marsha Hass, College of Charleston
Clay Hipp, Clemson University
William Honey, Auburn University
William Hughes, New Mexico State University
Sandra Hurd, Syracuse University
Jack T. Ingram, East Texas State University
J. Roland Kelley, Tarrant County Junior College
J. Scott Kirkwood, Wingate College
Mike LaFrance, Kirkwood Community College
Paul Lansing, University of Iowa
Murray Levin, University of Kansas
Hank Mallue, College of William and Mary
Nancy Reeves Mansfield, Georgia State University

John Norwood, University of Arkansas
Richard Perry, Santa Rosa Junior College
Francis Polk, Dundalk Community College
Jennifer Railing, Gettysburg College
J. Gregory Service, Broward Community College
Marcia Staff, North Texas University
Lawrence Stone, Boston University
Jesse Trentadue, University of North Dakota School of Law
William Vanderpool, Appalachian State University
Clark Wheeler, Santa Fe Community College
Mildred Whitted, St. Louis Community College
Katie Wolfe, University of Iowa
Murray Woodrow, Westchester Community College

Second Edition
Ben T. Allen, Humboldt State University
Ronnie Cohen, Christopher Newport College
Myron L. Erickson, University of Missouri-Columbia
H. Paul Garner, University of Miami
Susan E. Grady, University of Massachusetts
Mark Hefter, Northeast Louisiana University
E. Clayton Hipp, Jr., Clemson University
Dugald W. Hudson, Georgia State University
Arthur Marinelli, Ohio University
Thomas McCoy, Middlesex Community College
Lee. J. Ness, University of North Dakota
Sidney S. Sappington, York College of Pennsylvania
J. Gregory Service, Broward Community College
Paul Sukys, North Central Technical College
Ralph Washington, Hinds Junior College

Third Edition
William Halm, Ferris State College
Penny Herickhoff, Mankato State University
Scott Kirkwood, Wingate College
William Parks, Orange Coast College
Jean Volk, Middlesex County College

Finally, we wish to thank our editors, Kenneth MacLeod, Peitr Bohen, and Bernadette Boylan, for their dedication, insights, and encouragement with our fourth edition.

Lawrence S. Clark
Robert J. Aalberts
Peter D. Kinder

LAW AND BUSINESS

The Regulatory Environment

LAW AND SOCIETY

Murphy's Law, "If anything can go wrong, it will go wrong," appears on posters in many shops and offices. Fortunately, however, Murphy's Law is nothing of the sort. Life would be unbearable if, for instance, whenever you pushed the Coke button on a vending machine, you could not be reasonably sure that you would get Coke, not milk or water or grape juice. Our sanity depends on our ability to predict the course of everyday transactions, whether with a Coke machine, a bank, the registrar's office, or Sears Roebuck.

Business law is a course in prediction. Business law provides a basis for projecting what will happen, given a particular commercial situation. It enables you to make a reasoned appraisal as to how society—as represented by the courts . . . will treat a particular transaction. More importantly, business law allows you to predict the course of transactions which will never end up in court, because the law reflects how businesspeople expect to conduct their dealings.

THE NATURE OF PREDICTIONS

Each business day, Americans make and carry out hundreds of millions of contracts for the sale of goods ranging from ice cream to ice boxes. Only an infinitesimal number lead to a dispute between the parties, many fewer to lawsuits. Why? We all have a more or less developed sense of the way things do and should work, and we act accordingly. That sense is, at the same time, shaping and shaped by how business is actually practiced. Experience both creates and reinforces these expectations.

The role of experience

Experience is what allows you to predict with confidence. If you ran a chain of auto supply houses, you would have to contract with suppliers every day. You would learn what they expect of you and what you can expect from them. Courses of dealing would develop, and you would rely on them in predicting how other transactions would proceed.

The law reflects our common body of business experience while it shapes our expectations. The law's relationship to commerce is like a ladder, with the rungs and the rails providing communication links. One side of the ladder cannot function independently of the other, and alterations on one side require changes on the other.

In most instances, laws are directed at businesses in general, rather than at a particular industry. The same law which governs the sale of auto parts also regulates the sale of computer chips and potato chips. However, certain industries—railroads and electric power companies, for example—play such key roles in our economy that society has chosen to regulate some aspects of the way they operate much more closely than it regulates other businesses. As we will see in Chapter 3, these laws reflect America's historical experience with unregulated industries which once controlled transportation and energy supplies.

The practical and the ethical elements

Laws contain elements of how business actually is practiced and also of how it ought to be practiced. The "ought" element—the law's *ethical* or moral aspect —is reflected in the law's regular use of terms like "good faith," "fiduciary," and "reasonable." Such terms must be defined in a context. They are virtually undefinable in the abstract. For example, an agent has a fiduciary duty to her employer. It does not clarify matters much to say that a fiduciary relationship is one of trust.

Put in the context of a routine transaction, the meaning of the agent's duty becomes clear. Suppose you are looking for a house to buy. You find one you like, and you hire a lawyer, who is your agent, to handle the transaction for you. Realizing the house is underpriced, the lawyer buys it herself and resells it for a profit. The lawyer did not act in good faith, and she violated her duty of trust to you. You are entitled to the profit she made.

PREVENTION AND PREDICTION

For many years, courses in business law have emphasized what is called "preventive law." The idea behind this concept is that good planning can avoid lawsuits, particularly ones you probably will lose.

Lawsuits are a last resort. If the parties to a business dispute cannot resolve it themselves, they often bring the dispute to the courts. In our society, the courts apply the collective experience reflected in the law to particular sets of facts. It is their response with which the predictive aspect of business law is most concerned. Because it is possible to predict with considerable accuracy how the courts will decide most cases involving business disputes, the parties can avoid or minimize the possibility of a lawsuit by applying preventive law techniques.

The law and its makers

Students of the law must focus on the courts because under our system of government, judges have the last say on how the law is defined and interpreted. With a few minor exceptions, the courts act in the context of a lawsuit only. The last half of Chapter I and Chapter 2 will examine the American courts and the way lawsuits proceed through them.

Chapter 3 looks at perhaps the most important recent innovation in our system; administrative agencies. These departments of governments exercise control over certain areas of commerce or government. Examples include the Federal Trade Commission, a state public utilities commission, and a city zoning board. Administrative agencies often are hybrids; they make laws in the form of administrative regulations and decide disputes in their particular fields.

Legal wrongs

Chapters 1 through 3 describe the context in which business law is made and applied. Chapters 4 and 5 begin an examination of the substance of the law governing American commerce. The law of torts and crimes, which those chapters cover, has perhaps the most ancient origins of all that you will study. It is the law which developed to replace revenge and feuds.

Torts and crimes are legal wrongs. The person who commits a crime owes a debt to society. A checkout clerk who slugs a customer commits the crime of *battery,* the touching of a person without that person's consent. The clerk may serve a jail term or pay a fine or both. But that is not the end of his potential *liability,* or responsibility, for his act.

Torts are legal wrongs which give rise to an obligation to compensate the injured party. Thus, the checkout clerk may also have to pay the customer's hospital bills. Virtually all injuries caused by crimes can lead to tort liability. However, the reverse is not true; relatively few torts are crimes. While some statutes impose tort liability for violations, over the centuries the courts primarily have determined which wrongs require compensation.

For the businessperson, potential criminal liabilities are well defined because they are statutory. Tort liabilities are significantly less clear because the types of compensable legal wrongs change with the times. The manufacturer of a new consumer product, for example, must evaluate its potential liability for injuries defects in its product may cause. This prediction must be factored with the manufacturing and marketing appraisals in the decision to proceed with the product.

CONCLUSION

What you as a student should take from these chapters—and this course—was described some years ago by Mark DeWolf Howe. He was summarizing the views of U.S. Supreme Court Justice Oliver Wendell Holmes, Jr. (1841–1935):

> *If law in the final analysis is made by the decisions of judges, and those decisions are the consequence of many operating forces—customs, statutes, precedents, and public opinion—it becomes virtually impossible for the lawyer to say what the law on a particular matter "is." The best that he can usually do is make a more or less informed . . . prediction of how the matter . . . will be resolved through the judicial process. Law is made, not by the commands of [a] sovereign, but by judges, responsive at once to the dictates of tradition and to their own and the community's judgment of what is required by public policy.**

This course is an introduction to the customs, statutes, precedents, and public opinion which govern business.

KEY WORDS

administrative
  agency (7)
crime (1)

liability (2)
preventive law (2)
tort (3)

---

* M. DeW. Howe, "Introduction" to O. W. Holmes, Jr., *The Common Law* (Boston: Little, Brown & Co., 1881, 1963), p. xviii.

CHAPTER I

An introduction to American law

Lawyers predict, as previously noted, how the courts will resolve a particular matter. However, while lawyers can forecast a result by drawing on experience, they cannot say for certain what the law *is,* because the courts' interpretations change in response to society's judgment of what public policy requires. Public policy can also reflect society's ethical standards of behavior by enforcing what it feels is morally right and prohibiting what is wrong. Although some moral standards have changed little in thousands of years, ethical principles are being constantly debated and redefined. This chapter describes the principal means by which society expresses public policy: constitutions, statutes and administrative regulations, treaties, and judicial decisions. These four means are our society's principal sources of law.

If our social system were static, there would be no need for so many diverse sources of law. However, the United States itself came into existence because American colonists insisted on a fundamental change in the way in which they were governed. Our Constitution incorporates the Patriots' understanding of the need for change by guaranteeing Americans the right to alter laws as necessary. It is our institutionalized capacity for change which has enabled our system of government to prosper for more than twenty-one decades.

Continuity and change, then, are the two poles in our legal system. This chapter examines the institutions created to resolve the conflicts between these poles.

SOURCES OF THE LAW

In this book, the term "the law" refers to the body of philosophy, principles, standards, and rules which the courts apply in deciding cases brought before them. The four sources of law examined in this chapter—constitutions, statutes and administrative regulations, treaties, and judicial decisions—reflect and incorporate this body of concepts.

In the United States, "laws" come from several levels of government. All the states and the national government, for instance, have constitutions and enact statutes, while every level of government down to municipalities issues administrative regulations. We will discuss laws on the federal and state levels only, and we will omit some sources whose impact on business generally is not great.

The Constitution and the philosophy behind it

Our most important source of law is the U.S. Constitution and its amendments. Adopted in 1789, the Constitution is both a blueprint for national government and a general statement of the rights and liberties of American citizens. Both aspects reflect the prevailing philosophy of the Revolutionary era, which still dominates our political and legal thought.

The philosophy of the Enlightenment. Our national philosophy developed in the Age of Enlightenment (1650–1800), a period characterized by a strong belief in the perfectability of humankind and its institutions. The Declaration of Independence (1776) sums up the thought behind the Constitution in a very few words:

> *We hold these Truths to be self-evident, that all Men are created equal, that they are endowed by their Creator with certain unalienable Rights, that among these are Life, Liberty, and the Pursuit of Happiness—That to secure these Rights, Governments are instituted among Men, deriving their just Powers from the Consent of the Governed, that whenever any Form of Government becomes destructive of these Ends, it is the Right of the People to alter or to abolish it, and to institute a new Govern-*

ment, laying its Foundations on such Principles, and organizing its Powers in such Form, as to them shall seem most likely to effect their Safety and Happiness.

From this philosophical statement of the relationship between government and the governed, the founding fathers had to develop a mechanism to control its implementation. After considerable experimentation and debate, they settled on what we call simply the Constitution. A *constitution* establishes real boundaries—both positive and negative—on government. But like everything created by humans, it must provide room for growth and change. We have amended it twenty-six times in a little over 200 years. What is more significant, however, are the innumerable proposed amendments, over 10,000 since 1789, that have failed for one reason or another. For instance, the Equal Rights Amendment, a hot issue in the 1970s, fell just two states short of passage.

The relationship between state and federal governments. Before the U.S. Constitution was signed, the states functioned almost like independent countries. Our first constitution, the Articles of Confederation, established what amounted to an alliance among the former colonies. By contrast, our current Constitution is a *covenant,* a contract between states and the federal government in which the states give up some of their rights to govern themselves in exchange for the benefits of a national government.

The states did not give all their powers to govern to the national government. In the bargaining which produced the Constitution, the states gave the central government only limited authority, for instance, to pass laws and to hear lawsuits. The states retained the powers which they did not contract to give the federal government. The states themselves have constitutions which define the limits on their powers.

The nature of constitutional provisions. While a constitution is more specific than philosophy, it is still very general. Consider the First Amendment to the U.S. Constitution:

> *Congress shall make no law respecting an establishment of religion, or prohibiting the free exercise thereof; or abridging the freedom of speech, or of the press; or the right of the people peaceably to assemble, and to petition the government for a redress of grievances.*

Over the last 200 years, courts and scholars have filled thousands of volumes examining what those forty-six words mean in practice. For example, may Congress require an employer to violate its contract with unionized workers by altering its Saturday work schedule to accommodate an employee for whom Saturday is the Sabbath? May a law prohibit corporations from making expenditures in support of a political cause? Is a privately owned shopping mall a public place where political groups can distribute leaflets even though its owners object?*

All three of these questions involve issues the drafters of the First Amendment could not have anticipated. Yet it is the hallmark of our system that the courts can develop solutions to contemporary problems within the framework of the Constitution's statements of our shared values. Thus, the Constitution at once provides predictability by defining boundaries and flexibility by being able to meet new social and economic conditions.

Statutes, ordinances, and administrative regulations

The First Amendment also presents a technical problem. It refers to laws made by Congress, but Congress acting alone cannot make laws. It can only adopt *acts,* which are proposed laws. The laws to which the First Amendment refers are acts adopted by Congress which either are

---

* The answer to each question is no. *Trans World Airlines v. Hardison,* 432 U.S. 63 (1977); *First National Bank v. Bellotti,* 435 U.S. 765 (1978); and *Prune Yard Shopping Center v. Robins,* 447 U.S. 74 (1980).

not vetoed by the President or are passed over his veto. These laws are called *statutes.* State statutes come into being in the same manner. A statute must not contradict the U.S. Constitution *and,* if it is a state statute, that state's constitution.

A county, municipality, or other government subdivision may also have the power to enact laws. If they are subdivisions of the state, they must comply with the statutes the state legislature adopted prescribing how they are to be governed. The most common type of these laws are *ordinances,* laws adopted by the legislative branch of a municipal government.

The legislative branch in our system embodies the people's right, stated in the Declaration of Independence, to alter laws and governments to meet their needs. The state and federal regulatory structures we now have—like workers' compensation programs, the Federal Trade Commission, and the Environmental Protection Agency—concretely express that philosophy. The chief executive's power to veto an act is the principal check on the power of the legislative branch.

Often when dealing with specialized subjects like taxes or consumer lending, the legislative branch enacts a statute defining its goals. It directs an *administrative agency,* like the Treasury Department, the Interstate Commerce Commission, or the Power Authority of the State of New York to implement the goals by means of *administrative regulations.* Regulations have virtually the same force and effect as statutes. Also like the statutes that authorize them, regulations must not violate the Constitution. And the agency may not adopt a regulation not authorized by the legislative branch. As we will see in Chapter 3, no area of the law is growing faster in its importance to business than administrative law.

Treaties

Treaties are agreements between nations; like contracts, they create rights and duties between the parties. Treaties serve many purposes. They end wars; the Treaty of Versailles, for example, concluded World War I. Like the North Atlantic Treaty, which created NATO, some treaties create alliances. However, the vast majority of treaties define routine matters of international commerce. For instance, treaties govern fishing rights in U.S. waters, the imposition of taxes on foreign nationals, and duties on imported goods.

Under the Constitution, treaties are negotiated by the executive branch but require ratification by the U.S. Senate in order to take effect. Upon ratification, they have approximately the same effect as federal statutes. Individual states cannot negotiate treaties.

Judicial decisions

Courts make laws, too. Their main contribution comes in the form of decisions in lawsuits. The federal courts and most state courts have taken the position that a question of law is best resolved when it is raised in a lawsuit by parties with conflicting interests in a specific factual context. If adverse parties have a stake in a question's resolution, presumably their debate supported by their presentation of the facts and the law will clarify the issue for the court. This institutionalization of conflict is why our legal system is described as an *adversary system.* In the next chapter, we will see how this system works in practice.

In the context of deciding a lawsuit, the courts determine what the law is at a particular moment by interpreting statutes or constitutional provisions. If no statute governs and the parties do not raise a constitutional issue, the courts apply what is called the common law.

The common law. The *common law* refers to a body of judge-made law whose origins date to the fourteenth century or earlier. Then, England was made up of counties with very different legal systems. The common law was the law of the national courts and applies to all citizens alike. Thus, "common" in this phrase means "shared," not "ordinary."* British colonists brought the common law with them to America. Today, however, British and American common law differ in many respects.

Major portions of American law remain governed by the common law. As we will see in Chapter 4, the law of torts is primarily a matter of common law. However, throughout this book, you will encounter the phrase "at common law." It refers to what the law was on a particular point before statutes superseded the common law. For example, virtually every state has adopted statutes regulating the sale of goods, which was formerly a part of the common law of contracts. Thus, where a constitutional provision, a statute, or an administrative regulation applies, the common law does not.

The phrase "the common law" has a second meaning. It refers to the process by which courts look to earlier judicial decisions for guidance in deciding the cases before them. These earlier decisions often interpret constitutional or statutory provisions. The principles which guide the application of judge-made law developed in the common law but are now applied to all judicial decisions. These concepts order judge-made law and make it predictable.

Precedent. *Precedent* is a term used to describe a court's earlier holding on a question of law—never fact—which is similar to the issue in a pending case. Here is how precedent works. Suppose a court decided a contract between a football player and his team was one for personal services. Some years later, a contract between a tennis star and a tournament comes before another court. The second court would look to the earlier case for guidance and would probably hold the contract of the tennis star was also for personal services.

---

* See L. M. Friedman, *A History of American Law* (New York: Simon & Schuster, 1973) pp. 13–25, 29–32, 78–81. Because of its origins as a French colony, Louisiana is the only state not to follow the common law.

Lawyers look for precedents in *reporters,* which are published compilations of judicial decisions. They hope to find a case which precisely matches their case, but only rarely will they find such a case. More normally, they will have to predict judicial reaction by analogy to similar cases. We will look at digests of a number of court decisions in this book. Chapter 2 contains a reproduction of a case from a reporter and explains how to read it.

Stare decisis. The rule of *stare decisis*—a Latin term meaning "to stand by decisions"—determines how courts apply precedent to particular cases. In essence, courts faced with an issue similar to one in a reported case decided by a court of the same or higher rank in the same court system usually must follow the precedent.

Stare decisis gives the American legal system tremendous stability and predictability. In the tennis tournament example, the court would be bound by the earlier case if the reported case had been decided by the supreme court in its *jurisdiction* or court system. If the reported case had been decided by the supreme court in another state, the rule of *stare decisis* would not apply.

It is important to note that *stare decisis* applies only to certain decisions. Some decisions lose their value as precedent because of age, changing social conditions, or amendments to statutes, among many reasons. Other cases, the courts come to believe, are simply wrong.

Perhaps the classic example of a wrong decision is *Plessy v. Ferguson.* In that 1896 case, the U.S. Supreme Court had to interpret a clause in the Fourteenth Amendment which guaranteed all citizens equal protection under the law. A Louisiana statute required "separate but equal" accommodations for black and white railroad passengers. Plessy, a black man, challenged the statute's validity when he was arrested for riding in a coach reserved for whites. The Court upheld the statute and the principle of separate but equal.

For the next 58 years, the rule of *stare*

decisis applied to cases involving state laws which enforced racially segregated facilities. Citing *Plessy v. Ferguson* as authority, the Court, for instance, permitted Kentucky to fine Berea College for teaching black and white students together. Beginning in the 1930s, however, the Court began to face the reality that separate facilities rarely were equal. For instance, a law school for blacks was not equal when the law school for whites had a better faculty and a better law library. But it was not until 1954 that the Court signaled the end of the separate but equal rule.*

As *Plessy* and the cases which followed it show, the courts can say—on the basis of the Constitution, statutes, and precedent—what the law *is* in a particular case and thereby can affect what the law will be in the future. *Plessy,* however, also illustrates the evils that would accompany an absolute rule of *stare decisis.*

Although the courts have the power to overrule precedent, they do so reluctantly. They prefer to wait for the legislative branch to initiate changes in the law through statutes or constitutional amendments. So while the rule of *stare decisis* makes judicial decisions predictable, both the rule itself and our system ensure that change can be accommodated.

The civil law. The American and English common law legal system should be contrasted with the civil law legal system. The civil law originated in Rome and was later made the foundation of the legal systems of most continental European countries as a result of Napoleon's conquests. The source of law in civil law jurisdictions, however, is not judges. Instead statutes, codal articles, regulations, and even customary practices are the primary basis of

---

* See J. E. Nowak *et al., Constitutional Law,* 2d ed. (St. Paul, Minn.: West Publ. Co., 1983), pp. 627–639; *Plessy v. Ferguson,* 163 U.S. 537 (1896); *Berea College v. Kentucky,* 211 U.S. 45 (1908); *Missouri ex rel. Gaines v. Canada,* 305 U.S. 337 (1938); and *Brown v. Board of Education,* 347 U.S. 483 (1954).

law; a judge's main duties are to interpret them. Since laws are not judge-made, the essential common law concepts of precedent and *stare decisis* have little application in the civil law. Moreover, the conflict between parties (the adversary system), institutionalized in the common law, is not employed in the civil law. A less combative, more inquisitorial process is used; conducted primarily by a judge, it is similar to the quasi-judicial process discussed in Chapter 3.

The civil law system dominates most of Europe (except England), Latin America, and much of Africa and Asia. In North America it is the basis of the legal systems of the Canadian Province of Quebec and the state of Louisiana, both former French colonies.

Jurisdictions governed by either the common law or civil law legal systems are influenced by each other. Louisiana's tort law, for example, is predominantly based on common law precedents. Similarly, the marital property law of Louisiana, Texas, New Mexico, Arizona, California, Nevada, Washington, and Idaho, known as community property, has civil law origins and was introduced to most of those states by Spanish colonists.

TYPES OF LAWS

Every law is either substantive or procedural *and* either criminal or civil.

Substantive and procedural laws

Substantive law establishes *what* one can and cannot do, while *procedural law* defines *how* something is to be done. For example, someone holds up a Burger King restaurant. The description of the suspect matches that of Ken Pollet, a felon who the police know likes to rob fast-food restaurants. They obtain an arrest warrant and a search warrant and go to his apartment. When they enter, they immediately place Ken under arrest and read him his rights. While searching the apartment for Ken's gun and the money from the robbery, an officer finds 4 pounds of marijuana.

Substantive law defines the crime of robbery, which is what the police allege Ken committed. Substantive law also defines the crime of illegal possession of a controlled substance—in this case, marijuana.

Procedural laws define the steps the police took in obtaining the warrants, arresting Ken, and searching his apartment. But categorizing a law as procedural does not make it less important than one categorized as substantive. In this example, the procedures are required by the Constitution. If the police fail to observe them, a court may not admit the evidence the police found in Ken's house or, perhaps, may not permit Ken to be tried for either crime because the arrest was invalid. Procedural laws will also govern how the court system treats the case against Ken.

Full faith and credit. In a system with as many jurisdictions as ours, there are bound to be inconsistencies and outright contradictions in both procedural and substantive laws. The Constitution resolves this problem by requiring a state to give "full faith and credit" to the "acts, records, and judicial proceedings of every other State" [U.S. Const. Art. IV §1].

Here is how the "full faith and credit" clause might work in practice. Suppose the maximum interest rate on consumer loans or credit cards is 18 percent in state A and 21 percent in state B. A bank gets a judgment in state B against a borrower whose loan carried a 21 percent rate of interest. The borrower moves to state A. The bank attempts to use state A's courts to collect the money the borrower owes it. Those courts must enforce the judgment—assuming it is valid under state B's laws—even if state A's laws would have produced a different result.

The "full faith and credit" clause is critically important to the smooth operation of our federal system. Without it, people could avoid

part or all of an obligation simply by moving to a state with different laws.

Criminal and civil laws

Substantive *criminal* law defines duties citizens owe to society and prescribes penalties for violations. Procedural criminal law describes how violators are to be identified, arrested, and convicted. Substantive criminal law is discussed in Chapter 5.

Substantive *civil* law, our primary focus in this course, determines, among other things, private rights and obligations. A lease, a contract, a partnership agreement, and thousands of other business arrangements fall under the civil law. Of course, there are also procedural civil laws, such as laws which specify how to go about forming a corporation.

Some people contrast civil law* with criminal law as if by definition whatever is not criminal law is civil. Though accurate, that explanation understates two important differences between civil and criminal law.

First, substantive criminal law, although it originates in the judge-made common law, is today always *statutory*. Courts, of course, still look to precedent to guide them in interpreting statutes. However, the courts lack the power, under the Constitution, to create a criminal duty, as they may create a new obligation in a common law area. Civil law may come either from statutes or from the common law. Administrative regulations are never criminal, though a statute can make their violation a criminal offense. The agency itself cannot turn one of its rules into a criminal regulation.

Second, the Fourteenth Amendment to the U.S. Constitution guarantees "due process of law" before a state can deprive a person—which includes both individuals and business entities like corporations—of "life, liberty, or

---

* Civil law as a type of law should not be confused with the civil law legal system.

property." Due process requires the legislative branch to define carefully the elements of a crime so that citizens can know as precisely as possible when they may be subject to criminal prosecution.†

For example, a state legislature may not pass a statute which simply makes "robbery" a crime. What does "robbery" mean? To answer this question, the Constitution requires a statute like the following example from the Model Penal Code §221.1:

> *A person is guilty of robbery if, in the course of committing a theft, he:*
> (a) *inflicts serious bodily injury upon another; or*
> (b) *threatens another with or purposely puts him in fear of immediate serious bodily injury . . .*

The term "theft" is defined in the Model Penal Code as a wrongful but nonviolent taking of another's property—like stealing an unattended bicycle from a rack.

By contrast, a civil statute may state a goal and authorize an administrative agency to define how to achieve it. The federal Clean Air Act §231(a)(2), for instance, authorizes the administrator of the Environmental Protection Agency to:

> . . . *issue proposed emissions standards applicable to the emission of any air pollutant from any class or classes of aircraft engines which in his judgment causes, or contributes to, air pollution which may reasonably be anticipated to endanger public health or welfare.*

Third, criminal suspects are always prosecuted by the government. A citation of a criminal case might read "State of Louisiana," "People of California," or "The United States" versus the defendant. This is because historically, a crime was viewed as an affront to the sovereign. Civil law litigation, on the other hand, generally concerns a conflict between private individuals, although governments at all levels are routinely involved in civil lawsuits as both plaintiffs and defendants.

While the Constitution requires criminal laws to be more specific than civil laws, no society could operate if its members were not presumed to know the law. That is why a course in business law is a vital element in any businessperson's education.

OUR JUDICIAL SYSTEMS

The United States has fifty-three separate judicial systems. The fifty states, Puerto Rico, and the District of Columbia have their own systems, as does the federal government. Structurally, these systems are quite similar, but no two are identical.

Constitutional origins

Both historical and philosophical reasons account for this multitude of court systems. When the British ruled the thirteen colonies which became our first states, the crown limited the colonists' powers of self-government. This lack of self-rule helped cause the Revolution and was something the successful revolutionaries did not want to happen again.

The Articles of Confederation granted to the national government only those powers which the states agreed it should exercise. These powers were very limited. For example, even in wartime, Congress could not impose a tax without the unanimous consent of the states. The states were almost separate countries, which made development of national policy virtually impossible.

Checks and balances. Our present Constitution articulates a compromise between those who wanted a loose confederation and those who wanted a strong central government like Eng-

---

† The Fifth Amendment imposes the same duties on the federal government.

land's. That compromise is most clearly stated in our system of checks and balances.

The thirteen original states retained considerable power over their own affairs. They had their own constitutions and judicial systems before they adopted the U.S. Constitution. And in order to protect themselves from federal interference, the states reserved the right to keep their governments, including their judicial systems, while conferring limited powers on the national government. Congress granted similar rights to the states which entered the union later and to the District of Columbia and the Commonwealth of Puerto Rico.

The states act as a check on and a balance against the power of the national government. However, the Constitution's supremacy clause, Article VI §2, states that the "Constitution and the laws of the United States . . . shall be the supreme Law of the land." Still, the limitation on the power of the central government remains the critical factor in our constitutional arrangement.

Structurally, the federal government and the state governments parallel one another. In both the federal and state governments, each of the three branches—legislative, executive, and judicial—acts as a restraint on the others because the powers of government are divided among them. This concept is called the *separation of powers*.

Federal court jurisdiction

The framers of the Constitution, however, did not feel that preserving the states' judicial systems alone offered enough protection. They also limited the powers of the federal judicial system by restricting its jurisdiction.

Jurisdiction defined. In this context, "jurisdiction" has two meanings. First, it is used in a geographic sense. Every federal and state court except the U.S. Supreme Court has authority only within specific geographic boundaries.

These may be as small as part of a city or as large as several states. When lawyers speak of a case "arising" in a jurisdiction, they use the term in its geographic sense. Later in this chapter, some particular geographic limits are discussed.

The second meaning of "jurisdiction" refers to a court's authority to hear a particular case. A court "has jurisdiction" or "has *subject matter jurisdiction*" when it has the power to decide the questions presented in a lawsuit and to issue a decision which will bind the parties.* (As we will see in the next chapter, a court—federal or state—must also have a third type of jurisdiction: jurisdiction over the person of the defendant, meaning the ability to compel the defendant to appear.)

The party bringing a federal case must prove that the court has subject matter jurisdiction. The federal courts exercise jurisdiction over two types of cases of direct relevance to business: those involving a federal question and those involving diversity of citizenship between the parties.

Federal question jurisdiction. *Federal question jurisdiction* usually involves applications of the Constitution or federal statutes. For instance, a secretary whose employer did not promote her to a supervisory position because of her gender may file suit in the federal court to enforce her right to equal employment opportunities under the federal Civil Rights Act. If a case raises a federal question, a person bringing an action—a *plaintiff*—does not have to satisfy any other jurisdictional criteria.

State courts may enforce many, but not all, federal civil statutes. Employment discrimination under the federal Civil Rights Act of 1964

---

* Jurisdiction has nothing whatsoever to do with the *merits* of a case. A court which lacks jurisdiction for any reason does not have the power to decide which party is right and which is wrong. Having jurisdiction is a prerequisite to having the power to decide the merits.

and housing discrimination cases under the federal Fair Housing Act of 1968, for example, are commonly litigated in state courts. However, federal courts have *exclusive jurisdiction* over copyrights, patents, crimes under federal laws, bankruptcy, and lawsuits of any type involving the federal government. Highly specialized federal courts hear certain types of cases. The Tax Court, for example, hears cases involving only federal taxation questions.

Diversity jurisdiction. Diversity jurisdiction was established by Congress to circumvent the possible "hometown effect" of a state court favoring a litigant from its own state over a litigant from another state. There are two requirements to qualify for diversity jurisdiction:

- None of the plaintiffs can reside in the same state as a defendant. For example, a lawsuit brought by plaintiffs from Michigan and Minnesota against a defendant from Minnesota would *not* qualify for federal diversity jurisdiction.
- The amount in controversy must be $50,000 or more. For example, a lawsuit brought by a Virginia plaintiff against a defendant from Ohio for $75,000 in damages would correctly satisfy both requirements.

Federal diversity jurisdiction is an option, not a requirement. To illustrate, assume a New York driver negligently injures a Colorado pedestrian while driving in Denver. The injured Colorado citizen, *if* claiming to have suffered over $50,000 in damages, could choose to bring suit in either a Colorado state court or a federal court (located in Colorado), since diversity jurisdiction would exist. If the case was originally brought in a state court, the New York driver, the defendant, could have the case removed to a federal court (in Colorado). It is important to note that in *either* the state or federal court, the actual law which would be used to settle the dispute would be the law of Colorado. In other

words, federal law is not used to resolve what is otherwise a state law matter.

The Judicial Conference of the United States, an association of federal court judges, has continually asked Congress to abolish diversity jurisdiction. Diversity jurisdiction cases make up approximately 30 percent of the annual federal court case load. Without such cases, the backlog of federal cases would be greatly reduced and greater attention could be given to disputes involving federal law issues. The judges' position has been strongly opposed by trial lawyers desiring to maintain the strategic option of the federal courts. At this time, the probability that diversity jurisdiction will be eliminated appears slim.

The federal courts

Article III of the Constitution establishes the federal judiciary, but it mentions only the Supreme Court. However, it allows Congress to create other federal courts. Figure 1.1 shows today's federal court system.

U.S. district courts. Most lawsuits brought in the federal system begin in U.S. *district courts*. These courts are called *trial courts*. Like all trial courts, federal and state, the district courts hear witnesses, evaluate their testimony, and make findings of fact and law.

Although federal court jurisdiction is limited, as noted earlier, the district courts are termed *trial courts of general jurisdiction* because the cases they hear are not limited to a single subject area, as they are in the Tax Court. The diversity jurisdiction of district courts results in their hearing a broad range of cases.

District courts get their name from the fact that Congress has divided the United States into ninety-seven federal judicial districts. Each state contains one or more districts. Colorado, for instance, has only one, while California has four. Although only a single district court judge

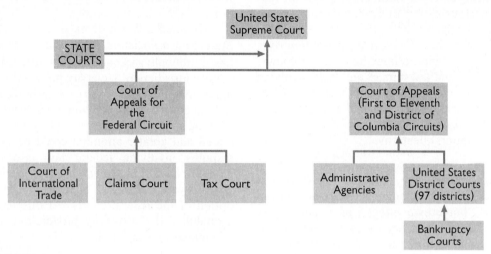

FIGURE 1.1

The federal court system. This is a simplified general outline of the federal court system. Note the point of intersection between the state and federal systems. The federal courts are superior to the state courts only when interpreting federal statutes or the U.S. Constitution. Figure 1.2 diagrams the state court system. Administrative agencies are discussed in Chapter 3.

normally hears a case, a district may have up to twenty judges assigned to it, depending on the number of cases filed in the district. The number of annual U.S. district court case filings has increased from 89,112 in 1960 to over 250,000 per year in 1990.*

U.S. courts of appeals. A party dissatisfied with a *judgment* of a district court may appeal to a U.S. court of appeals. The courts of appeals are termed *intermediate appellate courts* because they are between the district courts and the Supreme Court.

The courts of appeals hear cases in which the party appealing, the *appellant,* alleges (1) the trial court erred in applying the law or (2) the evidence presented to the court did not support the court's findings. Of course, the par-

ty who won in the trial court, the *appellee,* takes the opposite position. Appellate courts review the *record* of the proceedings before the trial court and hear arguments by the parties' lawyers. They do not admit new evidence or listen to witnesses.

Congress has divided the federal judicial districts among twelve appellate *circuits* and assigned a court of appeals to each circuit.† The state in which a judicial district is located determines which circuit the district is in. The Fourth Circuit, for example, passes on appeals from Virginia's federal district courts, while the Ninth Circuit covers Oregon. Usually, three judges hear an appeal.

---

† A thirteenth circuit, the Court of Appeals for the Federal Circuit, hears appeals from (1) federal trial courts of limited jurisdiction (the U.S. Claims Court and the Court of International Trade), (2) U.S. district courts in patent and trademark cases, (3) the U.S. Patent and Trademark Office, and (4) the Merit Systems Protection Board.

---

* *Time Magazine*, August 26, 1991, p. 91.

Because there are different federal courts of appeals, conflicting interpretations of federal law can occur, perhaps most commonly in federal labor law matters. The Supreme Court is commonly asked to resolve such conflicts. Until the Court hears and rules on a case, district courts within an appellate circuit are expected to decide similar cases consistent with the decisions of their circuit's court of appeals. Thus, if the Ninth Circuit Court of Appeals has ruled a matter to be a mandatory item for union-management bargaining, then a district court within the Ninth Circuit is expected to rule in a similar manner. If the Supreme Court should ultimately rule that the matter is not a mandatory item for bargaining, then this ruling would override the Ninth Circuit's position.

The U.S. Supreme Court. Nine justices sit on the U.S. Supreme Court. Normally, they all hear an appeal. Although *litigants* (persons engaged in a lawsuit) file more than 4700 cases with the Court each year, the number of matters actually argued before it averages between 150 and 175.

The U.S. Supreme Court, as the ultimate interpreter of the Constitution, can declare a federal or state statute to be unconstitutional. For instance, the Supreme Court voided a Massachusetts law limiting the amount of money corporations could contribute to a political campaign, because the law interfered with a corporation's right of free speech. Even so, the Court's power over the states is limited. The Court will not, for instance, interpret a state law unless it involves an application of the U.S. Constitution or federal statute. Otherwise, the state courts or the U.S. courts of appeals (in diversity cases) have the last judicial word.

Appeals reach the Supreme Court in two ways. In the first, an appellant has an *appeal of right*. An appeal of right most often arises when (1) a U.S. court of appeals has held a state statute unconstitutional or (2) a state court has found a state statute valid in a case where a party has claimed the statute violated the U.S.

Constitution. The Supreme Court decides more than 90 percent of the appeals of this type without a formal hearing.

The second way appeals reach the Court is by means of an appellant's application for a *writ of certiorari,* an order to a lower court to send the Supreme Court the record of the case for its review. The Court may grant the writ when (1) a case presents an issue which another U.S. court of appeals has decided differently, (2) the validity of a federal statute is in question, or (3) a party in a state supreme court case asserts a right under the U.S. Constitution. The Supreme Court has complete discretion as to whether to grant a writ of certiorari.

State court systems

State court systems have the same basic structure as the federal system (see Figure 1.2). They have trial courts of general jurisdiction and appellate courts. Many state systems include courts of specialized jurisdiction, such as *domestic relations courts.* However, no two state systems are identical. For this course, the particular details of one state court system are less important than the common structure and functions of the various levels of courts.

Trial courts of limited jurisdiction. Many states have two levels of trial courts. The lower-level courts, often called *municipal courts* or *justice courts,* have limited jurisdiction. *Small claims courts,* where they exist, often fit into this category. Geographically, the jurisdiction of these courts often extends only to a particular city or part of a county.

An amount in controversy, which may reach $10,000, usually defines the civil jurisdiction of such courts. Sometimes, these courts hear traffic cases and *misdemeanors,* crimes with penalties of less than a year in jail. Appeals from trial courts of limited jurisdiction go either to the trial court of general jurisdiction or to an intermediate court of appeals.

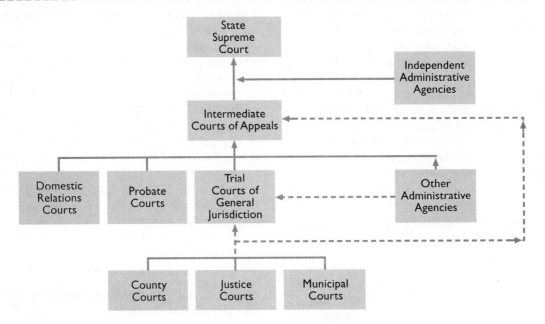

Figure 1.2
A state court system. This is a much simplified outline of a typical state court system. Each of the fifty systems differs from the others. The dotted lines indicate alternative routes of appeal, which vary from system to system. Figure 1.1 diagrams the federal court system. Administrative agencies are discussed in Chapter 3.

Trial courts of general jurisdiction. Apart from matters specifically reserved for specialized courts and trial courts of limited jurisdiction, trial courts of general jurisdiction may hear virtually any case—civil or criminal—a state court can decide within the bounds of the state and federal constitutions. These courts usually cover a district which may consist of a county or a group of counties.

Intermediate appellate courts. As in the federal system, the losing party in a trial court has a right to appeal to an appellate court. More than thirty states have intermediate appellate courts, while the others—mainly states with low population, like Nebraska and Alaska—have only a

supreme court. As in the federal system, state intermediate appellate courts are three-judge panels which hear cases coming usually from a number of trial courts.

Supreme courts. In states with intermediate courts of appeals, the supreme court usually chooses which appeals it will decide in much the same way as the U.S. Supreme Court. However, a comparison of Figures 1.1 and 1.2 reveals one important difference. In state systems, it is quite common for appeals from certain independent—that is, independent of the governor's direct supervision—agencies and commissions to go directly to the supreme court. For instance, appeals from the Ohio Public Utilities Commission bypass that state's intermediate court of appeals. These agencies are discussed in Chapter 3.

Judges

As we have seen in this section, a court consists of one or more judges. How these people become judges varies from judicial system to judicial system. These selection methods are highly controversial, and no consensus exists as to which is best.

Selection of federal judges. Article II §2 of the U.S. Constitution says, in part, of the President:

> . . . he shall nominate, and by and with the advice and consent of the Senate, shall appoint . . . judges of the Supreme Court, and all other officers of the United States, whose appointments are not herein otherwise provided for, and which shall be established by law. . . .

As subsequent laws have provided, all judges and magistrates of federal courts are nominated by the President, and their appointments are subject to the advice and consent of the Senate.

Despite protestations to the contrary, the judicial nomination procedure has always been an intensely political one. And, there is no evidence that the Constitution's framers ever thought it would be anything else. Intense controversy surrounded President Reagan's appointment of Robert Bork and several other judicial conservatives to the Supreme Court and the U.S. Courts of Appeals. Twenty years before, similar controversies surrounded President Johnson's appointments of liberals. And in the 1930s, no issue shaped President Roosevelt's second term more than his effort to remake the Supreme Court in the image of the New Deal.

Roosevelt's problem with the "six old men" on the Supreme Court arose from this part of Article III §1 of the Constitution:

> The judges, both of the supreme and inferior courts, shall hold their offices during good behavior. . . .

In other words, a judge of the federal courts is appointed for life. So unless a sitting federal judge is brought before the Senate in an impeachment trial, as happened twice in 1989, it is only during the nomination process that a judicial candidate is subject to public scrutiny and veto.

Selection of state judges. The states did not all follow the federal model. Many have chosen to elect judges who must face the electorate regularly. Ohio, for instance, elects judges of all courts to 4-year terms; in New York, terms range up to 10 years. Proponents of this system argue that judges' performance should be subject to electoral review, just like other important officials.

Texas also elects its judges. In the wake of the $11.1 billion judgment for Pennzoil against Texaco in 1986 and its affirmance by the Texas Supreme Court, many took note of the fact that all nine of the justices had accepted $6000 or more in campaign contributions from lawyers on both sides of the case. This led to calls for merit selection.

Merit selection of judges is supposed to remove the politics from the appointment process and lead to a highly qualified judiciary. The model varies from state to state, but typically the governor submits names to a screening panel which makes recommendations as to the nominees' suitability. The state senate then passes on the nominees.

In states like Massachusetts, judges serve for life as in the federal system. Some states, like California and Missouri, couple the merit selection process with the possibility of review by the electorate after a judge has served for a certain period. In 1987, California voters removed State Supreme Court Chief Justice Rose Bird from office in this way.

Which system of judicial selection is better? The answer is unclear. Great judges have been elected; appointed judges have been later impeached. To the extent there is an answer in anyone's mind, it probably depends on the individual's political philosophy.

CONCLUSION

This chapter examined the nature and types of laws and the structure of our judicial system. The next chapter explains how a dispute between two businesses might proceed through the system.

A NOTE TO ALL STUDENTS

Throughout this book you will find notes at the end of the chapters directed to future CPA exam candidates. These notes are primarily intended to help these students better focus on concepts historically emphasized on the CPA examination. However, we believe they may be of value to all readers, especially beyond Part I of this book.

A NOTE TO FUTURE CPA CANDIDATES

The CPA exam does not specifically test candidates on the material covered in Part I. However, you are expected to know the names of parties to a lawsuit and have a general awareness of the judicial system. For now, begin to build you legal vocabulary.

KEY WORDS

appellant (14)
appellee (14)
appellate court (14)
civil law (9)
civil law legal
   system (10)
common law (7)
court of appeals (14)
criminal law (10)
defendant (11)
federal question (12)
jurisdiction (8)
law (5)
plaintiff (12)
precedent (8)
procedural law (9)
stare decisis (8)
statute (7)
substantive law (9)
trial court (15)

DISCUSSION QUESTIONS

1. Why is an understanding of the philosophy underlying our legal system important to the study of business law?
2. Describe the relationship between the Constitution and statutes enacted by Congress.
3. How do civil statutes differ from administrative regulations? Can an administrative agency adopt a regulation that is not authorized by a statute?
4. How does the common law relate to statutes? Who makes common law?
5. Why is predictability a crucial factor in any legal system? How does *stare decisis* encourage predictability in our system? What are the disadvantages to relying upon precedent?
6. How does criminal law differ from civil law? What are the policy reasons underlying the different shape of criminal law?
7. What is the difference between substantive law and procedural law?
8. What are the jurisdictional limitations of the federal court system? Which types of cases can be heard only by a federal court? May a state court interpret the U.S. Constitution in a case in which it has jurisdiction?
9. Distinguish between diversity jurisdiction and federal question jurisdiction.
10. What are the characteristics of a trial court? What determines the differences between a trial court of limited jurisdiction and one of general jurisdiction?
11. What are the characteristics of an intermediate appellate court? Why would a judicial system not have an intermediate appellate court?
12. What are some of the differences between intermediate appellate courts and supreme courts?

CASE PROBLEMS

1. Suppose Antarctica has declared itself a sovereign nation and is about to hold a constitutional convention. You have been asked to present an explanation of how laws come into being under the American system of government. How will you describe this process?

2. The Supreme Court has consistently rules that organized prayer in public schools violates the First Amendment principle of separation of church and state. Suppose Congress is determined to allow organized prayer in the public schools. It enacts a statute if feels meets the First Amendment concerns. The statute provides that teachers may elect to incorporate organized prayer in their classrooms if dissenting students are given the option to be excused. What will happen if the Supreme Court determines that this statute, too, does not comply with the Constitution? Is there a way by which Congress could effectively circumvent the Supreme Court rulings in order to create such an option for teachers? Explain.

3. Over the past decade, various groups have proposed amendments to the U.S. Constitution. Their proposals have included amendments permitting prayer in public schools, requiring a balanced federal budget, prohibiting abortion, banning busing to achieve integration, and guaranteeing equal rights for women. Do these proposed amendments indicate our Constitution is not an effective blueprint for government in the twenty-first century? Explain how such proposed amendments affect your view of the Constitution.

4. Mayo brought suit in the U.S. District Court for the Western District of Pennsylvania, alleging that the defendants had "caused misery and unwarranted threats" and "placed deliberate obstacles in his path and . . . caused his downfall." What jurisdictional tests will the Court apply to Mayo's suit? If the defendants Mayo named were "Satan and his staff," how is the Court likely to deal with the jurisdictional questions?

5. As discussed in this chapter, the courts are a significant source of law. Some commentators object that the courts play too great a role in creating the law as opposed to enforcing it. As examples, they point to courts which required busing, permitted abortion on demand, terminated tax exemptions for private schools practicing racial discrimination, and prohibited prayer in schools. Should these decisions have been left up to the legislative branch? What of the argument that the Constitution required these decisions? Is there a need for courts to "legislate" when they perceive a failure to implement constitutional guarantees? Explain

6. Roger, a vegetarian, decided to use his car to block the entrance to a McDonald's restaurant and offer its would-be patrons a free vegetarian bag lunch. Unfortunately, Roger forgot to remove some recently harvested marijuana plants from the back seat of his car. When a police officer comes to tell Roger to stop blocking the driveway, she notices the plants and arrests him for illegal possession of drugs. She informs Roger of his rights and takes him to jail. What aspects of these facts give rise to procedural issues? What are those issues?

7. The Supreme Court of state A has declared that it is unconstitutional for a public university to force a student to pay fees when a part of those fees is allocated to the university health center to pay for elective abortions. The public universities in state B have similar fees. A student in state B files suit in the state court challenging the constitutionality of the university fees. Describe the precedential value of the state A Supreme Court decision in the B courts. Explain the effect on this action of a U.S. Supreme Court decision declaring such fees unconstitutional.

8. In state A, the divorce laws specify that whatever a spouse earns during the course of a marriage is treated in the property settlement as if half of the sum belonged to the other spouse. When Becky obtains a divorce in state A from John, the court orders John to pay her $25,000 as her share of his earnings. John does not pay Becky. He then moves to

state B, under whose divorce laws he would have owed Becky nothing. The state A divorce decree is valid, and Becky has brought suit in state B to enforce it against John. Can John rely on the state B law as a defense against the enforcement of the decree? Explain.

9. Real Issues. The Constitution provides that the President shall nominate and the Senate confirm appointments to the United States Supreme Court. Supreme Court appointments have always been political. However, more recently there has been growing criticism that the process has become too focused upon a potential justice's opinions on certain matters of significant dispute, such as abortion or prayer in the school. There is no one correct answer to the following question: If you were President of the United States, what would be your most important criteria for the nomination of a Supreme Court justice? Would you have a "litmus test" that a potential justice must agree with your position on certain issues in order to be seriously considered? Explain.

10. Real Issues. By constitutional provision, a justice is appointed to the Supreme Court for life. Supporters of this provision contend that it is needed to assure that justices will be truly free to decide what is best when considering issues before the Court. Some critics contend that periods of extended appointment, such as 10 years, would be preferable to lessen the "judicial imperialism" of the Supreme Court. There is no correct answer to the following question: What is your opinion on the best length of tenure for a Supreme Court justice? Explain.

CHAPTER 2
Ethics and Dispute Resolution

Ask anyone. They'll tell you that the state of ethics in this country is bad and getting worse. Just look, they might say, at the number of lawsuits filed each year. People don't trust each other, they don't deal fairly with one another. And, they'll take advantage of a minor injury to try to strike it rich in the court system.

That there are many more lawsuits filed today than 20 or 30 years ago should not surprise anyone. A larger percentage of Americans are over 18 than ever before in our history. More adults means more business transactions. Still, resort to *litigation,* or legal proceedings, seems to have increased out of proportion to the increase in the adult population.

Changes during this century in the way we live may help explain the phenomenon. When Americans lived mainly on farms and in small towns, people involved in disputes often knew one another in other contexts. Family, community, and church could all play roles in reaching a resolution. Today, telecommunications, mail order catalogs, and chain stores have limited the personal contacts which brought about settlements in the past. So the courts have had to play a greater role.

But if these modern innovations have limited personal contacts between buyer and seller, they have vastly increased the number of commercial transactions a person can expect to enter into. If you doubt this, imagine moving into a house or apartment that lacks even a single clothes closet. Until very late in the last century, even the rich could live out of a trunk or a dresser. The past was simpler in that people bought, sold, and had less.

More people, less personal contact between the principals of transactions, and a great many more transactions have led to an increase in disputes. So, people resort to the mechanisms our society provides for resolving conflicts. And these mechanisms are the focus in this chapter.

THE ROLE OF ETHICS

Ethics are standards of conduct or of moral judgment. The term is used to describe such standards whether they are held by an individual, a group, or a society. An individual's ethics often are unique to that person. All the major professions—for example, accounting, medicine, and law—have adopted codes of ethics as standards of conduct. However, the ethics of a group or a society require a consensus.

A free society imposes an enormous ethical burden on those who belong to it, because individuals have the duty to make choices about right and wrong. Part of this burden originates with the recognition that few situations are clear-cut. For example, consider the killing of one human being by another—*homicide.* Should a child who kills a molester in the course of an attack suffer the same penalty as an addict who kills a pharmacist in the course of a robbery? The answer to that question is not as simple as it seems. In our society, ethics play a critical role in our behavior and in the way we make decisions. And the ethical criteria brought to bear depend on the situation and on the specific parties involved.

Ethics Expressed in Laws

In many instances, legislative bodies express that consensus in laws which the executive branch and the courts then put into effect. The courts also independently express society's standards of conduct by refusing to impose results that offend the community's sensibilities—even though a strict application of the law would require such results. Courts have used words ranging from ''inequitable'' to ''shocking'' to ''unconscionable'' to describe situations in which they impose an ethical result as opposed to a strictly legal result.

The question of ethical conduct pervades the study of law. A book of this scope cannot define and treat separately all or even most of the ethical issues involved in the topics it covers. Indeed, treating them separately would give the mistaken impression that ethical issues arise in a vacuum, and they definitely do not. They arise in specific, concrete instances that real businesspeople must resolve.

Still, society does recognize and hold businesses responsible for a number of fundamental ethical duties. These include fairness, loyalty, maintaining promises, honesty, and avoiding the harming of others. Throughout this book you will analyze actual cases in which the law sought to enforce these duties. Likewise, you will study cases in which a business violated recognized ethical standards but was still not breaking the law. It is essential for one to recognize the dynamic relationship between law and ethics if one truly wishes to understand the law.

The State of Ethics Today

Hazy thought, inspired by nostalgia, has led commentators since the dawn of writing to claim that golden ages once existed in which all people acted morally and responsibly toward one another. We tend to look at the Victorian era of the last century as such an age. However, writers of that era referred to it as "the gilded age" and characterized its great business figures as "the robber barons." Both terms were and are apt.

There is no reason to believe that our ethics are any worse than those of our ancestors; indeed, there is much reason to believe that our awareness of ethical questions is considerably greater. A glance at Chapters 43 through 46 reveals how different our moral sensibilities are from those of the Victorians. Unfair trade practices, labor in conditions little better than slavery, and environmental degradation unimaginable today typified their era. The social safety net we assume protects Americans not only did not exist, it was inconceivable. The right to a

public education beyond grammar school was a matter of hot debate. However, even if we, as a society, have progressed, we have little reason to congratulate ourselves. We have a long way to go toward perfection.

People in business are increasingly in the public eye. In the 1980s, virtually every newspaper, magazine, and television station and network has expanded its coverage of business news. The public has demonstrated an increasing impatience with conduct it perceives as unethical. Business educators have responded by emphasizing ethics in their curricula. As implied in the introduction to this unit, the predictability and stability of our system depends on each individual's observation of ethical standards. Business depends on trust among parties who deal with one another. Disputes indicate a breakdown of trust.

LITIGATION: THE LAST RESORT

Reliance on the courts has its costs. Each year over 750,000 cases are filed in the federal court system, while over 25 million nontraffic cases are filed in state courts. Tax dollars must pay for courthouses, judges, support staff, libraries, security, and the like. But the bill for these is small in comparison with the costs to *litigants,* the parties to legal proceedings.

The Parties' Expenses

Each party to a civil case usually pays for its own lawyers and their expenses. Depending on their experience, lawyers charge fees that start at $35 an hour and can exceed $250 per hour. In addition, their secretaries prepare documents, and their clerks or paralegals may research the facts and the law. Telephone calls, photocopying, and travel add to the bill. Also, each phase of litigation has unique expenses associated with it. But what can be most costly of all is the diversion of attention and energy from the parties' other business ventures. So the costs of a lawsuit may exceed the value of winning.

Contingent fees. In certain types of cases, the injured party cannot afford to pay a lawyer's fee as it is incurred. This is especially true of personal injury suits where cases like those involving the Dalkon Shield birth control device or asbestos manufacturing can require 10 years or more of litigation. In these types of cases, lawyers sometimes work on the basis of a *contingent fee*—an arrangement between client and lawyer in which the lawyer agrees to take a percentage of the client's recovery, if any, as a fee. That percentage often ranges between 25 and 33 percent.

Whether contingent fee arrangements should be allowed is a matter of hot debate. Trial lawyers have a point when they argue that many plaintiffs—persons who file suits in court—could not afford to bring their actions otherwise, and they, therefore, would have no way to recover their losses. They are also correct that a contingent fee arrangement gives lawyers an incentive to achieve the best possible financial result for their clients.

Those opposed to contingent fees argue that this incentive leads to the filing of frivolous actions on behalf of unworthy clients. Opponents also contend that these arrangements protract disputes because they diminish incentives to settle quickly and actually result in more cases going to trial, since the lawyers hope to win a big jury verdict. And, the fear of liability inhibits product innovation for fear of large liability judgments.

Society's response to legal costs. As commonly happens when large sums and professionals' livelihoods are at stake, each side of the contingent fee debate has questioned the other's ethics. And clearly, the debate cannot be resolved on the terms in which it has been framed.

Many opponents of contingent fees point to the British system, in which contingent fees are almost unknown and losers pay the victor's legal fees. This has kept the level of litigation relatively low in the areas in which American lawyers rely on contingent fees. But, Great Britain also affords all its citizens comprehensive national health care and other social safety nets not offered in the United States. If our system is to be changed, we as a society acting through our lawmakers must decide whether to compensate those suffering injuries without reference to fault or traditional means of assigning financial responsibility and in what amounts.

In the short run, society's solution to the high costs of litigation probably will be statutes to force disputing parties into methods of resolution which do not involve courts and may not require lawyers. However, many companies are not waiting for statutes. They are developing their own methods or are using ones currently available. Three common forms of dispute resolution mechanisms, arbitration, mediation, and minitrials, are discussed below. This chapter, however, focuses on litigation because it affects everything you will study in this course. Also, lawsuits and the fear of them dominate the conflict resolution system today.

Preventive Law

Litigation costs come out of the litigants' pockets as either insurance premiums or direct cash outlays or both. Therefore, just as patients and doctors have begun to practice preventive medicine, businesses should practice "preventive law." The goal of preventive law is to try to manage legal risks. To be successful, a business must effectively identify and/or predict possible sources of future legal liability and then take appropriate action to avoid or lessen them. Examples of appropriate matters for a business to review might include the following:

- Contracts between customers and/or suppliers
- Employment handbooks
- Workplace accessibility for employees with disabilities
- Workplace compliance with environmental regulations

Just as a patient may still become ill even while practicing preventive medicine, preventive law practice does not assure against possible legal liability exposure. Some legal problems may occur which were simply not predictable, such as the impact from a new regulation concerning environmental waste. Other problems may occur even though the employer has carefully attempted to eliminate illegal workplace practices, such as sexual harassment. Finally, over time the mere fact of being actively engaged in business will likely result in exposure to frivolous lawsuits. While a business may prevail, ultimately the business may incur significant costs in time and legal expenses.

One means of managing legal risk is to anticipate the resolution of possible disputes. Today, a growing number of business contracts are written with alternative dispute resolution mechanisms to avoid the often more burdensome, expensive court system. The next section will discuss these mechanisms.

ALTERNATIVE DISPUTE RESOLUTION

Usually, the people involved in a business dispute settle it themselves. When they cannot reach a satisfactory resolution, they can drop the matter. Or, they can litigate. However, those are not their only choices. They have a number of other alternatives including arbitration, mediation, minitrials, rent-a-judges, and small claims courts. We will look at the first three of them in this section. But before we do, let's look at a hypothetical business dispute.

A Hypothetical Dispute

The best way to understand a system is to see how it operates in practice. So we will examine dispute resolution by watching two hypothetical companies attempt to resolve a business disagreement.

Pasta Corporation, Inc., agreed to supply Deli Company, Inc., with 60,000 pounds of pasta per month at $1 per pound. The negotiations consisted of a telephone call from Deli and an exchange of a purchase order and a confirmation by mail. Pasta and Deli each have only one place of business. Pasta is located in Los Angeles, California; Deli is in Chicago, Illinois. For 6 months, there were no problems. Then, Deli's purchasing agent contacted the Pasta sales office, claiming Deli had received a shipment of soggy pasta. Insisting nothing was wrong with the shipment when it left California, Pasta demanded payment.

Arbitration

Pasta and Deli may agree to arbitration. *Arbitration* is an arrangement in which the parties agree to refer a dispute to an impartial third party—the *arbitrator*—and to be bound by his determination. Often, contracts require the parties to submit disputes to arbitration and the courts enforce such contract clauses. However, nothing would prevent them from agreeing, after the dispute arose, to submit it. Businesspeople often resort to arbitration when negotiations aimed at resolving a dispute break down. Indeed, the American Arbitration Association alone handles more than 45,000 cases per year.*

In our hypothetical dispute, suppose Pasta and Deli agreed in their contract to arbitrate any disputes arising from it. Either Pasta or Deli may start the process by notifying the opposing party that it demands arbitration of the dispute. The parties must agree on an arbitrator, who may be a professor or businessperson with expertise in an area related to the dispute. Arbitration hearings proceed much like the trial described below. Howver, they are less formal, more private, and relatively inexpensive. In some arbitrations, a neutral party simply examines records and gives an opinion.

Normally, the parties agree that the arbitrator's decision, which is called an *award*, will

---

* K. Hannon, "Turnstile Justice," *Forbes*, December 15, 1986, p. 174.

bind them. While the losing party may take the matter to court, what it will dispute is the award, not the evidence before the arbitrator. So if the arbitrator agrees with Deli, Pasta cannot start the fact determination process over again in court. The courts will not interfere with an arbitrator's award unless it resulted from fraud or from a mistake which is so plain that the arbitrator would have corrected it had anyone pointed it out to him.

Mediation

Another litigation alternative is mediation. *Mediation* involves third party intervention—usually at the request of the disputing parties—to persuade those involved to settle the dispute themselves. Since *mediators* do not make binding decisions, their success depends on gaining the parties' trust and persuading them to look at the problem in new ways in order to find a compromise. Mediators have helped settle wars, international boundary disputes, baseball strikes, and contract disputes like the one between Pasta and Deli.

Minitrials

Arbitration and mediation are not the only formal alternatives to litigation. Large corporations—like ARCO, TRW, Gillette, Control Data, Texaco, and Shell—have used "minitrials." In these informal, off-the-record proceedings, the lawyers present their cases to a senior executive of each party. Given the opportunity to hear both sides, the parties often settle their dispute immediately after the hearing. This process has the benefit of being cheap, but it also keeps the relations between the parties on a less hostile level than litigation.

REMEDIES

When the parties submit a matter for, say, arbitration, they usually define the scope of the remedies the arbitrator may award. To an ex-

tent, that is also true when a *plaintiff*—a person who brings a dispute before a court—files a lawsuit. Figure 2.1 provides a list of nine questions which a potential plaintiff should consider in choosing a lawyer.

The description of remedies here is necessarily very general. Each part of this book contains detailed discussions of the specific remedies available for particular situations. For now, keep in mind that courts grant three basic types of remedies: legal, equitable, and declaratory.

Legal Remedies

As we will see below, a plaintiff like Pasta may obtain an order from the court awarding it the money the defendant owes. An award of money

---

CHOOSING A LAWYER: NINE QUESTIONS TO ASK YOURSELF

1. Do I understand the extent to which winning this case will benefit me?
2. Do I understand what this case will cost me in terms of lawyers' fees, my out-of-pocket expenses, and my time?
3. Is the lawyer interested in my problem?
4. Did the lawyer show that he or she understood and cared about my problem in our discussion?
5. Is my problem one that requires specialized expertise?
6. Did the lawyer indicate that he or she had experience with my type of problem?
7. What do I know about the lawyer's reputation for keeping matters confidential?
8. What do I know and how do I feel about the lawyer's ability to deal with me as an individual and a businessperson?
9. Does the lawyer have the kind of interpersonal skills required to deal with the people on the other side of my problem?

Figure 2.1 Choosing a lawyer: nine questions to ask yourself.
In the process of choosing a lawyer to handle a potential lawsuit, ask yourself these nine questions. You can devise a similar list for almost any legal problem.

is called *damages* or, because it developed in the common law, a *legal remedy*. Legal remedies are discussed extensively in Chapter 12.

Equitable Remedies

In some cases, damages alone will not resolve the dispute. Then, a party may seek an *equitable remedy,* which is generally a court order commanding a party to do or not to do something. The most common equitable remedy is an *injunction.* Suppose a waste disposal firm deposits toxic chemicals in a landfill next to a town reservoir. The town may seek a prohibitory injunction to stop the dumping and a mandatory injunction to force the company to remove the chemicals.

There are three types of injunctions. A *temporary restraining order* (TRO) is an emergency order issued by a court usually after a brief hearing that prevents a party from taking an action until the court can hold a hearing on a preliminary injunction. A court will issue a TRO only if the party seeking it will suffer an immediate and irreparable injury or loss. Usually, a TRO expires in 10 days, but the court or the parties may extend it.

A *preliminary injunction* is also an order issued by the court upon a showing that a party will suffer immediate and irreparable injury or loss. What distinguishes a TRO from a preliminary injunction is that, unless the parties agree otherwise, a court may issue a preliminary injunction only after the parties have had a chance to fully argue the issue. A preliminary injunction lasts until the court dissolves it or enters final judgment in the case.

A *permanent injunction* is an injunction that is part of a final order disposing of a case.

It is important to note that the courts will grant an equitable remedy only when a legal remedy is not sufficient or when a statute authorizes equitable relief in a particular situation. In other words, the norm is monetary compensation for an injury. Neither Pasta nor Deli would be entitled to injunctive relief in our hypothetical.

Declaratory Relief

Another important remedy for businesses in particular is the action for a *declaratory judgment.* Typically in these actions, the plaintiff asks the court to define the parties' rights and obligations under a statute or a contract. A request for declaratory relief may be accompanied by requests for an injunction or damages or both. Here, Pasta and Deli are not arguing about the contract's meaning, but rather whether the other has complied with it.

CHOOSING THE PROPER FORUM

For the balance of the chapter, suppose that instead of submitting the dispute to arbitration or mediation, Pasta told its *lawyer*—a person who has satisfied a state's educational and licensing prerequisites for the practice of law— to file suit. As you study the progress of Pasta's suit, you should refer to Figure 2.2, which outlines the stages of a civil suit.

But before filing suit, the lawyer must determine the matter's proper *forum*—place where the dispute may be resolved.

Cases, Controversies, and Standing

Courts make law, as Chapter 1 noted, when they decide cases. Civil cases usually come before courts when the parties cannot resolve a dispute between themselves. A person who wants to bring a dispute before a court must meet two tests.

The first test is that the plaintiff must present a "case or controversy" for the court to resolve. The term "case or controversy" has some very technical meanings, but for our purposes it means the dispute is one the court can legally or practically resolve. Both state and federal constitutions, for instance, commit certain matters exclusively to the legislative and executive branches. Whether particular legislation should be enacted or, if enacted, signed

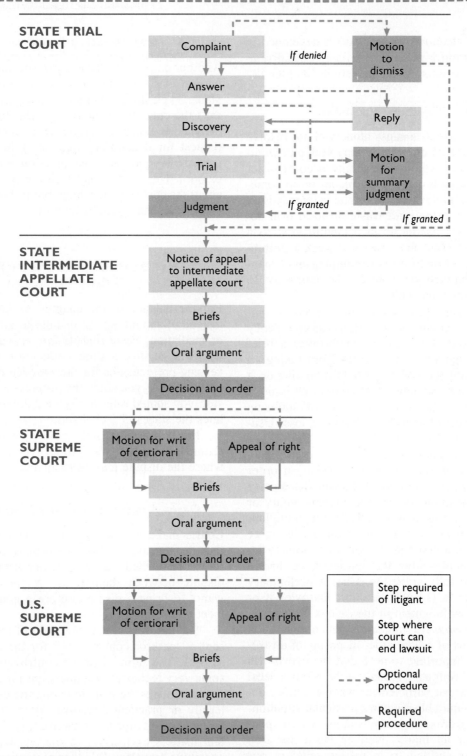

STATE TRIAL COURT

Complaint

Motion to dismiss

If denied

Answer

Reply

Discovery

Trial

Motion for summary judgment

Judgment

If granted

If granted

STATE INTERMEDIATE APPELLATE COURT

Notice of appeal to intermediate appellate court

Briefs

Oral argument

Decision and order

STATE SUPREME COURT

Motion for writ of certiorari

Appeal of right

Briefs

Oral argument

Decision and order

U.S. SUPREME COURT

Motion for writ of certiorari

Appeal of right

Briefs

Oral argument

Decision and order

Step required of litigant

Step where court can end lawsuit

Optional procedure

Required procedure

Figure 2.2 The path of a civil case through the courts.
This is a much simplified representation of a civil case's path through the courts.
Refer to it as you read Chapter 2.

into law are not matters for the courts. At the other extreme, a court cannot resolve a disagreement over who will win the National League pennant in 1995 or the dispute between Farmer MacGregor and Peter Rabbit over the vegetable garden.

The second test is that the plaintiff must have *standing* to bring the lawsuit. Standing refers to the plaintiff's capacity to assert a claim for relief in court. Suppose Al slips and falls on a wet spot on the floor of a grocery store. Al has standing to seek compensation from the store for his injuries. His neighbor, June, who hears about the accident, does not have standing to sue the market. The standing requirement is designed to ensure that the court hears both sides of an issue and that each side is presented as forcefully as possible.

Jurisdiction

As we saw in Chapter 1, before Pasta files suit, its lawyer must determine which courts have jurisdiction over the case. If more than one court can hear the case, the *plaintiff*—the party filing suit—can choose the one it prefers. Here, Pasta is the plaintiff.

Jurisdiction over the person. A court must have *jurisdiction over the person* of the *defendant*— the party being sued. Here, Deli is the defendant.

The *due process clauses* of the Constitution's Fifth and Fourteenth Amendments affect the determination of jurisdiction over the person. In most circumstances, they prohibit a court from hearing cases involving defendants (whether individuals or artificial persons like corporations) who have not lived or transacted business within the state in which the court is located. So the geographic scope of Deli's business activities will control where Pasta can file suit. Beyond that, Deli will have little say about where the case is heard.

Deli is an Illinois corporation, and Pasta is a California company. The pasta's value exceeds

$50,000. Therefore, the federal courts would have *diversity jurisdiction*. State courts in Illinois would also have jurisdiction, since Deli is located there.

Jurisdiction over the person of a defendant is the third meaning which has been presented of the word "jurisdiction."* Putting all three into one very loose definition, *jurisdiction* is the power of a court in a judicial system to decide a case involving a particular defendant.

Long-arm jurisdiction. *Long-arm jurisdiction statutes,* which all states have, allow a state court to exercise jurisdiction over the person of an out-of-state defendant. Suppose Deli's only California supplier is Pasta, and Deli neither advertises in California nor ships any products there. It has no other contacts with the state. Nevertheless, Pasta might be able to file suit against Deli in California under the long-arm statute.

Long-arm statutes permit jurisdiction if the defendant has sufficient contacts with the state, arising out of the transaction which gave rise to the suit. In many states, a single contract like the one between Pasta and Deli confers jurisdiction on the courts in the plaintiff's state.†

Whose law applies? In diversity cases, federal courts apply state law. In *Pasta v. Deli,* the

---

* Some other terms used in this chapter have several meanings. "Court" can mean a unit of the judicial system, like the U.S. Supreme Court or the Bexar County District Court. Or it can refer to an individual judge, as in "The court demanded that the lawyers stop talking to the press." The words "plaintiff" and "defendant" often refer not to a litigant but to the party's lawyer. For instance, "the plaintiff argued" means "the plaintiff's lawyer argued."
† In actions involving personal injuries or injuries to property—*tort actions*—the application of the long-term statute is considerably simpler. The courts of the state in which the injury occurs automatically have jurisdiction to hear a case arising from the injury. The courts of the state in which the defendant resides, of course, also have jurisdiction in such cases. Tort actions are the subject of Chapter 4.

court would have to decide whether the substantive law of California or of Illinois applied, depending on factors such as where the contract would be performed. State law also determines whether the district court has jurisdiction over the defendant's person. If California state courts did not have jurisdiction over Deli, a U.S. district court in California would lack diversity jurisdiction. By contrast, the Federal Rules of Civil Procedure, not those of the state, control the course of the proceedings. While differences between state and federal rules may not be great, they do exist. In this chapter, we will assume state and federal rules to be identical.

Just because diversity jurisdiction exists does not mean the parties will try the case in a federal court. If *Pasta v. Deli* were filed in a California trial court, Deli might decide to contest the case there. The California court would have to make the same choice of law determination as the federal court would. It might well decide Illinois law governed the transaction, in which case the California court would apply the law of Illinois. Every day, courts in one jurisdiction interpret, or *construe,* statutes and constitutional provisions from other jurisdictions. Figure 2.3 illustrates the potential choices.

COURT	PROCEDURAL LAW	SUBSTANTIVE LAW
Illinois State	Illinois	Illinois
Federal in Illinois	Federal	Illinois
California State	California	Illinois
Federal in California	Federal	Illinois

Figure 2.3 Choice of law.
This figure assumes the applicable state substantive law is that of Illinois. In every instance, the applicable rules of civil procedure would be those of the court hearing the matter.

Venue

Jurisdictional laws do not specify the particular courthouse where the plaintiff should file suit. Instead, they indicate which court systems have the power to determine a case and which type and level of court within each system is appropriate for a particular case. *Venue* laws determine which particular court will actually hear the case.

Venue laws protect people from having to appear in places where they have had no contact. Suppose Pasta's lawyer chooses to file in Illinois, since Deli is located in Chicago. Venue will be proper in either the state trial court for Cook County or the U.S. District Court for the Northern District of Illinois, both of which include Chicago. If Pasta filed in another county or district in Illinois, the court would have jurisdiction but Deli probably could have the case transferred to Cook County.

PLEADINGS AND RELATED MOTIONS

Lawsuits are not free-for-alls. Each American jurisdiction has either rules of civil procedure or a code of civil procedure which provides guidelines on how a civil suit is to be conducted in the trial court. The initial steps focus on the *pleadings,* documents which notify the parties and the court of what the case is about. The two main pleadings are the complaint and the answer.

The Complaint and the Answer

Pasta initiates the lawsuit by filing two documents with the trial court: a *complaint* (Figure 2.4) and a *praecipe*. The complaint is a pleading; the praecipe is not. The complaint is a short, plain statement notifying the defendant of the plaintiff's *cause of action,* or claim, and the *relief* the plaintiff demands. Here, Pasta demands $60,000 (the value of the pasta) with interest, as well as its court costs. The praecipe asks the court to issue a *summons* to the defendant. A summons simply orders the defendant to respond to the complaint.

THE UNITED STATES DISTRICT COURT
FOR THE
NORTHERN DISTRICT OF ILLINOIS

PASTA CORPORATION, INC.   :
  11 Upland Road   :
  Los Angeles, Cal.   90057   :
     Plaintiff   :

        v.   : Case No. 93-1014

DELI COMPANY, INC.   :
  151 O'Grady Road   :
  Chicago, Ill.   60628   :
     Defendant   :

COMPLAINT
----

    1.   The Plaintiff is a citizen of the State of California. The Defendant is a citizen of the State of Illinois. The matter in controversy exceeds, exclusive of interest and cost the sum of $50,000. Therefore, the court has jurisdiction over this case pursuant to 28 U.S.C. §1332.

    2.   On June 11, 1992, Plaintiff and Defendant entered into a contract wherein the Plaintiff agreed to supply the Defendant with 60,000 pounds of pasta per month at one dollar ($1.00) per pound.

    3.   On January 15, 1993, Plaintiff shipped Defendant 60,000 pounds of pasta.

    4.   On or about January 17, 1993, the Defendant received the said shipment of 60,000 pounds of pasta for which the Defendant wrongfully refuses to pay.

    WHEREFORE, the Plaintiff demands judgment against the Defendant in the sum of $60,000 and the costs of this action.

                         Pasta Corporation, Inc.
                         By Its Attorney

                         Paul Piper, Esq.
                         Nego & Poso
                         Attorneys At Law
                         1 Constitution Place
                         Los Angeles, Cal.   91779

Figure 2.4 A sample complaint.
Note that "28 U.S.C. §1332" is a reference to the section in the United States Code governing diversity jurisdiction. The reference to "costs" in the final paragraph is to items such as filing fees. It does not refer to the largest item of expense in litigation—attorneys' fees.

THE UNITED STATES DISTRICT COURT
FOR THE
NORTHERN DISTRICT OF ILLINOIS

PASTA CORPORATION, INC.   :
      Plaintiff   :

         v.   : Case No. 93-1014

DELI COMPANY, INC.   :
      Defendant   :

ANSWER AND COUNTERCLAIM

---

1.   The Defendant admits the allegations contained in paragraph 1 of the Complaint.

2.   The Defendant admits the allegations contained in paragraph 2 of the Complaint.

3.   The Defendant lacks information sufficient to form a belief as to the truth of the allegations contained in paragraph 3 of the Complaint regarding the data of the shipment. Otherwise, the paragraph is admitted.

4.   The Defendant admits that it received the said shipment but denies all other allegations coantained in paragraph 4 of the Complaint.

Second Defense

The Defendant received the shipment of pasta in such a condition that it was unfit for human consumption.

Third Defense

The Complaint fails to state a claim on which relief may be granted.

Counterclaim

1.   The Defendant purchased the pasta from the Plaintiff for processing into spaghetti.

Figure 2.5 A sample answer.

2.   The spaghetti ultimately was to be sold under contract to Air Waukegan, Inc. an Illinois corporation.

3.   As a result of Plaintiff's breach of its contract with the Defendant and the Defendant's consequent inability to perform its contract with Air Waukegan, Inc., Air Waukegan cancelled its contract with The Defendant.

4.   The Defendant has lost profits of $15,000.00 as a result of its loss of Air Waukegan's business.

WHEREFORE, the Defendant demands judgment against Plaintiff in the sum of $15,000.00 and its costs in this action.

```
                              Deli Company, Corp.
                              By Its Attorney


                              _____
                              Donna Draper, Esq.
                              Draper, Draper & Lobashevsky
                              Attorneys At Law
                              240 Maine Street
                              Chicago, Ill.   65638
```

Figure 2.5 (Cont.)

Service of process. The *clerk of court,* the court's administrator, attaches the summons to the complaint and either mails them to the defendant or has a law officer, like a sheriff or a marshal, deliver them personally. This delivery procedure is called *service of process.*

If the defendant is not a resident of the state or licensed to do business there, the state's long-arm statute will prescribe the methods of service. The principal method is service by mail. However, if the defendant is from another country, a treaty may specify or limit the means of service. For example, a treaty to which the United States and Germany are parties specifically rejects service by direct mail on German citizens. The documents must be served by the German government, according to its laws, and be written in or translated into German.

Responses to the complaint. The day Deli receives the summons and the complaint, it notifies its lawyer, who tells her client it has 20 days to respond to the complaint. If Deli does not respond, the court may issue a *default judgment* granting the plaintiff the relief it seeks. The response must be either an *answer*—a response to the complaint—or a *motion to dismiss*—a request that the court dispose of the case because of a technical insufficiency.

As Figure 2.5 shows, the answer responds to each of the factual allegations in the complaint. It must also state every defense Deli has to the complaint, whether factual or legal. A factual defense would be that the pasta arrived in an unusable condition. A legal defense would be that service of process was not proper. If Deli omits a defense in its answer, it probably will not be able to raise that defense later.

The answer also may include a counterclaim. A *counterclaim* is simply a cause of action the defendant has against the plaintiff. Suppose Deli bought the pasta for a noodle casserole supplied only to Air Waukegan, Inc., a commuter airline. When Deli failed to deliver the casserole because of Pasta's ruined shipment, Air Waukegan canceled its contract with Deli. As a result, Deli will lose profits of $15,000 this year. Deli would include its claim against Pasta in the answer.

Motions to Dismiss

Pleadings put the parties on notice of the claims and defenses in a lawsuit. *Motions,* by contrast, are the means by which a party asks the court to act. Courts act only by issuing an *order.* Thus, a motion is a request that a court issue an order (see Figure 2.6). An order in response to a motion for an extension of time to file a document may be as simple as the handwritten word "granted" followed by the signature of the judge. Figure 2.7, however, is a more typical order. (Below, Figure 2.8, an appellate court decision, also contains an order.) Almost all written motions (as opposed to oral motions made during a hearing or trial) follow the procedure described in this section.

Making the motion. The rules of civil procedure establish seven motions to dismiss. Six of these ask the court for an order disposing of the case in the defendant's favor for procedural reasons. These *defenses*—reasons why the plaintiff should not prevail—mainly relate to venue, jurisdiction, and the court's ability to decide the dispute as the plaintiff has presented it.

The seventh motion to dismiss alleges the complaint fails to state a claim against the defendant which the law recognizes (see Figure 2.6). This motion attacks the legal sufficiency of the complaint. Defense lawyers use this motion whenever possible because by doing so, even if they do not win the motion, they force the plaintiff to expose its legal theory of the case.

When the defendant makes a motion to dismiss, it must assume the facts alleged in the complaint are true. Thus, the motion does not lead to an examination of the merits of the plaintiffs claim. The rules of civil procedure do not require the defendant to file a motion. However, if Deli believes it has a nonjurisdictional defense of this type, it must assert the defense in either a preanswer motion or an answer, or it waives the defense.

Briefs and oral argument. The motion may be only a page long. But accompanying it is a *brief,* a memorandum containing legal arguments. Despite their name, briefs can run twenty-five pages or longer. Depending on the jurisdiction, Pasta will have from 10 to 21 days in which to respond to the motion with its brief. After Pasta files a response, Deli may file a reply brief.

After all the briefs are filed, the motion is submitted to the court for its consideration. Before deciding the motion, the court may hear *oral argument* from the lawyers, but quite often the judge will act on the documents alone. Most court rules do not specify when a judge must decide a motion, so the decision may take months. When the court does act, it issues an order (see Figure 2.6), sometimes accompanied by a memorandum discussing the applicable precedent and explaining the order, as in Figure 2.8.

If the court grants a motion to dismiss, the case is over in the trial court. The plaintiff may appeal to the intermediate court of appeals. If the court denies a motion to dismiss, the defendant must file an answer, and the case goes forward in the trial court.

THE UNITED STATES DISTRICT COURT
FOR THE
NORTHERN DISTRICT OF ILLINOIS

PASTA CORPORATION, INC.   :
          Plaintiff   :

                                 :

          v.   : Case No. 93-1014

                                 :

DELI COMPANY, INC.   :
          Defendant   :

MOTION TO DISMISS

    Now comes the Defendant, Deli Company, Inc., pursuant to Fed. R. Civ. P. 12(b) (6), and moves the Court for an order dismissing the Complaint in this action on the grounds that it fails to state a claim on which relief may be granted. Accompanying this motion is a brief in support which sets forth fully the grounds for this motion.

Deli Company, Corp.
By Its Attorney

Donna Draper, Esq.
Draper, Draper & Lobashevsky
Attorneys At Law
240 Maine Street
Chicago, Ill.   65638

Figure 2.6 A sample motion to dismiss.
"Fed. R. Civ. P." is the standard legal abbreviation for "Federal Rules of Civil Procedure."

THE UNITED STATES DISTRICT COURT
FOR THE
NORTHERN DISTRICT OF ILLINOIS

PASTA CORPORATION, INC.   :
        Plaintiff   :
                             :
                             :
        v.   : Case No. 93-1014
                             :
DELI COMPANY, INC.   :
        Defendant   :

ORDER

The Defendant in this action, Deli Company, Inc., has moved to dismiss the Complaint pursuant to Fed. R. Civ. P. 12(b) (6) on the grounds that it fails to state a claim on which relief may be granted. Having considered the motion and the briefs of the parties and having heard oral argument, after due deliberation it is

Ordered that the Defendant's motion to dismiss for failure to state a claim is denied, and it is further

Ordered that the Defendant answer the Complaint in this action within twenty (20) days of the date of this order.

_____
U.S. District Judge

Dated: _____, 1993

Figure 2.7 A sample order.

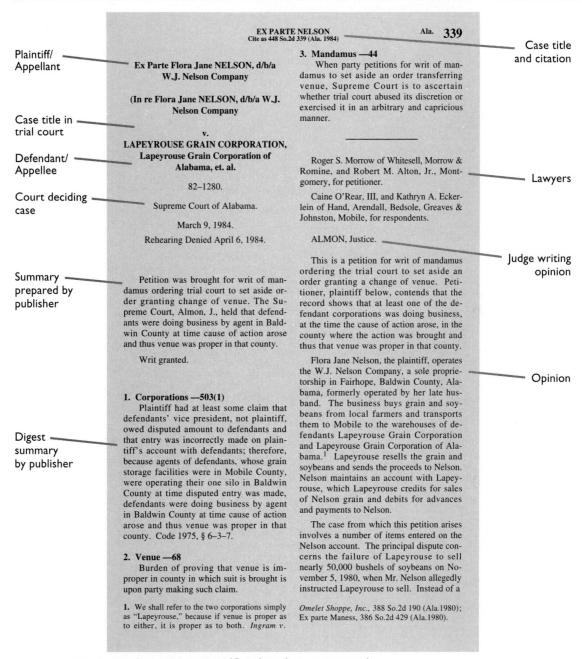

Plaintiff/
Appellant

Case title in
trial court

Defendant/
Appellee

Court deciding
case

Summary
prepared by
publisher

Digest
summary
by publisher

EX PARTE NELSON
Cite as 448 So.2d 339 (Ala. 1984)

Ala. **339**

Case title
and citation

**Ex Parte Flora Jane NELSON, d/b/a
W.J. Nelson Company**

**(In re Flora Jane NELSON, d/b/a W.J.
Nelson Company**

v.

**LAPEYROUSE GRAIN CORPORATION,
Lapeyrouse Grain Corporation of
Alabama, et. al.**

82–1280.

Supreme Court of Alabama.

March 9, 1984.

Rehearing Denied April 6, 1984.

Petition was brought for writ of mandamus ordering trial court to set aside order granting change of venue. The Supreme Court, Almon, J., held that defendants were doing business by agent in Baldwin County at time cause of action arose and thus venue was proper in that county.

Writ granted.

1. Corporations ⟶503(1)
    Plaintiff had at least some claim that defendants' vice president, not plaintiff, owed disputed amount to defendants and that entry was incorrectly made on plaintiff's account with defendants; therefore, because agents of defendants, whose grain storage facilities were in Mobile County, were operating their one silo in Baldwin County at time disputed entry was made, defendants were doing business by agent in Baldwin County at time cause of action arose and thus venue was proper in that county. Code 1975, § 6–3–7.

2. Venue ⟶68
    Burden of proving that venue is improper in county in which suit is brought is upon party making such claim.

1. We shall refer to the two corporations simply as "Lapeyrouse," because if venue is proper as to either, it is proper as to both. *Ingram v.*

3. Mandamus ⟶44
    When party petitions for writ of mandamus to set aside an order transferring venue, Supreme Court is to ascertain whether trial court abused its discretion or exercised it in an arbitrary and capricious manner.

———————

Roger S. Morrow of Whitesell, Morrow & Romine, and Robert M. Alton, Jr., Montgomery, for petitioner.

Caine O'Rear, III, and Kathryn A. Eckerlein of Hand, Arendall, Bedsole, Greaves & Johnston, Mobile, for respondents.

ALMON, Justice.

This is a petition for writ of mandamus ordering the trial court to set aside an order granting a change of venue. Petitioner, plaintiff below, contends that the record shows that at least one of the defendant corporations was doing business, at the time the cause of action arose, in the county where the action was brought and thus that venue was proper in that county.

Flora Jane Nelson, the plaintiff, operates the W.J. Nelson Company, a sole proprietorship in Fairhope, Baldwin County, Alabama, formerly operated by her late husband. The business buys grain and soybeans from local farmers and transports them to Mobile to the warehouses of defendants Lapeyrouse Grain Corporation and Lapeyrouse Grain Corporation of Alabama.[1] Lapeyrouse resells the grain and soybeans and sends the proceeds to Nelson. Nelson maintains an account with Lapeyrouse, which Lapeyrouse credits for sales of Nelson grain and debits for advances and payments to Nelson.

The case from which this petition arises involves a number of items entered on the Nelson account. The principal dispute concerns the failure of Lapeyrouse to sell nearly 50,000 bushels of soybeans on November 5, 1980, when Mr. Nelson allegedly instructed Lapeyrouse to sell. Instead of a

Omelet Shoppe, Inc., 388 So.2d 190 (Ala.1980); Ex parte Maness, 386 So.2d 429 (Ala.1980).

Lawyers

Judge writing
opinion

Opinion

Figure 2.8 A case from a reporter. (Continued on next page.)
Source: Reprinted by permission. West Publishing Co., St. Paul, Minn.

Reporter title

$465,262.66 credit for a sale at that day's market price, Lapeyrouse's books show a continuing storage fee and other charges.

Mrs. Nelson filed this action on January 26, 1983, in the Circuit Court of Baldwin County. Lapeyrouse filed a motion to transfer the action to Mobile County on the grounds that neither corporation was doing business by agent in Baldwin County "at any time relevant to the complaint." The court, after a hearing on the motion, entered an order finding that venue was improper in Baldwin County and transferred the cause to Mobile County. Mrs. Nelson brought this petition for writ of mandamus.

Statute citation

The parties agree that venue of the action is governed by Code 1975, § 6–3–7, which reads pertinent part:

"A foreign corporation may be sued in any county in which it does business by agent, and a domestic corporation may be sued in any county in which it does business by agent or was doing business by agent at the time the cause of action arose . . . ."

Both defendants are domestic corporations, and the dispute is whether they were doing business by agent in Baldwin County at the time the cause of action arose.

[1] Lapeyrouse's offices and storage facilities are in Mobile, except for one silo in Loxley, a community in Baldwin County. Lapeyrouse stopped using this silo in the fall of 1978 or thereafter, but continues to own and maintain it. Mrs. Nelson's complaint alleges that the first item in the account that is in dispute is dated April 14, 1978, in the amount of $36,000. She denies that she owes this amount, while Lapeyrouse contends that she does. Mrs. Nelson argues that because agents of Lapeyrouse were operating the silo in Baldwin County at the time this disputed entry was made, Lapeyrouse was doing business by agent in Baldwin County at the time the cause of action arose and thus that venue was proper in that county.

Lapeyrouse argues that the depositions and the evidence taken at the hearing clearly show that Nelson owes the $36,000.

This entry arises from a personal loan from Nelson to Ann Greenfield, vice president of Lapeyrouse. She repaid the loan with a Lapeyrouse check, and Lapeyrouse contends that Nelson's account was properly debited for this amount. Mrs. Greenfield's deposition, however, indicates that it was common practice for Lapeyrouse officers to informally borrow money from the company by drawing checks, and that Mr. Nelson had reason to know this when he accepted the Lapeyrouse check in payment for the personal loan to Mrs. Greenfield. Nelson thus has at least some claim that Mrs. Greenfield, not Nelson, owes this $36,000 to Lapeyrouse, and that the entry was incorrectly made on Nelson's account in 1978.

[2,3] The burden of proving that venue is improper in the county in which a suit is brought is upon the party making such a claim. *Ingram v. Omelet Shoppe, Inc.*, 388 So.2d 190 (Ala.1980); *Medical Service Administration v. Dickerson*, 362 So.2d 906 (Ala.1978); *Johnson Publishing Co. v. Davis*, 271 Ala. 474, 124 So.2d 441 (1960). When a party petitions for writ of mandamus to set aside an order transferring venue, this Court is to ascertain whether the trial court abused its discretion or exercised it in an arbitrary and capricious manner. *Ex parte Wilson*, 408 So.2nd 94 (Ala. 1981). Under the facts and circumstances of this case, the trial court erred in granting the motion to transfer.

Case citations

The writ of mandamus is therefore due to be granted, and the trial court is hereby ordered to vacate the order transferring the cause to the Circuit Court of Mobile County and to restore the case to the docket in the Circuit Court of Baldwin County.

WRIT GRANTED.

Court's order

All the Justices concur

Court's vote on decision

Figure 2.8 (Cont.)

DISCOVERY

Once Pasta and Deli have filed their pleadings, discovery begins. *Discovery* is a process which permits a party, for the purpose of preparing for trial, to obtain information from the other party. It has three major purposes: to preserve relevant information which otherwise might not be available at trial, to identify which issues the parties really disagree upon, and to determine what evidence exists on each disputed factual issue.*

Scope and Purpose of Discovery

A litigant may use the discovery process to get at information in an opponent's files. Pasta probably will ask Deli to supply all documents in its possession relating to the soggy shipment. The rules encourage a certain amount of "fishing." Besides asking for what Deli intends to use at trial, Pasta can request any documents or ask any question which might lead to evidence admissuable at the trial.

Nothing in the Federal Rules of Civil Procedure compels either party to conduct discovery. Discovery works on the assumption that the adversaries' desire to win will prod them to seek and produce the necessary evidence. However, a court can impose severe penalties on a party for failing to comply with a discovery request—in some cases, the court will enter judgment for the other party.

Discovery also simplifies presenting evidence at the trial. For example, admitted facts do not have to be proved through testimony or documents. The trial court has to resolve only real factual disputes. Also, the parties will have had an opportunity to organize the evidence they will introduce.

After seeing the shape of the case during discovery, the parties may decide to settle with-

out a trial. Deli's attorney, for instance, may realize after questioning Pasta's expert witness under oath—a process called *taking a deposition*—that she will have a difficult time justifying Deli's refusal to pay at least $5000 for the pasta. She may suggest to her client that she work out a settlement with Pasta. Thus, by exposing the strengths and weaknesses of their cases, discovery often leads the parties to compromise without further litigation.

Discovery Techniques

During discovery, a witness or a party answers all questions—written or oral—under *oath*. So, at trial, a party may use discovery material if a witness is unavailable or if there are inconsistencies in testimony. If Pasta's expert says at the trial that he found less than 4 percent of the pasta soggy, Deli's attorney will remind him he said 40 percent in his earlier statement.

Interrogatories. The rules do not require the parties to use discovery methods in any particular order. However, lawyers often begin the process with *interrogatories*—short, highly specific written questions requiring written responses. The lawyer for the opposing party usually drafts the answers to reveal as little as possible. Still, interrogatories are an effective tool for learning basic information, like who Deli's corporate officers are.

Requests for admissions. *Requests for admissions* ask a party to admit or deny facts. For example, Pasta could ask Deli to admit it did not return the soggy pasta. This inexpensive discovery method has an added advantage. If Deli refuses to admit this fact, the court may require Deli to pay Pasta what it costs at trial to prove the statement was true.

Requests for production. *Requests for production* apply to physical evidence. Pasta'a attorney might ask Deli to produce the pasta so that

---

* Adapted from J. J. Cound et al., *Civil Procedure,* 3d ed. (St. Paul, Minn.: West Publ. Co., 1980), pp. 643–644.

an expert can examine it. He might also ask Deli to produce its quality control reports on the pasta so that he can study them. This form of discovery can be quite expensive if traveling and copying massive quantities of documents are involved.

Depositions. By far the most expensive form of discovery, *depositions* offer an opportunity to ask questions directly of a party or a witness. Depositions require painstaking preparation by the lawyer asking the questions. The witness being deposed must also spend considerable time beforehand preparing for the questioning. A key deposition, like that of Pasta's expert, can last several days.

THE PRETRIAL PHASE

Motions for Summary Judgment

Even if discovery does not produce a settlement, it can lead to a resolution without a trial. Suppose Pasta and Deli trade interrogatories and subject some potential witnesses to depositions. After reviewing all the material generated during discovery, Deli's attorney decides no factual issues remain for trial. Her evaluation suggests that even Pasta agrees the shipment was soggy.

On that basis, she files a motion for *summary judgment*. A *judgment* is an order of the court which finally resolves a case. In this context, "summary" implies "shortened" because a summary judgment is one entered without a full-blown trial. In fact, this procedural device was created to eliminate trials of factual issues the parties were not really contesting. Either party can make a motion for summary judgment on one or more issues at any point before trial. It assumes no facts remain in dispute for resolution during a trial. In addition, Deli must show that the law entitles it to judgment in its favor. Pasta's attorney will respond by filing a brief in

opposition supported by *affidavits*—written statements of fact made under oath—or by documentary evidence proving that a factual dispute remains for trial. If he fails to support his brief in this way, the court likely will grant Deli's motion. Many of the cases you will read in this book were decided on motions for summary judgment.

Pretrial Conferences

If the court denies the parties' motions for summary judgment and Pasta and Deli do not settle the case, the parties begin to prepare for the trial. Still, the discovery process should have limited the number of disagreements over facts.

Judges, too, make every effort to limit the issues and evidence for trial. At the *pretrial conference,* the judge meets with the attorneys. If the facts are not really in dispute, but only the damages—here, the amount Pasta lost because Deli did not pay for the pasta—the judge will try to convince the lawyers to agree on the facts so that they will present evidence only on the amount Pasta claims Deli owes.

PROCEDURE AT TRIAL

Every lawsuit involves questions of law and questions of fact. In our system, the court—that is, the judge—decides questions of law. However, in many types of cases the parties have a choice as to the *trier of fact*. The trier of fact, which may be either the judge or a jury, applies the law to the facts.

Jury Selection

In some civil cases, the parties have a right to a jury trial. The jury acts as the fact finder after being instructed by the court on the legal standards it must apply. Either party can demand a jury. the number of jurors varies from five to twelve in civil cases.

The first order of business in a jury trial is selection of the jurors. All prospective jurors are assembled in the courtroom. The court asks them as a group a series of questions to determine whether it should excuse any because they cannot evaluate the evidence impartially. For instance, the judge will ask if any prospective juror has ever worked for Pasta or Deli and will excuse those who have. After the general questioning, the judge then calls each prospective juror for individual questioning. The judge may question each juror personally and then allow the lawyers to question jurors.

Pasta's lawyer might ask a prospective juror if he ever used Pasta's products. If he replies, "Yes, and they're always soggy," the lawyer will *challenge* the juror by moving the court to eliminate him and show *cause* why the prospective juror should be excused because of his prejudice. Additionally, the lawyer can assert a limited number of *peremptory challenges* to dismiss a juror she may not want. In a peremptory challenge the lawyer does not have to explain the prospective juror's removal.

Presenting the Case

A trial has a clear outline: (1) the plaintiff's opening statement, (2) the defendant's opening statement (see below), (3) the plaintiff's presentation of evidence, (4) the defendant's presentation of evidence, (5) the defendant's closing argument, and (6) the plaintiff's closing argument.

The plaintiff's lawyer speaks first and last because the plaintiff has the *burden* of proving its claim. In other words, the plaintiff must establish that the evidence in its favor is more convincing than what the defendant offers and that the evidence warrants granting the relief it seeks.

Opening statements. The presentation of the facts begins with the plaintiff's opening statement. Its lawyer outlines what he intends to prove. When he finishes, Deli's lawyer may make an opening statement. However, she may delay her statement until Pasta completes presenting its evidence.

Presentation of evidence. Following the opening statements, Pasta's lawyer begins questioning witnesses on *direct examination,* the questioning of witnesses by the party which called them. After he completes direct examination of a witness, Deli's lawyer may conduct *cross-examination,* the questioning of a witness by the opposing party. Cross-examination serves many purposes, ranging from simply clarifying statements made on direct examination to discrediting the witness. The plaintiff's lawyer may question the witness again on *redirect examination* to clarify points raised or obscured by the cross-examination.

When Pasta's witnesses have all appeared and all its evidence has been submitted, Deli presents its case and the process is reversed. Following the close of the defendant's case, the court occasionally permits the plaintiff to present rebuttal witnesses if the defendant has introduced evidence the plaintiff wishes to clarify.

Motions for a directed verdict. Following presentation of Pasta's case, Deli may move orally for a *directed verdict.* This motion asks the judge to direct the jury to find in favor of the requesting party because the other party has offered no evidence to support a judgment granting the relief it sought. Pasta might make a similar motion at the close of Deli's case.

Closing arguments. If the motions are denied, the lawyers present their closing arguments— the defendant's case first, then that of the plaintiff. These arguments examine the evidence and suggest the factual conclusions to be drawn from it. The case is then submitted to the trier of fact for decision.

Objections

Objections play an extremely important role in the legal process. An objection lets the court know that it may be making a mistake on a particular point and gives it a chance to correct the situation. Simply saying "I object" is not enough; the lawyer must explain why. For example, Pasta may offer evidence to which Deli's lawyer objects. She tells the court the evidence is of a type the law does not permit the trier of fact to consider because it is not reliable. If the judge sustains her objection, the jury will be told not to consider the evidence. If the court overrules her, the jury may consider Pasta's proof.

The objection and the lawyer's rationale for it also create a record of where the trial court may have erred, which an appellate court can review later. If an attorney fails to make an objection or to explain it clearly, the client loses the right to cite the trial court ruling as an error on appeal, regardless of the importance of the point.

In more than 90 percent of the cases you will read in this book, an appellate court was reviewing the record of proceedings before a trial court. (The appendix to this chapter explains how to read these cases.) The *record* an appellate court reviews usually consists of a typed transcript of the trial prepared from a court reporter's or a tape recorder's transcription *and* the evidence introduced at trial. It may also include the pleadings and other court papers.

Submission

The way a case is submitted for decision depends on whether the trier of fact was a jury or a judge. In a jury trial, the judge instructs the jury on how to evaluate the evidence and on the law to be applied to the facts in reaching a finding, or *verdict*. ("Verdict" comes from a Latin phrase meaning "a true saying.") The lawyers suggest instructions, but the judge decides which to use.

After being instructed, the jury leaves the courtroom to deliberate, returning when it reaches its verdict. In federal courts, the jurors in a civil case must concur unanimously on a verdict unless the parties agree otherwise. Most state courts require only two-thirds or three-quarters of the jurors to agree on a verdict. If the jury cannot reaach a verdict, the case may be retried.

In a case without a jury, the trial ends with the closing statements. Often, the court requests posttrial briefs from the parties. Generally, the judge mails the lawyers her decision some weeks later.

Judgment

The lawsuit ends in the trial court when the court issues an order granting judgment for one of the parties. If the jury found that Deli had no obligation to pay Pasta because Pasta violated their contract, the court simply enters judgment for the defendant. But if the jury found that Pasta had violated the contract and that Deli had suffered damages—lost profits as a result of losing Air Waukegan as a customer—the court inlcudes in its judgment for Deli an award of monetary damages on Deli's counterclaim.

After the verdict or the decision, Pasta can make motions for modification or reconsideration. It can also move for a new trial. If, as usually happens, these motions are denied, the court enters its judgment on the court records and the case is over in the trial court.

APPELLATE PROCEDURE

A losing party in the trial court has a right to an appeal, but only 1 in 7 exercises this right. Normally, a party can appeal only from a judgment. With this rule, parties cannot tie up a case by appealing every trial court ruling. Thus, in our hypothetical case, if the court overrules Deli's objection to some evidence, Deli could not have the trial halted to appeal immediately.

Errors

The *appellant,* the party bringing the appeal, must point to specific errors made by the trial court. An appellate court reviews the written record of the trial court proceedings. It does *not* hear witnesses or admit new evidence. Unlike the trier of fact, it cannot evaluate the demeanor, sincerity, and credibility of the witnesses. An appellate court normally has very limited authority to review a trial court's findings of fact. Unless a finding is clearly erroneous, the appellate court may not set it aside. If the trial court findings are plausible and based on the oral or documentary evidence, a court of appeals may not reverse even though it would have weighed the evidence differently had it been the trier of fact.

Appellate courts focus on the law the trial court applied. For example, in order to win on appeal, Pasta may have to show that over its objection, the court allowed Deli to introduce irrelevant testimony on the private life of Pasta's expert witness which improperly swayed the jury. This is why it is so important for the lawyer to state the rationale for the objection. The lawyer is asking the trial court to make an evaluation of the law which applies to the matter, which an appellate court may later review.

Briefs and Oral Argument

Within 30 days after the trial court enters its judgment, the losing party must file its notice of appeal with the appellate court. Within a month or so, its lawyer files its brief with the court. About a month after the appellant files its brief, the *appellee,* the party that won in the trial court, files its brief. Approximately 2 weeks later, the appellant may file a reply brief.

After the court receives all of the briefs, it typically sets a date for *oral argument,* a presentation to a court almost always made by lawyers in a format much like a debate. The judge or jugdes hearing oral argument may interrupt a party's argument with questions. Often, responding to the questions takes up two-thirds of the 15 to 30 minutes allotted to each side.

Not all appellate courts hear oral arguments on every appeal, though most do. Because of the great increase in litigation in recent years, the Federal Rules of Appellate Procedure now permit the judges assigned to a case to determine that oral argument is not required. Thus far, only three circuits routinely dispose of appeals without oral argument.

Decision

An appeals court does not announce its decision at the conclusion of the oral argument. Some time passes before the court issues its *opinion* and order. Like the lawyers' briefs, the court's opinion evaluates the errors claimed by the appellant, cites legal authorities, and discusses the proceedings before the trial court. Selected appellate opinions and trial court decisions make up the precedent contained in *reporters* (see Figure 2.8).

The appellate court may decide the trial court made a harmless error which did not affect the outcome. If that is the case, or if it finds the trial court acted correctly, the appellate court will *affirm* the decision of the trial court. If it finds the trial court erred to the appellant's detriment, the appellate court may *reverse* the judgment of the trial court and *remand* the case for retrial of some or all of the issues. For instance, the appellate court might affirm the trial court judgment in favor of Deli on Pasta's cause of action and reverse its judgment in favor of Deli on the counterclaim.

Not all errors require a complete retrial. Often, the court of appeals tells the trial court precisely how to handle the remand, so all the trial court must do is follow the order. For instance, the trial court may have misinterpreted the law in finding for Deli, and the court of appeals may remand the case with instructions to enter judgement for Pasta.

Further appeals. A losing party in an intermediate appellate court may appeal to the next appellate level without returning to the trial court. These appeals differ procedurally from initial appeals only in that there are two rounds of briefs. The first round discusses whether the appeal is of such significance that the court must hear it. Most supreme courts in states having intermediate appellate courts take only those cases which require their attention. If the court decides to hear the appeal, the procedure follows that outlined above. Otherwise, the order of the last court to hear the case usually stands.

CONCLUSION

This chapter and the last have looked at how laws come to be, how the courts are organized, and how a case proceeds through the courts. These two chapters provide the framework, the backdrop, for the rest of the course.

This chapter began by pointing out the increasingly important role the courts have had to assume in our society. As other dispute resolution institutions have lost their effectiveness or disappeared, the courts have had to step in. Despite the creative approaches to avoiding litigation which are now appearing, only the creation of new social institutions will diminish the courts' role in the future.

As with so many matters of fundamental justice, the last words should be Abraham Lincoln's. They are drawn from some advice he gave to lawyers on practicing law.

> *Discourage litigation. Persuade your neighbors to compromise whenever you can.*
> *Point out to them how the nominal winner is often a real loser—in fees, expenses, and waste of time. As a peacemaker the lawyer has a superior opportunity of being a good man. There will be business enough.**

---

* "Lincoln on How to Become a Good Lawyer," *General Practice,* June 1989, p. 1.

A NOTE TO FUTURE CPA CANDIDATES

An understanding of professional ethics is very important on the CPA exam. The overview to ethics in this chapter is a starting point. The remainder of material in the chapter historically has not been tested on the CPA exam.

APPENDIX

Cases and Case Briefs

This book uses the authors' digests of reported cases—called "case briefs"—and, on occasion, short excerpts from judges opinions to supplement the text. Since, starting in the next chapter, you will encounter up to ten of these per chapter, a few words are in order on what they are and how they should be read.

Why case briefs? We use case briefs to give you real-life examples of how courts apply the principles we are discussing.

Typically, reported state cases run between five and ten pages. Federal cases tend to be longer; twenty-page opinions are common. With opinions of that length, the courts are not focusing, usually, on a single issue. That is a problem for textbook authors, since the other issues often have nothing to do with the point we want to make. So, in our briefs, we have eliminated all discussion of these other issues. We have also eliminated most citations to precedent, statutes, constitutions, and the like. And we have trimmed the courts' discussions of the facts so that they center on the issue relevant to our discussion. If you would like to read the entire opinion, the citation for each case appears in the brief so that you can look it up.

Figure 2.8 is a case reproduced as it appears in a reporter. We might have briefed it in Chapter 2 to illustrate proper venue. Read the case as it appears in Figure 2.8, and then read the case brief below. This comparison will reveal how we deal with cases throughout the book.

Ex parte Nelson
448 So. 2d 339 (Ala. 1984)

FACTS

In January 1983, Mrs. Nelson brought suit against Lapeyrouse Grain Corp. for money it allegedly owed to the grain business of her late husband. Nelson lived in Baldwin County, Alabama, which was where she filed suit. Lapeyrouse, an Alabama corporation which operated silos, had its offices in Mobile County. One of the transactions at issue had occurred in April 1978. Lapeyrouse, however, ceased operating its silo in Baldwin County in the fall of 1978, though it still owned and maintained it at the time of the suit's filing. Under an Alabama statute, an Alabama corporation can be sued in the trial court of any county in which it is doing business or was doing business at the time the cause of action arose. The trial court granted Lapeyrouse's motion to have the case transferred to Mobile County on the grounds of improper venue.

ISSUE

Was venue proper in Baldwin County?

DECISION

Yes. Reversed. The burden of proving venue is improper rests on the party asserting that claim. Here, the facts indicate Lapeyrouse was doing business in Baldwin County, at least when the cause of action arose.

The omissions. Note what is missing from our case brief. It omits the details of the transactions the parties were litigating, because the particulars do not clarify the principal issue. The trial court had yet to decide the merits of the case, so only the procedural point was before the Alabama Supreme Court.

Because it would involve a lengthy explanation of no relevance to the issue of venue, we also do not mention the writ of mandamus. The plaintiff used this procedural device to appeal the venue ruling before the trial court entered judgment. Granting the writ had the effect of overruling the order of the trial court.

Finally, we do not discuss the "by agent" aspect of the Alabama venue statute. The parties were not arguing about its application. Using the "by agent" language would distract attention from the main factual question: whether—not how—Lapeyrouse did business in Baldwin County.

Case brief format. The case briefs always have the same format. The case name and reporter citation (or citations)* are followed by the facts of the case. Since most of the cases you will read are appellate cases, we indicate in the facts what the trial court's disposition was.

Next, we state the issue which was before the court whose opinion we have briefed. The issue is always stated so that it can be answered "yes" or "no."

The first word following the "Decision" heading tells you how the court decided the

---

* You can tell that a state supreme court decided a case *either* by the abbreviation of the state name in parentheses following a single reporter citation, as in the case above, or by the first of two citations which use just the state abbreviation. For example, *Dwyer v. Farrell,* 193 Conn. 7, 475 A.2d 257 (1984) is a Connecticut Supreme Court case. The abbreviation "Ct. App." in the parentheses or "App." in the first citation would indicate a decision by an intermediate appellate court. Federal district court citations always have a state abbreviation in the parentheses—(D.Me. 1985), for example—while court of appeals citations always contain "Cir."—(10th Cir. 1986), for example. U.S. Supreme Court decisions are always cited to reporters whose abbreviations contain "U.S." or "S. Ct."

issue. Next, we indicate how the court disposed of the case in words you have encountered in this chapter, such as "affirmed," "reversed," or "dismissed." We then state the court's rationale for its holding on the issue.

A final thought. In the reported decisions, we see applications of law to real-world problems. Many times, however, a case has a significance beyond its surface holding. In *Ex parte Nelson,* for instance, the parties did not care about the abstract procedural point. Each wanted the case tried in a county where it thought it had an advantage. Thus, the key to understanding these cases and the way business law works in practice is the question: What are the parties really fighting about? As here, the answer may appear to be "a mere technicality," a venue statute. But these technicalities often express pragmatic solutions to questions of critical concern to litigants.

KEY WORDS

affirm (43)	judgment (40)
answer (30)	jurisdiction (29)
appeal (43)	litigant (23)
appellant (43)	motion (34)
appellee (43)	peremptory chal-
burden (41)	lenge (41)
cause of action (30)	plaintiff (26)
challenge for	pleadings (30)
cause (41)	record (42)
civil procedure (30)	remedy (26)
complaint (30)	trier of fact (40)
defendant (29)	venue (30)
dismiss (33)	verdict (42)
ethics (22)	

DISCUSSION QUESTIONS

1. How do arbitration and mediation differ from litigation?
2. What are the three aspects of "jurisdiction," and how do they interrelate?
3. Describe the distinctions between judrisdiction and venue.
4. What are the rules of civil procedure, and what do they regulate?
5. Which documents comprise the pleadings, and when are they filed? What purposes do pleadings serve?
6. Describe the differences between motions and pleadings.
7. What are the principal forms of discovery? Describe the goals of the discovery process.
8. What are the differences between a motion to dismiss and a motion for summary judgment?
9. Compare and contrast an order and a judgment.
10. What matters will appellate courts consider on appeal?

CASE PROBLEMS

1. Miracle Microchip, a small computer company, sued Complex Computers, alleging Complex had stolen some of its designs and tried to drive it out of business. Miracle demanded a jury trial. The jury—composed mainly of retirees—heard 8 months of technical testimony from electronics engineers, economists, and numerous other experts. After some days of deliberation, the jury reported it could not reach a verdict because of the complexity of the factual determinations. What should the judge do? Would a judge necessarily be better able to determine the facts? State the policy reasons for your answer.
2. Colossal Cars introduced a new engine in its 1992 models. It was an immediate success and Colossal sold 800,000 cars equipped with it. Unfortunately, after 12,000 miles, the engines usually fell apart. The Federal Trade Commission refused to make Colossal recall the cars. Instead, it permitted Colossal to arbitrate individual consumer complaints. The hearings will be private, and the results of one will not serve as precedent in another. You own one of these lemons. Your lawyer tells you to sue, rather than to arbitrate, because the combina-

tion of precedents in your favor and discovery techniques makes a large recovery probable. However, litigation may take at least 2 years, even without an appeal, and discovery will be expensive. Which remedy will you choose? Why?

3. Arnie lives in Arizona. He decides to drive to Seattle for his vacation. While Arnie is stopped for gas in Jackson, Wyoming, the sheriff serves him with a summons and a complaint in a case brought against him in a Wyoming court by one of his many creditors. Arnie had never been in Wyoming before; he and his creditor had done their business in Texas. What would be Arnie's best legal recourse? Explain.

4. At trial, Munchausen's testimony for the defense directly contradicted Lincoln's testimony for the plaintiff. In order to find for the defendant, the jury had to accept the testimony of Munchausen and reject that of Lincoln. The court of appeals has reviewed the record and heard oral argument. It finds Munchausen's testimony incredible, but it can find no errors committed by the trial court. What can the court do? State the policy reasons for your answer. How would your answer be different if it were the trial judge who found Munchausen's testimony incredible and who had before him the plaintiff's motion for judgment notwithstanding the verdict?

5. Isabel Archer sued Henry James for breach of promise which she said resulted in $7500 in damages. She filed suit in a U.S. district court, alleging diversity of citizenship as the sole ground for jurisdiction. Henry's lawyer wants to file a motion to dismiss. Does he have good grounds for one? Explain.

6. Eileen brought suit against her employer after he promoted a less qualified male, instead of her, to be sueprvisor of her department. A prospective juror when asked what he thought about women working in offices, said, "A woman's place is in the home." Explain what Eileen's lawyer should do.

7. While driving in Cincinnati, Jack Peterson was severely injured when his car was struck by a car negligently operated by Glenn Men-ovich. Menovich lives in Illinois and Peterson in Iowa. Assuming at least $50,000 in damages is alleged, list the state and federal courts that might appropriately hear Peterson's suit against Menovich and which jurisdiction's substantive law each court would apply. Then, assume that a passenger in Menovich's car may have caused the accident when he jokingly grabbed the wheel while the car was moving. The passenger, Dick Shuldt, lives in Illinois. Explain how and why Shuldt's status as a defendant affects the list.

8. Tom Lillie sued Boyden's Tire Co. for its failure to deliver 100 tires he had ordered. Boyden received the complaint but decided to ignore it, since Lillie was completely in the wrong and Boyden did not have the time or money to waste on a lawsuit. A few months passed. One day, Boyden received notice that the court had entered judgment in favor of Lillie and awarded him danages. Boyden got angry and put in a call to his attorney. What is his attorney likely to tell him? If Boyden decides to appeal, what is an appellate court likely to hold? Explain your answer.

9. Real Issues. It is estimated that the United States has almost 800,000 licensed lawyers, one for every 300 Americans. In addition, there is an estimated 281 lawyers per 100,000 population versus 111 for Great Britain, 82 for Germany, and 11 for Japan. (Source: *Time Magazine*, August 26, 1992, p. 54.) As a result, some commentators claim that the United States legal system is undermining our country's ability to be more competitive in today's global economy. Others argue that the business successes of Toyota, Honda, and other Japanese firms in the United States seriously undermine this common assertion. They contend that many United States companies, such as General Motors, IBM, or Westinghouse, have lost their competitive edge more from management lapses than legal entanglements. Your thoughts?

10. Real Issues. In Great Britain, and many other industrial nations, the loser in a civil suit is required to pay the victor's legal bill. This approach, called the English system of advo-

cacy, has been advocated for the United States legal system. In support of this position, advocates point out that the United States has 30 times as many malpractice claims and 100 times as many product claims as does Great Britain. (Source: *Forbes Magazine*, March 18, 1991, p. 96.) Do you believe that the English system might effectively discourage people from filing suits without a strong, definite case? Does it seem fair? Your thoughts.

CHAPTER 3

The Constitution and Government Regulation of Business

What would you call a local, state, or federal unit in the executive branch that may have legislative, judicial, *and* law enforcement powers? An impossibility? After all, separation of the legislative, judicial, and executive branches—the *separation of powers*—is essential to our system of government. Yet such government units exist. They are called *administrative* or *regulatory agencies*.

Administrative agencies affect virtually every area of commerce. Consider these examples in your immediate surroundings:

- A local building department probably approved the plans for the building in which you are sitting.
- A state public utilities commission determined the rates for the electricity used to light the room in which you are sitting.
- The chair in which you are sitting had to meet federal Consumer Product Safety Commission standards.
- The U.S. Department of Agriculture set production quotas on the peanuts you may be snacking on.

It is nearly impossible to make useful generalizations about the substantive functions of a class of entities which includes the Justice Department, the National Aeronautics and Space Administration (NASA), the Utah Public Service Commission, and the Boston Water and Sewer Commission. For that reason, this chapter concentrates not on what administrative agencies do but on what they are, how they came to be, what powers they commonly have, and how they operate.

In order to understand the role of agencies in our legal system, some knowledge is necessary of the historical and constitutional forces which shaped the agencies. To a large extent, their history is the history of modern business regulation, which is part of our focus in this section of the book. But before looking at how agencies came to be what they are, let us first explore their nature today.

THE NATURE OF ADMINISTRATIVE AGENCIES

All administrative agencies are created by constitution or statute—never by the common law —and have defined, limited purposes. Beyond those characteristics, we can identify a number of functions which *may* be delegated to agencies. We can also describe three structural models common among agencies. In this section, agencies' authority, functions, and structures are our main concerns.

Agency Authority

An administrative agency receives its authority to act from a statute referred to as its *enabling act*.* An enabling act delegates certain tasks to an agency, as in the case of state workers' compensation boards, which award disability benefits for injuries suffered on the job. While later statutes can expand, shrink, or abolish its powers, the agency itself cannot take on anything aside from what the law assigns it. Other aspects of an agency's authority are discussed below in the context of conflicts between federal and state programs.

Functions

Administrative agencies can have quasi-legislative, quasi-judicial, and administrative functions. An agency's enabling act can assign the agency one, two, or all three of these functions.

Quasi-legislative activities. Many statutes authorize agencies to issue, or *promulgate*, rules and regulations. "Rules" and "regulations" are synonyms. Administrative rules read like stat-

---

* Often, a single agency is assigned substantive functions by more than one act. However, when an agency's power and responsibilities are discussed, the singular "enabling act" is used. It is important to note that administrative procedure acts, which are discussed in the last half of this chapter, are not enabling acts.

utes and—with an important exception—can be categorized in the same manner as statutes were in Chapter 1. The exception is that all regulations are civil. However, by statute the legislative branch can prescribe criminal penalties for willful violations of agency regulations. The regulation itself remains civil in nature.

Since the agency's enabling act usually gives rules the force of law, their adoption fulfills a *quasi-legislative* function. The courts give great weight to rules, though not as much as to statutes, because they reveal how the agency charged with administering a statute defines its responsibilities. The way agencies adopt regulations is discussed below.

Quasi-judicial activities. Some agencies, such as the Federal Communications Commission (FCC), have *quasi-judicial* powers to conduct trial-like hearings to resolve disputes or to enforce their enabling acts. Their jurisdiction is, of course, limited by their enabling acts and is strictly civil. Usually, the agency's staff initiates enforcement proceedings. Thus, as we will see below, different elements of the same agency can act as plaintiff and as judge.

An administrative agency does not necessarily have quasi-judicial powers to resolve disputes arising under its enabling act. A state division of forestry may have authority to regulate the use of state timberlands but may have to file court actions to resolve disputes. The Securities and Exchange Commission (SEC), which regulates the issuing and trading of stocks and bonds, falls into this category. This chapter closes with an examination of quasi-judicial proceedings.

Administrative activities. Even agencies authorized to decide disputes or adopt rules may devote relatively little time to performing these functions compared with the time they spend carrying on their other responsibilities. These activities are so varied that they cannot be categorized. In this part, they will simply be called "administrative activities." For instance, the primary efforts of the Social Security Administration go toward sending out millions of checks each month, conducting investigations and medical examinations of claimants, providing advice to prospective beneficiaries, and processing vast quantities of information.

A business law course focuses on the quasi-judicial and quasi-legislative functions of administrative agencies because these functions are what shape the law. But keep in mind that these activities often make up a very small part of what an agency does.

Three Structural Models

Already in this chapter we have mentioned entities called administrations, agencies, authorities, boards, commissions, departments, and divisions. We could have cited others called bureaus, offices, and services. You might logically—but wrongly—assume each of these ten words describes a particular type of agency structure. Most jurisdictions apply these names to agencies without regard for their structure or their relationships to other agencies.

Because administrative agencies perform such varied functions, it is impossible to fit them all into one structural model or even into the three we have devised. Thus, when we refer below to the department, authority, and independent agency models, we are drawing clear distinctions for comparison's sake where few pure examples exist.

The department model. The U.S. Constitution calls for the President to head an executive branch consisting of a number of departments. Each department is in the charge of a cabinet officer whom the President appointed to serve during his administration. The Constitution left the number, structure, and functions of the departments up to Congress.* State constitutions,

---

* The U.S. Constitution mentions only the Treasury Department by name.

by contrast, have tended to be more specific as to which departments shall exist.

The department model is the oldest of the three models. On the state and federal levels, departments also tend to be the largest agencies. As needs arose, Congress assigned to departments duties which more or less fit with what they were already doing. Over the years, some have received a bewildering mix of assignments. (The states have done a much better job of maintaining the functional integrity of departments.) The U.S. Department of Commerce, for instance, contains offices dealing with international trade, the Bureau of the Census, and the National Weather Service. It also shares responsibility with the Interior Department for administration of the Endangered Species Act.

This list of Commerce's responsibilities reveals what is perhaps the crucial characteristic of departments: they usually contain smaller agencies. However, the ultimate decision-making authority rests with the head of the department.

The authority model. The most significant difference between the authority model and the department model is that authorities are more narrowly focused. Some, like the U.S. Environmental Protection Agency (EPA), have a number of related functions, while others, like electric power authorities, do only one thing. For that reason, unlike departments, authorities do not normally function as a group of agencies under one head.

Like a department, however, an authority is hierarchical. Ultimate responsibility in EPA, for instance, rests with its administrator, appointed in the same manner and for the same term as the secretary of a department. But not all authorities have a single individual at their head. Many port, mass transit, and public building authorities are headed by boards of directors or by commissioners chosen by the chief executive and confirmed by a legislative body.

The independent agency model. The third structural model is the independent agency, so called because it is not in the chain of command of the executive branch. In other words, an independent agency is not under the direct control of the chief executive. Also, its enabling act usually attempts to insulate the agency from politics.

An independent agency is usually called a *board* or *commission*. The board of regents of a state university system, the Interstate Commerce Commission (ICC), the Federal Trade Commission (FTC), and a state public facilities commission are examples. These agencies have the most specific jurisdiction and virtually never have subdivisions which function like agencies.

In virtually every case, multimember boards or commissions head independent agencies. Federal law and most state laws require that appointees to multimember panels be split between the political parties. So a statute might require that of the five members of a state public facilities commission, no more than three may belong to the same party. Also, their terms of office are usually staggered so that a president or governor cannot replace all the members of a board at once.

In theory, party quotas and staggered terms make multimember boards less subject to partisanship and provide continuity in regulation. In practice, a new chief executive often has the power to designate the chair of an independent agency. The chair controls agendas and hiring. Early resignations and the passage of time often allow wholesale changes. A quick glance at the discussion of the National Labor Relations Board in Chapter 45 will illuminate this point.

Agency structures in the future. No trend exists toward one model or away from one. Agencies are created in forms which satisfy political needs. For example, President Carter kept his 1976 campaign promise to demonstrate his commitment to education by creating a Department of Education. He convinced Congress to move responsibility for education from what is now the Department of Health and Human Services to the new department. An authority would not have had the symbolic prominence of a cabinet department.

Political necessity has always been the reason for establishing new administrative agencies. Thus, agencies symbolize our government's capacity to respond to changing social and economic conditions. Historically, Congress created independent agencies—like the ICC, SEC, NLRB, and FTC—in response to demands for regulation of the marketplace. Today, regulation permeates every area of business. To see how this came about, let us turn now to how agencies gained their position and power in our system.

THE POWER TO REGULATE

Administrative agencies have become such a part of the fabric of our society that it is difficult to imagine our government without them. Yet 100 years ago, when the first independent agencies appeared, the entire concept seemed foreign and, many people strongly argued, unconstitutional.

As noted in the beginning of this chapter, the quasi-legislative and quasi-judicial functions of modern administrative agencies simply do not fit the model dictated by the separation of powers doctrine. But the controversy over the power of the legislative branch to create such agencies was not theoretical.

The modern administrative agency came into existence as a counterbalance to the rising power of transportation companies and other concentrations of economic power. Thus, the question of the proper role for agencies was part of a much larger controversy over the scope of government regulation of business. It is no exaggeration to say that the results of this

ongoing debate have reshaped American government.

Delegation

In order to put the debate over administrative agencies in proper perspective, we must go back another 100 years to the drafting of the Constitution. Among other things, a constitution defines the relationship between the governed and their government. The Tenth Amendment to the U.S. Constitution describes it thus:

> *The powers not delegated to the United States by the Constitution, nor prohibited by [the Constitution] to the States, are reserved to the States . . . , or to the people.*

All power to regulate activity originates with the people, the governed. They delegate it—via constitutions—first to the states and then to the federal government.

Under all American constitutions, the power to initiate regulation rests with the legislative branch. The major battle over administrative agencies was fought over whether the legislative branch could redelegate a part of this power to agencies. And it was fought first in the states.

The Police Powers

A state's power to regulate business comes from what are called its *police powers* to protect the health, safety, morals, and general welfare of its citizens. In theory, a state's police powers are broader even than the powers conferred on the federal government by the U.S. Constitution.

Initially, many state courts found redelegations of quasi-legislative powers to administrative agencies impossible to accept constitutionally. Today, all state constitutions permit the enactment of statutes under the police powers which delegate quasi-legislative authority to administrative agencies. However, legislatures cannot delegate to these agencies the power to create law.

The issue of whether Congress can delegate its legislative power to agencies in the executive branch of the federal government also has been a disputed question. Broad powers can be delegated by statute to administrative agencies today to carry out certain specified, but often very general, commands. The following case is an extreme example of how broad and controversial these delegated powers can be.

Hirabayashi v. United States

320 U.S. 81 (1942)

FACTS

Gordon Hirabayashi was a University of Washington student and native-born American of Japanese heritage. On May 16, 1942, he was arrested for defying a military order which required all persons of Japanese ancestry to register for evacuation to relocation centers in California and Arkansas, and for disobeying a curfew order. Several months earlier, Congress had passed the Act of March 21, 1942 which approved an earlier executive order directing the military commander to protect war resources "against espionage and sabotage."

ISSUE

Was the broad command made by Congress in the Act of 1942 to the military commander an unconstitutional delegation of its legislative power?

DECISION

No, conviction affirmed. When standards are set up to guide the administrative officer, in this case the military commander, and when these orders conform to the legislative standards set forth by Congress, then there is no unconstitutional delegation of the legislative function. The standards must be based upon the disclosure of facts by a government representative. In this case, it was found that there are 112,000 Japanese-Americans concentrated in Washington, Oregon, and California. There is support for the view that their solidarity has prevented them from "assimilation as an integral part of the white population." In addition, it is generally believed that Japanese language schools are sources of "Japanese nationalistic propaganda, cultivating allegiance to Japan."

The *Hirabayashi* case, although deplorable in outcome, and severely criticized both at the time and since, must be evaluated in the context of its era—World War II. Often constitutional concerns are subordinated to the critical task of defense during wartime. Even so, very broad powers have and continue to be routinely conferred to administrative agencies in the executive branch of federal government to carry out policy objectives. Indeed, the immense and complex responsibilities of the federal government today require delegation. In peacetime, however, the actions of Congress and the agencies are given greater scrutiny by the courts when constitutional issues arise.

The Commerce Clause

The source of the constitutional power of Congress to regulate economic activity is Article I §8(3), the *commerce clause*. A more descriptive name for this clause would be the "interstate" commerce clause because it grants Congress the exclusive power to "regulate commerce with foreign nations, and among the several States." Thus, a state cannot constitutionally regulate rates on rail shipments which either originate at or are bound for a point beyond its borders.

Congress, however, felt the same political pressures as the state legislatures. In 1887, it responded by creating the Interstate Commerce Commission (ICC), whose original function was regulating interstate railroads. The ICC was the first important federal independent agency.

What is interstate commerce? Certainly, every business activity which crosses a state line is involved in *interstate commerce*. But congressional authority to regulate does not depend on the actual crossing of a state boundary. Rather, the test is whether an activity affects commerce among the states.

The affectation doctrine. Under the *affectation doctrine,* Congress may regulate an activity if it has some appreciable effect—whether direct or indirect—on interstate commerce. Thus, activities may still affect interstate commerce though they appear wholly *intrastate*—within a state's boundaries.

Congress often uses the number of persons employed by an enterprise as a benchmark of interstate commerce. For instance, under workplace antidiscrimination provisions of the 1964 Civil Rights Act, any employer of fifteen or more persons is presumed to affect interstate commerce. However, congressional use of the benchmark approach in some statutes does not mean that a definable minimum exists in all cases. The next case—a classic—shows that Congress can reach even the smallest commercial unit with an appropriate regulatory scheme.

Wickard v. Fillburn

317 U.S. 111 (1942)

FACTS   In 1938, Congress passed the Agricultural Adjustment Act, whose goal was to stabilize agricultural prices and thereby provide farmers with a reasonable return for their efforts. The Secretary of Agriculture (Wickard) set annual national acreage allotments for wheat, and the allotments were then apportioned by state and ultimately by farm. Fillburn raised cattle and chickens. In 1941, he also grew 23 acres of winter wheat, some of which he fed his animals and some of which he sold. However, Fillburn's 1941 allotment was only 11.1 acres. The Department imposed a penalty of $117.11. Fillburn sought an injunction against enforcement of the penalty, claiming his wheat production and consumption were purely local. The Secretary showed that wheat grown for a farmer's own use amounted to more than 20 percent of all the wheat grown nationally.

ISSUE

Was the wheat Fillburn raised for his own use beyond the reach of federal regulation?

DECISION

No. Reversed. The Act's goal was to stabilize market prices of commodities by limiting volume. Therefore, because of its effect on price and market conditions, Congress must have the power to regulate grain grown for a farmer's own consumption. Even though Fillburn's activity was local and might not be regarded as commerce, Congress could regulate it because of the cumulative effect of all the "Fillburns" on interstate commerce.

As *Wickard* established, merely characterizing an activity as "local" does not remove it from the regulatory reach of Congress. An activity cannot be evaluated in a vacuum. It must be placed in the context of similar activity nationwide.

Congress also can reach intrastate activities which affect channels of interstate commerce. For example, a small motel on a state highway, used mainly by residents of the state in which it is located, is involved in interstate commerce. A restaurant which serves food transported in interstate commerce is itself active in interstate commerce. And a gangster who used the mails to send an extortion note from downtown Chicago to one of its suburbs committed a federal crime because he used an interstate channel of communication. Even though Congress may reach this far in its legislation, it may choose not to. In the following case, the Supreme Court limited the ability of states to impose a use tax on sales from out-of-state firms engaged in mail order business.

Quill Corp. v. North Dakota

119 L. Ed. 2d 91 (1992)

FACTS

North Dakota passed a use tax on all property purchased for storage, use or consumption in that state. All "retailers," defined as "every person who engaged in regular or systematic solicitation of a consumer market in the state," must collect the tax from state consumers and remit it to the state. This definition included businesses which advertised three or more times in North Dakota within a 12-month period. Quill, a Delaware corporation, made annual sales of nearly $1 million to about 3000 North Dakotans, but had no offices, warehouses, or employees in that state. *All* business was transacted by mail or common carrier. The trial court ruled in favor of Quill. The North Dakota Supreme Court reversed, holding that the use tax did not violate the commerce clause of the U.S. Constitution.

ISSUE

Does North Dakota's law violate the Commerce Clause by imposing a use tax on sales from an out-of-state firm which conducts business in that state only by mail or common carrier?

DECISION   Yes. Reversed. North Dakota's law violates the commerce clause since the only
connection between North Dakota and Quill is by common carrier or the U.S. mail.
This relationship lacks the "substantial nexus" necessary under the commerce clause.
Some physical presence must exist in North Dakota for the use tax to be legal. The
framers of the Constitution intended the commerce clause to bar state regulations,
including taxes, which unduly burden interstate commerce.

The *Quill* case brings up a number of interesting issues. One is the desire by the Supreme Court to create a "bright-line" demarcation between a legal or illegal use tax imposed on out-of-state businesses. The Court conceded that the requirement of some physical presence, such as a small sales force, plant or office, might be artificial. However, it felt this admittedly spurious distinction was more than offset by the benefits of a clear rule for states and businesses to follow. Indeed, the Court contended that the "settled expectations" created by its rule, first articulated in 1967 and now reaffirmed in *Quill,* had greatly contributed to the enormous success of the mail-order business.

Regulatory Conflicts

Given the breadth of the police powers and the reach of the commerce clause, regulatory conflicts between the states and the federal government are inevitable. However, the commerce clause does not prohibit the states from regulating activities which affect interstate commerce. The Supreme Court has held that only those state regulations which unduly impede or restrain the free flow of goods and those which conflict with federal regulations are impermissible.

Conflicts between regulatory schemes. Regulatory schemes for different states can conflict without either being invalid. For example, some states—like Texas—require that children under a certain age be strapped into safety seats while a motor vehicle is moving. A valid exercise of the state's police powers, safety seat requirements protect children from serious injuries. But suppose state A required child seats and state B did not. A car registered in state B carries an infant not in a safety seat into state A. State A could prosecute the driver. Here, a uniform national policy would clarify an individual's duties, but it is not constitutionally required, even though the safety seat law may affect interstate travel.

The next case presents a variation on the infant seat example.

Healy v. Beer Institute, Inc.

109 S.Ct. 2491 (1989)

FACTS   The state of Connecticut discovered it was losing tax revenue because its residents
often bought liquor in an adjoining state. Beer in Connecticut consistently cost more
than in neighboring states. A 1984 Connecticut law required out-of-state shippers of
beer into that state to affirm that the prices posted each month with the state
Department of Liquor Control were no higher than prices in bordering states at the
time of posting. The statute also made it unlawful for distributors to sell beer in

Connecticut at a price higher than the price at which beer is or would be sold in any bordering state during the month covered by the Connecticut posting. A beer industry group challenged the statute's constitutionality. The district court upheld the statute, but the court of appeals reversed. The court of appeals held that the Connecticut statute's interaction with Massachusetts' pricing statute had the effect of controlling prices in Massachusetts. The distributors could tie their competitive pricing to the competitive realities of either Massachusetts or Connecticut, but not both, because the latter's statute tied prices to those of the bordering states. Since Massachusetts permits volume discounts but Connecticut does not, Connecticut's affirmation scheme discourages this pricing method because the lowest of the volume-discounted prices would have to be offered as the regular price for an entire month in Connecticut. Therefore, the court of appeals held, the statute was void because it had the effect of controlling commercial activity occurring wholly outside of Connecticut's borders.

ISSUE

Does a state statute that controls commercial activity in adjacent states violate the commerce clause of the U.S. Constitution?

DECISION

Yes. Court of appeals affirmed. The Constitution reflects a special concern with the maintenance of a national economic union unfettered by state-imposed limitations on interstate commerce and with the autonomy of the states within their borders. The Supreme Court's prior cases in this area stand for three propositions. First, a state statute may not apply to commerce that takes place wholly outside of the enacting state's borders, whether or not the regulated activity affects commerce within that state. In particular, a state may not enact laws that have the practical effect of setting prices in other states. Second, such a statute is invalid whether or not the legislature intended it to have its extraterritorial effect. And third, a court must evaluate the statute's practical effect by considering the consequences not only of the statute itself but also of the statute's interactions with regulatory schemes in other states. The court of appeals correctly applied all these tests in holding that the Connecticut statute violated the commerce clause.

The *Healy* case is an excellent example of how some states attempt to pass statutes which appear to promote a reasonable state goal under their police powers, when in fact they are really trying to protect their own businesses from another state's competition. Connecticut was not only seeking to protect its tax revenues, but was attempting to protect in-state businesses as well. Similar politically motivated regulatory schemes have been tried by a number of states, particularly to protect agribusinesses such as the state's dairy industry.

A vast area exists in which both the states and the federal government can regulate, so long as the state regulation is consistent with the federal goals. Where both a state and the federal government have regulated in an area and the regulations differ but do not conflict in purpose, the courts usually enforce the stricter regulation. For example, California has set stricter automobile emission controls than EPA has set for the rest of the country.

On the other hand, a state also may not always regulate in certain areas even though the federal government has not elected to do so. If state A decides that all trucks passing through it must submit to an expensive and time-consuming safety inspection, the courts may consider the state's regulation an "undue burden" on interstate commerce. The regulation will be deemed unconstitutional even though the state is promoting the legitimate goal of fostering safety under its police powers.

The supremacy clause and preemption. If state and federal regulations conflict, the Constitution's *supremacy clause*, Article VI §2, requires that the courts give effect to the federal requirement. The supremacy clause states:

> *This Constitution, and the laws of the United States which shall be made in pursuance thereof; and all treaties made, or which shall be made, under the authority of the United States, shall be the supreme law of the land; and the judges in every State*

> *shall be bound thereby, any thing in the Constitution or laws of any State to the contrary notwithstanding.*

The effect the supremacy clause can have on state regulatory powers is called *preemption*. Preemption occurs when Congress so provides or when the courts find state regulation to be inconsistent with federal regulation. It applies not only to state administrative regulations but also to statutes and common law. Local regulations, such as the New York City ordinance forbidding transportation of nuclear waste materials within the city's boundaries, can also conflict with federal regulations and be void. In the following case, the U.S. Supreme Court was asked to determine whether two federal statutes, requiring cigarette manufacturers to warn consumers about their product's health hazards, preempts a claim for damages under a state's tort law.

Cipollone v. Liggett Group, Inc.

112 S. Ct. 2608 (1992)

FACTS   Rose Cipollone began smoking in 1942 and continued to smoke until her lung was removed in 1983. She died in 1984. Before her death, Cipollone and her husband filed a complaint in federal court alleging that the defendant cigarette manufacturers had: (1) failed to provide adequate warnings about the dangers of cigarette smoking; (2) expressly warranted that smoking did not create significant health risks; (3) willfully, through their advertising, neutralized federally mandated warning labels and had ignored medical and scientific data about the hazards of cigarette smoking; and (4) engaged in a conspiracy to deny the public of the data. As one of their defenses, the cigarette manufacturers argued that two federal statutes, the Federal Cigarette Labeling and Advertising Act of 1965 and the Public Health Cigarette Smoking Act of 1969, both preempted the use of a state's common law claims for recovery of damages. Their contention was that these statutes established a uniform warning throughout the country that protects the manufacturers from being subjected to varying state laws. The district court ruled in the cigarette manufacturers' favor that these claims were preempted. The court of appeals affirmed the lower court.

ISSUE   Did the two federal statutes which required warning labels on packs of cigarettes preempt all of the Cippolones' common law claims?

DECISION   No. Reversed in part, and affirmed in part. The Supreme Court agreed with the lower court's ruling that the Cipollones' contention that the cigarette manufacturers had failed to warn adequately of the dangers of smoking was preempted by the 1969 act. This claim was preempted under the 1969 act, which stated that: "No requirement or prohibition based on smoking and health shall be imposed under state law with respect to the advertising or promotion of any cigarettes the packages of which are labeled." The other three claims, however, are not preempted. The claim of a breach of express warranties arises from a voluntary contractual duty and so is not a "requirement under state law." The claim of willful fraud by false representation and concealment of material facts is not preempted, since it involves a more general duty not to deceive and not a duty based only on smoking and health. Finally, the claim of conspiracy among the manufacturers to misrepresent or conceal material facts about smoking's hazards is not preempted because this state claim is also not based solely on smoking or health. There is a strong presumption against preemption of state police power regulations by federal law, permitting the above actions to be now actionable under state law.

After the Supreme Court issued the above decision on the issue of preemption, *Cippolone* was remanded (sent back) to the trial court to decide, based on the facts of the case, if any of the three permitted common law actions might apply. In November 1992 Rose Cippolone's case was unexpectedly dismissed by her son. After 8 years of intense and expensive litigation, Cippolone's estate apparently received nothing. Although no reason was given, commentators felt that the cost of continuing for the plaintiff attorneys, retained on a contingent fee basis, was too great. Indeed, Cippolone's law firm had incurred $1 million by the time of the dismissal. In another setback for the plaintiff, the federal district judge, who had originally presided over the case, was recused (disqualified) by the Third U.S. Circuit Court of Appeals for giving the appearance of partiality against the defendant tobacco companies. It is now quite likely that other plaintiffs and their counsel will follow suit, since the expense of taking on the tobacco industry in a protracted lawsuit is clearly a serious economic undertaking.

The *Cippolone* decision might also be construed by future courts to preempt certain state actions when other federal labeling statutes are involved. For example, federal statutes now regulate how insecticides, fungicides, and rodenticides are to be labeled, as well as the warnings that currently appear on alcoholic beverages.

Indirect preemption. The federal government can preempt even in those areas which clearly fall within the state's police powers. In these instances, the federal government achieves its goal indirectly, usually through financial penalties. When Congress became concerned about drunk driving, it did not legislate directly. Rather, it instructed the Federal Highway Administration and the Department of Transportation to cut off funds to states which did not adopt 21 as the drinking age. Still, indirect preemption does not deprive the state of the power to regulate. The state may decide to forgo the federal financial incentive and maintain its own regulations. In practice, of course, this rarely happens.

Quite often, Congress's informal preemption scheme requires the federal agency to issue rules to implement the statute. That brings us back to where we began: the administrative agency and how it operates.

The Administrative Procedures Act

Until 1946, no statute prescribed uniform procedures for federal agencies. Each agency went its own way within the limits of its enabling act. Rules of evidence, for instance, varied from agency to agency. Courts, scholars, and lawyers criticized this lack of uniformity, but it took almost a decade for a consensus to develop on what should be done. The result, the federal Administrative Procedures Act (APA), outlines basic procedures all agencies must observe. Individual agencies may adopt further procedures consistent with the APA to fit their particular needs.

Every state also has its own administrative procedures act. The older state statutes tend to follow the federal act closely, but recent amendments diverge from the model. Nonetheless, the APA and the case law interpreting it remain highly influential among the states. For that reason, in the following examination of how agencies promulgate rules and decide disputes, agency functions are discussed in terms of the APA.

THE QUASI-LEGISLATIVE PROCESS

The quasi-legislative process, as noted earlier, is the process by which agencies adopt rules. An agency can promulgate only substantive and procedural regulations authorized by its enabling act. (The APA is not an independent source of rule-making authority. Rather, it describes how an agency may exercise the powers Congress granted it.)

The APA defines a rule as ''an agency statement of general or particular applicability and future effect designed to compliment, interpret or prescribe law or policy.'' Thus, rules are like statutes. They usually affect all those subject to them and set standards for future conduct. By contrast, adjudications apply only to the parties before a court or agency and nor-

mally deal with events in the past. While the rule-making process often looks to past events and current conditions for guidance, the regulations themselves apply usually to conduct taking place after their adoption. These two characteristics—general applicability and prospective application—are the strongest arguments for agencies to rely on rules instead of adjudications.

The Notice Requirements

The key procedural requirements in all rule making center on notice to the public. Notice guarantees the public an opportunity to comment on proposed regulations and thereby to influence their content. Once the agency adopts a rule, it must publish the rule so that the public can know what the law is.

In most jurisdictions, an agency's failure to observe either pre- or postpromulgation notice requirements invalidates the rules which were the subject of the proceeding.

Notice of proposed rules. When a federal agency decides to promulgate a rule, it must place a notice in the *Federal Register,* a daily journal which is the official record of the executive branch. The notice must include:

- A statement of the legal authority for promulgating the rule
- The text of the proposed rule or a brief description of its subject matter
- The address to which the public should submit written comments and the deadline for their submission
- The date, time, and place of any hearings on the proposed regulations

Most states do not have publications like the *Federal Register.* Usually, they require that notices containing the information listed above be published in newspapers. These notices also indicate where the public can obtain copies of the proposed rules.

The prepromulgation notice requirements

open the quasi-legislative process to the kind of give-and-take which typifies the legislative process. Administrators are not elected and are not subject to the kinds of open exchanges with constituents that members of Congress and state legislators are. The right to comment assures the public of an airing of proposed rules while they can still be changed.

Notice of promulgation. After the period for public comment ends, a federal agency may promulgate a rule by publishing it in the *Federal Register*. Accompanying the final rule must be a statement of its basis and purpose. The rule may take effect no earlier than 30 days after the rule and the accompanying statement are published. With some very limited exceptions, a regulation not published in the *Federal Register* cannot take effect, since the public has no official notice of its existence. Annually, the changes in regulations are incorporated into the *Code of Federal Regulations,* which now consists of over 100 volumes.

Typically, the states publish notice of promulgation in newspapers. Many states, including Ohio, California, and Alaska, have codified their regulations.

Types of Rule-making Proceedings

Federal law recognizes four types of rule making: exempt, formal, informal, and hybrid.

Exempt rule making. Under the APA, *exempt rule making* is a process by which agencies promulgate rules without either prior notice to the public or a public comment period. Exempt rule making occurs primarily when an agency issues interpretive rules, general policy statements, or rules of agency procedure. The resulting rules must be published in the *Federal Register.* However, military and foreign affairs regulations and regulations relating to agency management are completely exempt from the APA's notice requirements.

Formal and informal rule making. In addition to exempt rule making, the APA describes two other types: formal and informal. These are the types of most importance to business.

Enabling acts indicate that an agency must use *formal rule-making* procedures by stating that rules are "to be made on the record after opportunity for an agency hearing." This means the agency must hold a hearing like the trial described in Chapter 2. Parties interested in the rule may engage in discovery, introduce evidence, and cross-examine witnesses opposed to their positions. The proceedings are recorded either on tape or by a court reporter so that a transcript of the hearing can be prepared for either the parties or a court to review. After the hearing, the agency must base its promulgation of the rule on the *record* developed at the hearing and on the written comments submitted during the comment period.

Unless an agency's enabling act expressly specifies otherwise, an agency may use the informal method. *Informal rule making* requires that the agency meet only the notice requirements discussed above. Agencies permitted to use informal rule-making procedures do not have to hold a hearing of any sort. However, the APA specifically authorizes agencies to hold hearings in informal rule-making proceedings if they wish.

The record of an informal rule-making proceeding is quite different from one in a formal proceeding. If no hearing is held, the record consists of evidence that the agency complied with the notice requirements and of all comments submitted during the comment period. If a hearing is held, it serves mainly as an opportunity to express views orally to an agency and to submit written testimony. The hearing may not be recorded at all, and cross-examination is almost never permitted.

Both informal rule making and formal rule making have serious drawbacks. Informal rule making provides a very limited airing of the issues surrounding a proposed rule. Parties concerned about the proposed rule do not have an opportunity to test its rationale through discovery or cross-examination of witnesses. However, if agencies always had to use formal rule-making procedures, they would drown in hearings.

Hybrid rule making. In response to these and other problems with the APA's rule-making alternatives, the courts and Congress began to experiment with what came to be called "hybrid rule making." A "hybrid" is the product of the mating of two different species. A mule, for instance, is a hybrid of a donkey and a horse.

Hybrid rule making is a cross between informal and formal rule-making procedures. In essence, it is the addition of procedural devices, such as discovery and hearings, to the informal rule-making approach.

Hybrid rule making developed because informal and formal rule making represented procedural extremes. First the courts and then Congress adopted the hybrid approach. However, in the case which follows, the Supreme Court put an end to courts requiring that agencies use procedures beyond the minimum specified by the APA and the agencies' enabling acts.

Vermont Yankee Nuclear Power Corp. v. Natural Resources Defense Council

435 U.S. 519 (1978)

FACTS

The Nuclear Regulatory Commission (NRC) licenses nuclear power plants. As part of the quasi-judicial process leading to a decision on a license application, the NRC must consider the plant's environmental effects. One of these effects, the disposal of spent nuclear fuel, is common to all licensing proceedings. To avoid repeated case-by-case determinations, the NRC adopted a rule specifying what the environmental effects of spent fuel disposal were and ordered the effects indicated by the rule to be factored into licensing decisions. The NRC's enabling act did not require any procedures beyond the APA's informal rule making, but the Commission did hold hearings on the spent fuel rule. Environmental groups, however, demanded additional procedures, including the right to cross-examine the NRC staff. The NRC rejected these demands. After adopting the rule, the Commission granted Vermont Yankee a license. In the process, the NRC refused to allow environmental groups to challenge application of the spent fuel rule. The environmentalists challenged NRC's action, claiming the NRC's rule-making procedures had not sufficiently aired the issue. The court of appeals agreed.

ISSUE

Does a court have the power to order an agency to use procedures beyond those required by the APA?

DECISION

No. Reversed. Without extremely compelling circumstances, which were not present here, agencies are free to fashion their own procedural rules beyond the APA minimum. Congress intended the agencies to exercise their discretion as to the types of procedural devices to be used. If the courts could require reconsideration of rules using additional procedural devices, agencies would feel compelled to use trial-type procedures in every instance simply to avoid later reversal.

ACTIONS REQUIRED	INFORMAL RULE MAKING	FORMAL RULE MAKING	HYBRID RULE MAKING
Do Administrative Procedures Act rule apply?	Yes	Yes	Yes
Must agency file proposed regulation for comment?	Yes	Yes	Yes
Hearing required?	NO	Yes	Yes
Right to present evidence at hearing?	NO	Yes	Yes
Right to cross-examine agency's expert witnesses?	NO	Yes	NO
"Arbitrary or capricious" standard on review?	Yes	NO	Yes
"Substantial evidence" standard on review?	NO	Yes	NO

Figure 3.1 A comparison of the three types of rule making.

Vermont Yankee has not put an end to hybrid rule making. Congress has continued to enact statutes requiring it. Also, shortly after *Vermont Yankee* was decided, President Carter issued an Executive Order instructing agencies to go beyond the APA's minimums in providing opportunities for public input. President Reagan issued a similar order.

Figure 3.1 compares the three principal types of rule making.

Judicial Review

Vermont Yankee focuses on the scope of a court's review of an agency's procedures. One rationale cited by the Supreme Court for its holding was that courts could use the threat of reversal for procedural deficiencies to compel agencies to reach substantive results which the courts wanted. Because Congress has delegated responsibility for a substantive decision to an agency, reviewing courts are not to substitute their views for those of an agency. Instead, the

courts are to determine (1) whether the agency satisfied the procedural requirements which apply to its rule making and (2) whether the administrative record indicates the agency had a basis for adopting the rule.

The arbitrary or capricious standard. The actual standard the courts apply under the APA to an agency's substantive decision depends on the type of rule-making proceedings. Except for rules subject to formal rule making, the courts may not set aside an agency action unless it is "arbitrary, capricious, an abuse of discretion, or otherwise not in accordance with law." In other words, the court must uphold a regulation unless there is no rational basis for it established in the administrative record.

In practice, persons challenging regulations have great difficulty satisfying this standard. For example, the Clean Air Act authorized the EPA to issue regulations banning fuel additives which endangered the public health. When the EPA issued regulations banning lead additives to gasoline, the additive manufacturers challenged the regulations. The EPA could not show a conclusive relationship between lead additives and health hazards, though it could establish the relationship between lead in general and health hazards. The court held the EPA did not need rigorous proof of cause and effect. Where regulations deal with health hazards, courts defer to the agency's judgment so long as it is based on more than hunches or wild guesses.*

The substantial evidence standard. If an agency uses formal rule-making procedures, the courts will uphold the agency's decision to promulgate the rules unless the decision is "unsupported by the evidence." This standard, which is called the *substantial evidence rule,* is virtually identical to that applied by courts of appeals to factual determinations made by a trial court sitting without a jury (see Chapter 2).

In practical terms, the substantial evidence standard means that if a reasonable person might reach the same conclusion as the agency, the court will uphold the regulations. Thus, the substantial evidence standard is not as difficult to meet as the arbitrary or capricious standard. Still, the burden for the party challenging the rule is hardly insignificant.

The record in a formal proceeding must contain evidence on which the agency could base its decision. If the agency relies on disputed evidence, the statement accompanying the promulgated rule must explain why the agency chose to rely on the evidence it did. However, if evidence is discredited, the agency may not rely on it.

The Quasi-legislative Process in Perspective

The standards of review applied to agency rule making can best be understood through the lens of the separation of powers doctrine. Rule making is a legislative function. If Congress enacted laws to the same effect as an agency's rules, *none* of the standards of review described in the last two sections would apply. The courts can invalidate laws only on constitutional grounds. But beyond the limits of the review set by statute, the courts must defer to the agencies' expertise and judgment.

The separation of powers doctrine also affects Congress's ability to affect an agency's regulations. Beginning in the 1930s, Congress attempted to control agency regulations by means of a "legislative veto." A single house could pass a resolution—which is not subject to the President's approval—vetoing particular administrative actions. Congress exercised this power, for example, when it rejected the FTC's regulations on used-car sales. In 1983, the Supreme Court ruled the practice unconstitutional, citing the separation of powers doctrine.*

In essence, the Supreme Court held that what Congress does by statute, it must undo by statute. In the Minnesota Railroad Commission case at the beginning of this chapter, the court held the legislative branch could delegate some decision-making powers to an administrative agency which otherwise would require legislation. The legislative veto permitted Congress to undo administrative actions without being subject to the check of presidential approval. Thus, no matter how blurred the lines separating an agency's various powers become, the separation of powers doctrine still governs the relationships among the branches of government.

ENFORCEMENT OF STATUTES AND REGULATIONS

Critics fault some administrative agencies for having at once the powers to create regulations, prosecute violators of them, and adjudicate the

---

* *Ethyl Corp. v. EPA,* 541 F.2d 1, 28 (D.C. Cir.) (en banc), *cert. denied,* 426 U.S. 941 (1976).

* *Immigration & Naturalization Service v. Chadha,* 103 S. Ct. 1247 (1983).

prosecutions. Yet this system seems to work. In this section we will look at the prosecutorial and adjudicatory functions of an administrative agency and the way the APA affects them.

Instituting Enforcement

In most circumstances, an agency's enabling act specifies how the laws the agency is to implement are to be enforced. The principal means are citizens' suits and agency-instituted quasi-judicial or judicial proceedings.*

Citizens' suits. Some statutes permit persons to file court suits against parties allegedly violating an enabling act or against the agency to compel enforcement of the law. These direct suits are called *citizens' suits*.

Citizens' suits are most often available to enforce health, safety, and environmental laws whose violation can have a broad public impact. Usually, the plaintiffs will seek an injunction prohibiting further violations of the law. Such suits have the advantage of permitting the citizen plaintiffs to control their course. This factor may be quite important when the potential plaintiffs doubt an agency's ability or willingness to enforce the law. In 1984, for example, environmentalists used a citizens' suit to force the Interior Department to agree to collect millions of dollars in penalties for violations of federal surface mining rules and regulations.

The major disadvantage of citizens' suits is economic. They are expensive to bring and maintain, even though many environmental and civil rights statutes authorize the courts to award attorneys' fees to the plaintiffs.

---

* The word "proceeding" has a technical, but very broad, meaning. It includes virtually every way in which courts or administrative agencies conduct their business. Thus, we speak in terms of an agency's rulemaking proceedings and enforcement proceedings. The term also includes "actions," which properly refers to only certain types of civil and criminal proceedings before the courts.

Where an agency adjudicates an individual's rights, as in a state workers' compensation claim, direct suits are not normally available. Proceedings of this type are discussed in Chapter 46, The Law of the Workplace.

Agency-initiated proceedings. An agency can initiate enforcement either by conducting a quasi-judicial proceeding within the agency or by filing a lawsuit in court. A person outside the agency, also, can initiate an enforcement proceeding by filing a complaint with the agency. The agency investigates the complaint and determines whether it should begin enforcement proceedings. In this instance, the complainant loses control of the case, since the agency acts as plaintiff.

Some administrative agencies—like the SEC, NLRB, and FTC—enforce their enabling acts and regulations in agency proceedings. However, many other agencies, such as the Small Business Administration, must prosecute civil cases in the courts. (No administrative agency has the power to hear or bring criminal cases. Such cases are referred to the Department of Justice.)

The balance of this chapter deals with enforcement proceedings instituted by an agency.

An Agency's Enforcement Structure

Most agency enforcement arms are similar. So, too, are the paths through agencies' quasi-judicial processes. As you read this section, you should refer to Figure 3.2, which diagrams the progress of a quasi-judicial proceeding through an agency.

Regional offices. Federal administrative agencies with enforcement powers often have regional offices located throughout the country. The FTC, for example, has ten. Normally, these offices begin enforcement proceedings. While they can start investigations of potential violations, far more often they respond to complaints. Suppose a union claimed a Shreveport

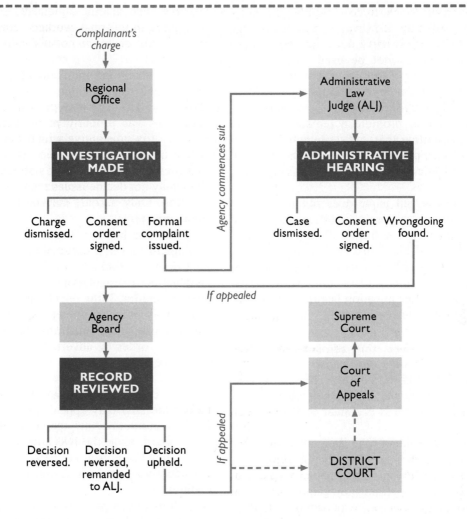

Figure 3.2 The path of a quasi-judicial agency proceeding.
This figure is based on federal practice. In the federal system, most appeals from agency adjudications go to a court of appeals. As Figure 1.2 indicates, where state appeals go depends on the jurisdiction and, sometimes, the nature of the agency.

construction firm was using unfair tactics to block its organizing efforts. The union would file a complaint with the NLRB regional office in New Orleans. If the office's investigation does not reveal a violation of the NLRB's enabling act or one of its rules, the office informs the union and the matter is dropped.

Where there is an apparent civil violation, the regional office normally notifies the alleged violator of its findings. At that point, the party charged with the violation may agree to a consent order.

A *consent order* can be either an agreement by the charged party not to commit particular acts, or an agreement to do something the party had declined to do. However, by agreeing to the order, the charged party does not admit guilt, and the order cannot be used as precedent against that party in another case. For instance, after an Equal Employment Opportunity Commission (EEOC) investigation, an employer may consent to promote a female employee without admitting that it discriminated against her. Other employees cannot cite the consent decree as evidence of their employer's discriminatory practices.

If the charged party does not agree to a consent order, the regional office may file a formal complaint. A formal complaint, which resembles a complaint in a civil action (see Figure 2.4), puts the case before the agency's quasi-judicial branch and an administrative law judge. (Even after litigation begins, the parties can agree to a consent order.)

Proceedings before the administrative law judge. *Administrative law judges* (ALJs) possess neither the powers nor the prestige of U.S. district court judges. Still, their role in the quasi-judicial process is similar to that of trial court judges.

An ALJ conducts the equivalent of trials within the agency to which he or she is assigned. The rationale for assigning ALJs to a particular agency is that they gain expertise in the agency's areas of responsibility. Critics have long complained, however, that this system leads to overly friendly relations between ALJs and their agencies.

A proceeding before an administrative law judge has the same format as a nonjury trial. The agency is the plaintiff, and lawyers on its staff present its case. The principal difference between a court trial and an agency proceeding is that the APA sets a very relaxed standard on matters concerning evidence. Some evidence admitted in administrative proceedings would not be admitted in a trial court. The APA emphasizes the informality of proceedings in order to develop as comprehensive a factual base as

possible. The hearings, themselves, often are conducted in informal settings such as conference rooms or rooms which resemble small classrooms.

Sometimes in enforcement proceedings, the charged party challenges the validity of a regulation. The ALJ may determine whether a regulation was properly promulgated but not whether it is substantively right.* Another limitation on ALJs, and on agencies in general, is that they can only interpret statutes and rules. They may not decide issues relating to the Constitution. Only a court may pass on constitutional questions.

After the hearing, the ALJ issues written findings of fact and conclusions of law. If the ALJ does not find a violation of the agency's enabling act or regulations, he or she will dismiss the matter. If the ALJ finds a violation, he or she may order the remedy specified by law. For instance, an administrative law judge at the FTC may order an advertiser to stop running deceptive ads.

Appeals to the agency head. The losing party before the ALJ may appeal. In some agencies there is an intermediate appeal to either an appeals board, as at the NRC, or to a deputy of the agency head, as at the EPA. Agencies have considerable latitude in formulating these procedures.

Ultimately, a party may take its case to the agency head. As noted earlier, the agency head may be either an individual or a board. An individual normally considers appeals on the record without granting an opportunity for oral argument.

An independent agency board operates like an appellate court. It listens to the lawyers' arguments about the ALJ's decision, but it does not hear witnesses or admit new evidence.

* A party wishing to challenge a regulation's substance must do so within the period specified by the enabling act. Often, the challenge must be filed within 60 days of a rule's adoption.

However, the APA does not require the board to give the ALJ's findings the weight an appellate court must give to the findings of a trial court. The board is free to reweigh the evidence and reach a totally different conclusion.

Like the ALJ, the board issues a written opinion and fashions an appropriate remedy. Alternatively, it can send the case back to the ALJ with instructions. For example, a board might instruct the ALJ to hold further evidentiary hearings on points which are unclear, or it may order a reevaluation of the record in view of a recent court decision.

Appeals to the Courts

If the agency head decides against the position taken by the agency staff, the staff cannot appeal. The charged party may appeal to the courts only if he or she has exhausted all administrative remedies. In other words, if the appellant has not exercised all of his or her rights to appeal within the agency, a court will dismiss the appeal.

After exhausting all administrative remedies, the charged party may appeal to the U.S. Court of Appeals either for the District of Columbia or, if the enabling act permits, for the judicial circuit in which the case arose. (See Chapter 1 for a description of the procedure before these courts.)

The standard of review of the appeals court is the substantial evidence test described above. (*Remember:* Formal rule making requires a trial-like proceeding.) The court will uphold the agency's decision if substantial evidence exists in the record to support the agency's decision and remedy. As with reviews of formal rule making, the courts will not substitute their interpretation of the evidence for that of the agency, even though the courts might have reached a different conclusion. Of course, they may reverse if their interpretation of the law is different from the agency's.

The losing party before the court of appeals may appeal to the U.S. Supreme Court. However, since the Court hears only about 4 percent of all the cases appealed to it, the court of appeals decision probably will be final.

Enforcing Agency Decisions

An agency order is not self-enforcing. An agency can order a party to stop doing something, but if the charged party does not comply, an agency does not have the power to force compliance. Instead, the agency must seek an enforcement order from a court of appeals. Suppose the SEC orders a firm to stop using deceptive methods to sell tax shelters and the firm does not comply. The SEC would have to seek a court order imposing a monetary penalty for the continuing violation. The unfortunate result is that the violator can delay compliance and put the agency and the court to considerable effort in order to secure compliance. Some commentators have proposed giving agencies contempt powers or the power to seize property in order to enforce their orders.

Rule Making Versus Adjudication

The APA assumes an emphasis within agencies on formulating rules which are then applied through quasi-judicial proceedings. It never intended that agencies act like common law courts in which precedents rather than statutes were the guide.

Yet some agencies have chosen quite deliberately to avoid issuing rules and regulations. The NLRB is the major case in point. Its principal interpretations of the National Labor Relations Act come in decisions of adjudicated cases. This fact leads to considerably less predictability in outcomes and to sweeping changes in the operative rules with little public input. (See Chapter 45 for examples of the NLRB's activities.)

Over the years, the NLRB has developed a number of rationales for its use of adjudication. For one thing, rule making is a time-consuming chore which would divert attention from the

Board's principal function: settling labor disputes. Also, adjudications eliminate procedural appeals based on deficiencies in the rule-making process.

It may be that Congress has accepted the NLRB's main justification—that the Board can respond more quickly to labor problems without rules. If so, this is a dangerous principle, for it permits agencies to formulate far-reaching policies without the public airing the APA was meant to guarantee.

STATE AND LOCAL REGULATION

The discussion in this chapter concerning administrative agencies primarily focused upon federal agencies and regulations. However, as you learned in the section on "The Power to Regulate," states and local governments also actively regulate business and society. For example, many of you will take the CPA examination and seek to become licensed to practice public accounting. Both matters are regulated by state law.

Process of Regulation

Each state is free to establish its own process of governance. However, states generally reflect the mirror image of the federal government, including the existence of state administrative agencies. Each state sets its own rules as to whether its state agencies must undergo review every so many years, the manner in which regulations are promulgated, and the manner in which administrative law judges, or their equivalent, shall rule. Common state agencies applicable to business include offices with such names as Secretary of State, Attorney General, Labor Enforcement, and Revenue Enforcement.

Scope of State Regulation

Like federal regulation, state regulation occurs as a result of legislative statutes and administrative regulation. Traditional state statutes or regulations applicable to business include the following:

- Incorporation statutes
- Consumer protection coverage
- Vehicle regulation and licensing
- Workman's compensation requirements

In addition, many states have gone beyond federal statutes or regulations by establishing, for example:

- Different minimum wage requirements
- Expectation of comparable pay for comparable work
- Parental leave for childbirth
- Mandatory health care coverage for employees

An ironic twist has occurred with the combination of federal deregulation and greater state regulation: multistate corporations which once strongly advocated federal deregulation are now seeking federal regulation for greater uniformity. If a business activity is to be regulated, it is much more cost effective for a multistate corporation to be concerned about compliance with only one set of laws.

Scope of Local Regulation

Local regulation generally refers to nonfederal, nonstate regulation. Local regulation may involve the actions of a municipality, county, school district, sewer district, part district, etc. Common regulations affecting businesses include the following:

- Zoning ordinances
- Requirements for building permits
- City vehicle stickers
- Blue laws (for example, the prohibition of the sale of alcoholic beverages or motor vehicles on Sunday)
- Nondiscrimination rules (for example, San Francisco forbids employment discrimination against gays and lesbians)

Local governments have felt the pressure to more effectively streamline their regulation of business so as to remain competitive in the retention and attraction of business.

Resolution of Conflicts

Earlier in this chapter we discussed the means of resolving conflicts between a state and the federal government. Conflicts are also inevitable between the state and local governments (for example, the regulation of billboards adjacent to highways). Local regulations must not be inconsistent with the state constitution, statutes, or regulations. In addition, local regulations must comply with federal law as provided by the federal constitution. Examples of common local government–federal conflict include oversight of still segregated school districts and environmental requirements for the treatment of water and sewage waste.

CONCLUSION

Administrative agencies have become a symbol of what some people call "big government." Critics have blamed these agencies for everything from causing economic recessions to stifling entrepreneurial spirit. From a historical perspective, however, it is difficult to take broad-scale attacks on agencies seriously. For example, given the nation's experience with an unregulated stock market before the great crash in 1929, it is difficult to imagine an honest marketplace for securities if the SEC did not exist.

Government regulation of business has existed as long as there have been governments. It is fair to assume that complaints from the regulated began with the first regulations. It is also fair to assume that in a country as complex as ours and in an era in which domestic and international trade is in constant flux, regulation is necessary. More important, elected lawmakers created these agencies to redress imbalances they perceived between business and individu-

als. That is why the first railroad commissions came into existence and why virtually every state today has consumer protection offices.

Nonetheless, some regulations and regulatory agencies have outlived their usefulness. The Civil Aeronautics Board was disbanded in the 1980s for just this reason. Many aspects of interstate trucking were deregulated under the Carter administration because the regulations no longer served any purpose.

Many administrative agencies were severely reduced in size and power under the Reagan administration in the 1980s. Although some of the agency cuts were made to trim government spending, others were decreased to "get the government off the backs of businesses." The proponents of deregulation contend that businesses are more efficient if they are not burdened by government red tape. This ideological reform of the federal bureaucracy sometimes resulted in various disfavored agencies being headed by people who were openly against the former policies of the agency. Thus, the EPA was initially led by a person many considered to be an anti-environmentalist. Many of these appointments became highly controversial and led to political repercussions for the Reagan administration.

The Bush administration added greatly to the regulatory demands on businesses. The number of federal enforcers, for example, exceeded that of the administrations of both Presidents Reagan and Carter. Far-reaching legislation such as the Americans with Disabilities Act, discussed in Chapters 27, 28, and 46, requires the promulgation of many regulations, and demands enforcement and interpretation by such agencies as the Equal Employment Opportunity Commission and the Justice Department for years to come.

Overall, administrative agencies have served us well. They have enabled the United States to adapt a governmental system designed for a mainly rural population of 3 million to the needs of a largely urban population of 250 million without a major constitutional revision.

A NOTE TO FUTURE CPA CANDIDATES

The material in Chapter 3 has not historically been tested on the CPA exam. However, you are expected to know that a state relies on its constitutional police powers to regulate professional licensing (see Chapter 9), while the Securities Exchange Commission relies upon the commerce clause to regulate interstate activity in securities (see Chapter 24).

KEY WORDS

administrative agency (50)
administrative law judge (68)
affectation doctrine (55)
commerce clause (55)
enabling act (50)
exempt rule making (62)
formal rule making (62)
hybrid rule making (63)

informal rule making (62)
interstate commerce (55)
intrastate commerce (55)
police powers (53)
preemption (59)
proceeding (66)
quasi-legislative (51)
regulations (50)
rules (50)
substantial evidence (65)
supremacy clause (59)

DISCUSSION QUESTIONS

1. What is an administrative agency? Give some examples of administrative agencies at each level of government.
2. Why are administrative agencies often called "government's fourth branch"? In fact, under which branch of government are they usually categorized?
3. Why is the commerce clause an important source of federal regulatory power? Why are the police powers of critical importance to state regulatory schemes? How would a state government operate if it did not have police powers?
4. Describe the three structural models of administrative agencies. Give examples of agencies fitting each model.

5. Describe the various results that might occur when a state law is found to conflict with a federal law.
6. What are the primary purposes of the Administrative Procedures Act? What is the purpose of the *Federal Register*?
7. Describe the four types of rule making and the standards of review which apply to them.
8. Contrast the arbitrary or capricious and the substantial evidence standards of review. Which applies to the quasi-judicial determinations of an administrative agency?

CASE PROBLEMS

1. Describe the progress of a case heard within an administrative agency through an appeal to the courts. What is the role of an administrative law judge? Do you think administrative law judges should have the same status and powers as U.S. district court judges?
2. At present, California is the only state with its own emission control standards for new vehicles sold within the state. The EPA also has emission control standards, but they are generally less strict than the California standards. With which rules must Chrysler Corporation comply when it sells cars in California? Why? Could a court determine that the California law is preempted by the federal rule even though the federal legislation does not expressly preempt the state's?
3. States and the federal government have argued for a long time as to who should have the final word on the regulation of businesses within a state. Advocates of states' rights often claim that the commerce clause, as it is currently interpreted, has made the Tenth Amendment a dead letter. Are these critics correct? If so, should the Tenth Amendment be revived? What practical effect would it have on the regulation of business?
4. Suppose a state has a rule limiting the size and weight of passenger buses on its highways. The federal government passes a law allowing larger buses on all interstate highways and

major state roads. In passing the law, Congress specifically preempted all state regulations regarding the size and weight of buses. Under what rationale would the state have originally enacted its law? Under what constitutional authority can Congress preempt the state law? Could Congress potentially preempt any state law, such as the requirement to be licensed in order to practice medicine? Explain.

5. Claxton Corp. has appealed an administrative decision to a federal court of appeals. Claxton claims that the rule it was found to have violated was improperly promulgated, since the agency did not change one word from the proposed rule to the final version, despite a mountain of evidence submitted in opposition to the proposed rule. If the rule is the product of informal rule making, what standard will the court apply? How is the court likely to rule if the court finds that the regulation was properly promulgated but is substantively defective? What will the court do if it finds the opposition evidence persuasive? Will Claxton be able to present witnesses to support its position before the court? Explain.

6. The Equal Employment Opportunity Commission, the federal agency charged with overseeing employment discrimination matters under Title VII of the Civil Rights Act of 1964, brought an action against Lusus, Inc., alleging gender discrimination in a management reorganization at Lusus. An administrative law judge found against Lusus, and the EEOC upheld the judge's decision and remedy. Lusus has refused to comply with the remedy. The EEOC is now seeking enforcement of its order from the federal court of appeals. The judges who have heard the appeal find the testimony of Lusus executives to be quite convincing on the facts of the dispute. However, the court finds no evidence of improper procedures, rulings, or award. Should Lusus expect to prevail? Explain.

7. Legislators in state X became concerned about news stories describing garbage barges and refuse trucks traveling America's waterways and highways looking for places to un-

load. To make sure that their state does not become another state's landfill, the legislature enacted a bill that permits state law enforcement officers to stop and turn back any out-of-state refuse barge or vehicle "apparently entering the state of X for the purpose of depositing its load within the state." Does this statute conflict with any provisions of the U.S. Constitution? What is the likely result of a constitutional challenge to this statute? Explain.

8. Real Issues. In *Quill Corporation v. North Dakota,* presented earlier in this chapter, states argued that direct-marketing businesses generate a potential of $3 billion in tax revenues per year. Retailers claim it makes it harder on them to compete with direct-marketing companies if customers of the latter can avoid sales taxes. States complain that direct-marketing companies like Lands' End or L.L. Bean deprive them of retail tax money which would otherwise be collected from sales in their state. Direct-marketing companies argue that keeping up with various complex, constantly changing sales tax regulations would be a costly nightmare to themselves and their customers. Congress could resolve the matter but it has not. Immediately after the *Quill* decision, the attorney for Quill, John E. Gaggini, predicted that direct marketers and the states would resolve their dispute outside of Congress with a voluntary tax collection agreement. Given the result in *Quill,* does this seem like a fair resolution? What about those direct marketers who refuse to voluntarily collect sales taxes? Explain.

9. Real Issues. Airline deregulation, begun in 1978, was supposed to provide consumers with greater number of flight choices and a more competitive price structure. Some once well-known airlines no longer exist, whether by merger or bankruptcy, such as Eastern, Pan American, and Braniff. Concerns have been raised about perceived poorer service, narrower margins of safety, higher airfares, and the impact of regional airline hubs. The domestic airlines argue that fliers are getting more service to more cities, at lesser cost, as a

result of deregulation. These airlines say that American fliers' primary concern should be in regard to foreign airlines, often foreign government–supported, possible gaining unfair access to our domestic markets through mergers with weaker United States airlines. Looking back on deregulation, from what you have experienced or know, do you think airline deregulation has worked? Explain.

10. Real Issues. During the Bush-Quayle administration, Vice President Dan Quayle chaired the President's Council on Competitiveness. The purpose of the Council was to screen proposed federal regulations to identify and prevent the issuance of regulations with an adverse impact on American competitiveness.

In previous administrations it had been the job of the Office of Management & Budget to screen regulations, although they seldom actually blocked many regulations. Democrats claimed that Mr. Quayle's council encroached on the freedom of independent regulatory agencies. Ralph Nader was more blunt: "Dan Quayle is just a tool of corporate interests."

The Council won praise from many business leaders who claimed that regulatory review is critical for American competitiveness. From your point of view, does it make sense that there should be some form of active central oversight of federal administrative agencies within the executive branch? Explain.

CHAPTER 4
Torts

What do the following situations have in common?

- Tom, a pedestrian, slips on ice accumulated in front of Tina's store and fractures his ankle.
- Sylvia's accountant carelessly prepares her tax return. As a result, the government requires her to pay a penalty.
- Due to a manufacturing defect, the ball joints on Eva's new car give out on the freeway. In the resulting accident she suffers severe injuries.

In each of these examples, a person was wronged by another's action or inaction. Tom, Sylvia, and Eva may file a civil suit seeking monetary compensation from the wrongdoer.

This chapter describes the law of legal wrongs, *torts*. "Legal" in this context refers to the fact that a wrong is not a tort unless it meets a number of prerequisites. Society has determined that conduct of the types in the examples above violates its standards of behavior. Not showing up for a date also falls below societal expectations, but it is not *tortious* conduct. The key distinction here is whether by law the injury suffered requires compensation. For that reason, think of the law of torts as "the law of compensation for legal wrongs."

WHAT IS A TORT?

The word "tort" comes from an Old French word meaning "twisted" or "wrong." "Torts" came to describe the wrongs which society has determined should be compensated. The law of torts developed in the common law, though legislation and the *Restatement of the Law, Torts** have affected it particularly in this century.

The law traditionally has classified torts according to the conduct of the person committing the tort—the *tortfeasor*. The first category, *intentional torts,* includes torts involving an act the defendant intended, even though she may *not* have intended the resulting injury. The second category, *negligence,* includes primarily acts of carelessness rather than intent. Most automobile accident cases are negligence actions. The third and final category is *strict liability*. In this category, the defendant's good intentions and lack of negligence are irrelevant. Instead, if the act—like selling a new car with a defective steering system—results in an injury, the defendant must compensate the injured party. This chapter examines each of these categories in detail.

The law of torts speaks in terms of "wrongs" and "culpability." That language reflects its common origin with criminal law, where the emphasis is on fault, blame, and punishment. Today, however, compensation is the principal goal of tort law. To put these concepts into proper perspective, let us first explore the nature of tort actions.

Relationship to Crimes

The language of blame used to describe torts makes it important to understand the distinctions between torts and crimes. A *crime* is a violation of a statutorily defined duty owed to society. Only the government prosecutes a criminal action, and one of its goals is punishment for an unlawful act. A tort, too, is a breach of a duty created by law, but the wronged party—an individual, not society—enforces the duty by seeking compensation from the wrongdoer.

---

* Early in this century, the American Law Institute (ALI) recognized the problems presented to a developing national economy by forty-eight separate common law systems. To introduce some uniformity to the law, scholars were brought together to formulate a series of codifications of such common law areas as torts, contracts, and agency. The *Restatements* do not have any official standing but have proved highly persuasive with state courts. We will refer to them often.

Because a tort is not a crime, liability in a tort action carries with it quite different sanctions. Tort liability does not bear the same social stigma a criminal liability nor does it ever result in imprisonment. Similarly, the proofs required to establish criminal liability and tort liability are quite different. In a criminal case, the government must convince the trier of fact that a defendant is guilty beyond any reasonable doubt. A person bringing a tort action, a *plaintiff,* has to prove his case only by a *preponderance of the evidence.* His evidence simply has to outweigh the evidence of the defendant —a burden which is significantly less than that of the government in a criminal action.

Nonetheless, the same conduct may provide grounds for both a tort and a criminal action. Suppose Nick manages Nora's restaurant. Every night, he pockets 10 percent of the cash receipts. He is guilty of the crime of embezzlement, and he is liable to Nora for the tort of *conversion.* The criminal action vindicates society's interest in preventing misappropriations of money. The tort action permits Nora to enforce her right, conferred by law, to recover the value of her property.

Relationship to Breaches of Contracts

A criminal act may result not only in tort liability but also in liability for breach of contract. However, liability on a contract is never described in terms of culpability. Rather, the question is whether the defendant must compensate the plaintiff. There is another major difference between tort and contract liability. Like crimes, torts are defined in terms of duties owed by all members of society. These duties are created by law, that is, by courts or legislatures. By contrast, a *contract* is an agreement between two parties which creates duties. A breach of contract is a violation of a duty established solely by a contract. For example, Bob's Bicycle Barn has no obligation to sell Norma Rae a ten-speed bike. But if it agrees to sell her one for $300, it will breach the contract by not

delivering the bike to her when she presents the $300. Fraud and product liability are the two principal areas of tort-contract overlap.

Fraud. "Fraud" is an extremely important term in business law. Generally, *fraud* consists of either making a misrepresentation intended to deceive—whether by misstating or concealing the truth—*or* making a statement with reckless disregard for whether it is true or not. A person who commits fraud is said "to defraud" another person. Fraud, as almost every chapter in this book reveals, takes in a wide range of wrongdoing. In the tort-contract context, Nick, the restaurant manager, violated his contractual duty as an employee to act in *good faith*— which means, at a minimum, not fraudulently— toward his employer when he embezzled from her. Thus, Nick's conduct could result in criminal, tort, and contract liability.

Product liability. *Product liability,* in contrast to fraud, often does not involve intentional wrongdoing. Instead, it refers to a seller's responsibility for a product put into commerce. As we will see in Chapter 34, a person injured by a product may sue in tort under either a strict liability or negligence theory or, if the seller made representations as to the quality or performance of the product, under a breach of contract theory. For example, Ben purchased a food processor for his catering business. Because of improper wiring, it short-circuited, giving him a severe shock. He may sue the manufacturer in tort for the injuries he suffered.

Culpability and Compensation

Today, as in contract law, compensation—not blame—guides courts and legislatures in assigning liability. (However, this does *not* mean there are no defenses to tort actions. There are, as we will see below.)

The law imposes liability on individuals who lacked any intent to do wrong. A drug manufacturer, for instance, may fully intend to benefit human beings with its new arthritis drug. Still, it will find itself liable for the injuries caused by the drug's unforeseen side effects.

This change in emphasis reflects the evolution from a rural economy to an urban one. It also reflects the development of multi-billion-dollar corporations and the almost universal availability of insurance against liability. These have made it considerably easier to spread the costs of compensation across society.

Damages. In most tort actions, plaintiffs must show that the injuries to themselves or their property resulted in their right to *damages*. "Damages" in this sense means a quantifiable amount of money which compensates for the injury. Thus, the law speaks of "recovering" damages, not "gaining" damages. Suppose Hal rear-ends Luz's car while it is stopped at a red light. His act causes an injury for which he is liable in damages—the repairs to the fender. If the impact causes Luz's head to strike the steering wheel, Hal would also be liable for her medical bills. What if Luz had a particularly thin skull, and instead of suffering a mild concussion, she died? Wrongdoers take their victims as they find them. Hal would be liable in damages for Luz's death, not just for the injuries a person with a normal skull would have suffered.

Tort liability can have a strongly punitive element, particularly in cases involving intentional torts or torts to which a strict liability standard applies. Thus, the heritage from criminal law is still visible. However, courts award punitive damages when the defendant's conduct is outrageous or particularly blameworthy. Punitive damages are awarded for intentional torts, in strict liability cases, and very rarely in negligence cases. Courts do not grant them routinely. The plaintiff must prove the conduct merits punishment in addition to compensation.

Injunctions. In rare cases, damages alone are inadequate—particularly where a plaintiff seeks relief from a continuing injury. Suppose

Cal's Campground is located in a rural area on a dirt road. Big Daddy's Drag Strip opens just down the road. The crowds drive by Cal's all day Sunday, leaving the campground in a pall of dust and noise and making it unusable. In addition to damages, Al might seek an *injunction,* an order compelling the defendant to do or not do something, to force Big Daddy's to control the dust generated by its customer's cars. (Injunctions and equitable remedies are discussed in Chapter 2.) If the defendants fail to obey the injunction, the court may order them jailed.

INTENTIONAL TORTS

The law of torts provides a far-from-perfect system for compensating injured parties. It retains many elements associated with assigning blame. Also, the view society takes of the importance of the right protected by a particular type of tort often determines what a plaintiff must prove in order to recover. In other words, the legal requirements for establishing liability bear no relationship to the severity of the harm. As we will see in this section and the next, this difference in the burden of proof distinguishes intentional torts and torts based on negligence.

Because they are traditionally held to be the most blameworthy, intentional torts do not require that the plaintiff prove quantifiable compensatory damages in order to establish the defendant's liability. Historically, plaintiffs brought the actions now classified as intentional torts to vindicate their rights. For that reason, compensatory damages often were of little concern compared with the assignment of blame. Where the plaintiff does not show compensatory damages, the trier of fact may award *nominal* damages of, say, a dollar.

An action by a plaintiff who cannot prove compensatory damages may seem pointless, but the availability of punitive damages makes it worthwhile. Many scholars disapprove of punitive damages which bear no relation to the compensatory damages the plaintiff proved, for example, an award of $1 in compensatory damages and $500,000 in punitive damages. Courts often significantly reduce such awards.

Intentional Torts Against the Person

Intentional torts against the person were once called "dignitary" torts because they affected an individual's dignity. That is still a useful way of thinking of them. The interest in protecting a person's dignity from injury here replaces the need for proving physical harm quantifiable as damages. If Moe shoves a pie into Curly's face, Curly suffers an indignity which probably cannot be translated into damages. Still, Moe would be liable to Curly. Thus, liability attaches not only to acts which cause real harm but also to those which are merely offensive.

In this context, "intent" refers to a voluntary act or omission designed to bring about a consequence. "Voluntary act" describes the muscle contraction it takes for Moe to slam a pie into Curly's face. It says nothing about Moe's *motive,* his thought before the muscle movement. Moe may only want to cover Curly's face with pie filling. Still, if he breaks Curly's nose, he will be liable for that injury. The law presumes people intend the probable consequences of their acts. But what if Curly ducks and the pie hits Larry instead? The intent follows the pie. Under the doctrine of *transferred intent,* Moe is liable to Larry for the actual injury and to Curly for the threatened injury.

Battery. A *battery* is an intentional tort consisting of an intentional, unauthorized contact with any part of another's body or anything attached to it or identified with it. When Moe hits one of his fellow Stooges, he commits a battery.

The plaintiff does not have to be aware of the contact at the moment it occurs. Suppose that before being anesthetized, a patient consents to surgery on her right ear. Instead, the doctor operates in her left ear. The doctor has committed a battery, since the patient did not consent to any work on her left ear.

The law does not provide a remedy for every offensive contact. The time, place, and circumstances determine the character of the contact. For example, people packed around you on a crowded bus will not be liable for touching you without your consent. No battery has occurred, because the people lacked the intent to touch you. But if you are standing in an open field and someone subjects you to the same kind of contact, that person has committed a battery.

Assault. An *assault* is an act by a defendant which puts the plaintiff in fear of an imminent battery. Unlike a battery, the victim must be aware of an assault when it takes place. A doctor cannot assault a patient under anesthetic.

The plaintiff's fear of a battery must be reasonable. A threat alone, without a threatening gesture like a raised fist, is not an assault. Still, the critical element of an assault is the plaintiff's perception of the situation. If the plaintiff reasonably believes that the combination of threatening words and an innocent gesture promises an imminent battery, the defendant has committed an assault. Also, the person threatening the battery must appear to be able to carry out the threat. A prisoner locked in a cell who threatens to "get" the district attorney when he is released lacks the ability to carry out the battery at that moment.

False imprisonment. *False imprisonment* is any intentional wrongful confinement or restraint of freedom of movement. A person can be confined wrongfully to a hotel room or a car, as well as a jail. The length of the confinement need not be great.

The tort of false imprisonment has three essential elements. First, the plaintiff must be aware of the imprisonment when it occurs. An unconscious person cannot be falsely imprisoned. Second, the confinement must be total. The plaintiff can have no reasonable, safe means of escape. For instance, a rope made out of sheets thrown out a fifth-floor window is not a reasonable means of escape, even if the plaintiff uses the rope successfully. Third, the defendant must intend to confine the plaintiff. Accidentally locking the plaintiff in a storeroom is not false imprisonment. Yet false imprisonment requires neither ill will nor a wish to injure the plaintiff.

People commonly think of false imprisonment in terms of the police. But anyone who unlawfully restrains another's movement commits this tort. For example, under the anti-shoplifting statutes in many states a merchant may detain a suspect for the time it should take the police to arrive. Any detention beyond that is a false imprisonment. Just questioning someone is not an imprisonment unless the merchant implies the suspect is not free to leave.

Intentional infliction of emotional distress. The *intentional infliction of emotional distress* is a relatively new tort. For a long time, courts have been awarding damages for emotional distress caused by another intentional tort. However, courts have been reluctant to impose liability where the sole injury is emotional. Because courts regard emotional injuries as easier to fake than physical ones, they require evidence of severe emotional harm before permitting recovery.

The conduct must be of a type which would produce a strong reaction in a normal person. Rather than being a violation of good manners, the defendant's conduct must be outrageous, extreme, and intolerable. Staging a realistic fake suicide as a practical joke may meet this standard.

The courts do not treat all plaintiffs alleging this tort the same. A grocery store checkout clerk who use profane and abusive language to an 85-year-old or who ridicules a disabled person will commit this tort. But the same language directed at someone who is not so vulnerable might well not be tortious.

Invasion of privacy. In one way or another, all intentional torts relating to the person protect the "right to be left alone." Few are so closely associated with that right than the four types of wrongs included under the heading *invasion of privacy*. They are:

- Appropriation of the plaintiff's name or likeness for a commercial purpose
- Publication of private facts relating to an individual
- Representation of the plaintiff or the plaintiff's product in a false light in the public eye
- Intrusion into a person's privacy

The first three principally result in damage to business or personal relations.

Appropriation most commonly deals with a celebrity's name or "trademark." Johnny Carson successfully sued a purveyor of portable potties called Here's Johnny Portable Toilets, Inc., which had billed itself as "The World's Foremost Commodian." A California trial court has extended the application of appropriation to an almost indistinguishable imitation of Bette Midler's singing style in a Ford commercial.

Publication of private facts usually applies to details about a person that, while true, are not newsworthy and might cause embarrassment. The classic case involved a former prostitute who had been convicted for her involvement in a notorious murder. Upon her release from prison, she took a new name and led a quiet, respectable life. A publication was held liable for revealing her new identity and the facts of her formal life.

False light resembles publication of private facts and defamation (discussed below) so closely that some commentators believe all false light cases should be categorized under those headings. In essence, false light plaintiffs complain that they have been embarrassed by representations made about them. What makes the false light category so confusing is that the representations causing the embarrassment may be true or false.

In contrast to the first three types of invasions of privacy, intrusion involves physically invading an individual's solitude. The classic cases involve photographers who relentlessly track celebrities like Jacqueline Kennedy Onas-sis. But, celebrity hounds are not the only people who must worry about this type of tort. Employers must be very careful not to violate their workers' rights in this area. The next case discusses an emerging trend in the workplace which some see as a serious infringement of these rights.

Jennings v. Minco Technology Labs, Inc.

765 S.W. 2d 497 (Tex. Ct. App. 1989)

FACTS   Minco Technology Labs, Inc. announced that all employees must consent when randomly asked to submit to urinalysis for the detection of illegal drugs. If the test was positive, employees would have to participate in a rehabilitation program. If they did not consent or refused the program, they might be discharged. Brenda Jennings sought a declaratory judgment to have the program enjoined because the tests constituted an invasion of privacy by unlawfully intruding into her privacy. The trial court ruled in Minco's favor, finding that there would be no illegal invasion into Jennings's privacy.

ISSUE   Would Minco unlawfully invade Jennings's right of privacy by having her consent to a random drug testing program?

DECISION   No. Affirmed. The appeals court agreed with the trial court that there would be no unlawful intrusion into Jennings's privacy, since she had the choice of either consenting to the company's random drug testing program or suffering the loss of her job. Jennings is an employee at will and so her employment continues at the mutual pleasure of Jennings and her employer. Minco was concerned about illegal drug use in its work force and felt that drug testing might lessen the harmful effects drugs might have had on its business, products, and the health and safety of its employees. The plan also had safeguards of accuracy, confidentiality, and modesty.

As in the *Jennings* case, many courts are now allowing random drug testing as long as the employee "consents" and if there are guarantees that testing procedures are reliable and respect the employee's personal privacy. Courts are also likely to consider whether im-portant interests, such as the safety and health of the workplace, need protection from the dangers of workers on drugs. You may question the court's assertion that an employee's consent is real when faced with the choice between submitting to a drug test or losing a job. Brenda

Jennings argued that because she was poor and needed her salary, her consent was only illusory.

Defenses to intentional torts against the person. As noted in Chapter 2, a *defense* is a reason why the plaintiff should not recover from the defendant. Defenses may be matters of either fact or law. Defenses to liability for intentional torts against the person fall into three categories. The first, *consent* negates the tortious character of an act. If Anna kisses Howard without his objecting, he cannot sue her later for battery, claiming he had not consented.

In some instances, the doctrine of *implied consent* removes the tortious character of an act. For example, one prizefighter cannot recover from another for injuries suffered in the ring. If a person arrives at a hospital unconscious and in need of emergency surgery, the doctors need not wait until a relative signs a consent form. The law implies consent.

The second principal defense, *self-defense,* also removes the tortious character of an act. Typically, the defendant tried to protect against a threatened battery and is now being sued for the battery he committed to avoid injury. The success of the defense depends on whether the act of self-defense bore a reasonable relation to the threat. That means the amount of defensive force cannot exceed the force to which it responds. If Bill hits Patrick in the mouth, Patrick may not kill to protect himself. Patrick may use only the force necessary to repel the attack and to escape. If, however, Patrick faces deadly force—Bill charges toward Patrick while waving a cleaver and swearing to kill him—he may respond with deadly force.

The third defense, *privilege,* has broader implications than the other two. It reflects society's need to protect the freedom of action of certain individuals. Members of Congress, for instance, are immune from suits based on what they say in a committee hearing.

The First Amendment insulates much that the media produce even when it is wrong. For example, a public official must show not only that a report is incorrect but also that those publishing it did so with actual malice toward the official. As a practical matter, this standard is exceedingly difficult to meet. In contrast, an individual who is not a public figure need only show the intentional statement.

The line between public figures and private individuals is not at all clear, however. Courts have had to struggle with whether high school football coaches in football-mad areas, unpaid members of local boards of education, and citizen participants in local politics are public figures. The answer has tended to vary according to the nature of the report: the closer the relationship to a public controversy, the more likely the person is to be found a public figure. Also, a soldier or an executioner, who in ordinary circumstances has to observe society's condemnation of homicide, is excused for killings necessitated by war or a valid death penalty.

Intention Torts Against Property

Trespass. A *trespass* is any wrongful entry onto real property. The only intent required is simply to cross a boundary. Trespassers may believe they have a right to cross when they do not, but the law does not require an intent to trespass. Suppose Adrienne tells Russell that he should feel free to come to her farm and chop down a Christmas tree. Russell goes to what he thinks is her farm and takes a tree. If the property belongs to Frank, Russell has trespassed. Even a good faith belief that one is not trespassing does not affect liability. An indirect entry also qualifies as a trespass. If Mary directs her sheep across McGregor's garden, she has committed a trespass.

However, where there is no intent to cross —directly or indirectly, there is no trespass. Suppose Bill runs Paul's car off a state highway, causing him to cross onto Melanie's farm. Paul would not have committed a trespass. However, Bill would be liable to Melanie for any damages caused by Paul's entry onto her property.

As with all torts, the principal remedy for trespass is damages. And, as with all intentional torts, if the actual damage is minor or nonexistent, the successful plaintiff will collect only nominal damages. If the trespass is a continuing one, the plaintiff may obtain an injunction. As we will see in Chapter 27, "Real Property," this assertion of the plaintiff's property interests can be critical in preserving title against a claim of adverse possession or of a prescriptive easement.

Conversion. *Conversion* is a wrongful act with respect to personal property, in which the defendant deals with the plaintiff's goods in a manner inconsistent with the plaintiff's ownership. Suppose a stationery company delivers to Evert Battery Corp. a prepaid shipment of pencils meant for Allan's Abacus Works. If Evert sells the pencils, Allan could recover the proceeds in a conversion action. If Evert kept the pencils for its own use, Allan would have a right to recover either the pencils or their value.

This emphasis on the value of the property distinguishes conversion from trespass and other intentional torts. The plaintiff's remedy is damages calculated on the goods' value. If the goods do not have a value, there can be no remedy.

Defenses to intentional torts against property. Consent is a defense to liability for intentional torts against property. If the plaintiff beckons to the defendant and the defendant then enters the plaintiff's store, the defendant has not trespassed. Given the right circumstance, a defendant can interpret silence as consent. If the defendant crosses the boundary in the plaintiff's clear view and the plaintiff says nothing, the plaintiff has consented.

Another defense, *necessity,* resembles implied consent. If a fire threatens a block of stores, fire fighters—whether volunteers or individuals paid by the public—may enter a store in order to protect it or its neighbors. That is a public necessity. When the necessity is private, such as the protection of one's home, the person entering will not be liable for trespass but only for the damage the entry caused.

A person in hot pursuit of stolen personal property may without liability enter another's property to recover the stolen goods. If Fenlon takes Dale's stereo and runs onto Peterson's land, Dale may chase him. But Dale will be liable for any damage caused by her entry. However, Dale may enter Peterson's land without liability if Peterson took the goods or if Peterson knows Fenlon has hidden the stereo on his property and refuses to let Dale on the property to recover it.

As for defending one's property, the law limits that right far more than it limits the right to protect oneself from the threat of imminent bodily harm. The following case illustrates those limits.

Katko v. Briney

183 N.W.2d 657 (Iowa, 1971)

FACTS The Brineys owned an abandoned farmhouse which vandals had raided repeatedly. Mr. Briney decided to rig a spring-operated gun trap for them. Katko and a friend broke into the house to steal antique bottles. When Katko opened a bedroom door, a blast from a 20-gauge shotgun nearly took his right leg off. The trial court awarded him both compensatory and punitive damages.

ISSUE   Did the Brineys have a right to use deadly force to defend their property against thieves?

DECISION   No. Affirmed. The law places a higher value on the human safety of a trespasser or a thief than on property. No right exists to use force capable of causing death or serious injury merely to protect property. Had Katko died, Briney might have been prosecuted criminally for manslaughter or murder.

Katko is not an exception to the rule on defenses. Rather, the law is evolving toward requiring persons like the Brineys to use peaceful means to protect or recover their property. To this end, the courts are narrowing the range of situations in which the use of force is permissible.

Intentional Torts Against Business

All the intentional torts discussed in this chapter can occur in a business context. However, the three discussed next uniquely affect business.

Inducing breach of contract. Breach of a duty created by contract is not a tort. But convincing someone to breach is a tort called *inducing breach of contract.*

This cause of action requires that a valid contract exist between two parties which a third party convinces one of the contracting parties to breach. The third party must know of the contract's existence and intend to cause the breach for his economic benefit. Suppose Dorothy had a contract to sell flour to Paul's bakery. Oscar, Paul's competitor, tells Dorothy that if she wants to continue selling flour to him, she has to cancel her contract with Paul. Since she sells more to Oscar than to Paul, she does so. Paul could recover damages in tort from Oscar as well as damages for breach of contract from Dorothy. Now suppose Oscar simply cancels his contract with Dorothy. She asks him why, and he tells her it is because of her contract with Paul. Dorothy decides she wants Oscar's business, so she cancels her contract with Paul. Oscar did not induce the breach. Now Paul has an action only for breach of contract against Dorothy.

The now famous case which follows demonstrates the potentially serious monetary consequences that can befall a business that induces another into breaching an existing contract.

Texaco, Inc. v. Pennzoil Co.

729 S.W. 2d 768 (Tex. Ct. App. 1987)

FACTS   Pennzoil offered to buy the controlling interest of Getty Oil. Getty's major stockholders, the Getty Museum, and Gordon Getty had agreed to the offer in a Memorandum of Agreement, subject to an approval by Getty Oil's Board of Directors. The Board, however, rejected Pennzoil's offer, submitted a counteroffer, and sought other potential buyers. Eventually Pennzoil did accept the Getty counteroffer. On January 5, 1984, the *Wall Street Journal* and other newspapers announced the news. Getty's investment banker, however, continued to solicit bidders while a final written agreement was being negotiated. Texaco subsequently made a bid, which Getty's Board of Directors accepted on January 6th. The trial court held that Texaco knowingly interfered, and therefore had induced a breach of a contract after Pennzoil accepted Getty's counteroffer.

ISSUE   Did Texaco knowingly interfere with the contract between Getty and Pennzoil?

DECISION   Yes. Affirmed. Even though there was no signed contract, one was in existence after the parties had agreed to all the material terms. Moreover, there was no understanding that a signed agreement was required before the parties would be contractually obligated. There was also a sufficient amount of evidence, from the *Wall Street Journal* article and other sources, to infer that Texaco, despite its denials, had known that there was a binding contract between Getty and Pennzoil.

Texaco's illegal actions resulted in a record judgment. The trial court awarded Pennzoil nearly $11 billion in compensatory and punitive damages. Following several more appeals, and Texaco's bankruptcy reorganization, the case was settled for $3 billion.

Injurious falsehood and defamation to business reputation. An *injurious falsehood* is a wrongful statement which injures a person's property interests. The essence of an injurious falsehood is that it relates to a property or business interest. The defendant does not have to say anything about the plaintiff's character. By contrast, *defamation* to business reputation consists of a wrongful statement which injures a person's reputation with respect to her business or livelihood. The examples which follow contrast the two torts:

- Knowing what he says is untrue, Xerxes, a restaurant critic, accuses Daria's restaurant of attracting "rats" as customers. As a result, the restaurant loses reputable patrons.
- Knowing what he says is untrue, Xerxes accuses Daria of serving rat meat. As a result, patronage drops drastically.

The first example illustrated an injurious falsehood. It applies solely to Daria's business and reflects on Daria herself only indirectly. The second makes a personal representation about Daria, as well as a representation about her restaurant. It is a defamation to her business reputation.

Defamation to business reputation is a subcategory of a larger intentional tort, *defamation,* which protects a person's interest in her good reputation. Defamation takes two forms: *slander* if it is spoken and *libel* if it is written. The defendant must publish the falsehood either by making the statement in the presence of a third party or by putting it in writing a third party will read.

Truth is an absolute defense to defamation actions. In certain contexts, defamatory statements are privileged; that is, the law immunizes their makers from liability. The First Amendment protections discussed above with respect to privacy apply equally to defamation. For businesspeople, the most important privilege relates to statements made in a business context.

NEGLIGENCE

In everyday language, "negligence" means "carelessness." In law, it has a similar, though

THE COURT OF COMMON PLEAS
FOR
FRANKLIN COUNTY, OHIO

BUCKEYE WIDGETS, INC.   :
   1111 High Street,   :
   Worthington, Ohio 44214   :
      Plaintiff   :

          v.   : Case No. 93-6-007WH

CARDINAL SKYHOOK CORP.   :
   21 East Broad Street,   :
   Bexley, Ohio   43211   :
      Defendant   :
                           :
DONALD H. DRIVER   :
   811 West 14th Avenue,   :
   Columbus, Ohio   43210   :
      Defendant   :

COMPLAINT
----

    1.   The Plaintiff is a citizen of the State of Ohio.

    2.   The Defendant Cardinal Skyhook Corp. is an Ohio corporation whose principal place of business is located in Franklin County.

    3.   The Defendant Donald H. Driver is a resident of Franklin County.

    4.   At all times relevant to this Complaint, Driver was employed by Cardinal Skyhook Corp. and was acting within the scope of his employment.

    5.   On May 14, 1992, at approximately 9:30 a.m. Driver was operating a van belonging to Cardinal Skyhook Corp. in an easterly direction on Main Street in Columbus.

    6.   While proceeding at a speed in excess of the posted limit, Driver negligently caused the van to cross the center line and strike a 1991 Ford truck owned by the Plaintiff which was lawfully parked on the north side of the street.

(continued)

7. The truck, valued at $19,000 and its contents, 35 crates of widgets valued at $35,000, were a total loss.

WHEREFORE, the Plaintiff demands judgment against Cardinal Skyhook Corp. or against Donald H. Driver or against both of them in the sum of $54,000 and the costs of this action.

Buckeye Widgets Corp.
By Its Attorney

_____
Lisa P. Hill, Esq.
McVay & Hill
Attorneys At Law
1 Post Office Square
Columbus, Ohio   43215

Figure 4.1 A sample tort complaint.
This hypothetical tort complaint involves a routine automobile negligence action. Can you identify all the elements necessary to state a negligence cause of action?

broader, meaning. It is the name given to a class of torts which do not require proof of an intent. Instead, the focus is on the existence of a duty and the defendant's failure to exercise due care in the particular circumstances. An action based on negligence requires proof of four elements:

- *Legal duty or duty of care:* the defendant's obligation to the plaintiff
- *Conduct:* the defendant's act or omission which breached the duty owed to the plaintiff
- *Causation:* the legal cause of the harm
- *Damages:* the harm done

All causes of action in tort require a plaintiff to establish duty, act or omission, causation, and injury. Negligence requires proof of damages, too. Figure 4.1 is a sample complaint in a negligence case.

Legal Duty

Legal duties are standards of care society imposed on reasonable persons. They are called legal duties because they are duties a court will enforce and because they must be distinguished from moral obligations, like giving blood to the Red Cross.

The reasonable person. In formulating standards, the law relies on the *reasonable person,* a judicial creation who always acts prudently and does the right thing. The law uses the reasonable person as an expression of the conduct society demands because of the impossibility of establishing a standard of care, either by statute or by precedent, for every situation in which an injury might occur.

The law does not impose duties which cannot be carried out. Suppose a paving company digs a trench across one lane of a highway and leaves it unmarked overnight. The company's duty relates only to conduct it is capable of performing, like ordering its employees to put up barricades with flashing lights. By failing to warn drivers of the hazard, the company breaches its legal duty to them.

Other standards. A statute may define a duty. For example, a state law may require that road contractors clearly mark hazards they create on and along highways. Quite often, statutes governing common carriers, such as railroads and airlines, specify the carriers' duties to passengers.

The common law has taken into account the relationship between the parties in defining duties. Landowners traditionally have had quite different duties toward persons invited onto their property and trespassers, though the wide availability of property insurance has caused this distinction to erode. As we will see later in this chapter, landlords have special obligations to their tenants.

The courts, too, in defining a duty may take into account an individual's condition or status. It would make little sense to apply the same standard to children or the mentally infirm as to the public at large. Similarly, the courts will hold a person with special skill or knowledge to a higher standard than an ordinary person. For example, a forester knows how a tree will probably fall when it is cut, but an ordinary person does not. The forester's duty will take that knowledge into account. Finally, the circumstances affect the definition of duty. The forester's duty will vary depending on whether he or she is cutting trees in the face of a forest fire for a firebreak—an emergency—or in the ordinary course of a logging operation.

Conduct

The plaintiff's injury must result from *conduct,* a particular action or omission, which breaches the defendant's legal duty. The defendant is usually able to control its conduct, but it may not be able to control whether its conduct will result in liability. Suppose Marjorie's car hit the unmarked trench and she was injured. Marjorie's accident is not within the control of the paving company. Of course, if no one's car hits the unmarked trench, there is no injured party to sue the paving company.

Intervention by third party. Even if a third party has an opportunity to prevent the injuries the negligent conduct might cause, the third party has no obligation to do so. In other words, the defendant cannot avoid responsibility for harm to the plaintiff by citing another's opportunity to prevent it. Suppose that Billy, while walking along the highway, sees Marjorie's car heading toward the ditch. He has no legal duty to flag her down, because he did not create the dangerous condition. His failure to stop Marjorie does not affect the duty owed to her by the paving company.

When someone decides to intervene to save another from harm, he must act prudently. Suppose Billy throws a rock at Marjorie's windshield to attract her attention. Startled, she swerves and hits a tree. Marjorie's injuries are caused by Billy's imprudent act, not by the dangerous condition left by the paving company.

When a rescuer reasonably risks himself to save another, the person who caused the original accident is liable for the rescuer's injuries. It is foreseeable that a rescuer would try to assist the original victim.

Res ipsa loquitur. The reasonable person standard works well when the court has a specific act to measure. However, in some cases it is impossible to determine the particular conduct which caused the plaintiff's injuries.

To avoid situations where an injured plaintiff could not identify the defendant's conduct and therefore could not recover, the law devised the doctrine of *res ipsa loquitur.* This Latin phrase means literally "the thing speaks for itself." In practice, it means that where the cause of the accident was under the control of the defendant or its employees, the event's occurrence indicates negligence on their part. In other words, the event does not normally occur in the absence of negligence.

When a court determines that *res ipsa loquitur* applies, the burden of persuasion shifts to the defendant to explain why its actions could not have caused the injury. The next case demonstrates how courts apply this doctrine.

Escola v. Coca Cola Bottling Co.

24 Cal. 2d 453, 150 P.2d 436 (1944)

FACTS
A Coca Cola driver delivered several cases of Coke to the restaurant where Escola worked as a waitress. He stacked them and then left. Thirty-six hours later, Escola removed the top case and began putting bottles in the refrigerator. One of them exploded in her hand. At trial, a Coca Cola driver testified he had seen other bottles explode and had found inexplicable broken bottles in the warehouse. The plaintiff admitted she could not show any specific acts of negligence and relied completely on the doctrine of *res ipsa loquitur*. Coca Cola introduced no evidence to show that anyone had tampered with the bottles between the delivery and Escola's injury. The trial court found for the plaintiff.

ISSUE
Was this an appropriate case for the application of *res ipsa loquitur*?

DECISION
Yes. Affirmed. The defendant had control over the cause of injury, and the nature of the accident indicates it would not have occurred in the absence of negligence by the defendant. Here, Coca Cola produced no evidence that anyone else damaged the bottle.

In sum, to warrant the application of *res ipsa loquitur,* the following criteria must be present:

- The circumstances surrounding the accident must create a presumption of negligence by the defendant.
- The defendant must have had exclusive control and management of the instrumentality that caused the accident.

Respondeat superior. The Latin phrase *respondeat superior* means "let the master respond." In tort law, this phrase expresses the doctrine that an employer takes responsibility for the

negligent acts its employees commit during the course of employment. In *Escola,* suppose the evidence showed that the driver chose a particularly bumpy route to the restaurant instead of a smoother route and that the vibration caused the bottle to explode. Even though the driver was negligent, under respondeat superior the company, too, would be liable to the plaintiff.

Respondeat superior is discussed in more detail in Chapter 14.

Causation

Negligence that is the proximate cause of an injury is an act that a person exercising ordinary caution and prudence could have foreseen producing an injury. It follows that *proximate cause* is a negligent act that as a direct and existing cause actively aids in producing an injury.

A legal duty exists if the reasonable person should foresee that damage or injury could result from particular conduct.

In order to determine duty under the reasonable person standard, a court looks forward from the time of the conduct. In the unmarked trench example, a court would look forward from the failure to mark the trench, not backward from Marjorie's injury. At the time the paving company failed to put up barricades, should it have foreseen that a car might hit the trench? If the reasonable person would have foreseen this, the paving company had a duty to mark the excavation. By contrast, the contractor would not be required to foresee that a pilot, mistaking the road for an airport, might land on top of his excavation.

Proximate cause and legal cause. When lawyers speak of the conduct which caused an injury, they often talk about the injury's *proximate cause*. In normal usage, "proximate" means "closely related" or "nearest" and implies an immediate relationship. However, the cause of a tort is not always proximate in this sense. Proximate cause does not refer to the usual notion of "cause and effect" or imply that one event follows another directly in time.

Proximate cause really means *legal cause,* or what the law regards as the cause of an injury. The legal cause concept limits liability to those consequences of an action which a reasonable person should have foreseen.

In the classic case, a man carrying a small package leapt onto a train that was about to leave. The guards at the door, noticing the man's unsteadiness, tried to help him on. In the process, the package, which contained fireworks, dropped to the tracks and exploded. The concussion caused a scale some distance down the platform to fall over and injure a Mrs. Palsgraf. She sued the railroad.

A sharply divided court held that Mrs. Palsgraf could not recover because her harm was not foreseeable. Foreseeability depends on the definition of a zone of danger within which the plaintiff must be. Mrs. Palsgraf was outside that zone, since the act consisted of the guards pulling the passenger on board. The dissent got to the heart of proximate cause when it noted:

> What we do mean by the word "proximate" is that, because of convenience, of public policy, of a rough sense of justice, the law arbitrarily declines to trace a series of events beyond a certain point. This is not logic. It is practical politics.*

Extent of liability. Nonetheless, if the relationship between an act and an injury is too remote, the act is not the legal cause and the defendant is not liable. The problem lies in determining what is too remote. For instance, legend has it that one night in 1871, when a Mrs. O'Leary went to her barn to milk her cow, she carelessly left her lantern too close to the animal; the cow knocked over the lantern, starting a fire which destroyed Chicago. Mrs. O'Leary should have foreseen the possibility that her carelessness might result in the destruction of a neighboring building. But what about buildings in the next block? Or ones a mile away?

Foreseeability is a question for the trier of fact. The evidence and the trier's own sense of what a person in the situation should be accountable for will determine whether the act is the legal cause of the injury or whether the relationship is too remote. In the next case, the California Supreme Court shed some light on the problem of determining causation.

---

* *Palsgraf v. Long Island R. Co.,* 248 N.Y. 339, 162 N.E. 99 (1928).

Weirum v. RKO General, Inc.

15 Cal. 3d 40, 123 Cal. Rptr. 468, 539 P.2d 36 (1975)

FACTS   In order to attract a larger audience, a Los Angeles radio station owned by RKO General staged a promotion called "The Super Summer Spectacular." It included a contest in which the station broadcast clues to the whereabouts of "The Real Don Steele," a disk jockey. Steele drove about the city, staying in any one spot for only a few minutes. The first person to reach Steele at a given location received a prize. Two teenagers separately spotted Steele and followed him in their cars. On the freeway, they jockeyed for position closest to his car. When Steele exited, the teenagers attempted to follow him. In the process, they forced Weirum's car off the road. Weirum died of his injuries. His family sued the teenagers and RKO. The trial court awarded the Weirums $300,000. RKO appealed.

ISSUE   Should RKO have foreseen that the Steele contest would create a hazard to others using the freeways?

DECISION   Yes. Affirmed.

> *While the question of whether one owes a duty to another must be decided on a case-by-case basis, every case is governed by the rule of general application that all persons are required to use ordinary care to prevent others from being injured as the result of their conduct . . . .*
>
> *While duty is a question of law, foreseeability is a question of fact for the jury. Their verdict in plaintiffs' [the Weirums'] favor here necessarily embraced a finding that decedent was exposed to a foreseeable risk of harm.*
>
> *. . . It was foreseeable that defendant's [RKO's] youthful listeners . . . would race to . . . the next site and in their haste would disregard the demands of highway safety.*
>
> *. . . The defendant invokes the maxim that an actor [a person whose conduct is in question] is entitled to assume that others will not act negligently. This concept is valid, however, only to the extent that the intervening conduct was not to be anticipated. If the likelihood that a third party may react in a particular manner is a hazard which makes the actor negligent, such reaction whether innocent or negligent does not prevent the actor from being liable for the harm caused thereby. . . .*

Causation is often described in terms of a "but for" test. In the last case, one might say, "But for the station's use of a contest which encouraged a chase, Weirum would not have died." The danger of the but for test is that it can be carried to extreme lengths. "But for the interstate highway construction program," one might say, "Weirum would not have been killed." It must always be understood that the but for test is limited by the foreseeability of the particular occurrence.

The court does not have to identify a single

wrongdoer or a single legal cause—much less a single relationship between them and the injury—in order to impose liability. More than one person can be liable for a single injury. In *Weirum,* the two teenagers and RKO were all liable. Also, a particular injury can have more than one legal cause. The conduct of the teenagers made them liable, regardless of the station's liability. Their actions did not eliminate RKO's liability, even though the teenagers were the immediate cause of the accident. Of course, the reverse is true, also. RKO's liability does not remove the teenagers' responsibility.

Common presumptions. The law makes some important presumptions about causation. An important one, implied earlier, is that tortfeasors take their victims as they find them. As in the "thin skull" cases, a tortfeasor cannot reduce his or her liability by claiming that a preexisting condition aggravated the injury.

Another presumption follows from that one: tortfeasors are liable for injuries caused by diseases victims contract because of their weakened condition. For example, a tortfeasor

will be liable for the additional expenses incurred when a hospitalized accident victim contracts pneumonia.

Finally, as we have already seen, "negligence invites rescue," and the tortfeasor is responsible for the injuries suffered by a rescuer who is not reckless.

Damages

In negligence actions, a plaintiff must establish an actual injury which resulted in damages. Damages, of course, are a quantification into dollars of the compensation required for the injury. Punitive damages are not awarded for torts classified under the negligence heading, as they may be for intentional torts. So compensatory damages are the only damages available in practice. The rationale for not permitting punitive damages in negligence actions is that the conduct leading to the injury is not a culpable as that in intentional torts, regardless of the extent of the injury. However, in the next case, the Wisconsin Supreme Court affirmed the trial court's award of punitive damages.

Brown v. Maxey

124 Wis. 426, 369 N.W.2d 677 (1985)

FACTS   Dr. Maxey owned Apollo Village, a low-income apartment complex that had critical security problems. Brown, who was disabled, lived in the complex. A neighbor's grandson set a fire outside Brown's door, and Brown was critically burned. At trial, Brown showed that Apollo Village had a history of arson and lack of fire safety. His building suffered six fires in the 8 months before he was injured, including one that was set outside his door. The locks on the building entrances, the fire doors on each floor, and the basement door were usually broken. The manual fire alarm system was commonly disabled because of regular false alarms—as it was on the night of the fire. There were no backup alarm systems or smoke detectors. The complex did not have a security force, and none of Maxey's maintenance staff was on duty the night of the fire. Maxey knew of these conditions, but he would not remedy them permanently. The trial court awarded compensatory damages and $200,000 in punitive damages to Brown. The court of appeals reversed the punitive damages award.

ISSUE	Should punitive damages be available as a remedy in cases where the negligent conduct is outrageous?
DECISION	Yes. Court of appeals reversed. The availability of punitive damages should not depend on the classification of the cause of action but on whether the conduct is such that the defendant should have reason to know that there is a strong probability that harm will result. If, nevertheless, he proceeds in reckless or conscious disregard of the consequences, such conduct is outrageous. Dr. Maxey's conduct here reveals a conscious disregard for and an utter indifference to the safety of his tenants.

The Wisconsin Supreme Court holding would not find favor in many jurisdictions. Indeed, it raises troubling questions about the extent and the degree of a landlord's responsibility for the consequences of the criminal behavior of a tenant or an unknown third person. We will consider this problem again in Chapter 28, The Relationship between Landlord and Tenant.

Defenses

Until the 1950s, there were significant legal defenses available to negligence suits. Increasingly, however, the courts have dismantled these defenses to make compensation for injuries more likely. Today, the only sure defense is non-negligence. In the next paragraphs, four remaining defenses are examinined.

Contributory negligence. Under the *contributory negligence rule,* if the plaintiff's negligence contributed in *any* way—no matter how slight—to his or her injuries, the plaintiff could not recover from a negligent defendant. Suppose Paul is driving north on North Street and Dorie is driving south. They reach a red light at the same time. Paul's car stops slightly left of the centerline. Dorie runs the red light, and her car sideswipes the left side of Paul's car. Under the contributory negligence rule, neither could recover from the other.

Last clear chance. The *last clear chance doctrine,* which exists in some states, is an excep-

tion to the contributory negligence rule. It holds that even if the plaintiff negligently placed himself in danger, the defendant is liable if the defendant could have avoided causing the injury by exercising due care. Suppose Don gets drunk and falls asleep in his car in the middle of the road. The posted speed limit for the stretch is 35 miles per hour, and had LaVerne been going 35 instead of 70 she could have avoided hitting Don. The doctrine would probably apply, and LaVerne would be liable.

Comparative negligence. Few states still observe the contributory negligence rule. Most have moved to *comparative negligence.* Under that approach, the trier of fact decides whether the defendant was negligent and, if so, the amount of the plaintiff's damages. Then, it compares the negligence of the parties and reduces the award by the percentage of the plaintiff's fault. In the last example, if Paul proved damages of $100,000 and the jury found him to be 30 percent at fault, he would receive $70,000.

Assumption of risk. *Assumption of risk* is the legal shorthand for the principle which states that if a party knowingly took the risk of injury, loss, or damage, she may not recover from the party who ordinarily would be responsible. Suppose Cathy goes to a riding stable and insists on taking a horse she knows bucks at unpredictable moments. She could not recover from the stable for her injuries.

In determining whether assumption of risk

applies, the courts apply a subjective test, not the objective reasonable person test. The classic assumption of risk example is that of a spectator at a baseball game. A spectator assumes the risk of injury from baseballs hit into the stands during the course of the game. Presumably, every American knows of the dangers in watching the national pastime. But what of a visitor from Greece who has never heard of baseball? He does not assume the risk until he learns what it is and has a chance to remove himself from the danger area.

STRICT LIABILITY

Strict liability is a legal doctrine that imposes responsibility for the consequences of activities involving abnormally dangerous activities or unreasonably dangerous products without reference to fault. In effect, strict liability represents a social policy which holds that even a well-intentioned, nonnegligent party who creates such a risk must bear its consequences.

Strict liability does not depend on a finding of any particular fault but rather on the nature of the activity. Thus, it is significantly different from negligence actions, in which the imposition of liability requires a determination that the defendant breached a duty.

Abnormally Dangerous Activities

If, for instance, a person keeps an animal of a type known to be dangerous, like a guard dog in a store, the law holds the owner responsible for any injuries caused by the animal, without any consideration of negligence. The risk of loss, as in the next case, falls on the person who exposes others to this abnormal risk.

Franken v. City of Sioux Center

272 N.W.2d 422 (Iowa, 1978)

FACTS	The city purchased Stubby, a 300-pound tiger, for its zoo. Temporarily, it stored him in a cramped but secure cage in Franken's warehouse. While he was there, a number of people patted him without ill effect. However, Stubby became increasingly "hyper" because of his cramped quarters and the fact that sheep were being kept close to his cage. One night, Franken went to his warehouse with some friends. Although Stubby was clearly agitated, Franken tried to pat him. It took a steel bar and a board with a nail through it to remove Franken's hand from Stubby's mouth. Franken sued the city but lost in the trial court.
ISSUE	Should the trial court have applied a strict liability standard?
DECISION	Yes. Reversed. The owner of a wild animal is subject to strict liability for harm it causes even though the incident would not have happened except for the unexpectable, negligent conduct of another party. The possessor may incur this liability without any negligence on its part. Still, assumption of risk may be a defense to liability if it can be shown that the plaintiff willingly subjected himself to the danger.

The rule on animals is ancient. However, late in the last century, courts began to apply its logic to human activities which were abnormally hazardous or were not normal in a particular location.

Many jurisdictions have adopted the standard stated in *Restatement (Second) of Torts* § 519(1):

> *One who carries on an abnormally dangerous activity is subject to liability for harm to the person, land or [property] of another resulting from the activity, although he has exercised the utmost care to prevent the harm.*

For example, crop-dusting close to a residence or storing large quantities of gasoline in the middle of a city might be classed as abnormally dangerous.

Abnormally dangerous activities today usually take place in a business context. Thus, the courts long ago adopted the attitude that since a business wished to profit by its activity, the business stood in a better position to bear the unusual risk than did the victim. So by imposing strict liability, the law deals with these activities more in the manner of allocating loss rather than assigning guilt.

A common example of an abnormally dangerous activity is blasting. The vast majority of courts have held that no matter how careful blasters are, they will still be responsible for any damage caused by either concussion or flying debris. In some jurisdictions, just storing explosives is an abnormally hazardous activity, particularly if it occurs in an inhabited area. But even strict liability as to explosives has its limits, as the next case illustrates.

Washington State University v. Industrial Rock Products, Inc.

37 Wash. App. 586, 681 P.2d 871 (1984)

FACTS
Industrial Rock Products employed an 18-year-old man as a blaster's helper at its rock quarry. The man's girlfriend had just moved across the state to attend Washington State University. Sensing he was losing her because of distance and new friends, the worker insisted she return. When she refused, he stole some dynamite from his job site and headed for the university. There, the woman told him to leave. He did so but returned with the dynamite and a detonator. An explosion resulted in his death, injury to two security officers, and $200,000 in property damage. The university brought action against Industrial Rock Products to recover property damages. The trial court entered summary judgment against the university on its strict liability cause of action.

ISSUE
Does the doctrine of strict liability in tort apply to the activities of Industrial Rock Products in this case?

DECISION
No. Judgment affirmed. One who carries on an abnormally dangerous activity is not strictly liable for every conceivable harm which might result from it. According to *Restatement (Second) of Torts* §519(2), "This strict liability is limited to the kind of harm, the possibility of which makes the activity abnormally dangerous." Here, the

Industrial Rock Products explosives did not harm anyone in the vicinity of its quarry. An employee's use of stolen explosives to blow up a college dormitory 300 miles away is not the kind of harm which makes storage of explosives by Industrial Rock Products abnormally dangerous.

Unreasonably dangerous products

The other major application of strict liability pertains to the manufacture or sale of unreasonably dangerous products. We will take a close look at this area and warranty liability in Chapter 34.

For now, you should be aware that strict liability for products (or as it is called, simply "product liability") applies only to sellers who are engaged in the business of selling the type of good involved in the sale. It does not apply to, say, someone selling a lawnmower at a garage sale.

The product must be in a defective condition and be unreasonably dangerous when it is sold. A manufacturer would be liable for injuries caused by a lawnmower that is manufactured with a defective skirt around the blades to keep feet from coming in contact with them.

Finally, the product must not be substantially modified after its sale. The question of what is a "substantial modification" has been much litigated with inconsistent results. A manufacturer probably would not be liable for injuries caused by a machine a consumer radically altered in a way the manufacturer could not effectively guard against. Suppose Irv took a properly designed mower and used an acetylene torch to remove the skirt. The manufacturer probably would not be liable for injuries caused by Irv's modifications.

Defenses

As the blasting case shows, strict liability does not mean absolute liability. Defenses to it do exist and indeed have changed over the years. In recent times, the courts have tended to narrow the application of strict liability for dangerous activities. For instance, all airplane travel was once regarded as dangerous. As it evolved and became more safe, the courts saw less reason to impose strict liability. In contrast, we will see that the courts have expanded the reach of strict liability for abnormally dangerous products.

Among the traditional tort defenses, contributory negligence is not a defense to a strict liability cause of action. The application of comparative negligence principles to strict liability cases is a matter of debate. Assumption of the risk, however, is a defense. Suppose Sharon is a news photographer. To get pictures of a building that is to be demolished with explosives, she ignores signs and leaps barricades in order to move well inside the police lines. She has assumed the risk of injury from the blasting.

LEGISLATIVE TRENDS

Statutes have become the largest single source of "new" torts. Congress and the state legislatures have created numerous types of actions, often applying a strict liability standard to conduct. At the same time, they have attempted to move to a pure compensation system in some areas and have accordingly removed whole classes of cases from the courts. These are called "no-fault" systems.

Environmental Statutes

One area in which these statutory torts have had a great impact is the environment. Formerly, many pollution cases had to be tried as *nuisance* cases. Torts in the nuisance category require that the plaintiff prove an injury to himself or to the public. These injuries often were impossible to prove, given the prevailing attitudes at that time toward the use of natural resources. It was difficult, for instance, for a fisherman to demonstrate a real economic loss when his favorite stream was polluted. Today, most pollution laws provide for strict liability, though in some cases the nuisance remedies remain. Many of these statutes allow individuals to sue polluters on behalf of the public without showing real economic loss. These remedies are discussed in detail in Chapter 47.

No-fault Systems

The state legislatures and Congress have removed fault as a consideration in certain classes of torts, such as injuries to railway workers. When they removed fault as a consideration, they also tried to remove the injury from tort litigation. The systems designed to deal with these classes of torts focus on compensation for injuries instead of responsibility for the tortious conduct.

Workers' compensation. Workers' compensation is a form of insurance for companies against liability for injuries suffered by their employees while on the job. It also guarantees that workers will receive compensation for any injuries suffered in the course of their jobs. States administer the system, and every state has one. The federal government has created similar systems for railway and maritime workers.

Fault is not an issue in workers' compensation cases. Even a negligent employee can recover. An employer may contest a claim, usually on the grounds that the injury does not exist, or is not of the magnitude claimed by the employee, or is not work-related. An employer has an incentive to contest claims, since its insurance premiums, or assessed contributions to a state-managed fund, increase as the number of claims against it rise.

No-fault auto insurance. As a substitute for tort actions, a few state legislatures have adopted a no-fault system for compensating automobile accident victims. These plans vary, but one common goal is to reduce litigation surrounding routine claims by having the victims collect from their own insurance carriers. Often, victims may sue only if their damages exceed a certain minimum amount.

No-fault insurance has a goal similar to workers' compensation plans. By eliminating fault, insurance companies spread the costs of injuries across their insureds. Thus, society ultimately bears the cost, just as it does that of workers' injuries. These systems are discussed further in Chapter 30, Insurance.

CONCLUSION

The law of torts, the law of civil wrongs, is society's means of determining who is responsible for injuries and whether the person responsible must provide compensation. The principles developed in the common law of torts have had a broad application throughout the law, and both the federal and the state legislative branches continue to create new remedies at a rapid rate. Figure 4-2 identifies some of the other discussions of tort and tort-like remedies in this book.

This explosion of remedies has contributed to the increase in litigation discussed in Chapter 2. But weighed against that negative effect is the benefit that these remedies were created where there were inadequate or no remedies before. In this way, they have made our society fairer.

It is at least arguable that business has borne a disproportionate share of the expense of these remedies. Strict liability for consumer product safety, for instance, can result in huge judgments. Still, businesses are better able than individuals to insure against liability. Also, they and their insurers can spread the costs of compensation across society by increasing prices and premiums.

This imperfect compensation system has

CHAPTER TOPIC	SUBJECT	CHAPTER
Criminal law	Relation to tort law	5
Contracts	Fraud defenses	9
Agency	Respondeat superior	14
Partnerships	Respondeat superior	17
Securities	Private actions	23
Accountants	Malpractice and fraud	24
Personal property	Infringements Conversion	25
Landlord-tenant law	Liabilities in tort	28
Insurance	Liability insurance No-fault laws	30
Products liability	Products liability	34
Bankruptcy	Fraud	43
Antitrust laws	Unfair competition	44
Consumer protection	Unfair competition Product safety	45
Employment	Wrongful discharge Discrimination Workers' compensation	46
Environment	Citizens' suits	47

Figure 4.2 Torts and tortlike remedies discussed in other chapters.
This figure contains a representative sampling of the tort and tortlike remedies in the book.

characteristics which have served us well. It is a vastly flexible system which allows experimentation. Its principles—if not the results in particular cases—are generally accepted. Their acceptance has enabled courts and legislatures to develop remedies for new problems without having to stray far from existing laws. For these reasons, major alterations in the principles governing liability are unlikely. However, innovations are possible in the way compensation is delivered to those who require it.

A NOTE TO FUTURE CPA CANDIDATES

The CPA exam historically has not focused on the specific torts discussed in this chapter. Instead, the exam has covered applications of tort law in the following situations:

- An employer's potential liability for the tortious acts of its employees. An employer will generally be liable for nonintentional acts of its employees which occur within the scope of employment (Chapter 14).
- The conduct of officers and directors in regard to corporate governance (Chapter 20) or SEC matters (Chapter 23).
- The professional conduct of public accountants (Chapter 24).
- Product liability for the sale of an inherently dangerous product (Chapter 34).

Do not try to master the CPA tort applications now. You will have plenty of opportunity to do so in the chapters which follow.

KEY WORDS

breach (84)	fraud (77)
comparative negligence (93)	intent (79)
	libel (85)
compensation (76)	negligence (76)
contributory negligence (93)	privilege (82)
	proximate cause (90)
culpability (76)	reasonable person (87)
damages (78)	strict liability (94)
defense (82)	tort (76)
duty (87)	

DISCUSSION QUESTIONS

1. What is a tort? How does the law of torts protect the interests of society?
2. What elements must a plaintiff prove to prevail in a negligence action?
3. What is proximate cause? How do you distinguish between proximate cause and legal cause?
4. Name three broad categories of torts. What are the degrees of culpability which attach to each?
5. Which intentional torts do you believe affect society most? Why?
6. Distinguish the torts of injurious falsehood and defamation to business reputation. Should there be a distinction? Explain your reasoning.
7. What is the difference between contributory negligence and assumption of risk? Formulate examples to illustrate each.
8. What is the rationale for imposing strict liability on those who harbor dangerous animals or engage in abnormally hazardous activities?
9. Should the courts be free to develop new torts? Explain your reasoning.
10. Do you think a no-fault system should be devised to cover all torts so that anyone injured could recover from a state fund? Explain the pros and cons of such a proposal.

CASE PROBLEMS

1. David Green was jogging on the sidewalk. As he passed Miller's Tavern, its overhead sign fell and struck him. He suffered a broken clavicle. Green brought a negligence action against Miller. Miller admits that he owns the building and the sign, but he claims the sign was in good condition when it was checked a month before. The evidence shows a strong—but not exceptionally strong—spring wind was blowing at the time of the accident. Is this an appropriate case for the application of *res ipsa loquitur?* Is Green likely to prevail? Explain your answers.
2. While Marvin was walking along Carmel Drive, a robber stopped him, slugged him, took his money, and fled. As the mugger ran off, she dropped her pistol. Marvin, an expert marksman, picked up the pistol and shot the mugger three times in the back. She died instantly. Her parents sued Marvin for damages, and he defended on the grounds that he was acting in self-defense and was legally attempting to recover his property. Evaluate Marvin's chances of convincing a judge of the validity of his defense. Explain your answer.

3. As Bobby Smith jogged by Victory Lake, a small pond next to Victory University, he saw Jerry Parker in the lake screaming for help. He and Jerry had recently fought over Jerry's ex-girlfriend, whom Bobby was now dating. Although Bobby had worked as a certified lifeguard for the past three summers, he decided to pretend he didn't see Jerry and leave the rescue to someone else. After running another 300 yards, Bobby realized his error and rushed back to help Jerry. Unfortunately, it was too late. Jerry's family sued Bobby, alleging he negligently failed to save Jerry. In remorse, Bobby has admitted he should have tried to save Jerry when he first saw him in peril. What negligence element will probably determine this case's outcome? Describe how.

4. Central Bank decided to tear down an adjacent building it owned and use the lot for parking. The most efficient demolition method was blasting. Sandford & Son agreed to do the job in accordance with the bank's quite demanding specifications for safety precautions. Despite the wrecker's best efforts, the blast caused extensive damage to a building owned by Cascio Printing. Cascio sued Central and Sandford & Son. Central claims it is not liable, since it did not do the blasting. Sandford claims it is not liable, since it was not negligent. Will Cascio prevail against Central Bank? Sandford & Son? Why?

5. Prince and his friends were walking through a dark forest when they happened upon Sonia White, lying asleep behind a thorn hedge. Prince's friends dared him to kiss her, which he did. She did not wake up. But after Prince left, her friend S. N. Ezee woke her up and told her what had happened. Ezee, a new lawyer, offered to sue Prince on her behalf for assault and battery. Prince files a motion to dismiss, claiming he could not be liable for assault, since White was asleep. Also, he claims she impliedly consented by sleeping behind a thorn hedge in the middle of a dark forest. Is the court likely to sustain either defense? If so, which one and why?

6. *Sports America* magazine presented a shocking story on the usage of steroids by middle school students in a particular city. The cover of *Sports America* showed the team's quarterback just about to pass the football with the caption: "Central Middle School Players Pass Steroids and Footballs." The name of the player pictured on the cover, Michael Mitchell, was not stated there or inside the magazine. Michael has suffered severe criticism even though he was not in any manner involved in the illegal steroid usage. What would be the best course of action for Michael's parents, on behalf of Michael, against *Sports America*? Would they be likely to prevail? Explain.

7. By tradition, golfers on the Park Hills Course who reach the par-three second hole wave on the foursome behind them to hit their drives. Duffer was on the green, and while waiting for the other foursome to drive, he began looking in his bag for his putter. Duffer did not hear Brent Skowron yell "fore" as he addressed his ball. Duffer sued Skowron for the damages the ball caused to his skull, alleging both negligence and battery. Will Duffer prevail on either ground? Explain.

8. Carla Matthews was attending an outdoor pool party. When the soft drinks began to run low, Carla volunteered to go to the nearby 7-Eleven store for more. Carla drove barefooted to the store (which is not prohibited in the state involved). En route, another driver, Christie Cassels, negligently pulled out into the path of Carla's car. Carla attempted to stop but her foot, still wet from the swimming pool, slipped off the brake. Carla has brought suit. The evidence will show that had Carla's foot not slipped off the brake, she probably would have avoided the collision. Assume that the state where the accident occurred recognizes all common law tort defenses. Which defense would be the best for Cassels to raise? Is Carla likely to prevail? Explain.

9. Real Issues. Sports violence is a matter increasingly before the public and litigated in courts of law. Coaches and managers strongly

encourage vigorous athletic competition, especially in heavy contact sports like hockey or football. However, unnecessarily hard contact, especially when removed from the main play, can result in unnecessary injuries. To what extent should a player be considered to have assumed the risk of bodily contact? A growing number of courts recognize an injured player's claim when he can show the defendant player acted intentionally or in "reckless disregard" for the injured player's safety. Reckless disregard is said to exist when a player knows an act is harmful, such as a "clothesline tackle" of a quarterback, and intends to commit that act but does not intend to harm the player. The key to this analysis is whether the player's actions were "part of the game." Does this analysis seem like an appropriate approach to sports violence? Would you find this standard appropriate for all collegiate and professional sports events? Explain.

10. Real Issues. In spite of the large number of lawyers in the United States, there are still complaints that the legal system provides unequal standards of justice for the rich and poor. Lawyers often say this is not true in tort cases for which attorneys will generally take a solid case on a contingency basis, say 30 percent. This means that the lawyers will take the case without fee, with their remuneration to come only if they win on a basis of 30 percent of the settlement or court judgment. Your thoughts?

Criminal law

Every year, businesses lose billions of dollars due to crimes against them. Shoplifting, embezzlement, securities fraud, mail fraud, and theft of services are just a few of the crimes which affect business. This chapter provides an overview of criminal law. It focuses on what a crime is, on what excuses or justifications the law recognizes for behavior which is otherwise criminal, and on the nature of particular offenses against business.

CRIMES AND CRIMINAL LIABILITY

A *crime* is a public wrong, a breach of a duty to society. Society defines these duties by means of statutes. Therefore, a breach of duty is not a crime unless it is so defined by statute.

Criminal Prosecution

The government prosecutes criminal actions on behalf of society, not on behalf of the victim. The purposes of a criminal action are to punish the offender, incapacitate him or her in order to protect society, deter others from breaching the same duty and, ideally, to rehabilitate the criminal. Unlike a tort action, compensating a victim of the breach is not a goal of a criminal prosecution.

Suppose Burt and Harry are sitting in a bar discussing the New York Giants' chances of winning the Superbowl. When Harry tells him, "The Giants couldn't win the Ivy League because they'd choke," Burt becomes irate and tries to make Harry see the light by hitting him over the head with a beer bottle. As noted in the last chapter, Burt has committed the crime of battery, the unlawful striking of another person. He has also cost Harry, we will assume, $2000 in medical expenses.

Harry might file criminal charges against Burt. The district attorney might file a criminal action against Burt, depending on the evidence. It is not Harry who files the action: it is the state's representative on behalf of the state. That is why the title of criminal cases always contains a synonym for the state, such as "The People of the State of New York" or simply "People."*

Tort Remedies for Criminal Acts

As he could in a tort action, Burt could defend on the grounds that Harry consented to the blow, as in a boxing match. Burt might also claim he had an excuse or justification for the battery. Here, disparaging the New York Giants is hardly an excuse. But if Burt is found guilty, he will have to pay a fine, serve a jail term, or both. Compensating Harry normally would not be part of Burt's criminal penalty. Under most circumstances, Harry would have to sue Burt in tort to recover his hospital costs. In the next case, the U.S. Supreme Court considered whether penalizing some criminals, who are able to pay a civil judgment for their criminal acts, violates their First Amendments rights.

---

* Other words used in this context are "State" or "Commonwealth." By convention, the name of the state appears in the case title only when the case is before the U.S. Supreme Court, as for example, *Coolidge v. New Hampshire*, 403 U.S. 443 (1971). Otherwise, the case citation tells anyone interested which state prosecuted the action.

Simon & Schuster, Inc. v. New York Crime Victims Board

116 L.Ed 2d 476 (1992)

FACTS

New York's so-called "Son of Sam" law was passed to compensate victims of crimes. It requird such entities as publishers and movie companies, which had contracted with a person convicted or accused of a crime, to turn over any money the criminal may have earned from a book or movie describing the crime. The amount of money owed the victim would be determined in a civil judgment. The statute was, ironically never applied to the "Son of Sam," David Berkowitz, who paid his victims or their estates voluntarily. However, since its passage in 1977, the Crime Victims Board had sought to escrow money from such highly publicized criminals as Jean Harris, convicted killer of the "Scarsdale Diet" doctor; Mark David Chapman, John Lennon's assassin; and R. Foster Winans, the *Wall Street Journal* columnist convicted of insider trading. In the present case, Simon & Schuster had contracted with mobster Henry Hill to write a book about his life. The book, *Wiseguy,* sold over a million copies and was later made into a film called *Goodfellas.* Simon & Schuster sought a declaratory judgment that the law violated both its and Hill's First Amendment freedom of speech. The federal district court and court of appeals ruled that the "Son of Sam" law was consistent with the First Amendment.

ISSUE

Was New York's "Son of Sam" law a violation of the first Amendment?

DECISION

Yes. Reversed. The law singles out speech on a specific subject—crime—and financially burdens only it and no other form of speech or income. This kind of treatment creates a presumption that the law is not consistent with the First Amendment. To overcome the presumption, the State of New York must demonstrate that the "Son of Sam" law is necessary to serve a compelling state interest and is narrowly drawn to achieve that end. There was no compelling state interest for limiting the victim's compensation to the profits of a criminal's speech about the crime. The "Son of Sam" law is also not narrowly tailored to accomplish New York's objective of compensating victims. The law is significantly overinclusive, since it applies to work on any subject as long as it relates to a person's crime. For instance, a person who admits in his autobiography that he once committed a petty crime for which he was never convicted, could have the book's proceeds confiscated by the Board for up to 5 years.

The *Simon & Schuster* case illustrates how, in pursuing the beneficial goal of compensating a victim of both a crime and a tort, a law can violate the First Amendment. The Court did explain, however, that it may be possible to tailor a law narrowly enough to be constitutional, leaving open the possibility that there could be modified versions of the "Son of Sam" law in the future.

CLASSIFICATIONS OF CRIMES

All crimes, originally created in common law courts, are now defined by either state or federal law and are either felonies or misdemeanors.

State and federal crimes

Jurisdiction determines what criminal laws, if any, apply to conduct. State laws apply only within the geographic boundaries of a state. A person accused of a theft committed in Georgia is prosecuted in, and under the laws of, that state. Federal laws apply nationally and coexist with state statutes. However, federal laws control exclusively in federal enclaves like Fort Bragg or Edwards Air Force Base.

All crimes are defined by either a state statute or a federal statute, except treason, which is defined in the U.S. Constitution. Although we will examine some instances where state and federal statutes overlap, for the most part the federal statutes deal with matters of national importance—like counterfeit currency and mail fraud—while the states focus on protecting individuals and property.

Because the states prosecute the more common crimes, like burglary and homicide, they handle the vast majority of criminal cases. However, since the 1930s the federal role has expanded in fighting crimes traditionally under state jurisdiction, like kidnapping. Rapid improvements in transportation left state enforcement personnel at a disadvantage, since their authority ended at the state line.

For federal laws to apply to a common crime, some aspect of the crime must involve federal property or touch more than one state. For example, auto theft is primarily a state concern. But if a stolen car crosses state lines, the thief violates the federal Dyer Act, which forbids interstate transportation of stolen vehicles. It is important to note that the auto thief could be prosecuted both by the state for the original theft and by the federal government for the separate offense of interstate transportation of a stolen vehicle. Thus, statutes like the Dyer Act permit the federal government to add enforcement muscle and deterrence without affecting the primary responsibilities of the states.

Felonies and Misdemeanors

Crimes are commonly classified as *felonies* (more serious crimes) and *misdemeanors* (less serious crimes). The classifying characteristic of a crime is the length of imprisonment associated with it. Typically, felonies are acts punishable either by more than 1 year in prison or by death. Misdemeanors are usually acts punishable by less than a year in prison.

THE ESSENTIAL ELEMENTS OF A CRIME

All crimes require conduct—an act or omission—and intent.

Conduct

It would be impossible for the state to punish everyone who has evil thoughts or contemplates committing a crime. That is why an *act* is required. However, the term "act" includes *omission,* which is the failure to act when there is a duty to do so. In most cases where an omission seems to be a crime, the failure to act violates an ethical or moral duty. For example, a person jogging by a swimming pool has no duty under the criminal law to prevent a drowning. A lifeguard, however, who ignores a swimmer's cries for help may well be liable criminally.

Intent

A criminal violation requires both an act and an *intent,* the purpose or resolve to do an act. Of course, intent alone is not a crime.

Specific and general intent. Some crimes require a specific intent to commmit a particular illegal act, while others require only a general intent to do something which results in an illegal act. An example of specific intent appears in the definition of "theft" in the Indiana Code. It states:

> *A person who knowingly and intentionally exerts unauthorized control over property of another person with intent to deprive the other person of any part of its value or use, commits theft. . . .*

Just exerting unauthorized control over the property is not enough. The wrongdoer must intend to commit the specific criminal act of deprivation. As a rule, the more serious the crime, the more likely the requirement will be for specific intent. However, there are exceptions to that rule.

The key to general intent statues is that—as with strict liability in tort—the wrongdoer does not have to intend to commit the wrong. But it is essential that she intend to do that act which constitutes the crime. She is criminally liable for her act because, even though she did not intend the criminal harm her act caused, she is usually in a better position to prevent the harm with no more care or effort than society might reasonably expect. Suppose Diana goes duck hunting. She shoots into a flight and accidentally hits a swan, a protected bird. Diana will be criminally liable for her act without regard for her specific intent.

General intent statutes are especially common in areas which affect businesses. For instance, state statutes which make it a crime to sell liquor to a minor commonly do not require specific intent. The only intent required is that of selling liquor. Whether the seller knows the age of the purchaser is irrelevant. Specific intent is usually not required under statues prescribing criminal penalties in the environmental, health, and food areas, too.

Motive not required. "Intent" and "motive" are not synonyms. *Motive* is the reason, or moving cause, of an act, and it does *not* have to be proved in a criminal case. For this reason, a good faith mistake about the ownership of a path is not relevant if the question is whether the defendant had a general intent to trespass. When prosecutors submit evidence of a motive, they usually do so in order to establish intent.

Burden of proof

The prosecution in a criminal case must prove the defendant's guilt beyond a shadow of a reasonable doubt. If the trier of fact has any reasonable question as to the defendant's guilt, it must find her not guilty. By contrast, as noted earlier, a plaintiff's burden in a civil case requires that the plaintiff show only that a *preponderance,* or the weight, of the evidence supports its position.

The defendant does not have to prove she did not commit the crime. Rather, through cross-examination of the prosecution's witnesses and through presentation of evidence that calls into question the prosecution's evidence, the defendant must create a reasonable doubt about her guilt in the mind of the trier of fact. That is the defendant's factual defense. However, if the defendant tries to avoid liability by proving a legal defense, such as self-defense, she must prove her right to it by a preponderance of the evidence. Legal defenses are examined immediately below.

Lack of excuse or justification

When the prosecution shows the act and intent required by statute, it has established that a crime was committed. Even so, the defendant can avoid liability for a crime by establishing a legal *defense.* A legal defense is an excuse or justification available to someone who has committed a criminal act.

Mistake. A reasonable mistake of fact excuses criminal liability. Suppose Hal, a customer in a restaurant, intends to take his own coat but mistakenly takes an identical one. Hal is not guilty of theft because he reasonably interpreted the facts of the situation in such a way that if he had been correct, his act would not have been a crime.

A mistake of fact is not a defense when the accused intends to commit a criminal offense and the act produces a different, but foreseeable, result from the one intended. If Peggy intends to shoot Alice but kills John instead, she would still be guilty of murder.

Insanity. An insane person cannot formulate the intent necessary to commit a crime. The traditional standard for determining insanity rests on whether the accused was capable of distinguishing right from wrong at the time of the act. Beginning in the 1950s, some jurisdic-

tions experimented with what is called the "irresistible impulse" rule. Under this rule, even if a person can distinguish right from wrong, the act may still be excused if it resulted from an impulse beyond the actor's control. The new rule has proved quite controversial, and some jurisdictions which adopted it seem likely to return to the traditional standard of the ability to determine right from wrong.

Intoxication. When a crime requires a specific intent, intoxication by alcohol or drugs may make it impossible for the accused to form that intent. However, as the defendant in the next case learned, voluntary intoxication does not completely excuse a criminal act. Rather, it affects the defendant's degree of culpability.

State v. Hall

214 N.W.2d 205 (Iowa, 1974)

FACTS   When he turned himself in, Hall told authorities he had agreed to drive Meacham from Oregon to Chicago. As they passed through Iowa, Hall claimed, he took a pill to feel "groovy." Instead, it made him hallucinate. Meacham, who was sleeping in the passenger seat, appeared to him to be a mad dog. Hall killed Meacham, disposed of his body, and took his wallet and car. In the trial court, Hall unsuccessfully argued that temporary insanity caused by voluntary intoxication from drugs was a complete defense to a charge of first degree murder.

ISSUE   Is voluntary intoxication a complete defense to first degree murder?

DECISION   No. Affirmed. A temporary mental condition caused by voluntary intoxication from drugs does not constitute a complete defense to a crime. The only consideration, given intoxication at the time the defendant committed the homicide, is the determination of whether he was guilty of murder in the first or second degree. Nor will intoxication reduce a homicide from murder to manslaughter, because intoxication by itself will not "negate" the intent required for homicide.

Infancy. Where minors are concerned, states often adopt the rule of the three 7s. A child 7 but under 14 is presumed to be incapable of

forming the intent to commit a crime, but the state can rebut this presumption by introducing evidence to the contrary. A child over 14 is presumed to be capable of forming the required intent, but the child may rebut this presumption.

Consent. As noted earlier, consent is a defense to the crime of battery. It may also apply to theft and arson.

Duress. *Duress* consists of bodily harm or threats of such harm to oneself or others. It may be associated with restraint on movement or kidnapping. For example, if John's arm is twisted behind his back until he signs a draft on his employer's account, he is excused from criminal liability for embezzlement. John lacks the intent to commit the crime.

Immunity. In some instances, the state will grant *immunity* from prosecution to a person who has committed a criminal act. This is usually done in exchange for information about other crimes or for testimony against codefendants.

Statute of limitations. All states have *statutes of limitations*. These statutes excuse criminal conduct—except murder—if an action is not brought within a specified period. The periods vary from state to state and from crime to crime. A person, however, cannot avoid prosecution by fleeing the state or hiding for the period of the statute. The period is extended by the length of time the person is in flight or in hiding.

Entrapment. *Entrapment* occurs when the initiative for a crime comes from a law enforcement officer. The person committing the crime must not have been inclined to commit it in order for entrapment to be a defense. However, a trap set by the authorities for an unwary criminal already disposed to act is legal and does not constitute a defense. The next case examines just how far the government sometimes goes to arrest a suspected criminal.

Jacobson v. United States

118 L. Ed. 2d 174 (1992)

FACTS   Before the passage of the Child Protection Act of 1984, Keith Jacobson, a single, 56-year-old Nebraska farmer, had legally purchased from a bookstore two magazines which contained nude photos of preteen and teenage boys. After the act's passage, the government discovered Jacobson's name on the bookstore list. Two agencies, the U.S. Postal Service and the Customs Service, started to send Jacobson mail through five fictitious organizations and a phony pen pal to investigate his willingness to break the law. The organizations portrayed themselves as protectors and promoters of sexual freedom and freedom of choice, and as against censorship. Jacobson responded to some of the literature. After 2½ years of these mailings, he was solicited to order child pornography out of a catalog. Jacobson ordered one magazine and was arrested after a controlled delivery of it. A subsequent search uncovered only the government-sent material and the two original magazines. Jacobson was convicted and the court of appeals affirmed the conviction.

ISSUE   Was Jacobson entrapped by the government into committing a crime?

DECISION   Yes. Reversed. The government had to prove that Jacobson, predisposed and independent of the government's acts, would have committed the crime of receiving child pornography through the mails. The government, in its zeal to enforce the law, cannot conceive a criminal scheme, impart to the innocent suspect's mind the willingness to commit the crime, and then coax him into committing it so that the government may prosecute. Jacobson's possession of the original two magazines did not display a criminal inclination to commit a crime. At the time he bought them, it was legal to do so, and he testified that he didn't know what they would portray.

Self-defense. The most common justification for conduct which is otherwise criminal involves self-defense: the use of force to protect one's self or one's property. The principle applied here is roughly the same as that in tort law. A person may respond with force proportionate to the danger involved.

In the most extreme case, a person threatened with deadly force may respond in kind if unable to retreat safely. Suppose John points a gun at Nancy and says he is going to kill her. She may shoot him first. But if John is 5 years old and the gun he is holding is obviously a toy, Nancy is guilty of murder if she shoots him. Without the threat of deadly harm, a defendant cannot justify the use of deadly force.*

Police procedural error. A procedural error by the police in the development of evidence or in the way in which a defendant is arrested can lead to the dismissal of charges against him. Strictly speaking, these defenses are neither excuses nor justifications. Rather, they are assertions of violations of the accused's constitutional protections. A few of these are examined in the next section.

PROTECTING THE RIGHTS OF THE ACCUSED

In order to protect the liberty of an individual accused of a crime and to ensure a fair trial, the Constitution dictates much of our criminal procedure. All the protections it provides spring from one fundamental tenet: an accused is presumed innocent until the trier of fact finds him guilty. The subsections below touch on some of the more important constitutional protections.

Arrest

The Fourth Amendment to the Constitution provides:

> The right of the people to be secure in their persons, houses, propers, and effects, against unreasonable searches and seizures, shall not be violated, and no warrants shall issue, but upon probable cause, . . . and particularly describing the place to be searched, and the persons or things to be seized.†

The guarantee of the Fourth Amendment that persons shall be "secure in their persons" re-

---

* Massachusetts and some other states have enacted laws permitting the use of deadly force against intruders into dwellings, even though the occupants could safely retreat.

† In some if its most controversial decisions of the 1930s through 1960s, the Supreme Court held that federal constitutional protection of an accused also applied to the states. In effect, then, the Constitution states the minimum protection to which the accused is entitled. State constitutions can and do expand these protections. The discussion here focuses on the federal minimums.

quires a showing of probable cause before a court may issue an *arrest warrant,* which is an authorization to take a person into custody. To show *probable cause,* police must demonstrate a reasonable ground for suspicion, supported by circumstances which would justify a cautious person's belief that the defendant committed the crime. Suppose the police want to arrest Barbara for holding up a convenience store. They must convince a judge of the reasonableness of their belief that she participated in the crime—not that she is guilty.

In some instances, the police need not get an arrest warrant. For instance, if they caught Barbara in the act of holding up the store, they could arrest her without a warrant.

Search and seizure

The Fourth Amendment prohibits only unreasonable searches and seizures. A search is unreasonable unless it meets one of the following requirements:

- The police obtain a valid *search warrant*—an authorization issued by a court to search a clearly defined area for certain specified items.
- The owner of the premises consents to the search.
- The search occurs as part of a valid arrest.
- The officers limit their search to a vehicle which they have validly stopped.

For example, a person who permits the police to search his apartment for stolen property cannot claim an unreasonable search if the police arrest him for possession of the marijuana he left in plain sight—even if the police did not find any stolen property. In the following case, the Supreme Court held the search warrant provisions of the Fourth Amendment applied to routine government safety inspections of business places.

Marshall v. Barlow's, Inc.

436 U.S. 307 (1978)

FACTS

The Occupational Safety and Health Act (OSHA) permits agents of the secretary of labor to enter the work area of a business to inspect for safety hazards and violations of OSHA regulations. The Act does not expressly require a search warrant for inspections. An OSHA inspector tried to enter the working area of Barlow's, Inc. The company refused to admit the inspector, who did not have a search warrant. Barlow's successfully sought an injunction against the attempts by the secretary of labor to inspect without a warrant. The secretary appealed.

ISSUE

If an employer denies a government inspector access to its premises, must the government obtain a search warrant in order to enter?

DECISION

Yes. Affirmed.

[The] Fourth Amendment prohibition against reasonable searches protects against warrantless intrusions during civil as well as criminal investigations. . . . "[The] basic purpose of this amendment . . . which is to safeguard the privacy and security of individuals against arbitrary invasions by Government officials" [would be violated] if the Government intrudes on a person's property. . . .

The critical fact in this case is that entry over Mr. Barlow's objections is being sought by the Government agent. . . . Without a warrant [the agent] stands in no better position than a member of the public. What is observable by the public is observable, without a warrant, by the Government inspector as well. The owner of a business has not, by the necessary utilization of employees in his operation, thrown open the areas where employees alone are permitted to the warrantless scrutiny of Government agents. . . .

As *Marshall* indicates, the requirement of a search warrant is the citizen's principal protection against unreasonable searches. Without a valid warrant, a court may not allow the evidence seized during the search to be used against the defendant. However, it is important to note that it is the judge who protects the citizen's interest. Typically, the target of the warrant is not present, since advance notice would provide a clear opportunity to destroy evidence.

Due process

The Fifth and Fourteenth Amendments to the Constitution guarantee that neither the United States nor the states shall "deprive any person of life, liberty, or property without due process of law." Essentially, "due process" means "fairness" or "justice." But it really is a shorthand expression for the ways in which we protect an individual in a criminal proceeding from the potential abuses of government. It is due process which requires that a police officer inform someone he has just arrested of her constitutional rights to:

- Remain silent
- Have a lawyer
- Have a lawyer appointed and paid for if she cannot afford one*

The rights to remain silent and to counsel are discussed below.

"Due process" can never be defined satisfactorily because our concept of it continually changes. As you will infer from the following case, the due process clause permits the Supreme Court to fine-tune criminal procedures to meet contemporary standards of fairness.

---

* These are the "Miranda warnings" police are supposed to give all criminal suspects. See *Miranda v. Arizona*. 384 U.S. 436 (1966).

Rochin v. California

342 U.S. 165 (1952)

FACTS   The police suspected Rochin was selling narcotics. They illegally entered his dwelling and found him in his bedroom. He swallowed two capsules while resisting the officers' attempt to extract the capsules by force. The officers took him to a hospital where, at their insistence, a doctor forced an emetic solution through a tube into his stomach against his will. Based on the morphine capsules the police thus obtained, Rochin was convicted of illegal possession of narcotics. The California Supreme court affirmed.

ISSUE   Are police officers permitted under the Constitution to force a defendant to regurgitate evidence?

DECISION   No. Reversed. "[The] proceedings by which this conviction was obtained do more than offend some fastidious squeamishness or private sentimentalism about combatting crime too energetically. This is conduct that shocks the conscience." Under the due process clause of the Fourteenth Amendment, the states in their criminal prosecutions must respect certain decencies of civilized conduct. If the police may not coerce a confession from a defendant, they may not force critical evidence out of his stomach.

The exclusionary rule. The courts enforce the restrictions on government's abuses of the criminal process by means of the *exclusionary rule,* a principle of constitutional law that forbids the use of illegally or wrongfully obtained evidence in a criminal proceeding. This rule is often cited by those who regard the courts as "soft" on criminals, because the forbidden evidence might have led to convictions. However, no one has yet devised a better method for warding off consistent misconduct by prosecutors and police. Further, experience during the 150 years before the Supreme Court adopted this approach early in the present century offered little hope that self-regulation would work.

Double jeopardy

The Fifth Amendment also provides, "nor shall any person be subject for the same offence to be twice put in jeopardy of life and limb." The British had a habit of trying criminal cases in colonial courts and, if dissatisfied with the outcome, trying the defendant again.

The double jeopardy provision forbids retrial after an *acquittal,* a formal discharge of a person charged with a crime. If a jury finds a defendant not guilty or a judge dismisses a criminal complaint for lack of evidence, the government may not try again. However, the double jeopardy prohibition does not prohibit retrial if, on appeal, a higher court reverses a conviction.

The prohibition has another limitation. It applies to prosecutions by one government level only. In other words, an act may violate a federal law and a state law, but the double jeopardy prohibition will not prevent separate trials for each violation. A defendant who steals a car in Columbia, South Carolina, and drives it to Dallas, Texas, where he is arrested, may be prosecuted under the South Carolina law against auto theft and the federal statute prohibiting interstate transportation of stolen motor vehicles. (Stealing a car is not a federal crime unless it occurs in a federal enclave like a military base.)

The double jeopardy prohibition also does not restrict the government's ability to bring multiple charges aginst a defendant for what appears to be a single incident. Suppose the auto thief actually operated a gang that stole cars to order. He arranged to have five cars stolen, put them on a trailer, and drove them to Dallas. Each car theft would result in a separate criminal charge in both federal and state courts.

Finally, the prohibition does not affect multiple charges arising from the same criminal act. In Massachusetts, for example, a robber who uses a gun may be prosecuted for both armed robbery and the commission of a crime using a firearm.

Self-incrimination

Anyone who has seen a gangster movie knows about "taking the Fifth." The Fifth Amendment provides, in part, that no person "shall be compelled in any criminal case to be a witness against himself." Thus, persons have the right to remain silent if what they would say could result in their criminal prosecution. While persons may not be forced to testify against themselves, criminal defendants may be required to supply handwriting samples, to appear in lineups, to give blood samples, and to take breathalizer tests. However, *Rochin* indicates the limits on what a defendant can be compelled to do.

Right to counsel

The Sixth Amendment guarantees the accused "the assistance of counsel for his defense." As the courts have interpreted it, this is the right to have "effective counsel," meaning that the defendant must have counsel at a point when legal advice could affect the exercise of the defendant's rights. Also, "effective" refers to the quality of a defendant's representation. However, the courts have taken a very lenient view of counsel's competence and rarely reverse convictions because of the poor representation the defendant received.

Defendants can waive counsel and act as their own attorneys. However, that waiver must be an intelligent decision, and the judge hearing the case must agree to accept the waiver. Lawyers who have represented themselves know the truth of the adage: "He who is his own lawyer has a fool for a client." An adequate criminal defense demands an understanding of the procedural and evidentiary rules which the court will apply. Also, it requires at least a sense of when to object, since objections at trial define the scope of an appeal (see Chapter 2). Perhaps most important, a person whose money, freedom, or life is at stake cannot take the kind of dispassionate view of the case which a good advocate can.

Under ordinary circumstances, private conversations between a lawyer and a client are privileged. So long as the client does not authorize the lawyer to repeat them, they are not admissible or even discoverable. But, the privilege has concrete limits, as the next case shows.

In re Grand Jury Proceedings (Company X)

857 F.2d 710 (10th Cir. 1988)

FACTS   Company X was the subject of a grand jury investigation relating to possible violations of federal laws. The grand jury issued subpoenas to Company X and Law Firm Y, its former counsel, for the production of documents. The company filed objections to the subpoena, citing the attorney-client privilege. The prosecution sought an order from the district court compelling the production of the documents. The district court concluded that the government had made a sufficient showing that the company through its employees had committed crimes and then used Law Firm Y to cover them up and to perpetrate a second series of crimes. The district court ordered production of the documents on the ground that the attorney-client privilege does not apply to client consultations designed to further a fraud or crime.

ISSUE   Is there an exception to the attorney-client privilege for consultations that may further a fraud or crime?

DECISION   Yes. Affirmed. The "crime-fraud" exception applies when the client consults an attorney in order to further a crime or a fraud. Before the client loses the privilege, the government must show that there is evidence that the client communicated with the attorney for this purpose. Here the alleged criminal activity occurred during Law Firm Y's representation of Company X, and the documents subpoenaed related to that activity.

Right to a jury trial

The Sixth Amendment also guarantees the right to a jury in criminal cases, but that right is not unlimited. Typically, individuals charged with minor misdemeanors, like traffic offenses, are not entitled to a jury. However, the line between those charges which entitle a defendant to a jury and those which do not is not precisely drawn. The penalty which may be imposed is the best evidence of the seriousness of the offense and, therefore, of whether a defendant is entitled to a jury. Six months in prison, the Supreme Court has held, evidences a serious offense. Crimes with penalties exceeding 6 months require a jury trial.

Until recently, criminal juries consisted of twelve persons. And, it was thought, criminal juries must render a unanimous verdict. However, the Supreme Court has approved state systems wherein juries of fewer than twelve are used in criminal cases and unanimous verdicts are required only of juries of fewer than twelve. Such systems have now become the norm.

CRIMES AFFECTING BUSINESS

The remainder of this chapter looks at a number of crimes which affect businesses economically. Of course, virtually all crimes can affect a business. The rape of a key officer may profoundly alter how a company functions, for example. But crimes of violence are of less daily importance to business in general than are economic crimes.

Over the years, writers have distinguished between crimes committed by ordinary criminals, like muggers and shoplifters, and those committed by "white collar criminals." *White collar crimes* are crimes likely to be committed in a business context by members of the middle and upper classes. Securities frauds and antitrust violations are classic examples. The term also reflects the feeling of many critics that white collar criminals simply pay fines while other criminals—often for crimes involving fewer victims and significantly less money—go to jail. Organized crime has discovered how lucrative white collar crime can be. In fact, white collar crime is widely estimated to generate $100 billion a year for crooks. Of course, in terms of the cost of white collar crime to society, that figure represents only the part of the iceberg above the water. Insurance fraud alone raises policyholders' premiums an estimated $13.75 billion per year.* So "white collar crime" is now really a misnomer for illegal acts in a business context committed by means of concealment or guile, usually without the threat of force.

This section examines examples of both ordinary and white collar crimes. Other crimes are discussed throughout the book (see Figure 5.1).

---

* *National Law Journal.* October 13, 1986, p. 29.

CHAPTER TOPIC	SUBJECT	CHAPTER
Adminstrative law	Rule violations	3
Torts	Relation to crimes	4
Contracts	Illegal contracts	9
Agency	Agents' crimes	14
Partnerships	Partners' crimes	17
Corporations	Illegal actions	21
Securities	Securities acts	22
Accountants	SEC/IRS	23
Landlord-tenant law	Landlord liability	28
Negotiable instruments	Stolen paper	37, 38
Bankruptcy	Fraud	43
Antitrust laws	Monopolies, price fixing	44
Consumer protection	Product safety	45
Employment law	OSHA violations	46
Environmental law	Water, air, surface mining acts	47

Figure 5.1 Crimes and criminal behavior discussed in other chapters.

Ordinary crimes

The last chapter introduced the concept of intentional torts. Many intentional torts are also classified as crimes. In other words, both civil and criminal liability can exist for the same act.

The elements of the intentional torts parallel those of the crimes. For example, in both instances a battery is a touching of another without that person's consent. The most common of the intentional torts that are also crimes are: assault, battery, false imprisonment, trespass, and conversion. This section looks at some other common crimes that may affect businesses.

Arson. *Arson* is the crime of starting a fire or causing an explosion for the purpose of destroy-ing a structure belonging to another or of destroying or damaging any property, whether that of the arsonist or of another, to collect insurance. Landlords, for instance, have burned down their own problem buildings for this purpose.

Many states created a special offense called "burning to defraud an insurance company" because earlier definitions of arson did not include the burning of one's own home for this purpose.

Forgery. In the ordinary case, *forgery* consists of signing another's name to a document with the intent to defraud. Marvin commits forgery when he signs Alice's name to a check, intending to cash it and keep the proceeds for himself. Forgery also includes any unauthorized alteration of a writing for the purpose of unlawfully obtaining money. Suppose Alice makes out a check to Marvin for $100. If Marvin adds a zero to the amount, he commits forgery. Now suppose Marvin receives a check with Alice's signature on it, but he knows Don forged the signature. If Marvin's attempts to cash the check, he commits forgery.

Larceny. *Larceny* is a theft of property which does not involve force or the threat of force.

Essentially, "theft" and "larceny" are synonyms. Larceny can range from stealing a lawn mower from someone's front yard to inducing gullible consumers to buy subscriptions to nonexistent magazines. Some types of larceny, such as automobile theft, constitute distinct crimes. In the next case, a court had to determine whether a modern invention was property for the purposes of a larceny statute.

People v. Zakarian

121 Ill. App. 3d 968, 460 N.E.2d 422 (1984)

FACTS   Zakarian owned a record store in Chicago which specialized in Iraqi music. Wiggins manufactured recordings by Iraqi artists for distribution in the United States. Chicago police officers bought two tapes from Zakarian's store which were by Wiggin's artists but which Wiggins had not authorized Zakarian to sell. Zakarian had bought copies of Wiggin's tapes, duplicated them on machines in his store, and then sold the copies. The trial court found Zakarian guilty of theft.

ISSUE   Did Zakarian's duplication and sale of the recordings constitute theft?

DECISION   No. Reversed. The Illinois theft statute requires that the stolen property be capable of being taken and carried away. Only property which is measurable or detectable by the senses or by mechanical means can be the subject of theft. The exclusive right to produce sound recordings cannot be taken away or moved. Therefore, the state did not prove beyond a reasonable doubt that Zakarian took property from Wiggins.

It is important to note that other laws do protect Wiggins in cases like these. As we shall see later, in Chapter 25, the copyright laws offer Wiggins some civil and criminal measures of relief. Also, theft statutes are not uniform. In some states, Zakarian's acts may constitute thefts.

Receiving stolen goods. A person who knowingly accepts stolen goods is guilty of *receiving*

stolen goods. Without proof to the contrary, a court presumes the required knowledge or belief in the case of a dealer in any of the following situations:

- The dealer is found in possession of property stolen from two or more people on separate occasions.
- The dealer received stolen property in another transaction within the prior year.

- As a dealer in property of the sort received, the dealer acquired the stolen property for an amount he or she knows to be far below its reasonable value.

Suppose Rich bought a typewriter from Stella's pawnshop. Later, the police confiscated it because it was stolen. Rich did not know it was stolen, so he is not guilty of receiving stolen goods. However, Stella would be guilty if she knew or believed the typewriter had been stolen or believed it probably had been.

Obtaining goods by false pretenses. One of the most common crimes against business is *obtaining goods by false pretenses*. The wrongdoer must make a false representation intending to relieve an owner of property, and the owner must rely on the pretense in parting with the goods.

If the seller intends to pass only possession—not ownership—at the time of sale, the buyer commits the offense of larceny by trick. If the seller intends to transfer ownership, the buyer obtains property by false pretenses. Ordinarily, ownership passes from seller to buyer on delivery, without regard to when payment is due. But when an implied promise to pay for goods delivered accompanies an intention not to perform, the promise is a fraudulent representation or pretense.

Mail fraud. As noted in the last chapter, "fraud" is a broad term meaning deception or trickery designed to induce someone to part with property or a legal right. *Mail fraud* has two necessary elements. First, the defendant must help organize a scheme to defraud or obtain property by false pretenses. Second, the defendant must mail or have someone else mail a writing for the purpose of carrying out the scheme. If Helen sends phony invoices to 500 large corporations, expecting that some will pay without checking to see whether they actually owe the money, she commits mail fraud. Mail fraud is a federal crime because the U.S. government operates the postal service.

White collar crimes

Typically, white collar crime involves an employee who misappropriates money from a firm. It differs from larceny in that the embezzler is in a fiduciary relationship, a relationship of trust, to the possessor of the property. If a bank teller takes $1000 out of the till, he embezzles because he is in a relationship of trust with his employer, the bank. But if he fishes $100 out of a customer's purse as it lies on the counter, he commits larceny.

Embezzlement. An *embezzlement* is the fraudulent appropriation of property of another by a person to whom such property has been entrusted or into whose hands it has lawfully come. The prosecution must establish that the defendant was not lawfully entitled to use the property for the purposes to which it was put. It is harder to distinguish embezzlement from breach of contract. The next case shows why this is important in a civil context.

In re Belfry

S62 F.2d 661 (8th Cir. 1988)

FACTS   Pursuant to a written contract dated November 14, 1980, Christopher Cardozo paid $19,500 in advance to Richard Belfry for the restoration of a BMW 633. The contract specified Belfry's responsibilities as to: (1) equipping the car; (2) the quality of delivery; (3) the terms of the warranty; (4) resale of the car and refund of the purchase price if Cardozo was unhappy with it; (5) the date of delivery, April 15, 1981; and (6) the guarantee of the paint job. At the time Cardozo gave Belfry the money, Belfry told him that he was having cash flow problems. Nonetheless, Cardozo later testified, it was his understanding that the money was to go exclusively for the BMW's restoration. Belfry did not deliver the car and later filed for bankruptcy. The Bankruptcy Court found that Belfry had embezzled the $19,500 and therefore his debt to Cardozo was not dischargeable.

ISSUE   Did a fiduciary relationship exist between Belfry and Cardozo?

DECISION   No. Reversed. The Bankruptcy Code provides that a discharge does not free an individual debt from any debt for "fraud or defalcation while acting in a fiduciary capacity, embezzlement, or larceny." Absent Cardozo's alleged "understanding." Belfry's diversion of the funds would not be embezzlement. Payment of a contract price in exchange for an undertaking of an obligation of future performance transfers ownership of the money to the recipient. One cannot embezzle one's own property. The question then becomes whether the terms by which the recipient came by the money created particular obligations that would support a claim of embezzlement. These obligations are ones that would make the recipient's discretionary use of the money improper. Here, the contract reveals no such obligations. In fact, Belfry's obligations could be performed without any reference to how he used the money. And, the contract does not require him to segregate the funds or to use the actual funds for the car's restoration.

Bribery. Three types of bribery affect business. Commercial bribery is perhaps the most common. People offer bribes to cover up their misdeeds, to secure information about the products of another company (industrial espionage), or to secure new business. If a company's purchasing agent tells a vendor to kick back a percentage of each order if he wishes to continue getting the company's business, the purchasing agent is soliciting a bribe.

Bribes to public officials, of course, receive enormous publicity when they are uncovered, because of the recipients' positions of public trust. Under federal law (the states have similar laws), it is illegal to give money or anything else of value to a government employee. The U.S. Code describes two separate offenses. The first involves payments in exchange for official action. The second involves a *gratuity*, any payment or promise of something of value, whether or not designed to prompt government action.

The third class of bribes, bribes to foreign officials, is forbidden by the Foreign Corrupt Practices Act. That Act makes it a crime to offer anything of value to an official of a foreign government for the purpose of influencing that official's acts for business reasons. The Act has proved highly unpopular among multinational corporations. They argue it fails to recognize the cultural differences in doing business around the globe. In some countries bribes are an accepted part of transactions.

The Foreign Corrupt Practices Act does, however, exempt "grease" payments. These are disbursements made to lower ministerial officers, who have no discretionary powers, in exchange for performing routine governmental actions. Examples of grease payments include money paid for obtaining permits and licenses, processing governmental papers, providing police protection, and supplying water or power. The argument for allowing these kinds of exceptions is that it is customery in some countries to make these payments, otherwise the services might not be performed.

Computer crimes. The term "computer crimes" refers to two quite different types of crimes: computer sabotage—crimes against a computer as property—and computer-assisted crimes—ones committed using a computer. (See Figure 5.2.)

Computer sabotage takes a number of forms, ranging from alterations to programs to actual destruction of the hardware. Often, the

saboteurs are persons who feel their jobs are threatened by the machines.

Computer-assisted crime is an emerging field because the limits on the computer's potential use for criminal purposes are unknown. For example, a bank employee reprogrammed the bank's computer to direct any odd fractions of interest on other accounts to his own account. If interest on an account was $112.893, the employee's account was credited with $0.003. Since this embezzler worked for a major bank, the fractions mounted up rapidly. Smith, in the last case, may have used a computer to assemble data for his "clients." Certainly prominent among computer-assisted crimes are those involving the sale of information. The next case illustrates the most common type of computer crime: theft of services.

Figure 5.2 Common computer crimes.

State v. McGraw

459 N.E.2d 61 (Ind. Ct. App. 1984)

FACTS   McGraw worked as a computer operator for the city of Indianapolis. McGraw used the city's computer in his private business—selling a diet product called "Nature Slim"—for client lists, inventory control, word processing, and other functions. He was discharged from selling Nature Slim on city time and for poor job performance. After his discharge, he asked another operator to print out all the Nature Slim data and then to erase it from the computer's memory. The other operator reported McGraw's request to his supervisor, and his activities came to light. Before being sentenced on two counts of theft, McGraw filed a motion to dismiss the two counts on the grounds that the facts did not show an offense. The court trial denied his motion.

ISSUE   Is it theft to engage in unauthorized use of another's computer for private business?

DECISION   Yes. Affirmed. McGraw argued that "use" of the computer was not property subject to theft. New York and Virginia courts had held under their statutes that computer time was not property subject to theft. However, Indiana defines "property" as "anything of value," and its statute expressly includes "services."

> Computer services . . . are a part of our market economy in huge dollar amounts. . . . Computer time is "services" for which money is paid. Such services may reasonably be regarded as valuable assets to the beneficiary. Thus, computer services are property within the meaning of the definition of property subject to theft. When a person "obtains" or "takes" those services, he has exerted control [over the property]. . . . Taking without the other person's consent is unauthorized taking. Depriving the other person of any part of the services' use completes the offense.

Indiana's statutory definitions of "theft" and "property" permitted successful prosecution of McGraw. Other states either do not have such comprehensive statutes or, like Illinois, have not revised them recently to take into account new forms of property. As computer literacy increases, the creative use of computers for criminal purposes will put legislatures to the severe test of drafting laws to fit crimes committed by means of an emerging technology.

Securities fraud. As we will see in Chapter 23, sales of securities to the public are strictly regulated. Basically, the federal law requires full disclosure of all relevant information relating to the company offering the security and to the security itself. An intentional misrepresentation or omission of a material fact relating to the company or the offering is a criminal violation of the federal Securities Acts. The states have similar statutes, called "blue sky laws," regulating security sales within their boundaries. The term "blue sky" was borrowed from a practice of real estate promoters who peddled a vision of "building lots in the blue sky in fee simple."

Crimes committed by corporations

The law considers corporations to be artificial persons. As such, corporations cannot harbor criminal intent. However, they may be criminally liable if the penalty is a fine, if specific intent is not an element, or if intent can be implied. For example, a corporation convicted of criminal price fixing under the federal antitrust laws (see Chapter 44) can be fined up to $1 million. Violations of the Foreign Corrupt Practices Act carry a similar penalty for the corporation.

A corporate officer can be prosecuted for a crime committed while she is acting for the company. A price-fixing violation may result in a fine of up to $100,000 and imprisonment for up to 3 years. Some people have argued that prosecution of corporate officers is a far more effective means of ensuring compliance with regulatory statutes than are criminal actions against companies. The implications of the next case support that view.

United States v. Park

421 U.S. 658 (1975)

FACTS

Park was president of Acme Markets, Inc., a national retail food chain. The Food and Drug Administration (FDA) found that food stored in two Acme warehouses was exposed to contamination by rodents. The FDA notified Park of these conditions. He delegated responsibility for remedying the situation. When conditions did not improve, the FDA brought criminal charges against him. The jury found Park guilty, but the court of appeals reversed.

ISSUE

Did Park have the power to eliminate the danger to the public posed by the contamination?

DECISION

Yes. Court of appeals reversed. The only way in which a corporation can act is through the individuals who act on its behalf. The Food and Drug Act forbids the transportation in interstate commerce of adulterated food. In providing sanctions which reach the individuals who execute a corporation mission, the Act imposes not only a positive duty to seek out and remedy violations when they occur but also a duty to implement measures that will ensure that violations will not occur. The Act does not make criminal liability depend on awareness of wrongdoing or on conscious fraud. However, it also does not authorize a conviction based solely on the defendant's position. If the defendant was powerless to prevent or correct the violation, he would not be guilty. Here, Park had the power.

When it was decided, the preceding case was almost unique. Today, an increasing number of prosecutors have targeted corporate officers for prosecution. In a notable case, three executives of one firm were convicted of the murder of an employee who inhaled cyanide fumes while on the job.

RICO

Prosecutors have often noted that it takes at least 5 years for them and other law enforcement personnel to fully integrate new legislation into their war against crime. It took almost twice that long for them to appreciate that Congress had given them, in the Racketeer Influenced and Corrupt Organizations Act (RICO), an atomic bomb to use against organized crime and other repeat violators. But, like a nuclear weapon, RICO is not a precision instrument, and companies that have never considered themselves to be racketeers have found themselves prosecuted under this Act.

Scope of the Act

In 1970, Congress enacted the Organized Crime Control Act. RICO is a part of that Act. Congress intended that this legislation would enable law enforcement agencies to attack the investment of organized crime revenues—from drugs, prostitution, gambling, and other sources—in legitimate businesses.

Enterprise liability. What makes RICO such a powerful weapon is that it targets the fruits of illegal enterprises. While RICO does prescribe fines and jail sentences, it also provides a means for both prosecutors and private individuals in effect to confiscate ill-gotten gains—and sometimes more.

RICO focuses on patterns—as opposed to instances—of criminal behavior. It applies to individuals or businesses that are involved in an interstate enterprise and in any 10-year period engage more than once in criminal activities, ranging from mail or stock fraud to extortion or murder. The language of the statute is so broad that every transaction involving the mails, telephones, or any other interstate communications device contains the potential for a RICO violation.

Relationship to antitrust. That RICO resembles the antittrust laws (which are examined in Chapter 44) is no accident. Congress intended to integrate the two statutory schemes. Thus, prosecutors and civil litigants may recover from firms or individuals that improperly resort to:

- Violence or the threat of violence (RICO)
- Deception (RICO)
- Market power (antitrust)

Criminal Actions

Although at least twenty-five states have "little RICO" statutes modeled on the federal statute, only the U.S. Department of Justice can initiate a criminal prosecution under RICO.

Establishing a RICO violation requires proof of three elements:

- Commission of racketeering offenses
- A pattern of prohibited activity
- Acts involving an enterprise

Racketeering activities covered by RICO include thirty state and federal crimes. These range from traditional mob-related crimes, such as arson, gambling, bribery, and extortion, to crimes often listed under the white collar heading—securities fraud, commodities fraud, and mail fraud. A pattern of prohibited activity simply consists of proof of commission of two racketeering offenses within a 10-year period.

An enterprise may be a corporation, a partnership, or an unincorporated association. Acts involving an enterprise include using income derived from a pattern of racketeering activity to acquire or maintain an interst in an enterprise, conducting or participating in the affairs of an enterprise through a pattern of racketeering activity, or conspiring to commit such acts.

RICO's criminal penalties include fines of up to $25,000 per violation, imprisonment for up to 20 years per violation, and the forfeiture of any interest gained in an enterprise as a result of a prohibited activity.

Civil Actions

The Department of Justice or an individual injured by activity forbidden by RICO may bring a civil action against the individuals or the enterprise that committed the offense. The elements of a cause of action are essentially the same as those for a criminal case, though, of course, a plaintiff in a civil suit does not have to prove guilt beyond a reasonable doubt.

Among remedies a plaintiff may choose are:

- Treble damages
- Forfeiture and divestiture
- Attorney's fees
- Seizure of assets
- Constructive trusts
- Injunctions

Plaintiffs have brought RICO civil suits in the following areas: commercial transactions, industrial espionage, securities and commodities trading, government contracting, labor relations, and insurance fraud by companies, as well as many other areas. In one particularly "hot" area, professional services, RICO suits have been brought against individuals such as accountants and stockbrokers. The next case involved a top-level manager.

Beth Israel Medical Center v. Smith

576 F.Supp. 1061 (S.D.N.Y. 1983)

FACTS   The Federation of Jewish Philanthropies (FOJP) formed FOJP Service Corporation to investigate potential medical malpractice claims against the more than fifteen health-related facilities it sponsored in or near New York City. Smith supervised the legal services FOJP Service offered and had access to all information it gathered. Immediately after he was hired in October 1979, he began selling information to several plaintiffs' lawyers. The scheme came to light in June 1981 as a result of a complaint by a patient solicited to sue one of the hospitals. Smith pleaded guilty to receiving a commercial bribe. FOJP Service and the FOJP-sponsored facilities then brought suit against Smith and the plaintiffs' lawyers involved in the scheme under the Racketeer Influenced and Corrupt Organizations Act (RICO). RICO authorizes a court to award triple damages to the victim of a pattern of racketeering activity. Smith filed a motion to dismiss.

ISSUE   Did Smith's scheme amount to a pattern of racketeering activity as defined to RICO?

DECISION   Yes. Motion denied. A racketeering activity consists of any act which is indictable under federal statutes specified in RICO—including mail or wire fraud—and certain state violations—including acts involving bribery. A pattern of racketeering activity consists of the commission of two or more acts of this type within 10 years of each other. The civil remedy of triple damages is available to anyone whose business or property is injured by a pattern of racketeering activity. RICO does not require the plaintiff to establish any connection between the activity and organized crime.

The Controversy Over RICO

It is easy to guess the main objection to RICO: the courts have interpreted it far too broadly. Legitimate businesses were never intended to be targets of RICO civil suits. Plainly, businesses also resent being accused of "racketeering," especially since less than 10 percent of the complaints in such cases allege a mob-type crime.

However, as the Supreme Court has pointed out, it may be that Congress did not intend RICO to be read so broadly, but what it enacted plainly requires an expansive, inclusive interpretation. Also, both the Ninety-eighth and Ninety-ninth Congresses had before them bills to limit RICO's reach, but none was passed. Nonetheless, the lobbying for reform continues.

It seems clear that Congress should provide business with effective remedies against frivolous RICO actions. However, it bears noting that considerably more than 50 percent of all private RICO suits have an independent basis for being in federal court.

CONCLUSION

Criminal law is a means by which government enforces the duties people owe to society as a whole. Its goals are principally punitive and preventive; that is, criminal law seeks to punish the criminal while deterring other people from committing crimes. Like the law of torts, it has had to respond to rapidly changing technologies. However, since criminal law is ultimately a matter of constitutional and statutory law, its response to change has not been as rapid or as satisfactory as one would hope.

This chapter is the only one which focuses on criminal laws. While additional criminal statutes are noted in other units (see Figure 5.1), the rest of the book focuses on civil law.

A NOTE TO FUTURE CPA CANDIDATES

The CPA exam historically has not focused upon the specific criminal law offenses discussed in this chapter. Instead, the exam has covered applications of criminal law in the following situations:

- In employment. An employer will ordinarily not be liable for the criminal actions of his employee (Chapter 14).
- In regard to officer or director responsibility relating to corporate governance (Chapter 20) or SEC matters (Chapter 23).
- In the professional conduct of public accountants (Chapter 24).

Do not now try to master the CPA criminal applications.

KEY WORDS

act (105)
bribery (118)
crime (103)
due process (111)
embezzlement (117)
felony (105)
forgery (115)
fraud (117)
intent (105)
larceny (116)
misdemeanor (105)
motive (106)
omission (105)
probable cause (110)
RICO (122)
theft (120)
white collar crime (114)

DISCUSSION QUESTIONS

1. What is a crime? Whom does it harm? Who enforces criminal duties?
2. What are the elements of a crime, and what are their functions?
3. How may crimes be classified? What purposes do such classifications serve?
4. When does a government officer with police powers require a search warrant to enter a place of business? Explain.

5. When is a person entitled to a jury trial, as guaranteed by the U.S. Constitution? When is a person entitled to have counsel appointed by the court? Explain.

6. Under what circumstances may a police officer make a lawful arrest without a warrant? Explain.

7. List five ordinary crimes, and discuss how each affects business.

8. What is white collar crime, and how does it differ from other types of crime?

9. Under what circumstances may an officer in a corporation be liable for a crime even though he or she lacks any awareness of the wrongdoing or lacks the intent to commit fraud?

10. Describe Congress's intent in passing RICO. Summarize the controversy surrounding RICO today.

CASE PROBLEMS

1. Without receiving proper legal warnings, Scott Perkins was arrested for the burglary of a residential home. Scott's request for a lawyer during police questioning was denied. During this interrogation Scott admitted the burglaries and told police the stolen property could be found at 1257 West Lunt. Police went there and found the stolen items and further evidence linking Scott to five more burglaries. Is a judge likely to permit the recovered stolen items to be admitted as evidence at trial? Does the failure of the police to give Scott proper legal warnings prevent his being convicted of burglary? Explain.

2. A hunter, mistaking Jim Smith's prize hunting dog for a fox, shot it. When he checked his quarry, the hunter realized his mistake and immediately started to flee. Jim had witnessed the entire incident at a distance. Highly distraught, he ran into his house, grabbed a rifle, and began firing in the direction of the fleeing man to stop him. Unfortunately, Jim did not see his neighbor, Sam Hollis, whom one of his bullets struck. In a criminal action brought against Jim, would mistake be a successful defense? If this jurisdiction recognizes the irresistible impulse standard, can Jim escape criminal liability by claiming temporary insanity? Explain your answers.

3. Roy Loran owned a car dealership. Business was bad and he faced bankruptcy. Two men he had never seen before approached him and offered to sell him 10 pounds of cocaine on credit, saying they would wait until he sold it before demanding payment. Loran figured the deal would net him enough money to avoid bankruptcy, so he agreed. As soon as the two men handed him the cocaine, they revealed they were undercover drug enforcement officers and arrested him. What defenses will Loran raise? Will any of them be successful? Explain your answer.

4. Peabody watched The Diamond Company for several weeks. He noted that an armed courier arrived every day about 10 A.M. to pick up diamonds for delivery to jewelry stores in the area. Peabody created a uniform and an identification card roughly identical to those of the courier. At 9:50 one Friday morning, he entered The Diamond Company in his uniform and showed the security officer his identity card. Peabody told the security officer that the regular courier was ill and that he was the replacement. Peabody ultimately left the firm with $500,000 in diamonds. If he is caught, what crime is he likely to be charged with? Explain your answer.

5. Robin Ragin flew to Florida for spring break. When Robin got off the plane she went to the luggage claim area and claimed a gray suitcase which she mistakenly thought was hers. As she was preparing to leave the airport she was stopped by airport security persons who were alerted by the real owner of the bag. Robin opened the suitcase in an attempt to prove that it was her bag. As she did so a kilo of marijuana fell out. The real owner quickly fled. Robin was immediately arrested for theft and possession of illegal drugs. Is Robin likely

to prevail on the theft charge? On the illegal drugs charge? Explain.

6. Bobby Elliott also flew down to Florida for spring break. As a joke, several of his fraternity brothers called the Miami airport and gave them an anonymous tip that "drug-pin Elliott" was about to pass through. Elliott was spotted and approached in the airport by police. When approached, Elliott began to run but was immediately caught. Police searched Elliott, found a small amount of marijuana on him, and arrested him. Elliott denies knowing how the marijuana got into his traveling bag, claims he was stopped without probable cause, and charges the airport police with entrapment. Did the police have probable cause to stop Bobby? Is Elliott's entrapment defense likely to hold up in court? Explain.

7. ABC Widgets and XYZ Widgets, two major, competing widget producers, entered into an agreement whereby the two companies agreed not to compete against each other for state widget purchases in Iowa. The companies alternated submitting the "low" bid on five different occasions before arousing suspicions. The state estimates that it has lost at least $100,000 on account of the ABC–XYZ agreement. Assuming the federal government brings a RICO suit, would a court be likely to find the elements for a RICO violation? Assuming the companies were found guilty under RICO, what remedy(ies) would a federal court be most likely to levy? Explain.

8. Rocky the Great, a professional wrestler, was to wrestle at Hirsch Coliseum. A local television newscaster, Peter Smith, persuaded Rocky to be interviewed live during the 6:00 newscast. During the interview, Rocky became incensed when Smith asked if pro wrestling was all fake. Rocky got out of his chair, punched Smith in the nose, applied a murderous head-lock, stomped on Smith's right foot, and walked out of the studio. Rocky was later arrested and charged with battery as he attempted to enter Hirsch Coliseum. Is Rocky likely to be convicted of battery? Assuming that Rocky is acquitted of criminal battery, would Rocky be able to assert a defense of double jeopardy if Smith were to institute a tort action alleging battery against Rocky? Explain.

9. Real Issues. The federal government has found an important tool to fight drug, money-laundering, and racketeering crimes: property seizures. In 1985, the federal government seized $27.2 million dollars of property related to criminal arrest and/or conviction. By 1991, the figure was up to $634.6 million. Former junk bond racketeer king Michael Milken has been the biggest contributor to date: $176 million. However, the most seizures (around two-thirds of the 31,087 seizures in 1991) occur in relation to drug enforcement activities, such as the seizure of a rare, valuable Tucker automobile allededly being used as a display decoy to traffic drugs. To recover their property upon seizure, owners must prove their innocence. The "innocent-owner defense" can be difficult to prove, especially when the property is money. Ultimately the seized property will be returned if no criminal conviction or settlement is secured. However, there are growing concerns about issues of fairness and abuse. For example, should a person caught with $1000 in illegal drugs in a $35,000 sports car while attempting to close a drug deal forfeit the car? Law enforcement officials often respond by saying "if you play the game you play to lose." In your opinion, are property seizure laws an appropriate device for law enforcement? Should the sports car owner "be out" the $35,000 sports car? Explain. (Statistics from *USA Today,* March 26, 1992, p. 3A.)

10. Real Issues. The Racketeering Influenced and Corrupt Organizations Act (RICO) was enacted in 1970 as a weapon against organized crime. Under RICO, a person must be found to have engaged in a "pattern of racketeering" for certain defenses before being prosecuted. Such a pattern is defined as two offenses committed within 10 years of each other. Perhaps most common is the RICO allegation of mail fraud involving securities. The ability of the government to freeze assets pending trial, discussed in the previous ques-

tion, gives the government terrific clout in gaining quick settlements, sometimes not necessarily the most fair of settlements. Perhaps more alarming to opponents is the extent to which the reach of RICO has been extended well beyond its original mobster intent, especially for civil RICO matters. One proposal is to raise the requirements for a RICO conviction from the current "preponderance of the evidence" to a "clear and convincing" standard. Supporters claim this would more fairly match the gravity of seized property with clear wrongful conduct. Even many opponents of RICO fail to get excited about this, since the potential reach of RICO would not otherwise be limited. Your thoughts?

PART I PROBLEMS

The end-of-part problems serve three purposes. First, some require practical applications of legal knowledge to everyday situations. Second, they are summative, bringing together many of the issues treated individually in the chapters of a particular part. Third, the last question presents an ethical problem which, as in real life, may not have an unqualifiedly right or wrong solution. Rather, its goal is to prompt two questions: What would I do in this situation? What *should* I do in this situation?

I. A PRACTICAL PROBLEM

Chapter 2 introduced pleadings, documents which place the parties and the court on notice of the issues in a civil case. This problem's purpose is to integrate what you learned about pleadings in Chapter 2 with what you learned about the elements of a cause of action in tort in Chapter 4. It is also designed to highlight the differences between the proof of facts and the law which applies to those facts. This problem asks you to pretend you are a paralegal assigned to draft pleadings based on the following facts.

Rusty Hinges, the Chicago Cubs star pitcher, has an excellent fast ball, but on occasion he has serious control problems.

Last summer in a game against the New York Mets at Wrigley Field, Hinges had a particularly bad day. After walking one batter in each of the first three innings, Hinges accidentally hit the Mets' second baseman, Louis Litehit.

The Mets' next hitter, Frank "The Enforcer" Nasty, shouted from the on-deck circle, "You come close to me, and I'm gonna rearrange your face." Hinges was well aware of Nasty's reputation and tried to place his first pitch low and over the outside corner of the plate. He missed but fortunately, he thought, the ball cleared Nasty's kneecap by an inch.

Nasty was not so pleased. Bat in hand, he headed toward Hinges. Hoping at least to slow Nasty down, hinges threw his glove at the onrushing "Enforcer." Nasty caught Hinges, knocked him to the ground, and hit him three times with the bat before an umpire and a Mets coach tackled him.

Hinges spent 3 days in the hospital recovering from head injuries. His eyesight was temporarily affected but eventually returned to normal. Nonetheless, Hinges has found it psychologically impossible to throw as fast or as freely as he once did. Hinges has decided to sue Nasty for both his physical and psychological damages, including his loss of earning power. He plans to demand $1 million.

The National League president suspended Nasty for the remainder of the season. Nasty publicly apologized "for losing my temper" but added, "Hinges is just one of those Cub crybabies. He don't mind hitting a batter but he gets mad if somebody tries to protect himself." In the same press conference, Nasty announced that if Hinges sued him, he would sue Hinges just to prove he was telling the truth about Hinges.

Hinges has retained Walter Sandberg of the firm of Altgeld & Darrow, located at 210 La Salle Street, Chicago 60604. Nasty has hired Fred Burke of the firm of Moran & Capone, located at 2122 N. Clark Street, Chicago 60614. Hinges is an Illinois resident and Nasty a New York resident. Sandberg plans to file in federal court.

Using the pleadings in Chapters 2 and 4 as a model, prepare the complaint in *Hinges v. Nasty*. You may assume that Chapter 4 reflects the tort law of Illinois.

2. A SUMMATIVE PROBLEM

The following problem contains a number of potential legal issues. Identify and resolve each of them. Please provide reasons to support your answers.

George Potter, a college professor at Victory University in Illinois, decided to run for state representative. Potter's campaign announcement met with a fair amount of student opposition. One student, Angie Allen, attended Potter's first public speech. As he approached the stage, Angie hit Potter squarely in the face with a pie to protest his stand on nuclear energy. Angie was arrested for battery. Angie wants to defend on the ground that no part of her body touched Potter.

The convertible in which Potter was riding in Victory's homecoming parade was in an accident caused by the negligence of the other driver, Ben Bradley. Bradley, who lived in Cleveland, was just passing through Illinois on his way to San Francisco for a vacation. Potter's brother practices law in San Francisco, so Potter asked his brother to file a $25,000 tort action against Bradley in the federal court there. Bradley was served in San Francisco. Bradley has been advised: (1) the court probably lacks personal jurisdiction, but (2) if the district court should rule otherwise, Bradley would have the benefit of California precedent that favors his case. Bradley has doubts about this advice.

Potter was invited to speak to a Rotary Club at the Croydon Hotel. While speaking, a chandelier came lose, fell, and struck Potter, injuring him. Potter's lawyer has suggested that he sue the hotel on a strict liability theory. Later that afternoon Potter was struck by a car and injured while walking between lanes of busy traffic on Rush Street handing out campaign literature to passing drivers. The driver of the car that hit Potter, Dan Davis, suffered $5000 in damages from the accident and Potter, $10,000. Evidence shows that Potter was 50 percent at fault and Illinois is a comparative negligence state. Potter believes his net recovery should be $5000 in damages.

A robber stopped Potter's father, who suffered from heart disease, as he walked from his car to attend a speech his son was giving. The robber pulled a gun and said, "Your money or your life." When the robber became momentarily distracted, Potter's father attempted to get away by dashing into the street. Unfortunately, a bus struck him. The police chased the robber into the unlocked house of an uninvolved third party, where he was arrested. Unknown to Potter's father at the time of the mugging, the robber's gun was actually a water pistol. The robber claims he has no liability for assault (since the gun was actually only a water pistol) or battery (since Potter's father foolishly ran into the street) and the arrest was improper, since the police had no arrest and/or search warrant to enter the house.

Just before the election, Potter went sailing with Earl Eason. Potter had never sailed before, and Eason failed to explain the workings of the Southcoast sailboat before they set sail. Potter quickly recognized that the horizontal boom to which the mainsail was attached could suddenly and forcefully move from one side of the boat to the other. A person on a passing boat recognized Potter and yelled some political encouragement. Potter stood up, and while waving in appreciation, was struck by the boom, which a sudden change in wind had swung toward him. Dumped into the lake, his body bruised and aching, Potter threatened suit as soon as Earl pulled him from the water. Earl told Potter he was all wet in more ways than one; getting hit was his own fault.

One of Potter's opponents, Frank Farley, took advantage of Potter's spill by running political advertisements claiming that he was "clumsier than Jerry Ford and an idiot besides." The advertisement recounted Potter's spill and asked voters if this was the image they wanted for their district. Potter has sued Farley for invasion of privacy and defamation, pointing out that he is a member of Phi Beta Kappa and MENSA (a national association for people of the highest intelligence).

Somehow, Potter fooled the pollsters and won. To prove all his detractors wrong, Potter developed and submitted five bills in his first week in the legislature. The five bills were designed to:

a. Bolster the state's lagging economy and reduce unemployment, by requiring at least 25 percent of the parts in every new car sold in the state to be manufactured in the state.

b. Reduce the impact of imported cars on the local auto industry by assessing a 15 percent sales tax surcharge on each sale of a new import.

c. Reduce the possibility of young children being exposed to partially or unclothed women in nonadult magazines by banning the sale or distribution by mail of the *Sports Illustrated* "swimsuit edition" within the state.

d. Fund expansion at Metro Airport, a major regional hub, by compelling the airlines to collect a $2 head tax from every arriving passenger at Metro.

e. Reduce air pollution in the state by requiring all new vehicles sold in the state to meet clean air standards more stringent than the federal government's.

An opponent in the state legislature, Grace Gibbons, has told Potter that all his proposed bills are both stupid and unconstitutional. Potter disagrees on both counts.

3. A SUMMATIVE PROBLEM

Waldo Smith owns and operates Waldo's Tourist Bus Line in Phoenix, Arizona. Waldo's is a one-man operation, and Waldo is the man who sells tickets, takes tickets, drives the bus, keeps the books, and answers the phones. A number of things have happened to Waldo during the last few months which have legal ramifications. From the description of the events below, identify the issues they present and determine Waldo's rights, duties, and liabilities.

One morning, Waldo overslept and consequently reached his bus too late to sweep it out before his first load of tourists arrived. Anna Aldrich discovered a banana peel left on the floor by a passenger the previous day. Unfortunately, she found it by slipping on it, falling, and breaking her wrist.

Anna's fall delayed the trip, and Waldo began to get impatient. Betty Baker, a heavy-set older woman, was getting onto the bus very slowly. From the driver's seat, Waldo yelled at her, "Come on, Fatso. Get a move on." Baker burst into tears, backed off the bus, and refused to get on.

"Have it your way, nutso," Waldo told her as he tried to close the door. He could not close it because Casey Carver, a passenger, had blocked the door. "If you weren't so decrepit, I'd punch your lights out for what you did to that old lady,'' Carver threatened. Waldo stepped off the bus. ''Go ahead. Make my day,'' he taunted Carver. Carver knocked Waldo to the ground and then turned to walk away. Waldo felt a loose brick. He picked it up and heaved it at Carver's back. He missed Carver's back but did hit him in the head. Carver suffered a severe concussion.

A police officer saw Waldo hit Carver and arrested him, even though Waldo protested loudly that he was just protecting himself.

The following week, Waldo was conducting his usual tour when he noticed a couple in the back seat engaged in a torrid embrace. Thinking he would amuse his passengers, he adjusted the inside mirror so everyone in the front of the bus could watch. When the couple realized the other passengers were cheering their performance, they abruptly broke apart—so abruptly that the man, Donald Denton, suffered a whiplash injury to his neck.

Denton has sued Waldo in the state Superior Court. There is no Arizona law on point. However, in Denton's motion for summary judgment, he noted that a California Court had held that a bus driver who adjusted a mirror so other passengers could watch a couple engaged in amorous conduct was liable for damages for the couple's public embarrassment. Waldo's attorney, Edna Elmose, is worried that case precedent and the rule of *stare decisis* will now compel the court to find against Waldo. She is considering removing the case to federal court where state law, she believes, will not apply.

A few days after the mirror incident, Waldo started his bus at the terminal, left the bus, closed the door, and went for some coffee. A group of teenagers standing nearby noted Waldo had not locked the door. On a dare, one of them, Frankie Feldman, opened the door, hopped into the driver's seat, put the bus in reverse, and backed it out of the terminal at high speed.

When Frankie got to the street, he rammed a passing car driven by Ginger Grant. Ordinarily, Grant would have been able to avoid the accident, but she had left a swimming pool moments before and her wet foot slipped off the brake pedal.

At the sound of the crash, Waldo raced out of the coffee shop. When he saw what had happened, he yelled at a beat cop, ''Arrest that punk! He robbed my bus!''

Waldo decided he needed better protection for the bus. He settled on an ingenious device which turned the driver's seat into an electrified hot seat for anyone attempting to drive the bus without disconnecting the device. Harry Harrier, a wino, stumbled into the bus one afternoon when the hot seat was on. Apparently he did not notice the warmth of the seat when he sat down. In fact, he sat on it so long, it short-circuited, turning itself into an electric chair. Waldo was arrested and charged with manslaughter.

The following day, Ike Ibert, a local talk show host, opened his program with a lengthy monolog on Waldo. ''Some people on the city payroll just aren't doing their jobs when a half-crazed hothead like Waldo Smith can terrorize Phoenix with his violent antics and booby traps. The guy ought to be put away,'' Ibert shouted. Waldo has sued Ibert for defamation. Ibert claims that his statements were truthful and that his remarks were made without any malice toward Waldo, a public figure.

4. AN ETHICAL PROBLEM

It is not necessarily true that an ethical question has been resolved just because it is old. The two halves of this problem raise questions which have vexed lawyers, judges, citizens, and legislators for at least 140 years. Yet controversies involving the issues posed below are still making the front pages.

In both instances, the starting point is rule 1.6(a) of the American Bar Association's Model Rules of Professional Conduct (1983). It states, in part:

> *A lawyer shall not reveal information relating to the representation of a client unless the client consents after consultation, except for disclosures that are impliedly authorized in order to carry out the representation. . . .*

Rule 1.6(b) does permit a lawyer to reveal information to prevent the client from committing a criminal act which is likely to result in imminent death or bodily harm. For the purposes of the two questions below, you may assume that the law offers little guidance beyond rule 1.6 and that the courts recognize it as a correct statement of the law.

a. *A criminal case.* Ruth Judd retained the law firm of DeSalvo & Packer to defend her on a charge of first degree murder of her boyfriend's wife.

During the lawyers' interview of Judd before surrendering her to the police, she asked if everything she told them would be "just between them." DeSalvo told her precisely what rule 1.6 said. "O.K.," she said, "I did it and here's the knife I did it with." The lawyers placed the knife in their safe.

Judd eventually pled guilty to a charge of second degree murder and was sentenced to life imprisonment. During sentencing, she told the court that she had turned the knife over to her lawyers.

The lawyers now face criminal charges of concealing evidence. They have defended on the grounds that their conversation with their client and the evidence it produced was confidential. Should the rule of confidentiality apply when the client gives the lawyer evidence of the commission of a crime or admits to committing it? What if Judd had insisted on pleading innocent and on telling the court she had had nothing to do with the killing? What if she had pled not guilty but had exercised her constitutional right not to testify?

b. *A civil case.* On paper, O.P.C. Corporation leased mainframe computers to businesses. In reality, its principals, Insul and Ponzi, generated O.P.C.—"Other People's Cash"—for their high living by forging titles and lease agreements for nonexistent computers. They used these documents to convince banks to lend them money.

O.P.C.'s counsel, Whitney & Cornfeld, prepared the loan agreements but learned of the fraud by accident only after it had been going on for 4 years. Tearfully, Insul and Ponzi admitted as much of their wrongdoing as the lawyers had discovered and promised never to forge another document. They also promised to pay off the loans so no one would be hurt.

On the basis of those representations, Whitney & Cornfeld agreed to continue representing O.P.C. Six months later, the lawyers discovered that Insul and Ponzi had lied to them and had continued their fraud. Whitney & Cornfeld immediately resigned as O.P.C.'s counsel and were replaced by Goodheart & True.

Whitney & Cornfeld told the new lawyers nothing about their clients' fraudulent activities. A year later, thanks to an inquiring young accountant, Goodheart & True discovered the fraud and immediately confronted their clients with the evidence. When Insul and Ponzi refused to authorize the lawyers to attempt to resolve the frauds with the banks and the government, the lawyers reported O.P.C.'s activities to the proper authorities.

Goodheart & True lost more than $300,000 in billings due from O.P.C. It has sued Whitney & Cornfeld for that sum, alleging that law firm had a duty to tell it of Insul and Ponzi's activities. Did Whitney & Cornfeld have such a duty? Under rule 1.6, did Goodheart & True act ethically in reporting the frauds to the banks and the authorities? If not, who should have a remedy against them and what should be the measure of damages for the breach of the duty?

CONTRACTS

The subject of this part, contracts, will affect your business and personal life more directly than any other you will study in this course. In fact, you are reading these words as a result of contracts—your contract with your school and the contract you made to buy this book.

When students first approach the subject, they think of contracts as long documents full of words like "whereas," "above referenced," and "but for." They associate contracts with big deals, but we have already seen that contracts are the basis of the most ordinary transactions. And only a few types of contracts have to be in writing. No one would expect a written contract for the sale of a hamburger or a movie ticket or a bicycle. If you join an exercise class, you probably would not expect a written contract either. Yet the basic principles which govern these ordinary transactions also govern a merger between two multi-billion-dollar corporations.

This part explores the basic principles of contract law: what contracts are, how they are formed, how they are fulfilled, and what they mean when parties do not fulfill them. At least 80 percent of what follows in succeeding parts rests on contract law.

WHAT IS A CONTRACT?

A *contract,* essentially, is a promise or set of promises a court will enforce. The key here is that the courts will enforce the promises. That means the promises are legal contracts, not illegal ones like "contracts" to commit arson. It also means that legal contracts do not include social obligations, like going out with someone if you accept a date. When we use the term "contract" in this book, we will always mean "legal contract" unless we specifically state otherwise.

All contractual relationships start with the fulfillment of a simple equation:

$$\text{Offer } + \text{ acceptance } = \text{ mutual assent}$$

Without *mutual assent*—consisting of both an offer and an acceptance—the relationship between the parties is not contractual.

The parties to a contract are the *offeror,* who makes the offer, and the *offeree,* who accepts it. An *offer* is the offeror's proposal stating what he is willing to do or not do in exchange for a specified action or promise by the offeree. If the offeree accepts the offer, the parties have a contract. If the offeree rejects the offer, no contract results.

The law categorizes contracts according to the type of acceptance—a promise or an action—which the offeror requires. If the offeror has specified a promise as the acceptance, this is said to be a *bilateral contract.* "Bilateral" comes from the Latin and means "two-sided." The term refers to the fact that in such contracts both the offeror and the offeree make promises. Suppose Kurt says to Linda, "I promise to sell you my Walkman if you'll promise to pay me

$20." If Linda responds, "Sure, I'll pay you $20 for it," then she and Kurt have formed a bilateral contract.

In contrast, a *unilateral* ("one-sided") *contract* is one in which only the offeror makes a promise. In return for the promise, the offeror wants a specified action from the offeree. Now, suppose Kurt says to Linda, "I promise to sell you my Walkman if you hand me $20." Linda immediately hands Kurt a $20 bill, thereby accepting his offer of a unilateral contract. The act does not have to occur immediately. The offeror can specify a time by which the act must be done.

Unilateral contracts are exceptional. Most contracts are bilateral.

THE ELEMENTS OF A CONTRACT

A contract always requires the presence of four components, but sometimes requires five. The five are:

- Mutual assent
- Consideration
- Possession of contractual capacity by the parties
- Legal objectives
- A writing, if required by statute

Mutual assent, the essential prerequisite for every enforceable contract, has already been discussed. Its elements, offer and acceptance, are examined in Chapters 6 and 7. What the parties mutually assent to is a bargained for exchange of things having a legal value. *Consideration,* which is discussed in Chapter 8, is the term used to describe the legal value each party brings to a contract. Suppose Harry offers to sell Jane his cassette deck for $300. Jane accepts his offer. Harry's consideration is his promise to sell the deck. Jane's is her promise to pay $300. A court will enforce their promises.

The law of contracts does not require that the consideration of each party be of equal value. Its only requirement is that the consideration have legal value, that is, some economic value no matter how slight. As we will see, courts have upheld transactions in which the parties exchanged considerations of vastly different values, like a house for $5000. Cases involving such unequal economic values are not exceptional.

A frequent question in cases involving disproportionate consideration is the *capacity* of the parties to contract. "Capacity" means "competency," or the ability to understand the nature of the contract. Note that the term refers to the ability to understand, not to whether a party actually understood. In other words, the capacity requirement does not protect people who misunderstand a bargain or who do not read contracts. Rather, the law permits certain categories of persons—minors, the mentally ill, and the intoxicated—to *disaffirm,* or void, their contracts. Contracts with persons whom a court had declared legally incompetent before the time of contracting are automatically void. Capacity and related concepts are the subject of Chapter 9.

By definition, a contract must have legal objectives, since a court will not enforce illegal ones. Some contract-like arrangements are prohibited by law. Agreements to fix prices or to purchase illegal drugs are just two examples. If Sam offers to sell Helen a pound of marijuana and Helen accepts his offer, no court would enforce their promises.

The final requirement, a *writing*—a written contract—only comes into play only when a statute actually requires one. Written contracts are not the norm; oral contracts are. As we will see in Chapter 10, writings are required in only six instances, among them contracts for the sale of *real property,* like land or a condominium, and for the sale of *personal property* or *goods* worth more than $500.

PERFORMING AND ENFORCING CONTRACTS

Virtually always, a party entering into a contract expects to fulfill her end of the bargain. The law terms this fulfillment *performance*. Sometimes, however, it is not the original parties to a contract who fulfill it but rather *third parties*. This term refers to the fact that such a party was not the original offeror or offeree, one of the first two parties. The law of substituted performances is covered in Chapter 11.

In the vast majority of contracts, the parties perform their duties. However, occasionally parties do not perform. They may have run into financial difficulty or decided to defraud their creditors, but the reason for the *breach,* or violation, of the contract is not nearly as important as the fact that it happened.

Now, whether the contract satisfies all the elements described in the last section becomes critically important to the performing party, because he or she may be asking a court to enforce the contract. Until enforcement becomes an issue, the way the parties chose to do business probably has no importance to anyone but themselves. But if, for instance, nonperformance by one party is justified because she lacked capacity to contract, the other party may suffer severe losses. That is why it is vital to apply preventive law principles at the time the contract is made.

In contract law, money damages are the normal remedy granted to a non-breaching party. As noted in the last unit, *damages* are a monetary valuation of the effects of a party's injury. However, unless a statute specifically authorizes *punitive damages* in a particular action based on a contract, a court may award only *compensatory damages*. Such statutes rarely exist outside the antitrust and consumer protection areas, both of which are examined in Part IX. On occasion, injunctive relief will be necessary to protect the interests of the nonbreaching party.

In two instances—the sale of real property and of unique personal property, like a painting or an heirloom—damages are presumed to be an inadquate remedy for a seller's breach. A buyer who is willing and able to perform may obtain an order for *specific performance,* which compels the seller to do what he or she agreed to do.

Performance and remedies are examined in Chapter 12. For now, keep in mind that contract remedies are compensatory.

THE SOURCES OF CONTRACT LAW

This part focuses on the common law of contracts which, like the law of torts, developed somewhat differently in each state. The commercial confusion caused by the states' varying interpretations of contract law led the American Law Institute to develop the *Restatement of Contracts,* published in 1932 and revised in 1979. When we refer to the *Restatement,* we mean the 1979 revision, formally cited as the *Restatement (Second) of Contracts*. The *Restatement* contains the general rules of contracts gleaned from generations of case law with broader discretionary principles more appropriate to today's society. As previously noted, the *Restatements* lack the force of statutes or precedent, but the courts routinely rely on them.

At the same time that the American Law Institute was developing the first *Restatement of Contracts,* a related group introduced the Uniform Sales Act, which applied only to the sale of goods. This Act, which was adopted in most states, standardized the law while adapting the common law to twentieth-century needs. The Act's successor, Article 2 of the Uniform Commerical Code (UCC), further modified the common law. Since its introduction in the 1950s, Article 2 has been adopted in every state except Louisiana. While a few of its effects are noted in this part, Article 2 will not be discussed in detail until Part VI.

It was the intent of the framers of the UCC that there be uniformity in regard to the UCC. However, it was never mandatory that states have identical statutory wording. In fact, the UCC is *not* the same in all states, not even any two. "The" UCC can be modified by any state legislature for that state as it sees fit. The major impetus for a state to closely adhere to "the" UCC is to avoid thwarting, or the appearance of thwarting, trade or commerce with the state. The model act version of the UCC, "the" UCC, is discussed throughout Part II and can be found in its entirety in Appendix 1. It is this version which is tested on the national CPA exam.

KEY WORDS

acceptance (135)
bilateral contract (135)
breach (137)
capacity (136)
compensatory damages (137)
consideration (136)
contract (135)
damages (137)
disaffirm (136)
mutual assent (135)

offer (135)
performance (137)
Restatement (Second) of Conracts (137)
specific performance (137)
Uniform Commerical Code (138)
unilateral contract (136)
writing (137)

CHAPTER 6
Offer

The Part II overview gave you a practical definition of a contract: a promise, or set of promises, which a court will enforce. This chapter begins a sequence of five chapters which examine the essential elements of a contract: offer, acceptance, consideration, capacity to contract, legality, and proper form. When these elements are present, the parties have a contract which a court will enforce. Offers are the subject of this chapter.

THE ROLE OF AN OFFER

To form a contract there must be *mutual assent* between two or more parties. Mutual assent requires an offer and an acceptance. The parties to a contract are the *offeror,* the party who makes an offer, and the *offeree,* the party to whom the offer is made. (See Figure 6.1.)

An *offer* is the offeror's proposal stating what the offeror is willing to do or refrain from doing in exchange for a specified action or promise by the offeree. If the offeree accepts the offer there is said to be a "meeting of the minds" and a contract exists. If not, no contract can exist. To illustrate, suppose John, the offeror, writes a letter to Margaret, the offeree, offering to sell his VCR to her if she promises to pay him $100. Only if Margaret accepts can there be mutual assent and a contract.

You will learn in this unit that there could be many different reasons why an offer from John to Margaret is not accepted. These might include:

- She never receives the offer.
- He revokes his offer before she accepts.
- She responds by saying no.
- She responds by proposing something different.
- She simply never responds.
- He dies before she accepts.

As discussed in the Part II overview, the law categorizes contracts according to the type of acceptance—promise or action—which the offeror requires. A *bilateral contract* involves a promise for a promise. For example, John's promise to sell his VCR to Margaret required a return promise from her, her promise to pay him $100. Here each party's actual performance of the contract, the VCR being exchanged for the $100, will occur after the point of mutual assent.

In contrast, a *unilateral contract* involves a promise for an action. For example, John might have promised to sell his VCR to Margaret if she pays him $100 when she comes to work this Saturday. It is important to note that here Margaret's acceptance of the offer and her performance under the contract will occur simultaneously. John's duty to perform his promise would occur immediately thereafter.

The next section focuses on the primary requirements of an offer.

REQUIREMENTS OF AN OFFER

For an offer to be enforceable a court must find that there is a legal offer, meaning an actual, genuine offer. In most cases the existence and/or genuineness of a supposed offer will not be at issue. However, sometimes this is the very focus of a lawsuit. In the following sections you will learn that for an offer to be enforced by a court there must be some objective evidence of a present intent to form a contract. Primary evidence of this intent is the fact that an offer was communicated to the offeree with sufficient

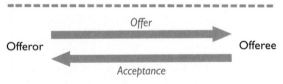

Figure 6.1 The relationship between offer and acceptance.
The only term which definitely appears more often in this book than the four terms in this figure is "law." Remember the basic equation of contract law:
offer + acceptance = mutual assent.

definiteness of terms to be able to form a contract.

A contract cannot exist unless someone has made an offer to enter into a contract. An *offer* states what the offeror will do and what he expects in exchange. For an offer to be valid, the offeror must intend to make the offer and must communicate it to the offeree. Sol says to Barbara, "I'll promise to sell you this model boat if you will promise to pay me $150." Sol, the *offeror,* has made an offer to Barbara, the *offeree.*

An offer also gives the offeree the power to accept the offer and thereby create an agreement between the parties. In the last example, all Barbara has to do to accept is say "OK." (See Figure 6.1.) This section, however, focuses on the intent of the offeror, the way offers are communicated, and the terms an offer must include. Acceptance is covered in Chapter 7.

Intent to Make an Offer

The test of an offeror's *intent* to make an offer is an objective one: that is, would a reasonable person believe the offeror was making an offer to the offeree? For example, Barry's 1966 Mustang will not start in wet weather. One day while trying to get it going, he yells, "I'll give this heap to the first person who hands me $40!" A passerby instantly hands him the cash and demands the keys. A reasonable person would realize that the value of the car greatly exceeded $40 and that Barry's "offer" was a cry of frustration. The circumstances hardly indicate an intent to contract.

Subjective intent—what the offeror was thinking at the moment he made the alleged offer—will not affect a court's determination of whether the offer is enforceable. Suppose Barry gets the Mustang home and decides he really does want to sell it. He writes a letter to a Mustang collector, offering to sell her the car for $4000, but puts it aside to think about it. By accident, he mails the letter, and the collector accepts his offer. A reasonable person receiving

Barry's letter would believe she had the power to accept, and a court would enforce the contract.

It is important to note that the same tests of intent apply to an offeree's acceptance.

Communication of an Offer

To be legally effective, an offer must be communicated to the offeree. Without actual communication, the offeree cannot accept. Suppose Roger offers to sell his watch to Reggie for $25. Tina, a passerby, hears the offer and says, "I accept." Since Roger did not communicate the offer to Tina, her acceptance has no legal effect. Tina is not the offeree, and there is no contract between Roger and her. Only Reggie, the intended offeree and the one to whom the offer was communicated, can accept.

The offeree must be aware of the offer in order to accept. Suppose Diane puts a sign on the bulletin board in the student union, offering a $100 reward for the return of her purse. Stan, who did not see the sign, finds the purse and returns it to Diane. She does not give him the $100. Contractually, he is not entitled to it because he did not know about the offer.

Finally, communication of an offer does not depend solely on spoken or written words. Conduct may constitute an offer. At commodities exchanges, for instance, brokers buy and sell using an elaborate system of hand signals to communicate offers and acceptances. At auctions, merely raising a finger or glancing at the auctioneer could signal an offer.

Not every representation made by a potential offeror to a potential offeree is an offer. Some, like the examples in the following paragraphs, may sound like offers but are not.

Statement of Future Intent. A statement of *future intent* is not an offer. If Tom says, "I'm going to sell my record collection for $100," he has not made an offer. Rather, he has stated a future intent to sell, since he does not intend to sell now, in the present. Tom must have a *present intent* to sell in order to make an offer.

Preliminary negotiations. Negotiations preliminary to making an offer do not constitute an offer. Inquiries as to the potential cost of an item, the availability of a warranty, the time for delivery, etc. are often a part of the bargaining process. For example, while attending an automotive flea market Randy spots an old radiator shell he has been seeking and states to the vendor, "What would you have to get on the shell?" An offer? No, an inquiry. The vendor responds, "Give me $25." An offer? Yes. The next case illustrates the hazards of misinterpreting negotiations as an offer.

Pacific Cascade Corp. v. Nimmer

25 Wash. App. 552, 608 P.2d 266 (1980)

FACTS

Pacific Cascade Corporation (PCC) negotiated with Nimmer to lease some property. PCC sent Nimmer a letter outlining three options for the terms of the lease. Nimmer responded, indicating his preference for one option but also stating additional terms. The parties exchanged further correspondence and met twice. After the second meeting, at PCC's request, Nimmer prepared a letter of intent to lease his property to PCC. In it, he specifically stated that the terms must remain subject to an appropriate written agreement and to the parties' signatures. Believing it had a deal, PCC began to negotiate for financing and prepared for construction. However, Nimmer terminated the negotiations. PCC sued Nimmer, contending his breach of their agreement forced the corporation to pay substantially more for a site than under the proposed lease. The trial court dismissed PCC's complaint.

ISSUE

Did Nimmer make PCC an enforceable offer?

DECISION

No. Affirmed. An offer consists of a promise of a stated performance in exchange for a return promise. However, an intention to do a thing is not a promise to do it. The fact that the parties intend to make a subsequent agreement is strong evidence they do not intend the previous negotiations to amount to an offer or an acceptance.

Auctions. An *auction* is a method of a sale in which a person, the auctioneer, invites offers called *bids* from prospective buyers. In an *auction with reserve,* the auctioneer may reject bids if they are below a predetermined minimum and may withdraw the goods at any time until he lowers the gavel or otherwise announces acceptance of a bid. In an auction with reserve, the bidding normally starts at or above the minimum or reserve price.

In an *auction without reserve,* after the auctioneer calls for bids, the article cannot be withdrawn unless no bid is made within a reasonable time. In this type of auction, the auctioneer is considered to be making an offer to the highest bidder. Auctions are presumed to be with reserve unless they are expressly stated to be without.

If a bidder withdraws his high bid before the auctioneer accepts it, the next-highest bid is not revived. Once a higher bid is made, the earlier bids are void. Suppose Earl bids $2000 for a used car. Jean then bids $2050, but she withdraws the bid immediately. The auctioneer must invite another bid, since neither Earl's nor Jean's bid is in effect [UCC §2-328].*

---

* This is a citation to the Uniform Commercial Code (UCC), which is reprinted in the Appendix. The sign § means "section." The sections run sequentially *but* not all numbers are used. For example, there is a §2-327 but

Advertisements. Generally, advertisements and price quotations are statements of a future intent to sell. Courts treat them as invitations to make offers. Suppose Jim places an ad in the newspaper which states, "For sale. Huffy 10 speed. Like new. $70." Lynn calls and says, "I saw your ad. I'll take it." No contract results.

not a §2-329; the next section is §2-401. The UCC is divided into nine articles. The article number precedes the hyphen. These citations throughout the text will allow you to look up the exact wording of appropriate sections of the Code.

Lefkowitz v. Great Minneapolis Surplus Store, Inc.

251 Minn. 188, 86 N.W. 689 (1957)

FACTS Lefkowitz responded to two Saturday advertisements in which several kinds of fur pieces were offered for sale in a newspaper advertisement for the Great Minneapolis Surplus Store. On the first occasion, three brand new fur coats, worth up to $100 were advertised for sale for $1. On the second Saturday, two "Brand New Pastel Mink 3-Skin Scarfs," normally selling for $89.50, were advertised for sale for $1 each. One "Black Lapin Stole," worth $139.50 was also advertised for a price of $1. The end of both ads declared "First Come, First Served." Lefkowitz was the first person present at the correct counter at the store and insisted on purchasing the coat and the stole at the price of $1. On both occasions, he was denied the merchandise because the defendant argued that it was a "house rule" that only women could accept the offer even though the ad was aimed at the general public. The trial court awarded Lefkowitz damages.

ISSUE Did the Great Minneapolis Surplus Store make an offer which Lefkowitz could accept?

DECISION Yes. Affirmed. In distinguishing in a newspaper advertisement between a legal offer and an invitation to make an offer, the court looks at the intent of the parties and surrounding circumstances. Here the defendant's "offer was clear, definite, and explicit, and left nothing open for negotiation." Since Lefkowitz was first to be served, the defendant should have performed its obligation to sell the merchandise. The defendant's argument that the offer was revised by the "house rule" was arbitrary, since it was not in the ad. To legally modify an offer, it must be done before, instead of after, the acceptance.

Jim would have to say something like, "It's yours," to form the contract. A similar principle, applies to a catalog or an advertising circular.

The common law considered advertisements too indefinite or uncertain to be offers. (The concept of definiteness is discussed below.) Unless an advertisement unequivocally indicated an intent to contract—for example, an advertisement listing a car by its stock or serial number—the courts hold to the notion that a seller is simply soliciting offers from buyers. The *Lefkowitz* case, discussed earlier, is a classic case of how under the common law an advertisement can be definite enough to create an offer. Such explicit terms as the quantity of fur pieces for sale, their value and price, plus the important words "First Come, First Served," identified the actual goods in the ad and demonstrated an intent to contract.

Today, consumer protection statutes and regulations, which supersede the common law when they apply, have made advertising much more like an offer. For example, stores now are required to have a reasonable quantity of the advertised goods on hand to meet reasonably

---

Hotel del Coronado Corp. v. Foodservice Equipment Distributors Ass'n

783 F.2d 1323 (9th Cir. 1986)

FACTS

The Hotel del Coronado is a well-known luxury hotel. On July 12, 1979, the hotel's sales representative sent a letter to the executive director of the Foodservice Equipment Distributors Association (FEDA) confirming a reservation for 240 rooms for March 2 through 8, 1984. The letter listed the hotel's current rates but noted that the hotel would state firm rates 1 year before the meeting. The letter concluded:

> If your plans are firm and the foregoing meets with your approval, we ask that you sign the enclosed copy of this letter in the space provided and return it. . . . This will serve as notice . . . of your approval of the arrangements, terms and provisions set forth herein and your agreement to have your meeting here. . . .

On July 20, 1979, FEDA's executive director signed and returned the copy to the hotel. On March 31, 1983, he notified the hotel that FEDA was canceling the reservation. The hotel brought suit for damages. The trial court granted summary judgment to FEDA on the grounds that an enforceable contract did not exist between the parties.

ISSUE

Did the lack of a price term in the proposal letter indicate the absence of an agreement between the parties?

DECISION

No. Reversed. Generally, if the parties reserve an essential or material term for future agreement, no legal obligation arises until they settle on the term. However, when the term is not essential, a court may force the parties to accept a reasonable determination of the unsettled point. Here, FEDA's selection of a luxury hotel suggests that room rates did not factor greatly in its choice. It bound itself to pay what the hotel chose in good faith to charge for the rooms.

anticipated demand. Federal Trade Commission (FTC) consumer protection legislation is discussed in Chapter 45.

Definiteness of Terms

In order for a contract to be legally binding, it must be reasonably definite as to all *material*—that is, important—terms and it must set out the rights and duties of the parties. Since the contract must be definite to be enforceable, the offer leading to it must also be definite.

At common law. Historically under the common law, courts have taken the position that since the parties—not the courts—made contracts, it was up to the parties to cover such material terms as:

- Price
- Quantity
- Time for delivery and payment
- Place for delivery and payment
- Manner of delivery and payment
- Names of the contracting parties

If any one of these was missing, the contract was usually unenforceable because it was not sufficiently definite. Many critics saw this approach as the ultimate triumph of form over substance, since it was often possible to infer what the parties intended even if they failed to state it.

Today, a court is more likely to emphasize the reasonable expectations of the parties. It will often attempt to give a contract the effect the parties intended even though the contract is imperfect by common law standards. Still, the courts are not inclined to remake contracts or to create them where they did not exist. In the *Hotel del Coronado* case, a court had to decide whether the omission of a price from the offer meant the parties had not contracted.

The UCC gap fillers. One of the reasons for this change is the development of the UCC. Its drafters rejected the traditional common law approach in favor of inferring terms to give effect to the intent of the parties.

Under the UCC, a court will enforce a contract for the sale of goods if the parties intended to contract and if a reasonably certain basis exists for framing an appropriate remedy [UCC §2-204(3)]. In many instances, the UCC supplies "gap fillers," provisions which specify how courts should supply missing terms. Suppose that on June 1 Harry Merchant and Bob Farmer agree that Farmer will deliver 10,000 pounds of potatoes to Merchant on November 1. Because of fluctuations in the potato market, they agree to set the price at the time of delivery. But when November 1 arrives, they cannot agree. Under the UCC a court could enforce their agreement and fix a reasonable price—usually the market price—as of the date of delivery.

Similarly, should a contract omit the place for delivery, a court could designate the seller's place of business, or if the seller has none, the seller's residence [UCC §2-308]. The time for delivery, if omitted, would be determined as a reasonable time [UCC §2-309(1)]. Should the parties fail to specify the time for payment, a court would require payment at the time and place the buyer is to receive the goods [UCC §2-310]. Figure 6.2 tabulates the gap fillers and compares the treatment of each type of missing term at common law and under the UCC.

Note in Figure 6.2 that the common law and the UCC treat a missing quantity term the same way. There is no contract. If the quantity term is completely omitted, a court would not have a basis for calculating damages in the event of a breach. Suppose Farmer agrees to deliver "a number of bags of potatoes to Merchant." If Farmer fails to deliver the bag of potatoes, a court would lack a basis for determining Merchant's damages.

The UCC approach to ambiguous or missing terms has influenced courts' interpretations of contracts not dealing with the sale of goods. However, it has not superseded the common law. Figure 6.3 compares the two approaches.

POTENTIALLY MISSING TERM	IF STATED COMMON LAW OR UCC	IF NOT STATED COMMON LAW*	UCC
Quantity	Amount stated; output or requirements contract OK	No contract*	No contract*
Price	Price amount stated	No contract*	Reasonable price at time for delivery [§2-305]
Time for delivery	As stated	No contract*	Reasonable time after contract is formed [§2-309]
Place for delivery	As stated	No contract*	Seller's place of business unless good is known to be elsewhere [§2-308]
Time for payment	As stated	No contract*	Time for delivery [§2-310]
Place for payment	As stated	No contract*	Place for delivery [§2-310]

*Past practices of parties or custom and usage may suffice.

Figure 6.2 Missing terms: treatment under the common law and the UCC.

The *Restatement* approach. The Part II overview introduced you to the *Restatement (Second) of Contracts,* a product of American Law Institute. You will recall that the *Restatement* is an attempt by leading legal scholars to blend the general rules of contracts gleaned from generations of case law with broader, discretionary principles more appropriate to today's society. As the *Restatement* often does, here it has taken an approach similar to that of the UCC. When the parties' intent to form a contract is reasonably clear and the terms are reasonably certain, the *Restatement* permits enforcement even when some terms are missing. Terms are reasonably certain if they provide a basis for determining the existence of a breach and for fashioning an appropriate remedy. As for missing terms, the *Restatement* allows a court to provide "a term which is reasonable in the circumstances" [*Restatement (Second) of Contracts* §204].

There will be further information about the *Restatement* approach to the definiteness problem later in this chapter, in the discussion of estoppels.

Output and requirements contracts. The major exceptions to the UCC definiteness of quantity requirement are requirements and output contracts, which never specify specific quantities. A *requirements contract* is an agreement to buy all goods of a specified type needed during a specified time from a particular seller. For example, McDonald's has a requirements contract with Coca-Cola for Coke to meet all of McDonald's soft drink requirements. McDonald's outlets do not sell Pepsi because of this agreement.

An *output contract* is the reverse of a requirements contract. An output contract is an agreement to sell all production, if any, during a specified time to a particular buyer. For example, Grover's Market agrees to purchase all the corn grown by Farmer John on his 300-acre farm. Under a contract like this one, Farmer John cannot legally sell his corn to anyone else.

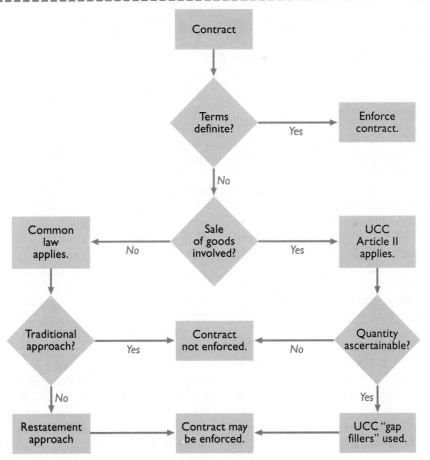

Figure 6.3 The definiteness problem: the common law and the UCC approaches compared.
At common law, a contract was not enforceable if it was incomplete or indefinite. The UCC Article 2 approach is much more flexible. However, it is always better to be as definite as possible.

However, this does not prevent Grover's Market from purchasing corn from other farmers.

Neither party may intentionally increase its supply or demand in order to burden the other party unreasonably. The UCC ties the quantity to the reasonable expectations of the parties [UCC 2-306]. So, Grover's Market, in the example above, would not have to purchase the output from an additional 300 acres of corn if Farmer John unexpectedly doubled the size of his crop.

Output and requirements contracts are fairly common. They serve several purposes, including guaranteeing a source of supply and ensuring product quality and consistency. Such arrangements are also simply convenient. Imagine how complex it would be to stock the concessions at a rock concert or a football game without requirements contracts with suppliers. In some cases, however, as we will see in Chapter 43, output and requirements contracts violate the antitrust laws.

TERMINATION OF AN OFFER

An offer does not stay open forever. The offeror may state a time when his offer expires. If he does so, that deadline controls. However, an offer may terminate in a number of other ways.

Termination by the Parties

Terms of the offer. The offeror has the power to control the manner and time in which the offeree may accept. Thus, an offer may require that an acceptance be received by the offeror at a stated place and time. For example, "acceptance must be received at our home office by 5:00 P.M. on March 27, 1994." The fact that the postal service unexpectedly delayed delivering the acceptance until the following day will not alter the fact of a terminated offer. As a practical matter, of course, the parties could subsequently agree to a new agreement with similar contractual terms.

Revocation. A *revocation* is the offeror's withdrawal of an offer. A revocation is effective only when it is actually communicated to the offeree before the offeree accepts.

A letter withdrawing an offer is not effective until delivery to the offeree's address. The offeree does not have to read the revocation. Suppose that at 10 A.M. the mail carrier places a revocation in the mailbox for Alma's Apiary. At 2 P.M., before she picks up her mail, Alma delivers her acceptance of the offer. The revocation took effect at 10, so there is no contract.

The rationale for the revocation on delivery rule is that any alternative would pose problems of proof. If the rule required actual receipt, the offeror would have to prove when Alma picked up her mail. If the rule required actual notice, the offeror would have to prove Alma understood she had received a revocation.

A similar logic applies to situations where the offeree learns by reliable means or from a reliable source that the offeror has taken actions inconsistent with the offer. Suppose Randy is offering for sale a rocking chair at a garage sale. Randy offers to sell it to Carla for $45. While walking around considering the purchase, Carla's friend, who has accompanied her to the sale, tells Carla she just saw Randy take money from a third party and mark "sold" on the chair price tag. Randy's offer to Carla is effectively terminated.

The offerer may revoke an offer made to the public, but he must do so in the same manner as the offer was made. Suppose Alvin places an ad in five newspapers, offering a reward for the return of his snowmobile. He must place the revocation in the same newspapers so that it has the same exposure the offer had.

The following case contains perhaps the most famous application of the revocation rule.

Shuey, Executor v. United States

92 U.S. 73 (1875)

FACTS   On April 20, 1985, immediately following President Lincoln's assassination, the secretary of war published notice of a reward of $25,000 "for the apprehension of John H. Surratt, one of [John Wilkes] Booth's accomplices." On November 24, 1865, President Andrew Johnson published notice of the revocation of the offer of a reward for Surratt's apprehension. The notice of the withdrawal was given the same publicity as the notice of the offer. In April 1866, Henry Ste. Marie was serving in a

Papal military unit in Rome. He recognized Surratt, who confessed his role in the Lincoln plot. Ste. Marie notified an American diplomat, and after a complicated process Surratt was apprehended. Neither Ste. Marie nor the diplomat knew of the withdrawal of the reward offer until after Surratt's capture. By act of Congress, Ste. Marie received a $10,000 reward. But, Ste. Marie believed himself entitled to the full $25,000 and brought suit. The court of claims dismissed the suit.

ISSUE

Is a notice of revocation of an offer of a reward effective as to a person who does not see the notice?

DECISION

Yes. Affirmed. The offer was revocable at any time before it was accepted or before anything was done in reliance upon it. There was no contract until the offer's terms were complied with. That Ste. Marie did not learn of the withdrawal until after Surratt's arrest is irrelevant. The offer was not made to him directly, so Ste. Marie should have known that the offer could have been revoked in the same way that it was made.

Rejection. A *rejection* is a notice the offeree communicates to the offeror that the offeree will not accept the offer. It terminates the offer. Like a revocation, a rejection takes effect when communicated. Suppose 37th Street Camera offers to sell Phil's Photos 100 cameras at $100 each. Phil rejects the offer in writing, but 37th Street Camera does not receive the rejection for 3 days. If he changes his mind, Phil still may accept so long as 37th Street Camera receives the acceptance before the rejection.

While a rejection often is *express*—that is, written or oral—it can also be communicated by conduct. Suppose both Pete and Marcia have offered to buy the same horse trailer from Equine Equipment, Inc. As Marcia pulls into the parking lot, she sees Pete pulling out with the trailer. She has notice that her offer was rejected.

Rejection also can occur when the offeree fails to accept after the lapse of a reasonable time. We will have more to say about the timing of acceptances and rejections when we discuss the *medium of acceptance* in the next chapter.

Counteroffer. An offeree's *counteroffer* simul-taneously rejects the original offer and presents the original offeror with a new offer. Suppose a salesperson for Crazy Freddie's Sound offers Regina a stereo for $495. Regina says, "I'll give you $395." Regina has rejected the offer and made a new offer which the salesperson may accept or reject.

An inquiry, however, is not a counteroffer. Suppose Regina replies, "I'll consider it, but would you take $395?" The test of a counter-offer is whether a reasonable person would conclude from the circumstances that the original offeree intended to make a counteroffer. Where an offer sets a specific time in which the offeree must accept, a late acceptance is a counter-offer.

Until this century, any deviation from the original offer was a counteroffer. If the offeree accepted but added a term—for example, that the offeree would take delivery at the offeror's warehouse immediately—the law construed the new term as a counteroffer. As we will see in the next chapter, courts have tended to relax the exact response rule, particularly in UCC cases. However, as the next case shows, the rule still has considerable vitality.

Gregory & Appel, Inc. v. Duck

459 N.E.2d 47 (Ind. Ct. App. 1984)

FACTS

Donald Duck and his family wanted to sell an apartment building. In his capacity as family lawyer, Donald sent a letter to Gregory & Appel, stating the terms of an offer the family would find acceptable. Gregory & Appel responded with a document headed:

CONTRACT FOR PURCHASE OF REAL ESTATE
OFFER TO PURCHASE REAL ESTATE

The Ducks rejected the contract, which contained terms materially different from those in Donald's letter. Gregory & Appel made minor changes and resubmitted the contract with a check for $10,000 as a down payment. The Ducks rejected it and returned the check. Gregory & Appel brought suit to compel the Ducks to transfer the apartment building. The trial court granted the Duck's motion for summary judgment.

ISSUE

Did Gregory & Appel accept the Ducks' offer?

DECISION

No. Affirmed. The Ducks' letter solicited an offer from Gregory & Appel. Even if the Ducks' letter were an offer and the proposed contract were an acceptance, the acceptance would have to correspond with the offer in every respect, point for point. An acceptance which varies the terms of the offer is a rejection and amounts to a counteroffer.

Termination by Operation of Law

In four instances where it would be unjust, impossible, or illegal to enforce an offer, the law treats it as terminated even though the offeror has not withdrawn it.

Destruction of subject matter. An offer automatically terminates if its particular subject matter is destroyed before the offeree accepts. Suppose Bertha offers to buy Garrison's cat, Puff. Before Garrison can accept, Puff dies. Bertha's offer terminates on Puff's death.

Incompetence or death. An offer also automatically terminates if a party becomes legally incompetent or dies, whether or not the offeree has notice of the event, since *incompetents* and *decedents* do not have the capacity to revoke their offers. Any other rule would place their estates at an unfair disadvantage. However, note that incompetency or death *after* acceptance does not necessarily void the contract. Incompetence is discussed further in Chapter 9.

Illegality. An offer which was legal when made terminates if it becomes illegal. For example, a French company, A. Deloir & Cie., offers to sell Monsieur Henri Wines, an American company, 3000 cases of Bordeaux. Before Monsieur Henri can accept, the U.S. government forbids the importation of French wine. That event terminates the offer. Chapter 9 examines illegality in some detail.

Lapse of time. If the offeree fails to accept an offer by the time stated, the offer terminates. If the offer does not state a time, the offeree must accept within a reasonable period. The particular circumstances of the offer determine reasonableness. These include the subject matter of the contract (for example, is it perishable?), business and market conditions, and the language used in the offer. In the following case, the trial court failed to make findings of fact as to the duration of each offer and its language.

Champagne Chrysler-Plymouth, Inc. v. Giles

388 So. 2d 1343 (Fla. Dist. Ct. App. 1980)

FACTS

Champagne Chrysler-Plymouth sponsored *Miami All Star Bowling,* a local TV show. Up to mid-January 1978, Champagne advertised on each show that it would give a new Plymouth Arrow to anyone who bowled a 300 game on the program that day. Giles entered a tournament leading up to the February 17, 1978, show.

> Giles qualified for the finals and . . . threw 12 strikes in a row for a 300 game. Although otherwise rewarded with cash prizes, free Pepsi and the like, Giles called upon Champagne for his just deserts.
>
> Not bowled over by this request, Champagne responded that it had made no offer of an automobile on February 17 and, for that matter, had not been offering such a prize for over a month of Saturdays. Its position, simply stated, was that Giles was aiming at the wrong pocket. Giles sued.

Champagne claimed its offer of a prize on and for a particular Saturday television show meant that it made an offer only for that show. Giles claimed Champagne placed flyers and posters containing its offer in nearly every bowling alley and some of these were still posted when he appeared on television. However, the only example presented to the court specifically stated the offer was limited to a particular show. The trial court granted summary judgment to Giles.

ISSUE

Did the trail court have sufficient facts before it to enter summary judgment for Giles?

DECISION

No. Reversed.

> We agree with Champagne that the mimeographed flyer offering a car as a prize for any 300 game bowled on the television program, even if it remained posted on February 17, 1978, expired by its own terms. . . .
>
> The television commercials and printed posters present a different problem. The . . . record does not reflect whether these were unilateral offers limiting the time of acceptance by their express terms or were offers requiring revocation. While the trial court was correct that there was no genuine issue of material fact that appropriate revocation did not occur, the issue as to whether revocation was required remained.
>
> If . . . the television commercials were unilateral contracts, it would not have

been necessary for Champagne to take any steps to revoke the offers made by it on prior television programs, since these offers would have expired by their own terms on the dates made and would not have been outstanding as of February 17, 1978.

Irrevocable Offers

Commonly, an offeror specifies a period within which the offeree must accept. In most cases, the offeree has no problems if he or she accepts within the specified period. However, suppose an offeror who promised an offeree 5 days in which to accept revokes the offer 2 days later. The revocation normally is effective, and the offeree has no recourse. Only in the three instances discussed below do the courts bind an offeror to his promise to hold an offer open.

Option contracts. An *option contract* keeps an offer to contract open for a specified period. In other words, it guarantees the offeree the right to accept during the period. But note that the option contract and the contract resulting from the offer held open are separate matters.

A court will enforce an option contract if it meets all the requirements of a contract, including the exchange of consideration. Suppose Harold offers to sell Paula a trampoline. Although he tells her, "I'll keep the offer open for ten days," he could revoke the offer at any time. If Paula paid him something, even $1, to keep the offer open, he would breach their option contract by revoking during the period.

Firm offers. Under UCC, some promises to keep an offer open are enforceable even though not supported by consideration [UCC §2-205].

Specifically, a *firm offer* to buy or sell goods in a writing signed by a *merchant*—one who customarily deals in the goods—cannot be revoked. However, the recipient of a firm offer does not have to be a merchant in order to enforce it. The UCC limits the irrevocability of a firm offer to the time stated, or if no time is stated, to a reasonable time—which in no event exceeds 3 months. Suppose Dysart Trampolines, Inc., offers in writing to sell Paula a trampoline for $400 and states the offer is firm for 10 days. Even though Paula pays nothing for this right, she can enforce it. If Dysart had stated, say, a 120-day period, a court would cut it down to 3 months. Of course, the parties could enter into an option contract in order to keep the offer open for longer than 3 months.

As with all UCC liberalizations, the goal of the firm offer provision is to ease the flow of commerce. If a business always had to make a separate option contract in order to guarantee an offer would stay open, uncertainty would be introduced into every transaction where an offeree required time to decide whether to accept.

Figure 6.4 outlines the differences among these types of offers.

Estoppel. Under most circumstances the offeror controls its offer. However, the offeror must leave an offer open when it can foresee that the offeree will rely upon the offer without accepting it. In legal terminology, the offeror is *estopped* from revoking the offer. Though the words come from different roots, "estop" means "stop." In this context, *estoppel* describes a situation in which one person has led another to do something the other would not ordinarily have done. The first person may not subject the other to an injury by destroying the expectations upon which that person acted.

The estoppel principle has a particular application where a contractor must rely upon the bids of subcontractors in formulating its own bid. Suppose Construction Company plans to bid on a new power plant. Subcontracting Corporation offers Construction 1 million tons of cement at $2 a ton, and Construction uses this figure in its bid on the project. Construction has relied on the offer; therefore, Subcontracting

TYPES OF OFFER	REVOKE WITHIN 10-DAY PERIOD?	MUST OFFER INVOLVE SALE OF GOOD?	MUST OFFEROR BE A MERCHANT?	MUST OFFEREE BE A MERCHANT?	CONSIDERATION REQUIRED?	SIGNED, WRITTEN OFFER REQUIRED?
NORMAL OFFER *Sell trampoline* *10 days to accept* Harold ⟶ Paula	YES	No	—	—	—	—
OPTION CONTRACT *Sell trampoline* Harold ⟶ Paula *10 days to accept* *trampoline offer* ⟶ Harold ← *$1.00* Paula	No	No	No	No	YES	No
FIRM OFFER *Sell trampoline* *10 days to accept* Dysart ⟶ Paula	No	YES	YES	No	No	YES

Figure 6.4 Comparison of a normal offer with option contracts and firm offers.
Firm offers affect only the sale of goods under UCC Article 2. If the contract is not for the sale of goods or if the offer is to be held open for more than three months, the parties must enter into an option agreement—just as under common law.

must leave it open for a reasonable time— which would be until either Construction's bid is rejected or, if its bid is accepted, the project is completed.

The *Restatement,* unlike either the common law or the UCC, applies a type of estoppel to indefinite agreements. It permits a court to consider whether to grant full or partial enforcement of a promise on the basis of the principle of promissory estoppel [*Restatement (Second) of Contracts* §34(3)]. *Promissory estoppel* is a doctrine which permits a court to enforce a promise when it is reasonable to hold that the promisor* should have anticipated that the promisee would act or not act in reliance on the promise and when the promisee did in fact act or not act. However, the doctrine applies only when it will avoid an injustice. Some commentators have strongly criticized the *Restatement* approach because, in effect, it requires

---

* A *promisor* is a person who makes a promise; a *promisee* is a person to whom a promise is made. Promissory estoppel is an important concept and finds applications in many areas of commercial law. It is next discussed in Chapter 8.

that a court make a contract—something the courts traditionally have refused to do.

Another term to describe the estoppel situation is "detrimental reliance." Partial performance in response to a unilateral offer is another example of detrimental reliance. If a newspaper offers $100,000 to anyone who swims across Lake Michigan, the newspaper cannot revoke its offer when a swimmer is halfway across the lake.

CONCLUSION

An offer is only the first step in creating a binding contract. Though lengthy negotiations may precede it, only the offer creates the possibility of an agreement.

The rules explored in this chapter as to communication and definiteness apply equally to acceptances. While the common law's rigidity has largely disappeared as to definiteness, it is a serious mistake to assume that a court will do the parties' work for them. The courts will not create a contract where none exists. They will only determine what the parties reasonably expected.

The next chapter explores acceptance, the other half of mutual assent. With gap fillers and similar devices to fill in the details omitted by the parties, one can lose sight of the essential concept expressed by the term "mutual assent": both parties must agree to the same material terms in order to form a contract.

A NOTE TO ALL STUDENTS

Probably every business law author team ends up spending a good amount of time debating to what extent, if at all, they should include a discussion of provisions from consumer protection legislation, the *Restatement (Second) of Contracts,* or the UCC, Article 2, in chapters primarily dealing with common law contract law. Today all three play a major role in the resolution of contractual disputes.

We decided our major focus in Part II should be common law contract law. Generally, we have deferred our discussion of consumer protection legislation, although very important, to Chapter 45, *Consumer Protection.* We decided not to emphasize the *Restatement* except for situations where it significantly departs from the common law. As to the UCC, we decided to follow the lead of the national CPA exam. On the business law portion of the CPA exam, the "Contracts Law" section includes common law contract law and those Article 2 provisions relating to the formation of a sales contract. The "UCC" section of the exam covers the remaining Article 2 provisions. We believe this is a conceptually sound approach. We focus on Article 2 in Part VI, Sales. Some instructors prefer to go directly to Part VI upon completion of Part II, Contract Law.

A NOTE TO FUTURE CPA CANDIDATES

To be successful on the CPA exam, it is important that you know and understand the basic contract terms and definitions. You should also begin now to master your ability to characterize a contract. Most contracts on the CPA exam will be for services, land, or goods. If the latter, the UCC will apply.

You must also know when and for how long an offer is effective. For example, an advertisement is generally not an offer. At common law, the offer is to be specific. In contrast, the UCC is much more flexible with its gap fillers. The latter is commonly tested on the CPA exam.

At common law, consideration, something of value, is required to prevent the offeror from revoking her offer. When given, it is said that an irrevocable offer or option contract results. If not present, the offeror can revoke her offer even though she said she would not. Under the

UCC, a firm offer by a merchant offeror needs no consideration. On the CPA exam it is important for you to fully understand the requirements of a firm offer.

You are expected to know how an offer might terminate by operation of law. The most common exception is death of the offeror or offeree.

Finally, the Part II Appendix, at the conclusion of Part II, provides you with a listing of Article 2 matters generally covered in the "Contract Law" portion of the CPA exam. You may wish to refer to this appendix while studying the material in both Parts II and VI.

KEY WORDS

counteroffer (149)	offer (140)
estoppel (152)	offeree (140)
express (149)	offeror (140)
firm offer (141)	option contract (152)
intent (141)	rejection (149)
material (145)	revocation (148)
mutual assent (140)	

DISCUSSION QUESTIONS

1. Who makes an offer? To whom is an offer made?
2. Define the following terms: offer, preliminary negotiation, output contract, requirements contract, and estoppel.
3. Under what circumstances does an advertisement constitute an offer?
4. In what ways is the common law requirement of definiteness relaxed by the UCC? By the *Restatement?*
5. Give illustrations of the termination of an offer by operation of law.
6. How may an offeree terminate an offer? How may an offeror terminate an offer?
7. Under what circumstances would an offeree desire to make a counteroffer? What is the effect of a counteroffer?
8. How does an implied revocation occur?

9. Must a person actually read an offer for it to be considered communicated? Explain.
10. How do you suggest that the risk of translation problems in international business transactions be minimized?

CASE PROBLEMS

1. The following ad in the morning paper caught the attention of Nancy Hutchinson:

   For sale. Wooden ice box. Original condition. Exc. appearance. First $300 or best offer takes. See Mr. Lawrence, 9238 Hillside Ave., 688-9238, after 8:00.

   Hutchinson arrived at Lawrence's home promptly at 8 and immediately presented her $300. Lawrence told her the paper had made an error and the price was actually $400. Seeing that no one else was there, Hutchinson offered $300, which was obviously the best offer Lawrence had. Lawrence again refused. Should Hutchinson bring suit against Lawrence, would a court find that she and Lawrence had a contract at $300 on the basis of the original ad? At $300 on the basis of Hutchinson's "best offer"? Why?
2. One Monday, Dustin received a telephone call from his oil supplier. The supplier offered him 1000 barrels of heating oil at $18 per barrel, the current price in a rapidly changing market. Dustin said he wanted to think about the offer. The next day, the price rose to $20 per barrel. Late that afternoon, Dustin sent the supplier a letter, accepting the offer at $18 per barrel. On Thursday, the letter arrived at the supplier's office with its usual mail delivery. By that afternoon, the price per barrel had risen to $26. Before the close of business, the supplier telephoned Dustin and told him it would not accept his order. Dustin insists that they have a contract. Who is correct? Explain.
3. Pritchard accepted Widget Works' offer to become its chief executive officer. Widget's board set Pritchard's salary at "$150,000 plus something from the bonus pool, if sales per-

mit.'' At year's end, Widget showed a small profit, but the board decided sales projections did not warrant bonuses. Pritchard became furious about the lack of a bonus and quit. If he sues Widget Works, is a court likely to award him any additional compensation? Explain.

4. Don Wells is the owner of Freeport Hardware. On hardware store stationary, Wells mailed to Sissy Phillips an offer to sell to her his home at 109 North Mernitz Avenue for $75,000 and/or a specific store lawn tractor for $1200. In the offer Sissy was given 10 days to accept. Three days later, Sissy went to the hardware store. Before she could tell Wells she was accepting his offer, he told her that he had changed his mind on both items. Sissy objected, stated he promised to keep his offers open, and that she was accepting the offer for both the house and the lawn tractor. Wells claims there is no contract. Is he correct in regard to the house? The lawn tractor? Explain.

5. By letter, Sanderson offered to sell Esposito his golf clubs for $350. In the letter Sanderson asked Esposito to write or call with his response. Esposito decided the clubs were too expensive, so on May 6 he mailed Sanderson a rejection. By the next morning, he had changed his mind. He called Sanderson to accept. Sanderson told him his acceptance was too late. Sanderson had mailed Esposito a revocation of his offer that morning. On May 8, Sanderson receives Esposito's rejection and Esposito receives Sanderson's revocation. Do the parties have a contract? Explain.

6. Unger had always admired Madison's 1956 Corvette. One night, Madison told his wife he planned to play a joke on Unger by offering him the $15,000 car for $9600. Madison gave him the offer in writing. It specified Unger had to accept within 3 days. Unger borrowed the cash and took the acceptance to Madison's house. Madison took the acceptance from him but shortly thereafter told Unger to keep his money since it was all a joke. Suppose Unger sued Madison for breach of contract.

7. Schwartz & Company distributed a running

shoe sales catalog showing an Asics Gel-120 running shoe for a special sale price of $39. When Chuck Parks telephoned the 800 number to order a pair he was told by a Schwartz sales rep that the price was a mistake, the actual sale price was $55. Parks hung up. He then called Vaughan's Sporting Goods, a local store. Glenn Vaughan, the proprietor, quoted Parks a price of $49 for the shoes "through Saturday." Parks said he would consider the price. When Parks visited the store later that day he was told that the price was actually $55. Parks, who has studied business law, believes that the Schwartz catalog obligated them to their $39 price. Correct? He believes that Glenn Vaughan's quote, as a merchant, obligated him to the $49 price. Correct? Explain.

8. The Sports Majesty sporting goods store widely advertised the $5000 bonus it would pay any runner who broke the course record in that year's renewal of the Majesty Marathon Run. Elton Morris, the store's owner, made the offer to gain publicity. He never thought he would have to pay the bonus because all the top runners were in another marathon that weekend. Only after the race had started did he realize that Billy Smith, a top competitor, was in the race. Morris hurried to the 10-mile mark, where he hoisted a hastily painted sign which read''

OUR $5000 BONUS OFFER
HAS BEEN REVOKED.
HAVE A GOOD RACE.
SPORTS MAJESTY

Smith won the marathon in record time. When Sports Majesty failed to pay the bonus, he brought suit. Sports Majesty claimed the original ads were not legal offers, Sports Majesty had revoked the offer. Who will prevail? Why?

9. Chris Martin was the auctioneer for an estate sale. The auctioneer asked for a $300 bid for a dining room set. Donna Mitchell bid $300. Peter Smith bid $310. While the auctioneer was seeking further bids, Smith's wife told him to revoke his bid, as the set cost too much

for them. Just seconds before the auctioneer slammed his gavel indicating a sale, Smith yelled out, "Forget my $310 bid." The auctioneer told Smith he could not revoke his offer and that the set was his. Was Smith's revocation effective? Assuming it was, would Mitchell now be liable to pay $310 for the set? Explain.

10. Noel's Christmas Tree Farm entered into a 3-year contract to sell all its annual Christmas tree harvest of 5-, 6-, and 7-foot trees to Slusher's Garden Store. The contract specified a price for each size. Several days later Slush-er's entered into a similar agreement with another Christmas tree supplier but the price scale exceeded that in the Noel-Slusher contract. Realizing that he might have underestimated the market prices for Christmas trees, Noel informed Slusher's that their second supplier contract breached his contract with them. Would a court be likely to agree? Also, would a court be likely to agree with Noel if he claimed that the contract is unenforceable because the number of trees to be harvested each year is not set? Explain.

CHAPTER 7
Acceptance

MUTUAL ASSENT AND THE INTENT TO ACCEPT
"Meeting of the Minds"
Genuineness of Assent

WHO MAY ACCEPT?

WHAT TERMS ARE ACCEPTED?
The Mirror Image Rule
The UCC Modifications
The Problem of Unread Terms
    The receipt cases
    Common law and legislative remedies
The End of Contracts?

METHODS OF ACCEPTANCE
Acceptance by Promise
Acceptance by Performance
Acceptance by Silence
    Prior dealings
    Implied acceptance
    Exercise of dominion

WHEN AN ACCEPTANCE TAKES EFFECT
Express and Implied Agents
Means of Acceptance
    The authorized means test
    The reasonable means test
Revocation of an Offer

CLASSIFICATIONS OF CONTRACTS
Formal and Informal
Executory and Executed
Express, Implied in Fact, and Implied in Law (Quasi-Contract)

CONCLUSION

A NOTE TO FUTURE CPA CANDIDATES

Key Words
Discussion Questions
Case Problems

Jane and Steve found a condominium they liked and could afford. The realtor urged them to make an offer on it immediately because at least one other couple was interested. Though their lawyer had told them not to sign a contract until he had looked it over, they submitted an offer the owners accepted. In a very good mood, Jane called the sellers to clarify a few points not covered in the offer. Of course, she said, they would leave the appliances and the built-ins. Sure, said the sellers, for a price. Only then did Jane and Steve learn:

Offer + acceptance = mutual assent

They also learned *mutual assent* usually means the parties have formed a contract.

This chapter examines how and when an acceptance binds both parties to an agreement. And, getting the other party to agree to modifications to a contract can be expensive.

MUTUAL ASSENT AND THE INTENT TO ACCEPT

Without the offeree's assent to the terms of the offer, the parties have not agreed, and there can be no contract. Suppose the offeree says, "I accept," and then repeats the offer word for word. A court will have no difficulty finding an acceptance and, therefore, a mutual assent to the terms. The problem comes when either the offeree's response is unclear or the parties omit some of the terms of the agreement.

"Meeting of the Minds"

Courts sometimes refer to mutual assent as a "meeting of the minds" of the parties. "Meeting of the minds" is a useful metaphor for the kind of agreement on the material elements of a contract which courts are willing to enforce. Taken literally, the phrase suggests a subjective analysis of the parties' intentions. But as noted in the last chapter, it is the parties' *objective intent*—that is, how a reasonable person would interpret the parties' actions—which determines the presence of mutual assent.

The courts look to the circumstances surrounding the alleged agreement and any *manifestations*—the outward signs—of the parties' intent for an indication of a meeting of the minds. Manifestations of intent include correspondence between the parties, their actions at the alleged time of contracting and afterward, and the reasons the case was brought into court. As the next case indicates, an offeree who reasonably believes the offeror has made him an offer may accept it, regardless of what the offeror later says he intended.

Lucy v. Zehmer

196 Va. 493, 84 S.E.2d 516 (1954)

FACTS   The Lucys and the Zehmers went out drinking one night. Toward the end of the evening, the two couples began discussing the Zehmers' financial situation. During the conversation the Zehmers handed Mr. Lucy what appeared to be a good faith offer to sell their farm for $50,000. Lucy accepted their offer. Shortly thereafter, Lucy raised the $50,000, but the Zehmers refused to convey the land. Lucy filed suit, seeking specific performance. At trial, the Zehmers testified that when Mr. Zehmer asked his wife to sign the offer, he whispered to her that it was a joke. So, they argued, there was no contract. The trial court found for the Zehmers.

ISSUE Did the Zehmers make an offer Lucy could accept?

DECISION Yes. Reversed. If the words or acts of one of the parties have but one reasonable meaning to the other party, subjective intent is not important. Lucy did not understand the Zehmers' offer to be a joke but considered it a serious business proposition. In contracts, courts look to a person's outward expression rather than to his secret, unexpressed intent. The law imputes an intention corresponding to the reasonable meaning of a person's words and acts.

Genuineness of Assent

The presence of an offer and an acceptance creates the presumption of a manifestation of mutual assent, a meeting of the minds. However, you will learn in Chapter 9 that what appears to have been mutual assent will sometimes be challenged by a party to the contract on grounds that there lacked a true genuineness of assent. For example, Mabel agrees to purchase what she is told is a Chicago Bulls scorecard signed by her favorite player, Michael Jordan. Later, Mabel learns that the signature is a clever forgery. In popular language, it might be said that Mabel ''got ripped off.'' In Chapter 9, you will learn that Mabel probably has a defense to her performance of the contract on grounds of fraud. Duress, undue influence, and innocent misrepresentation are the other three types of conduct which can lead a court to conclude a party did not truly assent. For the remainder of this chapter you should presume that if the objective test of assent is met, the assent is genuine.

In *Lucy v. Zehmer,* Lucy originally had the *burden of persuasion.* As plaintiff, he had to show that a binding, legal contract existed between him and the Zehmers. When a plaintiff establishes the existence of a contract, he is said to make a *prima facie* case, meaning that on the fact of what he presented, the defendant is liable.

Once Lucy met his burden—which the defendants may test with a *motion for a directed verdict*—the burden shifted to the Zehmers to show that such a contract did not exist. After all, the Zehmers' refusal to perform in effect denied the existence of the contract, so shifting the burden does nothing more than make them convince the court of their point. Still, as defendants, they did not have to prove anything at trial until Lucy made a prima facie case that they were liable. Here, the Zehmers did not meet their burden of persuasion, because their interpretation of the offer contradicted normal commercial practice. They failed to rebut Lucy's case, which persuaded the Virginia Supreme Court on appeal that a reasonable person would have interpreted the offer as he did.

WHO MAY ACCEPT?

Only the specific person or class of persons to whom an offer is made may accept it. Suppose Mr. Shutter, a photography instructor, offers to sell a camera to Harry for $350. Cathy cannot accept the offer, since she is not the intended offeree. Similarly, if Shutter offered the camera to anyone in his class who wanted it, the dean could not accept the offer.

A poorly worded description in the offer to the intended offeree can result in unanticipated and unnecessary liability. Now suppose Mr. Shutter offers to sell his camera to anyone who writes ''I accept'' on a postcard, signs it, and places it under his door before classes the next day. He has only one camera to sell, so if more than one student accepts, he can fulfill his contract with one but must breach his contracts with the rest.

The offeror controls the terms of his offer. Therefore, unintended multiple acceptances need never happen, but they do sometimes occur. In this case, all Mr. Shutter had to do to avoid the problem was to say he was inviting offers to buy his camera and would decide which, if any, he would accept.

Occasionally, an offeror will intend to make an offer to a particular offeree but by mistake communicate it to another. Suppose Fran intends to offer to sell some rugs to Carl. By mistake, she mails her offer to Bob, who accepts. If a reasonable person in Bob's position would believe that an offer in the form he received it was meant for him, his acceptance was effective. A court, for instance, would enforce the contract if the offer was addressed to Bob and he had no reason to know he was not the intended offeree. However, if the envelope was addressed to Bob and the letter to Carl, Bob could not take advantage of Fran's mistake.

WHAT TERMS ARE ACCEPTED?

The offeree's addition, in his acceptance, of terms not in the offer is a more common problem than misdirected offers. Generally, if the offeree adds terms, there is no contract. Keep the general rule clearly in mind while studying the exceptions to it discussed below.

The Mirror Image Rule

Formerly, under the common law, an acceptance had to be a mirror image of the offer. Suppose Anderson sends Baker an offer to sell her 100 widgets at $5 each, delivery to be by Rabbit Transit. Baker accepts but specifies delivery by Air Alabama. At common law, the parties would not have contracted.

The advantage of the mirror image rule was that a court had an easy time determining whether a contract existed. Its disadvantage was that people have never done business in so precise a fashion. Thus, the rule permitted per-

sons who might have intended to contract at the time of the agreement to escape their obligations later. The rule also impeded commerce by emphasizing the form of a transaction over its substance and by not giving effect to trade practices, usages of trade, or courses of dealing.

As *Gregory & Appel v. Duck* revealed in Chapter 6, the mirror image rule is far from dead. However, it, too, has felt the liberalizing influence of the UCC.

The UCC Modifications

The UCC's drafters rejected the common law position that any new or additional terms in an acceptance constitute a counteroffer. Instead, under the UCC a definite acceptance which adds or omits nonmaterial terms forms a contract. Whether these additional terms become part of the resulting contract depends upon whether it is a contract between merchants. The UCC rules will be discussed in detail in Chapter 31, Formation of Sales Contracts.

The Problem of Unread Terms

The common law presumed that both parties had read and fully understood the terms of a written contract. When parties later claimed that they had not read or understood what they signed, courts seldom relieved them of duties under the contract unless the parties could establish some other grounds for relief, such as misrepresentation or fraud.

The Receipt Cases. In many instances, the common law presumption remains valid today, especially when businesses or businesspeople contract with each other. But particularly in cases involving consumers, the courts have tended to place great emphasis on whether consumers have actual or reasonable notice of the contract terms contained in the offer. This view arose from what might be called the "receipt cases."

The receipt cases typically involved a person who had received a receipt at, say, a coat-check counter and dropped it in a pocket without reading the terms on it. The receipt represented an offer, and leaving the article signified acceptance. The coat, valued at $220, was not returned when the receipt was presented. Only then did the consumer look at the ticket and learn that the establishment disclaimed all liability for lost or stolen articles. Cases of this type have also involved tickets for sporting events and the small print on repair shop order forms.

Common Law and Legislative Remedies. Although many jurisdictions, starting early in this century, granted relief in receipt cases, consumers had to go to court to vindicate their rights and even then were not assured of winning. The inflexibility and arbitrariness of the common law spurred government at all levels of devise consumer protection legislation which required that more and plainer notice be given of disclaimers and the like. We will look at aspects of this legislation in Chapter 37. Negotiation and Holders in Due Course, and Chapter 45, Consumer Protection.

Even with the new protections in place, preventive law principles still dictate: Read the contract *before* you enter into it. If you are uncertain about its meaning, get professional advice. *Remember:* No court will excuse a person from reading the terms of an offer when they are adequately and reasonably presented.

The End of Contracts?

The UCC gap fillers (discussed in Chapter 6) and the presumptions of the UCC as to additional terms have led some scholars to claim they mark the end of mutual assent. Instead, they argue, the courts are now making contracts and the common law rules therefore are now dead. That argument is simply wrong.

Although the UCC has influenced the law of contracts generally, except in one area it has not replaced the common law. The UCC applies to the sale of good only; it does not, for instance, apply to sales of land or services. So the common law still lives.

More important than its continued existence is the continued validity of the common law approach to contracts. *Remember:* The UCC gap fillers and presumptions are tools for courts to use in resolving disputes. If the terms of a contract are clear and definite, they control. For example, contracts often contain provisions calling for delivery of goods within a reasonable time after signing. But what is a reasonable time? A day? A week? A month? If the buyer demands immediate delivery and the seller cannot ship for 2 weeks, the seller may face a lawsuit and liability which a specific delivery date would have avoided. Thus, even if the common law did not dictate definiteness, preventive law principles and common sense do.

METHODS OF ACCEPTANCE

An offer gives the offeree the power to form a binding, legal contract. The binding event is the *acceptance*. An offeror, of course, may specify how and when the offeree must accept. If the offeror does so, the offeree must comply or forgo the offer. This section examines how acceptances are made.

Acceptance by Promise

A bilateral contract, as noted above, is a promise for a promise. Suppose the offeror says, "I'll sell you my Yamaha guitar if you promise to give me $300." The offeree can accept by saying something like "OK" or "I promise." Note that the offeror is really asking for two distinct things from the offeree. She is asking for a return promise, which will bring the contract into existence, and for performance, which will fulfill or *execute* the offeree's end of the bargain.

If follows that an offeree's manner of acceptance cannot turn an offer of a bilateral contract into a unilateral contract. Suppose Jan offers to pay Ralph $50 a month if he promises to remove snow from her driveway during the winter. Ralph must promise to do so in order to accept. Even though Jan does not specify a time and place for acceptance, she has still asked for a promise. Ralph does not make the return promise, but he does shovel her drive after the first snow. Ralph has not accepted the offer and would not be entitled to the contract price. (He may, however, be entitled to the value of his services—see Chapter 12.) Jan wanted Ralph's promise. Since she did not get it, she may have hired someone else.

Acceptance by Performance

If the offeror states his offer in such a way that it can be accepted by an action only, the performance of that action must occur in order for a contract to be formed. Thus, if Todd offers $100 to the person who locates his lost watch, Sara's promise to find it would not result in an enforceable agreement. Ordinarily, the offeree need not inform the offeror of his intention to perform. However, if the offeree knows the offeror lacks an adequate means of learning of the actual performance, the offeree must diligently try to notify the offeror unless the offer indicates notification is not required.

Once the offeror knows the offeree has commenced performance with the intent to accept the offer, the offeror will generally be estopped from revoking the offer. Suppose Champion Sports Shop promises to give a $500 bonus to any entrant who breads the course record for their Super Derby 10K run. As a possible record-breaking runner approached the finish line, Champion would not be allowed to revoke its offer after the run had begun.

In one instance, the UCC allows acceptance either by promise or by performance. An offer to buy goods "for prompt or current shipment" invites acceptance "either by a prompt promise to ship or by the prompt or current shipment." Suppose Barteley Markets places an order with Cal Orange Corp. for immediate shipment of 10,000 bushels of oranges. A promise by Cal Orange to ship within the week would accept the offer, as would the actual shipment [UCC §2-206(1)(b)].

Acceptance by Silence

A bilateral contract if formed upon the offeree's communication of a return promise to the offeror. But what if the offeror says that she will interpret the offeree's lack of response as a manifestation of his acceptance. The general rule is that an offeror cannot force the offeree to take affirmative action to avoid accepting. Suppose Gina offers to sell Ted a 1-year subscription to *Life* magazine. "If you don't notify me to the contrary." she tells him, "I'll assume you want it." Ted's failure to notify Gina does not accept her offer.

The rationale for the general rule is that a contrary rule would provide too great an opportunity for misunderstandings or fraud. Book and record clubs are, perhaps, the most common situations where the offeror may take silence for an acceptance. In many instances, members agree to notify the club if they do *not* want the month's selection. The club may interpret their failure to respond as an acceptance of its offer of that month's selection.

The agreement between the club and its members is usually in writing, so it is not difficult to find an acceptance by silence. But when the parties have not expressly agreed, proof of a pattern of past dealings becomes crucial, as the Vermont Supreme Court held in *J.C. Durick Ins. v. Andrus,* presented below.

An extreme case might involve an offeree who had ignored an offer he felt was ridiculous and who later found he was liable on a contract. However, there are three exceptions to the general rule, which are discussed next.

Prior Dealings. Prior dealings between the parties may make it reasonable for the offeror to interpret silence as an acceptance. In the next case, the Vermont Supreme Court defined the limits of the prior dealings exception.

J.C. Durick Ins. v. Andrus

139 Vt. 150, 424 A.2d 249 (1980)

FACTS   Andrus insured his apartment building for $40,000 with Durick. The parties had never dealt with each other before. The policy did not contain an automatic renewal provision. Two months before it expired, Durick wrote Andrus recommending an increase in his coverage to $48,000. Andrus replied he wished to insure his building for only $24,000. Shortly before the expiration date, Durick sent Andrus a new policy with a face amount of $48,000. The policy contained a provision that the defendant could "cancel" the new policy by returning it. Otherwise, the new policy would automatically go into effect. Andrus did not respond. Durick sued him for the premiums due under the new policy. The trial court found for Durick.

ISSUE   Did Andrus accept the new policy?

DECISION   No. Reversed. Silence gives consent only where a duty to speak exists. Andrus had no such duty. The prior contract was a separate, independent agreement. It did not contain an automatic renewal clause and therefore did not bind the parties in any way after its expiration. The past dealings of the parties established no course of conduct.

There are many unanswered questions regarding this case. For example, why would Andrus want to reduce his insurance coverage? Was it wise for Durick to send a bill to a new customer that was different from the one he requested? Even if Durick won, what would Andrus do? Most likely, Andrus would have simply canceled the policy and selected a new agent. In summary, there is reason to question whether Durick's lawsuit was a reflection of smart business practices. Good business practices sometimes may mean forgoing legal rights.

The key to the prior dealings exception is an established course of conduct. Suppose that for 20 years Durick had sent Andrus an annual renewal policy and a bill. Each year, Andrus paid the premium. However, this year Andrus neither rejected the policy nor paid the premium. A court would hold that in light of the parties' prior dealings Andrus had accepted the policy.

Implied Acceptance. Silence or inaction also operates as an acceptance if the offeror has given the offeree reason to understand that silence will be taken to manifest acceptance and if the offeree remains silent, intending to accept. The next case illustrates a common situation where a court implies an acceptance from silence.

Anderson Chevrolet/Olds, Inc. v. Higgins

57 N.C. App. 650, 292 S.E.2d 159 (1982)

FACTS   Higgins signed a truck lease with Anderson in which she agreed to pay for all "maintenance and repairs to keep [the] vehicle in good working order." Less than a year later, when the truck broke down, Higgins called Anderson to tow the vehicle to its garage. Higgins permitted Anderson to disassemble the engine, which revealed that Higgins had put 25,000 miles on the truck but had not so much as changed its oil. Anderson informed Higgins of its repair estimate. Twenty-two days later, without hearing anything from her, Anderson's employees repaired the vehicle. The bill came to almost $1400. After receiving notice that the repairs were complete, Higgins sent employees to get the truck. Anderson refused to give them the truck without payment for the repairs. Anderson then sued Higgins for the value of the repairs and for its losses under the lease contract. Higgins claimed the parties did not have a contract for the truck's repair, but the trial court found for Anderson.

ISSUE Did Higgins's silence as to the truck's repair manifest an acceptance?

DECISION Yes. Affirmed. The relationship between the parties may justify the offeror to assume silence indicates assent. Here, Higgins's silence manifested assent in three ways. First, she had a reasonable opportunity to reject the offered services, which a reasonable person would expect to pay for. Second, the lease gave Anderson reason to understand that Higgins's silence manifested assent to the repairs. Third, Higgins sent her employees to the garage for the purposes of accepting and taking possession of the repaired vehicle.

Notwithstanding the fact that Higgins did not perform even minimal maintenance on the vehicle, it is important to note that many consumers find the whole experience of finalizing the purchase or lease of a new car to be very confusing, even traumatic. A dealer wishing to exercise good business practices and lessen the possibility of unnecessary litigation would be wise to review its sales practices and legal contracts to try to be more consumer-friendly.

Exercise of Dominion. An offeree may accept an offer by exercising *dominion*—control or possession—over the offered property. For example, Peggy offers to sell Mike her automobile for $3500. Peggy leaves it with Mike to test-drive. Mike drives the car to work every day for the next week and then takes it on vacation. Mike's exercise of control over the automobile operates as an acceptance of the offer.

Before 1970, this rule had unpleasant consequences for consumers. At that time, some companies would send unsolicited merchandise to a consumer and, if it was not returned—at the consumer's expense—force payment re-

gardless of whether the consumer wanted the goods. For example, suppose David received a package in the mail containing a set of luggage accompanied by a letter stating, "If you like the luggage, send $150; otherwise, return it." David's use of the luggage would amount to acceptance by exercise of dominion. Today, as a result of federal legislation, those who receive unordered merchandise through the mails from a commercial sender may do what they please with it without obligation to the sender.

WHEN AN ACCEPTANCE TAKES EFFECT

An acceptance takes effect when it is communicated to the offeror or to the offeror's *agent*.

Express and Implied Agents

The offeror's agent, if any, may be express or implied. Assume Ann is a food broker. She calls Ken and offers to sell him 100 crates of grapes at $4 per crate. Key says, "I'll take them." He has communicated his acceptance directly to the offeror. Suppose, however, when Ann

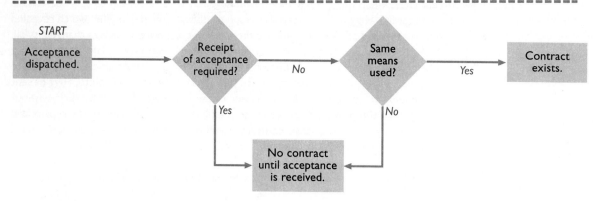

Figure 7.1 The common law "mailbox rule."
The danger of the mailbox rule to the offeror is that the offeree's acceptance takes effect upon its proper transmission whether or not it ever reaches the offeror.

made the offer she said, "I'll be out of the office for the next few hours, but if you want the stock, just tell Len, my salesman." Len is Ann's *express agent* for the purposes of receiving Ken's acceptance.

An offeror is said to use an implied agent to receive the acceptance when he or she does not specify an express agent. An *implied agent* is a third party that either (1) the offeror used to transmit the offer to the offeree or (2) the offeree could reasonably use to transmit the acceptance in view of the circumstances of the transaction. Implied agents include mail, telegraph, cable, and the like. At common law, the implied agent was the means used by the offeror to transmit the offer. When the offeree delivered the acceptance to the implied agent, it took effect.

The term "implied agent" refers to the fact that there is no agreement between the offeror and the agent that the agent will act on the offeror's behalf. In fact, like the postal service, all an implied agent agrees to do is transmit the message. For that reason, the term *means of acceptance*—the way the offeree is to transmit the acceptance to the offeror—better describes the implied agency concept.

Means of Acceptance

An offeror always has the right to stipulate that an acceptance will not be effective until the offeror actually receives it. By doing so, in the event of a dispute, the burden rests on the offeree to prove receipt. The offeror also has the right to stipulate the means of acceptance. However, offerors rarely do so. The common law courts therefore developed rules that defined when acceptances took effect in terms of the means the offeror used to transmit the offer.

The Authorized Means Test. At common law, an acceptance by an authorized means took effect when it was dispatched. The authorized means was either the means the offeror specified or, if none was specified, the same means as that used by the offeror to communicate the offer. Suppose Sears mails Karen an offer of employment that does not specify a means of acceptance. At common law, Sears would have impliedly authorized acceptance by mail. Thus, when Karen places her written acceptance—properly stamped and addressed—in a mailbox, she and Sears have formed a contract. Even if her letter is delayed, lost, or destroyed while in the hands of the U.S. Postal Service, her acceptance is effective. Because the mail is so often the express or implied authorized means of acceptance, this rule became known as "the mailbox rule" (see Figure 7.1). The next case, decided by the U.S. Supreme Court, is one of the earliest statements of the mailbox rule.

Tayloe v. Merchants' Fire Ins. Co.

50 U.S. (9 How.) 390 (1850)

FACTS   Tayloe asked an insurance agent to apply for fire insurance for his house. The agent made the application. The company replied it would undertake the risk on payment of the premium. On December 2, the insurance agent wrote Tayloe, who was away from home, advising him of the terms. Because of a misdirection, the letter did not reach Tayloe until December 20. On December 21, Tayloe mailed the agent his assent accompanied by a check for the premium. The agent received the letter on December 31. On January 1 he wrote Tayloe, declining to put the insurance into effect because Tayloe's house had burned down on December 22. Tayloe brought suit for the proceeds of the policy.

ISSUE   Did Tayloe's insurance contract come into existence as of the time he mailed the acceptance?

DECISION   Yes. Judgment for Tayloe. When negotiations are carried on through the mails, the offer and acceptance cannot occur at the same moment. An acceptance must follow the offer after a lapse of time. The party to whom an offer is addressed has a right to regard it as intended to continue until it reaches him. The risk of nondelivery and of a lapse of time in notification falls on the offeror. The unqualified acceptance by the offeree of the terms proposed by the offeror, transmitted by mail, closes the bargain from the time of the transmission of the acceptance.

Cases like *Tayloe* can cause fits for a court. Did Tayloe really mail the check on December 21, the day *before* his house burned down? What could Tayloe do to convince the jury that he really had dispatched his acceptance on December 21? The case is a good example of why an offeror might consider requiring that an acceptance must actually be received to be effective.

Under traditional common law, when the offeree uses and unauthorized means, the acceptance is not effective until the offeror actually receives it—provided it arrives within the time period in which an authorized means of acceptance would have arrived. Suppose Karen had asked her friend Michelle to deliver her written acceptance to Sears. It would not be effective until Sears actually received it; even then, it would be effective only if it arrived by the time Sears would have received Karen's acceptance had it been mailed. Had Karen attempted to accept Sears's offer orally—say, by telephone—the common law would treat her attempted acceptance as a counteroffer. Although the national CPA exam continues to recognize the traditional rule, few states still do.

The Reasonable Means Test. Today, most courts have adopted the view of the *Restatement (Second) of Contracts* §30 and the UCC §2-206(1) that an offer authorizes acceptance by any reasonable means if the offer does not specify a means and the circumstances do not indicate otherwise. Thus, Karen might transmit her acceptance by Federal Express or telex instead of the U.S. Postal Service, since they are at least as reliable and are commonly used for the same purposes. But suppose she chose to use a carrier pigeon or another unorthodox means to communicate her acceptance. Then it would not be effective until Sears actually received it.

Revocation of an Offer

Determining whether and when there is an acceptance becomes complicated when an offeror attempts to revoke the offer. Under the implied agency rule, a revocation takes effect on its delivery to the offeree. However, an offeree can accept at any time before the offer is revoked.

Suppose that on January 3 Ed mails Kristin an offer to sell her his home. Kristin receives the offer on January 4 and immediately deposits her acceptance in the nearest mailbox. On January 5, Ed changes his mind and tells Kristin he has revoked his offer. On January 6, Ed receives Kristin's acceptance. Ed's revocation has no legal effect because a contract came into existence on January 4, the day Kristin deposited her acceptance with Ed's implied agent. Obviously, Kristin must be able to prove when she mailed her acceptance in order to win.

CLASSIFICATIONS OF CONTRACTS

This chapter completes the discussion of mutual assent. From now on, we will be looking at contracts. So it makes sense at this point to look at the categories which classify contracts.

All contracts, as previously explained, are either bilateral or unilateral. That, however, is just one way of classifying contracts. All contracts are also either formal or informal; either executory or executed; *and* express, implied in fact, or implied in law (see Figure 7.2). An express, informal, executed bilateral contract is perhaps the most common of all contracts.

Formal and Informal

A *formal* contract is one which the law requires to be written in a particular form with certain characteristics in order to be enforceable. Only three classes of formal contracts exist today: *recognizances,* which are acknowledgments in court that persons will pay a certain sum unless they perform a specified condition—usually appearing in court; *negotiable instruments,* which are discussed in Part VII of this book; and *letters of credit,* which are also discussed in Part VII.

All other contracts are *informal,* meaning they do not have to be in a particular form. "Gimme a 'burger, two fries, and a Pepsi" can lead to a contract just as easily as an offer written in the finest legalese. The contracts discussed in this part are informal.

A *notarized* contract is an informal contract whose maker certifies under oath the genuineness of his or her signature before a notary public. The notary then affixes his or her certification, seal, and signature to the document. This procedure permits the use of the document in court as evidence of the facts contained in it. Many states require transfers of automobile titles to be notarized.

Executory and Executed

An *executory* contract is one the parties have not yet performed. Suppose Arcticana agrees to deliver 1000 cases of frozen orange juice to Super Market on July 1. Super Market agrees to

VALIDITY	= Valid	= Void	= Voidable	= Unenforceable
FORMALITY	= Formal	= Informal		
NATURE OF PROMISE	= Unilateral	= Bilateral		
EXTENT OF PERFORMANCE	= Executory	= Executed	= Partially executed	
NATURE	= Express	= Implied in fact	= Implied in law (Quasi contract)	

Figure 7.2 Characteristics of contracts.
The validity category is discussed in detail in Chapter 9.

pay $10 per case on delivery. Until July 1, the contract is executory if neither party has performed.

An *executed* contract is one the parties have performed. If Arcticana delivers the juice on July 1 and Super Market hands the driver a check, they have executed their contract. A contract, of course, can be partially executed. If Arcticana delivers the juice but Super Market does not pay, Arcticana has executed its part of the contract but Super Market has not executed its part.

Express, Implied in Fact, and Implied in Law (Quasi-Contract)

An *express* contract is one whose terms are actually stated, whether orally or in writing. If Erin offers to buy Sean's stereo for $200, they have entered into an express contract.

Contracts implied in fact and contracts implied in law are not really contracts at all. They are remedies devised by the courts. Courts apply them when the common law requirements for contract formation did not occur, but it would be grossly unjust to permit one party to benefit—without paying—from what he or she received from the other.

A contract *implied in fact* is not expressly stated. Rather, a court, examining the facts and circumstances, implies the existence of the contract from the acts or conduct of the parties. If a farmer asks a veterinarian to treat a sick horse, a court will infer that the farmer agrees to pay a reasonable fee, although neither party says anything about it. The parties may not have thought consciously that they were forming a contractual relationship. Still, it is only common sense that the farmer and the veterinarian agreed to an exchange of services for money. And, that is why the courts devised contracts implied in fact.

A contract *implied in law,* also called a *quasi-contract,* is an obligation imposed by a court to do justice between the parties even though they never exchanged, or intended to exchange, promises. In this instance, a court implies a contract to prevent one party's unjust enrichment at the other's expense. Suppose a house painter begins painting Judy's house. She knows he is at the wrong house but lets him go ahead. When he finishes, she refuses to pay. The painter will be able to recover the reasonable value of his services. However, if Judy was not at home when the painter arrived and did not return until after he had finished, she would owe him nothing. In fact, the painter would either have to return the house to its previous condition or pay damages to Judy if she suffered any.

Thus, a contract implied in law is really a remedy for wilful conduct on the level of fraud. A court imposes a "contract" on the wrong-doer in order to provide a basis for granting the other party fair compensation.

Contracts implied in fact and contracts implied in law are remedies courts apply when no contract exists, but justice demands redress. Chapter 12 describes remedies available for the nonperformance of a contract.

CONCLUSION

The basic contractual equation is:

Offer + acceptance = mutual assent

Once a party establishes that mutual assent is present, a court will presume a contract exists. But it is important to remember that a contract is an agreement that the courts will enforce. Not all agreements are contracts. The next chapter examines the element which normally makes an agreement enforceable in a court—consideration.

A NOTE TO FUTURE CPA CANDIDATES

The "mailbox rule" has been a favorite test item on the CPA exam. The exam still recognizes the common law approach, not the reasonable means approach, for non-UCC contracts. A word of caution: Before you presume the mailbox rule applies, make sure the offeror did not specify that the acceptance must actually be received by the offeror to be effective. This is often the case on the CPA exam. Remember, silence does not ordinarily act as an acceptance unless the parties expressly agree that it does.

The CPA exam has also heavily emphasized questions like Case Problem 10. We find the best approach in answering such questions is to sketch out the various transactions and then attempt to solve the problem. Remember

that when the mailbox rule applies, it is the only exception to the general rule: An offer, acceptance, revocation, rejection, or counteroffer must actually be received to be effective. Do not forget: When you mail carrier delivers a revocation letter to your mailbox, you have received it even if you do not then know of its receipt.

KEY WORDS

acceptance (162)
dominion (165)
executed contract (169)
executory contract (168)
express agent (166)
formal contract (168)
implied agent (166)
informal contract (168)
intent (159)
manifestation (159)
means of acceptance (166)
mutual assent (159)
prima facie (160)
quasi-contract (169)

DISCUSSION QUESTIONS

1. Describe the difference between the subjective and objective theories of contract formation.
2. How is "acceptance" defined in the law? What is the significance of a valid acceptance?
3. Who controls the terms of the offer? Who has the power to create a contract?
4. When does a contract come into existence?
5. Who may accept an offer? What is the reason for the limitation on who may accept an offer?
6. Explain the common law rule requiring an acceptance to "mirror the offer."
7. Will silence ever constitute an acceptance? If so, when?
8. What is "the mailbox rule"? Does either the *Restatement* or the UCC vary it? If so, how?
9. What is meant by the medium of acceptance? Name three, and explain when you would use each.

CASE PROBLEMS

1. Nash listed his home with Adams Real Estate Agency. Lollar, a prospective purchaser,

made an offer which Nash rejected as too low. Nash made some alternations to Lollar's offer and wrote at the bottom of the form, "Acceptance of this counteroffer must occur by Friday, November 29." He transmitted it to Lollar via Adams. Lollar signed the counteroffer and returned it to Adams on the 28th. Adams, however, failed to tell Nash of this until the 30th. Nash has told Lollar his acceptance was untimely and that he has decided to keep the house. Do Nash and Lollar have a contract? Explain.

2. Professor Wyatt told the 45 students in her Sociology 105 class she wanted to sell her used personal computer. She offered to sell it for $750. Any student who wanted it could accept by placing a written acceptance under her office door by 8 A.M. the following Tuesday. When Professor Wyatt opened her office the next Tuesday, she found seven acceptances. She chose to accept the first one she picked up. She informed the other six persons that she was rejecting their acceptances. One of the six, Red Matson, has sued Wyatt, alleging breach of contract. Is Matson correct? Explain.

3. Water Works, Inc. had a long-standing policy of offering its employees $100 for suggestions which the company put into effect. Because of inflation and the declining quality of suggestions, Water Works decided to increase the award to $500. At the time that management made this decision, several suggestions were under consideration. They included one made by Farber, an employee. Two days before the new award was to be announced, management accepted Farber's suggestion and awarded him $100. Within the year, Farber's suggestion saved Water Works $10,000 and will save the company at least that amount annually for the foreseeable future. Farber now wants an additional $400 and is considering a lawsuit.

4. On January 15, Lena Risker entered into an agreement with Home Cooked Soup Inc. whereby Lena would supply Home Cooked with 10,000 bushels of home-grown tomatoes that "Home Cooked needs over the next year." In accordance with the agreement, the price of the tomatoes was omitted "due to the fluctuating market over the year." Nothing was said as to where the tomatoes were to be delivered. Risker failed to perform and Home Cooked sued, alleging breach of contract. What arguments could you make on behalf of Risker? What arguments could you make on behalf of Home Cooked?

5. Taylor placed a classified advertisement in the newspaper offering to sell a used canoe for $450. Besser called Taylor and asked him if he would consider $350. Taylor responded: "The lowest I will go is $375. I'll be away from my office for a while. If you call and I'm not in, just let my associate, Randy Lefler, know if you want it for $375." Taylor called back and told Lefler that he had decided to buy the canoe for $375. Lefler said he knew nothing about the canoe but he would leave the message for Taylor. Unfortunately, Lefler got very busy immediately after the call and forgot to leave the message. Taylor, finding no message, sold the canoe to Cooper later that evening. Besser claims Taylor breached their contract. Taylor claims that they never had a contract. Is Besser correct? Explain.

6. Crosley wrote Packard, offering to purchase Packard's estate home at 1110 University Boulevard and an adjacent lot for $200,000. Wrote Crosley, "I came to the price of $200,000 because I figure the estate home is worth $175,000 and the lot $25,000. Together they equal $200,000, my offer." Packard wrote back to Crosley, "I accept your offer to purchase my estate home for $175,000. I am still considering whether to sell you the lot for $25,000." At this point in time, do the parties have a contract for the estate house? Explain.

7. For many years Joyce Petrie had attempted to purchase from Jimmy Wynn an old scorecard with the autograph of her favorite former baseball player, Roberto Clemente. Wynn finally mailed Petrie an offer to sell the scorecard, for $45. As Petrie was licking the envelope containing her return acceptance, she saw her mail carrier approaching her house. Petrie ran out to meet him. The carrier handed Petrie her day's mail and she then gave him her acceptance letter. As the carrier

drove off, Petrie discovered a revocation letter from Wynn. Petrie claims she has a binding contract as a result of the "mailbox rule." Wynn disagrees. Is Wynn correct? Explain.

8. Barnes saw a large sign on a vacant lot which read, "Lot for Sale. $60,000. Dawn Wells, 116 Campbell Street. 232-2343." Barnes was very eager to acquire the lot for a fast-food restaurant, so he mailed Wells a letter in which he said he accepted her offer and would consider their contract to be binding if he did not hear from her within 5 days. Wells simply ignored his letter. Six days later, Barnes called her, insisting they had a contract. Wells has asked you whether she is bound. Is she? Explain.

9. Delbert agreed to have surgery on his knee for damage from an old football injury. While Delbert was on the operating table under anesthesia, Dr. Honeycutt, the surgeon, performed the procedure on his knee. Noticing the bumps in Delbert's nose where it had been broken, Dr. Honeycutt decided to straighten it. When Delbert awoke and learned about his nose job, he told the doctor that he would pay him nothing. After all, they had never discussed the cost of the knee surgery. What is Dr. Honeycutt's best theory for recovering the cost of the knee surgery? The nose surgery? Describe the doctor's chances of prevailing under each theory.

10. Bennett mailed Kelly an offer to sell her his Texas vacation home. His offer specified that he must receive her acceptance by August 1. On July 20, Kelly mailed her acceptance. Unfortunately, the postal service delayed the acceptance, and it did not reach Bennett until August 2. On July 28, Kelley had received a letter from Bennett revoking his offer because he had changed his mind about selling. Does Kelly have an enforceable contract with Bennett? Assuming a court could not find an express contract here, would it be likely to find a contract implied in law? Explain.

CHAPTER 8
Consideration

You have learned that mutual assent requires an offer and an acceptance. Mutual assent is needed to form a contract. However, in this chapter you will learn that not all situations involving mutual assent result in an enforceable contract. It is also necessary to have consideration, the "glue" that holds the contract together. Years ago in a United States Supreme Court case involving pornography, Justice Stewart stated that he might not be able to define pornography but he knew it when he saw it. For totally unrelated reasons, consideration is often also something difficult for students to define and explain practically. Ideally, you will soon be able to recognize the existence of consideration.

WHAT IS CONSIDERATION?

We gave you a very simple definition of consideration: the "glue" that holds a contract together. The legal definition of consideration is "a bargained for exchange of value." To be even more precise, "consideration is that which is a legal benefit (to gain a legal right) to the promisor and/or a legal detriment (to owe a legal duty) to the promisee." We will further discuss these definitions shortly, but for now you might think of consideration as being similar to the traditional handshake—a means of formalizing a deal between contracting parties.

Basic Principles of Consideration

There are three basic principles to keep in mind when learning about consideration. One is that "a bargained for exchange" essentially means something for something, not something for nothing. Suppose John asks Sandy if she would like to have his chemistry textbook after he completes his course. Sandy says yes. There is mutual assent but no bargained for exchange. Why? Because Sandy has received a promise of a gift without making a commitment to do any-thing in return. In short, she is to get something for nothing.

The second basic principle to keep in mind is that legal sufficiency has nothing to do with adequacy of consideration. Stated another way, the law requires an exchange of things with value but the things need not be of similar economic, market, value. To illustrate, suppose Sandy has a snapshot of her golden retriever, Tucker. Does the snapshot have economic value? If so, probably very little. Does it represent legal value? Yes. For example, we could not use the snapshot in this textbook without Sandy's consent. Assume that John's used chemistry textbook is worth around $35, while Sandy's snapshot is without any clear market value. If John agrees to exchange his textbook for Sandy's snapshot, would this agreement be legally enforceable? Yes. Their exchange of promises involve an exchange of legal rights even if the actual items to be exchanged have significantly different values. As such, a court would find legal sufficiency.

Finally, the analysis for legal sufficiency is the same regardless of whether a bilateral or unilateral contract situation exists. To illustrate, Sandy's snapshot would support John's promise to convey his textbook, regardless of whether he required her response to be the conveyance of her snapshot, resulting in a unilateral contract, or her return promise to convey the snapshot, resulting in a bilateral contract. As Figure 8.1 shows, in both situations there is a *consideration,* a bargained for exchange of value. If you understand Figure 8.1, you will appreciate that it is not simply the exchange of promises in a bilateral contract situation which creates a contract. You must also understand why sufficiency of consideration does not require that it be equal in value to the goods or services exchanged.

Consideration is what a party to an agreement receives in return for his act or promise. It is required in the formation of both common law and UCC contracts. As such, determining

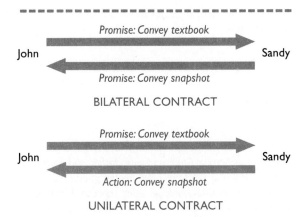

Figure 8.1 Consideration must exist for both bilateral and unilateral contracts.

whether consideration for a contract actually exists requires an analysis of each party's promise or action. The *Restatement (Second) of Contracts,* §71, lists four types of consideration which can exist:

- A promise for a return promise
- An act other than a promise
- A forbearance
- The creation, modification, or distinction of a legal relationship

These four types of consideration are discussed later in the chapter.

Sufficiency

Consideration must not only be present; it must also be sufficient. Courts and lawyers often refer to sufficient consideration as "good consideration," meaning that it has a legal value or is a legal detriment. Both concepts, as already noted, are distinct from economic value or economic detriment.

Legal value, for instance, implies an economic value, but it need not be great *or* equivalent to the consideration of the other party. Suppose Walter promises to sell his ten-speed bike to Mary in exchange for her promise to pay

him $75. His bike is worth $150. However, it is January, they live in Buffalo, and Walter needs money. Walter's promise is supported by consideration, since he will receive $75 he was not entitled to before—even though it does not represent the bike's actual value. But what if he bargained for and received $50? $25? $1? In all three cases, a court could find consideration present, even though a reasonable person might not have entered eagerly into such a contract.

Generally, if the consideration has some legal value, a court will not question its adequacy. So long as there is some potential value or detriment present, the court will find the consideration legally sufficient. Still, a very great disparity in economic value will cause a court to study a transaction for factors calling into question the reality of a party's assent to the contract. As we will see in the next chapter, such a disparity may signal assent brought about by duress, fraud, or the like, which may void the contract.

Louisiana, the only state whose laws primarily derive from the French civil law tradition, also requires that consideration support a contract. However, unlike the common law, Louisiana law requires that a court consider the adequacy of consideration before enforcing a contract. Many consumer advocates believe Louisiana's approach reduces the likelihood of the imposition of unfair burdens on one party.

An act other than a promise. An act, of course, can also be sufficient consideration, since it is the manner of accepting a unilateral contract. Suppose Nellie offers to pay L-K Tree Service $100 if it removes a tree from her backyard. In return for her promise to pay, Nellie gets an act. That act has legal value, since it is not something L-K previously had a legal duty to do. In return for its act, L-K is to receive $100, which also is good, or legal, consideration.

Forbearance. Forbearance may also be sufficient consideration. *Forbearance* is the giving up of something one otherwise has a legal right to do. The next case, a classic, presents a very difficult question relating to forbearance as consideration.

Hamer v. Sidway

124 N.Y. 538, 27 N.E. 256 (1891)

FACTS

It appears that William E. Story, Sr., was the uncle of William E. Story, 2d; that at the celebration of the Golden Wedding of Samuel Story and wife, father and mother of William E. Story, Sr., . . . in the presence of the family and invited guests, he promised his nephew that if he would refrain from drinking, using tobacco, swearing and playing cards or billiards for money until he became 21 years of age, he would pay him the sum of $5000. The nephew assented . . . and fully performed the conditions including the promise.

Almost 6 years later, when the nephew reached 21, he wrote his uncle, informing him that he had performed his part of the agreement. The uncle replied, stating that he had put the nephew's money in the bank and that "you can consider this money on interest." The nephew consented to this arrangement and the money remained with the uncle until his death in 1887. The uncle's personal representative denied a claim against the estate for the $5000 with interest. The trial court held the debt was valid, but the intermediate appellate court reversed.

ISSUE

Was sufficient consideration present to support the promise?

DECISION

Yes. Trial court judgment reinstated.

[The] promisee used tobacco, occasionally drank liquor and he had a legal right to do so. That right he had abandoned for a period of years upon the strength of the promise . . . that for such forbearance he would give him $5000. We need not speculate on the effort which may have been required to give up the use of those stimulants. It is sufficient that he restricted his lawful freedom of action within certain prescribed limits upon the faith of his uncle's agreement, and now, having fully performed the conditions imposed, it is of no moment whether such performance actually proved a benefit to the promisor . . . ; but, were it a proper subject of inquiry, we see nothing in this record that would permit a determination that the uncle was not benefited in a legal sense.

In *Hamer*, should the law provide a remedy to the nephew? How can the nephew prove the existence of their contract?

Hamer has proved difficult for students and commentators alike. Many do not believe the benefit to the uncle was legal consideration. But few have challenged the court's holding that the

nephew's detriment was sufficient consideration.

Forbearance can also refer to giving up a good faith cause of action. Suppose Harold slips on the ice in front of Vita's house. He suffers $1000 in damages. He agrees not to sue Vita for his damages in exchange for her promise to pay his hospital bills. Harold's forbearance from filing suit is sufficient consideration for Vita's promise. He had a right to sue Vita which he gave up. However, suppose Vita's neighbor, Virginia, threatens to sue Vita because of Harold's injuries unless she receives $1000 not to. Virginia's forbearance would not be good consideration for Vita's promise to pay because Virginia suffered no compensable loss.

Bargained for Exchange

As already noted, a major disparity in value may signal a lack of mutual assent. It may also indicate that there was no bargained for exchange of consideration. To be good, the consideration must be bargained for voluntarily and given up in exchange for a promise, an act, or a forbearance. The following case illustrates the reason for this requirement.

O'Neill v. DeLaney

92 Ill. App. 3d 292, 415 N.E.2d 1260 (1980)

FACTS Mr. and Mrs. DeLaney had a large art collection, including a painting attributed to Peter Paul Rubens. Unauthenticated, it was worth approximately $100,000 and, if authenticated, many times that. In 1970, Mr. DeLaney purportedly sold the painting to his friend, Mr. O'Neill, for $10 and "other good and valuable consideration." Mrs. DeLaney did not sign the contract. Mr. O'Neill alleged the other consideration was his friendship and affection for Mr. DeLaney. For the next 4 years, the painting remained in the DeLaney apartment. It spent only a few days in O'Neill's apartment. O'Neill never insured the painting. In 1974, Mrs. DeLaney began a divorce proceeding in which she claimed an interest in the picture. O'Neill brought this action to determine the painting's owner. The trial court held that the contract was void because of inadequate consideration.

ISSUE Was the O'Neill-DeLaney transaction a bargained for exchange?

DECISION No. Affirmed. Persons sometimes say that they have bargained when their conduct shows they have not. A gross inadequacy of consideration supports the conclusion that the parties did not actually agree upon an exchange, that the promisor did not in fact bargain for the consideration. If it was not bargained for, it was not consideration. By finding inadequate consideration, a court does not attempt to protect a party from the consequences of his bad bargain. Rather, it questions the existence of the alleged contract. Here, the purchase price of $10 for such a valuable work of art is grossly inadequate.

Why would DeLaney ever agree to sell the valuable Rubens painting for a mere $10? The answer, of course, is that the sale was a sham designed to cheat Mrs. DeLaney out of her half of the painting. Although the court decision is expressed in terms of consideration, the court was really saying there was no intent to transfer title. As *O'Neill* indicates, one of the principal purposes of the bargained for exchange requirement is to prevent frauds on third parties, such as DeLaney's ex-wife. Spouses in the process of divorce, tax authorities, and creditors are among the types of third parties most often affected by such frauds.

CONTRACTS INVOLVING MUTUAL OBLIGATION

For a bilateral contract, each promise must be sufficiently certain and binding so as to obligate the promisor. If so, it is said that *mutuality of obligation,* mutual binding, exists: for example, a promise by Sanders to sell his bike to Baker in return for Baker's promise to pay him $175. Note that each promisor has promised to do something at the request of the other party. Consideration would also be present if a contracting party agreed to refrain from doing something, such as agreeing not to bring suit in regard to damages incurred in an automobile accident in return for a promise of settlement.

There is a situation where a promisor appears to be making a binding promise but actually is not. Such a promise is called an *illusory promise,* a promise which does not actually bind the promisor to do, or refrain from doing, something: for example, a promise by Sanders to Baker to sell him his bike for $175 "if he feels like it when he completes the Victory biathlon competition." Since an illusory promise does not bind the promisor, there is *no* mutuality of obligation. Therefore, Sanders could not enforce their "contract" if he decided after the biathlon to sell his bike to Baker.

In the next sections we present situations which at first may appear to be illusory but actually are contracts involving mutuality of obligation and legally sufficient consideration.

Output and Requirements Contracts

Output and requirements contracts may at first seem to involve illusory promises because they lack quantity terms, but they are not illusory. As explained in Chapter 7, an *output contract* is an agreement to sell all production or output during a specified period of time to a single buyer: for example, a farmer selling all output of his pumpkins to a particular market. A *requirements contract* is an agreement to buy all production needs for a particular period from a single seller: for example, Pepsi Cola's agreement to supply all the cola for the Taco Bell restaurant chain. As also discussed in Chapter 7, in both situations the parties are bound to good faith limitations [UCC §2-306(1)].

Exclusive Dealing Contracts

Where a manufacturer of goods gives a distributor an exclusive right to sell the manufacturer's goods in a specified territory, unless otherwise agreed, the manufacturer impliedly agrees to use its best efforts to supply the goods and the distributor impliedly agrees to use its best efforts to promote the sale of the goods [UCC §2-306]. Suppose Ryan becomes a distributor of Saturn cars. Ryan would be held to impliedly agree to use his best efforts to sell Saturn cars. In contrast, Saturn would be held to impliedly agree to make good faith efforts to supply needed cars to Ryan. Saturn is used in this example because Saturn Corporation has made a conscious attempt to locate Saturn dealers sufficiently apart from each other to reduce competition among Saturn dealers.

Exclusive territorial licensing situations are quite common in the retail clothing industry. A retail store or chain receiving such a license will more readily invest money to specially merchandise exclusive clothes, such as a boutique within a department store that sells Polo clothing. In turn, Polo expects the department store to promote the sale of Polo clothing vigorously.

Exclusive dealing contracts between parties other than the manufacturer and distributor may be violative of federal antitrust laws, to be discussed in Chapter 44.

Conditional Contracts

It is quite common for parties to a contract to agree that the performance of one party is not to occur unless and until a specified event occurs.

A condition not controlled by either party—even if it appears unlikely that performance will occur—will not render a promise illusory.

Suppose Hodges enters into a contract to supply a department store with Chicago Cubs World Series mugs if the Cubs play in the World Series this year. Neither Hodges nor the department store controls the condition. Such a contract allows the department store to plan for the possibility of the Cubs being in the World Series without having to wait until it would actually occur. Mutuality of obligation exists because both parties are obligated to perform if the Cubs make it into the World Series.

PROMISES UNENFORCEABLE BECAUSE OF LACK OF CONSIDERATION

Some contracts appear to be supported by good consideration but actually are not. These are contracts in which a party promises love and affection, or one party's consideration is past services, or a party promises to do something he is already obligated to do. Contracts resting on these forms of consideration are not enforceable if the defense of lack of consideration is raised.

Love and Affection

By themselves, love and affection generally are not good consideration because they do not constitute legal value which people typically bargain for. Suppose a father promises his daughter a Toyota for her twenty-first birthday in exchange for her promise to accept it. The contract lacks consideration because the daughter's promise requires her to do nothing more than accept the car. Therefore, there is no bargained for exchange.

In contrast, love and affection can be the motivation for a contract so long as there is an exchange of legal value. If the father in the last example had offered the Toyota to his daughter if she graduated from college, the contract

would be supported by sufficient consideration. Why? Here, the daughter is doing more than just accepting the car. By going to college, she is forgoing other possibilities in her life, and that is a legal detriment.

The same principle applies in sales between family members where love and affection is a part of the consideration. Parents, for example, may sell a piano to a child for, say, one-tenth of its market value. The parents are receiving more than just the pleasure of giving the piano.

Past Consideration

Contracts are not enforceable if one party's promise is supported solely by *past consideration,* that is, by something which occurred or was transferred in the past. "Past consideration" is really a misnomer, since the law regards contracts supported by it as lacking consideration.

As in the case of love and affection, past consideration simply involves a promise to accept something. Suppose an employer calls in a retiring employee and tells her, "In consideration of your faithful service, the company will pay you a pension of $200 a week for the rest of your life." The employee has already performed, and the employer is not asking for a promise to do something in the future.

To be sufficient, consideration must relate to something the promisor agrees to do at the same time as or after the creation of the contract. Now suppose the employer promised the pension to the employee in exchange for a promise of an additional year's service. They have an enforceable contract because the employee agreed to do something in the future which he had no obligation to do before making the contract.

The question of past consideration often arises where a family member cares for aged parents. The services may begin gratuitously, but later the parents make a promise to pay for what the child has done for them in the past. This is not good consideration because the child has not provided any new consideration. However, an individual can make enforceable gifts in a will if they are based on love and affection or past consideration. The transfer of property by will is discussed in Chapter 29.

Preexisting Legal Duty

A promise to perform a *preexisting duty,* something one is already legally obligated to do, is not sufficient consideration. Such duties include those imposed by law on a contracting party at the time of contracting. Much of the case law in this area centers on the duties of law officers in regard to rewards. In most states, police officers cannot accept rewards for capturing criminals because of the officers' preexisting statutory duty to arrest them. The next case, however, raises an interesting question as to the applicability of the preexisting duty rule to a police officer who arrests criminals outside his jurisdiction.

Denney v. Reppert

432 S.W. 2d 647 (Ky. 1968)

FACTS — Three armed men robbed the First State Bank in Eubank in Pulaski County, Kentucky, of over $30,000. Later that day, the three were arrested by State Policemen Godby and Simms and by Deputy Sheriff Reppert of Rockcastle County. All the money was reclaimed. The bank, as a member of the Kentucky Bankers Association, had an ongoing advertisement which stated that there would be an award of $500 for the arrest and conviction of anyone who robbed its member banks. Three employees of the robbed bank, Denney, McCollum, and Snyder, all claimed the award and were denied it by the trial court. Although Deputy Sheriff Reppert was not employed by Pulaski County, where the crime occurred, he was given the award.

ISSUE — Did the trial court err when it awarded Reppert the money and not the bank's employees?

DECISION — No. Affirmed. Denny, McCollum, and Snyder, as bank employees, had a preexisting duty to protect and conserve the bank's money and protect the interests of its employer. They were "recompensed in commendation, admiration and high praise, and the world looks on them as heroes." Reppert was out of his jurisdiction and so did not have a preexisting duty to make the arrest. Thus, he is eligible to receive the award.

Illusory Promises

As previously discussed in this chapter, an *illusory promise* is a promise which does not actually bind the promisor to do, or refrain from doing, something. For example, suppose Warren says to Mrjenovich, "I promise to sell you my auditing textbook for $20 after my final if I think I passed the course." Here the decision to sell or not to sell is entirely at Warren's discretion. There is no mutuality of obligation between Warren and Mrjenovich.

MODIFICATION OF EXISTING CONTRACTS

The question of the presence of consideration often arises in the context of the modification of an existing contract. The parties commonly do not realize that when they discuss changing their agreement, they are negotiating a new contract which requires new consideration. Suppose Rodger Dodger, a major-league pitcher, is in the second year of a 4-year contract bringing him $1.5 million per year. Rodger feels underpaid and demands a raise to $2.5 million per year. If the baseball club simply gave him what he asked, the contract would be unenforceable. Rodger would not be agreeing to do anything except what he had already committed

himself to do. To make the new contract enforceable, Rodger must agree to do something beyond the terms of the old contract, like extend the period of the contract.

The requirement of new consideration reduces the possibilities of unfair demands being placed on a party. The classic case involved the captain of a fishing trawler who hired a crew at a certain wage. When the boat reached the fishing grounds, the crew refused to work unless he increased their hourly rate by $2.50. Having no alternative, he agreed. The crew could not enforce that promise because they offered no consideration for the pay increase other than performance of their existing duty. It should be noted that there is an important exception to this rule. Under UCC §2-209(1), no consideration is necessary for the modification of a contract for the sale of goods. This will be discussed in the UCC exemptions section of this chapter.

At first, the next case may look like the classic case, but it is not.

Linz v. Schuck

_____ Md. _____, 67 A. 286 (Md. 1907)

FACTS
Schuck was a contractor. He agreed to excavate and finish a cellar under Linz's property after inspecting Linz's adjacent property to determine the condition of the soil. Almost immediately after starting the job, Schuck unexpectedly discovered that the house sat on a "hard crust about three feet thick." Beneath that lay "a swamp-like—the bottom of an old creek, black, muddy stuff and soft." The house began to crack. With Linz present, the city building inspector checked the site and was of the opinion that the cellar should not be built. Schuck stopped work. Nonetheless, Linz pressured Schuck to build the cellar. Schuck agreed, but only if Linz would pay the additional cost and assume the consequences. In the meantime, an adjacent landowner sued Linz for damages to her property caused by the excavation, and he had to buy her house. Linz refused to pay Schuck, and Schuck brought suit. The trial court entered judgment for Schuck.

ISSUE
Is a contractor's promise to finish a job which proved to have substantial and unforeseen difficulties sufficient consideration to support the other party's promise to pay additional compensation?

DECISION   Yes. Affirmed. The conditions of the site were altogether different from what they appeared on the surface or what were anticipated.

> When two parties make a contract, based on supposed facts which they afterwards ascertain to be incorrect, and which would not have been entered into by one party if he had known the actual conditions which the contract required him to meet, . . . the fair course for the other party to the contract to pursue is either to relieve the contractor of going on . . . or to pay him additional compensation. . . . [The] parties can rescind the original contract and then enter into a [valid] new one, by which a larger consideration for the same work and materials that were to be done and furnished under the first contract. . . .

As a practical matter, courts tend to scrutinize an agreement to modify an existing contract for indications of conduct invalidating assent. If such conduct occurred, the courts will refuse to enforce the contract as modified. A more complete discussion of such conduct appears in Chapter 9.

Settlement of an Undisputed Debt

A party to a valid contract who owes an amount under it and who does not dispute either the debt's existence or amount is said to owe a *liquidated debt.** In such situations, even if the parties agree that the debtor may fully satisfy the obligation with a partial payment, the debtor cannot enforce the agreement unless the debtor supplied new consideration in exchange

* "Liquid" comes from a medieval Latin word which meant "pure" or "clear." "Liquidate" came to mean "make clear" or "set out clearly." From the nineteenth century on, it has had two definitions in legal and financial writing. First, it means "clear off a debt," and is used in this sense in bankruptcy proceedings (see Chapter 43). Second, it means "set out the liabilities of" a person. Thus, a liquidated claim is one which is agreed to by the parties, is established by law, or can be computed mechanically. It is in this second sense that we have used "liquidate" here and in our later discussions of contractual remedies under the common law and the UCC. See *The Oxford Dictionary of English Etymology.* (Oxford: Oxford Univ. Press, 1966, 1969) and *Black's Law Dictionary,* 5th ed. (St. Paul, Minn.: West Publ. Co., 1979).

for the creditor's promise. Suppose Lana types a paper for a professor and, as they had agreed, submits a bill for 20 hours' work at $7 per hour. The professor says he is short of cash and offers Lana $120 as full payment, which she accepts. Unless the professor reasonably disputes the existence or the amount of the debt represented by the original invoice, he could not enforce the agreement if Lana brought suit for the remaining $20.

The liquidated debt rule often is invoked when a party decides unilaterally to pay less than the liquidated amount. Suppose Webster charges a $24 dictionary at a bookstore. There is no dispute about the price or about the book's being as represented. So the $24 represents a liquidated debt. If Webster sends the bookstore a check for $12 marked "payment in full," in most states the bookstore could ignore the notation, cash the check, and recover the remainder from Webster.

Settlement of a Disputed Debt

Agreements to accept partial payments of *unliquidated* debts are enforceable. An unliquidated debt is one whose existence or amount a debtor reasonably and in good faith disputes. When the parties agree to a partial payment of an unliquidated debt, the agreement is called an *accord.* The full payment of the amount specified in the accord is called a *satisfaction.* For that reason, the resolution of an unliquidated

Figure 8.2 Liquidated versus unliquidated debts.

debt is often called an "accord and satisfaction."

The existence of an unliquidated debt also changes the effect of a unilateral attempt to satisfy it. In this instance, a check marked "payment in full"—if cashed—will keep the creditor from recovering the balance allegedly due, even if the creditor crossed out the words. The creditor must return the check to the debtor uncashed in order to recover the full amount. Otherwise, the creditor will be held to have accepted the partial payment as a complete satisfaction of the debt.

Suppose Anna agreed to buy a new cable-ready VCR from Stellar Stereo for $350, using her Stellar Stereo credit line. Unfortunately, the VCR was not compatible with the cable in Anna's town—even after Stellar's repeated efforts to make it work. Anna had to buy a cable adapter for $75 to make the VCR functional. Anna sent Stellar a check for $275 marked "payment in full satisfaction," accompanied by a letter explaining the deduction. Stellar cashed the check and then sued Anna for the balance. In this case, Anna would win, because Stellar knowingly accepted and cashed the check. The check is the accord and the satisfaction is of the original $350 debt. (See Figure 8.2.)

The payment in full problem aside, accord and satisfaction is an extremely useful and popular method of private dispute resolution. Businesspeople commonly use it, for example, when goods are damaged or deteriorate during shipment. Accord and satisfaction is discussed

in another context in Chapter 12, Performance and Remedies for Nonperformance.

Extension of Time for Third Party Payment

A creditor who grants to a third party an extension of time in which to pay another's debt receives sufficient consideration in the form of the third party's promise to pay. Suppose Brenda purchases a small boat from Stewart for $750, which is due on October 15. She takes immediate possession of the boat. On October 15 she convinces Stewart to accept $450 that day and $300 in a month. Since Stewart did not receive any new consideration for the extension, their agreement is not enforceable.

Now suppose that when Brenda paid Stewart the $450, Sheila agreed to pay the $300 balance if Stewart granted the extension. Stewart and Sheila have an enforceable contract because Stewart is getting something he did not have before: Sheila's contractual obligation to pay Brenda's debt.

FAILURE OF CONSIDERATION

When a promise lacks consideration, no contract can be based on it. In contrast, *failure of consideration* occurs when the parties have entered into a valid contract but the consideration does not materialize as expected.

Suppose The Video Shoppe hires the accounting firm of Bartleby & Heep to perform an audit. As a term of the firm's engagement, Video Shoppe specifies that the audit report must be in their hands by July 1 so that it can be used for a bank loan application. Through no fault of Video Shoppe's, the report does not reach the company until August 15, too late to be used in their loan application. In this case, the parties' contract is valid, but the consideration for which the Video Shoppe bargained—an audit report on July 1—did not materialize.

Failure of consideration is an *affirmative defense*.* An affirmative defense to a breach of contract action is one which essentially admits the sufficiency of the contract but offers an excuse for the defendant's failure to perform. In the last example, if Video Shoppe brought suit to recover damages on its contract for the plaques, its customer could raise failure of consideration as an excuse for not paying for them. It is important to note that if a defendant does not plead failure of consideration as a defense, it may waive its right to raise the defense at all.

PROMISES REQUIRING NO CONSIDERATION

Generally, to be enforceable, a promise must be supported by consideration. But over the centuries, a group of exceptions to that rule have developed which have little in common except that they are contracts not requiring consideration. Three of the exceptions originated in the common law, while two appear in the UCC.

To separate contracts enforceable by courts from other agreements, the early common law required that contracts be executed with certain formalities. These included placing a seal on the document. The promisor prepared hot wax, dripped it onto the bottom of the document, and pressed a signet ring into the wax, leaving the seal's impression. If the promisor went to that trouble, the courts recognized he or she was serious and they were willing to enforce the contract.

Contracts under seal were common in the United States until the nineteenth century. However, forms of communication which made it possible for parties to deal at considerable distance made such contracts obsolete. Also, the development of exchanges where oral contracts had to have effect—among many other causes—compelled the courts to revise their methods for determining which agreements to enforce. Today, in almost all instances consideration—not a seal—marks enforceable agreements.

Debt Barred by the Statute of Limitations

As we will see in Chapter 12, every state has *statutes of limitations,* laws that define the periods within which a lawsuit must be filed. If a claim for a breach of contract is made after the statute runs, the obligation is unenforceable and the debtor is under no legal obligation to pay.

However, after the statute runs, a debtor is liable on the obligation if he or she:

- Makes a voluntary, unqualified admission of debt
- Makes a partial payment of the debt
- Does not plead the statute of limitations as a defense

The rationale for holding a debtor liable in these three circumstances rests on the presumption that a debtor who willingly shuns protection from an unenforceable debt should not be allowed to retreat later. Nor should such debtors expect new consideration for doing what they should have done in the first place.

Debts Discharged in Bankruptcy

A similar rationale applies to debts *discharged,* or released, following an adjudication of bankruptcy. As we will see in Chapters 12 and 43, bankruptcy proceedings are designed to resolve debtors' obligations and provide debtors with new starts.

Nonetheless, a debtor discharged in bank-ruptcy can renew obligations without receiving new consideration. A renewal requires that an agreement to do so be executed before the Bankruptcy Court grants discharge. The debtor must be fully informed of his or her rights and voluntarily agree to the renewal. If a consumer and consumer debt are involved, the Bank-ruptcy Court must approve the renewal prom-ise. The standard the court applies is whether the renewal agreement is in the best interest of the debtor. Of course, a debtor can always re-pay such debts without making an enforceable promise to do so.

Promissory Estoppel

Sometimes, courts have cited *promissory es-toppel* as a grounds for enforcing charitable pledges. A promissory estoppel is the result of a promise, lacking consideration, which the promisor reasonably should expect will cause an action or forbearance by the promisee or a third person [*Restatement (Second) of Con-tracts* §90(1)]. If the courts can avoid an injus-tice only by enforcing the promise, the promisor is bound. Suppose Walter owes Mary $2500. He asks her to accept $2000 in satisfac-tion of the debt because he needs the $500 for his daughter's operation. She agrees. After the surgery, Mary demands the remaining $500. A court might well hold her claim was barred by promissory estoppel even though she received no new consideration for her promise.

As we will see, promissory estoppel affects a number of areas of law. For now, it is impor-tant to note that courts will enforce a promise made without consideration when the promisor should have foreseen it would induce a person to rely on it. The promisee's reliance must be real, justifiable, and detrimental. The next case illustrates how courts determine whether a promissory estoppel exists.

Hoffman v. Red Owl Stores, Inc.

26 Wis. 2d 683, 133 N.W.2d 267 (1965)

FACTS   In early 1961, Red Owl Stores promised Hoffman that for $18,000 it would establish him in a store by Fall. Hoffman was to sell his grocery store and purchase a site in another town, which he did in June. After he made a $1000 payment on the lot, Red Owl changed the $18,000 price to $24,100. Matters dragged on. In November, Red Owl assured Hoffman the deal would go through if the $24,100 were increased by $2000 and if he sold a bakery he and his wife were operating while waiting for their new store. However, Red Owl increased the price once again and demanded other terms Hoffman could not meet. Negotiations ended in February 1962, and the Hoffmans sued for damages. The trial court found for the Hoffmans.

ISSUE   Did the Hoffmans rely to their detriment on the representations made by Red Owl?

DECISION   Yes. Affirmed. Courts use promissory estoppel to enforce honesty and fair represen-tations in all business dealings. Originally, at common law, promissory estoppel—actually, the acts in reliance—served as a substitute for consideration. Here, however, Red Owl argued the parties never reached an agreement because they had not specified such things as the store's size, cost, design, or layout. A promise leading to a promissory estoppel does not need to cover all the details of a proposed transaction. All the law requires is that the Hoffmans relied to their detriment on the representations made by Red Owl.

Hoffman v. Red Owl Stores, Inc. has troubled a generation of students. It marks, perhaps, as far as a court may go in finding *justifiable* reliance, since Red Owl gave the Hoffmans so many indications that they should not rely. The case leaves unanswered the questions of why Red Owl would keep increasing the price of the store and why it would insist that Hoffman sell his bakery. Faced with the company's changing positions, a more conservative interpretation of the law would indicate that the Hoffmans should have ceased relying on the company's representations long before they did. In a slightly different context, the First Circuit has recently noted:

> *Confronted by [a conflict between two statements,] a reasonable person investigates matters further; he receives assurances or clarification before relying. A reasonable person does not gamble . . . , he suspends judgment until further evidence is obtained. Explicit conflict engenders doubt, and to rely on a statement the veracity of which one should doubt is unreasonable.**

Charitable Organizations

Every day, people make promises to charitable organizations without receiving any consideration in return. Pledges to a religious organization, the Red Cross, or a college alumni fund are just a few examples. Although there was a split among American jurisdictions, the common law tended to treat a pledge to a charity as

a promise to make a gift, which made it unenforceable against the promisor.

Today, courts are much more likely to enforce a charitable pledge on the grounds of detrimental reliance or promissory estoppel by the charity. The rationale is that the charity relied on the pledge in planning and/or it was a basis to be able to solicit other pledges. For example, semiannually public radio effectively solicits pledges from its listeners by building pledges toward a campaign goal. If public radio sought to enforce a non-paid pledge, a court would most likely cite promissory estoppel in finding against the pledgor's claim of no consideration.

UCC Exemptions

Like the common law, the UCC generally requires consideration to support promises. However, in two instances the UCC exempts contracts from the consideration requirement.

Firm Offers. As noted in Chapter 6, a merchant may not revoke a *firm offer* to buy or sell goods. Firm offers routinely lack consideration [UCC §2-205]. For example, Ace Manufacturing Co. sends a written offer to Pitkins Corp. in which Ace gives Pitkins 30 days to accept its offer of 2000 Super Widgets for $10 each. At common law, Ace could revoke the offer at any time, unless the parties entered into a separate option contract. But under the UCC, if Ace makes a firm offer, the offer remains open for the full period.

Contract Modifications. The UCC also exempts agreements modifying contracts for the sale of goods [UCC §2-209(1)]. If, for instance, the par-

---

* *Trifiro v. New York Life Inc. Co.*, 845 F.2d 31 (1st Cir. 1988).

ties to a contract for the sale of plant stands agree to change the delivery terms from prepaid to cash on delivery, that agreement does not require consideration. In this case, the UCC does not require either party to be a merchant.

CONCLUSION

Consideration is what a party to a contract receives for its promise, act, or forbearance. Over the years, legal writers have used many terms to describe consideration. Some have called it the "glue which binds the contract." Others, in the phrase we favor, have called it the "litmus test" of an enforceable agreement.

Except for the five instances noted immediately above, all contractual promises must be supported by consideration. That is the first and primary litmus test. The second is whether the consideration is grossly disproportionate. A great disparity will not invalidate a contract, but, as we will see in the next chapter, it may signal fraud or another impropriety which voids the contract.

Under normal circumstances, the presence of offer, acceptance, and consideration indicates an enforceable agreement. The next two chapters examine the defenses a person may assert against enforcement of a contract.

A NOTE TO FUTURE CPA CANDIDATES

The CPA exam follows the common law rule that it is legal value, not economic value, that determines whether consideration exists. This means that a court is *not* concerned with whether the consideration exchanged by the parties to the contract was of approximately equal value or was truly fair and reasonable under the circumstances. Consideration must be for future action or promise(s) of action, not past. Mutuality of obligation must exist, not an agreement based on an illusory promise.

Questions dealing with modification of existing contracts have been quite common. It is necessary to remember that an unliquidated debt essentially means undisputed. An agreement to pay a lesser amount for an undisputed debt without new consideration will not be binding.

Finally, remember that under the UCC, new consideration is *not* required to modify a contract for the sale of goods. However, good faith must exist. The requirement of good faith lessens the possibility of economic coercion when they have no other practical alternative. For example, finding an appropriate substitute wedding cake may become very difficult just hours before the wedding reception. Given this fact, a bakery might be able to extract a different promise or concession which the purchaser would not otherwise have agreed to.

KEY WORDS

accord and
    satisfaction (182)
consideration (174)
firm offer (186)
forbearance (175)
illusory promise (180)
liquidated (182)
past consideration (179)
preexisting duty (180)
promissory
    estoppel (185)
unliquidated (182)

DISCUSSION QUESTIONS

1. Why will the courts generally not enforce a promise unless consideration is present?
2. How is "consideration" defined?
3. Give an example of each of the following: (*a*) a promise for a promise, (*b*) a promise for an act, (*c*) a promise for a forbearance.
4. Why is love and affection insufficient consideration?
5. Explain the preexisting duty rule.
6. When will an agreement to accept partial payment as full satisfaction of a debt be sufficient consideration?
7. What is an illusory promise? Give two examples.

8. Explain the doctrine of promissory estoppel. What is the basis for its application?

9. In what ways has the UCC altered the rules for consideration?

10. Should the doctrine of consideration be abolished in favor of the enforcement of all promises? Explain.

CASE PROBLEMS

1. Bunker's son Michael wanted a job as account executive at Harrison & Co., a brokerage firm. The firm deliberated for several weeks and finally decided to hire him. On April 12, it offered him the job by telephone, and he accepted on the spot. Bunker did not know Michael had gotten the job when, on April 13, he wrote Harrison's president, committing himself to give Harrison $50,000 in commissions business if Michael was hired. Is Bunker's promise supported by consideration? Would promissory estoppel apply here? Explain.

2. Dean was thinking about buying a new sailboat for the upcoming racing season. He wrote Jayne, "You've been wanting to buy my sailboat, *Champion*. I promise to sell you it if I buy a new boat on the 15th, if you agree to pay me $4500." Jayne wrote back accepting his offer. Dean purchased a new boat before the 15th, did not tell Jayne, and sold *Champion* to another person for $4800. Did a binding contract exist between Dean and Jayne for the sale of *Champion?* If so, is Dean in breach of contract? Explain.

3. Fuller sent Blue a written offer to sell his tract of land, located in Cape City, for $75,000. The parties were engaged in a separate dispute. The offer stated it was irrevocable for 60 days if Blue would refrain from suing Fuller during that period. Blue promptly delivered her promise not to sue and to forgo her suit if she accepted the offer. Subsequently, Fuller decided Blue's suit was groundless. So 15 days after making the offer, he telephoned Blue and revoked it. Five days later, Blue mailed an acceptance to Fuller. Fuller did not reply. Under the circumstances, was Fuller's revocation valid? Explain your answer.

4. Marshall Motors offered to hire Jay Edmonds, a prominent race car driver, to drive their race car for the upcoming racing season. Edmonds initially said no to Marshall Motors because he was hoping to be hired by the Ford Motor Company factory racing team. Marshall Motors kept insisting and ultimately persuaded Edmonds to agree. Three weeks later, Ford, unaware of Edmond's contract with Marshall Motors, offered him a spot on their racing team. Edmonds called Marshall Motors to tell them he was sorry but he was going to accept his dream offer from Ford. Marshall Motors immediately counteroffered with a more competitive compensation package. Edmonds decided to forgo his dream of racing with Ford and accepted the counteroffer. Is the new contract enforceable? Explain.

5. Luther owned a drugstore. Because it kept him so busy, he decided to sell his boat, which he did not have time to use. He advertised it in the local newspaper. Richard answered the ad and asked Luther whether he would give him a signed offer allowing him 10 days in which to accept Luther's offer to sell the boat for $2500. Luther did so. Several days later, Luther told Richard he had changed his mind and was keeping the boat. Richard has filed suit to enforce what he regards as Luther's firm offer. Will a court uphold Richard's position? Explain.

6. Old Siwash College was engaged in a fundraising campaign to restore Alumni Hall. Kelly DuBois, an alum, agreed to make a $600 gift over 3 years. When the successful campaign was completed, work began on Alumni Hall. After making her first payment, DuBois became upset with a particular decision made by the president of Old Siwash College and informed them she would make no further payments. Assuming Old Siwash College wished to try to enforce her agreement, would a court likely side with the college? Explain.

7. Boyer was retiring from Colby Corp. At her retirement dinner, the corporation's president told Boyer he was authorized to offer her $300

per month in additional pension benefits if she would agree to be available for consulting services. Boyer agreed. However, Boyer's replacement proved so exceptionally capable that the corporation never called on her. Fifteen months later, Boyer received a letter informing her that since her advice was not needed, the $300 per month increase in benefits was being withdrawn. Boyer has brought suit against the company, seeking a declaration that she is entitled to a continuation of the extra pension benefits. Is she likely to win? Explain.

8. Don Wells agreed in writing to buy a Toyota from Georgia Adams for $4500, of which $2000 was due on January 9 and the remainder on March 17. Wells made the January payment, but on March 17 he found himself short of money. He asked Adams if she would agree to take $1900 instead. Adams was worried that if she did not take the $1900, she would get nothing from Wells. So she agreed. If Adams sued Wells for the remaining $600, would she win? What if Wells had offered the $1900 on March 3, and Adams had accepted on that date? What if Adams, on March 27, had accepted not only the $1900 but also a painting of Wells's golden retriever? Explain.

9. A storm caused extensive damage to the roof of Sherman's home. Sherman hired Plato, an architect, to prepare architectural drawings and a report on the roof's condition and repair. They agreed that Plato would receive $100 per hour and that Sherman would have the report by noon, March 15. Plato's secretary went home sick, and Plato had to finish typing the report himself. A slow typist, Plato took 2 hours to type the last two pages, for which he billed Sherman $200. When Sherman learned of the typing charge, he objected to the bill, deducted $200 from the total, and wrote a check for that amount which bore on its face "in full satisfaction." Plato cashed the check. He also sent Sherman a new bill for $200. Sherman claims that his debt to Plato was unliquidated. Is he correct? Given the facts, is he free of further liability to Plato? Explain.

10. While visiting Jack Peterson's dorm room, Dick Schuldt spotted a rock concert program signed by Madonna. Schuldt exclaimed, "Jack, I'll give you $100 for that program out of my next paycheck." Jack agreed. Later, Dick learned Jack had planned to throw out the program. Also, other programs signed by the rock star were changing hands on campus for $20. So, Dick refused to go through with his deal with Jack. Assuming a court would not find an express contract here, would it be likely to find a contract implied in fact or one implied in law? Explain.

CHAPTER 9
Lack of consent, incapacity, and illegality

Would a court enforce any of the following agreements?

- After Don threatens to break Paul's arm, Paul agrees to sell Don his mint-condition 1990 Mustang for $450.
- Margaret, whom a court has declared insane, contracts to buy twelve office computers from eight different vendors.
- Sharon agrees to pay Norm $50 if he promises to drop a water bomb on the dean during the commencement procession.

Despite the presence of mutual assent supported by consideration, none of these agreements is enforceable. The law of contracts is designed to encourage persons to act ethically, to do the right thing when given a choice. For this reason, courts do not enforce agreements built upon duress, fraud, undue influence, incapacity, or illegality.

Normally, the question of enforceability comes before courts in one of two ways. Most commonly, a party against whom enforcement of the contract is sought raises lack of enforceability as a *defense* in its *answer* or *motion to dismiss* (see Figures 2.7 and 2.8). Less commonly, a party asserting an agreement's invalidity brings an action seeking to have the agreement declared illegal or requesting damages or restitution. Nonetheless, the grounds for denying enforceability which are discussed in this chapter are normally referred to as "defenses."

A party seeking to enforce a contract does not have to plead or prove the absence of any defenses. The burden of raising and proving unenforceability virtually always rests on the party asserting the right to void, or *rescind,* the contract. This chapter describes what constitutes unenforceability and how it is proved.

Before we turn to the defenses, a word of caution is in order. As you study this chapter, keep clearly in mind that the defenses are not mere escape hatches for people who make bad bargains. They do not protect the careless.

Rather, contract defenses are a means of ensuring the integrity of our economic system.

LACK OF ASSENT

The presence of an offer, an acceptance, and consideration creates a presumption that each party voluntarily assented to the contract. On occasion, however, one party will contend that his or her assent was not voluntary and therefore that the alleged agreement lacks mutual assent. In other words, some action of the other party invalidated the assent of the first party.

Contracts subject to a lack of assent defense are *voidable*. A voidable contract is one the party having the defense can rescind. However, if that party intentionally waives the defense or neglects to raise it, he must perform the contract.

When a party raises a lack of assent defense, the courts do not apply the *objective test,* the reasonable person test, they use in determining the presence of an offer or an acceptance. Instead, they apply a *subjective test*. Because what is at issue is the voluntariness of the offer or acceptance, the subjective test evaluates conduct in light of what the party actually believed.

This section examines four types of conduct that can lead a court to conclude a party did not assent: duress, undue influence, fraud, and innocent misrepresentation. Figure 9.1 diagrams the process by which a court examines such allegations.

Duress

Duress is improper pressure or coercion used by one party against another in the bargaining process. Duress takes two forms: physical compulsion and improper threats.

Physical compulsion. If one party uses physical compulsion to gain the assent of another, the

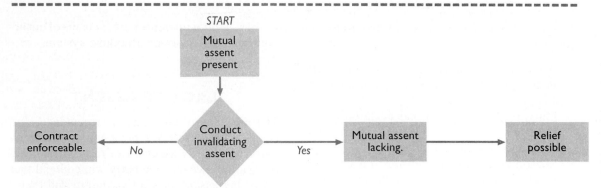

FIGURE 9.1 Conduct Invalidating Assent.
As this figure indicates, while such conduct is usually discussed in terms of
defenses, plaintiffs may also assert it as grounds for recovering damages or for
voiding the contract.

assenting party lacks the free will necessary to form the contract. If Sara holds a gun to Anna's head until she agrees to sell Sara her tape deck, a court will not enforce their agreement.

Improper threat. An *improper threat* may be expressly stated or inferred from words or conduct and must induce the assent of the person who claims to be its victim. Attaching the adjective "improper" to "threat" may seem like overkill, but many threats are proper. If Mike's car rams Alice's at an intersection, it would be proper for Alice to threaten a tort action to recover her damages. Alice could enforce a contract by which Mike agreed to pay her damages in exchange for her agreement not to bring suit against him. Insurance companies make this kind of contract routinely.

Using the subjective test, courts appraise threats from the victim's point of view. The victim must perceive the threat to leave no alternative but assent. The key element, of course, is the victim's feeling of compulsion. If a particularly timid person assents because of fear aroused when the other party gestures as if to slap him on the back, a court might void the contract.

The law also prohibits some threats not involving physical harm. For instance, a person may not threaten another with criminal prosecution in order to induce assent. Suppose Sandy sees a stereo shop owner buy stolen goods. She threatens to report him to the police if he does not sell her a $2000 system for $100. The contract is voidable. Such agreements misuse the criminal justice system. Society has an interest in punishing those who buy stolen goods, not in facilitating blackmail.

Economic duress. Some courts recognize that economic duress, under extraordinary circumstances, may justify rescission. To warrant relief, a party must show three facts:

1. One party involuntarily accepted the terms of another.
2. Under the circumstances, no other feasible alternative existed.
3. The coercive acts of the other party created the circumstances.

Economic duress often is found in "follow-up" contracts. For example, Victor runs an antique car museum. The museum's centerpiece, a 1930 Packard, needs restoration. Victor agrees to pay RESTO Co. $8000 for the job. Midway through the project, RESTO notifies

Victor it cannot complete the job unless Victor pays an additional $4000. RESTO agrees to do some extra, minor trim work. Despite the presence of new consideration, a court would permit Victor to rescind the second contract.

Tough bargaining by one party does not give the other grounds to claim economic duress later. Now suppose that in the original negotiations Victor had offered to pay RESTO $8000 for the job. RESTO refused to discuss a price lower than $12,000. Reluctantly, Victor agreed. A court will not permit him to rescind. Courts reach the same result when faced with economic duress defenses by consumers who claim salespeople persuaded them to buy products they now do not want.

Undue Influence

Undue influence is the improper use of a position of trust and confidence one party has in relation to another. Where it exists, undue influence permits the adversely affected party to rescind the contract. Most instances of undue influence involve the elderly, minors, or spouses—those whose wills are particularly subject to being overcome by a dominant party in a relationship of trust. Close family members, nurses, paid companions, friends, and trusted advisors—like lawyers, doctors, and accountants—often have relations of trust to a weaker party.

Suppose that for years Hal, a nurse, has cared for Walt, who is now in his eighties. One day, Hal convinces Walt that he is "not long for this world" and that out of gratitude he should sell his $250,000 house to Hal for $50,000. Although Hal did not threaten or use physical force on Walt, a court will view his conduct with great suspicion. Hal will bear the burden of showing he did not use his relationship of trust and confidence to exert undue influence on Walt. He will probably have to show that he made Walt aware of the true value of the house. However, as the next case proves, it is a mistake to assume that undue influence is involved when a very old person contracts with a person who might be in a position of trust.

Bruno v. Bruno

10 Mass. App. 918, 411 N.E.2d 1324 (1980)

FACTS

Mary Bruno was 99 years old. After her nephew Robert made $2500 worth of repairs to her property. Mary asked him if he wanted to buy it for $5000, a price he had offered her many years before. Robert retained an attorney to prepare the deed, which Mary signed without consulting anyone. Mary then brought suit to rescind the contract of sale, claiming undue influence. At trial, the evidence showed that despite Mary's age, she was of sound mind, lived alone, and was self-sufficient. In conducting her business affairs, she did not depend on the judgment of her nephew or anyone else. Nonetheless, the trial court ordered rescission.

ISSUE

Did Robert exercise undue influence over Mary?

DECISION

No. Reversed. Mary argued that because of their kinship, Robert owed her a greater duty to ensure she understood the consequences of her act. But whether a relationship of trust and confidence exists is a question of fact. Such a relationship does not arise merely from family ties. Undue influence destroys free agency and causes a person to do something contrary to her wishes. Here, Robert was not in a position of trust, did not exercise any influence on Mary, and did not exploit her advanced age.

Fraud in the Execution

Fraud, as noted in Chapter 4, is an extremely broad term. It is also one for which the courts have never attempted to formulate an all-inclusive definition. As a contract defense, the courts have divided fraud into two categories: fraud in the execution and fraud in the inducement.

Fraud in the execution generally involves a deceptive act with respect to the contract's formation. Suppose Randy is about to sign a contract to purchase a new Camaro for $15,000. The salesperson distracts Randy for a moment and substitutes a contract by which Randy would trade his $125,000 house for the Camaro. The contract Randy signs is *void,* not voidable.

Fraud in the execution is not as common as fraud in the inducement, partly because it is a much more specific defense. Unless we use the term "fraud in the execution," any reference to "fraud" in the context of contractual defenses refers to fraud in the inducement.

Fraud in the Inducement

Fraud in the inducement is an intentional misrepresentation of a material fact which induces justifiable reliance and causes a legal injury. It occurs when one party knowingly conceals or misrepresents facts, intending to induce another's assent. Each of these elements is considered below.

Intentional misrepresentation. An intentional misrepresentation occurs when a party either states something which is not true or leads someone to believe something is true by concealing the facts. Suppose Mike wants to sell Pearl his old guitar. He tells her, "This guitar once belonged to Elvis Presley," even though he knows he bought it new. That is an intentional misrepresentation.

Material fact. Fraud requires an intentional misrepresentation of a material fact. A *fact* is a true statement as to something's present or past condition. If the representation involves the future, it is an opinion, sales talk, or puffing—not a statement of fact.

The dividing line between a statement of opinion and one of fact often depends on who makes the representation. A used car salesperson who says "This car is a jewel" ordinarily states an opinion. However, statements made by experts induce more justifiable reliance than the same statements made by laypersons. If an antique dealer makes the statement that a vase is worth $250, it may be relied upon; the same statement made by a seller at a yard sale probably cannot be relied upon. Still, not every representation made by an expert is of a fact. Representations of fact include only those which would lead a reasonable person to believe that the expert, like a computer technician analyzing a machine's problems, has based the representation on specialized knowledge.

To establish a fraud defense, a party must show that the misrepresentation is of a *material fact,* a fact which is important to the party's decision to do or not to do something. The materiality of the fact is a subjective matter. As to Mike's guitar, the misrepresentation is material if Pearl is an Elvis Presley fan, but might not be if she just wants a guitar.

Concealment or nondisclosure. At common law, silence as to a material fact normally did not give rise to a fraud defense. Today, the courts do recognize a defense based on concealment or nondisclosure.

The most common application of this defense involves the sale of new or used homes. If the seller knows of a latent defect which a reasonable inspection would not discover, she must reveal it. Suppose Helen wants to sell her house. Her living room wall has a big hole caused by a leak in the roof. She puts a cabinet in front of the hole so that prospective buyers cannot see it. Her concealment is fraudulent. However, does a seller have to disclose *everything* she knows about what she is selling? In the next case, the court, presented with a bizarre set of facts, was asked to decide just how far disclosure should go.

Reed v. King

145 Cal. App. 3d 261, 193 Cal. Rptr. 130 (1983)

FACTS King sold his home to Reed, but failed to inform her that a woman and her four small children had been murdered there 10 years ago. After learning about the murders, Reed sued for recission of the sale, claiming that the house possessed a bad reputation and so was not worth what she paid for it. The trial court, in a summary judgment, ruled in favor of King.

ISSUE Were there sufficient facts for the court to enter a summary judgment preventing Reed from proving that silence as to the murders was a material fact which should have been disclosed?

DECISION No. Reversed. Generally, a seller of real estate has a duty to disclose facts, known to him, which materially affect the value of the real property. These facts are usually physical or legal barriers to the enjoyment of the property. The murder of innocents, although not physical or legal in nature, is highly unusual and has the potential for upsetting future buyers and depressing the property's value. Accordingly, Reed should be allowed to prove, if she can, that the multiple murders have a significant effect on her house's market value and so is a material fact that should have been disclosed.

Justifiable reliance. To be entitled to relief, a person must be justified in relying upon the misrepresentation. Suppose Nat tells Kim, "Here's an original handwoven quilt made in Pakistan." While examining it, Kim notices a tag which says, "Machine washable—made in Taiwan." Kim would not be justified in relying on Nat's statement, since her examination showed that she should not do so. However, the court in the next case and others have relaxed the justifiable reliance requirements, making it easier to rescind.

The issue of what a seller must disclose when selling a house has the potential to expand in its application. For example, after Rock Hudson died of AIDS in 1986, his home was listed

Pacific Maxon, Inc. v. Wilson

96 Nev. 867, 619 P.2d 816 (1980)

FACTS

Wilson wanted to sell her brothel. She furnished her real estate broker with a copy of an independent appraisal report. The original report valued her property at $195,000, but Wilson had altered this figure to read $405,000. After an officer of Pacific Maxon observed the brothel's operations and examined financial data Wilson prepared, Pacific Maxon purchased the property for $400,000. When the company learned of the fraud, it sued for rescission. The trial court found for Wilson.

ISSUE

Was Pacific Maxon justified in relying on the falsified appraisal report?

DECISION

Yes. Reversed Total reliance upon a misrepresentation is not required for rescission. It is enough that the misrepresentation is part of the inducement. When a party asserts misrepresentation as grounds for rescission, actual fraud—that is, an intentional false representation which is relied upon in fact—is all that is required.

for $7.5 million but eventually sold for $2.95 million. Many speculated that is was because of the disease, which was viewed with virtual hysteria at that time by a public quite ignorant of how it was spread. Since then California and other states' laws have made it clear that a seller does *not* have to disclose whether an AIDS victim resided in the house.

Legal injury. Generally, a person must suffer some legal injury in order to recover damages for a fraudulent misrepresentation. The injury occurs when a party receives less than she bargained for. However, many courts do not require evidence of injury when an innocent party seeks rescission.

When injuries are real, the injured party has to make a choice. She can either rescind the entire transaction or keep the property and sue for damages. Let's look at Pearl and the guitar again. If it is Elvis Presley's guitar, it is worth, say, $4500. If it is just Mike's old guitar, it is worth $100. If Pearl paid $4500 for it and its

only other owner was Mike, she can either keep the guitar and sue for $4400 or seek to return the guitar and regain all her money.

Misrepresentation

The defense of *misrepresentation* arises from (1) a party's assertion that was not in accord with the facts, that was material, and that was relied upon by another party to the contract and (2) the justifiable reliance of the other party on the assertion. In some, but not all, jurisdictions, the party seeking to void the contract must also prove the reliance led to a legal injury. In this context, misrepresentation is also called "innocent misrepresentation" to distinguish it from the fraud element.

Here, the false statement is made without an intent to deceive. Still, the law presumes that a person who misstates a material fact—even unintentionally—should be responsible for the statement. In other words, a person should be sure before making such a representation.

Nondisclosure can also amount to a misrepresentation when not to disclose would be a failure to act in good faith. As we will see in Chapter 27, nondisclosure amounting to misrepresentation is most often found in real estate cases in which sellers fail to inform buyers of serious defects.

Now suppose that Mike deals in rock 'n roll memorabilia. He represents to Pearl that the guitar belonged to Elvis. The person from whom he bought the guitar had said so, and Mike believed him. A quick check with Graceland, a rock 'n roll historian, or a guitar expert would have revealed Elvis could not have owned this model because it was not made until after his death. Pearl's contract with Mike is therefore voidable.

The legal injury and justifiable reliance required to establish the defense of misrepresentation are identical to the fraud elements of the same names. So if a person like the defendant in the next case has reason not to rely on a representation, he cannot use misrepresentation as a defense.

The remedy for misrepresentation is *rescission,* an equitable remedy that discharges the parties' contractual obligations. Damages are not available. Rescission is designed to return the parties to where they were at the time of contracting. Rescission is based on the notion

---

Miller v. Noel

51 Or. App. 243, 624 P.2d 1105 (1981)

FACTS   Noel had owned businesses which required him to keep books. He agreed to buy the Millers' donut shop, contingent on their producing "an actual profit and loss statement for 1974." The Millers were incapable of preparing one. Instead, Mr. Miller prepared a handwritten, wholly inaccurate "Tentative Profit and Loss Statement for 1974," based on his checkbook. After receiving the document, Noel bought the donut shop, signing a promissory note for part of the purchase price. Noel remodeled the shop into a Mexican restaurant. The business failed, and the Millers sued on the note. Noel defended on the grounds of reliance on the Millers' misrepresentation. The trial court found for the Millers.

ISSUE   Did the profit and loss statement amount to a nonfraudulent misrepresentation justifying rescission?

DECISION   No. Affirmed. Even if Noel did rely on the misrepresentation, his reliance was not justified, since the document was plainly marked "tentative" and lacked the information someone with Noel's experience would have expected to find. Also, the fact that Noel intended to change the nature of the business makes it unlikely he relied upon the misrepresentation. Anyone intending to change the nature of a business would place little weight on its prior profitability.

DEFENSE	BASIC SITUATION	STATUS OF RESULTING CONTRACT	DAMAGES GENERALLY AVAILABLE?
Duress	Physical compulsion, improper threat	Voidable	Yes
Undue influence	Violation of trust and confidence	Voidable	Yes
Fraud in the execution	Deceived as to the nature of the contract	Void	Yes
Fraudulent in the inducement	Knowing misrepresentation of a material fact, reliance	Viodable	Yes
Innocent misrepresentation	Unknowing misrepresentation of a material fact, reliance	Voidable	No*

*May only rescind contract.

FIGURE 9.2 Principal Lack of Assent Defenses.

that the parties acted in good faith, that the seller did not knowingly misstate or omit a material fact. Thus, the buyer who thinks she is buying Elvis's guitar is entitled to her money back, and upon rescission the seller is entitled to his guitar. (Rescission is discussed in greater detail in Chapter 12.)

Figure 9.2 tabulates the principal lack of assent defenses.

Mistake

A *mistake* is a belief not in accord with existing facts. The law recognizes two types of mistakes—mutual and unilateral—but attaches quite different significance to them.

Mutual mistake. A *mutual mistake* occurs when both parties to a contract are mistaken as to a material fact. The mistake must affect a fundamental assumption which motivated the parties to enter into the contract. Suppose Sandy's Soda Shoppe buys 100 cases of cola from a bottler, which it then sells. Both the

store and its customers assumed cola to be the subject of their transactions. If the cans contain soda water instead, either Sandy's or its customers may rescind, since the contract lacks genuine mutual assent.

Mutual mistakes which warrant rescission usually arise from the quality or characteristics of the subject matter, its existence, or its identity. An example of a mistake as to the existence of the subject matter would be a transaction involving a horse which—unknown to the parties—had died that morning. As for identity, if Pet Palace thinks you want a guinea pig of each sex and you thought you had made it clear that you wanted two females, you and Pet Palace have not agreed on the subject matter.

Even though the parties make a mutual mistake as to an item's value, rescission is not in order. Value is not considered a material fact. The seller, by placing a value on the subject matter, and the purchaser, by buying it, allocate the risk of a mistake in value. Suppose a museum buys a Rembrandt etching from a gallery at a price which turns out to be far above its market value. A court would not rescind their contract.

Unilateral mistake. Generally, a *unilateral mistake* occurs when one party makes a mistake as to a material fact. Ordinarily, a unilateral mistake is treated like a mistake as to value, and the mistaken party is not entitled to relief. Suppose you buy a shirt for a loved one at J.C. Penney. Unfortunately, there is more of the loved one than you thought, and the shirt does not fit. The common law does not provide you with a remedy.

If the rule on unilateral mistakes were different, many have argued, parties who make unfavorable contracts would find it too easy to avoid their obligations by claiming a mistake. Such an escape mechanism would reduce the law's incentives to use care in negotiating contracts. It is the parties' interests in protecting themselves which make our economic system essentially self-regulating.

Despite the policy in favor of the general rule, the trend today is to depart from it in two circumstances: if the other party had reason to know of the mistake at the time of contracting and if enforcement would cause extreme hardship.

A party that has reason to know the other party has made a mistake before the other party suffers any loss must at least permit the other party to withdraw from the contract. The courts regularly grant rescission in these circumstances. In one case, a court granted rescission when a company inadvertently omitted the cost of steel in its bid for a municipal sewer contract. In the past, the municipality could have "snapped up the offer," as it tried to do. However, the city officials should have recognized that the great disparity between the company's bid and the next higher bid—as well as the estimate of the city engineer—indicated the company had made a fundamental mistake. Today, one cannot snap up what is obviously a mistake.

The courts apply a similar rationale to unilateral mistakes which would impose an enormous hardship on a party. Again, the courts are more likely to rescind an executory contract. Suppose that in the example above the bid was not obviously out of line. Still, it contained a serious error which would impose a severe hardship on the bidder. If the other party had not yet relied on the bid, the court might permit rescission.

Contracts to Which the UCC Applies

The UCC applies somewhat different standards than does the common law. The UCC actually specifies, "Every contract or duty within this act imposes an obligation of good faith in its performance or enforcement" [UCC §1-203]. "Good faith" is defined as "honesty in fact in the conduct or transaction concerned" [UCC §1-201(19)]. Lack of good faith is grounds for voiding a contract.

Another key UCC concept is unconscionability [UCC §2-302]. The test of unconscionability is whether the terms, when placed in the context of transactions of the same or a similar type, are so one-sided as to be oppressive.

Let's look at an example. We saw, at the end of the last chapter, that the parties can modify an existing sales contract without new consideration. Nonetheless, unconscionable conduct in negotiating the modification would nullify the contract. Suppose Better Bear Corp. sells the "Buffy Bear," a stuffed animal. Demand for the toy increases rapidly. To take advantage of the demand, Better Bear decides to increase its prices by 20 percent to all retailers, including those with whom it already has contracts. One of the retailers, Toyland, accedes to the new terms because it needs the hot toy in stock to remain profitable. If Toyland sued Better Bear, a court would probably hold the actions of Better Bear to be unconscionable.

INCAPACITY

Capacity refers to a person's ability to comprehend and understand contractual obligations. Generally, the law presumes parties have the capacity to contract. Only *minors,* usually defined as persons under 18, and persons declared by a court to be insane before the time of contracting are presumed not to comprehend contractual obligations. All others who assert the defense of lack of capacity must prove it.

Minors

Minors have the legal power to enter into contracts. In order to protect them, the law gives minors the right to *disaffirm* a contract and make it void. Even so, if the subject of a disaffirmed contract is a necessity of life, a minor must pay its reasonable value.

The right of disaffirmance. The power to disaffirm applies only to contracts made while a person is a minor. However, persons may disaffirm for a reasonable time after achieving the age of *majority,* or adulthood.

Minors disaffirm by using language or conduct demonstrating their unwillingness to be bound by the contract. Then, the minor is entitled to a return of the full consideration she gave, and she must return the part of the consideration she still possesses. Suppose Jerri, age 16, purchases a bicycle for $250. After a week she becomes bored with it and returns it to the store where she purchased it. In most jurisdictions, the store would have to return Jerri's $250 even if the bike was damaged. But suppose the store refused to recognize Jerri's right to disaffirm because of damage to the bike. Through one of her parents or her guardian, she would have to sue the store.

A minor may also reclaim consideration he or she sells while a minor. Suppose Joey sells his ten-speed to Wally. Some weeks later, Joey misses his old bike and calls Wally to ask for it back. Joey is entitled to his bike. The common law extended this right to situations where the original purchaser had sold the minor's property to a third party who bought in good faith for value. Now suppose that Wally had traded in Joey's bike for a new bike at Spoke & Wheel Bicycle Works. Joey spots his old bike after the store has reconditioned it, and he demands it. Under the common law, the store must return it.

When a minor is a party to an executed real estate contract, the minor may not disaffirm the contract until coming of age. This rule is different from the general common law rule on the grounds that real property is of a permanent nature, which means that it should still be intact when the minor comes of age. To illustrate, assume that in a particular state a minor becomes of age at 18. If Laura, 16, sells her real estate lot to Harvey, she will not be able to disaffirm the sale until turning 18. However, it should be noted that if the contract between Laura and Harvey is executory, meaning the parties have not yet performed, then Laura could disaffirm the contract and not be forced to sell the lot to Harvey.

The UCC has modified the common law with regard to third party purchasers. A good faith purchaser for value will prevail over the minor's voidable title to property he or she has sold. Thus under the UCC, Spoke & Wheel—a good faith purchaser for value—would have no obligation to return Joey's bike to him.

If the minor no longer has the consideration, generally she has no duty to return the person with whom she dealt to the *status quo,* the position he was in before they contracted. However, as in the next case, some courts in particular circumstances compel minors to restore the other party to the status quo.

Valencia v. White

134 Ariz. 139, 654 P.2d 287 (Ct. App. 1982)

FACTS
In 1976, Valencia was a 17-year-old high school sophomore who lived at home with his parents. They furnished his food, clothing, and housing. His father gave him two tractor-trailer rigs. Valencia hired drivers, found jobs hauling produce, and managed the business at a profit—$26,000 in 1978. White repaired trucks and regularly did business with Valencia. In December 1976, White agreed to replace the engine in one of Valencia's trucks, delivering it in May 1977. Shortly thereafter, Valencia damaged the engine, which led to his dispute with White. Valencia had paid $7100 on his account with White, leaving a balance of approximately $12,900 when he stopped paying. The trial court held Valencia, who reached 18 shortly after this action was filed, had disaffirmed and ordered White to refund Valencia the $7100 he had paid on account.

ISSUE
May a minor operating a successful business disaffirm contracts for its expenses?

DECISION
No. Reversed. A minor who disaffirms a contract may be held liable for benefits he received. Here, no evidence suggested that White took advantage of Valencia because of his age or lack of experience or judgment. Likewise, no evidence suggested that the contract was disadvantageous to Valencia. The repairs enabled Valencia to operate his trucking business successfully and they cannot be returned in kind to White. Nor can the engine, since Valencia damaged it.

The court in *Valencia v. White* obviously took notice of the fact that Valencia was operating a fairly sophisticated business and had made a contract with White for a necessary repair to maintain the operation of his fleet. The result in this case is very similar to situations involving necessaries, discussed next.

Liability for necessaries. The general rule, as you have learned, is that a minor can disaffirm a contract in its entirety because of lack of capacity. The common law established an exception for a minor's contracts to purchase *necessaries,* the necessities of life, such as food, clothing, medicine, and shelter.

In all states, minors may disaffirm executed contracts for necessaries, but they are liable for the reasonable value of the items. Suppose Jill

bought a winter coat, and 3 months later disaffirmed the contract. She would still be liable for the reasonable value of the coat. If this rule did not exist, businesses would be extremely reluctant to sell minors anything, including items needed for survival.

While a contract for necessaries is executory, the minor may disaffirm it and avoid any further responsibility. Suppose Jill contracts with the store to place the coat on layaway for 2 months in exchange for a $50 deposit. Jill may disaffirm at any time before her performance is required. Of course, she is also entitled to her deposit.

Precisely what constitutes necessaries often poses a problem for courts. A minor needs one winter coat. But what about two coats? Or five? Or ten? Courts treat the question of necessaries as one of fact. Some courts have extended the concept to include trailer homes, services of an employment agency, cars, and educational expenses. As in *Valencia,* the extent of the minor's emancipation from parental controls often figures in a court's determination.

Misrepresentation of age. Minors often pretend to be older than they are. When they do so in order to buy something they want, they pose a difficult problem for businesses—and the courts. The common law permitted the minor to disaffirm such contracts, but many commentators, courts, and legislatures found this notion indefensible. However, there is no consensus among the jurisdictions on this topic.

Some states have permitted minors who have misrepresented their age to be sued in tort for deceit. A successful plaintiff must show:

- The minor misstated his or her age as being above the age of majority

- He or she made the misstatement with the intent of defrauding the plaintiff
- The plaintiff relied on the misstatement
- The reliance caused the plaintiff to suffer damages

Even in jurisdictions permitting such suits, the courts expect businesses at least to try to verify age. Checking a driver's license or school identification card will often suffice.

Ratification. *Ratification* is an indication by a person who has reached majority that he intends to be obligated under a contract he made as a minor. A person may expressly ratify by just saying so. However, the law implies a ratification if a person fails to disaffirm within a reasonable time after reaching majority or if his conduct indicates a ratification. For example, Wally buys a home computer on credit before he turns 18 and continues making payments after he reaches majority. A court would imply a ratification.

Boyden v. Boyden

9 Met. 519 (Mass. 1845)

FACTS   The Boyden brothers, both 20, bought a horse and plow, giving the seller a promissory note in exchange. [At this time, the age of majority was 21.] A year later, they traded the horse, which they had used, for another. The Boydens had evidently kept and used the plow. At no time did they offer to return the horse and plow to the seller nor did either give any notice of an intention to rescind the transaction. Almost 5 years after the transaction, the seller brought suit on the note; the Boydens claimed it was void because they were minors when they entered into the contract. The trial court entered judgment for the seller.

ISSUE   Does retaining goods bought as a minor without giving notice of rescission to the seller for a substantial period after reaching majority operate as a ratification of the transaction?

DECISION   Yes. Affirmed. A minor's contract is voidable. However, only the minor can void it, and only the minor can ratify it after he or she reaches majority. Until the minor gives some indication of voiding the contract, the seller cannot reclaim the goods. So, if after coming of age, a purchaser does not give any notice of an intent to disaffirm the contract, he or she manifests a determination to keep the property. Further, a decision to keep the property for his or her own use or for resale can only indicate an assumption that the contract of sale is valid. Here, the buyers kept the plow for between 2 and 3 years after they came of age.

Preventive law with minors. The practical reality of everyday life is that businesses sell goods to minors every day. A business concerned about the possibility of a minor disaffirming a contract may elect to require a parent or guardian to be the purchaser of record or to become a surety. A surety is a person who agrees to pay the debt of another if the debt is not paid. A common phrase associated with becoming a surety, especially with the purchase of a car, is for a parent or guardian "to cosign the note." Becoming a surety will be discussed in the next chapter and Chapter 40.

The Mentally Infirm

Virtually all legal systems assume that the mentally infirm require protection from their own actions. The type of protection, however, varies. Our laws distinguish between persons whom a court has declared insane—their contracts are void—and those who suffer from a mental disability—their contracts may be voidable.

Mental illness or defect. Mere weakness of intellect or mind is not grounds for voiding contracts. In general, the person must lack the mental capacity to comprehend the nature, purpose, and consequences of the transaction. A mental infirmity does not have to be long-standing, nor does it have to be permanent. It can be almost momentary. For example, a person who has just received a blow on the head in an automobile accident may not be competent, while still groggy, to contract with a towing company.

A person with an insane delusion has contractual capacity so long as the contract's subject matter does not touch on the delusion. Also, a person may be quite eccentric yet comprehend a transaction and hence may be legally competent. Sometimes the reverse is true. As in the following case, a person may appear quite rational and seem to understand the transaction but may still be incompetent.

Faber v. Sweet Style Manufacturing Corp.

40 Misc. 2d 212, 242 N.Y.S.2d 763 (N.Y. Sup. Ct. 1963)

FACTS   From April until July 1961, Isidore Faber experienced a depression. A psychiatrist, Dr. Levine, had been treating him, but in August, Faber refused to see the doctor again. Previously frugal and cautious, he suddenly began to buy expensive gifts and to speculate in real estate. On September 23, he contracted with Kass, Sweet Style's president, to purchase property for a discount mart. Between September 23 and October 8, Faber hired Leonard Cohen, promising him $150 a week and a Lincoln Continental when the project was complete; arranged for a title abstract and title insurance policy; hired an architect; initiated a mortgage application; hired laborers to begin digging a month before title was to pass; filed plans with city officials; and when told by them that State Labor Department approval was required, insisted on driving to Albany with the architect and Cohen to obtain it. On September 25, Faber complained to Dr. Levine that his wife needed help because she was stopping him from doing what he wanted. Faber was committed to a mental institution on October 8, after he purchased a hunting gun. His wife brought suit, seeking rescission of the land purchase contract. At trial, the psychiatric testimony was split on whether Faber suffered from abnormalities in his thinking and judgment on September 23.

ISSUE

Does mental incompetence require a complete lack of understanding of the nature and consequences of a contract?

DECISION

No. Judgment for Mrs. Faber. Lack of capacity to understand is not the sole criterion of incompetence. Mental incompetence also exists when a party enters into a contract under the compulsion of a mental disorder. Since psychiatric testimony often results in different opinions, courts tend to give greater weight to objective behavioral evidence, including an evaluation of whether, by usual business standards, the transaction is normal or fair. Here, Faber's acts—all before title passed—were abnormal. They indicated he contracted with Sweet Style under the compulsion of his psychosis.

Adjudication of incompetency. At the time that Faber contracted with Sweet Style, a court had not passed on his legal capacity. The tests described in *Faber* apply only where a party has not been adjucated an incompetent before contracting. After a court has declared a person incompetent and has appointed a guardian to manage his affairs, the incompetent cannot contract. However, the guardian can make contracts on her ward's behalf.

Disaffirmance. The rules which apply to an incompetent's disaffirmance are essentially the same as those which apply to a minor's disaffirmance, including the rules on necessaries. However, in some jurisdictions, a court will not permit disaffirmance if the following situation exists:

- The contract is fair to the incompetent.
- The competent party had no reason to believe the person lacked contractual capacity.

- Voiding the contract would be unjust to the competent party.

Other courts faced with this situation permit disaffirmance so long as the competent party is restored to the status quo.

Incompetents may ratify contracts and treat them as valid upon being restored to competency. Also, a guardian may ratify the incompetent's contracts.

Intoxication. The contracts of persons who are intoxicated by alcohol or drugs when they decide to contract are voidable. However, the contracts of persons who get intoxicated in order to gain the courage to contract are not voidable. In any case, a person can claim this defense only if intoxicated at the time of contracting. Merely being an alcoholic or a drug addict is not enough.

A common test of competence in intoxication cases is whether the person asserting the defense could understand the nature and consequences of his actions when making the contract. Or a court may ask whether a person could act in a reasonable manner with respect to the transaction. In both instances, the inquiry centers on whether the intoxication was so extreme as to prevent a valid manifestation of assent. Often, if they grant rescission, courts require that the intoxicated person return the other party to the status quo.

Because of the voluntary nature of intoxication, courts tend to extend less protection to persons claiming this type of mental infirmity. A court may place more emphasis on whether the sober party took advantage of the condition of the other party.

ILLEGALITY

To be enforceable, a contract must consist of an agreement supported by consideration between parties who possess the capacity to contract. However, even if a contract meets all these requirements, a court will not enforce it if the subject matter of the bargain is not legal.

An "illegal contract" is a contradiction in terms, since by definition a contract is an agreement the courts will enforce. It is more accurate to refer to an illegal bargain or an illegal agreement. For example, a heroin importer may "contract" with a hit man to "eliminate" one

of his competitors. But no court would enforce an agreement to commit murder.

Questions of legality are not always so clear-cut. In some cases, a contract's illegality is based on public policy, on what society regards as fair play and simple justice. This section examines the defense of illegality in the context of agreements which are contrary to criminal statutes, which violate civil regulatory statutes, and which violate public policy.

Agreements Contrary to Criminal Statutes

Agreements to commit crimes or to facilitate their commission violate statutes, since all crimes are defined by statute. Such agreements are void.

Drug paraphernalia statutes. The U.S. Department of Justice and the states have targeted the sale of drug accessories and paraphernalia as a means of discouraging drug use. The Model Drug Paraphernalia Act, which was interpreted in the next case, imposes criminal liability on "any person or corporation, knowing the drug related nature of the object" who sells, displays for sale, or uses with an illegal drug any drug-related paraphernalia. The next case also reveals how broadly courts in a civil case can give effect to the policy behind criminal statutes.

A Better Place, Inc. v. Giani Investment Co.

445 So. 2d 728 (La. 1984)

FACTS

In 1980, when Louisiana enacted the Model Drug Paraphernalia Act, Giani ran a store in New Orleans which prominently displayed pipes, smoking accessories, and the like. A Better Place (ABP) was one of its principal suppliers. Between December 29 and January 20, 1981, ABP sold Giani a large quantity of merchandise which the police confiscated as drug paraphernalia. ABP sought to recover the contract amount. At trial, Giani established that many of the items on the ABP invoices were defined in the statute as drug paraphernalia and argued that therefore the contract was unenforceable. The trial court, however, refused to accept the defense and entered judgment for ABP. The intermediate appellate court affirmed, holding that Giani had failed to show ABP's criminal intent—that ABP intended the goods to be used with illegal drugs by the ultimate purchaser.

ISSUE   Did Giani establish the defense of illegality?

DECISION   Yes. Reversed. Giani did not have to establish criminal intent in a civil action. The intent important here is that of the manufacturer or distributor. The key question is whether a businessperson of ordinary intelligence would understand that the ultimate use of the goods would be drug-related. Here, the statute listed as contraband many of the items described in the same terms in the ABP catalog.

Two points about *A Better Place* bear emphasizing. First, the Act itself does not void wholesale contracts for the sale of drug paraphernalia. The Louisiana Supreme Court interpreted the Act as a statement of public policy and refused to enforce a contract which the Court interpreted as facilitating violations. Second, the standard applied to the allegedly illegal conduct is objective, not subjective as in the lack of capacity defenses.

Usury statutes. Virtually all states place limits on the amount of interest which a lender can charge. These laws are called *usury statutes*. If a lender charges 25 percent in a state where the legal limit is 18 percent, the agreement—at least as to the excess 7 percent—is illegal and cannot be enforced.

Wagering agreements. Virtually all states regulate or prohibit gambling. For that reason, a bookie cannot use the courts to enforce a bettor's agreement to pay him. Even in Nevada, where gambling has been legal for over 60 years, the courts would not enforce gambling debts until a 1983 statute was passed. Now that legalized gambling is rapidly spreading throughout the United States, many states will likely follow Nevada's lead.

The law also forbids another type of gambling: gambling on collecting insurance proceeds. If the law permitted gambling on a calamity's befalling another person, the incentive to see that a calamity actually occurred would be too great for some to resist.

To prevent this, virtually all states have adopted a rule requiring a party taking out an insurance policy to have an *insurable interest* in the life or property being insured. As we will see in Chapter 30, an insurable interest is one created by a family or business relationship or by an interest in property. For instance, partners in an accounting firm have insurable interests in their partners' lives. Partnerships often buy life insurance so that they will have sufficient funds to purchase a deceased partner's interest in the firm. By contrast, a court would not enforce a contract of insurance issued to a fan on the life of his favorite baseball star.

Sunday laws. In days gone by, many states prohibited entering into contracts or transacting business on Sundays. Since World War II these laws have largely disappeared, although some remnants exist. A related body of law, "blue laws," prohibited certain businesses from opening on Sundays. These laws still have vitality in only a few states today.

Contracts in Violation of Licensing Statutes

Every state has a wide array of licensing statutes. Doctors, accountants, lawyers, sports promoters, nurses, beauticians, and dozens of others must obtain licenses in order to do business. Licensing statutes typically serve either of two purposes: regulating an enterprise or raising revenue for the state. The standards courts apply to contracts which violate licensing statutes often depend on the purpose of the particular law.

Regulatory statutes. A *regulatory statute* is one whose purpose is to protect the public's health, safety, morals, or general welfare.* The courts will not enforce a contract where a party has breached a regulatory requirement. Regulatory licensing requirements usually involve applicants who must meet certain qualifications. For example, in order to become an architect, an applicant must fulfill educational requirements and pass a qualifying test. An unlicensed architect could not recover a fee in a lawsuit. Nor can an unlicensed realtor, as the woman who brought the next case discovered.

---

* For a discussion of this power and of its constitutional context, see the section on *police powers* in Chapter 3, The Constitution and Government Regulation of Business.

Shehab v. Xanadu, Inc.

698 S.W.2d 491 (Tex. Ct. App. 1985)

FACTS   Margaret Shehab had worked as a licensed real estate broker in Michigan for Liberty Financial Corp. Its president offered her a job as sales manager of a subsidiary, Xanadu, Inc., which owned a condominium development in Texas. He told her she would not need to be relicensed in Texas. She agreed to relocate. During the next 3 years, she sold and received commissions on 140 units. Fifty-four remained unsold when she introduced Williston Clover to Xanadu. Clover proposed to buy all the remaining units but instead bought Xanadu. Shehab claimed a commission on the fifty-four units, which Liberty refused to pay. The trial court entered summary judgment for the defendants on the grounds that Shehab was not entitled to commissions on real estate transactions because she was not licensed.

ISSUE   Did Shehab's lack of a real estate license make her contract with Liberty unenforceable?

DECISION   Yes. Affirmed. The Texas real estate license act requires that anyone who deals in real estate on a commission basis within the state must have a valid Texas license. In order to recover in an action for a commission, the plaintiff must prove her possession of a valid license. The existence of the contract requiring the payment of commissions Shehab could not alter the statutory bar to recovery.

Revenue statutes. A *revenue statute* imposes requirements simply to raise money. Vendors' licenses and fees associated with foreign corporations doing business in a state fall mainly into this category. Unlike the case with regulatory statutes, a party that violates a revenue-raising statute may still enforce a contract. If a licensed engineer forgets to pay his annual registration fee, he may be able to enforce his agreements because the statute has nothing to do with competency.

Contracts Subject to Public Policy

On rare occasions, courts refuse to enforce contracts because they violate public policy. But what is public policy? Civil and criminal statutes contain statements of public policy—at least by inference. For that reason, one can speak of public policy as societal ethics and goals as expressed by the legislative branch. However, it has a considerably broader meaning when used in the sense of fair play. As we will see in this section, courts have refused—citing this ground—to enforce contractual provisions which unreasonably restrain trade or unreasonably relieve a party from liability under a contract.

Restraints of trade. Our system encourages free competition. Agreements which unreasonably restrain trade are contrary to public policy, since they interfere with this basic philosophy.

Every contract, in a sense, restrains competition. Whether an agreement which restrains trade is enforceable depends on the reasonableness of the restraint. Suppose Alice agrees to buy Bill's car. As a result of this contract, presumably Alice is no longer in the market to purchase a car and Bill is no longer in the market to sell one. In that sense, the agreement between Alice and Bill restrains trade. However, this restraint is reasonable and usual.

Now suppose Alice and Bill are automobile dealers. They agree to locate their lots at differ-ent ends of the city and not to sell the same makes of cars. Again, their agreement restrains trade. But since it has no legitimate business purpose other than to restrict competition, it is unreasonable and unenforceable. Restraints on trade of this type are discussed in more detail in Chapter 44, Antitrust.

Restrictive covenants. Employment contracts and contracts for the sale of a business often contain *restrictive covenants,* promises which place a direct restraint on competition. All other restrictive covenants are contrary to public policy and unenforceable. Even in these two types, if the clauses are not narrowly drawn and if they do not protect legitimate business interests, the courts will not enforce them and they may violate antitrust laws.

To be enforceable, a restrictive covenant must be reasonable as to both time and distance. A clause which prohibits Bill from competing with Alice for the rest of his life is too restrictive. Although a dealership is particularly vulnerable to competition from the previous owner, the protection of such a clause exceeds Alice's legitimate need to protect her dealership while it takes root. The permissible length of the restriction depends upon the type of business involved, the nature of the industry, and the length of time the previous owner ran the business.

As with the restriction's duration, the validity of its geographic limits depends upon the circumstances. In a recent case, Roger Lamp signed a contract with American Prosthetics, Inc. (AP), agreeing that should he leave his sales position with its Mason City, Iowa, branch, he would not compete with AP anywhere within 100 miles of one of its Iowa sales offices. Because of the number of AP offices, in effect Lamp could not sell in the state. The Iowa Supreme Court held that this restriction was unreasonable and therefore unenforceable.* Although the Court did not address the

---

* *Lamp v. American Prosthetics, Inc.,* 379 N.W.2d 909 (Iowa, 1986).

issue, it probably would have enforced a covenant not to compete within the sales territory of the Mason City branch.

In the following case, a federal appeals court was unwilling to give a restrictive covenant a broad reading.

Atlanta Center Ltd. v. Hilton Hotels Corp.

848 F.2d 146 (11th Cir. 1988)

FACTS

Atlanta Center owned a hotel in downtown Atlanta which Hilton had contracted to manage. The contract, executed in 1973, included this clause:

> Hilton agrees that until the expiration . . . of this Agreement, it will not operate a hotel . . . located within a radius of ten miles from the [downtown] Hotel, either as owner or lessee, or under a management agreement, or permit its name to be used in connection with such operation, other than (i) the Hotel, (ii) the Hilton Inn located at the Atlanta Airport, and (iii) [a franchisee in Tucker, Georgia].

The airport inn had 373 rooms. In 1986, Hilton decided to tear it down and build an upgraded 500-room hotel. Atlanta Center brought suit, alleging Hilton's operation of the new inn would violate the restrictive covenant in the 1973 agreement. The trial court dismissed the action.

ISSUE

Did the restrictive covenant preclude Hilton from operating the new inn on the site of its airport inn?

DECISION

No. Affirmed. The dispute here really centers on whether the restrictive covenant excepts a particular structure or a particular site. The language of the exception makes no reference to the size of the airport inn or what services Hilton might offer there. When a court has a choice between two reasonable interpretations of a restrictive covenant, public policy dictates that it choose the one that least restricts competition and not read in restrictions the parties' sophisticated lawyers did not state.

Exculpatory clauses. An *exculpatory clause* is a clause which relieves a person of liability for nonwillful torts. It is not enforceable as to willful or intentional torts. For instance, a health club has an exculpatory clause in its contract with its members. The clause would likely provide a valid defense for the health club if a member slips and is injured while participating in a step aerobics class. By contrast, the clause would probably not be recognized when a member is injured by improper chemicals put into the whirlpool or from being slapped by a club attendant without justification or excuse. Generally, parties to a contract are free to negotiate such clauses so long as the contract does not involve an item of necessity, like housing, and so long as a gross disparity of bargaining power does not exist between them. Some courts, for example, have refused to enforce the exculpatory clauses used in telephone company contracts for Yellow Pages advertisements. These clauses state that if the company makes an error, it will only be liable to return the advertiser's fee. The courts have reasoned that advertisers have no real alternative to the Yellow Pages. Such "take it or leave it" propositions violate public policy.

Where a party has an alternative to accepting a contract with an exculpatory clause, the courts usually will enforce the clause. For instance, car washes sometimes limit their liability for broken antennas. By shopping, customers can locate car washes which will assume greater responsibility. In general, courts are more inclined to enforce clauses which limit liability but do not eliminate it. Such agreements are examined in Chapter 12.

Exculpatory clauses negotiated between parties of equal bargaining power do not violate public policy. But even between commercial venturers, courts may refuse to enforce the clauses where the disparity in bargaining power is great.

Surrogacy contracts. The law of contracts has proved itself over the centuries to be adaptable to situations only science fiction writers of prior generations dreamed of.

Perhaps the most notorious example of this adaptability from the 1980s was the "Baby M" case. There, the New Jersey courts had to decide the validity of a contract in which a woman agreed to have a baby for a childless couple. But to the public, the "Baby M" case had much more to do with emotional issues, such as the right of a mother to keep her child versus the right of a biological father to his progeny.

As a matter of public policy and of law in some states, the courts have not sanctioned baby buying. Surrogacy has inspired seven state statutes banning the practice altogether. (Only Nevada has expressly permitted it.) In 1989, the American Bar Association endorsed two model statutes, one of which bans surrogacy while the other regulates it in a manner similar to adoptions. As science makes delegating conception and childbearing easier, one can expect that more issues surrounding surrogacy will come before courts and legislatures.

Cohabitation agreements. Thirty years ago, most people would have found couples living together without being married (*cohabiting*) as scandalous as surrogate parenting. The courts shared this view. Public policy, they held, strongly favored marriage and frowned upon cohabitation by either heterosexual or homosexual couples. Therefore, the courts would divide property between former partners according to who paid for it.

The effect of holdings like this sharply limited what a nonworking cohabitor could take away from a relationship. Suppose that Grant is an actor and Leigh is a scriptwriter. They move in together just as Grant's career takes off. For 10 years, Leigh gives up her career to manage Grant's now complicated personal life. They then decide to split up. Until very recently, the courts would let Leigh take only what was clearly hers alone. Today, however, Grant and Leigh's situation would likely be decided much like it was in the next case, involving a famous Hollywood actor. As you will see, society's mores have changed greatly regarding cohabitation. Most courts now enforce agreements between live-in couples, at least in regard to their property rights.

- -

Marvin v. Marvin

134 Cal. Rtpr. 815, 557 P. 2d 106 (1976)

FACTS   Michelle Marvin claimed that she and Lee Marvin, her live-in lover, had orally agreed that they would combine their efforts and earnings and share equally in all the property they accumulated. She also claimed that they had agreed to hold themselves out to the public as husband and wife and that she would provide services to him as a companion, homemaker, housekeeper, and cook. Soon thereafter, she quit a career as an entertainer and singer to devote her time to these duties. Six years later, the couple parted. Michelle's complaint stated that Lee Marvin had breached express and implied contracts. He countered by claiming that the contracts were unenforceable. The trial court dismissed her claims.

ISSUE

Can Michelle Marvin be allowed to prove that she and Lee Marvin entered into enforceable contracts?

DECISION

Yes. Reversed. Adults who voluntarily live together and engage in sexual relations can legally enter into contracts regarding their property rights and earnings. This is distinguishable from a contract for performing sexual relations, which would be illegal prostitution and against public policy. There should not be any judicial barriers imposed on cohabiting couples who wish to execute contracts regarding the reasonable expectations of the relationship. Society's standards have changed so profoundly that a moral standard on cohabitation can no longer hold.

After years of legal maneuverings and appeals, the courts ultimately decided that no express or implied contract existed between Lee and Michelle Marvin. In the end, Michelle received no money.

Cases like this one have led some couples to execute *cohabitation agreements,* contracts defining the property rights of unmarried cohabiting parties. These agreements may cover how property will be divided when the relationship ends and what rights the parties have to property they receive during the relationship. Cohabitation agreements often resemble antenuptial agreements, which are discussed in the next chapter.

CONCLUSION

Defenses are exceptions to the rule that an offer and an acceptance—each supported by consideration—form a contract. The burden of proving a defense rests firmly on the person raising it. Because defenses are not simply convenient ways to avoid bad bargains, that burden is sub-

stantial. At once, the law wants to encourage the parties to a contract to engage in tough, wary bargaining while discouraging frivolous assertions of defenses in contract actions. Our extensive coverage of the defenses is designed to serve the same purposes.

The next chapter examines another potential defense, the Statute of Frauds. The Statute works quite differently from the defenses examined here. It is designed to protect people who have *not* made contracts, as opposed to those who have. And its protection must always be claimed before a contract is executed.

A NOTE TO FUTURE CPA CANDIDATES

The CPA exam expects candidates to be able to distinguish the five types of conduct which can nullify mutual assent: duress, undue influence, fraud in the execution, fraud in the inducement, and innocent misrepresentation. Remember that each of these is evaluated on a subjective basis, not necessarily on what a reasonably prudent person might think or do. The conduct complained of must be material and actually induce assent. Remember that the remedy for innocent misrepresentation is rescission. Rescission means a court will cancel the contract and restore the parties to their original positions.

Incapacity has not generally been stressed on the CPA exam. You should keep in mind that a minor has the right to disaffirm a contract until a reasonable amount of time after coming of age. For a minor to disaffirm, the minor must disaffirm the whole contract (and return all remaining held consideration, if any, which was originally received). Intoxication is a possible defense only if involuntary; in other words, the decision to enter into the contract came *after* drinking too much, not before.

The CPA exam has often asked questions concerning covenants not to compete between an employer and employee. Remember that these covenants are legal if the agreement is necessary to protect a legitimate business interest. However, they must be reasonable as to the length of time and geographic scope of limitation. A court may consider an employee's ability to get another job.

Finally, questions concerning contracts in violation of licensing statutes have been quite common. Remember that noncompliance of a statute primarily with a regulatory purpose means *no* recovery. A partial recovery cannot be awarded under a quasi-contract or promissory estoppel theory. In contrast, violation of a revenue purpose statute does not affect rights and duties under the contract.

KEY WORDS

capacity (200)
defense (191)
disaffirmance (200)
duress (191)
fraud in the execution (194)

justifiable reliance (195)
material fact (194)
misrepresentation (196)
mistake (198)
necessaries (201)
ratification (202)

fraud in the inducement (194)
illegality (205)
improper threat (192)

rescind (191)
restrictive covenant (208)
undue influence (193)

DISCUSSION QUESTIONS

1. What is the requirement for proof of duress by improper threat? How does duress differ from undue influence?
2. List and describe the elements of fraud.
3. How does an innocent misrepresentation differ from a fraudulent misrepresentation? When would nondisclosure of information constitute a misrepresentation?
4. What is a "mistake" in the legal sense?
5. How does a mutual mistake differ from a unilateral mistake? Under which doctrine is a court more likely to allow rescission? Why?
6. What is the rationale for finding a contract voidable because of a lack of capacity to contract? What classes of individuals are likely to be protected?
7. Describe a minor's right of disaffirmance. Under what circumstances will the minor be prevented from disaffirming?
8. What standard is used by a court in determining the contractual capacity of a mentally ill person? Why would a court be less inclined to recognize the defense of incapacity due to drunkenness?
9. What is the general rule in regard to illegal bargains? What is the rationale for such a rule?
10. What is meant by a finding of "contrary to public policy"? What factors will be considered prior to making such a finding?

CASE PROBLEMS

1. Kemp contracted to sell Ward a parcel of land. Kemp knew Ward was buying the land with the intention of building a high-rise office tower. Kemp also knew that a subsurface soil condition would prevent construction of this

type. The condition was extremely unusual and was not readily discoverable in the course of normal inspections or soil tests. Kemp did not disclose the existence of the condition to Ward, but Ward did not ask Kemp about the suitability of the land for a high rise. While the contract was still executory, Ward learned of the soil condition. Kemp, however, claims Ward made a unilateral mistake; Ward terms Kemp's actions "fraud." Must Ward complete performance under the contract? Explain.

2. Jessica Austin, 17, went to a used-book store to look for a book by her mother's favorite author, Karen Douglas. Jessica found one that bore on the flyleaf a signature that read, "Karen Douglas." The store owner, Jim Sabin, told her he believed the signature was genuine because of what the book's prior owner had told him. So Jessica bought it, paying more than twice what she would have if it had been unsigned. Ten days after her eighteenth birthday, Jessica attempted to rescind the transaction because she had learned the signature was a forgery. If the age of majority in her state is 18, may Jessica disaffirm the transaction because she lacked capacity? If she cannot, does she have any other grounds for demanding her money back?

3. The public accounting firm of Good & Better had just hired Maurice. He decided to sell his used BMW and buy a new car. Anthony, a former classmate, answered Maurice's ad and offered $4000 for the car—$5000 less than its book value—and his promise not to tell Good & Better that Maurice was a homosexual and had used drugs. Maurice reluctantly agreed. Before the transaction was completed, the managing partner of Good & Better told Maurice the firm was aware of rumors about his past, but so long as neither practice became an issue on the job, his position was secure. Maurice immediately called Anthony and told him the deal was off. Anthony has sued for breach of contract. He has responded to Maurice's defense of duress by asserting he never threatened to tell the firm and, in any event, the firm knew. Will Anthony prevail? Explain.

4. Hiram Walker & Sons, breeders of Angus cattle, contracted to sell "Rose 2d of Abelone" to Sherwood for $80. At the time of the sale, both parties believed Rose to be infertile. A fertile cow of Rose II's caliber was worth between $750 and $1000. Subsequently, Walker discovered that the cow was "with calf." Walker refused to accept Sherwood's money and deliver the cow. Did Walker have a right to rescind the contract? Explain.

5. George Kemp, a building subcontractor, submitted a bid on an aspect of a construction project. Because of his haste in putting the bid together, Kemp did not discover a math error which he had made. In submitting his bid to the prime contractor, Green, Kemp stated that he had submitted a very competitive bid, as he really wanted this job. Kemp's bid was $4500. The five other bids ranged from $6200 to $6625. It was not unusual in the trade for bids to vary as much as 15 percent from the mean of clustered bids, here $6400. Green accepted Kemp's bid without mentioning the bid variance. Upon acceptance, Kemp discovered his mistake. Green has refused to release Kemp from his bid. Would a court likely find for Kemp? Explain.

6. Sam entered into a $75,000 contract with Orr, Inc., to do some plumbing on one of Orr's buildings. After Sam satisfactorily performed the work, Orr discovered Sam had failed to obtain a plumbing license, which state law required that he have. The licensing statute was enacted solely to raise revenue. An independent appraisal of Sam's work indicated that it increased the building's value by $70,000. Sam used $35,000 in materials on the Orr project. If Orr refuses to pay Sam, what, if anything, can Sam recover? Explain.

7. Laura Pincus was running late to teach her class in downtown Chicago. Finding no better parking spaces in the area, she went to Al's Parking Garage. Al's has a large sign in the entryway which says, "Not responsible for personal items left in your car." This warning

is also printed on the customer's receipt. Customers receive the receipt when they leave their car and car keys with an attendant. Pincus asked the attendant if stealing was a problem, as she had a spinnaker sail in the back seat of her car. She was told not to worry, as "no one would likely want something like that." When Pincus later returned to her car the sail was missing. Pincus later learned that the garage parked the car unlocked in an area easily accessible to the public. Pincus first contends the clause is ineffective, as she had no practical choice but to "accept" it. Correct? She also claims the garage's actions effectively negated the clause. Correct? Explain.

8. Adrienne Critcher sold her very successful gourmet luncheon restaurant, "Critcher's," to Al McKinny. The sales contract specified that Critcher would not be involved in or open another gourmet restaurant within a 150-mile radius for 5 years. Within a year, Adrienne opened a new business, "Adrienne's Bakery," directly across the street from Critcher's. Although the luncheon offerings were limited to bakery goods and the seating was more restricted than it was at Critcher's, the new restaurant attracted so many of Adrienne's old customers that Critcher's closed. McKinny has brought a breach of contract suit against Adrienne. Adrienne has defended on the grounds that she is not operating a gourmet restaurant and, even if she were, the covenant not to compete is too broad to be enforced. Is McKinney likely to prevail? Explain.

9. While eating in a Chicago restaurant, Gail Dart recognized Bruce Fallsteen, a rock singer. Gail and her friends leapt up, went over to Fallsteen, and asked him to give them something to remember him by. Fallsteen told them, "I'll sell my Cubs hat to any one of you who pays me $75 in cash." Gail immediately agreed, saying she would be right back with the cash. As she left to look for an ATM machine, her friend Julie Oschner said, "You're a big dummy to pay $75 for a beat-up Cubs hat. He's taking advantage of you." Gail laughed and agreed, and the two friends headed for a department store. If Fallsteen brought a breach of contract action against Gail, would a court be likely to find her liable? Explain.

10. Casey Dikkers, a minor, bought a new Schwinn racing bike from DeSalvo's Bike Shop. One day while riding the bike, he saw Sarah Goebel, also a minor, walking to her gymnastics class. Hoping to win her favor, Casey gave Sarah his bike. Sarah wanted a different-colored bike, so she sold it to a good faith purchaser, Jeff Rutter. Under the common law, would Casey have a right to compel DeSalvo's to return his money. Alternatively, could Casey compel Jeff to return his bike? Explain.

CHAPTER 10
Written Contracts and Their Interpretation

The general rule of contract law is that oral contracts are enforceable. One can only imagine the lines at noontime at a McDonald's if every order had to be reduced to a written contract. However, for contractual agreements of matters with more importance than the purchase of a cheeseburger, it is often advisable to create a written contract. With a written contract, ideally there will be fewer misunderstandings. If a dispute under the contract ends up in court, a written contract will provide the best evidence of what you agreed to do or to refrain from doing.

This chapter initially will focus on six types of contracts which must be in writing to be enforceable in court. These six types of contracts are exceptions to the general rule that oral contracts are enforceable. The acronym MY LEGS may help you remember that the six are:

- **M**arriage: contracts to marry, which include other promises.
- **Y**ear: contracts not to be performed within 1 year
- **L**and: contracts to transfer interest in land
- **E**xecutor: contracts by executors
- **G**oods: contracts for sale of goods over $500
- **S**urety: contracts by sureties

This chapter is about written contracts: when the law requires them, what they must contain, and how a court interprets them. Before turning to the six types which must be in writing, let us take a look at how these exceptions came into the law.

STATUTES OF FRAUDS

Originally, English courts did not enforce oral contracts. Once they began, problems of *perjury*, which is lying under oath, arose. To remedy this situation, in 1677 Parliament adopted an "Act for the Prevention of Fraud and Perjuries," or, as it came to be called, the *Statute of Frauds*. This Statute, which covered a number of topics, specified those contracts which were unenforceable if not evidenced by a writing. After American independence, the portion dealing with writings became a part of our common law of contracts.

The Common Law and the UCC Statutes

Today, virtually all states have a Statute of Frauds. In fact, most have at least two. One is general in nature, covering all contracts within specific categories. The second, adopted as part of the Uniform Commercial Code (UCC), relates solely to the sale of goods—the "G" in MY LEGS. However, the two are simply referred to as "the Statute."

A contract which is said to be "within the Statute of Frauds" must be evidenced by a writing *unless* an exception to the Statute makes it enforceable for other reasons. These are, of course, exceptions to the exceptions to the general rule that oral contracts are enforceable! *Note:* The word used in the Statute is "unenforceable," not "void." A party to an executory oral agreement within the Statute may not enforce the agreement in court. But if the parties execute it, the courts will recognize its validity. The Statute's purpose is to protect persons who do *not* enter into contracts of one of the six types, not to void the contracts automatically.

Preventive Law

The emphasis above on the validity of oral agreements may obscure an important preventive law point. When it comes to protecting oneself, a written contract is always superior to an oral contract. To enforce an oral agreement, the plaintiff must prove it exists and what its terms are. Proving what two parties agreed to in, say, a telephone conversation months or years before is not always easy.

A written contract which records the expectations of both parties as to performance is called an *integrated agreement* because it merges, or incorporates, the expectations of both parties into a single contract. An integrated agreement supersedes oral agreements covering the same subject matter which the parties made before or at the time they executed the integrated agreement. In fact, a court will not even listen to evidence that relates to the other agreements or that contradicts the integrated agreement unless a party raises one of the defenses to mutual assent discussed in the previous chapter.

In sum, the general rule is that oral contracts are enforceable unless they fall into one of the Statute's MY LEGS categories. But the commonsense, preventive law rule is, "If it matters, get it in writing."

MARRIAGE

Any agreement to marry which goes beyond a simple exchange of promises to marry must be in writing to be enforceable. Suppose Bob asks Carol to marry him, and she says yes. Their agreement does not have to be in writing. However, if anything else is involved, the agreement must be in writing. Suppose that in exchange for Carol's promise to marry him, Bob agrees in writing to give her a new car or to write an irrevocable will leaving all his property to her. Since the promises are in writing, they are enforceable if the marriage takes place.

An *antenuptial agreement* is within the Statute. This kind of contract usually deals with the disposition of property in the event of death or divorce. It is entered into before, and in anticipation of, marriage. Antenuptial agreements are quite common between retirees who marry. Under the laws of most states, a surviving spouse is entitled to a specific percentage of the estate of the dead spouse regardless of what the will provides. (This aspect of estates is discussed in Chapter 29.) An antenuptial agreement may void the effect of that provision, thus permitting the retirees to ensure their estates go to their children.

Agreements between a cohabiting couple are not covered by the Statute's marriage provision. If Ted and Alice, who are unmarried, agree to live together and share their income, their agreement does not require a writing. However, many courts have found public policy reasons for not enforcing such agreements. (Public policy as a ground for not enforcing such contracts is discussed in Chapter 9.)

YEAR

Under the Statute of Frauds, oral contracts are not enforceable if they cannot be performed within 1 year. The Statute's application depends on whether, at the time the parties agreed, the contract was performable within 1 year. Its application has nothing whatsoever to do with whether it *was* performed within a year, nor does it depend on the actual course of events, the parties' expectations, or the specification of a date in the contract. Rather, its application depends on whether it was *possible* to perform the contract within 1 year from when the contract was created.

The Statute's application depends on the possibilities of performance at the time the parties reached their agreement. Suppose that on December 1, 1993, Nicolla Construction Corp. orally offered Dana a job for 1 year, beginning December 12. The contract would not be enforceable. However, suppose Sean agrees to employ Erin for life. Their contract does not require a writing to be enforceable, since Erin may die within the year. The next case takes a similarly broad reading of what is outside the Statute.

Hodge v. Evans Financial Corporation

823 F. 2d 559 (D.C. Cir. 1987)

FACTS
Hodge was hired by Evans Financial Corporation to be vice president and general counsel. Because he was 54 and concerned about job security, Hodge accepted the job after he was assured orally by the president of the defendant company that he could work there until his retirement. Hodge was fired 1 year later. In an action for breach of contract, Hodge won at the trial level.

ISSUE
Was the agreement between Hodge and Evans Financial Corporation unenforceable under the Statute of Frauds, since it was made orally?

DECISION
No. Affirmed. The employment contract between Hodge and Evans Financial Corporation did not indicate that there was a specific time period. Hodge could have fully performed the contract within a year's time if he had chosen to retire or if he would have died during that time period. Thus, the oral contract is enforceable and the Statute of Frauds is not applicable.

Some courts have held that if one party to an oral contract which is not performable within 1 year actually performs within the year, the contract is enforceable. Such situations are rare.

LAND

Transfers of Interests

The Statute of Frauds requires any contract for the transfer of an interest in land to be in writing. "Land" in this context means the ground as well as anything that is attached to it, like a barn or trees. An interest is any right one has in the land itself and may be acquired through any of the following:

- A sale of land
- An easement
- A mortgage
- A lease, except for short-term leases

Thus, the Statute of Frauds requires that a contract to buy a house be in writing. But a landowner does not have to contract in writing to have, say, a garage built.

Mortgages and leases. A *mortgage* is a writing which creates an interest in land, usually to secure a debt. A bank, for instance, holds a mortgage on a house to protect itself when it loans the money to buy the house.

Leases are contracts to rent property. Real property leases, whether for an apartment or for a store, must be in writing. However, many states exempt short-term leases (1 year or less). Suppose Tom and his landlord agree he will rent an apartment for 9 months. Neither Tom nor the landlord may void the agreement on the grounds that it is not in writing.

Partnerships and joint ventures. One large class of cases to which the Statute does not apply consists of *partnership* or *joint venture* contracts whose subject matter is land. (These business entities are discussed in Part IV.) An oral contract between two persons to go into the business of buying and selling real estate as partners or joint venturers is enforceable. However, if the contract contains a provision for the transfer of specific land from one partner to the other or if it falls under another MY LEGS exception, it is not enforceable.

Part Performance Exception

The *part performance exception* permits a court, under certain circumstances, to enforce an oral contract for the transfer of an interest in land. The party seeking enforcement must have performed part of the contract and have changed her position because of reliance on it. Suppose David & Jonathan, Inc., orally agrees to sell land to Diana. She pays part of the price, moves onto the land, and builds a house—all with David & Jonathan's knowledge. Plainly it is unfair not to enforce their agreement just because there was no writing. Under the part performance exception to the Statute's land provision, this contract would be enforceable. The promisor is estopped from asserting the Statute of Frauds as a defense. However, as the plaintiff in the next case found out, not every type of reliance estops the promisor.

Lance J. Marchiafava v. Haft

777 F.2d 942 (4th Cir. 1985)

FACTS   Lance Marchiafava ran a hair salon. A local real estate developer asked him if he was interested in assuming a lease in a mall. Marchiafava indicated he was if the developer would write a new lease incorporating several terms he wanted. Under one of those terms, the developer was to agree not to rent space in that mall to any competing hairstylists. According to Marchiafava, he initially refused to sign the lease because it did not contain this clause. However, the developer orally agreed to this condition, and Marchiafava signed. About 3 years later, the developer leased mall space to a competing salon and Marchiafava brought suit for breach of contract. The trial court awarded damages to Marchiafava.

ISSUE   Did the Statute of Frauds bar enforcement of the developer's promise?

DECISION   Yes. Reversed. The developer was not estopped from asserting the Statute as a defense. Estoppel does not apply where, as here, the party asserting the estoppel suffered harm solely from the refusal of the other party to perform an obligation under the alleged oral agreement. Further, where a party asserts an estoppel related to land use, the representation on which it is based must relate to an existing or past fact. It cannot be a promise of future performance.

Many courts insist that for the part performance exception to apply, the promisor's representations must relate directly to the land. Suppose Roy orally agreed to take care of Barbara for the rest of her life in return for her promise to leave him her land and house. However, Barbara never makes a will. Roy sues her estate to enforce her promise. Since Roy's promise did not relate directly to the land, most courts would not enforce their agreement. However, if Roy treated the property as his own, by maintaining the land and renovating the house, his actions would relate to the land and would not be explainable in the absence of a contract. On this basis, some courts would enforce the agreement.

EXECUTOR

After a person dies, someone must gather the assets of the *decedent*, the person who died; pay outstanding liabilities; and distribute anything that remains to the heirs. The person who takes charge of these matters is called, variously, a decedent's *executor, administrator,* or *personal representative.* In this book, we will use the term "personal representative." But we have used "executor" in MY LEGS because it makes the acronym work.

Under the Statute, an oral promise by a personal representative to pay the decedent's obligations out of the representative's own funds is not enforceable. Quite often, the promise by a personal representative takes the form of a guarantee of payment if the estate does not pay.

The key to determining whether the personal representative must make her promise in writing is whether the debt existed at the decedent's death. If it did, it is the decedent's debt, and the representative's promise to pay the debt personally must be in writing. This rule prevents creditors from shaming the personal representative into paying bills. Although a personal representative may be quick to agree orally to pay a bill, she may be much more reluctant to do so in writing.

If the debt did *not* exist at the decedent's death, it is the debt of the decedent's estate, and the promise by the personal representative to guarantee the debt does not require a writing. Suppose a personal representative contracts with an undertaker for funeral services and

promises, "I guarantee payment personally." The executor's promise does not have to be in writing, since the obligation to the undertaker did not exist at the decedent's death.

The executor exception is closely related to the surety exception discussed below and in Chapter 40.

GOODS

Today, the goods exception is usually defined by the UCC Statute of Frauds [UCC §2-201].

The parties to transactions involving the sale of goods worth $500 or more may not enforce their contracts unless a writing exists sufficient to indicate they made a contract *and* unless the party against whom enforcement is sought or his authorized agent signed the document [UCC §2-201(1)].

The UCC Statute of Frauds applies only to contracts for the sale of *goods.* As noted earlier, the UCC defines "goods" in the broadest possible terms. Goods include wood, garbanzo beans, cars, and almost anything else that is movable other than the money with which their price is to be paid. Still, the term is not all inclusive. Goods are not services, such as repairing an office typewriter. Land is not goods, nor are securities such as stocks and bonds [UCC §2-105(1)]. The definition of "goods" is examined in more detail in Part VI of this book.

UCC Exceptions

The UCC Statute of Frauds permits enforcement of four types of oral contracts which would otherwise be subject to the requirement of a writing: confirmatory memorandum, contracts involving specially manufactured goods, those whose existence is admitted in court, and those which are partially performed.

Confirmatory memorandum. Under UCC §2-201(2) an oral sale of goods of $500 or more which is followed by a written confirmatory memorandum is an enforceable exception under the Code's Statute of Frauds provision. The transaction, however, must be *between* merchants. The *Goldkist v. Brownlee* case, which follows, is a good illustration of the need and efficiency of this exception when there is a sale of goods.

Specially manufactured goods. A seller may enforce an oral contract for goods to be specially manufactured for the buyer if they are unsuitable for sale to others in the ordinary course of the seller's business. For instance, glasses embossed with a restaurant's name will not usually be suitable for resale.

In order to enforce a contract under this exception, a seller must demonstrate that before it received notice of repudiation it had made either a substantial beginning on the goods' manufacture or commitments to procure them [UCC §2-201(3)(a)]. Suppose Pizza Shack sponsored a children's soccer team. It ordered 100 specially dyed T-shirts at $6 each, bearing the name of Pizza Shack on the back and "Sharks," the name of the team, on the front.

After the T-shirt company completed dying and labeling the shirts, Pizza Shack canceled the order. Assuming it can offer proof of the oral contract, the T-shirt company may enforce the contract even if no writing evidences it.

Admission in court. An admission in a court proceeding that an oral contract within the Statute existed between the parties permits the court to enforce it up to the quantity of goods admitted [UCC §2-201(3)(b)]. This particular liberalization of the common law avoids a situation where a defendant could admit the existence of an oral agreement but claim the protection of the Statute.

Partially performed contracts. An oral contract for goods whose value exceeds $500 is enforceable as to goods for which payment has been made and accepted or as to goods which have been received and accepted. As the next case illustrates, this "part performance" exception to the UCC Statute prevents parties from abusing the Statute.

Goldkist, Inc. v. Brownlee

355 S.E. 2d 733 (Ga. Ct. App. 1987)

FACTS   The Brownlee Brothers were farmers who sold their crops themselves. Barney Brownlee agreed, in a telephone conversation with Goldkist, to sell 5000 bushels of soybeans at $6.88 per pound and to deliver them in a month. On the day of the phone conversation, Goldkist sent the Brownlees a written memorandum confirming the above terms of the deal. Although the Brownlees received the memo, they didn't respond to it and didn't deliver the soybeans. Goldkist was subsequently compelled to "cover" the breached contract by buying from another farmer at a higher price. At the trial, the Brownlees prevailed, since there was no written contract signed by either of them as required under UCC §2-201(1).

ISSUE   Does Goldkist's confirmatory memorandum fall under the UCC §2-201(2) exception for enforcing an oral contract against the Brownlees?

DECISION   Yes. Reversed. Both Goldkist and the Brownlees are merchants, and the crop is a "good" under the UCC's definitions. It would be fraudulent to permit a farmer who routinely deals in crops, like the Brownlees, to back out of a confirmed oral sale of its crop. If this were allowed, a farmer could simply sell as agreed when the price stays the same or drops, or sell to a higher bidder if the price later rises.

SURETY

Quite often parents sign agreements with banks to pay off auto loans which the banks make to their college-age children should their children default. This arrangement is called a *suretyship contract*, a contract in which the *surety*—the first party—binds himself to pay the debt of the *obligor*—the second party and primary debtor—to the *obligee*—the party to whom the obligor is primarily liable (see Figure 10.1). In other words, suretyship contracts are ones in which the surety promises to be secondarily liable if the obligor fails to pay.

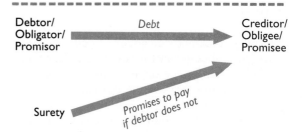

Figure 10.1 Suretyship Illustrated.
Note the multiple names for the principal parties. It is the surety's promise which always must be in writing.

The Leading Object Rule

The *leading object rule* is an exception to the Statute's requirement of a writing to evidence suretyship contracts. It excepts surety agreements whose primary purpose is to benefit the surety. Suppose OurGlo Electric Co. contracts with Time Warp Construction to build its new store. Time Warp purchases its building materials from Grossinger's Lumber. When Time Warp falls behind on its bills, Grossinger's refuses to deliver any more material unless OurGlo agrees to pay for the deliveries if Time Warp does not. OurGlo orally agrees. OurGlo's primary interest lies in getting the building up, not in keeping Time Warp in business. Therefore, a court would enforce OurGlo's oral suretyship agreement.

As this example shows, a more accurate term for the leading object rule might be ''the primary purpose doctrine.'' However, both terms accurately reflect the fact that a surety may have more than one reason for entering into a suretyship agreement. The next case points out why determining the leading object, or primary purpose, of a suretyship promise can be a very difficult problem.

Hudson v. Ashley

411 A.2d 963 (D.C. 1980)

FACTS   Ashley's son was arrested for assault with intent to kill and commission of a crime while armed. Ashley retained Hudson's law firm to represent his son, allegedly stating he would be responsible for the fee. The law firm negotiated a plea, and the son received 6 months' unsupervised probation. The firm repeatedly billed both Ashleys, who failed to pay. The law firm sued the father, alleging he was liable for the debt. The trial court granted a directed verdict for Ashley on the grounds that the agreement was within the Statute's suretyship provision.

ISSUE   Should the trial court have heard evidence on whether only the father made a promise to the law firm?

DECISION   Yes. Reversed. The distinction between the promise to answer for the debt of another person, which is within the Statute, and an independent obligation of the promisor, which is not, is a difficult one. The mere fact that someone other than the promisor received the benefit of the consideration does not bring the contract within the Statute. A court may enforce a nonwritten promise to answer for another's debt if the promisor's main purpose was to obtain a direct, personal benefit. The test for a suretyship's existence is whether the parties intended that credit would be extended solely to the promisor or to both the promisor and the party who was to receive the services. These questions are essentially ones of fact, and the jury should have decided them.

In *Hudson*, the court strongly implied that if the senior Ashley made the promise to pay, he was bound by it whether he was a surety or not. The goal of the leading object rule is to prevent parties who benefit from an obligee's performance from avoiding payment for what they received.

Figure 10.2 tabulates the MY LEGS contracts and the exceptions to the Statute of Frauds.

THE *RESTATEMENT*'S PROMISSORY ESTOPPEL EXCEPTION

The *Restatement (Second) of Contracts* §139 takes a unique position on the application of the Statute of Frauds. It states that the courts may enforce an oral promise that would ordinarily not be enforceable if the following conditions exist:

1. It induces action or forbearance.
2. The reliance was foreseeable by the party making the promise.
3. Injustice can be avoided only by enforcing the promise.

Neither the common law nor the UCC has adopted this position. Indeed, many reviewers of the *Restatement* objected to this section.

They argued that the Statute has a legitimate purpose, which is to serve as a fairly consistent guide to when a writing is necessary. This consistency should not be sacrificed to remedy the tiny number of cases each year in which an injustice might occur.

Plainly, those who object to the *Restatement*'s promissory estoppel exception sense that it will swallow the rule. Suppose Al sees a classified ad for a 1989 Mazda RX-7 for $5500. He calls and, after listening to the owner describe the car, offers to buy it sight unseen for $5000. The seller agrees. Later in the day, Al calls again, this time to tell the seller he has changed his mind. In the meantime, the seller had told several prospective buyers that he had sold the car. Do those facts warrant the finding of a promissory estoppel under *Restatement (Second) of Contracts* §139? If not, what more would the plaintiff have to show? Is it worth the time and effort required for fifty jurisdictions to draw this line?

CREATING THE WRITTEN CONTRACT

Until this point, our focus has been the Statute of Frauds exceptions to the general rule that oral contracts are enforceable. As noted earlier, the MY LEGS contracts, which must be in

	MARRIAGE	YEAR	LAND	EXECUTOR	GOODS	SURETY
Mutual exchange of promise to marry	X					
Admission in court	X	X	X	X	X	X
Part performance		X	X		X	
Leading object rule						X
Specially manufactured goods					X	
Relating to payments made and/or received and accepted					X	

Figure 10.2 The Statute of Frauds: MY LEGS and the Exceptions.
This table illustrates the relationship between the MY LEGS contracts—which must be in writing—and the exceptions to the Statute of Frauds—which may be oral. The admission in court and the part performance exceptions apply to more than one category.

writing, are far from the only ones which should be in writing. This section explores the rules of form governing written contracts.

If the rules of form are not observed, even a written contract may be unenforceable. However, the rules are not so complex that a lawyer must draw up each contract. In fact, the formal requirements can be stated in one sentence. A *written contract* must be a writing signed by or on behalf of the party to be charged that reasonably identifies the subject matter of the contract, sufficiently indicates a contract exists between the parties or was offered by the signer to the other party, and fairly states the essential terms of the contract's unperformed promises. The components of this sentence are examined below.

Writing

The courts have defined a "writing" very broadly. A notation on a check, a receipt, a court document, a letter between friends, a will —any of these satisfy the writing requirement.

In fact, any writing may suffice. A court, for instance, may recognize a real estate contract in a notation on a check which reads, "In part payment for Dairylea farm—balance due $50,000." The courts often refer to a writing as a "memorandum." The terms are interchangeable.

Several writings. A court may even piece together a sufficient writing from several writings, such as letters exchanged between two parties discussing various terms of their agreement. Courts also have found contracts in much more unusual circumstances. Suppose Fern and George enter into an oral contract not performable within 1 year. The only evidence of their agreement Fern can produce is two unrelated sheets of paper fastened together by a paper clip. Although the sheets' contents do not show they belong together, a court may find their proximity and their relationship to the contract sufficient to form a writing. Some courts, like the one that decided the next case, have refused to go this far.

Cohen v. McCutchin

554 S.W.2d 844 (Tex. Ct. Civ. App. 1977)

FACTS

McKnight acquired a 25 percent working interest in an exploratory oil and gas well. He then sold part of his interest to the three McCutchins. McKnight's name did not appear on the agreements but did appear as the addressee of the cover letters sent with them. The cover letters referred to both the agreements and the checks which accompanied them. Later, McKnight sent invoices on his letterhead to the McCutchins, which they paid by check. After McKnight's death, his administrator sought to recover payments due from the McCutchins. The McCutchins alleged the agreements did not identify McKnight as a party and did not contain a promise by them to pay. The trial court entered summary judgment for the McCutchins.

ISSUE

Did the agreements fail to meet the Statute's requirements for sufficient writing?

DECISION

Yes. Affirmed. McKnight's estate argued that all the writings, taken together, satisfied the Statute and that, when considered together, they necessarily identified McKnight as the unnamed party to the agreements. However, the agreements do not identify the seller of the interest in the well or the recipient of the sums the McCutchins were to pay. McKnight was not named in any capacity.

Subject Matter

So long as the parties themselves can understand what the subject matter of the contract is, a general description in a writing is sufficient. Suppose Will agrees orally to sell Hal a wheel alignment rack. A memorandum from Hal to Will confirming their agreement describes the subject matter as "the rack in your garage." This description will suffice, since both parties know the rack to which the memorandum refers.

The courts will give effect to loose descriptions, like the one in the last example, if they can determine to what the descriptions refer. Preventive law principles, however, dictate a much more specific approach to defining a contract's subject matter. *Remember:* A court's job is to enforce the parties' contract, not to make it for them.

Signed Writing

Under both the common law and the UCC, a written contract is unenforceable unless it is clear that the parties have adopted it as their own. Normally, their signatures on the writing establish that fact. Thus, an agreement written on a cocktail napkin and signed by both parties is enforceable.

Signature. Normally, people think of a *signature* as someone's full name written in his or her handwriting. However, a signature has to be sufficient only to authenticate the memorandum as that of the signer. A court may accept initials, a nickname, a special symbol, or any of a variety of other means of identification. The signature need not even be in writing. Signatures may include notations appearing in pencil, typescript, or printing. They can be made with a stamp. Contrary to *Cohen*, some courts have held a letterhead constitutes a signature.

The party to be charged. Sometimes, a party seeks to enforce a contract not signed by both parties. If the party to be charged—meaning the defendant, usually—signed the writing, a court will enforce it. Put differently, the party seeking to enforce the contract does not have to have signed it.

Here is how the party to be charged rule works. Suppose Rhonda is selling her house. She and Bruce agree on terms, but only Rhonda signs the sales contract. Bruce now refuses to perform, and Rhonda sues Bruce. Bruce is the party to be charged. The contract is not enforceable against him, since he did not sign it. But if Rhonda refused to perform, Bruce could enforce it against her, since she signed it.

The rationale for the party to be charged rule is sometimes stated in terms of the party asserting the contract, in effect, signing the contract by raising it in the context of a lawsuit. Really, what that party has done is admit the existence of the contract. Thus, both parties have acknowledged the contract. From a preventive law standpoint, the key point is that a party should always insist on the other party's signing the contract as a condition to the contract's taking effect.

The UCC exception. The UCC contains an exception to the party to be charged rule. Under the exception, a signed written confirmation of an oral contract sent from one merchant to another is considered to be a written contract between them unless the merchant receiving the confirmation objects within 10 days [UCC §2-201]. The next case illustrates how the confirmation process works. It also deals with a much-litigated question: Is a farmer a merchant?

Terminal Grain Corp. v. Freeman

270 N.W.2d 806 (S.D. 1978)

FACTS

Wheeler, a trucker, often negotiated contracts between wheat farmers, like Freeman, and Terminal Grain Corp., a grain dealer, in order to obtain the contract to haul the grain. Terminal Grain mailed confirmations of two contracts—both exceeding $500—which it believed Wheeler had negotiated for it with Freeman. Freeman did not object to the confirmations. When he refused to deliver the grain, Terminal brought suit. Terminal argued that Freeman was a merchant for the purposes of their transaction and was bound to respond to the confirmations. The trial court held a farmer was not a merchant in grain transactions, and the jury found for Freeman.

ISSUE

Was Freeman a merchant and therefore required to respond to the confirmations?

DECISION

No. Affirmed. The UCC assumes that transactions between professionals in a given field require special and clear rules which may not apply to a casual seller or buyer. The inexperienced are not to be held to the same standards as those set for the professional. The average farmer with no particular experience in commodity transactions, who sells only the crops he raises to local elevators for cash or places his grain in storage under one of the federal loan programs, is not a merchant under the UCC.

Some courts faced with the same question as to a farmer's status have reached the opposite conclusion. For instance, the Ohio Court of Appeals said of a farmer asserting nonmerchant status, ''[His attorney] would represent defendant as a simple tiller of the soil, unaccustomed to the affairs of business and the marketplace. Farming is no longer confined to simple labor. Only an agribusinessman may hope to survive.''* The wise merchant will assume he is dealing with a nonmerchant whenever there is any question as to the status of the other party.

---

* *Ohio Grain Co. v. Swisshelm*, 40 Ohio App. 2d 203, 318 N.E.2d 428, 430 (1973).

INTERPRETATION OF WRITTEN CONTRACTS

Even when contracts are in writing, disputes occur as to their meaning. Over the centuries, the courts have developed rules, called *rules of construction*, for interpreting written contracts. At the same time, however, the *parol evidence rule* developed, which limited or eliminated the introduction of evidence tending to contradict the plain meaning of a writing. This section examines these two sets of rules.

Obligation to Read the Contract

Before looking at the rules of construction and the parol evidence rule, you should first note the oldest of all rules concerning written con-

---

In re Cajun Electric Power Cooperative

791 F.2d 353 (5th Circ. 1986)

FACTS   Cajun Electric Power Cooperative ordered two coal-fired steam generators from Riley Stoker Corporation at a cost of over $75 million. The project did not go as planned, and 8 years later Cajun sued Riley for $200 million in damages. Riley moved to stay the proceedings on the grounds that the contract between the parties compelled arbitration. The trial court granted the stay.

ISSUE   Did the undisputedly present arbitration clause bind the parties?

DECISION   Yes. Affirmed.

The arbitration clause was not hidden or "buried" in the complicated . . . contract documents compiled by Cajun and Riley. The page on which the arbitration clause appears is clearly listed in two separate indexes. . . . The arbitration clause appears under the heading "ARBITRATION," on the signature page . . . directly above the required signature of the "authorized officer of the company." . . . If the arbitration clause was indeed the "blooper" Cajun says it is, then even a mildly attentive legal aide should have been able to spot it easily ("from across the room," we are tempted to add). . . . Understandably, the trial judge had difficulty concealing his skepticism: [']Well, then I say 'Shame on them' for a corporation this big to take a document in a two hundred million dollar contract, having a clause that is right above the signature line, and say they didn't know it. I don't believe them. . . . [']

tracts: Read before you sign. Study the document to make sure it fairly represents your agreement. If it does not or if you do not understand a clause, the burden is on you to have the contract altered *in writing* before you sign. The following case is a fair example of cases in which a corporation claimed not to have read a contract.

Rules of Construction

The word "construction," not surprisingly, comes from a Latin verb, *construere*, meaning "to build." But the verb's earliest adaptation in English was into the word "construe," meaning "analyze the structure." Lawyers still use "construe" as a verb, with the added meaning of "interpret." Thus, when lawyers use the phrase "rules of construction," they mean rules of interpretation, not rules of building.

Plain English. The courts will not construe written contracts at all if a "plain English" interpretation is available. In that case, a court probably will not permit the introduction of evidence about the parties' subjective intentions. Instead, a court will give priority to an objective analysis of what the writing says, looking to the plain meaning of the words contained in the contract. "Oranges" means oranges, not apples, for example.

A court will interpret a contract as best it can. However, when confronted with two parties who have contracted in good faith, a court will construe a contract against the party who wrote it. Even so, preventive law principles dictate that when the party who does not author the contract notes a point that requires clarification, he or she should insist upon it before signing. What may seem unclear to a party may look crystal clear to a judge or may be subject to the parole evidence rule.

Integration clauses. As noted earlier in this chapter, the best protection a party can have is an integrated agreement. Some written contracts make the fact of their integration express

by means of an *integration clause*. These clauses are found commonly in printed order forms. They signify that the writing is the final expression of the parties' agreement and that it supersedes any earlier statements or documents. A typical one might state, in part, "This is the complete and final understanding of the parties."

To be integrated, however, a contract does not have to have an integration clause. In fact, without contrary evidence, a court usually assumes in a writing to be the complete expression of the parties' intent.

The types of writing. The courts also have rules as to the precedence given to forms of writing in a contract. Handwritten clauses take precedence over conflicting typed clauses. Typed clauses prevail over printed form material. These rules reflect the courts' desire to give effect to the parties' intent, which is more likely to be reflected in handwritten or typed provisions.

The Parol Evidence Rule

Like the rules of construction, the parol evidence rule developed in the common law to ensure that the courts gave effect to integrated agreements. The rule excludes *extrinsic evidence*—evidence from outside the four corners of the writing—of prior or contemporaneous agreements that alter or contradict a written contract intended to be the final and complete expression of the parties. Although the word "parol" comes from the French word for "oral," extrinsic evidence may be either oral or written.

Here is how the rule works. Mike and Nancy orally agree that she will lease his store. They also agree that since the electrical supply is inadequate, they will share the costs of bringing it up to standard. Mike's lawyer draws up the lease, which states that Nancy will bear the entire cost of the electrical conversion. Nancy signs the lease without reading it closely. A court will not admit evidence of the earlier,

---

THE PAROLE EVIDENCE RULE:

1. Applies to written contracts where the writing is intended as a final, integrated agreement.
2. Generally *prohibits* the introduction of evidence prior to or contemporaneous with the creation of the written contract which would vary, alter, or contradict the contract.
3. Does *not prohibit* evidence offered to:
   a. Explain an ambiguity.
   b. Prove no genuine mutual assent occurred.
   c. Prove the contract was subject to a condition.
   d. Prove the contract was subsequently modified or replaced.

Figure 10.3 Summary of the Parole Evidence Rule.

---

contrary agreement, and Nancy will have to bear the full cost.

As Figure 10.3 shows, parol evidence is admissible in certain cases. A court will admit it to determine whether a contract actually is integrated, that is, whether it is the complete agreement of the parties. A court may also look to outside evidence to clarify the meaning of individual terms which are ambiguous or otherwise need clarification. Suppose Ice Cream Co. contracted with Steve to buy "your ice cream." Steve both manufactures his own and deals in ice cream manufactured by others. A court would look to the negotiations leading to the contract for clarification of the phrase.

The parol evidence rule will not bar proof of illegality, fraud, mistake, duress, or any other fact which would invalidate the contract. If a 14-year-old signs an integrated contract, a court will allow evidence of her lack of capacity. A party may also challenge an integrated agreement on the grounds that it lacked considera-

tion. For instance, a party might claim that a promise to pay was based purely on love and affection or on past services, either of which would invalidate the contract.

Finally, it is important to note that the parol evidence rule applies to evidence relating *only* to events or writings which took place before or at the same time as the agreement was executed. It does not exclude evidence of subsequent writings or events. Suppose Al's Haulage contracts with ABC Construction to remove all the rock from a job site. According to their integrated agreement, the amount of rock removed was to be measured by ABC engineers. As the job progressed, this procedure became burdensome, so the ABC field supervisor orally notified Al that field personnel would do the measurement. Al consented to the arrangement. In a breach of contract action, the court would accept evidence of the later agreement. But in the following case, the court rejected parole evidence.

A. Kemp Fisheries, Inc. v. Castle & Cooke, Inc.

852 F.2d 493 (9th Cir. 1988)

FACTS A. Kemp Fisheries needed a boat to fish for herring in Alaska. Kemp signed a letter of intent with Castle & Cooke, incorporating certain telexes they had exchanged, which was their agreement pending "preparation and execution of final documentation required for the bareboat charter and option to purchase." After reviewing drafts of the agreement with Kemp's attorney, Castle & Cooke sent the final agreement to Kemp's president. The final agreement was different from what he had understood the agreement to be. Specifically, he understood Castle & Cooke had warranted that the engines would be in good working order and that the freezing system would meet Kemp's needs. The agreement, however, disclaimed all warranties, express or implied, and stated that once Kemp took delivery of the boat, Castle & Cooke's responsibility for its condition ended. Nonetheless, Kemp's president executed the agreement without calling the discrepancies to Castle & Cooke's attention. During the herring season, two of the three engines used for freezing failed, and Kemp suffered losses on the herring catch. Kemp brought suit against Castle & Cooke. The trial court held that the agreement Kemp signed was ambiguous on the warranties question and admitted evidence of the parties' negotiations. Based on that evidence, she found that Castle & Cooke had warranted the engines to be in good repair and held Castle & Cooke liable.

ISSUE   Is evidence of prior negotiations admissible when the parties have expressed their intention that a writing serve as the exclusive embodiment of their agreement?

DECISION   No. Reversed. The agreement was complete and comprehensive. The contract did not contain an integration clause, but the letter of intent shows that the parties intended the agreement to be the "final documentation." The alleged agreements about the freezing system were not ones usually made in collateral documents. Further, they directly contradicted the agreement's waiver of all warranties. Finally, Kemp had had ample opportunity during the negotiations leading to the final agreement to express its understanding of the deal, yet it did not.

The UCC rules. The UCC parol evidence rule prohibits the contradiction of terms by extrinsic evidence where the parties' confirmatory memoranda agree and where the parties intend a writing to be a final expression of their agreement.

However, the UCC *does* permit terms to be explained or supplemented by evidence of the parties' course of dealings, of the usages of their trade, or of the course of the parties' performance. It also permits the introduction of consistent additional terms—not in writing—unless the court finds that both parties intended the writing to be a complete, exclusive statement of all the terms [UCC §2-202].

The drafters of the UCC rejected the assumption that because a writing is final on some

matters, it is final on all matters. For that reason, the rule speaks of "terms." Also, by permitting evidence of transactions between the parties and of the usages of their trade, the framers of the UCC intended that a court should apply to the terms the meaning which arises in the contract's commercial context. They insisted on a commercial—not legal—interpretation of the contract. Further, the UCC permits evidence relating to a contract's commercial context even when the language used in the contract appears unambiguous.

Course of dealing and usage of trade. When the UCC gap fillers (discussed in Chapter 6) do not apply, courts look to the course of dealing between the parties or to a usage of trade to imply the terms. The *course of dealing* is the way the parties have conducted business in the past, thus establishing a common understanding for interpreting their statements and conduct. A *usage of trade* is a practice or method of dealing which is used regularly in a certain place, location, or trade [UCC §1-205]. For example, in the thoroughbred horse business, a reference in a contract to a ''horse'' would clearly mean to people in the trade an unneutered male animal

at least 5 years old. The following case illustrates how a court uses these tools to determine the intentions of the parties and the terms of their contract.*

---

*For another view of the *Frigaliment* problem, see *A. J. Cunningham Packing Corp. v. Florence Beef Co.*, 785 F. 2d 348 (1st Circ. 1986), briefed in Chapter 31.

Frigaliment Importing Co. v. B.N.S. International Sales Corp

190 F. Supp. 116 (S.D.N.Y. 1960)

FACTS

A New York poultry processor negotiated in German a contract to sell chicken to a Swiss company which used a Czech middleman. The contract called for the poultry processor to supply frozen chicken in two weight classes. When the chicken arrived, it was not what the Swiss expected, and they sued for damages.

ISSUE

What is "chicken"?

DECISION

Plaintiff [the Swiss company] says "chicken" means a young chicken, suitable for broiling and frying. Defendant [the New York poultry processor] says "chicken" means any bird of the genus that meets contract specifications on weight and quality, including what it calls "stewing chicken." . . . Assuming that both parties were acting in good faith, the case nicely illustrates [U.S. Supreme Court Justice Oliver Wendell] Holmes' remark "that the making of a contract depends not on the agreement of two minds in one intention, but on the agreement of two sets of external signs—not on the parties' having meant the same thing but on their having said the same thing." I have concluded that plaintiff has not sustained its burden of persuasion that the contract used "chicken" in the narrower sense. . . .

Since the word "chicken" standing alone is ambiguous, I turn first to see whether the contract itself offers any aid to its interpretation. Plaintiff says the 1 1/2-2 lbs. birds [specified in the contract] necessarily had to be young chickens since older birds do not come in the size, hence the 2 1/2-3 lbs. birds must likewise be young. This is unpersuasive—a contract for "apples" of two different sizes could be filled with different kinds of apples even though only one species came in both sizes. Defendant notes that the contract called not simply for chicken but for "U.S. Fresh Frozen Chicken, Grade A, Government Inspected. . . ."

Defendant's witness Weininger, who operates a chicken eviscerating plant in New Jersey, testified, "Chicken is everything except a goose, a duck, and a turkey. Everything is a chicken, but then you have to say, you have to specify which category you want or that you are talking about. . . ." Sadina, who conducts a food inspection service, testified that he would consider any bird coming within the classes of "chick-en" in the Department of Agriculture's regulations to be a chicken. . . .

[Defendant] believed it could comply with the contract by delivering stewing chickens in 2¹/₂-3 lbs. size. Defendant's subjective intent would not be significant if this did not coincide with an objective meaning of "chicken." Here it did coincide with one of the dictionary meanings, with a definition in the Department of Agriculture Regulations to which the contract made at least oblique reference, with at least some usage in the trade, with the realities of the market, and with what plaintiff's spokesman had said. . . .

Modification and Rescission

An oral modification of a contract which the Statute requires to be in writing would have to be confirmed in writing if the *resulting* contract falls within the Statute. Suppose a buyer contracts for a printer at $450. The buyer later orders a $100 tractor feed to be added to it. The resulting contract for the printer plus tractor feed must be in writing. By contrast, if the buyer had ordered the two items together and then deleted the tractor feed, the resulting contract would not require a writing, though in this case it would certainly be a good idea to have one.

The parties to a contract may agree orally to rescind it unless the contract is for the transfer of an interest in land. The parties to the printer transaction can call it off. Again, if the transaction is of sufficient importance to require a writing, a written rescission is the best approach.

CONCLUSION

After reading this chapter, you might easily lose sight of the general rule that oral contracts are enforceable. Imagine, however, what it would be like if every contract required a writing. Every time you bought something at a grocery store, gas station, or discount store you would have to draw up and sign a contract. The inefficiency and frustration of such a requirement would cause great harm to our economic system.

Restricting the kinds of contracts which require a writing makes sense. Casual, everyday transactions normally do not result in disputes. Usually, little time passes between the contract's formation and its execution, minimizing the likelihood of problems.

In the absence of a writing, however, some contracts lend themselves to fraud and disputes of fact. The Statute of Frauds requires that these contracts, in particular, be evidenced by a writing. For example, purchasing or selling land is often the biggest monetary transaction in which the parties are ever involved. Much emotion is associated with such transactions. Also, considerable time often passes between the agreement and the performance, and dozens of problems can occur in the interval. The time lag and the emotions may cause the parties to forget the oral terms regarding details like furnishings. In the absence of a writing, it often becomes the word of one person against that of another. A writing avoids this type of dispute.

A third classification includes contracts which are neither casual nor covered by the Statute of Frauds, for example, contracts between a car owner and a mechanic to fix a car, between an interior decorator and a homeowner to remodel a home, or between two friends to venture into a partnership together. These transactions ordinarily do not require a writing. Nonetheless, in retrospect many parties to such contracts wish they had stated their agreement in writing because of later disagreements, conflicts, and legal expenses. So, if it is important, get it in writing!

A NOTE TO FUTURE CPA CANDIDATES

We encourage you to remember the Statute of Frauds by the MY LEGS acronym. The CPA exam has traditionally focused upon the Y, year, and G, goods over $500. Remember that whether an employment contract for 1 year must be in writing is dependent upon whether performance can be completed within 1 year of the date the contract was created. If the hired person can begin today or tomorrow, there is no problem. If the person is to begin later than this, the oral agreement is unenforceable. Do not forget that the Statute of Frauds is an exception to the general rule that oral contracts are enforceable.

The parole evidence rule frequently is tested on the CPA exam. Remember that the rule applies to all written contracts, not just those required to be in writing because of the Statute of Frauds. Be sure you understand Figure 10.3, and especially the fact that the Statute generally prevents the introduction of evidence prior to or contemporaneous with the creation of the written contract.

KEY WORDS

antenuptial agreement (217)
construe (228)
executor (220)
extrinsic (228)
integrated agreement (217)
leading object rule (220)
obligee (222)
obligor (222)
parol evidence rule (227)

part performance exception (219)
personal representative (220)
rules of construction (227)
signature (225)
Statute of Frauds (216)
suretyship (220)
writing (228)

DISCUSSION QUESTIONS

1. What is the purpose of the Statute of Frauds?
2. Name the six types of contracts which fall within the Statute of Frauds. Do they have anything in common? If so, what? Explain.
3. When does a sale of goods fall under the Statute of Frauds? Under what circumstances is a case removed from this prong of the Statute?
4. Construct a hypothetical case which fits under two categories of the Statute of Frauds. Construct one which fits under three.
5. What is the doctrine of part performance, and when is it applicable?
6. What is the leading object rule? When does it apply, and what is the rationale for it?
7. What are the rules of contract construction?
8. What is the parol evidence rule? What reasoning lies behind it?
9. If a written contract, after it is modified, is no longer within the Statute of Frauds, must the modification be in writing? Is an oral rescission of a written contract effective?

CASE PROBLEMS

1. The Erewhon College Pep Club entered into an oral contract with Marts Paper Co. for 1000 plastic cups with the club's name and college logo printed on them. The cost of the cups was $600. Midway through the manufacturing run, the Pep Club canceled its order. If Marts sues the Pep Club, is a court likely to find the Pep Club liable? Explain.
2. Debbie Kent owns Kent Kennels. Debbie called Charlottesville Supply Company and ordered five new kennel cages on credit, to be delivered. The supply company sent a written confirmation saying they had ordered eight cages from a manufacturer to be delivered directly to her. Debbie received the notice, noted the discrepancy, but decided to wait 3 weeks until delivery was due to see what actually was delivered. A carrier arrived with eight cages and told Debbie she had to take all or none of them. Debbie received all eight. Will Debbie's ability to return the extra three

cages turn on whether she is considered a merchant or not? Is whether the original agreement was for $500 or more a key factor in resolving this problem? Explain.

3. Reed entered into an oral contract to buy Smith's vacant building for $50,000. He gave Smith a $5000 deposit. They intended to reduce their agreement to writing later. Pursuant to their oral agreement, Reed took possession of the building with Smith's permission and made permanent and substantial improvements. Due to a rise in the price of similar real estate, Smith served notice on Reed to vacate the premises. Smith contends that the sales contract is unenforceable and that therefore Reed must vacate. Is Smith correct? Explain.

4. Lynn Judd entered into an oral contract with McKee Builders to have a cottage built on her lot at Cross Lake. The contract price was $89,000. McKee fell behind in its payments to Pilot Lumber Co. for lumber and supplies. Pilot notified Judd that it would not make any more deliveries to the site unless Judd agreed to pay for them if McKee did not. Judd reluctantly agreed, since the cabin had to be completed before winter. Which, if either, contract must be in writing to be enforceable? Explain.

5. Dick and Jane wanted to get married. However, both had concerns in regard to their personal situations. Dick had inherited money from his rich uncle. Jane was a successful CPA with a significantly greater income than Dick. Dick and Jane orally agreed that Dick would always retain the outright ownership of his inheritance and Jane's income would be considered her separate income during their marriage. Assuming the marriage later fails and a dispute about their agreement arises in divorce court, how would the court likely resolve the issue? Explain.

6. Berton agreed to buy Vassar's truck for $8000. Their written contract contained a clause stating the contract represented their final understanding, and it was signed by both parties. After paying Vassar and taking possession of the truck, Berton realized that Vas-

sar had removed the CB radio. The contract did not mention the CB radio, but Berton has brought suit for its value, alleging Vassar orally promised to leave it in the truck. Is Berton likely to win? How will Vassar defend?

7. Mike Vargo, a painter, entered into a written contract with Howard Katz to paint his four-story apartment building in Chicago. Because it was late fall, the parties agreed that Vargo would be paid on the basis of the percent of the total windows completed before winter set in. However, "window" was not defined. The parties subsequently agreed when it was impossible for Vargo to continue his fall painting. However, a dispute arose as to how many windows Vargo had painted. Katz claimed a window is an opening in the wall that is not a door, regardless of how many panes might be involved. In contrast, Vargo claimed that a window is the framework surrounding each separate pane of glass. Vargo brought suit for payment. Would the parole evidence rule apply in regard to the dispute as to the definition of a window? How would the court ultimately resolve this dispute? Explain.

8. On April 1, Dot Cady signed and mailed a letter containing an offer to sell Lyle Cook vacant land for $50,000. The letter stated the offer would expire on May 3. On the morning of May 3, Cook learned a major shopping center was to be built on the land next to Cady's lot. Cook immediately called Cady and accepted her offer. Three days later, he signed her offer and sent it back to her. Cady now refuses to transfer the land at the price stated in the offer. Explain.

9. Lorraine Krajewski hired Mel Harju to manage her restaurant, Spinach Greens. On June 25, Mel orally agreed to a 1-year contract and was to begin work on July 1. On June 28, Mel got a more lucrative offer to manage Camp Marigwen, a romantic restaurant on Lake Bisteneau. Mel accepted that offer and sent his regrets to Lorraine. Lorraine sent her lawyer to see Mel. Mel claims his contract with Lorraine is unenforceable. Is he correct? Explain.

10. Barney Brannon wrote and signed an offer to Byrd Eastham offering to purchase Eastham's

estate, Valencia. Eastham called Brannon and said he agreed to the offer. Before the closing and before Eastham signed and returned his offer, Brannon changed his mind. When Brannon failed to attend their closing, Eastham brought suit against him. Brannon claims he is not liable, since he and Eastham have no written contract. Is he right? Assuming Brannon and Eastham have an enforceable contract, would Brannon have a right to a countertop microwave oven that Eastham was supposed to leave in her house if their contract says nothing about it? Explain.

Third Parties

Under some circumstances, third parties have an enforceable interest in the performance of a contract. Suppose Herb is a painting contractor. His daughter, Carol, is a college student. Shortly before a new quarter starts, Herb contracts to paint Virginia's small house for $600, which they agree Virginia is to pay Carol. Although Carol has not promised performance, she is a third party beneficiary of their contract and she can enforce her right to the $600 against Virginia.

Now suppose Herb's contract to paint Virginia's house for $600 does not specify payment to Carol. He could later assign his right to receive the $600 to Carol. The assignment does not affect Virginia's duty to pay for Herb's services or Herb's duty to paint her house. When Carol informs Virginia of the assignment, Virginia must pay Carol when Herb finishes the job. But, Virginia could not assign her right to receive Herb's services to Scott, who needs his mansion painted. Since such an assignment would alter Herb's duty under his contract with Virginia, a court would not enforce the assignment against him.

It is important to note that normally no one other than the contracting parties has any rights or duties under a contract. But in some circumstances—as in the hypothetical situation above—a third party may have enforceable rights or may have to perform duties. This chapter considers instances in which such third parties are involved.

THIRD PARTY BENEFICIARIES

A *third party beneficiary* is a stranger to a contract who stands to benefit from it in some way. The contracting parties may intend to benefit the third party, in which case the third party is an *intended beneficiary*. For example, in the hypothetical situation above, Carol can enforce her right to the $600 against Virginia.

However, an *incidental* or *unintended beneficiary* has no right to enforce the contract because the parties did not intend to benefit this third party. Suppose Virginia's house is an eyesore. Her neighbor, Vince, wants her to paint it so that he can sell his for a better price. If Herb breaches his contract with Virginia, Vince cannot enforce the contract even though he will lose some profits on the sale of his home. Neither Virginia nor Herb intended to benefit him.

Intended Beneficiaries

Only intended beneficiaries have rights under contracts. Therefore, the contracting parties' intent at the time they contract determines a third party's status. Intended beneficiaries fall into two categories: creditor beneficiaries and donee beneficiaries.

Creditor beneficiaries. When a promisee's purpose in making a contract is to satisfy a debt or a duty owed to a third party, the third party beneficiary is a *creditor beneficiary*. The next case has exemplified the creditor beneficiary relationship for generations of students.

Lawrence v. Fox

20 N.Y. 268 (1859)

> Holly lent Lawrence $300. He told Lawrence that he owed Fox that sum, and Lawrence agreed to pay Fox the $300 the next day. Lawrence failed to pay Fox, and Fox brought suit. The jury found for Fox and the intermediate appellate court affirmed.

ISSUE   Could Fox enforce the contract between Holly and Lawrence?

DECISION   Yes. Affirmed. Lawrence argued that he made his promise to Holly, not to Fox, and therefore Fox could not enforce it. However, Lawrence's obligation as the promisor does not rest on any relationship between him and Fox. Rather, the law gives effect to the parties' agreement creating the duty to pay Fox. When a promise is made to one for the benefit of another, the beneficiary may bring an action for its breach.

For a third party to become a creditor beneficiary, the debtor-creditor relationship must already exist. The debtor (Holly) makes a contract with the promisor (Lawrence) by which he intends to discharge his debt to the third party (Fox). Although not a party to the Holly-Lawrence contract, Fox is a creditor beneficiary and can enforce the contract against the promisor. (See Figure 11.1.)

The creditor beneficiary situation is quite common in two instances involving consumers. The first is loan assumptions. Suppose a home buyer pays 20 percent down and assumes the seller's mortgage to Dixie Bank. Dixie becomes the third party beneficiary to the contract between the buyer and the seller and, if the loan is not repaid, may collect from either party. The second instance is apartment lease assumptions. Suppose John assumes Mary's lease at the Canterbury Apartments. Canterbury is the third party creditor beneficiary of their agreement and may look to either John or Mary for payment should John default.

Donee beneficiaries. When the promisee's intent in making the contract is to confer a gift on a third party, the third party beneficiary is a *donee beneficiary*. Traditionally, the law has lumped into this category all enforceable third party beneficiary contracts which do not involve a preexisting duty.

A donee beneficiary has enforceable rights against the promisor. The most common donee beneficiary contract is a life insurance policy. Suppose Judy buys a policy from New Caledonia Life, naming her children as beneficiaries. She intends the proceeds to provide for their needs when she dies. On her death, her

---

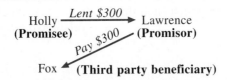

STATUS OF FOX	COULD FOX RECOVER FROM HOLLY?	COULD FOX RECOVER FROM LAWRENCE?
Creditor beneficiary	Yes	Yes
Donee beneficiary	No	Yes

Figure 11.1 Third Party Beneficiary Recovery. Although the case of *Lawrence v. Fox* involved a recovery by Fox against only Lawrence. Fox could have recovered in the alternative from Holly.

children can require New Caledonia Life to pay the proceeds according to the terms of its contract with Judy.

Another common type of donee beneficiary contract is a child support agreement when couples separate or divorce. As the next case indicates, the donee beneficiaries' rights survive the promisor's death.

Mitchell v. COMBANK/Winter Park

429 So. 2d 1319 (Fla. Dist. Ct. App., 1983)

FACTS   Richard S. Patrick and his wife entered into a child support agreement when they divorced. Richard agreed to pay "all reasonable college expenses" for their children. All four of their children attended college before Richard's death, but he had not paid their expenses. The children filed a claim with Richard's personal representative, who denied it. The trial court upheld the denial.

ISSUE   Could the children enforce the college expense provision of the support agreement?

DECISION   Yes. Reversed. In the absence of an agreement to do so, parents have no legal obligation to provide a college education for their children. However, Richard agreed to do so. The children incurred those expenses, and Richard breached the agreement by failing to pay them. The children are third party donee beneficiaries of their father's executory agreement. They may enforce their rights, subject to any defenses which their father had.

Incidental Beneficiaries

Unintended or *incidental* third party beneficiaries of a contract have no enforceable rights because the original parties did not intend to give them any. An unintended beneficiary stands in the same position as any other stranger to the contract, regardless of how great an incidental benefit she may gain from it. Suppose George decides to install a swimming pool in his backyard. He tells Harriet that she may use it when Pools, Inc., finishes it. However, Pools breaches its contract with George and does not complete construction. Harriet has no rights against Pools. The next case presented a court with a much more difficult determination of whether a person was an intended beneficiary.

Paradiso v. Apex Investigators & Security Company, Inc.

91 A.D. 929, 458 N.Y.S.2d 234 (N.Y. App. Div. 1983)

FACTS   Paradiso managed a Pathmark Supermarket. Pathmark contracted with Apex to supply unarmed guards for Paradiso's supermarket. One evening shortly after closing, the uniformed guard got permission from Paradiso to go to the bathroom. Allegedly the guard failed to lock the door to the supermarket properly before he left. A few minutes later, two armed robbers burst into the room where Paradiso was counting the day's receipts. One of them shot him in the arm. Paradiso brought suit against Apex, claiming that he was a third party beneficiary of its contract with Pathmark. However, the Pathmark-Apex contract, the guards' job descriptions, and Apex's rules and regulations did not specifically create an obligation to store managers.

ISSUE   Was Paradiso a third party beneficiary of the Apex-Pathmark contract?

DECISION   No. Before an injured party may recover as a third party beneficiary, the contract provisions must clearly show that the parties intended to confer a direct benefit on him. As a matter of law, it could not be said that the parties intended to provide for Paradiso's protection.

The *Paradiso* decision raises a number of questions. What was the supermarket's real intent in creating the contract? The store could have made it clear that the manager and other employees were intended beneficiaries, but apparently it did not. Should the store owner be forced to protect employees? Do anything at all? If not, should the owner be able to choose whom or what to protect? These are obviously ethical, not legal, questions.

Vesting of beneficiary's rights. A person's rights under a contract are said to *vest* when they become fixed and enforceable by a court. However, vesting is one concept that is easier to understand than to apply.

Parties creating a third party beneficiary contract may specify when and how a third party beneficiary's interest will vest. The easiest vesting case is one in which the contracting parties specify that vesting is to occur upon creation of their contract. In contrast, life insurance contracts usually reserve to the *insured,* the person whose life is covered by the policy, the right to change the intended beneficiary at any time. Upon the insured's death, the right to the policy proceeds vests in the person whom the insured last named as beneficiary.

When a contract fails to specify the time of vesting, the courts have a range of options available to them. And, there is no consensus as to which is preferred. The most common choices are:

1. The interest vests at the contract's creation.
2. The interest vests on the third party learning of the promise.
3. The interest vests when the third party does something in reliance on the promise.

Lawrence v. Fox is an example of the first choice. *Mitchell v. COMBANK/Winter Park* is an example of the third.

ASSIGNMENT OF RIGHTS

A third party beneficiary's interest comes into existence when the contract is created. In an assignment the assignee's interest is created after the original contract and is not a part of it.

The Elements of an Assignment

In analyzing an assignment, the place to start is the original contract. An ordinary bilateral contract contains two sets of rights and duties.

Suppose Maryann agrees to buy a $1000 system from John's Stereo Store. They sign a contract which contains two promises, each involving a right and duty. In this example, the rights and duties are:

Maryann's right:	Receive stereo
Maryann's duty:	Pay $1000
John's right:	Receive $1000
John's duty:	Supply stereo

Thus, an *assignment* is a transfer of an existing contractual right from a party to a contract to a third party. Now John's Stereo Store wants to assign its right to receive the $1000 to AME Electronics in exchange for inventory. John,

the person making the assignment, is the *assignor*. AME, the person to whom the assignment is made, is the *assignee*. AME is also the *obligee*, the person to whom a duty is owed—in this case, Maryann's duty to pay. Maryann is the *obligor*, the person who owes a duty. Once Maryann has the stereo, AME has a right to the $1000. John has no more rights to it. (See Figure 11.2.)

Assignability

In order to transfer contract rights, the assignor must intend to extinguish his or her rights under the contract. The assignment must clearly iden-

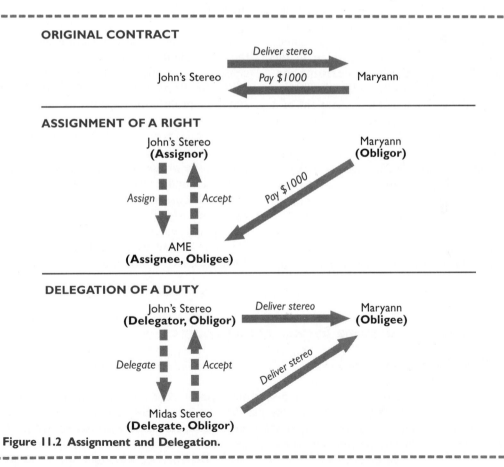

ORIGINAL CONTRACT

John's Stereo — Deliver stereo → / Pay $1000 ← Maryann

ASSIGNMENT OF A RIGHT

John's Stereo **(Assignor)**   Maryann **(Obligor)**

Assign / *Accept*   Pay $1000

AME **(Assignee, Obligee)**

DELEGATION OF A DUTY

John's Stereo **(Delegator, Obligor)** — Deliver stereo → Maryann **(Obligee)**

Delegate / *Accept*   Deliver stereo

Midas Stereo **(Delegate, Obligor)**

Figure 11.2 Assignment and Delegation.

tify the contract's subject matter. And, the terms of the assignment must be communicated to the assignee, who must accept them.

An assignment does not require consideration, though consideration must be present if the assignee is to have the right to enforce the assignment against the assignor. Finally, as with all contracts, assignments within the Statute of Frauds must be in writing. For example, an assignment of an interest in land requires a writing.

Most contract rights are assignable. However, there are a number of categories in which rights are not assignable.

Future Contracts. An assignment is a transfer of an existing right in a contract. Rights under a contract to be formed in the future are not assignable. Since no contract exists at the time of the assignment, there are no rights to be assigned.

Contracts which are to be formed in the future should not be confused with existing contracts which are to be performed in the future. Most assignments, such as an assignment of a right to receive payment for services, are to be performed in the future.

Increased burden. Rights may not be assigned which would increase the burden or risk assumed by the obligor. Assume that each month, Generic Corp. agrees to deliver to its plant in Cincinnati all the widgets Queen City Manufacturing needs. Queen City cannot assign its right to receive them to Boomerang Ltd., whose Australian plant needs five times as many widgets per month. This assignment would impose an increased burden on Generic, the obligor.

Personal or unique services. When a contract involves highly personal or unique services, those rights may not be assigned. Suppose Ralph hires Susan to give him ten piano lessons at $20 per lesson. He then assigns his rights under the contract to Ivan. Ivan may not enforce the assignment because it changes Susan's duties. Ivan's talent may be quite different from Ralph's. However, once Susan has executed her portion of the contract by performing, she may assign her rights. So, if Susan gives Ralph the ten lessons and all that remains to be performed on the contract is his payment, she may assign her right to receive the $200.

Statutory prohibitions. A statute may prohibit the assignment of a particular right. Liquor licenses, government pensions, alimony, and child support payments are common subjects of statutory prohibitions against assignment.

Contractual prohibitions. If a contract states that it may not be assigned, courts usually will enforce the provision. But, where assignments do not fall under any of the exceptions or prohibitions discussed in this section, some courts view nonassignment provisions with disfavor, particularly where the promisee has no valid objection to the transfer. The next case brief illustrates such a situation.

Pino v. Spanish Broadcasting System of Florida, Inc.

564 So. 2d 186 (Fla. Ct. App. 1990)

FACTS   Beatriz Pino signed a 5-year employment contract with two radio stations—WCMQ, Inc. and Great Joy, Inc. Pino was a disc jockey and radio announcer. In her contract there was a covenant not to compete clause which stated that if she left before the end of her contract, she could not engage in the broadcasting business in Dade or Broward Counties, Florida. The contract also contained an assignment clause. A year later, the two stations sold and assigned their assets to Spanish

Broadcasting Systems of Florida, Inc. (SBS). The sale involved Pino's employment contract. Pino worked for SBS for 3 years and then left to work for Viva, an SBS competitor. SBS sought to enforce the covenant not to compete. Pino asserted that the covenant was not assignable. SBS won at the trial level.

ISSUE

Was Pino's contract assignable and therefore enforceable by SBS even though it contained a covenant not to compete clause?

DECISION

Yes. Affirmed. Pino had agreed to both the covenant not to compete and the clause permitting assignment when she signed her contract. The law strongly supports the policy of upholding contracts to create uniformity and assurance that commercial transactions will be enforced.

The above case brings up several important issues. Covenants not to compete, which restrain a person's future employment prospects, are generally enforceable if they are reasonable as to their restrictions in geography and time. Thus, if the contract has stipulated that Pino could *never* work as a disc jockey anywhere in the southeastern United States, the clause would have been illegal as an unreasonable restraint in trade. Of course, the clause in Pino's contract, which was legal, remained legal once it was assigned. Restraints in trade will be discussed in greater detail in Chapter 44, Antitrust.

Could Pino have gotten out of her contract at the time it was assigned to SBS by arguing that her services were personal and unique and therefore not assignable? The answer is no as long as SBS, the assignee, could perform its end of the employment contract with Pino without negatively altering her interests and duties in that job. The fact that she remained with SBS 3 years after the assignment strongly suggests that her employment duties must not have changed materially. Keep in mind that Pino possessed contract rights that were legally assignable by her employer. These rights must be distinguished from Pino's duties as a disk jockey and announcer which, in her case, would almost certainly not be *delegable* to anyone; another person might not be as talented as Pino. You will learn more about the concept of delegable duties later in this chapter.

Rights and Obligations of Parties

An assignee stands in the same legal position as his assignor. To illustrate, suppose under a contract that Alan agrees to pay Beth $400 on May 15. On May 1, Beth assigns her right to receive the $400 to Calvin. On May 5, she assigns the same right to Debbie. A majority of states hold that the first assignee, Calvin, will prevail upon notice to the obligor, Alan. A minority of states holds that the first assignee to notify the obligor will prevail. Thus, Debbie would prevail if she provided first notice to Alan. Assume, for example, that the stereo Maryann bought from John's Stereo did not work right. She could raise this defense against John's assignee, AME, in an action for the balance due on the contract.*

Notice of assignment. An assignee has the legal burden of notifying the obligor regardless of any promise by the assignor to notify the obligor.

---

* In Part V, you will learn that in some instances an assignee is *not* subject to most of the obligor's potential defenses, including failure of consideration. Contracts of this type are called *negotiable instruments* and are the subject of UCC Articles 3 and 4. Examples of negotiable instruments include checks and certain types of loan agreements. Quite often the note evidencing a student loan or an auto loan is a negotiable instrument. A firm grasp of the principles of assignment law is critical to an understanding of Articles 3 and 4.

Thus, if AME does not notify Maryann of the assignment and she pays John, AME could look only to John for payment—not to Maryann.

Successive assignments. Sometimes an assignor assigns the same rights to two or more assignees. Jurisdictions have split on how to deal with this problem. Put another way, the assignee "steps into the shoes of his assignor" and gains whatever rights his assignor had and is subject to any defenses the obligor could have raised against the assignor.

DELEGATIONS OF DUTIES

Rights are assigned; duties are *delegated.* An effective *delegation* requires an expression of an intent to transfer a clearly identified duty to a *delegate,* the person to whom the duty is delegated. The delegate must manifest a willingness to assume the duty. Generally, the obligee does not have to be notified of the delegation or consent to it. Again, let's suppose Maryann buys a stereo from John's Stereo Store. John does not have the stereo in stock, so by contract he transfers his duty to provide the stereo to Midas Sounds. Thus, John has delegated his duty to Midas, probably accompanied by an assignment of his right to receive $1000 from Maryann.

At this point, John is the *delegator,* the person transferring a duty, and Midas is the *delegate,* the person assuming responsibility for performance. However, it is critically important to note that *both* the delegator and the delegate are liable for performance to the obligee—Maryann. Midas Stereo, as delegate, is also the obligor, since it has the duty to fulfill John's obligation. (See Figure 11.2.)

It should be noted that the delegate's agreement to assume the duties under an assigned contract results in a third party creditor beneficiary contract in regard to the creditor. Why? Because an assignment agreement is a separate, new contract. The creditor is the beneficiary of the delegate's promise to pay the debt on the original contract. To illustrate, in our stereo example, Maryann is the third party beneficiary of Midas's promise to accept payment responsibility of John's contract with Maryann.

Unique Skills, Training, or Abilities

Duties are not delegable if performance by another person would vary the performance due to the obligee. In particular, duties involving unique skills, training, or abilities are not delegable. Contracts to manufacture specialized goods, to provide personal services, or to do unique construction work are not delegable. Similarly, contracts to perform professional services are not delegable because they are founded on the client's trust and on the provider's discretion.

Duties which do not depend on the obligor's unique qualifications may be delegated. Simple construction project contracts, for instance, normally are delegable, since reputable contractors are accustomed to building in accordance with specified plans. Similarly, duties to pay money, to manufacture standard goods (like nails), or to supply standard goods (like blank 20-pound bond paper) are delegable.

Rights and Liabilities After Delegation

A valid assignment ordinarily ends the assignor's rights. However, a delegation does not relieve the delegator of the obligation to perform until performance is complete.

After an effective delegation, the delegate is primarily liable to the obligee, but the delegator remains secondarily liable. So, if the delegate does not perform, the delegator must. In that event, the delegator may recover damages from the delegate. Suppose Eleanor buys Fritz's home. As part of the deal, she agrees to assume Fritz's obligations under his mortgage with Third Savings & Loan. Should Eleanor fail to pay off the mortgage, Fritz will be liable on it. If the rule were otherwise, Fritz would have no incentive to delegate to a responsible person and thereby protect the obligee's interest. Thus, the law balances the delegator's interest in being able to delegate against the obligee's interest in performance. We will discuss mortgage assumptions in Chapter 42.

Novation. The delegator can avoid all liability if the obligee agrees to substitute the delegate's promise of performance for the delegator's. This agreement is called a *novation*. In the last example, if the savings & loan agrees to accept Eleanor as its obligor and to release Fritz's obligation under the original mortgage, it has agreed to a novation. Novations are discussed in more detail in the next chapter.

Assignments which include delegations

Sometimes an assignment includes a delegation of duties. Suppose Al assigns to Charlene "all my rights and interests in a contract between Bob and me for the purchase of his farm." It seems clear from this language that Charlene is getting Al's right to buy the farm. Also, she would seem to be obligated to perform Al's duties to Bob in accordance with the contract. In this case, that probably means paying the purchase price. However, until recently, the common law construed language like that in Al and Charlene's contract as only assigning rights, not delegating duties.

The UCC takes the modern approach. It provides that an "assignment of 'the contract' or of 'all my rights under the contract' or an assignment in similar general terms" also constitutes a delegation of the duties under the contract, unless the circumstances indicate otherwise [UCC §2-210(4)].

If a contract provision, however, bars assignment of "this contract" or "the contract," under the common law rights under the contract could be assigned but duties could not. Thus, if a contract to build a house contained a provision barring assignment, the contractor could assign its right to receive payment but not its duty to build the house. The UCC has adopted this approach [UCC §2-210(3)]. This rule probably reflects a recognition that when laypersons contract, they are often unaware of the distinction between assignment and delegation, and that it is delegation which really concerns them.

CONCLUSION

The key to distinguishing between third party beneficiary relationships on the one hand and assignments and delegations on the other lies in identifying when the third party's interest in the contract comes into existence. If the contract itself creates the interest, the third party is a third party beneficiary. If the interest is transferred after the contract is in existence, the third party is either an assignee of a delegate.

Third party beneficiary contracts are common, but they are not of critical importance to the businessperson. The law of assignments and delegations, however, is. It is a critical building block in business law.

Assignments are commonly utilized in:

- Agency and partnership relationships.
- Real estate transactions.
- Landlord-tenant relationships.
- Sales contract situations.
- Commercial paper (checks and notes).
- Documents of title (warehouse receipts and bills of lading).
- Secured transactions.

A NOTE TO FUTURE CPA CANDIDATES

Figure 11.1, illustrating the *Lawrence v. Fox* case, is an important figure for you to understand. Only a creditor or donee beneficiary can recover from a breaching promisor. An incidental beneficiary cannot. To illustrate, if Hawkins is hired by the City of Erewhon to conduct training courses for unemployed citizens, an unemployed citizen would not be able to recover against Hawkins for his breach of contract, his failure to actually perform such services. Why? Such a citizen would be considered an incidental beneficiary, someone not directly related to the contract.

A party can normally assign a contract unless the contract specifically prohibits assignment. Generally the right to receive compensation under a contract can be freely assigned. The delegation of duties under the assigned contract is subject to greater scrutiny. An architect could not unilaterally assign to another architectural firm a contract to design a ten-story building. However, under the law it would be acceptable for Sears Home Improvement to assign to another firm the duty to install gutters on a home.

It should be remembered that without a release or a novation, the assignor will remain liable on the contract. Also, the assignee generally holds no more rights than those held by the assignor. The major exception of this rule is tested on another portion of the CPA exam, Commercial Paper (UCC, Article 3), in regard to the holder in due course. We cover commercial paper in Part VII. Finally, a party who makes payment to an assignor in good faith and without notice of an assignment is not subsequently liable to the assignee. The assignee must be sure to notify the obligor party of the assignment.

KEY WORDS

assignee (241)
assignment (241)
assignor (241)
creditor beneficiary (237)
delegate (244)
delegation (244)
delegator (244)
donee beneficiary (238)

incidental beneficiary (237)
intended beneficiary (237)
obligee (241)
obligor (241)
third party beneficiary (237)
unintended beneficiary (237)

DISCUSSION QUESTIONS

1. Name two ways in which a third party can obtain rights from a contract to which he or she is not a party, and briefly describe each.
2. Describe three types of beneficiaries. Which had enforceable rights, and why?
3. What is the difference between an assignment and a delegation? When is an assignment also a delegation?
4. What are the requirements for a valid assignment?
5. What is the majority rule when there have been successive assignments of the same right? What is the minority rule? Explain.
6. Why are rights which are personal in nature nonassignable?
7. What are the requirements for an effective delegation?
8. Give an example of nondelegable duty.
9. What are the rights and liabilities of the parties after delegation?
10. Generally, how are nonassignment clauses viewed by the courts?

CASE PROBLEMS

1. Robert Leitz owns a parcel of land encumbered by a mortgage securing Leitz's note to State Bank. Leitz sold the land to Bloom, who assumed the mortgage note. Bloom did not execute any paperwork with State Bank. However, she did begin making the monthly mortgage payments. Although she had the resources to continue making the payments, Bloom decided to stop when she moved to another city. Leitz claims he has no liability to the bank because Bloom agreed to stand in his place. Bloom claims she is not liable to State Bank because she never directly promised to pay the bank. State Bank has brought lawsuits against both Leitz and Bloom. Would Leitz have liability to the bank? Would Bloom? Explain.
2. Charley MacAdams entered into a written contract with Bobby Critcher to restore his

valuable 1967 Corvette. Critcher selected MacAdams because of his excellent reputation in working with collector cars made of fiberglass, like the Corvette. MacAdams became heavily backlogged and assigned the restoration contract to Eric Smith, a well-known restorer of pre–World War II cars. The contract is silent as to assignment. Critcher has objected to the assignment and taken back his car. Did MacAdams breach his contract with Critcher? Explain.

3. Ruckelman entered into a contract with Treese to paint Treese's house in return for Treese paying Ruckelman's niece, Morley, $1500. The payment to Morley was intended as a gift to celebrate her graduation from college. Ruckelman properly completed his painting, but Treese has yet to pay Morley. Treese contends that Morley is merely an incidental beneficiary, since under the contract she had nothing to do with Ruckelman's duty to paint or his duty to pay. If Morley brings suit for payment, will Treese likely be found to have liability? Will Ruckelman? Explain.

4. Barr entered into a contract with Gray which required that Gray construct a warehouse on Barr's land. The contract specifically provided that Gray had to use Apex Corp. pipe fittings for all plumbing. Gray did not use Apex fittings. Apex had learned of the provision in the Barr-Gray contract and, in anticipation of receiving the order, manufactured additional fittings. Is Apex entitled to damages resulting from Gray's breach? Explain.

5. Debbie Burt is a beauty queen. She agreed to appear for a day at LeBarron's Furniture Store to promote a sale on waterbeds. Burt sprained her ankle the day before she was to appear. She called her friend, Madge Sullivan, and asked her to fill in. While Sullivan, too, is pretty, LeBarron's customers were very disappointed. After an hour, LeBarron's sent Sullivan home. Sullivan now wants to recover her full fee from LeBarron's, but LeBarron's is only willing to pay her for an hour. If Sullivan brings suit, will LeBarron's prevail? Explain.

6. The Chicago Winds basketball team drafted Carlos Spaht, a college all-American. The team sent Carlos a $2 million offer, but he decided to go to divinity school instead. So he assigned the offer to his favorite professor, Dick Spears. Spears contacted a political science professor, who served as the college pre-law advisor, who told him the assignment was proper. Spears immediately signed the offer and mailed it back to the Winds, quit his teaching job, and headed for Chicago to begin his pro career. The team claims it has no obligation to Spears. Spears cannot reclaim his university job because of a hiring freeze. Will the Winds prevail in a breach of contract lawsuit brought by Spears? Explain.

7. Laurie Morrow owed Raines Corp. $1000 on a sales contract. Raines assigned the contract to State Bank. Raines had given the bank an address and phone number for Morrow that were incorrect. While the bank attempted to secure correct data, Morrow paid Raines the $1000 ahead of time. On the day the sum was due, State Bank reached Morrow, who told the bank of the payment. Meanwhile, Raines had filed for bankruptcy. If State Bank sues Morrow for payment, will State Bank win? Why?

8. Harry Wright bought a new stereo system from Herb Huskie. Wright gave Huskie a $1000 note. Huskie assigned the note to Ike Illini. Ike forgot to notify Harry. Not knowing of the assignment of the note, Harry made three payments to Herb, who then disappeared. Ike has demanded the three payments from Harry. Would Ike be likely to prevail in an action against Harry for the three payments? Would your answer be different if Herb had promised Ike that he would notify Harry of the assignment but had intentionally not done so? Explain.

9. Carl Eberle bought a blue 1966 Mustang convertible from Delores Rinke. Rinke had indicated to Eberle that the car's prior owner had completely restored its drive train. Rinke took as partial payment Eberle's personal note for $4000. Rinke assigned the note to Ahmed

Rifai. Later, Eberle learned that the car's engine had only been painted, and she is now confronted with a major overhaul expense. Eberle has notified Rifai that he is reducing his payments on account of Rinke's innocent misrepresentation. Under contract law, can Eberle raise this defense against Rifai? Must Eberle first raise this defense against Rinke? Explain.

10. Charley Bartels took out a life insurance policy on himself with Liberty Life. Bartels named his girlfriend, Eileen Dolan, as the beneficiary. Bartels did not tell her about the policy. Several months later, Dolan broke up with Bartels. Shortly thereafter, Bartels changed the beneficiary to his business partner, Dennis DiMarzio. Two weeks later, Charley died in a car crash. Eileen now claims she has a right to the proceeds of the insurance policy. Is a court likely to agree? Explain.

Performance and Remedies for Nonperformance

Our system of doing business based on contracts works well. Of the millions, if not billions, of contracts made each year, only a very few end up in court. The system is essentially self-regulating. People make a contract and then carry it out. But, when one party fails to perform, the courts stand ready to provide a remedy, since a contract is by definition an agreement that the courts will enforce. This chapter describes performance and the remedies a court may provide in the event of nonperformance.

CLASSIFICATIONS OF CONDITIONS TO PERFORMANCE

Often, one party's performance takes place at the same time as the other party's. For instance, an agreement whereby David will buy Kathi's calculator would be understood to call for simultaneous performance. However, the parties could make performance dependent on an event or circumstance happening or not happening. Such contracts are termed *conditional*.

The presence of the word "if" normally reveals the presence of a condition. Suppose David told Kathi that he would buy her calculator for $15 if the professor let him enroll in the advanced statistics course. The contract is conditional.

All conditions are categorized as:

- Concurrent, precedent, or subsequent
- Either express or implied

We will examine all five categories in this section.

Concurrent Conditions

A *concurrent condition* exists when the parties are to exchange performances simultaneously. Each party's obligation depends upon the other party's performance. If Kathi simply sells her calculator to Dave, the conditions are concurrent.

Unless the parties specify otherwise, the courts treat promises as mutually dependent, so that performance will occur simultaneously. In essence, the courts imply concurrent conditions. Suppose Kathi and Dave agree on the sale of the calculator, but fail to specify when delivery and payment will occur. The court will imply concurrent conditions. Concurrent conditions are the norm for express contracts, which include virtually all consumer transactions.

Conditions Precedent

When parties agree on a *condition precedent* as a part of a contract's terms, the condition must exist or occur before either party must perform. If the condition remains unsatisfied, the parties' obligations never come into existence. In the hypothetical situation above, David's obligation to buy Kathi's calculator does not mature unless the instructor admits him to the course (see Figure 12-1).

Many real estate purchase contracts contain conditions precedent. A clause might read, "The buyer's obligation under this contract is conditional upon the buyer obtaining a mortgage loan in the amount of $90,000 at 12% per annum for a period of 25 years. The buyer's obtaining the loan is a condition precedent to the parties' obligations to perform the terms of the contract.

However, if performance depends on the arrival of a certain time in the future, its occurrence is not a condition precedent. It is simply the time at which performance is to occur. Suppose Liquidators, Inc., agrees to buy all of a store's remaining stock and fixtures when its going out of business sale ends. If the store fails to turn over the goods and fixtures, the only question before the court would be whether the sale has ended, not whether the store was obligated to perform. Similarly, if the performance were set for September 28, 1994, the arrival of that date is not a condition precedent.

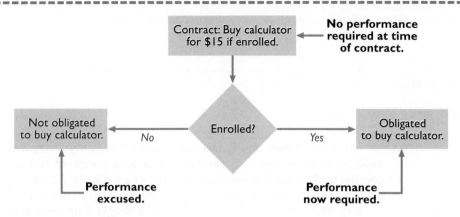

Figure 12.1 Condition Precedent.

Conditions Subsequent

A *condition subsequent* discharges a party's duty to perform and terminates the contractual obligations if a specified event occurs at any time during the period covered by the contract. Now suppose David agrees to pay Kathi $15 for her calculator. They also agree that if the course is canceled, he can return the calculator to her and get his money back. The cancellation of the course is the condition subsequent (see Figure 12-2).

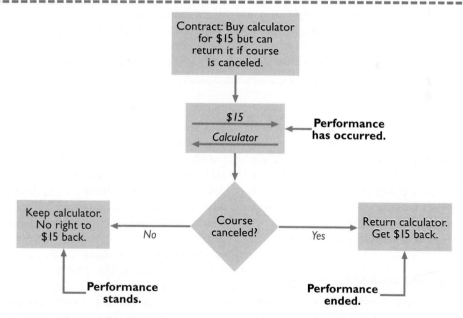

Figure 12.2 Condition Subsequent.

Courts do not regard conditions subsequent with great favor. Often, as in the next case, these clauses produce such great inequities that courts refuse to enforce them.

Burger King Corp. v. Family Dining, Inc.

426 F. Supp. 485 (E.D. Pa. 1977)

FACTS

In 1963, Family Dining and Burger King agreed that Family Dining would have an exclusive territorial right to develop Burger King franchised restaurants in two counties for 90 years if it built approximately one a year, for a total of ten or more by 1973. For reasons that were not entirely its fault, Family Dining did not construct its tenth restaurant until 1975. Until late 1973, Burger King never interpreted the development rate literally. At times Family Dining had fallen behind or gone ahead of that rate. Burger King sought a declaratory judgment that it was no longer bound by the exclusivity provision of the agreement.

ISSUE

Would giving effect to the condition subsequent result in an unjust forfeiture of Family Dining's rights under the contract?

DECISION

Yes. The development rate was a condition subsequent, not a promise. The territorial provision, however, promised long-term exclusivity to induce Family Dining to develop the two counties within a certain time. Giving strict effect to the condition involves divesting Family Dining of exclusivity, which would amount to a *forfeiture*, the loss of a right as a penalty for nonperformance. Family Dining would lose something of incalculable value, based on its investment in developing the area, the significant risks it assumed, and the fact that some 76 years of exclusivity remain. Yet, the breach caused Burger King only a relatively modest injury.

Why would Burger King suddenly want to get out of the exclusivity clause? A more conservative court might have chosen to ignore Family Dining's potential economic harm. Should it be considered? To speculate, it would appear that Burger King was looking for an out to gain new opportunities for the sale of franchises, possibly for more money and with less exclusivity.

Express and implied conditions

If the parties impose a condition by words in the contract, it is an *express condition*. Express conditions—we have seen a number of exam-

ples already—often begin with words like "if," "on condition that," "subject to," or "provided that." Express conditions are an important preventive law tool because they permit parties to avoid liability when they know in advance that the occurrence of some event would make performance burdensome or impossible.

Sometimes, we have seen, contracts omit key terms, such as the time and place of delivery and payment. In this case, the courts imply concurrent conditions. Such conditions are called *conditions implied-in-law* because the law supplies the term.

In other cases, the language of the contract, the conduct of the parties, or the circumstances indicate that a condition exists. When a court implies conditions based on evidence of conduct or circumstance, they are *conditions implied-in-fact.* Suppose Randolph's Upholstery, Inc., contracts with Shreve's Antiques to reupholster twelve Victorian chairs in whatever color leather they specified in exchange for $2800. The chairs are for resale in Shreve's store. Because the value of the chairs depends on the quality and authenticity of their upholstery, Randolph would be justified in treating Shreve's choice of a color as a condition implied-in-fact. In other words, it has no duty to perform until Shreve fulfills the condition. (*Note:* A court could impose an implied-in-law condition that Shreve has only a reasonable time in which to choose the color.) The following case is a fairly typical example of a court imposing an implied-in-fact condition.

Merrill Lynch, Pierce, Fenner & Smith, Inc. v. B.C. Rogers & Sons, Inc.

696 F.2d 1113 (5th Cir. 1983)

FACTS

Rogers began negotiating with a local bank for a $5 million loan, which would be partially guaranteed by the Farmers Home Administration. While willing to make the loan, the bank did not want to retain the guaranteed portion. For that reason, Rogers contracted with Merrill Lynch to place or purchase the guaranteed portion of the loan. Rogers was to pay a fee based on the amount of the guaranteed portion of the loan. Two days before the closing, the bank announced that it had decided to retain the guaranteed portion. Rogers had no influence on its decision, which resulted in his paying a significantly higher interest rate on the loan. As a result of the bank's action, Merrill Lynch's services were unnecessary. Rogers refused to pay the fee to Merrill Lynch, which brought suit. The trial court denied recovery.

ISSUE

Was the contract subject to an implied condition that the guaranteed portion of the loan would be available for placement?

DECISION

Yes. Judgment affirmed. Certain events excuse performance. They are not within the contract because the parties would not have contracted had they thought at the time of contracting that such events would occur. Thus, a party's duty to perform is excused if: (1) the parties contracted on the basis of the continued existence of a specific state of things which has ceased to exist by the time for performance, (2) the promisor was not at fault, and (3) the promisor could not have anticipated the crucial event. Here, Rogers's contract with Merrill Lynch centered on placing the guaranteed portion of the loan. Both parties assumed that it would be available for that purpose. Therefore, the contract's purpose ceased to exist when the bank decided to retain the guaranteed portion.

The bank was undoubtedly concerned about the associated regulations tied to the government guaranteed loan. Merrill Lynch, an international brokerage house, is in the business of spreading investment risks for a fee. However, in this case the fee was to come from brokering the guaranteed loan to investors. As *Merrill Lynch* indicates, occurrence of an event unforeseen by the parties which alters the essence of the contract ends it without liability. The occurrence of such an implied-in-fact condition discharges the parties' obligations.

DISCHARGE OF CONTRACT

A *discharge* is a release from or the termination of an obligation. Usually, it is performance which discharges the parties. However, in earlier chapters, we discussed discharge of contractual obligations—without so labeling it— due to a party's ability to void the contract or by reason of the other party's misconduct, such as exerting duress. This section covers discharge in a number of other settings.

Performance

Complete performance in accordance with the contract's terms is, of course, the ideal. It discharges the party who performed from any further obligations and entitles the party to the promised consideration. Assume Texaco agrees to buy 1 million Champion sparkplugs for $1 million. Champion delivers the plugs to Texaco in accordance with the contract. When Texaco accepts them, Champion is discharged from any further obligation and is due the $1 million.

The law recognizes that people are not always able to perform their obligations perfectly. In some cases, particularly with respect to building contracts, courts use the term *substantial performance* to describe the level of performance which discharges a contractual obligation. Under this standard, minor deviations from a contract's specifications will not bar recovery, although they may require an adjustment in the contract price. The next case illustrates how courts apply the substantial performance standard to an unusual conflict.

Russell v. Salve Regina College

890 F.2d 484 (1st Cir. 1989)

FACTS   Sharon Russell was an obese woman whose weight fluctuated between 280 and 300 pounds. When Salve Regina College first admitted her, her weight was not made an issue. Once she entered the nursing program her sophomore year, however, conflicts arose when an instructor publicly ridiculed her about her weight. In the beginning of her junior year, Russell refused to agree to attend Weight Watchers and lose weight. She later failed a clinical course. Russell signed a contract to avoid dismissal. In the second semester of her junior year she agreed to lose two pounds a week. Russell attempted to fulfill her part of the agreement by proving that she was attending Weight Watchers, but she was unable to lose weight consistently. During the summer she lost touch with the college and did not lose additional weight. Consequently Russell was asked to withdraw voluntarily from Salve Regina, which she did. She started another nursing program but had to repeat her junior year because of a residence requirement. She eventually graduated and became a registered nurse. Russell sued for breach of contract, claiming she had substantially performed her side of the contract with the college. The jury at the trial court found that Salve Regina had breached the contract with Russell.

ISSUE   Was it a reversible error to apply the substantial performance standard to this case of first impression?

DECISION   No. Affirmed. It was not a reversible error to allow the jury to decide whether Russell had substantially performed her end of the bargain. The jury found that her relationship with Salve Regina College was contractual. Russell substantially performed her contractual requirements by obeying the disciplinary rules, paying tuition, and maintaining a good academic record. Salve Regina was required to furnish her with an education until she graduated. Despite the fact that Russell did not perform the contract fully, the jury found that she had substantially performed her end of the deal. Salve Regina breached the contract by not allowing Russell to finish the program.

Personal satisfaction. Some contracts specify performance to the personal satisfaction of a party. Because of the potential for injustice in their enforcement, the courts give them a very narrow reading. When a contract requires one party to perform to the satisfaction of the other, courts must determine whether a party has an unqualified right to reject performance or whether it should apply an objective, "reasonable person" standard. Unless the parties make it quite clear in the contract that one or both of them has an unqualified right to object on the basis of personal dissatisfaction, the courts usually apply an objective standard.

Even so, when something as personal as a portrait is involved, the courts may imply a right to personal satisfaction. Suppose George Washington hired Gilbert Stuart to paint the portrait by which we all know him. Washington, however, did not like being portrayed as if his false teeth did not fit, so he refused to pay for the portrait. A court might well find for Washington, even if the contract was ambiguous on the subject of personal satisfaction. By contrast, if Stuart was whitewashing Mt. Vernon's walls, a court would never imply a personal satisfaction standard. Rather, it would apply an objective standard—what a reasonable person would expect from a professional wall painter.

Nonperformance. *Nonperformance* is a failure to sufficiently or substantially perform. The

term includes defective performance as well as the absence of performance. In order for nonperformance to be a breach, all of the following conditions must exist:

- The time for performance must have arrived or passed.
- Performance must not have occurred.
- Performance must not have been excused.

Material breach of contract. Nonperformance is, of course, just one way in which a breach can occur. A *breach of contract* is any failure to perform the terms of the contract without legal excuse.

A *material* or substantial breach may discharge the innocent party's remaining obligations. For example, Unfinished Furniture, Inc., contracts with Knotty Pine Corp. for ten tables to be delivered on October 1. Unfinished Furniture is to pay Knotty Pine $400 on October 15 and $400 on November 1. If Knotty Pine has not delivered by October 15, Unfinished Furniture is not obligated to make the payment. A material breach may also entitle the nonbreaching party to one of the remedies discussed in the last section of this chapter.

Anticipatory breach. An *anticipatory breach* consists of an act or statement clearly revealing an intent not to perform when performance is due. The innocent party may treat the contract as breached and sue immediately. Alternatively, the innocent party may wait until performance is due and sue, or rescind the contract and sue to recover whatever payments have already been made.

Where an innocent party alleges an anticipatory breach as a result of an act, that act must be unequivocal. Suppose Alma offers to sell Baker her car. They agree on a price and that delivery is to take place the following week. Two days later Alma sells her car to Carla, who takes immediate delivery. Alma's act is an anticipatory breach. The next case was resolved on the basis of the substantial performance standard, but note how Witvoet, the plaintiff, attempted to have the court find an implied personal satisfaction expectation.

Morton Bldgs., Inc. v. Witvoet

90 Ill. App. 3d 316, 413 N.E.2d 202 (1980)

FACTS   Morton erected a building for Witvoet. Witvoet refused to pay the remaining $5460 due under the construction contract on the grounds that Morton had failed to perform satisfactorily. Witvoet alleged a number of minor problems, but could prove only that Morton had failed to properly notch a board in the sliding doors. The cost of replacing this board was $50.

ISSUE   Did Morton substantially perform?

DECISION   Yes. Affirmed on this ground. "In building contracts a literal compliance with the provisions of the particular contract and the plans, specifications and drawings is not necessary to a recovery by the contractor. . . . [Recovery] for work may be had notwithstanding slight defects or mere technical and inadvertent omissions. Where a contractor is permitted to recover on the ground of substantial performance, the other party is entitled to an allowance for the sum required to remedy the omissions or defects and to complete the building or work as agreed." The court ordered judgment entered for Morton for $5410.

Under the Uniform Commercial Code (UCC), a party with reasonable doubts about the other party's willingness or ability to perform may demand assurance of performance and may suspend his own performance until he receives it. If the other party does not respond within a reasonable time—no more than 30 days—the law assumes an anticipatory breach [UCC §2-609]. For example, if there are rumors in the trade about a firm's impending bankruptcy, one of its vendors could request assurance of payment. If the vendor received no response, its obligations under the contract would be discharged. This topic is discussed further in Chapter 33.

Delay. Whether a delay in performance is a breach of contract depends on the contract's language and on the circumstances surrounding the agreement. Suppose Clark agrees to buy McCullogh's house for $100,000. Under the terms of the contract, McCullogh is to give Clark possession on June 1. However, Clark does not actually take possession until June 3 because McCullogh's movers did not arrive until then. Does that 2-day delay amount to a breach of contract which will excuse Clark from paying the purchase price? No. The 2-day delay has little or no adverse effect on Clark. However, any damages Clark sustains as a result of the delay—bills for temporary lodging, for example—would be deducted from the purchase price.

In the agreement, the parties can provide that "time is of the essence," meaning that the time of performance is an essential term of the contract. Under such a clause, even 1 day's delay might amount to a breach which would entitle the nonbreaching party to relief if time actually was of critical importance.

Sometimes courts find that time is of the essence even in the absence of an express statement. Suppose a municipality contracted for the delivery of display fireworks not later than July 3. Their arrival on July 6 would discharge the municipality's duty to perform. Where Fourth of July celebrations are concerned, time obviously is of the essence, even if the parties did not say it in so many words.

Agreements to Discharge

Parties who have the capacity to make contracts may subsequently agree to terminate them. *Agreements to discharge* are contracts to terminate an existing contract. They must meet all the requirements for a valid contract. Normally, the consideration for agreements to discharge is that each party relieves the other of the obligation to perform under the earlier contract. If one party has already performed, clearly the nonperforming party will have to supply some other consideration.

Agreements to discharge normally take one of four forms, discussed below:

- Accord and satisfaction
- Mutual rescission
- Release
- Novation

Accord and satisfaction. In Chapter 7's discussion of consideration, we noted that an *accord* is an agreement to accept a substituted performance. *Satisfaction* is the fulfillment of the substituted performance. An accord suspends the original duty until the new promise is either performed or breached. If the substituted duty is performed adequately, it discharges both the original and the new duty. However, if the accord is breached, the innocent party may choose between enforcing the original duty or enforcing the duty under the accord.

An accord and satisfaction as to a debt is possible only where the claim is *unliquidated*. In other words, the amount or the existence of the debt must be in question. If the debt is *liquidated,* there can be no accord and satisfaction. These concepts are more fully developed in Chapter 8.

Note that the parties to an accord and satisfaction are the same parties who entered into the original contract. Only the performance of one of the parties changes. Thus, the essence of accord and satisfaction is substituted performance.

Mutual rescission. The parties to a contract may agree to rescind it. This is called *mutual rescission*. Suppose Lang agrees to buy a car from Beck Chevrolet which will be delivered in 2 months. Just before the car arrives, Lang loses her job. She asks Beck if she may cancel their contract. Beck may agree, but nothing requires him to, even though the buyer faces a severe hardship. Also, while mutual rescission would be sufficient consideration in itself, the seller in this situation may demand additional consideration.

A mutual rescission does not have to be express. In the absence of an express intention to abandon a contract, a court may find that the parties' conduct reveals a mutual rescission. For instance, Henry contracts with Brooke to model his line of spring clothes. He never calls her to set a date, and she takes on other jobs which would make it impossible for her to model Henry's line. Their contract reveals an intent to abandon the contract. That is an extreme example. The following case presents a more typical one.

Economy Leasing Co., Ltd. v. Wood

427 N.E.2d 483 (Ind. Ct. App. 1981)

FACTS

Economy leased Dickey a plane valued at approximately $105,000. He had paid over $25,000 as advance rent when, 2 months later, the plane crashed, killing him. The lease provided that in case of loss or damage, Dickey should repair or replace the plane. However, in its negotiations with Dickey's heirs, Economy only expressed an interest in the insurance Dickey carried on the plane. Economy had collected the insurance proceeds, which approximated the plane's value. Dickey's heirs brought suit to recover the advance rent, claiming that the parties had mutually rescinded the replacement provision. Economy argued that the parties could not rescind the lease because the plane's destruction made it impossible to restore the parties to the status quo. The trial court held that Economy should restore the advance rent to the heirs.

ISSUE

Did the parties mutually rescind the lease provision relating to replacement of the plane?

DECISION

Yes. Affirmed on this issue. Neither party expressed an intent to enforce the replacement term that implied a continuation of the lease. When a rescission occurs but exact restoration is impossible, a court will restore the parties to as close to the status quo as possible. Payment of the insurance proceeds accomplished that goal. Until the plane's destruction, the lessor provided the aircraft to the lessee, who paid rent. Rescission terminated the lease prospectively. Consequently, if there is any unpaid rent, it should be paid; if there is any unearned rent, it should be refunded.

Release. A *release* is a statement by one party to a contract which relieves another party of any further obligation to perform.

As with all discharges, everything required to make a contract is required of a release. However, a party granting a release without requiring consideration may know that the other party will rely on it. If in fact she does rely on the release, a court is likely to hold that the party granting the release is estopped from asserting lack of consideration or any of the defenses as to form. Suppose Jane borrows $10,000 from her uncle for the down payment on her home. Some years later, he tells her he is forgiving her debt in honor of her daughter Susan's twenty-first birthday. Jane then uses her increased equity in the house to borrow to meet Susan's business school expenses. If Jane's uncle sues her on the debt, he will be estopped from asserting a lack of consideration for the release.

Novation. As noted in Chapter 11, the essence of a *novation* is the substitution of one contract for another. A novation creates a contractual relationship between the obligee and the new obligor while releasing the old obligor from liability under the original contract. Thus, it stands distinct from a delegation or an accord and satisfaction whose essence is a substituted performance—though, of course, substituted performance may be an element of a novation.

Discharge by Operation of Law

In some instances, a party's obligation to perform under a contract is discharged by law.

Statute of limitations. *Statutes of limitations* define the time during which an action can be brought in court to enforce an obligation. The purpose of these limitations on actions is to spur collection efforts and, failing that, to see that suit is filed before evidence becomes stale or lost. These statutes vary from state to state for common law actions and from statute to statute for statutory actions. Under the UCC, a plaintiff must bring an action for the breach of a contract for the sale of goods within 4 years after the cause of action arises unless the parties have agreed otherwise. In any case, the period cannot be less than 1 year or more than 4 years [UCC §2-725(1)]. The statutory period begins running when one party fails to perform.

Statutes of limitations normally begin to run from the moment the defendant breaches a duty to the plaintiff, not from the moment the plaintiff suffers an actual loss or discovers the breach. (There are important exceptions to this rule, particularly in the area of medical malpractice.) Unless a cause of action arises from a specific event on a certain date—such as a letter received on a particular day that terminated a contract—it is rarely wise to delay filing a suit until what appears to be the cutoff date.

Impossibility. *Impossibility* of performance discharges the parties to a contract. Assume Smith agrees to lease his horse barn to Dale for $1000 per month. Before Dale can move her animals in, the barn burns down. The fire ends Smith's obligation to provide the barn and Dale's duty to pay the rent.

Frustration of purpose. Generally, the law presumes that the parties to a contract take into account the risk that the contract may become burdensome or unprofitable. However, the *frustration of purpose* concept permits a court to discharge a party's performance if an extraordinary event or condition so alters its nature that it becomes vitally different from what the parties originally expected. The frustration must be so severe that the party seeking discharge would not have assumed its risk. Also, the parties must have based their contract on the implicit assumption that the frustrating event would not occur. The English case which follows is the classic example of frustration of purpose.

Krell v. Henry

[1903] 2 K.B. 740

FACTS   The processions in connection with the coronation of King Edward VII were scheduled for June 26 and 27, 1902. On June 17, Henry noticed an announcement that the windows of Krell's flat, which overlooked the procession route, could be rented for those 2 days. After negotiating with Krell's lawyer, Henry agreed to pay $25 as a deposit and $50 on June 24th. By June 24, the procession had been cancelled. Henry refused to pay the $50 due that day. Krell sued Henry for the balance due. The trial court entered judgment for Henry.

ISSUE

Did the cancellation of the coronation procession frustrate the purpose of the contract?

DECISION

Yes. Affirmed. The purpose of the contract was not to lease the flat but to use its rooms for a particular purpose. Both parties assumed that the procession would take place on the days announced along the established route. Neither can reasonably be supposed to have considered, at the time the contract was made, that the coronation would not be held as scheduled or that the parades would take a different route.

The UCC has adopted the principle of *commercial impracticability,* which is roughly the same as the frustration of purpose concept in common law. We will examine commercial impracticability in Chapter 33.

Discharge in bankruptcy. A *discharge in bankruptcy* bars most claims against the bankrupt that are in existence at the time of the discharge. If the bankrupt chooses to make partial payment of a discharged debt, that payment will not revive the original obligation. However, under the Bankruptcy Reform Act of 1978, a discharged debtor may reaffirm a debt only with the federal Bankruptcy Court's approval. For a further discussion of bankruptcy, see Chapter 43.

REMEDIES FOR BREACH OF CONTRACT

Once a party has proved a breach of contract, it must then establish the relief to which it is entitled. Traditionally, courts have spoken of *legal remedies* and *equitable remedies.* The ancient procedural differences in how plaintiffs obtained these remedies have largely disappeared. However, the categories still describe distinct types of remedies, and that is how we have categorized them in this section.

Legal remedies usually involve awards of monetary *damages* to the injured party. Based upon the evidence, the court places a dollar value on the injury. Equitable remedies usually attempt to return the parties to their approximate positions before the agreement. This may involve allocating funds between the parties but would not place a dollar value on the injury. Also, in certain very limited circumstances, a court may order the performance of a contract under its equitable powers, particularly where the sale of land or unique personal property is involved.

In learning the various remedies you should keep in mind one very important principle: a plaintiff can recover only for those loses which can be proved with reasonable certainty. A court will not speculate as to potential future gain or profits "that might have been" where there is not an established basis for prediction. To illustrate, suppose at issue is the probable volume of sales for a restaurant for the next 6 months. Given the high failure rate for new restaurants, a court would be unlikely to speculate on the probable volume of sales for a restaurant not yet open for business. In contrast, the court might be very willing to consider the likely future volume of sales for a well-established restaurant.

Legal Remedies

The damages the injured party may recover in an action based on a contract depend on the circumstances of the case. This section looks at the types of damages which are ordinarily awarded (compensatory), sometimes awarded (consequential), and virtually never awarded (punitive).* Then, we will glance at the forms these damage awards have taken.

Compensatory damages. *Compensatory damages* are always available to the injured party. Compensatory damages are intended to put the injured party in the position he would have been had the breaching party properly performed, to make the plaintiff whole. They are generally measured by the difference between the contract price and the cost of securing substitute goods or performance. Suppose that Doug agrees to sell Catherine his calculator for $25. He changes his mind, and Catherine has to buy one at the bookstore for $40. Catherine's compensatory damages are $15.

Compensatory damages may also include the plaintiff's reasonable incidental damages, expenditures arising directly out of the breach. To illustrate, assume Barker breaches his contract to purchase a vacant home from Simon. Simon could recover the cost of insurance nec-

essary to cover against loss or damage while trying to sell the home to another person.

Consequential damages. *Consequential damages* arise from the injured party's special needs or unique position. They are an indirect, but foreseeable, consequence of the original injury.

Consequential damages are rarely awarded because for generations courts have held that a party must be able to foresee the consequences of a breach in order to be liable for them. For that reason, they usually limit recovery to instances in which the defendant had notice of the plaintiff's special circumstances at the time of contracting. Also, the plaintiff must be able to quantify the damages with reasonable certainty. Much litigation has focused on the concepts of foreseeability and reasonable certainty.

Parties often limit or eliminate consequential damages in their contracts. For example, many photo labs limit their liability for film they process to the replacement cost of the film roll.

In the classic case of *Hadley v. Baxendale,* discussed below, the requirement that damages for a breach of contract can be awarded only if the consequences are fairly and reasonably foreseeable by both parties was first articulated by the common law courts of England.

---

* It bears repeating that the damages available in a contract action differ significantly from those available in tort actions. A review of the discussion in Chapter 4 of the differences between damages in tort and contract actions is strongly recommended.

Hadley v. Baxendale

9 Exch. 341, 156 Eng. Rep. 145 (1854)

FACTS   The Hadleys operated a flour mill. A crankshaft which ran the steam engine in the mill broke, and the mill was forced to close down. Baxendale, a common carrier, was hired to transport the broken shaft from Gloucester, where the mill was located, to Greenwich, so that a new shaft could be fashioned to fit the engine. The Hadleys claimed that they had told Baxendale that the shaft must be dispatched at once, since the mill was not operating. Baxendale agreed to deliver the shaft the next day. It took Baxendale several days to deliver it, however, causing the mill to remain inoperative during that time. The Hadleys sued for the lost profits for the several days' delay. Baxendale defended by claiming that he had not been told of the mill closing and that the lost profits were not a foreseeable consequence of the breach. The Hadleys won at the trial level.

ISSUE

Was the closing of the Hadley's mill a foreseeable consequence of Baxendale's delay in delivering the new shaft?

DECISION

No. Reversed. Damages that arise as a consequence of a breach of contract can be awarded only if the loss can be fairly and reasonably contemplated by both parties at the time they make the contract. The Court of the Exchequer, which heard the appeal, concluded that the only facts communicated to Baxendale were that the Hadleys were millers and needed one of their mill's shafts taken to Greenwich for repair. In most cases, the fact that a shaft has broken does not necessarily mean that the entire mill will be shut down. The fact that it had closed in this case should have been communicated, since it was not reasonably foreseeable.

Punitive or exemplary damages. *Punitive* or *exemplary damages* are really tort remedies, and they are discussed in Chapter 4. However, it is worth noting again that because they are imposed to punish a party, they do not mesh with the theory of compensation which governs contract liability. In the following case, the court refused to award punitive damages in a case involving a breach of contract.

Stamps v. Southwestern Bell Telephone

667 S.W.2d 12 (Mo. Ct. App. 1984)

FACTS

The Stamps had been in the sewer cleaning business for 20 years, and had used Yellow Pages advertising throughout that time. Between 1965 and 1970, the Stamps and Southwestern Bell were involved in litigation over charges for Yellow Pages advertising. In June 1975, the Stamps signed a Yellow Pages advertising contract for the November 1975 directory. The ad copy showed two numbers to call for service. These numbers were reserved for Yellow Pages advertisers and were connected when the advertiser requested. The advertising charges were then billed monthly. Shortly after entering into this contract, the Stamps began disputing the accuracy of the presentation of their advertisement in the 1974 directory. In January 1976, the Stamps asked the telephone company to activate the lines. The telephone company agreed to do so if they paid an outstanding bill and signed a form attesting the accuracy of the earlier ad. The Stamps paid the bill but refused to sign. The telephone company then demanded the total annual payment in advance. The Stamps refused to pay; the telephone company refused to turn on the numbers; and the Stamps brought suit for breach of contract. The trial court dismissed their claim for punitive damages.

ISSUE

Could the Stamps recover punitive damages in a breach of contract action?

DECISION   No. Affirmed on this issue.

The general rule is that punitive damages are not recoverable for breach of contract. An exception to the general rule allows punitive damages to be recovered when plaintiff alleges and proves an independent and willful tort founded on breach of contract. [The Stamps] . . . failed to allege or prove the necessary independent and willful tort. Therefore, punitive damages were not recoverable.

Nominal damages. Any injured party has a right to sue and a right to a verdict and costs in his or her favor for any breach of contract, no matter how slight. However, in keeping with the principle of compensation, when the damage is slight, the court may award *nominal damages*—often $1 or $10. While they merely symbolize the plaintiff's successful vindication of a legal right, they do entitle the successful litigant to recover the court *costs,* which can amount to $1000 or more.

In a now famous antitrust case in 1986, the struggling, new United States Football League sued the National Football League for $1.69 *billion* dollars. After 40 days of testimony, 35 witnesses, and nearly 6500 pages of trial transcript, the USFL was awarded $1.00 in nominal damages!

Liquidated damages. *Liquidated damages* refers to an amount the parties agree at the time they contract will compensate for a loss suffered as a result of a breach. A common example appears in contracts for the sale of real estate, which often specify that 10 percent of the purchase price represents the liquidated damages should the buyer default. Courts have

generally accepted this amount as a fair representation of actual damages.

Where no percentage is commonly accepted, the courts allow the injured party to recover the stipulated amount if he or she establishes all of the following:

- The amount is reasonable considering the parties' expectations at the time of contracting.
- The actual damages are difficult to determine.
- The amount is reasonably tailored to the circumstances of the contract.

The courts have developed these tests to prevent liquidated damage clauses from becoming penalty clauses—which the courts will not enforce. Without this protection, the party with greater bargaining power might insist on a clause setting liquidated damages at an unreasonably high figure in relation to the potential loss. On the other hand, liquidated damages clauses sometimes protect the breaching party, as in the case of the photo lab limiting its liability to replacement of the film. Photo labs, as the next case shows, are not the only businesses using such limitations on liability.

Alcom Electronic Exchange, Inc. v. Burgess

849 F.2d 964 (5th Cir. 1988)

FACTS   Burgess was BellSouth's authorized sales representative for South Central Bell's 1986 Gulf Coast Yellow Pages. Acting on BellSouth's behalf, Burgess entered into a written contract with Alcom, a Mississippi corporation that provided for publication of Alcom's advertisement. The contract executed by Alcom provided in part:

*[BELLSOUTH'S] LIABILITY, THE LIABILITY OF ITS AUTHORIZED SALES REPRESEN-
TATIVES AND THE LIABILITY OF THE TELEPHONE COMPANY (IF ANY) ON
ACCOUNT OF ANY OMISSION OF OR ERRORS IN SUCH ADVERTISING SHALL IN
NO EVENT EXCEED THE AMOUNT OF CHARGES FOR THE ADVERTISING
WHICH WAS OMITTED OR IN WHICH THE ERROR OCCURRED IN THE THEN
CURRENT DIRECTORY ISSUE AND SUCH LIABILITY SHALL BE DISCHARGED BY
ABATEMENT OF THE CHARGES FOR THE PARTICULAR LISTING OR ADVERTISING
IN WHICH THE OMISSION OR ERROR OCCURRED.*

Alcom's ad did not run. Alcom brought suit seeking $250,000 in damages. The trial court held that the limitation of liability clause was valid and awarded Alcom $15, the amount it paid for the ad.

ISSUE   Is a limitation of liability clause valid when the parties to the contract are in unequal bargaining positions?

DECISION   Yes. Affirmed. Under Mississippi law, parties to a contract may define the amount of compensation in the event of breach, and the courts will enforce such agreements so long as the provision is not in the nature of a penalty. Many states have held enforceable such provisions in directory advertising contracts, including two United States district courts in Mississippi.

From the standpoint of precedent, *Alcom* was correctly decided. But, such outcomes—especially in directory cases where the consequences of omission to small businesses can be devastating—trouble many who are concerned with ethics and the law. These concerns led the Alabama Supreme Court to invalidate a similar clause.*

The duty to mitigate damages. A party injured by a breach of contract has a duty to minimize or *mitigate* the damages he or she might suffer. Mitigation is a very practical concept. It means, for example, that after a customer's breach, a building contractor must stop purchasing supplies and sell or use materials already purchased for a job. The contractor's recovery from the customer will be limited by the value of those items which he could shift to other projects or return for credit.

The same principle applies when an employer wrongfully discharges an employee before her employment contract expires. The employee has an obligation to look for another job. She need not take any job that comes along, but rather only one of approximately equal rank with similar duties and which offers comparable working conditions. The employee's efforts to mitigate may also affect entitlement to unemployment compensation (see Chapter 46).

Equitable Remedies

Equitable remedies today fill the niches where damages are not adequate relief. It cannot be emphasized strongly enough that damages are the norm, not the exception. Equitable relief is available only when money damages are not adequate.

Injunction. As discussed in Chapter 2, an *injunction* is an equitable remedy by which a

* *Morgan v. South Cent. Bell Tel. Co.*, 466 So. 2d 107 (Ala. 1985).

court orders a party to do or not do specific acts. Under ordinary circumstances, injunctions will issue only upon a showing that without it the party seeking the order will suffer irreparable harm. Irreparable harm means, in practical terms, that a later judgment awarding damages would not be sufficient to make the injured party whole. Whether irreparable harm would occur was the question the court in the next case confronted.

Frank's GMC Truck Center, Inc. v. General Motors Corporation

847 F.2d 100 (3d Cir. 1988)

FACTS   Frank's began selling GMC trucks in 1937 and added heavy-duty trucks to its line in 1973. In 1986, GMC notified Frank's that it was forming a joint venture, Volvo/GM, to manufacture and market heavy-duty trucks in the United States. GM, itself, would no longer be in the heavy-duty market. Volvo/GM then notified Frank's that Frank's had not been selected to market the new trucks and that orders for part would be considered on a case-by-case basis. Frank's brought suit seeking, among other relief, an injunction ordering GM to continue Frank's supply of parts. At the hearing on the preliminary injunction, Frank's argued that it would lose sales because sales of trucks are directly related to service. And without parts, it could not offer full service. Although the trial court was "unclear [as to] the irreparable nature of the damage," it granted Frank's a preliminary injunction that would remain in effect until final judgment.

ISSUE   Is loss of sales an irreparable injury that therefore justifies the issuance of a preliminary injunction?

DECISION   No. Reversed. All Frank's stands to lose are profits. Loss of income is not irreparable harm that cannot be compensated in money damages.

Injunctions requiring someone to do something positive are far less common than ones preventing a change in the status quo. In 1988 to 1989, the commissioner of baseball was investigating Cincinnati Reds Manager Pete Rose's alleged gambling activities. Rose obtained an injunction prohibiting the commissioner from taking any action against him until a court determined whether the commissioner could give him a fair hearing.

Injunctions are commonly issued in cases where former employees have signed agreements not to compete or not to disclose information. However, courts do not issue them automatically. They carefully scrutinize the agreement and the alleged violation to determine whether the agreement protects a legitimate business interest, is drawn as narrowly as possible, and is not simply designed to keep the former employee from working.

Specific performance. *Specific performance* involves precisely what its name implies: specific enforcement of a contract. The remedy is granted only in the cases of real estate and unique personal property, like a custom-made sports car or a family heirloom.

The reason for this limitation on the remedy's availability is that historically the courts have preferred compensation in the form of damages to ordering parties to do something they obviously do not want to do. That is also why there is no circumstance under which a court may order specific performance of a personal services contract. For instance, when the Yankees fire a manager, the manager cannot seek specific performance of the remainder of his contract. He is, of course, entitled to damages. By the same token, if he quits, the team cannot force him to remain.

The most common actions for specific performance involve the breach of contracts for the sale of land. Suppose Helen contracts with George to buy a lot in the Florida Keys. Just before the closing, George changes his mind. If Helen seeks specific performance, a court will grant it. No lot is precisely the same as another. Therefore, neither money damages nor another lot is adequate compensation if the buyer still wants the property.

Rescission and restitution. Rescission and restitution are remedies which return the parties to the position they occupied before forming the contract. A court grants rescission (which we discussed above and in Chapter 9) when it cancels contracts involving mutual obligations. *Rescission* presumes a contract's enforceability in the absence of conduct justifying the granting of the remedy. Rescission is often the remedy when the parties have made a joint mistake in forming the contract or when one party induced the other's assent through fraud or duress.

The same sorts of circumstances can justify *restitution,* a remedy mandating the return of consideration. Restitution is commonly described as a remedy to prevent a party's unjust enrichment by retaining consideration. However, unlike rescission, restitution is available when there is no enforceable contract between the parties. For example, two parties enter into an oral contract for the sale of land. The buyer pays the seller, who then refuses to transfer the title. Their contract is not enforceable because the Statute of Frauds requires a writing. However, a court will grant restitution to the buyer.

A party seeking rescission or restitution— or any other equitable remedy—must have acted in good faith. Courts say such a party must have "clean hands."

Reformation. A court may *reform* a written contract when the writing does not accurately describe the agreement between the parties. For example, a buyer and seller have agreed on the buyer's purchase of a particular farm. Their written contract contains an error in the legal description of the property. A court will reform the description to reflect their agreement.

Except when fraud is involved, reformation applies only to mutual mistakes. A victim of fraud may seek either reformation or rescission. Otherwise, a court will not rewrite the parties' agreement. Thus, as the next case illustrates, it is crucial to know the difference between rescission and reformation and when each is available.

Maryland Port Administration v. John W. Brawner Contracting Co., Inc.

303 Md. 44, 492 A.2d 281 (1985)

FACTS   John W. Brawner Contracting Co., Inc., was the low bidder on a Maryland Port Administration (MPA) construction project. After the contract was awarded to Brawner, the company discovered a $10,000 error in its bid, caused by an error in a subcontractor's quotation. Although it went ahead with the project, Brawner asked the MPA for a change in the contract amount. The MPA refused, citing the statute governing contracts with the state, which permits corrections or withdrawals of bids after they are opened only if the regulations of the state agency allows the changes. Under the MPA regulation, "changes in price are not permitted" in order to correct mistakes discovered after the award of a contract. The State Board of Contract Appeals reversed the MPA decision and an appellate court affirmed the Board's decision.

ISSUE   Did Brawner have a right to have its contract reformed?

DECISION   No. MPA decision reinstated. The regulation meant what it said. Brawner's remedy was rescission of the bid.

CONCLUSION

Whatever remedies the law provides in the event of a breach, they cannot fully compensate in most cases. When the parties must resort to the courts, they are trying to make the best of a bad situation. Neither damages nor specific performance compensates successful parties for the costs of litigation, much less for the distraction from profit-making enterprises.

No businessperson can eliminate the possibility of litigation completely. However, by using preventive law techniques such as conditions precedent, it is possible to limit potential liability. Still, the best protection is a hard-driven, fair bargain which satisfies the requirements we have outlined in this unit.

In Part VI, Sales, we will look closely at how—in connection with the sale of goods—the UCC has replaced the common law of contracts. Nonetheless, the common law of contracts is the foundation on which the UCC rests. In fact, with the definite exception of one and the possible exception of another, all the remaining chapters require an understanding of the common law of contracts.

A NOTE TO FUTURE CPA CANDIDATES

Agreements to discharge and discharge by operation of law have traditionally been heavily tested on the CPA exam. Release and novation have generally been tested in connection with an assignment, discussed in Chapter 11. An accord and satisfaction is an agreement between the parties to resolve a dispute. However, be aware that the CPA exam has used the term to describe a situation where no dispute exists but the parties subsequently enter into a second contract to discharge performance owed under the first contract. For example, suppose as a result of a sales contract Alex owes Baker $400 on April 1. On March 5, Baker needs cash and tells Alex that if Alex will pay him $250 this day, Baker will cancel the duty to pay $400 on April 1. Alex agrees. Note that this agreement is binding because of an exchange of new consideration (receipt of $250 on March 5, when no money was then due, in exchange for release of the later obligation to pay $400).

Do not confuse discharge of performance by operation of law with termination of an offer by operation of law. They are different. Death of an offeror always terminates an offer. Death of a party to an existing contract does not discharge the decedent's estate unless the decedent's performance was critical to the performance of the contract, for example performing future accounting services. If the required performance is nonpersonal in nature, such as an agreement to deliver a boat to you in exchange for $450, then the agreement is still binding on the decedent's estate.

To be excused from a performance as a result of frustration of purpose requires a change of circumstances which could not have been readily contemplated. Examples of such circumstances are: crop failure as a result of a lack of rain, a flood, or insect infestation; less need for heating oil as a result of a warmer-than-expected winter. A better solution is to structure such contracts as requirements or output contracts, depending upon which is appropriate. An output contract would relieve a farmer with crop failure problems; a requirements contract would relieve a business of having to purchase unneeded heating oil.

The statute of limitations is the time period in which a party must commence a breach of contract lawsuit or be denied a recovery. Time begins to run from the time *of breach,* or when the breach should have been discovered, *not* from the time that the contract was signed or action commenced under the contract. UCC Article 2 presumes the statute of limitations to be 4 years, but the parties may agree to reduce it to as little as 1 year.

In regard to damages, if money damages are appropriate then specific performance will not be ordered by a court. Specific performance is appropriate to direct the *seller* to go through with a contract to sell unique property, such as land or a rare item of personal property. Remember that liquidated damages must be reasonable in relationship to the probable loss which could have been anticipated when the agreement was originally made.

KEY WORDS

accord (257)
anticipatory breach (255)
compensatory damages (261)
concurrent condition (250)
condition implied-in-fact (253)
condition precedent (250)
condition subsequent (251)
consequential damages (261)
discharge (254)
express condition (252)
liquidated damages (263)
mitigation of damages (264)
performance (254)
reformation (266)
release (258)
rescission (266)
satisfaction (257)
specific performance (265)
statute of limitations (259)
substantial performance (254)

DISCUSSION QUESTIONS

1. Describe the three types of conditions that differ on the basis of time. What is the difference between an express condition and an implied condition?
2. What constitutes substantial performance? In what instances would full performance be required?
3. What is meant by accord and satisfaction? How does it differ from a novation?
4. Under what circumstances can increases in costs excuse a party from performance? How does frustration of purpose differ from impossibility? Create an example distinguishing the two.
5. Define anticipatory breach. What conditions must the breaching party's actions meet in order to justify the nonbreaching party's reliance?
6. What kinds of damages are available in contract actions? Briefly explain when each is available.
7. When does a party have a duty to mitigate damages?
8. When are liquidated damages clauses enforced by the court?
9. When will a party be able to recover lost profits?
10. What equitable remedies are available to a party who is injured by a breach of contract?

CASE PROBLEMS

1. Parsons sold a guitar to Pierce for $1800. During the course of negotiations Parsons showed Pierce an old sales receipt for the guitar which showed that it had once been owned by Elvis Presley. Because Pierce was a Presley fan, this fact clinched the sale. Later both Parsons

and Pierce discovered that the receipt was a fraud and the guitar was never owned or used by Elvis. Parsons claims he is free of any liability or responsibility, since he sold the guitar to Pierce in good faith. What remedy, if any, is available to Pierce? Explain.

2. Rogers entered into a contract with Burke to buy Burke's home for $90,000. A clause in the contract stated: "Contract is subject to Rogers's obtaining conventional mortgage financing of $75,000 at 10 percent or less interest for a period of 30 years." Because of rising interest rates, Rogers was not able to get financing for less than 10.5 percent. Will Rogers be in breach as a result of his failure to obtain financing? Explain.

3. The New York Bonkers, a baseball team, hired Ken Purdy as manager for one season at $250,000. Purdy had resisted the offer because he knew the team's managers generally did not have long tenures and usually suffered embarrassments on their way out. As a result, Purdy demanded and received a clause in his contract which required that the Bonkers pay him $15 million if the team improperly discharged him. At midseason, the Bonkers fired Purdy. Purdy immediately brought suit, seeking either reinstatement or the $15 million in liquidated damages. The Bonkers claim Purdy is entitled to only the remainder of his salary. Is the team correct? After his discharge, could the Bonkers prevent Purdy from managing for the Chicago Chokers for the remainder of the season? Explain.

4. Knoble & Company hired Radford, a public accountant, for $5000 to audit its company books to assist in getting a loan from Central Bank. Radford agreed to complete the work before March 27. Because he became backlogged with income tax preparation work for other clients, Radford did not complete his work for Knoble & Company until May 1. By this time, for various reasons, the audit proved to be of no use to Knoble & Company. Recognizing the tardiness of his report, Radford offered to reduce his bill to cover only his actual costs involved in the audit: $2500. Knoble & Company has refused to pay anything.

If Radford brings suit to collect for his work, will a court be more likely to award $5000, $2500, or nothing? Explain.

5. Sklar bought two computers from Wiz Corp. Ten months after taking delivery, Sklar discovered material defects in the computers. Three years after discovering them, Sklar brought an action for breach of warranty against Wiz. Wiz has raised the statute of limitations as a defense. Their contract contained a conspicuous clause stating that the statute of limitations for breach of warranty actions would be limited to 18 months. Sklar claims he should prevail because the UCC statute calls for a 4-year period measured from the date of delivery. Is Sklar correct? Explain.

6. Ketchum Builders, Inc., contracted with Sampson to construct an office building for $800,000. Ketchum inadvertently used materials that were not in accordance with the contract. Although the breach resulted in only minor damages, Sampson has refused to pay Ketchum the $100,000 balance due on the contract. Ketchum claims it is entitled to the entire $100,000 because it has substantially performed. Is Ketchum correct? Explain.

7. Kent Construction Co. contracted to build four garages for Magnum, Inc., according to Magnum's specifications. Wherever it believed it could do so without being detected, Kent deliberately substituted two-by-fours for the more expensive two-by-sixes called for in the contract. Magnum, however, discovered the substitutions and has withheld the final installment on the contract. The final installment is for $25,000 of the total price of $100,000. The estimated damages are $15,000. In a lawsuit seeking the balance due, Kent claims it should receive the final installment less the damages. Magnum claims Kent forfeited all rights to the final installment. Will Magnum prevail? Explain.

8. Sigle Computer Works sent its only assembly robot to its manufacturer for repairs. It hired Jimes, a local trucking company, to redeliver the robot to Sigle promptly upon completion of the repairs. Although the trucking company

did not know it, Sigle's entire plant had to shut down while awaiting the robot's return. The trucking company delayed returning the robot for several days. During the period it expected to be without the robot, Sigle expected to lose $5000 in profits. At the end of that period, Sigle rented a replacement robot at a cost of $250 per day. Is Sigle entitled to lost profits for the period beginning when it expected the robot to return? Compensatory damages? Punitive damages? Explain.

9. Crae Tate entered into a contract with Johnson Sportswear to represent them at racquetball tournaments for the next 6 months, provided she won the Sunset Hills Pro Tournament. Tate won. On winning, she received a better offer from Theus Sporting Gear to represent them, which she accepted. Johnson has brought suit to enforce their contract with Tate. Tate claims their contract is illusory. Is Tate correct? Assuming it is not, would a court force her to represent Johnson? Explain.

10. Paul Hoefer hired Powers McGuire, a contractor, to build a new office complex for his roofing company. McGuire agreed that the new building would be completed by March 15. Hoefer had a contract to turn over possession of his existing offices to a third party on April 1. Hoefer and McGuire agreed to a liquidated damages clause providing for damages of $250 per day for each day after March 15 that the building was not habitable. McGuire did not complete the building until April 15. Hoefer has brought suit seeking to recover an additional $150 per day because of higher-than-anticipated costs of moving into temporary facilities. Will Hoefer prevail? Explain.

PART II APPENDIX

Uniform commercial code Article 2 sections covered in Parts II or VI

As you have seen in this part, Article 2 of the Uniform Commercial Code has a major impact on the law of contracts. In the following table, we have assembled the concepts from Article 2 discussed in this part and in Part VI, Sales. You may want to refer to this table when you are studying the UCC in Unit VI.

Those planning to take the Certified Public Accounting (CPA) examination should take note of this table. The UCC Article 2 matters discussed in this unit are almost always tested in the contracts portion—not the UCC portion—of the CPA examination in business law.

In the table, chapter references are to the first chapter within Unit II or Unit VI where the concept is discussed. The UCC sections can be found in Appendix I at the back of the book.

The unit appendix at the end of Unit VI provides a listing of special rules involving a merchant or between merchants. You may wish to review this list at this time.

Concept	UCC section	Part II chapter	Part VI chapter
"Gap fillers" (see also §§2-305, 308, 309, and 310)	2-204	6	31
Firm offer	2-205	6	31
Auctions	2-328	6	31
Course of dealing	1-205	7	31
Usage of trade	1-205	6	31
"Battle of the forms"	2-207	7	31
"Prompt or current shipment"	2-206	7	31
"Reasonable medium" rule	2-206	7	31
Contract modifications	2-209	8	31
Good faith	1-203	9	Part overview
Unconscionability	2-302	9	Part overview
Voidable title, third party	2-403	9	32
UCC Statute of Frauds	2-201	10	31
Merchant confirmations	2-201	10	31
UCC parole evidence rule	2-202	10	31
UCC assignment rule	2-210	11	Not covered
Anticipatory breaches	2-609	12	33
UCC statute of limitations	2-725	12	35

PART II PROBLEMS

The end-of-part problems serve three purposes. First, some require practical applications of legal knowledge to everyday situations. Second, they are summative, bringing together many of the issues treated individually in the chapters of a particular part. Third, the last question presents an ethical problem which, as in real life, may not have an unqualifiedly right or wrong solution. Rather, its goal is to prompt two questions: What would I do in this situation? What *should* I do in this situation?

I. A PRACTICAL PROBLEM

Involving a lawyer seems to contracting parties like so much wasted time and effort if a contract involves a relatively small sum. When they feel the need for a writing, quite often the parties produce it themselves.

Lawyers might argue that self-help is always a bad idea when a transaction is anything more than routine. But, in reality, nonlawyers draft contracts all the time. This problem is designed to show you what drafting a contract involves. It should also make you think about the potential hazards in even an ordinary transaction, like the one in this problem

George Williams saw an ad for his dream car, a 1955 Chevrolet convertible, for only $3500. He contacted Arlene Adams, who had placed the ad, drove the car, and immediately opened negotiations with Arlene for its purchase.

George has a number of concerns he wants resolved before committing himself to buy the car. First, he wants to have his mechanic check the car's mechanical and electrical systems. Second, he has to check with his credit union to see if he can borrow $1000 toward the purchase price. However, he wants to be able to cancel his deal with Arlene if the credit union will not lend him the $1000 for less than 11 percent interest per year and for a term of not less than 1 year. Also, he wants to make certain that Arlene leaves the CB radio in the car, does not remove the original wheel covers, and delivers the original convertible top bag with the car. Finally, George wants Arlene to guarantee that she knows of no major defects in the car's condition or performance.

Arlene will allow George to have his mechanic check the car and to check on financing. But, she will give him only 3 days in which to do this, after which she will negotiate with other potential buyers. George has agreed, but he wants their agreement in writing.

Assume that you are George and that you must draft a contract reflecting the terms of your agreement with Arlene. Use today's date as the date of the contract.

2. A SUMMATIVE PROBLEM

Charley White just opened the business of his dreams, Crazy Charley's Classic Cars Company. Charley plans to sell antique, vintage, and sports cars.

Charley was offered a 1947 Buick Roadmaster convertible which, the seller stated, actor Tom Cruise drove in the movie *Rainman*. Charley quickly bought it and offered it for sale as the "Cruise Buick." Kathy Freer, a devoted fan of Cruise's, purchased it. Sometime later, Kathy was disappointed to learn that the car was never used in the movie and that she probably paid $5000 too much for the car, based on what comparable 1947 Buicks went for. When she threatened to sue Charley for the difference, he promised to pay her $1000 if she did not. Said Charley, "This is blackmail but I can't afford bad publicity at the outset of my business." Later Charley changed his mind and refused to pay Kathy.

Charley sold a 1929 Ford Model A Roadster to John Sheldon. Prior to the sale, Charley told Sheldon that he would provide free servicing for the car for the first 30 days after the sale and that it was "the best roadster in the valley." The final written contract stated neither of these things and Charley subsequently refused to honor the 30-day servicing promise because "he could not remember saying anything like that."

Charley's competitor, Scoop Daniel, announced plans to open for business a block from Charley. He and Charley met, and they agreed that this competition would hurt both of them. Daniel agreed not to relocate within 5 miles of Charley's for 5 years in return for Charley agreeing not to relocate within 5 miles of Daniel's location during the same period. They agreed that if either breached the contract the other party would be entitled to $50,000 in liquidated damages. Daniel broke the agreement several months later but refuses to pay Charley the $50,000.

Charley mailed Ed Way a written offer to sell him a 1965 Ford Thunderbird for $3500. Charley's business was located just across Lake Georgia from Way's home. In the offer, Charley instructed Way to raise the American flag on his dock by 7:00 A.M. on April 1 if the deal was satisfactory. Way did, but Charley could not see the flag because of fog. By the time the fog cleared, around 9:00 A.M., the flag had been lowered. Assuming that Way had not accepted, Charley sold the car to Dorothy Gross for $3300. When Way demanded damages for breach of contract, Charley refused. Said Charley, "You failed to communicate your acceptance, which would not have been any good anyway because it was not in writing."

Charley decided to create a dramatic television advertisement by taping a person bungee jumping off the Barksdale Highway bridge while wearing a Crazy Charley's T-shirt. Charley hired Cindy Brix to do the jump for $600. Several days before the jump was to occur, the state's legislature passed a law prohibiting persons from bungee jumping off state bridges. Cindy is willing to bungee jump from the top of a high crane at a construction site, but Charley has rejected the idea and has told her the deal is off. As a result, Cindy claims she has a right to the $600. Charley claims she does not as a result of the Statute of Frauds and the impossibility of performance.

Charley instead decided to film an advertisement featuring parachutists wearing Crazy Charley's T-shirts. Charley hired five persons to do the advertisement and had them sign an agreement not to hold him liable for possible injuries suffered during the jump. During the filming of the jump, one parachutist, Showalter, collided with another jumper, preventing the other jumper's parachute from opening. Showalter's insurance policy states that "injuries arising out of the use of an aircraft" are not covered. An aircraft was defined as "any contrivance used or designed for flight except model aircraft of the hobby variety not used or designed to carry people or cargo." Both the insurance carrier and Charley contend that they are not responsible for injuries resulting from the accident.

Charley discovered a 1949 Packard Henney Hearse that a schoolteacher, Sharon Hodges, had inherited from her uncle, a funeral home owner. Charley sent her a written offer to purchase it for $350. Said Charley in the note, "I cannot imagine anyone around here who would give you much for the old 'dreary,' but it has some sentimental value to me because my daddy was also a funeral director." Charley knew but did not tell Sharon that the national market value of the hearse was at least $6000. Sharon called Charley and said, "If you think the price is fair I will accept, as you deal in cars and I do not know what it is worth." Charley responded, "I'd rather you ask someone else." Not knowing who would possibly know such a value, Sharon responded, "I guess your offer is probably fair. Okay." Before Charley paid Sharon, she learned the real value and has now refused to go through with the deal "on account of Charley's fraud." Charley is ready with the $350.

Charley's niece, a first-year law school student, has pleaded with him to hire legal counsel. Charley feels she means well but says, "Why do I need a lawyer? The law's with me 100%. Besides, I've got an employee who just finished business law." You're that person. Assuming there is no law against your giving legal advice, how would you advise Charley on each of the problems raised above? Fully explain your advice.

3. A SUMMATIVE PROBLEM

Bob Kirby is the owner of Kirby's Real Estate Development Company. Kirby's both builds houses and serves as a broker firm for the sale of real estate owned by others. Bob Kirby has overseen the building of some 100 hours, and his firm has sold over 750 houses in a 10-year period of doing business. During the last year Kirby has encountered some potential legal problems which may need addressing. Please advise him.

Kirby showed a house owned by Brown to Radford. While negotiating the contract, Brown orally agreed to include with the sale of the house the counter-top microwave oven, the furniture in the sun room, and the dining room chandelier. The resulting written sales contract failed to include these items. However, Kirby has assured Radford that if a problem develops a neutral third person who was present during negotiations could clarify the matter in court.

Kirby had a listing for a house owned by Hepburn. George Lawson wished to make an offer. Because Hepburn was vacationing elsewhere, Kirby mailed Lawson's offer to her. Hepburn responded with a different price and stated that acceptance could be "by certified mail, return receipt requested" only. Lawson accepted the counteroffer but sent the response by Federal Express Overnight Delivery. Hepburn refused to accept Lawson's means of acceptance. Kirby claims Hepburn's actions were ridiculous; an acceptance is an acceptance. The state court which would hear the case is bound by the traditional common law rules of offer and acceptance.

Bill Stampfli inherited a house owned by his grandmother, in the community of Erewhon. Stampfli lived in Boston and had no idea of the house prices in Erewhon. He called Kirby, a former friend of his grandmother's, about listing the house for sale. Kirby suggested a list price of $65,000, since "Erewhon values are only a fraction of those in Boston." Kirby then offered to buy the house for $60,000 to use as a rental house. Being pressed for time and living far away, Stampfli agreed. After getting the house, Kirby quickly sold it to White, a good faith purchaser, for $80,000. Stampfli has just learned of the above facts and has threatened to sue both Kirby and White for the $20,000 difference. Both have claimed no liability.

Kirby is developing home sites adjacent to Cross Lake. A prospective lot buyer and friend, Tremulis, was interested in purchasing Lot 42. Tremulis asked Kirby, "Since I am an old friend, how about if I let you use my box tickets for next month's Cubs-Cardinals series in return for you giving me a ten-day option to purchase at $45,000?" Kirby responded, "I would do this only for a friend. Put it in writing." He did, and both signed it. A week later, Kirby signed a contract to sell the lot to Karsten for $55,000. Tremulis learned this the following day when he attempted to purchase the lot. Said Kirby, "My agreement was a joke. Besides, you gave me no money to keep the offer open." Tremulis has threatened suit.

Offutt already owned a lot on Cross Lake. He invited Kirby to his lot to talk about Kirby building a house for him. Offutt showed Kirby a picture of the house of his dreams adjacent to a lake. Offutt asked, "Do you think you can build this for me, complete with the basement?" Kirby responded, "If it worked at that lake, it should work here. We can do it." A week later Kirby began and the basement floor was poured. Water seepage began almost immediately. An engineer told Offutt and Kirby that the floor would have to be raised 3 feet. Kirby sent Offutt a supplemental bill for the $3000 it took to raise the floor and fix the problem. Offutt claims it is Kirby's problem.

Kirby later showed a house to Leabu. Leabu said he heard there were rumors about some house in the neighborhood being haunted. Said Kirby, "Surely you do not believe silly talk like that. There is no need to call "Ghostbusters" about this house." In fact, Kirby had read in a *Reader's Digest* article that the house was a supposed "playground for poltergeists." After agreeing to purchase the house, Leabu learned that three ghosts were rumored to frequent this house. Leabu has demanded a return of his $5000 deposit and a release from the purchase contract.

Kirby got into another dispute with Pearson, a newspaper reporter. Pearson had written in the local paper that "Bob Kirby of Kirby's Real Estate Development Company" had filed bankruptcy previously and was about to file again. The impact on Kirby's business was immediate. Unfortunately, Pearson was referring to the wrong Bob Kirby. Kirby threatened to sue the newspaper and Pearson for defamation. The newspaper offered Kirby $10,000 if he would agree not to sue. He agreed. Before the newspaper paid Kirby the $10,000, he talked to a lawyer who told him he should have insisted upon at least $100,000. Consequently, Kirby has now told the newspaper he has changed his mind, will not accept the $10,000, and plans to sue.

Kirby repossessed a house owned by Campini. Toulmin, a worker for Kirby, asked to buy the house. Kirby orally agreed to a price of $45,000, since the house was in disrepair. Toulmin gave Kirby $500 and was permitted to move in and began to make major improvements. A few weeks later Kirby got an offer to sell the house to someone else for $60,000. Kirby accepted. Kirby has offered to reimburse Toulmin for his repair expenses but has pointed out that they had no enforceable contract which would prevent the sale to a third party. Toulmin has disagreed.

Kirby was building a house for Rausch. Their contract included a clause which specified the installation of Red Dog pipes in the walls because Raush's father had once owned that company. Kirby hired a subcontractor to do the plumbing. The subcontractor, Sakuyama, used Badger pipes, an equivalent-grade pipe. Raush has insisted that all the internal pipes be removed and replaced with Red Dog pipes. Kirby has rejected the request on the grounds of excessive cost and that the internal Badger pipes are not defective. Kirby claims the final payment is owed, since the work on the house is otherwise satisfactorily completed.

Hanson Brown has contacted Kirby about his home that Kirby built 9 years ago at 1257 West Lunt. Brown claims a foundation problem has caused a major shift of his house. An investigation by an engineer found that the foundation problem could have been reasonably discovered 6 years ago. Brown claims he did not discover it because he seldom entered the back room of the basement, the area where the problem began. The applicable statute of limitations in the state is 3 years from the time of breach or when the breach should have been discovered. Kirby told Brown, "Your complaint comes way too late for me to be responsible. Sorry."

Please advise Kirby about these situations.

4. ETHICS AND THE LAW

The doctrine of *caveat emptor*—let the buyer beware (or take care)—was a fundamental maxim of the common law. The doctrine placed on the purchaser the burden of knowing, understanding, and judging the merits of a proposed bargain and exchange. A weaker party might possibly be able to establish conduct of the stronger party that would invalidate consent, such as duress or fraud, but such cases were, and are, not prevalent.

During the nineteenth century, most state and federal legislators, like most judges, tended to have business-oriented backgrounds and accepted the fairly rigid rules of construction and interpretation of the common law. It appears that most householders of that era, whom we would today call consumers, accepted the workings of caveat emptor as the fate of those lacking economic strength. Caveat emptor and ethics need not have been exclusive matters, but in practice they often were.

The *Restatement (Second) of Contracts* incorporates a number of new provisions reflecting the ideal of fair dealing between parties and the fulfillment of reasonable expectations. However, adoption of several of these provisions has been controversial. Consider the issues below from both an ethical and a legal perspective.

a. At the common law a court would find a misrepresentation only where a false statement was involved or when there was a failure to respond to a specific question. In contrast, *Restatement (Second) of Contracts* §161 states that non-disclosure can also be misrepresentation where the nondisclosure amounts to a failure to act in good faith. The effect of this section, if accepted by the states, would be to provide new affirmative duties for all contracting parties.

Today, the affirmative duty of disclosure is being widely adopted by courts in relation to the sale of residential homes. Does the *Restatement* reflect appropriate ethical expectations of contracting parties? Should the seller of a used house be under a duty to provide a prospective buyer with a complete history of all defects that the seller knows about—or should know about? Should a prospective buyer be under a corollary duty to point out the strong selling points of a house before being able to purchase the house at what appears to be a below-market price? Would your expectations of the ethical behavior of a seller or prospective buyer be altered if either or both were represented by a real estate agent?

b. Restatement (Second) of Contracts §139 permits a court to enforce an oral contract that falls within the Statute of Frauds *if* the promise induces action or forebearance, reliance occurs, the reliance was foreseeable by the person making the promise, and injustice can be avoided only by enforcing the promise. Some commentators believe that §139 goes too far in relaxing the requirements of the Statute of Frauds. Others contend that the *Restatement's* approach provides a resolution in keeping with society's ethical expectations. Consider the following:

- An attractive feature of the Statute of Frauds under the common law is that it is relatively clear which contracts are considered sufficiently important to warrant a writing. The *Restatement* approach, while being more flexible in both law and ethics, is likely to cause more problems—not fewer—if people become less concerned with the need for a writing and bring more lawsuits in hopes of being protected by the *Restatement* exception. Your thoughts?
- Part of the rationale for the *Restatement's* approach is an attempt to reduce the opportunities for the Statute of Frauds to be used as a sword rather than—as intended—a shield. Does the *Restatement* appear to achieve a better balance between ethical and legal approaches to the law?

c. In Chapter 7, you saw that Louisiana's French-derived civil law requires that courts consider the adequacy of consideration in reviewing contracts. This approach is designed to promote fair dealing between contracting parties. In addition, Louisiana recognizes defenses similar to the common law defenses based on conduct invalidating assent. Does the Louisiana approach seem to compel a more ethical approach to bargaining between parties? Is the goal of fair dealing in contract law likely to be better promoted under the Louisiana approach or the common law approach?

The Uniform Commercial Code does not require consideration of the adequacy of consideration, but it does impose a duty of good faith on all parties to a sales contract and provides the defense of unconscionability. Does this seem to be an appropriate ethical and legal approach to unfair dealing?

AGENCY AND EMPLOYMENT

Stories about professional athletes' agents and the multimillion dollar contracts they negotiate seem to dominate the sports pages. To many readers, the concept of an agent seems exotic, exciting, high-powered. That notion may have some truth where sports agents or movie agents are concerned, but it is not generally true. There are thousands of types of agents. The manager of your local McDonald's, for instance, is probably an agent, as are many sales representatives.

An *agent* is simply someone who represents another person, called a *principal*. The law of agency is primarily concerned with the agent's authority to create contractual relationships with third parties on behalf of the principal. For example, a baseball player hires an agent to negotiate a contract with his club. A McDonald's manager hires counter help on behalf of his or her principals, the franchise owners.

This part examines the legal effects of an agent's acts.

DEFINITION OF AGENCY

Agency is the relationship between the principal and the agent. The law terms the relationship *fiduciary,* a word which comes from the Latin *fidere,* meaning "to trust." In fact, trust and trustworthiness must characterize the agent's activities.

The agent must consent to the relationship and to the control of her actions on his behalf by the principal. But, generally the law does not require any formalities, such as a writing, to create an agency relationship. So, if Barbara agrees to sell Alvin's furniture through her store but they never discuss whether she will act as his agent, a court could find that she is.

Normally, the parties agree on compensation for the agent's services. However, the parties can create an agency relationship without agreeing on compensation. Compensation is not a necessary part of an agency relationship.

TYPES OF PRINCIPALS

Principals are categorized as either disclosed, partially disclosed, or undisclosed. What the third party dealing with the agent knows determines how a court will categorize the principal. Remember: The agent *always* knows who the principal is. The third party may not.

The principal is said to be *disclosed* if at the time of the transaction with the agent, the third party knows of the existence *and* the identity of a principal. Quite often, however, a principal prefers not to be identified, although his agent is free to tell those with whom she deals that she is representing a principal. In this case, the principal is said to be *partially disclosed* because the third party knows of his existence, though not his identity.

If the agent does not reveal the principal's existence, the principal is *undisclosed.* Representing an undisclosed principal places the burden of performing the contract on the agent, as we will see in Chapter 13. However, there is nothing morally wrong with representing a partially disclosed or undisclosed principal unless the principal has reason to know that the third party would not deal with him or someone in his line of business.

AGENTS' ROLES IN BUSINESS

Both individuals and businesses employ agents. The most common situations in which individuals employ agents are for real estate and securities (i.e., stocks and bonds) transactions. Every type of business employs agents, and their roles are almost uncountable. In fact, businesses as we know them could not operate without agents.

Businesses employing agents

Agency law affects every form of business. However, to help you conceptualize the agency relationship, the examples in this unit primarily involve sole proprietorships. A *sole proprietorship* is the simplest form of business, being essentially an individual in business alone. Its owner, the *sole proprietor,* may employ an agent, say, to manage an office.

In a partnership, each partner is a principal. But when a partner acts on behalf of the partnership, that partner is an agent for the partnership. When Davenport signs an office lease on behalf of his partnership, Davenport & Lucy, he acts on the partnership's agent.

Corporations work quite differently from partnerships. The corporation itself is a "legal person." No one person or group—including its shareholders—*is* the corporation. Thus, a corporation can operate only through its agents. Its agents are its officers and any other employees—like purchasing agents and salespeople—to which its board of directors gives the power to *bind* the company by contracting on its behalf.

Types of agents

There are two types of agents. A principal authorizes a *general agent* to conduct a series of transactions over time. The key here is the agent's continuity of service. By contrast, a principal employs a *special agent* to conduct only a single transaction or a limited series of transactions. A residential real estate agent usually is a special agent.

Agents are also characterized by whether they are independent, like a real estate broker, or employees of the business, like a corporate officer or a purchasing agent. We will discuss employees below.

TYPES OF EMPLOYEES

Every form of business can hire persons to work for it. In employment matters, the principal is called the *employer.* Every agent is an employee of the principal in the sense that the agent works for the principal. But, not all employees are agents—in fact, far from it. Agency law divides employees into three categories: agents, servants, and independent contractors.

Agents

Agents have management discretion to bind their employers. For instance, the person who buys office supplies for a corporation often has the title "purchasing agent." Such agents have authority to make contracts for and to change the legal relationship between the principal and third parties. However, as we will see in Chapter 14, their power to bind the principal is not unlimited.

Servants

At common law, employees without management discretion were called *servants,* and their employers, *masters.* While today most courts use the word "employees'' rather than ''servants,'' it is useful to think of the employee-employer relationship as that between master and servant. Servants generally have little, if any, managerial discretion. Typically, a master retains control over the servant's activities during working hours. Among the categories of servants are laborers, clerical help, store clerks, and maintenance personnel.

Independent contractors

Independent contractors are persons engaged in a business distinct from the employer's. In this type of employment, the principal hires the independent contractor for a specific purpose, but the independent contractor has the discretion to determine how to accomplish the desired result. Ordinarily, and independent contractor does not have the power to contract on an employer's behalf. For example, manufacturers commonly hire an independent trucking company to make deliveries. That relationship does not authorize the trucking company to order, say, office supplies on the manufacturer's behalf.

RIGHTS OF EMPLOYEES

Chapter 15 takes a close look at employees other than independent contractors. These employees fall into two categories: those who are employees at will and those who are not.

Employees at will

An *employee at will* is an employee who has no fixed term of employment and who may be terminated at any time with or without cause. Of course, such an employee may quit at any time, too. But reports of cases by employers against at will employees who quit are exceedingly rare.

Suits by terminated at will employees against their former employers are becoming increasingly common. The economic realities of late-twentieth-century America are such that people on established career paths who lose their jobs in midlife or later have an extremely difficult time finding comparable employment. They have every incentive to sue, and the courts have not been unsympathetic to their plight.

Over the last 20 years, the courts have carved a series of exceptions out of the employment at will doctrine to provide employees with more protection. No consensus has emerged as to what the exceptions should be. But courts on every level have grappled or are grappling with the problem of redefining the at will employment relationship.

Employees not at will

The majority of American employees are employees at will. Those who are not may be employees for a term. If you are hired as a summer lifeguard at an outdoor pool in Duluth, you are an employee for a term. An employee for a term is *never* an employee at will.

Similarly, an employee who may be terminated only for cause is never an employee at will. The most common examples of such employees are unionized workers, because their contracts provide elaborate grievance procedures to test the validity of terminations. We will examine these procedures in Chapter 46.

The law in flux

As noted earlier, the law relating to employment at will is in a state of flux. However, the same is true of most aspects of the law relating to the employment relationship. Drug tests, polygraph tests, AIDS tests, and the like have made employee privacy a controversial subject. Nonenforcement of workplace health and safety laws has become a political issue. And the shifting positions of the National Labor Relations Board have roiled union-management negotiations.

In Chapter 15, we will look generally at the common law of employment relations and at some statutes that have begun to modify it, particularly in the area of privacy. Later, in Chapter 46, we will examine government regulation of employment, which ranges from antidiscrimination laws to health, safety, and benefit laws.

CONCLUSION

The key to solving many agency problems lies in identifying the third party's perceptions. In many instances, if a third party reasonably perceives agency authority, the agent can bind the principal. Thus, a major preventive law theme of this unit is the need for the principal to communicate the scope of the agent's authority to all those with whom the agent might deal.

This unit has three overlapping topics:

- How, when, and why an agent can bind a principal contractually
- How, when, and why a principal will be responsible for an agent or employee's tortious acts
- The nature of the contractual relationships between principals and agents and between principals and third parties

In Chapter 13, we will explore the relationship between a principal and an agent. In Chapter 14, we will examine the liabilities of the parties to a transaction in which an agent participates and the liabilities for torts committed by agents and employees. And, in Chapter 15, we will focus on the nature of the employment relationship.

KEY WORDS

agent (279)
disclosed principal (279)
employee at will (281)
employer (280)
fiduciary relationship (279)
general agent (280)
independent contractor (281)

master (280)
partially disclosed principal (279)
principal (279)
servant (280)
sole proprietorship (280)
special agent (280)
undisclosed principal (279)

CHAPTER 13

The Relationship Between Principal and Agent

The law of agency centers on relationships. First it defines the consensual relationship between the principal or employer and the agent or employee. Second, it determines the effect of that relationship on actions affecting third persons.

This chapter examines the relationship between principal and agent. It focuses upon four issues: how an agency relationship comes into existence; the duties the agent owes the principal; the duties the principal owes the agent; and termination of an agency relationship.

FORMING AN AGENCY RELATIONSHIP

Agency is a consensual relationship. It can be formed simply by mutual assent between the principal and agent, *without* consideration. As such, although the formation of an agency relationship is generally contractual, it need not be. Suppose Glenda asks her neighbor to receive an expected delivery of a package to her apartment today. When her neighbor accepts a consensual relationship, an agency relationship, for the purposes of receiving the package, has been established even though consideration is absent.

Where an agency relationship is created by contract the principal and agent must comply with all the requirements of a common law contract:

- Mutual assent (offer + acceptance)
- Consideration
- Legality of purpose
- Capacity
- Writing (in some cases)

The following sections discuss these elements.

Mutual Assent

Agency is a consensual, voluntary relationship. Thus, both the principal and the agent must agree to form the relationship. Aside from the occasional need for a writing, which we will discuss below, no particular requirements are necessary to demonstrate mutual assent. Suppose Bob said to Barb, "I want you to be the marketing director for my radio station. I will pay you $3000 per month. Will you do it?" In order to form an enforceable agency agreement, all Barb has to do is say, "Yes."

Quite often, the principal and agent will elect to create their agency relationship by written contract, sometimes called a *power of attorney*. A power of attorney authorizes the agent to act on behalf of the principal. Figure 13.1 is an example of a power of attorney from Gutman to Spade. The grant of the power of attorney from Gutman to Spade has *nothing* to do with whether Spade is or is not a lawyer, an attorney at law. Power of attorney is simply a common law term describing a written grant of agency authority.

Figure 13-1 is a very formal example of a power of attorney, but these documents do not have to be in any particular form. As with virtually all writings, the key lies in stating the agreement's terms clearly. The following is a perfectly valid power of attorney.

> *To Whom It May Concern:*
>   *I hereby authorize Jane Smith to sell my 1987 Pontiac Fiero for not less that $7500.*
>   */s/Barbara Davis*

Consideration

As previously discussed, since agency is a consensual relationship *no* consideration is necessary to form an agency relationship. However, where the formation of the relationship is contractual, consideration is required. In these cases, generally, the exchange of value consists of the agent's promise to do something or to act on the principal's behalf in exchange for compensation.

Some powers of attorney, such as Figure 13-1, do not state any consideration. They are not legally enforceable against the agent if the

Spade & Archer
Private Investigators
21187 Embarcadero Plaza
San Francisco, California   99881

July 28, 1990

To Whom It May Concern :

Know all men by these presents that I, Casper Gutman, of San
Francisco, California, hereby make, constitute, and appoint Samuel
Spade of San Francisco, California, my true and lawful attorney
for me and in my name to negotiate the purchase of a certain gold
Maltese falcon, giving my said attorney full power and authority
as fully as I could do if personally present. In the event of my
death or incapacity, this appointment shall remain in effect, and
shall bind my heirs or my duly appointed guardian, until my said
attorney receives notice of that event at which time this appointment
shall terminate.

_____
Casper Gutman

Figure 13.1 Sample Power of Attorney.

agent decides to do nothing *and* the principal has not reasonably relied upon the agent's promise. If the principal has reasonably relied, a court may find the agent to be bound on a promissory estoppel theory. Suppose the Maltese falcon comes on the market, and Spade leads Gutman to believe he is negotiating for the bird, but in fact he is not. Spade may be liable to Gutman if the falcon eludes him.

If an agent does act on the principal's behalf, the principal is liable both to the agent for his customary compensation and also to the third party with whom the agent contracted. Thus, if Spade contracts to buy the falcon on Gutman's behalf, Gutman is liable on the contract with the seller and on his contract with Spade.

Legality and Capacity

As with any contract, the purpose of an agency contract must be legal. In regard to the power of attorney in Figure 13-1, if it should become illegal to acquire a gold Maltese falcon then the authorization would become void.

Where capacity is concerned, the rules are somewhat different. Essentially, the agent has the principal's capacity to contract. For that reason, a third party dealing with an agent need worry only about the principal's capacity. If the principal is an adult and the agent a minor, the principal may not void contracts because the agent lacked capacity. For example, Boyce pays his 12-year-old newspaper carrier, Arne, each month. If Arne loses Boyce's payment, the newspaper may not make Boyce pay again because the carrier was a minor.

Writing

The *Statute of Frauds* applies to agency contracts just as it does to all other contracts. As you will recall, the Statute identifies the exceptions to the general rule that oral contracts are enforceable. Those exceptions must be in writing.

Contracts Not to be Performed Within 1 Year. Agency or employment contracts not to be completed within 1 year of the creation of the contract must be in writing. Suppose on a Friday Lemon hires Reiser to manage his marina for 1 year, to begin the following Monday. Although the contract is for only 1 year of performance, performance cannot be completed within 1 year of the creation of the contract. Therefore, the contract must be in writing. In contrast, if Reiser could have started the performance by the next day, a writing would not

have been necessary. Contracts of agency or employment for an indefinite time need not be in writing.

Contracts to Sell Real Estate. Authorization for an agent to sell the principal's interest in real estate must be in writing. Suppose Charlie West, a warrant officer in the Army, is transferred overseas before he is able to sell his home. He might want to give somebody a power of attorney to sell and convey his home in his absence. This situation, while not uncommon, should not be confused with a much more common practice in real estate: listing a property for sale with a real estate broker. The latter, often referred to as a listing contract, authorizes the broker to find a ready, able, and willing buyer for the principal's interest in the real estate. It does *not* authorize the actual sale of the property.

A power to sell specific real property is considered to be a *special power of attorney,* a power of attorney for a specified purpose. As the next case illustrates, courts strictly construe such agreements.

King v. Bankerd

303 Md. 98, 492 A.2d 608 (1985)

FACTS   Howard and Virginia Bankerd owned a house. In 1966, Virginia moved out. In 1968, Howard left and began wandering the west. Virginia moved back in. For the next 12 years, Howard made no contributions toward the mortgage, taxes, or upkeep on the house. Before Howard left, he gave attorney King a power of attorney. From 1971 to 1974, King did not hear from Howard. In 1975, for valid business reasons, King sent Howard a revised power of attorney permitting King "to convey, grant, bargain and/or sell" his interest in the house. After receiving the executed power of attorney, King did not hear from Howard again until 1978. In 1977, Virginia, nearing retirement, felt saddled with a property she could neither mortgage nor sell. She contacted King. Over 9 months, King attempted unsuccessfully to trace Howard. Believing that Howard didn't care about the property or might even be dead, King transferred the property to Virginia. Virginia paid nothing for the property, and King received nothing for executing the conveyance. In 1981, Howard brought suit against King for breach of his fiduciary duty. The trial court awarded Howard $13,555 in damages and an appellate court affirmed.

ISSUE	Does a power of attorney authorizing an agent to "convey, grant bargain and/or sell" the principal's property authorize the agent to give the property away?
DECISION	No. Affirmed. Powers of attorney are strictly construed. They grant only those powers outlined in them. Indeed, the courts discount or disregard all-embracing expressions found in them. Also, where an ambiguity exists, it is normally resolved against the party who drafted the instrument. The agent's main duty is to be loyal to his principal's interests. The power to make a gift of the principal's property is a power potentially hazardous to the principal's interests. Therefore, such a power will not be inferred from a broad grant of power to the agent.

King was obviously placed in a difficult position by Howard Bankerd. However, he was Howard's, not Virginia Bankerd's, agent, and the problem in regard to the house was ultimately Virginia's, not King's. As you will learn later in this chapter, although King had the best of intentions, he failed to fulfill his fiduciary duties owed to Howard Bankerd.

In the next chapter, we sill see that what a third party believes about an agent's authority often has more to do with the principal's liability than what in fact was an agent's authority. It is important to keep in mind—as attorney King should have—that in determining the agent's liability to the principal, authority is defined as narrowly as possible.

DUTIES THE AGENT OWES THE PRINCIPAL

The law characterizes the duties an agent owes to a principal as *fiduciary,* or ones of trust. However, "fiduciary" does not characterize a single duty so much as it describes the way an agent performs the duties described in this section. It is important to note that these duties apply to all types of agents, whether special agents or full-time employees.

To Use Proper Care and Skill

An agent owes a duty to a principal to use proper care and skill in carrying out the duties

under their agreement. Suppose that before he leaves on a business trip, Morton asks Chin, his neighbor, to feed and care for his dog in his absence. Chin agrees. Chin thinks the dog is too fat and decides not to feed the dog so that it will lose weight. If the dog becomes ill as a result, Chin will be liable for veterinary bills.

While courts often impose a lower standard for an uncompensated agent, like Chin, the agent still must exercise a reasonable degree of care and skill. Where an agent offers particular services for hire, the degree of care and skill demanded by a court will be greater. For example, the law will charge a professional moving company with a higher duty of care than it would seven students hired through the college employment office.

Normally, agents do not guarantee the success of their undertakings. A professional football coach in the middle of a multiyear contract does not guarantee that his team will make the playoffs. As we will see at the end of this chapter, the owners have the *power* to fire him for a losing record. But since they would not have the *right* to do so, they would breach the coach's contract.

To Obey Legal Instructions

The agent must obey all the principal's legal instructions. Unless a major change in circumstances makes it clear that the principal now would want the agent to act otherwise, the agent may not deviate from the principal's instructions. Suppose Faraway Farms hires Wright to buy a race horse from Fitzsimmons. The horse goes lame just before Wright completes the purchase. Wright would be justified in not following the Farm's instruction to purchase the horse.

But, what if the principal orders the agent to commit a crime or a tort, or to otherwise break the law? If there is no alternative to carrying out the employer's wishes, the agent must terminate the relationship. Suppose the owner of a 'hotel instructs its manager never to rent rooms to nonwhites. The manager must not honor this instruction.

To Account for Money and Property

An agent has a duty to keep accurate records of, and account for, the principal's money and property. If a store manager misplaced the day's receipts on the way to the bank, he would be liable to the store's owner. Also, as the next case establishes, an agent may not make a secret profit as a result of a transaction initiated by a principal.

Johnson v. Hand

377 S.E.2d 176 (Ga. App. 1988)

FACTS Johnson approached Hand, offering his services as a real estate agent to sell a specific piece of property owned by Hand. Hand agreed and they set a price. A short time later Johnson returned with an offer for the price they had just set. The offer, however, was from Johnson's father-in-law, which he never disclosed to Hand. After the title passed to Johnson's father-in-law, Johnson sold the land again for a much greater price. Most of the profit from this second sale went to Johnson. The trial court ruled that Johnson had breached the fiduciary duties he owed Hand.

ISSUE Did Johnson breach his fiduciary duties to Hand, his principal, when he made a secret profit from the land sale?

DECISION Yes. Affirmed. Agents owe a fiduciary duty of trust to their principals. An agent who collects a secret profit at the expense of his principal breaches that trust. Johnson owed a duty to disclose the information to Hand that he was buying the property for himself. Because Johnson was, in reality, the buyer of Hand's property, his interests at the time they set the price were contrary to Hand's. As a consequence he was able to reap a secret profit from his position as an agent.

An agent may not take or use a principal's property for nonagency purposes. *Comingling,* or mixing a principal's funds with an agent's, often leads the agent to grief, even if the comingling is innocent. In some states, lawyers' licenses are almost automatically suspended for comingling. Agents always should establish trust accounts for their principals' funds.

To Communicate Information

The law assumes that the principal receives information communicated by a third party to an appropriate agent. Therefore, such an agent has the duty to communicate information to a principal. For example, a tenant may tell a landlord's rental agent that she will not renew her lease. The rental agent's job includes communicating that information to the landlord. However, the same message given to the landlord's maintenance manager would not be effective because receiving such notices is not a part of his job.

As the next case illustrates, if an agent fails to communicate information to a principal, the agent may be liable for damages that result.

Rookard v. Mexicoach

680 F.2d 1257 (9th Cir. 1982)

FACTS

The Rookards, whose accents identified them as English, wanted to travel through Mexico. They approached Mexicoach, an American bus company which provided tickets for Mexican buses. Mexicoach's brochures described the company as "agent for the passengers in all matters relating to . . . transportation." However, the tickets Mexicoach issued contained disclaimers printed in Spanish regarding Mexican limitations on tort liability and certain insurance problems. Mexicoach did not provide a translation, nor did it warn the Rookards of the significant risks of bus travel through Mexico. The bus the Rookards took crashed due to its driver's gross negligence. They sued Mexicoach for damages, alleging that, as their agent, it had a duty to warn them about Mexican travel. The trial court granted summary judgment in favor of Mexicoach. The Rookards appealed.

ISSUE

Did Mexicoach, as the Rookard's agent, have a duty to warn them of the risks of Mexican bus travel?

DECISION

Yes. Reversed. Although the question ultimately was for a jury, the evidence indicated that Mexicoach was the Rookard's agent.

The remaining question is whether Mexicoach was under a duty to disclose the facts known to it given the totality of the circumstances:

1. *limited [tort] liability under Mexican law;*
2. *tickets . . . with disclaimers in Spanish;*
3. *knowledge that the Rookards were foreign visitors;*
4. *poor safety record of Mexican bus companies; and*
5. *lack of even a de minimis investigation into the safety record of [the Mexican bus company].*

. . . The rule in California "charges an agent with the duty of fullest disclosure of all material facts concerning the transaction . . . which might affect the principal's decision. . . ."

The scope of this duty of disclosure will be limited, naturally, to what is reasonable in any given instance. A travel agent is not an insurer, nor can he be reasonably expected to divine and forewarn of an innumerable litany of tragedies and dangers inherent in foreign travel. . . .

. . . All travelers, foreign or not, could reasonably expect to be informed of such risks before booking passage. The duty to warn . . . does not represent an extension of tort liability upon an agent. Rather, it results from an exposition of the preexisting duty of care owed a principal by his agent.

It is important to note that many employees who fall into the servant category have the job of accepting communications for their employers. Insurance companies, for instance, often have clerks who are authorized to accept notice of accidents. However, they lack any authority to bind the company to pay claims.

To be Loyal

Many of an agent's duties to a principal could fall into the general category of a duty of loyalty. An agent must avoid even the appearance of a conflict of interest. Suppose Vivien works as an independent casualty appraiser. An insurance company hires her to evaluate fire damage to Pangloss Pumpkin Products' factory. After she submits her report to the insurance company, she cannot offer to help Pangloss press its claim with the insurance company.

An agent may not make a secret profit out of any transaction involving the agency. Suppose Curran has hired Swalve to sell her boat for at least $4000. Swalve finds a buyer for $4300. Swalve cannot secretly keep the $300. If Swalve did and it was later discovered, he would owe the principal the $300 *plus* the return of any associated commission or payment he might have received.

It follows that an agent may not undermine the principal's interest or position. For instance, without the principal's permission an agent may not tell a third party to offer a very low price for the principal's property because the principal is in the midst of a cash flow crisis. An agent who does something like this, and whose principal discovers it, risks losing the commission on the sale.

The duty of loyalty is broader than simply avoiding conflicts of interests. An agent may not either use himself or disclose a principal's confidential information—customer files, financial condition, trade secrets, and the like during or immediately after employment. However, without a covenant not to compete, discussed in Part II, a former agent is free to compete against his former employer and use general knowledge and skills acquired in employment. The next case illustrates that a court may take a rather limited view of what confidential information includes.

Woodward Ins. Co. v. White

437 N.E.2d 59 (Ind. 1982)

FACTS   White began working for Woodward Insurance, Inc., in 1930. Forty-nine years later he left Woodward to join the May Agency. Of the 106 customers he served during his 8 months at the May Agency, 77 percent were former Woodward customers. Of the $120,000 in premiums his clients paid, $110,000 came from former Woodward clients. Woodward sued White, alleging improper use of its trade secrets and confidential information. The trial court found for White on this issue and the Court of Appeals affirmed.

ISSUE

Is information about a customer's insurance confidential?

DECISION

No. Affirmed. Whether a former employer's customer information is confidential depends upon:

1. The extent to which the information is known outside of the business and the ease with which others could properly acquire it
2. Whether the information was confidential or secret
3. The extent and manner in which the employer guarded its secrecy
4. The former employee's knowledge of customers' buying habits and other customer data and whether the employer's competitors know this information

Here the allegedly confidential information included customer names and policy expiration dates, coverages, and costs. While White worked for Woodward, he had access to this information. However, through a variety of legitimate means, other insurance agents could get the same information. And, the Woodward Agency had no established policy defining it as confidential.

As the case points out, very often an employer's definition of confidential information is much broader than what the law will protect. An employer should be realistic in identifying confidential information to be protected. Where a covenant not to compete is appropriate, the restrictions must be reasonable in scope. If not, an employer, like Woodward Insurance, may waste valuable time and money in later fruitless litigation.

DUTIES THE PRINCIPAL OWES THE AGENT

A principal does *not* owe fiduciary duties to an agent because the principal does not act on the agent's behalf. *Only* an agent owes fiduciary duties. Nor does the principal deal with the agent's money or property, except to the extent that the principal compensates the agent. How-

ever, the principal has a duty to cooperate with the agent and to comply with the agency contract.

To Compensate for Services

Where the parties have so agreed, the principal must compensate the agent. Difficult problems arise when the agreement is silent on the subject, but the agent claims the parties had an understanding as to compensation. Then, the agent must prove the agreement's existence in court based on the relationship between the parties and the circumstances surrounding it.

Where only the amount of compensation is at issue, the courts will evaluate the services provided. Assume Clapp hires Johnston to find a buyer for his stamp collection. Johnston finds a buyer who is ready, willing, and able to purchase the entire collection. At that moment, Johnston earns her commission. If she and

Clapp had not set her commission, she would have the burden of proving the agreement and of establishing the fair value of her services. Normally, that value would be based on commissions paid on sales of similar collections.

Of course, as *Johnston v. Hand* showed, an agent may forfeit his right to compensation—as well as any illicit gain—if she breaches her duties to the principal. Suppose Johnston sold Clapp's collection for $13,000 but told her she sold it for $10,000, keeping $3000 for herself. A court would force Johnston to pay Clapp the $3000 and return his commission to him.

To Reimburse and Indemnify

Unless they agree otherwise, the principal must reimburse the agent for any reasonable expenses incurred on his behalf. However, the transactions resulting in those expenses must lie within the scope of the agent's employment. In other words, they must relate directly to the purpose of the agency. If the principal sends the agent to Los Angeles to purchase some new manufacturing equipment, the principal normally would reimburse the travel expenses. However, it would not pay for a weekend excursion to San Francisco.

Should the agent incur personal losses while acting within the scope of his or her authority, the principal must *indemnify* or reimburse the agent. Assume Sarah employs Nick to sell a painting she inherited. She chooses to be an undisclosed principal. Nick sells the painting and pays the proceeds, less his commission, to Sarah. Later, the buyer obtains a judgment against Nick for $10,000 because the painting is a fraud. Sarah would have to indemnify Nick's losses associated with the lawsuit.

TERMINATION BY ACTS OF THE PARTIES

An agency relationship can come to an end by acts of the parties or by operation of law. Acts

of the parties include expiration by lapse of time; fulfillment of agency purpose; mutual agreement; and unilateral termination.

Lapse of Time

Authority granted to an agent for a specified period of time will expire by its own terms. If Clayton is hired to manage a seaside cafe from Memorial Day to Labor Day, his agency authority will terminate on Labor Day. If no specified period of time is stipulated, the agency relation will terminate after a reasonable time.

Where the parties create an agency relationship to accomplish specified objectives, the relationship terminates upon completion. Normally, this situation involves a special agent, such as a realtor engaged to find a buyer for a farm.

Fulfillment of Agency Purpose

Some agency relationships terminate upon the occurrence of a specific event. The Tofu Corporation has the food service contract for a university. Its contract with Mary states that she will manage the cafeteria so long as Tofu has the contract. If Tofu loses the contract, Mary loses her job.

Termination by Mutual Consent

No matter how long the contract specifies that an agency relationship will last, the parties at any time may agree to terminate the relationship. As in any other contract termination, the agreement must not be based upon fraud, coercion, duress, or any other unlawful means.

Termination by a Party's Unilateral Action

A principal ends the relationship with an agent by a *revocation of authority,* while an agent terminates by a *renunciation of authority.* Either the principal or the agent may end the agency relationship at any time, though termination may result in liability for breach of contract. (The sole exception to this rule, "an agency coupled with an interest," is discussed below.)

Even if the termination breaches the agency contract—and quite often it does not—the terminating party has the power to end the relationship. Power in this context means "ability." It does not mean that the breaching party is justified or that he or she will avoid liability. For that reason, a party whose termination would breach an agency agreement is said to have "the power buy not the right" to terminate.

The Power But Not The Right. The perplexing phrase "the power but not the right" reflects a most important concept in American law. The law will not compel parties to fulfill agency or any personal services contracts against their will. The remedy for the nonbreaching party is damages, not specific performance. Assume that the manager of the California Angels quits with 2 years to go on his contract. The Angels may prevent him from managing another team during the period the contract remains in force. However, the law will not force the ex-manager to continue working for the Angels. Of course,

the team may sue him for any damages resulting from his breach of contract.

Employees at Will. Earlier in this chapter, we discussed the application of the Statute of Frauds to agency agreements. We noted that an agency contract which is not to be performed within 1 year must be in writing. Such a contract is breached if it is terminated before the expiration date. But, as we noted there and in Chapter 9, an employment contract with no ending date does not have to be in writing because it can be performed within 1 year. Persons employed under such contracts are called *employees at will.*

An employee at will is one who may rightfully terminate employment at her discretion or whose employer may rightfully terminate her at any time. Generally, an employee at will lacks any grounds for recovering from her employer or principal for discharge unless a collective bargaining agreement protects her, or a specific contract between her and the employer exists, or the law affords her special protection from discharge. (For discussions of the particular protections the law offers, see Chapter 15.) In the next case, an employee tried to disprove his employer's claim that he was an employee at will.

D'Angelo v. Gardner

819 P.2d 206 (Nev. 1991)

FACTS D'Angelo was employed by GEMCO for 12 years. During that time he had risen from sales clerk to department manager. One day he was fired for reducing the price of several roles of expired film from $3.97 to $2.00. In a letter to the state labor commissioner, GEMCO stated that D'Angelo was fired for violating work rule number 6: "accepting or extending unauthorized discounts or credit to anyone," which was contained in GEMCO's Employee Handbook. The handbook also included provisions for discharge for "proper cause," and stated that "*any* discharge based on an employee's failure to perform work as required . . . must be preceded by written notice to the employee."

ISSUE   Did the trial court judge have sufficient facts to determine that D'Angelo was an employee at will?

DECISION   No. Reversed and remanded. There are facts in this case which might lead a jury to conclude that GEMCO and D'Angelo intended to be bound by the terms of the handbook. The fact that D'Angelo's dismissal was based on a handbook violation supports the argument that the two parties meant the handbook to serve as a contract of employment. Thus, the case must be remanded for trial to decide if D'Angelo's discharge was an illegal breach of contract.

Agency coupled with an interest. The only exception to the rule that either the principal or the agent may terminate an agency relationship at any time occurs in the case of an *agency coupled with an interest.* This concept protects the agent's interest in specific property belonging to the principal. Suppose Morgan borrows $1000 from the Last National Bank. She *pledges* (puts up as security) 100 shares of stock, which she authorizes the bank to sell to satisfy her obligation if she defaults on the loan. If the bank sells the stock, it acts as Morgan's agent. She may not terminate its agency authority except by paying off the loan. The bank's interest in the collateral is worthless without this rule's protection.

TERMINATION BY OPERATION OF LAW

Where a significant change of circumstances alters the original rationale for the agency relationship, a court may hold the agency relationship terminated "by operation of law." The most common situations of termination by operation of law are discussed next.

Death

Because an agency relationship is a personal, consensual relationship, the death of either the principal or the agent terminates the agent's authority. Suppose that Clara hires Darrow, a

lawyer, and Darrow dies. Their agency relationship automatically terminates because Clara contracted for a particular person's services.

Bankruptcy

When a principal files bankruptcy after the creation of the agency relationship, a trustee in bankruptcy normally will terminate the principal's existing agency contracts (see Chapter 43). The bankruptcy of the agent, when critical to the performance of the agency agreement, will also terminate the agent's authority.

Incapacity of Principal

When a principal is declared legally insane after the creation of the agency relationship, the relation will automatically terminate. If Clara, above, is adjudicated insane then Darrow's authority to represent her is automatically terminated. A court could subsequently reappoint the agent, Darrow, to act on behalf of the principal's, Clara's, estate.

Performance Becomes Impossible

When an event or circumstance occurs after the creation of the agency relationship which makes performance impossible, the relation will terminate. If Darrow loses his license to practice law his relationship with Clara is terminated for loss of qualification. A destruction of the subject matter of the agency relationship would similarly terminate the relationship. If Darrow had been hired to find a buyer for Clara's racehorse, the death of the racehorse will terminate Darrow's authority.

Change of Law

When a change in the law occurs after the creation of the agency relationship which makes performance of the agency purpose now illegal, the relation will terminate. Suppose Carlisle is hired by Stone to purchase and bring back particular artwork from Russia. Before doing so, the Russian government makes it illegal to export such works from its country. Carlisle's authority will be terminated.

Outbreak of War

When a declared war occurs after the creation of the agency relationship, and the principal and agent are on opposite sides at war, the relation will terminate. This result is not unique to agency law.

Notice of Termination

The principal has a duty to notify third parties with whom the agent might deal of the agency's termination. The one exception to the notice rule occurs when the relationship ends by operation of law. Then, the principal does not have to notify anyone and no later act by the agent will bind the principal. As we will see in the next chapter, the agent may be personally liable to the third party on a contract made after the agency relationship has terminated.

Persons to be notified. The principal must give actual notice to all creditors who have dealt with the agent and constructive notice to everyone else who might have dealt with the agent. *Actual notice* means that the principal must inform the third parties of the termination directly, by letter or telephone. *Constructive notice* or legal notice usually takes the form of a classified ad in the legal column of an appropriate trade journal or newspaper.

Effect of improper notice. If the principal fails

Burch v. Americus Grocery Co.

125 Ga. 153, 53 S.E. 1008 (1906)

FACTS   Burch fired the manager of his grocery store. However, following his discharge, the manager ordered goods from the Americus Grocery Co., which he kept for himself. The grocery company had no notice of the manager's firing. The grocery company brought suit against Burch to recover the value of the goods. The trial court found for the grocery company.

ISSUE   Was Burch liable for his former manager's order?

DECISION   Yes. Affirmed. Whenever parties establish an agency, all persons who know of the agency or have dealt with the agent and are likely to deal with him have a right to presume that his authority will continue until they receive notice of its termination. Creditors must receive "actual notice," which should not be confused with "actual knowledge." Notice is actual when one either has knowledge of a fact or is conscious of having the means of gaining knowledge of a fact, although one may not use those means.

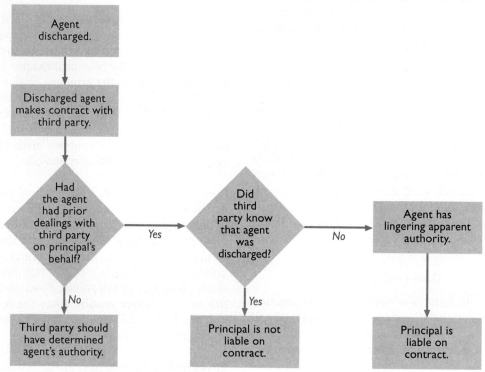

Figure 13.2 Liability After Termination.

to give the third party appropriate notice, it will be liable on a contract made by a former agent with a third party. That was the holding in the next case.

Figure 13-2 diagrams how liability is determined after the termination of an agency agreement.

CONCLUSION

Agency or the appearance of agency depends almost as much on the perceptions of third parties as it does on the actual agreement between principal and agent. For that reason, in analyzing whether an agency exists, one must examine not only the arrangement between the principal and the agent, but primarily how the third party views their relationship. In the next chapter, we will look at the relationships among parties to transactions involving principals or employers and agents or employees.

A NOTE TO FUTURE CPA CANDIDATES

The concepts you will learn in Chapters 13 and 14 are heavily tested on the CPA exam in three areas: principal-agency law, partnership law, and corporation law.

Agency is a consensual relationship. Although the formation of an agency relationship is generally contractual, it need not be. Where it is, the common law requirements to form a contract apply, including consideration. A power of attorney is a written authorization of agency from the principal to the agent. Remember that it need be signed only by the principal.

It is important to remember that an agent owes fiduciary duties to the principal, not the reverse. An agent must act in good faith, use care, account for all agency funds owed the principal, obey all reasonable, legal instructions, and be loyal. An agent must not secretly benefit. Where agreed, a principal must compensate an agent. In addition, the principal must reimburse and indemnify the agent for costs or losses incurred while carrying out duties as agent for the principal.

An agency relationship is considered to be highly personal. As a result, an agency relationship automatically terminates, by operation of law, upon the death of either the principal or agent, the bankruptcy of the principal, or the principal being declared legally incompetent.

KEY WORDS

actual notice (295)	indemnify (292)
agency coupled with an interest (294)	power of attorney (284)
agency (284)	renunciation of authority (292)
comingling (288)	revocation of authority (292)
constructive notice (295)	
fiduciary duty (287)	

DISCUSSION QUESTIONS

1. What are the essential requirements of an agency relationship?
2. What is a "fiduciary relationship"? Explain.
3. When is a written agency contract required?
4. What is a "power of attorney"?
5. Why is it a good idea to put an agency agreement in writing? Explain.
6. Describe the duties an agent owes a principal.
7. Explain what is meant by an "employee at will."
8. Describe the duties a principal owes an agent.
9. Explain the various ways in which an agency relation may terminate.

10. What is meant by "the power but not the right" to terminate an agency relationship?

CASE PROBLEMS

1. Jerry Godwin is employed as a regional sales representative for Grayson Manufacturing Company. Jerry, a baseball legend, learns that Mayfield's Sporting Goods Store is for sale. He buys it, changes its name to Jerry Godwin Sports, Inc., and arranges for his daughter to manage it. Jerry does not inform Grayson before purchasing it. The store immediately becomes a huge success. Although Godwin continued to devote full-time attention to Grayson, he was fired. Grayson has now brought an action asking the court to find that Godwin violated his fiduciary duties. Is the court likely to agree with Grayson? Assuming the court agrees, what would the court be likely to do? Explain.

2. Cleatis Voss hired Margie Hamilton to purchase a racehorse for the upcoming racing season at Red River Downs. Unknown to Cleatis, Margie owned a racing horse called Gilda's Star. Gilda's Star was worth approximately $12,000. Margie used a third person to sell the horse to Cleatis for $11,500. Margie received a 10 percent commission ($1150) from Cleatis. After Gilda's Star had a very successful first season, Cleatis learned the truth. Cleatis now demands the return of the commission paid Margie. Margie claims that he is due nothing, as he obviously got a good deal. Would a court be likely to require Margie to return the $1150? Explain.

3. Eileen Dolan worked as a salesperson for Bob Flemming in his delicatessen. On January 9, Flemming's landlord, Marty Kron, saw Dolan during half-time at a Chicago Bulls basketball game and told her to tell Flemming that he was going to terminate their lease on April 30. Dolan promised that she would remember to tell Flemming. She did not. Flemming did not personally learn of the planned termination until a subsequent discussion with Kron on March 27. Flemming claims he has not gotten "at least 90

days' personal notice of termination" as required by his lease. Would a court be likely to agree with Flemming? Explain.

4. Hawley, Inc., appointed Dan Heine as its agent to market its various product lines. Heine entered into a 2-year written agency contract with Hawley which provided that Heine would receive a 10 percent sales commission. After 6 months, Heine was terminated without cause. Heine asserts that his agency was coupled with an interest. Is he correct? Heine also asserts that the agency relationship may not be terminated without cause prior to the expiration of its term. Is he correct? Finally, Heine asserts that he is entitled to damages because of the termination of the agency relationship. Is he correct? Explain.

5. The *Morning Herald* hired Molly Chambers, 13, to deliver newspapers in her neighborhood. One of Molly's duties was to collect monthly payments from subscribers on her route. Molly's family was moving to another city, so Molly made her final collections from customers and gave the money to Andy Young, also 13, to drop off at the *Morning Herald* office. Instead, Andy spent the money on a new tennis racquet. Citing her age, could the *Morning Herald* recollect from customers that had paid Molly? Explain.

6. Shirley Kelly was a sales representative for ABC Copier Company. Shirley lost sales opportunities because ABC added several new representatives in Shirley's region. ABC had never had more than one representative in her region. Unable to sustain her lifestyle representing just ABC, Shirley began representing XYZ Computers, Inc., also. ABC and XYZ do not compete against each other. When ABC learned of Shirley's dual agency status she was fired and not paid her remaining earned commissions. In a suit to recover her commissions, Shirley claims that she should recover, since ABC breached its fiduciary duties to her. Is she correct? Is ABC likely to prevail in the suit? Explain.

7. Baker Corp. dismissed Abel as its general sales agent. Baker notified all of Abel's known customers by letter. Fam Corp., a retail outlet located outside Abel's previously assigned sales territory, had never dealt with Abel. However, Fam knew of Abel as a result of various business contacts. After his dismissal, Abel sold Fam goods, to be delivered by Baker, and received from Fam a cash deposit for 25 percent of the purchase price. It was not unusual for an agent in Abel's previous positions to receive cash deposits. In an action by Fam against Baker on the sales contract, will Fam prevail? Explain.

8. The Erewhon Captains hired Ollie Mathews to manage the team for the upcoming season. Mathews knew that the team's owner, Jorge Stanky, had a reputation for firing managers in the middle of the season in embarrassing ways. To protect himself, Ollie added this clause to his contract: "I, Jorge Stanky, hereby make an irrevocable commitment to retain Ollie Mathews for the entire playing season." In the middle of a game 7 weeks into the season, the large screen on the scoreboard blinked: "Say good night, Ollie. You are hereby notified that you are a part of the Captains' history." Ollie claims that Stanky's promise prevents his termination. Would a court be likely to agree? Explain.

9. In a telephone conversation on June 15, Jim Heno hired Molly Garza to manage his golf shop for 1 year beginning July 1. On July 27 Heno learned that a retired golf pro. Bill Mayfield, was available and hired Bill without a specified term of employment. Heno immediately informed Molly that her services were not going to be needed. Molly claims that Heno had neither the right nor the power to terminate her. Correct? Bill has gotten a little nervous because Heno has not yet provided him a power of attorney. If Heno now changes his mind and wants to hire a different manager, does he have the right and power to do so? Explain.

CHAPTER 14

The Liability of Principals and Agents to Third Parties

In the last chapter, we looked at the relationship between principal and agent. In this chapter, we will focus on how principals and agents deal with third parties. Up to this point, we have considered the principal-agent relationship in the context of contracts the agent makes on the principal's behalf. In the second half of this chapter, we will see how agency affects the principal's tort liability for the agent's acts.

THE AGENT'S AUTHORITY

In situations involving an agent entering into a contract on behalf of his principal with a third party, the third party has the ultimate responsibility to (1) determine whether a person is in fact an actual agent of the principal; and, if so, to (2) determine whether the agent has the authority to bind the principal in the particular contractual transaction. *Authority* describes the legal ability of an agent to act for another. There are three common types of authority which can directly bind a principal: express, implied, and apparent authority. We begin with express authority.

Express Authority

Express authority is what the principal specifically communicates, either orally or in writing, to the agent. Assume Paul hires Alice to manage his bar. Paul tells Alice, "You can hire live entertainment appropriate for the bar." Paul has given Alice express authority to hire entertainment. He might also give her authority to hire other employees, enter into contracts with suppliers, and the like.

Specific grants of authority, of course, are likely to reduce misunderstandings or disagreements in the future. So, too, are specific limitations on an agent's authority. For instance, Paul may tell Alice she may not hire more than three waiters. Problems arise when the limitations on the agent's authority are ones that persons who deal with agents of the same type would not

anticipate. If Paul told Alice never to order Blech's beer for the bar, a beer distributor would probably not expect a bar manager's authority to order to be so restricted. We will look at this problem more closely later in this chapter.

Implied Authority

When they form their agency agreement, a principal and an agent may try to anticipate all the eventualities in which the agent would require authority to contract. Even so, situations may arise in the context of the agent's duties that require the exercise of discretion or an interpretation of the scope of authority. In such situations, the agent may rely upon *implied authority,* that authority reasonably necessary to implement the grant of express authority.

To illustrate, suppose when Paul hired Alice as his bar manager nothing was stated about her authority to hire entertainment. Would Alice have implied authority to hire entertainment? If so, to hire a band like R.E.M.? To hire a comedy act? To stage silly contests for prizes? To advertise the entertainment?

The *Restatement (Second) of Agency,* a compilation of the common law applicable to agency, in §§ 50 and 73, provides guidance as to Alice's scope of implied authority. Section 50 states:

> *Unless otherwise agreed, authority to make a contract is inferred from authority to conduct a transaction, if the making of such a contract is incidental to the transaction, usually accompanies such a transaction, or is reasonably necessary to accomplish it.*

Section 73 states:

> *Unless otherwise agreed, authority to manage a business includes authority:*
> *(a) to make contracts which are incidental to such business, are usually made in it, or are reasonably necessary in conducting it;*
> *(b) to procure equipment and supplies and*

to make repairs reasonably necessary . . .
(c) to employ, supervise, or discharge employees as the course of business may reasonably require;
(d) to sell . . . in accordance with the purposes for which the business is operated;
(e) to receive payment . . . and to pay debts due . . .
(f) to direct the ordinary operations of business.

In determining implied authority, a court will attempt to determine what is usual and customary in such a situation.

A court will ask: Would an agent *with similar express authority* in a similar business of a similar size be expected to have the power to *implement* the same action? If so, the agent had implied authority, and the principal may not assert the agent's lack of authority as a defense.

The scope of an agent's implied authority is always a matter of a third party's reasonable expectations—based on the powers of agents with similar express authority—as to what an agent with her express authority may do. So, Alice's implied authority to hire entertainment would be what a reasonable third party would expect managers of bars of a similar size and character and in a similar location to have. If Paul's bar seats fifty-five, it would not be reasonable to expect Alice to have authority to hire a twelve-piece band.

In regard to Alice's authority to advertise, it would probably be customary for a manager of a larger bar with live entertainment to be able to advertise. Her choices of when and where to advertise would be limited by what similarly situated bars would be expected to do. An ad in a college newspaper might be perfectly appropriate, while one in *USA Today* would probably be questionable. In contrast, a marketing director for Ford Motor Company would be expected to be able to place an advertisement in *USA Today*.

In regard to Alice's authority to stock the bar, it would be very unusual for a principal to specify precisely what brands of beer, wine,

and spirits the manager might order. The salespeople with whom the manager deals would expect her to have authority to choose what to order. This implied authority is implementation authority, that authority necessary to carry out the express authority the principal grants the agent.

Apparent Authority

Apparent authority is authority an agent possesses as a result of representations from the principal to a third party. Unlike express or implied authority, an agent who acts with apparent authority has no actual authority from the principal. In fact, an agent who binds his principal by apparent authority may have a duty to reimburse the principal.

When Paul informs third parties of his appointment of Alice as the bar manager, she is presumed to have the same authority that other bar managers enjoy in businesses of similar type and size. In other words, her position title gives her the appearance of authority, apparent authority. Suppose, for whatever reason, Paul has told Alice to never order Blech's beer for the bar, but she does. Alice clearly had no express authority so she could not have acted with implied, implementation, authority. However, she did have apparent authority from her position as manager, the appearance of authority by title; thus, the bar will not be able to assert the agent's lack of actual authority as a defense. See Figure 14-1.

The agency example with Blech's beer provides some key learning points about apparent authority.

1. Apparent authority is that which does not in fact exist, but third party reasonably concludes that it does exist. For example, Alice had no authority to order Blech's beer.
2. The principal is held liable because he permitted this misunderstanding to occur or failed to fulfill his duty to dispel this erroneous understanding. As manager, Alice had

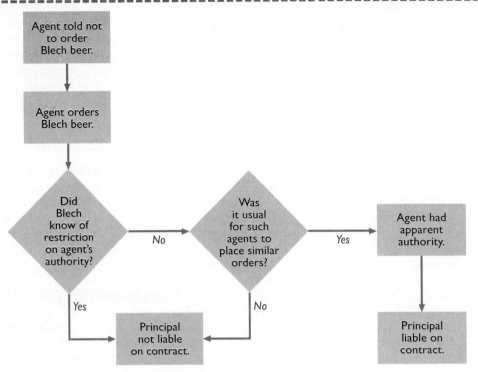

Figure 14.1 Effect of Secret Instructions.
The law presumes that an agent has the same authority as any other agent acting in a similar capacity in the same line of business. The agent may be liable to the principal for violating secret instructions, but the principal may not rescind a contract with a third party for their violation—assuming the agent had apparent authority.

the appearance of authority to order any brand of beer. The bar should have directly told the distributor of Blech's beer about Alice's specific limitation of authority.

3. The question of apparent authority arises because the third party wishes to hold the principal liable and the principal prefers to decline this honor. Blech's beer will be attempting to enforce the order of their beer.

4. It is always the third party who alleges apparent authority, not the agent. If Alice had told the distributor she had no actual authority to order Blech's beer, then the resulting contract clearly would have been unenforceable by Blech's beer.

5. The agent may have a duty to indemnify, pay

back, the principal. In regard to the bar and Alice, Alice could be made to take the beer and cover the costs which the bar ultimately must pay the Blech's beer distributor.

6. Since apparent authority results from actions or communication of the principal, *not* the agent, to the third party, it is impossible for an agent to act with apparent authority in an undisclosed principal situation. This will be discussed further later in this chapter.

Principal's action or inaction. Apparent authority can arise out of the principal's words or conduct. The test is what the words or conduct would lead a reasonable person to believe. Suppose Paul is present in the bar one night when

Alice tells Mario she wants to buy his stock car for advertising the bar. Mario turns to Paul and asks, "Can she do that?" Paul laughs, "Sure, she can." Paul may have been joking, but unless that is clear, Mario is entitled to rely on the plain meaning of what Paul told him. Now suppose that Paul sits silently while Alice and Mario agree on the sale of the stock car. Paul's inaction may result in liability if a third party would reasonably have expected him to intervene.

A principal has no duty to intervene when he is not aware of an assertion of authority or, as the following case illustrates, if he has expressly revoked the agent's apparent authority.

Rudolph v. Lewis

418 So. 2d 296 (Fla. Dist. Ct. App. 1982)

FACTS   Lewis wanted to buy a yacht through Rudolph's marina. He signed a contract with Blake, an employee of the marina. The contract stated, "This order is not valid unless signed by the dealer." Directly below appeared two lines, the first marked "Dealer" and the second, "Salesman." Blake, whom Lewis knew was not the dealer, signed the line marked "Salesman," leaving the "Dealer" line blank. Rudolph refused to accept the contract, and Lewis sued for damages. The trial court held that Blake had authority to bind Rudolph and entered judgment for Lewis.

ISSUE   Did Blake have apparent authority to bind Rudolph?

DECISION   No. Reversed.

> [The] presence of the acceptance clause in the agreement prevented the creation of an enforceable contract. An acceptance clause specifically limits the authority of an agent and reduces the agreement to the status of an unaccepted offer. Only when the agent's principal accepts the offer does a contract arise. The claim of apparent authority is negated on the face of the instrument.
>
> When Blake did not sign the agreement as dealer, Lewis was on notice that he lacked the authority to create a binding contract. In any event, Lewis . . . knew Blake was not the dealer. . . . Since there was no contract, Rudolph may not be held accountable for a breach.

Restrictions on authority. Notice destroys apparent authority. If a third party has notice of a restriction on the agent's authority, no act or representation by the agent will permit the third party to assert that he relied on the agent's apparent authority.

However, third parties will not be held responsible for what they have no reason to know. If the third party would expect an agent in a similar position to have authority which the principal has limited by secret instructions, the principal will be bound by a contract which violates those instructions. Our earlier discussion of Alice's purchasing of Blech's beer and Figure 14-1 dealt with restrictions on authority by secret instructions.

Apparent agents. Up until this point, we have described situations in which an agent does something not directly related to her express authority. But, apparent authority can also justify a court's imposition of liability on a person as a principal for the acts of someone who is not his agent.

A person who holds out another as his agent—whether by actions, words, or silence—will be liable for the "agent's" acts because he has given the "agent" apparent authority to act. Suppose that while Paul, the bar owner, is present, Von tells a beer salesman that he has authority to order beer for the bar. If Paul fails to contradict Von when he has the chance, Paul will be liable for Von's orders from the salesman.

A similar rationale leads courts to impose liability on principals who fail to notify third parties that an agent no longer has authority to represent them. The reason for the termination of the agent's authority is not important, nor is who terminated the relationship. What is important is the principal's duty to notify third persons with whom the agent might have dealt on his behalf that he no longer employs the agent. Until such third parties receive notice, the agent retains what is called "lingering apparent authority," as discussed at the end of the previous chapter.

Emergency Authority

The fourth type of agency authority is *emergency authority,* which exists in the absence of other authority. The law presumes that an agent has a certain amount of authority to handle an emergency for the principal. In most respects, emergency authority resembles apparent authority, but, unlike apparent authority, it extends to employees who normally lack contractual authority. Suppose neither Alice nor Paul is at the bar when a water pipe breaks. A waitress normally would not have authority to hire a plumber. However, in this situation she would in order to protect Paul's property.

The principle of emergency authority may seem obvious today, but the issue was bitterly fought in the nineteenth century.

Terre Haute & Indianapolis R.R. Co. v. McMurray

98 Ind. 358 (1884)

FACTS

Frankfort was a way station on the railroad's line some miles from its headquarters. At 1 A.M. on July 2, 1881, a brakeman had his foot crushed by the wheel of the train on which he was working. The injury required immediate attention. The conductor asked the local surgeon to take care of the brakeman, promising him that the railroad would pay his bill. When the conductor took this action, the railroad had no employee superior to him in Frankfort. The railroad's resident agent in Frankfort was fully informed about the injury and the surgeon's employment. Although the resident agent could have contacted headquarters by telegraph, he did not. When the railroad refused to pay the surgeon, he brought suit. The trial court found for the surgeon.

ISSUE

In the absence of superiors in an emergency, does an agent have authority to take an action to protect his employer's interests that would ordinarily be outside the scope of his authority?

DECISION   Yes. Affirmed. A court determines the authority of an agent from the facts of the particular case before it. Facts may exist that greatly broaden or greatly lessen an agent's authority. Under normal circumstances, a conductor has general authority to control the train and the trainmen on it. In the absence of a superior, the conductor is the railroad's general agent as to the management of the train while it is on the road. Specifically, he has the duty of using reasonable care for the safety of his subordinates. That duty does not ordinarily extend to hiring surgeons. But here, an emergency arose that required the conductor to take action to save a life or prevent a great injury. And, he was the highest official of the railroad available to take action. If the conductor lacked authority in this instance to hire a surgeon, then a train operates without any representative of the owner.

Ratification

A *ratification* is an act by which a principal accepts responsibility for an unauthorized action taken by the agent, or by a person purporting to act as an agent, which would otherwise not have bound the principal. Stated another way, ratification may occur when a person purports to act on behalf of a principal without possessing express, implied, apparent, or emergency authority.

For example, Al has authority to buy only late model cars for Pat's used car lot. Al sees a choice vintage car, a 1929 Model A Ford, and buys it in Pat's name. It is clear that Al has no express, implied, or emergency authority. Since it is doubtful that such a transaction would be considered customary, the third party would probably not prevail on the grounds of Al's apparent authority. As a result, Pat would be bound only if he were to ratify Al's purchase.

For a principal's ratification to be effective:

- The agent must indicate that he is acting on behalf of a principal. This would be met if Al had said he was a buyer for a car dealer without actually identifying Pat.
- The principal must have the capacity to authorize the act both at the time of the act and at the time of ratification.
- The principal must manifest an intent to be bound with knowledge of all material facts. An agent's knowledge will ordinarily be imputed to his principal.
- The principal must ratify all or none of the transaction. If the purchase of the Model A was a package deal that included a special trailer, Pat could not ratify the transaction only as it pertained to the car.
- Since the ratification relates back to the time of the agent's contract, no significant intervening event shall have occurred since then: for example, a material change in circumstances or the third party's death, loss of capacity, or withdrawal from the contract.

A principal's ratification can be express, written or oral, or implied, by the principal's conduct. If Pat puts the Model A on his lot for several days to see how marketable it is, he will probably be considered to have ratified the purchase. A principal cannot revoke a ratification.

CONTRACTUAL LIABILITY IN AN AGENCY CONTEXT

The main reason principals use agents is to make contracts for them. The basic rules relating to contracts do not change simply because a principal uses an agent. For the most part, the law treats contracts made by agents for their principals as if the principals had contracted directly with the third parties.

Accordingly, the third party does not have the option of not performing simply because an agent signed the contract for the principal. Unless the principal specifically reserves the power to accept the agent's act, the third party is bound as if the principal had actually signed the contract.

The exceptions to this rule—the focus of this section—often relate to whether the third party knows that he or she is dealing with an agent. As with the scope of the agent's authority, the third party's reasonable expectations play a large role in defining who is liable on contracts made by an agent.

The Third Party's Duties in General

The third party has two duties when contracting with someone claiming or appearing to be an agent:

- To determine whether the person is in fact an agent
- If the person is an agent, to determine the limits of the agent's authority

The third party's duty to inquire contains an implicit "reasonableness" qualification. There are some transactions in which the third party need not make these inquiries. A cash purchase by the agent, for instance, would not require an exploration of an agent's authority. But, if the purchase is on credit or if a contract calls for performance over time, the third party acts at his peril if he does not make these inquiries.

Once a third party has determined that someone is an agent and over a course of dealing determines the limits of the agent's authority, the third party may presume that the agent's authority continues until he is notified or learns otherwise. Of course, the principal has the responsibility to communicate to third parties any extraordinary restrictions on the agent's authority.

Third parties are also presumed to know the normal scope of an agent's authority, if the agent is of a type with whom they normally deal. Such an agent's assertion of authority beyond the normal limits triggers the third party's duty to inquire.

Gunn v. Schaeffer

567 S.W.2d 30 (Tex. Civ. App. 1978)

FACTS   The Schaeffers owned an apartment house. They hired Nick Bikos to manage the building. Bikos allowed some tenants to pay a year's rent in advance in exchange for a discount on their monthly rents. From this money he paid the Schaeffers only 1 month's rent, using the rest to pay gambling debts and other expenses. The prepayment plan caught on among the tenants. However, Bikos needed to keep up the rent payments for those who had already paid. So, he began selling tenants short-term savings certificates in the name of the apartment building. The scheme collapsed, and Bikos was arrested. The tenants sued the Schaeffers for $20,200 which they had paid for the certificates. The trial court granted summary judgment to the Schaeffers.

ISSUE   Did Bikos have the apparent authority to issue the savings certificates?

DECISION   No. Affirmed. The manager of an apartment complex with authority to collect rent does not have the apparent authority to issue savings certificates in the name of the apartment complex. No manager of a business has the apparent authority to borrow money in the name of the principal unless the business involves borrowing money.

While third parties have a duty to ask whether the person with whom they are dealing is an agent, agents do *not* have a duty to say who their principals are. In fact, a term of an agent's agreement with her principal may forbid her to reveal the principal's identity. Nonetheless, the agent's potential liability on the contract will depend on the extent of the third party's knowledge.

Contracts with a Disclosed Principal

When the third party knows the identity of the agent's principal, the principal is said to be *disclosed*. Generally, an agent will not be liable on contracts made on behalf of a disclosed principal so long as the agent acts within her realm of authority. The principal has the duty to perform under the contract. Suppose a principal sends an agent to rent a front-end loader, but before the agent returns, the principal finds another one. The principal cannot avoid the rental obligation incurred by the agent simply because he now does not need the first machine. Figure 14-2 illustrates liability combinations where a disclosed principal exists.

Principal's liability for an agent's representations. A principal is liable for an agent's representations in negotiating a contract if they are representations normally made by agents in that business. Thus, if an agent makes false representations which are of a type normally made in the principal's business, the principal would be bound. For example, a computer company's sales representative will bind her principal when she makes representations about her product's capacity. Even if the agent made the representation without the principal's knowl-

edge or authorization, the principal will be liable for the misrepresentation. (Of course, the agent will be liable to the principal for any injury caused by the misrepresentation. The agent's liability is discussed in more detail below.)

However, a principal will not be liable for a misrepresentation when the third party knows or should know that the agent could not be in a position to making binding representations. Suppose Mimi bought a stereo at a self-serve discount warehouse. She would have considerable difficulty showing that a warehouse employee had authority to make a representation about it. A full-service store is far more likely to face liability for employee statements about products than a self-serve store because the full-service store's employees presumably are familiar with the goods they sell.

Exculpatory clauses. The principal may try to limit liability to a third party by using an *exculpatory clause* in a written contract. An exculpatory clause disclaims the principal's liability for any of the agent's representations not stated in the written contract. A typical clause reads, "The agent has no authority to expand the representations made in this contract." Often, such contracts also contain a clause requiring approval of the contract by the principal.

Exculpatory clauses are designed to ensure that the contract is *integrated* in the form in which it is submitted to the principal for approval. They are meant to trigger the application of the *parol evidence rule* and thereby prevent the buyer from introducing evidence of representations not included in the contract.

Courts view exculpatory clauses with disfavor because such clauses are often presented to consumers on a "take it or leave it" basis

TYPE OF AUTHORITY FOR ACTION(S)	AGENT NORMALLY LIABLE TO THIRD PARTY ON CONTRACT?	AGENT POSSIBLY LIABLE TO PRINCIPAL ON CONTRACT?	PRINCIPAL NORMALLY LIABLE TO THIRD PARTY ON CONTRACT?
Agent acts with express authority	No	No	Yes
Agent acts with implied authority	No	No	Yes
Agent acts with apparent authority	No	Yes	Yes
Agent acts with emergency authority	No	No	Yes
Agent acts without authority, not ratified by principal	Yes	No	No
Agent acts without authority, principal ratifies	No	Yes	Yes

Figure 14.2 Liability Where Disclosed Principal.
These are the six most common combinations of agent-disclosed principal actions.

after a salesperson has made extensive representations. Also, exculpatory clauses have tended to be buried in form contracts where the buyer would not notice them. For these reasons, the courts have refused to enforce exculpatory clauses when their effect is tantamount to fraud.

Agent's liability to third parties. An agent normally will not be personally liable on a contract made on behalf of a disclosed principal if she has clearly stated her agency or representative capacity and identified her principal. Then, if the principal does not perform, the agent is not liable unless the agent guaranteed performance to the third party. After all, the contract benefits the principal, not the agent.

Nonetheless, the agent must make it clear that she is entering into a contract in her capacity as an agent, not as an individual. If she does not make her agent's status known to the third party, she may be liable on the contract. For that reason, the agent must be certain to sign contracts on behalf of the principal so as to leave no doubt that she is acting in a representative capacity. Otherwise, she will be treated as if she were a party to the contract, not the representative of a party. If she signs contracts, "Margaret Harty, Agent for Charles Ford," she has protected herself against personal liability.

In the next case, the signers of a note might have saved themselves some litigation expenses had they been clearer about their status as agents.

Federal Deposit Insurance Corp. v. Tennessee Wildcat Services, Inc.

839 F.2d 251 (6th Cir. 1988)

FACTS

The Federal Deposit Insurance Corporation (FDIC) held two notes on which it was trying to collect from the individuals and corporations who had signed them. The first was signed:

Maker s/ By: Jack Creech   Maker Tennessee Wildcat Services, Inc.

The second was signed:

Signature Troxel Motors, Inc.

Signature s/ By: Keith A. Jeffers

The individual signers denied liability, asserting they had signed the notes as agents for the corporations. In both instances, the FDIC argued that the signers were required to show their representative capacity by using words in addition to "by." The trial court disagreed and entered judgment for the individual defendants.

ISSUE

Does the use of the word "by" before a signature establish that the signature is made in a representative capacity when the principal is fully disclosed?

DECISION

Yes. Affirmed. UCC §3-403, which applies in this case, does not require that an agent designate the precise capacity in which he or she signs. Nonetheless, the official comments to the UCC indicate that the best way to avoid personal liability is to show the principal's identity, use the word "by" before the signer's signature, and follow the signature with a designation of the signer's capacity. However, this is not the only way to indicate a representative capacity. The test should be whether a person who takes the note would reasonably believe, on the basis of what appears on its face, that the signer was personally responsible for payment. Absent some showing of fraud or another circumstance requiring the court to look beyond the note's face, where the principal is identified and shown on the face of the note as the maker and "by" precedes the signature of the signer, the note is not ambiguous and the signer is not personally liable.

We will look much more closely at the issues in this case in Part VII, which deals in part with the negotiability of commercial paper.

An agent impliedly warrants that she has a principal and authority to represent him. If she falsely represents that a principal exists or if she has no authority to represent her alleged principal, she will be liable.

For example, we noted in the last chapter that the principal's death terminates the agency relationship. But what happens if, unknown to the agent, the principal dies and the agent subsequently enters into a contract? The agent no longer has the authority to bind the principal. Even though the representations of agency status and authority were made in good faith, the agent would be liable to the third party for false representations. The agent could avoid this result if she and her principal had agreed that her appointment would bind both him and his heirs. The following clause in a power of attorney would insulate the agent from liability: "The actions of my agent, Margaret Hardy, shall be binding on my heirs, assigns, and estate as they are binding on me unless and until she receives notice of the termination of her agency." See Figure 13-1, the sample power of attorney, in the last chapter.

To avoid the harshness of the common law rule, today, some states find the principal's estate liable when neither the agent nor the third party knew of the principal's death at the time the contract was "properly executed" and the contract did not require the personal services of the decedent. For example, a contract for the decedent to present a speech obviously would not be enforced.

Contracts with an Undisclosed Principal

An *undisclosed principal* is one whose existence and identity are both unknown to the third party. The principal is liable on the contract as if he were disclosed.

Agent's liability. Where the principal is undisclosed, the agent is liable on the contract because as far as the third party knows, he is dealing only with the agent. If the third party obtains a judgment against the agent, the principal must indemnify the agent for the amount of the judgment and any associated expenses.

Suppose Alicia represents Irving, an undisclosed principal. Alicia makes a contract with Beauregard on Irving's behalf to purchase 1000 bales of cotton. If Irving fails to purchase the cotton as stipulated in the contract, Beauregard may sue Alicia for damages. He may also sue Irving, if he learns of his existence. Of course, Beauregard is only entitled to a single recovery.

Unless the agent's nondisclosure of the principal amounts to fraud, either the principal or the agent may enforce the contract. In the next case, the nondisclosure was fraudulent.

Casteel v. King

201 Or. 234, 269 P.2d 529 (1954)

FACTS
Casteel—an undisclosed principal—sought specific performance of a land purchase contract in which King agreed to sell his property to Coleman, Casteel's agent. Casteel brought King and Coleman together for the sale. Casteel and King had had some difficulty over earlier business transactions. King asked both Casteel and Coleman whether Casteel had any interest in the sale. Both said no. Irving signed the contract with Coleman on that basis. Later, Coleman told King that he had lied to him, and they canceled the contract. The trial court refused to grant Casteel specific performance of the King-Coleman contract.

ISSUE
Is an undisclosed principal entitled to specific performance of a contract the third party would not have made had he known of the principal's interest in the contract?

DECISION
No. Affirmed. Specific performance is an equitable remedy. The courts are guided by the maxim that "one who comes into equity must come with clean hands." Casteel asked the court to enforce a contract which had its inception in his wrongdoing.

TYPE OF PRINCIPAL	APPARENT AUTHORITY POSSIBLE?	AGENT NORMALLY LIABLE ON RESULTING CONTRACT	PRINCIPAL NORMALLY LIABLE ON RESULTING CONTRACT
Disclosed	Yes	No	Yes
Partially disclosed	Yes	Yes	Yes
Undisclosed	No	Yes	Yes

Figure 14.3 Contract Liability to Third Party.

Apparent authority. An agent acting for an undisclosed principal cannot have apparent authority, since apparent authority comes from the principal's action or inaction or from the agent's position. Where principals are undisclosed, third parties know nothing of the principals' actions, nor do they know that they are dealing with an agent.

Contracts with a Partially Disclosed Principal

Where the third party knows that a principal is involved but does not know his or her identity, the law characterizes the principal as *partially disclosed*. In this situation—which is quite common in real estate transactions—the usual rules applying to contracts with disclosed principals apply.

However, because the third party does not know the identity of the principal, the third party cannot rely on the principal's performance. Therefore, both the agent and the principal are liable for performance of the contract, just as in the case of an undisclosed principal. (Figure 14-3 compares contracts involving partially disclosed principals with those involving undisclosed principals.) In the next case, the third party knew that the agent represented someone else, but the agent did not make clear who it was.

New England Whalers Hockey Club v. Nair

1 Conn. App. 680, 474 A.2d 810 (1984)

FACTS Nair operated a one-man advertising agency out of his home. He executed three advertising contracts with the Whalers, each of which named Grinold Auto Parts, Inc., as the client. There was no such corporation. Rather, Grinold Auto Parts was a chain of stores operated by R. W. Grinold Realty Co., Inc. Nair used his address as the billing address and, after the accounts were past due, promised to pay the outstanding bills. The Whalers brought suit against Nair, and the trial court entered judgment for the team.

ISSUE Did the contracts identify the principal sufficiently to exempt the agent from liability?

DECISION No. Affirmed. To avoid personal liability, it is the agent's duty to disclose both the fact that he is acting as an agent and the identity of his principal, since the party with whom he deals is not required to discover or make inquiries to discover these facts. An agent's use of a trade name under which his principal does business is not a sufficient identification of the principal to protect the agent from personal liability.

At the beginning of this section, we noted the third party's obligation to determine whether she is dealing with an agent and, if so, what the scope of the agent's authority is. That duty applies only when the third party has reason to believe she is dealing with an agent and wishes to hold the principal liable.

New England Whalers presents almost the mirror of that rule. It stands for the proposition that if the agent does not disclose both the scope of his agency and the *precise* identity of his principal, he will be liable. For agents, the preventive law lesson is: either disclose the terms of your agency and the name of your principal or make sure you are fully indemnified against liability.

A special rule covers *negotiable instruments*—checks and notes. Suppose an agent signs a note "Walter Fletcher, Agent," and the identity of the principal is not clear from the instrument. A third party cannot hold the principal liable on it. The third party's only recourse is against the agent. We will discuss negotiable instruments in Part VII.

TORT LIABILITY IN AN AGENCY CONTEXT

As we have seen, the law of agency determines the contractual rights and responsibilities of principals, their agents, and third parties. Agency law simply allocates rights and responsibilities under a contract. It does not vary the principles of contract law.

Similarly, the law of agency does not affect the principles of tort law. Rather, it specifies under what circumstances a principal must pay damages to a third party for a tortious act by his agent. However, while the principal's liability in contract generally involves only the acts of an agent, his liability in tort extends to any employee, whether a servant or an agent. For that reason, in this section, we refer to employers and employees—instead of principals and agents—because those terms are more inclusive.

Respondeat Superior

The law refers to the imposition on an employer of liability for an employee's torts in terms of the doctrine of *respondeat superior*. This Latin phrase means "let the master respond."

Respondeat superior often imposes liability even where the employer is blameless. The rationale for employer liability is that the principal has "deeper pockets" than the employee and that, since the use of employees is a privilege, the employer has a social responsibility to stand behind an employee's action. In the next case, two of the seven judges who heard it argued that the employer's social responsibility required imposing liability. The majority disagreed.

Totem Taxi, Inc. v. N.Y. State Human Rights Appeal Bd.

65 N.Y.2d 1075, 480 N.E.2d 1075 (1985)

FACTS

Four black women had been visiting a relative in a hospital. They called Totem Taxi for a cab when they finished. The white driver became belligerent when the women indicated they wanted to go to different addresses. First the driver and then the women uttered racial epithets. The driver left without the women. They then called another Totem cab and reached home without further trouble. When Totem's owner learned of the incident, he apologized profusely to the women and suspended the driver for several months. Totem's policy was to treat all persons with decency and courtesy regardless of color or religion. Nonetheless, the women filed complaints with the state Division of Human Rights, which held the taxi driver to be guilty of discriminatory conduct and Totem responsible for its driver's acts. An appellate court affirmed the Division's judgment awarding each passenger $500, reduced to $250 because of the mitigating circumstances—the owner's responsible actions.

ISSUE

Is an employer responsible for the discriminatory acts of its employees even though it did not approve of or acquiesce in the conduct?

DECISION

The New York antidiscrimination law does not provide that one who employs a person who commits a discriminatory act also violates the act, regardless of fault. The employer cannot become liable for such an act unless the employer becomes a party to it by encouraging, condoning, or approving it. Here, no evidence indicated Totem in any way became a party to the act.

The employer's liability does not eliminate or even reduce the responsibility of the *tortfeasor* (the person who committed the tort). The employer and the employee are *jointly and severally liable:* When the court awards damages, the victim may collect the full award from either the employee or the employer, or a percentage of the total from each. Suppose a lumberyard owner instructs her forklift operators not to go more than 5 miles per hour in public areas of the lumberyard. While driving at 15 miles per hour in the yard, an employee hits a third party. The owner and the employee are liable.

Scope of employment. Respondeat superior does not make an employer responsible for every tort his employees commit. An employer is liable only for those which occur within the employee's *scope of employment*. The employee's tortious act must relate directly to the manner in which the employer conducts his business. The employee's act must be of the same essential nature as the authorized work and have a reasonable connection in time and place with that work. For respondeat superior to apply, the act need not have to benefit the principal. Indeed, a principal may be responsible for an employee's intentional torts committed within the scope of employment despite the lack of any benefit. However, as the next case establishes, respondeat superior has limits.

White v. Hardy

678 F.2d 485 (4th Cir. 1982)

FACTS   While on 24-hour active duty with the Army, Sergeant Hardy—without authorization—left his post, borrowed a government vehicle, and left the fort, supposedly to make a telephone call. Even had Sgt. Hardy received authorization to leave his post and borrow the vehicle, the scope of his authorization would have been limited to the time and place necessary for the telephone call. In any event, he never placed the call and remained away from his post for several hours before his vehicle collided with the cab in which White was riding. White brought suit against Hardy and the United States, seeking damages. The trial court granted summary judgment in favor of the United States.

ISSUE   Did the accident occur while Hardy was acting within the scope of his employment?

DECISION   No. Affirmed. To establish that respondeat superior applies, the plaintiff must prove (1) an injury by the negligence of the wrongdoer, (2) the employer-employee relationship, (3) a wrong committed in the course of employment or within the employee's scope of authority, and (4) an employee going about the business of his superior at the time of the injury. Here, the evidence showed that Hardy did not act within the scope of his employment.

Frolics and detours. The law calls Hardy's excursion a *frolic,* a substantial departure from, or abandonment of, the employer's business. Hardy's jaunt clearly exceeded the scope of his employment. The result would have been the same if his commanding officer had sent him for some equipment and Hardy had gone off on his own after picking it up.

The result may vary if the employee's accident occurs after the frolic ends. Some courts have held that an employee resumes employment when he begins his return from the frolic's end point. Other courts have held that the employee does not resume employment until he returns to the point at which he started on his frolic.

Not every deviation from the employer's business is a frolic. If, on his way back to the fort from an authorized errand, Hardy went two blocks out of his way to cash his paycheck, the law would call that a *detour,* a brief digression from his duties. If the accident occurs while the employee is on a detour, the employer would be liable, since the employee mainly has been on the employer's business.

In the examples above, Hardy is away from the fort. What happens if Hardy takes a jeep on a joy ride around the fort and strikes a pedestrian? Hardy's presence on the fort's grounds is irrelevant. So long as Hardy is on a frolic, his employer is not liable. However, it may make a significant difference if, instead of negligence, Hardy committed an intentional tort.

Intentional torts. In general, under the doctrine of respondeat superior, an employer is not liable for an employee's intentional tort unless it relates closely to the purpose of the business or to the scope of the employee's employment.

At common law, the courts did not tend to

impose liability on the employer unless the intentional tort was clearly part of the job. For example, a bar owner would be liable for assaults or batteries committed by a bouncer in the course of his duties.

Today, because of the employer's capacity to insure himself, the courts are more inclined to find a relationship between the employer's purpose and the employee's act in order to avoid an unjust loss to an injured third party. For instance, courts routinely impose liability on employers whose truck drivers get into fights following accidents. Still, as the next case shows, this trend toward employer liability for intentional torts has its limits.

Simmons v. Baltimore Orioles, Inc.

712 F.Supp. 79 (W.D. Va. 1989)

FACTS   Simmons attended a baseball game between the Bluefield Orioles, a Baltimore Orioles farm team, and the Martinsville Phillies. Simmons, disappointed with Bluefield's performance, began to heckle the players in the bullpen. After the game, two players, Champ and Hicks, encountered Simmons in the parking lot. Simmons claims that he was attacked by both men with a baseball bat for no reason, and that they broke his jaw. Champ and Hicks maintained that Simmons had threatened to shoot them, and that Hicks broke his jaw with his fist only after Simmons persisted in going after them. The defendant Orioles made a motion to dismiss at the trial level, claiming they were not responsible for the torts committed by Champ and Hicks.

ISSUE   Under the doctrine of respondeat superior, were the Orioles liable for the torts of their employees, Champ and Hicks?

DECISION   No. Motion granted. To prove respondeat superior, the plaintiff must demonstrate that (1) the tort was committed at the time the employee was going about his employer's business, and (2) that the employee was operating within the scope of this employment. In this case, Champ and Hicks had left the locker room and the scuffle occurred outside the ballpark. Thus, they were not engaging in Oriole business at the time of the dispute. It is also absurd to suggest that fighting was within the scope of their employment. Accordingly, Simmons cannot recover damages from the Orioles based on respondeat superior.

Nonemployees. Up to this point, we have focused on the employer's liability for employees' tortious acts. However, sometimes an employer will be held liable under the doctrine of respondeat superior for acts of persons who are not actually employees. These cases typically arise in two instances in which a person is temporarily under the control or direction of the employer.

In the first instance, the tortfeasor is a volunteer who does something for the employer. Suppose, for example, that Jack is a medical technician at Seaside Hospital. When Jack drops his car off at Harvey's Auto Repair for some body work, Harvey asks Jack to move another customer's car away from the garage door. In the process of doing so, Jack negligently backs into Mildred, severely injuring her. Seaside Hospital would not be liable, since the accident had nothing to do with Jack's employment. Of course, Jack would be liable, since he committed the act. And, Harvey would be liable, since moving the car would have benefited his business.

In the second instance, *borrowed servant* cases, the tortfeasor's employer actually lends him temporarily to another employer. The borrowing employer will be liable for the borrowed servant's tortious acts if they occur within the scope of the borrowing employer's business. Suppose Seaside Hospital lends Jack to Ocean General because it is shorthanded that day. Jack negligently misreads a test, with dire consequences for an Ocean General patient. Ocean General, not Seaside, would be liable for Jack's act.

Independent contractors. In general, an employer is not liable for torts committed by independent contractors when the employer does not control the means or methods used by the independent contractor. Determining whether a person is an independent contractor requires a detailed examination of the relationship between principal and agent.

Not long ago, the U.S. Supreme Court had to determine whether a sculptor hired to create a monument to the homeless was an independent contractor or an employee of the nonprofit advocacy group that commissioned the sculpture. The sculptor, the Court held, was an independent contractor because:

- He engaged in a skilled occupation
- He supplied his own tools
- He worked away from the group's premises
- He worked without daily supervision by the group
- He was retained for a relatively short period
- He had absolute freedom to decide when and how long to work to meet the group's deadline
- He had total discretion as to the hiring and paying of his assistants

The Court also considered the relationship from the employer's point of view, noting that it paid the sculptor as independent contractors usually are, did not provide him with any of the benefits normally conferred on an employee, did not have the right to assign him any other projects, and did not engage in the business of creating sculptures—or any other business.*

It is important to keep in mind that what an agent calls himself or herself does not necessarily affect what a court will determine his or her status to be. In the next case, the agent considered himself an independent contractor, but the court found he was not one when it came to determining liability for negligence.

* * * * *

* *Community for Creative Non-violence v. Reid,* 109 S.Ct. 2166 (1989).

Massey v. Tube Art Display, Inc.

————*Wash. App.*————, 551 P.2d 1387 (1976)

FACTS   McPherson Realty Co. decided to move an outdoor reader board to its new branch office location in a residential-commercial building. Tube Art, which owned the sign, agreed to remove it and reinstall it. Tube Art obtained a sign installation permit from the city. The next morning, Tube Art's service manager went to the new site and took photos and measurements. Later, an employee returned to mark in yellow paint the exact site for the excavation—a 4-foot by 4-foot square which was to be dug to a depth of 6 feet. Tube Art hired backhoe operator Richard Redford to dig the hole. Redford was essentially self-employed, paying his own income and business taxes. During the 3 prior years, he had worked exclusively for sign companies, and spent 90 percent of his time working for Tube Art. Nonetheless, he did not participate in any of the company's employee programs. Further, when he worked a job for the company, he did not pull the permits and excavated holes only to his employer's precise specification. In fact, Redford had no discretion as to their size or location. While digging the hole at the McPherson site, Redford struck a small gas line. He inspected the line and found no indication of a break or leak. He concluded the line was not in use and left the site. He was wrong. That night, an explosion and fire hit the building served by the line. Two people were killed and the building's contents destroyed. Massey, a tenant in the building, brought suit to recover damages for the loss of his business records. The trial court held as a matter of law that Tube Art bore responsibility for Redford's actions, and entered judgment on a verdict for Massey.

ISSUE

Did Tube Art control Redford's physical activity to such a degree that Redford became its agent?

DECISION

Yes. Affirmed. The issue in liability cases involving alleged independent contractors often is the employer's right to control the other's physical conduct relating to the details of the work. The control exercised does not have to be total for a court to impose liability. Here, Tube Art, controlled all significant decisions which related to the size and location of the hole. Given its control, it would not be unreasonable to expect Tube Art to suspect that a gas line might be located near the board's new location. And, Tube Art had a duty to determine where these pipes were.

Figure 14-4 diagrams employer tort liability under respondeat superior.

Other Sources of Employer Liability

Respondeat superior is not the sole theory for imposing liability on an employer for an employee's acts. In this section we will examine two others.

Negligent hiring and supervision. If the employer negligently hires or supervises an employee, a court may impose liability. Assume that Turtle Courier hires Don as a messenger. Turtle accepts his statements on its employment application form without checking them. If a simple check would have revealed that Don had spent 2 years in jail for embezzlement, Turtle will be liable if Don steals from one of its customers.

Nondelegable duties. A *nondelegable duty* is one for which the employer remains liable even if she turns the work over to an independent contractor. Traditionally, such duties were ones considered to be inherently dangerous or ultrahazardous, but the trend is toward broadening the liability of those who employ independent contractors.

The phrase "nondelegable duties" has different meanings in contract law and tort law. Under the law of contract assignments (dis-

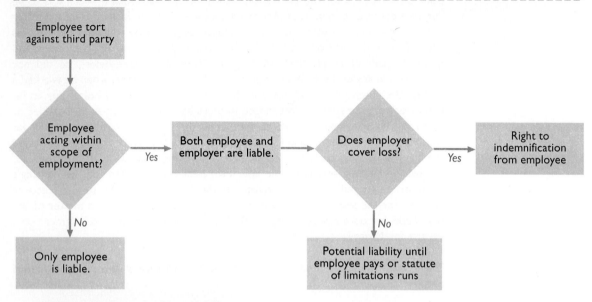

Figure 14.4 Employer Tort Liability.
While this figure correctly indicates that an employee has joint liability with his or her employer, as a practical matter liability falls exclusively on the employer because of greater net worth or insurance coverage or both.

cussed in Chapter 11), a nondelegable duty is one which cannot be delegated because of the unique nature of the service or of the skills required to perform the contractual obligation. A portrait painter may not delegate his duty to perform to another painter. A lifeguard cannot delegate her duties to someone not trained to swim.

Tort law is not concerned with who does the work. Its concern is solely with who is responsible for it. The employer *can* delegate the work to an independent contractor, but, like the sign company in the last case, it continues to be liable for any tortious conduct. Thus, in tort law, "nondelegable duties" means "nondelegable potential liabilities."

An employer may not delegate duties with respect to inherently dangerous or ultrahazardous activities. The most common situation involving nondelegable duties occurs when the

employer has a duty to provide safety for the public. In most jurisdictions, for example, city property owners must keep their sidewalks clear of snow. A property owner may hire a snow removal crew to do the job. However, if a passerby falls and is injured on the walk before it is cleaned, the property owner is liable. Otherwise, the property owner could shirk his social responsibility by arguing that the accident was the fault of those hired to shovel the walks.

The classic example of hazardous activity involves blasting. When an employer contracts to have blasting done, particularly in an inhabited area, the employer cannot avoid liability for its consequences. The employer has only two means of limiting his financial exposure: obtaining insurance or requiring the independent contractor to show proof of having insurance.

Employee's Liability to Third Parties

As we have already noted, an employee is liable to a third party for the results of her actions. She may be liable even if she acts in good faith and is not aware that the act is wrongful. An employer, by mistake, might send an employee to harvest apples in the wrong orchard. The employee would be liable for trespass even though she was acting in good faith.

If an employer fails to inform the employee of a crucial fact, the employee would be able to use that fact as a defense. Assume that Marcia agrees to sell Mel's car for him. Mel tells Marcia that the car runs perfectly, but he knows that the car has a cracked engine block. If Marcia does not know about the car's defect when she sells it, she would be liable to a third party for a *false representation,* but not for *fraud in the inducement.* In this situation, the employer may be liable for fraud, but the agent will not be unless either she knew of the misrepresentation or the law imputes that knowledge.

CRIMINAL LIABILITY IN AN AGENCY CONTEXT

Ordinarily an employer is not liable for his employee's criminal acts. Usually, commission of a crime requires intent, and if the employer has not authorized the crime, he has not formulated the necessary criminal intent. For that reason, the employer in *Scott v. Commercial Union* would not be criminally liable for the battery Scott suffered.

An employer will be held criminally liable for an employee's act done to further the employer's illegal business. In some instances, an employer will be criminally liable for an illegal transaction conducted as part of a legal business. This is particularly true in the case of ''strict adherence'' laws. For example, statutes like those regulating the sale of liquor to minors often impose liability not only on those who actually commit the act but also on the person who owns the business.

CONCLUSION

This chapter has focused on the liabilities of principals and agents to third parties. In contract matters, the principal issues are whether a person is an agent and, if so, what the scope of the agency authority is. Normally, a contract made by an agent on a principal's behalf binds only the principal and the third party. However, agents who do not clearly state their representational capacity and identify their principal run a serious risk of personal liability.

In tort matters, the principal issue is whether the tortfeasor was acting within the scope of employment when the tort occurred. However, the tendency here is to impose liability on the employer if there is some connection between the employment and the tortious activity. Similarly, courts are increasingly likely to hold an employer criminally liable for the acts of its agents, especially when the principal is a corporation and the agent, one of its officers.

In Part IV, Business Organizations, we will have occasion to explore how particular types of agents relate to the business organizations they represent.

A NOTE TO FUTURE CPA CANDIDATES

Questions about an agent's authority to act are among the most commonly asked on the CPA exam. A third party first encountering a supposed agent has the duty to ascertain whether in fact the agent is an agent and, if so, with what authority the agent may act. If not, a third party potentially acts at their peril.

Two types of agency authority are heavily covered on the CPA exam: implied and apparent authority. Implied authority flows from a grant of express authority. Implied authority is, in essence, implementation authority. In contrast, apparent authority results from manifestations made by the principal to a third party. Most often the manifestation results from the position or title given to the agent. Apparent authority is, in essence, appearance authority.

For both implied and apparent authority, a court will inquire whether an agent of a similar type and size of business would be expected to have the power to take the same action. For example, the manager of a large retail store would be presumed to have much greater authority concerning advertising than would a manager of a small retail boutique.

It is important to remember that a person may be an apparent agent. This concept is also found in partnership law in regard to apparent partners (see Chapter 16). Upon the termination of an agency relationship, as with a partnership relation (see Chapter 17), it is necessary to give actual notice to actual creditors, constructive notice to everyone else.

A principal is normally liable for the negligent, unintentional tortious acts of his employees if they are acting within the scope of their employment. If the possibility of the use of force is a normal part of the job, such as the job of a bouncer, or the employer was negligent in hiring or retaining an employee prone to violence, an employer may have liability. A principal is generally *not* liable for an employee's criminal actions.

Remember, the CPA exam tests agency principles in one of three situations: agency, partnership, or corporation law applications.

KEY WORDS

apparent author-
  ity (301)
borrowed servant (316)
disclosed (307)
detour (314)
express authority (300)
frolic (314)

implied authority (300)
joint and several lia-
  bility (313)
nondelegable
  duties (317)
partially disclosed
  principal (311)

ratification (305)
respondeat supe-
  rior (312)

undisclosed princi-
  pal (310)

DISCUSSION QUESTIONS

1. What are the two things a third party must do when first encountering and transacting business with an agent? Why?
2. What are the types of authority under which an agent might operate? How do they differ from one another?
3. How does apparent authority differ from implied authority? Give some business examples of apparent authority.
4. "The law may find that a person is an agent of another even though this simply is not factually correct." Explain why and give a practical business example.
5. "An agent will not normally be liable to a third party on a contract involving a disclosed principal." Do you agree? Explain.
6. John Smith is an agent for Mary White. How would you advise Smith to sign contracts he enters into on White's behalf? Negotiable instruments (checks, notes, etc.)? Why?
7. How does the existence of an undisclosed or partially disclosed principal alter the potential contract liability of the principal, agent, and third party? Explain.
8. What is meant by respondeat superior? How does this relate to "scope of employment"? Explain.
9. Describe the general characteristics of a servant. How does a servant principally differ from an agent?
10. How does an independent contractor differ from an agent? Explain.

CASE PROBLEMS

1. Dick Schuldt was hired to manage the new Holiday Tennis Club. The club owner, Joe Northshield, instructed Schuldt that he could purchase any brand of tennis balls for the tennis shop except Gripper. Northshield ex-

plained that Gripper balls were unacceptable because Northshield had lost a major tennis match because of defective Gripper balls. Schuldt thought that Northshield had to have been kidding, since the infamous match had occurred back in 1971. Months later, Schuldt ordered 200 cans of Gripper balls for the club. When Northshield saw the invoice for the Gripper balls, he immediately called the Gripper sales representative and told him not to send the balls, as Schuldt had no authority to order them. Is Northshield likely to prevail? Explain.

2. Barton, a wealthy art collector, engaged Deiter to obtain a painting from Cumbers. Cumbers did not know that Barton had engaged Deiter because, as Barton told Deiter, "that would cause the price to skyrocket." After Deiter and Cumbers agreed on a contract, Cumbers found out that Barton was the actual buyer. What type of principal is Barton? Would Cumbers prevail in a lawsuit she brought to rescind the contract? Explain.

3. Kent works as a welder for Mighty Manufacturing, Inc. Mighty specially trained him in the procedures for safely installing replacement mufflers on automobiles. One rule of which he was aware prohibited the installation of a muffler on any auto which had heavily congealed oil or grease or which had any leaks in the gas tank. Kent disregarded this rule, and as a result a customer's auto caught fire and was extensively damaged. Is Mighty liable to the customer? Is Kent? Explain.

4. Janice Ackerman decided to have a new bathroom built onto her home. Ackerman hired Nate's Plumbing Service, a licensed plumber, to do the plumbing work. Nate attempted to swat a mosquito while carrying some new 8-foot pipes up Ackerman's driveway. He lost control of the pipes, which then hit Mike McWilliams, Ackerman's neighbor, who was cutting a hedge on his property. Assuming Nate was negligent, if McWilliams should bring suit against Ackerman, would Ackerman prevail? Explain.

5. Tommy, a minor, worked for Hot Sam's Pizza. One night Sam's friend Lucky called. He asked if he could borrow Tommy the next day for a special sale at his store, Lucky's Sporting Goods. Sam agreed. The next day Tommy reported directly to Lucky's. Lucky told Tommy not to demonstrate any sporting goods items. Around midmorning a young customer, Angie White, came into the store and asked Tommy for some help in choosing a tennis racquet. Wishing to impress Angie, Tommy demonstrated the smooth swing of the racquet. Unfortunately, during the backswing portion, Tommy negligently struck another customer, Mrs. Hurt. If Hurt should sue Sam, would Sam be held liable for Tommy's actions? Would Lucky? Explain.

6. Metropolitan Department Store employed Joe Walters to drive one of its delivery trucks. Under the terms of his employment, he was to make deliveries along a designated route and bring the truck back to a garage for overnight storage. One day, instead of returning to the garage as required, he drove the truck 20 miles north of the area he covered to attend his girl friend's birthday party. En route to the party, his negligence caused an accident in which Richard Bunt was injured. Bunt filed suit against the store for damages. Metropolitan claims it is not liable because Walters was an independent contractor or, if Walters is classified as an employee, because he had abandoned his employment. Do you agree? Explain.

7. Marilyn Brinkman was a sales representative for Norman & Wolford, Inc. Although Brinkman did a good job, the firm had to release her because of difficult economic times. The firm provided appropriate notice to third parties. Brinkman decided to try to get more sales so that she might be rehired. Brinkman contacted a former customer, Gary Schleich. Brinkman assured Schleich she had been rehired. Schleich gave Brinkman an order. Although Brinkman intended to submit the Schleich order to the firm, she forgot it when she accepted another job. Schleich has demanded the order be completed by the firm. Is the firm liable to Schleich on the contract? Explain.

8. Kristie Kevern, a popular rock singer, hired Ken Howell to be a bodyguard at a rock concert. During the concert a fan, Louie Chappas attempted to run on stage to get a picture autographed by Kristie. Seeing him approaching, Howell stopped Louie, took the picture, and ripped it up. As Louie was walking away, he told his friend that Howell was a "fat jerk." Overhearing this, Howell charged after Louie, hit him, and broke his nose. Assuming that Howell is Kristie's employee, would Kristie be liable to Louie for Howell's actions? Explain.

9. Dottie Murray, an agent, managed Leach's Restaurant. Dottie decided that it would be good advertising if Leach's had a sailboat entered in the spring regatta on Cross Lake. On behalf of Leach's, Dottie signed a contract to buy a sailboat with trailer from Pam Schmidt for $4500. When the restaurant owner became aware of the purchase, he immediately called Pam and told her that Dottie had had no authority to bind the restaurant. Assuming this is true, what liability, if any, does the restaurant have? What liability, if any, does Dottie have? Assuming the restaurant owner wishes to retain the trailer but not the boat, could he ratify the transaction only as to the fair market value of the trailer? Explain.

10. Bob Wayne was an agent for Mary Lee. As instructed, Bob signed a negotiable promissory note to Jesse Gregerson. Bob signed the note, "Bob Wayne, Agent." Gregerson negotiated the note to Stella Adams. The note has come due and Adams has demanded that Bob pay it. Bob refuses. In court Bob attempts to establish that Mary Lee is really the person responsible, but the court rejects his offer of proof. Was the court correct? What remedy, if any, does Bob have? Explain.

CHAPTER 15
Employee Rights and Benefits

The last two chapters introduced servants and agents, who are called *employees* in today's employment terminology. Thus far, the primary focus has been on the role of the principal and the principal's relationship with the agent and third parties. In this chapter the focus shifts to the role of the employee and the employee's rights and benefits. Here, the term "employee" refers to anyone who works for an employer, other than an independent contractor. From the lowest-paid maintenance worker to a store manager to the chief executive officer, all have basic rights and benefits under the law.

The range of topics in this chapter is bounded by the principles of contract and agency law that we have been discussing. While both state and federal laws apply in this area, not surprisingly state laws predominate. We will defer, until Chapter 46, a major discussion of the federal laws that apply to employment discrimination and union-management relations.

EMPLOYMENT AT WILL

In the absence of evidence to the contrary, the law presumes that the relationship between an employer and an employee is an *employment at will*, a contractual relationship whose subject matter is personal services that either party may terminate at any time with or without cause. Thus, an *employee at will* is a person hired without an established term of employment and subject to discharge without cause.

Characteristics of the At Will Relationship

An employee hired for a specific term is never an employee at will. For example, the Los Angeles Dodgers hire a manager for a particular baseball season. So he is not an employee at will. If the team breaches its contract with him by firing him before the end of the contract term, it is liable to him for damages.

An employee who may be discharged only

for cause or who is entitled to appeal the discharge by means of a procedure specified by contract is also not an employee at will. Normally, these elements are found together. For example, a unionized employee cannot be an employee at will because he or she may be discharged only for cause and may appeal termination through a multistage grievance procedure. Even an employee caught stealing from his or her employer has a right to test the validity of the termination through the process specified in the union contract. For similar reasons, a tenured civil servant or a college professor is not an employee at will.

Note that whether an employee is an at will employee does not, in and of itself, determine whether an employer has the power to discharge an employee. The fact that the Dodgers hired a manager for the whole 1988 season does not prevent the club from firing him.

If that is so, what significance does nonemployee at will status have? Ultimately, it comes down to whether the employer has the right to terminate the employee under the terms and conditions of the contract that apply to that employee. Stated another way, the distinction between employees at will and non-employees at will rests on whether the discharged employee has a right to recover compensatory damages or to be reinstated or both.

Returning to our examples, the fired Dodger manager has no right to retain or recover his job because of the highly personal nature of his former position, but he does have a right to the remainder of his salary under the contract —assuming the club dismissed him for the usual reason, lack of success on the field. By contrast, a unionized employee might be able to recover his job if he was discharged in a manner other than that provided in the collective bargaining agreement. Likewise, a government employee might get both damages and her job back if she was terminated without due regard for regulations and policies.

Finally, it should be noted that the United

States is currently one of the few major industrialized countries left in the world that has retained employment at will as its presumptive rule in employment law. Today, nearly sixty nations, including the entire European Community, Japan, Canada, and most of South America, provide their workers with some legal protections from wrongful terminations.

Forming an At Will Relationship

As with any other contractual relationship, forming an employment at will relationship requires:

1. Mutual assent
2. Consideration
3. Legal object
4. Capacity
5. Writing (in some cases)

These elements were discussed in Part II and in Chapter 13.

As a practical matter, most employees at will do not have personal written contracts of employment. In those rare instances when they do, the contract, of course, does not have a specified term.

THE TRADITIONAL VIEW OF AT WILL EMPLOYEE RIGHTS

Under the common law, beginning in the late nineteenth century, at will employees had the right to terminate their relationship with their employers at any time and for any reason. The employer was said to have a reciprocal right.

"Wood's Rule"

The employment at will concept probably originated in 1877 when a legal commentator named Wood published a highly influential treatise, *Master and Servant*, in which he identified it.* Whether "Wood's Rule" accurately described American common law at the time has become a matter of hot scholarly debate. Beyond any question, however, is the fact that because of, or simultaneously with, the publication of Wood's book, the at will doctrine gained rapid and virtually universal acceptance.

In 1884, the Tennessee Supreme Court wholeheartedly endorsed Wood's Rule:

> [Men must be left] to discharge or retain employees at will for good cause or for no cause, or even for bad cause without thereby being guilty of an unlawful act per se. It is a right which an employee may exercise in the same way, to the same extent, for the same cause or want of cause as the employer.†

In the following case, the court many regard as America's premier common law court adopted the reasoning of the Tennessee court.

---

* H. Wood, *Master and Servant*, Sec. 134 (1877).
† *Payne v. Weston, Atl. Ry. Co.*, 81 Tenn. 501, 518-19 (1884).

Martin v. New York Life Ins. Co.

148 N.Y. 117, 42 N.E. 416 (1895)

FACTS   Martin began working for New York Life in 1881. He did not have a written contract. As head of the real estate department, his salary was $5000 per year. On January 1, 1883, he received a raise to $6500, and a year later to $10,000. No changes occurred in his employment relations until April 13, 1892, when the company president terminated him, effective April 30. Claiming that he had a contract for the year. Martin brought suit for 8 months' wages. The trial court found for the company, but the appellate court reversed.

ISSUE   Does an ordinary hiring import employment by the year?

DECISION   No. Trial court judgment reinstated.

The present condition of the law as to the legal effect of a general hiring is thus stated by Mr. Wood. . . .

> *"In England it is held that . . . a hiring for which no term is fixed is a hiring by the year. . . . With us the rule is inflexible that a general or indefinite hiring is . . . a hiring at will. . . . [The] fact that the compensation is measured at so much a day, month, or year does not necessarily make such hiring a hiring for a day, month, or year, but that in all such cases the contract may be put an end to by either party at any time. . . ."*

As a result of cases like *Martin,* the courts began to presume that all employment contracts were at will unless the parties expressly agreed otherwise. The burden of defeating the presumption rested on the employee. In contrast, the English rule was and is the reverse: the employer had to establish that an at will relationship existed.

The effects of Wood's Rule soon spread. With the courts' support, employers quickly extended the same approach to the hiring and promotion of all employees.

The Justification for the Rule

As a concept, employment at will offers symmetry. Employees and employers have mutual obligations and rights. It also affords protection to employers that other rules do not. No employer should have to employ a person whom the employer no longer wishes to associate with. If an employee can leave an employer at any time, an employer should be able to shed an employee just as easily.

Further, many employees do not accept positions in good faith, yet employers generally do not seek damages from them. It is quite common for a person to take a permanent job while waiting to hear from a prospective employer. If the offer comes through, the employee quits.

The Rule Under Fire

The quotation from the Tennessee Supreme Court highlights a common criticism of the at will rule. The court acknowledges that an employer can be legally right in terminating an employee but ethically and morally wrong. Should the law take an approach other than an ethical or moral one? That question has troubled even the defenders of the employment at will concept.

Perhaps the strongest argument against the at will concept attacks its apparently symmetrical fairness. What the rule fails to acknowledge is that in most instances an employee has far less market power than an employer. In some areas only a few employers may be in the market. A common complaint in areas of high unemployment is that employers will hire only part-timers in order to avoid paying any benefits.

Also, while a fair number of employees do not deal fairly with their employers, this fact does not warrant the heavy effect of the at will rule on the vastly greater number of faithful employees.

The rule might make sense where the owner is also the employer-manager and the business has relatively few employees. In these situations, a more personal relationship develops. However, a General Motors assembly line

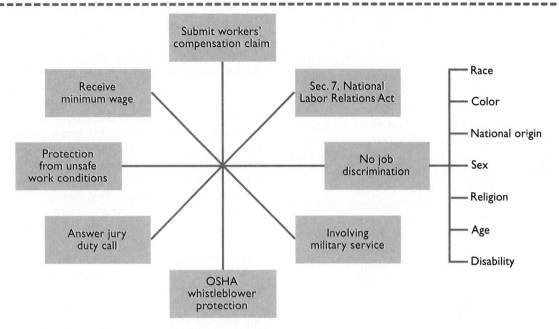

Figure 15.1 The Statutory Rights of Employees.
As this chapter and Chapter 46 reveal, many statutes confer rights on employees. This figure depicts a few of them.

worker in Framingham, Massachusetts, clearly would not have a personal relationship with the top management in Detroit.

The Statutory Rights of All Employees

Over the past 40 years, state and federal legislation has drastically limited the ability of an employer to hire, promote, retain, or discharge an employee for any reason at any time. For example, when you study employment discrimination in Chapter 46, keep in mind that before the statutes were enacted employers could—and many did—make employment decisions taking into account the gender, color, age, physical appearance, disabilities, and religion of a job applicant or an employee.

Other statutes prohibit discrimination against veterans. Some employers terminated employees for taking time away from their jobs to perform social duties, such as serving on a jury or appearing as a witness in a lawsuit. Statutes in most states now forbid punitive action against employees in these circumstances. More controversial are *whistleblower statutes,* which protect employees who report an employer's violations of the law. The most visible of these laws apply to defense contractors and violators of the Occupational Safety and Health Act, which is discussed later in this chapter. Figure 15-1 illustrates several of the protections against employment discrimination that exist for all employees, whether at will or not.

Predictably, many employers and employer associations claim that the law now places too many restraints on personnel matters. These arguments, it is important to realize, are part of a much larger debate over the role of business in society that has dominated political life since before Wood's Rule appeared.

EMERGING TRENDS IN AT WILL EMPLOYMENT

As we have implied, the fact of the employment at will doctrine is changing. In 1991 The National Conference of Commissioners on Uniform State Laws, in its proposed Model Employment Termination Act, estimated that forty to forty-five states had or were soon likely to approve modifications to the employment at will doctrine.* The emerging exceptions, however, represent piecemeal alterations—not a repudiation—of the doctrine. Nothing better reflects the haphazard changes going on in fifty jurisdictions than the lack of a uniform categorization of the exceptions. For convenience sake, we have divided the exceptions into three classes: public policy torts, implied contracts, and the covenant of good faith and fair dealing.

Public Policy Torts

Public policy is an extremely vague term referring to the principle that no member of society may act in a manner that threatens the common good. Most commonly, the phrase appears in the negative, as "a violation of public policy."

The nature of a violation. Courts have difficulty with this class of exception because they prefer to leave the determination of what public policy should be and how it should be implemented to the legislative branch. When compelled to make a determination in this area, they tend to struggle first to define what public policy should be and then to determine whether the employer's conduct violated it. In other words, did the conduct constitute a tort? That the public policy exception rests on tort rather than contract principles benefits a plaintiff, since it opens the possibility of punitive damages.

Deference to the legislative branch. The jurisdictions recognizing the public policy exception differ as to whether the plaintiff must rely on a statute in order to prove that a public policy exists and whether, if a statute does exist, it should provide the employee's exclusive remedy—if any. Other jurisdictions, such as Arizona, have stated that public policy for determining "bad cause" for termination can be articulated not only by statute, as it was in the *Wagenseller* v. *Scottsdale Memorial Hospital* case that follows, but also by the state's constitution and common law courts.

In Florida an employee was fired for refusing to do work that violated environmental statutes. A state appellate court refused to provide a remedy, since the statute provided none.* By contrast, in the case of a South Carolina employee who was fired for obeying a subpoena after he had been told that to obey would cost his job, the state Supreme Court has held that the firing violated public policy even though no statutory policy specifically provided a remedy.†

Types of violations. As should be apparent by now, the approach to the public policy exception is not uniform among the forty-two states that recognize it. What the states do seem to agree upon, however, is that the interest that the employee seeks to vindicate must be a public interest, not a personal or private interest. Thus, being discharged for answering a call to jury duty violates public policy in most states. (Indeed, it may be the most common, judicially recognized violation.) But being discharged for missing work as a result of a car accident is not likely to be a violation.

While the courts passing on the question

---

* 9A *Labor Relations Reporter* (Washington, D.C.: Bureau of National Affairs) IERM 540:21 (December 1991).

---

* *Hartley v. Ocean Reef Club, Inc.,* 476 So. 2d 1327 (Fla. Dist. Ct. App. 1985).
† *Ludwig v. This Minute of Carolina, Inc.,*___S.C.___, 337 S.E.2d 213 (1985).

have not always agreed, it seems safe to say that the more important the public interest, the more likely the employee is to find relief. Generally, the public policy will involve a citizen's obligations to society, such as the duty to tell the truth in court or before a legislative committee.*

Refusal to violate a criminal statute. Penalizing an employee who refused to commit an illegal act or to omit something the law required that the employer do is often a violation of public policy. In addition to the examples cited earlier, employee actions of this type include:

- Refusing to commit perjury to protect an employer

- Refusing to mislabel a food product
- Reporting an employer's violations of federal securities laws
- Refusing to falsify a pollution control test

In the next case, the Arizona Supreme Court had to confront the problem of an at will employee who was discharged for refusing to violate the law.

---

* It must be reiterated that not all jurisdictions agree with these generalizations. Nothing better illustrates this fact than the disagreement among them over whether an employer can legitimately discharge an employee for not lying to a legislative committee on the employer's behalf.

Wagenseller v. Scottsdale Memorial Hospital

147 Ariz. 370, 710 P.2d 1025 (1985)

FACTS   Wagenseller was a nurse and an employee at will at Scottsdale Memorial Hospital. Wagenseller and Kay Smith, her managing nurse, and a group from the hospital went on an 8-day camping and raft trip down the Colorado River. Smith and others in the group engaged in heavy drinking and lewd activities during the trip, including a parody of the song "Moon River" which concluded with the actors "mooning" the audience. The skit was later repeated two more times at the hospital. Wagenseller refused to participate in these activities, which strained her relationship with Smith. About 6 months after the rafting trip, Wagenseller was terminated. Up to the time of the trip, she had consistently received favorable ratings from Smith. In a suit for wrongful discharge, Wagenseller lost at the trial level. The appeals court affirmed the trial court.

ISSUE   Was Wagenseller's termination for refusal to violate Arizona's criminal statute outlawing indecent exposure a basis for a claim of wrongful discharge?

DECISION   Yes. Reversed and remanded. Wagenseller on remand is entitled to a jury trial to prove that her discharge was caused by her refusal to engage in the unlawful act of indecent exposure. Public policy is defined as something the constitution, the legislature, or common law courts of the state have forbidden. Arizona's indecent exposure statute was enacted to protect public privacy and decency. Thus, the termination of a worker for refusal to publicly expose "one's buttocks" is contrary to the state's public policy.

Exercising legal rights. Some employers have forced employees to choose between continued employment and the exercise of their legal rights. As we will see later in this chapter, some employers have penalized employees for filing workers' compensation claims for injuries suffered on the job or making claims under the Fair Labor Standards Act. Others have discharged employees who file for bankruptcy despite the fact that the federal Bankruptcy Code, discussed in Chapter 42, protects such employees.

Also, employers have often disciplined workers engaging in union activity although the workers are protected by the National Labor Relations Act, discussed in Chapter 46. Refusing to take a lie detector test as a condition of employment was until recently a hotly litigated public policy issue.

The range of examples here seems endless, for employers persist in developing novel ways to provoke confrontations on the issue, as the next case illustrates.

Western States Minerals Corporation v. Jones

819 P. 2d 207 (Nev. 1991)

FACTS   Robert Jones was a miner and employee at will for defendant Western State Minerals Corporation. Jones recently had been hospitalized and returned to work with an unclosed surgical wound in his lower abdomen. He was told by his supervisor to enter a cyanide leach pit to work. He respectfully refused, since he had learned at a required Western States' safety course that it was contrary to company policy to do so because of the potentially fatal consequences of cyanide absorption in the body through unhealed wounds. Jones was told to go home and the next day was fired for insubordination. Jones prevailed at the trial level.

ISSUE   Could Western States legally terminate Jones for exercising his rights under the state's occupational safety and health act, which guarantees a safe and healthy work environment?

DECISION   No. Affirmed. Nevada law requires that employers guarantee safe employment and do whatever is necessary to protect the lives, safety, and health of its employees, including prohibiting a worker from entering an unhealthy place. Jones's termination for exercising his rights to seek a safe and healthy work environment is contrary to the state's public policy.

Performing a legal duty. As noted earlier, the most common violation of public policy involves disciplining an employee for reporting for jury duty. The courts reason that our judicial system depends on having qualified jurors readily available and, therefore, that a court should decide whether an employer's need for the employee at work outweighs jury duty.

Similarly, most courts have held that an employer's disciplinary action against an employee for obeying a subpoena violates public policy. Though a subpoena may have nothing to do with the employer's business, such as one in a child custody dispute, the employer's ability to penalize workers for obeying it affects the ability of the court system to render proper decisions.

Military duty. Another common public policy exception forbids discharge for participating in activities required by state or federal military service. For example, many states have statutes forbidding the firing of an employee who reports for mandatory weekend National Guard duty rather than reporting for work.

Whistleblowing. Protection for whistleblowing employees occurs in two basic settings. First, some statutes—such as OSHA, the 1964 Civil Rights Act, and many federal environmental laws—provide a specific remedy if an employer retaliates against an employee for reporting a violation. Moreover, both the Civil Service Reform Act of 1978 and the Federal Whistleblowers Protection Act of 1989 protect whistleblowing employees who divulge governmental fraud, waste, and abuse of power. In some cases, state and federal government workers are also protected under the First and Fourteenth Amendments of the Constitution.

As of 1992, thirty-three states had general whistleblowers statutes. All these laws cover workers in the public sector, while approximately fifteen of them also protect those in the private sector.* Michigan enacted the first of these statutes in 1980, with Maine, New York, and California following shortly thereafter.

There is no consistency among these state statutes. Some broad generalizations are discernable, however. Most of the statutes list specific kinds or wrongdoing that a worker can disclose and still be protected, although the kinds of reportable wrongs vary greatly—from violations of environmental regulations only to

general governmental mismanagement, waste, and abuse of authority. All the statutes indicate that the wrongdoing must be relatively serious. Thus, if a worker whistleblows concerning an issue that is neither specified under state law nor grave enough, she could be legally terminated. The statutes also normally require the worker to report the wrongdoing in good faith. An employee who is reckless or malicious in his accusations would thus be left to the mercy of his employer. Most of the statutes also allow a whistleblower to file a civil suit, either directly or after the exhaustion of administrative remedies. The victim would assume the burden of proving that the "terms and conditions" of his employment were changed detrimentally (such as termination, denial of a promotion, etc.) due to the whistleblowing incident. Most statutes also afford the employee some equitable remedies, such as reinstatement. Only a handful allow for actual damages; four states permit punitive damages.

It should be noted, too, that the public policy exceptions, discussed above, also function as protection for whistleblowers even when the states do not statutorily protect them.

Do whistleblowing statutes actually protect workers from retaliation? At this time there is no convincing evidence that they work. For example, results from a 1987 study of the Michigan, Maine, and Connecticut statutes were not promising.†

Implied Contract

As we saw in Chapter 7, an *implied* contract is one a court infers from the parties' conduct rather than from their expressions of mutual assent. At least thirty-seven states permit a discharged at will employee some form of recovery on the basis of an implied contract theory.

As with the public policy tort, the states do

---

* T. Barnett, "Overview of State Whistleblower Protection Statutes," *Labor Law Journal,* July 1992, pp. 440–448.

† T. M. Dworkin and J. P. Near, "Whistleblowing Statutes: Are They Working?" *American Business Law Journal,* vol. 25, 1987, pp. 241–260.

not agree on what constitutes an implied contract in these circumstances. Also, when an employee expressly accepts at will employee status as a condition of employment, the states do not agree on what effect this acceptance has upon a later termination without just cause. These issues and the implied contract theories of recovery are best understood when examined in terms of employer and employee actions.

Employer actions before hiring. An implied contract based on an employer's action can result from oral representations or from company actions. What an employer does before or at the time it hires an employee can determine the result—many years later—of a wrongful discharge suit. Put differently, the state of the law gives a discharged employee's lawyer excellent reason to examine carefully what the employer advertised when it listed the position, what it represented during the employment interview, what it said on its job application form, and what it states in materials given to applicants before they accept employment.

For instance, does the employer's help-wanted advertisement make reference to "permanent employment" upon completion of a probationary period? Some courts have held that employers who create "probationary" and "permanent" employee status implicitly make a greater commitment to employees who become permanent. To avoid this situation, many employers are abolishing these categories. The general rule would appear to be: the greater the permanence of position that is implied or expressed, the greater the likelihood that a court will find conditions prohibiting the employee's discharge.

If an employer represents to a prospective employee that it has a procedure for making personnel decisions, a court may hold that the employer improperly discharged the employee if it ignored or misapplied the procedure.

Employer actions at hiring. The greater the employee's justifiable reliance upon the employ-

er's assertions before accepting employment, the greater the employee's chance of proving an implied contract.

For obvious reasons, what the employer says and does when it hires plays a critical role in how a court will view the employment relationship. That is why, for example, Sears requires all new workers to acknowledge that they are being hired as at will employees in the following language: "my employment and compensation can be terminated, with or without cause, and with or without notice at any time, at the option of either the Company or myself." A written employment contract that creates an at will relationship lessens or eliminates the employee's opportunity to introduce parole evidence to vary or contradict it. However, it can be important *when* the written employment contract is introduced to the employee. In the 1989 case of *Bullock v. American Automobile Association of Michigan,** the Michigan Supreme Court ruled that an employee could obtain an enforceable oral lifetime employment contract even though the employment handbooks expressly stated that all employees were classified at will. The reason was that the oral promise was made to the employee at the time he was hired, while the at will handbook provision was created later.

Employer actions and employee manuals. Some courts are especially interested in employee manuals or handbooks provided prior to the employee's acceptance of the job. Employee handbooks often assemble all pertinent information for employees, such as procedures for leave time and vacations. They also often cover matters that give the employer cause for termination.

The courts in several states have held that the contents of an employee manual created an implied contract with the employee. (However, courts in ten other states have held that a manual does not create such a contract.) The courts

---

* 432 Mich. App. 472, 444 N.W.2d 114 (1989).

are most likely to find an implied contract when the employee received the manual before hiring, but at least one court has held that whether the employee read the manual or not does not affect the existence of the implied contract. In effect, then, the manual becomes part of the employment contract.

As in all implied contract situations, the burden of proving reliance on the manual or handbook rests on the employee. However, even when an employee establishes that the publication altered the standard employment at will, it does not follow that the employer will lose the wrongful discharge action.

Courts have taken references in manuals to "probationary"—as opposed to "permanent"—employees as implying lifetime employment in return for satisfactory work. This may result in a standard under which the employer, to defeat a wrongful termination action, must show that an employee is not doing quality work.

Procedures for notifying an employee of subpar work or for considering and implementing corrective or punitive actions may modify the contract with the at will employee. An employer with such procedures may face liability for ignoring them or not following them in good faith. Suppose a company president sees an employee arrive 15 minutes late on three consecutive mornings. On the third morning, he meets the late arriver at the door and fires her on the spot. If the handbook outlines procedures for corrective or punitive actions and the procedures were not followed, the company may have breached its implied contract with the employee.

Some companies have codes of behavior for their employees that specify disciplinary actions for particular offenses. A court may use such a code to compare the disciplinary actions under dispute to those specified for other offenses. If it concludes the punishment is disproportionate, it may find for the plaintiff. For example, the late arriver may show that the company's Employee Conduct Code prescribes dismissal for theft, gross insubordination, in-

competence, and the like, which may convince the court to find a breach.

Discharges limited to "good cause" are common in collective bargaining agreements between a union and an employer but are not very common in an employee handbook primarily intended for nonunion members. Yet, where it does appear, the good cause stipulation will prevent an employer from discharging an at will employee without cause.

Employee actions and promissory estoppel. The courts that have found an implied contract exception based upon employee actions have tended to apply the doctrine of promissory estoppel discussed in Part II. Typically, the courts confront an employer action followed by an employee action taken in reliance on the action of the employer. A Minnesota appellate court found a lifetime contract where an employee relinquished 27 years of prior employment.* Similarly, where an employee incurs personal costs and relinquishes a job to make a move on behalf of a new employer, the employee may be found to have more than at will term if he or she was discharged almost immediately after commencing work.

Courts that find for the employee sometimes do so on the ground that the employer should have foreseen such reliance and that justice requires enforcement even though the contract lacks some essential element such as consideration. Suppose an employer gives its employees a memorandum detailing disciplinary procedures for all at will employees. The employer may be held to these procedures if it discharges a worker using different procedures or no procedures.

Implied Covenant of Good Faith and Fair Dealing

The *implied covenant of good faith and fair dealing* is the most liberal exception to the employment at will doctrine. It presumes that an

---

* *Ecklund v. Vincent Brass and Aluminum Co.*, 351 N.W.2d 371 (Minn. App. 1984).

employer has a duty of good faith to an employee and, as a corollary, a duty not to terminate an employee unjustly. This exception recognized in eight states, focuses upon the relationship between the employer and the employee. It does not depend on legislative action or a judicial decision as to what constitutes "public policy."

The reasonable employer standard. Determining whether an employer owes such a duty to a given employee requires a determination of what a reasonable employer would do and of what just cause would be for termination. Undoubtedly, courts will look for guidance to labor arbitration cases which review terminations of unionized employees to determine whether the employer acted in good faith.

Good faith. The common law recognized that in certain situations the conduct of a contracting party negated the assent of the other party. In these circumstances, a court might excuse performance. However, the common law did not impose an implied condition of good faith. Look again at the Tennessee holding quoted earlier, affirming the employer's right to discharge a worker for "good cause or for no cause, or even for bad cause."*

By contrast, the drafters of the Uniform Commercial Code (UCC) expressed their goal of promoting fair dealing and higher standards

in the marketplace by requiring that parties to transactions governed by the UCC act in good faith. The UCC defines "good faith" as "honesty in fact" and requires that each party observe "reasonable commercial standards of fair dealing" [UCC §2-103(1) (b)].

The *Restatement (Second) of Contracts* has adopted the UCC good faith standard. "Every contract imposes upon each party a duty of good faith and fair dealing in its performance and its enforcement" [§205].

One can see some movement toward a duty of good faith and fair dealing that is not limited to sales contracts. California was the first state to recognize a duty of good faith and fair dealing.*

This exception to the employment at will doctrine may grow in acceptance as courts and legislatures persist in their tendency to adopt and expand the rationale of the UCC and the *Restatement*. However, the highest courts in some states—New York, for instance—have had the opportunity to adopt the implied covenant but have refused to do so, holding the decision was a legislative one.† Moreover, the next case examines the reasons California, the first state to recognize this exception, has now backpedaled to its application.

---

* *Payne v. Western & Atlantic R.R. Co.*, 82 Tenn. 507, 518–19 (1884).

---

* *Seaman's Direct Buying Service, Inc. v. Standard Oil Company of California,*__Cal. 2d__, 206 Cal. Rptr. 354, 686 P.2d 1158 (1984).
† *Murphy v. American Home Prod. Corp.*, 58 N.Y.2d 293, 58 N.Y.S.2d 232, 448 N.E.2d 86 (1983).

Foley v. Interactive Data Corporation

254 Cal.Rptr. 211, 765 P.2d 373 (1988)

FACTS Daniel Foley, the plaintiff, worked for Interactive Data Corporation, the defendant, for nearly 7 years, rising to the rank of branch manager. During that time he consistently received salary increases, bonuses, promotions, awards, and superior performance evaluations. The incident that caused Foley's termination stemmed from a complaint he made to one of Interactive's vice presidents concerning his supervisor, Robert Kuhne. Foley discovered that Kuhne was being investigated by the FBI for embezzlement (Kuhne later pleaded guilty to it) when he had worked for the Bank of America. Foley feared that the reputations in the financial community of both Interactive and its parent company, Chase Manhattan Bank, might be tarnished. He was told to "forget what he heard" about Kuhne. After a series of demotions, Foley was fired. He sued defendant for, among other actions, breach of the implied covenant of good faith and fair dealing and sought tort remedies. The trial court ruled for the defendant. The court of appeal affirmed.

ISSUE   Does a breach of the covenant of good faith and fair dealing in employment contracts give rise to an award of tort damages?

DECISION   No. Affirmed. The covenant of good faith and fair dealing arose in contract law and creates a duty enforcing promises contained in an agreement. The duty is recognized by most U.S. jurisdictions in the *Restatement* and the UCC. However, because the covenant is part of contract law, compensation for its breach should not be based on tort law, but should be limited to contract damages. Moreover, due to concerns about economic policy and stability, and in view of the other protections employees now have for wrongful termination, tort damages should not be awarded for breach of this duty.

The *Foley* case is considered by many to be a watershed in the area of wrongful termination. California, a state which has historically influenced other states' courts and legislatures, was the first to create the covenant of good faith and fair dealing. Thus, it is probable that other jurisdictions which have adopted it will similarly embrace the *Foley* modification.*

The implications of *Foley* are noteworthy, since the difference between tort and contract damages is significant. As discussed in Chapter 12, contract damages generally are limited to compensation of the victim of the breach for actual economic losses. Tort damages, on the other hand, can be potentially great. Under the implied covenant of good faith and fair dealing both substantial compensatory as well as puni-

tive damages have been awarded in some of the more reprehensible cases. In a 1987 Nevada case, for example, a faithful 10-year K-Mart employee, with excellent evaluations, was unceremoniously fired on the pretext of spraying the battery cover of his forklift with a gray primer. The jury concluded that he was terminated so that K-Mart would not have to pay him retirement benefits. He was eventually awarded $383,120 in compensatory damages and $50,000 in punitive damages.*

THE FUTURE OF EMPLOYMENT AT WILL

As stated earlier, about forty states recognize at least one exception to the employment at will doctrine. Thus, the common law approach is under siege, if not altogether losing favor. How-

----

* R. J. Aalberts and L. Seidman, "The Employment At Will Doctrine: Nevada's Struggle Demonstrates the Need for Reform," *Labor Law Journal*, October 1992, pp. 651–662.

* *K-Mart Corporation V. Ponsock*, 732 P.2d 1364 (Nev. 1987).

ever, it is not at all clear what position most states, and perhaps the federal government, will ultimately take regarding at will employment.

More Employer Successes

There is some evidence that employers are beginning to win more termination cases even under the exceptions. Several factors have contributed to this.

Employers are beginning to get smarter about what employee handbooks should appear to promise employees. Anything that looks like an implied promise of lifetime employment is disappearing.

More employers insist on employment contracts in which the new employee specifically acknowledges his or her employee at will status. However, some courts may disregard this clause and imply a covenant of good faith and fair dealing.

In the next case, former employees could not convince a federal court to do that.

International Klafter Co., Inc. v. Continental Casualty Co., Inc.

869 F.2d 96 (1989)

FACTS

The three plaintiff corporations served as general insurance agents for continental Casualty under contracts called "general agency agreements." Paragraph 8 of the agreements provided that the agreements

> shall continue in force until either party . . . shall give the other party thirty (30) days prior written notice of intention to terminate it for any cause other than as specified in paragraph 18 (in which case the provisions of paragraph 18 shall apply).

Paragraph 18 eliminated, among other things, the 30-day notice for terminations on account of an agent's fraud, loss of state license, or breach of contract. On December 20, 1983, Continental gave the plaintiffs notice of termination and subsequently terminated the contracts. Continental never specified any reason for the terminations. Although the insurance company made all payments that were due the former general agents, they brought suit alleging breach of contract. The principal of the three corporations, Leonard Klafter, had been a salaried employee of Continental for 12 years when he left to become a general agent in 1967. He testified that when he hired general agents for Continental, he told them that Continental had an unwritten policy of not terminating agents so long as they performed satisfactorily and lawfully. He assumed that the policy had continued. Continental did not rebut Klafter's testimony. The trial court, however, granted Continental's motion for summary judgment on the grounds that the only reasonable interpretation of the contract was that either party could terminate at will. Since the meaning of the contract was plain. there was no reason to look beyond the document.

ISSUE

Does a contract clause permitting termination for any cause also permit termination for no cause?

DECISION

Yes. Affirmed. The literal meaning of "any cause" in paragraph 8 is "any reason." Thus, the agents' argument that they could be discharged only for "valid reasons" fails. Paragraph 18 broadly covers the range of legally valid reasons for termination. The agents would have paragraph 8 interpreted so as to require the courts to ignore the words "any cause" and then to try to determine whether the decision to terminate was made arbitrarily or for a "valid reason." But the contract is specific: Only terminations under paragraph 18 require any statement of reasons.

Many employers are using more caution and documentation in regard to termination. Also, many courts are reluctant to expand the at will exceptions without legislative guidance. Finally, as potential plaintiffs have become aware of the possibility of winning wrongful termination cases, the number of less worthy cases has increased. But the courts have shown a reluctance to find against an employer where a termination was marginally improper.

The Possibilities for Legislation

Periodically, legislative proposals appear at both the state and federal levels for protecting the at will employee from wrongful discharge. As of 1992, three American jurisdictions had passed statutes modifying the employment at will doctrine, while at least fourteen had drafted and/or considered legislation. Moreover, a proposed model statute, the Model Employment Termination Act, was submitted to the state legislatures in 1991 for their consideration.

Organized labor's position. For example, few would argue that the loss of one employee—assuming he or she is not a key employee—will jeopardize an organization. But the loss of a job can have a disastrous impact upon the employee and his or her family. So shouldn't an employer be required to show just cause or economic necessity before discharging an employee, especially one who has been with a company for a number of years?

That argument has equally little appeal to management and organized labor. After all, one of a union's strongest selling points is its ability to secure from an employer contractual recog-

nition that employees will not be discharged without cause and that layoffs compelled by economic necessity will affect employees in reverse order to seniority.

Legislative expansion of the implied covenant exception could remove an incentive for nonunion workers to organize. This disincentive is especially critical now, as the percentage of organized employees has declined with the loss of jobs in the "smokestack" industries. To make matters worse, in this decade unionized employees have realized lower percentage increases in wages than nonunion employees.

At present, an employee covered by a collective bargaining agreement must look to that agreement and its judicial machinery for settlement of a retaliatory discharge dispute that an at will employee might now take directly against the employer.

Management's position. Understandably, management has not favored national legislation providing at will employee exceptions. However, this may change as states fashion more exceptions. A hodgepodge of state laws will create great difficulties for multistate corporations. Keeping centralized personnel managers abreast of the many state laws and attempting to avoid "new law" created retroactively by judicial decisions will challenge even the most sophisticated management.

Statutory modifications. Only three American jurisdictions, Montana, Puerto Rico, and the Virgin Islands, have at this time passed statutes modifying the traditional employment at will doctrine. Montana's is the most comprehensive and has been considered by other jurisdictions as a model. It provides that a discharge is wrongful if it occurs in one of the following three situations:

- In retaliation for refusal to violate or report a violation of public policy
- When an employee successfully completes his probationary period and the discharge was not for "good cause"
- When an employee is discharged in violation of an express term of a written personnel policy

A number of key provisions of the Montana statute need to be more fully explained. Public policy, under the first provision, is defined as "a policy in effect at the time of the discharge concerning public health, safety, or welfare established by constitutional, statute, or administrative rule." Under the second circumstance, "good cause" is specified as "reasonable job-related grounds for dismissal based on a failure to satisfactorily perform duties, disruption of the employer's operation, or other legitimate business reasons." The third situation would occur if there is a written personnel policy in, say, an employee handbook. Thus, it appears that implied contracts, discussed earlier, could now not arise under Montana law, at least under a strict interpretation of the statute.

Despite the bold legislative effort made by Montana, courts will continue to be closely involved in employment at will cases in that state. As is quite evident, there are still many aspects of the statute that will need to be interpreted.

Model Employment Termination Act. In 1991, the National Conference of Commissioners on Uniform State Laws approved the Model Employment Termination Act. The Act, which is now being reviewed by the state legislatures, would protect a worker from wrongful termination. The Act creates trade-offs between the competing interests of employers and employees, much like in workers compensation laws, with the hope of creating a fairer and more productive workplace. This means workers can

be dismissed for only "good cause," defined as the "exercise of business judgment in good faith by the employer." In exchange for these protections, workers give up their common law actions for wrongful termination, such as the actions discussed in this chapter, for sharply reduced remedies. The remedies would include reinstatement, with or without back pay and severance pay if reinstatement is not viable, and reasonable attorneys' fees. Finally, arbitration is contained in the Act as the preferred method for dispute resolution.

Proponents of the Act maintain that employers, employees, and the U.S. economy would all be beneficiaries if the states adopted it. Employees would no longer have to fear arbitrary firings, which now are estimated to be 200,000 annually. Moreover, there would be uniformity in the legal expectations of the millions of workers who seek new jobs in other states. Employers also would likely save money. In California, for example, a study found that plaintiffs in wrongful termination cases have enjoyed a 70 percent success rate, with awards averaging $300,000 to $500,000. A few of the verdicts have reached into the millions of dollars. In addition, a standard case was found typically to cost about $80,000 in attorneys' fees and costs.* The U.S. economy (and employers) may profit by savings that now go into the cost of adhering to intricate personnel procedures, internal grievance systems, and the retention of unproductive workers by fearful employers. Indeed, a recent study by the Rand Corporation found that in states which allow wrongful termination suits, risk-averse employers lay off fewer of the poorer workers but have reduced their employment levels by 2 to 5 percent.† Thus, employers' fears and perceptions of potential lawsuits may actually be causing higher unemployment rates.

---

* 9A *Labor Relations Reporter* (Washington, D.C.: Bureau of National Affairs) IERM 540:21, December 1991.
† J. Dertouzos and L. Karoly, *Labor Market Responses to Employer Liability* 1991 Santa Monica, CA: Rand Corp.

The Act has not been without its critics. Various trial and employment lawyer associations have argued that tort damages, particularly punitive damages, are one of the few disincentives employers have for wrongfully treating their workers. They believe the threat of worker reinstatement and back pay simply does not deter employers from illegal and unethical behavior in the workplace.

Employee pacts. Another recent development surrounding employment at will has been the introduction of employee pacts.* In an employee pact, a worker surrenders her right to sue for wrongful termination and other kinds of discrimination. In return, the business must provide mandatory arbitration of disputes. The pacts would then protect the employer from costly lawsuits, while the employee would have a neutral forum for handling her grievances. The pacts greatly resemble the provisions of the Model Employment Termination Act, but because they are privately executed, they do not require legislation.

Legal challenges are expected because some view these pacts as unjust and coercive, due to the unequal bargaining positions of the parties. It is possible, for example, that courts could rule that the pacts impose a form of economic duress on prospective workers and so are unenforceable. After all, if a worker needs a job, he will likely sign whatever is necessary in order to get it. The 1991 U.S. Supreme Court case of *Gilmer v. Interstate/Johnson Lane Corp.*† strongly supported the legal viability of these pacts. In that case, the Court gave its approval to an arbitration clause contained in an employment contract after a terminated employee in the securities industry had sued for age discrimination under the Age Discrimation in Employment Act. Since *Gilmer,* at least six other federal cases have upheld and strongly

favored arbitration clauses in settling discrimination cases under federal law. Thus, it is quite likely that state actions for wrongful termination will be treated in a similar manner in the future.

EMPLOYEE RIGHTS TO RECORDS AND PRIVACY

In an age when computers and data accumulation techniques enable the construction of detailed files on individuals, it is critically important that individuals have a means of protecting themselves from false information and protecting their privacy from unnecessary intrusions. Those are the goals of a rapidly growing field of legislation. As you would expect, the states have adopted the major and more generally applicable statutes. Nonetheless, Congress has provided employee rights and protections in specific employment areas.

Right to Inspect Personnel Records

Seventeen states have given employees a right to inspect their own personnel records and to correct them. Some statutes, like that of Illinois, cover all private and public employees and all employers with one or more employees. Others are more limited in scope.

Invoking the right. Typically, a person who is currently employed, is on layoff status will recall rights, or has been terminated within the past year has the right to inspect his or her personnel record at least twice in any calendar year. The employee normally must make the request in writing on a form provided by the employer.

Within a certain period, the employer must provide the employee with access to the file. The Illinois statute sets 7 working days as the period, with the possibility of a 7-day extension, if needed. Actual review takes place on the employer's premises during work hours, unless employee and employer agree otherwise.

* W. Lambert, "Employee Pacts to Avoid Suits Sought by Firms," *Wall Street Journal*, Oct. 22, 1992, p. B1.
† 114 L.Ed 2d 26 (1991).

If the employee demonstrates an inability to review the record during the time allotted the employer can make copies of the record for the employee at the employee's cost.

An employer's failure to comply with an employee's request can result in the imposition of a civil penalty and the award of actual damages to the employee.

Using agents. The employee may delegate the inspection to his or her agent if the employee is engaged in or anticipates a grievance with the employer. The agent might by a lawyer or a union official. A union may have a separate right to seek information under federal labor laws.

What is a record? An *employee record* includes any information which has been or could be used in determining:

- Promotion
- Transfer
- Additional compensation
- Disciplinary action

Employers often complain of the logistical problems entailed in assembling and providing so much information, especially when there are likely to be multiple files on an employee.

The employer's strategy. Preventive law principles dictate an employer strategy centering on eliminating unnecessary materials. Further, management should not color the facts of allegations contained in a personnel file. Also, before allowing the employee to examine the file, a responsible manager should carefully cull the items the law permits the employer to keep confidential. Such items include letters of reference, test documents other than scores, materials used by management for planning, recommendations on future salary increases and other wage matters, information of a personal nature about another employee which would clearly constitute an unwarranted invasion of the privacy of another person, and security files.

If there is a possibility of litigation, an important consideration weighs against an aggressive approach to excluding documents. In some states in a judicial or quasi-judicial proceeding, an employer cannot use information against an employee which the employer should have given to the employee pursuant to a request but did not supply.

It is also important to note that an employer's right to accumulate information on its employees is not boundless. For example, under Illinois law an employer cannot gather information on an employee's political and nonemployment activities without the employee's consent unless the activities are considered harmful to the employer's interest or constitute criminal conduct.

Postinspection disputes over contents. After inspection, if the employer and the employee cannot agree on the removal or correction of a record relating to a disciplinary matter, the employee usually has a right to submit for inclusion in the file a written statement expressing his or her viewpoint. The employer must include this statement if the disputed portion of the file is released to a third party.

Releasing information to third parties. Under many statutes, the employer may not release to a third party information about disciplinary reports or actions without prior written notice to the employee. This rule does not apply if:

- The employee waived the right in an employment application with another employer
- A court or an arbitrator required disclosure
- A government agency requested the information pursuant to the employee's complaint or as a part of a criminal investigation

Under the Illinois statute and others like it, an employer may not give anyone records that are more than 4 years old.

Recent Legislation Protecting Privacy

Congress and several state legislatures have moved recently in several other areas to protect employees' privacy. The reaction by employers to this legislation has often been less than enthusiastic.

Polygraph tests. For years, civil liberties groups, unions, and employees complained about employers administering *polygraph*—lie detector—tests without nay safeguards for an employee's rights. After forty-one state legislatures had acted to restrict these practices, Congress stepped in, virtually banning polygraph, voice-stress, and other mechanical testing as an employment screening device.

The Employee Polygraph Protection Act of 1988 forbids employers to:

- Suggest that an employee or job applicant take a lie detector test
- Ask about a lie detector test an employee or applicant has taken
- Take any action against an employee for either refusing to take a test or failing one
- Take any retaliatory action against an employee who files a complaint or testifies about the employer's use of polygraph tests

The Act exempts some limited uses of polygraph examinations among employers generally. For example, tests administered in the course of an ongoing investigation relating to an embezzlement would be permitted under the Act. However, the circumstances under which the tests may be given are so narrow and the conditions surrounding the tests are so strict that most employers have concluded that the risks of lawsuits far outweigh the tests' benefits.

The Act also exempts armored car, security guard, and alarm companies hired to protect state government functions or national security. Also exempt are employers who manufacture, distribute, or dispense controlled substances.

The Department of Labor has issued regulations implementing the Act. If anything, they make the use of polygraphs even more difficult for employers.

Drug testing. Testing employees for substance abuse has become a popular cause among some politicians. However, it has proved extremely difficult to implement. Often, employees who have no contact with drugs oppose testing. Many employees find the experience humiliating, since reliability usually depends on the subject urinating in the presence of another person. Some employers have tended to be rather indiscriminate about who they tested—secretaries as well an engineers.

While employees and civil libertarians complain about random testing—testing without any reason to believe an employee is a substance abuser—the trend appears to be toward more drug testing. The U.S. Supreme Court has approved drug testing in certain circumstances, and it appears that private employers are embracing the tests at least as an employment screening device. The following case illustrates the problems of drug-testing requirements.

Skinner v. Railway Labor Executives Association

109 S.Ct. 1402 (1989)

FACTS   The Federal Railroad Administration (FRA) has authority to issue safety regulations for railroads. In response to evidence indicating that drug and alcohol abuse had contributed to several train accidents, the FRA adopted regulations that required blood or urine testing of railroad employees following certain major train accidents and permitted, but did not require, testing following violations of certain safety rules. Several railroad labor unions brought suit challenging the regulations on the grounds that they violated their members' Fourth Amendment right to be secure from unwarranted searches and seizures. The district court upheld the constitutionality of the regulations, but the Ninth Circuit reversed, holding that the Fourth Amendment requires before testing a warrant or a reasonable suspicion that a particular employee was under the influence of a controlled substance.

ISSUE   Does the government's interest in ensuring the safety of the traveling public and of railway employees outweigh the employees' privacy concerns?

DECISION   Yes. Court of appeals reversed. The Fourth Amendment applies to the drug and alcohol testing authorized by the FRA regulations. The action is not private action outside of the reach of the Fourth Amendment which constrains government actions, because the FRA has compelled the railroads to take it. Blood and urine tests are clearly searches within the meaning of the Fourth Amendment, since they intrude on the employees' expectation of privacy on medical matters. And, these tests are reasonable under the Fourth Amendment even though the regulations do not require a warrant or a reasonable suspicion that any particular employee may be affected by drugs or alcohol. The government's interests in safety outweigh the employees' interest in their privacy. Imposing a warrant requirement is not necessary to make the searches reasonable. The regulations narrowly define the circumstances in which the testing may be conducted, so there are no facts for a neutral magistrate to weigh. Similarly, an individualized suspicion requirement is not necessary because the intrusion into the employee's justifiable privacy expectations is very limited, given the pervasive federal safety regulation in the industry. Further, the government's interest in testing without a particularized showing of impairment is compelling in view of the harm such employees can cause. And, the regulations put employees on notice of the likelihood of testing in the event of an accident.

The federal Drug-Free Workplace Act of 1988 has added an impetus to drug testing. The Act requires federal government contractors to certify that they will provide a drug-free workplace before they can receive contracts exceeding $25,000. All federal grants recipients must make a similar certification. The Act requires employers to:

- Maintain a drug-free workplace by banning the use or possession of controlled substances
- Put employees on notice of the prohibition and the consequences for its violation
- Require notification by employees convicted of a criminal drug violation based on conduct in the workplace

- Notify the federal agency or agencies with which they have contracts of these criminal violations
- Discipline workplace drug violators or require them to enter a rehabilitation program as a condition of further employment

The proliferating use of drug testing in the private sector has resulted in the passage of a growing number of state statutes for regulating how the tests are administered. These statutes differ significantly. In Utah, for example, a private sector employer can randomly test an employee as long as there is a safety or productivity reason for the test. Rhode Island, on the other hand, is very strict about when and how the tests are used. An employee in that state can be tested only if there is reasonable suspicion that he is on drugs. Also, the guidelines for administering drug tests in Rhode Island are rigorous. For example, if the employee's urine sample initially tests positive, there must be a reliable and expensive follow-up test of the first sample.

Arrests and convictions. In certain instances, an employee does not have to reveal arrests or convictions. Indeed, the law typically limits access to conviction records because, as we will see in Chapter 46, reliance on arrest records can result in unlawful discrimination. Among the restrictions on the use of arrest and conviction records are state statutes providing the following:

- An applicant need not disclose an expunged or pardoned conviction
- An applicant does not have to list convictions for misdemeanors unrelated to the job
- An applicant does not have to disclose a conviction record unless the circumstances of conviction relate to circumstances of the job

Disclosure of private information. Recent enactments restrict the private information an employer may release about employees. For instance, a California law states that an employer must accommodate employees wishing to enroll in alcohol and drug abuse programs by using reasonable efforts to safeguard the fact of their program enrollment.

Developments in Privacy Torts

The courts have also acted to protect employees' expectations of privacy. (These torts were defined in Chapter 4.)

Defamation. The law of defamation recognizes a qualified privilege that permits the communication of otherwise defamatory information. Suppose an employer acting in good faith communicated inaccurate information about a for-

mer employee's unemployment compensation claim to the state Bureau of Employment Services, the employee's union, and a prospective new employer. In that instance, the employer probably would not be liable to the employee. However, if the employer spread the misinformation out of spite or with reckless disregard for the truth, the employer would lose its qualified privilege.

Invasion of privacy. One type of privacy tort involves the appropriation of an employee's name and likeness. In this case, the employer might use an employee's name or picture for its benefit without compensating the employee. For example, a bank was liable to thirty-eight employees for using their photographs in a trade show without their consent.

Another type of privacy tort involves the public disclosure of true but private facts. (It is worth noting that the fact that a statement is true does not mean you have a right to say it.) For example, an airline's medical examiner told the results of an examination of a flight attendant to her husband and a male flight supervisor. A court held that neither had a need to know.

This class of tort also includes intrusions into the employee's seclusion. In a 1984 case, a K-Mart store provided lockers for its employees, who supplied their own locks. The employees' use of their own locks made the lockers "private places" and gave the employees an expectation of privacy and freedom from intrusions that they would not have had if K-Mart had provided the locks. When unlocked or locked with K-Mart's locks, the lockers were subject to legitimate, reasonable searches.*

Intentional infliction of emotional distress. Most states recognize a tort described as the intentional infliction of emotional distress. For many years, the courts resisted the concept

---

* *K-Mart v. Trotti,* 677 S.W.2d 632 (Tex. Ct. App. 1984).

because, it was feared, the injuries could be faked and the damages phonied. Today, however, an employer will be liable for deliberately engaging in outrageous conduct that he or she knows or should know will result in severe emotional distress to another. The classic case involved the manager of a Howard Johnson's restaurant. He could not figure out which employee was stealing money from the cash register. So he announced that he would fire employees one by one, from A to Z, until the culprit admitted his or her wrongdoing. The first employee fired brought suit. The manager's conduct, the court held, was outrageous and was intended to bring about emotional distress.*

CONCLUSION

It should come as no surprise that the law of employment is controversial and changing. Almost nothing so directly affects our sense of self-worth as our jobs. This chapter had addressed only some of the questions bound up in the employment relationship. Chapter 46 will survey the nature of government regulation of the workplace.

The "right" to a particular job or to the continuation of employment cuts across many unexpected areas of law. In the next part, Business Organizations, we will see how questions of employment can lead to strife that makes a business enterprise not viable.

A NOTE TO FUTURE CPA CANDIDATES

The CPA exam has never tested candidates over the law covered in Chapter 15. However, the exam does cover other employment matters found in Chapter 46: payroll taxes, employee

---

* *Agis v. Howard Johnson,* 371 Mass. 140, 355 N.E.2d 315 (1976). Although it has never expressly modified *Agis,* the Supreme Judicial Court has since implied that claims for such injuries may be made only under the worker's compensation program.

safety, employment discrimination, wage and hour and pension and other fringe benefits.

KEY WORDS

employee (324)
employee at will (324)
employee record (340)
implied contract (331)
implied covenant of good faith and fair dealing (333)
public policy (328)
whistleblower statutes (327)
Wood's Rule (325)

DISCUSSION QUESTIONS

1. Define "employee at will." What is the significance of this employment status, as compared with an employee for a term, in regard to termination?
2. What was the original rationale for the employment at will doctrine? Who has the burden of establishing that an employment relationship is other than an employment at will?
3. Give examples of several instances of statutory protection available to *all* employees.
4. What are the three primary classifications of exceptions to the employee at will doctrine? Which is considered to be the most liberal exception?
5. What are the four subcategories of the public policy tort? What are the primary factors which may cause a court to recognize the implied contract exception?
6. What is the purpose of right to information statutes?
   What tort law rights might an employee have in regard to his or her employment? Explain.

CASE PROBLEMS

1. Anita Curran, an employee at Conter Tool Works, Inc. had unsuccessfully attempted to have smoking banned around her office area. Anita called a local talk show and complained about the unwillingness of Conter management to listen and learn about the dangers of secondhand smoke from smokers. The next day the Conter personnel manager met Anita at the

door of the office and told her that she was fired for defaming Conter Tool Works. Anita's statements were not inaccurate, but Conter refuses to consider reinstating her. What rights, if any, does Anita have at common law? If her state recognizes the public policy tort exception, would she be likely to recover under this exception? Explain.

2. Mike McWilliams was a commercial loan officer for First Bank. One day, while jogging during his lunch hour, Mike witnessed an accident in which a fellow jogger, Bill Holm, was hit by a car. Mike stopped to provide assistance to Holm. An arriving police officer asked Mike to remain so that he could ask Mike questions about the accident. By the time Mike returned to the bank, he discovered that he had missed his appointment with an important bank customer. The customer, offended by Mike's tardiness, canceled his planned major transaction with the bank. Mike's supervisor, a person who despised joggers, told Mike that since he obviously considered jogging to be more important than the bank, he was fired. If Mike's state recognized the public policy tort, would he be likely to prevail for damages against his former employer? If his state recognized only the implied contract exception? Explain.

3. Dave and Doug Marskie, identical twins, were high school students at Victory High and worked summers as groundskeepers at the Rolling Meadows Country Club. They were excellent workers, but there was some confusion among the supervisors as to which twin was which. Tired of always guessing incorrectly, the club manager told the twins to flip a coin and terminated the loser. Dave, the loser, wants to know if he would prevail under the implied covenant of good faith and fair dealing. Explain.

4. Ellen Bubolz received a 3-year contract to coach the Victory College women's tennis team. Although Ellen worked hard, the team never became a big winner. At the end of her second year, the athletic director told Ellen she was fired for the "lack of a significant contribution to Victory College." Setting aside any sex discrimination considerations, what would be Ellen's best argument to recover against Victo-

ry College for breach of contract? Would she win? Explain.

5. Gerald Brown was the sports announcer for Channel 8. Gerald always signed off his section of the news by saying. "This is Gerald Brown, this has been Channel 8 Sports." Gerald decided to change his name to Jabari Abdul-samad and use his new name on the sports program. Fearing adverse public reaction, Channel 8 management told Jabari that he was free to use his new name in his personal affairs but that he would be discharged if he insisted upon using it on the air. Jabari ignored the warnings and was discharged. Assuming that no employment discrimination law applies, what exception to the employment at will doctrine would be Jabari's best choice to prevail in an improper discharge suit against Channel 8? Explain.

6. Judy Green was passed over for promotion by her employer, Fyock Distributing Co. Judy is concerned that a fired former employee, who was always jealous of the fact that Judy was a former beauty queen, might have wrongfully implicated her in an internal theft racket. Judy's employer showed Judy her file and admitted that there was something in the file concerning her and the theft racket but refused to let her know what. Judy now demands to be told what is in the file and, if necessary, to include a rebuttal statement. If the state has a public records law similar to the Illinois Personnel Records Act, would Judy have a right to further information? To provide a written rebuttal for her file? Explain.

7. Rick Gleason, human resource manager for Miller Manufacturing, convinced management to implement a random drug-testing program. Gleason installed a suggestion box for employees anonymously to tip the company about probable drug users. One of these cards named Don Savage. Gleason found Savage and demanded that he take a drug test immediately or face dismissal. Savage reluctantly agreed. When Savage failed the test be was dismissed. Savage has brought a judicial action seeking his job back. Savage's neighbor, Dan Ford, has told him that he would probably have a much better chance of prevailing if it was a govern-

mental employer that was involved. Is Ford correct? Explain.

8. Bud Low owns Bud's Taco City. Bud's has recently experienced some fairly significant losses of food and money. Bud hires Moffatt Security to come to Bud's on an irregular schedule to administer lie detector tests to all employees working a particular shift. Wilma Miller, a kitchen worker, and J. J. Burek, a security guard, refused to take the tests and were discharged. Both seek damages and the return of their job. Is Wilma likely to prevail? J. J.? Explain.

PART III PROBLEMS

The end-of-part problems serve three purposes. First, some require practical applications of legal knowledge to everyday situations. Second, they are summative, bringing together many of the issues treated individually in the chapters of a particular part. Third, the last question presents an ethical problem which, as in real life, may not have an unqualifiedly right or wrong solution. Rather, its goal is to prompt two questions: What would I do in this situation? What *should* I do in this situation?

1. A PRACTICAL PROBLEM

A power of attorney is often the means parties use to establish a principal-agent relationship. This problem requires you to consider many aspects of this relationship as you draft a power of attorney.

Charles West's employer gave him only 2 weeks' notice of his transfer to Tokyo. Of course, in that period he did not have time to sell his house at 514 Market Street in University City. Charles has asked you to be his agent in finding a buyer for his house and in actually conveying the property. You have decided that you should have Charles's power of attorney for the sale of the house. Your notes from your conversation with him indicate that the document should cover the following matters.

- Charles insists on a purchase price of at least $95,000.
- He wants your agreement to last only 6 months.
- With the proceeds, you are to pay the mortgage Fidelity Bank holds on Charles' house and mail the remainder to him.
- Charles's Tokyo address is c/o Mercury Micro Circuitry, Inc., Drawer 3465, Central Post Office, Tokyo, Japan.
- You are not a licensed real estate broker and will have to hire one to assist you in finding a buyer.
- Charles has had a series of serious illnesses, and the last time you saw him, he was not the picture of health. You are worried whether he will survive the stress of foreign travel and living.

2. A SUMMATIVE PROBLEM

Marty Dybicz owns University Health and Fitness Club, a medium-sized health club in a city of 150,000. Marty has agreed to leave management of the center to his nephew, Wiley Dybicz, while Marty spends the summer in Europe. Wiley, a bodybuilder, is a marketing major at nearby Veritas University. Marty left the following note for Wiley:

> *Do not change anything with the Club. Don't buy any new equipment.*
> *Keep your bodybuilding friends out of here. No free memberships to anybody for any reason.*

Wiley read the note and then tossed it away. No silly note was going to limit his opportunity for entrepreneurial adventure.

Wiley's first big change was for the first time to open membership to women. He hired Alvin Adams to build a women's locker room and accommodations in a former storage area. Wiley told Adams he would be paid as soon as Marty returned.

The women members initially caused a number of men to quit the club. However, the number of new members increased so quickly that soon the club reached an all-time high in membership. Wiley decided it was time for an addition to the building and hired Bill Byers to do the job. Wiley told Byers he, too, would be paid when Marty returned.

The new members began demanding aerobics classes. Wiley did not know much about aerobics classes, so he asked Cindy Culbertson, a star women's basketball player at Veritas University, if she knew how to teach aerobics. Cindy told Wiley she regularly did high-impact aerobics to a Jane Fonda video-tape and knew she could lead just like Jane. Unfortunately, at least five class participants have suffered serious injuries from attempting high-impact aerobics without proper conditioning. Wiley claims the club has no liability for "wimps" and points to signs all around the club that warn, "Members Assume Risk of Injury."

A sales representative for American Sporting Goods came to the club and showed Wiley a new machine: "The Stair Machine." Since several clubs in town had each bought one and club members were constantly asking for one, Wiley decided to purchase three machines, payable in September. The machines proved to be extremely popular and helped Wiley to secure even more new members.

A club sales representative, Don Dvonch, was showing a new member the equipment. Don meant to change a stack of weights on a multiple station exercise machine for an overhead pull. Instead, he accidentally changed the weight level for the leg extender machine which Edie Eastham was using. As a result, Eastham suffered an injury to her right knee ligaments. Wiley fired Don on the spot and told Edie the club would pay for her injuries regardless of the "Members Assume Risk of Injury" signs. Several weeks later Wiley sent a postcard to Edie saying that since the club was not at fault and he lacked authority for his promise, the promise was void.

While preparing to leave the club after being fired, Don retaliated by selling three special memberships for half price. The club had heavily advertised this promotion, but it had ended 1 week earlier. Don told the three prospective members he would still honor it for them. They quickly offered cash, Don took it, gave them membership cards, and departed. Wiley discovered the new members as he helped Edie limp out the door. Said Wiley, "You three better get Don to return your money; you have nothing with us."

Wiley's bodybuilding friends talked him into sponsoring the "First Annual Summer Flex" competition at the club. The weight/sex division winners were given free 1-year memberships at the club. Free club memberships were also given to winners of the Sports Spectrum Triathalon, sponsored in part by the club. For the fastest male and female participants, Wiley announced that the club would sponsor and pay all expenses for them to compete in next year's Chicago competition. Susan Gray won free memberships in both competitions and was the fastest woman triathalon competitor. Wiley told her that Marty would provide her with everything just as soon as he returned.

Because of Wiley's tremendous success in running the club a competitor, Lambert's, suffered severe member and income losses. Lambert's owner offered to give Wiley a one half interest if he would become a partner and begin managing Lambert's. Since he wanted his own club when Marty returned, Wiley agreed. Wiley began spending about a quarter of his time generating sales strategies with which to make Lambert's highly profitable again.

Meanwhile, Wiley's bodybuilding friend, Buddy Orloff, offered to supply him with protein pills for sale to members at Marty's club. Wiley agreed and set up a display area. A club employee, Jack Gaggini, learned that the pills were actually illegal steroids and told Wiley. Buddy denied Jack's allegations, so Wiley continued to sell them. When Jack told the police, he was fired. With a valid search warrant, the police raided the club and confiscated the protein pills. Testing proved them to be illegal steroids. Buddy and Wiley were arrested. Jack has written a letter to Marty demanding his job back.

Marty learned of Wiley's arrest and cut short his summer in Europe. Marty is wearing a shirt that says "Don't Worry, Be Happy," but he looks worried. Please advise him on each of the problems his beloved nephew left him with.

3. A SUMMATIVE PROBLEM

While passing through town, Brenda Anderson visited Victory University. She saw a number of students looking at a poster put up by ABC Rentals, a company which rented small refrigerators for dorm use. Recognizing a way to make a quick—if dishonest—buck, Brenda went to an ABC Rentals showroom and stole a number of its brochures. Next, she forged an authorization letter, supposedly from ABC Rentals to Brenda Bauer, designating Bauer as ABC'S Victory University representative. Finally, she spent 2 hours tracking down all of ABC's posters and taping the following notice on the bottom of each:

SEE Brenda Bauer at the ABC Rentals Booth
Waterloo Room, Student Union
THIS AFTERNOON ONLY 1 P.M. to 6 P.M.

During registration for each quarter, Victory permitted local businesses to set up booths in the Student Union. It did not encourage this practice, but permitted it as a service to its students. Vendors sold everything from restaurant coupon books to ski vacations. Brenda fit right in.

If a student asked Brenda a question whose answer she did not know, she said she had just transferred to Victory and took the job to meet her fellow students. But, she had rented from ABC at her last school and liked their service. Most students stopped their questioning there and took time to welcome her to Victory.

Seven of the students who signed up for refrigerators from Brenda had rented from ABC before. They had been to ABC's store and seen all of its personnel in Day-Glo orange vests with "ABC" in pink letters across the back. Brenda wore jogging pants, a Victory U. T-shirt, and a gold-on-green Oakland A's hat.

One of the seven previous ABC customers, Jenny Linsky, asked Brenda for proof that she actually represented ABC. Brenda produced the forged letter while other students standing in line made fun of Jenny. Jenny signed up.

By 4:00, Brenda had signed up 75 students, each of whom had paid the $25 rental fee and $25 deposit in cash. Then, Bernie Fenster appeared. Bernie became very upset when Brenda insisted on cash, refusing to take either a check or any of the credit cards listed on the ABC poster. Bernie left, promising Brenda that he would call ABC about its false advertising.

Brenda appeared ill after this encounter. She told the people in line to wait for her while she went to the rest room for a moment. That was the last anyone saw of Brenda or the money she collected. At 4:30, Bernie, a campus policeman, and an ABC representative arrived at the now vacant card table.

The 75 students Brenda defrauded have brought suit against ABC to recover the money they lost. Based on the facts above, should any of them recover from ABC? Explain your answers.

4. ETHICS AND THE LAW

Agency law and ethical considerations are tightly bound together. Consumers expect honesty and fair play in matters of agency status and authorization. For that reason, they are often not on guard against false representations, like Brenda's in the last problem. An unscrupulous person can find herself the beneficiary of the rule that a third party has the duty to determine the agency status and authority of the alleged agent.

Ethical considerations also have a significant impact on how an agent implements her express authority. Has the agent made a reasonable effort to understand the principal's instructions? Has she considered the totality of the implications which could be drawn from the principal's instructions, conduct, or past actions or course of dealing?

The agent's duty is to follow the principal's reasonable wishes, not to follow her own concept of how the matter should be handled. Thus, the agent must not only follow the principal's actual secret instructions, but also try to implement any implied restrictions or reservations which might apply. The fact that a court might ignore the effect of secret instructions on an innocent third party does not affect the agent's duty to carry them out.

a. Analyze the behavior of the persons in the three preceding problems from an ethical standpoint. In particular, considering the following:

- In Problem 1, should the seller, Charles West, list the instruction to the agent not to sell for less than $95,000? The agent is likely to have to show the power of attorney to third parties interested in buying the house. They are unlikely to offer more than $95,000 if they know that that is the seller's price. If the seller does not state the amount in the power of attorney, he has communicated the limitation to his agent only in the form of a secret instruction. What if the seller gave the agent three or four powers of attorney, each stating a different minimum price, which could be shown to prospective purchasers?
- In Problem 2, how might a principal better protect himself against an agent who does not follow instructions? How can a principal assure himself that his agent will act ethically as to both himself and third parties?
- In Problem 3, do you believe that the law of agency allows an unscrupulous person to defraud those who reasonably believe in her good faith?

b. Suppose that Professor Smith accepted a position at another university. For weeks, he had no luck selling his house for $75,000. One Tuesday, he came up with what he thought was a brilliant idea.

Through his real estate agent, Gallant Realty, he lowered his asking price to $71,000. But, he offered a $1000 bonus to any broker who sold his house for $71,000 within 10 days. This word quickly passed to all local brokers.

On Friday, Chuck Hobbs called a broker, Velda Anderson, to see what investment properties were on the market. Velda told Chuck there was a great opportunity available. She told him about Smith's house, but left out any mention of the bonus. Chuck liked the house when she showed it to him, but balked at the price. "I've never paid the asking price for anything I've bought," he told her. Velda told him Smith's price was firm. After much talking, Hobbs offered $71,000, and Smith accepted.

Before the closing at which the title to the house was to pass, Velda asked Smith to pay the bonus separate from the actual closing with Chuck. The closing papers showed that Smith had paid a 6 percent commission and made no mention of the bonus. Smith paid the additional $1000 to Gallant, which in turn, paid Velda after Hobbs left the room at the end of the closing.

Hobbs never learned of the bonus and has used Velda on several other transactions. What legal duty, if any, did Velda have to Hobbs with respect to the bonus? What are her ethical duties, if any? Explain.

BUSINESS ORGANIZATIONS

In 1991, there were over 20.4 million non-farm business entities in the United States. Of these, 14.2 million were sole proprietorships, 1.8 million were partnerships, and 4.4 million were corporations.* Perhaps the most important lesson you can draw from the statistics about business entities in this country is that few are large and impersonal. Indeed, only 13 percent of American businesses have twenty or more employees.†

Sole proprietorships, by far the most common business form, are also the simplest to form, operate, and terminate, since they are essentially individuals in business for themselves. For that reason, they do not receive the special attention more complex forms do. Our focus in this unit will be on the more complex forms.

STATE
REGULATION AND
CONTRACTUAL
RELATIONSHIPS

State laws define the organization and operation of partnerships, corporations, and the variations on these forms, such as limited partnerships and close corporations. If two persons want to start a business together, the laws of their state will define their relationship. Federal statutes, however, affect partnerships and corporations, particularly as to taxation and financing.

Fundamentally, business organizations consist of contractual relationships. The relationships among their owners and the organizations' obligations to their creditors and investors are all matters of contract. However, it is the law of agency—an outgrowth of contract law—which defines how business organizations function.

In fact, this part continues the examination of the two central questions addressed in the Agency part: First, who has authority to act on behalf of others, and what is the scope of that authority? Second, what fiduciary duties accompany the authority to act, and to whom do these duties run? Every chapter in this part addresses those questions and variations on them.

The importance of these questions in a part entitled Business Organizations emphasizes the fact that such organizations can act only through people. A corporation cannot execute a contract; an agent of the corporation executes a contract on its behalf. For that reason, mastering the details of the various organizational structures is important because they define the boundaries of the relationships of the people involved to one another and to the world.

These structures determine how the law will evaluate a problem, but they do not address why the people involved acted in a particular manner. Thus, evaluating business organization problems requires both a knowledge of the law and a shrewd eye for human motivation.

---

* *The State of Small Business: A Report of the President* (Washington, 1991), pp. XV.
† Ibid., p. 86.

SOLE
PROPRIETORSHIPS

As its name implies, a sole proprietorship has only one owner. However, that owner may have any number of agents or employees. Nonetheless, 81.7 percent of the 13.2 million sole proprietorships have five or fewer employees. Interestingly, that group accounts for only 45.6 percent of sole proprietorship receipts and employs only 39.5 percent of the employees who work for sole proprietorships.*

The principal advantage of sole proprietorships is that since there is only one owner, management and financial decisions can be made more simply than in a partnership or corporation. The major drawback of a sole proprietorship is that its one owner must furnish the business capital or borrow it personally. In other words, all the risk rests on the proprietor, as does the tax liability on any profits.

Most of the discussion of principals and agents in Part III was presented in the context of sole proprietorships. Accordingly, it will not be repeated.

PARTNERSHIPS

Chapters 16 and 17 analyze partnerships. Like sole proprietorships, partnerships tend to be small. Only 2.4 percent of the 1.8 million partnerships have fifty or more employees, but this group accounts for 33.6 percent of all partnership assets and 37.4 percent of all partnership employees.†

A *partnership* is a voluntary association of two or more persons to carry on a business for profit as co-owners. Generally, partners need only shake hands to establish their partnership. Still, they would be well advised to negotiate a written *partnership agreement,* a contract between them that states the terms of their agreement to become partners. A written contract can avoid confusion, disputes, and litigation later. However, a partnership agreement does not have to be in writing unless the Statute of Frauds requires it.

The partners' contributions to the firm's assets may come in various forms —services, skills, and property as well as money. Since partners are co-owners, the law presumes that they share profits and losses equally. However, they may agree on a different division.

For income tax purposes, the state and federal governments treat partners like sole proprietors. The partners must divide—according to their partnership agreement—all partnership profits and losses for the year and report their shares on their personal tax returns.

Mutual agency

Sharing of profits and losses is the primary test courts apply to determine whether a partnership exists. However, they place almost equal importance on the existence of *mutual agency* authority—each partner's power to bind himself, his partners, and their partnership. Where this relationship does not exist, one rarely finds a partnership. Of course, with agency authority comes fiduciary duties.

The death of a partner dissolves the partnership. Thus, another major reason for a written agreement is that a partnership business can survive the death of a partner if the articles allow the other partner or partners to continue it. Otherwise, like a sole proprietorship, the partnership business terminates after its affairs are wound up.

Corporations, and in some instances partnerships, are treated as distinct

---

* *The State of Small Business: A Report of the President* (Washington, 1986), p. 291.
† Ibid., p. 292.

entities, or beings. The law treats them as if they have an existence and identity independent of their owners. A partner, for instance, is the agent of her partnership, not of her partners as individuals. (However, the partners may be liable individually for her acts as a partner/agent.) Similarly, a corporation's treasurer is an agent of the corporation, not of each of its owners or *shareholders.*

Limited partnerships

The *limited partnership* is a hybrid of a corporation and a partnership. As Chapter 18 points out, it grants its investors, the limited partners, the privilege of limited liability while imposing unlimited liability on its general partners, the business's actual managers. In other words, a limited partnership operates like a partnership as to the general partners and as a corporation where the limited partners are concerned. For tax purposes, limited partnerships are treated like partnerships.

CORPORATIONS

The word "corporation" brings to mind General Motors, RCA, Exxon, and the other mammoth businesses whose products dominate our lives. Large entities dominate the corporate statistics, as one might expect. Of the 3 million corporations, only .2 percent employ more than 1000 people, yet they manage 60 percent of all corporate assets and almost 50 percent of all corporate employees. In contrast, 38.3 percent of all corporations employ fewer than five employees, and they account for only 2 percent of corporate assets and 2.7 percent of corporate employees.* Still, a corporation with $50 million in sales and one with $50,000 in sales have the same basic form. Chapters 19 through 21 explore the general nature of corporations.

Whatever its size, a *corporation* is a group of individuals who have organized themselves according to a state's statutes and received a *certificate of incorporation* from that state. Size, though, does make a difference in how a corporation operates. For instance, the larger the business, the greater the government supervision. Suppose a corporation hires its sixteenth employee. It automatically becomes subject to the federal antidiscrimination laws. Or, assume it grows to have more than 500 shareholders and more than $1 million in assets. Then, it must file periodic reports with the Securities and Exchange Commission. We will examine some of the effects of increased size in later chapters.

Independent existence

Except in some very limited circumstances, a corporation exists independently of its shareholders. It may go on forever without any special provision in its *articles of incorporation,* a document describing the corporation's powers and organization which is filed with the state as part of the incorporation process.

As a separate entity, the corporation has many of the powers and privileges of real persons. It can sue and be sued; it can buy and sell property of all types; and it must pay income taxes. Unlike a sole proprietorship or a partnership, whose individual owners pay taxes on their shares of its earnings each year, a corporation pays income taxes as an entity. Usually, a shareholder pays taxes only on cash dividends he or she receives.

Limited liability

Another benefit of incorporation is the shareholders' limited liability. Limited liability refers to the fact that under most circumstances a shareholder's liability

---

* Ibid.

in the event the corporation goes bankrupt or is unable to satisfy a judgment may not exceed what she paid for the share. That loss may be large, but at least it is finite—unlike a partner's or sole proprietor's potential liability.

Limited liability also means limited management rights and responsibilities. It enables the corporation to sell shares to persons who are not going to participate in the business other than financially. All partners, by contrast, are presumed to have equal rights in the management and conduct of the partnership business.

Method of operation

In fact, the shareholders' principal management function is the election of the board of directors which actually runs the company. It is the board, not the shareholders, that hires and fires corporate officers. By law, the officers are agents of the corporation. The board can create additional agents, including its own members, but neither directors nor shareholders as such are corporate agents.

Nonetheless, directors owe fiduciary duties to the corporation and to its shareholders, as do its officers. In some instances, independent agents, like accountants and lawyers, may also have fiduciary duties to the corporation. The shareholders, however, do not owe fiduciary duties to anyone except in some relatively narrow cases.

Corporations with a very few stockholders—*close* or closely held corporations—tend to operate more like partnerships, and so the duties of their owners resemble those of partners. As Chapter 22 notes, this is particularly true when the shareholders are also officers or directors, or both.

VARIATIONS ON CORPORATIONS

For some purposes, the generic forms of corporations and partnerships are not adequate. Chapter 22 describes the variations on the generic forms which fill special needs.

A *close corporation*—a corporation with less than fifty shareholders—whose owners, officers, and directors are two brothers simply will not function like Tenneco or Raytheon. Either by case law or by statute, many states have acknowledged this fact and have made special provisions for these corporations. The federal government also allows some close corporations to elect to be treated as if they were partnerships for tax purposes. These corporations, called *S corporations,* are discussed in Chapter 22.

A second state corporation variation is the *limited liability company (LLC)*. LLCs, well-known and utilized in Europe and Latin America, are a cross between a partnership and a corporation. The goal in forming an LLC is to secure limited liability for all owners, be taxed like a partnership, and secure flexibility in management. LLCs are discussed in Chapter 22.

COMPARISON OF BUSINESS ENTITIES

This part overview has given you a very general introduction and comparison of the different forms of business entities. In Chapter 22 we provide a more detailed comparison. We would urge you to quickly review Figures 22-1 and 22-2 now and return to them as you study the chapters in Part IV.

SECURITIES

The word "securities" brings to mind stocks and bonds and the New York Stock Exchange. But, as Chapter 23 points out, securities take dozens of other forms.

For example, a person who buys a limited partnership interest in a venture building a new mall has purchased a security. A person who has an interest in a syndicate which owns and breeds a thoroughbred stallion owns a security.

The state and federal securities laws do not define the term. Rather, when confronted by something which appears to be like a security, the courts ask whether the investor is expecting a return on capital based solely on the efforts of others. In other words, the test is, "Is the investor doing anything significant besides putting up money?" If not, the investment is a security.

The states and the federal Securities and Exchange Commission (SEC) police the markets primarily through reporting requirements. These reports give investors access to financial and other significant information—such as key personnel changes—about the issuers of securities.

These reporting requirements have a significant impact on many accountants. As Chapter 24 notes, the SEC has imposed a new, significantly greater burden on accountants who audit corporations subject to its reporting requirements. As a result of the SEC's influence, the profession and the courts have made accountants more accountable to those who rely on their work, not just to the corporation. This part closes with an examination of accountants' responsibilities for their work.

Chapter 24 is geared toward accounting students. However, it contains important lessons for nonaccountants. For them, Chapter 24 defines when they may rely on audited financial statements and when they may not.

CONCLUSION

This part begins with the structure of business organizations. The rules governing these structures are fairly straightforward. But, as the cases in this part reveal, the personal dynamics of business organizations are rarely so uncomplicated.

The problems which arise in business organizations rarely pit faceless masses of shareholders against impersonal corporate structures. Rather, family members or former friends fight civil wars of great intensity. The battlefields may be matters of corporate law, securities questions, or issues relating to the adequacy of the accountants' services. Thus, as with most legal problems, the place to start in analyzing a business organization's problem is with the facts—what is at issue and what is motivating the parties.

The preventive law challenge of this area lies in matching the organizational form to the personalities involved and in designing safety valves and releases to protect those whose money and livelihoods are at stake.

KEY WORDS

articles of incorporation (355)
certificate of incorporation (355)
close corporation (356)
corporation (355)
limited liability company (356)
limited partnership (355)
mutual agency (354)

partnership (354)
S corporation (356)
Securities Exchange Commission (357)
shareholders (355)
sole proprietorship (354)

CHAPTER 16
Forming and Managing Partnerships

The concept of partnership has existed for perhaps 4000 years. However, partnership law as we know it today originated in the English common law. In 1914, the American Law Institute, the moving force behind the *Restatements,* introduced the Uniform Partnership Act (UPA), which codified much of the common law. Since then, the UPA has shaped the law of partnership in every state, though the effect is not totally uniform because the states have made many changes in it.

In 1992, the National Conference of Commissioners on Uniform State Laws issued a revision of the UPA, the Revised Uniform Partnership Act (RUPA). RUPA is intended to replace the UPA completely. It reflects many of the changes to the UPA made by the states of Georgia and Colorado, among others. We will still focus on the UPA, since it currently reflects the basic partnership law in most states and is the law tested on the national CPA examination. We have developed a chapter appendix at the end of Chapter 17 to present, summarize, and contrast the major points of RUPA. Where appropriate, we have mentioned RUPA within the text of Chapters 16 and 17.

THE NATURE OF PARTNERSHIPS

The UPA Definition

The UPA defines *partnership* as "an association of two or more persons to carry on as co-owners a business for profit" [UPA §6(1)]. Such partnerships are sometimes called *general partnerships* to distinguish them from limited partnerships, a subject of Chapter 18. Let's look at the elements of the UPA definition.

An "association" is an act of individuals who join together for a particular purpose. In the context of a partnership, the association is consensual, similar to an agency relationship. This means the law will neither force people to be partners nor force a partnership upon them without their consent. However, it is possible that the law will hold them liable as if they were partners in situations parallel to those of the apparent agent. Such persons are called "apparent partners," the subject of discussion later in this chapter.

The UPA uses the word "persons" to describe the co-owners, but the word encompasses not only individuals but also other partnerships, corporations, and associations.

The sharing of profits or losses is the UPA's principal test of a partnership's existence. The UPA definition reflects that fact in its use of the word "co-owners," indicating that every partner has a right to share equally in the management and profits or losses of the partnerships. However, as we will discuss below, the partners can agree to divide management responsibilities and profits or losses unequally.

The UPA also requires that a partnership be a "business for profit." If two churches jointly operate a secondhand clothing store whose entire proceeds go to the poor, their operation would not qualify as a UPA partnership.

The definition uses the term "carrying on a business" in its broadest possible sense. The sole qualification is that the business be active and ongoing. The next case illustrates how a court approaches this issue.

Travis v. St. John

176 Conn. 69, 404 A.2d 885 (1978)

FACTS   St. John and the three plaintiffs agreed to purchase land for investment purposes. They agreed to share equally its cost, its maintenance expenses, and the profits or losses upon resale. They bought the property for $8000 in cash, assumed an existing mortgage, and took out a further mortgage. The title to the land was in St. John's name. The assumed mortgage turned out to be unassumable. St. John, the only member of the group who could obtain refinancing, paid off both the existing mortgages. For a short period after the sale, the plaintiffs paid their shares of the expenses, but then for 5 years they paid nothing. St. John kept up all payments. In 1969, St. John notified the plaintiffs that the venture was terminated and offered to return their original investment if he sold the property at a profit. At that time, St. John had not marketed the property. Two months late he sold it for $100,000. The plaintiffs brought suit, each seeking a quarter of the proceeds. The trial court limited the plaintiffs' recovery to their contributions to the venture.

ISSUE Were St. John and the plaintiffs partners?

DECISION No. Affirmed. Partnerships carry on a general business. This venture was limited to a single transaction. Co-ownership of property does not establish a partnership whether or not the co-owners share profits from the property. Under the UPA, a mutual agency relationship must exist; every partner must be an agent of the partnership for its business. Here the parties established their association to invest in a single parcel. They did not intend to carry on a trade, occupation, or business, or to create an agency relationship among themselves. The only indication of a partnership in this case was the agreement to share profits or losses.

Two Theories of Partnership

In looking at the nature of partnerships and joint ventures, we have emphasized that they are associations of persons. Their members define their existence. By contrast, the law treats corporations as entities separate from, and independent of, the persons who own them. During the last several decades, partnerships have begun to be treated as separate entities in certain circumstances. These two views of the nature of partnerships significantly affect how partnership property is regarded, how the partners relate to one another, and how the partnership interacts with others. The UPA incorporates both theories.

The aggregate theory. The common law viewed a partnership as the sum or *aggregate* of the individual partners. A partnership had no legal existence apart from the co-owners. The UPA adopts the aggregate theory in a number of instances. For example, upon the departure of any partner, the partnership is dissolved [UPA §29]. Also, one partner may not simply sell her partnership interest to another. No person can join a partnership without the consent of all the partners [UPA §18(g)].

Both state and federal income tax laws adopt the aggregate theory. A partnership does not pay income taxes as a partnership. Rather, the partnership allocates income—whether or not it is actually paid out—to the individual partners, who report it on their personal tax returns. Thus, partners pay taxes even on income retained in the partnership for research and development.

The entity theory. The UPA also reflects the entity theory, the partnership as a whole. For instance, every partner is an agent of the partnership, not of every other partner—a critically important distinction [UPA §9(1)]. Also, the

UPA permits partnership property to be held in the name of the partnership [UPA §8]. Suppose that as a part of his capital contribution to the partnership, John supplies it with a truck. At common law, John would have continued to hold its title because the partnership could not hold property in its name. Today, the partnership can and should have the title changed into its name to make it clear that the truck is partnership property.

Where income taxes are not involved, taxing authorities treat partnerships as entities. Thus, when the partnership incurs liabilities for Social Security taxes, unemployment assessments, or workers' compensation obligations, the authorities will regard the obligation as the partnership's, though the partners are still ultimately liable.

Alternative Business Associations

After corporations, partnerships are the most common form of multiple ownerships of business ventures. Partnerships of the type discussed in the next two chapters are often referred to as "general partnerships" to distinguish them from some related forms of multiple ownership. The most common of these alternative forms are joint ventures and limited partnerships.

Joint ventures. The relationship between St. John and the plaintiffs is called a joint venture. *Joint ventures* resemble partnerships in every respect except two. First, joint ventures do not involve ongoing businesses. They normally are formed for a single purpose, like constructing an office building or co-ownership of a duplex for rental income. As in *Travis v. St. John,* the coventurer's enterprise is often oriented toward an investment. In other cases, coventurers join to minimize exposure in high-risk operations, as when oil companies agree to jointly explore an offshore area. Still, as the next case indicates, a joint venture requires more than simply a business relationship between the parties.

Hispano Americano Advertising, Inc. v. Dryer

112 Misc. 2d 936, 448 N.Y.S.2d 128 (Civ. Ct. 1982)

FACTS	In October 1976, Hispano Americano Advertising, Inc. ("Hispano"), rented office space in Manhattan. Rhoda Dryer, an attorney, agreed to occupy one room in the suite and to pay Hispano two-thirds of Hispano's monthly rent and utility charges. In January 1981, Dryer stopped paying rent. In this action, Hispano attempted to evict Dryer. Dryer claimed she was not Hispano's subtenant, but rather a cotenant. She claimed that her agreement to pay rent actually reflected her status as a joint venturer.
ISSUE	Does an agreement between an advertising firm and a lawyer to share office space make them joint venturers?
DECISION	No. Judgment for Hispano. A joint venture is a combination of two or more persons who in some specific venture jointly seek a profit without an actual partnership or corporation designation. It requires a mingling of property, profits, or other interests which the parties hold jointly. Here Hispano and Dryer became commercial roommates, not joint venturers.

The second way in which joint ventures differ from partnerships is that a coventurer's apparent authority to bind the other joint venturers is generally far less than a partner's. This limitation flows logically from the one-time nature of the coventurers' relationship. The limitation's main effect is to restrict a single venturer's ability to borrow money on behalf of the enterprise.

Limited partnerships. Limited partnerships are a special type of partnership that is ideally suited for situations in which some of the owners will be passive investors rather than the active manager-owners characteristic of general partnerships. Hence, in a limited partnership, there are two types of partners: limited partners—the investors—and general partners—the managers.

As discussed in more detail in Chapter 18, the general partner's role, duties, liabilities, and authority are similar to those of a partner in a general partnership. A limited partner, however, has limited personal liability for the venture's debts and has a very restricted role in management. The law also imposes much more specific requirements for the formation of a limited partnership than for a general partnership or a joint venture.

TYPES OF PARTNERS

In the previous section you were introduced to two types of partners: general and limited partners. The UPA does not further characterize types of partners. However, it is not uncommon for courts to describe certain types of general partners by their common law designations: secret, silent, or dormant partners.

- A *secret partner* is a general partner whose membership in the firm is not made known to third parties.
- A *silent partner* is a general partner who has

no voice and does not actively participate in the management of the firm.
- A *dormant partner* is a general partner who is both a secret and silent partner of the firm.

It is important to recognize that although secret, silent, and dormant partners are essentially only investors in the firm, they are still general partners without limited liability protection. Today, many such investors prefer to become limited partners in a proper limited partnership, discussed in Chapter 18.

The final type of partner, an *apparent partner,* is a person who has held herself out, or consented to her being held out, as a partner, whether or not she is an actual partner. This type of partner, sometimes called an ostensible partner, will be discussed later in this chapter.

PARTNERSHIP FORMATION

Partnership agreements generally may be either written or oral. But, partnerships which begin on a handshake often end with shaking fists. This sad fact has less to do with ill will than with the many possibilities for misunderstandings over responsibilities and rights. In many cases, misunderstandings would not have occurred had the partners adopted a written agreement, called *articles of partnership,* before shaking hands.

The UPA prescribes no specific manner, method, or place for creating a partnership. It focuses on partnership operations, not their formation. Some states, such as Louisiana and Oregon, have statutory procedures governing the creation of a partnership.

Whether state law requires one or not, the parties should execute articles of partnership. "Good fences make good neighbors," New England farmers used to say. The same logic applies to agreements between partners. Consider the cases in this chapter and the next as object lessons in what can happen when either no fences are erected or they fall into disrepair.

What Articles of Partnership Should Contain

A partnership should have articles of partnership in order to minimize misunderstandings and to better define the business's objectives. A good partnership agreement covers the following:

- The partnership name
- The start-up date and duration of the partnership
- The partnership purpose
- Capital contributions per partner
- What property of a partner used in the business is to be considered partnership property
- Partners' duties and time owed to the partnership
- Formula for division of profits and losses
- Partners' authority to bind the partnership
- Partners' rights to salaries and advances or draws on profits
- Procedures for settling disputes among partners

- Manner of terminating the partnership
- Restrictions on competition, if any, after termination of the partnership

This list alone is a persuasive argument for articles of partnership.

Partnership Agreements and Contract Law

A partnership agreement is a contract. Therefore, common law contract principles apply to it where the UPA has not superseded them.

Consent. All partners must consent to the partnership agreement. Otherwise, they obviously lack the intent necessary to form the partnership. Alleged partners may assert all the common law reality of consent defenses, such as fraud or duress. In the next case, the court had to deal with a claim of undue influence.

Ferguson v. Jeanes

27 Wash. App. 558, 619 P.2d 369 (1980)

FACTS   Jeanes, a Christian Science practitioner, assisted in the healing process and maintained a confidential and spiritual relationship with his patients. He met Ferguson in 1972, when she was considering making a commitment to Christian Science. They fell in love and considered marriage. In 1973, Ferguson asked Jeanes to help her buy an apartment house. Jeanes agreed, but urged Ferguson to make him her partner. She declined. Jeanes became abusive, asserting that her refusal violated Christian Science tenets. He prevailed, and she acknowledged their partnership in writing. However, for what he said were tax reasons, he asked not to be listed on the deed or the two mortgages. Ferguson contributed nearly $13,000, Jeanes approximately $3500. Ferguson alone managed the property. Their personal relationship continued until 1975. In 1977, Jeanes asked Ferguson for title to the property. Ferguson instead offered to return his contribution. In 1978, she filed this action to establish her sole ownership of the property. The trial court rescinded the partnership, left title in Ferguson's name, and ordered her to return Jeanes's contribution plus interest.

ISSUE   Did Jeanes exert undue influence over Ferguson?

DECISION   Yes. Affirmed. A transaction induced by unfair persuasion is voidable. Where, because of their relationship, one party may justifiably assume that the other will not act inconsistently with her welfare, persuasion is unfair when the will of one overcomes the other's, in effect destroying her free will. Undue influence makes assent involuntary and warrants rescission of the partnership agreement.

Legal Purpose. A partnership agreement must have a legal purpose. No court will enforce a partnership agreement for an illegal object. Suppose Al and Sal run a bookie shop as partners. No court will enforce their partnership agreement against one another or a debt owed to them by one of their "clients."

Capacity. We noted in the last part that a minor may be an agent. Similarly, a minor may be a partner.

The courts have held that a minor may withdraw from a partnership at any time. A minor's liability for partnership debts extends only to the amount of his *capital contribution,* the amount of property or cash or both provided in exchange for a partnership interest. Further, if the partnership is dissolved, the minor has a right to the return of whatever remains of his capital contribution after the payment of partnership debts. While the minor partner may void his partnership agreement, the partnership may not void its contracts with third parties of its minor partner.

Where a court declares a partner insane or a partner is shown to be of unsound mind, another partner may seek dissolution of the partnership [UPA §32]. Because partnerships require a mutual agency, a lunatic may not be a partner, since he or she cannot act as an agent.

Writing. A partnership agreement which cannot be completed in 1 year must be in writing because the Statute of Frauds applies to it. Suppose a partnership is formed for 10 years. The partnership agreement would have to be in writing because it could not be performed within 1 year. By contrast, a partnership of indefinite duration would not require a writing, since conceivably the agreement could be performed within a year.

PROVING A PARTNERSHIP EXISTS

At times, even when a writing exists, it is not clear whether those involved intended to form a partnership. In these instances, the courts apply three tests to the facts surrounding the relationship between the partners. In order of importance, these tests are the sharing of profits; the intent of the parties; and the amount of activity and its duration.

Sharing Profits

By far the most important test of a partnership is the sharing of profits. In fact, under the UPA, receipt of a share of the profits establishes a rebuttable presumption that the recipient is a partner [UPA §7(4)]. However, that presumption is not absolute, and the alleged partner may prove that no partnership existed.

A person may share profits and not be a partner. The UPA states that a court should draw no inference of partnership if a person receives a share of the profits as payment of a debt or a loan [UPA §7(4)]. An employee who receives a percentage of the profits as wages is not a partner either. Salespersons and managers, although not partners, often receive a salary plus a percentage of profits. Also, articles of partnership often provide that should the firm continue after a partner's death, the partnership will pay a share of the profits as an annuity to the partner's heirs—who do not become partners. Finally, if a share of the profits is assigned as rent, the lessor is not a partner. Stores in shopping centers often pay a base rate per square foot plus an amount attributable to gross sales or profits.

The Intent of the Parties

The sharing of profits is the first test a court applies in determining whether a partnership exists. If a court still has doubts, it then asks: Did the parties intend to be partners? Did they call themselves partners? Do their words and actions indicate that they related to one another as partners? As the next case indicates, the intent to be partners must be plain.

Montana Bank of Red Lodge v. Lightfield

771 P.2D 571 (Mont. 1989)

FACTS
Lee Lightfield was in the used car business. In order to get a line of credit to finance the business, his parents Aileen and Gilbert pledged a CD and signed as guarantors. Gilbert died shortly thereafter and Aileen went into the used car business both to learn about it and to be near Lee. She also bought her own used cars to sell on the lot. Several months later she left because she felt Lee was not teaching her about the business. Lee continued selling cars but later was found guilty of defrauding the bank. After his conviction, he and his wife went bankrupt. The bank subsequently sued Aileen, arguing that she was her son's partner and therefore liable for all partnership debts. The trial court granted a directed verdict in Aileen's favor.

ISSUE
Did a partnership exist between Aileen and Lee Lightfield?

DECISION
No. Affirmed. A partnership is defined as "an association of two or more persons to carry on as co-owners a business for profit." The parties must also manifest their intent to associate themselves in a partnership. When there is no written agreement, intent is proved by looking at the facts, circumstances, and conduct of the parties. The facts in this case support the position that Aileen was not a partner. Aileen never shared in the profits or losses of Lee's auto sales. She also did not control either Lee's or her cars in the lot, and she was not permitted to look at the books. The fact that Lee and Aileen operated under the same license and bond and shared a bank account does not, in light of all the facts, overcome the bank's burden of proving there was a partnership.

Title to property. Sometimes courts evaluate intent by examining the manner in which the parties hold title to property used in the venture. Suppose Maggie and Enzo operate their Italian deli in a small building. If the title to the building lists the owner as "Maggie & Enzo's Italian Deli," a court will take this as a strong indication of a partnership.

When intent does not control. Sometimes, the parties' intent will not control. Suppose it is clear that the parties intended something other than a partnership—like a corporation. But a court finds that they failed to comply with the state's incorporation statutes. The court may treat their venture as if it were a partnership or joint venture. In reality, the court has no other option, since the venture could not be a sole proprietorship, and all other forms require fulfillment of statutory prerequisites.

Amount of Activity and Duration of Relationship

As noted above, the UPA describes a partnership as an ongoing, active business. The UPA does not define this phrase. However, it covers situations in which continuous, regular business activity is taking place, such as operating a hardware store, or farming, or practicing law. It does not include a refreshment stand run by two college students for the duration of the county fair.

It has already been noted that coventurers are involved in a business association primarily for investment purposes. They may refer to their relationship—incorrectly—as a partnership, as when two friends buy a 1957 Thunderbird to restore and sell. But at some point, the joint venture may evolve into a partnership by becoming an ongoing, active business. The two friends may buy a 1956 Chevrolet, then a 1961 Corvette, and find themselves in business. Similarly, real estate coventurers may find that they have accumulated so much rental property that they have created a full-time business.

The line between joint ventures and partnerships is not a clear one. So as a practical matter, the courts tend to emphasize the purpose of the association more than the form in determining what it is.

Apparent Partnership

An *apparent partnership* or a *partnership by estoppel* results when a person, termed an *ap-*

parent partner, either represents himself as, or consents to having another represent him as, a partner, though he is not in fact a partner [UPA §16(1)]. The principles a court applies in such cases are essentially the same as those in which courts find a promissory estoppel or apparent agency.

Reliance. The third party must rely on the representation of partnership in order to assert an apparent partnership. If the person to whom the representation was made acts on it by giving credit to the actual or apparent partnership, the apparent partner is liable to the creditor. If the representation was made in public or in a public manner, the apparent partner is liable to the creditor whether or not the representation was communicated to the creditor or the apparent partner knew that the creditor had learned of the representation. See Figure 16-1.

Liability. In effect, an apparent partnership means that the apparent partner may not raise the fact that there was no partnership as a defense. Apparent partners are liable to a third party who reasonably relies on the representation. For example, in Berton's presence Reed tells Charles that he and Berton are partners. Berton does not deny the statement. Charles lends money to Reed, believing he is actually lending money to their partnership. Berton may not deny his partnership status when Charles sues to recover the money from him. Thus Charles can hold Reed and Berton liable as partners even though they are not. See Figure 16-1.

A person holding out another as a partner gives the apparent partner agency powers as if they were partners. Under the UPA a person held out as a partner in an existing partnership can bind only those partners who consent to the representation. Suppose Norma tells Henry that Margot is a partner in Norma and Ken's partnership. Ken does not know about the representation or consent to it. Margot has apparent authority to bind Norma. But, Margot could

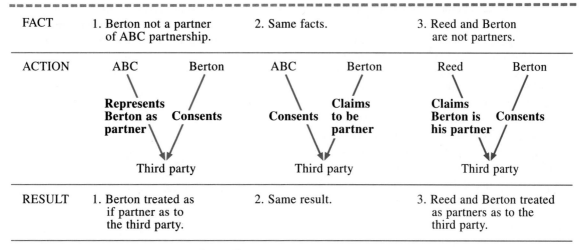

Figure 16.1 Apparent Partnerships: Three Situations.
Note that apparent partnerships are sometimes called partnerships by estoppel.

not bind Ken. Thus, an apparent partnership requires all of the following:

- A representation—either a statement or an act—by an apparent partner inconsistent with the defense later asserted
- Reliance by the other party on the representation
- An injury to the other party if the apparent partner is allowed to contradict or repudiate his representation.

We will look further at apparent authority and third parties in Chapter 17.

PARTNERSHIP PROPERTY

Partnership property is real or personal property the partners contribute to the partnership. The partner may have acquired the property either before or after the partnership came into existence [UPA §§8, 10].

Identifying Partnership Property

A partnership does not have to own property. Also, the fact that a partnership uses property does not necessarily mean that it is partnership property. But, if the partnership uses property, it is extremely important for the partners to identify what is and is not partnership property. Practically, the partners can keep track of partnership property by such means as identifying it in the articles of partnership or in a ledger or in periodic inventories.

The reasons for clearly identifying partnership and nonpartnership property are numerous. For instance, property taxes can be assessed to the wrong party. On credit applications, whether for the partnership or a partner, the bank will want to know what assets it can look to in the event of a default. And, partnership property left in the name of an individual partner may leave that partner with apparent authority to dispose of it to a good faith purchaser.

Perhaps the time when the importance of identification becomes most clear is on the termination of the partnership. Then, claims by creditors or the partners' faulty memories can lead to disputes and even lawsuits.

At times, it is not clear whether a party

intends to make a loan to a partnership or to become a partner by making a capital contribution. In family businesses this issue quite often leads to disputes. In one case, two brothers inherited the family farm they had operated with their father. Later, one brother claimed that some farm machinery belonged to the partnership, while the other claimed that their father had given it to him. Since the court lacked any firm indication as to its ownership, it left the property with the brother claiming ownership. A written partnership agreement with a provision covering equipment contributions could have averted this litigation.

In instances where ownership is disrupted, the courts often apply the following tests:

- Were partnership funds used to acquire the property?
- Were partnership funds used to maintain, improve, and/or repair the property?
- Is the property used for partnership purposes?
- How is the property titled, if it has a title?
- How is the property treated on the partnership books?
- Whose funds are used to pay the property taxes, if any?

The following case illustrates what evidence became important in resolving a conflict between another pair of brothers in a family business. The case exemplifies the all too familiar problems that arise between partners who rely on trust instead of formal, legal protections.

Mehl v. Mehl

786 P.2d 1173 (Mont. 1990)

FACTS   The Mehl brothers, Eugene and Marlowe, were partners in a family farm. The partnership was very informal with no written agreement. Partnership property included money in an account in a local bank, from which all the bills were paid, and farm equipment. The Mehls shared profits equally and withdrew money from the account when it was required for partnership business by simply informing each other. After years as a partner in the farm, Eugene and his wife Bonnie decided to buy a bar. Eugene withdrew money from the partnership account to purchase it. Seven years later, the couple were divorced and Bonnie received the bar in the property settlement. Marlowe, several years after Eugene's divorce, sued to dissolve the partnership, claiming the bar was partnership property. Marlowe won at the trial level.

ISSUE   Was Eugene and Bonnie's bar partnership property?

DECISION   Yes. Affirmed. Under UPA §8(2), property that is procured with partnership funds is presumed to be partnership property. Eugene argued that it was not partnership property, since title and various business records pertaining to the bar were in his and Bonnie's name. Marlowe produced tax records and Eugene and Bonnie's property settlement, which reported that the bar was partnership property. Marlowe's evidence, together with the presumption of partnership property under the UPA, is substantial evidence for upholding the trial court's findings.

A Partner's Interest in the Partnership and in its Property

A partner has an ownership interest in the business as a whole, not in its individual assets. For this reason, a partner's interest in the firm is considered to be personal property even if the firm owns only real property [UPA §26].

Tenancy in partnership. A partner's interest in the partnership's property is known as a *tenancy in partnership,* meaning that a partner has the right to use all partnership property for partnership purposes but has no rights in specific items [UPA §25(1)]. Partners often agree that one will use a particular car, office, or dictating machine, but such agreements do not confer an ownership interest [UPA §25(2)(a)].

Upon a partner's death, his or her estate has a right to the value of the ownership interest in the partnership, but not to individual partnership assets. Thus, the estate has no rights as to the desk the decedent occupied, but it does have rights as to the value of the decedent's interest in the partnership [UPA §25(2)(d)].

Assignments. With or without the other partners' consent, a partner may assign her interest in the partnership assets, but not her rights to manage the firm and to act as her partners' agent [UPA §27(1)]. The assignment of a partnership interest only entitles the assignee to receive profits due the partner. It does not:

- Dissolve the partnership
- Make the assignee a partner without the other partners' consent
- Give the assignee the right to interfere with the partnership's management or administration
- Grant the assignee the right to information about partnership transactions
- Give the assignee the right to inspect the partnership's books

Assume that Sarah wants to retire from her accounting partnership. She may not sell her interest as freely as she could her IBM shares.

The other partners must approve any purchaser of an entire partnership interest. By contrast, if Sarah wishes to continue as a partner but wants to assign part of her rights in partnership profits to secure a home mortgage loan, she could do so without her partners' approval.

Charging order. A partner's partnership interest is subject to a *charging order,* the imposition of a judicial lien obtained by a partner's personal creditors against his property [UPA §28(1)]. To illustrate, suppose a court finds Paul liable in a personal injury case. A court might issue a charging order allocating a percentage of Paul's partnership profits to the plaintiff to help cover payment of the judgment.

A charging order neither requires Paul's consent nor results in a dissolution of the partnership. If such a lien proves insufficient to pay the claim, a creditor can seek a court order to foreclose and sell Paul's interest. A purchaser at a foreclosure sale may ask the court to dissolve a partnership at will, a partnership with no specific term length. The remaining partners can always pay the charging order off to free the partnership from any lien.

PARTNERSHIP OPERATIONS

Unless the partnership agreement otherwise specifies, the law makes six basic presumptions about a partnership's operation:

- Every partner is, and acts as, an agent for the partnership.
- Partners share equally in profits and losses.
- Every partner potentially is personally liable for all the partnership's debts.
- Admission of a new partner requires unanimous consent of the partners.
- The partners have equal management rights.
- No right to a salary, unless surviving partner winding up the partnership affairs.

We have considered aspects of these presumptions above. In this section we will look at some more specific applications.

Application of Agency Law

Agency law principles apply to transactions a partner undertakes on behalf of the partnership. The partnership is the principal. A partner acting on its behalf acts as its agent. Thus, a partner possesses the same express, implied, and apparent authority as a general agent. We will examine a partner's agency powers in Chapter 17.

Fiduciary duties. The partner owes to his fellow partners fiduciary duties equivalent to those an agent owes to a principal [UPA §21]. (See Chapter 13 for a discussion of an agent's duties.) For instance, a partner may not compete against the partnership without its approval. If the partnership owns a Mercedes dealership, a partner may not start selling Cadillacs on his own without the partnership's consent.

A partner must also communicate information which may affect the partnership and may not use it for private gain [UPA §20]. Finally, a partner must use reasonable care, account for partnership money and property, observe the articles of partnership, and remain loyal to fellow partners.

Management Rights

The UPA presumes that every partner has an equal voice in management regardless of the amount of the partner's capital contribution. That is: one partner, one vote [UPA §18(e)]. Suppose Joe puts up 60 percent of the partnership's capital, while Rose puts up 40 percent. Unless their partnership agreement specifies otherwise, Rose and Joe have an equal voice in the partnership's management. In a corporation, Joe, as a 60 percent shareholder, would outvote Rose.

As a practical matter, partners often agree that day-to-day business decisions do not require a majority vote. The partners delegate these decisions to a partner sometimes called a *managing partner*. For example, the partners in a hardware store may designate one partner to handle the books, one to handle inventory and stock, and the third to manage the retail operation. This happens routinely where most of the partners are essentially investors or where the partnership—particularly in law and accounting firms—is quite large.

Financial Relations Between Partners

Sharing profits and losses. Unless the partnership agreement provides to the contrary, the law presumes that partners will share profits and losses equally [UPA §18(a)]. That presumption applies *regardless* of the amount of capital contributed by the partners. Thus, if Janet contributes 40 percent and Jack 60 percent, a court will award Janet 50 percent of the profits.

This presumption provides another strong argument for preparing articles of partnership. In many, if not most, partnerships, the shares are not equal by agreement. Architectural, law, and accounting firms rarely assign equal shares to their partners.

Except in one instance discussed in the next chapter, a partner does not have a right to a salary. Even if a partner will have to operate the business alone for a time because of another partner's illness, he will not be entitled to a salary. Suppose Nida suffers severe injuries in a car crash and cannot work for 7 months. Her partner, Bernie, has no right to a salary during this period, even though he must do all the work.

The absence of a right to a salary has become controversial in recent years. One highly respected committee has proposed amending the UPA to allow a court to authorize compensation when one or more of the partners devote substantial time to the business while the other partners are inactive or if they have abandoned the partnership.*

---

* *Should the Uniform Partnership Act Be Revised? A Report of the UPA Revision Subcommittee of the American Bar Association Partnership Committee, Corporation, Banking & Business Law Section* (April 1986), pp. 71–72.

TOTAL PARTNERSHIP PROFIT	PROFIT RETAINED BY PARTNERSHIP	PARTNER A's PROFIT PERCENTAGE	PARTNER A's DISTRIBUTION AMOUNT	PARTNER A's TAX LIABILITY
$120,000	0	33⅓%	$40,000	$40,000
$120,000	0	40%	$48,000	$48,000
$120,000	$30,000	33⅓%	$30,000	$40,000
$120,000	$30,000	40%	$36,000	$48,000

Figure 16.2 Examples of Partner Tax Liability Assuming a Total Partnership Income of $120,000.

Capital contributions. Partners do not have a right to interest on their capital contributions [UPA §18(c)]. However, they do have a right to interest on loans to the partnership. When making a loan, the partner should make sure it is clearly documented as such. Otherwise, a court may presume it to be a capital contribution. As a result, if the partnership goes bankrupt, the creditor-partner could lose both her capital contribution and the amount of the loan.

Tax allocation. Unlike a corporation, a partnership, as such, does not pay income taxes to either the state or federal government. Instead, the partnership files an informational return with both and indicates how it allocated its profits and losses among the partners. Each partner must report the profit or loss allocated to her on her personal income tax forms.

Because profits and losses pass through the partnership to the individual partners, partnerships are of most tax benefit when they produce losses which can offset the partners' other income. They are an extremely poor choice as a business form if the venture needs to retain profits to reinvest in, say, plant and equipment. As we will see later in this part, corporations pay considerably lower rates than individuals and can retain earnings. For that reason, a corporate form is better for a profitable business which wishes to retain earnings. See Figure 16-2, which illustrates a partner's potential tax liability.

Reimbursement and indemnification. A partner has a right to be reimbursed for payments made on behalf of the partnership, as when a partner pays a freight charge from his own pocket.

Partners also have a right to indemnification for personal liability reasonably incurred as a result of the partnership business [UPA §18(b)]. Suppose a partner has put up her IBM stock as collateral for a loan to the partnership. If the bank sells the stock when the partnership defaults, the partner is entitled to indemnification by the partnership.

Right to financial information. A partner always has the right to inspect and copy the partnership books. Unless the partners otherwise agree, the books are to be kept and maintained at the partnership's place of business [UPA §19].

Auctions and judicial sales. Ordinarily, when partnership property is sold at auction, a partner may bid on it without disclosing in advance to the other partners that he or she plans to do so. A partner has to disclose such an intention only when bidding on the property might adversely affect the partnership's interests or would amount to a breach of a fiduciary duty.

The rule is somewhat different in the case of a *judicial sale,* a court-ordered auction, following an order dissolving the partnership. (Dissolution is discussed in the next chapter.) The law presumes that all partners have an equal opportunity to bid. Therefore, so long as valid grounds exist for dissolving the partnership, the judicial sale is conducted properly, and the partner does not violate any fiduciary duty owed the other partners, the partner is free to bid at the sale.

Legal Actions Between Partners

The general rule is that a partner may not sue the partnership for damages, or vice versa. Suppose a partner's negligence causes a large loss. The nonnegligent partners may reduce the negligent partner's share of the profits to cover the loss but may not sue him for the amount. If the negligent partner disagrees, a court could settle the matter on termination of the partnership.

A partner may sue another partner for reasons unrelated to the partnership business, such as for personal injuries received while riding in a partner's car.

A partner's principal remedy against her partners or the partnership is a suit for an accounting. An *accounting* is a formal audit and report on the financial condition of the partnership. Usually courts order an accounting when the partners have wrongly excluded a partner from the partnership business or from possession of partnership property [UPA §22]. Where it appears that one partner has not dealt fairly with another, a court may require an accounting or grant other relief, as appropriate. That occurred in the next case.

- -

Marsh v. Gentry

642 S.W.2d 574 (Ky. 1982)

FACTS   Gentry and Marsh formed a partnership to buy and sell race horses. In November 1976, they purchased a mare named Champagne Woman and her foal, Excitable Lady, for $155,000. In November 1978, the partnership put the mare in an auction, and Gentry bought her for $135,000. Although Gentry could have told Marsh before the sale that he intended to bid on Champagne Woman, he did not. Eleven months later, Marsh discovered that Gentry had bought the mare. In the interim, Gentry told Marsh that he had sold Excitable Lady to a third party in California. Marsh asked who had bought the filly, but got no answer. Marsh learned that Gentry owned Excitable Lady on the day of the 1980 Kentucky Derby, when she won the Debutante Stakes. Marsh brought an action for conversion and for an accounting against Gentry. The trial court found for Gentry.

ISSUE   Did Gentry violate his fiduciary duties as a partner?

DECISION   Yes. Reversed. The Uniform Partnership Act provides:

> *Every partner must account to the partnership for any benefit, and hold as trustee for it, any profits derived by him without the consent of the other partners from any transaction connected with the formation, conduct, or liquidation of the partnership or from any use by him of its property [UPA §21(1)].*

In both instances here, the seller was the Marsh-Gentry partnership and the purchaser was Gentry. Gentry did not inform Marsh of the true nature of either sale. Partners scrutinize buyouts by their partners in an entirely different light from an ordinary sale to a third party. Even though Marsh received the stipulated purchase price, a partner has an absolute right to know when his partner is the purchaser.

Figure 16-3 summarizes partnership management duties.

CONCLUSION

Benjamin Cardozo served as Chief Judge of New York's highest court. In 1928, the future U.S. Supreme Court justice had occasion to examine the duties of coventurers to one another. Although his language is somewhat old-fashioned, what he said is as true today as it was when he wrote.

Joint adventurers, like copartners, owe to one another, while the enterprise continues, the duty of finest loyalty. Many forms of conduct permissible in a workaday world for those acting at arm's length, are forbidden to those bound by fiduciary ties. A [person

with fiduciary duties] is held to something stricter than the morals of the market place. Not honesty alone, but the punctilio of an honor the most sensitive, is then the standard of behavior. . . . Uncompromising rigidity has been the attitude of courts of equity when petitioned to undermine the rule of undivided loyalty by the "disintegrating erosion" of particular exceptions [to this rule], . . . Only thus has the level of conduct for fiduciaries been kept at a higher level than that trodden by the crowd.*

Despite the high standard of conduct the law demands of partners, only those with enormous faith in their fellow humans should forego a written partnership agreement. Like any but

---

* *Meinhard v. Salmon,* 249 N.Y. 458, 164 N.E. 545 (1928).

ITEM	UPA PRESUMPTION OR POSITION REGARDING PARTNERS	CAN BE ALTERED BY AGREEMENT?	COMMONLY ALTERED?
Sharing of profits	Equal	Yes	Yes
Voice in management	Equal	Yes	Yes
Agency role	General agent	Yes	Sometimes limited
Fiduciary duties	Owed to partnership	No	No
Usage of partnership property	Equal	Yes	Yes

Figure 16.3 Partnership Management.

the most routine contracts, a partnership agreement is best formulated in the kind of negotiations which go into the preparation of a writing. In the next chapter, when we discuss dissolving partnerships, the importance of a comprehensive writing will become quite clear.

A NOTE TO FUTURE CPA CANDIDATES

The CPA exam presently assumes that candidates know the Uniform Partnership Act (UPA), not the Revised Uniform Partnership Act (RUPA).

The CPA candidate should keep in mind that partnership law is basically a combination of contract and agency law. You should know the UPA definition of a partnership: "An association of two or more persons to carry on as co-owners a business for profit" [§6(1)]. Remember that the association is consensual. The definition has been tested often on the CPA exam as an example of the aggregate theory. In contrast, the eligibility of a partnership to own property and sue or be sued as a partnership is an aspect of the entity theory of partnership.

The concept of apparent partnership must be understood. Remember that the concept is similar to the apparent agent, discussed in Part III. In the next chapter, note that if a partnership fails to give a third party appropriate notice of the departure of a partner, the departed partner may be found to be an apparent (ostensible) partner.

A partner owes fiduciary duties to fellow partners and the partnership. When a partner acts, a partner acts as an agent of the partnership. The most commonly tested UPA presumptions, subject to partnership modification, are that partners share profits and losses equally; have an equal voice in management; and have no right to a salary (except that a surviving partner is entitled to reasonable compensation in winding up the partnership affairs).

Keep in mind that a partner ultimately may be responsible for all the debts of the partnership, a major drawback to the partnership form of business. This will be discussed further in Chapter 17.

KEY WORDS

accounting (372)
aggregate (360)
apparent partner (362)
articles of partnership (362)
capital contribution (364)
charging order (369)
dormant partner (362)
entity (360)
joint venture (361)
judicial sale (372)
partnership (359)
partnership by estoppel (366)
secret partner (362)
silent partner (362)
tenancy in partnership (369)

DISCUSSION QUESTIONS

1. What requirements does the UPA state for the formation of a partnership? What contract law requirements apply?
2. Do partnership agreements generally have to be in writing? If not, why should partners go to the trouble of drawing one up?
3. What are articles of partnership? What information should they generally include and why?
4. What is the UPA's principal test for determining whether a partnership exists? How does it work?
5. What is meant by the phrase "one partner, one vote"?
6. Will the parties' intent to form a partnership control a court's determination as to one's existence? Under what circumstances will it not? Give an example where it will not.
7. What does "partnership by estoppel" mean? Illustrate two ways in which it may occur.
8. Describe a partner's interest in partnership property.
9. May partners sell or assign partnership interests? Do assignees automatically become

partners? If not, what status do they assume? What are their rights?

10. What duties does a partner owe to the partnership and to his or her partners?

CASE PROBLEMS

1. Ed Way and Peter Daniel, friends, each owned a collector car. They decided to jointly purchase and own for investment a 1968 Shelby Mustang. Soon after they purchased the car, Ed purchased a 1967 Camaro convertible. When Peter saw the car he immediately offered Ed one half the purchase price. Ed refused the money, claiming he had bought the car for himself. Ed claims there was never serious discussion or actual agreement to go beyond the original purchase of the Mustang. Peter claims they became partners with the purchase of the Mustang and that the Camaro should be considered partnership property. Would a court likely agree with Peter? Would your answer be the same if Ed and Peter had together purchased over ten cars before Ed purchased the Camaro? Explain.

2. Allison Ward and her sisters, Connie and Rebecca, formed a partnership to open a bookstore, Bookends. It was agreed that Allison would manage the business. The other two sisters were to be investors, and agreed that Rebecca's involvement would not be disclosed to the public. After succeeding initially, the partnership ultimately went bankrupt. Creditors have now learned of the ownership involvement of all three sisters. Given the facts above, would Connie and Rebecca be considered limited partners? Dormant partners? Ultimately as personally liable as Allison? Explain.

3. Ken Fritz was a partner in OPQ, a partnership. He decided he wanted to leave OPQ and travel around the world. Ken suggested several persons who might purchase his interest and take his place in the partnership, but each time the remaining partners refused. Finally, Ken decided to assign his partnership interest to his cousin, Rick Roglis. The assignment permitted Roglis to take Ken's office in the company, speak on Ken's behalf, and protect Ken's interest in the firm until Ken returned. After Ken left, the remaining partners changed the door locks and barred Rick from entry. If Roglis were to bring a court action to enforce his assignment of interest, would a court be likely to find in favor of the partnership? Explain.

4. On August 1, Koenig, Isham, and Mills orally agreed to form a partnership and open KIM Travel Service. Because they were not sure just how successful the business might be, they agreed that they would open the business to the public on September 1 and operate the partnership for 1 year. In November, an irate customer, Peter Garrity, demanded the return of $2500 that he had paid for a trip to Europe. Unfortunately for Garrity, Koenig had forgotten to book his prepaid land accommodations. Garrity has brought suit against the firm and all partners. Mills claims that there can be no partnership liability, since written articles of partnership were never formed or signed. Is a court likely to agree with this assertion? Explain.

5. Gingrich, Hollister, and Hill formed a partnership to operate an antique business. Gingrich contributed her illustrious name, Hollister managed the partnership, and Hill contributed the capital. Without an agreement to the contrary, does Hill have the majority vote with respect to a new business idea being discussed by the partnership? Suppose Hollister has been sidelined after being struck by a bus and Hill has had to step in and manage the business. Would Hill have a right to a salary? Explain.

6. Charles Norman and Walter Rockwell did business as Norman & Rockwell Company. Their relationship was very informal, and neither considered himself to be the other's partner. Their stationery carried the name "Norman & Rockwell Company." Donald Quirk loaned Rockwell $10,000 for the business. Rockwell told Norman about the loan. Norman told him, "That's your responsibility. I've got nothing to do with it." Rock-

well has defaulted, and Quirk now wants to hold Norman liable on the debt as Rockwell's partner. Would Norman's comment to Rockwell preclude liability to Quirk? Are Norman and Rockwell partners by estoppel? Explain.

7. Arms, Balk, and Clee formed a partnership to operate a retail drug and sundries shop under the name Drug Shop. The firm hired Dell, a pharmacist, for a 5-year term and agreed to pay him a fixed annual salary plus 10 percent of the profits. Fricke, a supplier of fixtures, indicated to the partners that he would sell fixtures to the firm on credit only if Dell, the pharmacist and a wealthy man, was a partner. Dell, who was present, said that he was a partner, and the sale was made. Dell, however, later notified all others dealing with the firm that he was not a partner. If Fricke were to bring suit, would he be likely to recover from Dell? Explain.

8. Judy Green was the proprietor of the Green Thumb Floral & Gardening Store. Sally Burck, a friend, asked Judy if she would like to share a floral booth with her during the town's Tutty Baker Days celebration. Judy said yes. They agreed that Judy would provide all the flowers, display containers, and carts, while Sally would provide and set up a tent, secure temporary help, and manage the booth. A shopper, Stephen Marks, was severely cut by a broken container while he was visiting the booth. Marks has brought a tort action against Judy and Sally, alleging joint and several liability. Sally claims that she has no liability. What type of business arrangement did Judy and Sally have? If a court finds negligence in the usage of the broken container, is the court likely to hold Sally liable? Explain.

9. The Internal Revenue Service claims that Chris Goebel, a partner in C & J Goebel Company, has underreported his federal income for the past year. Chris denies the charge. Partnership records show that the firm made an $80,000 profit after expenses. However, the partners drew only $30,000 each from the business, as $20,000 was left in the partnership to accumulate money to purchase a building. Chris reported $30,000 in income for federal tax purposes from the partnership. Was he correct? Explain.

10. Al Soldatz was a partner in Knox Buick, a retail car dealership. Although Al was a full-fledged partner, his actual role in the business was that of an investor. He maintained a separate, noncompeting business, seldom visited the business, and never attempted to participate in daily management activities. Without partnership approval, Al became a partner with his brother Jim in a new Hyundai car dealership. The dealership was an immediate success. Al's partners in Knox Buick are now claiming that they have a right to share in Al's income from the Hyundai dealership. Are the partners correct? If Al has breached any duties to his Buick partners, describe them.

CHAPTER 17

Partnerships: Relations with Third Parties and Dissolution

The law of partnerships involves a combination of contract and agency law with only a few new concepts added. The last chapter focused on how contract law controls the formation of partnerships and noted the importance of mutual agency as a key element of partnership. This chapter first explores how the law of agency governs a partnership's relations with third parties. Then, it examines the interaction between the law of contracts and some statutes in the process of dissolving, winding up, and terminating partnerships.

AGENCY AND RELATIONSHIPS WITH THIRD PARTIES

The law of agency defines the potential liability of partners to third parties. The partnership is the principal, and each partner is its agent. Generally, a partner has the same range of express, implied, and apparent authority as a general agent.

Contracts by Partners

When a partner has apparent authority. A partner apparently carrying on a partnership's usual business may bind it to a contract unless the partner lacks authority to act on the particular matter *and* the person with whom she is dealing knows it [UPA §9(1)]. In the following case, a partner attempted to avoid liability under a contract made by another partner.

Ball v. Carlson

641 P.2d 303 (Colo. Ct. App. 1981)

FACTS Carlson and Teegardin developed and sold real estate as C.I.T. Construction Company (C.I.T.), a partnership. The Balls contracted to buy a house in a C.I.T. subdivision. The contract, which Carlson signed, called for a closing date of May 10, 1978, "contingent upon approval of subdivision by county commissioners." As the closing approached, Carlson realized that the plan would not be approved in time. He asked the Balls to wait, and they agreed. In June, Teegardin told the Balls that their house would cost between $7000 and $8000 more than the contract price. The Balls did not indicate that they would pay the difference. In July, the commissioners approved the subdivision plan. On August 1, C.I.T.'s real estate agent notified the Balls that C.I.T. considered their contract terminated and returned their deposit. The Balls sued the partners for damages for breach of contract. The trial court entered judgment for the Balls.

ISSUE Did Carlson bind Teegardin when he signed the construction contract with the Balls?

DECISION Yes. Affirmed. UPA §9(1) provides, "every partner is an agent of the partnership for the purpose of its business." A partner is both principal and agent of the partnership with complete authority as to acts which are apparently within the usual course of the partnership's particular business. Here, C.I.T. developed and sold real estate. Therefore, Carlson bound Teegardin by signing the contract in C.I.T.'s name.

Thus, as *Ball* illustrates, a partner has apparent authority to make contracts which are normal in the partnership's business. This is so even if the partner lacks express authority. Assume that three partners vote two to one not to renew a store lease. However, the dissenting partner renews it anyway. The partnership would be liable to a lessor who did not know of its decision.

Trading and nontrading partnerships. The kind of business in which a partnership engages often defines the extent of a partner's apparent authority.

The law categorizes partnerships as either trading or nontrading partnerships. *Trading partnerships* engage in commercial or merchandising businesses. Essentially, these are partnerships which maintain an inventory and make profits from buying for and selling from it. A *nontrading partnership* is usually a service-oriented business, like an accounting firm, though the courts apply the term to any partnership which is not a trading partnership.

Partners in trading partnerships have broader apparent authority than those in nontrading firms because such trading partnerships routinely borrow to finance their operations. For example, clothing stores often seek financing for new seasonal stock. Therefore, it would not be unusual for a partner to borrow on the partnership's behalf. However, a partner in a nontrading partnership—like a law firm—would not borrow on its behalf as a normal part of its business.

Whether a partnership is a trading or nontrading partnership generally becomes an issue when a lender seeks to hold the partnership liable on the signature of a single partner, as agent. If the partnership refuses liability and proves its nontrading partnership status, then the creditor's only recourse will be against the partner who borrowed the money. This is why lenders, as a preventative law measure, often require a partnership resolution authorizing the borrowing of money before lending to a partnership.

When partners lack apparent authority. A partner lacks any apparent authority when the transaction does not relate to carrying on the partnership's business in its usual fashion [UPA §9(2)]. This limitation minimizes a partner's ability to shift liability for personal obligations to the partnership. If a partner signs a note on behalf of the partnership as a *surety* for the purchase of his vacation house, the partnership will not be liable if he defaults.

The UPA limits the scope of a partner's apparent authority in five specific instances [UPA §9(3)].

First, a partner does not have apparent authority to dispose of the business's goodwill. For instance, a single partner may not sell the rights to the company logo, since it identifies the business.

Second, a partner may not do anything which would make it impossible to carry on the ordinary business of the partnership. So, a partner in a bar lacks any authority to sell its liquor license.

Third, a partner may not assign partnership assets in trust for the benefit of the partnership's creditors. Often, an assignment for creditors so ties up partnership assets that carrying on the business is virtually impossible. We discuss assignments for the benefit of creditors in Chapter 42.

Fourth, similarly, in a lawsuit, a partner may not make a written admission of liability on the partnership's behalf. Suppose Peter, of Peter & Paul Paint Projects, rams Virginia's car with the partnership's truck. Peter's admission of liability in her suit against him and the partnership will bind only him personally, not Paul or the partnership.

Fifth, a partner lacks apparent authority to unilaterally submit a partnership claim or dispute to arbitration. (Remember: Arbitration is binding on the parties.) Peter may agree to arbitration of the question of his personal liability, but he lacks authority to do so on behalf of Paul or the partnership.

Each of the five actions in the list requires the other partners' authorization, unless they have abandoned the business. Otherwise, the single partner's act will not bind the partnership.

The following case is an example of how two of three partners lacked apparent authority to sell a business asset that would have made it impossible for the partnership to continue.

Patel v. Patel

260 Cal. Rptr. 255 (Cal.Ct.App. 1989)

FACTS L. G. Patel and his wife, S. L., were owners of the City Center Motel in Eureka, California. They later formed a partnership for the purpose of owning and operating the motel, and added their son, Raj, as a third partner. In the written partnership agreement, Raj had to approve any sale of the motel building. L. G. and S. L., however, never did record a legal instrument to reflect Raj's interest in the building. L. G. and S. L. Patel subsequently contracted to sell the motel building to P. V. and Kirit Patel, who did not know about Raj's partnership interest. Raj resisted when he learned of the sale and would not approve of it. The buyers sued for specific performance of the agreement. The trial court ruled that the sale was not enforceable.

ISSUE Did L. G. and S. L. Patel have apparent authority to sell the motel building?

DECISION No. Affirmed. The general rule is that every partner is an agent of the partnership and can legally bind it when carrying out partnership business. UPA §9(3)(c) is an exception to the rule. It states that any partners acting without the approval of any remaining partners may not do anything that would make it impossible to carry on the ordinary business of the partnership. The purpose of this partnership was to operate a motel. Obviously, selling it would make it impossible to perpetuate it.

RUPA changes. RUPA has eliminated the listing of the five limits on the scope of a partner's apparent authority. Colorado has led a number of states which previously removed the UPA prohibition against unilateral submission of disputes to arbitrators. Because of the increasing reliance on arbitration to resolve all types of disputes—a phenomenon noted in Chapter 2—this RUPA deletion seems a welcome one.

Partners' Liability

Partners have a dual nature. Every partner is an agent of the partnership for the purpose of its business. As such, each partner possesses authority to bind the partnership. As a co-owner of the partnership, each partner has potential liability for the debts of the partnership.

Tort liability. A partnership's tort liability is *joint and several*, meaning that a plaintiff may sue the partnership and one partner, all the partners, or any combination of the partners [UPA §§13 and 15(a)]. Suppose Karl injures himself when he trips on a throw rug in the offices of L&M Productions. Karl may sue L&M and Leo or Max, or both of them.

Of course, agency law dictates that the

partnership, and therefore the partners, will be liable for torts committed by employees—whether partners, agents, or servants—acting within the scope of their authority. As Chapter 15 notes, liability is more likely to be imposed for negligent acts than for intentional torts.

However, if the intentional tort is sufficiently related to the employee's duties, the partnership will be liable. A bouncer for a bar is the classic example here. The following case may mark an outer limit of partnership liability for intentional torts.

Soden v. Starkman

218 S. 2d 763 (Fla. Dist. Ct. App. 1969)

FACTS   Mr. and Mrs. Soden operated an apartment house as a partnership. Mrs. Starkman, then 74, occupied one of their apartments. On July 2 and again on July 3, Mrs. Soden asked Mrs. Starkman for her July rent. Mrs. Starkman refused to pay it because repairs Mr. Soden had promised had not been made. On July 5, Mr. Soden left on a 10-day trip. On July 11, Mrs. Soden again asked Mrs. Starkman for the rent. When Mrs. Starkman refused, Mrs. Soden beat her with a broom. Mrs. Starkman sued both Mr. and Mrs. Soden. The jury awarded Mrs. Starkman $15,000 in compensatory damages against both Mr. and Mrs. Soden. Mr. Soden appealed.

ISSUE   Was Mrs. Soden acting within the scope of her authority when she struck Mrs. Starkman?

DECISION   Yes. Affirmed. Agency principles determine the liability of one partner for the acts of the other. One partner is not liable for the intentional tort of another if she did not commit the tort within the actual or apparent scope of the agency or common business or at the first partner's direction or with his approval or ratification. Here, the trial judge told the jury he thought the evidence indicated that Mrs. Soden assaulted Mrs. Starkman not in furtherance of the business but from personal jealousy and malice. However, he believed the question was a close one and correctly instructed the jury to resolve this question of fact. Its verdict indicated that it found that Mrs. Soden acted within the scope of her agency.

Contract liability. A person bringing a breach of contract action against a partnership must sue the partnership and all the known partners. Partnership contracts with third parties create joint liability among the partners [UPA §15(b)]. *Joint liability* is a phrase used to describe those limited cases in which the law permits one defendant to insist that the plaintiff join another as a defendant. Suppose Leo and Max are partners in L&M Productions. They breach their contract with Karl to produce his play. Karl must sue the partnership and both Leo and Max, though if he is successful he may collect his judgment from either partner.

RUPA change. RUPA has eliminated the distinction between tort and contract law liability for partners. Under RUPA, all partners have joint and several liability for both contract and tort actions. At least ten states, primarily in the south and southwest, have adopted such a rule.

Incoming Partner's Liability for Partnership Debts

A new partner entering an existing partnership has unlimited liability for future partnership debts. As to preexisting partnership debts, a new partner has liability but it is limited to the partnership's assets [UPA §17]. If a partnership goes bankrupt the new partner will have no further liability.

Suppose Katherine joins an existing partnership, to which she contributes $25,000. The partnership goes bankrupt. Katherine will have no further personal liability if her share of the prior debts exceeds the remaining partnership assets. It should be noted, however, that Katherine may in effect waive the UPA limitation of liability provision if she agrees to assume the position of a withdrawing party, discussed next.

Withdrawing Partner's Liability for Partnership Debts

A *withdrawing partner* is one who leaves the partnership for any reason. Possible reasons include retirement, ouster by the other partners, a wish to enter another business, or death.

Prior debts. Withdrawing partners are personally liable for partnership debts existing at the time of withdrawal unless they receive a release from the partnership's creditors. Chapter 11, "Third Parties," discusses in more detail the principles which apply here.

Suppose John sells his partnership interest to Ray with the partnership's consent. If John does not obtain releases from the firm's existing creditors, he remains liable for the firm's debts. That does not mean that the firm's creditors will pursue John. They may seek satisfaction from the partnership. But if the partnership were to fail, they might well seek a judgment against John. The principle involved here is no more than this: if A owes B $10, A cannot discharge that debt by telling B that C has agreed to pay it.

However, now assume that the partnership creditors agree to a *novation*, the substitution of a new contract for an existing one. They release

John in return for Ray's agreement to assume John's partnership liabilities. The novation frees John of potential liability. At the same time, Ray in effect waives the UPA's limitation on an incoming partner's liability [UPA §17]. He is now in John's position and is potentially liable for *all* partnership debts.

Without a novation, whether the incoming partner has agreed to stand in the place of the retiring partner does not matter to the creditors. If John and Ray made such an agreement, the creditors would not be bound, since they were not parties to it. However, if John had to pay the creditors, he could enforce the agreement against Ray.

Later debts. A withdrawing partner is potentially liable for partnership debts incurred after withdrawal unless she gives actual notice to creditors and constructive notice to all others dealing with the firm [UPA §35(1)(b)].

The principles applied in this situation are essentially the same as those which determine the principal's liability for contracts made by terminated agents. For example, Julia retires from a partnership. Neither she nor the partnership gives notice to creditors, who extend further credit to it. If the partnership goes bankrupt, Julia will be personally liable to the creditors.

Retiring partners will not be liable if they can show that creditors knew of the withdrawal, even though they lacked proper notice. Suppose a creditor heard of Julia's retirement from a reliable source in the trade. Julia would not be liable to him for later debts. But assume that, in response to the creditor's inquiry, a remaining partner, Henry, tells the creditor that Julia is still with the firm. Despite the fact that Henry lied, Julia would be liable. Had she given proper notice, she would not have been in a position to have Henry misrepresent her status. If the creditor obtains a judgment against her, Henry must reimburse her.

Prompt notice is as important to the partnership as to the withdrawing partner. Until the creditors receive it, the withdrawing partner

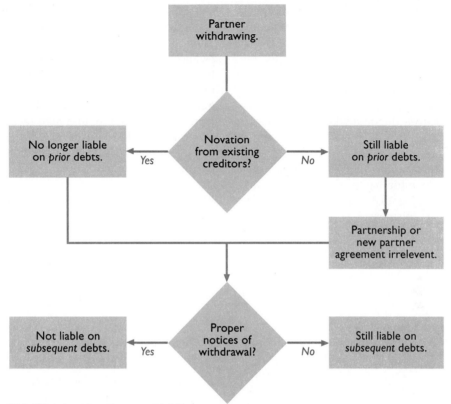

Figure 17.1 Withdrawing Partner Liability.
Notice of a partner's departure can prevent liability for *subsequent* partnership debts. However, only a novation extinguishes liability for *prior* debts.

retains apparent authority to bind the partnership. Assume that Julia retires from the partnership without giving notice to any creditors. Later, she charges a suite of office furniture to her former partnership's account. Her old firm would be liable if Julia regularly engaged in this type of transaction before she retired.

Figure 17.1 summarizes a withdrawing partner's potential liability.

DISSOLUTION, WINDING UP, AND TERMINATION

The law uses three terms to describe the process by which partnerships end: dissolution,

winding up, and termination. Though these three terms sound as if they should be synonyms, they are *not*. Rather, they refer to three stages in the process of ending a partnership.

The Process of Ending a Partnership

Dissolution is ''the change in the relation of the partners caused by any partner ceasing to be associated in the carrying on . . . of the business'' [UPA §29]. Dissolution is best thought of as the firing of a starter's pistol. It ends the partnership's normal operation and signals the beginning of the process of closing it. Suppose Jean and Jim were partners in an accounting firm. Jean dies. Jim must begin bringing the business to a close. (As we will see, the articles of partnership may permit the surviving partners to continue the business, or the remaining partners may agree to do so.)

Upon dissolution, the partnership must begin *winding up*—that is, going out of business. The firm may not enter into any new transactions unrelated to that process. Suppose a partnership ran a store. It could take out newspaper ads for a "going out of business" sale, but it could not order more stock.

The partnership is said to be *terminated* when the partnership has paid all its debts and distributed all its assets. Now, nothing remains of what was its business.

Proper Dissolutions by Partners

Because a partnership is based upon agency principles, a partner cannot be forced to remain in a partnership against his or her will. At any time, a partner has the power—if not the right—to dissolve the partnership. Thus, some dissolutions are proper and some improper.

Proper dissolutions do not breach the partnership agreement. Improper dissolutions do. As we will see in the following sections, improper dissolutions can carry a heavy penalty, since the withdrawing partner is not entitled to share in the value of the business's goodwill. Because of this and other consequences, many former partners have litigated whether dissolution was proper.

Partnerships at will. A partner may dissolve a *partnership at will* at any time without breaching the partnership agreement [UPA §31(1)]. In a partnership at will, the partnership has no set term, or its term has elapsed, or the particular undertaking specified in the partnership agreement has occurred. Suppose Carla and Leroy form an accounting firm as a partnership. Their agreement says nothing about the duration of the partnership. It is a partnership at will, and either partner may elect to dissolve it without violating their agreement. By contrast, suppose

two people agree to be partners to run a concession at a world's fair. Their agreement would terminate at the end of the fair.

Assent of the partners. The partners may agree to dissolve the partnership [UPA §31(1)]. Suppose that, because of her ill health, Patricia asks her fellow partners to allow her to withdraw from the partnership, although its 10-year term has not expired. They agree. Her departure dissolves the partnership but does not breach the partnership agreement.

Expulsion. A partnership agreement may provide for expelling a member who violates it. A proper expulsion dissolves the partnership without liability to the remaining partners. The expelled partner has a right to the value of his partnership interest—determined by an *accounting*—as of the date of his expulsion, less any goodwill interest [UPA §31(d)]. Essentially, the expelled partner receives his portion of the partnership's book value.

Dissolution by Operation of Law

A partnership terminates by operation of law without any action taken by the partners themselves if:

- A partner dies
- A partner or the partnership goes bankrupt
- Any event makes it unlawful to carry on the partnership's business or for its members to carry it on in partnership

However, as we will discuss below, the partnership agreement may contain a clause which permits the business to start again immediately following a partner's death or bankruptcy [UPA §31].

Dissolution by Court Decree

In five instances, a partner—without breaching the partnership agreement—may apply to a court for an order dissolving the partnership. If the partner proves one of the following conditions, the court may decree a dissolution despite the fact that the partnership's term has not elapsed or that its purpose has not been achieved [UPA §32].

Insanity. The court may dissolve a partnership if a court has declared the partner to be a lunatic or if the partner is shown to be of unsound mind.

Incapability. Incapability to perform the partnership agreement is a proper ground for dissolution. If a partner develops a disabling but not fatal disease, dissolution is proper. Or, in a medical partnership, if one doctor lost her license to practice, that would be sufficient grounds.

Prejudicial misconduct. A partner's misconduct which has been prejudicial to the business warrants dissolution. A partner's misappropriation of partnership funds would be grounds for dissolution.

Willful breaches of partnership agreement. A partner who willfully breaches the partnership agreement or who makes it impossible for the other partners to work with him also provides grounds for dissolution. Suppose that in forming a partnership, each partner commits to working full time on partnership business. A court may properly dissolve a partnership where one partner spends only 3 hours a day, 3 days a week on partnership activities.

Proving a breach of a partnership agreement requires the plaintiff to establish the agreement's terms. If the partnership agreement was oral, the defendant may be the only other person who can say what its terms were. In short, articles of partnership are a necessity.

Equitable causes. The courts may dissolve a partnership for equitable reasons, that is, where it would be unfair to compel a partner to continue. Irreconcilable differences between the partners as to how—or whether—the business should be conducted are a common equitable ground. For example, Frieda and Fred made a decent living operating a diner on a town's main street. Then, an Interstate bypassed the town. The partners now have to work 15 hours a day to make what they made in 8 hours before. A court may dissolve the partnership on Fred's motion, even though Frieda wants to continue.

The law will not require a partnership to continue if it has no prospect of turning a profit. Suppose Al and Alberto's Brussels sprout farm has not shown a profit for 5 years. Worse, the Albanians have just flooded the world Brussels sprout market. Alberto wants to dissolve the partnership and sell the farm, but Al does not. A court probably will grant a dissolution.

Effects of Dissolution

Generally, a dissolution requires that the partnership be *liquidated*—its assets turned into cash—and each partnership contribution returned. In the case which follows, the trial court had ordered a somewhat different remedy.

Taylor v. Bryan

664 S.W.2d 52 (Mo. Ct. App. 1984)

FACTS   Taylor and Bryan had been partners but had never executed articles of partnership. Taylor brought suit seeking dissolution and damages, alleging that Bryan had breached his fiduciary duties. Bryan counterclaimed, alleging fraud and seeking damages. The partnership's debts had all been paid, and the only partnership property remaining was a bulldozer. The trial court denied both damage claims, dissolved the partnership, and awarded the bulldozer to Taylor. It also ordered Taylor to pay Bryan $10,000, half the value it placed on the bulldozer. Taylor appealed.

ISSUE   Should the trial court have ordered the bulldozer sold and the proceeds divided between the ex-partners?

DECISION   Yes. Judgment modified. Upon dissolution, each partner "unless otherwise agreed, may have the partnership property applied to discharge its liabilities, and the surplus applied to pay in cash the net amount owing the . . . partners" [UPA §38]. One partner cannot be forced to buy out another partner. When they cannot agree, as here, the property is to be sold and the proceeds divided.

As we have already seen, where the dissolution results from a breach of the partnership agreement or a proper expulsion of a partner, the remaining partners may continue the business. Now, let's examine the effects on various parties of a decision to continue or terminate the partnership.

Effects of Dissolution: Partnership to Continue

Not all partnerships terminate on the withdrawal of a partner. Some, in fact, have remained in existence for well over a hundred years. After all, it would make little sense for the remaining partners to abandon a profitable, ongoing business. They would lose their jobs and, perhaps, the goodwill they had built up in the business.

When the remaining partners continue, the partnership is dissolved and wound up only as to the withdrawing partner. Upon the conclusion of the winding up, the withdrawing partner's interest is terminated.

Continuation statements. Partnerships continue either because the partners decide to keep the business going upon dissolution or because the articles of partnership provide for it. A provision in the articles permitting the remaining partners to continue the business is called a *continuation statement*. Often, in a continuation statement, partners agree to buy out the withdrawing partner. Often the partnership takes out life insurance on each partner with the partnership as beneficiary. The policy's proceeds are used to buy out the insured's interest.

Making provision, when the partnership is formed, for buying out withdrawing partners can avoid unpleasant choices later. If the remaining partners lack sufficient funds to buy the withdrawing partner's interest, they may be forced to bring in another partner. Or, they may have to sell the business altogether. Or, the withdrawing partner, in order to get the full value of his or her investment, may have to stay on as an inactive general partner.

Valuing the withdrawing partner's interest. If the withdrawing partner has not breached the partnership agreement, the remaining partners must pay him or his estate the fair market value of his partnership interest. If the partnership continues without a settling of accounts, the withdrawing partner or his estate may elect the more favorable of the following formulas:

- The value of the partnership interest at dissolution plus interest until the date of payment
- The value of the partnership interest at dissolution plus a share of the profits until the amount is paid [UPA §42]

Goodwill. If the withdrawing partner has breached the partnership agreement, the remaining partners may deduct from his share the enterprise's goodwill value.

Goodwill is the difference between a business's fair market value and its book value, or what its balance sheet shows. It is additional value which cannot be assigned to any particular asset. Suppose Evelyn is one of three equal partners in DEF Office Supplies. DEF's book value is $45,000, but it could be sold as a going concern for $150,000. If Evelyn breaches the partnership agreement, she has a right to only $15,000 on termination.

By permitting them to retain the business's goodwill value, the UPA attempts to protect the remaining partners from the unreasonable demands of a partner who has been acting in bad faith. This provision also does much to explain the large quantity of litigation involving whether a dissolution was proper.

Most businesses are worth more if sold as going concerns than they are if sold asset by asset. That is why most partnerships if possible sell their businesses rather than liquidate them.

Effect on creditors. When the partnership business continues, the dissolved partnership's creditors automatically become creditors of the person or partnership continuing the business [UPA §41(6)]. As we have already noted, unless the withdrawing partner obtains a release or a novation, existing creditors may still recover from him for the partnership's past debts.

Effects of Dissolution: Partnership to Terminate

Absent an agreement to the contrary, whether a business will continue or not is entirely up to the remaining partners. Also, if the withdrawing partner's breach of the partnership agreement led to the dissolution, the remaining partners can bring an action for breach of contract against him. The next case examines why one partner was ordered to pay damages for trying to use the bankruptcy laws to wrongfully dissolve the partnership.

Walters v. Sawyer

130 B.R. 384 (Bkrtcy. E.D.N.Y. 1991)

FACTS Walters and Sawyer formed a partnership and opened the Southern Taste Restaurant. Although the business was doing very well, Sawyer decided to oust Walters by using the bankruptcy laws. First, Sawyer secretly leased the restaurant premises and other assets to a close friend. Next, he initiated Chapter 7 (total liquidation) bankruptcy proceedings without telling Walters. The bankruptcy schedules did not list the partnership agreement, its assets, or Walters as a creditor. Shortly before the bankruptcy proceedings were to end, Sawyer told Walters he was going bankrupt and that Walters' participation in the business was over. Sawyer, however, continued the business as if nothing had happened. Walters, alerted now to the fact there was a bankruptcy proceeding, intervened in the suit.

ISSUE Did Sawyer breach the partnership agreement and wrongfully dissolve the partnership by filing for Chapter 7 bankruptcy?

DECISION Yes. Under New York state law, a partnership automatically dissolves when one of the partners files for Chapter 7 bankruptcy. Sawyer used the bankruptcy laws, not to reorder his affairs and get a fresh start, but to dissolve the partnership and oust Walters. Walters is entitled to his monetary contribution to the partnership plus any lost profits due to the wrongdoing and the breach of the partnership agreement.

Winding Up the Partnership

Once a partner initiates dissolution, the partners must begin winding up the partnership business, if they decide to terminate it.

The partners' fiduciary duties. The scope of the partners' fiduciary duties to one another under-goes a subtle change upon dissolution. As the next case points out, the withdrawing partner's fiduciary duties to her partners continue until the winding up is completed—but only as to business matters which existed before the dissolution.

Woodruff v. Bryant

558 S.W.2d 535 (Tex. Civ. App. 1977)

FACTS   The plaintiffs and Bryant were partners in the Flour Bluff Finance Company, which made loans up to $100. In February 1971, after a dispute, Bryant resigned as the loan company's manager and offered to sell her quarter interest to her partners. They took no action on her offer. Thereafter she continued to receive her share of the partnership profits but did not participate in its management. In January 1972, Payday Loans, which made the same type of loans, opened 100 feet from Flour Bluff. Bryant managed and owned a quarter interest in Payday. Her former partners sought an accounting of her Payday profits, but the jury in effect found that Bryant's fiduciary duties to them ended upon her notice of dissolution.

ISSUE   Did Bryant's fiduciary duties continue until termination of the Flour Bluff partnership?

DECISION   Yes. Reversed. The fiduciary relationship between partners ends on dissolution as to new business but continues as to business begun before dissolution. Thus, a partnership continues during the winding up until the relationship terminates. Since a partner cannot carry on another business in competition with her partners, Bryant is accountable to her former partners for any profit from Payday.

Right to wind up and liquidate. A partner who has not wrongfully dissolved the partnership has the right to wind it up. However, a bankrupt partner may not wind up the partnership. Any partner may seek a court-appointed receiver to wind up the partnership [UPA §37].

If a partner's death causes the dissolution and only one partner remains, the sole surviving partner winding up the business may claim a salary for the work involved [UPA §18(f)]. Otherwise, unless the partnership agreement provides for it, the partner winding up a partnership's affairs does not receive compensation.

During the winding up, the partnership may enter into new contracts only if they are necessary to complete unfinished business [UPA §33]. For instance, Bonnie and Dave operate a construction equipment leasing business. Bonnie causes the partnership to be dissolved. While they wind up, Dave may not order new machinery. However, he can order parts to repair a damaged grader in order to obtain a better price when they liquidate their inventory. But, what happens if the partners cannot agree on how to wind it up? That was a question the court faced in the next case.

Dreifuerst v. Dreifuerst

90 Wis. 2d 566, 280 N.W.2d 335 (1979)

FACTS   The parties were three brothers who operated two feed mills. They had never adopted articles of partnership. Cletus and Roy served Claude with a notice of dissolution. Four months later, Cletus and Roy filed suit because the brothers could not agree on how to wind up the partnership. Claude demanded that the two mills be sold and the proceeds divided among the partners. Cletus and Roy, however, successfully sought a decree dividing the property among the parties.

ISSUE   Did the trial court have authority to order an in-kind distribution of the partnership property?

DECISION   No. Reversed. Since no written agreement existed, there could be no provisions governing distribution of partnership assets upon dissolution. In that event, the UPA requires distribution of assets in cash [UPA §38]. The statute does not permit an in-kind distribution unless the partners agree to it.

Payment of liabilities. A partnership's assets include all partnership property, including the partners' capital contributions. If necessary, the partners may have to contribute additional sums to satisfy the liabilities.

The UPA specifies payment of liabilities in the following order of priority:

1. Liabilities owed to creditors other than partners
2. Liabilities owed to partners other than for capital contributions and profits
3. Liabilities owing to partners with respect to capital contributions
4. Liabilities owing to partners with respect to profits [UPA §40(a)]

The partners may not alter the order of payoff as to outsiders. However, they may alter the order as to themselves and as to whether capital contributions will be repaid in the event that partnership losses exceed capital contributions.

When the partners have satisfied their creditors and the partners' interest have been accounted for and satisfied, the partnership terminates.

Let's look at how payment on termination works in practice. Assume that Scott, Herb, and Virginia are partners in a commercial real estate firm. At formation, Scott was new to the business but had ready cash. Herb's name carried great weight in the commercial real estate world. Virginia, too, was well known and had extensive management experience. Their capital contributions were as follows: Scott, $25,000; Herb, $15,000; and Virginia, $0. Liabilities to creditors other than partners at dissolution were ABC, $15,000; and XYZ, $10,000. Partner loans at dissolution: Herb, $15,000. The two examples are based on UPA §§18(a) and 40(b). Figure 17.2 contains the math.

Case 1 presumes that the partnership has a profit of $30,000 upon termination of the partnership. As a result, the partners will each receive $10,000, as shown.

Case 2 presumes that the partnership was able to repay all creditors but not to return all the capital contributions. The partnership lacks $30,000 to pay back the $40,000 owed to Scott ($25,000) and Herb ($15,000). Stated another way, the partnership has negative profits of $30,000 to cover the return of capital. The partners will split this loss. Because the loss occurs at the time of partnership termination, Virginia will have to pay into the partnership her share of loss, $10,000. The $10,000 loss for Scott and for Herb will be reflected in their respective return of capital: Scott will get $15,000 (versus $25,000) and Herb $5000 (versus $15,000).

Effect of bankruptcy. If the partnership goes bankrupt, the partnership creditors have first rights on the partnership property. Any assets remaining after their claims are satisfied are distributed to the partners. If the assets are not sufficient to satisfy the creditors, the partners are individually liable.

If a partner goes bankrupt, his secured personal creditors have first right to his individual assets. Thereafter, partnership creditors and unsecured personal creditors are on an equal footing.

CONCLUSION

If Chapters 16 and 17, we have examined the law of partnership. Partnerships are popular because they are easy to form and manage, do not require—in most states—any legal formalities, and can have attractive tax consequences. They also have the virtue of being easily dissolved, so, if the venture matures, the partners can convert it into a corporation.

A partnership operates on trust. Partners must trust one another because of the extensive apparent authority each has to bind the partnership. The necessity for trust is perhaps the form's greatest weakness. Also, the presumption that all partners are going to be active in the business can cause problems when one shirks his or her responsibilities.

The corporate form or the limited partnership may offer a better solution than the general partnership when a number of owners, with varying commitments of skills, cash, and time, are to be involved. The choice of the proper business form is not easy. It requires a careful analysis of the owners' contributions and the type of venture.

A NOTE TO FUTURE CPA CANDIDATES

The CPA exam frequently covers the "Agency and Relationship with Third Parties" material. If you keep in mind how an agency issue would be resolved in a sole proprietorship setting you should arrive at the correct answer in the partnership setting. Why? Remember that when a partner acts, a partner acts as an agent of the partnership. A partner, as an agent, should be presumed by a reasonable third party to have that authority which an agent would generally have for such a business and business issue.

		Case 1	Case 2
Total remaining assets at termination:		$110,000	$50,000
1. Pay outside creditors:		25,000	25,000
		85,000	25,000
2. Pay back partner loans:		15,000	15,000
		70,000	10,000
3. Pay back capital contributions:		40,000	40,000
		30,000	(30,000)
4. Profits (losses) to be divided:		30,000	(30,000)
5. Profits (losses):	Scott	$10,000	($10,000)
	Herb	$10,000	($10,000)
	Virginia	$10,000	($10,000)

Figure 17.2 Payment on Termination of a Partnership.
Case 1 assumes the partnership showed a profit. Case 2 assumes a loss.

Therefore, just as under agency law, a partner of a large bar would be expected to have greater implied and apparent authority than a partner of a significantly smaller bar.

It is important to remember for the exam that a withdrawing partner continues to have personal liability for partnership debts prior to dissolution unless he receives a release or a novation. An incoming partner, who must be approved by all existing partners, has potential liability for the debts prior to his becoming a partner only to the extent of his capital contribution (a similar situation for limited partners, the focus of Chapter 18).

A partner who improperly dissolves or who is involuntarily removed from the partnership forfeits the right to share in the value of goodwill. Goodwill value can constitute a significant value and is often not reflected on the books of a business.

If the exam presents a problem concerning the winding up of a partnership, do not terminate your payout process too soon. Unless stipulated in the articles of partnership, partners have the right to a return of their capital contributions. On the CPA exam this often means one or more partners will have to come up with new personal money to complete the final capital payout step. Figure 17-2 illustrates this point.

KEY WORDS

dissolution (383)
joint liability (381)
joint and several liability (380)
liquidated (385)
nontrading partnership (379)

novation (382)
partnership at will (384)
termination (384)
trading partnership (379)
winding up (384)
withdrawing partner (382)

DISCUSSION QUESTIONS

1. When a partner acts on behalf of the partnership, is he or she acting as an agent of the partnership or as a principal?
2. What authority, if any, does a partner have to bind the partnership to contracts with third parties? To what extent may a partnership be liable when the partner does not have express authority? Explain
3. How, if at all, might a partnership be liable for the tortious act of a partner?
4. What are the differences between a trading partnership and a nontrading partnership?
5. Contrast the liability of an incoming partner to an existing partnership with that of a retiring partner.
6. Why is notice of retirement important for both the retiring partner and the partnership? What happens if it is not provided?

7. What is a dissolution? Name at least five ways in which dissolution may occur.

8. What are the characteristics of a partnership at will?

9. Are "dissolution," "winding up," and "termination" synonyms? If so, for what? If not, define each.

10. What is the order of payout when winding up a partnership?

CASE PROBLEMS

1. Arms, Balk, and Clee formed a partnership to operate a retail drug and sundries store under the name Drug Shop. They agreed that Arms would have the sole right to purchase merchandise on credit. They also agreed that Balk was to manage the store. Balk ordered merchandise for resale by the store on credit from a wholesaler in the firm name. The partnership claims that it is not liable for this order. Is the partnership correct? Explain.

2. In the ordinary course of business, John Gagginni, a partner in Gaggini & Ternes Sports Shop, accidentally injured a customer while moving some cross-country skis. Is Ternes potentially liable for Gaggini's negligence? If Ternes is liable, would her liability be joint or joint and several?

3. Chuck Tamminga retired from PDT Company, a partnership. The two remaining partners decided to continue the business and to admit Al Greenwald as a new partner. At the time of Chuck's withdrawal, the total partnership assets were $300,000, while liabilities were $180,000. Since the partners shared profits and losses, Chuck received $40,000. Al paid $50,000 to purchase a one-third partnership interest. Past creditors were properly informed of Chuck's retirement. What potential liability, if any, does Chuck have to creditors prior to his departure? What potential liability, if any, does Al have to creditors prior to his joining the partnership? Explain.

4. Greg Smith, a partner in Smith, Massey, & Wiegert, renewed an existing supply contract which the other partners had formally voted to terminate. The supplier did not know of the partnership vote. In addition, he submitted a long-standing dispute regarding a partnership claim against a customer to arbitration. The other partners claim that under the UPA, the partnership is not liable for Smith's acts. Are they correct? Explain.

5. Marty Kron, one of four equal partners in Baltic Produce Company, died. His widow, Amy, informed the partnership that she wished to assume Marty's role in the partnership, a right she claims Marty passed on to her in his will. Two of the three remaining partners agree that Amy should be allowed to assume Marty's partnership role. The third partner refuses to admit Amy and claims she is not entitled to partnership interest when Marty died. What rights, if any, does Amy have in regard to Marty's partnership interest? Explain.

6. Alden, Balsamo, and Collier originally contributed $100,000, $60,000, and $20,000, respectively, to form the ABC Partnership. Profits and losses of ABC are to be distributed one-half to Alden, one-third to Balsamo, and one-sixth to Collier. After operating for 1 year, ABC's total assets on its books are $244,000, total liabilities to outside creditors are $160,000, and total capital is $84,000. The partners made no withdrawals. ABC has decided to liquidate. If all the partners are solvent and the assets of ABC are sold for $172,000, how much additional money, if any, will Collier have to contribute? Explain.

7. Holm, Johnson, and Snidtker formed a partnership, agreeing to contribute $100,000 cash. Johnson and Snidtker each contributed $100,000 cash. Holm contributed $75,000 cash and agreed to pay an additional $25,000 2 years later. After 1 year of operation the partnership is insolvent. The fair market value of the assets of the partnership is $200,000. The liabilities total $410,000. Because of additional bad luck, both Johnson and Snidtker are personally insolvent. Holm has a net worth of $750,000. What is Holm's maximum potential liability? Explain.

8. Brill, Rutter, and Pierce were all partners. Pierce decided to resign from the partnership in order to engage in world travels. However, in his hurry to begin his travels, Pierce forgot to

give notice of his resignation to the partnership creditors. When asked of Pierce's whereabouts, Brill and Rutter told the business creditors that Pierce was just traveling and would be back soon. Without Pierce's management skills the business soon ran up extensive debt, and it ultimately went bankrupt. Pierce, now back from his trip, claims he has no liability beyond his termination date since Brill and Rutter have admitted falsely representing his continued relationship to the business to third parties. Is Pierce correct? Explain.

9. Mark Van Pernis worked for Petro Products Company, a partnership owned by Hawkinson and Zager. Mark was warned numerous times not to smoke in a loading area containing gas fumes. One day, while on break, Mark lit a cigarette in this area and caused a major explosion which severely injured Mark Fiocchi, a delivery person for XYZ Transit, Inc. Fiocchi has brought a lawsuit for $250,000 against Mark and the partnership. Mark and Zager have both filed petitions for personal bankruptcy since the accident. To what extent, if any, could Hawkinson be personally liable? Explain.

10. Tom Turner, a partner in ABC Company, withdrew from the business to form his own company in another state. ABC Company continued in business. Turner had formerly represented his firm when it brought computers from Garver Office Computers. By mail, Garver was given notice of Turner's departure. However, this information has not been conveyed to Martha O'Bannon, a Garver sales representative who had been Turner's contact person. O'Bannon sold two computers to Turner, who took delivery and directed the bill to ABC Company. ABC Company has refused to make payment. Does ABC have liability? Explain.

APPENDIX: RUPA

The Revised Uniform Partnership Act (RUPA) is a new model act intended to completely replace the Uniform Partnership Act (UPA). However, as of early 1993, no state had yet adopted RUPA. This appendix compares key RUPA sections with the UPA.

§103 Provides nonwaivable partnership provisions. RUPA retains the expectation of fiduciary duties between partners and a partner and the partnership. Section 103 permits partners to agree on greater flexibility concerning individual partner activities outside the partnership and less restrictive fiduciary duties. However, partners still cannot completely eliminate the duty of loyalty, the obligation of good faith and fair dealing, or unreasonably reduce the duty of care owed by a partner.

§201 States that "a partnership is an entity." RUPA emphasizes the entity approach,

the partnership as a business, more than does UPA.

§202 Retains the base UPA § definition of a partnership: "An association of two or more persons to carry on as co-owners a business for profit." However, it adds: " . . . creates a partnership whether or not the persons intended to create a partnership." The latter emphasizes what was implied in the UPA.

§204 "Property is presumed to be partnership property if purchased with partnership assets, even if not acquired in the name of the partnership. . . . " The UPA places greater focus on title versus the source of funds which bought the property.

§301 "Each partner is an agent of the partnership." RUPA retains the same approach to apparent authority but deletes the listing of "no authority" acts of UPA §9(3) (including the former prohibition against submitting a partnership claim to arbitration).

§303 Under RUPA, a partnership can now publicly file a "statement of partnership authority" which provides public notice of grants or restrictions of authority to partners of the firm. However, except for transfers of real property, a third party "who gives value without knowledge" is not bound. In contrast, the UPA provides for no "statement of actual authority."

§305 Retains the UPA approach that a partnership is liable for a partner's actionable conduct in the ordinary course of business of the partnership.

§306 Under UPA, a partner potentially has joint liability for contract actions, joint and several liability for tort actions. Under RUPA, a partner potentially has joint and several liability for all partnership actions and debts.

§307 Under RUPA, a partnership creditor is required to follow more steps to try to collect from the partnership before being able to seek collection from an individual partner. As such, RUPA treats a partner more like a guarantor, not a surety (the approach of the UPA).

§308 New term, "purported partner." Similar to apparent (ostensible) partner under UPA.

§309 Liability of incoming partner similar to UPA.

§401 The basic rights and duties between partners are not changed. RUPA still requires consent of all partners for an admission of a new partner. Partners are still presumed to share profits and losses.

§404 Under general standards of partner's conduct, partners can now agree that certain specified types or categories of activities can be done, in possible competition with the partnership and in furtherance of a partner's own interest, without breaching the duty of loyalty. However, obligation of good faith and fair dealing cannot be eliminated by agreement.

§406 Legal actions between a partner and the partnership or another partner are possible (no longer need wait until a dissolution of partnership as you do under the UPA.)

§501 Partner's interest in partnership property is still not transferable. However, a partner's interest in the partnership itself is still assignable.

§504 Like the UPA, a charging order against the partnership interest of an individual partner does not require partnership liquidation. Treated like a lien.

§601 New term and status, "partner disassociation," provides an intermediary step for changes of partnership composition without dissolution. May be voluntary (example: resignation or retirement) or involuntary (example: expulsion).

§701 A partner may be disassociated without it resulting in dissolution and winding up of the partnership business. Buy out provisions can be triggered by disassociation.

§801 With the new disassociation status, the RUPA listing of events causing dissolution of a partnership business is much shorter than that of the UPA. Essentially, dissolution is now intended for partnerships actually bringing their business to an end.

§901 RUPA now provides a process for conversion of a general partnership to a limited partnership.

CHAPTER 18

Limited Partnerships

LIMITED PARTNERSHIPS

A limited partnership is designed to meet the needs of investors who want the tax advantages of being a partner, do not want to be active in management, and require the limited liability of a shareholder. Those are the principal characteristics of limited partners.

THE NATURE OF LIMITED PARTNERSHIPS

Although unknown at common law, limited partnerships are not a recent creation. New York enacted the first limited partnership statute in 1822. Until then, courts had held that where a lender to a partnership took a share of the profits instead of interest, the lender became a partner with liability to other creditors for partnership obligations. The New York statute insulated creditors from that liability.

By the early twentieth century, many states had limited partnership acts. However, the acts varied widely. In 1916, the American Law Institute proposed the *Uniform Limited Partnership Act* (ULPA). Over the following 60 years, every state except Louisiana adopted at least part of the ULPA. While it did not attain its goal of national uniformity, the ULPA has dominated construction of limited partnerships.

To remedy flaws in the ULPA, the National Conference of Commissioners on Uniform State Laws, which took over from the American Law Institute, endorsed the *Revised Uniform Limited Partnership Act* (RULPA) in 1976. More than twenty-five states have adopted parts of it. While the RULPA may bring greater uniformity to the field, states continue to deviate from the uniform acts. In this chapter, limited partnerships are discussed within the framework of the ULPA, but changes introduced by the RULPA are also noted.

Finally, it should be recognized that RULPA, like other uniform laws, is neither federal law nor applicable to the federal government. RULPA governs limited partnerships within a given state.

Characteristics

Limited partnerships have characteristics of both corporations and partnerships. A *limited partnership* consists of one or more general partners who actively manage the business and one or more limited partners who, by law, may do little more than invest in it. *General partners* have the same powers and duties as a partner in a *general partnership*, discussed in Chapters 16 and 17. Although *limited partners* have a role similar to that of shareholders, they have considerably less ability to influence business policy.

The general partners function as both the officers and the board of directors, but they have the unlimited liability of partners. (A general partner may also be a limited partner, but this added status has no effect on liability.) Limited partnerships tend to be organized to undertake a particular venture, like drilling for oil on a specific leasehold, erecting an office building, or operating a restaurant.

Limited partnerships were dealt a severe blow as a business entity by the Tax Reform Act of 1986 (commonly called the TRA). Since limited partners are not actively involved with the management of the limited partnership, their income is now categorized under the TRA as "passive income." This means that any losses cannot offset other forms of "active income" such as salaries, although the losses may be carried forward indefinitely. This has hit the real estate industry particularly hard, since before the TRA much commercial real estate was, as stated above, owned by limited partnerships. It was common, for example, for professionals with high incomes, like doctors, dentists, and lawyers, to invest as limited partners and be shielded from personal liability while reaping substantial tax benefits through interest deductions and depreciation on the buildings. Indeed, many economists and others partially blame the real estate collapse and deflation of the late 1980s because of the new tax treatment imposed on limited partnerships.

MECHANICS OF LIMITED PARTNERSHIP FORMATION

Like corporations, limited partnerships can only come into existence by meeting statutory requirements. If these are not observed, a court may find that the partners have formed a general partnership, and the limited partners would lose their limited liability.

Compliance with Statute

The ULPA provides, "A limited partnership is formed if there has been substantial compliance in good faith with the requirements [for its creation]" [ULPA §2(2)]. One of those requirements was the filing of a *certificate of limited partnership* with the secretary of state for the state in which the limited partnership was organized.

The RULPA adopted the substantial compliance rule, but it added a *condition precedent:* the certificate must be filed with the secretary of state before the limited partnership can come into existence [RULPA §201(b)]. The following case contrasts the ULPA and RULPA filing requirements.

Franklin v. Rigg

143 Ga. App. 60, 237 S.E.2d 526 (1977)

FACTS

Dimentia Corp. and its president, Ronald Wilson, had contracted to buy land from Rigg. In November 1973, Dimentia and Wilson, as general partners, executed a certificate of limited partnership with Franklin and others as limited partners. In December 1973, Wilson and Rigg closed. The deed and the promissory note for the purchase price described "Dimentia Limited, a limited partnership" as the buyer. On April 1, 1974, the limited partnership defaulted on the first installment on the note. In a letter dated April 18, Rigg demanded payment of the entire debt. On April 19, Dimentia Ltd. filed its certificate of limited partnership. Rigg obtained a judgment against Dimentia Corp. and Wilson, from whom he could not collect. Rigg then sued the limited partners, alleging they were liable on the note as general partners because of the delay in filing the certificate. The trial court found for Rigg.

ISSUE

Was the limited partnership in existence when Rigg demanded full payment?

DECISION

Yes. Reversed. The RULPA provides, "A limited partnership is formed at the time of the filing of the certificate of limited partnership in the office of the Secretary of State" [RULPA §202(2)]. Georgia, however, had not adopted the RULPA. Under the ULPA, where there has been substantial compliance with the law, limited partners will not be liable as general partners. Late filing in and of itself will not enlarge their liability. Here, Rigg was not harmed by the late filing. Rigg dealt initially with a corporation and its president, who became the general partners of the limited partnership. In addition, the documents plainly indicate Rigg was dealing with a limited partnership.

The Certificate's Contents

The key element in *Franklin* is that Rigg did not rely on the records of the secretary of state for information about the entity with which he was dealing. As in the filing of a corporation's articles, the purpose of the certificate's filing is to place those dealing with the limited partnership on notice as to its existence and powers.

Creditors need this information because, as with corporations, the range of sources to which the creditor can look for satisfaction is much narrower than with general partnerships. For that reason, limited partnerships may not be created with the same informality as general partnerships.

The certificate filed with the secretary of state must contain the following information about the limited partnership:

- Its name, which must include the words "Limited Partnership" but not the surname of a limited partner unless one of the general partners has the same name [ULPA §5(1)]
- Its purpose
- The location of its principal place of business
- All partners' names and addresses
- Its duration
- The contributions made by each partner, including descriptions and agreed-upon values of property contributed in lieu of cash
- Whether the general partners may admit additional limited partners and, if so, under what conditions
- Whether a limited partner may sell an interest and substitute another as a limited partner
- Whether the remaining general partners have the right to continue the business on the death, retirement, or insanity of a general partner.

Amendments

Under some circumstances, the limited partnership must amend its certificate. Any change in the amount or character of any partner's contribution requires an amendment. The admission of a new partner, the withdrawal of a partner, and the continuation of business after the withdrawal of a general partner also require certificate amendments. In the absence of amendments, creditors lack notice of these changes. For example, without the filing of an amended certificate, the liability and apparent agency of a retired general partner would continue unchanged.

False Statements in Certificate

Any party to the certificate—whether a limited or a general partner—who knows it contains a false statement will be liable to persons who suffer a loss because they relied on that statement. Parties will be liable if they were aware of the falsehood at the time of the certificate's signing or if they became aware of it before third parties relied on it.

A party to the certificate who later learns it contains a false statement has a duty to have it canceled or amended. Filing a petition in court to have the certificate canceled or amended insulates a party from liability. Suppose a limited partner discovers that the certificate grossly overstates the assets of the limited partnership. If a creditor has already relied on the false statement, the limited partner is not liable. But suppose that after discovering the falsification, the limited partner does nothing and a creditor subsequently relies on the certificate's representations. In that case, the limited partner would be personally liable.

Application of Securities Laws

Under both state and federal laws, the sale of a limited partnership interest is considered to be a sale of a security. The promoters of the limited partnership or the limited partnership itself, if it is in existence, may have to receive state or federal clearance before marketing limited partnership interests. Also, the law may require that the promoters or the limited partnership disclose certain information about the investment to prospective purchasers before they buy. Among the information to be disclosed, for example, is the business history of the general partner. These requirements and others are examined in Chapter 23.

THE ROLE OF THE GENERAL PARTNER

General partners essentially have the same duties, obligations, agency authority, and liabilities as partners in an ordinary partnership would have if there were no limited partners [ULPA §9, RULPA §403].

Management

At the outset of a venture, general partners play a role like that of a corporation's promoters. Once the limited partnership is formed, they function as the managers of the business.

General partners are potentially liable for the entire amount of the partnership's debt. The law imposes unlimited liability on them because investors and creditors normally place great emphasis on the management role of general partners in evaluating the investment opportunity or business risk.

Capital Contributions and Compensation

A general partner is not required to make a capital contribution. A general partner may contribute capital in the form of services or his or her name, rather than cash or property. In the field of tax shelters, where companies like Callon Petroleum may act as a general partner for a dozen or more limited partnerships, the name and track record of the general partner can prove quite valuable.

Usually, general partners receive a percentage of ownership in compensation for assembling the limited partnership. Also, general partners often receive salaries and sometimes a percentage of the venture's profits. General partners may purchase limited partnership interests in ventures they manage.

Fiduciary Duties

General partners owe both the other general partners and the limited partners the same fiduciary duties as a partner in an ordinary partnership owes. The next case explains these duties.

Boxer v. Husky Oil Co.

429 A.2d 995 (Del. Ch. 1981)

FACTS   The limited partnership agreement of Husky Exploration Ltd. granted the general partner, Husky Petroleum Corp., an option to purchase the interests of the limited partners. The general partner could assign this option to another. On the date the partnership terminated, the assets of the limited partnership included an interest in Husky Canadian Exploration Co. and an interest in Husky Minerals Ltd. The general partner assigned the partnership's interest in Husky Canadian—which it valued at $10 million—to Husky Oil Operations, Ltd. It assigned the partnership's interest in Husky Minerals Ltd.—valued at $78,480—to Husky Oil Co. Husky Oil Co. owned the general partner and controlled Husky Canadian. The limited partners brought suit, claiming the general partner breached its fiduciary duty to them by selling their interests at an inadequate price.

ISSUE

Did the circumstances of the sale of the assets of Husky Exploration indicate that the general partner breached its fiduciary duties to the limited partners?

DECISION

Yes. Judgment for the limited partners. The general partner in a limited partnership has all the rights and powers, and is subject to all the restrictions and liabilities, of a partner in a partnership without limited partners [ULPA §9]. The UPA makes a partner accountable as a fiduciary [UPA §21]. The general partner in a limited partnership has the same duty to exercise the utmost good faith, fairness, and loyalty toward the limited partners. Here, Husky Oil stood on both sides of the transaction.

As indicated earlier, a major difference between limited and general partnerships is that general partners in limited partnerships quite often are general partners in other limited partnerships, particularly in the oil and gas, real estate, and equipment-leasing fields. Multiple general partnerships may breach the fiduciary duties of the general partner if they are not fully disclosed to the limited partners before they invest.

THE ROLE OF THE LIMITED PARTNER

The principal role of limited partners in the venture is to make financial contributions. Like shareholders, they have virtually no voice in management and few other responsibilities. While each limited partnership interest may represent an equal share in profits and losses— up to the amount of capital contributed per interest—those interests usually are not in the same percentage as the interests of the general partners.

Agency Authority and Fiduciary Duties

Limited partners have no actual or apparent authority to represent the limited partnership. The general partners are its only agents and managers.

Like a shareholder, a limited partner does not owe fiduciary duties to the partnership or the other limited partners. Suppose David owns a limited partnership interest in a Mama & Mia's pizza shop. Without violating any fiduciary duties, he may also own a limited partnership interest in a Pervasive Pizza outlet, Mama & Mia's main competitor.

Capital Contributions

Under the ULPA, the capital contribution of a limited partner must consist of cash or other property, not services [ULPA §4]. In exchange for a limited partnership interest in an oil and gas partnership, Alvin may contribute the use of a drilling rig but not his services as a master driller.

The RULPA varies the ULPA by permitting limited partners to contribute services either past or future. The certificate of limited partnership must state the value placed on these services [RULPA §101]. A limited partner's capital contribution creates a property right in the limited partnership. The contribution must be indicated in the limited partnership certificate. As the next case implies, no reason—including death—excuses limited partners from contributing what they pledge, in the form of either the services or their stated value in cash.

Indiana Mortgage & Realty Investors v. Spira-Mart

115 Mich. App. 141, 320 N.W.2d 320 (1982)

FACTS Spira-Mart, a limited partnership, defaulted on its loan from Indiana Mortgage. Spira-Mart had no assets, so Indiana Mortgage turned to its limited partners. The certificate of limited partnership indicated that three of the four limited partners had contributed $50,000 each, while the fourth had contributed $100,000. In reality, each contributed approximately one-third of the amount pledged. The limited partners contended Spira-Mart had canceled their remaining obligations. However, the certificate was never amended to reflect the waiver. The trial court found for Indiana Mortgage.

ISSUE Are limited partners liable for the amount of their stated contributions to the partnership?

DECISION Yes. Affirmed.

> [For] the purposes of determining the rights of plaintiff, a judgment creditor of Spira-Mart, the differences between the capital contributions as listed in the certificate of limited partnership and as actually made by limited partners were obligations owed to Spira-Mart. . . .
>
> [Plaintiff] extended credit to the limited partnership . . . after the filing of the certificate. . . . The certificate was not canceled or amended to reflect the . . . waivers and assignments. By its terms, [ULPA §17] preserves the rights of partnership creditors in plaintiff's position to enforce the liability of limited partners . . . regardless of a waiver or compromise of that liability.

Rights of Limited Partners

The rights of limited partners are essentially the same as those of general partners and are similar to a partner's rights under the UPA. Thus, limited partners have a right to receive the profits and compensation specified in the limited partnership agreement. They also have a right to reasonable access to the partnership's books for the purpose of inspecting and copying them. When appropriate, they have a right to a formal accounting.

Assignability of Interest

Limited partners may assign their interests to anyone at any time. However, general partners may not admit new general or limited partners without the unanimous consent of the present limited partners unless they are authorized to do so in the certificate [ULPA §19]. Without this agreement, the assignee cannot assert the rights of a limited partner. Therefore, an assignee may not require an account of the partnership's transactions and may not inspect the partnership's books. An assignee may share only in the profits or other compensation and the return of capital contributions.

CONTROL

A major flaw in the ULPA is its lack of a definition of the extent to which limited partners may be involved in the venture's management. Instead, it states: "A limited partner shall not become liable as a general partner unless, in addition to the exercise of his rights and powers as a limited partner, he takes part in the control of the business" [ULPA §7]. The ULPA does not define "control." However, it clearly states the price of exercising control: loss of limited liability.

Involvement in Management

The courts have agreed that participation in the day-to-day management of the firm constitutes the exercise of control. For instance, if Carol is a limited partner in an equipment-leasing venture, she can talk about the firm's plans with the general partners. However, she probably will be exercising control if she directs what equipment it buys.

Beyond the relatively clear case of day-to-day management, courts in ULPA states have not agreed on what amounts to control. Jurisdictions have reached different answers to questions like:

- What is the difference between making "suggestions" to the general partners and exercising "control"?
- When may limited partners vote on matters affecting the partnership's management?
- Under what circumstances may limited partners exercise a veto over the actions of the general partners?

All that can be said is that under the ULPA, the answers to these questions depend on the facts of each case.

Under the ULPA, a limited partner may do business with the limited partnership without exercising control. The ULPA even provides that a limited partner lending money to the partnership will be treated as an outside creditor in dissolution [ULPA §13]. Partnership employees may be limited partners so long as they hold nonmanagement positions. If Carol works as a bookkeeper for the firm sponsoring the limited partnership, she probably can be a limited partner.

The following case points out that wielding some control does not mean that the limited partner will necessarily become a general partner.

Alzado v. Blinder, Robinson & Co., Inc.

752 P.2d 544 (1988)

FACTS   A boxing match was scheduled between Mohammed Ali, former heavy weight champion, and Lyle Alzado, former National Football League star. A limited partnership, Combat Associates, was set up to finance the match. Combat Promotions, Inc., a corporation, was formed to be general partner, and Blinder, Robinson & Co, Inc., was the limited partner. The boxing match proved to be a financial disaster. Alzado sued Blinder, Robinson for damages, claiming it exercised sufficient control over the fight to be considered a general partner and therefore was liable under the contract between him and Combat Associates. Alzado's argument relied on the following facts: Blinder used its Denver office as a ticket outlet, entertained at two parties to promote the fight, and furnished a meeting room for the limited partnership meetings; also, Blinder personally participated in media events to promote the match. The trial court ruled for Alzado, but the ruling was reversed on appeal.

ISSUE

Did Blinder, Robinson & Co., the limited partner, exercise the control necessary to be a general partner?

DECISION

No. Affirmed. A limited partner can be liable as a general partner if it exercises control over the limited partnership. What constitutes the necessary control is determined on a case-by-case basis. Courts look to such factors as the partnership's purpose, the administrative activities taken on, how the partnership functioned, and how frequent the limited partners' control activities were. Blinder may have helped in promoting the fight. However, it made no accounting, investment, or other financial decisions, and it did not discharge any other functions of management or control.

It is interesting to note that the general partner in this limited partnership was a corporation. This is commonly done to shield the general partner from personal liability. In these cases, who becomes liable if the general and limited partners' investment is exhausted? Generally, creditors require a guarantor for the general partner if it is a corporation. In this case, the event was partially guaranteed by Alzado, who, after losing a great deal of money, was attempting to recoup part of his loss by demonstrating that Blinder, Robinson was a general partner.

RULPA Changes

RULPA §303(b) permits more active involvement by limited partners but not control. Without losing the protection of limited liability, a limited partner may:

- Be a contractor for or an agent or employee of the limited partnership of a general partner

- Consult with or advise the general partner about partnership business
- Act as a surety for the partnership
- Vote on changes in the partnership agreement, dissolution and winding up of the partnership, changes in the nature of the business, removal of a general partner, sale of all or substantially all the assets of the partnership not in the ordinary course of business, and incurrence of debt not in the ordinary course of business.

WITHDRAWAL AND DISSOLUTION

Withdrawal by Limited Partners

Unlike partners under the UPA, limited partners may withdraw from a limited partnership without causing a dissolution. Withdrawing limited partners may demand return of a capital contribution, so long as they give 6 months' notice and the partnership agreement does not forbid it. The withdrawing partner is not entitled to interest on his or her capital contribution. A limited partner may not withdraw his capital contribution unless there is sufficient limited partnership property to pay all its general contractors.

Causes of Dissolution

A limited partner has the right to demand a dissolution and the winding up of the partnership. Also, the withdrawal, bankruptcy, death, insanity, or substitution of a general—but not a limited—partner causes a dissolution unless the other general and limited partners agree otherwise or unless the certificate provides otherwise. The withdrawal of all the limited partners also causes a dissolution.

Both limited and general partners may seek a court decree of dissolution for the same reasons as a partner in a general partnership may. A court may dissolve a limited partnership "whenever it is not reasonably practicable to carry on the business in conformity with the partnership agreement" [RULPA §802]. The next case shows how courts deal with such a situation.

Mandell v. Centrum Frontier Corp.

86 Ill. App. 3d 347, 407 N.E.2d 821 (1980)

FACTS   The Mandell brothers were limited partners in a partnership Centrum organized. The partnership's sole asset was a fifty-six story apartment building which the partners had agreed to convert to condominiums. However, disagreements between the limited and general partners prevented not only the building's conversion but also its sale. The Mandells brought suit and convinced the trial court to dissolve the partnership and order the building's sale.

ISSUE   Is dissolution the appropriate remedy when partners cannot agree on the course of the business?

DECISION   Yes. Affirmed. When a deadlock defeats the purposes of a business relationship, a court can terminate the business relationship. As under the UPA, the established procedure in winding up a limited partnership is to convert its assets into cash, discharge its liabilities, and distribute the surplus, if any, to its members. If the partners cannot agree on a method of liquidation, a public judicial sale is the only appropriate method.

Distribution of Assets

The winding up of a limited partnership results in a distribution of assets which is somewhat different from the distribution specified in the UPA [ULPA §23]. The order of priority is:

1. Loans by limited partners and outside creditors
2. Liabilities to the limited partners with respect to profits
3. Liabilities to the limited partners with respect to capital contributions

4. Liabilities to the general partners other than for capital contributions or profits
5. Liabilities to the general partners with respect to profits
6. Liabilities to the general partners with respect to capital contributions

CONCLUSION

Unlike general partnerships, limited partnerships are not a business form that can evolve through dealings between individuals. Forming one requires close attention to the applicable state statute, including the filing of the certificate of limited partnership. Thus, a partner in a general partnership whose partners agree that she will have a reduced role in the business is not a limited partner.

Limited partnerships are a statutory variation on a partnership law unknown in the common law. The major differences between general and limited partnerships lie in the treatment of the limited partners, as you can see in Figure 18.1. Limited partnerships are used mainly for investment purposes. The form's advantages are limited personal liability for the investor who does not want control and treatment as a partnership for federal tax purposes. Although limited partnerships are not as old a form as corporations, the may be thought of as a kind of way station between partnerships and corporations—our next topic in this unit.

A NOTE TO FUTURE CPA CANDIDATES

CPA candidates often comment that the emphasis upon limited partnerships in the business entities portion of the exam seems disproportionate. We tend to agree. However, it is the reality and you must be sure to understand the basic rules concerning limited partnerships.

We believe that three comparative figures of our book should be well understood before

	GENERAL PARTNER	LIMITED PARTNER
Right to take part in control?	YES	No
Fiduciary duties?	YES	No
Agency authority?	YES	No
Death, bankruptcy, or insanity cause dissolution?	YES	No
Right to transfer interest without consent?	No	No
Subject to personal liability for partnership debts?	YES	No
Right to reasonable access to partnership books?	YES	YES

Figure 18.1 General Partners and Limited Partners Compared.

taking the CPA exam: Figure 18.1, 22.1, and 22.2. The latter two figures compare limited partnerships to other forms of business entities, a common emphasis on the CPA exam.

Keep in mind the basics of a limited partnership. You must form a limited partnership, like a corporation, through a filing with the state. Limited partners have limited liability so long as they do not cross the line of active managerial decision making. Unlike a corporation, a limited partnership cannot be forever. Remember that it will be dissolved upon the death of a general partner and for other causes discussed in this chapter.

KEY WORDS

certificate of limited partnership (397)
general partner (396)
limited partner (396)
limited partnership (396)

DISCUSSION QUESTIONS

1. What is a limited partnership? How does it differ from a general partnership?
2. What model act applies to limited partnerships? What is its goal? Has it achieved that goal?
3. Were limited partnerships possible at common law? What must you have to create a limited partnership in any state?
4. Briefly describe the role of the limited partner.
5. What legal requirements must be met in order to form a limited partnership?
6. How does RULPA alter the ULPA contribution rule?
7. What role may limited partners take in the management of the partnership? What happens if they exceed this? How has RULPA clarified the matter of ''control''?
8. How do the rights of a limited partner compare with the rights of a partner in a general partnership?
9. How might a limited partnership be dissolved?
10. What rights, if any, does a limited partner have in leaving a limited partnership?

CASE PROBLEMS

1. Fox, Harrison, and Dodge are the general partners of Great Expectations, a limited partnership. The general partners unanimously vote to add two more general partners and to sell additional limited partnerships to the public. The limited partners are not consulted, and the limited partnership certificate is silent as to whether the current general partners have the power to take these actions. Is the vote to admit the new general partners effective? What about the new limited partners? Explain.
2. Stanley, a retired movie star, purchased a limited partnership interest in Terrific Movie Productions. Terrific has three general partners, who also purchased limited partnership interests. Terrific has 1000 limited partners located throughout the United States. May Stanley permit his name to be used in connection with the business? May the general partners own limited partnership interests? Explain.
3. Beth McGregor and Ginger Parrish, partners, wish to significantly expand their partnership import business. Their business advisor has suggested that they consider a limited partnership form of business, since they could retain control as general partners but offer investment opportunities to limited partners. Can the partners form a limited partnership simply by declaring such status and selling limited partnership interests? Does a limited partnership seem to make sense for them? Explain.
4. Ross Wiegert, Greg Smith, and Mark Massey were limited partners in Savanna Pizza. Mark was also the general and managing partner. Because of a bad storm the usual delivery drivers failed to report to work. Ross happened to be in the restaurant and agreed to make a round of deliveries. While doing so, Ross negligently struck a car driven by Alvin White. White has sued Savanna Pizza, Ross, Greg, and Mark. Ross, Greg, and Mark all claim they have no personal liability exposure, as they each have limited partnership protection. Is Ross correct? Greg? Mark? Explain.
5. Dave Schmidt was a limited partner in both Red Badger Co. and Blue Fox Co., limited partnerships that are both involved in mortar mix manufacturing. Red Badger hired Schmidt to become general manager after Red Badger began losing significant sales to Blue Fox. Primarily because of Schmidt's new management ideas, Red Badger made a very strong recovery against Blue Fox. Blue Fox has now brought a legal action to divest Schmidt of his Blue Fox ownership interest. Blue Fox claims that Schmidt breached fiduciary duties that he owed to it. Schmidt has responded that limited partners owe no fiduciary duties to the limited partnership and that he still is simply a limited partner in both businesses. Would a court agree that Schmidt is simply a limited partner in both businesses? Disregarding any possible antitrust considerations, is a court likely to find that Schmidt has breached any duties owed to Blue Fox? Explain.

6. Barb Carroll, Bob Collier, and Jeff McKinney have been partners in Lebanon Bike Works, a retail motorcycle shop. The shop has fifteen employees, but the partners represent the only management persons. The three partners run a successful business even though they have been consistently unable to develop and/or adhere to a well-defined managerial approach. The partners have become quite concerned about their potential personal liability from lawsuits involving three-wheel off-road vehicles which they sell in great numbers. The partners cannot agree on the form of business that they should adopt. They do agree that they very much like the tax advantages of a general partnership. Carroll has recommended a limited partnership. Assuming all business ownership entities and elections are possible, would this be a good choice? Explain.

7. Joe Heumann rounded up some old college friends to form a limited partnership to restore and operate the Raub Hotel. Joe became the general partner and manager. The hotel enjoyed a fine reputation for quality until Joe booked professional wrestling matches in the hotel's ballroom. One limited partner, David Pacelli, became so angered that he demanded the immediate return of his capital contribution with interest. Another, Jack Gaggini, remained a limited partner but purchased the adjacent Griffith House Hotel. Joe claims that since the Raub Hotel limited partnership agreement is silent as to repurchase of interests, it has no duty to do so. Correct? Joe also claims that Jack has breached his fiduciary duties by going into competition with Raub Hotel. Correct? Explain.

8. Steve Persinger, a limited partner in Geneva Limited, wishes to withdraw from the partnership. The partnership has suffered financial setbacks the past few years and expects to post a loss this year. Persinger claims that his right to a return of capital is not conditional on the financial strength of the limited partnership and that he has a right to interest until paid. The general partner disagrees and has refused to return Persinger's capital contribution, since there is not sufficient limited partnership property to cover full claims of its general creditors. Is the general creditor correct? Assuming the limited partnership should be dissolved, would Steve's return of capital come before the repayment of a partnership loan owed to a general creditor? Explain.

Until the mid-nineteenth century, forming a corporation, or *incorporating*, required an act of a state legislature. One of that century's great legal reforms was to make corporate status available to anyone fulfilling specific statutory requirements. Forming a corporation became a function of private organization followed by registration with, and regulation by, the state—although the federal government now regulates some activities, particularly those relating to financing.

With some very minor exceptions, all U.S. corporations are incorporated under state laws.* As with partnership laws, fifty jurisdictions make for fifty different treatments. However, major portions of the Model Business Corporation Act (MBCA)—which provides the focus for our discussion—have been adopted in

---

* Some federal, nonstate jurisdictions do grant corporate charters, e.g., District of Columbia, U.S. Virgin Islands, Commonwealth of Puerto Rico.

thirty-seven states, and it has influenced the laws of every jurisdiction since its introduction in 1946.

In 1984, the MBCA received a thorough overhaul. The Revised Model Business Corporation Act (RMBCA), which is under consideration for adoption in nearly a third of the states, will be our focus here. It is important to note that some important states—including California and Delaware—have not adopted the MBCA in any form. Still, the MBCA has profoundly influenced the law of even these states.

WHAT AND WHO ARE CORPORATIONS?

Today, the question of whether an entity is a corporation rarely comes up because contemporary statutes, as we will see below, make the matter so clear-cut. However, this question did arise in the next case, which outlines the hallmarks of a corporation.

In re. Armed Forces Cooperative Insuring Ass'n.

5 Kan. App. 2d 787, 625 P.2d 11 (1981)

FACTS   Since 1887, the Armed Forces Cooperative Insuring Association (AFCIA) has operated a mail order insurance business from the Fort Leavenworth reservation. A nonprofit organization which limits its membership to active and retired officers, it has no certificate of incorporation. Its members annually elect a governing board, but the board members serve at the pleasure of Fort Leavenworth's commanding officer. AFCIA has no authorized or issued stock. It distributes income only as a credit against premiums due from its members. The county attempted to tax AFCIA's personal property under a statute permitting it to tax corporate property within its boundaries. AFCIA appealed.

ISSUE   Is AFCIA a corporation?

DECISION   No. Judgment for AFCIA. Until the state grants authority to incorporate, there can be no corporation. AFCIA never applied for this status nor did it pretend to exercise it. The most commonly accepted corporate characteristics, few of which AFCIA had, include: the use of an adopted corporate name; issued and paid for transferable units of ownership interest held by stockholders; a board of directors, elected and vested with powers delegated by the stockholders, which manages the business of the corporation; *bylaws*—rules governing a corporation's operation—adopted by the stockholders, or by the board of directors if the stockholders delegated that power to them; officers elected by the board of directors; and the conducting of business in the name and on behalf of the corporation.

A *corporation* is an entity which comes into existence when, upon an application by one or more persons, the secretary of state of a state issues a *certificate of incorporation*, and whose owners' liability for its debts ordinarily is limited to the amount of their investment. Formulating a more specific definition of "corporation" is virtually impossible because, as we will see in the next three chapters, this business form takes many different shapes.

By law, a corporation is an independent entity, a "person." It has a life of its own, separate and apart from its owners, officers, and employees. Unlike a partnership, its life does not depend on the existence of any individual or group. If a corporation's sole owner dies, no dissolution occurs. The corporation's life continues.

Still, without people—shareholders, directors, officers, and employees—the corporation could not exist. Each of these groups has its own relationship with the corporation. These relationships are the principal subjects of Chapters 19 to 21 and 23 and 24.

A clear discussion of these relationships requires isolating these groups and their functions. However, particularly in small corporations, the distinctions between them tend to blur. Quite often one person will be a shareholder, a director, and an officer. In some large corporations, all employees together hold substantial quantities of stock.

The interests of these groups can conflict. For example, an officer-shareholder may oppose the other shareholders' plan to sell the company because she would lose her job. Or, shareholders may want the board to declare a dividend, which the board opposes because it believes the company needs the money for research and development. Often, as the cases in these chapters reveal, competing groups resort to the courts to define the relationships between them and the corporation. In the next case, a federal appellate court had to deal with the relationship between an officer-shareholder and the corporation in almost unique circumstances.

Palazzo v. Gulf Oil Corp.

764 F.2d 1381 (11th Cir. 1985)

FACTS   In 1978, when they filed their antitrust suit against Gulf Oil Corp., Frank and Tina Palazzo were respectively president and vice president of the third plaintiff, Advanced Sales Corp. By 1981, when the case was set for trial, Frank and Tina had divorced, and their lawyer had withdrawn as counsel for both the corporation and the individual plaintiffs. Upon receiving counsel's notice of withdrawal, the court ordered Advanced to obtain substitute counsel and notified the individual plaintiffs of their right to proceed *pro se*, i.e., as their own counsel. Frank, who was not a lawyer, moved for permission to appear as "counsel *pro se* for the plaintiffs," including Advanced. He noted in his motion that Tina had assigned all her claims to him as part of their property settlement and that, as the largest creditor and shareholder of Advanced, he was entitled to represent the corporation's claims, too. For the next 2 years, the trial court repeatedly told Frank to find counsel for Advanced. Finally, the court dismissed the complaint.

ISSUE

Does a corporation's largest creditor, who is also a shareholder and an officer, have a right to represent the corporation in a legal action?

DECISION

No. Affirmed. By their natures, corporations and partnerships cannot represent themselves; they can act only through agents. In legal actions, their only proper representatives are licensed attorneys, not laypersons, no matter how close an individual's association is with the entity.

TYPES OF CORPORATIONS

The word "corporation" immediately brings to mind companies like American Express, Chrysler, IBM, and the like. However, the most common corporations are small businesses, such as your neighborhood drugstore. Corporations come not only in various sizes but also in various types. In several instances, the names of these categories imply precisely the opposite of the true nature of the corporations within them. But whatever their classification, virtually all share the characteristics outlined in *Armed Forces Cooperative Insuring Ass'n*.

Public Corporations

Public corporations are created by acts of Congress or of state legislatures. They serve a special purpose, like the Corporation for Public Broadcasting, which funds public radio and television, and usually are not expected to make a profit. Public corporations retain many characteristics of government units, such as management which answers ultimately only to a government-appointed board, not to stock-holders. For instance, many public school districts are incorporated.

In contrast, a corporation whose stock is publicly traded on a stock exchange is a private corporation whose goal is profits. This unit focuses on private corporations.

Quasi-Public or Public Service Corporations

Quasi-public or *public service* corporations also have misleading names. Also called *public utilities*, these are private for-profit corporations which receive privileges from the government in return for providing special services to the public. Examples include electric power companies, natural gas distribution companies, and telephone companies. Their privileges may include insulation from competition from other companies providing the same service. Public service companies, too, fall outside the scope of this book.

Private Corporations

A *private corporation* is one organized by private parties, not by a public body. Private corporations are by far the most numerous. And, they themselves fall into a number of sub-categories.

Nonprofit. A *nonprofit* corporation is usually a charitable entity, such as a hospital, college, or religious congregation. Typically, non-profit corporations are headed by boards of trustees—not directors—and do not have shareholders. Although they are often run like businesses whose goals are profits, they have characteristics requiring special treatment which are outside the scope of this book.

For-profit. Corporations established to make profits for their shareholders are called *for-profit* corporations. These are our focus.

For-profit corporations may be classified as either publicly traded or non-publicly traded. A *publicly traded* corporation is one whose ownership interests, called *stock* or *shares*, are bought and sold in interstate commerce. The Securities & Exchange Commission, which we will discuss in Chapter 23, regulates the issuing and trading of stock in interstate commerce.

Publicly traded corporations tend to be the largest and best-known corporations. But, non-publicly traded corporations are many times more numerous. The most common type is the *close* or *closely held* corporation. Such a corporation usually has fewer than thirty owners—called *shareholders*—who often are friends or are related to one another. The MBCA does not recognize the close corporation. However, many states have enacted statutes which permit shareholders in close corporations to function like partners while remaining a corporation.

An increasingly important form of non-publicly traded corporation is the *professional corporation*, a corporation whose shareholders have joined together to offer legal, medical, architectural, or other professional services. Virtually unknown before 1961, this business form was created to permit professionals to establish the kinds of pension and retirement plans available to corporate employees. Today,

all states have statutes which permit at least some professionals to form corporations. Ironically, changes in the federal tax laws in the 1980s broadening the availability of Individual Retirement Accounts (IRAs) and Keogh plans eliminated much of the rationale for professional corporations. In regard to malpractice liability, most states hold that practitioners are still individually liable for their own malpractice.

Our focus in this chapter and the next two will be on MBCA requirements which affect virtually all corporations. We will examine close corporations and other variations on the normal corporate form in Chapter 22. Figure 19.1 charts the characteristics of the different types of corporations.

Domestic and Foreign Corporations

People who incorporate do so under the laws of a particular state. A court in one jurisdiction will refer to a corporation created under the laws of another as a *foreign corporation*. For example, Northwest Energy Company is a Utah corporation. To the Utah courts it is a domestic corporation, but to the California courts it is a foreign corporation.

When a foreign corporation wishes to do business regularly in a state, it usually must obtain a certificate of authority to do business with that state's secretary of state. Foreign corporations which fail to file may not be able to enforce contracts they made in that state with its residents.

Application of the long-arm statute. Even if that penalty did not exist, it would be important for a foreign corporation to know when the courts would consider the corporation to be doing business in a state.

You will recall from Chapter 2 that every state has a *long-arm statute* which permits the state courts to assert personal jurisdiction over individuals and business entities that have more

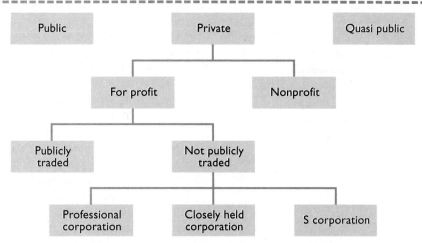

Figure 19.1 Types of Corporations. An S corporation is one which elects under the federal tax laws to be taxed like a partnership. This form is discussed in Chapter 22.

than minimal contacts with the state.* In practical terms, a long-arm statute can force a defendant to appear in courts in a quite distant state. Such appearances can be extremely costly and can put a defendant at a tactical disadvantage. As might be imagined, the extent of long-arm jurisdiction has been much litigated. However, today the most minimal contacts are considered sufficient, particularly where businesses are concerned.

The RMBCA view of doing business in a state. RMBCA §15.01 attempts to redress this balance somewhat. It offers a list of examples of activities that do *not* constitute sufficient contacts with a state for personal jurisdiction. For example, merely participating in interstate commerce will not suffice. Thus, if the Maine outdoor outfitter L. L. Bean sends a catalog to Kentucky residents, that action alone will not amount to doing business in Kentucky.

Conducting an isolated transaction which is completed within 30 days will not confer jurisdiction on a state's courts unless the transaction is one of a series of similar transactions. Suppose a prefabricated-home manufacturer is located in Oregon. It goes to California to build a house, which it does within 30 days. If the California house does not represent an isolated event, that state's courts will have jurisdiction over the company.

The RMBCA would also exempt sales contracts which are solicited within the state but which must be accepted outside its boundaries. Thus, the sales representative of a Minnesota pharmaceutical house could solicit orders in Iowa without subjecting the company to the jurisdiction of the Iowa courts so long as the actual acceptance took place in Minnesota.

FORMATION: THE PROMOTERS' ROLE

Promoters develop a business idea and take the initial steps to organize and finance a corpora-

---

* The commerce clause of the U.S. Constitution [Article 1 §8(3)] limits a state's power to legislate in this area. The commerce clause is discussed in Chapter 43.

tion. Anyone can become a promoter, and no set number of promoters is required. If Allan and Belinda decide to form a corporation to manufacture computers, they become promoters when they begin developing ideas and negotiating contracts in anticipation of incorporation.

Organizing the Corporation

After developing a business plan, the promoters assemble investors by selling subscriptions. *Subscriptions* are contracts to purchase shares. When promoters sell subscriptions, what they are really selling is the concept behind the corporation. Subscribers buy into the idea because they see an opportunity to make money. (As we will see in Chapter 22, the promoters must comply—when selling subscriptions—with federal and, if applicable, state securities laws.)

The subscribers may consist of the promoters alone or may include third parties. Subscribers may not revoke their subscription agreements for 6 months unless the agreements specifically state otherwise or unless all other subscribers consent [RMBCA §6.20]. If the subscription is oversubscribed, the corporation must prorate the shares.

While arranging the corporation's financing is probably their most important function, the promoters also negotiate the contracts necessary to enable the corporation to begin business. For example, Allan and Belinda might lease a building for the company's plant.

Finally, the promoters must arrange to incorporate the business. They retain a lawyer to prepare the articles of incorporation, the bylaws, and any other documents which state the rules by which the corporation will operate. These documents are described below.

The Problem of Stolen Ideas

Promoters face a highly practical problem in selling a new corporation: someone may steal their ideas. This presents a particular risk when the promoters lack sufficient capital to start the corporation themselves.

Of course, the promoters may sue someone who steals their ideas, but proving the theft of an idea is often impossible. Even if it can be proven, because of the impossibility of estimating the profits of a business which never got started, a court will probably not award substantial damages.

In an effort to protect their concepts, promoters may try to limit the information they disclose to potential subscribers. This tactic risks later charges by subscribers of failing to disclose information necessary to make an informed judgment about investing—a breach of the promoters' fiduciary duties. It may also cause the promoter to violate federal Securities and Exchange Commission rules, discussed in Chapter 23.

The Promoters' Fiduciary Duties

Promoters owe a duty of full disclosure and fair dealing to other promoters, subscribers, and the corporation which is to be formed. They must disclose any potential conflicts of interest. Allan, for instance, must reveal to Belinda and all potential subscribers if he is a partner in another computer company.

Promoters may not make secret profits from their arrangements for the corporation. They may profit from a contribution of property or services to the corporation only if, after the corporation is formed, an independent board of directors approves the contribution or all the shareholders approve the transaction. Suppose Belinda, as a promoter, arranges to sell the new corporation a building which cost her $125,000. She sets its price at $200,000, its fair market value, and an independent board approves the transaction. The board's approval minimizes the possibility of a successful action against her for breaching her fiduciary duty. The next case illustrates what can happen if the promoters fail to follow these rules.

Whaler Motor Inn, Inc. v. Parsons

372 Mass. 620, 363 N.E.2d 493 (1977)

FACTS For more than a year, the promoters of the Whaler Motor Inn studied its feasibility, siting, and financing. In February 1967, they established the corporation, and 6 months later the corporation transferred to them 52 percent of its shares, valued at $432,000. The promoters later claimed that they paid for the shares with their promotional services and expenditures. The promoters did not disclose to the subscribers how they paid for the stock. The outsiders brought suit to compel the promoters to return their shares to the corporation without compensation. The trial court granted this relief. The court of appeals reversed. It remanded the case for a determination of the credit due the promoters for their services toward the purchase of the shares.

ISSUE Did the promoters' violation of their fiduciary duty warrant compelling them to return their shares to the corporation?

DECISION Yes. Court of appeals judgment modified. To merit the extreme penalty of returning the shares without compensation, the promoters' breach must be conspicuously blameworthy. Even where courts require promoters to return unpaid-for shares, they have allowed the promoters to recover not only their actual promotional expenditures but also the value of their services in launching the venture. These promoters should have disclosed how they bought the stock, or secured ratification by the shareholders or by an independent board. The trial court correctly held that the promoters had to return the shares to the corporation. But, the appellate court was correct that their slipshod activities did not merit the extreme sanction.

The Promoters' Contracts

It may seem logical that the promoters would be the corporation's agents. However, the corporation cannot be a principal because it does not exist yet. So, promoters face another practical problem. Third parties want assurance that a new corporation will fulfill the contracts the promoters make on its behalf. But, the promoters cannot bind the corporation even if they will be its controlling shareholders.

To avoid liability, promoters may seek to sign contracts as individuals and make them conditional upon the corporation's coming into being and adopting the contract. However, third parties may not be willing to wait for an event that may never occur. If they have failed to so condition their contracts, they can seek a novation, but they will have to convince both the other party to the original contract and the new corporation to agree to it.

A corporation is not liable for a promoter's preincorporation contract unless it adopts it after incorporation. A corporation must adopt all or none of a contract. In most situations the decision to adopt a preincorporation contract will be express—the corporation states it does or does not adopt a given contract. However, a corporation can be found to have impliedly adopted a preincorporation contract where it knowingly accepts benefits of the contract after incorporation, such as utilizing software subject to a preincorporation contract.

A promoter is liable on a preincorporation contract whether or not the corporation adopts the contract. This places the promoter in a difficult legal situation. Where the corporation does adopt a preincorporation contract the promoter may seek a novation, the third party agreeing to substitute the corporation in place of the promoter. The promoter may anticipate this situation by including in the preincorporation contract an automatic novation clause, which automatically substitutes the corporation for the promoter at the time of adoption. Of course, the third party must still agree.

A promoter can avoid personal liability by making a preincorporation contract which is conditioned upon acceptance by the new corporation. The drawback to this approach is that the third party is also not liable until adoption and can withdraw prior to adoption. Also, a third party may be unwilling to suspend sale of an item, perhaps a piece of real estate, where there is no obligated party.

The next case illustrates what can happen when the promoter fails to take steps to protect him- or herself.

TIN CUP PASS LIMITED PARTNERSHIP v. DANIELS

195 Ill. App.3d 847, 553 N.E.2d 82 (1990)

FACTS

Pat and John Daniels and William Mandell sought to purchase a tavern and restaurant. Although not yet incorporated, the three signed a lease in January 1987 in the proposed corporation's name, D & M, Inc., with Pat Daniels as president and Bill Mandell as secretary. The lessor also knew that D & M, Inc., had not been incorporated, although the lease was not conditioned on a successful incorporation. The three later discovered that the name D & M, Inc., was already in use in Illinois, so they incorporated in the name of the Lodge at Tin Cup Pass, Inc., in March 1987. It then ratified the lease. In December 1988, the three defendants were personally sued as promoters of D & M, Inc., for back rent of over $12,000. The plaintiffs won at the trial level.

ISSUE

Were the defendants Daniels and Mandell personally liable as promoters?

DECISION

Yes. Affirmed. Promoters create and organize a business idea which later becomes a corporation. When the defendants entered into the lease they were acting as promoters of D & M, Inc. The fact that the final name of the corporation was the Lodge at Tin Cup Pass, Inc., does not change the fact that they were that corporation's promoters, since the intent of the parties was for the defendants' yet-to-be-formed corporation to ultimately lease the premises. Moreover, even though the corporation did ratify the lease, the lessor never released the defendants through a novation.

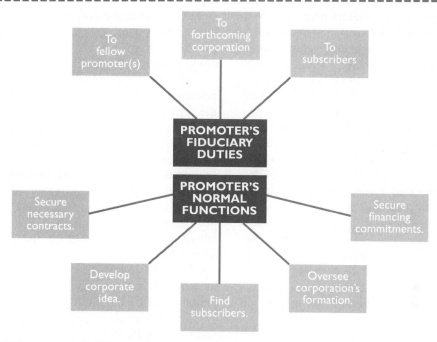

Figure 19.2 Promoter's Fiduciary Duties and Functions.

Given the possibility of personal liability, the promoter often will attempt to incorporate a business before making any contracts for the new corporation. By doing so, the promoter will have no personal liability. However, a third party may be unwilling to enter into such a contract without the original promoters assuming a guarantor position. Figure 19.2 summarizes the promoter's ultimate rights and responsibilities.

FORMATION: THE PROCEDURAL REQUIREMENTS

Forming a corporation is not like forming a partnership. It cannot be done with a handshake. The promoters must have *articles of incorporation* drawn up for the corporation which describe its organization, powers, and authority. Unlike articles of partnership, this document is not optional. The secretary of state will not process an application for a certificate of incorporation unless the articles accompany it.

As we noted in our definition of "corporation," one cannot come into existence until it receives a certificate of incorporation. When it does, its board of directors must meet to elect officers, adopt bylaws, and generally organize the company.

Choosing State for Incorporation

The selection of the state for incorporation often turns on whether the business is likely to be primarily intrastate. To illustrate, it would make sense for a small retail store in Milwaukee intending to conduct business primarily in Wisconsin to incorporate in Wisconsin. Why? The costs of organizing and maintaining the corporation are likely to be less with just one state. In addition, an important preventive law consideration for smaller businesses is that the opportunities for inadvertent errors in compliance with specific corporation laws should be reduced.

A much larger Wisconsin retailer, say Land's End, might be more interested in other issues, such as shareholder rights, greater freedom from shareholder intervention, greater rights of managerial discretion, the ability to restrict stock, or the ability to operate as a close corporation, discussed in Chapter 22. To illustrate, traditionally Delaware has been a popular state for incorporation because of perceived greater flexibility for management. As a practical matter, the selection of the state for incorporation is likely to have little impact on whether the corporation is ultimately successful.

Articles of Incorporation

Every corporation must have articles of incorporation which describe the corporation.

Contents. Both the MBCA and the RMBCA set minimum requirements for what the articles of incorporation must contain. Let's look first at the MBCA requirements. The articles must state the name of the corporation. Its name may not be deceptively similar to that of an existing corporation. ''Macdonald's Hamburgers, Inc.'' is too close to ''McDonald's.'' The name must include one of the following words: Corporation (Corp.), Company (Co.), Incorporated (Inc.), or Limited (Ltd.).

The articles also establish the duration of the corporation. Usually, the duration is stated as perpetual, but it can be limited.

The articles state the purpose of the corporation. Historically, corporate purpose clauses were quite specific, and the courts interpreted them narrowly. Today, purpose clauses often say simply that the corporation may engage in any lawful business or activity. Under such a clause, a corporation which operates a tire store could acquire a lemon grove.

The types and quantities of shares the corporation is authorized to issue must appear in the articles. We will discuss this requirement in the last part of this chapter.

Finally, the articles must list the names and addresses of the persons who will serve as the corporation's board of directors until the first annual shareholders' meeting or until their successors are elected and qualified. Often, the persons listed are members of the promoter's lawyer's firm so as to cloak the firm's initial ownership.

We will note other items which may be included in the articles in the course of this chapter and Chapters 20 and 21.

The RMBCA minimim requirements are somewhat different. A corporation must specify:

- The corporation's name
- The number of shares the corporation has authority to issue
- The address of the initial registered office of the corporation
- The name of its initial registered agent
- The names and addresses of all the incorporators

Signing and filing. An individual or an agent may act as an *incorporator* on behalf of a corporation. An incorporator's sole functions are to sign the articles and file them with the secretary of state [MBCA §55]. If the articles conform to legal requirements and the incorporators have paid the required fees, the secretary of state will issue a certificate of incorporation [MBCA §56]. The corporation comes into existence when the certificate is issued. The incorporator's status comes to an end with the initial meeting of the board of directors.

The Organization Meeting

At its first meeting, the board must adopt by-laws and elect the corporation's officers. In addition, the new board will usually issue stock to the subscribers, set salaries for the officers, and ratify promoter contracts [MBCA §57].

The RMBCA [§2.05] calls for an organization meeting which either the incorporators or the initial board of directors may call. Either group has the authority to adopt the initial bylaws and to complete the corporation's organization. If the incorporators meet first, they may elect the initial board of directors. The incorporators can leave the adoption of bylaws to the board.

Corporate Bylaws

A corporation's bylaws regulate the corporation. Normally, the articles describe the corporation's operations in broad terms, while the bylaws contain more detailed internal regulations. The bylaws must be consistent with state statutes and the articles of incorporation, but do not have to be filed with the secretary of state.

Bylaws frequently describe:

- The duties and agency authorities of corporate officers
- How and to whom notice of shareholder and director meetings is to be given
- The formalities of shareholder voting
- Where and by whom corporate records are to be maintained
- Procedures for issuing and transferring stock
- The duties and compensation of the directors

Unless the articles reserve the right to the shareholders, the board of directors may freely adopt or amend the bylaws [RMBCA §10.08].

The RMBCA also specifies that the shareholders always have the right to amend or repeal bylaws, regardless of the board's rights. The shareholders may specify that only they can amend or repeal certain bylaws. For in-stance, they may restrict the board's ability to define its duties and compensation.

Defective Incorporation

In the past, much litigation concerned whether an entity was properly incorporated and therefore was actually a corporation. All jurisdictions had extensive and contradictory rules for determining whether articles sufficiently complied with the law. At stake—if the entity was not a corporation—was the personal liability of the shareholders of the challenged entity, which of course was usually insolvent.

Common law. At common law, a *de jure* corporation was one formed in substantial compliance with the corporate statute. Once formed, the corporation was considered appropriately formed and free from challenge of its corporate status.

A *de facto* corporation occurred where organizers in good faith attempted to form a corporation properly but somehow failed to comply substantially with the corporate statute. If the organizers subsequently exercised corporate powers, acted as if it were a corporation, then it was considered to be incorporated properly. In such a situation only the state could challenge its deficiencies in incorporation. Such status could not be challenged by a third party or raised as a defense by the corporation. In contrast, a defective corporation occurred when the attempt to incorporate was defective or nonexistent, resulting in no corporation status.

The common law recognized one additional status: corporation by estoppel. This occurred where a nonincorporated business represented itself as a corporation and a third party reasonably relied. The business was not permitted to seek refuge in its lack of corporate status. This situation might occur when, for example, a partnership represents itself as a corporation, able to borrow money from a lender at an interest rate reserved to corporations. This business cannot later deny its loan liability on grounds that it is not an actual corporation.

Approach of MBCA and RMBCA. The MBCA and RMBCA have sought to avoid the confusion of the common law by taking the following approach: ''No charter, no corporation.'' The MBCA resolves disputes over defective incorporation by providing that the secretary of state's issuance of a certificate establishes an irrebuttable presumption of compliance with the state's incorporation laws [MBCA §56]. A few states have not adopted this approach, but most have.

Under RMBCA §2.03, a corporation comes into existence when its incorporators file the articles and receive an official receipt from the secretary of state. In effect, this section, too, creates an irrebuttable presumption of proper incorporation.

It is difficult for a corporation to claim its own defective incorporation as a defense to liability on a contract, but that is what the defendant in the next case tried to do.

Conway v. Samet

59 Misc. 2d 666, 300 N.Y.S.2d 243 (Sup. Ct. 1969)

FACTS The Conways signed a contract with Trend Set Construction Corporation for home remodeling work. Samet, as its president, signed on behalf of Trend Set. The Conways sued Trend Set for breaching the contract, and the court entered a default judgment against the corporation. Some time later, they discovered that Trend Set lacked a certificate of incorporation and brought this action against Samet personally as the real party in interest.

ISSUE Was Samet insulated from liability by Trend Set's status as a corporation?

DECISION No. Judgment for the Conways.

> [Samet] alleges that she hired an attorney to file all papers necessary for incorporation, paid a fee, received a seal, and did business as a corporation, and that "The failure to file the Certificate of Incorporation was not my fault. . . . I had every right to assume that the attorney hired for this purpose would . . . [file] the Certificate of Incorporation." Unfortunately for [her] those allegations evidence a malpractice claim against the attorney involved, but do not constitute a defense to the claims made against her in the present action. More is required to establish the . . . corporation defense than giving instructions to an attorney; there must have been a colorable attempt to comply with the statutes governing incorporation. . . . And "without any Certificate of Incorporation having been prepared or acknowledged" there can be no . . . corporation. . . .

FINANCING THE CORPORATION

Any business venture can be financed in three ways: sale of ownership, borrowing, and—after it has started business—earnings. In this section, we will examine what kinds of ownership interests corporations sell and what kinds of vehicles they use to borrow.

Corporations normally finance their long-term operations by selling ownership in the form of shares or *equity securities*, or by borrowing in the form of *debt securities*. In both cases, the corporation is said to *issue* the securities, and the corporation is called the *issuer*. Any change of ownership after a security's issuance is called a *transfer*. Securities which have been issued are termed *outstanding*.

As we will see in Chapter 23, the issuing and transferring of publicly traded shares are matters of intense state and federal regulation. Here, we will focus on the types of funding mechanisms.

Equity Securities

Equity securities are intangible personal property, ownership of which is usually represented by a *share certificate* or *stock certificate*. (The terms are synonymous, but the UCC and the RMBCA use the former.) A certificate represents an ownership interest. However, only the corporation's shareholder records reflect actual ownership.

Most people who buy equities do so for one reason: to make money. What varies is how they intend to make money.

The value of equities. Equities have two distinct values. First, they have a value as an investment. That value depends on how much the company earns *and* on whether it pays dividends and whether the stock can be sold for its fair market value. As we will see in Chapter 21, the last two factors are particularly difficult to compute when the corporation's stock is not publicly traded.

Normally, investors buy shares in older, established companies, like telephone companies or public utilities, if they want earnings. If they are interested in the price at which they can ultimately sell the stock, they look to growth companies, like hot, young computer peripheral manufacturers. Stock prices of publicly traded issues are purely a function of supply and demand.

The second value of equities is as ownership interests in a corporation. In small companies, particularly closely held corporations, shares represent control. Control means the ability to determine dividends, to hire and fire employees and officers, and to assign prerequisites. Even where large, publicly traded corporations are involved, one share in a large block of stock is worth more than one share alone to someone seeking control.

Except in the situation in which a publicly traded corporation is about to be taken over by another, control value is of little relevance to the ordinary investor. It is of critical, day-to-day importance to individuals who own stock in the corporations for which they work and whose jobs depend on who controls the company. Chapter 21 examines the value of control and how it is maintained.

The articles of incorporation authorize the issuance of equity securities by type, class, and amount. Equities come in two types: common stock and preferred stock.

Common stock. All corporations must have *common stock*. Of the securities we will examine in this section, common stock has the lowest priority when the corporation pays interest or dividends. *Dividends* are distributions of the earnings of the company to its owners, the shareholders. The corporation's board of directors must determine that earnings are sufficient to pay a dividend, and then vote to pay one. Normally, dividends are paid quarterly.

While dividends are important, for many investors in common stock, appreciation in value as a result of the company's success may be far more important. That is why investors typically pay several times what a successful company earns per share. They are betting on a continued appreciation in the value of stock.

Many companies pay no dividends, preferring to reinvest their earnings in the business. For example, Tandy Corp. and Digital Equipment Corp. (DEC) have never paid a dividend. Prior to the Tax Reform Act of 1986, investors who looked to the sale of their stock for their return found such companies attractive. The Act, however, eliminated favorable tax treatment for the proceeds from the sale of stock. Now both dividends and realized appreciation receive the same treatment.

Preferred stock. *Preferred stock* has priority over common stock as to dividends or to asset distributions if the company is dissolved. If the corporation pays a dividend to any of its shareholders, it must pay the preferred holders first.

Because preferred stock usually pays a fixed dividend, say $10 a share per year, it appeals to investors who want a flow of income from their investments rather than an appreciation in value, or who want greater security in lean times. If the company does not pay a dividend during a particular quarter, the articles of incorporation and the stock certificate itself will state whether the preferred shareholder has a claim on subsequent earnings for the amount of the omitted or *passed* dividend. For example, suppose that in 1990 Sky Hook Corp. could not pay the $2 per share quarterly dividend on its preferred stock. If its preferred was *cumulative*, the shareholders would have a continuing claim on Sky Hook for the passed dividend. Most preferred is noncumulative, and shareholders simply lose passed dividends.

Preferred stock rarely has any control value, since it normally has voting rights only on matters which directly affect it, such as whether the corporation will be liquidated.

Classes of stock and voting rights. A corporation may issue as many classes of common and preferred stock as it wishes. Not all stock need be equal in terms of the rights of ownership that shareholders assume upon purchasing it. However, one class of common stock must have the right to elect directors and to vote on shareholder resolutions. For example, Wang Laboratories, the computer manufacturer, has issued two classes of common stock, class B and class C, with different voting rights.

The rights of ownership must be consistent within classes of stock. For instance, every holder of Wang class B has the right to one vote for directors for every 10 shares held, while those holding class C have one vote per share. Usually, corporations create classes of common stock to preserve control of the company in the hands of a particular group. Many corporations have adopted schemes involving stock with unequal voting rights as a means of warding off takeover bids. These include Cincinnati Milacron, Hershey Foods, J. M. Smucker, and United Artists Communications.*

Stock with unequal voting rights has proved extremely controversial not only because of its use to thwart tender offers but also because it creates a strong potential for abuse by the shareholders with voting control. Accusations of this type led to litigation between holders of the two classes of stock in the casino operator Resorts International† and, as we will see in Chapter 21, the New England Patriots Football Club.

Par value and stated value. *Par value* is the value printed on a stock certificate. In the past, the articles of incorporation would state a par value for the corporation's stock. The corporation could not issue its shares for less than the amount indicated in the articles. If A&B's stock

---

* B. Ingersoll, "One-Share, One-Vote Controversy Comes to Head in SEC Hearings," *Wall Street Journal*, December 16, 1986, p. 37.
† M. Mahar, "No Class Act," *Barron's*, December 15, 1986, p. 18.

Figure 19.3 A Typical Share Certificate. This certificate is quite typical of those issued today. Note the signatures on either side. These banks actually transfer the stock from the seller to the buyer and maintain the records identifying company stock owners. For the history of the company which issued this certificate, see *Escott v. BarChris Construction Corp.*, 283 F. Supp. 643 (S.D.N.Y. 1968), which is briefed in Chapter 23.

has a par value of $5 per share, A&B must sell the shares for $5 or more. The board is liable to the corporation for issuing shares at less than par or stated value.

Many corporations set par at $1 per share or some other amount far below what the shares will actually sell for. In Figure 19.3, which shows a typical stock certificate, the legend or notation across the fact of the certificate indicates a par value of 50 cents. Today, stock is often sold at its *stated value*, an amount the board of directors deems appropriate. This is what is known as *no-par* stock.

An advantage to the corporation in issuing low or no-par value stock is that it frees up money from the capital account to "capital in excess of par." This allows the corporation to pay future dividends or fund larger operating losses without creating an impairment of capital. Whether this is an actual benefit to shareholders is debatable. A shareholder's rights to dividends is discussed in Chapter 21.

Issuing stock. Corporations may issue stock in exchange for cash, past services, or personal or real property [MBCA §19]. As we saw in *Whaler Motor Inn, Inc. v. Parsons*, promoters may receive stock for their services and expenses before the corporation comes into existence.

A corporation may not accept IOUs or promises of future services in exchange for stock. Subscribers may pay for shares in installments if the opportunity is offered to all subscribers. However, the corporation may not issue stock to a subscriber before it is fully paid for [MBCA §23]. Stock issued before it is fully paid for is termed *watered stock*.* The holder of watered stock is liable to both the corporation and its creditors for the difference in value between the price paid and the subscription price.

The RMBCA [§6.21] permits the issuance of shares in exchange "for consideration of any tangible or intangible property or benefit to the corporation, including cash, promissory notes, services performed, contracts for services to be

performed, or other securities of the corporation." Thus, the RMBCA significantly broadens the range of consideration. This provision is likely to be controversial when states consider adoption because of the possibility of misrepresenting true corporate worth by jiggling the valuation of noncash consideration.

Treasury stock. *Treasury stock* consists of issued shares which the corporation has reacquired but does not *cancel* or destroy. A corporation may reacquire stock for more or less than its original issue price without specific authorization in its articles of incorporation. The corporation may resell treasury stock for less than its par or stated value. The officers or directors of the corporation may not vote treasury shares in shareholder meetings.

The MBCA has eliminated the concept of treasury shares. Under it, shares reacquired by a corporation and not canceled are to be considered shares authorized but unissued [MBCA §6]. For instance, assume that the articles of A&B Computer Corp. authorize 500 shares of stock. A&B sells 400 shares and reacquires 50 of those shares as treasury stock. A&B now has 350 shares outstanding and 150 shares authorized but not issued.

Despite the MBCA, the treasury stock concept is likely to remain in use in many states.

The following case discusses the difference between issued and treasury stock. The distinction can be crucial when the consideration for the stock is a promissory note.

---

* This term has a colorful origin. A cow's live weight determines the price a butcher pays. In the nineteenth century, unscrupulous dealers fed cattle salt and then gave them all the water they wanted just before they were weighed at a stockyard. A practitioner of this technique, Daniel Drew, adapted it to stock in railroads. Hence, the term and the pun. See M. Klein, *The Life and Legend of Jay Gould* (Baltimore: The Johns Hopkins University Press, 1986), p. 77.

BRUMFIELD v. HORN

547 So.2d 415 (Ala. 1989)

FACTS   Horn owned stock in South Central Holding Company, Inc. (SCHC). Horn subsequently transferred his stock to Bonner. Bonner pledged the stock to Farmer's & Merchant's Bank as collateral for a loan. Bonner later defaulted on the note and went into bankruptcy. After a successful lawsuit challenging the transfer to Bonner, an agreement was drawn up in which SCHC reacquired the stock from Bonner and the bank. Also as part of the agreement, Horn regained title from SCHC to the shares he originally transferred to Bonner. He was also permitted to assign the stock to Old Towne, a company he owned and controlled, for $140,000. At a shareholders' meeting, Horn's right to vote his Old Towne stock was challenged, since Old Towne had paid for it with a promissory note. The trial court ruled in Horn and Old Towne's favor.

ISSUE

Can a promissory note be given in exchange for treasury stock?

DECISION

Yes. Affirmed. There is a long-standing rule of law that worthless or watered stock cannot be issued to the public. The stock must represent something of value or it is fictitious and fraudulent. Issued stock also is intended to ensure that the stated capital account of a corporation is an accurate indication of the money contributed to it. Treasury stock, on the other hand, does not affect the stated capital account. The legal protections afforded issued stock do apply to treasury stock, since it is a resale of stock that had once been purchased for actual consideration.

Restricted stock. Corporations sometimes restrict the transfer of their shares. Restricted stock certificates must bear a *legend*—a notation on the certificate—stating the terms of the restriction, so that anyone handling the stock has notice of it. The corporation may refuse to recognize the transfer of restricted stock if the transfer is not in accordance with the restriction. A good faith purchaser without notice of the restrictions is not bound by them.

The restrictions may not be so arbitrary as to make the stock in effect nontransferable or transferable only at an unconscionably low price. Ultimately, the holder must be able to sell the stock to someone.

Shareholders in small corporations often restrict transferability by providing for a *buy-out* in the company's articles or in a shareholders' agreement. Buy-out provisions permit the remaining shareholders to preserve their existing proportional ownership and to control who might come into the corporation. The next case illustrates how courts may treat restricted stock and buy-out agreements.

F H.T., Inc. v. Feuerhelm

211 Neb. 860, 320 N.W.2d 772 (1982)

FACTS

In 1972, Feuerhelm and Thompson, F.H.T.'s only shareholders, adopted a resolution requiring a deceased shareholder's estate to offer its shares first to the company at their book value. The purchase price was to be paid by the purchaser with a promissory note carrying a 4 percent annual interest rate, with both principal and interest payable in 15 years. Feuerhelm died in 1980. F.H.T. tendered a promissory note for $2.7 million in exchange for the stock. Feuerhelm's estate refused to transfer the shares. F.H.T. sued. The trial court ordered the estate to transfer the stock to F.H.T.

ISSUE   Was the resolution unenforceable because it unreasonably restricted transfer of the shares?

DECISION   No. Affirmed. In close corporations, stock restrictions ensure that management control remains with the same group of investors or with people well known to them. The F.H.T. restriction constituted a reasonable restraint—not an absolute restriction—on the power to transfer its shares. Where no question of a bona fide purchaser without notice is involved, the stockholders of the corporation may restrict stock in order to retain control.

Why would a corporation like F.H.T., Inc., adopt such a plan involving restricted stock? The most common reason is to maintain the balance of power, especially where there are more than two shareholders. It also guarantees a market for the shares, often purchased from the proceeds of a key person life insurance policy which the corporation held for the decedent shareholder/officer. Finally, restrictive stock prevents unwanted persons from becoming shareholders, in effect adopting a partnership approach to ownership whereby consent for an incoming partner is required.

Uncertificated shares. Both the MBCA and the RMBCA look forward to the day when corporations will not issue share certificates but will instead simply record ownership on the corporation's shareholder records. The benefits to corporations of such a switch would include not having to pay for the issuance of a new certificate every time shares change hands. It would also eliminate paper handling in the securities industry.

The practical effect of uncertificated shares on shareholders would be minimal. Indeed, the U.S. Treasury issues some types of debt without certificates. As noted earlier, certificates simply evidence ownership, and the form that evidence takes has no impact on ownership rights. Suppose Alice gives her alma mater 100 shares of IBM stock. Her school would have to ask IBM to alter its shareholder records to indicate the changed ownership. However, whether the school received a certificate or a receipt would not alter the fact that it now owned the 100 shares.

The mechanics of transfer: UCC Article 8. Article 8 of the Uniform Commercial Code also anticipates uncertificated securities. Article 8 governs the mechanics of transferring shares, as we will see in Chapter 38.

Debt

By definition, corporations must have shareholders, and those who own companies must put up sufficient money to capitalize them. But, the sale of ownership is only one of the ways in which to finance a corporation. The corporation may borrow money, in addition to its shareholders' capital contributions.

Many corporate borrowings take the form of securities, called *debt*. As a type of security, the issuance and transfer of debt are subject to the federal and state statutory schemes described in Chapter 23. Still, debt is essentially a contract between the corporate issuer and the holder.

Debt takes three forms. First, *bonds* evidence long-term loans (generally at least 10 years) which are backed or *secured* by particular assets. If A&B Computers decides to issue bonds to finance a new facility, normally its land and buildings secure the bonds. If the company defaults on the bonds, their holders may seek a court order allowing them to sell the property backing the bonds to satisfy the company's obligation to them.

Second, *debentures* evidence unsecured loans to the corporation. Debentures ordinarily are not issued for more than 15-year terms. *Commercial paper*, which represents loans with terms of less than 9 months—*short-term loans*—is a form of debenture.

Third, *convertible bonds* and *convertible debentures* both pay interest and give the holder the right to exchange debt for a certain number of shares of common stock. Investors typically pay for the convertibility feature by accepting lower interest rates than nonconvertibles would pay.

CONCLUSION

This chapter has contained more than its share of mechanics and definitions. However, in most cases forming a corporation *is* mechanical. Some secretaries of state even provide checklists to ensure that incorporators observe all the formalities.

Financing a corporation, however, is *not* mechanical. Yes, a for-profit corporation must have shareholders who contribute capital in exchange for ownership interests. But, how are these contributions to be valued when one shareholder contributes cash; another, real property; another, inventory and cash; and yet another, services? If the corporation requires outside financing, what *vehicles*, as the various financing options are called, will optimize the company's chances for success?

No computer program can provide answers to those questions or others like them because it cannot factor in intangibles like employee-shareholder enthusiasm for the company. Where money is concerned and where a value must be placed on noncash contributions, emotion and negotiating skills play a larger role in getting the corporation off to a good start than intellectual appraisals of financing mechanisms. Many ventures never recover from this start-up

process because it destroyed the trust the venturers needed.

As in the agency and partnership chapters, the following chapters will have much to say about *fiduciary* duties, or duties of trust. Such duties are relatively easy to define, and the term itself makes them seem impersonal. Yet, the cases we will examine in the next chapters reveal how wrong that impression is. Trust is what makes a business succeed. Without it, those involved are reduced to picking over the bones in lawsuits.

A NOTE TO FUTURE CPA CANDIDATES

The CPA exam's corporation section has been based upon the MBCA. The examination has moved away from the common law applications such as de jure and de facto corporations.

It is important to understand the basic purpose and function of the articles of incorporation, sometimes called the corporate charter, and the corporate bylaws. The exam recognizes the MBCA approach to incorporation: "No charter, no corporation."

The role of the promoter should be understood. The promoter has personal liability on contracts formed before incorporation unless it is specifically agreed in the contract that it is conditioned upon the corporation being formed or a novation from the third party has occurred effective after incorporation.

The distinction between equity and debt instruments should be understood. In addition, the candidate must be able to distinguish common stock from preferred, know what treasury stock is, and understand the effect of restricted stock.

KEY WORDS

articles of incorporation (417)

bond (426)

bylaws (419)

cancel (424)
convertible (427)
cumulative (422)
debenture (427)
debt (426)
equity (421)

issue (421)
preferred stock (422)
promoter (413)
subscription (414)
treasury stock (424)
watered stock (424)

DISCUSSION QUESTIONS

1. What is the role of the state in the formation of a corporation?
2. What is the role of a promoter in the formation of a corporation?
3. What fiduciary duties does the promoter owe? To whom?
4. Who is bound by a promoter's contract? Why?
5. What are articles of incorporation? What is generally included in them?
6. Contrast articles of incorporation and bylaws.
7. Contrast common stock and preferred stock.
8. What is treasury stock? What is the new MBCA position concerning it?
9. Contrast the investment characteristics of common stock and bonds.
10. Would you expect to pay a higher price for a bond or a debenture? Why?

CASE PROBLEMS

1. Bixler obtained an option on a building he believed was suitable for use by a corporation he and two others were organizing. After the corporation was successfully promoted, Bixler met with the board of directors, who agreed to acquire the property for $200,000. Bixler deeded the building to the corporation. When the directors later learned that Bixler paid only $155,000 for the building, they demanded that he return the $45,000 profit. Bixler refused, claiming that the building was worth far more than $200,000 both when he secured the option and when he deeded it to the corporation. Must the directors prove that the building was worth less than $200,000 in

order for Bixler to be obligated to return any profit? Assuming that Bixler has a problem here, what would you have advised him to do to avoid it? Explain your answers.
2. Haynes Corporation, a manufacturer of roller bearings, is incorporated in Indiana. It wishes to establish a distribution center in Toledo, Ohio. A recent note from the company legal counsel to the CEO included the following: "Because we will be a private, for-profit, foreign corporation in Ohio we will need to file a certificate of authority before we open our Toledo center." The CEO responded: "I'm confused. Our stock is publicly traded, we are an American company, and we have always shipped roller bearings through Ohio free of Ohio regulation. Are you sure?" Is the corporate counsel correct? Explain his note.
3. Fenton Publishing Corp. fears a takeover by Polaris, Inc., a competitor. To reduce the number of shares outstanding, Fenton has begun to repurchase a large number of $25 par value shares held by the public. Fenton's strategy is to reduce the number of shares available to Polaris and to increase the number of treasury shares that Fenton management will have to vote. Shelley Halvorson, a Fenton stockholder, claims the voting strategy by Fenton management is against the law. She has also urged the corporation to resell the treasury stock immediately. Fenton management has responded that it cannot resell the treasury shares, even if it wanted to, as the market would not currently support a selling price of $25 or higher. Is Halvorson correct about management's inability to vote the treasury shares? Is management correct about its inability to resell the treasury shares? Explain.
4. Bill Ford signed a subscription agreement to purchase 200 shares of stock in Ade, Inc., a new corporation. Six weeks after signing the agreement Bill notified the promoter that he would be unable to purchase the shares because of a personal business reversal. What continued liability, if any, would Bill have? Another investor, Kevin Murray, signed an agreement to purchase fifty shares but has

since learned that subscribed shares for Ade stock outnumber shares to be issued by twice the number. The Ade promoters have announced that they intend to hold a lottery to determine who will be able to purchase Ade stock. Kevin claims he is entitled to at least twenty-five shares of stock. Is Kevin correct? Explain.

5. Daniel Leiby is a promoter for a corporation to be formed and known as Star Corp. Leiby entered into several supply and service agreements with Schweder Supply Company. These agreements were executed in Star's name, expressly contingent upon adoption by Star, when formed, and were based solely on Star's anticipated financial strength. Within 2 weeks after the signing of the agreements, Star was duly formed and operating. Shortly thereafter, Star, by its board of directors, rejected the preincorporation agreements entered into by Leiby and Schweder Supply, stating that it could obtain more beneficial contracts elsewhere. If Schweder Supply should bring suit, would it recover against Leiby? Against Star Corp.? Explain.

6. The articles of incorporation of Siwash, Inc., require shareholders to give the corporation the right of first refusal to purchase outstanding shares being resold. By mistake, some of the stock certificates were not stamped with a restrictive stock legend. A dissident shareholder, Joyce Petrie, has sold fifty shares of Siwash stock, without legend, to Jon Kimmel. Kimmel had heard that Siwash stock was restricted, but Petrie showed him her stock certificate, which did not bear a legend. Kimmel was unaware of Petrie's disputes with the corporation. Siwash, Inc., has refused to recognize the sale of the stock. Is Kimmel likely to prevail? Explain.

7. John Austin wanted to form a corporaton to develop a business computer system. Austin approached Jena Hoyt about investing in his new firm, Intergalactic Business Mechanics, Inc. Three times, after listening to Austin, Hoyt asked for—and received—further information about the product and the market. Then, she said no. Shortly thereafter, Busi-

ness Mechanix, Inc., opened its doors with Hoyt as its majority shareholder. Her corporation, which was well financed, largely with her own resources, seemed to be following Austin's business plan to the letter. However, his corporation never came into existence because Hoyt's product made his redundant. What remedies does Austin have? If he sues, is he likely to prevail? Explain.

8. Stuart Morse was the promoter for a new corporation, Madison Products, Inc. Prior to incorporation, Morse leased a building for the new corporation from Peggy French in the name of Madison Products, Inc. Upon formation, the board of directors of the new corporation decided not to adopt the building lease, gave Morse 250 shares of stock for his services rendered as promoter, and gave 100 shares of stock to singer Janet Louise to do future singing commercials on behalf of Madison Products. French claims the corporation is liable, since Morse is a shareholder of Madison Products and the lease is in the name of Madison Products. Is the corporation liable to French? Does Morse have a right to his stock? Does Janet Louise have a right to her stock? Explain.

9. Whiting Hall, Inc., is a winery. Kelly Bubois and Bev Eatman, members of the board of directors, are concerned that the winery CEO, Bradley Downing, is considering establishing a chain of restaurants. The board members wish to limit Downing's authority by amending the bylaws. At a special board meeting called for this purpose, Downing objected on the basis that the articles of incorporation did not give to the directors the power to amend the bylaws. In addition, Downing claimed that such a bylaw change would probably not be effective to nullify a contract with a good faith third party. Is Downing correct? Explain.

10. Kathi Barth purchased stock in Moffatt Computers, Inc., a new corporation. Kathi received her stock certificate for 100 shares and a cash dividend after the first year. During the second year the corporation lost sales and ended up in bankruptcy. Kathi was disap-

pointed to have lost her money in the corporation but was later shocked to learn that the company had never actually been incorporated. Bud Low, the promoter and another shareholder, had not realized that the attorney hired to file the corporate paperwork and articles had not done so. Kathi and Bud claim they should be treated as if they were shareholders—that is, as if they had limited liability—because they acted in good faith. Would a court be likely to agree? Explain.

Operating Corporations

The corporate form allows great flexibility in the kinds of daily business decisions which officers, directors, and shareholders may make. Corporation law prescribes the structure and the authority for acting upon and implementing them. In short, it provides operational boundaries. Beyond that, the internal laws established for the company in its articles of incorporation and bylaws control the way a decision is made.

This chapter examines two interrelated topics. First, what authority does management have to act in the day-to-day operation of the corporation? Second, what are the legal relationships between and among directors and officers?

A CORPORATION'S POWERS

When we speak of a corporation's "powers," we are using the word in the same sense as we did in describing an agent's powers. *Powers* refers to the corporation's authority to act.

Sources of Corporate Power

A corporation's sources of powers are threefold: statutory powers; express corporate powers from the articles of incorporation; and implied powers, those powers reasonably necessary to fulfill the corporation's objectives.

Statutory powers. State incorporation statutes, such as the Revised Model Business Corporation Act (RMBCA), give a corporation broad powers to enact business. To illustrate, §3.02 grants the corporation "the same powers as an individual to do all things necessary or convenient to carry out its business and affairs." This broad grant puts the burden on shareholders to specify what the corporation may *not* do. For instance, under RMBCA §3.02(13) a corporation may make charitable contributions. Nonetheless if a company's shareholders vote to amend its articles to forbid contributions, they may.

Unless the articles of incorporation provide otherwise, under RMBCA§302, a corporation has the following powers:

- Perpetual existence
- To sue and be sued
- To make and amend bylaws not inconsistent with state law or the articles of incorporation
- To purchase and own personal and real property
- To sell, mortgage and lease property
- To own interests in other corporations
- To make contracts and guarantees, incur liabilities, borrow money, and put up property as collateral
- To lend money and invest funds
- To elect directors and officers and to lend officers and directors money and credit
- To pay pensions and establish pensions for any or all of its present or former employees, officers, and directors
- To make charitable donations

The MBCA did not specifically authorize the lending of money to directors or the establishment of pension plans for former employees, officers, and directors.

Express corporate powers. Express corporate powers are those that the articles of incorporation grant to the corporation. The articles state the corporation's objectives. Rather than list each action management may take, they are more likely to contain a provision such as the following:

The purpose for which Leary's Drug Store, Inc., is organized is the transaction of any and all lawful business for which corporations may be incorporated.

Thus, the articles may grant all the powers the law permits a corporation to exercise.

The law presumes that anyone dealing with a corporation has notice of what its articles say because it is a matter of public record. This presumption that everyone knows what is in the public records is called *constructive notice*. (On payment of a copying charge, the secretary of state's office will supply a copy of the articles of any corporation licensed to do business within the state.) The presumption of constructive notice means that a person dealing with a corporation rarely can enforce a contract which exceeds a company's express powers— something the plaintiff in the next case discovered to his loss.

Newberry v. Barth, Inc.

252 N.W.2d 711 (Iowa, 1977)

FACTS Mrs. Barth, Secretary-Treasurer of Barth, Inc., owned 465 of its 490 common shares. The corporation's principal asset was an apartment complex, which she managed. The Federal Housing Administration (FHA) was its sole preferred stockholder and mortgagee. Under Barth, Inc.'s, articles, it could not transfer any real or personal property without the FHA's permission. Mrs. Barth listed the apartment complex with a a real estate agent, indicating that the seller was Barth, Inc. Subsequently, Mrs. Barth agreed to sell Newberry the complex. When Barth, Inc., could not convey the property, Newberry successfully sought an order compelling specific performance of the contract.

ISSUE Did Mrs. Barth have authority to sell the apartment complex?

DECISION No. Reversed. A person who deals with a corporation is charged with constructive notice of the recorded articles of incorporation. Their adoption creates the corporation, and they form the very basis of its existence. Everyone who deals with it or its stock is charged with knowledge of their contents. They expressly indicated that Mrs. Barth lacked any authority to convey without the FHA's prior consent.

The *Newberry* case is unusual because of the role of the corporation's creditor, the FHA. Ordinarily a lender would secure a mortgage against the property, not become a preferred shareholder with the right of approval for the transfer of any real or personal corporate property. As a policy matter, it could be argued that if the FHA fears its financial position might be so perilous without an equity interest, then it should not make or guaranty the loan in the first place.

Implied powers. In addition to its express powers, a corporation has *implied powers* to perform any acts reasonably necessary to fulfill the corporation's objectives. Of course, what the corporation does must be legal and must not be prohibited by its articles or bylaws.

Ordinarily, the articles do not restrict corporate activity. As a result, those who deal with corporate management have reason to believe it has fairly wide latitude in which to operate, since state corporation statutes tend to be quite permissive.

Thus, one oil company may form a joint venture with another for the purpose of exploring a new field, even though its articles and bylaws do not cover the point. Nonetheless, the burden is on the person doing business with the corporation to determine the limits on its authority stated in its articles.

Ultra Vires Transactions

The law terms unauthorized corporate transactions *ultra vires*, a Latin phrase meaning "beyond the powers." Historically, such transactions were considered to be unenforceable as null and void. Unfortunately, this defense often worked more as a sword, not a shield. Although the defense could be raised by either the corporation or the other contracting party, more often unscrupulous corporations would endeavor to accept the other party's performance and then claim ultra vires to excuse their return performance.

Today, application of the doctrine of ultra vires has been greatly reduced. The MBCA, §7, states the following:

> *"No act of a corporation and no conveyance or transfer of real or personal property to or by a corporation shall be invalid by reason of the fact that the corporation was without capacity or power to do such act or to make or receive such conveyance or transfer. . . ."*

The practical effect is that an executed contract, even if beyond the authority of the corporation, cannot be challenged by the corporation or other contracting party.

Under both MBCA, §7, and RMBCA, §3.04, the defense of ultra vires can be raised in three situations:

1. A proceeding by a shareholder in the name of the corporation, called a derivative suit, to enjoin (prevent) the corporation from performing an ultra vires *executory* (nonperformed) contract
2. A proceeding against an incumbent or former director, officer, employee, or agent of the corporation
3. A proceeding by the Attorney General leading to judicial dissolution

To illustrate, assume the articles of ABC, Inc., prohibit charitable contributions. A completed charitable gift by ABC, Inc., to the University of Virginia could not be reversed. However, a shareholder could bring a derivative suit to prevent payment of the charitable gift if the pledge were still executory.

The fact that the doctrine of ultra vires has all but been eliminated does not mean a corporation can engage freely in any form of business activity. An illegal contract, whether or not it is an ultra vires act, is still void. In addition, a corporation potentially faces criminal and tort liability for improper business activity.

Tort and Criminal Offenses

Like any other principal, a corporation may be liable under the doctrine of respondeat superior for the acts of its agents and employees. The corporation may also be liable on a strict liability in tort theory. These topics are discussed in Chapters 4, 15, and 34.

As to criminal liability, courts once took the position that corporations could not commit crimes involving intent because they could not form the required criminal state of mind. Today, it remains extremely difficult—where it is not impossible—to prove a corporation's intent, say, to commit murder.

Courts are more likely to find corporations guilty of crimes where fraud is involved or where the law imposes a strict liability standard. Many criminal statutes specifically govern business behavior. These include statutes governing securities law infractions (see Chapter 23), antitrust violations (see Chapter 44), and air and water pollution (see Chapter 47).

Officers and directors may be criminally liable for authorizing or participating in violations. As we saw in *U.S. v. Park* in Chapter 5, they may also be liable for criminal violations which they could have acted to prevent. In *Park*, the defendant, as president of Acme Supermarkets, could have ordered its warehouses to take steps to avoid contamination of food by rodents.

A court will not excuse criminal conduct by officers and directors on the grounds that their illegal actions were meant to benefit the corporation and that they derived no personal gain from them. The corporate defendant in the next case put forward a variation on this defense.

United States v. Cincotta

689 F.2d 238 (1st Cir. 1982)

FACTS

Cincotta was Mystic Fuel Corp.'s treasurer and Zero its dispatcher. Both were major shareholders in Mystic. In Mystic's name, Cincotta and Zero billed the Department of Defense for oil which was supposedly delivered to Fort Devins, but which Mystic actually sold to others. The jury found Mystic, Cincotta, and Zero guilty of conspiracy to defraud and a variety of other charges.

ISSUE

Could Mystic be criminally liable for the acts of one of its officers and one of its agents?

DECISION

Yes. Affirmed.

A corporation may be convicted for the criminal acts of its agents, under a theory of respondeat superior. But criminal liability may be imposed on the corporation only where the agent is acting within the scope of employment. That, in turn, requires that the agent be performing acts of the kind which he is authorized to perform, and those acts must be motivated—at least in part—by an intent to benefit the corporation. Thus, where intent is an element of a crime . . . a corporation may not be held strictly accountable for acts that could not benefit the stockholders, such as acts of corporate officers that are performed in exchange for bribes paid to the officers personally.

. . . [Mystic] contends that the government failed to produce evidence of Cincotta's and/or Zero's intent to benefit the corporation through their scheme to defraud the United States. This argument may be rejected out of hand. The mechanism by which the fraudulent scheme worked required money to pass through Mystic's treasury. . . . Mystic—not the individual defendants—was making money by selling oil that it had not paid for.

THE BOARD OF DIRECTORS

The ultimate responsibility for seeing that the corporation acts within its powers rests on the board of directors. Logic would seem to dictate that that responsibility should be the shareholders' because they own the corporation. However, the principal responsibility of those holding stock with voting rights is to elect the directors. As we will see in the next chapter, shareholders play a vital role in the corporation, but not in its day-to-day management. Figure 20.1 outlines the basic structure of corporate governance.

Powers and Responsibilities

As the RMBCA [§8.01(b)] puts it, "all corporate powers shall be exercised by or under the authority of . . . the board of directors." "Ex-

---

SHAREHOLDERS: Owners

Elect and remove

- Are not agents of corporation
- Have no fiduciary duties (except majority shareholder in some cases)

DIRECTORS: Set policy

Appoint and remove

- Are not agents of the corporation
- Do have fiduciary duties to corporation
- "Business judgment" standard applies

OFFICERS: Implement policy

- Are agents of the corporation
- Do have fiduciary duties to corporation
- Principal-agent rules apply

Figure 20.1 Basic Corporate Governance.
One of the great public policy debates of the last 25 years has centered on the public's role in corporate governance. Should the public have a role? If so, what should it be?

---

ercised by" means that the board is actually involved in the making of corporate decisions and policy. "Under the authority of" refers to the fact that the board may delegate authority to its committees—particularly, as we will see, to its executive committee—and to corporate employees. Thus, the board of directors actually sets the corporation's policy and steers the corporation's business. The directors select the officers, who manage and implement board policies. Also, the board has the power—in accordance with state law, the articles, and the bylaws—to grant agency authority for the corporation.

Compensation. The board sets its own compensation, unless the articles reserve this right to the shareholders. Directors normally receive their out-of-pocket expenses. In some corporations, they receive compensation for their services or malpractice insurance, or both [RMBCA §8.11(a)].

Board structure. Although, as we will see, some powers assigned to the board may never be delegated, to a large degree the board may shape its own role in the corporation. In part, a board will tailor its role to fit the structure and size of the company. For example, the General Motors board must operate as a guide of corporate strategy. Involving itself in the day-to-day corporate transactions, even at the highest level, would be impossible. In contrast, as will be discussed in Chapter 22, some small corporations may elect to dispense with the board altogether.

Eligibility and Elections

The MBCA permits a corporation to have just one director [RMBCA §8.03(a)], but a number of states require a minimum of three. The articles of incorporation must name the corporation's initial board members and set their terms. The articles also specify when the shareholders will meet to replace the initial directors. Thereafter, elections take place at the shareholders' annual meeting.

Candidates and terms of office. The RMBCA does not establish qualifications of membership on a board. If the shareholders want to set some, they may do so by amending either the articles or the bylaws.

Ordinarily, a committee of the board proposes a slate of candidates to the shareholders, and those candidates are elected. A director often is a major shareholder or an officer or both, but a director does not have to be either. Directors who are officers of the corporation are called *inside directors*. Those who are not are called *outside directors*. Corporations commonly draw outside directors from companies or lenders with which they do business. Large, highly visible corporations often draw their boards from the top strata of other corporations. Celebrities and former political figures—like former President Gerald Ford and his Secretary of State, Henry Kissinger—can make small fortunes by lending their prestige to corporate boards. In contrast, Japanese corporations rarely have outside board members because their boards have many more hands-on management responsibilities. On American boards, minorities and women are not well represented. In 1988, only 6.4 percent of the board seats of the *Fortune* 1000 companies were occupied by women.

The shareholders elect directors to specific terms of office. Directors' terms are usually staggered to provide continuity on the board, and also to limit the ability of insurgent candidates to take control of the board, because a majority of seats is never up for election at any one time. If a board has six directors and its articles provide for staggered 3-year terms, then only two directors are elected annually.

The straight election method. For board elections, a corporation uses either the *straight* or the *cumulative* election method. If the articles do not specify a method, the corporation must use the straight method [RMBCA §7.28(a)].

In the straight method, a simple majority of votes cast elects a director. Typically, the shareholders are entitled to one vote per share for each seat to be filled. In effect, a separate election is held for each open seat on the board.

Let's look at an example. At the annual meeting, the shareholders of D&L Corporation are to elect three directors. The nominating committee has selected Ray, Sue, and Tom for the three seats. Dan holds 350 of D&L's 1000 outstanding shares and wants to sit on the board. He decides to contest all three seats. If the other shareholders vote against him, the vote on each seat would be 650 to Dan's 350. Clearly, straight voting does not favor representation of minority interests.

The cumulative method. A corporation may choose to use a cumulative voting system. However, the articles must specify its use [RMBCA §7.28(b)].

Cumulative voting was devised to provide board representation for minority shareholders. In this system, a shareholder is entitled to one vote per share for each director to be elected. All the directors are elected in one ballot, and shareholders may cast all their votes for one candidate or split them among as many as they choose. The formula used to determine the number of shares necessary to win a board seat is

$$x = \frac{yz}{t + 1} + 1$$

where x = number of shares necessary to elect desired number of directors
y = number of directors desired to be elected
z = the number of shares voting
t = total number of directors to be elected

Now look at Dan's situation under cumulative voting. Dan holds 350 of the 1000 shares

---

FACTS
1. Three board seats to be chosen.
2. Dan has 350 of 1000 shares outstanding.
3. Dan wishes to elect himself and Don.
4. Majority wishes to elect Ray, Sue, and Tom.

TYPE OF VOTING	STRAIGHT	CUMULATIVE
Results of first vote	Ray 650, Dan 350	Dan $(251 \times 3) = 753$ Don $(99 \times 3) = 297$ Ray $(251 \times 3) = 753$ Sue $(251 \times 3) = 753$ Tom $(148 \times 3) = 444$
Results of second vote	Sue 650, Dan 350	None
Results of third vote	Tom 650, Dan 350	None
Final results	Ray, Sue, and Tom win.	Dan, Ray, and Sue win.

Figure 20.2 Methods of Voting for Directors Compared.

---

and therefore has 1050 votes to cast. In order to determine how many *shares* he needs to vote in order to elect a director, he would perform the following computation:

$$X = \frac{(1)(1000)}{3+1} + 1$$
$$= 251$$

By casting all the votes of 251 shares (i.e., 251×3) for himself, Dan is assured of election. He may vote his other 99 shares as he chooses. Figure 20.2 charts this example.

Removal and replacement. The shareholders may remove directors with or without cause at a special meeting called specifically for that purpose [RMBCA §3.08]. However, the articles may provide that a director may only be removed for cause. Also, the shareholders may consider other business at the special meeting called to remove a director. The key requirement, though, is that the notice of the meeting specifically place removal of a director on the agenda.

Under the straight voting methods, removal normally requires just a majority vote. Suppose Dan was elected to D&L's board. Under the straight voting method, he could be removed if a simple majority of the votes cast favored removal.

If the corporation's articles require cumulative voting, removal is a more involved procedure. Unless all the board members are being removed, the shareholders may not remove a director if the votes cast against that director's removal would be sufficient to elect him if they were cumulatively voted at an election of the entire board of directors. Again, suppose D&L's other shareholders wanted to remove Dan. If Dan voted 251 of his shares against his removal, he would remain on the board regardless of how many shares were voted against him. Thus, cumulative voting protects incumbent directors as well as offering a greater opportunity for minority representation.

If a director is removed, either the shareholders or the remaining board members elect a new member to fill the vacancy until the next annual meeting. The same rule applies if the number of directors is increased, say, from seven to nine [RMBCA §8.10].

Board Meetings

Corporate boards take action by adopting *resolutions*, positions adopted after a formal vote. The subject matter of a resolution can be as simple as congratulations to the sales representative of the month or as complicated as an employee pay schedule. Because of the responsibilities the law assigns boards, resolutions are not to be adopted casually, but rather after full discussion. For that reason, boards are required to meet. And, except in extraordinary and limited circumstances, they may adopt resolutions only in those meetings.

Types of meetings and notice. Board of directors' meetings are of two types: regular and special. The two words carry their ordinary meanings.

The corporate bylaws should prescribe what notice of regular meetings of the board or any of its committees' directors are to receive. Often, the bylaws require the board to establish a schedule of regular meetings for an entire year. The secretary of the board is assigned the responsibility of giving the directors specific notice of the time, place, and agenda for the next meeting between 10 and 30 days before it is to take place. Special meetings, too, require notice, and again the bylaws may prescribe what form the notice will take.

The law presumes that a director who attends a meeting had notice of it. A director's participation in a meeting amounts to a waiver of notice unless the director attends expressly to object to the transaction of any business because the meeting had not been lawfully called [MBCA §43]. Suppose the bylaws of Asteroid, Inc., require that notice of special meetings be telephoned to all directors. The board's majority wants to ratify a contract for a new plant, a project to which Arlene, a board member, strongly objects. They deliberately do not notify her of a special meeting called to ratify the contract. She learns of it and attends. Unless she clearly states her objection to the meet-

ing, she will waive notice of it, and the contract ratification will be valid. If she does object, Asteroid must call another meeting—properly—to ratify the contract.

Quorum. A *quorum* is the minimum number of qualified members of a body who must be present in order to take an action which binds that body. In the corporate setting, to be adopted, a resolution must receive the votes of a majority of the number of directors fixed as a quorum by either the bylaws or the articles of incorporation. An act of the majority of the directors present at the meeting is the board's act—assuming that a quorum is present and that the articles or bylaws do not require a larger number.

Physical presence not required. The board need not meet by sitting around a boardroom table. The MBCA allows meetings by conference call or by similar telecommunications equipment. It requires only that everyone participating in the meeting be able to hear each other at the same time [RMBCA §8.20(b)].

If the articles or bylaws permit and if all directors agree in writing, the board may take action without actually meeting. All the directors must sign the consent to an action, and it must fully describe the action to be taken [RMBCA §8.20(b)]. Suppose a corporation is invited to participate in a joint venture forming to bid on a government contract. The opportunity will not wait for the next regularly scheduled board meeting. If all the directors agree in writing to approve pursuing the venture, then the board does not need to meet formally in order to act on it. The board's action takes effect when the last director signs the consent, unless the consent specifies a different date [RMBCA §8.21(b)]. Thus, the consent amounts to a unanimous vote.

Delegation of Board Powers and Duties

Individual board members may not delegate their responsibilities to act on proposed resolutions. However, the board of directors as an entity may delegate its powers. Primarily, these delegations are to committees of the board whose actions the board ratifies and to corporate officers whose job it is to implement board policy and whose performance the board monitors.

Proxies. A director may not use a *proxy*, a person authorized to represent and vote for another.* Such a delegation is improper because a board member has an obligation to attend meetings and consider resolutions put before the board.

Board committees. A board may create an executive committee and any other committees authorized by the corporation's articles or bylaws [RMBCA §8.25]. While a board may delegate significant duties to committees, it cannot delegate fundamental decisions, such as whether to declare a dividend.

An *executive committee* has authority to act on matters delegated to it between meetings of the entire board. Typically, these are matters which require board approval, but on which decisions can be made that are consistent with established board policy. For example, the board may have voted to spend $2.5 million for a new plant site and left the choice between site A and site B to its executive committee. Often, the executive committee prepares proposals for action by the entire board on particularly nettlesome issues, such as executive compensation. With duties such as these, it is easy to see why an executive committee can have enormous power.

In response to a New York Stock Exchange requirement, many large corporations have board audit committees which oversee the company's annual independent audit. The Securities & Exchange Commission requires corporations under its jurisdiction to disclose whether their boards have audit, compensation, or nominating committees. Because of the enormous influence these committees can wield, corporations must reveal their membership and their scope of authority.

The MBCA specifically forbids committees to assume certain functions. In other words, the MBCA requires the board itself to take the following actions—if they are to be taken at all:

- Authorize dividends and other distributions to shareholders.
- Recommend how shareholders should vote on proposals submitted for their approval.
- Designate candidates for directorships (many states have not followed the MBCA on this).
- Amend the bylaws.
- Take any extraordinary actions relating to the company's securities [MBCA §42].

In addition to these and the MBCA's other restrictions on committee actions, the articles or the bylaws may further restrict committee authority.

CORPORATE OFFICERS

A board must appoint a president, a vice president—or more than one, if permitted by the bylaws—a secretary, and a treasurer for the corporation. Under the MBCA [§50], one individual may hold any two of these offices, except that no one person can be both president and secretary. The board may appoint other officers, assistant officers, and agents when necessary. Either the articles or the bylaws define the duties of those the board appoints. The RMBCA [§8.40] allows one person to hold all the corporate offices. However, as a preventive law strategy, it would seem the MBCA rule is a better one, since it builds in a check on the officers.

The board also has the duty and right to fire its appointees with or without cause [RMBCA

---

* In the next chapter, we will see that *proxy* can also mean the *power of attorney*, which authorizes a person to act in another's place, particularly with respect to issues put before the shareholders. Shareholders *may* use proxies.

§8.43(b)]. Accordingly, the shareholders could not vote to fire the company's president at the annual shareholders' meeting.

Express and Implied Authority

Unlike directors and shareholders, officers are agents of the corporation by virtue of their positions.

Officers' express authority comes from the state's incorporation statutes and the corporation's articles, its bylaws, and its board's resolutions. Officers also have the implied authority reasonably necessary to fulfill a grant of express authority. For instance, in order to carry out a board's charge to purchase a plant site, a corporate officer would have the implied authority to hire an appraiser, employ an attorney, order a title search, and do all the other things necessary to protect the corporation.

The next case illustrates why a state's incorporation statutes as well as the corporation's own bylaws are sometimes invoked to rein in corporate officers who abuse their positions of power.

SQUAW MOUNTAIN CATTLE COMPANY v. BOWEN

804 P.2d 1292 (Wyo. 1991)

FACTS

The Two Bar-Muleshoe Water Company (Muleshoe) owned land underneath a reservoir which it leased out to Wheatland Irrigation District (Wheatland). In exchange for the lease, Wheatland delivered irrigation water from the reservoir to Muleshoe shareholders. The Squaw Mountain Cattle Company (Squaw Mountain) owned 59 percent of the stock in Muleshoe. Jones was president and sole owner of Squaw Mountain and also president of Muleshoe. Muleshoe authorized Jones to sue Wheatland over an ongoing water dispute. To drop the suit, Wheatland offered Muleshoe $1 million for its land and $250,000 to settle. Jones lied to the Muleshoe shareholders, telling them that $116,000 was an offer for the land but that the rest of the offer was made to Jones and his relatives for "physical and emotional stress, embarrassment and loss of reputation" caused by the dispute. The Muleshoe shareholders rejected the offer, but Jones voted Squaw Mountain's 59 percent of the shares and declared the offer accepted. He then signed the settlement on behalf of Muleshoe. Muleshoe, in a shareholders' derivative suit, sued Jones, asserting that he lacked the authority to bind Muleshoe to the settlement. Muleshoe prevailed at the trial level.

ISSUE

Did Jones have the authority to accept the settlement offer on behalf of Muleshoe?

DECISION

No. Affirmed. Corporate officers must act within the scope of their authority. Jones's authority to act on behalf of Muleshoe flowed from two sources. First, Muleshoe bylaws stated that the president presides at all meetings and shall have general charge and control *subject to the board of directors*. This was violated when Jones did not receive the board's permission to make the settlement. A second source was a state statute which requires that *two-thirds* of the shareholders must approve a sale of substantially all the corporate assets. In this case Jones voted 59 percent of Squaw Mountain's shares to sell Muleshoe's sole asset, which means the sale was unauthorized.

Apparent Authority

As with all agents, corporate officers have apparent authority to carry out functions normally associated with their positions. For instance, a corporate vice president for marketing may have authorized rebates to dealers in the past. After a board resolution relieves her of that power, she will have apparent authority to bind the corporation to a rebate she later offers to a dealer who lacks notice of the board resolution.

Ratification

Like any principal, the corporation's board may ratify a transaction of one of its agents. As the following case indicates, the normal agency rules apply.

Molasky Enterprises, Inc. v. Carps, Inc.

615 S.W.2d 83 (Mo. Ct. App. 1981)

FACTS   Herbert and Emile Carp, directors as well as, respectively, president and executive vice president of Carps, Inc., applied for a $267,000 personal loan from Lindell Trust. Lindell Trust required a cosigner on the loan. The Carp brothers asked Molasky to cosign, which he did after the brothers executed the loan in their personal capacities and after Herbert had cosigned it in the corporation's name. Molasky did not ask for Carps' board's resolution to guarantee the loan, nor did he ask whether Herbert had authority to bind the corporation. Herbert lacked authority, and the board never ratified his endorsement. The brothers defaulted on the note, and Carps, Inc., refused to pay. Molasky paid the balance due and brought suit against Carps, Inc., for reimbursement. The trial court entered judgment for Carps, Inc.

ISSUE   Did the brothers have authority to bind the corporation as a guarantor of their personal obligations?

DECISION   No. Affirmed. A corporation's president normally has authority to bind the corporation by executing and transferring negotiable paper in the ordinary course of company business. However, that authority is limited to transacting business for the corporation's benefit. It does not include authority to sign as surety for a third person. The board must specifically give that authority. The Carp brothers had no actual authority to bind the corporation. They could not have apparent authority because the principal creates the appearance of authority, not the agent.

STANDARDS OF CONDUCT FOR DIRECTORS AND OFFICERS

Directors and officers owe fiduciary duties to the corporation. These duties generally resemble those owed by any person in a fiduciary capacity.

As agents of the corporation, officers' fiduciary duties are very similar to those of agents generally. Directors, however, are a different matter. Their duties closely resemble those of agents and employees, but when they act as directors, they are neither. Directors must perform their duties in good faith and in a manner they reasonably believe to be in the best interests of the corporation [RMBCA §§8.30, 8.41].

Duty to Use Due Care

Corporate directors and officers do not ensure the corporation's profitability. Thus, if the corporation suffers a loss from a transaction the board authorized, the directors are not personally liable to the shareholders unless they violate the business judgment rule.

The business judgment rule. Courts generally defer to the board's business judgment unless they find a clear lack of good faith, fraud, or an abuse of discretion. Sometimes disputes arise over a board's failure to declare dividends some shareholders consider to be sufficient. Courts seldom reverse a board's judgment in this area.

Directors and officers must discharge their duties in good faith and exercise the care that an ordinarily diligent and prudent person would be expected to exercise in a similar position. In other words, if the directors were sole proprietors, would they have taken a particular action? If their actions satisfy this test, they will not be liable for errors of judgment, short of clear negligence.

This is known as the *business judgment rule*. For example, when a large company goes bankrupt, the directors will not be personally liable if they acted in good faith, even though better management might have avoided the bankruptcy.

Another area in which controversy often arises is *tender offers*. These offers to purchase stock—usually for the purpose of gaining control—are made either to the company or directly to the shareholders.* Quite often, as in the next case, a critic might question whether the business judgment rule always works in the shareholders'—as opposed to existing management's—best interests.

---

* The SEC's role in regulating tender offers is discussed in Chapter 23.

Panter v. Marshall Field & Co., Inc.

646 F.2d 271 (7th Cir. 1981)

FACTS   Beginning in 1975, Marshall Field received inquiries about mergers from other retail chains. In 1977, Carter Hawley Hale made a tender offer. Because, among other reasons, Marshall Field's board believed the merger posed antitrust problems, it rejected the offer. Panter and other shareholders brought suit against the board for not accepting the tender offer, claiming that the offer was rejected to maintain current management's control. The trial court granted the corporate defendants' motion for a directed verdict.

ISSUE   Was the directors' action shielded by the business judgment rule?

DECISION   Yes. Affirmed. An allegation that one purpose of rejecting the tender offer was the board's desire to retain control will not shift the burden to the directors to show a rational business purpose for their judgment.

If directors were held to the same standard as ordinary fiduciaries, the corporation could not conduct business. An ordinary fiduciary may not have the slightest conflict of interest in any transaction on behalf of the principal. Yet by the very nature of corporate life, directors have some self-interest in everything they do. Directors want to enhance corporate profits partly because they want to keep shareholders satisfied so that they will not be ousted. The business judgment rule alleviates this problem by assuming that if directors take an action that is arguably for the benefit of the corporation, they are exercising their sound business judgment rather than responding to personal motivations. The plaintiff must show that impermissible motives predominated.

In cases like *Panter*, the test, loosely stated, is whether the board fairly and reasonably exercises its business judgment to protect the corporation and its shareholders against any injury a corporation might suffer should the tender offer prove successful. The presumption of good faith is heightened when the majority of the board consists of independent outside directors. But that presumption is far from absolute. Indeed, 5 years after *Panter*, the Seventh Circuit again had a tender offer case before it in which five of the eight directors were outsiders. This time, however, the Court reached precisely the opposite result, as the next case shows.

Dynamics Corp. of America v. CTS Corp.

794 F.2d 250 (7th Cir. 1986)

FACTS   Dynamics Corp. owned 9.6 percent of CTS's stock. On March 10, 1986, Dynamics made a tender offer for another million shares, which would bring its stock holdings up to 27.5 percent and give it effective control of CTS. At the time that it announced its tender offer, Dynamics also announced it was fielding a rival slate of directors for election at the annual meeting on April 24. The same day, without studing the tender offer, CTS's directors adopted a *poison pill*, "a family of shareholder rights agreements which, upon some triggering even such as the acquisition by a tender offeror of a certain percentage of the target corporation's common stock, entitle the remaining shareholders to receive additional shares of common stock (or other securities) at bargain prices." The purpose of a poison pill is to kill the tender offer. Dynamics sought and was granted an injunction against implementation of the poison pill.

ISSUE   Did the business judgment rule insulate the actions of the CTS board from judicial review?

DECISION   No. Affirmed.

The market price of publicly traded stock impounds all available information about the value of the stock, and anyone who tenders a higher price [as Dynamics did] thereby offers an unequivocal benefit to the shareholders of the target firm, which management if it is really a fiduciary of the shareholders should embrace rather than oppose. . . .

[The business judgment rule] expresses a sensible policy of judicial noninterference with business decisions made in circumstances free from serious conflicts of interest between management . . . and the corporation's shareholders. When however there is a serious conflict of interest, and in particular when management is making decisions that may thwart the operation of the market in corporate control, the judicial role . . . is less deferential. When managers are busy erecting obstacles to the taking over of the corporation by an investor who is likely to fire them if the takeover attempt succeeds, they have a clear conflict of interest. . . .

After reading *Panter* and *Dynamics Corp.*, one would be forgiven for feeling about the business judgment rule and tender offers as former Treasury Secretary Michael Blumenthal did about the nation's economy: "Anyone who isn't schizophrenic about it isn't thinking straight." Indeed, in the space of 7 months in 1985, the Delaware Supreme Court—the nation's most influential court on questions of corporate law—appears to have flipped from *Panter* to *Dynamics Corp.* and back to *Panter.**
For almost 10 years, tender offers have dominated the national news. Like the public, the judiciary has not made up its mind about the ethical questions surrounding such offers. And there is no consensus in sight.

One of the Delaware cases, *Smith v. Van Gorkom*, may mark the line below which directors may not go. In that case, the Delaware Supreme Court upheld a judgment for $23.5 million against directors and key officers of a corporation who agreed to a surprise merger proposal in a brief meeting just before the chairman's party inaugurating the opera season. They took matters so casually in approving the

---

* See *Smith v. Van Gorkom*, 488 A.2d 858 (Del. 1985); *Unocal Corp. v. Mesa Petroleum Co.*, 493 A.2d 946 (Del. 1985), and *Moran v. Household Int'l. Inc.*, 500 A.2d 1346 (Del. 1985).

transaction that they did not even take detailed minutes, much less seek the advice of an outside lawyer or an investment banker. Perhaps the bottom line is that directors must exercise their judgment—not just make a decision.

Reliance on corporate data. Outside directors, however, have a problem. They have to rely on management for data on the company's performance and outlook. Still, by law, the outside directors have a duty to monitor management and pass on its performance.

Directors have the right to inspect corporate records to enable them to set policy and to carry out their fiduciary duties. However, they may rely on information, opinions, reports, or statements, including financial statements and other financial data, prepared by corporate employees, legal counsel, public accountants, and the like [RMBCA §8.30].

A court will not consider directors to be acting in good faith if they know or have reason to believe that reliance on these documents is unwarranted. Also, as discussed in Chapter 23, even good faith reliance on reports prepared by corporate officers may not excuse directors from liabililty under the federal securities laws.

Bad faith. A director or officer found by a court to have acted in bad faith or in a clearly negligent manner may be liable to the corporation. Courts may find negligence in selecting or approving employees, as, for instance, if the board appoints a disbarred lawyer as general counsel. A board may also be held liable for appointing inadequate supervisory employees. Appointing the chairman's playboy son president of a subsidiary might fall into this category. A lack of vigor in defending claims against the corporation may lead to a verdict against directors. If the corporation loses a major case because management failed to refer the matter to corporate counsel in a timely fashion, those responsible should expect someone to file suit against them.

An officer's or director's liability for violating the business judgment rule extends only to those losses flowing directly from the breach of duty. It does not extend to speculative losses, such as shareholder profits had the directors not rejected the tender offer.

Duty of Obedience

Directors and officers must act within their respective authorities. Officers who exceed their authority in contracting may be liable to the corporation for the damages which result. However, directors or officers involved in an ultra vires act will not be liable if they believed in good faith that the action was proper.

Duty of Loyalty

In their relations with the corporation, directors and officers have but one master—the corporation. Their loyalty must be undivided. They must be honest and act in good faith in their dealings with it.

Corporate opportunity doctrine. The rule that directors are not corporate agents has an exception. Under its power to appoint corporate agents, the board may give a director special powers to represent the corporation. Suppose the corporation authorizes Linda, a director, to negotiate with a realty company to buy an office building. She acts as an agent of the corporation and owes it the same duties an agent would. If Linda buys the property on her own behalf and sells it to another company, she breaches her duty to the corporation. This is known as the *corporate opportunity doctrine* because the director deprived her corporation of the opportunity to profit from a venture. The same rule applies to officers. In the next case, the defendant was the corporation's president and a director.

Klinicki v. Lundgren

67 Or. App. 160, 678 P.2d 1250 (1984)

FACTS   Klinicki and Lundgren were laid off Pan Am pilots stationed in West Germany. In April 1977, they incorporated Berlinair, Inc., in Oregon. Berlinair was to provide air taxi service to West Berlin. Lundgren and his family held 66 percent of the stock; Klinicki held 33 percent. As president, Lundgren had duties including developing business for Berlinair. Through 1982, Berlinair had not shown a profit but was never insolvent. In late 1977, Lundgren began negotiating with a consortium of travel agents on behalf of Berlinair for a contract to operate charter flights. When the contract was nearly in hand, Lundgren announced to the consortium that he would make a new proposal on behalf of Air Berlin Charter Co., a corporation he owned alone. In September 1978, Air Berlin won the contract. When Klinicki learned what Lundgren had done, he brought suit, alleging that Lundgren had usurped a corporate opportunity. Lundgren defended on the grounds that Berlinair did not have the financial capacity to undertake the charter contract. The trial court found for Klinicki.

ISSUE
Is a corporation's financial ability to undertake a business opportunity relevant to proving the usurping of a corporate opportunity?

DECION
No. Affirmed. A corporation's financial ability to undertake a business opportunity is not a factor in determining the existence of an opportunity unless the defendant demonstrates that the company was insolvent. Otherwise, the determination of whether the opportunity existed for the company is the company's. If a fiduciary is uncertain as to whether an opportunity is corporate or whether the company has the financial ability to pursue it, all he has to do is disclose this to the directors and let them decide. Disclosure resolves the question for all concerned and avoids later litigation. Here, Berlinair was never insolvent and Lundgren never made a disclosure to its directors.

Competition with the corporation. If directors and officers may not usurp a corporate opportunity, then logically they may not compete directly with the corporation either. If a retail furniture company vice president owns an interest in a furniture chain active in the same locale, she has a conflict.

Business dealings with the corporation. Under early corporation law, an officer or director could not do any business with the corporation. Today, officers or directors may do business with the corporation if:

1. They fully disclose their personal interest in the matter and the contract is fair and reasonable to the corporation.
2. An independent board majority or all shareholders approve the contract [MBCA §41].

The law recognizes the practical reality that outside directors often will be doing business with the corporation, either individually or as representatives of other corporations. It is both common and natural for companies with close business ties to have representatives on each other's boards. However, an outside director must never forget that when she acts as a company's director, she owes undivided loyalty to that company.

Disqualification. Board members must disqualify themselves when the board votes on a matter in which they have a personal interest. That is one clear meaning of *Weiss Medical Complex*, briefed above. In addition, board members must disclose the nature of the conflict of interest. Suppose a corporation is considering purchasing insurance through the Annapolis Agency. A board member must disclose any immediate family connection to the agency and, if one exists, disqualify himself from voting on the contract.

Insider trading in securities. As we will see in Chapter 23, the federal securities laws forbid persons who have access to information which may affect the price of a corporation's securities to trade in those securities if that knowledge is not available to the general public. This prohibition applies to *all* directors, officers, employees, and significant shareholders.

Indemnification for Breach of Duty

Angry shareholders have been suing directors at record rates. And today many people who ordinarily would serve on boards will not. Indeed, one study revealed that claims against directors had soared 257 percent between 1974 and 1984. *

By 1988, bondholders had joined the litigation merry-go-round. They saw junk bond financing as a threat to the quality of their investments. Institutional investors—pension funds, university endowments, and the like—were not suing but they were clearly expressing their concerns in the face of corporate restructurings that traded equity for debt. As a result, the always controversial subject of indemnification of directors and officers for judgments arising from a breach of their duties has become a white-hot topic. Not the least important element fueling the controversy is the rising cost of indemnification insurance—when it can be obtained at all.

Right to indemnification. Unless the articles of incorporation provide otherwise, the RMBCA [§8.52] requires that a corporation indemnify a director who successfully defends a suit arising from his or her status as a director. Suppose a plaintiff has named the directors of Enormous Auto Maker Corp. in a product liability suit against the corporation. The complaint alleges the directors negligently approved the sale of a car with a faulty brake system. The action is dismissed against the directors, but the plaintiff obtains a judgment against the corporation. The directors have a right to be indemnified for their litigation expenses.

Voluntary indemnification. Unless the articles prohibit it, a corporation may voluntarily indemnify a director who unsuccessfully defends a suit arising out of his or her status as a director. The director may be indemnified for his or her reasonable litigation expenses if the director:

1. Acted in good faith
2. Reasonably believed his or her conduct was in the best interests—or at least was not opposed to the interests—of the corporation [RMBCA §8.51(a)(1), (2)]

Suppose the plaintiff in the last example prevails against the directors, but the directors had acted in good faith and believed that their actions would further the company's interests. The corporation could indemnify the directors' expenses.

A corporation may even indemnify a director's expenses in defending a criminal action under the same circumstances as a civil action. However, the director must also have had no reasonable cause to believe his or her conduct was unlawful [RMBCA §8.51(a)(3)].

Court-ordered indemnification. Under RMBCA §8.54, a director may bring an action against the corporation to secure indemnification when mandatory indemnification rights exist and the corporation has not observed them.

Indemnification prohibited. In addition to those circumstances in which the articles prohibit indemnification, a corporation may not indemnify a director where the director is found to be liable to the corporation or to have received an improper benefit from the corporation [RMBCA §8.51(d)].

Indemnification for nondirectors. Nondirectors—including officers, agents, and employees—have the same indemnification rights as those of directors. However, a corporation may expand the rights of nondirectors beyond those of directors "to the extent consistent with public policy" [RMBCA §8.56(3)]. The act offers no guidance as to what that extent is.

CONCLUSION

This chapter has focused on the duties of directors and officers. Analytically, these duties may

* D. Sellers, "Too Many Hot Seats on the Boards," *Insight*, February 2, 1987, pp. 40–41.

be separated and explained. They seem relatively clear cut, but in practice they may be anything but.

The directors' fiduciary duties are geared toward preserving and enhancing the shareholders' interests. Outside directors in particular have a duty to be watchful for the interests of those who cannot guard their own. However, the honorary nature of their position and their close relationship with, and need to rely upon, management makes independent judgment extremely difficult.

Nonetheless, in almost all corporations, whether big or small, the board and management tend to identify their own interests with those of the corporation. This is the complaint many shareholders raise against management resistance to lucrative tender offers.

When corporate officers and others who work for the corporation identify their own interests with those of the corporation, this can give the corporation great strength. Still, corporate officers owe the corporation fiduciary duties which may require them to put the shareholders' interests ahead of their own where these interests conflict.

Plainly, the potential for ethical dilemmas among directors and officers is great. *Panter v. Marshall Field* has foreshadowed much of the discussion in the next chapter on shareholder rights. Shareholders are not defenseless against the board and management, but their opportunities to protect their interests are far fewer than those of officers and directors.

The price of limited liability for shareholders, we noted in Chapter 19, is a limited role in management. In some cases, that may be too high a price for the privilege.

A NOTE TO FUTURE CPA CANDIDATES

The doctrine of ultra vires was once commonly tested on the CPA exam, but modern corporation statutes, containing provisions similar to the MBCA and RMBCA, have resulted in less

test emphasis. However, it is still necessary to understand the doctrine and its most common remaining application, enjoining the performance of an executory contract.

You need to understand fully the basic relationships between the shareholders, directors, and officers which are illustrated in Figure 20.1. Remember that shareholders, as shareholders, are considered investors without agency authority and fiduciary duties.

An officer or director of a corporation is expected to exercise due care when acting on behalf of the corporation. The business judgment rule is the standard which measures this conduct. Under the business judgment rule good faith usually is sufficient to prevent personal liability. In contrast, the SEC's due diligence standard, noted in this chapter and discussed in Chapter 23, requires more than mere good faith. As a result, on the CPA exam you must be careful to note whether the question involves a potential SEC violation.

The fiduciary duties owed by an officer or director to the corporation are similar to those previously encountered in the study of agency and partnership law.

KEY WORDS

business judgment rule (443)
constructive notice (433)
corporate opportunity doctrine (446)
cumulative voting (437)
executive committee (440)

powers (corporate) (435)
proxy (440)
quorum (439)
resolution (439)
tender offer (443)
ultra vires (434)

DISCUSSION QUESTIONS

1. For the officers of a corporation to act, there must be proper authority. What are the sources of that authority?
2. Where is the corporation's official declaration of purpose to be found? What limits do the

MBCA and the RMBCA place on a corporation's activities?

3. Compare the straight and cumulative voting methods for electing directors. Which method is favored by minority shareholders? Why?

4. May shareholders directly remove the president of a corporation? Explain.

5. What is an ultra vires act? In what circumstances is it likely to be raised as a defense, and by whom?

6. What is a director's role in a corporation? Can a director have agency authority? Does a director owe fiduciary duties to the corporation?

7. What is an executive committee? What is its purpose?

8. How might a board delegate its authority concerning matters that arise between regular board meetings? Why would it do so? What restrictions would normally be placed on the delegation?

9. Give five examples of basic duties owed to the corporation by both directors and officers.

10. What is the business judgment rule? Under what circumstances is it likely to be at issue?

CASE PROBLEMS

1. Virginia De Vita was president of Stipp Corp. At the annual shareholder's meeting De Vita was questioned about the company's donation of land to a local college. De Vita angrily chided the shareholders for their narrow point of view. One shareholder stood up and made a motion that De Vita be fired as CEO and removed from the board for showing utter disrespect to the shareholders. The motion was quickly seconded and approved. As security personnel dragged her from the room, she yelled that she would prevail in court. Assuming no other relevant facts, did the shareholders have the legal power to remove De Vita as CEO? To remove her as a director? Explain.

2. Janice Maynard, chairperson of the board of directors of Mayco, Inc., wishes to call an immediate special board meeting to consider a takeover offer from Kendle-Hawley Department Stores. One board member, Morrow, cannot attend because he is traveling in Europe, while another, Guenzler, is hospitalized. If Mayco's articles and bylaws neither authorize nor prohibit actions taken by directors without an actual meeting, would it be sufficient for Maynard to conduct a telephone poll by calling each director individually? If not, what additional requirement(s), if any, would be necessary to sustain a proper board action? Explain.

3. The directors of Powerhouse Racquetball Club voted to double the number of racquetball courts. The directors knew that a competitor was to open soon in the area, but they felt that the market was so strong it would support both of them. The demand for racquetball courts fell off greatly in the following years, and the expanded facilities proved to be a large financial drain on the corporation. The directors have now been sued by a group of shareholders, who claim that the directors should be held personally liable for the losses attributable to the expanded courts. What test will the court use to evaluate the directors' performance? How will it be applied? Will the shareholders be likely to prevail? Explain.

4. Eagle Corporation decided to move its company headquarters from a small city, Erewhon, to Metropolis. Because of the much higher housing costs in Metropolis and the depressed real estate market in Erewhon, a number of Eagle officers have indicated that they will not move without some sort of financial assistance beyond moving expense reimbursement. The directors are contemplating whether they should offer to purchase any officers' homes in Erewhon that are not sold at fair market value within 90 days and to provide company financing assistance on homes purchased in Metropolis. An Eagle shareholder, Carl Kruse, has objected to this plan on the basis that there is no provision for such assistance in either the articles or the bylaws. Would a court uphold such a plan by the board of directors? Explain.

5. Peter is attempting to get elected to the board

of directors of Sirrah Corporation. Three seats are being voted on. Of the 1200 shares authorized, 1100 have been issued and 200 have been reacquired as treasury shares. Peter holds 180 shares. Assuming that all outstanding shares are voted and Peter is assured of only his own votes, will he win a seat if the corporation uses the cumulative voting method? Explain.

6. The board of directors of Marskie Corporation wishes to purchase a tract of vacant land for a new store. The land is owned by Sue Dikkers, the mother of one of the directors, Cory Dikkers. Does this preclude the corporation from acquiring the vacant land? What, if anything, should Cory do? Explain.

7. Fantana Corp., a retail shoe store chain, decided to sell its store in Red Oak, as the store was too far from its distribution center. Ella McNair purchased the store. Later, McNair successfully sued Fantana's treasurer, Thomas Frakes, and the board of directors because of the inaccurate financial statements for the store which Frakes had negligently prepared and the board had negligently approved and provided to McNair. The articles and bylaws are silent about indemnification. Would a board, without shareholder approval, normally be able to grant indemnification for an employee who acts within the course of employment but who is negligent? On what grounds, if any, could a court order indemnification for the board members in this case? Explain.

8. Rodney Davis was the CEO of Brown Imports, Inc., an import company specializing in Spanish-made products. While traveling on behalf of the company, Davis learned of a Chinese import company, Mikiso Hane, Inc., which was for sale. Davis purchased the company and installed John Sauter as CEO. Within a few years, Mikiso Hane was doing so well that Davis left and joined the firm. Brown Imports, learning of the facts above, has now brought an action against Davis claiming that Mikiso Hane should be considered the property of Brown Imports. Davis has countered that he never offered the opportunity to the Brown board of directors, since Mikiso Hane was involved in Chinese imports, not Spanish. Would Brown Imports be likely to prevail? Explain.

9. Sutton Corporation's board of directors established an executive committee to handle important board matters between board meetings. Sutton had an excellent sales year, and the executive committee decided that it would be appropriate to award a bonus cash dividend for the year. A shareholder, Momcilo Rosic, has demanded that the board of directors cancel this dividend because it was improperly declared. The board held a meeting at which four of the seven board members were represented by proxy. The board voted unanimously to affirm the special dividend. Was the original special dividend declaration legally declared? Was the ratification of the declaration legally made? Explain.

10. Donald Blanchard was CEO of Melville Publishing, Inc. Melville received an offer of merger from Pillsbury Publishing, Inc., a well-respected rival. Blanchard strongly urged the board of directors to consider the offer. The board refused, on the grounds that Melville should continue its independent status, and fired Blanchard. A shareholder, Lewis Salter, demanded that the board reconsider both decisions, but the board refused. Within a year the corporation encountered financial difficulties and ended up in bankruptcy. The directors have now been sued for their actions regarding the Pillsbury merger. The directors claim they complied with the spirit of the business judgment rule. Is a court likely to agree? Explain.

CHAPTER 21

Shareholders and Extraordinary Transactions

Since the 1970s, the business stories which have dominated the business news involve takeovers, buyouts and mergers of large, publicly traded corporations. For example, Philip Morris bought General Foods and Kraft, Beatrice was purchased by Kohlberg Kravis Roberts in a leveraged buyout and Nation's Bank acquired a number of failed banks around the country.

The media portrayed these stories—rightly—as titanic wars between corporate armies. Each side marshaled regiments of bankers and lawyers, who then did battle in the financial markets and the courts. Some of these wars ending in victory for one company and defeat for the other. Some ended with peace treaties.

Much of the media coverage of these wars focused on the leaders of the competing armies. It tended to identify the interests of the target company with those of its management, not of its shareholders. It therefore obscured the reason why particular takeover attempts succeeded or failed. In the end, the shareholders determined whether the takeover was in their best interests as owners.

The preceding chapters have noted how limited the shareholders' role is in the day-to-day operation of corporations. The real power of shareholders comes from their right to elect directors and to determine ultimate questions relating to the corporation, such as whether to liquidate it.

This chapter explores the rights and liabilities associated with owning interests in corporations. In the process, it corrects a distortion in perception which the media's coverage of the takeover wars has unintentionally created. The public has come to think of such wars as unique to large, publicly traded companies. Every day, however, similar wars of equal or greater intensity break out among far smaller companies.

SHAREHOLDER DUTIES AND RIGHTS

A person becomes a shareholder in one of two ways: either by buying stock from the company or by receiving a transfer of stock from an existing shareholder. With some minor exceptions, discussed below, shareholders holding the same class of stock have the same duties, rights, and liabilities regardless of the number of shares held. For instance, everyone holding a share with voting rights may vote in the annual election of members of the board of directors.

Chapter 19 examined the range of *equity* financing—financing by the sale of ownership—available to a corporation. This chapter focuses on the duties, rights, and liabilities which come with shares, particularly shares with voting rights.

Fiduciary Duties

No shareholder in his or her capacity as a shareholder has fiduciary duties to either the corporation or other shareholders. However, shareholders who are also directors, officers, or agents *do* have fiduciary duties to the corporation and other shareholders. Those duties arise from the individuals' status as directors, officers, or agents, not from their status as shareholders. Shareholders acting as shareholders never have agency authority to bind a corporation.

Since shareholders normally do not owe fiduciary duties, they may engage in transactions which might be closed to someone who did owe such duties. For instance, an investor may own stock in two major automobile companies without any question of a conflict of interest. That shareholder probably can do business with the two companies. If, however, the investor were an officer of, say, Chrysler, the propriety of owning stock in Ford would be questionable.

There are two exceptions to the rule that shareholders as shareholders do not owe a fiduciary duty to the corporation they own. The first exception applies primarily to close corporations. Because such corporations have very few shareholders and because they tend to operate more like partnerships than corporations, their shareholders may have fiduciary duties to both the corporation and their fellow shareholders. The next chapter examines how those duties might arise.

The second exception applies to a shareholder with a controlling interest in a company. This exception is discussed below.

The Right to Vote

One class of common stock must carry with it the right to elect directors and to vote on those matters for which either the law or the articles of incorporation require shareholder approval. Normally, shareholders only vote in the context of shareholder meetings.

Who may vote. A shareholder's right to vote depends on whether the stock held is nonvoting or voting stock. Generally, nonvoting stock is preferred stock,* although some classes of common stock may not have voting rights either. See Chapter 19 for the distinction between the two types of equities.

Shareholders who own voting stock as of the record date may vote. A *record date* is a date—usually within 2 months of the meeting—picked by the board. Those shown on the corporate books as owning stock on that date are eligible to vote their shares. The record date mechanism is a necessity where companies have actively traded stock, since it would be impossible to determine at the annual meeting precisely who owned stock.

Shareholder meetings. A corporation must hold an annual meeting of its shareholders at which the shareholders elect directors and vote on matters of corporate policy. A corporation may also call special shareholder meetings when urgent matters arise which require a vote of the shareholders [RMBCA §7.02].

A corporation is required to hold an annual meeting within the earlier of the following periods:

- Six months after the end of the company's fiscal year
- Fifteen months after the last annual meeting

If it does not, a court may order the corporation to hold the meeting [RMBCA §7.03(a)(1)]. However, the corporation's failure to hold the annual meeting at the time indicated in the bylaws does not affect the validity of any corporate action [RMBCA §7.01(c)].

The corporation must notify shareholders of the meeting's time, place, and agenda. They must receive this notice not more than 60 but not less than 10 days before the meeting [RMBCA §7.05(a)]. But shareholders, like directors, waive improper notice if they attend the meeting and stay on after protesting the lack of notice. Shareholders may also waive notice by signing a waiver [RMBCA §7.06].

A quorum at a shareholder meeting is not defined by the number of persons present but rather by the number of shares represented. Unless the articles specify a different percentage, a simple majority of shares must be represented. If an action requires the approval of more than one class of stock, a simple majority of each class constitutes a quorum. However, when a vote is actually taken, a quorum does not have to be represented—unlike the case with a board meeting [RMBCA §§7.25, 7.27].

Shareholders ordinarily meet together formally. However, like boards of directors, shareholders may act and vote outside a formal meeting. The shareholders must consent in a writing setting forth the action to be taken, and all the shareholders entitled to vote on the matter must sign the document [RMBCA §7.04].

---

* As will be discussed below, the holders of preferred stock ordinarily do have the right to vote on extraordinary transactions which affect their interests.

This mechanism, clearly, is of use only to corporations with very few shareholders.

Proxies. A shareholder may attend a shareholder meeting and vote in person or may vote by *proxy*, which is a *power of attorney* authorizing another to vote shares. Generally, a shareholder is free to revoke a proxy either by making a new proxy or by attending the shareholder meeting in person. In short, shareholders can revoke executed proxies at any time up to the meeting. Unrevoked proxies are valid for 11 months unless the appointment form specifically provides for a longer period [RMBCA §7.22(c)].

If a corporation falls under the jurisdiction of the Securities and Exchange Commission (SEC), the SEC rules govern the way proxies are solicited. These rules are discussed in Chapter 23. The corporation will always solicit proxies in favor of the board's proposals and candidates. However, it is important to note that proxy solicitations are also the principal instruments used in shareholder efforts to change corporate policies or management.

Voting trusts and pooling agreements. Shareholders may aggregate their stock's voting rights and vote their shares as a block. This arrangement is called either a *voting trust*, in which the stock's legal ownership is transferred to a trustee who votes it, or a *pooling agreement*, in which the stockholders simply bind themselves to vote as a block. Often, the purpose of these arrangements is to ensure continuing control of the corporation by a particular group or management. The major drawback of voting trusts and pooling agreements is that these arrangements are irrevocable during the period of their existence, which may be up to 10 years [RMBCA §7.30]. The stock's ownership may be transferred, but the voting rights remain subject to the trust or pooling agreement. For that reason, such stock often brings a lower price than it would if its new owner could vote the shares.

Courts void trusts or pooling agreements devised for improper purposes, such as those designed to suppress the rights of minority shareholders. Courts have routinely voided voting trusts used in schemes which violate the antitrust acts, as well as those which encourage fraudulent activity or the looting of corporate assets.

Matters Requiring Shareholder Approval

Control over the corporation's policy and direction lies with the board of directors. However, the shareholders are not powerless. They have the right to vote on many matters which directly affect their ownership interests. These include:

- Electing and removing directors [RMBCA §§8.03, 8.08]
- Mergers [RMBCA §11.01]
- Amendments to the articles of incorporation [RMBCA §10.03]
- Extraordinary transactions—those not in the ordinary course of business. [RMBCA §12.02]
- Amendments to the bylaws, if reserved to the shareholders by the articles [RMBCA §10.20]
- Voluntary dissolution [RMBCA §14.02]
- Sale of substantially all assets [RMBCA §12.01]

Some of these have been discussed earlier. Others deserve additional comment.

Amending the articles of incorporation. Any amendment of the articles of incorporation requires shareholder approval. That fact is a major reason why the articles today normally grant the corporation the broadest possible express powers.

The shareholders may not offer amendments to the articles. The board of directors must adopt a resolution proposing an amendment. Then, the amendment must receive the affirmative vote of the holders of a majority of the shares entitled to vote. Suppose a corporation has 5000 shares eligible to vote. The holders of 3000 shares vote on the amendment, and the vote is 2000 to 1000 to approve the amendment. Since 5000 shares are outstanding, the amendment requires 2501 votes. So it fails. If the shareholders approve an amendment, the corporation must file amended articles with the secretary of state.

If an amendment to the articles involves a change in the rights of a type or class of stock not ordinarily entitled to vote, like preferred stock, holders of that type or class have a right to vote on the amendment.

Extraordinary transactions. The shareholders must approve any *extraordinary transactions*, that is, those transactions which are not in the ordinary course of business. This would clearly cover situations involving a proposed management buy-out of the corporation, a quite common corporate phenomenon of the past 10 years.

Mergers and *consolidations*, for instance, are extraordinary transactions requiring shareholder approval. Mergers and consolidations have the same effect: two businesses join together to form one. The creditors of the two corporations become creditors of the new corporation. In a merger the name of the new corporation usually is that of one of the two former corporations. For example, it would be a merger if Calzone Corp. and Italian Foods, Inc., joined together to form Italian Foods, Inc. In contrast, a name such as Calzone Foods, Inc., would indicate a consolidation. The RMBCA has dropped the distinction between

mergers and consolidations which had seemed artificial to many commentators.

Like the procedure for amendments to the articles, the board must approve and propose a merger or a consolidation. The proposal then must receive an affirmative vote equivalent to a majority of the shares entitled to vote on it. Ordinarily, that means the common shareholders. However, if a company has sold stock without voting rights, holders of that stock have a right to vote on extraordinary transactions [RMBCA §11.03].

Voluntary dissolutions. A resolution proposing a *voluntary dissolution*—going out of business—follows the same pattern as other extraordinary transactions.

Sale of assets. The sale, lease, exchange, or other disposition of all or substantially all the property or assets of a corporation—if not in the ordinary course of business—is treated as an extraordinary transaction and requires shareholder approval.* It must receive the votes of a majority of the shares entitled to vote. However, as the next case indicates, it is not always clear when the sale of assets requires shareholder approval.

---

* As to when a sale of substantially all the assets of a business dealing in goods is in the ordinary course of business, see the discussion of bulk transfers of inventory in Chapter 31.

- -

Story v. Kennecott Copper Corp.

90 Misc. 2d 333, 394 N.Y.S.2d 353 (Sup. Ct. 1977)

FACTS   In 1968, Kennecott purchased the Peabody Coal Co. for $600 million. By 1977, it had invested an additional $530 million in Peabody. However, the Federal Trade Commission obtained an order under the antitrust laws compelling Kennecott to sell Peabody. Kennecott, whose assets excluding Peabody exceeded $1 billion, agreed to sell it to Newmont Mining Corp. for approximately $1.2 billion. Kennecott's management did not seek shareholder approval for this sale. Story brought suit, contending that the sale to Newmont required shareholder approval because Peabody was Kennecott's only profitable operation during the preceding 2 years and because Peabody's assets were Kennecott's sole income-producing assets.

ISSUE   Did the sale require shareholder approval?

DECISION   No. Judgment for Kennecott. Like the MBCA, the New York Business Corporation Law requires shareholder approval for a sale of all or substantially all the assets of the corporation, if not made in the regular course of the business conducted by the corporation. That section does not apply here because Kennecott's interest in Peabody does not constitute all or substantially all its assets.

As in many cases brought by shareholders, it is worthwhile probing for Story's motive. Clearly, he could not prevent Peabody's sale. So he had targeted this particular sale. Adding Kennecott's purchase price to its subsequent investment in Peabody and then factoring in an annual inflation rate of, say, 2.5 percent reveals the real point of Story's suit.

Right to Dividends

A *dividend* paid on stock is a portion of the company's earnings distributed *pro rata* among the shares outstanding in a class of stock. In most publicly traded corporations, the directors decide each quarter whether to declare a dividend. When it declares a dividend, the board determines which shareholders will receive it by establishing a record date for the distribution. That is, the board declares a dividend of, say, $2 per share for holders as of February 10, 1987.

The right to dividends is qualified by the fact that the board must authorize their payment. The board has almost absolute discretion as to whether to authorize payment of a dividend.

Preferred stock shareholders have priority rights over common stock shareholders as to liquidations and dividends. Holders of cumulative preferred stock, if any, must have their entire unpaid dividends from past years, if any, cumulated (paid) before common shareholders may receive any dividends. Any additional rights, such as the right to convert preferred shares to common shares, to participate with common shareholders in a dividend distribution made after preferred dividends are paid, and to vote if dividend payments are in arrears, must be *granted* specifically in the articles of incorporation.

Actions to compel payment of a dividend. If the board does not elect to pay a dividend, a shareholder's lawsuit to compel the board to vote one stands almost no chance of success.

So long as the board can show it has a reasonable purpose for retaining earnings, a court will defer to the board's business judgment. Building a new plant or funding research are usually considered valid purposes. Only if the board acts in bad faith or abuses its discretion might a court overturn a board's decision. A board, for instance, may not retain earnings in order to force a minority shareholder in financial straits to sell stock to the majority. Because close corporation shareholders often lack a ready market for their shares—other than selling to their fellow shareholders—cases brought to compel the payment of dividends usually involve small corporations. The case which follows is typical.

Iwasaki v. Iwasaki Bros., Inc.

58 Or. App. 543, 649 P.2d 598 (1982)

FACTS

The three Iwasaki brothers each owned one-third of the shares in the family's nursery. Each served on the board. In June 1978, the board removed Arthur from his position as president and general manager and replaced him with the son of another brother. In 1979, the corporation distributed $12,000 in earnings to each shareholder, while retaining $144,000 which the board determined the business needed to smooth out seasonal cash flow problems. Arthur sued, alleging, among other things, that the board breached its fiduciary duties by not declaring a greater dividend. The trial court dismissed the case.

ISSUE

Did the board's action constitute a breach of its fiduciary duties?

DECISION

No. Affirmed. Those in control must decide in good faith whether to declare a dividend. Unless it is extremely serious, a single breach of the fiduciary duty of good faith and fair dealing owed by majority to minority shareholders may not warrant a court's intervention. Even continuing conduct may not unless it causes a disproportionate loss to the minority or unless those in control are so incorrigible that they can no longer be trusted to manage the corporation. Arthur's contention did not satisfy these criteria. Arthur did not dispute the plausible business purpose which the board established for retaining the earnings.

Tax considerations. One of Arthur's main grounds for complaint was that he had paid taxes on his share of the retained earnings but they were not available to him. Iwasaki Bros. was an *S corporation*, that is, a corporation which has elected under the federal tax laws to be taxed as a partnership. This election is examined in the next chapter.

The Internal Revenue Service (IRS)—or, rather, the fear of it— plays a critical role in the decision about paying a dividend. The IRS cannot compel corporations to pay cash dividends. However, it applies harsh penalties to earnings retained beyond the corporation's reasonable current or anticipated needs, regardless of whether the corporation routinely declares and pays dividends. As a practical matter, tax penalties more effectively deter boards from retain-ing earnings than does the threat of shareholder suits.

Noncash dividends. Occasionally, corporations make noncash dividend distributions of property or stock.

Property dividends consist of corporate assets *or* of stock in another corporation. For instance, Alpha Corp. considered taking over Beta, Inc., but decided against it after acquiring 12 percent of Beta's stock. Alpha might distribute two shares of Beta's stock for each outstanding Alpha share as a property dividend.

A *stock dividend* is a distribution of additional shares of the corporation's own stock. Alpha might distribute, say, one share of its stock for every share outstanding. Some commentators refer to stock dividends as "psychological dividends," since shareholders have the same equity interest after the distribution as they had before. In essence, a stock dividend is an accounting transfer whereby the corporation moves retained earnings into the capital, or shareholder equity, account.

In contrast, a *stock split* is not really a dividend. Instead, the corporation simply exchanges an existing share for two or more new shares. Publicly traded corporations do this to make their shares easier to sell on the stock market. If Alpha's shares sell on the American Stock Exchange for $60 per share, smaller investors may not purchase them. They prefer stocks selling at $15 to $35 per share, which they can afford to buy in 100-share multiples. (They save on brokers' commissions by buying in 100-share multiples, because brokers charge more on odd-lot sales.) If Alpha announces a 3-for-1 split, a holder of 100 old shares will now hold 300 new shares. Unlike a stock dividend, a stock split does not increase the capital account. Rather, it reduces the shares' stated value. If the old stock had a stated value of $6 per share, the new will have a stated value of $2.

An illustration best reveals the differences between the types of dividends. Suppose ABC Corporation is considering what type of dividend to offer its shareholders. Its stated capital (shareholder equity) is presently $500,000; its earned surplus (profits made but not paid out) is $100,000. ABC currently has 50,000 shares outstanding at a stated value of $10 per share. Figure 21.1 reflects the considerations the corporation will take into account as it makes its decision. Which option ABC will choose, however, may depend on factors not shown on the chart, such as pressure from shareholders to declare a cash dividend or the desire to decrease retained earnings to make it a less attractive takeover candidate.

Obligation to pay dividends. The corporation must pay a cash dividend which the board has declared unless doing so would make the corporation insolvent [RMBCA §6.40(c)]. The MBCA states alternative tests of insolvency. A corporation may not declare a dividend if, as a result, it would be unable to pay debts as they came due. In other words, a corporation may declare a dividend only if its assets are greater than the sum of its liabilities plus the maximum amount payable to any outstanding shareholders having preferential rights, such as preferred stockholders. The directors may be personally liable for the amount of an illegally paid dividend.

If the corporation must pass a declared cash or property dividend, the shareholders become unsecured creditors of the corporation.

ABC CORPORATION	ACTION	STATED CAPITAL	RETAINED EARNINGS	NUMBER OF SHARES	STATED VALUE
Before	—	$500,000	$100,000	50,000	$10/share
After: cash dividend	$50,000 cash dividend	$500,000	$50,000	50,000	$10/share
After: stock dividend	$50,000 capitalized	$550,000	$50,000	55,000	$10/share
After: stock split	2 for 1 stock split	$500,000	$100,000	100,000	$5/share

Figure 21.1 A Comparison of Dividend Types.

However, the board may reverse a decision to declare a stock dividend. After all, failing to pay a stock dividend does not alter the shareholders' interest in the corporation.

Right to Inspect Books and Records

Perhaps the shareholders' most important rights in terms of protecting their investment is that of inspecting the corporation's books and records. These documents include shareholder lists, minutes of board and shareholder meetings, and financial books and accounts.

Proper purpose doctrine. Shareholders have an absolute right to inspect the shareholder voting list at shareholder meetings [RMBCA §7.20]. However, they have only a qualified right—as opposed to the directors' unqualified right—to inspect general books of accounts, minutes of director or shareholder meetings, and the shareholder list other than at a shareholder meeting.

In order to inspect these documents, shareholders must show a *proper purpose*, which means some purpose relevant to their status as shareholders. Examples of a proper purpose would include:

- To commence a stockholder's derivative suit
- To solicit stockholders to vote for a change in the board of directors
- To investigate possible management misconduct

In contrast, a corporation could properly deny access to its books to a shareholder whose purpose was to obtain customer lists for his business. Shareholders denied access must seek a court order compelling management either to permit access or to disclose the information the shareholders sought.

Procedure. Under the MBCA [§52], the shareholder must make a written request stating a proper purpose for the inspection. If a shareholder has owned shares for the preceding 6 months or if a shareholder owns 5 percent or more of the outstanding shares, the corporation must comply with the request. The RMBCA eliminated the 6-month/5 percent qualification. It requires only that the shareholder give written notice of the inspection at least 5 business days in advance [RMBCA §16.02(a)]. This change is likely to encounter opposition when the RMBCA enters the legislative process.

The corporation must maintain the books and shareholder records at its official office, which is where the inspection takes place. An accountant, an attorney, or another agent of the shareholder may assist in the inspection [RMBCA §6.03(a)]. An officer who improperly denies a shareholder access may be liable in damages. The next case illustrates why this penalty exists.

CM&M Group, Inc. v. Carroll

453 A.2d 788 (Del. 1982)

FACTS   Carroll owned 51 percent of the stock in Carroll, McEntee & McGinley, Inc., and served as its president and chairman. Personality conflicts with the company's key employees led Carroll to resign his posts and sell some of his shares to the corporation. He remained its largest shareholder, with approximately one-third of the company's shares. After the company was reorganized into CM&M, other shareholders organized a voting trust controlling 47.9 percent of the shares. Carroll decided to sell his stock. Under the bylaws of CM&M, the corporation has a right of first refusal on the shares. In order to value them, Carroll made a written demand to inspect certain financial records. CM&M denied his request. The trial court ordered CM&M to produce them.

ISSUE   Did Carroll state a proper purpose for inspecting the books?

DECISION   Yes. Affirmed. When a shareholder seeks inspection of records, he has the burden of proving a proper purpose. Once a shareholder states a proper purpose—such as valuing stock—a court may deny inspection only if the corporation can show that the shareholder made the request out of sheer curiosity, unrelated to any legitimate interest, or that the inspection's sole purpose is to harass the corporation.

Preemptive Rights

The articles of incorporation may grant shareholders a *preemptive right* on shares which the company plans to issue to the public. This right permits shareholders to maintain their proportionate equity interest in the company by purchasing the same percentage of a new issue before the corporation offers it to the public [MBCA §26]. For instance, Henry owns 3 percent of Theta Corp. If Theta's articles grant shareholders a preemptive right, Henry may subscribe to 3 percent of any new offering before it is made to the public.

Generally, preemptive rights only attach to new issues. Sales of treasury stock usually are exempt. However, a court has held that preemptive rights applied where control of the corporation depended on the sale of treasury stock. The exercise of preemptive rights would confront large, publicly traded corporations with enormous logistical problems. Imagine the investment of time, money, and resources required for 3M—manufacturer of Scotch tape— just to notify the holders of its 114.5 million shares of the opportunity to exercise their rights. And several other corporations have at least twice that number of shares outstanding. For that reason, preemptive rights are common only in small, closely held corporations where questions of control often supersede most other questions.

Right to Sue

Shareholders have the right to sue the corporation to enforce their rights and to sue others on behalf of the corporation to enforce rights it has neglected to enforce. There are three types of shareholder actions: individual, class, and derivative. They are compared in Figure 21.2.

	WHO BRINGS THIS SUIT?	BROUGHT ON BEHALF OF WHOM?	USUAL DEFENDANT?	RECOVERY GENERALLY GOES TO WHOM?
Individual action	Shareholder	Self	Corporation	Self
Class action	Shareholder	Other shareholders	Corporation	Shareholders
Derivative action	Shareholder	Corporation	Officer, director, third party	Corporation

Figure 21.2 A Comparison of Shareholder Actions

Individual actions. Shareholders may bring individual actions against the corporation where an injury occurs to their interests as shareholders. Grounds for such suits include:

- Refusal to permit the exercise of preemptive rights
- Refusal of permission to inspect corporate books and records
- Performance of ultra vires acts (discussed in Chapter 20)
- Failure of corporate insider to disclose material information when trading corporate stock (discussed below and in Chapter 23)

Note that the list does not include a shareholder's right to sue in his or her behalf because of a real or threatened injury to the corporation.

Class actions. A *class action* is a suit against the corporation which the shareholder brings on behalf of all shareholders in his position. Shareholders could bring any of the causes of action listed above as a class action. If a personal or class action suit results in a judgment for the plaintiffs, the sums recovered usually go to the shareholders because the action is brought on their behalf, not on behalf of the corporation.

Derivative actions. Shareholders may bring *derivative actions* on behalf of the corporation to enforce a corporate right or to recover a corporate loss. The term refers to the fact that the shareholders' right to bring suit derives, or originates, from their status as shareholders.

Enforcing the corporation's rights in court is not normally a power exercised by shareholders. For that reason, before filing suit, shareholders must exhaust all their means to convice the board to enforce the corporation's rights. Because a derivative suit is brought on behalf of the corporation, any damages awarded go to the company.

A derivative action might follow a corporation's decision to write off a loss on a contract when it could recover something from the customer. Shareholders also bring derivative actions where officers divert corporate assets for their personal use, like buying "corporate getaways" in the Bahamas. Minority shareholders have brought derivative actions against majority shareholders who take advantage of their status for personal gain. If a corporation decides not to pursue a promising research idea and the major shareholder forms an independent company to produce the product, the other shareholders may have a cause of action.

One problem confronting shareholders attempting a derivative suit is what to do when the officers engaged in the wrongdoing are actually working for a wholly owned subsidiary of a holding company. The shareholder owns stock in the holding company, but the holding company is simply a corporate body that is set up to own the stock and take control of the subsidiary. From a technical point of view, the shareholder should not derive any enforceable rights by owning stock in a company that owns another company. The following case demonstrates how one court handled this formality by using a *double* derivative suit.

Brown v. Tenney

125 Ill.2d 348, 532 N.E.2d 230 (1988)

FACTS   Pioneer Commodities, Inc., was formed in 1975 by Brown, the plaintiff, Tenney, the defendant, and Farnsworth. In 1982, the shareholders set up T/B Holding Company to act as Pioneer's holding company. Pioneer's shareholders, including both Brown and Tenney, exchanged their Pioneer stock for an equal share of T/B stock, with the Pioneer stock representing the principal asset of T/B Holding. A year later, Tenney obtained control of T/B Holding as an officer and director and began to waste Pioneer corporate funds, and to convert the funds to his personal use. Brown, on behalf of Pioneer, sought damages from Tenney in a double derivative suit for breaching his fiduciary duties to Pioneer. Tenney prevailed at the trial level, but the decision was reversed by the intermediate appellate court.

ISSUE

Does Illinois corporate law recognize a shareholder's right to maintain a double derivative suit?

DECISION

Yes. Affirmed. The shareholders' derivative suit was devised to protect shareholders from exploitation from a corporation, its officers, and its directors and to secure corporate accountability. A holding company is a corporation which owns the stock of another company and exerts control over the policies and management of its subsidiary company. It has been recognized that holding companies have created many new problems for shareholders from the impropriety of the holding company's directors. Even though a shareholder of a holding company cannot technically maintain a derivative action on behalf of the holding company's subsidiary, the law cannot be deluded by deceptive and illusory disguises. To prevent this from happening, the court will allow Brown, the shareholder of the holding company, to enforce a right belonging to Pioneer, the subsidiary, against the defendant Tenney.

Dissenting-Shareholder Rights

Where a dispute involves an extraordinary transaction, shareholders have remedies besides filing suit. If a shareholder, for instance, disapproves of a proposed merger or of a proposed liquidation, the MBCA grants minority shareholders the right to have the corporation purchase their shares at an appraised price. This is termed a right of *appraisal*.

The appraisal is designed to establish the shares' fair value immediately before the effectuation of the corporate action, say, the shareholder meeting at which a merger was approved. For conceptual convenience, most courts use the day before the corporate action as the date of valuation. The calculation excludes any appreciation or depreciation in anticipation of the corporate action [RMBCA §73.01(3)]. Shareholders who may wish to exercise their appraisal rights must file a written objection to the proposal either before or at the shareholder meeting, and they must vote against it [RMBCA §13.01(2)]. The next case illustrates how an appraisal works.

Sarrouf v. New England Patriots Football Club, Inc.

397 Mass. 542, 492 N.E.2d 1122 (1986)

FACTS

In 1959, William Sullivan bought an American Football League franchise for $25,000. Despite retaining less than 25 percent of the stock, Sullivan controlled the team until 1974, when he was removed from office. With a $5.3 million bank line of credit, Sullivan began acquiring voting stock and a year later held it all. He quickly voted out the board and took charge. Over the years, the Patriots had sold almost 140,000 shares of nonvoting stock. The banks now insisted that the corporation assume responsibility for Sullivan's loans, and that meant the nonvoting shareholders' interest had to be eliminated. So Sullivan decided to set up a new corporation into which the old one would be merged. Most nonvoting shareholders voted for this transaction, which resulted in payments to them of $15 per share as compared with $102 per share for the voting stock. The plaintiffs in this action exercised their right of appraisal. The trial court valued their shares at $80 per share.

ISSUE

Did the trial court properly appraise the stock?

DECISION

Yes. Affirmed on this issue. Normally, a court must consider three approaches: the shares' market value, their earnings, and their net asset value. Here, the stock was not traded on a recognized exchange, so market value was not a valid measure.

> The judge found that the Old Patriots had a proven earnings capacity. He did not base his valuation on the earnings value of the stock, however, because he found it to be of little consequence in the over-all valuation of this type of corporation. The true value [of corporations of this type] is difficult to measure by the usual indicia of stock value. . . . It is not only a business venture, but . . . a sportsman's endeavor. A team owner is a celebrity, a member of an exclusive club. . . . Most teams are owned outright by extremely wealthy individuals. The value they place on ownership of an NFL team is discernible in the prices they are willing to pay which are largely independent of earning potential. Thus, the judge used the prices paid for new franchises as a starting point. . . .
>
> No single stockholder [except possibly Sullivan] could obtain the true value of his stock. The unreliable market for shares in the corporation did not reflect those values easily comprehended in the hypothetical sale of the entire assets. . . .

Based on a price of $12.5 million for the most recent new franchises (Tampa Bay and Seattle) and the additional assets the Patriots held—a stadium lease, a monopoly in New England, and the like—the valuation of the shares by the trial court was conservative and supported by the evidence.

Right to Change Corporate Policy

Some dissident shareholders have goals other than getting the maximum return on their investment. In the last 20 years some religious and social action groups have claimed that a corporation's relationship to the economic, social, and natural environments should be a matter of direct concern to its management. Using a variety of devices, members of the movement for corporate social responsibility applied pressure to many large, publicly traded corporations.

No company met all the varying demands these groups made upon them. Standard Oil of Indiana, for instance, became deeply involved in urban renewal projects targeted to benefit low-income groups. At the same time, however, it appeared for 3 consecutive years among an environmental group's "filthy five," the leading corporate polluters and contributors to anti-environment members of Congress.

Proxy resolutions. Some of these groups took their causes to the shareholders by buying stock themselves and then placing resolutions reflecting their concerns before the shareholders at annual meetings. These issues included divestiture of South African holdings, improved minority hiring, elimination of trade with Communist block countries, and a multitude of other matters.

The actual proxy form is a computer card which the shareholder fills out with instructions—usually by checking boxes—as to how the shares are to be voted. With the proxy form, the shareholder receives a *proxy statement*. This booklet describes candidates for the board and contains the full text of the resolutions to be voted on by the shareholders, a statement of the proponent's rationale for each resolution, and the board's recommendations on each resolution.

Questions posed for shareholder approval must allow for a yes or no answer, though state law generally permits a shareholder to grant full discretion to the proxy holder. Note that the question in shareowner proposal 5 in Figure 21.3 is whether General Electric should prepare a report.

In order to put a resolution on the ballot, a shareholder must own at least 1 percent or at least $1000 worth of the stock to be voted. The shareholder must request that the corporation place the resolution on the ballot 120 days before the proxy statement is mailed to the shareholders. The purpose of the resolution must be significantly related to the corporation's business—at least 5 percent of its assets. If the corporation rejects a resolution, it must tell both the proponent and the SEC why. The SEC may order a resolution onto the ballot. A resolution must receive at least 5 percent of the vote in order to be presented to the shareholders the following year.

To date, such resolutions have rarely received 10 percent of the vote. However, they have served an educative function and, in some cases, actually affected corporate policy.

Normally, a publicly traded corporation solicits its shareholders' proxies. Of course, other groups may do so, too.

Direct actions. Some groups took more direct action to make corporations responsive to what they believed society demanded. The following case shows what happened when a corporation decided to fight a group which had bought its shares. As you read this case, keep in mind that publicly traded corporations with fewer than 500 shareholders are exempt from many of the SEC's reporting requirements. As we will see in Chapter 23, those reports contain detailed information about the company's operations.

Loretto Literary & Benevolent Inst. v. Blue Diamond Coal Co.

444 A.2d 256 (Del. Ch. 1982)

FACTS

The plaintiffs are certain religious organizations and individuals who are members of a Coal Company Monitoring Project Coalition. This Coalition actively advocates social and environmental reform within the coal mining industry [in Appalachia]. They believe that Blue Diamond is one of the principal offenders of what plaintiffs perceive to be an enlightened social and environmental policy. . . .

The vehicle chosen by the plaintiffs to advance their ideas was the purchase [of a block] of Blue Diamond stock in the open market in the hopes that by exercising their shareholder rights they would be able to lobby their social and environmental views to management. [When they bought the stock, the plaintiffs concealed their identities from Blue Diamond.]

> *Shortly thereafter, plaintiffs decided that if Blue Diamond could be forced to register with the Securities and Exchange Commission, mandatory disclosure requirements would facilitate their monitoring the company. [If] they fractionalized their block of shares among the individual members of the coalition, Blue Diamond would reach the 500 shareholder threshold which mandates registration with the Securities and Exchange Commission. . . . [But] upon learning that plaintiffs had been the beneficial owners of this block of stock all along, Blue Diamond refused to record [the transfers of the stock into the plaintiffs' names].*

The coalition brought suit to compel Blue Diamond to record the transfers. Blue Diamond defended on the grounds that the plaintiffs had conspired to alter the business operations of Blue Diamond to the detriment of its shareholders. Five months after the suit was filed, Blue Diamond voluntarily recorded the transfers. The plaintiffs then sought their costs and attorneys' fees.

ISSUE   Were the plaintiffs entitled to attorneys' fees because they had to bring suit to have the transfers recorded?

DECISION   Yes.

> *The record clearly shows that the plaintiffs simply intended to exercise routine shareholder rights in order to lobby their views to management with the expectation of enhancing, not injuring, Blue Diamond. Shareholders have the inherent right to assert their individual interests within their Company, however bizarre, unpopular or unusual they may be.*

Even if the plaintiffs did conspire to alter its business practices, Blue Diamond was not justified in refusing to transfer the shares and putting the plaintiffs to the expense of a lawsuit.

SHAREHOLDER LIABILITIES

Every corporation's name must include one of the following words: "corporation," "company," "incorporated," or "limited" [RMBCA §4.01(a)]. Those words put a person dealing with an entity on notice that it is a corporation and that, as such, the liability of its shareholders is limited to the amount of their investment. In other words, a person dealing with the corporation can look only to the corporation's assets to satisfy its obligation.

Under ordinary circumstances, shareholder liability is limited. But, in the extraordinary circumstances examined in this section, shareholder liability can be extensive and, in some cases, unlimited except by the shareholder's personal worth.

Liability on Subscriptions and Watered Stock

Chapter 19 noted that subscription contracts generally are irrevocable for a period of 6 months. The subscriber must fulfill the agreement or be liable to either the company or its creditors for up to the amount of the unpaid subscription [RMBCA §6.20(d)].

Shareholders who are issued *watered stock*—stock sold for less than its par, or stated, value—must reimburse the corporation for the difference between the price they paid and

Share Owner Proposal No. 5

Leo. A. Drey, 515 West Point Avenue, University City, MO 63130, has notified the Company that he intends to present the following proposal at this year's meeting:

"Whereas General Electric is the proprietor of the only commercial nuclear waste storage depot receiving high level nuclear waste (irradiated fuel rods from nuclear reactors) at Morris, Illinois;

"Whereas the Morris facility is located in a flood plain above prime drinking water aquifers serving a large population, above an earthquake fault, and only 50 miles southwest of Chicago;

"Whereas many nuclear reactors' on-site storage facilities are near capacity, indicating that greater quantities of irradiated fuel rods will need interim storage in the near future;

"Whereas the Morris facility is also approaching capacity; and

"Whereas the manifest failure of the West Valley, N.Y. storage facility, particularly with regard to technical difficulties and court decisions against the operators, highlights the hazards implicit in such an operation;

"Therefore be it resolved that Management prepare a report to stockholders within three months detailing:

"1. An assessment of the risk to the Company and the public in the operation of the Morris facility;

"2. The extent and nature of any Company liability to operating and maintenance personnel and the public, of the Morris storage facility;

"3. A report of routine radiation exposures during the last three years to employees, and the amount of radioactivity released to the public by air and water;

"4. A description of the monitoring procedures for employees, the Morris community and communities along transportation routes, regarding possible radiation contamination;

"5. The number and nature of accidents involving radioactivity that have occurred within the Morris facility or during transportation of irradiated fuel rods to the facility;

"6. The training and education requirements for accident personnel and the emergency facilities and support systems for dealing with radiation accidents on site or en route;

"7. GE's plans for the ultimate disposition of the irradiated fuel rods and related radioactive waste which is stored there;

"8. Upgrading modifications in the Morris facility bringing it to conform with NEPA requirements for its use as a *long term* irradiated fuel storage facility; and

"9. The nature of any plans for expanding the Morris operation, and Management's best estimate of when its involvement in this facility will cease."

The statement submitted in support of this proposal is as follows:

"Continuing public concern about health effects of nuclear radiation, the increasing stockpiles of nuclear waste, lack of a scientific solution to permanent storage of this material, and the potential financial liability to the Company because of its involvement, point out serious problems that need to be addressed.

"Many people living near the Morris facility are concerned about reported and potential leakage of radioactive liquids and other accidents at that facility. They and those living along the transportation routes nationwide are also concerned about over-the-road transportation of irradiated fuel elements en route to Morris.

"When a federal waste repository is designed, it is likely that radioactive wastes stored at Morris will have to be shipped out again, creating an extra over-the-road hazard.

"Stockholders are entitled to be informed on these issues which may have direct effects on their interests."

Your Board of Directors recommends a vote AGAINST this proposal.

General Electric's Morris facility is meeting a necessary and important national need for the interim storage of commercial spent fuel. Further, GE is contractually obligated to electric utility company customers for storage of much of the fuel now at Morris.

The Morris facility was originally constructed as a spent fuel reprocessing facility; accordingly, more stringent safeguards were included than necessary for the storage-only function it now performs. Morris is licensed by the Nuclear Regulatory Commission. The NRC monitors facility operation and its reports are a matter of public record. Morris has had 13 years of experience as a passive warehousing operation meeting GE obligations as the government moves toward its recommendations on site selection and the adoption of satisfactory long-term disposal methods.

General Electric has communicated and held meetings with interested and concerned share owner groups to discuss Morris operations and other nuclear power questions and will continue to do so.

Figure 21.3 General Electric's 1985 Proxy Statement: A Shareholder Resolution.
Shareholder resolutions like this one very rarely prevail against the board's opposition. Their purpose usually is to bring attention to issues. (*Source: 1985 General Electric Proxy Statement, pp. 33–35.*)

the stocks' par, or stated, value. In addition, shareholders will be liable for the value of stock received in exchange for a promise to perform services in the future or for a promissory note is they do not perform the services or pay the note.

Liability for Receipt of Illegal Dividends

While the primary personal liability for paying illegal dividends rests on the directors who authorize the payment, shareholders, too, are potentially liable. The directors have a right of contribution from each shareholder for the amount the shareholder accepted knowing that the distribution was made in violation of either the act or the articles [RMBCA §8.33(b)(2)]. Under the bankruptcy laws, if the corporation is insolvent, shareholders must return the illegal dividend, regardless of whether they knew when they received the dividend that it was illegal. If the corporation is solvent, shareholders unaware of the dividend's illegality may retain the dividend.

Liability of Controlling Shareholder

Generally, shareholders do not owe fiduciary duties to the corporation or to other shareholders. However, an exception applies to controlling shareholders. As *Iwasaki* reveals, minority shareholders sometimes feel the majority has not dealt fairly with them. In this situation, some jurisdictions—but not all—have held controlling shareholders have a fiduciary duty to minority shareholders to exercise their control for the good of the corporation. In some instances, courts have imposed liability even where the controlling shareholder did not hold a directorship or a corporate office.

Types of wrongdoing. The types of wrongdoing which may result in personal liability include the sale or transfer of control to individuals known to be unreliable or corporate looters. A controlling shareholder may not destroy the interest of minority shareholders by leaving them defenseless against such purchasers.

Controlling shareholders may not divert or usurp corporate opportunities. Here, the same rules apply as those discussed with respect to directors. Finally, a controlling shareholder may not make changes in the corporation's structure which benefit her to the detriment of the minority. For instance, under some circumstances controlling shareholders may not exercise their right to liquidate the corporation. In the next case, the controlling shareholders froze out the minority from a lucrative professional football team.

Coggins v. New England Patriots Football Club, Inc.

397 Mass. 525, 492 N.E.2d 1112 (1986)

FACTS	This case presented the same essential facts as *Sarrouf v. New England Patriots Football Club, Inc.* Nonvoting shareholders who voted against the merger brought this action to have the merger rescinded. The trial court held the merger was illegal, but too much time had passed to undo it. The court awarded the nonvoting shareholders damages.
ISSUE	Did the Patriots' directors fulfill their fiduciary duties to the minority nonvoting shareholders?
DECISION	No. Affirmed. The duty of a corporate director must be to further the legitimate

ends of the corporation. Here, the controlling shareholder instituted a *freeze-out merger*, a merger designed to eliminate public ownership of the corporation by means of corporate processes and corporate assets. The corporate directors who benefit from this transaction must show how it furthered the ends of the corporation. Here, the freeze-out merger had no legitimate business purpose. The Patriots were under no legal obligation to eliminate public ownership. Instead, the merger's purpose was to benefit Sullivan.*

---

* The Supreme Judicial Court equated Sullivan's fiduciary duties to the holders of the nonvoting shares to those of a controlling shareholder in a close corporation. The Court relied upon *Wilkes v. Springside Nursing Home, Inc.*, 370 Mass. 842, 353 N.E.2d 657 (1976), which is briefed in the next chapter.

Premium for controlling interest. The controlling interest in a corporation is usually worth more than a minority interest. The reason is obvious: purchasers may run the company as they see fit, rather than having the company run for them.

Until recently, no one questioned whether the *control premium*—the additional value per share of majority shares—should go to the majority holder. However, in a few juridictions, minority shareholders have argued successfully that all stock is equal in value and that control has an independent worth which belongs to the corporation. In addition, the Williams Act, an amendment to the Securities Exchange Act of 1934, provides specific rules which apply to bidders making tender offers to shareholders of a corporation regulated by the Act. These rules will be discussed in Chapter 23.

Piercing the Corporate Veil

Providing limited liability to a corporation's owners is one of the principal reasons to incorporate. However, in extreme circumstances courts will deny shareholders the benefits of limited liability. They do so by disregarding the corporation's separate entity and holding the shareholders personally liable. This is called *piercing the corporate veil.*

The alter ego doctrine. Piercing the corporate veil most commonly occurs when shareholders in a small corporation treat it as their *alter ego* (a Latin phrase meaning "other self").

Here, the interests of the corporation so intertwine with those of the shareholders that the shareholders do not maintain the corporation's separate entity. They treat it as an extension of themselves by, for example, commingling their personal funds with corporate funds. They may also not observe the basic corporate formalities such as issuing stock, keeping careful minutes of board meetings, or ratifying transactions between officers or shareholders and the corporation. In short, the shareholders act as if the corporation did not exist.

These are not the only circumstances in which individuals treat the corporation as an alter ego. In the next case, the defendant was a director who did not own any stock.

LaFond v. Basham

683 P.2d 367 (Colo. Ct. App. 1984)

FACTS Charles Basham was president, general manager, and a director of Colorado Patio & Awning and of its wholly owned subsidiary, Colorado Builders of Englewood. Basham's wife and son held all the stock of Colorado Patio. They and Basham were the only directors for both companies. The LaFonds contracted with Builders to remodel their home. They gave Builders a $9500 down payment. After completing $2800 worth of work, Builders stopped work. Shortly thereafter, the companies became insolvent. The LaFonds brought suit against the companies and Basham personally for the balance of the down payment. At trial, Basham testified that "the rule was that I owned the corporation" and that only the board could overrule his decisions—something it had never done. Basham dominated his wife and son. He determined when the corporations would pay him and loan him money. He also determined that the corporations should rent space in a building he owned, and he used corporate funds for the building's upkeep. When the companies approached insolvency, Basham insisted on payment of notes due him and took corporate assets which might have been used to satisfy the creditors. The trial court held Basham personally liable to the LaFonds.

ISSUE May a corporate director who owns no stock be held personally liable for the debts of the corporation?

DECISION Yes. Affirmed. A court may impose personal liability on a director where, as here, to do otherwise would protect fraud, promote injustice, and defeat a legitimate claim. A director who used assets of a corporation for his own gain may not hide behind the cloak of the corporation to defeat a creditor's valid claim.

Domination of a corporation or failure to maintain its separate identity are not in and of themselves wrongs. By themselves, they hurt no one. What a plaintiff must show when he or she wishes to pierce the veil is that the domination of the company was used to commit a wrong, a fraud, a breach of a legal duty, or a dishonest and unjust act that violated his or her legal rights *and* that the domination and the breach of duty proximately caused the injury of which the plaintiff complains.

Abuse of limited liability protection. When shareholders who are actively involved in a cor-

poration use limited liability as a sword instead of as a shield, courts will disregard the corporate entity. Virtually always, the corporations involved in such cases are small.

For example, shareholders of a corporation which sells home care products door-to-door normally would not be personally liable for damages resulting from a defective cleanser container. However, if the shareholders are intentionally using the corporation to sell defective goods, a court will hold them personally liable. Usually in these cases, the shareholders have also underinsured or undercapitalized the corporation.

Inadequate capitalization. In some states, the courts may pierce the corporate veil if the shareholders did not provide sufficient capital to meet the corporation's normal obligations, even though the shareholders did not intend to defraud those dealing with the corporation. More commonly, as in the following case, a court must at least sense fraud before it imposes liability on the shareholders.

Inryco, Inc. v. CGR Building Systems, Inc.

780 F.2d 879 (10th Cir. 1986)

FACTS
Between 1980 and 1983, CGR Building Systems incurred $39,999 in debts to Inryco, Inc. The three Reiman brothers owned CGR Building Systems. CGR began operations in May 1980 as a partnership with $7500 in capital. When it was incorporated 14 months later, CGR had $1500 in the bank, no assets of significant value, and accounts payable far in excess of the combined value of its assets and capital. Inryco had no notice of the incorporation. Inryco brought suit to recover the debt from the Reiman brothers personally. While the brothers were clearly liable for that portion incurred while CGR was a partnership, they asserted their limited liability as to the portion incurred after incorporation. The trial court held the Reimans personally liable.

ISSUE
Did the level of capitalization justify piercing CGR's corporate veil?

DECISION
Yes. Affirmed. Ordinarily, the corporate form shields investors from personal liability for the debts of the corporation. However, a court may ignore the separate corporate existence where necessary to promote the ends of justice. When a corporation is capitalized this meagerly at the time of incorporation, protecting the shareholders would promote injustice.

The shareholders of a corporation which lacks either sufficient capital or insurance, or both, to cover an ordinary, known risk of its particular business may find themselves personally liable. For example, a court might pierce the corporate veil if it found a demolition company could not pay for repairs to the foundations of an adjacent building it damaged.

It is important to note that inadequate capitalization generally does *not* warrant piercing the corporate veil. Inadequate capitalization is a normal risk assumed by those doing business with corporations, and as you will see in Part VIII, creditors have many means by which to protect themselves.

Abuse of parent-subsidiary relationship. A *subsidiary* is a corporation in which most or all of the stock is owned by another corporation, called the *parent*. Many corporations have subsidiaries. For instance, Electronic Data Systems, Inc. (EDS) is a subsidiary of General Motors. As a result of the 1992 presidential campaign, most students might recognize EDS as having been Ross Perot's former company. After acquiring EDS, GM later purchased

Perot's individual holdings on condition that he remove himself from GM's board of directors. Perot enjoyed telling America that General Motors ought to have listened to him.

Generally, a parent corporation is not liable for the debts of its subsidiary. If the subsidiary is properly incorporated and financed and is separately operated, a court will treat it as an entity distinct from its parent.

However, a court will disregard the separate entity where the parent generally ignores the distinction between it and the subsidiary and the subsidiary's only purpose appears to be to shield the parent from liability. For example, in a product liability case, a corporation set up a subsidiary whose only function was to sell the parent's products. The subsidiary had no assets or inventory and merely passed on orders from third parties. The court found the subsidiary to be, in effect, a corporate sales division rather than an independent entity and allowed recovery from the parent.

Sometimes, a parent deliberately undercapitalizes a subsidiary, preferring to make loans to it in an effort to further limit the parent's liability. Suppose Day Care Centers Corp. sets up its twenty-three day care centers as separate corporations. Instead of capitalizing each so that it would be self-sufficient, Day Care loans each center start-up expenses and money for capital improvements. Should one go bankrupt, the loans made by Day Care would normally be *subordinated*—given a lower priority—to those made by other creditors. The bankruptcy court might also impose liability on Day Care for its subsidiaries' obligations.

It is important to note that where a court pierces the corporate veil of a subsidiary, it will impose liability on the parent, not on the parent's shareholders. Imposing liability on the parent's shareholders would require a finding of an abuse which warranted disregarding its corporate status, too.

CONCLUSION

The price of limited liability, as noted in Chapter 19, is limited participation in management.

But this chapter has shown that "limited" does not mean "absence of." Shareholders have distinct and important responsibilities which the law imposes on them. When shareholders abuse their limited liability privileges, the law will permit plaintiffs to pierce the corporate veil and reach the shareholders' personal assets.

The shareholders also have responsibilities whose neglect carries less severe penalties. Shareholders ultimately decide corporate policy and the corporation's very existence. In both instances, they can evade responsibility by not voting for directors and by not paying attention to the issues put before them in shareholder meetings.

The traditional response to dissident shareholders was, "If you don't like management's policies, sell your stock." In today's business, social, and economic environments, that response is far too simple. It also denies the simple fact which began this chapter: shareholders own their corporation and, ultimately, control its fate. The board and the management it selects work for the shareholders. The law rarely requires shareholders to exercise their ownership rights. Nonetheless, it provides them with the power to do so.

A NOTE TO FUTURE CPA CANDIDATES

The CPA candidate must understand the role of the shareholder in the corporation. There are certain things which must be approved and proposed by the board of directors for shareholder vote. These include nontechnical changes to the articles of incorporation and proposals for merger. Shareholders also have a right to vote on all extraordinary transactions, for directors and sale of substantially all the assets of the corporation. The candidate should understand how appraisal rights work for the shareholder opposed to a merger.

It is important to know the basics in regard to the declaration of dividends. Once declared, a shareholder becomes an unsecured creditor. Preferred shareholders are to receive cash dividends before common stock shareholders. Cumulative preferred shareholders have a right to be paid past dividends declared but not paid prior to common stock shareholders receiving any dividend. The candidate should remember that a corporation cannot pay cash dividends if to do so would cause the corporation to be unable to pay its debts as they come due.

All shareholders have basic rights which include the right to inspect the books and records of the corporation. Remember that a purpose for inspection is proper if related to the corporation even if the purpose is to challenge management. A personal purpose, such as to gain names of shareholders for one's own business, is not proper. A shareholder may be able to retain her percentage of ownership by prescriptive rights.

A shareholder is said to have limited liability. However, remember that a shareholder who has not fully paid for his stock from the corporation will have liability for the deficiency amount. In certain situations, a court will pierce the corporate veil of a corporation and hold all active shareholders personally liable. Commingling personal and business assets, undercapitalization, and abuse of limited liability protection are the most common reasons a court might pierce the corporate veil.

KEY WORDS

alter ego (469)	pooling agreement (455)
appraisal (463)	proper purpose
class action (462)	doctrine (460)
control premium (469)	proxy (455)
derivative action (462)	stock dividend (458)
piercing the corporate	stock split (459)
veil (469)	voting trust (455)

DISCUSSION QUESTIONS

1. Are shareholders agents of the corporation? Do they owe fiduciary duties to the corporation or their fellow shareholders?
2. Give four examples of matters on which shareholders have an exclusive vote.
3. What is a proxy? How is it given? How is it voided? How is it exercised?
4. What is a pooling agreement? A voting trust?
5. Do shareholders have a right to a dividend? What is the difference between a stock dividend and a stock split?
6. What rights does a shareholder have to inspect the corporation's books?
7. What is a preemptive right? Why is it important?
8. Compare a class action to a derivative action.
9. What is the "book value" of shares? Does book value have any relation to the real value of the shares?
10. Under what circumstances will a court disregard corporate status? What are the public policy arguments for and against routinely disregarding corporate status when a corporation's assets are insufficient to meet its obligations?
11. Should shareholders have the right to attempt to change corporate practices to meet their ethical standards? What limits, if any, should apply to that right? Should the regulation of corporate activities be left up to government?

CASE PROBLEMS

1. Wiley Embry owns 100 shares of $7 preferred stock of McLeod, Inc. Embry claims preferred stock shareholders are vested with the following rights *unless* the articles of incorporation state otherwise: right to convert preferred shares to common shares, to participate with common shareholders in a dividend distribution made after preferred dividends are paid, and to vote if dividend payments are in arrears. Correct? Two years ago $7 preferred cash dividends were declared but not paid. Last year no preferred dividends were declared or paid. Embry claims that he has a right to $7 per share for dividends for both past years. Correct? Explain.
2. A group of shareholders of Jax, Inc. brought a derivative suit on behalf of Jax, Inc. to sever a personal services contract with Connell Lashley, a financial advisor to the corporation. The shareholders claimed that Lashley failed to

disclose a substantial conflict of interest with the corporation. They filed their suit without first seeking remedial action from the board. The shareholders contended in court that it would have been fruitless for them to have sought board action since it was the board that had originally approved the contract. The trial court dismissed the suit on the basis that the shareholder group should have first demanded action by the board of directors. Would a court of appeals be likely to reverse the trial court's decision? Explain.

3. Starkey, Inc., a manufacturer, has decided to sell all its manufacturing plants and operations and to begin specializing in financial services. The directors of Brown Corporation have voted to acquire all the Starkey manufacturing plants and operations. Starkey's directors have approved the Brown offer. Neither corporation sought or received shareholder approval. Susan Etnyre, a Starkey shareholder, has demanded that a shareholder vote be taken. Are the Starkey shareholders entitled to such a vote? Likewise, Steven Heitter, a Brown shareholder, has demanded a shareholder vote. Are the Brown shareholders entitled to such a vote? Explain.

4. Claudia O'Neal is a consumer rights activist and the owner of one share of stock of Fizz Corp., a soft-drink bottling company. O'Neal has threatened to sue Fizz's management for mismanagement for its approval of the expenditure of a large sum to sponsor a regetta. O'Neal has objected to numerous other management actions in the past 5 years, including sales in South Africa and pollution by company plants. A regular Fizz Corp. shareholder meeting is coming. O'Neal has demanded access to the company's shareholder list and the minutes of the past two shareholder meetings. Management has refused O'Neal's requests on the basis that it believes her motive continues to be to publicly embarrass the company. Does O'Neal have a right to the information she has requested? Explain.

5. Rhonda owns 100 of 1000 shares outstanding of Berton, Inc. The board has voted to sell 250 new shares to the public. Rhonda claims

should should be able to purchase a minimum of 25 shares before the public offering. The board of directors claims the articles do not grant the shareholders preemptive rights and, even if they did, the stock to be sold is treasury stock. Will Rhonda prevail in an action to enforce her preemptive rights? Would your answer be different if the shares were new shares? Explain.

6. Pat Almdale and Alan Asche are the sole shareholders of Almco Transit Company, Inc., an intrastate bus company. Chuck Waller, a passenger injured in an accident involving an Almco bus, has brought suit against Almco and the two shareholders. Almco's buses and equipment are badly deteriorated; the corporation's assets have been continually depleted by the shareholders; and the firm carries only minimal insurance. In addition, the corporation and its shareholders do not maintain separate bank accounts and records; there has never been a shareholder or director meeting; and Almdale and Asche have consistently bragged that they formed the corporation to be able to avoid personal liability for business debts. If the intent to avoid personal liability for business debts were the only circumstance that existed, would a court be likely to pierce the corporate veil? Would a court be likely to pierce the corporate veil under all the circumstances given here? Explain.

7. Gragham Tool Works, Inc., and Fyock Corporation have agreed to a consolidation to form Gragham-Fyock, Inc. Although the stocks of the two companies have fallen in price since the announcement, the shareholders of the two corporations have approved the consolidation. Kurt Dikkers voted against the consolidation and has demanded that his shares of Fyock stock be purchased at their fair value, which he claims is above the present stock trading value. The new corporation is willing to pay Dikkers for his stock only at the stock's value when the shareholders approve the consolidation. What right is Dikkers attempting to exercise in his objection to the consolidation? Is it possible that

Gragham-Fyock will have to pay Dikkers more than the stock's market price? Explain.

8. Plimpton subscribed for 1000 shares of the Billiard Ball Corporation at $10 per share. The stock's par value was $1. Plimpton paid $1000 upon Billiard's incorporation and $4000 later. The corporation is now in bankruptcy. The creditors of the corporation are seeking to hold Plimpton personally liable for his failure to pay the full subscription price. Plimpton claims he has no liability, since he paid the corporation more than the par value of the shares. What will the result be? Explain.

9. Borden and Francois purchased the Orange Cab Company. They decided to divide the 100 cabs into 50 newly created subsidiary corporations. Drivers were assigned to one of the 100 cabs by the parent company. Barbara Dunn was injured by a driver of one of the cabs and has brought a legal action seeking to pierce the corporate veil of all the subsidiary companies. Borden and Francois claim that forming a subsidiary to limit investor liability is not an illegal motivation. They also claim that the corporate veil should not be pierced, since each subsidiary carried the minimum insurance coverage required by law. Would a court be likely to agree with them? Explain.

10. In 1987, Sloan, Ladner and Sodetz formed a voting trust, as authorized by the RMBCA, to vote their shares of stock at Delta Corporation. The trust worked effectively until Sloan died in 1989. Sloan's heir, Harvey Moore, is opposed to the positions previously taken by the trust, and he claims that his stock is unmarketable because of the trust agreement. Moore further claims that the trust should be treated like a partnership and that the death of Sloan should dissolve the trust. Ladner and Sodetz claim the trust is irrevocable until 1997 but have offered to buy Moore's stock at a major discount to the price of Delta's publicly traded stock, which is not subject to the trust. Would a court be likely to uphold the voting trust? Explain.

CHAPTER 22

Choosing a Form of Business Organization

"What business form is right for me?"

Lawyers and accountants hear that question all the time. As you probably have guessed, the answer is, "It all depends."

We have already seen that partnerships and corporations are highly versatile forms of business organization. And, we have also seen that limited partnerships have characteristics of both. In this chapter, we will focus on the attributes of sole proprietorships, partnerships, and corporations that you would consider when making a choice of form. We will also look at close corporations. And, we will examine franchises, which are not a business form but do have a substantial impact on their owners' choice of one.

CHOOSING AMONG THE MAJOR FORMS

The discussion of the forms of business began in Part III, "Agency and Employment." Agency and employment law were discussed mainly from the perspective of the sole proprietor. But, no matter what form your business takes, the principles of agency and employment law apply. The manager of Matt's sporting goods store will have apparent authority to engage in the types of transactions such managers usually make, regardless of whether the store's form of organization is a sole proprietorship, a partnership, or a corporation.

There is at least a theoretical progression from sole proprietorship to corporation. In fact, many—though not most—businesses do evolve from one form to another. Suppose Matt owns his sporting goods store as a sole proprietor. When his business grows beyond his ability to manage it, he asks Lisa to become his partner. The business continues to grow, and over time Matt and Lisa invite key employees to join them as partners. Finally, the partners decide to incorporate so they can sell stock to investors and obtain the benefits of limited liability.

Factors Influencing the Choice of Form

Just as no single business form fits all, no single method of determining which to choose suits all. The choice often requires weighing several factors. For example, the limited liability afforded corporate shareholders in the context of contracts may be of little importance to entrepreneurs forced to cosign corporate notes individually. But suppose their business is manufacturing and selling a product that can be hazardous if misused, like swimming pool chemicals. Limited liability in a tort context will be very important.

Surveys of new business owners have shown that they had various reasons for choosing the forms they did. Many of these reasons revealed misunderstandings of the law. For instance, business owners often do not appreciate the individual partner's liability for partnership debts.

Similarly, some choose one form over another because they believe the government interferes with their type less than it does others. The fact is, of course, that no business form liberates its owners from government regulation. Just look at Figure 15-1, which tabulates common statutory rights employees enjoy regardless of their employers' business form. Most environmental regulations apply with equal rigor to sole proprietorships and *Fortune* 500 companies—and that has been one of the great criticisms of them.

The most common, valid considerations to be weighed in choosing a business form are:

- Ease of creation
- Management process
- Potential liability of the owner
- Transferability of ownership
- Treatment by taxing authorities

We will examine each of these below.

Ease of Creation

"Ease of creation" refers to the process of bringing the business into a legal form.

Sole owners. For sole owners of a business, the choice usually is between a sole proprietorship and a corporation. For sheer ease of formation, the sole proprietorship wins hands down because there are no statutory requirements, filings, and the like. Millions of people run part-time businesses (like furniture refinishing) as sole proprietors without ever giving the form a second thought.

In contrast, we have seen that forming a corporation requires a good deal of paperwork and probably the services of an attorney. Even without an attorney, there are costs involved in preparing the filings, and these costs can be significant to the start-up.

Multiple owners. For businesses with multiple owners, a general partnership often will be easier to form than a corporation. The Uniform Partnership Act (UPA) does not require any formal partnership agreement, unless one is required by the Statute of Frauds, and does not require a filing with the Secretary of State. Nonetheless, preventive law principles *strongly* dictate that the partners should execute a written partnership agreement. If the owners are going to that trouble of preparing a formal partnership agreement, the balance may shift to another form.

Management Process

Who will control the business and who will manage it are always concerns in choosing a form of organization. The factors that go into the choice include:

- Complexity of the business
- Number of agents and employees
- Number of business locations
- Nature of business
- Need for external financing
- Competition and the demands of the market
- Government regulations

Some of these substantive business concerns can dictate a particular legal form. For example, a combination of the nature of the oil business and the Internal Revenue Code dictates limited partnerships as the form for oil exploration and drilling ventures.

In most cases, however, the owners have a choice. Thus, given their substantive concerns, they must choose an organizing principle. That organizing principle—the form of business—is chosen to enable the owners *procedurally* to control the operation of the business. So, ultimately, the choice may come down to an evaluation of the business's decision-making process.

Sole proprietorships. Of course, the decision-making process is simplest for the sole proprietor. A sole proprietor has the legal authority to make decisions without having to adhere to any particular procedures, notices, forms, or the like. In other words, the sole proprietor has the legal authority to bind the business without anyone else's approval or ratification. The sole proprietor is the business.

Partnerships. When a business has multiple owners, partnership is generally the most flexible form. A partnership requires two or more persons carrying on a business for profit. The Uniform Partnership Act permits a great degree of flexibility in management. For example, the UPA presumes that each partner has an equal voice in management, but it permits the alteration of this presumption by agreement of the partners. This occurs quite routinely in large partnerships, like law and accounting firms where management is delegated to particular partners.

Maintaining control of management functions becomes increasingly difficult as the number of ''owners'' in a general partnership increases. Conversely, it becomes difficult to design procedures to deal with partners who are not actively involved in the business, as in the case of investor-owners. Since the UPA presumes equal management rights in all partners, the partnership must devise a partnership agreement covering the nonmanagement partners. Ironically, such general partners are not likely to accept a diminution of their potential right to manage because of their potential full liability for partnership obligations.

When investor-owners are involved and a corporation is not an option, a limited partnership may be the solution. It offers the general partners the flexibility of the general partnership and the investor partners—the limited partners—the protection of limited liability for partnership obligations in exchange for a much reduced right to manage.

Corporations. By its nature, a corporation involves the most complicated management process of any of the three principal forms of business organization. Shareholders, directors, and officers have their own distinct roles.

Shareholders have no management or agency authority. A shareholder—in his or her capacity as a shareholder—is merely an investor. But, investors have their say in their power to elect the board and to vote on extraordinary transactions.

A single owner may choose to incorporate, but that choice will depend on nonmanagement considerations, usually. But single owners must be careful to observe the procedural requirements, like maintaining the separateness of the corporate identity, so as to avoid losing the protection afforded by the "corporate veil."

Some states provide an option for the single owner (and others) of a corporation: the statutory close corporation. This variation on the standard corporate form grants owners the protections of limited liability and the flexibility of management usually found in partnerships. Close corporations in general will be discussed below.

Potential Liability of Owner

Of the ownership forms, corporations and limited partnerships offer owners the greatest insulation from liability. Their liability extends only to their investment, under normal circumstances. Suppose Margaret buys 100 shares of Widget Corp. at $35 per share. If the corporation fails, her total loss is $3500. Potentially, a general partner is liable for all the business's debts. If worse comes to worst, the sole proprietor or partner can face personal bankruptcy.

Torts. An active owner of a business—regardless of its form—will always be vulnerable to personal liability for torts in which he is involved. Suppose Lisa, the shareholder-manager of Matt's sporting goods store, accidentally hits a customer in the head with a tennis racket while demonstrating it. She will be personally liable.

Limited liability does cut off the tort liability of passive shareholders at the amount of their investment. Thus, if Lisa's negligence bankrupts the business, the other shareholders will lose only their investments. They will not have to dig into their pockets to pay the judgment as they would if they were general partners.

Contracts. Shareholders as shareholders have no liability on corporate contracts beyond the amount of their investments.

But as noted previously, third parties may not enter into contracts with corporations—especially start-ups and small businesses—without guarantees from one or more shareholders. Banks often make this a condition of their loans to such businesses. They will evaluate the net worth and creditworthiness of the shareholder-guarantor as carefully as they will the business's.

A shareholder-guarantor of a corporate obligation has a potential liability that probably exceeds the value of his or her investment. But that potential liability arises from an act performed outside of his or her status as a shareholder. Guarantors are discussed in Chapter 40, "Suretyship."

Transferability of Ownership

Consideration of the transferability of ownership requires the addressing of two distinct issues: the ability to sell an ownership interest, and the procedural aspects of how a transfer of an ownership interest can occur.

The ability to sell an ownership interest will depend more on the business's commercial viability and its owners' access to buyers than on its form. For example, the shareholders of a family-owned and -run corporation may have great difficulty selling the business on the death of the only family member actively involved in its operation. The business has lost at least some degree of viability, and the inexperienced family members lack ready access to buyers. These are the types of issues that should be addressed in a succession plan, something every closely held business of any value should have.

From a purely procedural standpoint, a sole proprietorship is the easiest business in which to sell an ownership interest.* No particular form, filing, or procedure is required. In contrast, selling stock involves exchanging the transferred certificates for new ones. If the stock is restricted, the buyer must satisfy the terms of the restriction and may have to go through an approval process similar to that of an incoming partner.

Treatment by Taxing Authorities

In considering the tax implications of the choice of a business form, the key element will be whether the business requires the retention of earnings to fund research or growth. If it does, a corporate form is indicated. If not, any form will probably do.

Corporations. Previous chapters have emphasized the differences in the Internal Revenue Code's treatment of corporations and other forms of business. Corporations pay taxes directly on corporate profits. If the corporation

then distributes those profits in the form of dividends, the profits are taxed again as income to the shareholders. As logic dictates, this is referred to as "the double taxation of dividends."

As a practical matter, small corporations with active shareholder-managers rarely pay dividends. They prefer transactions that provide the corporation with legitimate business expense deductions, such as salaries and employee benefits.

Other business forms. All other business forms file an informational tax return. The taxes on business income are reported and paid by the owners in proportion to their interests. Suppose ABC is a partnership. Its income is $120,000 for the year of which it pays out $30,000 to each of its three equal partners. Nonetheless, the partners' income tax liability would be $40,000 each.

As discussed below, under the Internal Revenue Code a corporation's owners may elect S corporation status, which permits them to treat the corporation as a partnership for tax purposes.

Statutory Variations

The choice of the right form of business organization may be somewhat more complicated than described here because there are significant variations on the three major forms.

Part IV has mentioned five major variations on the theme of business organizations: limited partnerships (discussed in Chapter 18), professional corporations (discussed in Chapter 19), statutory close corporations, limited liability companies, and S corporations. All five are creatures of statute: the first four, state; the last, federal. The next sections will examine the latter three.

CLOSE CORPORATIONS

Because there is no commonly accepted model close corporation act there is no single, univer-

---

* As will see below, from a practical standpoint the sale of any closely held business can be very complex, if for no other reason than the difficulty in placing a value on it.

sally accepted definition of a *close corporation*. Each state which has enacted legislation permitting close corporations has created its own definition appropriate to the scope of its act. It is safe to say that a close corporation is not publicly traded and that its shares are held by one person or a small number of persons. That is an extremely broad definition when one considers that of the 2,700,000 corporations in the country, only 10,000 are publicly traded. Also, the states vary widely in what they consider to be a maximum number of shareholders in a close corporation—from ten to fifty. The usual example of close corporations is the family or single-shareholder corporation.

However, it is correct to think of close corporations as small only in terms of the number of shareholders involved. Close corporations can be extremely lucrative.

Shareholders in a close corporation, typically, are deeply involved in its management and operation. Their main tax concern may lie in being able to retain earnings in the business for investment and growth without paying personal income taxes on their portions. (S corporations, also discussed below, have different tax consequences.) The close corporation laws meet the requirements of such shareholders by permitting them to cross the "alter ego" line, which would normally cost shareholders their limited liability protection.

The Role of Shareholders

In many respects, the general incorporation laws are inappropriate for close corporations. Most importantly, the role of shareholders in publicly traded corporations and privately held corporations is quite different.

These statutes reflect a division between ownership of shares and management of the corporation. In publicly traded corporations, the shareholders are generally far removed from everyday operations. For example, the typical IBM shareholder does not work for IBM, much less manage it. Few shareholders of publicly traded companies know one another.

This is hardly surprising when you consider, for example, that General Electric has more than two shares outstanding for every living American—and it is not the nation's largest issuer of stock!

In contrast, shareholders in privately held corporations usually know one another. Often, they work for or manage the company or are related to someone connected with it. These corporations rarely have outside directors, so shareholders tend to run them at all levels.

Because shareholders in privately held corporations wear so many hats at once and because they typically deal with one another daily, they often ignore the formalities of corporate governance. They act more informally, like partners, and often without a formal vote. Also, unlike shareholders in larger corporations, they regard their holdings less as an investment than as a part of their employment. Finally, they have a direct, intense personal interest in who buys into their company.

Statutes Governing Close Corporations

Generally, close corporations are subject to the provisions of state corporation laws, like the Model Business Corporation Act (MBCA). Gradually, however, the courts and state legislators have come to the realization that the general corporation laws do not deal with the realities of these corporations.

General corporation statutes. A principal reason for the development of close corporation statutes lies in the philosophy behind the MBCA and other general corporation statutes. These statutes were designed to accommodate companies with direct management structures rather than the shareholder management structures found in most close corporations.

The orientation of the general corporation statutes is most clearly expressed in their clear definitions of the respective roles of shareholders, directors, and officers. Also, they emphasize formal requirements such as notice of meetings and the size of a quorum. These sharp

definitions of functions and formal requirements are not observed in close corporations,
and it would be unrealistic to expect them to be.

Close corporation statutes. In case law, some
states recognized that close corporations were
different from other corporations. However,
until New York modified its corporation code in
1948 to recognize close corporations as unique,
no state had adopted particular legislation in
regard to them. Since then, at least fifteen
states have adopted special close corporation
legislation.

The principal feature of a close corporation
statute is that it permits such companies to operate like partnerships without losing their
shareholders' limited liability protection. The
California statute, for instance, states:

> The failure of a close corporation to observe
> corporate formalities relating to meetings of
> directors or shareholders in connection with
> the management of its affairs. . . . shall not
> be considered a factor tending to establish
> that the shareholders have personal lia-
> bilities for corporate obligations [Cal. Corp.
> Code §300(e)].

In 1982, the American Bar Association's
Committee on Corporate Law completed the
Model Statutory Close Corporation Act, which
is designed to supplement the MBCA. This
Model Act has a close resemblance to the state
acts currently in force.

Governance of Close Corporations

Normally, a corporation must elect to be
treated as a close corporation. Either a newly
created corporation or one already in existence
may make the election. However, the shareholders of an existing corporation must agree
unanimously on the change in status. The
shareholders can also vote to end the corporation's status as a close corporation.

Fiduciary duties. The most notable characteristic of corporate governance under close corporation statutes is that the corporation's
management is recognized as operating more
like a partnership. Even dissolution is based on
the partnership model. It follows that the shareholders should have duties to one another like
those of partners.

Quite often, close corporation statutes require all shareholders to observe duties of utmost good faith and loyalty to each other.
These fiduciary duties resemble those owed by
partners. The rationale is simple: if a close corporation acts as a partnership, its shareholders
should behave like partners. As the next case
illustrates, the courts of some states without
close corporation statutes have imposed the
same duties.

Wilkes v. Springside Nursing Home, Inc.

370 Mass. 842, 353 N.E.2d 657 (1976)

FACTS In 1951, Wilkes invited Riche, Quinn, and Pipkin to join him in converting a hospital
to a nursing home. Each was to be a director and receive money equally from the
corporation as long as each actively participated in the business. In 1965, the
corporation sold some real estate to Quinn. Wilkes insisted on a higher price than
Quinn wanted to pay, and their relationship deteriorated. In January 1967, Wilkes
stated his intention to sell his interest. The directors than established salaries,
omitting Wilkes's salary while increasing Quinn's and continuing the amount paid to
the others. At the annual meeting, Wilkes was not reelected as a director or an

officer. Wilkes sued to recover the salary that would have been due him had he continued as a director and officer. The trial court dismissed the action.

ISSUE   Did the majority breach its fiduciary duties to Wilkes?

DECISION   Yes. Reversed. Majority stockholders have an opportunity not present in larger corporations to oppress, or "freeze out," the minority. Those in control must have some room to maneuver in establishing business policy. But when minority stockholders bring suit alleging a breach of the majority's strict good faith duty, a court must ask whether the controlling group can demonstrate a legitimate purpose for its actions. Denying employment is especially dangerous, since a job may have been a basic reason for a stockholder's investment in the firm.

The technical term for what Wilkes's fellow shareholders attempted is a *freeze out*, the denial of a minority shareholder's rights by the majority in violation of its fiduciary duty. We saw in the last chapter another type of freeze out in *Coggins v. New England Patriots Football Club, Inc.*, but there the frozen-out shareholders in a publicly held corporation were losing only a part of the increase in the value of their investments. Wilkes was losing his livelihood.

Stock offerings. As noted earlier, statutes often restrict the number of shareholders a close corporation may have. At the extremes, the Model Act permits a close corporation to have fifty shareholders, while the Arizona statute sets the number at ten. Several states prohibit public offerings of close corporation stock. Virtually all require that the stock bear a *legend*, that is, a plainly printed notation of the transfer restrictions on the stock, which often include buy-out provisions or rights of first refusal. Should stock not be transferred properly and in accordance with the legend, the corporation may refuse to register the stock.

Shareholder agreements. Close corporation statutes permit much greater shareholder participation in the actual operation of the company than do general corporation statutes. The

Model Act and others permit the shareholders to adopt a *shareholder agreement*, a document which resembles bylaws and can be used in their place. Under the Illinois Close Corporation Act, shareholders can agree on:

- Methods of managing the corporation's business
- Means of declaring and paying dividends
- Appointment of individuals as officers and directors
- Restrictions on the transfer of shares
- Vetoes on particular matters for certain shareholders
- Arbitration of matters which produce a deadlock among the shareholders

As in *Wilkes*, the shareholders commonly agree to the long-term employment of their fellow shareholders.

The role of directors. The list of matters which may be included in a shareholder agreement contains several items normally assigned to the board of directors. So at least in some respects directors are redundant. The Model Act permits the shareholders to eliminate the board. The shareholders will then assume all the board's normal functions.

The disadvantage of eliminating the board is that it imposes on the shareholders the same liabilities directors have. Therefore, if a corporation is going to have some nonmanaging shareholders, it should retain its board.

Limited liability. Close corporation statutes generally guarantee limited liability for shareholders. However, like any corporation, the shareholders of a close corporation may have its corporate veil pierced if shareholders are commingling personal and corporate funds, if the corporation is thinly capitalized, or if the shareholders are abusing its limited liability protection. See the discussion in Chapter 21 for a greater discussion of piercing the corporate veil.

S CORPORATIONS

S corporations or *Subchapter S corporations* are close corporations which elect, under Subchapter S of the Internal Revenue Code, to have their shareholders treated as if they were partners for federal income tax purpose.

Subchapter S corporations are created under and governed by state law. The only difference between them and any other corporation similarly organized in the same state is their federal tax treatment. All matters of corporate organization not related to federal income tax questions are controlled by state law. If the state in which the corporation is organized has a close corporation statute, a Subchapter S corporation can elect to be treated as one. Otherwise, it is subject to the general corporation laws.

Shareholders and Voting Rights

Under the Internal Revenue Code, Subchapter S corporations may have no more than thirty-five shareholders and no more than one type of stock. However, within that type—which of course must be common stock—classes of stock can have different voting rights. For example, a Subchapter S corporation can have Class A common, which has voting rights, and Class B common, which does not.

Election of Tax Status

The corporation must elect, and the shareholders must approve the election of, Subchapter S status by the fifteenth day of the third month of the corporation's current taxable year.

All shareholders who own stock in the current year up to the date the shareholders vote on the election have a right to vote. An example will clarify this. SubS Corp.'s tax year begins January 1. It must elect Subchapter S status for 1994 by March 15, 1994. Jodi, one of the thirty-five shareholders of SubS, sells her stock on February 1, 1994. She has a right to vote on the 1994 Subchapter S election, since she held stock during that fiscal year and the status of SubS will affect her tax liability.

Passive Income

A Subchapter S corporation may not receive more than 25 percent of its gross receipts for 3 consecutive tax years in the form of passive income. *Passive income* is income from rents, interest on loans, dividends on stock, and the like. A corporation which exceeds the passive income level for 3 years will not be allowed to elect Subchapter status again. Still worse for its shareholders, they will have to pay the highest corporate tax rate on the amount of the annual excess.

Congress intended that the passive income limit would keep the Subchapter S election from being used simply to pass on investment losses to the shareholders. Unlike a limited partnership, a corporation normally cannot pass on its investment losses to the shareholders for them to claim on their personal income tax returns.

Future of S Corporations

In 1991, an estimated 1.4 million businesses filed Subchapter S income tax returns. However, the number of closely held businesses choosing to operate under Subchapter S appear to be declining because of perceived "nit-picking rules and draconian penalties" of the IRS.* A new Model Subchapter S Act has been developed to assist states in helping close corporations become more compatible with the expectations of the federal tax law. However, it has been criticized as actually further burdening S corporations. As of 1991, only Hawaii and North Carolina have adopted the Act. It is because of major dissatisfaction with the S corporation status today that limited liability companies (LLCs) have begun to become quite popular. LLCs are discussed next.

LIMITED LIABILITY COMPANIES

A hybrid business entity, well-known and utilized in Europe and Latin America, is now gaining wide acceptance among the states: *limited liability companies* (*LLCs*). The goal in forming an LLC is to secure limited liability for all owners, be taxed like a partnership, and secure flexibility in management.

An LLC is a cross between a partnership and a corporation. It shares some legal and tax similarities to both limited partnerships and S corporations but is ultimately different from both. For example, unlike a limited partnership, all LLC owners, called *members*, have limited liability protection. Unlike an S corporation, there are no restrictions or limitations on the kinds or number of members. You may recall that an S corporation is limited to thirty-five or fewer owners.

Formation of an LLC

An LLC can be formed only if a state recognizes such an entity. As of July, 1992, nineteen states recognized LLCs and thirteen more were then considering recognition.* Requirements to

---

* *Forbes*, April 29, 1991, p. 78.
* ABA Section of Taxation, Subcommittee on Limited Liability Companies, Survey of Limited Liability Legislation, July 9, 1992.

form and operate an LLC vary greatly by state, as there currently is no uniform or model LLC statute.

An LLC is formed by filing *Articles of Organization* with the state. Requirements vary, but most states require two or more members. As previously stated, generally there are no restrictions on the type or character of members which permit members to include individuals, partnerships, corporations, foreign investors, pension plans, and corporate joint ventures. While there could potentially be an unlimited number of members, most LLCs will limit the number to under 500 to avoid coverage by the Securities Exchange Act of 1934.

In addition to the Articles of Organization, members create an *operating agreement* which serves a function similar to the articles of partnership: an agreement on the purpose and operation of the business. The operating agreement, like articles of partnership, is a source of authority.

Management of an LLC

Members are considered to be of equal status. What this actually means is that they are all of the same kind or type. For example, all shareholders are of the same status: shareholders. In contrast, in a limited partnership there are two types of owners: general and limited partners. As such, they have different status with different legal and tax attributes.

Unlike a partnership, members are not presumed to have an equal voice in management. Instead, a member's "voice" is dependent upon its proportionate ownership interest. Although not required, most LLCs choose to designate one of its members to be the *manager*, the head of the LLC. The manager generally serves in a role similar to that of the managing general partner of a limited partnership. The significant difference is that the *manager*, like all other members, has liability limited to its LLC capital contribution.

Although a manager is generally designated to lead the LLC, other members may also be actively involved in the management of the LLC. Those who are so involved do so without risking a loss or change of status for legal or tax purposes. This is another significant difference from a limited partnership, where a limited partner risks losing this status if he or she is too actively involved in management.

It is the ability of members, as members, to actively participate in management which causes an LLC to be different from a corporation. In a corporation, shareholders, as shareholders, have no right of management.

Transferability of Interest

To maintain its hybrid status and not risk being classified as a corporation, LLCs have limitations on transferability of interest. Some LLCs are similar to a partnership, requiring unanimous consent to admit a new member. Some more closely resemble a limited partnership where approval of the managing general partner must be obtained to be able to transfer a limited partnership interest. For an LLC, this would mean approval by the manager.

Continuity of Life

A corporation may have perpetual life. All other business entity forms, including the LLC, have less than perpetual life. This creates a practical problem for an LLC. Since most LLCs will be created to serve investment goals, continuity of business is desirable. However, if the LLC is structured to obtain perpetual, or near perpetual, existence it will risk being classified as a corporation.

Because there is no commonly adopted uniform or model law for LLCs, the requirements concerning continuity of life for LLCs vary from state to state. Some LLC statutes specify a maximum length of life for an LLC. For example, Colorado and Florida limit the life of an LLC to no more than 30 years. Most states stipulate certain events which will cause dissolution of an LLC.

The State of Wyoming, which enacted the first LLC statute in 1977, has dissolution provisions which track very closely to those of a general partnership. These include expiration of the term specified in the articles of organization and certain events which terminate the continued membership of a member, such as death, bankruptcy, expulsion, etc. Wyoming, like most other states, does allow the LLC to continue after dissolution by unanimous vote of all remaining partners if authorized in the LLC's articles of organization.

Exploring ideas on how an LLC can gain greater continuity and flexibility without risking LLC status is currently a hot topic among business lawyers and state legislators. It is expected that LLCs may move to majority, versus unanimous, vote for continuation. Preagreement to continue may be made a part of the articles of organization and/or operating agreement for matters like death or disability of a member.

Futures of LLCs

The greatest strengths of LLCs are their flexibility of ownership and management and limited liability for all members. An LLC may have almost any combination of owners with unlimited proportionate ownership interests. All members, not only pure investors, have liability limited to their capital contribution.

The future of LLCs is highly dependent on how the Internal Revenue Service ultimately treats them. The IRS has recognized LLCs and has issued various Revenue Rulings providing some guidance. However, the IRS has not yet formalized regulations fully describing eligibility for LLC tax status or taken a position on whether LLCs are to be treated like a partnership for all tax purposes. This has left significant unresolved issues. For example, it is not presently clear how, if at all, passive income and loss regulations may apply. For now, owners contemplating an LLC do so with some risk and uncertainties.

| | SOLE PROPRI-ETORSHIP | GENERAL PARTNER-SHIP | LIMITED PARTNERSHIP | | GENERAL CORPO-RATION | CLOSE CORPORA-TION (BY STATUTE) | SUB-CHAPTER S CORPORA-TION | LIMITED LIABILITY COMPANY |
			GENERAL PARTNERS	LIMITED PARTNERS				
Formal state filing require-ments?	No	Generally not	Yes	Yes	Yes	Yes	Yes	Yes
Minimum number of business owners?	One	Two	One	One	Usually one	One	Usually one (state law)	Usually two (state law)
Maximum number of business owners?	One	None	None	None	None	10 to 35 common	35 (federal law)	None
Maximum number of employees?	Unlimited	Unlimited	Unlimited	Unlimited	Unlimited	Unlimited	Unlimited	Unlimited
Partnership–style management psooible?	Not applicable	Yes	Yes	No	No	Yes	Not unless also close corpora-tion	Yes
Payment of federal income taxes by entity?	No	No	No	No	Yes	Yes unless also Sub-chapter corporation	No	No

Figure 22.1 A Comparison of Business Entities.

MAKING THE CHOICE

Now that the overview of the principal business forms and the main variations on them has been completed, you can see why the answer to, "What is the best business form?" always begins, "It depends."

What the answer depends on varies because different types of businesses require different organizations. For a college student's part-time landscaping business, a sole proprietorship is probably ideal. For a family grocery store, a close corporation may be the answer. For a real estate developer targeting a prime downtown parcel, a limited partnership may be the best investment vehicle. Figure 22.1 compares the business entities that have been examined and can serve as a checklist of their requirements.

As important as fitting the form to the enterprise is fitting the form to the personalities of the owners of the enterprise. *Wilkes* and the cases in Chapter 21 reveal that much of business life is a matter of personalities and personal relations. Figure 22.2 compares the types of owners involved in the various business forms that have been examined.

Still, no matter how carefully owners make

	SOLE PROPRIETOR	PARTNER	LIMITED PARTNER	SHARE-HOLDER	CLOSE SHARE-HOLDER (BY STATUTE)	MEMBER
Does owner status bestow inherent agency authority?	Owner is principal	Yes	No	No	No	Can vary by state
Equal voice in management?	Is management	UPA presumption	No	No	Not unless so agreed	No
Limited liability for business debts?	No	No	Usually yes	Usually yes	Usually yes	Usually yes
Can ownership interest be freely transferred?	Yes	No	Usually no	Usually Yes	Usually no	Usually no
Does death cause dissolution of business?	Yes	Yes	No	No	No	No

Figure 22.2 A Comparison of Owners of Business Entities.

a choice of form, virtually no business can succeed without the critical element identified in the conclusion of Chapter 17: trust. The franchising relationship highlights the importance of that element for a venture because there must be a strong element of trust between the franchisee and the franchisor, as well as between and among the franchisee's owners.

FRANCHISES

A *franchise* is a license to sell another's products or to use another's name in business, or both. It is not a form of business organization. Rather, almost any type of business entity can hold a franchise. Franchising accounts for 7.2 million jobs and $650 billion in annual retail sales, nearly half of all retail sales in the United States.* As a result, it is understandable why one sees so many in a commercial zone: McDonald's, Computerland, Wendy's, Midas Mufflers, Budget Rent-a-Car, and dozens of others.

The relationship between the *franchisor*,

the entity granting the franchise, and the *franchisee*, the person buying the franchise, can be quite complicated. They may have competing interests. For instance, the franchisor may wish to expand rapidly in an area by granting a number of franchises, while the franchisee may view additional franchises in its service area as competition diminishing the value of its investment.

Choosing Among Franchises

Industries appropriate for franchising usually have more than one company offering franchises. For instance, many companies offer fast-food franchises. Choosing the right franchisor involves a detailed appraisal of what the franchisor offers.

For the franchisee, the advantages are that a franchise provides immediate access to established goodwill and advertising. For instance, Roto-Rooter is a household name reinforced by extensive national advertising. Marketing ability and willingness to promote the franchisor's products are major factors in choosing a particular franchisor. Particularly for persons who have never operated a business before, the

* *Nation's Business*, July, 1992, p. 46.

management assistance offered by the franchisor can be a critical elements. Some offer extensive ongoing training courses in management and operations, but few furnish consulting services for particular problems.

Franchisor-Franchisee Relations

Relations between franchisors and franchisees are not always happy. The causes of the unhappiness are vaired and are not one-sided. For example, in early 1989, Exxon franchisees were extremely upset about the company's ham-handed handling of the *Exxon Valdez* disaster in Alaska. For a time, their gasoline sales dropped as customers boycotted Exxon stations to protest the 11 million–barrel spill. Gas station franchisees have generally been unhappy for nearly 20 years because, they claim, the oil companies have been squeezing them out of business.

Franchisees are matters of contract. In view of the statistics on new business success quoted above, it is easy to see that the franchisor has the upper hand in negotiating the franchise agreement. Many franchisees come to feel that they were presented the contract on a take-it-or-leave-it basis. Much of the government regulation discussed below is aimed at this problem.

A second problem posed by franchise agreements involves the application of the antitrust laws. If the franchisor attempts to control some of a franchisee's practices, such as the franchisee's pricing of products, the franchisor may violate the antitrust laws. These issues are discussed in Chapter 44.

One of the problems of success is greed. More than a few courts have heard lawsuits brought by franchisees against franchisors in which the issue was not fair dealing or antitrust violations but how the franchisee could gain a larger percentage.

Federal Regulation

Disputes between franchisees and franchisors have led to government intervention and regulation. The first legislation governing franchises was the federal Automobile Dealer's Day in Court Act of 1956. This act makes manufacturers liable for terminating a dealer's franchise for failing to comply with the manufacturer's arbitrary or unreasonable demands. Similar legislation, the Petroleum Marketers Practices Act of 1979, was adopted when many oil companies terminated service station franchise agreements. The Act requires that suppliers establish "good cause" before terminating. In the following case, the court had to determine whether "good cause" was present.

Portaluppi v. Shell Oil Co.

869 F.2d 245 (4th Cir. 1989)

FACTS   Shell canceled Charles Portaluppi's franchise to operate a gasoline station. Portaluppi had pled guilty to a criminal charge of possession of cocaine and marijuana. In its notice of cancellation, Shell cited his conviction as a "relevant event" included as a grounds for termination in both the Petroleum Marketing Practices Act (PMPA) and the lease the parties had executed. The PMPA permits termination under specified conditions on the "occurrence of an event which is relevant to the franchise relationship and as a result of which termination of the franchise . . . is reasonable. . ." The PMPA contains a list of examples of relevant events, including "conviction of a franchisee of any felony involving moral turpitude." Portaluppi brought suit seeking both dammages and injunctive relief. The trial court entered summary judgment for Shell.

ISSUE   Is conviction on a criminal drug charge sufficient grounds for termination of a franchise agreement under the PMPA?

DECISION   Yes. Affirmed. The PMPA protects franchisees from arbitrary termination or nonrenewal of their franchises. Portaluppi argued that his narcotics conviction did not involve moral turpitude and had no relevance to his ability to run the service station. Therefore, it could not be the sole basis for termination of his franchise. However, even assuming that a narcotics law violation is not a felony involving moral turpitude, possession of cocaine in and of itself can relate to the operation of a service station in such a way as to justify the franchisor's termination of the franchise agreement under the PMPA.

In 1979, the Federal Trade Commission (FTC) issued regulations which require that franchisors supply franchisees with a disclosure statement at least 10 days before the franchisee enters into the franchise agreement. This statement should give the franchisee full, fair, and detailed information about the franchisor's operations, finances, and relations with its franchisees and about the performance of the franchisee. The statement must disclose the cost the franchisee must bear, both initially and during the course of the franchise agreement. It also must disclose conditions under which a franchise may be renewed, terminated, or canceled.

The information must be relevant to the particular prospective franchisee. For example, data for a fast-food restaurant next to the Cal Berkely campus would have little relevance to a prospective franchisee in a small, noncollege town in eastern Oregon.

The FTC disclosure document is not a guarantee against fraud and misrepresentation, but inaccuracies and deception are less likely to occur because the franchisor has prepared and attested to his statement in the document. A franchisee may recover for losses caused by the franchisor's misrepresentations or failure to disclose material information. The FTC itself may issue a cease and desist order or seek an injunction against a franchisor which violates its regulations.

State Regulation

Some fifteen states have separate regulations governing the sale and/or operations of franchises in their state. Some legal commentators have argued that these state regulations provide minimal, if any, additional benefits to the franchisee over the FTC franchise regulations. However, the regulations do represent an additional attempt to balance the many inequities between the franchisor and franchisee.

The Iowa Franchise Act, enacted in 1992, is an example of a more recent state franchise law. It prohibits a franchisor from granting another franchise in "unreasonable proximity" of an existing unit of the same franchise system. This rule will require a franchisor like McDonald's, for example, to seriously consider the impact of any new frannchise it grants in an area already having a McDonald's Restaurant.

A franchisor cannot terminate, refuse to renew, or deny a transfer of the franchise to another qualified owner except for "good cause." This provision is intended to reduce the situations where a franchisor unreasonably terminates a franchise or refuses to allow a franchisee to transfer ownership to a qualified buyer.

An additional major provision deals with postterm noncompetition clauses. Franchisors routinely place such clauses in the franchise agreement, which prevents a franchisee from competing with the franchisor in the same system after the contract expires. For example, if Ralph's Burger King franchise had such a clause and his franchise was not renewed, he could not open a competing restaurant for a period of time specified in his franchise agreement. As a result, Ralph would be unable to use personally or lease his building for a different restaurant, say an Arby's. The Iowa law declares noncompetition clauses unenforceable unless the franchisor offers to purchase the assets of the business for fair market value.

As even more retail business is done by franchise in the future, it is probable that more states will choose to follow the lead of Iowa in attempting to secure a fairer balance of interests between franchisors and franchisees.

CONCLUSION

Franchises illustrate how little really depends on the form of the enterprise. The form is simply a means to facilitate an end—making money. It is hard to conceive of a venture which could not be operated using any of the forms we have discussed. What dictates form is a combination of tax laws, individual personalities, and the nature of the business.

While success or failure rarely depends on choosing the right form of business organization, one form is not to be chosen over another haphazardly. And the potential liabilities in each must always be kept in mind.

A NOTE TO FUTURE CPA CANDIDATES

The business law portion of the CPA exam has not focused on close corporations by statute, Subchapter S corporations, limited liability companies, or franchise law. However, any future CPA candidate would do well to understand these topics.

The main focus for a CPA candidate should be to know and understand both the basic differences and similarities between sole proprietorships, partnerships, limited partnerships, limited liabilities companies, and corporations. Figures 22.1 and 22.2 should help you achieve this goal.

KEY WORDS

close corporation (481)
franchise (488)
franchisee (488)
franchisor (488)
limited liability company (485)
member (485)
S corporation (484)

DISCUSSION QUESTIONS

1. What are some of the major concerns to be considered in deciding which business form to adopt?
2. Why is the sole proprietorship the least difficult to form?
3. Why will a creditor of an incorporated small business be likely to require one or more shareholders to sign as sureties before lending money to the corporation?
4. "The most critical factor in the sale of a business will likely be the type of business entity that it is." Do you agree?
5. Contrast the federal income tax treatment of a sole proprietorship, partnership, and corporation.
6. What is a close corporation? How does it differ from a general corporation? How will such a corporation be treated for federal tax purposes?
7. What is an S corporation? How does its management process vary from that of an MBCA corporation?
8. "A shareholder holding restricted stock in a small corporation may find that he is not too unlike a partner attempting to sell his ownership interest in a partnership." Agree?
9. What is a franchise? What type of business entity may a franchisee select?
10. What is the role of the federal government in the sale of franchises?

CASE PROBLEMS

1. Jere Hatcher is preparing to open a new business manufacturing and selling tree-mounted hunting stands. The stands are portable and can be erected temporarily to assist hunters to spot game during hunting season. Hatcher has patented his new design for tree stands and expects to be able to avoid the type of lawsuits which have been directed against manufacturers of traditional hunter tree stands. Hatcher would like to operate as a sole proprietorship until his daughter, Kaye, can join him as a partner in the business in a few years. From these limited facts, how would you advise Hatcher about the most appropriate business form for his purposes. Explain.

2. Heritage Bank is considering a loan to Hoefer Roofing Company. The bank is concerned that the company is not making enough profit, pays rent that is too high for its facilities, and has loans outstanding that are too great for the firm's capital. The company's president, Paul Hoefer, has shown the bank that the firm's apparent income is understated because of relatively high salaries to shareholder-officers, that the rent is being paid to a separate corporation owned by the same shareholders, and that the shareholders are the primary creditors of the firm. Said Hoefer, "In essence, you must consider us as something other than a corporation." Does this seem true? How might Heritage Bank best protect itself in making a loan to the corporation?

3. LeBarron and Clark have decided to establish an antique car restoration business. Each will put up an equal amount of capital, but LeBarron's role is to be primarily that of an advisor. LeBarron does not want the risky restoration business to jeopardize the financial stability of his separate, successful retail furniture business. Clark does not want the red tape of a corporation and dislikes the "double taxation" which occurs when a shareholder receives a cash dividend. What form of business ownership would you recommend? Explain.

4. Spataro, Inc., is a new real estate investment firm. The shareholders elected to assume S corporation status for federal income tax purposes so that the firm could pass investment losses through to the owners. The owners elected against a partnership because of their potential liability exposure and against a limited partnership, since all the owners are actively engaged in operating the business. For their first tax year, passive income (basically rent receipts) constituted over 50 percent of the firm's total gross receipts. What federal tax problems, if any, might the firm have? Explain.

5. Odyssey Cola Corporation was established under close corporation laws. Odyssey has no board of directors, has eight shareholders, and has restricted stock. Selber, a shareholder of Odyssey, got into a disagreement with the other shareholders when they decided to delay marketing a new cola drink that he had devised. Selber thereafter sold both his stock in Odyssey and his new cola formula to Vantage Soda Pop Company, which began selling the cola drink in record numbers. Selber claims that, because he is a minority shareholder and not an officer, he owed no fiduciary duties to Odyssey preventing him from selling either the cola formula or the stock to Vantage. Is Selber correct? Explain.

6. Eleanor Guerin purchased an outdoor sports clothing store franchise from Glacier Hiking Corporation. Eleanor had been quite skeptical of the chances of success for a Glacier Hiking Shop in a small southern town until Glacier "proved" that success was assured by providing sale figures from ten franchises located in other small towns. Glacier failed to tell Eleanor that the ten franchises were located near very popular mountain hiking areas and/ or major metropolitan areas. Although well managed, Eleanor's franchised shop went bankrupt within 6 months of operation. Would Eleanor be likely to prevail in a lawsuit against Glacier for improper franchise disclosure? Explain.

7. Chris Goebel is interested in opening a sporting goods store with his son, Brian, and daughter, Sarah. Their goal is to open three

more stores within the next 3 years. To do so, they will have to borrow a large amount of money. They would like to operate as a partnership. But, they are concerned about their potential tort liability from the sale of football helmets to scholastic teams. Their state does not have a close corporation statute. They are considering having Sarah be the sole proprietor with Chris as the general manager to reduce Chris's personal liability exposure. To do this, Chris would loan $50,000 to Sarah or the sole proprietorship instead of making a direct capital contribution. A lawyer has suggested the corporate form to avoid personal liability. Is the lawyer's advice correct? What is likely to be the best form of business for them? Explain.

8. Jim Fennema offered a 25 percent discount for the purchase of one of his Jimbo Burger Restaurant franchises if it was bought during a 3-day franchise fair in Chicago. Fennema hired a famous football player, Johnny Soldwedel, to give a personal testimonial about his franchise in Canton. The financial information about the Canton franchise was accurate, but Johnny has never been involved with it. Barb Jastrem was so impressed that she purchased a franchise at the fair. Unfortunately, Jastrem's Jimbo Burgers franchise failed within a year. Jastrem claims that Fennema violated the franchise disclosure laws. Disregarding Jastrem's potential remedy, if any, is she correct? Explain.

9. A group of investors is preparing to form a new business to develop and sell specialized medical field software. Knowing that doctors would be naturally interested in their product, the group is also seeking to attract them as potential outside investors. Although the long-term future of their product looks very promising, the company is likely to suffer 3 to 5 years of moderate annual losses while they attempt to penetrate existing national markets. Assuming all possibilities shown in Figure 22-1 are available, what would you advise these investors? Explain.

10. Assume you have won a major state lottery and now wish to invest money in several business ventures. You are very capable, have a basic understanding of business, want some voice, but still expect to pursue independent business interests. An old high school friend has approached you about helping form a company to purchase, restore, and operate an old theater. Having once had a minor role in the play *Lil' Abner*, this appeals to you. However, being no stage dummy, you want to be assured that you will have limited liability protection. Assuming all possibilities shown in Figure 22-1 are available, is there any one possibility which would assure you against any loss of your *initial* investment? Explain.

CHAPTER 23

Securities and Their Regulation

Mention ''securities and the arcane world of the New York Stock Exchange (NYSE) comes to mind. But the stocks *traded*—bought and sold—on the NYSE make up only about half of the securities traded on national exchanges every business day.

Although the NYSE is only a part of the securities market, a few statistics relating to it will put the market in perspective. Only 10,000 of the 3 million corporations have issued *publicly traded securities*, which are securities bought and sold on a stock exchange or in the so-called over-the-counter market. Of those 10,000, about 16 percent have issued shares listed on the NYSE. In 1988, the NYSE recorded more than 17.7 million transactions involving almost 41.1 billion shares. By comparison, in 1982 only 16.4 billion shares changed hands. Also in 1982, the NYSE set a single-day trading record of 149.4 million shares. Just under 5 years later, 608.1 million shares were traded in a single session.

Plainly, no agency could hope to monitor every stock transaction on the exchanges, much less the millions of other off-exchange securities transactions that occur annually. Even an agency as highly respected as the federal Securities and Exchange Commission cannot keep up with the seemingly ever-growing tidal wave of securities when its staffing level decreased by 3 percent between 1981 and 1986.

Legislators and regulators have focused their attention on the information an investor should have in order to make an informed analysis of the opportunities and risks of a particular security. Disclosure of this information is the principal means used by both state and federal regulators to police the marketplace. Nonetheless, where fraud occurs—especially when it involves the use of information which places ordinary investors at a disadvantage—the regulators can impose substantial civil and criminal penalties.

This chapter focuses primarily on federal disclosure requirements under the Securities Act of 1933 and the Securities Exchange Act of

1934. As you study these regulations, it is important to keep in mind that they affect contracts to buy and sell stock. However, they do not govern the actual transaction, the manner in which the parties exchange consideration. Article 8 of the UCC governs the transactions themselves, as we will see in Chapter 38.

THE REGULATORS AND THEIR AUTHORITY

The New Deal reformers under President Franklin Roosevelt were determined to provide an honest marketplace for securities. By means of two statutes, the Securities Act of 1933 and the Securities Exchange Act of 1934, they permanently altered the way that publicly traded corporations had to treat the purchasers and holders of their securities. They also changed both the ethical and the operational aspects of buying and selling securities. The principal instrument of that change was the Securities and Exchange Commission (SEC), a regulatory agency created under the 1934 Act to police the securities marketplace. Nonetheless, then and now, the states play an important role in securities regulation.

The Securities and Exchange Commission

The SEC investigates possible wrongdoing and provides civil enforcement of the security laws and rules.

The Securities Act of 1933 primarily regulates *new issues*; the original sale and distribution of securities. It requires that sellers of new issues—the *issuer*—provide adequate, accurate, and truthful information to prospective purchasers. To accomplish its goals, the 1933 Act requires that issues *register*—file a report describing the offering—with the SEC. The registration requirements are detailed below.

The Securities Exchange Act of 1934 has a different and much broader application. It regulates the trading of securities after their original distribution. For instance, the 1934 Act applies every time anyone buys or sells through a *broker-dealer*, a person who deals in securities issued by others. The 1934 Act, too, has reporting requirements. Unlike the requirements of the 1933 Act, these apply to all publicly traded companies with more than 500 shareholders and $3 million in assets. These reporting requirements are discussed below.

Both the 1933 Act and the 1934 Act authorize the SEC to issue *administrative regulations* or rules. As discussed in Chapter 3, regulations are statute-like interpretations of the statutes an administrative agency is charged with carrying out.

In 1990, the SEC was given significantly broader powers to enforce securities law violations without the need for a court hearing and ruling. The SEC has broad powers to impose stiff penalties for stock manipulation, records falsification, insider trading, and other security law violations. In addition, it can order violators to return illegal profits, issue cease and desist orders to halt illegal wrongdoing, and exercise debarment powers (disqualifying persons from involvement with securities matters).

The SEC cannot itself prosecute criminal violations of the federal securities laws. Instead, the SEC refers cases to the Department of Justice for prosecution. Both the 1933 and 1934 Acts provide for persons injured by illegal securities activities to bring civil suits for damages.

State Securities Regulation

The states, too, have securities laws. They are called *blue sky laws* because they were designed to prevent the sale of "air" to unknowing investors. Most states enacted these laws before the federal government entered the field, but this regulatory scheme proved inadequate in the 1920s as national markets for securities became the rule.

Today, blue sky laws generally serve the same purposes and use the same definitional framework as the federal securities laws. Blue sky laws, too, aim to prevent fraud and manipulation by ensuring that investors have sufficient data to evaluate the merits of an investment. A seller of securities must comply with both the state and the federal regulatory schemes. Where the reporting requirements are different, the issuer must comply with the stricter requirement, that is, the one requiring greater disclosure. As discussed below, where securities are to be sold only within one state, often the offering is exempt from SEC regulation.

WHAT IS A SECURITY?

In the discussion of financing a corporation (Chapter 19), "security" was not defined beyond noting that there were equity and debt securities. And, for good reason.

The Securities Acts Definitions

The federal securities laws do not really define the term either. Instead, as in the 1933 Act [§2(1)], they list the types of items which may be securities. These include:

> *[any] note, stock, treasury stock, bond, debenture, evidence of indebtedness, certificate of interest or participation in any profit-sharing agreement, collateral-trust certificate, pre-organization certificate or subscription, transferable share, investment contract, voting-trust certificate, certificate of deposit for a security, fractional undivided interest in oil, gas or other mineral rights, or, in general, any interest or instrument commonly known as a "security," or any certificate of interest or participation in, temporary or interim certificate for, receipt for, guarantee of, or warrant or right to subscribe to or purchase, any of the foregoing.*

With that list to go by, one might think little controversy would surround the definition of "security." The opposite is true. In an article examining devices designed to protect large investors from wide swings in the markets, *Forbes* identified more than seventy-five new types of securities in this narrow category devised between 1971 and 1986. Over seventy of these first appeared after 1980!*

---

* S. Lee, "What's with the Casino Society?" *Forbes*, September 22, 1986, pp. 150–153.

The *Howey* Test

The next two cases deal with the question of what a security is in terms of "investment contracts," another undefined term. In the first of the two cases, the U.S. Supreme Court stated what has come to be the classic test of a security. In the second case, a federal appellate court applied that test.

SEC v. W.J. Howey Co.

328 U.S. 293 (1946)

FACTS
W. J. Howey Co. and Howey-in-the-Hills Service, Inc., had common management and ownership. W. J. Howey planted 500 acres of orange groves in Florida. It offered 250 acres to the public. Howey offered each prospective customer a land sales contract and a service contract. The customers were told it was not feasible to buy into the grove without contracting with someone to manage it. Of course, W. J. Howey emphasized the superiority of Howey-in-the-Hills, and 85 percent of those buying acreage also retained the service company. The 10-year service contracts were not cancelable by the customer and granted the service company full possession of the acreage. Most purchasers were not Florida residents and lacked the knowledge, skill, and equipment necessary to run the groves. The SEC sought an injunction against Howey, alleging Howey was marketing investment contracts required to be registered with the Commission. The district court denied the injunction and the court of appeals affirmed.

ISSUE
Was Howey selling an investment contract required to be registered with the SEC?

DECISION
Yes. Reversed. An investment contract means

> a contract, transaction, or scheme whereby a person invests his money in a common enterprise and is led to expect profits solely from the efforts of the promoter or a third party, it being immaterial whether the shares in the enterprise are evidenced by formal certificates or by nominal interests in [its] physical assets. . . .
>
> [All] the elements of a profit-seeking business venture are present [in the Howey operation]. The investors provide the capital and share in the earnings and profits; the promoters manage, control and operate the enterprise. It follows that the arrangements whereby the investors' interests are made manifest involve investment contracts, regardless of the legal terminology in which such contracts are clothed. . . .
>
> This conclusion [that Howey was offering securities required to be registered with the SEC] is unaffected by the fact that some purchasers choose not to accept the full

offer of an investment contract by declining to enter into a service contract with [Howey-in-the-Hills. The 1933 Act] prohibits the offer as well as the sale of unregistered . . . securities. . . .

Should the purchasers of orange grove parcels in **Howey** have been surprised at the outcome of the case? What primarily motivated them to purchase a parcel? To become farmers themselves? No, most likely parcels were purchased with the intent to make money from an investment. Would the result be the same if the contracts had instead dealt with the purchase of to-be-mined gold ore? Rental condominiums? The case highlights an important learning point—securities are not limited to stocks and bonds.

Three points in *Howey* bear emphasis. First, "securities" include many types of investments, many of which do not fall into the categories of debt and equity. Second, the 1933 Act applies not just to transactions in securities but also to offers to sell. Third, the "efforts of others" standard has become the basic test of a security.

The "efforts of others" test has its limits. In 1979, the U.S. Supreme Court held that an employee's interest in his pension plan was not a security when only the employer made contributions to it. The contributions were not investments by the employee but rather were part of his compensation. Also, the value of the pension benefits depended less on the skill of the fund's managers than it did on the flow of the employer's contributions.* It is not clear how the Court will treat interests in employee pension funds to which employees may contribute.

The Ninth Circuit has held that a prepaid investment in gold coins was not a security because the world market for gold—not the seller's efforts—determined whether the coins appreciated in value. The fact that the buyer paid for the coins before delivery did not make the contract for their purchase a security because the buyer's risk in that regard was that the seller would not perform—a risk run by any buyer of goods who pays in advance.†

Before leaving *Howey*, let's look at a case that is almost its polar opposite.

---

* *International Brotherhood of Teamsters v. Daniel*, 439 U.S. 551 (1979).
† *SEC v. Belmont Reid & Co., Inc.*, 794 F.2d 1388 (9th Cir. 1986).

Mace Neufeld Productions, Inc. v. Orion Pictures Corp.

860 F.2d 947 (9th Cir. 1988)

FACTS Before 1982, Neufeld had produced the television series *Cagney and Lacey*. In 1982, he contracted with Orion and a producer, Barney Rosenzweig, who were to take over production of the show. Neufeld was to invest cash in the venture. Orion was required to consult "with regard to the exercise of Orion's approval over all substantial matters" relating to the business. Neufeld was to receive 50 percent of all fees Orion paid Rosenzweig and 72 percent of all profits—above a specified level—from the show. Neufeld brought suit against Orion and Rosenzweig, alleging breach of contract and violation of the federal securities laws. The trial court dismissed the securities claim.

ISSUE   Was the contract a security for the purposes of the 1934 Act?

DECISION   No. Affirmed. The 1934 Act was intended to protect public investors and to restore
                 public confidence in the securities markets. The Act was not intended to cover
                 ordinary, private agreements negotiated directly and individually between the par-
                 ties. All uncommon instruments found to be securities have been offered to a
                 number of potential investors, not just to one. In *Howey*, for instance, forty-two
                 persons had bought interests in the orange grove. Further, Neufeld's contract is not
                 the type of instrument that is commonly thought of as a security. Neufeld was to
                 remain involved with the business aspects of *Cagney and Lacey* while being entitled to
                 a percentage of fees and profits. Finally, the control the contract gave Neufeld over
                 the venture is not characteristic of a security, which is expected to bring a profit
                 from the efforts of others.

THE SECURITIES ACT OF 1933

The 1933 Act requires that issuers register their securities with the SEC before the securities may be offered to the general public. However, it exempts from registration certain types of securities and certain types of transactions. For example, securities issued by government units or charitable organizations are exempt. So if your school were to sell bonds to raise money to build a new laboratory building, it would not have to register the offering with the SEC. Other exemptions are discussed in the next section.

Deciding Whether to Go Public

Corporations do not find the decision of whether to go public an easy one. Sales of securities to the public have distinct advantages and disadvantages.

The advantages. A public securities offering provides working capital and access to a larger capital market than that available through private arrangements. If the issue is of equities, a public offering broadens the corporation's equity base, which in turn gives it more borrowing power. Apple Computer and Lotus cited this fact in justifying their decisions to go public.

Publicly traded securities also function as a sort of corporate currency that large corporations use to acquire other companies and to reward management. GM used stock to acquire Hughes Aircraft and EDS, while the favorite tool of the corporate raider has been the *junk bond*, a debt security that is not of investment grade. Also, a publicly traded corporation has more credibility with creditors, customers, and the public simply because its name is recognized.

Finally, and sometimes most importantly, going public allows the owners of a successful, or even a merely promising, company to "cash in."

The disadvantages. A public offering generally costs at least $200,000—primarily attributable to about 3 months of attorney, accountant, and management time. That expense dictates a sale of at least $5 million in securities, so public offerings are not for small companies. And, after going public, there are the costs of complying with SEC rules and making the required reports.

However, financial costs make up only a portion of the drawbacks of going public. Management must become more professional and more responsive to investors and financial analysts. The potential liabilities of officers and directors increase accordingly. With some rare but notable exceptions, such as Cummins Engine, publicly traded corporations cannot operate like family businesses. The personal touch disappears, in no small part because investors demand that their stocks defy the laws of physics and always go up.

Finally, federal securities regulators require a level of ongoing reporting that a corporation can manage only by instituting rigorous controls and reporting systems. The various reports listed in the next sections demand thousands of hours of preparation time. If they are not done right, the corporation and its employees may be liable for civil or criminal penalties. And the ever-present specter of lawsuits and all their costs haunts those preparing the reports.

Registration of Public Offerings

Because registration requires extensive documentation and financial information, the registration process is expensive. A $200,000 bill is not uncommon. A company making its first offering to the public will have to meet all the requirements described in this section.

The registration process is best explained in terms of a hypothetical new issue. Suppose Quasi Computer Corporation, a for-profit corporation incorporated in California, wants to offer common stock to the public. Its offering is not exempt, so it must register its offering with the SEC.

Registration statement and prospectus. To register, Quasi must file a *registration statement* and a *prospectus* for SEC review. The prospectus essentially summarizes the registration statement. The emphasis in a registration statement is on disclosure. The statement must contain:

- Information about the company's management and its experience
- Current financial statements
- Descriptions of the company's property and business

- Disclosure of any options or rights in favor of promoters or insiders—major shareholders, directors, or officers
- Information about the purposes of the sale of the securities

Potential investors must receive a copy of the prospectus before they purchase the new stock.

Normally, a registration statement and prospectus are valid for only one issue of securities. If the company decides not to go through with the sale, it must start the process over again. Suppose that after receiving SEC clearance, Quasi decides market conditions are not favorable, and it does not proceed with the sale. When it decides the time is right, it may have to start all over again.

If all the securities in an issue are not sold within 9 months of SEC clearance, the issuer must update both the registration statement and the prospectus. The update triggers another SEC review. Similarly, the company must revise both documents if developments—like significantly lower sales figures than Quasi had publicly projected—affect representations made in them. The expense and inconvenience of revision and rereview ensure that the issuer will try to sell the securities a fast as possible after SEC clearance.

In the early 1980s, the SEC adopted what it called "shelf registration." This system permits an issuer to file a registration statement with the SEC and let it "lie on the shelf" until market conditions are right. During the 2 years following shelf registration, the issuer may make as many offerings as it wishes without registering each offering individually. Large, periodic issues of debt found this system quite advantageous. One-time issuers, like Quasi, were not affected by it.

Standard of review. The SEC has 20 days to review Quasi's registration statement and prospectus. The SEC does *not* evaluate the merits of the prospective offering. Rather, it reviews the adequacy of the disclosures. In contrast, many states do evaluate the merits of an offering; especially to prevent excessive dilution of existing ownership, cheap stock, or likely misuse of proceeds.*

The SEC determines whether the company has supplied enough information to enable the investing public to make a sound, reasoned judgment about the new offering. Suppose Quasi Computer stated that a prime purpose of its new offering was to secure working capital to diversify by building a downhill ski facility in Georgia. The SEC may not think this is a well-reasoned business decision, but the agency will not prevent a public sale so long as the offeror adequately presents the risks. If necessary, the SEC could extend the 20-day review period in order to have Quasi clarify its plans for the proceeds. However, the SEC ultimately would not prohibit the public sale if Quasi supplied sufficient information for prospective investors to evaluate the offering's merits.

Contact With the Public

The SEC closely regulates the manner and content of the registrant's communications with the public prior to the effective date of the registration statement. Different restrictions apply in each of three periods:

- Prefiling period
- Waiting period
- Posteffective period

We will examine each of these below.

Prefiling period. Before filing the registration statement and prospectus, the issuer must avoid publicity about the forthcoming issuance of the securities. In other words, the issuer may not prime the market. However, the issuer may put out a press release that gives a basic description of the securities and of the offering. It

may not mention the price of the securities. Quasi might issue the following release:

> Quasi Computer Corp. announced today that it would seek SEC clearance for a $12 million issue of preferred stock.

During the prefiling period, the issuer may not sell any of the securities that will be registered. The SEC's regulatory scheme hinges on investors having adequate information in front of them on which to make an investment decision. Clearly at this stage, they would not have it.

Waiting period. The waiting period is the time after filing while the SEC is reviewing the registration statement and the prospectus. During the waiting period, the issuer is still prohibited from conditioning the market for the securities. Unlike companies softening up the market for new product rollouts, securities issuers must observe tight restrictions on whom they may offer the securities to.

The key word here is "offer." The issuer may not actually sell the securities. Even these offers must be made under tight restrictions. Thus, during the waiting period Quasi may offer its securities by means of:

- Face-to-face offers (including telephone calls) in which potential investors have the opportunity to ask questions about the securities.
- A written offer accompanied by a preliminary prospectus ("red herring").
- A "tombstone" advertisement announcing the sale of an issue of securities (see Figure 23.1).

A written offer must omit the price of securities. The names listed at the bottom are the *underwriters*, securities firms that will distribute the issue to broker-dealers who, in turn, will sell the securities to the public.

Posteffective period. The posteffective period is the time following the SEC's clearance of the

---

* The SEC does engage in a form of merit review in its supervision of mutual funds. Some argue that mutual funds are safer investments because of extensive regulation.

1,100,000 Shares

Walt Disney Productions

Common Stock
(no par value)

Price $66⅞ a Share

MORGAN STANLEY & CO.
Incorporated

BLYTH EASTMAN PAINE WEBBER
Incorporated

GOLDMAN, SACHS & CO.

KIDDER, PEABODY & CO.
Incorporated

LEHMAN BROTHERS KUHN LOEB
Incorporated

MERRILL LYNCH WHITE WELD CAPITAL MARKETS GROUP
Merrill Lynch, Pierce, Fenner & Smith Incorporated

SHEARSON/AMERICAN EXPRESS INC.

SMITH BARNEY, HARRIS UPHAM & CO.
Incorporated

WERTHEIM & CO., INC.

DEAN WITTER REYNOLDS INC.

January 28, 1983

Figure 23.1 A Typical Tombstone.

registration statement and the prospectus. Now, the issuer can make statements to condition the market. The issuer can also offer the securities to the public by means of the prospectus. It is important to note, however, that market conditioning is allowed only to the extent that the statements are true and not misleading.

Exemptions From Registration

All securities issues must be registered before they are sold to the public unless they fall into one of the Securities Act's exemptions from registration. These exemptions may be sorted into two classifications: exempt transactions and exempt securities. The next two sections will discuss exempt securities and exempt transactions.

Regardless of which type of registration exemption may be involved, the antifraud provisions of the 1933 Act may still apply. These are discussed later in this chapter.

Exempt securities. Exempt securities never have to be registered with the SEC. The exempt securities under the 1933 Act are:

- Government-issued or -guaranteed securities
- Securities issued by religious or charitable organizations
- Securities issued by banks or savings and loans, i.e., certificates of deposit
- Insurance policies and annuity contracts
- Promissory notes maturing in 9 months or less
- Securities issued by issuers regulated by the Interstate Commerce Commission (ICC)

These securities touch your lives in many ways. For instance, in all likelihood the classroom building in which your business law class meets was financed with bonds issued by either a government agency or a religious or charitable organization.

Commercial paper—corporate debt, usually with a face amount of $100,000 and with a maturity not exceeding 9 months—does not have to be registered. Most insurance policies need not be registered. Stock issued as part of a stock dividend or new shares issued as a result of stock splits are also exempt. Finally, usual stock exchange transactions are exempt so long as they do not involve a new issue. For that reason, when an individual buys 100 shares of Quasi Computer through a broker-dealer, like Merrill-Lynch, under most circumstances the transaction is exempt from registration under the 1933 Act. However, such transactions are covered by the 1933 Act.

Exempt Transactions

The exempt transactions described in this section and the next are quite common. But, that does not mean that they are commonly understood. On the contrary, they are difficult to understand, hard to distinguish, and complicated to apply. So, beware.

The best way to understand the exemptions is to keep in mind their purpose, which is to regulate three types of transaction:

- Intrastate offerings
- Small offerings
- Private offerings

As we look at each of these, it may help to know how the regulations covering the last two are structured. The SEC has published two major compilations of rules covering small offerings and private offerings: Regulation A and Regulation D. Within these regulations are numbered rules. Three exemptions are referred to by the numbered rules—Rules 504, 505, and 506—in which they are found in Regulation D.

However, transactions exempt under the 1933 Act may be subject to state regulation. As of 1990, almost half the states had adopted the Uniform Limited Offering Exemption Act, which covers Regulation D offerings within a state.

Intrastate offerings. Under SEC Rule 147, an *intrastate sale* is one in which the corporation offering the securities and *all* persons to whom they are offered reside in the same state.

Quasi Computer, which is incorporated in California, might be able to structure its offering to meet the criteria of Rule 147 if it:

- Is incorporated in the state of the sale
- Does 80 percent of its business there
- Plans to use at least 80 percent of the proceeds within the state
- Has not offered or sold the securities to any out-of-state buyers

If Quasi offers or sells to a single non-Californian, it will lose the exemption and all the purchasers could demand their money back. Because of the great risks attached to this exemption, it is not commonly used.

Small offerings generally. Under SEC Regulations A and D, small offering exemptions allow issuers to sell securities without registration where the amount of the issue or the number of purchasers, or both, is not great. In exchange for the ability to make such offerings, the issuer must agree to a number of restrictions as to the type of purchasers, the type of information that must be disclosed, and the length of time the securities must be held before resale.

Regulation A small offerings. Regulation A was revised substantially in 1992 to make it possible for more small business issuers to take advantage of Regulation A. The key changes are a significant reduction in the amount of "red tape," authorization for an issuer to "test the waters" to solicit indications of interest prior to SEC approval to sell, and an increase in the permitted dollar ceiling from $1.5 to $5 million.

Regulation A is available to any issuer who is *not* required to report to the SEC under the 1934 Act.* Stated in the reverse, an issuer subject to the 1934 Act reporting requirements cannot utilize Regulation A. A qualifying issuer is permitted to issue up to $5 million in securities within a rolling 12-month period of time.*

A Regulation A issuer must file with the SEC an *offering statement* which includes completion of a notification report of the intent to issue securities, 2 years of unaudited financial statements, and an *offering circular*, a summarized description of the issuer and the offering for prospective purchasers. If no problems are encountered, an offering statement is approved on the twentieth calendar day after submission. Until then, no sale can be consummated.

The costs of undertaking a public sale under Regulation A can be quite substantial to a small business. As a result, Regulation A has been changed to permit a potential issuer to first "test the waters" to evaluate demand and raise investor interest. Issuers are allowed to broadcast, publish, or deliver written solicitation of interest materials that have been filed concurrently with the SEC to prospective investors. This allows an issuer to gauge investor receptiveness before spending greater money developing and submitting the offering circular. Once an offering circular is filed with the SEC no other solicitations of interest may be distributed.

Issuers must report sales and use of proceeds every 6 months until substantially all the proceeds from the offering have been applied. In addition, notice must be given to the SEC within 30 days of termination or completion of the offering. Issuers who substantially and in good faith comply with Regulation A will gain exemption for all sales. Issuers are still subject to the SEC's antifraud provisions.

Regulation D offerings overview. An issuer that can satisfy the requirements of a Regulation D exemption does not have to file a registration statement and prospectus with the SEC. Instead, the issuer files less detailed documents

---

* "Blank check" companies, those without specific business plans, cannot use the Regulation A exemption.

* The $5 million cannot include more than $1.5 million offered by all selling security holders other than the issuer. These would be sales by controlling persons.

(to be discussed shortly) to secure SEC approval to sell exempt securities. However, the issuer may not publicly offer the securities for sale and must still comply with any applicable state regulations.

The failure of an issuer to comply with specific Regulation D offering requirements will disqualify exempt status for the securities. No general advertising or offer of Regulation D securities can be made. An issuer must notify the SEC no later than 15 days after the first sale of securities under Regulation D.*

Rule 504 small offerings. Under Rule 504 of Regulation D, a company which is not required to report to the SEC under the 1934 Act may issue up to $1,000,000 in securities within a 12-month period without registering the offering. By definition, a company which does not report under the 1934 Act is not publicly traded. So if Quasi Computer is not publicly traded and if it plans to offer only $275,000 in debt within the next year, it would qualify for a Rule 504 exemption.

Rule 505 small offerings. Rule 505 of Regulation D applies to small offerings, which in this case are defined as $5 million in securities offered within a 12-month period. Rule 505 applies to any issuer, not only to companies not required to report under the 1934 Act.

The Rule 505 small offering exemption closely resembles the Rule 506 private offering exemption (discussed below) except for its dollar limitation. Under both rules there can be an unlimited number of accredited investors but a limit of only 35 unaccredited investors. An accredited investor is an investor presumed by the SEC to be so sophisticated that he is not in need of special issuer disclosure rules. The SEC presumes that the following are accredited investors:

- Institutional investors, like banks, savings and loans, or pension funds
- Insiders, such as the issuer's officers, directors, or major shareholders
- Individual investors (''fat cats'') who have either a personal income of at least $200,000, or joint income of $300,000, or a net worth of more than $1 million

There are no special issuer disclosure rules under either Rule 505 or 506 if all investors are accredited investors. However, if a sale includes any nonaccredited investors then Rule 502 requires that all investors be given ''material information'' which includes audited financial statements.

Rule 506 private offerings. As already noted, Rule 506 of Regulation D applies to private offerings. Rule 506 varies from Rule 505 in the absence of a dollar limitation. Also, under Rule 506 the issuer must reasonably believe that each nonaccredited investor is a sufficiently sophisticated investor, as a result of experience and knowledge, to be capable of evaluating the investment.

Figure 23.2 summarizes the registration alternatives under the 1933 Act.

Rules 144 and 144A. Securities issued pursuant to Regulation A or D are considered restricted securities, securities which cannot be publicly resold for a period of time. Rule 144 provides specific rules concerning how such securities can be ''dribbled'' out, slowly sold, after 2 years of time. A noninsider can sell all his securities after a 3-year holding period. For an insider, only faster-paced dribbling is allowed.

Rule 144A was implemented in 1990 to allow institutional investors holding restricted securities to sell them at any time, in any amount, to other qualified institutional investors. The National Association of Securities Dealers (NASD) has established the *Portal Market*, an exchange market for the trading of restricted securities, to facilitate such trading. The potential impact of the Portal Market could be quite

---

* An issuer's failure to provide timely notice is considered a procedural defect and will not disqualify exempt status.

	SEC REGISTERED SECURITIES	INTERSTATE EXEMPTION (RULE 147)	REGU-LATION A	REGULATION D		
				RULE 504	RULE 505	RULE 506
Dollar limit per 12-month period?	No	No	$5 million	$1 million	$5 million	None
Limit on number of unaccredited investors?	Not applicable	Not applicable	Not applicable	Not applicable	35	35‡
General solicitation, advertising allowed?	Yes	In-state only	No	No	No	No
Required information for investor?	Prospectus	By state law	Offering circular*	None	None†	None†
Do 1933 insider rules apply to sales?	Yes	If out-of-state offer	Yes	Yes	Yes	Yes
Is notice required to SEC about sales?	Not applicable	No	Yes	Yes	Yes	Yes
1934 Act company eligible?	Yes	Yes	No	No	Yes	Yes

* Only if offering exceeds $100,000.
† Rule 502 required that all offerees be given "material information" if there are any unaccredited investors.
‡ Unaccredited investors must be knowledgeable and sophisticated.

Figure 23.2 A Comparison of 1933 Act Alternatives.

significant, since institutional investors are thought to hold over $160 billion of restricted securities annually.

For the seller to secure Rule 144A exemption, the purchaser must be a *qualified institutional buyer,* or QIB. Essentially, a QIB is defined as an institution that owns and invests on a discretionary basis at least $100 million in securities of issuers not affiliated with the institution. In addition, banks or savings and loans with audited net worth of at least $25 million can qualify. In short, Rule 144A is only for "big league players."

Sellers will have to disclose enough information to satisfy a buyer, but no specific SEC disclosure rules apply. Rule 144A will for the first time permit freer trading of foreign debt and equity issues that do not meet the stringent requirements of the 1933 Act.

Rule 144A will likely have a major impact in the trading of restricted securities between institutional investors.

Controlling Person

Chapter 22 noted the obligations a person with a controlling interest in a corporation has to the other shareholders. The 1933 Act also imposes particular obligations on controlling persons when they sell a significant portion of their holdings. Such persons are required to comply with the registration provisions of the 1933 Act. They cannot simply sell the shares as an ordinary shareholder would.

A *controlling person*, according to the SEC, is someone who can greatly influence decisions within a corporation. Case law indicates such persons can hold as little as 5 percent of the corporation's shares if they are also officers or directors.

The 1933 Act treats sales by controlling persons as if they were new issues. The rationale for the rule is the controlling persons have an advantage over others in the marketplace because of their knowledge of the corporation and should, therefore, be under an obligation to disclose what they know. In effect, controlling persons are the corporation, and the 1933 Act treats them accordingly. (For that reason, controlling persons may use Regulation A or Regulation D offerings to sell part or all of their holdings.) Investors, for instance, would be greatly influenced by the fact that Quasi's controlling shareholder was selling his stock because of a bitter management struggle.

LIABILITY FOR 1933 ACT VIOLATIONS

The 1933 Act imposes liability in two common situations involving the offering or sale of securities:

- Violation of procedural rules (§5)
- False registration statements (§11)

Most violations of procedural rules that become the subject of litigation relate to securities that were not registered but should have been. The remedy is recision or damages.

Compared to cases involving false registration statements, those involving violations of procedural rules are fairly uncommon. In the following sections, we will look at the consequences of filing an improper registration statement.

Basis for liability. A purchaser of securities issued under the 1933 Act who suffers a loss because of a misstated or omitted material fact in the registration may bring an action for damages. To recover, the plaintiff must establish:

- The plaintiff bought the securities
- The registration statement either omitted or misstated a material fact
- The plaintiff suffered a loss

Potentially liable parties. If a registration statement contains false or misleading statements, the 1933 Act permits a securities purchaser to recover damages from, among others, those who sign the registration statement or who allow their names to be used to give authority to the statement.

A registration statement must be signed by the issuer, a majority of the board of directors, the issuer's principal executive officer (who is often also a director), and the issuer's chief financial officer. In addition, all the remaining directors, any actual signer, and any experts who allow their names to be used in the registration statement may be liable. This last category may include the corporation's accountants or lawyers. Chapter 24 examines the particular effect of the 1933 Act on accountants.

Defenses. The issuer will prevail if it can prove that at the time of purchase the plaintiff knew of the false statement or of the omission. The issuer also may avoid liability by showing that the loss occurred for reasons unrelated to the false statement or omission.

For defendants other than the issuer, the principal defense is that they exercised due diligence. *Due diligence* means the defendants made a reasonable investigation into the truth of what the registration statement said and they reasonably believed, in good faith, that what it said was true. Courts measure reasonableness by what prudent persons would do in managing their own property. A defendant in the next case claimed he exercised due diligence.

Escott v. BarChris Construction Corp.

283 F. Supp. 643 (S.D.N.Y. 1968)

FACTS

Beginning in 1956, BarChris Construction Company built bowling alleys and then sold them. In a number of instances, BarChris financed the purchases for the buyers. By 1961, a number of alleys had defaulted on the mortgages BarChris held, and BarChris took over their operation. In order to gain more cash flow, BarChris decided to issue convertible bonds. The registration statement and prospectus contained a great number of misrepresentations and omissions, which ultimately led the purchasers to file this suit.

One defendant, Auslander, became a director less than a month before BarChris filed the registration statement and prospectus. Auslander had the mistaken impression that Peat, Marwick & Mitchell, which had audited BarChris in 1960, was responsible for all the figures in the two documents. Peat, Marwick had always done reliable work at the bank where Auslander was chairman. Had he done more than glance at a preliminary draft of the registration statement, Auslander would have discovered that Peat, Marwick had not verified significant portions of it. But when Auslander signed the registration statement, two BarChris officers told him it was proper and correct.

ISSUE

Did Auslander establish a due diligence defense?

DECISION

No. Judgment for the purchasers. Auslander made no investigation of the accuracy of the registration statement. Under the 1933 Act, a director can escape potential liability only by using the same reasonable care in investigating the facts as a prudent man would employ in the management of his own property. A prudent man would not act on an important matter without any knowledge of the relevant facts, relying only on representations of persons who are comparative strangers. To hold that such a minimal effort measures up to the statutory standard would absolve new directors from responsibility just because they are new.

Auslander's fate illustrates a key difference between the due diligence rule and the business judgment rule. The business judgment rule, which does not apply to questions under the Securities Act, places the burden of proof on the plaintiffs and gives directors every benefit of the doubt. The due diligence rule places the burden on directors claiming its protection.

Figure 23.3 illustrates the plaintiff's case and potential defenses under both the 1933 and 1934 Acts.

Damages. In some situations a court may require the issuer to return the purchasers' entire payment, as when an issuer violates a condition of the intrastate offering exemption. Generally, however, the measure of damages is the difference between the price paid for the stock and its price either at the time of suit or at the time the buyer sold it.

Suppose Quasi's stock sells initially for $50 a share. Later, a newspaper reveals that the financial statements in the registration state-

TIME FRAME FOR POTENTIAL LIABILITY	1933 ACT UNTIL REGISTRATION STATEMENT BECOMES EFFECTIVE	1934 ACT AT TIME OF COMPLETION OF WORK (AUDIT)
Is mere negligence sufficient to constitute violation?	Yes	No
Must plaintiff establish scienter?	No	Yes
Must plaintiff show reliance?	No	Yes
Plaintiff's case	1 False statement(s) or omission of material fact(s). 2 Plaintiff purchased security. 3 Plaintiff suffered loss.	1 False statement(s) or omission of material fact(s). 2 Plaintiff purchased or sold security. 3 Plaintiff relied. 4 Scienter (defendant knew of falsity).
Possible defenses	1 No reliance. 2 Loss for different reason. 3 Due diligence (free of negligence). 4 Statute of limitation period has run.	1 Good faith. 2 Lack of knowledge. 3 Action constitutes "mere negligence." 4 Loss for different reason. 5 Statute of limitation period has run.

Figure 23.3 SEC Liability.
A comparison of suits against defendants under the Securities Acts of 1933 and 1934.

ment contained false and misleading statements. The market price for Quasi stock immediately drops to $20 per share, where it stays. The original purchasers of Quasi's stock would have a cause of action at least against the persons who signed the registration statement. The damages would be $30 per share, assuming the shareholders did not sell their stock before filing suit.

Criminal penalties. If the U.S. Department of Justice can show actual knowledge of the misrepresentation or an intent to defraud, the corporation and the signers could be subject to fines of up to $10,000 or imprisonment for up to 5 years, or both.

THE SECURITIES EXCHANGE ACT OF 1934

The 1933 Act deals primarily with issuing securities. The 1934 Act applies to the exchange, or trading, of securities after their initial distribution. In essence, Congress sought to free the market of abusive practices, like trading by corporate management based on inside information. Through its reporting requirements the 1934 Act attempts to ensure that investors have the information necessary to make informed decisions about particular investments.

Registration and Reporting Requirements

An issuer whose equity securities (stock) are publicly traded on a national securities exchange, like the NYSE, or who has $5 million or more of assets and 500 or more stockholders of stock sold in interstate commerce is considered a 1934 Act company. These companies must register their stock and provide specific disclosures, including profit-sharing arrangements, the financial structure, nature of the business, and names of officers and directors. In addition, these companies, and any issuer who has made a registered offering under the 1933 Act, are considered reporting companies and must file periodic reports with the SEC in order to keep both the agency and the investing public informed of their activities. These reports include:

- Certified annual reports (10-K report)
- Unaudited quarterly reports (10-Q report)
- Current reports (8-K report), which must be filed monthly if significant changes (such as election of new directors) have occurred since the 10-K or 10-Q report

Each year, the SEC receives over 80,000 annual reports alone.*

The Foreign Corrupt Practices Act. In 1977 Congress enacted the Foreign Corrupt Practices Act as an amendment to the 1934 Act. The Act prohibits any U.S. corporation—whether registered under the Securities Acts or not—from bribing foreign officials to obtain business. The Act also requires that any corporation registered under the 1934 Act establish internal accounting controls so that it can maintain accountability for the control of its assets, whether the company engages in international trade or not. In fact, the failure to keep records is, itself, a criminal offense.

The Act requires that companies disclose in their reports to the SEC any illegal or questionable transactions of this type. Chapter 24 discusses the impact of the reporting requirements on accountants.

Rule 10b-5 Fraudulent Practices

Section 10(b) of the 1934 Act prohibits fraud in the purchase or sale of securities. SEC Rule 10b-5, which implements §10(b), is perhaps the most widely known of the SEC regulations. It prohibits any deceptive or manipulative practices regarding securities:

> *It shall be unlawful for any person, directly or indirectly, by the use of any means or instrumentality of interstate commerce, or of the mails, or of any facility of any national securities exchange,*
> *(1) to employ any device, scheme, or artifice to defraud,*
> *(2) to make any untrue statement of a material fact or to omit to state a material fact necessary in order to make the statements made, in light of the circumstances under which they were made, not misleading, or*
> *(3) to engage in any act, practice, or course of business which operates or would operate as a fraud or deceit on any person, in connection with the purchase or sale of any security.*

Coverage. When it drafted Rule 10b-5, the SEC intended to cover every conceivable kind of fraud. And the courts uniformly have given the Rule a very broad reading. If, for instance, the Motherlode Gold Company spreads false rumors among brokers about its new gold strike, the company would violate this rule.

Rule 10b-5 applies to anyone involved in securities transactions. Thus, corporate officers, directors, and employees, as well as broker-dealers, outside lawyers, and accountants, have potential liability. Chapter 24 explains an accountant's liability under Rule 10b-5. Rule 10b-5 also applies to insider transactions, which are discussed in the next section.

Rule 10b-5 applies to *all* securities, whether registered or unregistered, and to all persons

---

* 1934 Act reporting companies are required by SEC proxy rules to attach an annual report with proxy solicitations for the annual meeting. This report need not be, and seldom is, the 10-K report.

involved in interstate transactions regardless of the application of the 1933 Act. Suppose Motherlode's common stock was exempt under the 1933 Act. As the company went into bankruptcy, Nan, an original purchaser, sold her stock to Robert by lying to him about Motherlode's gold strike. Nan has violated the 1934 Act.

Proving a case. Either the SEC or an injured party may bring a civil action under Rule 10b-5. In order to establish a fraudulent practice, the plaintiff must show a misrepresentation or a deceptive omission of a material fact in connection with the purchase or sale of securities. The plaintiff must also establish *scienter*—actual knowledge of the falsity or reckless disregard of the truth by the defendant.

Private plaintiffs do not have to establish *privity* of contract, that is, that they bought the stock directly from the company or person making the misrepresentation. They need only show an injury where there was an affirmative misrepresentation. Suppose a company and its officers release false financial information. The plaintiffs rely on it in buying the company's stock through their brokers. They could recover from the company and its officers even though a firefighter in Kansas City or a dentist in Seattle sold them the stock. It follows that plaintiffs need not show that the defendant specifically intended to injure them.

Defenses and liability. A defense will fail if it is based on the fact that no one could possibly attach any importance to an omission or that no reasonable investor would believe a particular misrepresentation. Suppose a corporation claims it has actually developed a widget. No one can say it is reasonable to believe such a representation. But if someone relies on the representation and buys securities in the corporation, the company has committed fraud under Rule 10b-5.

Essentially, defendants have only two defenses. First, they can prove the purchasers knew the truth and so were not affected by the misrepresentations or omission. Second, they can try to show that no one relied on the misrepresentation or omission. In the next case, the defendants tried to prove that the plaintiff could not have relied on the misrepresentation.

Pidcock v. Sunnyland America, Inc.

854 F.2d 443 (11th Cir. 1988)

FACTS   John Pidcock and Dude Harvard each owned 50 percent of Sunnyland. Harvard and his sons, Joe and Bryant, ran the business; Pidcock did not participate in its daily operations. The two owners became concerned about losses in the business and in 1982 decided to sell. After a buyer backed out, the Harvards offered to buy out Pidcock. Pidcock knew that the $2.2 million the Harvards offered was a bargain price, but family concerns and doubts about the Harvards' management convinced him to sell. In accepting their offer, Pidcock wrote that he was relying on their representation that finding a third party buyer was doubtful. Indeed, he had repeatedly asked whether any third parties were interested, and Joe Harvard had made no mention of any. Joe was not telling the truth. Before the Pidcock-Harvard transaction closed, the Harvards had listed the company for sale at $16 million and had received an expression of interest. The Harvards specifically asked their agents to say nothing to Pidcock about Sunnyland being on the market. The sale did not occur, but 2 years after Pidcock sold his interest, Sunnyland was sold for $7.3 million. Pidcock brought suit under Rule 10b-5, seeking the difference between the fair market value of his stock and the $2.2 million he received. The trial court held that the misrepresentations were material under Rule 10b-5, that the Harvards made the misrepresentations with scienter, and that Pidcock justifiably relied on them. However, the court denied Pidcock damages because he failed to prove they were proximately caused by the Harvards' fraud.

ISSUE

Is a plaintiff who proves a material misrepresentation under Rule 10b-5 entitled to a presumption of proximate causation?

DECISION

Yes. Reversed. In Rule 10b-5 actions, the measure of damages proximately caused by a defendant's fraud is the difference between the value of the stock at the time of the fraudulent transaction and the price received. But where the purchaser receives more than the seller's actual loss, the damages are the purchaser's profits. And, the rule is that a defrauding purchaser's profits must be disgorged. The defrauded seller is entitled to a presumption that the damages he suffered are equal to the profits realized. He is entitled to this presumption because, as in this case, the buyer is in a better position than the seller to explain how the profit came about. Thus, the buyer may rebut the presumption by presenting evidence that the profit is attributable to some cause other than the fraud. Here, the Harvards would have to show that some effort of theirs—beyond the end of divided control that they obtained fraudulently—led to part of or all the profit.

As *Pidcock* states, the principal remedy in a private action under Rule 10b-5 is disgorgement of profits. The remedies the SEC can seek are more varied. They include:

- Reimbursement of the losses incurred by those trading in the stock
- Loss of trading profits
- Injunction against further practices of the same type
- Suspension or loss of a license issued by the SEC, such as a broker's license
- Censure, a public reprimand by the SEC usually administered to someone in the securities business
- Criminal penalties include a fine up to $2.5 million or imprisonment up to 5 years, or both

Insider Trading

Rule 10b-5 also covers insider trading. Between 1934 and 1978, just over forty cases were brought alleging insider trading. In 1987 alone, the government brought that many.

An *insider* is a person—typically an officer, director, or major shareholder—who has information about a publicly traded corporation which is not available to the public. An insider may not purchase or sell that corporation's securities if the transaction is based on information not available to other shareholders and the investing public. If Ditto Corp. develops a new copier, its insiders may not buy shares in anticipation of a sharp rise in price when the new copier is announced. The insiders have to wait until the announcement. Thus, the most typical types of insider trading are:

- The trading done by an insider for direct profit just before a public announcement of a major development
- The passing of valuable information by officers or directors to someone who trades in the company's stock and subsequently repays the source in some fashion

- The buying of stocks and options by insiders through overseas financial institutions.

Insiders and tippees. In this context, the term "insider" can apply to many others besides officers or directors. It includes particularly those persons an insider "tips" to confidential information. In a recent case, the SEC cited a secretary employed by a law firm which represented an investment banker involved in a number of new issues. Also prosecuted in the same case were the secretary's two brothers. From the documents he typed, the secretary gathered information which he then gave to his brothers, who made the actual investments. The secretary was an insider. His brothers, the "tippees," are treated as if they were insiders, too.

A tippee assumes the insider's fiduciary duty to the corporation's shareholders when (1) the insider has breached his fiduciary duty by disclosing the information to the tippee *and* (2) the tippee knows, or should know, that there has been a breach. However, not all disclosures are inconsistent with the duty insiders owe to shareholders. The disclosure's purpose determines whether there is a breach of duty. The test is whether the insider personally will benefit, directly or indirectly.

For some time, the SEC had given that test a broad reading. However, in a case decided the same week the SEC filed charges against the secretary of the law firm representing the investment banker, the Supreme Court put a limit on the SEC interpretation of who is a Rule 10b-5 insider.

Dirks v. SEC

463 U.S. 646 (1983)

FACTS Dirks provided analyses of insurance company securities to institutional investors. On March 6, 1973, a former officer of Equity Funding of America told Dirks the company had fraudulently overstated its assets in its financial statements. Various regulatory agencies had failed to act on similar charges by other Equity Funding employees. Dirks investigated the charges, which proved accurate. Neither Dirks nor his firm owned or traded any Equity Funding stock. Throughout his investigation, he openly discussed the information he obtained with *The Wall Street Journal* and with a number of clients and investors, some of whom sold their Equity Funding holdings. On March 27, the NYSE halted trading in Equity Funding after the company's stock fell from $26 per share to less than $15 in 2 weeks. A few days later, California insurance authorities and the SEC took action against Equity Funding, but only on April 2 did *The Wall Street Journal* reveal the fraud to the public. The SEC censured Dirks for aiding and abetting insider trading violations under Rule 10b-5. The court of appeals affirmed.

ISSUE Was Dirks an insider or the tippee of an insider?

DECISION No. Reversed. A violation of Rule 10b-5 arises not from the possession of nonpublic information but from the existence of a fiduciary relationship to the corporation. An individual must take unfair advantage of information intended to be available only for corporate purposes and not for anyone's personal benefit, and the individual must make secret profits. There can be no duty to disclose such information before trading where the person who has traded on inside information—which Dirks did not—was not the corporation's agent, a fiduciary, or a person in whom those selling the securities had placed their trust and confidence.

Misappropriation theory. Since the early 1980s, there has also been a notable expansion of Rule 10b-5 liability under the so-called *misappropriation theory*. Under this theory, first established in the case of *United States v. Newman,** a person is liable if he steals or misappropriates private, nonpublic information belonging to another, and then uses that information to trade for individual profit. Up to this time, there have been only a few cases in which this theory has been applied. Each time, the courts have generally stated that a fiduciary duty of trust and confidence must have been breached and that someone must be harmed by the fraud. For example, in *S.E.C. v. Materia,†* a proofreader for a financial printing company profited by using information he gleaned off of financial documents he was reviewing. In another case, *United States v. Carpenter,‡* a financial columnist for the *Wall Street Journal*, R. Foster Winans, was found liable under Rule 10b-5

---

*United States v. Newman, 664 F.2d 12 (2nd Cir. 1981).
†*S.E.C. v. Materia* 745 F.2d 197 (2nd Cir. 1984).
‡*United States v. Carpenter* 791 F.2d 1024 (2nd Cir. 1986).

when he advanced information to certain brokers about securities that were yet to be reviewed in his column. Relying on Winans's information, the brokers purchased a particular security before the column appeared, and then sold it for a tidy profit (which was shared with Winans) after the favorable review influenced the stock's rise in value. In both of these cases, an employee was breaching duties of trust he owed to his employer by appropriating nonpublic information for personal gain.

It should be noted that the *Carpenter* case, on review to the U.S. Supreme Court, failed to establish the misappropriation theory as law of the land. This was a result of a split vote of four to four; although in the Second Circuit, the origin of the case, the vote meant that *Carpenter* was upheld by default for that circuit. The Court did, however, uphold unanimously the convictions based on the misappropriations theory as long as the convictions are based on federal mail or wire fraud statutes. The following case also discusses the misappropriation theory in the highly confidential setting between a doctor and his patient.

United States v. Willis

737 F.Supp. 269 (S.D.N.Y. 1990)

FACTS

Sanford Weill, former CEO of Shearson, Loeb, Rhodes and former president of American Express, sought in 1985 to become CEO of BankAmerica. To enhance his chances of securing the job, Weill received a commitment from Shearson to invest $1 billion in BankAmerica. While Weill was negotiating for the position, BankAmerica stock was trading low, based on negative reports by Moody's Investors' Services. On February 20, 1986, BankAmerica announced that Weill's offer to be CEO would not be accepted. The next day the stock went up in value. While the secret negotiations were transpiring, Weill's wife had been under the care of a psychiatrist, Dr. Willis. During their confidential sessions, Mrs. Weill had been telling

Dr. Willis about her husband's ambition to be CEO and his offer of $1 billion to BankAmerica. Relying on the information, Willis acquired stock during this time ranging from $12 to over $14 per share. On the day after Weill's announcement, Willis sold his stock for over $15 a share and made $27,475 in profit. Willis, indicted for violation of Rule 10b-5, moved to dismiss the indictment.

ISSUE

Was Dr. Willis's use of material nonpublic business information confided to him by his patient a basis for liability under the misappropriation theory?

DECISION

Yes. Motion denied. The misappropriation theory is applied when information is taken by someone holding a position of trust and confidence in connection with the purchase or sale of securities. Dr. Willis, as a psychiatrist, held himself out as a professional with well-recognized duties of confidence and trust. By appropriating the private information from Mrs. Weill, he was defrauding her of the tacit representation of confidentiality he gave her as her doctor.

Statute of limitations. A person must bring a claim under Rule 10b-5 within 1 year of discovering a fraud and no longer than 3 years after the underlying securities were bought or sold. To illustrate, someone discovering fraud 30 months after purchasing stock of ABC, Inc., would have to initiate suit within the next 6 months or lose her claim. There continues to be strong political pressure for Congress to substitute a 2-year/5-year rule.

Insider trading legislation. As a result of cases involving people like Dirks, Ivan Boesky, Michael Milkin, and others, Congress enacted legislation in 1984* and again in 1988† to give the SEC greater enforcement authority to deal with insider trading of existing securities. In addition, in 1990, Congress gave the SEC significantly broader administrative powers to act without court approval, discussed earlier in this chapter.‡

Although both the 1984 and 1988 Acts were passed to address insider trading, neither act defines the term. There are two reasons for this. First, there were too many differences of opinion about the definition. Second, some feared a definition would give inside traders a standard to work around.

The 1984 Act approached insider trading from the standpoint of defining the offense. Under the Act, a person may not buy or sell a security while in possession of material nonpublic information. Congress rejected a considerably weaker provision which would have imposed liability only on those who actually traded on the basis of material nonpublic information. It is considerably easier to prove that someone is in possession of inside information than it is to prove that someone made a decision to trade on the basis of that information.

The 1984 Act specifically includes aiders and abetters who pass on inside information to clients. The SEC now takes the position that someone in possession of inside information has a duty to disclose it to the person on the other side of the transaction.

The 1988 Act puts yet more enforcement muscle into both private and public actions against insiders.

The Act expanded the range of possible defendants who may improperly participate in

---

* The Insider Trading Sanctions Act of 1984.
† The Insider Trading and Enforcement Act of 1988.
‡ The Stock Reform Act of 1990.

insider trading. *Contemporaneous traders*—persons who can show they bought or sold during the time of illegal trading activity by an insider—may bring civil actions against controlling persons, insider traders, tippees, or investment advisors. They may also sue *controlled persons*, persons who work directly for a controlling person, including financial advisors, brokers, and the like. Thus, the Insider Trading and Enforcement Act makes clear that for the purposes of insider trading actions, "insider" has a much broader usage than under §§10(b) and 16(b).

A controlling person's defenses are limited to good faith or lack of knowledge of the illegal conduct by a controlled person. Suppose Webster is a controlling person. Suppose Webster is a controlling person of Revelation Motors Company. He tells his broker to buy 1000 shares in Revelation immediately after the third-quarter earnings are made public. The broker tells some of his other clients about Webster's instructions, and they buy ahead of the public announcement. The broker would be liable to contemporaneous traders, but Webster would not be.

The sanctions available against insider traders were dramatically broadened by the acts. The insiders may be subject to fines up to three times the amount of profits made or losses avoided on each prohibited transaction. In addition, the insiders are still liable for compensatory damages under traditional civil suits.

Like the IRS, the SEC can now reward informants with up to 10 percent of a fine levied against a violator. Fines for individuals have a ceiling of $1 million, corporations $2.5 million. Maximum prison sentences were increased to 10 years. There is a 5-year statute of limitations under these acts.

Short-Swing Profits

Section 16(b) of the 1934 Act affects certain insiders who buy and then sell, or sell and then buy, securities in the firm within a 6-month period. These particular insiders, Congress presumed, traded on inside information if the transactions came within 6 months of each other.

The §16(b) definition of "insider" is narrower than the Rule 10b-5 definition. Under §16(b), the insider must be an officer, a director, or a "10 percent shareholder" (one who owns 10 percent or more of the firm's outstanding stock). In calculating the 10 percent, the SEC adds in what it calls "beneficial ownership," which refers to shares owned by the shareholder's immediate family.

The definition of an officer has been narrowed to executive officers who play a direct role in policy making. This eliminates persons who have officer status but do not have significant managerial or policy-making duties and customarily do not have access to inside information. To illustrate, the vice president and head of marketing would be covered; the vice president in charge of security would probably not be covered.

With some very limited exceptions, §16(b) insiders must turn over to the issuer all profits on such transactions.* If the transactions take place within the 6-month period, the insider has no affirmative defense—including good faith—to an action under §16(b). Because §16(b) liability is absolute, few cases involving it come to trial. The following is one that did.

---

* The two exceptions under the SEC's Rule 16(b) are an odd-lot transaction—one involving less than 100 shares—and a transaction involving less than $10,000.

Feder v. Martin Marietta Corp.

406 F.2d 260 (2d Cir. 1969)

FACTS
Feder brought this derivative suit on behalf of Sperry Rand Corp. to recover short-swing profits Martin Marietta Corp. made while George M. Bunker, Martin's president and CEO, was a Sperry director. Martin's board had approved Bunker's membership on Sperry's board but did not designate him as Martin's representative. During the 3 months Bunker served on Sperry's board, Martin bought 101,300 shares of Sperry. Within 45 days after Bunker resigned, Martin sold its Sperry stock. At trial, Bunker testified that he was responsible for Martin's total operation. He approved the firm's investments, including those in Sperry. The evidence showed that, as a Sperry director, Bunker could acquire inside information and that he could use it without disclosing it to any Martin personnel. However, Bunker denied using any inside information for investment purposes. The trial court held that since Martin's board had not made him its representative on Sperry's board, Martin was not liable as an insider.

ISSUE
Was Martin an insider under §16(b)?

DECISION
Yes. Reversed. The trial court should have held Bunker represented Martin on Sperry's board. Liability does not depend on proof of an insider's intent to profit from unfair use of information or upon proof that the insider had access to confidential information. Rather, liability is automatic and attaches to any profit by an insider on any short-swing transaction within the time limits fixed by the statute.

While 10 percent shareholders must be such at both ends of the transaction, that is, when they buy and when they sell or vice versa, an officer or director need not be one at both ends. Thus, Martin was liable.

Figure 23.4 tabulates the key "persons" under the Securities Act.

Takeovers

The period from 1967 to 1970 saw a wave of mergers and acquisitions much like the one that lasted from 1981 through 1987. Congress responded by adopting the *Williams Act of 1968*, a series of amendments to the 1934 Act designed to make corporate acquirers or raiders reveal their positions.

Five percent disclosure rule. The Williams Act added §13(d) to the 1934 Act. Under the requirements of that section, when anyone acquires more than 5 percent of any class of equities of a company registered with the SEC, he or she must file what is called a *Schedule 13D* statement. It must describe:

- The purchaser's identity and background
- The source of the funds for the purchase
- The purchaser's reasons for acquiring the securities and intentions as to the issuer

Tender offers. The Williams Act also added §14(d) to the 1934 Act. That section applies to *tender offers*. A tender offer is an offer to acquire stock at a stated price made either to an issuer or to its shareholders. A tender offer

TERM	DEFINITION	ACT	IMPORTANCE
Controlling person	Individual with great influence on corporate decisions; officer or director with 5% interest or more	1933	May be required to register own securities for sale as if the issuer.
Accredited investor (Regulation D)	Institutional investor, officer, director, or "fat cat"	1933	"Person" under Regulation D who is considered sophisticated and knowledgeable. Does not count against 35-investor limits.
Q. I. B. (Rule 144A)	Qualified institutional buyer	1933	Permitted under Rule 144A to freely purchase restricted securities
Insider [§10(b)]	Person in possession of material, nonpublic corporate information	1934	Cannot use such information for private gain or pass it to another for the person's private gain.
Insider [§16(b)]	Officer, director, or 10%-interest shareholder	1934	Cannot engage in "short-swing" transactions during any 6-month period.

Figure 23.4 Important "Persons" under the Securities Acts.

always has a fixed expiration date, though the offeror may extend it. In any case, tender offers must be open to shareholders for 20 days. The offer may be for all the stock in the parent company or just the amount required to give the offeror control. In the latter case if the offer is oversubscribed, the offeror must accept tendered shares on a pro rata basis. A shareholder may withdraw his or her tender within 15 days of making it.

Section 14(d) requires that tender offerors disclose in filings with the SEC all the information required under §13(d) as well as some additional data. Section 14(e)—added at the same time—is a broad criminal provision which prohibits misleading or fraudulent conduct, statements, or omissions in connection with tender offers. A target company may enforce the Williams Act disclosure requirements, as it did in the next case.

Florida Commercial Banks, Inc. v. Culverhouse

772 F.2d 1513 (11th Cir. 1985)

FACTS   By October 1981, Hugh F. Culverhouse, Sr., had acquired 5 percent of Florida Commercial Banks, Inc. He filed Schedule 13D with the SEC, which he amended twelve times over the next 3 years. In October 1984, Culverhouse made a tender offer in which he sought a controlling interest in Commercial. At that time, he also filed Schedule 14D-1, the tender offer statement. Commercial filed suit against Culverhouse, alleging he had made misrepresentations and omissions on both schedules—twenty-three alone on Schedule 14D-1. Commercial sought an injunction halting Culverhouse's tender offer until he made corrective disclosures. The trial court dismissed the complaint on the grounds that Commercial did not have a right to enforce the Williams Act disclosure requirements.

ISSUE

Does a target company have a right to bring a suit to compel accurate Williams Act disclosures by a tender offeror?

DECISION

Yes. Reversed. In determining whether a target corporation has a private cause of action under the Williams Act, a court must balance the likelihood that the shareholders will benefit by obtaining the information against (1) the likelihood that management may misuse the cause of action in order to thwart the takeover, thereby harming the shareholders, and (2) the likelihood that other aspects of the relief sought will harm the shareholders. Where, as here, the remedy sought is corrective disclosures, the shareholders will not be harmed by the remedy. As to the misuse of the cause of action to thwart the takeover, again the remedy would not seem to halt the takeover. Further, in most cases the shareholders lack the ability and resources to confirm the accuracy of the schedules, and the SEC cannot police every tender offer. So the target stands in the best position to seek corrective disclosures that will significantly benefit the shareholders.

In order to put this case in perspective, it is worth reviewing the business judgment rule in Chapter 20. There, we saw that management can violate its fiduciary duties to the shareholders by preventing a takeover. Here, however, management did not try to block the takeover—at least not directly.

The 1934 Act requires disclosure in order to make the marketplace, the agency, and securities issuers and their shareholders aware of the takeover attempt. Those making the tender offer must disclose it when the tenders or other acquisitions of voting stock would give the offeror 5 percent or more of the target's stock. An offeror may not keep shares "in street name"—that is, in the name of the brokerage through which the stock was bought—to avoid disclosure.

The role of the SEC in tender offers is strictly informational. It is solely concerned with ensuring that investors know what is af-

fecting the purchase price of the securities of the companies involved. However, the Federal Trade Commission and the Department of Justice perform what is called a "premerger" antitrust review, which may result in action being taken against the merger by one of those agencies. Antitrust laws are the topic of Chapter 43.

Proxy Solicitations

Proxies can be solicited by either management or shareholders. The 1934 Act requires a proxy solicitor for a 1934 Act company to furnish by proxy statement full disclosure of all material facts concerning issues on the proxy. The proxy or proxy statement must be submitted to the SEC for approval at least 10 days prior to its being mailed to shareholders. 1934 Act companies are required to furnish shareholders with an annual report in conjunction with the solicitation of proxies for the annual meeting.

Effective as of 1993, both corporations and shareholders are allowed to circulate their views to shareholders and announce how they intend to vote on proxy proposals without filing a formal solicitation with the SEC. Proxy statements must now be made available to the public as soon as they are filed with the SEC. Finally, shareholders have been given easier access to companies' shareholder lists. These changes are expected to give shareholders significantly greater voice in possible proposed merger or buy-out situations.

The new rules also address executive pay. Executive compensation for the five highest paid senior executives must now be disclosed to shareholders in one location in the proxy statement. This report must include and list base salaries, bonuses, and any other compensation. In addition, the corporate performance factors used by the board compensation committee must be disclosed.

Shareholder proposals on executive compensation must now be allowed at shareholder meetings. Although such proposals are not binding on the corporation, they are expected to have an impact on corporate compensation policies.

The executive compensation measures are a result of public outcry at the perceived excessive salaries paid to corporate executives. For example, the 19991 total compensation packages of the CEOs of IBM and General Motors, $2.5 and $1.3 million respectively, were highly criticized given the simultaneous terrible financial conditions of both companies. The CEOs at Exxon, Reebok, and Chrysler were among other CEOs receiving sharp shareholder scrutiny.*

Chapter 21 noted that shareholders could vote their shares by *proxy*, that is, by authorizing someone else to vote their shares for them. In small corporations, proxies are a convenience. In large corporations—like IBM, which has half a billion shares outstanding—proxies are a necessity.

Time, May 4, 1992, p. 47.

OTHER SECURITIES MATTERS OF PRACTICAL NOTE

This chapter has primarily focused on federal securities law, the public sale and trading of stocks, and larger corporations. As a practical note, there is a much bigger world of securities, securities trading, regulation, and law than what we could possibly cover in one chapter. Some of these matters of importance include the following:

- State blue sky laws play a substantial, important role. Although they closely parallel much of the federal law, there are important differences which can vary from state to state. Evaluation of an offering, as previously discussed, is one common difference from federal law.

- Besides government regulation, there is self-regulation within the securities industry. For example, the National Association of Securities Dealers (NASD) and the stock exchanges have their own regulations and reviews to protect the public.

- Investors sometimes have disputes with their investment brokers. It is common for such disputes to be resolved by arbitration. The Securities Investor Protection Corporation (SIPC), a nonprofit, private corporation, guarantees protection for investors against a brokerage firm going bankrupt while holding or owing customer securities or cash. The SIPC limits protection coverage to $500,000 in securities, including $100,000 cash.

- International securities trading is becoming very important, especially with increasingly sophisticated technology and new securities markets. SEC Regulation S, adopted in 1990, provides definitive rules enabling American companies to gain 1933 Act securities registration exemption for offshore (foreign) offerings.

- The trading of commodities, such as wheat futures, has become increasingly important in the United States capital markets. This is another example that securities include far more than just stocks and bonds.

CONCLUSION

Prosecuting civil fraud and insider trading cases is the most visible function of the SEC. However, for the investing public, the SEC is far more important as a means of forcing companies to report their finances accurately and to reveal what they are doing.

In fact, Congress never intended the SEC to be, principally, a prosecutorial agency. The primary purpose of the SEC was, and is, to ensure that investors have access to sufficient accurate information so that they can make an informed appraisal of a security's merits. Congress presumed that if the investing public had accurate information, the market would reward those who deserved success. Thus, the Securities Acts express a fundamental confidence in an unmanipulated market. To a remarkable degree, 60 years' experience with these Acts has proved the wisdom of their drafters.

A NOTE TO FUTURE CPA CANDIDATES

The CPA examination extensively tests candidates over securities law matters. It is important that you understand the terminology of securities law. To this end, you should be sure you know and understand both Figure 23.4 and the key words listed at the end of this chapter.

It is critical that you be able to identify and distinguish the purposes of the 1933 Act from those of the 1934 Act. The 1933 Act deals with the issuance (sales) of new securities. A "security" is not defined by statute or regulation. The *Howey* case continues to provide the best guidance to understand that a security is an investment.

The CPA exam traditionally focuses on the exempt securities and transactions, especially Regulations A and D. However, before you can effectively understand them you must know basics concerning what is normally required: a registration statement, a prospectus, a 20-day waiting period from time of filing for SEC ap-

proval to sell, and a prohibition of actual sales before approval. Remember, the SEC reviews the registration statement and prospectus to determine if sufficient information is available for the prudent investor to decide to invest in the new security. The SEC does *not* pass judgment on whether it is a good or bad investment risk.

Regulations A and D have been continuously emphasized on the CPA exam. We regret to tell you that we know of no better way to prepare for the exam than to learn and understand *all* the information presented in Figure 23.2.

For the 1934 Act, applicable to the purchase or sale of existing securities, you should focus on insider trading. However, it is still important to know the requirements to be a 1934 Act company and the basic reports due to the SEC. It is important to understand additional portions of the Act dealing with takeovers and proxies.

It is important to understand the potential civil and criminal liabilities under the 1933 and 1934 Acts. Figure 23.3 is important to know for the exam, especially the role of the due diligence defense. The information in Figure 23.3 is sometimes tested in the context of accountant legal liability, discussed the next chapter.

KEY WORDS

accredited investor (496)
blue sky law (496)
due diligence defense (507)
insider (512)
issuer (496)
offering (504)
misappropriation theory (514)
prospectus (500)
registration statement (500)
restricted security (505)
security (496)
small offering (504)
tender offer (517)

DISCUSSION QUESTIONS

1 What are the basic objectives of the federal securities laws?

2 Briefly describe how the focus of the 1993 Act differs from that of the 1934 Act.

3 What is a security? Give some examples.

4 What are the purposes of a registration statement? A prospectus? An offering statement?

5 What is the purpose of the SEC review of a registration?

6 Give some examples of security sales which would be exempt from registration. Why does the law permit exemptions?

7 What are the major purposes of the Foreign Corrupt Practices Act?

8 What does Rule 10b-5 address? What must the plaintiff show to prevail?

9 What is insider trading? Compare the effects of Rule 10b-5 and §16(b) on insider trading. How do these relate to a director's or an officer's fiduciary duties, discussed in Chapters 20 and 21?

10 What are the basic requirements for proxy solicitation? For tender offers?

CASE PROBLEMS

1. Suppose Theobald Construction Company, Inc., is planning its first public offering. It wishes to raise $2.0 million by a common stock offering and is considering making an offering pursuant to Regulation A. Is there a limitation as to the potential number of offerees? Does Theobald's planned offering qualify? If so, would a prospectus be required? Explain.

2. Given the facts represented in problem 1, now suppose Theobald wishes to consider using Rule 505. What kinds and number of investors may participate? Are audited financial statements required? What restrictions apply to the way the securities may be sold? Explain.

3. Jim Graves, a 15 percent shareholder and cofounder of Oscar Computer, Inc., a publicly traded corporation, was removed as president in a special meeting of the board of directors. Graves has decided to sell all his Oscar stock, except those shares purchased 2 months ago, and to form a new private corporation. (All other shares that Graves wishes to sell he has

owned for more than 6 months.) Five major investment firms have agreed to purchase all the stock that Graves wishes to sell without any financial disclosure information. However, Graves's attorney has now warned Graves that the sale could violate the SEC laws. Is the proposed sale likely to violate the 1933 Act? The 1934 Act? Explain.

4. Issuer, Inc., a New York corporation which sells goods at retail in New York City, wanted to raise $1.6 million by selling 15-year debentures. Through personal letters, it contacted eighty-nine people in New York, New Jersey, and Connecticut and then followed up positive responses with face-to-face negotiations. As a result, nineteen people bought the debentures after extensive discussion in which Issuer fully disclosed all the information the people requested. Issuer did not limit its offer to insiders, their relatives, or wealthy or sophisticated investors. The investors' annual income averaged $200,000, their net worth $1 million. Is the offering exempt as a private placement? As an intrastate sale? What should Issuer do now? Explain.

5. Gary Eilders is an office clerk at Gemini Computer, Inc., a 1934 Act company. While delivering a file within a company, he happened to overhear two important managers talking about a major product which would be publicly announced later that week. When Eilders returned to his work area, he called a good friend, Robert Zunker, and told him. Zunker immediately purchased 250 shares of Gemini stock. Another person, Theresa Farr, purchased 50 shares after she overheard Zunker telling another person on a bus that he had "the inside scoop that Gemini stock was about to take off." Farr had no more specifics about Gemini and she did not know Zunker, but she felt that he looked both knowledgeable and lucky. By the end of the week the product announcement was made and Gemini stock rose dramatically in value. Would a court be likely to find that Zunker has 1934 Act liability? Farr? Explain.

6. Taylor is Reflex Corporation's executive vice president for marketing and a member of its board. From information obtained during the

course of his duties, Taylor concluded Reflex's profits would fall by 50 percent for the quarter and by 30 percent for the year. He contacted his broker and sold 10,000 shares of Reflex at a profit. He had acquired some of the stock within 6 months of the sale. Reflex's profits did not fall, but its stock price declined for unrelated reasons. What liability, if any, has Taylor incurred under the 1934 Act? Explain.

7. Ron Byrd, an accredited investor and a controlling person in Lusus, Inc., wishes to sell restricted shares of stock he purchased under a Rule 506 sale of securities. Investor's Choice Mutual Fund, a major international mutual fund corporation, wishes to purchase his Lusus stock. What is required under Rule 144A for Byrd to avoid his sale being classified as a "distribution"? Is it possible that Byrd could still have insider trading liability? Explain.

8. The Foreign Corrupt Practices Act of 1977 prohibits bribery of foreign officials. The president of Star Corporation claims the Act does not apply to the corporation, as its securities are not registered under the Securities Exchange Act of 1934. Star's comptroller claims the Act applies to all domestic corporations engaged in interstate commerce. Who, if either, is correct? Explain.

9. The movie *Tucker: The Man and His Dreams* (Paramount Pictures, 1989) depicts real-life problems that the creator of the Tucker Corporation, Preston Tucker, had with the SEC. One SEC concern was the sale of Tucker automobile franchises before even a prototype car was available. The SEC was concerned that potential franchise holders would be totally at the mercy of Tucker as to whether they ever had a viable franchise with actual cars to sell. In fact, only fifty-one cars were ever produced, and franchise holders lost their money. In order to assert jurisdiction, what did the SEC have to show about the franchises? Describe the SEC's probable line of argument.

10. *Tucker* later depicts Preston Tucker's criminal trial. He was charged with securities fraud under the 1933 Act. The SEC alleged that Tucker never actually intended to build and sell a new car but rather used the launching of a new automobile manufacturing company as a front to sell stock and divert the proceeds to personal gain. In the movie, Preston Tucker says:

They [prosecution] say all I wanted was to take the money and run. But according to the law, if I tried to make the cars, even if they turned out no good, even if I didn't make them, if you believe I tried, really tried, I'm not guilty.

Does this seem like an appropriate, if simple, explanation of the law? Explain.

CHAPTER 24

Legal Liabilities of Accountants

This chapter is written especially for those students intending to become accountants. When we speak of an *accountant* here, we are referring to someone who has passed the test administered by the American Institute of Certified Public Accountants (AICPA) and satisfied a state's educational and experimental requirements. Such persons are commonly known as "certified public accountants," or "CPAs."

This chapter deals with the liabilities of only those accountants who provide services for someone other than their employer. These accountants would include sole practitioners and those working for a firm such as Peat, Marwick, Main & Co. This chapter does not address the liabilities of an accountant—whether a CPA or not—who works as an in-house auditor for, say, American Electric Power or Montgomery Ward.

ACCOUNTING AND ACCOUNTABILITY

Accounting's function is to accumulate, record, evaluate, and communicate financial data. For the most part, this chapter does not deal with the "hows" of accounting. Rather, it concentrates on accountability, which:

> . . . has clearly been the social and organizational backbone of accounting for centuries. Modern society and organizations depend upon intricate networks of accountability which are based on the recording and reporting of [their] activities. . . . Accounting, therefore, starts with the recording and reporting of activities and their consequences, and ends with the discharging of accountability. . . . [A]ccountability is what distinguishes accounting from other information systems. . . . *

---

*Y Ijiri, Theory of Accounting Measurement," *Studies in Accounting Research*, No. 10 (American Accounting Association, 1975), p. 32.

Accountability creates trust if the system is generally accepted as fair. Since that is the case today, accountants enjoy high prestige among the public.

The concept of accountability is closely related to that of *liability*, the assignment of financial responsibility for the violation of a legal duty. It is the logical end of the accountability process.

Neither federal statutes nor those of any state set general standards for the practice of accounting. The most common bases for imposing liability on accountants are violations of:

- Common law contract or tort duties
- Securities laws or regulations
- IRS tax-preparer guidelines

While this chapter focuses on these three areas,* it also touches on the issues of confidential communications and the protection of the accountant's working papers.

CPAs and Other Accountants

CPAs are not the only type of accountants, as previously noted. However, only CPAs can perform certain accounting activities, in particular, auditing of others. The preceding chapter discussed two common situations in which the Securities and Exchange Commission (SEC) requires audited financial statements. These are the financial statements that accompany a registration statement under the 1933 Act and the financial statements that are included in an annual report on Form 10-K under the 1934 Act. Lenders often require audited financials, even though they are not required by law, before they commit to lend money.

---

*Other state and federal regulatory schemes affect the accounting profession. For instance, the Interstate Commerce Commission prescribes special accounting rules for auditing interstate truck lines. However, these special rules tend to be of less general application to the profession than are the SEC and IRS rules.

The distinction between CPAs and non-CPAs is one that the AICPA aggressively protects. It has launched an educational campaign directed at convincing the public that CPAs are held to higher competency and ethical standards than other accountants. As the next case shows, this campaign is not restricted to public information.

Accountant's Society of Virginia, Inc. v. Bowman

860 F.2d 602 (4th Cir. 1988)

FACTS   Accountant's Society of Virginia is an organization composed of practicing accountants, most of whom are not CPAs. The defendants include the members of the Virginia State Board of Accountancy, a government agency set up by statute to license and regulate the profession in the state. The Board's enabling act restricts the words non-CPAs may use to describe their work. For instance, they may not give "assurances" and may not indicate that they prepared financial statements in accordance with "generally accepted accounting standards." The statute also forbids non-CPAs from holding themselves out as, among other things, "certified public accountant, CPA, public accountant, PA, certified accountant, CA, chartered accountant, licensed accountant, LA, registered accountant, RA, independent auditor, or auditor." The Accountant's Society of Virginia brought suit seeking a declaratory judgment that, among other things, Virginia may not constitutionally prohibit non-CPAs from assuming the title "public accountant" and its abbreviation "PA." The district court found the statute to be valid and entered judgment for the Board.

ISSUE   Does the First Amendment protect non-CPAs' use of "public accountant" to describe themselves?

DECISION   No. Affirmed. "Public accountant" and "PA" are business or trade labels analogous to advertising. These words are commercial speech. The First Amendment protects commercial speech unless the communication is false, deceptive, or misleading. If the use of the terms "public accountant" and "PA" by non-CPAs is misleading, it may be prohibited. The similarity of the title "public accountant" to "certified public accountant" is self-evident, and the use of the former by non-CPAs would be inherently misleading.

There may be a price attached to the continuing effort to emphasize the competency and higher standards of CPAs. That price may be courts that hold CPAs to a greater duty of care and higher standard of competence.

ACCOUNTING PRACTICE STANDARDS

Before looking at the potential sources of an accountant's liability, let us look briefly at the types of rules which apply to reporting financial information of a public corporation and therefore govern the accountant's accountability.

Accounting rules are not like chemical laws. They are neither natural nor absolute. The rule that debits go on the left and credits on the right, for instance, lacks the immutability of the law that one part oxygen mixed with two parts hydrogen makes water. Accounting rules are made by people, so they can be changed.* Their recent history—particularly the role of the SEC in their development—is important to an understanding of an accountant's liability.

The SEC and the AICPA

Accountants, their clients, and more sophisticated investors have always understood financial statements to be management's responsibility. Until 50 years ago, an auditor had no independent duty to verify what management reported.

This duty came about as an indirect result of the great stock market crash of 1929. The Securities Act of 1933 authorized the SEC to prescribe the forms of the balance sheets and income statements filed with it. At that time, the AICPA had not taken a position on whether auditors should independently verify either inventory or receivables. Five years later, a major scandal broke when it was discovered that the financial statements of McKesson & Robbins, Inc.—a publicly traded company—were overstated by about $20 million. The fraud involved fictitious inventory and receivables, which the McKesson & Robbins auditors had never tried to verify.

This scandal led the SEC to threaten to impose its own general auditing standards on all publicly traded companies—a threat it periodically revives whenever it wants the profes-

sion to adopt a particular standard. The AICPA responded by establishing in 1938 what is now the Auditing Standards Executive Committee. The Committee has issued more than seventy-five statements of auditing standards. These standards are interpretations of *generally accepted auditing standards (GAAS)*. An accountant must justify any deviations from them.†

In addition to GAAS, public accountants acting as auditors are expected to prepare financial statements in accordance with *generally accepted accounting principles (GAAP)*. The GAAP are a collection of broad statements of accounting principles amounting to aspirational norms as well as more specific guidance and illustrations. Like the GAAS, they are also issued by the AICPA.* The purpose of following the GAAS and GAAP is to present fairly a client company's financial position.

The Financial Accounting Standards Board

Its origins. For 35 years, an AICPA committee set auditing standards. During that period, however, the profession's duties to the public remained a point of controversy. Meanwhile, the SEC established its role in setting standards by issuing more than 150 Accounting Series Releases relating to financial reporting by companies under its supervision. Also during this period, some more and some less successful attempts to formulate statements of generally accepted accounting principles highlighted the need for them.

By 1972, public and SEC demands for an independent authority which would set accounting—not just auditing—standards became

---

*However, in the west, the debits-left, credits-right convention is at least 4000 years old. "Sumericalc," *Forbes,* 5 Nov. 1984, pp. 228–229.

*AICPA Code of Professional Ethics, Rule 202. The preceding section was drawn from D. R. Herwitz, *Accounting for Lawyers* (Mineola, N.Y.: Foundation Press, 1980), pp. 108–109.

†GAAP are issued after review and approval by the AICPA's Committee on Accounting Procedure, the Accounting Principles Board, and the Financial Accounting Standards Board.

overwhelming. In 1973, the Financial Accounting Standards Board (FASB) was created. The FASB consists of five CPA's and two non-CPAs drawn from industry, government, and Wall Street. Since its founding, the FASB has issued more than eighty Statements of Financial Accounting Standards, which are referred to as ''FASBs.''

Criticism of the FASB. The FASB has its critics both outside and inside the profession. Some will not be satisfied until the government assumes complete control over financial reporting. While no government agency is likely to take on this burden soon, both the SEC and the IRS use their regulatory powers to move reporting requirements in the directions they want.

A more serious criticism is that the FASB has an impossible task. In addition to setting standards for public accounting, it is attempting to develop a conceptual framework for current and future accounting rules. These efforts, in its critics' view, have led to standards which are issued very slowly and which are exceedingly difficult to understand and implement. Some new standards have required additional standards just to implement them.

Despite these criticisms, the FASB probably will remain the principal source of uniform accounting guidelines. Its pronouncements, with those of the IRS and the SEC, will be the standards against which an accountant's performance—and therefore liability—will be measured.

Effect on CPAs and their clients. For individual accountants, the FASBs establish standards which they must apply. Of course, they must also observe GAAP and GAAS. GAAP and GAAS are considerably more inclusive than the FASBs, and they incorporate the FASBs. In addition, accountants must observe the AICPA Code of Professional Ethics and the rules issued by regulatory agencies to which their work is submitted. An accountant's failure to observe these guidelines where they apply may result in liability either in contract or in tort.

For all publicly traded companies required to file an annual report under the Securities Exchange Act of 1934, the FASBs have the force of law. The SEC will not approve financial statements which do not conform to the standards of the FASB. This deference by a government agency to an independent board is unique to the United States. In Germany and Japan, for example, the government actively controls the rules for such companies.

COMMON LAW LIABILITY

Accountants may be liable to their clients or third parties in either contract or tort. In the wake of the savings and loan failures of the 1980s, accountants faced greater liability exposure than ever before. Federal regulators and others are looking closely at how auditors performed their duties at the institutions that the government has had to buy out or salvage.

Contract Liability

An accountant who does not perform the services he or she contracted to perform may be liable for breach of contract.

Basis of understanding. A CPA usually agrees to perform accounting services for another on the basis of an engagement letter. An *engagement letter* is a contract. As such, it should specify what service are to be performed, when they are to be completed, and for whom they are to be done. In engagement letters for audits, it is especially important to specify precisely what the accountant is to analyze, review, and test.

Because it calls for unique personal services, an engagement contract is not delegable. As discussed in Chapter 11, a promisor cannot delegate contracts based on his or her special abilities, experience, or expertise. The law presumes accountants have unique skills on which basis clients select them. Similarly, a client cannot assign his or her right to an accountant's services, because the assignee's problems presumably would be different from those of the assignor. Of course, accountants may assign the right to receive payment for services provided to clients.

Failure to perform. An accountant who fails to perform is subject to the same damage remedies as any breaching party to a contract. In addition, if the breach is substantial, he may forfeit any remuneration due him under the contract *and* be liable for any consequential damages suffered by the client. For example, Smith's client needs its audit completed by March 1, as Smith's engagement letter states. Smith does not submit the audit until May 5, long after it had lost its value to the client. Smith could not collect any compensation for his work and would be liable for, say, his client's lost business opportunity.

Discovering fraud. If an audit is properly performed, an accountant generally will not be liable for failing to discover fraud. Accountants do have a duty to look for fraud and *defalcations*—embezzlements—and they will be liable in their negligence or failure to comply with the engagement letter results in their failure to detect these diversions of assets. For instance, an accoun-

tant's failure to examine a travel expense reimbursement account might result in liability if an employee was routinely submitting obviously false vouchers. By contrast, the accountant will not be liable if a routine audit fails to discover a novel computer-assisted scheme to skim money from corporate accounts.

When accountants are instructed specifically to look for fraud or defalcations, they must use greater-than-normal care in performing their duties. This assignment may occur in the context of either an annual audit or a special audit to identify such losses. In either case, the client must tell the accountant what type of fraud it suspects. The engagement letter should cover this point specifically, since clients ordinarily are charged more for this service.

An objective standard defines the standard of care when an accountant is retained to identify frauds or defalcations. It is that care which a reasonable accountant with a similar charge would use in those circumstances.

Nonnegligent accountants will not be liable for their failure to identify a fraud or defalcation if the client hinders their discovery of it (see Figure 24.1). In the next case, a company sued

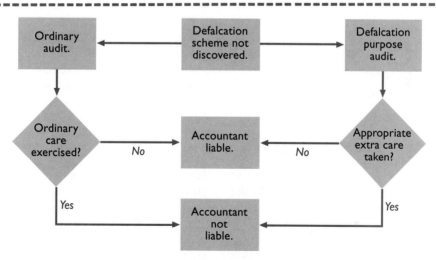

Figure 24.1 Accountant's Liability for Defalcation Schemes.
The accountant's liability extends only to losses from the time of the audit to the time the scheme is discovered.

its auditors when they failed to discover a fraud perpetrated by the company's former chief executive officer and various members of upper management.

Cenco Inc. v. Seidman & Seidman

686 F.2d 449 (7th Cir. 1982)

FACTS From 1970 through 1975 member of Cenco's management inflated the value of the company's inventory far beyond its actual worth. They thereby increased the company's apparent worth and, not incidentally, the value of its stock. The inflated stock was used to acquire other companies. Cenco's overvalued inventory was also used as collateral for loans. Cenco also filed insurance claims based on the inflated value whenever inventory was lost or stolen. Thus, the fraud benefited the company, not the individual perpetrators. When a newly hired financial officer disclosed the fraud to the SEC, the stock's price declined 75 percent. Shareholders who purchased stock during the fraud sued the company and its auditors, Seidman & Seidman, for their stock's lost value. The company also sued the Seidman firm for breach of contract, basing the suit on the auditor's failure to discover the fraud. On the day after the trial began, Seidman settled with the stock purchasers. In the case brought by Cenco, the jury found for Seidman.

ISSUE Was wrongdoing by Cenco's officers a valid defense?

DECISION Yes. Affirmed. A judgment in Cenco's favor would benefit all its shareholders alike. However, the settlement of the suit brought by the stock purchasers compensated the losses of those who purchased during the fraud period, and they are not entitled to two recoveries. To allow the other shareholders—the owners of a corrupt business—to shift the costs of wrongdoing entirely to the auditors would remove any incentive to hire honest management. Also, the primary costs of a fraud on a corporation's behalf are borne by outsiders, not by the corporation. Unlike fraud against the corporation where shareholders are the principal victims, here the shareholders were its beneficiaries—at least until the fraud was unmasked.

An accountant's liability for not discovering a defalcation extends only to losses which the client suffers between the time the audit in question was conducted and the time the scheme was discovered.

Third party actions. A major procedural question in third party actions against accountants is whether the third party has standing to sue the accountant.

Standing refers to the interest a plaintiff must have in a suit. Under our adversary system, the courts require that a plaintiff have a sufficient stake in a case's outcome to ensure that the issues are sharply drawn for the court. The standing requirement for third parties filing a contract action against an accountant is quite stringent. In order to avoid having the case dismissed, the third party must establish that he was the primary beneficiary of the accounting services contract *and* that the accountant knew that at the time of contracting.

In practice, this standing requirement—as opposed to the one for tort actions, discussed in the next section—produces clear-cut results. Suppose that in order to qualify for a loan, Greenacres engages Ziffel & Haney to audit its financial condition. The accountants know First Federal Bank will use their audit to evaluate Greenacres' creditworthiness. Therefore, First Federal would have standing to sue them in contract. However, if First Federal agreed to accept Greenacres' annual outside audit in support of a loan application, the bank would not have standing to sue the accountants in contract.

Tort Liability

An accountant may be liable in tort for negligence, which in this context is called *malpractice*, or for fraudulent work. The key distinction between a tort action and a contract action is that in order to prove a contract claim, the plaintiff does not have to prove a negligent or fraudulent act. However, note that a negligent or fraudulent act also usually causes a breach of contract. The reason for trying to prove a cause of action under a tort theory is that the amount of damages may be greater and the standing requirements for third party suits are less stringent than in a contract action.

Accountant's duty. An accountant has a duty to the client to exercise reasonable professional care, which means the accountant must follow the normally accepted accounting practices discussed above. An honest error in judgment, however, will not result in liability so long as the accountant was acting with reasonable care. For example, an accountant would not be liable if a forged authorization led her to conclude mistakenly that an employee was entitled to travel expense reimbursement.

Fraud. An accountant will be liable for the actual or constructive frauds he commits. *Actual fraud* occurs when the accountant knowingly misrepresents the facts or covers up information to cast the work product in a false light. For instance, while performing an annual audit, an accountant realizes he made a serious mistake in calculating depreciation on plant in the previous year's audit. Rather than correct the mistake, he tries to cover his error. He has committed actual fraud.

Constructive fraud, which in this context is also called "gross negligence," occurs when the accountant's actions are an extreme, flagrant, or reckless departure from the profession's standards of due care and competence. In such cases, because of the nature of the accountant's act, the plaintiff does not have to prove an intent to deceive. Suppose an accounting firm is running far behind schedule on its annual audit of a small corporation. To save time, it accepts the client's accounts receivable figures after minimal testing, rationalizing that the client's figures had always been valid in the past. If accounts receivable are the client's principal assets, their certification may be constructive fraud. By contrast, if the accounting firm discovered the client's figures were actually wrong and still certified them as correct, that would be actual fraud.

The distinction between actual fraud and constructive fraud is far from academic. Generally, accountants' malpractice insurance policies do not cover actual fraud. Since courts can award punitive damages in fraud cases, an accountant may be personally liable for a large judgment in an action based on the actual fraud.

Third party actions. An accountant found to have engaged in constructive fraud or fraud will have potential liability to all foreseeable users of his work product. An accountant's potential liability to third parties for negligence in the preparation of a work product is not so clear. There are three major approaches to third party liability: traditional ("*Ultramares* rule"), *Restatement Second*, and "foreseeable user" approaches. To make matters more confusing, there are deviations among the various states within the three major approaches.

Most states originally followed the rule first voiced in 1931 by the New York Court of Appeals in *Ultramares Corp. v. Touche, Niven & Co.** The Court held accountants liable for negligence only to their clients and to those they know will be using their work product. However, the opinion, written by future Supreme Court Justice Benjamin Cardozo, stated that an auditor had a duty not to certify financial statements tainted by fraud that extended to all foreseeable users.

The auditor's defense against liability to third parties became known as the "privity defense." While its name is technically incorrect, it had the same effect as the privity defense in contract law. To illustrate, assume Chumley is hired to perform a year-end audit for Champion Ford, a car dealership. Nothing is said about any external usage of the audit by Champion Ford. Chumley negligently performs the audit. Champion Ford later uses the audit to secure a loan from Pioneer Bank. Pioneer Bank would not be a known third party beneficiary and would be barred by the privity defense.

In 1985, the New York Court of Appeals, the court that decided *Ultramares*, revisited the issue of accountant's negligence liability to third parties. Many speculated that the court might move away from the privity test. They were wrong. Instead, the court retained the privity rule but added a new linkage element between the accountant and the third party. The court ruled that a third party plaintiff must establish:

1. The accountants were aware that the financial reports were to be used for a particular purpose.
2. A known party or parties was intending to rely on the reports to further those purposes.
3. Some conduct on the part of the accountant

shows their understanding of the reliance of that party or parties (the linkage element).†

As of 1992, some thirteen states are known to actively follow the *traditional ("Ultramares rule") approach* in some form, most without the linkage element.

The traditional ("*Ultramares* rule") approach has been criticized sharply for its failure to recognize that "audit reports are very frequently (if not almost universally) used by businesses to establish the financial creditability of their enterprise in the perceptions of outside persons, e.g., existing and prospective investors, financial institutions, and others who extend credit to an enterprise or make risk-oriented decisions based on its economic vitality."‡ In addition, the emphasis on a privity relationship is inconsistent with the usual rule of legal accountability for negligence. Ordinarily, a person is held accountable for reasonably foreseeable injuries caused by their faulty conduct.

The compilers of the *Restatement (Second) of Torts)*, §552 (1977), took heed of the objections to the traditional ("*Ultramares* rule") approach and attempted to strike a balance between it and the usual foreseeability rule of negligence. The result is accountant liability to a known and an intended user *or class of users* of information. This is recognized as a compromise approach. What this means is that if Champion Ford, above, used the audit to secure a loan from Commercial Bank, not Pioneer Bank, Chumley would still have liability. Why? Commercial Bank is part of the intended class of users: commercial bankers. However, Chumley would not have liability to a prospective shareholder relying upon the audit. As of 1992, some seventeen states are known to follow the *Restatement* approach actively.

---

† *Credit Alliance v. Arthur Andersen & Co.*, 65 N.Y.2d 435 (1985).

‡ *Bily v. Arthur Young and Co.*, 834 F.2d 745, 751 (Cal 1992).

---

*255 N.Y. 170, 174 N.E. 441 (1931).

APPROACH	KNOWN STATES*	TEST	LIABLE TO THIRD PARTY IF:			
			GENERIC AUDIT?†	KNOWN PARTY?	CLASS OF KNOWN PARTY?	FORESEEABLE USER?
Traditional ("*Ultramares* rule")	13	1. Accountant aware of particular purpose(s) of audit? 2. Know foreseeable user(s)?	No	Yes	No	No
Restatement second	17	Above plus: 3. Known class of foreseeable users?	No	Yes	Yes	No
Foreseeable user	3	Was injury to third person using report foreseeable?	Possibly	Yes	Yes	Yes

*Survey of states reported in *Bily v. Arthur Young and Co.*, 834 F.2d 745 (Cal. 1992).
†Generic audit is where no third party is intended by the client or accountant at the time the audit is performed. *Bily* is a generic audit case.

Figure 24.2 Third Party Negligence Approaches.
This figure illustrates the three primary approaches to determine potential third party negligence liability for accountants.

Three states have extended an accountant's potential legal liability to the usual standard of negligence. These states hold that negligent accountants should be held accountable for reasonably foreseeable injuries caused by their faulty performance of their professional duties in auditing financial statements. These states would hold Chumley, above, liable to the prospective shareholder, as the usage of certified financial statements to attract prospective investors is a foreseeable usage of the report.

Figure 24.2 illustrates the three major approaches to an accountant's negligence liability to third parties. In 1992, the California Supreme Court, in a major decision which follows, moved from the *Restatement (Second)* to the traditional ("*Ultramares* rule") approach.

Bily v. Arthur Young & Company

11 Cal.Rptr.2d 51, 834 P.2d 745 (1992)

FACTS   The Osborne Computer Corporation, founded in 1980, introduced the first portable computer to the mass market. In 1983, the company planned an initial public offering of stock. Due to delays, the company issued warrants and common stock to investors to obtain "bridge" financing. Bily, one of the plaintiffs, bought stock.

Arthur Young & Company was hired to perform audits on Osbourne's 1981 and 1982 financial statements. It issued unqualified or "clean" audit opinions on the two statements. After the warrant transactions closed in April 1983, the company quickly declined, due to manufacturing problems with its new model computer and the introduction of IBM's new personal computer and software. It went bankrupt in September 1983. Bily and other plaintiffs who had purchased the warrants and stock sued Arthur Young under several theories of recover, including professional negligence. The trial court ruled for the plaintiffs. The appellate court affirmed.

ISSUE

Does an auditor's liability for negligence on an audit extend beyond a client to a third party who is not a specifically intended beneficiary?

DECISION

No. Reversed.

(W)e hold that an auditor's liability for general negligence in the conduct of an audit of its client financial statements is confined to the client i.e., the person who contracts for or engages the audit services. Other persons may not recover on a pure negligence theory. There is, however, a further narrow class of persons who, although not clients, may reasonably come to receive and rely on an audit report and whose existence constitutes a risk of auditing that may be fairly imposed on the auditor. Such persons are specifically intended beneficiaries of the audit repot who are known to the auditor and for whose benefit it renders the audit report. While such persons may not recover on a general negligence theory, we hold they may . . . recover on a theory of negligent misrepresentation. The sole client of Arthur Young in the audit engagements involved in this case was the company. None of the plaintiffs qualify as clients. Under the rule we adopt, they are not entitled to recover.

The court in *Bily* stated three compelling reasons for its rule. One is the potential multi-billion-dollar professional liability that is not in balance with the fault of the auditor and the third party's injury. Second, the court discounted the argument that third party liability is important for deterring auditor mistakes, since it was not supported by any empirical data. Finally, if a third party fears faulty audits, the court said he can "privately order" the risk by engaging in contractual arrangements with the client, such as spending his own money for a verification of the financial statement.

The *Bily* case was seen by many observers as a very timely and important morale-booster for the beleaguered accounting industry. As one commentator observed, the condition of auditors in the 1980s was that, "the deep pocket [had come] to replace the greenshade as an emblem of the profession."* Indeed, suits against small and mid-size accounting firms doubled in the period from 1986 to 1991, according to a survey by the AICPA. Big Six accounting firms reportedly paid out $404 million in 1990 and $477 million in 1991 to litigants and lawyers. Those figures represented a stunning 7.7 percent and 9 percent of those firms' accounting revenues in 1990 and 1991, respectively. Finally, in late 1992, Ernst & Young settled all claims against it by agencies of the federal government responsible for the massive S & L cleanup, for $400 million.

---

* Gail Diane Cox, "Unlimited Liability," *The National Law Journal*, December 21, 1992, pp. 1 and 22.

As the judge in the *Bily* case explained, "[a]n auditor is a watchdog, not a bloodhound." With the accounting industry under ongoing attack by both private parties and the federal government, both seeking to recoup enormous losses suffered in the last decade, the more conservative approach enunciated in the *Bily* case might spare the accounting industry from the fate many of its clients endured.

THE SECURITIES ACT OF 1933

As discussed in the last chapter, the Securities Act of 1933 applies to initial public offerings of securities in interstate commerce. Unless an offering is specifically exempted, the issuer must file a registration statement with the SEC for review. The registration statement must include financial statements audited by independent public accountants.

Basis of Liability

Any false statement or omission of a material fact in the audited financial statements may subject an accountant to liability under §11 of the 1933 Act.

An accountant is potentially responsible for incorrect statements or omissions in the audited financial statement until the registration statement's effective date. That does not mean her liability ends on that date. Rather, she may be liable for any errors which reveal themselves during that period. Thus, the accountant must monitor the issuer's financial statement from the time she completes the audit until the SEC permits the securities to be sold. Should an accountant develop reasonable doubts about the accuracy or completeness of the financials, she has a duty to notify the SEC.

The plaintiff's case. In order to recover, the plaintiff must prove:

- The registration statement contained a false statement or omitted a material fact.

- The plaintiff bought the security covered by the registration statement.
- The plaintiff suffered a loss as a result of the purchase.

Potential plaintiffs include any actual purchaser of securities covered by the registration statement. However, the false statement or omitted information must be of a type which a reasonably prudent investor would consider important in making an investment decision.

What the plaintiff need not prove is almost as important as what he must prove, and it reveals the broad potential for accountant liability. The plaintiff does *not* have to prove:

- He relied on the false statement or omitted information.
- The false statement or omission was the proximate cause of his injury.
- He was in privity of contract with the accountant.
- The accountant was negligent or committed an actual or constructive fraud.

A comparison of this list with what a plaintiff has to prove in either a contract or tort action reveals the heavy responsibilities the 1933 Act handed accountants.

Damages. The measure of damages is the difference between the amount paid and the market value of the securities at the time of the suit. For instance, an investor pays $45 per share for stock covered by financials the accountant prepared. At the time of suit, the price is $15, so the investor could claim damages of $30 per share. If the investor sold the stock before filing suit, the measure of damages is his actual loss. In neither case could the investor recover damages in excess of what he actually lost.

Statute of limitations. The plaintiff must bring his action under §11 of the 1933 Act within 1 year of the time when he discovered, or should have discovered, the false information or omission. However, in no event may the plaintiff file more than 3 years after the effective date of the registration statement.

The Accountant's Defenses

An accountant is not defenseless in an action under the 1933 Act. However, once the securities buyer establishes the false statement or omission, the burden of proof shifts to the accountant to show why she should not be liable.

Lack of reliance. The accountant can prevail if she establishes that the plaintiff did not rely at all on the registration statement in making his decision to invest. For example, she might show that the plaintiff never read the registration statement or that the plaintiff had actual knowledge of the true information when he invested. Obviously, the lack of reliance defense is difficult to establish if the plaintiff is at all wary.

Unconnected loss. There must be some connection between the plaintiff's loss and the false statement or omitted information. If the accountant can show the loss resulted from an entirely unconnected reason, the accountant may prevail. Suppose the registration statement of Antarctic Refrigeration clearly says the company's business is selling freezers to settlers on McMurdo Bay. But the company's CPA significantly overvalued Antarctic's accounts receivable. The accountant may prevail by demonstrating the investors' loss resulted from the harebrained nature of Antarctic's scheme, not from her negligence.

Due diligence. The accountant's principal defense in §11 cases is due diligence. *Due diligence* means:

- The accountant made a reasonable investigation of the issuer's financials.
- She had a reasonable basis for believing the information they contained was true.
- She believed in good faith the financials fairly represented the issuer's condition.

In essence, the due diligence defense is one of nonnegligence. For instance, an accountant who significantly overvalued fixed assets because of the issuer's ingenious scheme would assert this defense. However, note how much greater the accountant's burden is than that of the plaintiff even when this defense is available.

THE SECURITIES EXCHANGE ACT OF 1934

The scope of the Securities Exchange Act of 1934 differs from that of the 1933 Act in that the 1934 Act applies to transactions in existing securities, not just new issues. Figure 24.3 tabulates the differences between the two Acts as they affect accountants.

As Chapter 23 indicated, the 1934 Act is a monitoring act whose purpose is to keep the public informed of the condition of a publicly traded corporation by means of reports to the SEC. From the standpoint of an accountant's legal liabilities, the most important of these reports is a corporation's annual statement to the SEC, called a *10-K* after the number of the SEC form. A 10-K contains much of the same information provided in an annual report to shareholders, including auditing financials certified by a public accountant.

The Accountant's Liability Under §10

Under §10 of the 1934 Act, the certifying accountant is potentially liable for any fraudulent acts or misstatements or omissions of facts in their preparation. As the discussion of §10 in Chapter 23 implies, the 1934 Act does not apply particularly to accountants but to all professionals involved in securities transactions or with reports to the SEC.

The plaintiff's case. Under §10 of the 1934 Act and Rule 10b-5 of the regulations issued under it, an accountant will be held liable if he engages in any device, contrivance, or scheme to de-

TIME FRAME FOR POTENTIAL LIABILITY	1933 ACT UNTIL REGISTRATION STATEMENT BECOMES EFFECTIVE	1934 ACT AT TIME OF COMPLETION OF WORK (AUDIT)
Is mere negligence sufficient to constitute violation?	Yes	No
Must plaintiff establish scienter?	No	Yes
Must plaintiff show reliance?	No	Yes
Plaintiff's case	1 False statement(s) or omission of material fact(s). 2 Plaintiff purchased security. 3 Plaintiff suffered loss.	1 False statement(s) or omission of material fact(s). 2 Plaintiff purchased or sold security. 3 Plaintiff relied. 4 Scienter (accountant knew of falsity).
Accountant's defenses	1 No reliance. 2 Loss for different reason. 3 Due diligence (free of negligence). 4 Statute of limitation period has run.	1 Good faith. 2 Lack of knowledge. 3 Action constitutes "mere negligence." 4 Loss for different reason. 5 Statute of limitation period has run.

Figure 24.3 A Comparison of Suits Against Accountants Under the Securities Acts of 1933 and 1934.

fraud or makes any untrue statement or omits a statement of an important fact. For example, an accountant who falsifies a client's financial condition at the client's request will be liable.

In order to prevail in a suit against an accountant under the 1934 Act, a plaintiff must show:

- The annual report or Form 10-K contains a false statement or an omission relating to a material fact.
- The plaintiff bought or sold the stock in question.
- The accountant had *scienter;* that is, the accountant knew or should have known of the misstatement or omission.
- The plaintiff relied on the misstatement or omission.

- The plaintiff suffered damages.

The plaintiff's burden under the 1934 Act is much greater than under the 1933 Act. The plaintiff, for instance, must rely on the misstatement or omission under the 1934 Act. The rationale for imposing under the 1934 Act a greater burden on plaintiffs in order to recover from accountants is based on investor expectations. The law presumes that a prudent investor will read the prospectus carefully and rely on the certified financial statements before making a decision to buy a new issue of securities registered under the 1933 Act. In contrast, fewer prudent investors make their decisions to buy publicly traded securities based upon the certified financial statements required under the 1934 Act.

The scienter requirement means that, in effect, the accountant must have been grossly negligent or must have committed fraud. In the next case, the Supreme Court put the scienter requirement into context.

Ernst & Ernst v. Hochfelder

425 U.S. 185 (1976)

FACTS	From 1946 through 1967, Ernst & Ernst audited First Securities Co., a small brokerage. During the 1950s, Nay, the brokerage's president, induced Hochfelder and the other plaintiffs to invest in high-yield escrow accounts. These transactions were not handled like the brokerage's other dealings. All checks were made out to Nay or his bank, and the accounts did not appear on the customers' monthly statements or on the firm's books. In fact, the escrow accounts did not exist. Nay used the money for his own purposes, a fact his suicide note revealed. The plaintiffs sued Ernst, seeking damages under §10(b) on the grounds that Ernst aided and abetted Nay's scheme by negligently failing to inquire into the state of the company's books. The trial court dismissed the case because the plaintiffs failed to allege scienter. The court of appeals reversed.
ISSUE	Was scienter required under §10(b) to establish a cause of action for aiding and abetting?
DECISION	Yes. Trial court judgment reinstated. Ernst's negligence, if any, would not be a sufficient basis for an action under §10(b). Section 10(b) proscribes manipulative or deceptive devices or contrivances. These words strongly imply intentional or willful conduct to deceive or defraud investors. In fact, the legislative history of the 1934 Act indicates Congress intended §10(b) to be a catchall, giving the SEC regulatory power over new techniques to manipulate the securities markets.

The accountant's defenses. It follows from *Ernst & Ernst* that an accountant can avoid liability under §10 by showing that he acted in good faith or that he had no knowledge of the falsehood or omission—so long as his ignorance was not produced by a reckless disregard for the truth. Under the 1934 Act, "mere negligence" is a defense to liability. Under the 1933 Act, however, an accountant would be liable for negligent acts.

As under the 1933 Act, the accountant may defend successfully on the ground that the plaintiff's loss arose for a reason not connected to the misstatement or omission. Of course, the statute of limitations may also bar as suit against an accountant; the statute of the 1934 Act is the same as that of the 1933 Act.

The Foreign Corrupt Practices Act

As noted in Chapter 23, the Foreign Corrupt Practices Act of 1977 prohibits the bribery of officials of foreign countries to obtain business. The Act also imposes a system of internal accounting controls to ensure that covered companies accurately reflect any suspect transactions. Any such transactions must be reported to the SEC, and an accountant may be liable for omitting this information from a 10-K.

The SEC's Power to Discipline Accountants

Violations of the laws enforced by the SEC can lead to another form of liability. Rule 2(e) permits the SEC to bar from practice before it any person who is unqualified, who violates ethical standards, or who violates the securities laws. In the following case, an accountant challenged the SEC's power to adopt this rule.

Davy v. SEC

792 F.2d 1418 (9th Cir. 1986)

FACTS Russell Davy, an experienced CPA, had audited SNG Oil & Gas Co. in 1977 and 1978. The closely held SNG corporation had few assets and almost no ongoing business activity. In 1979 its controller told Davy there would be some minor changes relating to the contribution of new assets by a new shareholder. The controller provided only a journal entry and an unexecuted contract to confirm these transactions. Davy did not inquire further about them. The statements Davy then certified showed a ninefold increase in shareholders' equity and an elevenfold increase in total assets between 1978 and 1979. The statements also included "Sales," "Cost of Sales," and a note on "Inventory" even though Davy knew they created the false impression that SNG had an ongoing business. Afterward, Davy received documents which showed that SNG did not own what had been listed in the statements. Despite this evidence, Davy did not investigate the discrepancies. With Davy's knowledge, SNG used the statements as part of a registration statement for SNG's stock. The stock was traded only briefly before it was suspended because of inadequate financial information about SNG and unusual and unexplained market activity in the stock. The SEC found that Davy had engaged in improper professional conduct and had willfully violated the Securities Acts by certifying inaccurate financial statements used to register, market, and sell stock. Basing its decision on its Rule 2(e), the SEC barred Davy from practicing before it.

ISSUE Did the SEC have authority to make Rule 2(e)?

DECISION Yes. Affirmed. The SEC's authority comes from §23(a)(1) of the 1934 Act, which empowers its members to "make such rules and regulations as may be necessary or appropriate to implement the provisions of [the Securities Acts] for which they are responsible or for the execution of the functions vested in them." Like other administrative agencies with similar grants of power, the SEC has authority to police the conduct of those who practice before it.

THE INTERNAL REVENUE CODE OF 1954: TAX-PREPARER LIABILITY

Congress and the IRS have become concerned about large sums of undeclared income and tax shelter abuses on federal income tax returns. With each tax reform act since the mid-1970s, Congress has progressively increased the burden on tax preparers and tax shelter advisors to substantiate the legitimacy of claims for deductions and exemptions. There is no indication that we have seen the end of this type of legislation. This section deals with the more common type of accountant liability under the Internal Revenue Code (IRC): tax-preparer liability.

Scope of Regulations

The IRC defines a "compensated income tax preparer" as a person who for compensation prepares income tax returns for third parties or as one who employs one or more persons to prepare returns. Thus, the term includes anyone from a sole practitioner to H. & R. Block. We will refer to anyone in this category simply as a *preparer*.

The Duties of the Compensated Preparer

The IRC provisions dealing with tax return preparation apply only to preparers. So, the regulations would not apply to a tax student who fills out a friend's tax return as an act of friendship. Suppose a tax student does a friend's return and makes an error due to his lack of knowledge. He will not be liable if he did not accept compensation. However, if the student does his friend's taxes in exchange for tickets to a Madonna concert, then a penalty might attach.

As long as the preparer exercises due professional care in the performance of his duties, she will not incur penalties for understating a client's tax liabilities. Suppose a Christmas tree farmer fails to report income received from selling firewood on the side. If the preparer has no reason to suspect that the woodsman has omitted this income from his firewood business, the preparer will not be liable.

The preparer's duty is to present the taxpayer's tax information fairly, fully, and accurately. An explanation of the way that duty applies to substantive problems under the IRC is beyond the scope of this book. Instead, the paragraphs below examine the procedural requirements which apply to preparers.

Signed return. The preparer must sign every return he prepares. If the preparer is self-employed, he must also include his address and IRS identification number. (The IRS will provide a number to anyone registering with it as a preparer. No tests or standards exist for achieving preparer status other than asking for a number.) If the preparer works for another, he must put his name and his employer's name, address, and identification number on the return.

Taxpayer copies. The preparer must give the taxpayer a copy of the prepared return. The copy does not have to be signed. The preparer must keep either a copy of the actual returns he prepares or a list of the names and addresses of all taxpayers for whom he prepared returns. The rationale for this record-keeping requirement is that if the IRS discovers that a particular preparer has improperly claimed a deduction for one of his clients, it wants to be able to monitor the preparer's other returns for similar claims.

Preparer annual reports. Each preparer and each employer of preparers must submit an annual report to the IRS. The report provides a list of all preparers by identification number and states the number of returns prepared. The preparer is to maintain a log of all returns, which the IRS may inspect.

Refund checks. The preparer must not cash another person's income tax refund check.

Understatement of liability. Whether it results from negligence or from an intentional violation of the rules, the preparer is liable if he understates the taxpayer's liability on the return. For example, a preparer who accidentally consults last year's regulations volume and misses a recent change regarding depreciation allowances would be subject to a fine if his error resulted in an understated taxpayer liability. Similarly, the preparer may not knowingly prepare a return in which the taxpayer understates her liability. For instance, Susan is a manufacturer's representative. She uses her home computer for word processing when her husband is not using it to play games. If her accountant knows how the machine is used when Susan claims an investment tax credit for its full value, he will be liable.

Liabilities Under the IRC

Under the IRC, the preparer may be subject to civil and criminal penalties. Should the preparer fail to fulfill any of the duties discussed in this section, she may be subject to a fine.

In addition to imposing fines, the IRS may seek injunctive relief against preparers who violate the IRC or IRS regulations. The IRS may ask for an injunction to prohibit the preparer from engaging in a particular practice or it may —in the worst cases—seek an order prohibiting the preparer from offering any tax return preparation services at all. The IRS, for example, might seek to permanently enjoin a preparer from working on returns after it discovered he had systematically prepared fraudulent returns. As with all injunctions, the IRS enforces these orders by seeking contempt of court citations against those who violate them.

The IRS, however, cannot suspend a CPA's license to practice, since it is granted by the state.

Trends in Liability to Clients

In addition to liabilities imposed on preparers under the IRC, the client may have a remedy against the preparer for breach of contract or negligence, or both, if the preparer's action should subject the client to penalties or other sanctions.

With the increasing emphasis on forcing taxpayers to report their liabilities honestly, accountants can expect ever-increasing IRS regulation of preparer activities. It is no longer enough—as it was in the past—for a preparer to rely upon accepted practice, as reflected in secondary source materials such as tax services, to justify a matter's treatment on a return. Instead, the preparer must have authority in the form of an IRS pronouncement or cases. Also, the preparer now must substantiate with facts the taxpayer's right to claim a benefit.

The practical effect of an IRS spotlight on preparers may be a substantial increase in malpractice suits against accountants. Taxpayers who are audited and ordered to pay additional taxes and penalties will bring these actions against preparers who relied on disputed authorities in claiming tax benefits. In addition to normal tort and contract damage remedies, a preparer may be subject to punitive damages if the client proves gross fraud or intentional conduct.

CRIMINAL LIABILITY

Like any other person, an accountant can incur criminal liability—fines or imprisonment—only by committing an act which violates a specific criminal statute (see Chapter 5). While few, if any, criminal statutes apply only to accountants, an accountant, while acting in her professional capacity, could violate a number of state and federal statutes. This section focuses on the laws discussed above: the two Securities Acts and the IRC.

The Securities Acts

An accountant may face criminal liability if he willfully makes false statements or omissions as to a material fact in a registration statement or any other report, document, or application filed with the SEC. For example, some days after giving the Frodco International financials a clean certification, Pamela discovers the inventory's value was vastly overstated. Frodco's registration statement is being reviewed at the SEC. Realizing what a mistake of this magnitude could do to her professional future, Pamela decides to say nothing and hope for the best. Pamela's failure to report her discovery could lead to her criminal prosecution.

An accountant's compliance with generally accepted accounting principles will not insulate her from liability in every case. While her actions may persuade a court that she did not intend to violate the law, she must show that she acted in good faith. In other words, she cannot blindly follow accepted procedures and ignore lurking problems or intentionally look the other way.

The Internal Revenue Code

An accountant who acts as either a preparer or a tax shelter advisor may be subject to criminal penalties under the IRC. The IRC describes three criminal violations to which an accountant may be subject: tax evasion, perjury, and bribery.

In this context, *tax evasion* consists of willfully aiding or assisting another to evade federal taxes. For example, an accountant knowingly provides false financial statements which she knows her client will use in filing its income tax return.

Perjury involves willfully preparing or assisting in preparing a false return for another. An example might be an accountant who accepts her client's false claim to a depreciation allowance on the family car.

Bribery is an attempt to evade or defeat tax liability by means of an illegal payment to an IRS official. In this instance, the government does not have to prove the client knew of or authorized the accountant's act, since the accountant may have been covering up her own mistake.

State Provisions

A number of state criminal provisions relating to securities and taxes may affect accountants. For example, a knowing violation of state securities laws may lead to prosecution. As noted in Chapter 23, the states have reporting requirements, and the submission of false information can result in criminal liability. Most state tax codes contain criminal provisions similar to those in the IRC. Some have additional remedies such as prohibitions against destroying books of accounts to avoid sales tax liability.

Other provisions in the state criminal code which may affect accountants include those prohibiting embezzlement and criminal fraud. An accountant may commit a criminal fraud if he assists a business in preparing false financial statements to be submitted to a bank as part of a loan application.

ACCOUNTANT COMMUNICATIONS AND RECORDS

In recent years, the nature of communications between accountant and client and the status of the accountant's working papers have been debated quite extensively. The debate has focused on what is confidential or privileged and when the accountant may or must disclose. While the debate is not yet over, it is possible to outline current thinking on disclosure.

Communications with Clients

Voluntary disclosure. An accountant who voluntarily discloses confidential communications without the client's consent generally breaches his fiduciary duty and may be liable to the client. Both the AICPA Code and the state codes of ethics prohibit such disclosure in order to protect the client's expectation of privacy.

Of course, an accountant may not use confidential information for his personal gain. And his voluntary disclosure must not work to his client's detriment. For example, Walter let slip to a friend that his client, a major department store chain, was considering a site near their town. The friend knew the person who owned the site and told her. Walter may be liable to the department store chain for any additional sums it had to pay in order to acquire the site.

Involuntary disclosure. Sometimes in the course of litigation a court may order an accountant to testify as to his conversations regarding particular financial matters. These orders are usually valid.

Earlier editions of this book said that unlike a lawyer's communications with his client, an accountant's communications are not *privileged*, that is, they are not exempted by law from disclosure in court. While it is still basically correct, that statement must now be qualified. A trend appears to be developing for courts to disregard the attorney-client privilege when the lawyer performs essentially accounting or tax-preparation functions. However, a lawyer's communications with a client about the client's tax fraud case remain unquestionably privileged.

Neither the common law nor federal statutes permit an accountant to cite the confidential nature of a communication in order to avoid testifying about it. However, some states have granted this privilege to accountants' clients. Even where it exists, as the next case shows, the privilege is quite limited, particularly when the client is a corporation.

Neusteter v. District Court

675 P.2d 1 (Colo. 1984)

FACTS   The Neusteters owned the controlling interests in two closely held, family businesses—a real estate company and a store. The Lackners were the principal minority shareholders. The Lackners brought a shareholders' derivative suit against the Neusteters, alleging they had wasted the assets of the realty company in several specific instances by shifting resources to the store. The Lackners sought to depose accountants retained by the realty and store companies and to examine documents in the records of the accounting firm. Citing Colorado's accountant-client privilege, the firm refused to cooperate. The trial court, however, ordered compliance with the Lackners' discovery requests. The Neusteters sought an injunction against enforcement of the trial court order.

ISSUE   Does the accountant-client privilege bar the accountant's testimony in shareholder derivative actions where the client is a closely held corporation?

DECISION   No. Injunction denied. A Colorado statute provides:

> A certified public accountant shall not be examined without the consent of his client as to any communication made by the client to him . . . , or his advice, reports, or working papers given or made thereon in the course of professional employment. . . .

The privilege encourages full and frank communications so that CPAs can advise clients on the basis of complete information, free from the consequences of disclosure. But when the client corporation is in a lawsuit brought by its shareholders on charges of mismanagement, the shareholders have a right to demonstrate why the privilege should not be invoked. Management acts as a trustee for the shareholders, and accounting information records its transactions. Here, the Lackners' allegations established good cause for not permitting the control group to withhold financial information from the minority.

Where a state does not recognize the privilege, an accountant must testify when a court orders it whether the client consents or not. For instance, an accountant may have to testify against a client charged with systematically underreporting its sales when the state attempts to recover the taxes due. In this instance, the accountant does not breach his fiduciary duty to the client.

Where a privilege does exist, an accountant cannot refuse to provide information if his client waives his privilege. The privilege is the client's, not the accountant's. And remember that the Supreme Court has stated: "No confidential accountant-client privilege exists under federal law, and no state-created privilege has been recognized in federal cases."*

Working Papers

Disputes sometimes arise between accountants and their clients or between an accountant and a court or regulatory agency as to the ownership of an accountant's working papers. *Working papers* are the internal documents, tests, memoranda, and accounts developed in creating the final work product for the client. For instance, a test sampling of the client's accounts receivable from an audit would be a working paper.

Authorized disclosure. At common law, an accountant's working papers belonged to her unless the engagement letter specified otherwise. Today, about half the states have codified the common law rule to make clear precisely what is protected.

The right to retain working papers is not a right to assign, dispose of, or publish them freely. Since they reflect the financial operations of the client, their content is confidential and not subject to disclosure without either the client's consent or a valid court order for their production.

Any accountant disclosing working records outside of those instances breaches her fiduciary duty to her client. For example, an accountant who turns over working papers to a bank which is considering her client's loan application would breach her fiduciary duty if she did not have the client's approval to do so. In the next case, the Supreme Court ended any question as to the privileged nature of the working papers of an independent auditor.

---

* *Couch v. United States*, 409 U.S. 322, 335 (1973).

United States v. Arthur Young & Co.

104 S.Ct. 1495 (1984)

FACTS   From 1972 through 1974, Arthur Young served as an independent auditor for Amerada Hess Corp. An IRS audit of Amerada's returns for those years revealed a questionable payment. The IRS issued an order to Arthur Young, instructing it to make its files available, including its tax accrual working papers. Amerada ordered the firm not to comply. The IRS sought enforcement of its order in the U.S. District

Court. That court refused to recognize any privilege which would shield the papers. The Court of Appeals, however, reversed. The working papers, it held, were privileged because they were prepared in the course of complying with federal securities law.

ISSUE

Can a publicly held corporation assert a privilege as to the working papers of its independent auditor?

DECISION

No. Reversed. The IRS can compel the production of items of even potential relevance to an ongoing investigation, without regard for whether the items ultimately would be admissible as evidence in court. The broad powers of the IRS in these circumstances are not limited by any sort of privilege. The auditor's function as a public watchdog demands total independence from the client. To insulate from disclosure its interpretation of the client's financial statements would ignore its public trust. The auditor's working papers are also available through discovery to the SEC or a private plaintiff in a securities case.

Unauthorized disclosure. Even though no privilege exists as to working papers, the client still has a right to have them treated as confidential. The client's remedy for an unauthorized disclosure of working papers is a malpractice suit. The accountant, however, can avoid liability by proving that the client's actions would have appeared to a reasonable person to have amounted to permission to disclose. Suppose an accountant's client tells her that he has applied for a loan from First Federal Bank and that the loan officer may call her for additional financial information. That instruction may be sufficient to justify disclosure.

When a court or an administrative agency has issued a valid subpoena for the working papers, the accountant's defense is absolute. A court order, for instance, to turn over working papers so that the client's wife can better assess his worth in her divorce action supersedes the client's right to confidentiality.

CONCLUSION

The accounting profession plays a critical role in business, and the importance of its reports to investors cannot be overstated. At one time, accountants' only legal liabilities were to cli-

ents. Today, contract and malpractice liability extends to any known or foreseeable beneficiary. Where gross negligence or fraud is established, the plaintiff has to prove only an injury due to the accountant's act or omission. This expansion of the class of persons to whom the accountant may be liable reflects a recognition that others besides the client may rely on the accountant's work.

Federal statutes—particularly the IRC and the Securities Acts—have, for a long time, exposed accountants to broad liability. In addition, federal agencies have played a critically important role in the formulation of accounting standards, both through new substantive reporting requirements, like the Foreign Corrupt Practices Act, and through procedural reforms brought about by leverage on the profession. It is unlikely that the federal government's influence on accounting practices will diminish in coming years.

A NOTE TO FUTURE CPA CANDIDATES

As would be expected, the material in this chapter is heavily tested on the business law portion of the CPA exam. It is important to understand the role and function of an accountant, especially an auditor. Remember, an accountant is expected to follow GAAS, GAAP, and applicable FASBs but does *not* insure an audit. Specific professional responsibility expectations, now tested in the business law portion of the CPA exam, should be reviewed from your auditing course.

An accountant's potential liability to the client is straight-forward and clear. Under contract law, an accountant has no right to compensation for a work product that is delivered late and is then no longer of value to the client. The accountant has liability for negligence, constructive fraud, and fraud. For fraud, there must be scienter (intent to act). Liability to clients is never based on strict liability.

An accountant's potential tort liability to a third party is clear as to constructive fraud or fraud: liable. As to negligence, an accountant's liability may be dependent on which of the three major approaches a state recognizes: traditional ("*Ultramares* rule") approach, *Restatement Second*, or "foreseeable user." You should study and understand Figure 24.2. The CPA exam recognizes the traditional ("*Ultramares* rule") approach.

An accountant's liability potential under the securities law is significantly more stringent. Figure 24.3 contrasts liability under the 1933 and 1934 Acts. Notice that the 1933 Act's period of potential liability is greater (until the registration statement and prospectus are approved by the SEC in contrast to the 1934 Act where it ends upon the accountant's submission of the final report to the client), the accountant generally carries the greater burden of proof in a 1933 Act case, and "mere negligence" is, in essence, a defense under the 1934 Act. Note that a plaintiff in a 1933 Act case against an accountant does *not* have to prove either scienter or reliance.

You need to understand that although an accountant's work papers belong to the accountant, she cannot freely transfer or disclose these to third parties. An accountant does not enjoy

accountant-client privilege rights unless the state has specifically provided such protection.

The CPA exam historically has expected the candidate to know the potential SEC and IRS penalties and punishment for an accountant.

KEY WORDS

accountant (525)
certified public
  accountant
  (CPA) (525)
due diligence (536)

engagement letter (528)
preparer (540)
traditional ("*Ultramares*
  rule") approach (531)
working papers (544)

DISCUSSION QUESTIONS

1. Must every person providing accounting services to the public be a CPA?
2. Are the guidelines and principles directing an accountant's manner of work generally created by the federal government?
3. What are the most common bases for liability in suits against accountants?
4. What must the client prove to be able to prevail against an accountant for breach of contract? For negligence?
5. Discuss the ability of third parties to recover from an accountant for work the accountant performed for her client.
6. What must a plaintiff show in order to prevail against an accountant under the Securities Act of 1933? Under the 1934 Act?
7. What is meant by due diligence? How does this relate to an accountant's duties under the 1933 Act?
8. Why is an accountant's potential for liability greater under the 1933 Act than under the 1934 Act?
9. What are the potential liabilities of the tax preparer? Are the IRS monitoring systems likely to achieve their goal of increased voluntary compliance?
10. What protections as to confidentiality can clients expect of their individual communica-

tions with their accountant? What if the client is a corporation?

CASE PROBLEMS

1. Glenn Mrjenovich, a CPA, was hired by Atlas Power Company to perform accounting services. Mrjenovich was asked to produce financial statements to be used internally for management purposes, and also to obtain short-term loans from financial institutions. No engagement letter was prepared. In the course of the review, some suspicious circumstances were revealed. Mrjenovich decided to accept the explanations of management, since the review was primarily for internal use and not a full audit. Unfortunately, had Mrjenovich not so relied, he might have discovered a material act of fraud committed by management. What is the role of an engagement letter? What is the duty of the accountant when suspicious circumstances are revealed during a review? Explain.

2. Hall, Inc., engaged Locke, a CPA, to audit Willow Co. Hall purchased Willow after receiving Willow's audited financial statements, which included Locke's unqualified certification. Locke was negligent in performing the Willow audit. As a result of Locke's negligence, Hall suffered a $75,000 loss. On what grounds, if any, could Hall recover from Locke? Explain.

3. Ella Hayes, a CPA, audited the financial records of Ajax Tool Co. Although Ella exercised reasonable care, she failed to discover a novel embezzlement scheme by one of Ajax's internal accountants. Ajax did not become aware of this scheme until after the audit, and it did not instruct Ella to watch particularly for thefts. Is Ella liable for not discovering the scheme? Explain.

4. Martin, a CPA, is engaged in an audit of the Becker Corporation in order to develop a certified annual report. Becker's president, Mary Lyons, has asked Martin to disregard loans made to certain officers. "They'll be repaid before the annual report comes out," she tells

him. "Anyway, they're no business of the stockholders." When Martin resists, she lets him know she might terminate his contract with Becker should he not comply. Explain what Martin should do.

5. Monica Seles, CPA, rendered an unqualified opinion on the financial statements of a company for the purpose of selling common stock pursuant to Regulation D of the 1933 Act. Seles failed to detect material acts of embezzlement by the company's president. Based on a false statement in the financials, a suit is being brought against Seles by an investor who purchased shares. Seles claims she can have no 1933 Act liability, since the sale of the stock was exempt from registration. Correct? Assuming an action can occur, what must the third party prove to recover? What must Seles prove? Explain.

6. Alice Frazier, CPA, rendered an unqualified opinion on the financial statements of a company for its annual report, 10-K, to the SEC. Frazier failed to detect material acts of forgery because of her inadvertent failure to exercise due care in the design of her audit of the company. Based on a resulting false statement in the financials, a suit is being brought against Frazier by an investor. The investor claims to have purchased shares of the company after reading the 10-K report. What must the third party prove to recover? What must Frazier prove? Is the third person likely to recover in this case? Explain.

7. Whitney prepared a number of tax returns in a fraudulent manner. The IRS and a number of his clients now wish to take legal action against him. What potential liability could exist for Whitney as to these parties? If Whitney is a CPA, could the IRS take federal action to deprive him of his right to practice? Explain your answer.

8. The CPA firm of Knox & Knox has been subpoenaed to testify, and to produce its correspondence and working papers, in connection with a lawsuit brought by a third party against one of the firm's clients. Knox considers the subpoenaed documents to be privileged communications and therefore wants to

avoid submitting to the subpoena. Under what circumstances would a court recognize a privilege here? Explain.

9. Brian Heurlin, a rich oil man, had Sue Billett, a CPA, prepare his personal tax return. Heurlin was a new client and Billett did not know—and was not told—that Heurlin had substantial horse racing winnings for the year. Prior returns—which Heurlin showed Billett—did not list any racing income. The IRS later audited Heurlin's return that Billett prepared and found that he owed some $20,000 in unreported taxes. The IRS has begun an investigation of Billett's role in the preparation of the return. Is it likely that Billett would be found subject to Internal Revenue Code penalties? Could the IRS suspend her CPA license? Explain.

10. Scott Boyden completed the biggest job of his young accounting career—preparing audited financial statements for inclusion in the registration statement filed by Lillie Products, Inc. After completing the audit he went on an extended vacation to the beaches at Kokomo. Between time he completed the audit and the SEC's clearance of the sale of the securities, the largest purchaser of Lillie's widgets filed for bankruptcy. This was never reported to the SEC. The bankrupt company accounted for approximately 30% of Lillie's accounts receivable. Soon after, Lillie's financial condition greatly deteriorated. A securities purchaser has included Boyden in a 1933 Act suit. Is the purchaser likely to prevail against Boyden? Explain.

PART IV PROBLEMS

The end-of-part problems serve three purposes. First, some require practical applications of legal knowledge to everyday situations. Second, they are summative, bringing together many of the issues treated individually in the chapters of a particular part. Third, the last question presents an ethical problem which, as in real life, may not have an unqualified right or wrong solution. Rather, its goal is to prompt two questions: What would I do in this situation? What *should* I do in this situation?

1. A PRACTICAL PROBLEM

Effective January 9, Sparta Sports Partnerships Aime, Bush, Clark, and Dowling have decided to form a general partnership, Sparta Sports Partnership, for the establishment and operation of a sporting goods store, Sparta Sports. The store is to be operated near the campus of Iliad University at 120 Priam Road in Troy, Texas.

The partners have asked you to draft a simple partnership agreement for them. They understand the Uniform Partnership Act (UPA) presumptions and are willing to live with them unless they have specified otherwise to you. Nonetheless, they would like you to include them in their agreement.

The partners, their primary roles, and their agreed contributions are:

- Jamie Aime (manager): $10,000
- Sherry Bush (assistant manager): $5000
- Jennifer Clark (treasurer): $1000 and knowledge
- Kevin Dowling (investor): $20,000

The partners have agreed to the following:

- Unless a unanimous vote is required under the UPA, partnership decisions not in the ordinary course of partnership business shall be by majority decision.
- Any sponsorship of athletic activities by the store shall be limited to $250, whether in cash, services, products, or a combination of them.
- Each partner shall have the right to draw up to 10 percent of partnership net income per month. Annual partnership allocation of income shall occur by December 15 of each year.
- All partners shall be expected to work full-time except for Dowling.
- The partnership shall last for 10 years.

2. A SUMMATIVE PROBLEM

This problem assumes the facts of problem 1. You should first read this problem for overall content and then begin resolving the problems of each paragraph in the order presented.

a. Sparta Sports became very successful. Soon it became the athletic shop of choice for leading area athletes. Sporting goods stores in Troy commonly spend as much as $1500 sponsoring local athletic events. Aime perceived that the store was beginning to lose its competitive edge by not sponsoring events. So, she agreed with a local running club to commit $1250 to sponsor its popular amateur track meet, renamed the Sparta Sports Spring Sprints Track Meet. Clark refused to pay the $1250 voucher when it was received.

b. Aime later provided $250 to Chris Conger to sponsor him in the Revel Regatta. Conger's sailboat had a Sparta Sports decal prominently placed near the bow. During the regatta Conger took a tack that resulted in a collision with a boat captained by Markus Clements. Clements was injured and has brought suit against Sparta Sports. Aime claims Conger was not an employee.

c. Recognizing the growing interest in triathalons, the partners agreed to expand their lines of merchandise to include racing bikes. Aime instructed all employees to be sure to demonstrate carefully the shifting features of their best bike, the Ulysses, since it had an unusual shifting feature. A well-known local triathlete, Joe Ferguson, was not told by a salesperson of the unusual shifting mechanism before he took a demonstrator bike for a ride. Joe was injured as a consequence of improperly shifting the bike. Joe has brought suit against the partnership and Dowling, the wealthiest partner. Dowling claims he has no personal liability because of the partnership agreement.

d. Rent as the Priam Road store rose each year. Finally, the partners voted three to one to move the store to a location farther from campus that offered a lower rent. Aime strongly disagreed for fear of losing important college customers. Aime decided to sign the Priam Road lease renewal letter and send it back to the landlord as she had done in earlier years. When the other partners learned of Aime's actions they immediately notified the landlord that she had acted without authority. The landlord has responded that a signed lease is a signed lease.

e. Sherry Bush was injured while performing in an area rollerblade competition. At year end, the partners voted three to one to award extra income to Aime and Clark because they had worked a minimum of 10 extra hours per week during the 6 months that Bush was out. Bush claims the partners cannot do this.

f. Bush decided to leave the partnership. Amy Broussard purchased Bush's interest and became a new partner. Broussard separately agreed to cover any possible claims against Bush arising out of her interest in the partnership. A lawsuit was filed against the partnership, Broussard, and Bush for an accident caused by a store delivery driver 5 weeks before Bush left the partnership. Bush claims that her agreement with Broussard exempts her from liability.

g. Before Broussard purchased Bush's interest, the firm had hired Covington & Herring, a CPA firm, to conduct an audit of the company. The accounting firm was told that the certified audit was necessary because a potential new partner wanted to evaluate the partnership's financial strength. However, the accountants were never told that Broussard was the potential new partner. The audit was conducted in a negligent manner, and Broussard bought in without realizing the company was steadily losing money. Broussard has brought a suit against Covington & Herring.

h. Aime, Clark, and Dowling bought out Broussard. The store began to make money again. The partners decided to incorporate and to expand to other locations. After the business was incorporated, they began running a small notice within their larger newspaper advertisements that Sparta Sports, Inc. stock was available for $50 a share only at the Priam Road store. The new corporation had hoped to sell $50,000 in stock, but the SEC secured an injunction to prevent sales pending a judicial review for violation of the 1933 Act. The *Troy Tribune* reported, "Paris, otherwise known as the SEC, has found Sparta Sports's Achilles heel: Its sale of unregistered stock."

3. A SUMMATIVE PROBLEM

Jupiter Tool Works stock was privately held. Its board decided to go public. To prepare the necessary paperwork for the Securities *and* Exchange Commission

(SEC), the board hired Castor & Pollux, a public accounting firm. On January 10, Castor & Pollux completed its work.

a. On January 16, the firm called Jupiter's treasurer to ask if anything significant had occurred since the tenth of the month. Despite the fact that Jupiter's largest customer, Pluto Distributors, had just declared bankruptcy, Jupiter's treasurer indicated nothing important had happened. Pluto accounted for 30 percent of Jupiter's accounts receivable. On January 18, Jupiter filed its registration statement, certified financial statements, and prospectus. On January 29, the SEC cleared the offering. Four days later, Castor & Pollux learned of Pluto's bankruptcy. Castor & Pollux reported the omission to the SEC on February 3.

Jupiter's stock rose on January 29 and 30 but then fell sharply on rumors of Pluto's debts to Jupiter. Polly Pluger bought at the top of the market. She has brought suit against Castor & Pollux for her stock's 30 percent loss in value since January 30. The accountants' defense is good faith. Who will win and why?

b. Soon after Jupiter went public, it held its annual shareholders meeting. A large shareholder introduced a resolution which would remove the company's president, Mark Mars, from office as a sign to investors that Jupiter would never misrepresent its position again. The resolution passed and the company's security guards took it on themselves to drag Mars—screaming—out of the building. The shareholders then voted Vanessa Venus in as president and chief executive officer. Who is president of Jupiter and why?

c. After the annual meeting the price of Jupiter's stock began to climb, albeit slowly. On April 1, Jupiter's director of research, Art Emis, called his brother Lyle and suggested he buy as much Jupiter stock as he could. "Your ol' brother's really hit paydirt this time," he chortled. Lyle mortgaged his house and on April 5 bought 3000 shares at $20 per share. On April 7, Jupiter announced a new laser which would revolutionize the production of fiber optics. By the time Art bought on April 9, the price was $35. Was either Lyle's or Art's purchase in violation of the federal securities laws? Explain.

d. On April 10, Jupiter's first vice president, Athene Pallas, bought 1000 shares at $40. She already held 1500 shares she had acquired gradually since the public offering. On July 15, her townhouse burned down and she needed to buy replacement goods immediately. To finance these acquisitions, she sold 400 shares at $55. She had acquired these shares in late January. Does this transaction violate any securities laws? If so, does Athene have any defenses? Explain.

e. The new laser attracted sharks, particularly in the form of Neptune Corp. By mid-July, Neptune had upped its offer for Jupiter from a straight exchange of stock to three shares of Neptune for one of Jupiter. Jupiter's board accepted, and their decision was ratified by the shareholders. But 12 percent of the Jupiter shareholders voted against the merger and have demanded that they be bought out for cash. Must Neptune buy them out?

f. The two companies formally merged in December. Within weeks, Neptune discovered that Jupiter's device would never work in practice. In conducting the year-end audit, auditors for Neptune's accounting firm, Romulus & Remus, were not told of the defect. Nor did the auditors note any evidence which indicated a serious product problem. The completed Form 10-K with Romulus & Remus's certified financials were filed with the SEC on February 10.

Neptune's stock had remained at about $25 per share following the acceptance of its proposed merger with Jupiter. But on March 1, when Neptune finally announced the laser was worthless commercially, its price per share dropped immediately to $15 and then slowly to $7.50. A shareholder who bought 1000 shares of Neptune on February 15 has brought suit against Romulus & Remus to recover her losses. Will she prevail? Explain.

4. LAW AND ETHICS

For a great many years after World War II, the financial pages of a newspaper were the source of fairly predictable news. No longer.

a. The release of Michael Milken from prison, in early 1993, was a reminder of the highly visible scandals and sensational cases during the 1980s involving insider trading. Milken was the star financier, the quarterback, of the powerful international brokerage firm of Drexel Burnham Lambert. Drexel provided financing for corporate raiders and other high fliers. Milken, and numerous others, demonstrated insatiable greed and a total failure of ethics in accumulating incredible illegal insider gains.

In 1988, Milken pleaded guilty to six criminal counts and agreed to pay a personal fine of $600 million and do prison time. At his release from prison in 1993, Michael Milken continued to be one of the richest persons in America. Said some, so much for the theory that crime does not pay.

Congress responded to these outrageous acts of insider trading by significantly tightening insider trading laws in 1984 and 1988.* Still, Congress has not ever actually defined insider activity. Said one commentator:

> Insider trading these days is a lot like pornography. Even though it's not clearly defined, prosecutors insist they know it when they see it. . . . The idea is that a vague law covers more abuses and stops clever lawyers from exploiting loopholes. . . . †

The real challenge for traders, prosecutors, and courts is to identify the moment when information crosses the line between market gossip and inside information. Without a clear definition, no one can predict or know for sure.

There are commentators who argue that Congress should move to do just the opposite: substantially, if not totally, eliminate insider trading bans. Noted economist Lester Thurow has pointed out that ordinary investors gain an impression from the illegality of insider trading that they can play the same game as professional investors. But, Thurow contends, "Amateurs aren't in fact privileged to the same flows of information as professionals. By making insider trading legal, amateurs would essentially be warned that financial investments are a game where the average investor is playing with a deck of cards effectively stacked in favor of the professionals."‡ It should be noted that within a couple of years of Thurow's remarks, Japan's investment markets, where insider trading is generally permitted, were stunned by evidence of the degree of widespread unethical behavior and inside trading.

---

* Insider Trading Act of 1984 and the Insider Trading and Enforcement Act of 1988.
† M. Galen, "Insider Trading: To Squelch It, First Define It," *Business Week*, May 21, 1990, p. 146.
‡ L. C. Thurow, "The Insider Wrangle," *Boston Globe*, December 16, 1986, p. 36.

From your point of view, would amateur investors be better served with lesser or no insider trading bans? Stated another way, should Congress continue its attempt to sustain the public's confidence in the financial markets by limiting insider trading activity? Should Congress define illegal insider trading activity to make it clearer when a violation occurs? Explain.

b. During the 1992 presidential campaign, Ross Perot enjoyed reporting that during the time he served as a director at General Motors, he had said that the only way to change the direction of GM was to "nuke the board of directors."

In 1992, after 2 consecutive years of losses totaling more than $7 billion, Robert C. Stempel was forced out as GM's chairman and CEO. The boardroom coup, led by GM board outsides, is consistent with a trend toward greater involvement by outside directors in the policy-making and goal-setting activities of the corporation. Ironically, this trend comes at a time when threats of potential personal legal liability for all corporate directors is also reaching a high point.

With the downfall of many banks and savings and loan institutions over the past 10 years, the federal government has aggressively pursued contributions for losses from a number of the former directors. Although the number of ex-directors who have actually been assessed personal liability may still be relatively small, the resulting tremors in corporate board rooms have been great. Potential directors are now well-advised to consider whether they will have sufficient time and expertise to be able to serve on a board effectively. The days of simply showing up at board meetings, automatically voting with the majority, and afterward going out to the golf course are over. Many businesspersons who formerly might have considered it an honor to serve on a board now have but one response: No thanks.

General Motors is a classic example of the need for active, independent board of directors to help set the priorities of the corporation. Some commentators have suggested that corporations should include a new breed of directors on their boards—professional outside directors. These directors would be persons who serve on one or more corporate boards of directors as their full-time professional occupation. In theory, they would be able to devote more time and be more industry-knowledgeable than traditional outside directors. In addition, such directors might better balance the interests of management and shareholders. Does this idea have merit for large publicly traded companies like General Motors? Is there a potential danger of having a board too independent from officers and/or shareholders? What should be a director's primary focus? To attempt to have the corporation return the greatest return of profit to the shareholders? If so, how should the rights and expectations of employees, suppliers, customers, consumers, etc., be factored? The potential risks to the environment?

c. As discussed in Chapter 23, the SEC has moved to require 1934 Act reporting companies to provide extensive data on CEO and high executive salaries to shareholders. This new regulation is in response to numerous shareholder complaints that CEO salaries have become excessive, especially in comparison with the pay of the average employee working within the corporation.

In January 1992, then President Bush took a trip to Japan with twenty-one American business executives, including the CEOs of Chrysler, Ford, and

General Motors. While the President attempted to focus discussion on freer trade between Japan and the United States, the Japanese pointed out the extravagant pay packages for United States CEOs.

To illustrate, the average CEO of a large U.S. company is paid 160 times as much as the average worker. In contrast, in Japan the average CEO is paid 10 to 20 times the average worker's wage. In 1990, Chrysler CEO Lee Iacocca made $4.5 million and GM's Robert Stempel made $2.1 million in contrast to the CEOs of Toyota and Nissan, who made, respectively, $740,000 and $592,000. Said one Japanese professor: "[President Bush couldn't have chosen a less appropriate bunch of business executives because they represent collectively what is wrong with U.S. society today."*

The Japanese way makes resolution of the issue of pay for U.S. business executives may seem clear-cut. However, executive wages are consistent with other salary extremes in the United States. Consider the recent extraordinary salaries and bonuses received by professional baseball players and performers. Is Barry Bonds, a baseball star, really worth $44 million on a long-term contract with the San Francisco Giants? Is Barbara Streisand really worth the $60 million long-term performance contract she signed in 1992 with Sony? Bonds's salary has very little relationship to the earnings of a ballpark vendor. Should it?

One legal commentator has stated, tongue in cheek, the probable response by most shareholders to CEO pay:

> *So long as earnings are good, stock prices increase and there are no "60 Minutes" camera crews hanging around corporate headquarters, no one really cares if the CEO makes enough to buy triple scoops of Ben & Jerry's (ice cream) every day.†*

Given all the above, is it appropriate for the General Motors CEO to make $2.1 million in a year of $750 million losses? What do you think of the argument that given all the responsibilities of the General Motors CEO, especially in comparison to other highly paid individuals in society, $2.1 million is not exorbitant? Does the new SEC role for shareholders seem balanced? Appropriate? Explain.

---

* *USA Today*, January 8, 1992, p. BI.
† M. M. Jennings, "A Funny Thing Happened on the Way to the Shareholder's Meeting," *Business Law Today*, September–October 1992, pp. 42, 57.

PROPERTY

The word "property" has many meanings. One way to think of it is as something that can be owned. If you buy a hamburger at McDonald's, it belongs to you. Sometimes "property" in a narrow sense refers simply to land, with or without buildings or other *improvements,* additions, or enhancements to land. But "property" also includes many things we cannot feel or eat, like an interest in a partnership. For that reason, it is best to define "property" very broadly as a right to possess, use, and dispose of something, usually to the exclusion of other people.

Earlier parts have examined the way people contract to buy and sell property. The last part also explored the nature or ownership rights in certain types of property—interests in business organizations. Part V looks at the ownership, use, protection, and transfer of property generally.

THE STATUS OF PROPERTY IN AMERICAN SOCIETY

For thousands of years in many types of societies, courts have protected property rights, interests, and expectations. For example, as early as the Middle Ages, English courts held that because every parcel of land is unique, *specific performance* is always available to enforce a contract for the sale of land.

The constitutional concept

In the American system, no right is more central than the right to own and use property. The Fifth and Fourteenth Amendments of the U.S. Constitution provide that no person shall be deprived by federal or state governments, respectively, of "life, liberty or property without due process of law." That language echoes the Declaration of Independence, drafted 11 years earlier:

> We hold these Truths to be self-evident, that all Men are created equal, that they are endowed by their Creator with certain unalienable Rights, that among these are Life, Liberty, and the Pursuit of Happiness. . . .

By substituting "property," the Constitution's framers implemented the philosophy so clearly stated in the Declaration. It also reflected their reaction to British rule. Taxes imposed without any colonial representation in Parliament, homes appropriated to house British mercenaries, and good confiscated without any form of judicial proceeding convinced the Founding Fathers that the pursuit of happiness necessarily involved the freedom to own and use property with a minimum of government interference.

The Constitution's framers did not specifically define "property." They intentionally used the term in its broadest sense so that it would include changes in the concept of property. In one critical respect, however, the framers' concept has been limited. Article IV §2 acknowledged slaveholders' property interests in their slaves. The Thirteenth Amendment, adopted after the War between the States, abolished involuntary servitude—including slavery.

A less dramatic example of the evolution of the property concept involves the ownership of land. Until this century, courts held that ownership applied not only to the surface of the land but to everything above and below it. With the coming of airplanes and space shuttles, this notion had to yield to the public's right to fly over land and to the fact that land ownership could not extend indefinitely into space.

Balancing individual and societal interests

The Constitution, you will note, does not say that individuals have an absolute right of ownership in property. Rather, it restrains the government's power to deprive an individual of property rights. Here are a few examples:

- You may keep flesh-eating fish as pets, but you cannot put them in a pond on your property whose runoff flows into a lake used for public swimming.
- You may develop a peach orchard, but the state may force you to sell it if the land is needed for a highway.
- You may practice the tuba in your backyard, but your neighbors can obtain an injunction if you "oompah" at 3 A.M.
- You may direct the transfer of your property at your death, but you may not cut your spouse off without a nickel.
- You may own a car, but state law may prohibit you from operating it without liability insurance.

These are the kinds of balances our society strikes between the individual's right to use and control property and society's need to regulate its use to protect the common good.

CLASSIFICATIONS OF PROPERTY

The major classifications of property are relatively clear-cut. All property is treated as either real property or personal property. Personal property, in turn, is either tangible or intangible.

Real property and personal property

Real property, or *realty,* is land and anything permanently attached to it. By nature, some things are permanently affixed to land. A grove of trees is considered permanent even though it can be cut down. Real property is the subject of Chapter 26.

Other things permanently attached to land do not start out that way, like bricks used to construct a building. These items are called *fixtures.* Fixtures, which are treated like real property, start out as items of personal property. Some commentators simply define *personal property,* or *personalty,* as anything that is not real property. A better sign of personal property or what evidences possession of it—like securities certificates—is that it is movable. A deck of cards, a check, a printing press, and an automobile are all items of personal property. Chapter 25 explores personal property and fixtures.

The common law still governs real property. However, statutes like the UCC and the Securities Acts have superseded much of the common law of personal property.

Tangible property and intangible property

Personal property is categorized as either tangible or intangible. The word "tangible" comes from a French word meaning "to touch." So items of *tangible property* have an existence. All real property is, by definition, tangible, as are fixtures, like built-in bookshelves.

Intangible property has no real physical existence. For instance, stocks, bonds, and patents are certificates which evidence property rights, but they are not the property itself. A business's goodwill value is called an *intangible asset*.

POSSESSION AND OWNERSHIP

You have heard the phrase "Possession is nine-tenths of the law." The speaker is usually claiming ownership of something she knows does not belong to her. Like all conventional wisdom, this phrase contains some truth, though it is not nine-tenths true. Generally, one does not have to possess something in order to own it, nor does one have to own something in order to possess it. A person who rents an apartment, for instance, has the right to possess it but does not own it. The principal focus of Chapters 25 through 30 is on how people come to possess or own property.

Title

Generally, ownership shifts when title to property passes from one person to another. The word "title" has both a broad meaning and a narrow meaning. It is used in its broad sense when someone says, "Karen has title to the pizza." Here, "title" is simply a synonym for "ownership." In its narrower sense, "title" refers to a document which evidences, say, ownership of a car or a parcel of real estate. Titles to cars are registered with a state's department of motor vehicles. Titles to real property are often placed on public record or *recorded* in the courthouse in the county in which the real property is located.

Title documents are the exception, not the rule. A grocer, for instance, does not give a title document to customers with each bag of potatoes. Thus, in the vast majority of cases, people establish ownership with evidence that they purchased goods or paid taxes on them. That is one reason why it is important to save receipts for major purchases.

Transfer of possession

Property owners may transfer full or partial interests in property with or without consideration, during life or after death. Many possessory interests may exist simultaneously in one parcel or item of property. Thus, a transfer of a property interest may involve less than the whole interest of the original owner. For example, a *lease* is an ownership interest which gives the tenant a right of possession superior to that of the landlord for the term of the lease.

The chapters which follow examine many of the ways in which possession of property may be transferred, including:

- *Sale:* a voluntary conveyance for consideration (Chapters 25 and 27)
- *Gift:* a voluntary transfer during life without consideration (Chapters 25 and 29)
- *Lease:* the temporary transfer of possession of real property (Chapter 28)
- *Bequest:* a voluntary gift at death (Chapter 29)
- *Intestate succession:* an inheritance in the absence of a will (Chapter 29)

Uses of property

A person's right to use property often does not include either the right to own it or the right to possess it. Sometimes a person uses property without any right to do so. Property is used in one of three ways:

- By the owner
- By another with the consent of the owner (e.g., when one rents a car)
- By another without the consent of the owner (e.g., when one trespasses or steals)

Perhaps the most common right to use real property without any possessory interest is the license. A person is said to have a *license,* or permission, to enter the premises of a business for business purposes. For instance, you had a license to enter the bookstore when you bought this book. Licenses are discussed in Chapter 27.

INSURANCE: THE PROTECTION OF PROPERTY

The last chapter in this part, Chapter 30, does not deal with the possession or transfer or ownership of property. It describes insurance, the principal mechanism our society uses to protect property interests against loss. Insurance provides indemnification against the loss of life or property or against liability for negligence, malpractice, or the like.

The two essential concepts of insurance are risk transfer and risk spreading. The person insuring property, the *insured,* shifts some of the costs of losing the property to the insurance company, the *insurer* (or carrier). The insurer spreads the risk of loss among its insureds by adjusting what it charges for insurance, the *premium.* The adjustment is based on its experience with claims.

CONCLUSION

A chapter on insurance is a fitting end to this part. Most of this part explores how possession and ownership change hands, so it necessarily devotes much attention to applications of contract law. While insurance, too, is a matter of contract, it is a reminder that where there is real or personal property, there is potential tort or sales warranty liability.

KEY TERMS

bequest (557)
gift (557)
intangible property (557)
intestate succession (557)
lease (557)
license (558)

real property (556)
sale (557)
specific performance (555)
tangible property (556)

Personal Property and Fixtures

Personal property is property which is not *real property*. It is all property which is not land or buildings. Perhaps a better definition is that personal property or what evidences possession of it—like securities certificates—is movable or starts out being movable. A checkerboard, a mantle piece, a mainframe computer, and an airplane are all items of personal property. *Fixtures,* too, start out as items of *personalty,* though, like kitchen cabinets, they become fixed to *realty.*

TITLE

This chapter concentrates on how *title* to personal property is acquired. "Title" means "ownership," but it does not necessarily include the right to use or consume the property. Suppose you buy a candy bar from a vending machine. In situations like this, where you obtain full title to personalty, you may—subject to some governmental and societal restrictions—possess, use, consume, divide, give, sell, lend, or even destroy the property (see Figure 25.1).

Title often comes with less than full rights to use or possess the property. If you buy a car with a bank loan, the bank retains a lien on the car, even though you have title. You cannot sell the car without the bank's permission.

The rights to possess and use property which a purchaser receives depend on what rights the seller had. Suppose you buy a truck which the seller had leased to WXY Trucking. Your rights, like those of the seller, depend on the terms of the lease. Similarly, a seller can transfer only the title he or she has. For example, a good faith purchaser of stolen goods from a good faith seller acquires the seller's rights— none—to the goods.

Multiple Ownership of Personal Property

Ownership rights in personal property can also be possessed by multiple parties. It is common, for example, for savings and checking accounts and automobiles to be owned by a husband and wife as joint tenants. In states utilizing the community property system of marital property, all personal (as well as real property) accumulated during marriage, such as a spouse's salary or the acquisition of stocks and bonds, is presumptively owned by both spouses as community property. Forms of multiple ownership are explained in detail in Chapter 27, Real Property.

Methods of Acquiring Title

A person may acquire title in one of a number of ways. These include:

- *Creation:* e.g., painting a picture or writing a book
- *Possession:* e.g., catching a fish
- *Gift:* e.g., receiving a dozen roses from a friend
- *Purchase:* e.g., buying land or goods (discussed in Parts II and VI and Chapter 27)
- *Inheritance:* e.g., receiving an heirloom from a grandparent's estate (discussed in Chapter 29)

This chapter focuses on the first three categories.

Acquisition of tile to fixtures does not fit into this list. This category marks the boundary between real and personal property. *Fixtures* are items of personalty, like downspouts, which have become permanently attached to real property. So title to them passes with title to the real property. Often, however, hard questions arise as to whether a particular item is a fixture or movable personal property. This chapter closes by looking at some of those questions.

Tangible and Intangible Property

Personal property may be either tangible or intangible. Items of *tangible property* can be touched: examples include this book, a computer, and a tape cassette. *Intangible property*

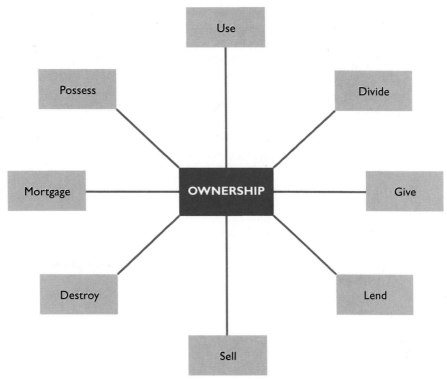

Figure 25.1 The Rights of Ownership.
An owner of property possesses at least eight major rights with respect to it.
All of them will be introduced over the course of this part of the book.

has no real physical existence. It includes many things we cannot see, feel, or eat. In the following case, the court had to determine whether a student had a property right in a scholarship to play football for his university.

Conard v. University of Washington

119 Wash. 2d 519, 834 P.2d 17 (1992)

FACTS   Conard and Fudzie were recruited to play football at the University of Washington. They received athletic financial assistance, or scholarships, which were renewable as long as the students maintained normal progress toward graduation and were in compliance with University, PAC-10, and NCAA requirements. Both were accused of violating NCAA rule 2(c), which revokes financial aid if the player "engages in serious misconduct warranting substantial disciplinary penalty." Among the improprieties they were accused of were stealing a student food credit card, punching out windows in the dorms, assaulting other students, attempting to extort money from a female student by blackmailing her with sexually explicit photos, and finally resisting arrest on the night before the Freedom Bowl, when they challenged police to a fight. After each incident, Coach James had warned them that they could lose their eligibility and financial assistance. However, it was not until after the Freedom Bowl episode that their scholarships were finally revoked. Only Fudzie requested a hearing, at which time his assistance was rescinded. Both later sued, claiming that their financial assistance was a property interest protected by the Fourteenth Amendment to the Constitution. They lost at the trial level, but on appeal the court ruled that they possessed a property interest.

ISSUE   Was Conard and Fudzie's athletic financial assistance a property interest protected under the Fourteenth Amendment?

DECISION   No. Reversed. The Fourteenth Amendment creates property interests under state law when it gives rise to rules or understandings that secure certain benefits or entitlements. A contract awarding financial aid to football players for three consecutive quarters did not establish a protected property interest in the form of a renewal of the aid, nor was it specific enough to create an entitlement.

State law creates many types of property interests which the owner cannot be deprived of under the Fourteenth Amendment unless he is afforded the due process of law. Due process has been interpreted in this context to be notice and a fair hearing, which must take place before the interest can be revoked. The form of the hearing depends on the extent of the interest. Thus, if a person's house is condemned and taken away under eminent domain, discussed in Chapter 27, she would likely possess more procedural protections than Conard and Fudzie would have received had their financial aid been declared a property interest. State law recognizes a variety of intangible property interests. A professor at a state college or university who has "tenure," for example, possesses a property interest in that status. Thus, to remove a tenured professor from her job, she must be accorded all the protections, such as a fair hearing, recognized under the Fourteenth Amendment. Since losing one's job and quite possible one's career is a serious matter, the procedures involved in removing a tenured professor are often complicated and extensive.

The law recognizes many intangible property rights, such as a celebrity's property interest in exploiting her fame or a corporation's interest in its good reputation. Some of these rights were dealt with in Chapter 4, Torts. The next section explores some others.

ACQUISITION OF TITLE BY CREATION

Personal property acquired by creation is produced by an individual, not an assembly line. It is the product of the application of a person's intellect and skills to a problem or a set of materials.

For the most part, the work of an artist or a craftsperson is unique, and the common law has always provided tort and contract remedies for its unlawful appropriation. Historically, however, the common law remedies were inadequate to protect created property consisting of an idea or the application of an idea. For that reason, the Constitution's framers charged the federal government with the protection of created property by means of patents, as on new types of machinery, and copyrights, as on books. In addition, Congress has enacted legislation protecting trademarks, such as "Coca-Cola."

Patents

By means of a *patent,* the federal government grants to creators an exclusive right for 17 years to exploit new processes, machines, and manufactured goods; new, useful, and not obvious improvements to existing processes; and the like. A patent is evidenced by its registration with the U.S. Patent and Trademark Office.

Under the common law, the mere fact of the creation gives the creator legal ownership of the idea's embodiment. A patent enforces those ownership rights through the granting of a monopoly on the creation's exploitation. By contrast, the common law does not protect the creator against someone who independently develops the same idea. Suppose Dialog Devices invents a new machine to code inventory. Working without knowledge of Dialog's invention, Quantum Products develops a similar machine. Under the common law, Dialog could not prevent Quantum from producing and marketing its encoder. Had Dialog patented its invention, Quantum could not market its machine.

A patent protects creations, not discoveries of natural phenomena. A chemist who isolates a new element has no patentable right to it, because it exists in nature. However, he may be able to patent the process by which he isolated the element.

An inventor receives a patent in return for public disclosure of the innovation. The disclosure takes the form of a descriptive filing made with the Patent Office. The goal here is to encourage others to apply the patent, thus advancing knowledge and material well-being and, perhaps, generating cash for the original patent holder.

During a patent's 17-year term, the patent holder has the exclusive right to license, sell, or assign the patent. But when the term expires,

anyone may use the innovation. For instance, General Motors (GM) held a patent on the cranking mechanism for automobile vent windows. When the patent expired, other manufacturers were free to adopt the idea without paying GM.

However, a patent does not grant absolute protection to its holder. A person may challenge a patent's validity on one of three grounds:

- The idea was not novel.
- The idea actually originated with another.
- The patent simply reflects the existing state of the art.

Henry Ford successfully challenged a patent on the automobile, citing the last ground.

A growing number of patents have been granted for medical applications of specific genes and other biological material. However, a controversy surrounds the patentability of gene fragments. In late 1992, the U.S. Patent and Trademark Office rejected an application by the National Institute of Health (NIH) stating that the 2700 segments of DNA, of which genes are made, are not novel, since the information is available in public libraries. The practical applications of gene sequences were also cited. These objections may soon be overcome, since many scientists believe that genes hold the key to the understanding of many diseases and that without patent protection businesses will not invest the money to develop medicines and other treatments for these diseases.

Copyrights

Whenever an individual creates an original work, she automatically secures a *copyright.* With the limited exceptions noted below, anyone copying or otherwise using copyrighted material must obtain permission from the copyright holder for the privilege. For instance, a band recording a song must obtain permission from the copyright's holders. Usually, obtaining that permission requires payment of a fee.

Common law copyright. The common law recognized copyright protection for publication of original works of authorship without prior filing of notice with the government. Copyright protection did not exist for facts, ideas, principles, or discoveries, although these could possibly be protected by patent or trade secret law. The Copyright Act of 1976 has incorporated common law copyright protection under the federal copyright rules. The safest means of protection, however, continues to be by formal filing, discussed next.

Federal copyright act. Under the federal Copyright Act, the creators of artistic or literary works have the exclusive right to their use. Such works include:

- Computer programs
- Literary works
- Musical works
- Dances and pantomimes
- Plays
- Photographs
- Motion pictures
- Audio and video recordings

For works created after January 1, 1978, a copyright will last for the life of the author plus 50 years. The author may assign or sell this interest during her lifetime or convey it upon her death.

Notice and registration. The creator of an original work must provide a public notice of the copyright on the property whenever possible. The notice must include:

- Use of the symbol © or the word "copyright"
- The year of the work's publication
- The copyright owner's name

The copyright notice for books appears on the page backing the title page.

Copyrighted material may be registered by submitting the work or documentation of it to the Library of Congress. Registration provides a public record of the claim of the copyright holder. While the Copyright Act does not require registration, it does penalize those who do not register by limiting their legal remedies in suits brought to protect copyrighted material against unauthorized use—*copyright infringement* suits. A court cannot award damages unless registration occurred within 3 months of publication. If registration did not occur within that period, a court may only issue an injunction against infringement.

The fair use doctrine. One of the most controversial areas of copyright law today involves the photocopying of books and magazines and the taping of records and television programs. The Copyright Act permits the public to make fair use of copyrighted materials without paying a fee to the copyright holder. Primarily, this doctrine applies to the use of such material in the course of scholarly research, teaching, criticism, and news reporting. However, even here, limits upon use exist. For example, a professor may distribute to her class a few copies of a copyrighted journal article without the journal's permission if she lacks sufficient time to obtain it. However, she would violate the act if she distributed the article every semester without permission.

Congress had hoped that its 1976 amendments to the Copyright Act would resolve the copying problems. However, technology's pace—particularly in audio taping, videotaping, and computers—has far exceeded the vision of Congress. As copying becomes easier and cheaper, the problem of protecting copyrighted property becomes increasingly acute.

A growing legal debate over the fair use doctrine revolves around a practice in the computer industry known as "reverse engineering." Reverse engineering is the process of taking apart a competitor's software to see how it works. However, in the 1992 case of *Atari Games Corp. v. Nintendo of America, Inc.** a

---

* 975 F.2d 832 (Fed. Cir. 1992).

federal appeals court stated that fair use does not extend to commercially exploiting copyrighted material. Atari replicated the Nintendo program by first procuring an unauthorized copy of the program and then acquiring its source code by chemically peeling layers from the Nintendo chips. Although the fair use doctrine allows, as the court stated, "the dissemination of ideas, processes and methods of operation," Atari had clearly exceeded this by engaging in considerable efforts to replicate the copyrighted program.

Commercial use. Commercial use of copyrighted material without permission generally violates the Copyright Act. A motion picture company, for instance, would have to obtain permission from a copyright holder to use his musical composition in a movie. The authors of this book had to pay several copyright holders for permission to reproduce their materials. In the case which follows, an author claimed that Jane Fonda infringed on her copyright in Fonda's Academy Award–winning movie, *Coming Home.*

Jason v. Fonda

526 F. Supp. 774 (C.D. Cal. 1981)

FACTS
Sonya Jason wrote her book, *Concomitant Solider—Women and War,* over a period of 20 years. The first printing of her book in April 1974 consisted of approximately 1100 copies. Between 200 and 700 copies were sold in Southern California. Jane Fonda first conceived of the movie *Coming Home* in the late 1960s and early 1970s. She commissioned a screenplay, whose first draft was completed near the end of 1973. Filming of the picture began in January 1977, and the movie was released in February 1978. Both works involved the effects of war on women, injured veterans, and soldiers. There was no evidence that anyone associated with the movie had read Jason's book.

ISSUE
Did Fonda infringe on Jason's copyright?

DECISION
No. Judgment for Fonda. In a copyright infringement suit, the plaintiff must establish that the defendant had access to the plaintiff's work and that there is a substantial similarity both of ideas and of the expression of ideas between the copyrighted work and the allegedly infringing work. Here, a comparison of the book and the movie showed that both dealt with the same general subjects. However, these ideas are not protectable in and of themselves. Countless works dating back over centuries have dealt with the same themes. What Jason cited as similarities consisted of similar but unprotectable ideas, commonly cited historical facts, and sequences which necessarily follow from a common theme. The copyright granted Jason's book extends only to its particular expression of ideas, not to the ideas themselves.

It is quite simple to see how a copyright infringement case can arise when there is a commercial film, as there was in the above case. But how about amateur-made films which have value? For example, in 1992 George Holliday, the man who videotaped the Rodney King beating, sued both the Los Angeles TV station he gave his video to and Turner Broadcasting, owner of CNN, for unauthorized use and copyright infringement. Holliday contended that only the station could use it, for which he was paid. However, the tape was subsequently fed to other stations. Spike Lee also settled with Holliday for his use of the footage in the movie "Malcolm X." The issue had not been resolved as of late 1992, due to its novelty. However, some commentators argue that the videotape may be used legally by the media under the fair use doctrine.

Right of Publicity

Clearly movies, computer programs, and such can be copyrighted. But can a celebrity's likeness, picture, or name be similarly protected? For example, what would happen if Don takes a picture of the Rolling Stones, places it on T-shirts, and sells them at a Rolling Stones concert for a profit? The Rolling Stones or, more likely, a company which has purchased the rights to make the T-shirts could easily halt Don's sales by proving the group's name and likeness has publicity value, that the Stones have "exploited" their likeness or name, and

that Don is making the T-shirt without consent for commercial reasons. Following this logic, the right, known as the *right of publicity,* has been extended to protect a flawless imitation of Bette Midler's singing voice in a commercial, a Woody Allen lookalike promoting a product, and Johnny Carson's name on a portable toilet called "Here's Johnny."

One legal controversy that has developed from the right of publicity is whether it can descend to heirs of the famous person. Indeed, the monetary implications are potentially significant, as witnessed by the enormous monetary success of the Elvis Presley Estate. Since the early 1950s, cases have been litigated by the heirs of such famous performers as Groucho Marx, Laurel and Hardy, Elvis Presley, Rudolph Valentino, Bela Lugosi, and Glenn Miller. Even the heirs of notorious criminals such as Al Capone and Jesse James have tried to exercise the right. Most of these celebrities commercially exploited their names and likenesses during their lifetime. However, what happens when a famous person does not seek commercial success and his likeness is exploited by another? The next case will discuss that issue.

Martin Luther King Center for Social Change v. American Heritage Products, Inc.

694 F.2d 674 (8th Cir. 1983)

FACTS

After Martin Luther King's death, American Heritage Products, Inc., began manufacturing and selling memorial busts of the slain civil rights leader. Commercials for the busts advertised the price as $29.95 with 3 percent set aside for the Martin Luther King Center for Social Change. Some money was tendered to the Center, but none was accepted. The Center and Coretta King, as executrix of the King Estate, sought a preliminary injunction. At the trial level the injunction was denied, since King had never commercially marketed himself during his lifetime.

ISSUE

Was it necessary for Martin Luther King, Jr. to have commercially exploited the right of publicity prior to his death in order for the right of publicity to be descendible?

DECISION   No. Reversed and remanded. Generally the right of publicity has been asserted by the heirs of actors, comedians, professional athletes, and other entertainers, all of whom commercially exploited their names and likenesses during their lifetime. Dr. King could have exploited his name and likeness during his lifetime but did not do so. Thus, to deny his heirs this right while according it to heirs of entertainers would place a premium on exploitation. There is no sound reason for making this distinction.

A number of states, such as Georgia in the *King* case, have either by case or by statute specified that the right of publicity is descendible. California, with its many Hollywood celebrities, passed a comprehensive statute in 1984 which guarantees this right to heirs for 50 years after the personality's death, as is done under copyright law. Texas passed a similar statute that is now known as the "Buddy Holly Statute" for the Lubbock, Texas, singer. California's law does provide an exception under the First Amendment, which protects freedom of expression. Thus, for example, if a fictional biography is made into a film about a famous person, the heirs could not assert their right even if the film made money.

Another related trademark issue involves the protection of a color. A number of businesses have fought hard to obtain trademark protection of a color which it contends is strongly associated with its product. The courts, however, have generally not responded favorably. Some examples include Procter & Gamble which attempted to secure a trademark for the color pink for its Pepto Bismol stomach remedy, and the NutraSweet Co., which lost its bid to trademark the blue on its packets of artificial sweetener. Recently, in at least two cases there has been a departure from this position. In 1985, the U.S. Court of Appeals for the Federal Circuit ruled that Owens-Corning Fiberglas Corp. could register the color pink as its trademark for its fiberglass insulation which it advertises featuring the Pink Panther cartoon character. Similarly, in early 1993, the 8th Circuit Court of Appeals permitted Master Distributors, Inc. to sue a competitor for using blue, which it uses in its "Blue Max" tape. The Court did emphasis that there must be a strong customer identification with the color and the protected hue must be specific. Thus, all shades of red, for example, could not receive a trademark. Critics of the case argue that if too many companies receive trademark protection, manufacturers may someday run out of colors.*

Trademarks

A *trademark* is an identifying word, name, or symbol used by a seller to distinguish its goods from those of another. For instance, Izod uses an alligator on its clothing, and Ford Motor Company uses the name "Ford" in script on a blue oval. Trademark protection permits the seller to identify goods readily to the public. At the same time, it permits the public, when purchasing goods, to rely on the mark as a sign of quality. Thus

> *[The] purposes underlying the Lanham Trademark Act of 1946 are to protect the public so it may buy a product bearing a particular trademark with confidence that it will get the product it wants and to protect the holder of the mark's investment in time and money from its misappropriation by pirates and cheats.†*

---

* Junda Woo, "Rulings Clash Over Colors In Trademarks," *Wall Street Journal*, February 25, 1993, p. B1.
† *Getty Petroleum Corp. v. Bartco Petroleum Corp.*, 858 F.2d 103, 105 (2d Cir. 1988).

An emerging variation of the trademark is protection of trade dress. To gain protection the product shape must have secured a clear secondary meaning. Protectable trade dress may include bottle shapes, candy shapes, shaker top cans for flower seeds, unusual packaging, greeting card design, and restaurant design.

Registration. As with copyrights, the common law recognized a property interest in trademarks. However, both state and federal statutes also protect trademarks. The principal difference between the federal Lanham Act and the state acts is the geographic scope of protection offered a trademark registered under their provisions. For that reason, this section focuses on the Lanham Act.

A trademark is registered with the U.S. Patent and Trademark Office. The registration must include a description of the product or services which will be offered under the trademark. Once a trademark is registered, its owner can prevent others from copying or using it. However, a company must actually use its trademark. It cannot simply register its trademark without presenting the mark to the public.

A trademark holder has the right to prevent usage of the trademark by others. To illustrate,

There are two R's in Xerox.

One is right in the middle.

But the really important one is the one you probably never notice.

It's the little R in a circle — like the one you see at the bottom of this ad — that tells you that Xerox is a registered trademark.

And it reminds you that our name — which is also our trademark — should only be used in connection with the products and services of our corporation.

Including everything from Xerox copiers to information processors to electronic printers.

So as you can see, our trademark is a very valuable one.

To us. And to you, too.

Because it ensures that when you ask for something you can be sure of what you're going to get.

Of course, we don't expect you to use the second R every time you use our name.

But we do hope you'll give it a second thought.

XEROX

XEROX® is a trademark of XEROX CORPORATION.

Figure 25.2 How Xerox Protects Its Trademark.
Xerox Corporation has zealously protected its trademark. This advertisement appeared in newspapers and magazines nationwide. (Reprinted by permission of Xerox Corporation.)

General Motors recently has become aggressive in policing the usage of its logo, car names, and car likenesses in such things as the manufacturing and sale of model car kits, calendars, parts for collector cars once made by GM, etc. "The General" claims it is trying to reduce public confusion and to earn royalties rightfully belonging to the GM shareholders.

Also, the trademark holder may not allow the trademark to become a *generic term,* one referring to all similar goods or services. If a trademark becomes a generic term, the holder loses its rights in the mark. That is why Xerox continually campaigns to keep the public from calling photocopying "xeroxing" (see Figure 25.2). Thermos, Zipper, Linoleum, Nylon, Cornflakes, Heroin, and Yo-Yo are trademarks which became generic terms. Unlike Xerox, Federal Express is flattered that its nickname, "fedex," has entered the language as a synonym for "courier."†

infringement actions. A company's trademark may not be so similar to another's mark that it causes confusion. In other words, a company may not clone its rival's trademark. Ralph Lauren, the clothier, has brought numerous trademark infringement suits against manufacturers or sellers who have used a design similar to its trademark, a mounted polo player. Disney and McDonald's aggressively pursue anyone they think infringes on any of their many trademarks. McDonald's, for instance, challenges almost anything that has "Mc" in front of its name. In the next case, a manufacturer sought to protect a trademark that in the 1960s was as common as the golden arches.

---

† "Shop Talk," *Wall Street Journal,* November 6, 1986, p. 35.

Volkswagenwerk A.G. v. Wheeler

814 F.2d 812 (1st Cir. 1987)

FACTS   Starting in 1949, Volkswagenwerk A. G. imported into the United States more than 7 million of its small sedan, the Beetle. It distributes auto parts only through an American subsidiary and licensed distributors and retail dealers. In Massachusetts, Volkswagenwerk has thirty-eight dealerships. It has invested large sums in promoting its goods and services and in helping its distributors and dealers improve their quality of service. Each dealer must identify its business as authorized to sell, repair, and service Volkswagen products by using its trademarks on stationery, advertising, and promotional material. Volkswagenwerk had registered "VW" and "Beetle" as service and trademarks. Beginning in 1968, it had also used "Beetle" in publications relating to servicing the cars. In 1972, the Wheelers began operating The Beetle Barn, an auto sales and repair service, located in a suburb of Boston. In addition to this name, the Wheelers used phrases like "VW Repair" and "Beetle Barn/Volkswagen Repair" on business cards, stationery, and advertising. The Wheelers, who had no affiliation with Volkswagenwerk or any of its subsidiaries or dealerships, chose the name Beetle Barn because of the public's association of "Beetle" with VWs. Volkswagenwerk brought suit against the Wheelers seeking, among other relief, a permanent injunction against their use of "Beetle" and "VW." The trial court entered summary judgment in favor of Volkswagenwerk.

ISSUE

Did the Wheelers's use of "Beetle" cause a likelihood of confusion among prospective purchasers of Volkswagenwerk's products and services?

DECISION

Yes. Affirmed.

The Court has examined eight factors to be used as guides in assessing likelihood of confusion: (1) the similarity of the marks; (2) the similarity of the goods; (3) the relationship between the parties' channels of trade; (4) the relationship between the parties' advertising; (5) the classes of prospective purchasers; (6) evidence of actual confusion; (7) the defendant's intent in adopting its mark; and (8) the strength of the plaintiff's mark. . . . No one factor is necessarily determinative, but each must be considered.

Here, Volkswagenwerk established all these factors except actual confusion. Since the evidence of the likelihood of confusion was overwhelming, proof of actual confusion was unnecessary.

The last case is relatively clear-cut. But consider the problem of Lyle Sardie, a small-business owner in Burbank, California. He opened a "New York style bar and grill" called "Sardie's" that catered to a nearby television studio. He soon found himself sued by Vincent Sardi, proprietor of the New York theater district landmark, "Sardi's." Was there a likelihood that patrons would confuse a typical Southern California neighborhood restaurant with the exclusive Gotham eatery? The courts said no. A simple similarity in names, even in the same general business, will not result in a trademark violation if other significant factors distinguish the litigants.*

Litigation can be avoided by compromise where both parties have a solid claim to the mark. The Universities of Texas and Tennessee had valid claims to "UT." They agreed that Texas had exclusive rights to "UT" west of the Mississippi, except in certain parts of Louisiana, and Tennessee, east of the Mississippi. Each could use "UT" in connection with bowl games regardless of where they were played.

Figure 25.3 compares patents, copyrights,

and trademarks. Chapter 45, Consumer Protection, looks in more detail at how trademarks protect the public.

ACQUISITION OF TITLE BY POSSESSION

Acquisition of title to personalty by possession occurs when someone rightfully takes actual physical control of the property.

Unowned Property

Unowned property is a misnomer because, by definition, property requires an owner. What the term really describes are items which are capable of being owned.

Wild animals. The traditional example of unowned property is wild animals. The common law considered them the common property of all until someone took control of them. Capturing or mortally wounding a wild animal accomplished this, but merely pursuing one or inflicting a nonfatal wound did not.

Abandoned property. *Abandonment* is the intentional giving up of property without any ref-

---

* *Sardi's Restaurant Corp. v. Sardie*, 775 F.2d 719 (9th Cir. 1985).

	PURPOSE	REQUIREMENTS	LENGTH OF PROTECTION	ABLE TO BE SOLD OR ASSIGNED?	"FAIR USE" ALLOWED
Patent	Protect idea	Useful, novel, and nonobvious idea	17 years	Yes	No
Copyright	Protect mode of expression	Original artistic work	Author's lifetime plus 50 years	Yes	Yes
Trademark	Protect identifying symbol	Distinctive, used, and nonsimilar symbol	While actively used	Yes	No

Figure 25.3 Comparison of Patents, Copyrights, and Trademarks Under Federal Law.

erence to a particular person or purpose. A person who throws an empty bottle out a car window abandons it. Someone who wants the bottle to sell it for recycling may acquire title simply by picking it up. Litter and garbage might seem obvious examples of abandoned property, but some prominent figures have questioned—in court—the right of reporters and law enforcement officers to pick through garbage cans put out at the curb for collection.

The question in abandoned property cases is whether the owner of the property actually gave up control over it. It is at least plausible that trash on the curb is not intended for evidence gathering and that the owner has not given up that control over it.

Lost or Mislaid Property

In everyday speech, "lost property" and "mislaid property" have about the same meaning. The law, however, makes a distinction between them which depends on the intent of the original owner.

Lost property. *Lost property* is property which was accidentally and casually lost; the owner had no intention of parting with it. The finder has good title to unclaimed lost property against anyone other than the true owner. Suppose Barbara unknowingly drops her ring on a dance floor in a bar. Chad finds the ring but refuses to return it to Barbara when she asks for it. Barbara would win a court action to have her ring returned to her.

In title disputes between the finder of lost property and the owner of the premises where the property is found, unclaimed lost property generally belongs to the finder. Sometimes though, in deciding between a finder and a premises' owner, courts make an exception when an item is found in a private portion of a public place. For example, items accidentally lost in a bank's safe deposit area are generally considered to belong to the bank, not to the finder. Also, as the treasure seeker in the next case found, a finder may not commit a trespass in order to recover lost property.

Favorite v. Miller

176 Conn. 310, 407 A.2d 974 (1978)

FACTS	On July 9, 1776, patriots in New York City toppled a lead statue of King George III. They hacked it apart and took the pieces to Connecticut to be turned into bullets. On their way, the patriots stopped for a few drinks. Some Tories recovered pieces of the statue, which were then scattered about the area. For the next 196 years pieces of the statue turned up occasionally. In 1972, Miller's research revealed that portions of the statue were probably on land he knew belonged to the Favorites. Using a metal detector, he located a large piece of the statue. Miller had to dig more than 10 inches below the surface to retrieve it. The Favorites did not learn of his discovery until they read about it in a paper. By that time, Miller had agreed to sell the fragment to a museum for $5500. The Favorites brought suit to recover it. The trial court found for the Favorites.
ISSUE	Was Miller's claim to the property as the finder superior to that of the Favorites as owners of the land where it was discovered?
DECISION	No. Affirmed. Miller trespassed on the Favorites' land. Except where the trespass is trivial or merely technical, it deprives the finder of his normal preference over the owner of the place where the property was found. Miller knew the land belonged to the Favorites, and he had to dig for the fragment. So his trespass was neither technical nor trivial.

Mislaid property. *Mislaid property* is intentionally place somewhere and then forgotten. Unclaimed mislaid property goes to the owner of the premises, not to the finder. The rationale is that the person mislaying the property is likely to remember where she left it and return to look for it. Suppose Tom puts his backpack on a shelf in a gym locker, and he forgets to take it when he finishes working out. If Arnie finds it, he will not be able to claim it legally.

Statutory modifications. Some states have abolished the common law distinction between lost and mislaid property—for good reason. It is often hard to determine which is which. In New York, for instance, all abandoned, lost, or mislaid property is treated as if it were lost. The finder prevails.

ACQUISITION OF TITLE BY GIFT

A *gift* is a voluntary transfer without consideration. Despite the absence of consideration, the person to whom the gift was given—the *donee*—has no duty to return the property if the giver of the gift—the *donor*—asks for it back. For instance, if Agatha gives Connie a bracelet but later changes her mind, Connie would have no legal obligation to return the bracelet.

Requirements for a Gift

In order to establish a valid, binding gift, the facts must show:

- Donative intent
- Capacity

- Delivery
- Acceptance

Each of these is examined below.

Donative intent. *Donative intent* requires that a donor intend to pass title at the time he makes the gift. Possession alone is not sufficient. A promise to pass title in the future will not satisfy the requirement. Suppose Vern lends Ida a book and says that if Ida likes it, he may let her keep it. He has not expressed donative intent.

Donative intent requires an immediate intention to make a gift.

Capacity. A donor must possess full contractual capacity. In the last example, Vern must not be a minor and must not suffer from any mental disabilities. In the next case, the heirs of a wealthy widow challenged gifts she had made before her death on the grounds of lack of capacity.

Bauer v. Lucich

6 Ark. App. 37, 638 S.W.2d 263 (1982)

FACTS

Agnes Bauer was born in 1900. When her husband died in 1974, she was inconsolable. The Lucichs began to care for her. Eventually she moved into their house. Beginning in 1974, Mrs. Bauer gave the Lucichs a number of expensive gifts, including a used Cadillac, furs, jewelry, and money. Their value exceeded $161,000. The Lucichs never solicited a gift from Mrs. Bauer. In fact, they repeatedly tried to return her gifts. Until August 1977, no one observed any mental infirmity in Mrs. Bauer. Then her bank noticed overdrafts of her accounts. After talking to her, the bank officers concluded she needed a guardian. One was appointed in November 1977, and no gifts were made after that date. After she died, Mrs. Bauer's heirs brought suit to rescind the gifts to the Lucichs. At trial, no testimony indicated Mrs. Bauer lacked capacity before the appointment of the guardian. Indeed, some testimony indicated she was competent after the appointment. No allegations of undue influence were made. The trial court found for the Lucichs.

ISSUE

Did Mrs. Bauer have the capacity to make the gifts to the Lucichs?

DECISION

Yes. Affirmed.

> *The law governing the validity of gifts . . . is well settled. . . . Ordinarily the burden is upon one who attacks such a gift to prove that the donor lacked the capacity to give the gift or was unduly influenced. . . .*

The appellate court then quoted the trial court decision:

> *It may sound sordid, to suggest that love, car and attention is to be put on a monetary basis, but I do not think this is unusual for wealthy, childless, septuagenarians; and it may be that some may conclude that it was a bad deal for Agnes Bauer, or amoral, or anti-social, or even evil, but once it is found that the donor is competent and acted with full knowledge and without undue restraint or fraud, the result of the act is not the concern of the law. The motive of the donor, whether*

virtuous or not, is not the interest of the law except as an explanation in a search for the truth. All that is needed is that the gift be the free and voluntary act of a mind having proper capacity. With the morals or justice of such gifts the court cannot deal.

Delivery. *Delivery* sounds like a simple concept. However, it is the most litigated aspect of gifts. One reason for this is that the law permits a symbolic or constructive delivery. The delivery does not have to be an actual, physical delivery. For instance, April's father hands her the keys to a car and tells her the car is now hers. The keys symbolize the car, and her father has made a valid gift.

The principal test for delivery is whether the donor has surrendered control and placed the gift beyond recall. Sometimes delivery occurs through a third person. If the third person is the donee's agent, delivery occurs when the agent receives the gift. If the third person is not the donor's agent, delivery does not occur until the donee takes possession. Often, it is not a simple matter to determine whose agent the third person is. Suppose Tom's mother gives his girlfriend, Tina, a check for him. A court would probably find delivery occurred upon transfer of the check to Tina. But if Tina acted as his mother's agent, Tom's mother has not surrendered control until actual delivery to Tom; she could revoke the gift at any time before then.

If the donor gives the donee property already in his possession—thus eliminating the need for delivery—a court will look closely at the transaction to find clear, convincing evidence of the donor's intent to make the gift.

Acceptance. The donee's acceptance is presumed where the gift would be beneficial to him. However, the donee always has the legal power to refuse a gift. Suppose Frieda leaves her priceless bearskin rug at Alan's house as a gift because she is grateful for his help during a family crisis. The law presumes that Alan accepts the rug. However, when he returns home, he may refuse to accept it.

Types of Gifts

There are three principal types of gifts: gifts inter vivos, gifts causa mortis, and *testamentary gifts* (gifts made by will). The first two categories are discussed here and the third is discussed in Chapter 29, Wills, Estates, and Trusts.

Gifts inter vivos. All the gifts described above are *gifts inter vivos,* that is, gifts made by one living person to another. ("Inter vivos" comes from Latin and means "between the living.") The distinguishing characteristic of a gift inter vivos is that the gift takes effect during the donor's lifetime. For example, a grandmother hands a vase to her granddaughter and says, "Take it; I want you to have it." The gift is complete and effective.

Bauer v. Lucich is an example of a challenge to a gift inter vivos. Although a gift may be challenged during a donor's lifetime, challenges come more commonly when the donor's *personal representative*—the person winding up the decedent's estate—analyzes gifts made shortly before death. This is particularly true where the recipient had a fiduciary or confidential relationship with the deceased donor. Contrast Mrs. Bauer's situation with that of Mr. Keiper in this case.

Estate of Keiper v. Moll

308 Pa. Super. 82, 454 A.2d 31 (1982)

FACTS

Both Keiper and his wife suffered from terminal diseases. Knowing this, Keiper opened a bank account to which he gave a power of attorney to his son-in-law, Lloyd Moll, a bank trust officer. After his wife's death and his hospitalization, Keiper signed a document Moll prepared, authorizing the transfer of assets to accounts held jointly by Keiper and his daughter, Luise Moll. By the terms of the accounts, on the death of Keiper or Luise, the proceeds went to the survivor. The accounts totaled almost $40,000—all Keiper's liquid assets. Keiper then executed a will, leaving specific sums to his three children, including Luise. Following Keiper's death, Lloyd, as personal representative, filed an inventory of the estate's assets, excluding the joint bank account. Keiper's other two children objected. The trial court ordered Lloyd to return the accounts' proceeds to the estate.

ISSUE

Because of Lloyd's relationship of trust with Keiper, did the Molls have the burden of proving the gifts' validity?

DECISION

Yes. Affirmed. Courts view with suspicion transactions in which a decedent practically strips himself of his property. Here, Keiper's trusted advisor effectively disposed of his assets contrary to the intent expressed in his will. This situation must be regarded with such suspicion as to shift the burden of proof to the recipient of the gift. Because of the relationship between Lloyd and Luise, it is fair to impose the same burden on them both.

Gifts causa mortis. *Gifts causa mortis* are gifts made by donors who anticipate imminent death. ("Causa mortis" is Latin for "by reason of death.") What distinguishes an inter vivos gift from a gift causa mortis is that the gift causa mortis is conditional on the donor's death.

Gifts causa mortis—which are usually made orally—serve as a substitute for, and supersede, a will. Because of the great potential for fraudulent claims and the exercise of undue influence, courts are quite strict in their applications of the requirements for a valid gift causa mortis. These requirements include the elements required for a gift inter vivos plus three others:

1. The gift must be made in contemplation of immediate, approaching death. For example, the donor may be about to undergo a complicated cancer operation which he knows he may not survive.
2. The donor must transfer the property to the donee or a third person on the donee's behalf. The donee, for instance, might hand his doctor a ring to give his daughter if he dies.
3. The donor must die of the peril he contemplated. If not, the donee must return the gift to either the donor or the estate. If, in the example above, the operation was successful, or if the operation was successful but the donor dies from injuries suffered in an accidental fall, the donee must return the gift.

Normally, the donor anticipates death from a disease or an injury. But can a person planning to commit suicide make a valid gift causa mortis? The New Jersey Supreme Court had to answer that question in the next case.

Scherer v. Hyland

75 N.J. 127, 380 A.2d 698 (1977)

FACTS

Before her death in January 1974, Catherine Wagner lived with Robert Scherer for 15 years. In 1970, Wagner suffered face wounds and a broken hip in an automobile accident. The hip injury significantly impaired her mobility, and she was forced to give up her job. Scherer cared for her and assumed sole financial responsibility for their household. On January 23, 1974, Wagner committed suicide by jumping from the roof of their apartment building. Just before her death, she endorsed a check for $17,400, placed the check with two handwritten notes addressed to Scherer on the kitchen table, and left the apartment. In one of the notes, she "bequeathed" to Scherer all her possessions, including "the check for $17,400." Scherer brought suit against Wagner's personal representative to enforce the gift. The trial court entered judgment for Scherer, and the appellate court affirmed.

ISSUE

Did Wagner's acts as to the check satisfy the delivery requirements for a gift causa mortis?

DECISION

Yes. Affirmed. Wagner's personal representative claimed there was no delivery because Wagner did not unequivocally give up control of the check before her death. She could have changed her mind, reentered the apartment, and reclaimed the check. However, the major purpose of the delivery requirement is to reduce the possibility that the evidence of intent has been fabricated. Since gifts causa mortis come into question only after the donor's death, the delivery requirement provides a substantial safeguard against fraud and perjury. Where unequivocal proof exists of the donor's deliberate and well-considered intent, the courts overlook technical requirements. They hold that a "constructive," or "symbolic," delivery is sufficient. Here, Wagner did everything she thought necessary and sufficient to effect the gift.

ACQUISITIONS WITHOUT TITLE

In many situations, possession does not confer title. In others, like leases, the legal interest of the rightful possessor is limited to possession. Sometimes, as in the instances covered in this section, possession is wrongful.

Conversion

Conversion is the taking or retaining of another's property without consent. It is a tort re-lated to trespass. (For an additional discussion of conversion, see Chapter 4.) Neither a thief nor someone who purchases from a thief—even in good faith—can hold good title to the property. In a conversion action against the thief or a subsequent purchaser, the rightful owner has a choice of remedies. He may seek either the return of the property or damage equivalent to the property's fair market value. In the next case, the true owner tried to double his money through a conversion action.

Baram v. Farugia

606 F.2d 42 (3d Cir. 1979)

FACTS Baram bought Foxey Toni, a racehorse, and turned her over to Dennis Fredellia for training. Fredellia owed Robert Farugia some money. Fredellia obtained the horse's registration papers. He then forged Baram's signature on the papers, thereby transferring the horse to Farugia. Farugia then filled out the registration documents so that he and Glenn Hackett appeared to own the horse. As a result of a criminal action against Fredellia, Baram received restitution of $3000, which Baram acknowledged was the horse's fair market value. Baram then filed this conversion action, seeking the same amount from Farugia and Hackett. The trial court entered judgment for Baram.

ISSUE Did Baram's recovery from Fredellia prevent a later recover from Farugia and Hackett?

DECISION Yes. Reversed. When Baram received the $3000 from Fredellia, it effected a forced sale, passing title from the legal owner to the converter retroactively to the time and place of the original conversion. Therefore Fredellia's transfer of Foxey Toni to Farugia was legally effective. As a result of the sale, Baram did not have a right of possession at the time of the alleged conversion. Without a right of possession, Baram could not maintain an action for conversion against Farugia and Hackett.

As *Baram* illustrates, the choice of remedies made by the rightful owner in a conversion action can have a profound effect on the subsequent purchasers of converted property. Had Baram chosen to reclaim his mare, Farugia and Hackett could have lost the horse and their money. The forced sale aspect of the conversion remedy .insulates the subsequent purchases.

Confusion

Confusion occurs when the goods of two or more owners are mixed together so that it is not possible to separate them and to restore the respective property interests. Ordinarily, the goods are *fungible,* which means they are so similar that they are interchangeable. If confusion occurs either by consent or because of an innocent mistake, each owner is presumed to own his proportionate share. For example, Fern stores olive oil in Velma's holding tank. The tank is 20 percent full. By accident, Velma allows Walter to store oil of the same grade in that tank. He fills the tank. Fern will own 20 percent of the mixed oil.

If the mixture was intentional and without consent, the innocent party becomes the owner of as much of the combination as is necessary to make him whole. Suppose Fern's oil is top-grade. Velma deliberately fills the balance of the tank with a much lower grade oil. Fern would be entitled to the amount of the mixture which would bring the same price as her high-grade oil would have brought.

Accession

An *accession* is an improvement or increase in the value of personal property attributable to another's labor or materials. When the other is a thief, accession does not pose a problem. The original owner retains title and may reclaim the improved property without cost. Suppose John steals Sara's sailboat and overhauls it. When he is caught, Sara would owe him nothing for the work he did.

Accession does pose a problem where innocent parties are involved. Suppose that in good faith Dick purchases Sara's sailboat from John. Dick makes substantial improvements to its navigation system. If Dick can remove the improvements—at his expense—a court will order that he do so and that the sailboat be returned to Sara.

If the value of the improvements is substantial when compared with the property's original value, then the court may grant the owner only the fair market value of the property at the time of the theft. If Sara's sailboat was in bad condition when John stole it and Dick invested in unremovable major improvements, Sara probably would receive only the boat's fair market value as of the time John stole it.

FIXTURES

The law treats fixtures as it does accessions. By definition, *fixtures* are items of personal property which have become so attached to real property that they are considered part of it. But some items are more attached or, conversely, more easily removed than others. The seller or lessee of real property often wants to remove items of personalty which the buyer or lessor believes should remain with the realty. Courts have had to decide cases involving items such as stoves, chandeliers, furnaces, and the like.

Importance of the Categorization

Because fixtures mark the border between personal and real property, the categorization of personalty as a fixture means it receives different treatment under the law. A brief survey of the effects reveals why the categorization is worth litigating.

Leases and conveyances. Improvements to leased real estate made by a tenant often lead to disagreements. Are the bookshelves which the tenant built the property of the landlord or of the tenant? If a tenant installs a ceiling fan in her apartment and removes it when she leaves, has she removed a fixture which belonged to the landlord? The tenant's time and expenses have to be weighed against the damage the improvement's removal will cause to the real property. Also, is it fair to force the landlord to pay for improvements he may not have wanted? A lease provision covering improvements is usually a necessity.

Similarly, an agreement to sell real property should specify the fixtures which are included. Litigation often arises, for example, when someone moves into a house only to find that items he regarded as fixtures—a window air conditioner or a television antenna—were removed.

Property taxes. Whether property is classified as personalty or real property makes a difference where a personal property tax exists. Taxpayers will claim that items of personalty are fixtures in order to avoid the tax, as the lessees of the *Queen Mary* attempted to do in a case that appears later in this chapter.

Remedies. The fixture categorization also determines whether personal property or real property remedies apply. The sales warranties described in Chapter 34 may apply to an item of personal property, but they never apply to real property. A lessee of real property has significantly less protection against defective conditions under the law of real property than he does under the law of sales. For that reason, the categorization question frequently arises with respect to heating systems and mobile homes.

Tests for Fixtures

Courts use a number of tests in order to determine whether something is a fixture. The clearest evidence comes from the parties' express agreement as to an item's status. Contracts for the sale of a home quite commonly specify which personalty will remain, like fireplace equipment, curtains, and appliances. They may also provide that, for example, a particular attic fan will not be conveyed and that a plate will be installed in its place.

Where a lease is involved, usually the parties agree on what the tenant may remove. For instance, they may agree that the tenant may substitute her chandelier for the landlord's fixture so long as she replaces the original fixture at the end of her lease.

Where the intent of the parties is not clear, courts look to three criteria to determine whether an item of personal property has become a fixture:

- The manner of attachment
- The relationship of the item to the real property
- The relationship between the parties

The manner of attachment. The more difficult it is to remove an item or the greater the probability of damage due to the removal, the more likely a court is to find the item is a fixture. If removal of cabinets in a family room would significantly harm the flooring, paneling, and doorways, a court will rule the cabinets are fixtures even though they are not built-in. Sometimes the difficulty of removal test is inconclusive. Different persons or courts may perceive the difficulty in different ways. For

example, courts have split on whether a backyard storage building is a fixture or not.

The relationship to real property. Sometimes even an item which could be removed without great damage is a fixture. These items are ones generally regarded as fixtures because they are integral or specially adapted to the property. For example, a built-in dishwasher, custom draperies which match the wallpaper in a room, and wall-to-wall carpeting sometimes fall into this category.

The relationship between the parties. The relationship between the parties often has an effect on a court's determination. Generally, the law tends to favor tenants over landlords, purchasers over sellers, and mortgagees over mortgagors.

Where a commercial lease or a lease for business purposes is involved, the courts are more likely to find that personalty used by tenants in their businesses, *trade fixtures,* are present. Generally, a tenant may remove trade fixtures, but the tenant must compensate the landlord for any damages resulting from their removal. A tenant may not remove trade fixtures if their removal would cause permanent structural damage. If a market's meat coolers could be moved only by knocking a hole in the outside wall, a court will not permit their removal unless the tenant repairs the damage.

The next case discusses the three tests for determining the character of a rather unique piece of property.

Specialty Restaurants Corp. v. County of Los Angeles

136 Cal. Rptr. 904 (1977)

FACTS   The ship the *Queen Mary* was leased to the Specialty Restaurants Corp. and the PSA Hotels, Inc., by the city of Long Beach. The *Queen Mary* was in an immobilized position alongside the docks in Long Beach's harbor. The County of Los Angeles assessed Specialty's and PSA's leasehold interests as interests in real property and levied real property taxes. Specialty and PSA protested the tax, arguing that the *Queen Mary* was personalty and therefore not subject to taxation. They prevailed in an appeal to the Assessment Appeal Board, but lost when the County appealed to the trial court.

ISSUE

Was the *Queen Mary* real property subject to taxation?

DECISION

Yes. Affirmed. In determining whether an object is real or personal property a three-part test is applied: (1) the manner of annexation; (2) the object's adaptability or relationship to the use and design for which the realty is employed; and (3) the intent of the party or parties making the annexation. The *Queen Mary* was annexed at great expense to the pier. Detaching it would have caused material damage to the ship, since the ship was annexed to land with steel mooring lines and an extensive gangway structure. In terms of the second test, the ship became an integral part of the land situated next to it with the development of paving, lights, strips, and landscaping, as well as access facilities. Thus, in light of all the above appearances, it is clear that the ship was intended by its owners to be permanent.

CONCLUSION

The examination of how persons acquire title to personalty began in Part II, Contracts, and continued in Part IV, Business Organizations. There the focus was on transfers by contract. This chapter and Chapter 29, Wills, Estates, and Trusts, fill in more of the picture. Purchase, creation, possession, gift, and inheritance are the five ways in which title to personal property is acquired.

Fixtures mark the border between personal property and real property. They are tangible personal property which has been incorporated into realty. An intangible fixture is as inconceivable as intangible real property. Chapter 26 describes how one acquires title to real property and, therefore, fixtures.

Acquiring title to property—whether personal or real—does not necessarily bring with it the right to use or consume it. In fact, there are a number of ways a person can have rightful possession of property and not have title. The most obvious of these is a lease. The next chapter explores another major form of possession without ownership: the bailment. As you study it, keep in mind that except in some very limited circumstances, rightful possession of property without ownership is a matter of contract.

A NOTE TO FUTURE CPA CANDIDATES

Since 1994, the CPA exam has returned to testing the types of personal property ownership. You should fully understand how personal property can be acquired, especially by gifts. You should also be able to clearly recognize and distinguish situations involving personal versus real property, especially fixtures.

Fixtures are items originally of personal property which have become so attached to real property that they are considered part of it. For example, wallpaper on the walls or bricks in a fireplace are clearly fixtures. Many other items commonly found in a home are not as obvious, such as a ceiling fan or a porch swing. The primary test is the manner of attachment. The more difficult it is to remove an item or the greater the probability of damage due to removal, the more likely a court is to find the item is a fixture.

The exam frequently has required candidates to resolve issues involving trade fixtures, a fixture installed by a tenant in connection with a business on leased premises. The presumption is that the tenant may remove a trade fixture unless the removal would cause substantial damage. If so, it is considered to have become part of the real property. To illustrate, a convenience store owner would most likely be able to remove cooler equipment, but a bank may be unable to remove a large, heavy security vault.

There are other areas on the exam which focus on specific personal property applications. These include:

- Contracts for the sale of goods, tangible personal property (involving Article 2 of the Uniform Commercial Code).
- Contracts for the sale of intangible personal property (involving common law contracts).
- The transfer of commercial paper, documents of title, and investment securities (involving Articles 3, 4, 7, and 8 of the UCC).
- The sale of securities (involving the Securities and Exchange Commission and state laws).
- A borrower giving a security interest in personal property to a creditor (involving Article 9 of the UCC).

KEY WORDS

abandonment (570)
accession (577)
capacity (573)
confusion (577)
conversion (576)
copyright (563)
delivery (574)
donative intent (573)
donee (572)
donor (572)

fixtures (578)
gifts causa mortis (575)
gifts inter vivos (574)
infringement (569)
lost property (571)
mislaid property (572)
patent (563)
personalty (560)
title (560)

DISCUSSION QUESTIONS

1. Give five examples of how title to personal property may be acquired.
2. What is the purpose of a patent? What are the basic requirements for being granted a patent by the federal government?
3. Coca-Cola has never patented its basic for-

mula. What business reasons could the company have for that decision?
4. What is the purpose of a copyright? What are the basic requirements for being granted a copyright by the federal government?
5. What is meant by "fair usage"? How does this apply to copyrights?
6. What rights does a person holding a patent or copyright have?
7. Contrast the rights of the finder of abandoned, lost, and mislaid property.
8. What are the basic requirements for a valid gift? If a valid gift is completed, can the donor later revoke the gift?
9. What is required to make a valid gift causa mortis?
10. How do courts determine whether or not an item of property is a fixture?
11. Why might a court be asked to determine whether something is or was a fixture?

CASE PROBLEMS

1. Professor Smart, an auditing professor, decided that the figures in the "Legal Liabilities of Accountants" chapter of *Law and Business* would be excellent for classroom discussion. Without securing approval from McGraw-Hill Book Company, Smart made and distributed copies of the material to each of his students. The figures proved to be so valuable to classroom discussion that he has continued to do so each semester, still without approval. Assuming McGraw-Hill has learned of Smart's practice, would Smart have any potential liability? Explain.
2. Sally Lenz purchased a state lottery ticket. When the week's winning number was aired over television, Sally misheard the number and thought that she had lost. She threw the ticket into her trash, which was latter picked up by the city refuse truck. The next week Sally realized that she had had the winning number. Sally went to the city landfill and began looking for the lottery ticket. When a local radio station told her story, several persons went out to the landfill to try their luck at

finding the ticket. The ticket was found by Dave Schmidt. Sally claims that Schmidt must turn the ticket over to her. Disregarding any property rights in the ticket which the landfill may have, is Sally likely to prevail? Explain.

3. John told his sister, Marlo, that he wanted a portrait of her which hung in her hallway. Marlo responded, "I'll give it to you if I move to New York next year." Marlo did move to New York but died in an automobile accident. John claims that the portrait belongs to him even though Marlo failed to give it to him before she moved. Marlo's personal representative has rejected John's claim because there was not a completed gift. What is your decision? Explain.

4. Wilbur told his nephew, Horace, "If I should die as a result of my cancer operation, I want you to have my old Packard, which you've always cherished." Horace told his uncle that he was quite pleased with his generosity and would love to have the car but that it would not matter as "the operation will go just fine." On the way to the hospital, Wilbur was killed in an automobile accident. Horace subsequently claimed the Packard. Will Horace prevail? Explain.

5. Robert was an avid believer in astrology. His astrologist told him that he should part with his personal belongings, as a great personal catastrophe was likely to occur to him within the month. Extremely concerned with this news, Robert began giving away his personal belongings, including his Elvis Presley music collection to Woody. Woody had initially resisted taking the collection, telling Robert it was stupid for him to part with his belongings on the advice of an astrologer. When Robert convinced him that he was going to give the collection to someone, if not Woody, Woody accepted. Two weeks later, Robert called Woody, told him his astrologer had been mistaken, and asked for the return of his Elvis collection. Woody refused. What would be Robert's best legal position in trying to regain the collection? Would a court likely order Woody to return the collection? Explain.

6. Wilmont owned a tract of waterfront property on Big Lake. While Wilmont owned the land, his tenants built several frame bungalows on it. In addition to paying rent, the tenants paid for the maintenance and insurance on the bungalows and repaired, altered, and sold them without permission or hindrance from Wilmont. The bungalows rested on surface cinder blocks and were not bolted to the ground. The building could be removed without injury to either the buildings or the land. Wilmont sold the land to Marsh. The deed to Marsh stated that Wilmont sold the land, with buildings thereon, "subject to the rights of tenants, if any." When the tenants attempted to remove the bungalows, Marsh claimed them. What factors should a court consider in resolving this dispute? How would you rule? Explain.

7. Aerobics Plus Health Club offers aerobic dance classes throughout the day. All classes begin with the club's theme song, "Trying to Win," written and sung by Carla Mathews. The club's classes are conducted to popular music by Carla and other rock musicians. Carla's agent has notified Aerobics Plus that they must either stop using Carla's music for their classes or begin to pay a small royalty fee for each time it uses one of Carla's songs. The club management believes that they are under no obligation to do so. Under what basis is Carla asserting the right to royalty payments? Explain.

8. Robin Ragan designed and secured a patent on a new process for cleaning crayfish. Without knowledge of Ragan's work or patent, Naquin Seafood, Inc. developed a similar cleaning process. Naquin Seafood spent a substantial amount of money converting its processing lines to the new technology and began a large media campaign emphasizing their new process. Ragan spotted one of the advertisements and had her attorney notify Naquin Seafood that they should either cease using the new process or secure permission and begin making royalty payments to Ragan. Given the facts above, is Ragan's demand justified under the law? Explain.

9. Mary Smith was shopping at Sawyer's Department Store. She went to the customer ser-

vice counter to make a payment on her credit card. As she left the area, she inadvertently left a package there. Another customer, Ben Parsons, found the package. Ben asked if anyone there had lost the package and no one claimed it. Ben looked inside the package, saw it contained two Willie Nelson compact diskettes, and said, "Looks like I've got myself some Willie music." The area manager disagreed and had a store security person take the package from Ben. Does Ben most likely have a right to the package? Explain.

10. Real Issues. Tabloid newspapers and personality magazines, ranging from the *National Enquirer* to *People Magazine,* seem fixated on covering the activities of Princess Diana. Circulation studies have proved that who or what is on the cover can have a significant impact on the sales of a particular issue, especially a cover that shows Princess Diana doing something like romping in the waters in a bathing suit. So long as there is no invasion of Princess Diana's privacy, discussed in Chapter 4, there is generally nothing she can do to prevent the appearance of such covers or to receive income for the covers. In contrast, if a company sought to use a picture of Princess Diana to help sell the company's bathroom products, for example, this activity could be stopped as an improper commercial exploitation. From an ethical or legal perspective, do you believe public figures should have the right to be able to control the usage of their picture or likeness in the media? Explain.

Bailments

CHAPTER 26

At one time or another, you have probably parked your car in a parking lot and left the key with the attendant, or you have left your stereo at a shop to be repaired, or you have loaned a radio to a friend. In each instance you entered into a legal relationship, called a *bailment*, based on the other party's responsibility for your property. This chapter examines the various types of bailments.

Bailments are quite common in business. Farmers often store grain in elevators; clothing stores deposit out-of-season merchandise in commercial warehouses; and manufacturers often ship equipment back to vendors for repair.

THE ELEMENTS

A *bailment* is a contract for the temporary transfer of possession of personal property from one person (the *bailor*) to another (the *bailee*) for the accomplishment of some purpose.

In a bailment, the transfer never grants title to the bailee. After the bailment's purpose is accomplished, the bailee has a legal duty to return the personalty to the bailor, to deliver it to the bailor's assignee, or to dispose of it in accordance with the bailor's instructions. Suppose Trudy leaves her black raincoat at Sparkle White Cleaners for dry cleaning. Trudy is the bailor, and the cleaner is the bailee. The bailee's duty is to return Trudy's cleaned coat. If her coat comes back zebra-striped, Sparkle White has breached its bailment contract.

Classification of Bailments

The scope of the duties a bailee owes to a bailor depends on how a bailment is classified. Bailments are classified first by whether they provide for compensation. The law terms those which do, such as equipment rentals, *bailments for hire*. Those which do not are called *gratuitous bailments*. Generally, compensated bailees owe a greater duty to the bailor than do uncompensated bailees. If Helen pays a furrier to store her fur coat during the summer, the furrier will owe her a greater duty of care than will Helen's next-door neighbor who agrees to keep the coat while Helen moves.

To this point, only ordinary bailments have been described. By contrast, *special bailments* generally are those in which the law imposes greater-than-normal duties on the bailee. This chapter discusses one type of special bailment, that involving hotelkeepers. Chapter 39 examines another type: warehousing under Article 8 of the Uniform Commercial Code (UCC).

Obligation to Return or Dispose

The fact that the bailee must either return the bailed property to the bailor or dispose of it in the manner the bailee specified, as the following case indicates, distinguishes a bailment from a sale.

H. S. Crocker Co., Inc. v. McFaddin

148 Cal. App. 2d 187, 112 P.2d 36 (1957)

FACTS H. S. Crocker Co., Inc., manufactured Christmas cards. Each January from 1952 through 1955, it took hundreds of thousands of unsold cards to City Dump & Salvage, Inc. Normally, after a driver dumped refuse, the employees of City Dump began salvaging any usable material for resale. A bulldozer operator covered what remained. For an additional fee, however, City Dump would dig a hole for refuse, deposit it there without any salvaging, and cover it. Crocker never requested this service. In January 1955, City Dump salvaged 220,000 Crocker cards and sold them to McFaddin for $25. Crocker sued McFaddin, seeking either the cards' return or their value, $8830. The trial court found for Crocker.

ISSUE

Did Crocker sell the cards to City Dump?

DECISION

Yes. Reversed. A transaction is a sale, not a bailment, and title to the property changes when the receiving party is under no obligation to return the property or account for it. In a sale, the transfer is absolute. Since Crocker and City Dump made no express agreement as to the cards' disposal, the nature of the obligation of City Dump holds the key. City Dump offered Crocker a choice. Crocker chose not to specify the dump's disposal method, thereby giving up all its rights to the cards. So McFaddin acquired title to the cards from City Dump.

In contrast to the situation in *Crocker*, bailors often deposit goods with a bailee intending ultimately—but not immediately—to pass title to a third party. For example, bailors may employ *factors*, bailees who take possession of goods from bailors for the purpose of selling them, for a commission. If, for instance, Leonard was selling a painting through an auction house, he might leave it with the auctioneer for display several weeks in advance.

The one exception to the bailee's duty to return or dispose of the same good the bailor deposited relates to *fungibles*, goods which are so similar that they are interchangeable. With fungibles, the bailee may return goods of the same type, grade, and quality as those bailed. Thus, the owner of a grain elevator may return wheat grown by someone else to a bailor.

Possession and Control

The important characteristic which all bailments have in common is that the bailee intends to take possession and control of the particular personalty. If the alleged bailee did not intend to take possession and control, there is no bailment even though the property is committed to another's possession. Without the intention to take possession and control, the possessor of the property does not have the duties of a bailee.

Bailees must actually receive the bailed property and accept possession of it. Thus, bailees must know they have the property and willingly accept responsibility for it. This rule protects bailees by limiting the property for which they are responsible. The owner of bus station lockers, for instance, rents storage space. The operator has no way of knowing what customers will put in it; they pay the same price whether they leave yesterday's newspaper or a rare book. In neither case is the locker owner a bailee. Similarly, if an establishment supplies its patrons with an unattended coatrack, the establishment is probably not a bailee. But as the next case shows, this rule has exceptions.

Laval v. Leopold

47 Misc. 2d 624, 262 N.Y.S.2d 820 (N.Y. Civ. Ct. 1965)

FACTS

Leopold practiced psychiatry in an office with two associates. No receptionist or other employee attended the office. Laval was Leopold's patient. On one of her visits to his office, in accordance with her usual practice, she put her fur coat in a clothes closet in the office reception room. At the end of her appointment, her coat was missing. She sued Leopold for the value of the coat.

ISSUE

Did Leopold have the duties of a bailee toward Laval?

DECISION

Yes. Judgment for Laval.

> *The maintenance of the closet in defendant's office created an implied invitation to plaintiff to deposit her coat there.*
>
> In Webster v. Lane *which involved the loss of a coat in a dentist's office, the court took judicial notice of the fact that patients of a dentist are not placed in a dental chair with their wraps on. This court likewise takes judicial notice that it is not the custom for a patient to lie on the couch or sit in the chair in a psychiatrist's office wrapped in her fur coat. . . .*
>
> *The defendant undertook voluntary custody of the coat as an accommodation to his patient and as part of the service for which he was being paid.*
>
> *Implicit in the relationship between the parties, the defendant became a bailee of plaintiff's coat, and it is for the trier of the facts to determine whether . . . reasonable care was exercised by the defendant with reference to plaintiff's coat. . . .*

Constructive bailments. Some bailments arise without the consent of the property owner. A *constructive bailment* occurs when the bailee takes possession of the article without the owner's knowledge and without intending to deprive the bailor of ownership. Found items fall into this category.

Container contents. A court will not hold bailees responsible for items they do not accept, but it will presume bailees know about items normally kept inside particular containers. Suppose you park in a garage where there is no notice that the garage's liability is limited. You turn your car and its keys over to an attendant, and that is the last you see of the car or its contents. The garage will be liable for the value of the spare tire in the trunk but not for your stamp collection, which you left in the glove compartment, because stamp collections are not normally kept in cars.

Termination

Action of the parties. If an agreement sets a specific period for the bailment, it terminates at the end of that time. If the agreement does not establish a term, mutual agreement or either party's demand ends the bailment.

Also, a material breach of the bailment agreement by either party terminates the bailment. If, for instance, Eva contracts with a garage to store her car during her vacation and one of the attendants takes it for a joyride, the garage has breached its duty.

Destruction of bailed property. When an *act of god* (e.g., fire, flood, or tornado), an act of a third party, or the nature or the bailed property (e.g., a perishable like fresh peaches) results in the property's destruction, the bailment terminates without liability to the bailee.

If, however, the bailee's negligence caused the destruction, the bailment technically does not end. For example, Hobbs stores 10,000 sheets of plywood in the Wood Products warehouse. An arsonist burns it down. If the Wood Products nightwatchman left the main gate open and went to sleep, technically the bailment relationship continues and Wood Products is liable. More is said about this below.

Operation of law. By law, bailments for hire and, sometimes, gratuitous bailments terminate on the death, insanity, or bankruptcy of the bailor or bailee. However, the parties may establish rights under their contract which would survive such events. For instance, the agreement of a typewriter leasing company may provide that in the event of the company's bankruptcy, the lessee-bailee may keep the machine until the lease's term expires.

THE BAILEE'S RIGHTS AND DUTIES
The Bailee's Rights

To possess. The bailee has a right to possess the property for the term of the bailment.

To use. The parties may spell out the bailee's right to use the bailed property in the bailment agreement. When Bill lends his car to Martina, he may say she can use it to go to the laundromat but not to visit her parents. In any event, her right to use it is far more limited than her right to use a car she rents. But whether she borrows or rents the car, her misuse or unauthorized use of it may result in liability for breaching the bailment agreement.

If the bailment agreement does not specify the uses to which the bailee may put the property, a court will consider the parties' intent, the nature of the property, and the type of bailment involved in determining permissible uses.

To insure. In a bailment for hire, the bailee has an *insurable interest*—a legal right or interest which is capable of being insured—in the use of the bailed property. In some instances, a bailment agreement may require that a bailee insure the property to protect the bailor against loss. In others, like the next case, the bailee should have insured the property.

Saf-T-Green of Atlanta, Inc. v. Lazenby Sprinkler Co., Inc.

169 Ga. App. 249, 312 S.E.2d 163 (1983)

FACTS On February 7, Saf-T-Green leased a scissors lift to Lazenby. The contract between the parties stated in part:

> You [Lazenby] agree that you shall be responsible from the time of the signing of this contract for all injury (including death) or damage to persons or property resulting from the use of [the] equipment. . . . You agree to hold [Saf-T-Green] harmless from loss for the value of any equipment rented . . . Which you do not return to this company for any reason whatsoever.

Shortly thereafter, the scissors lift was stolen from Lazenby's job site. Saf-T-Green brought suit for the value of the lift, but a jury found in favor of Lazenby.

ISSUE   Was Lazenby liable for the value of the lift?

DECISION   Yes. Reversed. In a bailment for the mutual benefit of the parties, the bailee is liable only for damages caused by its failure to exercise ordinary care. However, a contract which enlarges the bailee's responsibilities will be given effect. Here, the language of the contract was unequivocal in placing responsibility for the loss on Lazenby.

To receive compensation. The bailment agreement should specify the bailee's compensation and reimbursement of expenses. If the agreement does not mention them, a court must determine whether and in what amount the parties expected the bailee to be compensated.

To attach and sell bailed goods. Under the common law, persons who repair or enhance the value of goods may retain them until the bailor pays for them. Shoemakers, tailors, and many others enjoy this right, which is called an *artisan's lien*. Many states have extended this right well beyond its traditional limits. For instance, bailees for hire of motorcycles and airplanes now have the same rights as traditional artisans under New York law.

Most bailee's liens are *possessory liens*, which means they apply only so long as the bailee actually has the property. The bailee's possessory lien is superior to any other *security interest* in the property which arose before its lien. Suppose Bad Risk, Inc., stores its jet in a rented hangar at County Airport. When Bad Risk fails to pay the rent for 3 months, the airport can hold the plane.

If the airport allows the company to remove the plane, the airport loses its possessory lien, although it can sue Bad Risk for the money owed. Losing the lien can cost the airport a great deal. Suppose Bad Risk used a mortgage to finance the purchase of the plane. If the airport sold the jet to satisfy its lien, in many states its claim to the sale's proceeds would take precedence over the bank's claim.

Until very recently, statutes permitted bailees to sell bailed property with little or no no-

tice to the bailor and denied the bailor an opportunity to contest the lien's validity before the sale. The bailor's only choices were to pay the bailee or to watch the property be sold. After courts in California and New Jersey declared statutes of this type unconstitutional, amendments to several state statutes required notice of the sale to bailors and permitted bailors to prevent the sale and challenge the lien's validity by filing suit before the sale.

In our example, County Airport must try to notify Bad Risk of the coming sale. Usually, notice is by certified mail or by publication in a newspaper, or both. The airport's right to sell the plane will depend on its good faith effort to notify the bailor of the sale. If Bad Risk files suit before the sale and the court finds Bad Risk owes all or part of the lien's amount, the airport may go ahead with the sale. If the proceeds exceed the amount due the bailee, the excess goes to the bailor.

The Bailee's Duties

To perform. The bailee has an absolute duty to perform in accordance with the bailment agreement. Except under the most extreme circumstances, the law recognizes on excuses for nonperformance. For instance, a jeweler must repair your ring according to your instructions.

With respect to merchants, the UCC makes an exception to the rule that the bailee must return the bailed property to the bailor. If someone entrusts property to a merchant who deals in goods of that type, the merchant has the power to transfer all the entruster's rights to a buyer. That means a watchmaker can sell Bill's watch to a good faith buyer and Bill will not have any remedy against the buyer. His remedy is against the watchmaker [UCC §2-403(2)]. Entrustments are discussed in Chapter 32.

To repair. In the absence of an agreement as to who will repair bailed property, the general rule is that the bailee performs minor repairs, such as replacing the light bulb in a rented freezer, while the bailor handles major repairs, such as overhauling a cooling system. However, if the bailment is for the sole benefit of the bailee or bailor, the answer depends on the circumstances. Borrowing a neighbor's stereo for the day results in a lesser duty to repair than borrowing it for the summer.

To exercise reasonable care. Normally, a bailee does not act as an insurer of bailed goods. Rather, a bailee must exercise reasonable care toward them. Chapter 4 deals with this concept in detail. Reasonable care depends on the following:

- The nature and value of the bailed property
- The time and place of the bailment
- The special skills of the bailee
- The type of bailment involved

The kind of service offered and the type of equipment available to perform it will influence a court's determination as to what is reasonable care.

Tort Liability

Negligence. In a negligence action, the bailor must prove the bailee reached the duty of reasonable care toward the bailed property. However, if the bailee cannot return the goods or has returned them damaged, the bailor's proof of that fact establishes a *prima facie* case of negligence. In other words, if the bailee cannot introduce evidence to the contrary, the court will enter judgment for the bailor. Suppose Amy leaves her chairs with Seth for repair. When she picks them up, she discovers that they are broken in new places. If Amy proves

the existence of the new damage, Seth must establish his reasonable care toward the goods or be liable.

Conversion. The bailee's failure to deliver bailed goods may result in liability for the intentional tort of *conversion* if the bailee's actions in regard to the property are inconsistent with or deny the bailor's right to the property.

To rebut the bailor's case, the bailee has only to offer proof of what actually happened to the goods and need not show that she was free from fault. Once the bailee shows what happened to the goods, the burden of proving fault falls squarely on the bailor.

The last chapter showed that the plaintiff in a conversion action can elect one of two remedies. A court can either order the property returned or, in effect, order a forced sale. Both remedies presume the converted property remains in existence. In the next case, the property had disappeared, and the court had to decide whether the plaintiff could state a cause of action in conversion.

Limitation of liability. It is not unusual for a bailee to limit liability for items bailed to them. For a limitation of liability to be effective, the bailee must be able to prove that the bailor knew or had reason to know of the limitation of liability. Common forms of notifying the bailor of limitations in liability include warnings on a claim receipt ticket and/or prominent signs at the time and place that bailed property is surrendered to the bailee.

Limitations of liability are effective only as to general negligence. Such limitations generally are not effective where the bailee acts with wilful or gross negligence or intentionally acts to injure the bailed property. The various forms of negligence are discussed in Chapter 4. An example of gross negligence would be when an employee at a parking garage takes the keys and the car from the bailor and then leaves the car unlocked, keys inside the car, unguarded and adjacent to a busy sidewalk. The garage would have liability if the car was stolen.

I.C.C. Metals, Inc. v. Municipal Warehouse Co.

50 N.Y.2d 657, 431 N.Y.S.2d 372, 409 N.E.2d 849 (1980)

FACTS

In 1974, I.C.C. Metals, Inc., deposited with Municipal Warehouse three lots of indium valued at a total of $100,000. The receipt stated that Municipal's liability was limited to $50 per lot. A year and a half later, Metals requested one of the lots, but Municipal could not produce any of the indium. Municipal claimed someone stole it, but offered no proof. I.C.C. sued Municipal, alleging conversion. The trial court found Municipal liable for the full value of the three lots of indium.

ISSUE

Did I.C.C. establish a cause of action in conversion?

DECISION

Yes. Affirmed. A warehouse which fails to redeliver goods to the person entitled to their return upon a proper demand may be liable for either conversion or negligence, depending on the circumstances. Conversion, but not negligence, voids the contractual limitation on liability, since enforcing it would reward a misdeed. Since the bailee has sole control of the warehouse, the bailee is in the best position to explain the loss of, or damage to, the property. A bailee cannot avoid liability for negligence by pleading ignorance. In a conversion action, to allow a warehouse to offer no proof of what happened to the property while asserting the protection of a contractual limit on liability would encourage dishonesty.

THE BAILOR'S RIGHTS AND DUTIES

In most bailments, the bailor's rights and duties are the converse of those of the bailee. Many of them have been discussed above, but a few others merit further discussion.

The Bailor's Right to Compensation

The bailor has a right to compensation if the parties so agreed or if a court implies that it is due. If a restaurant asks its beer distributor for a keg tapper which it rented in the past, a court may hold that even if the parties did not agree on compensation, the distributor is entitled to its usual fee.

A bailor loses the right to compensation if the bailment terminates because of the bailor's negligence or if the goods are stolen or destroyed other than as a result of the bailee's negligence. The bailor's failure to make necessary repairs may suspend the right to compensation during the period when the bailee cannot use the goods.

The Bailor's Duties

To furnish in reasonable condition. The bailor must furnish the bailed goods in reasonable condition. What "reasonable" means may depend on whether the bailment is gratuitous or for hire. If the bailment is for the sole benefit of the bailee, the obligation is somewhat less than it would be if the bailment was for the sole benefit of the bailor or was a mutual benefit bailment. If you borrow a car from a friend one day in order to get to work, the bailment is gratuitous and solely for your benefit. For that reason, the car's reasonable condition is "as is" unless it has some obviously dangerous defect. But if you rent a car, you have every right to expect it to run well.

To inform. The bailor has a duty to protect the bailee from defects in the property. If Charlie knows Amy will use his extension ladder to reach her roof, he will be liable for any injuries that she suffers when the ladder collapses if he failed to warn her about its weak brace.

The bailor's obligation goes beyond reporting any known defects. The bailor must examine goods for defects, especially if the bailor knows great harm could result from their use. The type of bailment—gratuitous or for hire—will affect a court's determination of the kind of inspection a bailor must make.

Where the bailor's special expertise would reveal a defect which the bailee would lack the ability to recognize, the bailor must check the property to be bailed. A company renting a backhoe to a contractor must inspect it to ensure, for example, that its stabilizers work. However, the equipment bailor is not liable in every instance for injuries caused by the failure of its equipment. If the backhoe proves unstable and the contractor continues to use it, a court may find the contractor *contributorily negligent* and limit or deny recovery. In other situations, the court may find the bailee *assumed the risk* of using the equipment in its hazardous condition and may deny recovery.

The Bailor's Liability

Injuries to bailees. The bailor must exercise reasonable care to protect the bailee. Otherwise, the bailor will be liable for the bailee's injuries.

Various types of equipment leases have been mentioned in this chapter. With the rapid growth of this type of business has come a relatively new theory for imposing liability on bailors. Courts now imply a *warranty*, or guarantee, by the bailor that the equipment is fit for its intended use for the duration of the bailment. Suppose Roller, Inc., rents one of its steamrollers to Pavement Co. The brakes fail, causing the steamroller to crash into Pavement's grader. Pavement will recover because Roller's business is renting machinery and it should have foreseen Pavement would rely on it to have the steamroller in safe working condition. However, the implied warranty of fitness may not extend to gratuitous bailments.

Injuries to third parties. The general rule is that the bailor is not liable for injuries to third parties caused by his bailed property. However, there are a number of exceptions to this rule:

1. *Liability to employees*: If Phil, Pavement's employee, was using the steamroller in the course of his employment, a court will hold Roller liable for Phil's injuries *if* Roller is liable to Pavement. This rule is really an application of the law of agency, discussed in Chapter 15.
2. *Dangerous instrumentalities*: The bailor will be liable for injuries caused by his failure to exercise reasonable care in regard to dangerous instruments or substances in his charge. If the bailor entrusts nitroglycerine to a person with hiccups, the bailor will be liable to any third parties the bailee may injure. The lack of care lies in entrusting the bailee with the dangerous instrumentality.
3. *Injuries for which the bailor would be liable if suffered by the bailee*: The bailor will be liable for injuries suffered by a third party if the bailor would have been liable had the bailee suffered the injuries. Suppose Rent-a-Lemon leases a car to Felix. Because of Rent-a-Lemon's negligence, the front wheels come off and the car crashes into a wall, seriously injuring Felix's passenger. Rent-a-Lemon will be liable for the passenger's injuries.
4. *Statutorily imposed liability*: Many states have enacted statutes imposing liability on bailors in circumstances where bailors would not have been liable under the common law. One common statute holds the owner of a car liable for death or injuries caused by a bailee's negligent operation. The purpose of this statute and others like it is to

provide a solvent defendant from whom the injured party may recover. Some states have accomplished this result by judicial decision.

A rather bizarre twist on the issue of bailor liability to third parties was raised in 1993 after the imprisonment and death of Exxon Corp. executive Sidney Reso and the bombing of the World Trade Center. In both situations, self-storage facilities were used. Legal observers generally feel that there would be no liability unless the owner of the facility had some knowledge of what was occurring.

HOTELKEEPERS

The term "hotelkeepers" includes anyone who provides lodging for compensation to guests as a regular business. A *guest* is a transient member of the public and, by definition, is not a permanent lodger. The bailment aspect of the hotelkeeper-guest relationship relates to the guest's belongings.

Hotelkeeper-Guest Relationship

The hotelkeeper-guest relationship begins when the hotel receives the guest, normally when the guest checks in. The relationship ends when the guest either leaves or ceases being a transient by making the hotel his permanent residence.

Duties to guests and their property. At common law, a hotelkeeper acted as a virtual insurer of a guest's property. In other words, the hotelkeeper was absolutely liable for the loss.

Almost all states have changed this rule by statute. One common statute eliminates a hotelkeeper's liability for the loss of valuables, like jewelry or money, if she provides a safe to put them in and the guest does not use it. However, regardless of the value of the guest's property placed in the safe, the hotelkeeper's liability is often limited to $500 or less, unless the guest declares a greater value before turning his property over for safekeeping. And the hotelkeeper must agree in writing to store such goods. Statutes often limit liability for a guest's baggage and clothing to $500, too.

In general, both courts and legislatures regard with disfavor bailee's attempts to exempt themselves totally from liability. However, the courts do enforce statutory limitations on liability even though the amount of the loss often exceeds the possible compensation. As the following case indicates, however, courts have refused to expand the scope of statutory limitations.

Ross v. Kirkeby Hotels, Inc.

8 Misc. 2d 750, 160 N.Y.S.2d 970 (N.Y. Civ. Ct. 1957)

FACTS   The plaintiffs were to be married at the [Hotel] Warwick. . . . The husband, accompanied by his brother, arrived at the hotel in his car the morning of his wedding day.
[T]he car was placed in the care of the hotel doorman, with specific instructions to park it in the hotel garage . . . ; the doorman undertook to do so, and told the plaintiff husband to leave the keys in the ignition switch. . . . Later . . . , when the husband came . . . to arrange for the delivery of his car, he found it in the street and discovered that it had been broken into and that all its contents were missing. The doorman admitted that he had not placed the car in a garage, but had parked it across the street from the hotel.

[T]he plaintiffs did not register as guests of the hotel, . . . no room was assigned to them, and . . . the sole purpose of their visit was to participate in the wedding ceremony and reception.

The newlyweds sued the hotel for the value of the car's contents. The hotel claimed its liability was limited to the $500 statutory maximum.

ISSUE   Were the newlyweds "guests" to whom the statutory limitation on liability applied?

DECISION   No. Judgment for the plaintiffs.

The defendant urges, however, that the bailment was an incident of the relation of hotelkeeper and guest between it and the plaintiffs and that, because of this relation, it is entitled to the limitation of liability prescribed by section 201 of the General Business Law. This section provides:

"No hotel keeper . . . shall be liable for damage to or loss of wearing apparel or other personal property in the room or rooms assigned to a guest for any sum exceeding the sum of five hundred dollars, unless it shall appear that such loss occurred through the fault or negligence of such keeper. . . . "

. . . Section 201 refers . . . to "the room or rooms assigned" to the guest. Thus, the assignment of a room to be occupied is stressed as an element of the relation. . . .

This vital element of the relation is totally absent. . . . Their presence in the hotel for a purpose other than that of becoming guests did not make them guests. . . It follows that the defendant is not entitled to the benefit of the limitation of liability. . . .

Goods entrusted to third parties. If a hotelkeeper entrusts a guest's property to a third party, the hotelkeeper remains liable for loss or damage. If the guest knows the hotel has used a third party, the hotelkeeper's liability extends only to her negligence in choosing the third party. If, however, the guest does not know, then the hotelkeeper functions as an insurer.

In one case, Davidson registered at a hotel and asked the hotel porter to arrange to have her baggage picked up. The porter gave her ticket to a trunkman he knew, but after the trunkman retrieved her bag, someone stole it from him. Davidson sued the hotel and won because once she gave the ticket to the porter, the hotelkeeper had the duty to obtain her luggage; therefore, the hotelkeeper was liable.

Hotelkeeper's Lien

If a guest fails to pay his or her bill, hotelkeepers have a possessory lien on a guest's property. The rules which apply to hotelkeeper's liens are essentially the same as those which apply to the possessory liens described above.

CONCLUSION

Bailments are among the most common contractual arrangements relating to personal property. Lending goods, leaving goods for repair, renting goods—the list of bailments is nearly endless. As Figure 26-1 shows, these arrangements always have two parties and their subject

TYPE	POSSESSOR'S STANDARD OF CARE	EXAMPLE*
GRATUITOUS BAILMENTS		
Bailor's sole benefit:		
• Gratuitous storage	Slight care	E allows R to store her bike in E's garage.
• Gratuitous carriage	Slight care	E moves R's furniture in E's van.
• Storage for gratuitous service	Slight care	E offers to fix R's radio if she will leave it with him.
Bailee's sole benefit:		
• Gratuitous loan	Great care	R lends his calculator to E.
MUTUAL-BENEFIT BAILMENTS		
Ordinary bailments for hire:		
• Compensated storage	Reasonable care	R stores her plutonium inventory in a warehouse.
• Storage for service	Reasonable care	R leaves his suit at the dry cleaners to be cleaned.
• Hired use of a thing	Reasonable care	E rents a snow blower from an equipment leasing company.
• Pawn or pledge	Reasonable care	R leaves his stereo with a pawnbroker to secure a loan.
Special bailments:		
• Innkeepers as bailees	Insurer/ reasonable care	R, a hotel guest, leaves her sample case in the hotel safe.
• Common carriers as bailees (Chap. 39)	Insurer/ reasonable care	R ships his dog via E railroad.

Remember: You can only bail *personal* property.

*E = bailee; R = bailor.

Figure 26.1 A Classification of Bailments.

matter is always personalty. And one party or both benefits from the relationship.

A NOTE TO FUTURE CPA CANDIDATES

Since 1994, the CPA exam has returned to testing bailments. Figure 26.1 should be fully understood. In addition, situations involving documents of title, warehouse receipts, and bills of lading, covered in Chapter 38, should possibly be expected in this area of the exam.

KEY WORDS

act of God (588)   factor (586)
artisan's lien (589)   fungible (586)
bailee (585)   gratuitous bailment (585)
bailment (585)   guest (593)
bailment for hire (585)   hotelkeeper (593)
bailor (585)   possessory lien (589)
conversion (590)

DISCUSSION QUESTIONS

1. How is a bailment different from a sale?
2. What types of property may be bailed? What types of bailments are there?
3. What rights does a bailee have, if any, to use your property? What protections do you have against unauthorized use?
4. How does a mutual benefit bailment differ from a gratuitous bailment? From a bailment for hire?
5. What is an artisan's lien? Who may use it?
6. Explain how the warranty of fitness for an intended use applies in a bailment situation. Is this a common law warranty?
7. What is the difference between an action for conversion and one for negligence? Which provides a better opportunity for full recovery against a warehouse?
8. What public policy reasons might make courts and legislators reluctant to extend limited liability protection for bailees?

9. If a hotelkeeper seizes your luggage because you have not paid your bill, what are your rights?

CASE PROBLEMS

1. The Satterthwaites operated the Crystal Palace Barber & Beauty Shop. It consisted of three rooms: the back room, which was the barber shop; the middle room, which was the beauty shop; and the front room, which was the waiting room. There was no attendant in the waiting room, and people in the middle room could not see into it. A sign prominently posted in the waiting room stated, "Not responsible for hats, coats and purses." On a previous visit, Mae Theobold, a regular customer, had asked if her coat was safe in the waiting room. She was assured it was. One December day, she left her fur coat in the waiting room while she had her hair done. It was stolen and not recovered. Are the Satterthwaites liable for the value of her coat? Explain.
2. On a Friday, Feuer left some leather skins with Kilmer for curing. The following Sunday night, a fire broke out at Kilmer's plant which damaged the skins. Kilmer's watchman had checked the premises on Saturday and found nothing out of order, but when the firefighters arrived they found the door to the building unlocked. Kilmer's son was the last to leave the building before the fire. That is the evidence Feuer presented to the court. Is it sufficient to establish liability? Explain.
3. On Friday, the Modells arrived at the Concord Hotel. At check in, Mrs. Modell deposited her jewels in the hotel vault. On Saturday evening, she retrieved them and wore them to the hotel's nightclub. After midnight, she went back to the hotel desk to have the jewels returned to the vault, only to be informed the vault would not be open again until 8 A.M. That night, the jewels were stolen from her room. Will the state statute limiting the hotel's liability determine whether Mrs. Modell recovers the full value of her jewels? Explain.
4. Don Wells was transferred to Virginia. Wells

asked his friend, Mark, if he might store his antique car in Mark's garage. Mark agreed. Mark also volunteered to run the car from time to time. Wells thanked Mark but asked him to be sure not to drive the car out of the driveway. Mark agreed. However, one day Mark drove the car around the block to try to determine whether a noise might be a serious problem. While he was doing so an uninsured motorist struck the car. Mark claims that as a gratuitous bailee he is free from any possible liability for damages to the car. True? Wells claims that Mark assumed liability for any damages to the car by his driving the car on the streets. Would a court be likely to agree? Explain.

5. Mah checked a bag on a Greyhound bus. She was given a claim check which stated on its front in bold letters, "Baggage Liability Limited to $50 (See Over)." On the back was language indicating Greyhound's limited liability unless the passenger declared a greater value in writing at the time of checking the bag and paid an additional fee. Mah did not read the ticket or the posters on the bus station walls notifying passengers of Greyhound's limited liability. Her bag and its contents, which she valued at $1000.55, were lost. Can she recover their full value? Explain.

6. Morse was a jewelry salesman. On leaving the Piedmont Hotel, where he was a guest, he gave his sample case to a bellboy to put on the airport bus. When Morse reached the airport, he discovered the case had been stolen. His company's insurer covered the loss, but the company fired Morse because the insurance company would not cover him any longer. No other company would insure him either, so no jewelry company would hire him, though he had been a salesman for 40 years. Morse claims the shock of not being able to work caused a heart attack, which, in turn, further prevented him from working. Can Morse recover from the hotel the $100,000 in earnings he claims to have lost? Explain.

7. Shelley Halvorson, of Chicago, was moving to Boston. Shelley did not have enough room to pack everything into the U-Haul truck she had rented, so she took a box of keepsakes over to the house of a friend, Susan Wolfe. Susan was gone for the weekend, so Shelley left the box with a note on Susan's back porch. Unfortunately, the wind blew the note away. Susan discovered the box containing what looked like junk. When no one claimed it within a couple of days, Susan threw the box into the trash. Two weeks later Susan received a letter from Shelley about the box. If Shelley now seeks to recover her losses from Susan, would Susan be found liable? Explain.

8. Joe Dickens asked a college roommate, Scott Humphrey, to keep his stereo system over the summer. Scott agreed. Joe told Scott that he could use the stereo, but Scott decided to use his own and simply store the one belonging to Joe. Toward the end of summer school another dormmate, Pat Almdale, asked to use Joe's stereo because his had broken. Scott agreed. Several nights later Joe's turntable was ruined when someone accidentally spilled Coke on it. When Joe learned this, he demanded a new turntable from Scott. Is Joe entitled to one? Explain.

9. Greg Backofen parks his Honda each work day at Britt's Garage. Greg drives into the garage, gets a claim ticket from an automatic machine, and parks the car himself. He keeps the keys and locks the car himself. A sign at the entrance to the garage warns against leaving valuables in sight inside the car while the car is parked. However, it does not indicate a limitation of liability by the garage. A thief has broken into Greg's Honda and taken eight CDs which had been sitting on the front seat of his car. The garage claims no bailment liability on grounds that Greg maintained custody of his car. Is the garage likely to be correct? Explain.

10. Kim Sexton parked her car at the attendant side of Britt's Garage. Kim left her keys and car with the attendant, Josh Fairbanks. Josh gave her a claim ticket with a limitation of liability clause and also directed her attention to an overhead sign which stated: "Britt's Garage Not Responsible for Losses or Damages to Cars or Possessions Left in Cars While

at Garage." After Kim had left, Josh eagerly jumped into Kim's new V-8 Mustang convertible, floored it as hard as he could, and aimed for the ramp. Unfortunately, he lost control, hit the ramp wall, and severely damaged Kim's car. Britt's Garage has refused to pay for the damages on grounds of their disclaimer for liability. They claim Kim's only recourse is to try to recover personally from Josh. Is the garage likely to be correct? Explain.

CHAPTER 27
Real Property

For hundreds of years, legal theorists have described property ownership in terms of a "bundle of rights." The allusion is to a bundle of sticks.

With *real property*, which is land and anything permanently attached to land, the bundle of rights is considerably larger than it is with personalty because a greater number of types of simultaneous ownership are possible for realty. Suppose Sandy owns a farm, Green Fields. She does not live on it or farm it. Figure 27.1 shows five possible interests Sandy could convey while retaining ownership herself. Even with these interests in existence, Sandy may sell her ownership interest to Robert, but he will take Green Fields subject to the five interests. For that reason, he may not take possession of the house until Daniel's lease runs out.

As a practical matter, real estate ownership is rarely sold without a few of the "sticks" missing. For example, ownership of a city lot often is subject to *easements*, rights of way through land for power, gas, water, and sewer lines. A prospective purchaser must consider the ownership interests which will not pass with the property and value the property accordingly. That does not mean, necessarily, its value is reduced. Many times, a parcel is worth less without utility easements, since the land-owner may bear the cost of extending the utility lines.

This chapter describes the types of interests in land and the methods of transferring those interests. In this chapter, the transfers are of ownership. In Chapter 28, the transfers are of the right to possess real property but not to own it. This chapter also examines public restrictions on the uses of land.

RIGHTS AND INTERESTS IN REAL PROPERTY

Your right—if any—to be where you are as you read this book is defined by your property interest in that place. If you are reading this in your house, you have an ownership interest in the house. If you are married and bought the property with your spouse, you have a joint ownership interest. If you are reading this in your apartment, you have a leasehold interest to be there. If you are reading this over lunch at Pizza Hut, you have a license to be there while you eat. But if you are reading this in the library after hours, you are a trespasser and have no right to be there. This section explores the full range of property interests, from ownership to trespass.

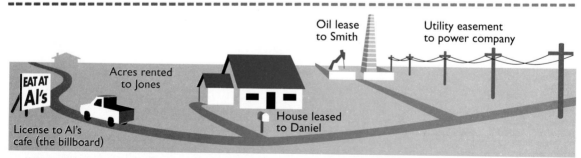

Figure 27.1 Multiple Property Interests in the Same Parcel of Land.

Fee Simple

A home buyer normally receives ownership in *fee simple*.* It is the greatest interest one can own on real property. Roughly, "fee simple" translates as "absolute ownership," or ownership of the full bundle of rights for that property. Transferring the ownership of real property generally means transferring the fee simple ownership. However, as a practical matter, very little real property is held in absolute ownership without a portion of the bundle of rights being held by someone else. For example, gas companies often have the right to bring their lines across land they do not own.

Adverse possession. Usually, an owner transfers a fee simple interest by sale or gift to the new owner. In rare instances, a person can acquire a fee simple interest in land by a process called *adverse possession*. Adverse possession occurs when someone

- Openly uses another's land
- In a manner contrary or adverse to the owner's interests
- Without the owner's permission or consent
- For a period prescribed by statute

The statutory period varies from 5 to 10 years, depending on the jurisdiction and the property involved.

The law does not favor adverse possession because it denies the right of the true owner. For that reason, courts tend to apply the requirements strictly. Suppose Tim and Teresa own adjacent parcels of land. Tim decides to put a fence along the property line. By mistake, he runs the fence 20 feet inside Teresa's proper-ty. If Teresa does nothing about it for the statutory period, Tim will own the strip of land. However, if Tim merely told people he owned the strip, without doing anything like erecting a shed on it or mowing it, his claim would not be adverse and open and a court would not uphold his claim. His use must make it apparent to Teresa if she inspects her land that he is claiming ownership.

Courts generally hold that where one enters property permissively, such as by originally renting the property, the person must disavow the title holder's ownership by unequivocal acts to begin adverse possession. The act of merely staying on after termination of a lease or after permission expires would generally not trigger adverse possession rights.

There is a growing debate as to whether a claim for adverse possession should or must begin in good faith. A court in the state of Georgia rejected an adverse possession claim because "to enter upon the land without any honest claim of right to do so is but a trespass and can never ripen into prescriptive title."* To date, this continues to be a minority position.

Forms of Multiple Ownership

Several persons may have interests in a single piece of property. Similarly, several people can share title to it. This is called multiple ownership.

The principal differences between the types of multiple ownership lie in the ability to convey the property interest or to direct its inheritance. However, in *all* instances discussed in this subsection, the law considers ownership to be of undivided interests. In other words, the owners together hold the whole bundle of rights. One does not own, for example, the subsurface mineral rights while another holds the surface rights. Still, the common owners together can sell these particular rights to other

---

* The word "fee" evidently comes from an Old English or French term meaning "property in cattle." During the early Middle Ages, cattle were the most important form of property. Later in the Middle Ages, "fee" came to mean "property interest in land," as land had replaced cattle in importance. The law has recognized various types of fees. A fee simple was and is essentially an unrestricted fee. For the most part, the other fees are of only historical interest.

* *Halpern v. Lacy Investment Corp.*, 379 S.E.2d 519 (Ga. 1989).

parties or to each other from their common bundle.

Tenancy in common. In a *tenancy in common*, the ownership interests may be unequal. Bill may own a one-third interest in the family farm, while Sarah owns two-thirds. At his death, Bill's interest passes to his heirs under either his will or the state's laws of *intestate succession*, laws designating heirs in the absence of a will. These laws are discussed in Chapter 29.

Each tenant in common has the right to use and possess the property. One tenant may not deny this right to another. Tenants in common may divide the property either by agreement or at the direction of a court. If a court divides the land, the division is called a *partition*.

Joint tenancy. In a *joint tenancy*, the ownership must be of equal and undivided interests. Joint tenancies are most commonly found where a husband and a wife own property together. If three persons own land as joint tenants, by definition each holds a one-third ownership interest.

Unlike the case in a tenancy in common, upon the death of a joint tenant, the surviving joint tenants automatically receive the decedent's interest. Suppose Herb and Virginia own property as joint tenants. Virginia's will states that her interests shall go to her daughter, Carol. If Virginia dies before Herb, the jointly held property will go to Herb regardless of Virginia's will. Likewise, if Herb should die first, the property goes to Virginia, who becomes the sole owner. If Virginia does not change her will, the property would pass on her death to Carol. The rights of use, possession, and termination are quite similar to those involved in a tenancy in common.

A joint tenant may convey his or her interest to a third party. The conveyance destroys the joint tenancy and creates a tenancy in common between the remaining joint tenant and the third party.

When it is not clear whether the parties intended a joint tenancy or a tenancy in common, a court will usually find a tenancy in common. This occurs quite often when courts must construe a will. Suppose Allen's will leaves his farm, Blackacre, to his daughters, Cathy and Paula. If Paula dies and leaves a child, the child will take Paula's share of Blackacre.

Tenancy by the entirety. *Tenancies by the entirety*, which are not recognized in some states, apply to property owned by a married couple only. They resemble joint tenancies except that neither spouse may convey an interest without the consent of the other. Upon the death of one, the property automatically passes to the other.

Figure 27.2 presents a comparison of tenancy in common, joint tenancy, and tenancy by entirety.

Community property. An increasing number of western and subwestern states have adopted *community property* as the standard governing property ownership between spouses. Under the community property concept, property acquired during marriage is presumed to be owned equally by the spouses. Any property owned by a spouse prior to marriage is that spouse's separate property. The wife, for instance, may later exchange her separate property for other property during marriage, but the new property remains separate and apart from the wife's community property or the husband's separate property. Suppose Norma purchased a summer home before she married Ken. The summer home or the proceeds from its sale will be considered Norma's separate property in a divorce settlement. The distinction can also be very important if Norma dies, since without a will her separate property generally would devolve, at least in part, to her children or other close heirs, while her community property would be inherited by Ken. Separate property also can be accumulated during marriage through an inheritance, as a gift to one

TYPE OF TENANCY	UNEQUAL OWNERSHIP INTERESTS?	UNDIVIDED INTERESTS?	RIGHT OF SURVIVOR-SHIP?	ASSIGNABLE INTERESTS?	TRANSFERABLE BY WILL?
Tenancy in common	Yes	Yes	No	Yes	Yes
Joint tenancy	No	Yes	Yes	Yes	No
Tenancy by the entirety	No	Yes	Yes	No	No

Figure 27.2 Comparison of Three Forms of Multiple Ownership.

of the spouses, or in a prenuptial contract in which both spouses agree that some or all property acquired during marriage will be separate.

After marriage, property acquired as a result of either spouse's efforts becomes community property. Regardless of who actually produced the money which bought it, the law considers the property to be owned equally. Suppose Norma earns $44,000 while Ken earns $20,000. Under the community property concept, each has a half interest in the $64,000 total.

The community property concept acknowledges contributions to marriage which are difficult to quantify. It was developed to protect the interests of a wife who stayed home to manage the house and family. Her contribution often made possible the success of the wage earner. Under the rules still in effect in the majority of states, these intangible contributions are greatly undervalued.

Life Estates

An owner of real property may grant an interest in it called a life estate. A *life estate* grants possession of real property for a period measured by the lifetime of either the recipient—the life tenant—or another person. At the end of the life measuring the estate's existence, possession reverts to the grantor of the life estate or to someone the grantor designated.

The interest in the property following expiration of the life estate is called the *remainder*. When former President Lyndon Johnson died, he left his wife a life estate in his ranch. Upon her death, the U.S. government will receive the ranch as a federal park site. Thus, the government has the remainder interest.

The holder of a remainder interest may transfer it. Thus, if the terms of President Johnson's will permitted it, the government could sell the remainder while Mrs. Johnson still lived.

A life tenant, too, may sell, lease, or give the life estate to another. However, regardless of how she transfers the life estate, the transferee's interest will not extend beyond the life measuring the estate. The principle is a familiar one: a possessor of property normally cannot transfer a greater interest than she herself has.

A life estate permits its holder to use and occupy the land. However, the life tenants may not commit *waste*, conduct which lessens the property's value. For example, a life tenant may grow and harvest crops, but she may not extract coal or oil. When nonrenewable resources are gone, the value of the remainder is reduced. A life tenant also commits waste if she fails to maintain the property she possesses.

An emerging trend in property law is the use of the trust as a replacement for the life estate. Trusts can be fashioned in a manner that makes them more efficient and adaptable to future events than life estates. For example, if Richard left property first to his wife Marilyn as the beneficiary of a trust instead of granting her a life estate, and then to his daughter Gretchen, as a remainder beneficiary, after Marilyn's death, Richard's trustee Barbara could oversee the property during Marilyn's lifetime according to Richard's wishes in the trust instrument. This might include the opportunity to sell the property even before Marilyn's death in order to take advantage of favorable market conditions. Trusts will be covered in more detail in Chapter 29.

Leaseholds

A *leasehold* comes into existence when the owner grants possession to another for a time. Chapter 28 discusses leaseholds.

Easements

An *easement* is a right to cross another's property. It can remain in effect either forever or for a period. When the owner of a fee simple interest grants an easement, she does not transfer either ownership or passive possession. The holder of an easement has a right to use the property which, often, is lost if not exercised. A utility easement, for instance, usually expires if the company does not use it. However, it is permanent if the company does.

Affirmative and negative easements. An *affirmative easement* is a right to do something with another's property. The most common examples involve rights of passage across property, whether by foot, boat, horse, car, or utility line. A *negative easement* is a right to restrict the use of the property in a particular fashion. For example, a solar easement may prevent a landowner from blocking the flow of natural light onto an adjacent parcel.

Creation of an easement. There are four ways to create an easement:

1. An *easement by grant* is one which is sold or given by itself. The granting of an easement to use a driveway would fall into this category.
2. An *easement by reservation* usually arises as part of the transfer of a fee simple interest. Here, the grantor subdivides a parcel of property, reserving at the time of sale a right of passage from the retained property across the sold parcel(s).
3. An *easement by necessity* occurs when someone divides property and sells a portion which lacks surface access. Without an easement, that portion would be landlocked. The transferor bears responsibility for access, since he divided the property. The owner of landlocked property may claim an easement by necessity only across the transferor's land, not across the land of anyone else. If the transferee's property becomes landlocked as a result of a natural occurrence, as when a river changes course, or because of the rerouting of a highway, she has no right to an easement by necessity over anyone's land.
4. An *easement by prescription*, or a *prescriptive easement*, arises—like adverse possession—from repeated, continuous, and open passage across land without the owner's consent. If Tina allows Mark to drive across her property to his, no prescriptive easement arises. Mark's crossing needs to be sufficiently open and notorious so that a prudent owner would know or be on notice of the continuous crossing.

The states differ on the amount of time required to establish a prescriptive easement. Occasional use or regular use broken by periods of nonuse will not suffice. But what if the use is continuous by successive owners of an adjacent parcel? That was the question in the following case.

Healy v. Roberts

109 Ill. App. 3d 577, 440 N.E.2d 647 (1982)

FACTS

The Healys and the Roberts lived on adjoining parcels. Their homes were two of ten built about 1900, all of which face south on Cottage Row. A gravel alley crosses the ten lots, beginning in the east at lot 1 and ending in the west at lot 10, where the Healys resided. The Healys purchased their home in 1970 from the Corleys, who had bought the house in 1951. The Corleys and the Healys used the alley continuously and without permission from the owners of lot 9. Before the Roberts bought the home on lot 9 in 1977, they told the Healys they intended to close the alley. However, they did not do so when the Healys objected. Sometimes, though, the Roberts blocked the alley with their cars or with piled snow. Once, they placed railroad ties across the alley. When the Healys sought to enjoin them from interfering with the use of the alley, the Roberts build a barricade across it. The trial court issued the injunction.

ISSUE

Did use of the alley by the Corleys and the Healys result in a prescriptive easement?

DECISION

Yes. Affirmed.

In order to acquire an easement by prescription, a claimant must show that the use of the land was adverse, exclusive, continuous and uninterrupted, and under [a] claim of right for a period of at least 20 years. . . . [Where] there has been privity between the users of the property, periods of use may be tacked together in order to satisfy the required prescription period. . . . [To establish a claim,] it is sufficient if the evidence shows that [the successive owners] acted in such a manner as to clearly indicate that they claimed the right to use the property and that its use was not a mere privilege or license. Further, to meet the requirements of adverse use, the use must be with the knowledge and acquiescence of the owner but without his permission. . . . Here the evidence showed that at least from 1951 to 1981, the Roberts or their predecessors in title knew that the Corleys and the Healys used the alley and acquiesced in that use, but never gave express permission.

Once established, a prescriptive easement may be lost if the holder affirmatively indicates an intent to abandon it. Nonuse alone is not sufficient. Suppose the facts in *Healy* showed that the Roberts erected a barricade across the alley as soon as they moved in and that the Healys did not object. If the barricade remained for a sufficient period, a court would hold the Healys had abandoned the easement.

Conservation easement A *conservation easement* occurs where a landowner donates certain rights on his property, such as the right to develop or mine the land, to a trust for perpetuity (forever). The landowner retains legal ownership to the land with all other bundles of rights, including the ability to sell it, bequeath it, or give it away. To illustrate, suppose John Austin owns 600 acres of undeveloped wetlands which are home to numerous birds and wildlife. Austin might be able to transfer his right to develop the land to a nature trust. Austin would gain an immediate, likely significant income tax deduction. His land would thereafter be reduced in value, which would likely reduce his current real estate taxes and, if later bequeathed, lower his estate taxes. Austin wins, and nature lovers win.

Licenses

A *license* is a temporary permission to use another's property for a limited purpose. Unlike an easement, a license is not an interest in land. Rather, it permits someone to use property without being a trespasser. A ticket to a football game is a license. A farmer who allows hunters on his land grants them a license. *Gratuitous licenses*—licenses granted without an exchange of consideration—are personal and may not be

assigned. The property owner can revoke one at any time.

Trespasses

Any use of another's land without consent is called a *trespass to property*.

As discussed in Chapter 4, a trespass is an *intentional tort*. In an action based on a trespass, the owner does not have to show actual injuries to obtain *nominal damages*—the necessary prerequisite to an award of *punitive damages*. The violation occurs when the trespasser intends to, and does, cross another's land, not when the trespasser intends to, and does, cross another's land without permission. Suppose Terry uses a boat launch he thinks he has permission to use. But, he mistakenly used the wrong one. He has committed a trespass. In the next case, the trespasser not only crossed a property line but also removed trees precious to their owner.

Roark v. Musgrave

41 Ill. App. 3d 1008, 355 N.E.2d 91 (1976)

FACTS   Roark bought 120 acres of rough, hilly land accessible only by horse or four-wheel-drive vehicle. He planned to build a retirement home there and to leave the rest of the land as it was. Musgrave was a logger and timber dealer. He cut Roark's fences and took down approximately 120 of Roark's trees, which he sold for lumber. Roark brought suit for damages to his property resulting from Musgrave's trespass. Musgrave argued that the amount should not include damage to the aesthetics of the property or any sums required to clean up the debris left by the logging operation. The trial court awarded damages to Roark representing the commercial price of the timber plus the loss of the aesthetic value of his property.

ISSUE   Should Roark's recovery have been limited to the trees' commercial value?

DECISION   No. Judgment affirmed. Trespass is a remedy designed to make the owner whole. An owner has a right to enjoy his property according to his own tastes and wishes. He has a right to hold it for his own use as well as to hold it for sale, and a court will calculate damages accordingly. In a case involving cutting down shade trees, for example, a court would not limit an owner to the value of the trees for lumber. Here, the trial court property awarded damages equaling the difference in value to Roark of his property before and after Musgrave's wrongful acts.

Two points need to be made about *Roark*. First, Roark's remedies were not limited to damages. He could have obtained an injunction forbidding Musgrave to cross his boundaries if he perceived a threat of continued violations. Second, the court did not calculate damages according to the land's potential resale value. It is important to keep in mind that courts can measure value in ways other than market value.

TRANSFER OF OWNERSHIP INTERESTS BY SALE

The majority of Americans buy or sell real property at least once during their lives. The usual steps in a transfer of ownership by sale are:

- The seller lists the property with a real estate broker.
- The broker locates a buyer who is ready, willing, and able to purchase.
- The buyer and seller sign a contract.
- The buyer obtains financing for the purchase.
- A lawyer performs a title search.
- The parties close the transaction, and the seller transfers the *deed*—the instrument conveying title—to the buyer.
- The buyer or the entity providing financing records the deed.

This section examines each of these steps.

The Role of the Real Estate Broker

The law does not require that a real estate broker or agent be involved in the transfer of real property. However, it is quite common for a prospective seller to hire one in order to find a ready, willing, and able buyer. The seller will owe the broker her commission when she locates the buyer, even if the buyer subsequently defaults.

In most cases, the broker does not have authority from the seller to sell the property or to make representations about it to potential buyers. The broker's role is to solicit offers. Buyers must keep the broker's role in mind, since courts almost universally have held that a broker's representations do not bind the seller and are not enforceable. See Chapter 13 and 14 for a discussion of the agency relationship.

The Real Estate Sales Contract

The real estate sales contract binds the parties to the terms of the sale. As this section demonstrates, the sales contract is *not* a contract to make a contract. The key preventive law principle here is that the sales contract should explicitly include all terms the parties have negotiated. No party who expects to negotiate further about a term should sign a real estate sales contract unless it explicitly reserves the matter for later resolution. Thus, both buyer and seller have good reason to have their attorneys examine the contract before they sign it.

Writing. The Statute of Frauds (discussed in Chapter 10) requires that a contract be in writing if its subject matter is the transfer of an interest in real property.

Real estate brokers often use standard form contracts for the sale of a home. They have a buyer sign it as an offer to the seller. Sometimes a buyer does not realize that if the seller accepts the form contract, it cannot be modified later without the seller's agreement. Since real estate sales contracts are written, a court will not admit *parol evidence* to show that the parties orally agreed to different terms.

The seller, too, must be careful. Because the law considers land to be unique, the buyer can obtain specific performance of a contract for the sale of an interest in land.

Terms. The sales contract should precisely describe the property's boundaries, the nature of the interest being conveyed, the disposition of the fixtures, and whatever warranties the seller makes as to the property's condition. Quite often, the contract will specify a *condition precedent*, such as the buyer's receiving financing on certain terms. Usually, a sales contract specifies the type of deed which the buyer will receive. The various types of deeds are discussed later in this chapter.

In addition to itemizing the fixtures that are included in the sale, the sales contract should specify the personalty that is to be sold with the house. Personal property that is not specified as accompanying the house may leave with the seller. For example, a fireplace mantel is a fixture and would be covered by a clause requiring the seller to leave all fixtures in place. The fireplace tools and the andirons are personalty, not covered by the fixtures clause. Preventive law principles would dictate a separately executed bill of sale for the personalty at the closing.

Marketable title. Even if it is not stated expressly, every real estate sales contract implies that the seller has a *marketable*, or *merchantable*, *title*, that is ownership which a reasonably prudent investor would accept. Suppose Sylvia signs a contract to buy a lot in fee simple from Stan. When her lawyer researches the title to the property, he discovers that Stan has only a life estate. Sylvia may void the contract and sue Stan for damages. The key to the concept of marketable, or merchantable, title lies in the seller's ability to transfer the ownership he or she has promised. That is the lesson of the next case.

Sinks v. Karleskint

130 Ill. App. 3d 527, 474 N.E.2d 767 (1985)

FACTS   In 1963, the Sinks purchased by an installment contract 40 acres of agricultural land. The contract required that the sellers, the Karleskints, supply a warranty deed and an abstract of title showing a merchantable title upon payment of the final installment in 1983.* Upon receipt of the abstract, the Sinks notified the Karleskints that it did not disclose a means of access to the land and that the surrounding landowners had denied them access since 1981. The Sinks demanded from the Karleskints an easement from some owner of the adjoining tracts, which the Karleskints did not supply. The Sinks elected to accept the title the Karleskints could convey and sue for damages. The trial court held the Karleskints' title was not merchantable.

ISSUE   Is title to real estate merchantable if the real estate is not accessible?

DECISION   Yes. Reversed. A marketable title is one that is not subject to such doubt as would create a reasonable fear as to its validity in the mind of a prudent and intelligent person guided by competent legal advice. Merchantability does not equate with market value, which may be affected by many factors, including lack of access. Unmerchantability arises only from defects in title. An abstract of title ordinarily will not reveal lack of access. The buyer, however, is charged with knowledge of matters that a cursory visual inspection of the real estate would reveal. Here, the buyer received what the seller promised to convey.

---

* An *abstract of title* is a condensed history of the title to real estate drawn from the appropriate county records.

An easement does not make a title unmarketable if it benefits the property—as in the case of an electric line which brings power to a house—and would be obvious to a reasonable person inspecting it before purchase.

Financing the Transaction

Occasionally a buyer pays cash for real property. Ordinarily, though, the buyer borrows either from a lender or from the seller to finance part of the purchase price.

The most common device used to finance the purchase of land is a mortgage. People commonly speak of "getting a mortgage," but that is the reverse of what actually happens. A *mortgage* is an interest in land often given by a buyer as security for a loan of the purchase money. Thus, a mortgage grants a *security interest*, a claim on the property for payment of a debt. A security interest in property is also called a *lien*.* Since a mortgage is an interest in land, the Statute of Frauds requires that it be created in a writing. Chapter 42 is devoted to mortgages.

Property Inspections

A buyer takes title to realty subject to the legal interests in it of those who are not parties to the

---

* The liens described in this chapter are *nonpossessory liens*, which means the lien holder does not have the property.

transaction. A preventive law approach to real property transactions emphasizes investigating the property's condition and title *before* the closing because it may be impossible to gain relief afterward. This section discusses what to look for in property inspections. The next section looks at what the public records may reveal.

Environmental inspections. In recent years, environmental laws have enhanced the importance of a property inspection prior to the closing. A buyer can be held liable for millions of dollars if the property he is purchasing contains leaking fuel tanks, asbestos, or other environmental threats. If the buyer exercises a thorough investigation of the property, however, he may be able to establish a defense or minimize his liability by demonstrating that he had no knowledge of the problem. This process, referred to as "due diligence," is becoming a routine and required step in transferring ownership of property, especially since lenders which have a security interest in the property can be held liable in some circumstances.

In some areas of the country, environmental inspections have also become important to detect the presence of radon. Radon is tasteless, colorless, odorless, chemically inert, nonflammable gas that is typically found in areas with high deposits of granite, phosphate, shale, or uranium ore. Radon typically enters a home or building by seeping into openings or cracks, generally in the foundation. Radon is a carcinogenic form of radiation which, over time, can trigger lung cancer in humans. Although the effects of radon are just now being understood, they are of legal concern for both sellers and buyers. Environmental law will be discussed in greater detail in Chapter 47.

Building inspections. If a building is involved, buyers quite often condition their offers on the receipt of a satisfactory report by an architect or engineer on its condition. If the inspection reveals structural defects which significantly reduce the building's value, the buyer may void the contract without penalty.

Unrecorded easements and adverse possession. The buyer should inspect carefully for interests which might not be on public record, such as an easement by necessity or a fee simple by adverse possession. Clues to other potential interests include paths, roads, structures, or any other improvements not reflected in the sales contract.

Buyers often have surveys taken of the property to determine boundary lines because in most states an adverse possessor will prevail against a buyer even though he or she has not recorded the now-legal title. A survey would show, for example, whether a neighbor has put a fence well inside the parcel's boundaries. A wise buyer never relies on fence lines.

Leaseholds. A tenant's right of possession normally prevails over that of a purchaser. Many sales contracts cover this situation by requiring that the seller convey the property free of tenants. This puts the burden on the seller to buy out a tenant's lease, if possible. Suppose Alice buys a house which the former owner rented to Bill. Bill's lease has 7 more months to run. Alice will have to wait until the lease expires before taking possession.

Mechanic's lien. New construction may signal the possibility of liens on the property.* Every state has a device called a *mechanic's lien*, which permits a contractor to assert a security interest in the property for work which was not paid for. The lien is effective only if it is *recorded*, that is, placed on public records, so that the public has notice of its existence. (The recording of interests and the public records are discussed below.) The work does not have to be done on a new building. Repairs to an existing structure also qualify.

Mechanic's liens are discussed more fully in Chapter 42.

Checking the Public Records

Often, an inspection will not reveal an interest in the property or a potential mechanic's lien. To guard against surprises, the buyer must check the public records relating to the property.

Real property records. A *title search* is the process of checking the real property records for the county in which the land is located. These records are usually maintained in the county courthouse by an official who is often called the *county recorder* or *registrar*. They contain all property interests of record.

A title search, of course, should reveal whether the prospective seller owns the property and can transfer a marketable title to the buyer. The buyer will also want to learn of any other interests in the property. Outstanding mortgages, leases, easements, or liens which are of record when the buyer takes title have

---

* It is critically important to note that mechanic's liens are just one of many types of liens, ranging from assessments for sewer lines to Internal Revenue Service liens for back federal taxes. Other types of nonpossessory liens are discussed below and in Chapters 40 and 42.

priority over the buyer's interest. In other words, because these are interests in the land, they become the buyer's responsibility if they are not removed before title passes. For that reason, real estate sales contracts usually specify that the seller will transfer a title free of liens or other similar *encumbrances*—burdens on the ownership interest consisting of rights or interests in land which would diminish its value to the buyer.

Title insurance is not required by law. However, in many instances, a lender will require that the buyer purchase title insurance. Title insurance guarantees that a lender will not lose the value of its security interest because of a defective title or any undiscovered interests. The title insurance company will perform its own title search, which the lender will review before making the loan. Title insurance policies are not transferable.

Personal property records. A seller of personal property which becomes a fixture may record liens against it. So a buyer must check the personal property records to determine whether any fixtures or other personal property which is to accompany the real property is subject to a lien. Suppose Carla contracts to buy Ken's house. The contract indicates that the dishwasher will stay with the house. A check of the personal property records should establish whether the company which sold Ken the dishwasher holds a lien on it pending receipt of Ken's final payment. These liens are discussed in Chapter 41.

Transferring the Deed

The closing. The closing marks the end of a real estate transaction. At the closing, the parties perform their promises under the sales contract. The buyer tenders the purchase money and the seller tenders a signed deed evidencing marketable title.

A *deed* conveys title to real property. It is a two party instrument: the *grantor* gives the deed, and the *grantee* receives it.* Because a deed transfers an interest in land, the Statute of Frauds requires that it be in writing.

If the buyer has mortgaged the property to secure the loan, immediately following the transfer the buyer will execute the mortgage and notes relating to it. Thus, many closings really involve two transactions: the sale of the property and the granting of the mortgage (see Figure 27.3).

Warranty deed. The *warranty deed* is the most common type of deed used in real estate transactions. A warranty deed both grants title and makes covenants about the property being sold. The grantor either expressly or impliedly promises to make the grantee whole if the grantee suffers any loss as a result of the grantor's breach of a covenant.

There are two types of warranty deed: general and special. The general warranty deed is commonly referred to simply as a "warranty deed." Normally, one contains three major covenants:

* The terms "grantor" and "grantee" are broader than "buyer" and "seller" and include, respectively, anyone transferring or receiving an ownership interest in real property.

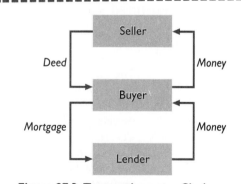

Figure 27.3 Transactions at a Closing.

- The grantor has good title to the land conveyed
- No encumbrances (e.g., a lien or an easement) have attached to the land other than those noted in the deed
- The grantee's possession will not be disturbed by a lawful claim by the grantor or a third party

Figure 27.4 is an example of a warranty deed.

A special warranty deed conveys title, but the seller warrants only that he or she has not encumbered the property, not that the property is unencumbered. For example, special warranty deeds are commonly used in the sale of commercial buildings where an exception is made for long-term leases made before the grantor owned the building.

A real estate purchaser is entitled to a warranty deed unless the real estate contract specifies otherwise. If the instrument leaves in doubt which type of warranty deed the grantor must supply, the buyer only has a right to a special warranty deed.

Quitclaim deed. With a *quitclaim deed*, the grantor conveys whatever title he has, if any. If the grantor has good title, that is what the grantee receives. Often, a quitclaim deed is used to clear possible defects of title. Suppose Kyle bought a farm from a married couple as joint tenants. Inadvertently, the wife failed to sign the original deed. Kyle should obtain a quitclaim deed from the wife so that her interest in the property ends.

Fraud in the inducement. At common law the doctrine of *caveat emptor*—let the buyer beware—generally governed the purchase of real property. Today, the doctrine is in retreat. Courts have granted relief for *fraud in the inducement* of the sale of a used home. Buyers of used homes can recover when the seller knew of a *latent defect*—one that is hidden or not obvious—and knowingly and expressly misrepresented the condition of the house. The seller's silence alone an amount to fraud. Indeed, because of the problems that can result from a failure to disclose defects in homes, at least twenty-four states have passed statutes either requiring or recommending disclosure of known defects. The next case will examine whether a lender which has seized and sold a home in a foreclosure proceeding must also disclose defects.

Karoutas v. Homefed Bank

232 Cal. App. 3d 767, 283 Cal.Rptr. 809 (Cal.App. 1991)

FACTS   The Lawrences defaulted on a secured note held by the Homefed Bank. Their property was sold in a nonjudicial foreclosure sale to the Karoutases, the plaintiffs, for $173,000. After the sale, the plaintiffs discovered that soil conditions and other defects would cost them over $250,000 to repair. Because it was sold in a foreclosure, the Karoutases did not and could not inspect the home. Homefed possessed reports which stated that repairs would exceed $350,000 and that the house should be demolished, but they did not tell the Karoutases about it. Homefed argued that under the nonjudicial foreclosure statutes of California it had no duty to disclose anything. Homefed won at the trial level.

ISSUE   Does Homefed, possessing knowledge of the defects, have a duty to disclose them in a foreclosure proceeding?

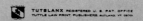

Know all Men by these Presents

That Thomas L. Thurber and Jeanette Y. Thurber
3755 Grant Street
Taft,
of Garfield *County, State of Ohio, for valuable consideration paid, grant*
with general warranty covenants, to

Elizabeth Appleton
whose tax mailing address is

998 Buckeye Way, Taft, Ohio 44444
the following real property:

Begining at a steel stake in the north side of Harrison Street
exactly 100 feet west of the intersection of the said north side
line of Harrison Street with the west side line of Grant Street,
in the City of McKinley, State of Ohio; Thence due north at right
angles to the north side line of Harrison Street 160 feet to
another steel stake; thence due west and at right angles to the
line just drawn 80 feet to another steel stake; thence due south
and at right angles to the line just drawn 160 feet to another
steel stake in the north side line of Harrison Street; thence
along the north side line of Harrison Street to the place
of begining.

Prior Instrument Reference: Volume 447, *Page* 345
wife/husband of the grantor, releases all rights of dower therein.

Witness *our* *hand* s *this* 25th *day of* February
19 90.

Signed and acknowledged in presence of

_____   _____

_____   _____

_____   _____

_____   _____

State of Ohio, } ss. *Before me, a* notary public
Garfield *County,* } *in and for said County and State, personally appeared the above named*

Thomas L. Thurber and Jeanette Y. Thurber

who acknowledged that they *did sign the foregoing instrument and that the same is* their *free*
act and deed.
In Testimony Whereof, *I have hereunto set my hand*
and official seal, at McKinley, Garfield County, Ohio
this 25th *day of* February *A. D. 19* 90

_____

_____

This instrument prepared by Edward Esquire, Attorney At Law
_____

Figure 27.4 A Warranty Deed.
The use of this form eliminates the need to specify the precise terms of the warranties, because the statute defines them. However, the parties may alter the warranties by agreement. A quitclaim deed form differs only in the elimination of the words "with general warranty covenants." The statutory form shown here is used in Ohio. (Reproduced by permission of Tuttle Law Print, Inc., Rutland, Vermont.)

DECISION   Yes. Reversed. Under the common law, there is a duty to disclose material defects known only to the defendant that the buyer does not or cannot reasonably discover. A lender, such as the beneficiary under a deed of trust, does have a common law duty to disclose such defects. The absence of such a duty being specified in the state nonjudicial foreclosure statutes does not deprive bidders at the sale from recovering damages. The doctrine of *caveat emptor* is also not applicable to such sales.

The implications of the above case are potentially great. Since the recession in the oil and agricultural regions of the United States in the mid-1980s, which has since spread to most of the country, thousands of homes have been sold in foreclosure proceedings. Although it is the norm for the lender to be the only bidder at the sale, those who do purchase homes at foreclosure sales often find these properties to be seriously damaged by their former owners as well as by vandals.

Home quality warranties. Fraud requires a determination of what a seller did or did not know about latent defects. Clearly, it is more difficult to prove what is in a seller's mind than to show the condition of the property.

To avoid this problem of proof, some (but not all) jurisdictions apply an *implied warranty of merchantability* to used homes. The seller affirms that he does not know of any serious latent defect which would impair normal use of the home. But the buyer can establish a breach by showing that the seller should have known of a particular defect.

At least forty states and the District of Columbia recognize an *implied warranty of habitability* on new homes. This warranty represents the builder's affirmation that the home is free of defects in design or workmanship which would impair its normal use. A septic system which cannot handle normal demands would breach this implied warranty. The New York Court of Appeals adopted this view in the next case.

Caceci v. Di Canio Construction Corp.

72 N.Y.2d 52, 526 N.E.2d 266 (1988)

FACTS   On November 29, 1976, the Cacecis contracted with Di Canio construction for the sale of a lot on which Di Canio was to build them a one-family ranch home. The contract price was $55,000. Di Canio guaranteed "for one year from title closing, the plumbing, heating, and electrical work, roof, and basement walls against seepage and defective workmanship." However, the guarantee was limited to "replacement or repair of any defects or defective parts." Title closed on October 14, 1977. Four years later, a dip appeared in the Caceci's kitchen floor. Di Canio tried to fix it by jacking up the basement ceiling. The dip soon reappeared. In November 1982, Di Canio again tried to repair the house, while assuring the Cacecis that ordinary settling was causing the problem. The Cacecis hired a soils expert who determined that the house's foundation was sinking because Di Canio had placed it on top of soil composed of rotting tree trunks, wood, and other biodegradable materials. The

Cacecis hired another contractor who, over the next 7 months, dug up the entire slab foundation, removed the wood and tree trunks, and poured a new foundation. The Cacecis brought suit to recover the cost of the repairs. The trial court entered judgment in favor of the Cacecis for $57,466. Di Canio had defended on, among other grounds, that the doctrine of *caveat emptor* applied to the sale of homes. The trial court and the appeals court, in affirming the judgment, rejected this argument.

ISSUE

Is a warranty that a house will be constructed in a skillful manner free of material defects an implied term in the express contract between a builder-seller and a buyer?

DECISION

Yes. Affirmed. The judicially created doctrine of *caveat emptor* once governed the sale of real and personal property. It grew out of the nineteenth-century political philosophy of *laissez-faire*. Almost immediately after the doctrine was articulated, judges created exceptions relating to the sale of inherently dangerous personal property. Those exceptions were not extended to real property until well after World War II. One writer noted the irony of a legal system that "offers greater protection to the purchaser of a seventy-nine cent dog leash than it does to the purchaser of a 40,000-dollar house." [Haskell, *The Case for an Implied Warranty of Quality in Sales of Real Property*, 53 Geo. L.J. 633 (1965)]. A growing awareness of a homebuyer's relative helplessness led courts to imply a warranty of quality. The justification for this rule is that the parties to a contract for the construction of a house do not bargain as equals with regard to potential latent defects from the contractor's faulty performance. The buyer, obviously, cannot inspect the house prior to signing the contract, while the builder-seller can prevent the occurrence of defects. Therefore, responsibility and liability should be placed on the party best able to prevent and bear the loss.

Like the court in the last case, most courts have not limited recovery to defects discovered shortly after purchase. Some permitted recovery several years later, but often only to those in privity with the builder.

Recording the Deed

A grantee records the deed in order to establish his ownership rights against all other potential claimants to title of the land. Between the grantor and the grantee, the grantee takes legal ownership upon the *passage* of the deed, not upon the recording of the deed. After all, the grantor knows she has transferred the property and does not require further notice of the fact. But, as to everyone else, the grantee establishes notice of legal ownership upon properly recording the deed.

The recording system is designed to protect those who properly record their property interests and those who rely on the public records. Given a choice between a person who has failed to record a property interest and a person who has relied in good faith on the public records, the law usually (but not always) favors the latter. For instance, Erin sells her farm to Jason; but before Jason records his deed, Erin sells the farm to Mary. Mary had checked the records and found no indication that Erin had conveyed the property. Mary has the deed recorded. In many jurisdictions, Mary will prevail against Jason in an action to determine the farm's ownership.

The recording statutes which determine when a grantee has good title against a third party fall into three categories.

In *notice* states, a later grantee never wins if she knew of the earlier conveyance when the property was deeded to her. However, if Mary, as the *last* buyer, is in good faith, meaning she has no knowledge of the prior sale, she will own the farm even if Jason records his deed in good faith *before* Mary does. Notice states greatly penalize those who do not record in a timely manner.

In *race* states, the race is to the recording office. The first party to record prevails. Good faith is not part of the race test. Knowledge of the prior transaction will not affect the validity of the title held by the first grantee to record. Suppose Mary knew of the earlier sale to Jason. If she files first in a race state she will prevail.

In *race-notice* states, the later grantee has title if she is the first to file and does not have notice of the earlier conveyance. If Mary filed first and did not know of Erin's conveyance to Jason, she would hold the title in a race-notice state.

Regardless of the statutory test a jurisdiction applies, the grantee who does not have good title has a cause of action against the grantor. Often, however, the multiple grantor is nowhere to be found.

Private Restrictions

A previous owner imposes *private restrictions* to limit the subsequent owners' use of the property. For example, in a subdivision private restrictions often specify the style, size, and cost of a home which may be built.

HYPOTHETICAL: A sells farm to B. B fails to file. Later, A sells same farm to C.

ISSUE: Who prevails in given situations below?

FILING ORDER	NOTICE STATUTE	RACE STATUTE	RACE-NOTICE STATUTE
B files, then C files			
• If C did not know of prior sale to B.*	C	B	B
• If C knew of prior sale to B.*	B	B	B
C files, then B files			
• If C did not know of prior sale to B.*	C	C	C
• If C knew of prior sale to B.*	B	C	B

*For each of these categories, focus on C's knowledge at time of purchase of farm, not time of filing deed for farm.

Figure 27.5 Contrast of Filing Statutes.
Note that if C knew of the prior sale at time of purchase, C will not prevail under a notice statute.

Often, the restriction appears in the deed. Restrictions may also appear in a *subdivision plat*—a developer's detailed property description of a subdivision or development—or in the articles of either a condominium or a homeowner's association. Restrictions can prevent the erection of structures as well as incidental usages. For example, a common restriction in a subdivision plat reads: "Lots will be for single-family residential purposes only."

Where property is owned in common, often the deed contains a restriction granting the other owners a *right of first refusal*, which is a right to have the first opportunity to buy when a co-owner decides to sell his or her interest.

Regardless of the type of document or restriction involved, the restriction's validity depends on whether it is in the grantee's chain of title. A *chain of title* is the history of the ownership of a particular piece of property. The term refers to what appears in the public record as of the time the grantee records. Documents placed on record after that are not in the grantee's chain of title because the grantee could not have had notice of them.

Only parties subject to the contract can enforce the private restriction. However, a court may deny enforcement if it finds the restriction to be unreasonable. For example, a right of first refusal may be so burdensome that selling one's interest for a fair price is impossible. Courts will not enforce restrictions against public policy. In the past, for instance, private restrictions were used to prevent the sale of real estate to blacks, Jews, and Asians. Today, such restrictions are unenforceable.

A court may also deny enforcement if the restriction was waived as a result of inaction. Suppose a subdivision plat forbids stockade fences, but many residents have erected them without objection from other residents. If a homeowner sought an injunction to prevent his neighbor from building one, the court probably would allow the neighbor to have her fence.

The courts do not favor private restrictions on real property. Historically, the courts have been reluctant to enforce any types of limitations—whether private or public—on land use.

The next case involves restrictions imposed by the developer of a famous resort and retirement community.

Sea Pines Plantation Co. v. Wells

363 S.E.2d 891 (S.C. 1987)

FACTS Wells bought three lots and a partly completed house in the Sea Pines Plantation subdivision on Hilton Head Island. When he bought, he knew that restrictive covenants appeared in his chain of title. He was also aware of the covenants' substantive provisions under which he could not, without the developer's approval, make any exterior alterations to his house or do any landscaping that might block a neighbor's view. The covenants expressly permitted the developer to reject proposed modifications on purely aesthetic grounds. During his negotiations to buy the property, Wells had received a set of plans for the house that had been approved by the developer's Architectural Review Board. After Wells began construction, the Board objected to specific unapproved modifications to the house and the site. When Wells did not cooperate, the developer obtained a temporary restraining order. The parties then agreed to modifications, and Wells resumed construction.

Again, Wells made unauthorized changes. After a trial, the trial court issued a mandatory injunction requiring Wells to: remove a flagpole, a jacuzzi, and satellite dish; remove a wrought iron fence, gate, beach walkway, shower, and no trespassing sign; remove all trees, bushes, walls, fences, and other structures he had placed in his neighbors' views; and relandscape the property.

ISSUE

Were the restrictive covenants enforceable?

DECISION

Yes. Affirmed. Wells argued that the law's historical disfavor of restrictive covenants required an interpretation in favor of free use of property. Where a restrictive covenant contains ambiguities, the courts do interpret them strictly and in favor of free use. However, the rule of strict construction does not preclude enforcement where, as here, the clear express language of the covenant states the party's intent. Unless such a covenant is indefinite or in violation of public policy, the courts will enforce it. This restrictive covenant was a voluntary agreement between the parties that was neither indefinite nor in violation of public policy.

PUBLIC RESTRAINTS ON THE USE OF PRIVATE PROPERTY

At the turn of the twentieth century, restraints on land use—other than private restrictions—were extremely limited by today's standards. In the last 70 years, public regulation of the uses of private property has increased dramatically. Zoning regulation, for instance, which we now take for granted, only received Supreme Court approval in 1926. Environmental laws, as we know them today, first began to appear in the late 1940s.

This section discusses three types of public restraints: nuisance actions, zoning laws, and eminent domain. Chapter 47 discusses their interplay with environmental laws.

Nuisance Actions

Either a private party or a government agency can bring a nuisance action. In either case, a *nuisance action* is a tort action to prevent the unreasonable interference by one party with the rights of others to use their property. A rock band practicing nightly in a backyard or a run-down house with a large population of rats might lead to private nuisance actions.

The word "nuisance" comes from a Latin verb meaning "to hurt." As the next case illustrates, the plaintiff in a nuisance action must establish a real harm, not just offended sensibilities.

Ness v. Albert

665 S.W.2d 1 (Mo. Ct. App. 1983)

FACTS

Ness and Albert lived next to each other in a rural area. On his property Albert kept rusted objects, pieces of broken concrete, parts of old sinks and stoves, and a partially burned house trailer. Ness brought an action for damages against Albert, alleging that these unsightly objects were a nuisance. The trial court entered judgment for Ness.

ISSUE

Does the use of one's property in such a way as to offend the esthetic sense of an adjoining property owner constitute a nuisance?

DECISION

No. Reversed. Unsightliness without any other harm is not grounds for a nuisance action. An owner's use of property cannot be restricted on the basis of purely esthetic considerations.

An official, such as the attorney general or a district attorney, may bring public nuisance actions which attack nuisances with broader effects—like fumes from a refining operation. Although many of the causes of these actions—like water pollution—now fall under environmental or public health laws, public nuisance remedies remain available in some instances.

Zoning Ordinances

Zoning ordinances classify property according to the uses to which it may be put. Usually, the state authorizes county or municipal governments to zone as an exercise of their *police powers*, the state's authority to protect the public health, safety, morals, and general welfare.

Prospective application. A zoning ordinance applies prospectively only. In other words, zoning ordinances do not affect uses which exist at the time the ordinances are adopted. Existing uses which do not conform with the zoning ordinance—*nonconforming uses*—are permitted to continue so long as they are continuous.

Suppose George operates a junkyard. His town adopts a zoning plan calling for one- and two-family housing on his land. George and anyone to whom he sells his property may continue the nonconforming use indefinitely. However, if George stopped using the property as a junkyard, he would lose his right to do so in the future. Usually, zoning laws permit the zoning authority to make *variances*, exceptions to the

overall zoning plan. George might seek a variance to allow him to start up again.

Regulating uses. Zoning laws permit a planned approach to the development of land so that, for example, homeowners have some assurance that a brewery will not go up next door.

Zoning restrictions are often strictest near residences, churches, and schools. Many zoning codes, for instance, do not permit bars or liquor stores near a school. However, the U.S. Supreme Court declared unconstitutional a Massachusetts statute which allowed churches to veto applications for liquor licenses within 500 feet of their doors. That power belongs solely to the government.

While zoning reduces the chances of inappropriate mixes of uses, it is easy to see how questions of land use can become heated and complex. Boundaries between particular development zones are often hard to justify to those whose properties bear greater development restrictions than others just across the line. Ultimately, defining an appropriate use requires some subjective judgment.

The courts uphold zoning classifications unless a property owner can show that a classification is arbitrary or unreasonable. The fact that land would be more valuable for one use does not ordinarily mean that a government unit cannot restrict it to a use which results in a lower value. Nor does it usually mean that the government has taken the land from its owner. However, in the next case, an Illinois court found that a restriction imposed too great a burden on a property owner.

Oak Park Trust & Savings Bank v. Village of Palos Park

106 Ill. App. 3d 394, 435 N.E.2d 1265 (1982)

FACTS | In 1963, Libert bought a 19.6-acre tract zoned for single-family houses. He obtained permission to build a nursing home on the tract, but it was never built. He then proposed to build multifamily housing, but his plan was rejected. Some years passed, and Libert renewed his attempts to have the parcel rezoned for 155 units of multifamily dwellings. The village rejected his request on grounds that it was inconsistent with the town's development plan and with the surrounding uses. The tract was bordered by a forest preserve on two sides; by single-family dwellings, a riding stable, and a restaurant on another; and by a major highway on the fourth side. Libert brought suit to have the village's zoning ordinance, as applied to his property, declared unconstitutional and to compel the village to permit him to develop the property in accordance with his plan. At trial, testimony established that the property would be worth between $300,000 and $400,000 for single-family lots but between $480,000 and $560,000 for multifamily dwellings. The testimony also established that Libert had received some expressions of interest in the property for single-family dwellings, but he had made no efforts to market the property for that purpose. The trial court entered judgment for Libert.

ISSUE | Did the village's zoning classification impose an undue hardship on Libert?

DECISION | Yes. Affirmed. The less substantial the relationship of the zoning to the public health, safety, comfort, morals, and welfare, the more likely the zoning is invalid and the more significant the reduction in value is as one of the criteria of invalidity. Zoning's confiscatory effect has no reference to the amount originally paid for the piece of property. Rather, it applies to the difference between the fair cash market value of the property as currently zoned and the value the property would have if it were put to the proposed use. Here, the loss could be as great as $260,000. The fact that the property has been vacant for a significant period under the present zoning classification strengthened Libert's argument.

A strong argument could be made that *Oak Park* was decided wrongly. Libert made no effort to market the land in accordance with the zoning classification, and the authorities had attempted to accommodate Libert on another proposal. In fact, *Oak Park* is an oddity; zoning decisions are rarely overturned on these grounds.

Development plans. Municipalities often have plans for development. These may consist of an overall scheme for an entire municipality or, in other instances, of standard specifications for subdivisions or planned-unit developments. Ordinances which restrict condominium conversions often affect zoning classifications as well. All these devices are designed to aid the municipality in planning its environment.

Restrictions on population density are also common. Zoning plans restrict certain areas to single-family homes, while they permit multifamily and high-rise apartment buildings in others. Particularly in multifamily and commercial areas, municipalities are requiring that developers provide off-street parking.

Esthetics. Zoning laws also affect many other less obvious problems of land use, like esthetics. While zoning on esthetic grounds is permissible, an ordinance cannot bar a legitimate use, like a landfill, solely on those grounds.

Some municipalities have designated historic areas in which the appearance of buildings must fit a particular architectural scheme.

Height and setback regulations are quite common. In Washington, D.C., no one may construct a building which is taller than the U.S. Capitol. However, just across the Potomac River, Alexandria, Virginia, permits buildings which greatly exceed the Capitol's height.

Zoning restrictions on signs have proved controversial because many people view signs as part of their First Amendment right of free expression. However, as the next case indicates, the Supreme Court has largely resolved that debate.

Harnish v. Manatee County

783 F.2d 1535 (11th Cir. 1986)

FACTS Manatee County, Florida, is a rapidly growing retirement and tourist-oriented community. In order to prepare its esthetically pleasing environment, the county commissioners adopted an ordinance banning portable signs. Its adoption followed a series of citizen complaints, which in turn prompted a series of public hearings and workshops. A vendor of portable signs and merchants who used such signs challenged the ban's validity. The trial court declared the ordinance unconstitutional, as it placed too great a restriction on commercial speech.

ISSUE Does a total ban on portable advertising signs violate the First Amendment to the Constitution?

DECISION No. Reversed. After the trial court entered its judgment, the Supreme Court issued two opinions dealing with speech communicated by signs. These cases stand for three propositions. First, esthetics is a substantial and valid government goal. Second, the governmental entity charged with the responsibility of protecting the environment has the discretion to determine the degree of protection necessary and the best method to achieve it. Third, the Constitution permits restrictions on commercial speech so long as they are narrowly tailored to achieve the esthetic goal and alternative means of communication remain available.

"American with Disabilities Act" Applications

The American with Disabilities Act (ADA) has applications for public accommodations—essentially any property used for commercial

purposes—including establishments that sell or rent goods of any type, provide a service, are restaurants, places of lodging, etc. Although technically not a public restraint on the use of property, the ADA has the practical effect of public constraint on commercial properties subject to the Act.

Under the ADA, persons or entities owning, leasing, or operating public accommodations are required to, among other things, remove architectural and communications barriers that are structural in nature, provided that the removal is "readily achievable." Readily achievable means "easily accomplishable and able to be carried out without much difficulty or expense." In addition, persons building or remodeling public accommodations must ensure such buildings are readily accessible.

The impact of the ADA is that any owner, tenant, operator, or potential buyer of public accommodations may have to widen doors or install ramps, low-density carpeting, or other things to help make the facility more accessible to disabled persons.

Environmental Controls

Since the early 1960s, environmental laws have prescribed limitations on activities which degrade the quality of the natural environment. These include, for instance, restrictions on pollutants released into the air. As Chapter 47 demonstrates, such restrictions directly affect land use.

Eminent Domain

Eminent domain is the government's power to take private property for public purposes in exchange for cash compensation to its owner. However, the government may take only that property reasonably necessary to complete a public undertaking.

The government does not have to ask for permission from a property owner to exercise the right. The only negotiations required between the government and the property owner involve the value of the property, not the decision to take it. Suppose the city decides to locate its new bus terminal where Margaret's

office building now stands. She will have no choice about selling to the city.

The Constitution expressly limits the exercise of eminent domain. The Fifth Amendment provides, in part, "nor shall private property be taken for public use without just compensation." Over the last 200 years, commentators have debated what the Constitution means by "just compensation," "taken," and "public use." There are widely different views of these terms. For example, in Louisiana "just compensation" requires that a business's goodwill value at the location must be factored into the compensation. Many states, however, restrict compensation to the property's market value.

Distinguishing between a "public use" and a "private use" has become very difficult. In urban renewal and similar programs, for example, government exercises its right of eminent domain in order to encourage new, private development of a type it regards as desirable.

As for what amounts to a "taking," some states, for example, have held that residences located near an airport were taken when the noise from jets made the homes uninhabitable. Other states have held to the contrary.

One of the issues currently stirring the most controversy is whether a regulation is a taking. Property owners are now aggressively asserting through litigation and other avenues the proposition that if their "property rights," including their right to develop their property, are profoundly diminished in value by state or federal regulatory actions, it constitutes a taking under the Fifth Amendment. Thus, if, under the law, a property is deemed a wetland or contains endangered species and can no longer be developed for residential use or be drained for farming, it is argued that the government is engaging in a regulatory taking for which the owner should receive just compensation. The following Supreme Court case, which some commentators feel is a landmark case for the proponents of property rights, discusses how a regulation could become a taking.

Lucas v. South Carolina Coastal Council

112 S.Ct. 2886 (1992)

FACTS

Lucas, a land developer, purchased two residential lots in 1986 on a South Carolina barrier island. His intention was to build two single-family dwellings on the lots sometime in the future. At the time of the purchase, Lucas's land was not zoned to exclude the building of dwellings. However, in 1988 the South Carolina legislature passed the Beachfront Management Act, to protect the state beaches from erosion, which prevented Lucas from building permanent habitable structures on the lots. Lucas argued that the Act was a "taking" under the Fifth and Fourteenth Amendments to the Constitution, since it divested him of all "economically viable use" of his property and demanded "just compensation." Lucas prevailed at the trial level. The state supreme court reversed on appeal.

ISSUE

Are state regulations which deny a property owner of all "economically viable use of his land" a regulatory taking for which the state must compensate the owner?

DECISION

Yes. Reversed and remanded. There are two situations in which a regulatory action requires the owner to be compensated. The first is when there is a "physical invasion" of the property, and the second is when a regulation strips the owner of all economically beneficial uses of the land. Because Lucas can no longer build any permanent or productive improvements on his land, the state law is a "taking" unless it can be determined on remand to the trial court that there are common law prohibitions, such as nuisance, that would have prevented Lucas from building the dwellings in the first place.

After the *Lucas* case was decided it was cheered by property rights advocates as a turning point in American property law. Many see the *Lucas* case as finally reversing the years of unabated regulation of property, particularly environmental laws, which seriously impair land development. It appears that now a state legislature cannot simply pass a law and deem that it is a right it can exercise under its police powers. Instead, the law may be construed by the courts as a taking, which can cost a state government a great deal when it must compensate the landowners. As a consequence, some environmentalist fear that state and federal governments will choose not to regulate at all.

The *Lucas* decision leaves a number of unanswered questions. First, to what extent must the property be rendered useless? Justice Scalia, who wrote the opinion, stated that it would be a mistake to assume that the deprivation must be complete. Does this mean 80 percent of its value must be lost, or 70 percent? No one knows, which means this will likely be resolved in the future on a case-by-case basis. On the other hand, in the dissent, Justice Blackman felt that Lucas did not suffer a taking, since he could still "picnic, swim, camp in a tent, or live on the property in a movable trailer." Clearly there is a wide divergence of judicial opinion on how much must be lost for a taking to occur.

However, the *Lucas* case already had an impact. In Michigan, an oil and gas company was awarded $51 million because it could not diagonally drill under its mineral leases. In New Jersey, owners of 12.5 acres of wetlands received a $5 million judgment because they now could not build on their land.

Does this mean that common regulations such as zoning laws require that the owner be compensated? Probably not, since zoning still allows economically viable uses of the land and because building a nonconforming land use, such as a factory in a residential neighborhood, could be construed as a common law nuisance.

CONCLUSION

Many commentators have complained about the growing restrictions on land use. They point to the rapidly growing regulatory frameworks as an indication of a loss of freedom. To an extent, they are correct.

The unregulated uses open to a landowner in 1890 considerably exceeded those available to the owner of the same land in 1980. However, this appraisal ignores the enormous population growth of our country. In 1890, the population approached 63 million. Its density was 21.2 persons per square mile. In 1980, the figures were 226.5 million and 64 persons per square mile. Cheap land, which fueled America's explosive expansion in the nineteenth century, no longer exists. With its end has come an awareness of the competing interests in land use decisions.

Increasing population density and the closing of the frontier have caused a radical change in the perception of appropriate uses for real property. What has not changed is the right guaranteed by the Constitution to own and possess land. While society has placed restrictions on some of the uses to which land may be put, that right remains undisturbed.

A NOTE TO FUTURE CPA CANDIDATES

The property portion of the CPA exam includes the material in this chapter, landlord-tenant law (Chapter 28), mortgage law (Chapter 42), and insurance (Chapter 30).

It is important to know and be able to distinguish the basic rights and interests in real property. The rightful owner of real property is said to have a fee simple. Figure 27.2 provides a useful comparison of the three forms of multiple ownership most commonly covered on the exam. You should note that for joint tenancy the undivided ownership interests are always equal (meaning that the fraction of ownership is one over the number of owners, e.g., four owners, $1/4$ ownership each). In addition, there is a right of survivorship with joint tenancy, which means the property passes automatically to the survivor(s). Stated another way, it means that the interest is not transferable by will. In contrast, tenants in common may have unequal ownership interests, and such interests never pass automatically.

Questions involving life estates are generally found in the trust section of the exam, not the property section. The focus of these questions is the proper allocation of income and expenditures between the life estate and the remainder beneficiaries. Trusts are discussed in Chapter 29.

Candidates should be sufficiently familiar with Figure 27.5 to be able to identify priorities between competing deed or mortgage claimants. In addition, candidates must understand the differences between a warranty and a quitclaim deed. You should note that the CPA exam often refers to a special warranty deed as a ''bargain and sale deed.''

The candidate should know the elements for adverse possession and a prescriptive easement. Process matters discussed in the chapter (except for filing the deed) and public restraints on the use of private property generally are not covered on the exam.

KEY WORDS

adverse posses-
sion (601)
deed (607)
easement (604)
eminent domain (622)
encumbrance (611)
fee simple (601)
implied warranty of
habitability (614)
latent defect (612)
license (606)
lien (609)
life estate (603)

merchantable title (608)
mechanic's lien (610)
mortgage (609)
nonconforming use (619)
notice statute (616)
nuisance (618)
private restrictions (616)
race-notice statute (616)
race statute (616)
recording (615)
remainder (603)
variance (619)
zoning (619)

DISCUSSION QUESTIONS

1. Define "fee simple." Does possession in fee simple mean the owner has absolute ownership rights?
2. What is a life estate? Give an example.
3. What is an easement? How may an easement be created?
4. What is a prescriptive easement? How does it compare with adverse possession?
5. What are the usual steps in a transfer of real property by sale?
6. Why is it important that the real estate sales contract reflect a party's true expectations?
7. What is a mortgage? Describe the parties to a mortgage.
8. What is the purpose of a deed? What types of deeds are there?
9. What is the purpose in carefully checking the title to property? In checking the property itself?
10. What distinguishes a public from a private nuisance action?
11. What is the difference between a variance and a nonconforming use?

CASE PROBLEMS

1. Jim Morrow is a co-owner of several parcels of property. Jim owns Blackacre with his wife Kathy in a tenancy by entirety. He is a joint tenant in Redacre with Gordon, Peter, and Jane. Finally, he is the remainder beneficiary of a trust for Greenacre wherein Jane is the life tenant and upon Jane's death Jim, if surviving Jane, is to take as a tenant in common with Peter. Jim and Jane were killed in a traffic accident, with Jim dying first. Under Jim's will Kathy is to take his share of Redacre and Greenacre only, not Blackacre. What property, if any, will Kathy have a right to at Jim's death? Explain.
2. Franklin's will left his ranch to his wife, Joan, for her life, and upon her death to his sons, George and Harry, as joint tenants. Can Joan convey her interest in the ranch to someone other than George and Harry? If George dies before Harry, will Harry obtain full title to the ranch on Joan's death? Explain.
3. Bill Murphy listed his home for sale with American Realty. American showed the house to Bea Quinn, who liked it so much that she offered to purchase it for $80,000—Murphy's asking price. Murphy refused the offer and decided to continue living in the house. Bea sued Bill for specific performance. American Realty has also brought an action against Murphy for its commission, which it claims he owes. Will either Bea or American obtain a judgment against Bill? Explain.
4. Paxton owned Blackacre. He obtained a $10,000 loan secured by a mortgage on Blackacre. The mortgage was properly recorded. Later, Paxton sold Blackacre to Rogers, expressly warranting that there were no mortgages on the property. Rogers was unaware of the bank's interest in the property. Paxton has disappeared, and the bank is about to foreclose. Is Rogers personally liable on the mortgage loan? Explain.
5. David Golden inherited Willow Ridge Farm from his grandfather. When the will was probated, Sean, David's half-brother, argued that he was to inherit the property jointly with David. The probate court held against Sean. Area residents regularly crossed a portion of the farm to get to Apple Lake. An oil well on

the property continues to be operated by Monk Oil under a mineral lease which expired in 1986. David has been told by his lawyer that he should seek to sell Willow Ridge by quitclaim deed, versus warranty deed, even if he will have to take less money. How does a warranty deed compare to a quitclaim deed? Why might a buyer of Willow Ridge seek to secure a quitclaim deed from Sean? Explain.

6. Stacy Capinger sold her farm, Blackacre, to John Miley for $450,000. Miley became critically ill right after the closing and did not register his warranty deed in the county courthouse. In the interim, John Hogg used the deed records to identify Stacy as the owner of Blackacre. Hogg contacted Stacy and offered to buy Blackacre. Realizing that Miley must not have filed his warranty deed, Stacy agreed. Stacy delivered a quitclaim deed to Hogg in return for $400,000. Miley discovered Hogg's quitclaim deed for Blackacre when he sought to file his warranty deed after he recovered from his illness. Assuming the state recognizes the race/notice rule, is Miley likely to prevail in a title suit against Hogg. Is Stacy likely to be liable to the loser of the Miley-Hogg dispute? Explain.

7. Curtis purchased a tract of land from Williams. To protect himself, Curtis ordered title insurance from Viking Title Insurance Company. Viking's title search revealed nothing which would constitute a defect in title. Soon after taking possession of the property, Curtis learned that McWilliams had an easement by prescription which was valid but unrecorded. Viking denies legal responsibility for this easement interest in the land. Should Curtis prevail against Viking for the failure to list the easement as a defect in title? Explain.

8. Gibson wants to build an auto dealership next to the city golf course. The city zoned the parcel as a multifamily residential area to take advantage of the setting. Gibson claims the many specialty stores and boutiques within a mile of the site have given it a business character. Also, since his dealership sells luxury and sports cars, it would benefit from a location near the golf course. The city has denied his variance application on the grounds that the proposed use was not compatible with the surrounding uses and was not the best use of the property for the city. What would Gibson's best argument be on appeal? Is Gibson likely to prevail? Explain.

9. In 1978, Roger Smith inherited from his grandfather a rural track of land thousands of miles away from his home. This year, Smith finally visited the property for the first time. He discovered Billy Becker living in an old mobile home on a back corner of the property. Billy's aunt originally had a lease for this area, but it expired in 1970. Roger learned that his invalid grandfather had repeatedly told her to vacate but she had always refused. Smith also learned that his grandfather had never sought a court eviction. Billy took over the trailer and area immediately upon his aunt's death, in 1976. Roger has now demanded that Billy vacate the land. Assuming the state law is that adverse possession occurs after 20 or more years of continuous occupancy, is Billy likely to prevail? Explain.

10. On August 1, Debra Byers deeded her farm to Susan Fortson for $250,000. Fortson did not record the deed. On August 9, Byers deeded the same farm to Sam Tuma for $230,000. Tuma was aware of the prior conveyance to Fortson. Tuma recorded his deed before Fortson recorded. Who would prevail under a notice statute? Race statute? Race-notice statute? Explain.

CHAPTER 28

The Relationship Between Landlord and Tenant

In the nineteenth century, writers and dramatists often made landlords their villains. To a degree, this view presented reality because the law offered more protection to property owners than to tenants—particularly poor tenants. This treatment was consistent with the prevailing philosophy, which emphasized the rights of property owners to control their property.

Today, the balance of power has shifted to favor tenants. If a tenant rents a store which subsequently burns down, no contemporary court would hold—as nineteenth-century courts would have—that the tenant was liable for rent on the now-vacant land. Similarly, statutes and precedent have limited the landlord's ability to evict tenants, even for nonpayment of rent. This chapter examines the relationship between tenants and landlords today.

TYPES OF TENANCIES

A *tenant* is a person who, under a lease, has the temporary right to use or occupy another's real property. A *lease* is a contract conveying an interest in land called a *tenancy* or *leasehold*. The lease usually describes the terms and conditions of the interest. One of the lease's principal functions is to specify the type of tenancy it conveys.

Tenancy for Years

Contrary to its name, a *tenancy for years* describes any leasehold with a set termination date. It may be for a very long time or a very short time. For example, both a 25-year lease and a 1-day lease—say, for a room at a Marriott Inn—convey tenancies for years.

Periodic Tenancy

A *periodic tenancy* is one which runs from one period to another; for instance, week-to-week, month-to-month, and year-to-year leases convey periodic tenancies. The lease automatically renews itself for the next period unless one party notifies the other of its termination. Normally, termination occurs at the end of the next full period following the one in which notice of termination is given. Suppose that when Rona rents her apartment, she agrees to pay the landlord $100 every Friday. She has a week-to-week periodic tenancy. One Friday, she pays the rent and notifies her landlord that she will move out by the next Friday. Rona has properly terminated her lease.

Tenancy at Will

At the beginning of a *tenancy at will*, the parties do not establish a termination date. Therefore, either party may terminate the leasehold upon notice to the other. If, over time, the parties establish a pattern of rent payments, many courts treat tenancies at will as if they were periodic tenancies. If a tenant at will pays rent each week, a court may treat the tenancy as one which runs week to week.

Tenancy at Sufferance

A *tenancy at sufferance* occurs when a leasehold has terminated but the tenant continues in possession. Since the lease has terminated, the tenant has no greater right of possession than a trespasser. Thus, a tenancy at sufferance differs from a tenancy at will in that the landlord has not consented to the tenant's continued possession. However, if the landlord continues to accept rent, a court may hold the parties have created a periodic tenancy.

THE LEASE AGREEMENT

A *lease* is the contract between a landlord and a tenant, and the common law contract rules (discussed in Part II) govern it. Thus, a court must find mutual assent, capacity, consideration, and legal purpose in order to enforce a lease agreement. This section examines some applications of contract law in the context of leases.

Mutual Assent

In order to create a contract, the parties must mutually assent, or agree, to its terms. Determining assent requires an examination of the facts of the case.

In *Weaver v. American Oil Company*,* the

---

* 257 Ind. 458, 276 N.E.2d 144 (1971).

oil company forced its filling station lessees to agree to indemnify it for damages caused by its own employees' negligence. The *Weaver* lessee had little education and business experience. The Indiana Supreme Court voided that provision of the lease because of a lack of mutual assent. The Court held that a company may not take advantage of its superior knowledge and bargaining position to force a person of little education and small means into an outrageously unfair indemnification provision. Ten years later, in the following case, a federal court in Indiana enforced an identical provision against a filling station lessee.

Price v. Amoco Oil Company

524 F. Supp. 364 (S.D. Ind. 1981)

FACTS
Fair leased a service station from Amoco. Under the lease, Fair was to indemnify Amoco for any damage claims resulting from equipment installed at the station. Fair took out an insurance policy to cover his liability under this clause. Price worked for Fair. On February 24, 1976, Price put a Pontiac on the hydraulic lift and began working on it. The car rolled off the lift and onto him. Price, now a paraplegic, sued Amoco and Fair. Amoco settled with Price and sought indemnification from Fair. Relying on *Weaver*, Fair claimed the indemnification provision was unconscionable and therefore unenforceable. The indemnification provisions here and in *Weaver* were identical. Both cases involved a filling station lessor who claimed Amoco presented a lease to him on a "take it or leave it" basis. Weaver, however, left high school after 18 months. Before becoming a service station operator, he was a laborer. Fair, a college graduate, had taken courses in business law. He spent 17 years with Amoco as a marketing representative responsible for negotiating service station leases and answering dealers' questions about lease provisions—including the one at issue.

ISSUE
Was the indemnification provision unconscionable as to Fair?

DECISION
No. Judgment for Amoco. *Weaver* held indemnification clauses *were* legal if the parties agreed to them knowingly and willingly. For that reason, determining unconscionability requires an examination of the facts. Weaver was not one who should be expected to know the law or to understand the meaning of technical terms which were not explained. Unlike Weaver, Fair had many opportunities to read and become familiar with the provisions of the lease. However, the most significant

evidence showing that Fair understood the provision was his insurance coverage for his indemnity obligation. Fair's actions were those of a person who understood the agreement's legal significance.

One lesson of *Price* and *Weaver* is that determining mutual assent to the terms of a lease requires a careful factual inquiry. As Fair discovered, what is unconscionable behavior in one instance may not be in another.

Oral Leases and Promises

The Statute of Frauds. Leases represent interests in land, so the Statute of Frauds requires that they be in writing. However, as Chapter 10 indicates, the law generally enforces oral leases so long as a lease's term does not exceed a year. The rationale for this exception is practical; many short-term lease arrangements are oral.

Even if a lease is in writing, the law does not require that it be in a particular form or that its provisions follow a particular order. For example, if Sam rents his house to Adrienne, the tenancy could be based on an agreement written on the back of a cocktail napkin.

Parol evidence. Because of the *parol evidence rule*, a court will not admit evidence of oral promises made to a tenant before or at the time the lease was signed. So the lease should reflect all the parties' promises. Quite commonly, for example, a lease will say "no pets." But the rental agent may tell a prospective tenant that a small dog "probably would be all right." If this assurance does not appear in the lease, the landlord later may require that the tenant either dispose of the pet or vacate the apartment. A court will not admit evidence of what the rental agent promised.

Typical Apartment Lease Provisions

Local or state real estate organizations prepare form leases for use by their members. Therefore, such leases tend to favor the landlord.

They usually cover the following:

- When, where, and how much rent is to be paid
- Timing of notice for lease renewal or cancellation
- Limit on the number of nonfamily guests
- Landlord's right to enter the apartment in emergency and nonemergency situations
- Tenant's right to assign or sublet
- Purposes for which the tenant may use the property
- Rights to use amenities such as a swimming pool, clubhouse, etc.
- Landlord's rights against the tenant for nonperformance of lease provisions

The parties may modify provisions in form leases by striking through paragraphs or writing in new ones and initialing the changes. Or they may attach an additional clause, called an *addendum*, reflecting other agreements. For instance, an addendum might waive a "no pets" clause. Another common modification is a *transfer clause*, which permits the tenant to terminate the lease if her company transfers her to another city. These clauses typically require prior notification to the landlord. Often, an addendum lists repairs the landlord will made before the tenant takes possession.

LANDLORD'S RIGHTS

Right to Receive Rent

The landlord has the right to receive rent from the tenant when it is due. Under the common law, the tenant's obligation to pay rent is a contractual promise separate from the landlord's promise to provide services to the tenant. For this reason, courts generally did not permit tenants to withhold rent even though the landlord had not performed his duties. Today, a number of states have statutes allowing residential tenants, under certain circumstances, either to withhold rent or to put their rent in escrow. Legislatures have now shown the same concern for commercial tenants, who, presumably, are better able than residential tenants to protect their interests.

Right to Possession at End of Term

The landlord has the right to receive the premises at the end of the lease's term in the same condition as they were in when they were rented. The tenant must pay for any repairs necessary to return the premises to their original condition. However, the tenant is not liable for reasonable wear and tear. Suppose Karen moved out of the apartment where she had lived for 4 years and her dog had ripped a part of the bedroom's wall-to-wall carpeting. Karen would be liable for the cost of replacing it. However, if she did not cause any extraordinary damage to the walls, she would not be responsible for repainting them.

Right to Evict

Among other causes, a tenant's failure to pay rent can result in her *eviction*, or dispossession of the leased premises. Normally, a landlord must seek an eviction order from a court. If possible, the landlord must provide the tenant with notice of the proceedings and of the proposed eviction date.

A landlord may not use "self-help" methods to evict a tenant, because such methods lead to damage to the tenant's possessions and, sometimes, to brawls. The law provides a means of evicting a tenant, and a landlord must use it unless the tenant has obviously abandoned the premises. A landlord could, for instance, remove a tenant's possessions from an apartment in order to rent the premises to another if the tenant has not paid rent or been seen for several months. Even then, the landlord

should obtain a court order granting him or her possession of the premises.

The landlord has a right to insist that the tenant observe the terms of the lease and not engage in behavior which amounts to a *nuisance*. For example, a landlord might evict a tenant who persistently plays loud music at all hours of the night, disturbing his neighbors. In addition, usage of the apartment for illegal activity, such as the sale and distribution of pornography or drugs, could result in a legal eviction.

LANDLORD'S DUTIES

Duty Not to Discriminate in Renting

Landlords sometimes argue that they have a right to rent to whomever they please. That may be true in theory, but the right is limited by various antidiscrimination laws. Under the Fair Housing Act, a landlord will get into serious legal difficulties by denying an apartment to a prospective tenant because of any of the following:

- Race
- Color
- National origin
- Gender
- Disability
- Marital status
- Parental status

Federal regulations now forbid landlords to discriminate against prospective tenants who have children. There is a very limited exception for retirement communities.

Many landlords prefer to rent only to individuals or married couples. They do not like to rent to unaffiliated groups of individuals, like roommates. Some courts, however, have refused to enforce lease provisions restricting occupancy to members of the tenant's immediate family.

One state permits discrimination on the basis of a profession. Because lawyers are notoriously troublesome tenants, New York permits landlords to refuse to rent to them.

One emerging problem between landlords and tenants is the sexual harassment of tenants by apartment managers and owners. Although there has been no thorough empirical study done, a number of commentators feel that the practice is quite pervasive. Most of the victims are thought to be single mothers with children, who fear losing their homes and so do not report it. The Fair Housing Act prohibits discrimination based on gender, but does this include sexual harassment of tenants? The following case established the precedent.

Shellhammer v. Lewallen

4 Eq. Opportunity in Housing Rep. (P-H) 15,472 (W.D. Ohio 1983)

FACTS   Tammy and Thomas Shellhammer rented an apartment owned by Norman and Jacqueline Lewallen. Norman, the manager, approached Tammy Shellhammer asking her to pose nude for him. Later he also solicited her to have sexual intercourse with him. She refused both requests. The Shellhammers were subsequently evicted under the pretext that they did not pay their rent. The Shellhammers, in this case of first impression, claimed that sexual harassment in employment, developed under Title VII of the Civil Rights Act of 1964, should be applied by analogy to Title VIII of the Fair Housing Act. The Lewallens countered that there is no legal basis for finding that sexual harassment is actionable under the Fair Housing Act.

ISSUE   Is the sexual harassment of tenants a form of illegal sex discrimination under the Fair Housing Act?

DECISION   Yes. Judgment for the plaintiffs. It is proper to apply the sexual harassment doctrine, as interpreted under Title VII of the Civil Rights Act of 1964, to Title VIII of the Fair Housing Act because of the similarity of purpose between the two statutes. Congress intended the Fair Housing Act to prohibit "all forms of discrimination, sophisticated as well as simpleminded." The Shellhammers' eviction was caused by Tammy's refusal to have sex with Norman Lewallen. This is known under Title VII as a "quid pro quo" claim, and it is now illegal as well under the Fair Housing Act.

The *Shellhammer* case also addressed several other important issues. One was whether Norman Lewallen's action constituted an "offensive environment" for his tenants, a concept which has been applied similarly to Title VII employment cases. The court stated that although this theory also pertains to sex discrimination under the Fair Housing Act, in this case discrimination did not occur because Lewallen's two offensive actions were not "pervasive and persistent" enough. Another issue was how sexual harassment should be ascertained by the victim; under a subjective or objective standard. The court ruled that it should be a subjective standard, meaning that the plaintiff must show that the conduct was personally offensive to her or him. This is in contrast to an objective standard, in which a reasonable person or victim standard would be applied. And finally, the court ruled that Mrs. Lewallen, as the owner, was also liable under the principle of respondeat superior. This is because she had known of her husband's actions, and as his manager and employer she did nothing about it. This last holding could result in significant damages for property owners who do not monitor the behavior of their managers.

Duty to Provide Peaceful Possession

The landlord warrants the tenant's peaceful possession of the premises. "Peaceful possession" means that the tenant may take possession at the time stated in the lease and maintain possession for its term free from claims to the premises by either the landlord or third parties. This duty is usually expressed in a lease clause called a covenant of quiet enjoyment.

The landlord also warrants that he will not enter the premises except in accordance with the lease or in response to an emergency. In other words, the landlord's ownership of the building alone does not give him the right to enter apartments without a legally justifiable reason.

Duty to Provide Safe Premises

Under the common law, the landlord had no obligation to provide safe premises. Today, landlords must provide safe premises in the sense that the premises must not be physically hazardous. In addition, a trend has developed toward requiring landlords to keep residential premises secure from criminal activity.

Common areas. The landlord's duty to provide safe common areas means that, for example, public hallways must have adequate lighting, stairways must not be rickety, and the building must meet fire safety code provisions.

Courts understand that problems with common areas often arise simply from the use and aging of a building. Nonetheless, landlords have the duty to identify and fix defects within a reasonable time—especially where landlords provide regular maintenance or janitorial services. Still, courts will not impose liability for an injury caused by a defect unless the plaintiff proves the landlord knew or should have known of the defect.

Minimizing opportunities for criminal activity. A landlord is not an insurer against criminal acts occurring on the premises. Some courts, though, have held that the duty to provide safe common areas includes a duty to minimize opportunities for criminal conduct by taking rea-

---

Aaron v. Havens

758 S.W. 2d 446 (Mo. 1988)

FACTS In March 1984, Aaron rented an apartment from Havens in a St. Louis neighborhood her complaint described as dangerous. At that time, the latch on her rear window was broken; a burglar could enter from the fire escape. Havens knew a burglar had entered her apartment through her balcony windows, which were also accessible from the fire escape. Aaron repeatedly reported the broken latch to Havens, telling him she feared for her safety. She claimed a particular danger to herself because Havens had designated her to collect rents from the other tenants. In September 1984, an intruder entered Aaron's apartment through the window with the broken latch and sexually assaulted her. Aaron brought suit, alleging Havens was negligent in not repairing the latch and in not taking precautions against an intruder's use of the fire escape. The trail court dismissed the complaint on the grounds that a landlord does not have a duty to make premises safe against the criminal conduct of an intruder.

ISSUE   Does a landlord have a duty to make the premises safe from unauthorized entry from a common area into a private area?

DECISION   Yes. Reversed. A complaint in a negligence case must state facts demonstrating a duty owed by the defendant to the plaintiff. The existence of a duty is a question of law. The law recognizes a duty of a landlord to make common premises safe against foreseeable risks. Here, the complaint alleged that the landlord knew or should have known of the dangerous condition of the fire escape, which allowed easy access to Aaron's apartment. The fire escape was part of the public premises under the landlord's control. As such, no tenant had the right to make modifications to it, and this gives rise to the landlord's duty to use due care to protect against dangerous conditions. If a private apartment can be entered from a common area through a window, injury to the occupant is foreseeable. There is, therefore, no logical reason why a dangerous condition of common premises, proximately causing injury on private premises, could not warrant liability. Nor is it necessary to allege that past crimes involving entry are of the same general nature. Where a burglar can enter, so can a rapist.

----

sonable preventive measures. These might include more effective lighting, better security locks, and even guard service, depending upon the location and size of a building or complex. Normally, for instance, courts require more security for buildings in an urban area than for those in a small town. The last case is a typical one involving an urban landlord.

In other jurisdictions, courts have reached results similar to *Aaron* by relying on the implied warranty of habitability, which is discussed below.

Disclosure of latent defects. Like the seller of a home, a landlord has a duty to disclose *latent*

defects on and about the leased premises. Normally, a landlord's duty applies only to significant concealed defects. A person inspecting an apartment would assume the oven worked unless told otherwise. By contrast, the leak which caused a large, damp water stain on the ceiling would not be a latent defect, since its existence should be obvious to anyone inspecting the premises.

Repairs. A landlord is liable for negligent repairs, even though the lease may not have required him to make them. As the next case illustrates, the landlord owes this duty both to tenants and to the tenants' social guests.

Brewer v. Bankord

69 Ill. App. 3d 196, 387 N.E.2d 3344 (1979)

FACTS   Margaret Brewer was visiting her son and daughter-in-law when she fell on the stairs of the house they rented from the Bankords. The Bankords had recently repaired the steps. Brewer brought suit against the Bankords, alleging the repairs had resulted in an unsafe condition not readily visible to her. The trial court dismissed her complaint.

ISSUE   In making repairs, does a landlord owe the same duty of nonnegligence to a tenant's guest as he owes to the tenant?

DECISION   Yes. Reversed. A landlord should expect a tenant's social guests to enter premises by using the staircase leading to the doorway. A landlord who voluntarily and without obligation repairs a staircase—by that act and by the reasonable expectation of future use—becomes subject to a duty of ordinary care both to a tenant and to a tenant's social guests.

Duties to the Disabled

Both the Fair Housing Act's 1988 amendments and the Americans with Disabilities Act (ADA) passed in 1990 prescribe new legal duties that a landlord owes her disabled tenants. As stated earlier, the Fair Housing Act prohibits discrimination on the basis of disability, including pregnancy, for the tenant and his family. The Act also has provisions which afford a disabled tenant greater access into and within a dwelling. For example, the Act states that a landlord must permit a disabled tenant to make reasonable modifications, such as building a ramp, although the ramp must be installed at the tenant's expense. Multifamily dwellings built after 1988, however, must be designed and constructed to accommodate the disabled. This includes accessibility to and within common areas, like hallways and lobbies. Light switches, outlets, and other controls must also be fashioned so that a disabled person can easily operate them.

Finally, bathrooms must be constructed in which wheelchairs can maneuver.

The Americans with Disabilities Act imposes potentially great legal obligations and expense on commercial landlords. Moreover, these duties may extend not only to tenants, but to the disabled in the general public. Under Title III, twelve categories of businesses and other facilities called ''public accommodations'' must now be accessible to the disabled. The categories include hotels and restaurants, retail establishments such as grocery stores and shopping centers, public transit stations, parks and amusement parks, recreational facilities and museums, libraries, and galleries. In fact, almost no facility which the public can normally enter is exempt from the ADA. Similarly, any new construction (excluding multifamily) made after the ADA's enactment must be made accessible to the disabled even if it is not deemed a public accommodation. This includes ''commercial facilities,'' such as office buildings,

Ralston, Inc. v. Miller

357 So. 2d 1066 (Fla. Dis. Ct. App. 1978)

FACTS Ralston, Inc., rented the Opa Locka Hotel from Miller. Paragraph 23 of the lease stated that Miller was responsible for maintaining the roof, the exterior of the premises, and the structure. If Miller failed to make repairs within a reasonable time, Ralston could make them and deduct their cost from the next rent payment. However, two other paragraphs stated that Miller was not responsible for water damage. During the lease's term, the hotel's dome sank into the roof, which then cracked. Miller did not shore up the dome or cover the cracks. Rainwater began leaking through these fissures. As a result, the city declared the premises unsafe for habitation and locked out Ralston, Inc. Miller brought suit against Ralston for failing to pay the rent. The trial court entered judgment for Miller.

ISSUE Did the damage which resulted from Miller's failure to repair the roof cause Ralston's constructive eviction from the premises?

DECISION Yes. Reversed. Any disturbance of the tenant's possession by the landlord which makes the premises unfit for occupancy amounts to a constructive eviction. No law requires a lessee to make repairs in the absence of the lessor's performance, even if the lessee has the right to do so. As for the apparently conflicting lease provisions, the provisions exempting the landlord from liability for water damage do not negate the landlord's duty to keep the roof sound and watertight.

which are not frequented by the public. To comply with the ADA, the commercial landlord must remove all architectural barriers to the disabled where removal is "readily achievable." In essence, readily achievable means affordable. Commercial landlords must conform to these obligations but are permitted to, and in fact commonly do, delegate duties under the ADA and other Acts to their commercial tenants, particularly those under long term leases.

It has been estimated that over 43 million Americans are considered disabled under the ADA's definition. This means that almost all businesses open to the public must now accommodate these millions or face legal action. Groups representing disabled persons, frustrated by years of discrimination and inaction, have been mobilizing privately to enforce the

accessibility requirement. For example, shortly after Title III went into effect in early 1992, hundreds of wheelchair-bound protesters entered New York City's Empire State Building and demanded entrance to the inaccessible viewing area on the top. On the other side of the argument, many feel that accommodating the disabled is simply good economics, since they will now be better able to enter and patronize these businesses. Indeed, many of the disabled are the elderly, who have money to spend but previously were limited in where they could shop because of physical barriers.

Implied Warranty of Habitability

The courts developed the *implied warranty of habitability* to provide recourse for both residential and commercial tenants when the defects of leased premises are so great that they make the premises uninhabitable. Lack of water or an uncontrolled rat population are examples of breaches of the warranty of habitability.

A tenant must give the landlord a reasonable time in which to correct the situation before moving out. Some courts have granted tenants an *abatement*, or a reduction, of their rent for the period during which they waited for a condition to be repaired. Suppose that one February a Chicago landlord could not fix the furnace in his apartment building for 4 days. A court might grant his tenants a rent abatement for those 4 days. However, it is important to note that courts often are unsympathetic to tenants who abate their rents without a court order. Unauthorized abatements can lead to eviction.

Constructive eviction. Should a landlord fail to remedy a substantial defect, the tenant has the right to vacate without further liability on the lease because the tenant has been *constructively evicted*. If the Chicago landlord could not replace the furnace until the following May, the residents would be considered constructively evicted. In other words, they moved out involuntarily, which, in effect, constitutes an eviction.

If a tenant abandons the premises claiming a breach of the implied warranty of habitability and the landlord subsequently sues for nonpayment of rent, a court will carefully examine the tenant's claim. The tenant could have reason to make self-serving characterizations of the condition of the premises. In the previous case, a court had to evaluate a constructive eviction claim by a commercial tenant.

Housing Standards Codes

Many municipalities have adopted housing standards codes for apartments. These standards apply in addition to any warranties a landlord makes under state law. Housing standards require that the landlord meet health and safety minimums such as:

- Supplying adequate heat, water, and sewer service
- Installing working locks on all outside doors
- Providing screens and storm windows
- Replacing broken or cracked glass
- Repairing structural defects

A landlord who fails to comply with a code provision may receive a fine. Violations may also lead a court to grant tenants a rent abatement—or to hold that the tenants were constructively evicted, if the violations are serious enough—or to bar the landlord from renting an apartment to the public until repairs are made.

TENANT'S DUTIES AND RIGHTS

The residential tenant's duties are the opposite of the landlord's rights and vice versa. In general, the tenant has the legal duties to observe the terms of the lease and to use ordinary care in occupying the premises.

Duty to Pay Rent

The corollary of the landlord's right to receive rent is the tenant's duty to pay rent.

The courts have generally held that a tenant's duty to pay rent is separate from a landlord's duty to provide promised services. For this reason, a tenant relying on constructive eviction to justify not paying rent must have a very strong case establishing landlord abuse or neglect. At common law, a tenant who rented an entire building continued to owe rent even if the building was destroyed. In contrast, destruction of the premises terminated the duty to pay rent of a tenant who rented only part of the building.

The duty to pay rent does not terminate with the tenant's death.

Duty to Repair

A tenant is also expected to make minor repairs, like changing lightbulbs and replacing burned-out fuses. Major repairs are usually the landlord's responsibility. If the tenant did not cause the damage, the tenant's major duty is to minimize the landlord's loss, where possible. If a water pipe bursts in the kitchen, the tenant would be expected to turn off the main valve to stop the flooding. However, repairing the pipe would be the landlord's duty.

Unless the landlord consents in advance, a tenant may not hire someone to perform non-emergency repairs. The tenant probably lacks the landlord's expertise in overseeing repairs. Also, the landlord may be able to do the work or may have an employee who can do the work for less than a contractor. Suppose a tenant's bathroom door will not close properly. It may be cheaper for the landlord to replace the door with an extra door on hand than to have the tenant's contractor attempt to rehang it.

Some states have adopted *repair and deduct* statutes. Generally, these laws permit a tenant to have someone repair a property problem and then deduct it from the rent. The tenant possesses the right only if he is in compliance with the lease or if he notifies the landlord and she fails to repair the problem in a prescribed number of days. Most of these statutes also limit the amount that can be deducted to a percentage of the rent or a dollar amount.

Modern Protections

Under the common law the tenant had few rights outside specific provisions made in the lease agreement. Today, however, state laws and courts have adopted a more liberal view toward tenants' rights. The development of the implied warranty of habitability and of housing standards codes reflects the new view.

Security deposit laws. Another legislative response to tenants' complaints deals with security deposits. A *security deposit* is a sum required by a landlord to cover damages to the premises or losses resulting from a breach of the lease. In the past, landlords *commingled*, or mixed, security deposits with their other funds, did not pay interest on them, and often arbitrarily refused to return them at the termination of the lease.

Today, a growing number of states and municipalities require landlords to place security deposits in interest-paying escrow accounts and to return the deposit with interest within a certain period following termination of the lease or to provide an explanation of why part or all of the deposit is being withheld. In some jurisdictions, landlords who fail to comply may be subject to triple damage—that is, three times the amount due the tenant.

Freedom from retaliatory evictions. A tenant's rights under state or municipal laws would not be worth much if the landlord could retaliate by evicting the tenant for exercising them. In the next case, a landlord claimed it had an absolute right to terminate a lease even if it did so in response to the tenant's complaints to the city housing department.

Sims v. Century Kiest Apartments

567 S.W.2d 526 (Tex. Ct. Civ. App. 1978)

FACTS Sims lived in the Century Kiest Apartments under an oral week-to-week tenancy. During his 9 years there, the building's condition steadily deteriorated. He repeatedly complained to the management and helped organize a tenants' council. He and the council reported numerous housing, building, and health code violations to the authorities. Finally, the landlord gave Sims 10 days' notice to vacate his apartment. When Sims refused, the landlord obtained an order granting it possession of the premises. Sims brought suit, alleging violations of his First Amendment rights and seeking recovery of moving expenses and other costs he incurred as a result of the eviction. The trial court granted summary judgment to the landlord on the ground that the landlord had the right to terminate a tenancy at will upon notice to the tenant.

ISSUE   Is a landlord subject to an action for damages if the landlord terminates a tenancy at will because the tenant reports code violations to the authorities?

DECISION   Yes. Reversed.

> *The tenant has a legal right to be free of interference with his reporting of violations of laws enacted for his benefit and . . . the landlord has a . . . duty not to interfere with the tenant's exercise of that right. If the tenant had no such right, the public policy to encourage reports of violations of the law would be substantially frustrated. Accordingly, although the landlord may have the legal power to terminate the tenancy, . . . the law recognizes no legal right to do so for the sole purpose of retaliation. . . . On this basis, we hold that retaliatory eviction is a legal wrong for which an action for damages will lie.*

Sims represents the trend in the law on retaliatory evictions. However, not all jurisdictions have adopted its logic.

TRANSFER OF LEASE INTEREST

A tenant holding a lease for a term may transfer that interest in the premises to another unless the lease or a statute restricts transfer. However, a lessee may not transfer the premises for a purpose which injures the property, is inconsistent with the original lease's terms, or increases the landlord's risk. This general rule has not changed appreciably over the centuries. However, the law applied to lease provisions prohibiting transfer has changed.

Methods of Transfer

Transfers of leaseholds normally occur either by means of an assignment of the tenant's interest or by the tenant's subletting of the premises.

The basic rules applicable to the assignment of contracts, discussed in Chapter 11, apply to the assignment of leases. In an *assignment*, the tenant transfers the entire possessory interest to another. The original tenant, the *assignor*, remains liable on the lease to the landlord unless the landlord grants a *novation* and thereby agrees to look only to the second tenant for performance. Suppose Ginger assigns her boutique's lease to Susan without a novation. Susan's venture does poorly, and she falls behind in the rent. The landlord may look to Ginger for payment. Figure 28.1 diagrams an assignment.

When a tenant *sublets*, he transfers part or all of his possessory interests for a specified period, but that interest reverts to him before the lease terminates. Suppose Jim's lease on his apartment expires September 30. He transfers his apartment to Jerry for July and August and plans to return September 1. Jim has sublet his apartment because he did not convey his entire

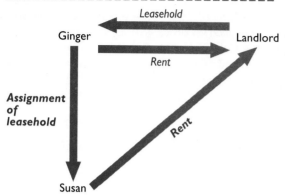

Figure 28.1 Assignment of a Lease.
A comparison of this figure with those in Chapter 11 reveals that the identical provisions of contract law apply here.

interest in the premises. As in an assignment without a novation, the sublessor (Jim) remains liable to the landlord for the sublessee's (Jerry's) nonpayment of rent. In essence, the original tenant is the sublessee's landlord. Figure 28.2 compares an assignment with a sublease.

Restrictions on Transfer

Until this century, courts often denied tenants the right to transfer if the lease prohibited it. Some simply said, "A deal is a deal." Others reasoned that the tenant had agreed to the lease

and that the landlord's interest in preserving the property was superior to the tenant's interest. By that, the courts meant the owner had a legitimate interest in controlling who possessed the property, because some tenants take better care of property than others.

Today, many courts will not uphold a total prohibition on transfer. Instead, such courts tend to balance the expectations of the tenant and the landlord. Still, they recognize that a landlord has a legitimate interest in ensuring that the character and creditworthiness of a successor tenant are similar to those of the landlord's other tenants. The successor tenant does not need to have creditworthiness equal to the original tenant so long as it is equivalent to that usually required of tenants in the same complex or building. The courts certainly will not permit a restriction on transfer to be used as a subterfuge for preventing transfer of the interest for discriminatory reasons.

Leases often specify a procedure for transferring the tenant's interest. If a clause prohibits assignment only, the tenant generally may sublet. If it prohibits subletting only, the tenant may assign the lease.

Commercial tenants, because of their greater bargaining power and presumed business sophistication, generally cannot assign or sublet their lease even if the landlord is unreasonable in withholding permission. The next case discusses this issue.

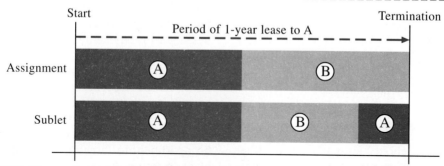

Figure 28.2 Comparison of Assignments and Sublets.

21 Merchants Row Corp. v. Merchants Row, Inc.

412 Mass. 204, 587 N.E.2d 788 (1992)

FACTS   The plaintiff-lessee, 21 Merchants Row, Inc., entered into a commercial lease which contained a clause prohibiting it from assigning or subleasing its leasehold interest without first receiving consent from the defendant-lessor. The plaintiff later sold its business, contingent on an assignment of its lease to the buyer. The defendant would not agree to the assignment for fear of losing control of its property. The plaintiff, which had an ongoing acrimonious relationship with the defendant, sued, claiming the defendant's withholding of the assignment was unreasonable. The plaintiff-lessee prevailed at the trial level.

ISSUE   Can a commercial lessor unreasonably withhold from the lessee its content to assign or sublet its lease?

DECISION   Yes. Reversed. A majority of jurisdictions, including Massachusetts, subscribe to the rule that there is no reasonableness requirement implied in the assignment or sublease clause of a commercial lease. This rule, however, would not apply to residential leases, since such tenants do not possess the bargaining power commercial tenants assert when drafting a lease.

Effect of Property's Sale

A landlord may transfer title to leased premises, but the buyer takes title subject to the tenant's interest. For example, if the tenant has a lease with 5 months remaining, the buyer will have to wait 5 months before she has a right to occupy the leased premises. If the tenant has prepaid his rent to the seller, the buyer cannot compel him to pay twice by paying her, too. Thus, before making a purchase, a prospective purchaser of rental property should determine the tenant's legal interest.

TENANT'S IMPROPER TERMINATION OF LEASE

While a tenant has the legal power to terminate a lease at any time during its term, he generally does not have the legal right to do so. In other words, a tenant may break his lease, but he may have to pay the remaining rent. Thus, the law protects the landlord's expectation that the tenant will be liable on the lease during its term.

A tenant who, without cause, abandons the lease, terminates possession, and stops paying rent remains liable for the full amount of the rent for the remainder of the term. Suppose Harvey leases a store for 5 years. After 3 years, he wants to move to a larger location. His landlord will not be able to prevent Harvey's move, but Harvey may be liable for the remainder of the rent.

If a tenant wrongly vacates before the end of the term, a landlord has a duty to mitigate her damages by attempting to relet the premises. Suppose Linda leases an apartment to Lex for 1 year at $300 per month. After 6 months, Lex stops paying rent and vacates the apartment. Two months later, Linda rents his apartment at the same rate. Had she not found a new tenant, Linda's damages would have been $1800 ($300 × 6). Now, her damages are $600.

While the landlord has a duty to mitigate her damages by reletting, she may give priority to renting premises she owns which were vacant before the breach. If Linda had four vacant units when Lex left, she may rent them before she tries to rent Lex's—without affecting her right to damages.

Quite commonly, landlords insert a clause in lease agreements establishing the tenants' continuing liability for rent if they abandon the premises. This clause requires the tenant to pay rent due while the premises are vacant or, if the premises are later rented, to make up the difference between any lower rent the landlord must accept and the rent specified under the lease agreement. These clauses usually require that the tenant pay any expenses which the landlord incurs in enforcing them. A court may grant a landlord her attorney's fees in this situation even without a clause in the lease to that effect.

Finally, in about 33 states, a landlord possesses a statutory lien or claim against any of the tenant's personal property left on the abandoned premises. If the tenant does not pay his rent the landlord can sell the property to recoup some or all of the arrears.

CONCLUSION

Under the common law, the courts were normally not sympathetic to tenants. The courts presumed tenants could protect themselves by negotiating appropriate provisions in the lease, since, like all contracts, a lease requires mutual assent.

During the last 30 years, that approach has been rejected or modified in view of the modern perception of the great disparity of bargaining power between landlords and tenants. While most of the country does not suffer from the shortages of rental housing which exist in New York, Boston, and San Francisco, landlords generally do have the power to offer "take-it-or-leave-it" terms.

As this chapter has indicated, the ferment in this area of law has led to considerable variations between jurisdictions. The area of landlord-tenant relations would benefit from a uniform act, but one is not likely to appear until more of a consensus emerges on the respective rights and duties of landlords and tenants.

A NOTE TO FUTURE CPA CANDIDATES

Questions concerning the relationship between landlord and tenant generally are found in the property section of the CPA exam. However, it is possible to have a contracts question concerning the Statute of Frauds for a lease not to be completed within 1 year.

It is important for the candidate to understand the types of tenancies. Remember, a tenancy for years describes any leasehold with a set termination date. A common situation is a tenancy at sufferance, in which the tenant continues in possession after a leasehold has terminated. Remember, the tenant is now considered a trespasser and the landlord may evict the tenant by instituting legal proceedings. No other form of tenancy is created.

To be enforceable, unless otherwise agreed, a residential real estate lease must entitle the tenant to exclusive possession of the leased property. The nonpayment of rent or the use of the leased premises for illegal acts can result in legal eviction. The CPA exam historically has not focused on other duties between landlord and tenant.

It is important to be able to distinguish a sublease from an assignment situation, as illustrated in Figure 29.2. In the absence of a provision in the lease to the contrary, a lessee ordinarily may sublease or assign the lease to another party without the consent of the lessor.

KEY WORDS

assignment (639)　　repair and deduct (638)
eviction (634)　　sublet (639)

DISCUSSION QUESTIONS

1. How did the common law look upon the landlord-tenant relationship?
2. Give examples of how landlord–tenant law has evolved from the common law.
3. List the four different types of tenancies discussed in this chapter.
4. A lease for 1 week would be what type of lease? Could it continue for a year? How?
5. When is a written lease necessary? Must any particular form be used?
6. What is meant by the implied warranty of habitability?
7. What are the basic rights and duties of the landlord?
8. What are the basic rights and duties of the tenant?
9. Explain the differences between assignments and subleases.
10. What are the landlord's rights upon a tenant's improper abandonment of the lease?

CASE PROBLEMS

1. Martinson Services, Inc., had rented two floors of office space in Jason's building for 15 years. The lease provided for a $2000-per-month increase in rent in the lease's fifth year. Near the end of the fourth year, Martinson's business was doing very poorly. Martinson told Jason that he could not stay in the building if the rent was increased. Jason agreed in writing to allow Martinson to remain at the prior rental, and Martinson did so. At the end of the fifth year, Martinson moved to another office building. Then, Jason sued Martinson for $24,000, the amount of the forgiven rent. What would the result be? Explain.

2. Grover leased an apartment in Buffalo from Bayley for 1 year, starting February 1. When Grover moved in, he discovered that there was no hot water and that the main radiator was broken, so the apartment got no warmer than 55 degrees. Grover demanded that Bayley make the necessary repairs. Bayley said he was "laid up from a fall" and would "make it up to Grover" by allowing him $25 off his March rent. After 2 weeks of these conditions, Grover moved out. Bayley brought an action for breach of contract against Grover. Will Bayley prevail? Explain.

3. Wilcox had an apartment in the Rock Hollow Apartment Complex. One night, she invited guests to her apartment for a retirement party. A guest, Jim Reed, slipped and fell on the common steps leading to the second floor, where Wilcox lived. Reed brought suit against the apartment complex, alleging his injuries were caused by poorly secured carpeting on the stairs. The complex claims it is not liable to Reed because he is not a tenant or, alternatively, because it was unaware of the defective condition of the carpeting. Is the court likely to accept either of these defenses? If so, which? Explain.

4. The Victory Apartments complex was designed as an adults-only complex with little or no provision for the use of its facilities by children. Upon enactment of the federal law prohibiting most adults-only complexes, Victory began leasing to tenants with children on condition that these tenants sign a release of liability for injuries which might occur at the complex. Jesse Gregerson, a minor, and his mother, Nancy, moved into apartment 149 after she signed the release. Later, Jesse was injured when he dove into the unmarked, shallow end of one of the complex's swimming pools. Nancy has brought suit on behalf of Jesse. She claims that the apartment complex breached its duty to provide safe facilities and that it violated the intent of the federal law by making her sign the release to be able to rent an apartment. Is a judge likely to be persuaded by her arguments? Explain.

5. Unlimited Fashions, Inc., leased a store in the Suburban Styles Shopping Center for 5 years

at $1500 a month. The lease prohibited assignment. After occupying the premises for 2 years, Unlimited sublet the premises to Fantastic Frocks for the balance of the lease's term, less 1 day, at $2000 per month. Has Unlimited breached its contract with Suburban? Is Suburban entitled to the additional $500 rent paid each month by Fantastic to Unlimited? Explain.

6. Missy Dagenhart was a dance major at Victory University. Missy practiced her routines several times a day in her apartment. Her third-floor apartment was in an older building which had hardwood floors and no acoustic insulation between floors. The noise from her dancing and musical accompaniment greatly disturbed the tenants below her. The apartment manager told Missy to stop dancing in her apartment or she would be evicted. Missy is willing to turn down her music but claims the noise from her dancing is a problem with the floors, not her. Is a judge likely to find Missy's dancing a nuisance which would justify eviction? Explain.

7. Val Maiewski operates a modeling school in the Kasten Shopping Center. On February 15, Hepner Development Corp. purchased the shopping center from Kasten. Kasten had told Hepner that no tenant had more than a 6-month lease and none had prepaid the monthly rent. Hepner wanted to raze the shopping center to build a new, larger center, so he notified all tenants that their leases would come to an end in 6 months. Val received an additional warning that if she did not pay her March rent, she would be evicted immediately. Val can show that she has 3 years remaining on her lease and that she had paid her March rent before the purchase. Will Val prevail against the new owner concerning her lease? Concerning her prepayment?

8. The decision in *Price v. Amoco Oil Co.* cen-

ters on the understanding of the lease's provisions by the service station lessor. How valid is *Price*'s distinction between those who should know the legal implications of their acts and those who cannot be expected to know them? What are the ethical and public policy implications of this distinction? If you were advising Amoco, what methods would you recommend to accomplish the same ends as the indemnification clause?

9. Bill Bickham has 2 years remaining on a 10-year lease for office space from Sonia Agouab. The lease specifically prohibits subletting but is silent as to Bickham's right to assign his lease. Bickham has moved to larger quarters in another building and assigned his lease to Elizabeth Calhoun. Calhoun has agreed to make the rental payments to Agouab. Agouab has notified Bickham that she wants Calhoun out and that he is liable for rent for the remainder of the lease. Bickham claims he had the right to assign the lease. Correct? He also claims that the assignment relieved him of further liability to Agouab regardless of what happens after the assignment. Correct?

10. Clyde Alexander, a tenant, brought suit against his landlord, Walter Fletcher, for injuries sustained by his son, Jason, when he fell from a second-floor window of their apartment. Jason, a minor, fell out of a bedroom window in which there was an aluminum screen. His father alleges negligence on behalf of the landlord for the failure to install and maintain window screens sufficiently strong to support the weight of a child who might lean against a screen. Fletcher has argued that he did not control the premises and he had no duty to install and maintain windows which could have prevented a fall from a window. Is a court likely to agree with Fletcher? Explain.

CHAPTER 29

Wills, Estates, and Trusts

"In this world, nothing is certain but death and taxes," wrote Benjamin Franklin, over 200 years ago. Because death and taxes are certain, people should plan for both. Yet, particularly where death is concerned, people show a remarkable reluctance to make even the simplest plans. Your chances of avoiding tax problems are better than those of avoiding death. Still, in both instances you can minimize the consequences through the application of preventive law.

This chapter is about the legal consequences of death and the principal tools available to plan for them.

THE DISPOSITION OF A DECEDENT'S PROPERTY

A *decedent* is a person who has died.

Most people own property at their deaths. The law of estates and wills primarily deals with what happens to that property.

The Estate

In general, a decedent's *estate* includes all her property, both personal and real, which her heirs will inherit. Figure 29.1 illustrates the kinds of property which might be found in an estate.

ITEM	PART OF ESTATE FOR ESTATE TAXES?	SUBJECT TO WILL?	CHAPTER DISCUSSED
Gift inter vivos	If within 3 years of death	No	25, 29
Gift in contemplation of death	If within 3 years of death	No	29
Tenancy in common property	Yes	Yes	27
Joint tenancy property	Yes	No	27
Life estate during lifetime	No	No	27
Testamentary trust	Yes	Fund by will	29
Life insurance when estate is beneficiary	Yes	Yes	30
Life insurance when estate is not beneficiary	Yes	No	29, 30

Figure 29.1 Potential Estate Property.
This figure summarizes the tax treatment of property which may be included in a decedent's estate. It also indicates which types may be transferred by will.

The definition of "estate" contains two important qualifications. First, an estate contains only property whose ownership will pass to *heirs*—persons who receive property from an estate. Some property is transferred on death but not to heirs. Therefore, it is not part of the decedent's estate. Suppose Sharon held land in a *joint tenancy* with her husband. On her death, her interest will go automatically to him and does not form part of her estate. Also, insurance with a beneficiary other than her estate, completed inter vivos gifts, or gifts in contemplation of death are not part of her estate.

Second, the general definition of "estate" is not the same as the definitions used by the federal and state taxing authorities. For example, Sharon's estate for federal tax purposes will include her interest in the joint tenancy, all gifts in contemplation of death, and inter vivos gifts made within 3 years of her death.

As the last two paragraphs imply, estate planning has a much broader focus than simply minimizing estate tax liability. It is a process for ensuring that a person distributes her property in accordance with her wishes and minimizes a whole range of taxes. In fact, because federal estate taxes do not apply (as of 1986) to estates under $600,000, most estates are not affected by them. If Sharon was fortunate enough to have potential estate tax liability, she could minimize it my making gifts of up to $10,000 per year to a person who would inherit. Thus, if Sharon had two children, she could give each up to $10,000 per year. Her husband could make similar gifts, so the total per child per year could reach $20,000. These gifts also would not be subject to the federal gift tax.

The Purpose of a Will

A person can make dispositions of property which take effect after her death. The principal means for making these gifts is the *will*, a document directing the disposition of a decedent's property upon death. Wills are critically important as estate planning devices not because they save estate taxes but because, by the use of devices such as trusts, the future tax consequences for the heirs can be minimized.

If Sharon dies leaving a valid will, she is said to have died *testate*, and she is termed the *testatrix*, the person who made the will. (A man who makes a will is called a *testator*.) If she dies without leaving a valid will, she is said to have died *intestate*. If Sharon dies intestate, her state's laws of *intestate succession* define how her estate will be administered. They specify who will inherit and in what proportion, without regard for what her wishes might have been.

Estate problems tend to be straightforward and easily remediable through the application of preventive law and estate planning. But only the living may plan their estates, and the key instrument in estate planning is the will. Once death comes, it is too late.

INTESTATE SUCCESSION

The state court which oversees the administration of all estates, often called the *probate court*, will appoint a personal representative, who is called an *administrator*, to dispose of an intestate's estate. (A woman appointed by the court is called an *administratrix*.) Many people think that since the courts will assume responsibility for their estates, they need not bother with a will. But consider just two possible consequences that might occur if a decedent does not leave a will:

- She has forfeited her right to determine who will receive her property and in what proportion.
- If she has children under 18, a person not of her choosing may obtain guardianship of them.

As this section demonstrates, there are other, equally negative, consequences of dying intestate.

Determining the Heirs

Each state has a law of intestate succession, which determines how the estate of a person who dies intestate is distributed among his survivors. These laws, which are also called *descent and distribution* statutes, vary from state to state. Still, they share the common goal of distributing the estate fairly. To this end, they provide a priority of heirship and percentage-share allotments which the courts *must* follow in distributing the decedent's property

The decedent's family and blood relatives. The law gives priority to the surviving spouse, followed by the decedent's children or grandchildren. Suppose Paul dies, survived by his wife Linda and they had no children. Under most states, Linda receives the entire estate. In some states, Paul's parents would receive a percentage of the estate if he died childless. But suppose Linda and two children survive Paul. Linda receives between one-quarter and one-half of Paul's estate. The balance is divided between the children. If Linda dies before Paul and they had no children, his estate passes to his blood relatives—his parents, brothers, sisters, and their children.

Collateral relatives. If no family member or blood relative survives, the estate passes to *collateral relatives*, or *next of kin*, that is, persons related to the decedent through a common ancestor. The search for collateral relatives begins with the decedent's grandparents. Thus, Paul's first cousin is a collateral relative.

The descent and distribution laws determine who the closest collateral relatives are and place a limit on how distant a collateral relative may be to inherit. If neither a family member nor a next of kin is to be found, the estate *escheats*, or forfeits to the state.

Qualifications for Heirship

The descent and distribution laws determine whether a person qualifies as an intestate decedent's heir. For instance, adopted children often—but not always—have the same standing as natural children. However, in-laws and other relatives by marriage, except a spouse, do not qualify. Thus, if Paul died intestate, Linda's brother would not be an heir.

Murderers. A decedent's murderer may not inherit under either the laws of intestate succession or a will. That does not mean that a person who kills the decedent may not be an heir. Many states distinguish between murder, which requires intent, and involuntary manslaughter, which does not. A California court has held that a person found not guilty of murder by reason of insanity could inherit her victims' estates.* As the next case shows, a somewhat different rule applies to the decedent's interest in a joint tenancy, which normally passes to the survivor.

---

* *In re Estates of Ladd and Ladd*, 91 Cal. App. 3d 219, 153 Cal. Rptr. 888 (1979).

In re Estate of Matye

645 P.2d 955 (Mont. 1982)

FACTS Mrs. Matye allegedly murdered her husband. His father petitioned the probate court for an adjudication of intestacy, a determination of heirs, and his appointment as administrator. Mrs. Matye agreed to her father-in-law's appointment but asked the court to order the sale of property she and her husband had held jointly so that she could use the proceeds from her interest for her defense. Her father-in-law, as administrator, opposed her request. The probate court found for Mrs. Matye.

ISSUE

Does a joint tenant who murders the other joint tenant retain an undivided half-interest in the jointly held property?

DECISION

Yes. Affirmed. A murderer has no right of survivorship in joint property. A joint tenant who murders another joint tenant causes the decedent's interest to be severed so that it passes into the decedent's estate as his property. Thus, if Mrs. Matye was found guilty of murder, she could not take her husband's interest under her right of survivorship in the joint tenancy. But her interest in the property came into existence when they created the joint tenancy. She had the right to convey her interest and sever the joint tenancy at any time. Thus, she was entitled to the proceeds from the sale of her half-interest.

Simultaneous death. For many years, courts were troubled by the application of the intestacy laws to situations where spouses died in a common accident or died within a very short time of each other. Besides the impossibility in some circumstances of establishing who died first, a choice often was unjust to one set of heirs. Suppose Paul and Linda were childless. They die in an automobile accident, and there is no evidence to establish that one survived the other even momentarily. If a court were to hold that Linda died first, her estate would go to Paul's family.

Today, most states have adopted the Uniform Simultaneous Death Statute, which directs a court, in effect, to find that each spouse died just before the other. This solution permits heirs on both sides of the marriage to inherit. Thus, in the example above, Paul's heirs would inherit his estate, and Linda's heirs would inherit hers.

Distribution

Descent and distribution statutes apply mechanical formulas for allocating the estate among qualified heirs. They make *no* provision for determining the decedent's preferences. Suppose Paul and his son John had many bitter fights. On many occasions people heard Paul say that John would inherit nothing on Paul's death. However, if Paul dies intestate, John is an heir.

A much more painful problem arises when the intestate decedent intended to allocate his estate to reflect his heirs' varying needs. Suppose Linda is in the early stages of cerebral palsy. She faces years of very high medical bills. For that reason Paul wished to leave her 90 percent and John 10 percent of his estate. A court could not carry out Paul's intent.

The courts distribute the intestate's real property under the law of the state in which it is located. Suppose Paul's residence was in California but his vacation cabin was in Nevada. California law would apply to the residence and Nevada law to the cabin.

Personal property, however, is distributed according to the laws of the state in which the decedent had his *domicile*. A person's domicile is the location of his permanent home. It is the place to which he ultimately intends to return when he is absent from it. Domicile and residence are not precisely synonymous. Paul could be in residence at his cabin but his domicile would be in California. Thus, California law would control the distribution of Paul's personalty in the Nevada cabin.

WILLS

A *will* is a document directing the disposition of a decedent's property upon death. Depending on the testatrix's circumstances, she may accomplish a number of things in her will—both related and unrelated to the disposition of her property. These might include:

- Establishing guardianship for her children
- Creating trust funds for their education
- Making *bequests*—gifts of personalty made by will—to charities or to nonfamily members
- Allocating her property among her heirs according to their needs

Figure 29.2 is a sample will.

The testatrix also may designate a personal representative, called an *executor* (masculine) or *executrix* (feminine), who will take charge of her assets and see that her estate is administered in accordance with her will. Quite often, the designated personal representative is the decedent's lawyer or spouse.

Requirements for a Valid Will

Formalities of execution. Wills are *formal* documents, meaning they must meet certain specifications. The law requires that a will must be in writing and be signed by the testator, usually in the presence of one or more witnesses who must also sign the document.

While wills must be in writing, few states restrict the form of that writing. It may be typed or handwritten. A will scrawled on the back of an envelope would be legal, so long as the testator signed it *and* it satisfied the state's requirements as to witnesses to the testator's signature. Some states permit *holographic wills*, unwitnessed wills in the handwriting of, and signed by, the testator. Courts regard these documents with suspicion because of the obvious opportunities for fraud and forgery.

The testator must sign the will. If he is physically incapable of signing it, as a quadriplegic would be, he may sign it by proxy. The person signing as proxy must do so at the testator's direction and in his presence. As with holographic wills, a probate court will review this procedure with great care.

The number of witnesses to the testator's signature varies. Illinois, for instance, requires two; many other states, three. In order to avoid questions of impropriety, an heir should not be a witness. Witnesses need not know the contents of the will nor even that the document being signed is a will. All they need to verify is that the testator was signing the document of his own volition and that he was competent to do so.

Testamentary intent. *Testamentary intent* refers to the testator's intention to dispose of his property by will. At the time of executing the will, he must have intended that the property covered by it pass upon his death to the persons he designated. So to have testamentary intent, a testator must know and approve of the will's contents.

Intending to make a will is not the same as testamentary intent. As the next case holds, a person must execute a document with the intention that that document be her will.

LAST WILL AND TESTAMENT

I, PETER J. HAMMERSMITH of Gibbsville, Appleton County, Erewhon, make this my last will and testament, and hereby revoke all earlier wills and codicils.

FIRST, except as provided in paragraph the SECOND, I give all my personal effects and all other tangible personal property I own at the time of my death, not including any cash, bank books, certificates of deposit, securities or other intangible personal property, to my wife, ROBERTA PIERCE HAMMERSMITH, if she survives me.

SECOND, I give all personal property inherited by me from my mother, Annette Holmes Hammersmith, to my wife, should she survive me, for her life, and then in equal shares to any of my children who survive her or to the issue surviving her of such deceased children, provided, however, that if none of my children or their issue survive her, the said personal property shall be distributed in equal shares to the lineal descendents of Annette Holmes Hammersmith.

THIRD, I give to my brother, ALLAN Y. HAMMERSMITH, if he survives me, all of my stock in Hammersmith Enterprises.

FOURTH, I give to ST. MARY'S CHURCH, Gibbsville, Erewhon, a sum equivalent to one tenth (1/10) of all the intangible personal property I own at the time of my death.

FIFTH, I give to my wife, should she survive me, all real property or interests in real property which I own at the time of my death.

SIXTH, I give the remainder of my property, of whatever type and wherever situated, as follows:

1. To my wife, if she survives me.

2. If my wife does not survive me, in equal shares to my children and to the issue of any deceased child.

3. If my wife does not survive me and if I am not survived by any children of mine or their issue, in equal shares to St. Mary's Church, THE AMERICAN RED CROSS, THE AMERICAN CANCER SOCIETY, and SOUTHEASTERN UNIVERSITY.

SEVENTH, I fully understand who my heirs at law would be upon my death and have intentionally not provided for those not specifically indicated in this will.

EIGHTH, I nominate my wife as executor of my will, or if she fails or ceases to serve, Allan L. Goldsmith, Esq. of Gibbsville, Erewhon.

I direct that any person appointed to serve as the executor or administrator of my estate shall be exempt from giving any bond, or if required to give bond, shall be exempt from furnishing any surety.

I direct my executor to pay my funeral expenses, the expenses of administering my estate in any and all jurisdictions, and all my just debts.

NINTH, I appoint my wife to be guardian of the person and property of each minor child of mine. If she fails or ceases to serve as guardian, I appoint Allan Y. Hammersmith to serve in her place.

IN WITNESS WHEREOF, I hereunto set my hand this _____ day of _____, 1990.

_____

Signed, published, declared and acknowledged by PETER J. HAMMERSMITH as and for his will in the presence of us two who at his request, in his presence and in the presence of one another subscribe our names hereto as witnesses.

_____   _____
(Name)   (Address)

_____   _____
(Name)   (Address)

Figure 29.2 A Simple, Hypothetical Will.
The formal requirements for wills vary considerably from state to state. Many wills contain detailed instructions to the executor as to the administration of the estate. Also, where minor children are involved, the testator will commonly create trusts for their care and education.

In re Will of Smith

108 N.J. 257, 528 A.2d 918 (1987)

FACTS   Esther Smith's husband died testate. As her husband's sole beneficiary, she worked closely with the family lawyer to settle the estate. Sometime between the death of her husband and her own death 7 months later, Esther Smith gave her lawyer the following writing:

> *My entire estate is to be left jointly to my step-*
> *daughter*
> *Roberta Crowley*
> *178 Tillotson Rd. Fanwood, N.J.,*
> *and my step-son*
> *David J. Smith*
> *112 Hillside Ave.*
> *Watchung, N.J.*
> *Extor—*
> *DAVID*
> *s/Esther L. Smith*
> *492 Mountainview Dr.*
> *No. Plainfield, N.J.*
> *07063*

Her attorney was then 84 years old and preparing to retire. He testified that Mrs. Smith told him, "This is my will, this is the way I want my estate to go." The attorney did not treat the document as he did wills. He kept wills in separately marked envelopes in a fire-proof safe. This document he attached to the file for her husband's estate. When the document was offered for probate, it was challenged by Mrs. Smith's first cousins. The objectors conceded that the document met the statutory requirements for a holographic will and expressed her intentions as to the disposition of her property. Nonetheless, the probate court concluded Mrs. Smith knew the formal requirements for a will and that she never intended the document to be her will. It denied probate for the will. The stepchildren appealed. The appeals court agreed with the trial court's factual findings. However, it held that even though Mrs. Smith had not intended the document to be her will, it should be admitted to probate because it would implement her probable intent. Mrs. Smith's cousins appealed.

ISSUE   In the absence of testamentary intent, may a writing that satisfies the other requirements for a holographic will be admitted to probate as an expression of the writer's probable intent?

DECISION   No. Trial court judgment reinstated. The issue here is not whether the document expresses Mrs. Smith's wishes as to her estate. Rather, the question is whether she intended the document to be her will. A formally executed will ordinarily declares that it represents the testator's last will, a declaration that is generally acknowledged by the witnesses in the attestation clause. Thus, the face of a formal will manifests its testamentary character. The holographic instrument at issue here does not manifest such an intent. The burden then fell on the document's proponents to establish that Mrs. Smith prepared it with testamentary intent. The trier of fact concluded that they had not borne this burden.

Testamentary capacity. *Testamentary capacity* is the capacity to make a valid will. Generally, states establish a minimum age—18 in many states—for making a will.

The testator must also have sufficient mental capacity to make the will at the time he *executes*, or creates, it by signing it. "Mental capacity" generally means that a person has a sound mind, an independent will, and the ability to understand the nature and effects of his acts.

Courts generally look for evidence of at least minimal mental capacity. For example, they often seek evidence that the testator knew who his immediate heirs were.

A testator may lack the ability to manage ordinary business affairs yet have testamentary capacity. The rationale for this minimal standard is that a will's purpose is simply to provide gifts upon death. The following case illustrates the application of this standard.

In re Estate of Rosen

447 A.2d 1220 (Me. 1982)

FACTS

Seymour Rosen was a certified public accountant. He had been married for 30 years and had a grown son. In 1973, doctors diagnosed Seymour as having chronic leukemia. In 1978 he abandoned his home and practice in New York City and moved to Maine with his secretary, Robin Gordon. There he set up an accounting practice. Despite his medical problems, Seymour continued his practice until 2 months before his death in December 1980. While in New York, Seymour had executed a will, leaving everything to his wife and son. However, in July 1980, after negotiating a property settlement with his wife, he executed a new will, leaving all his property to Robin. His wife and son challenged the will, alleging Seymour lacked testamentary capacity. At trial, the three witnesses to the new will—all of whom saw Seymour regularly before and after its execution—testified that he was of sound mind. The lawyer who drew up the 1980 will testified he consulted Seymour for tax accounting before and after its execution. However, the evidence also showed that the disease and the drugs used to treat it periodically eroded his mental capacity. Both Robin and the lawyer acknowledged that at times Seymour did not know what his assets were or their value. The trial court upheld the 1980 will.

ISSUE

Did Seymour have sufficient mental capacity to dispose of his property by will?

DECISION   Yes. Affirmed. The mental competence required to execute a valid will involves the exercise of only as much mind and memory as would enable a person to transact common and simple kinds of business. It is the intelligence which belongs to the weakest class of sound minds. A will will be upheld so long as the testator can recall the general nature, condition, and extent of his property and his relationships with his potential heirs.

Sometimes an otherwise competent testator may suffer from an *insane delusion*, a belief in something which a reasonable person would understand to be untrue or impossible. Suppose Baxter's son was killed in Vietnam. Baxter came to believe that another soldier was buried in his son's grave and that his son was still alive. Baxter's will contained a bequest to his son. A court would uphold the will if Baxter's insane delusion did not affect his mind in ways that would cause him to lack testamentary capacity. Also, Baxter must have made the bequest to his son in such a way that the court could ignore it without defeating the purposes of the will. The court, for instance, would reallocate a cash gift to the other beneficiaries. However, if the son was the sole beneficiary, the court could not reform the will. Then, it would declare that Baxter had left no valid will and would distribute his estate under the laws of intestate succession.

Revocation or Modification of a Will

A competent testator always has the power to modify or revoke a will. In some instances, a court may modify or nullify a will.

Codicils and later wills. The principal means of modifying a will is by an addendum, or *codicil*, to an existing will. The testator must execute this document with the same formalities and satisfy the same intent and capacity requirements as those for a will. A codicil may add totally new matters, or it may modify or revoke provisions. A later will, as its name implies, is one executed after an earlier will.

A codicil or a later will may expressly revoke part or all of an earlier will. Where the later document does not expressly revoke the earlier one, the court may find an implied revocation of those matters in the earlier document with which the later document conflicts. Thus, assuming both the earlier and the later documents are valid, the later one normally controls.

Physical act. A testator may revoke his will by a physical act, but it must leave no question in anyone's mind of his intent. He must rip, tear, burn, or otherwise mutilate the will. Scratching an X in a corner of a page is not sufficient.

In most states, a will which the testator has revoked may not be *revived*, or brought back into effect, after revocation. If a testator tears up his will and then attempts to tape it back together, a court will hold he revoked it. The testator must reexecute the will. Any other rule would lead to fraudulent claims.

Operation of law. In some instances the law revokes all or part of a will. The circumstances vary from state to state, although they usually involve events which the testator did not anticipate when he made his will.

As noted earlier, a person who murders the testator may not inherit from him. In allocating the estate, courts treat murderers as if they died before their victims did. If the testator marries after executing a will, the surviving spouse is usually guaranteed by law a percentage of the testator's estate. A divorce or an annulment usually revokes those provisions which favor the former spouse.

Normally, by statute, a child born after the execution of a will and whose birth the testator did not anticipate is entitled to a percentage of the estate. As for children alive when the testator makes his will, the law assumes the testator intends to provide for them. If a testator intends to disinherit a child, he must do so specifically.

Bequests and Devises

Gifts made by will are of two types. As noted earlier, a gift of personalty is called a bequest. A gift of realty is called a *devise*. When speaking generally of all gifts made by will, writers often refer to them as bequests. (The mechanics of distributing bequests are discussed later in this chapter.)

Just being named in a will confers no rights on the beneficiary because, up to the moment of death, the testator can change his will. The beneficiary's rights come into existence only at the time of the testator's death.

Conditions. Courts will enforce conditions imposed on heirs receiving bequests under a will so long as the restrictions are not against public policy or decency. One common restriction cancels a bequest to any individual who challenges the validity of the will. A court might enforce that condition, but it certainly would not enforce one requiring a son to divorce his wife in order to inherit.

Taking against the will. Virtually all states prohibit disinheriting a surviving spouse. Some testators attempted to evade this provision by making nominal bequests to their spouses. State laws now permit a surviving spouse to elect to renounce bequests made by the decedent spouse. This option, called *taking against the will*, gives the surviving spouse a statutorily prescribed percentage of the entire estate— usually between one-third and one-half, depending on whether any children survive.

Suppose Ken and Mary spent most of their married life battling. Ken decides to win the last round by leaving Mary only $5000 out of his $250,000 estate. Upon his death Mary can elect to renounce the bequest and take the statutory percentage instead. With some careful planning, however, Ken could have achieved his goal. All he had to do was dispose of all his property before he died. While legally feasible, such a course clearly poses ethical questions.

Disclaimers of inheritances. An heir or a legatee does not have to accept an inheritance. He or she can disclaim or renounce it. Valid reasons for disclaiming inheritances range from simply not needing the money to not wanting to accept anything from a person the heir despised.

Living Wills

In 1976, California became the first state to enact a statute recognizing the *living will*, a formal declaration by an individual stating that he or she wishes to "die naturally" rather than be kept alive by "heroic" or "artificial" means during a painful, terminal illness or while hopelessly comatose. By 1986, at least 36 other states had adopted living will legislation.

Goals. The idea of a living will evolved in response to advances in medical technology that allowed the continuation of bodily functions in individuals whose brains had stopped functioning and that prolonged the last illnesses of persons with loathsome or excruciating diseases, like cancer. It took, however, the nationally publicized case of Karen Anne Quinlan to give focus to the movement for living wills. After partying one night, Ms. Quinlan—then in her midtwenties—lapsed into a coma. She was "brain dead." For more than 2 years, her parents fought—and ultimately won—a landmark battle in the New Jersey courts to permit them to instruct the physicians to disconnect the respirator that they believed kept their daughter alive.

Advocates of the living will intended it to free physicians from liability if, acting under its terms, they used less than every method available to prolong the life of a terminally ill patient. Without a living will physicians often found themselves caught in the dilemma of whether to use every means to keep a patient alive or to respect the wishes of the family or the patient to allow nature to take its course.

Usual requirements. The legislation governing living wills is remarkably diverse. Generally, however, the formal requirements for a valid living will resemble those for an ordinary will, including the need to have at least two witnesses. Often, a critical additional element consists of designating someone to make treatment decisions in critical conditions. Quite commonly, that person is a spouse.

Some states require that a diagnosis of "terminal illness" made by the patient's physician must be confirmed by a second, neutral physician before the terms of the living will may be invoked. Several states require periodic renewals of the living will declaration.

The model act. Because of the great disparities among state laws, in 1985 the National Confer- ence of Commissioners on Uniform State Laws adopted the *Uniform Rights of the Terminally Ill Act*. This model act limits the availability of the living will to adults. The provisions of a living will apply only to a person who "is in an irreversible condition that will cause death in a relatively short time." Ironically, the Uniform Act would exclude the Quinlan situation, since Quinlan did not die until several years after she was disconnected from the respirator.

The Uniform Act contains some controversial provisions. First, it asserts the living will should apply in states other than the one in which it was executed. Second, health professionals are not required to observe the terms of the living will. Alternative model acts have covered patients in persistent vegetative states and required health officials to comply with the terms of a living will.

The tragic consequences of not writing a living will were powerfully revealed in the following highly publicized case involving another young woman, Nancy Cruzan. Like Karen Quinlan's parents, Cruzan's parents sought to permit her to "die with dignity" after she fell into a vegetative state.

Cruzan v. Director, Missouri Department of Health

110 S.Ct. 2841 (1990)

FACTS In 1983, 25-year-old Nancy Cruzan lost control of her car and crashed, leaving her severely brain damaged. Her condition, referred to as a "persistent vegetative state," required that her life be sustained through gastronomy feeding and hydration tubes. When it was obvious that Cruzan would never recover her mental faculties, her parents requested that the hospital discontinue the feeding and hydration procedures and allow her to die. The hospital refused unless a court approved. At the trial it was revealed that Cruzan had no living will, but her former roommate testified that Cruzan had told her that if ever she could not live at least "halfway normally," she would choose to die. The Cruzans prevailed at the trial level but were reversed by the Missouri Supreme Court on the grounds that no one can assume that an incompetent person would choose to end their life without "clear and convincing" evidence.

ISSUE	Can the state of Missouri establish procedures which require that the withdrawal of life-sustaining treatment be proved by a "clear and convincing" standard of evidence?
DECISION	Yes. Affirmed. States are free to establish procedures by which an incompetent's desire to withdraw from life-sustaining treatments must be proved by clear and convincing evidence. It is true that the due process clause of the Constitution protects someone who wishes to refuse life-sustaining medical treatment. However, if the person is incompetent and cannot make that decision, this deeply personal decision cannot be left solely to surrogates, who may not always protect the patient's interest. State law prohibits oral evidence in contracts under the parol evidence rule and the Statute of Frauds, and require that wills be in writing. These rules may also frustrate a party's true intent, just as Missouri's law may. However, the Constitution does not demand that general rules work perfectly.

Durable Powers of Attorney

The public awareness that the *Cruzan* case brought about also underscored the need for similar legal documents to deal with legal and health problems when a person is less impaired. One such document is called a *durable power of attorney*. As discussed in Chapter 13, in a power of attorney the principal confers to another person, the agent, called an attorney in fact, the expressed authority to perform certain acts on her behalf. In this case, the principal is often an elderly parent who grants her son the power to enter into transactions and other matters should she become disabled in some way. These may include allowing the son to use his mother's checking and banking accounts to pay bills, sell her real and personal property, and make investments for her.

Similar to the durable power of attorney, some states also permit *durable powers of attorney for health care*. These documents allow the attorney in fact, sometimes called a health care representative, to make health decisions concerning the principal. This could include endowing the attorney in fact with the authority over whether the principal can undergo surgery or be admitted to a nursing home. It should be emphasized that with both documents, the principal, while competent, can always revoke the power of attorney, the attorney in fact (agent) owes his principal the normal fiduciary duties of care, obedience, accounting, and loyalty and good faith. Trusts, examined later in this chapter, can also achieve the same goals as those realized by the foregoing documents.

Uniform International Wills Act

In recognition of our more global environment, a new uniform law, the Uniform International Wills Act (UIWA), has been established to make more uniform the requirements to create a valid will. UIWA requires that a testator, in the presence of two witnesses and a person authorized to act in connection with international wills, must:

- Declare that the written instrument (document) is his will and that he knows the content of the will.
- Sign the will on each page and at the end of the will.
- Himself witness the designated persons signing each page and the end of the will.

There are several additional procedural requirements charged to the authorized person, including the numbering of all pages of the will, inclusion of the date at the end of the will, and the attachment of a certificate, signed by the testator, which indicates that all the requirements of the act have been met.

States which approve the UIWA, such as Illinois, consider compliance with it to satisfy the existing state requirements for signature and attestation. The UIWA does *not* alter state laws in regard to any other facet of probate. As a result, a probate hearing might be necessary for such things as the supposed competency of the testator, clarification of the language of a bequeath, or a person's right to receive from the estate aside from those allocated in the will.

ADMINISTRATION OF ESTATES

Probate

Questions about a will's validity or intestate succession are litigated only after death. They arise as part of a process called *probate*, a word derived from a Latin word meaning "to prove" or "to verify." Probate originally referred only to proving that the will was the testator's and that it met all the state's formal requirements. Today, it includes all matters relating to the administration of a decedent's estate. Thus, probate is the mechanism by which the will is verified, the decedent's assets are assembled, the outstanding bills are paid, and, finally, the property in the estate is transferred to the heirs.

Whoever has the will at the time of the testator's death has a duty to submit it to the probate court. Its submission begins the probate process. If the decedent dies intestate, the probate process begins with a petition to the court for appointment of an administrator. Usually, the surviving spouse or a family member submits the petition.

The term *admission to probate* refers to the probate court's determination that a will is in fact the decedent's and that it was legally executed. Normally, this is a formality. If the will is regular on its face, it is presumed to be valid.

A will may be admitted to probate even though some provisions are invalid or require the court's interpretation. The testator's intention guides the interpretation of all wills. A court looks to the language the testator used and the sense in which it was used. The court will attempt, as nearly as possible, to put itself in the position of the testator at the time that he executed the will. This requires an examination of the relationships between the testator and the beneficiaries named in the will and of the condition, nature, and extent of the testator's property.

Will Contests

Will contests, which are challenges to a will's admission to probate, are not usual. The ultimate issue in a will contest is whether a competent testator executed a valid will or codicil. Aside from challenges based on the will's form, such as one alleging too few witnesses, most will contests focus on the testator's intent or capacity. The issues resemble those contract actions described in Chapter 9 which raise questions of *fraud, undue influence,* or *mistake.*

Fraud. Fraud normally requires proof that the testatrix was deceived when she executed her will and that, but for the fraud, the testator would not have executed either the will or the provision benefiting the defrauder. Suppose the testatrix's nephew tells her that her daughter has died in an automobile accident, knowing the daughter is alive. The nephew convinces the testatrix to make a new will, leaving all her property to him. The new will will fail. Or suppose the nephew hands the testatrix a document for her signature which he says is a letter but is, in fact, a will. The will is invalid because the testatrix did not have the intent to make a will.

Undue influence. Courts always view with suspicion beneficiaries who occupied confidential relationships with the testator. Lawyers, doctors, nurses, companions, and the like may find themselves under intense scrutiny if the bequests to them are out of proportion to the testator's other bequests. Their special relationships put them in a position to exert undue influence. In order to defeat the will, a contestant generally must show force, coercion, or overpersuasion by such a beneficiary. Mere persuasion is not enough.

Mistake. Courts are extremely reluctant to find that the testator made a mistake in his will. The law presumes that the testator designated the persons he wanted to benefit in the stated amounts. Suppose several people heard the testator say that he planned to leave a small gift to a neighbor in appreciation for her years of kindness. A court will not reform the will to give her what the testator promised. Any other approach, the courts have held, would lead to false claims. However, omission of heirs protected by statute is a different matter altogether.

Functions of the Personal Representative

A personal representative is called either an executor—if he is designated as such in the will and agrees to serve—or an administrator—if he is not designated in the will. In both cases, the personal representative must be appointed by the court. The personal representative, which may be a bank or trust company, takes control of the decedent's assets, pays the debts, makes distributions to the heirs and beneficiaries, and closes the estate.

The naming of an executor in a will does not mean the person will serve. He or she may decline to serve or may be dead.

Appointment. The court appoints a personal representative after an application is filed with the court stating the facts which give rise to the jurisdiction of that particular probate court over the estate and stating why a personal representative should be appointed. The court has the power to reject an executor named in the will, but the power is rarely exercised.

The personal representative may have to post a performance, or surety, bond to indemnify the estate for any losses which may result from his or her administration of it. Normally, the testator will exempt the executor from posting a bond.

Fiduciary duties. Personal representatives serve in a fiduciary capacity. While their role is analogous to that of an agent, their fiduciary duties are considerably greater. Personal representatives must act with due diligence and exercise utmost good faith. For example, an executor may not purchase a painting from the estate simply because he has the right to sell estate assets. In order to protect the estate, a personal representative may employ professionals such as accountants, lawyers, and appraisers, if necessary.

Personal representatives must file accounts with the court periodically until the estate is closed. They may be personally liable for estate assets which existed at the decedent's death but which later disappeared.

Personal representatives may not *commingle*—mix—estate property with their own. In some states, lawyers acting as personal representatives will be disbarred if money belonging to the estate appears in their personal bank accounts even though the commingling causes no loss to the estate.

Estate assets and debts. Personal representatives must discover, collect, and account for all the decedent's assets. Most states require that personal representatives file inventories of assets with the court.

Personal representatives must notify creditors of the decedent's death, since the law requires that they file their claims within a certain period. Personal representatives also settle the decedent's debts. In order to raise cash to pay the debts, personal representatives may sell estate assets—even if they are the subject of a specific bequest—generally starting with the personal property. They are also responsible for seeing that federal estate taxes and state inheritance taxes are paid.

Distributions. Where possible, personal representatives carry out the decedent's intentions as expressed in the will. If no will exists, they must determine which relatives will take under the laws of intestacy and distribute the assets accordingly.

Personal representatives distribute property in accordance with an order of distribution established by law. When the estate contains sufficient assets to cover all its obligations and the gifts specified in the will, the statutory scheme is of no great importance. However, when that is not the case, there is an *abatement*, the process of determining the distribution of the estate where the estate property is insufficient to pay all debts and gifts. Thus, after the personal representative has settled the estate's debts and administrative costs, the law establishes the following priority of distribution:

1. *Specific devices or bequests*, e.g., "100 shares of IBM stock to my daughter, Kate"
2. *General bequests*, e.g., "All my corporate bonds to my son, Harry"
3. *Residue*, e.g., "All remaining assets to my sister, Karin"
4. *Intestate property* (property not provided for in a will)

When the testator made a specific bequest in the will but the asset no longer exists or was not in the testator's estate, the gift fails. This is called an *ademption*. Suppose a bequest provides, "I give my Cadillac to my nephew, Henry." But a year before he died, the testator sold the Cadillac and bought a Lincoln. Henry will have no right to the Lincoln.

Personal representatives must obtain approval of their accounts from the probate court in order to make final payments and distributions and to close the decedent's estate.

TRUSTS

A *trust* is established when the person who creates the trust—the *settlor*—transfers title to property to a person or an entity—the *trustee*—to hold, manage, and invest for the benefit of the trust's beneficiaries. The trustee has the legal title to the assets in the trusts; the beneficiaries are said to have an equitable title. Figure 29.3 illustrates a typical trust arrangement.

A beneficiary may be a person or an institution, like a college, hospital, or church. Beneficiaries are classified as either income or remainder beneficiaries. An *income beneficiary* receives use or income, or both, from the property in the trust—the trust's *corpus*—for the period of the trust or until the purpose of the trust has been accomplished. A *remainder beneficiary* receives the corpus of the trust when the trust terminates. A very common trust arrangement specifies that income from the corpus should support a spouse for life. On his or her death, the corpus is to be divided among the settlor's children.

Why Create a Trust?

Settlors' purposes in establishing trusts vary widely. Trusts are popular devices for family financial planning. A trust allows the settlor to separate the burdens of managing property from the beneficial enjoyment of the property. In other words, it allows the settlor to place responsibility in the trustee's hands, freeing the beneficiaries of that duty.

Trusts are particularly useful for guaranteeing care for sick relatives, paying a child's college expenses, or ensuring a charity of income.

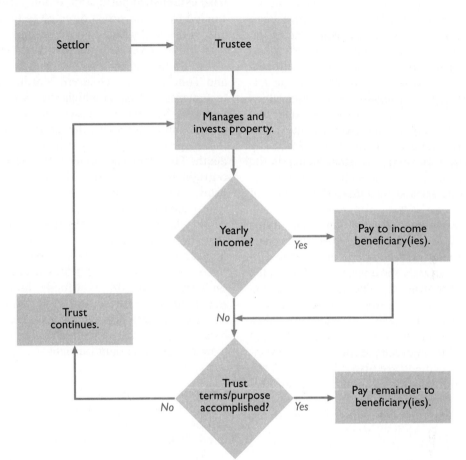

Figure 29.3 A Typical Trust Arrangement.

A trust may continue to implement the settlor's financial plan for the beneficiaries long after the settlor's death. If a settlor could implement his goals only by means of a bequest, the recipients would be under no obligation to carry out his ongoing directions. However, except for *charitable trusts*—trusts whose beneficiaries are churches, hospitals, medical research, or the like—trusts do not last forever. Every state has restricted their duration by statute.

Types of Trusts

Inter vivos trusts. A trust created during the settlor's lifetime is called a *living*, or an *inter vivos*, trust. Suppose Fred is 40 years old. His mother is 70 and in good health. Fred wants to ensure that she has a place to live and an adequate income. He buys her a condominium and places it and $100,000 in trust for her benefit, with the remainder of his estate to go to his daughter. The trust he created is an inter vivos trust.

Living trusts, in recent years, have been marketed aggressively on television and in the print media by law firms and estate planners. The trusts they are promoting are in effect a revocable, living trust. This means that the settlor, as trustee, can legally make inter vivos transfers of property in the trust to anyone. She can also vary any of the terms of the trust, including revoking it, at any time. When the trustee dies, a successive trustee, named in the trust instrument, distributes all the trust assets to the beneficiaries according to the dictates of the trust.

After removing all the hype, are living trusts really as good as their promoters say? Trusts are relatively complicated legal instruments; consequently the answer depends on the settlor's circumstances. The feature most extolled by those promoting them is that they avoid probate, a process that commonly takes as long as 2 years in states like California and costs from 3 to 5 percent of the estate's assets. Probate proceedings are also on display in the public record, which may embarrass some. Finally, trusts are simply harder to contest by disgruntled heirs than are wills. The disadvantages are that a skillfully written living trust is more expensive to set up than is a will. Those who buy a trust kit in the neighborhood drugstore may not pay much now, but their heirs will if the trust kit fails and is challenged. Living trusts also do not lower estate taxes, contrary to how some are promoting them. Last, under some states' laws, like New York's, living trusts may actually be less effective than wills. When all the pros and cons are factored in, those who might benefit most from a living trust are persons who own real property in more than one state, have complex estates, and live in states with high probate costs.

Testamentary trusts. A *testamentary trust* is a trust established during the settlor's lifetime but funded by estate assets directed to the trust by will. If the settlor fails to provide funding for the trust in his or her will, the trust goes unfunded.

Let's look at an example. Suppose Martha and Tom have two children. Martha sets up a testamentary trust to which she assigns in her will half her estate. Under the terms of the trust, Tom is to receive the income for life and the corpus is to pass to their children on his death. The other half of her estate Martha wills outright to Tom. Tom's will leaves his entire estate to his children.

Ultimately, Tom and Martha's children receive what remains of Martha's estate. Note that the funds which were not subject to the testamentary trust may be subject to estate taxes twice—first on Martha's death and then on Tom's death; the trust funds, however, are taxed only once (see Figure 29.4). Nonetheless, because of state and federal exemptions from estate taxes, it will make financial sense to give Tom a certain amount outright.

Constructive trusts. A *constructive trust* is an equitable remedy, not a trust established by a settlor. To prevent unjust enrichment, a court imposes a duty on a constructive trustee to transfer to others property he wrongly acquired or holds. Suppose a principal appoints an agent to deliver a sailboat to a customer and to receive $45,000 in payment from the customer. If the agent refuses to turn over the money, a court will hold the agent to be the constructive trustee of the money. In the next case, the court's task was complicated by fraud and the possibility that the beneficiary's right was barred by the statute of limitations.

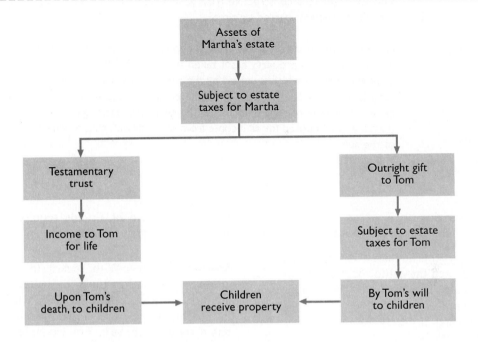

Figure 29.4 Martha's Estate and Its Distribution.

Stone v. Williams

970 F.2d 1043 (2nd Cir. 1992)

FACTS Just before his untimely death in 1952, singer-songwriter Hank Williams, Sr., executed a custody and support agreement for his illegitimate daughter Cathy Stone. In 1985, Stone commenced an action seeking to be declared the child of Williams, Sr., and therefore entitled to copyright renewals for his vast repertory of songs. Hank Williams, Jr., Roy Acuff, and others who had rights to the copyright renewals had the case dismissed at the trial level on grounds that it was barred by the passage of time. On a rehearing, Stone's right to sue for the copyright renewals was reversed, since it was found that the sister of Williams, Sr., as administratrix of the estate, and others had conspired to conceal Stone's true identity as the daughter of Williams, Sr. On appeal concerning several issues surrounding her right to receive the copyright renewals, Stone was seeking a right to set up a constructive trust as a remedy for the wrongful withholding of the renewals which the lower court found was barred by time.

ISSUE
: Was the right to a constructive trust as a remedy for the wrongful withholding of copyright renewals barred by time?

DECISION
: No. Reversed. A constructive trust is proper as a remedial device when a person who is entitled to property has it taken away wrongfully. A constructive trust is an equitable remedy which is barred by the running of a 3-year period. Stone's right to copyright renewals arises each time she does not receive her rightful share of the income from the renewals, not when the renewals first began. Thus, a constructive trust may be imposed for all income from the renewals that originate within 3 years of the suit.

Creating an Express Trust: the Seven Elements

An *express trust* is an inter vivos or a testamentary trust which the settlor declares in specific terms, usually in a writing. The settlor or a personal representative creates an express trust by transferring property to the trustee. The paragraphs below discuss the seven elements required to create an express trust.

Capacity. The settlor must have contractual capacity to convey property to the trust if the trust arrangements are made by contract, as they would be in a living trust. If the trust is created by will, then the decedent must have testamentary capacity.

Intent. The settlor must have a present intention to create a trust. While the law does not require that any particular form of words be used in creating a trust, the words must plainly reflect the settlor's immediate intention. If the settlor says, "This spring, I will put my farm in trust for my son," the wording indicates a future—not a present—intent to create a trust.

Writing. Although preventive law principles dictate that all trusts be evidenced by a writing, only those involving real property require one. If a settlor creates a trust which will hold real property, she must transfer the land to the trustee. Since she has transferred an interest in land, the Statute of Frauds requires that the trust be evidenced by a writing.

Specific property. With regard to the trust's corpus, the settlor must designate specific, identifiable, transferable property which exists at the time of the trust's creation and which he has a right to convey. For example, a settlor could not put in trust "the foal that Petit Etoile will have next spring." However, the settlor could place Petit Etoile in trust and specify that should she have a foal, it, too, would become a trust asset. Similarly, if the settlor wants to transfer stock to a trust, he must be specific as to which stock and how many shares. "All my stock" would be specific enough; "some of my Exxon shares" would not.

Trustee. It is necessary for a trust to have a trustee. However, it is not necessary in the creation of the trust for a particular trustee to be named or to provide a specific name for a successor trustee if a named trustee can no longer serve. In both situations a court can appoint an appropriate trustee. However, to avoid unnecessary court hearings and serve the wishes of the settlor, it is best that the trust designate a trustee and possible successor trustee(s).

A settlor can designate himself as trustee. However, for tax reasons this is generally not advisable. A beneficiary can also serve as a trustee. However, the trust will terminate if such a beneficiary should be or become the sole beneficiary of the trust. The trustee's fiduciary duties are discussed shortly.

Ascertainable beneficiaries. The settlor must either specifically identify the beneficiaries or make them identifiable by some objective standard. A settlor might state her desire to place certain assets in trust "for my grandsons, Tom, Dick, and Harry" if those were the only grandchildren she wished to benefit. If she intended that the trust benefit all her grandchildren—including those not yet born—she could simply say, "for all my grandchildren."

Proper purpose. The settlor must create the trust for a proper purpose. This requirement is similar to that in contract law. It means simply that the trust's purpose must not be illegal or contrary to public policy.

A restriction on a charitable trust may come to violate public policy. When this occurs, the *cy pres doctrine* permits a court to interpret the trust so that it does not violate public policy and as much as possible carries out the settlor's intent. Suppose a settlor in the 1890s established a charitable trust to pay the expenses of poor white children admitted to a particular hospital. A court today would hold that the trust benefited all poor children regardless of color.

The *cy pres* doctrine applies to other situations in which it becomes impossible or impractical for a trustee to carry out the settlor's charitable intentions. In these cases, the courts will reform the trust. But the courts will not apply the doctrine if the settlor clearly indicated he or she intended the funds to be used only for the purpose stated in the trust instrument. In that case, the court will dissolve the trust and distribute the corpus to the settlor's heirs.

The Trustee's Duties

The settlor usually selects the trustee on the basis of investment and managerial capabilities. The trustee may be an individual or a business which handles trusts, like a bank or a trust company. Normally, trustees are compensated.

Trustees serve in a fiduciary capacity. They must not benefit at the expense of the beneficiaries. Like the court in the next case, most courts give a broad interpretation to what benefits a trustee contrary to the interests of the beneficiaries.

Prueter v. Bork

105 Ill. App. 3d 1003, 435 N.E.2d 109 (1982)

FACTS   In 1939, Herman Prueter set up a trust for the benefit of his son, Ervin. In 1951, he set up a similar trust for the benefit of his daughter, Bernice Bork. In both cases, Herman was the sole trustee. In 1965, Herman asked Ervin to agree to revoke the trust because Herman had acquired real estate which he wished to include in a new trust. The new trust would benefit Ervin and Bernice equally. Ervin agreed and did not read the documents his father asked him to sign. Herman did not tell Ervin the new trust instrument contained provisions quite different from those in the 1939 instrument. Under the 1939 trust, Ervin had complete power over the trust assets and income. In the 1965 trust, Herman retained those powers. He also retained the right to terminate Ervin's interest in the trust, a right he later exercised. On

Herman's death, Ervin sued Bernice as Herman's successor trustee on the 1965 trust, seeking to establish his rights to certain trust properties. The trial court found for Bernice.

ISSUE

Did Herman, as trustee, breach his fiduciary duties to Ervin under the 1939 trust by convincing Ervin to revoke it?

DECISION

Yes. Reversed. Herman benefited from the transaction by gaining greater control over the trust. When a trustee benefits from a transaction with the beneficiary, the courts presume the transaction to be fraudulent. The trustee may rebut the presumption with clear and convincing proof that the transaction was fair and that the trustee did not breach his duty of loyalty to the beneficiary. Here, that burden fell on Bernice as the successor trustee. She failed to show that Ervin revoked the 1939 trust with full knowledge of the differences in his rights under the 1965 instrument.

Independent judgment rule. When possible, the trustee has the duty to carry out the settlor's intent. However, if the trustee acts under an inter vivos trust, she must be extremely careful not to become the settlor's puppet. If the Internal Revenue Service determines she is not exercising independent judgment as to the trust's management, the settlor may have to pay taxes on the trust income as if it were his own. Also, depending on the circumstances, he may have to pay significant tax penalties. If the trustee does not act independently, she may be liable to the beneficiaries for breach of her duties to them.

It follows that the trustee must fairly administer the trust for the benefit of the beneficiaries. If more than one beneficiary is involved, the trustee must act impartially toward them. Suppose a trustee approved the payment of educational expenses for one beneficiary but not for another who had an equal right to the funds. A court could order the trustee to pay the expenses, or it could remove her altogether.

Trustees may not delegate their primary duties to others. For example, a trustee could consult with the various beneficiaries of the trust as to their wishes on her investment policy. However, the responsibility for that policy is hers, and she may not defer to their wishes.

Managing the trust assets. A trustee must use the same degree of skill, judgment, and care in managing trust assets as reasonably prudent persons would exercise in the management of their own affairs.

The trustees normally may buy and sell trust property. However, state laws may restrict the type of investments she may make, and the settlor may forbid the sale of some assets—often a family farm or other real estate. The trustee usually must keep the trust assets diversified and productive. For example, it would not be prudent to invest all the trust assets in the stock of one company, even if the company is IBM. In fact, if the trust is a charitable trust, federal tax laws prohibit holding more than a certain percentage of the stock of any one company.

A trustee also may not engage in speculation which would deplete the trust assets. Trustees normally acquire stock in companies. However, investing a large portion of the trust's assets in new companies in rapidly developing fields, like genetic engineering, may be considered speculation.

Allocation of receipts. The trustee has the duty to allocate trust income and expenses between trust income and trust corpus. Rent, *cash* dividends, and interest are considered income. However, the proceeds from the sale of an asset, such as a building, are considered corpus, as are stock dividends or splits.

The trustee must allocate ordinary trust expenses against income and extraordinary expenses against corpus. Ordinary expenses include real property taxes, normal maintenance, and insurance costs relating to trust properties. In contrast, if the trust owned a building, the cost of major renovations would be charged against the corpus.

Trustee liability. Should the trustee breach her fiduciary duties under either a testamentary or an inter vivos trust, she will be liable in damages to the beneficiaries. If the trust is inter vivos, the trustee will also be liable to the settlor, if he is still alive.

A trustee may also be personally liable on contracts she makes on the trust's behalf, unless the contract specifies otherwise. The trustee would also be liable for torts committed during her administration of the trust and within the scope of her duties. However, the trust will indemnify the trustee if the trustee was not at fault. For example, if a customer slips on a wet floor in an office building owned by a trust and the trustee is held liable for the customer's injuries, the trust would indemnify the trustee.

Special Trust Situations

Once the trust comes into existence, many situations can arise that require the trustee's attention. Some clearly should be anticipated in the trust's creation, such as the settlor's powers, if any, to revoke, modify, or terminate the trust. But, some are not so obvious, such as the need of a young income beneficiary to invade the corpus should he need extraordinary health care.

Revocation. A settlor may reserve the right to revoke or modify the trust. If the settlor revokes, all the trust assets return to him or her. However, a court will prevent a settlor from revoking a trust unless the settlor has specifically reserved this right in the trust instrument.

The Internal Revenue Code taxes trust income to the settlor if the trust is not irrevocable for at least 10 years after the trust is funded. Normally, therefore, a settlor will not retain the power to unilaterally modify or revoke a trust during that period. If the settlor chooses to retain control of the trust, she will be taxed on the trust income as if it were her own.

If the settlor is dead, the trust may be modified or revoked only if all the beneficiaries agree and if it would not frustrate any material purpose of the trust.

Termination. Generally, a court will not terminate a trust simply because it has a sole beneficiary who wishes it terminated. Suppose Jane is to receive income from a trust until she reaches 35, when she is to receive the trust property. A court would not allow her to terminate the trust when she reached 31 simply because she consents to it.

However, if the trustee and the sole beneficiary are the same person, a court will merge the legal and beneficial ownerships and terminate the trust. Thus, if Jane were the sole beneficiary and the trustee, she could petition an appropriate court to terminate the trust.

The death or resignation of the trustee will not normally terminate the trust. A court will appoint a new trustee.

Invasion of principal. A court or the trust instrument may permit the trustee to make a partial invasion of principal—to pay out some of the corpus—in the case of a sole beneficiary who has genuine need. If Jane was critically injured at age 31, the trustee might invade the principal to meet extraordinary medical expenses.

If there is more than one beneficiary and the corpus is to pass to someone else after the death of the income beneficiaries, the courts generally will not permit income beneficiaries to invade the principal unless the trust instrument allows it. Quite commonly, a settlor will list in the trust instrument specific occurrences which might justify a partial invasion.

Transfer of beneficial interest. Normally, a trust beneficiary can transfer his or her beneficial interest in the trust without causing a modification or revocation. The term *beneficial interest* refers to a beneficiary's right to income or principal under a trust. For example, a beneficiary might pledge his right to trust income to a lender in order to secure a mortgage. Similarly, a beneficiary's interest is normally subject to claims by creditors, as would be any other income belonging to the beneficiary.

Spendthrift trusts are trusts whose instruments specifically deny beneficiaries the right to assign their interests in the principal. The purpose of spendthrift trusts is to keep beneficiaries from spending or committing trust assets before they receive them. In the past, creditors could not file claims against such trusts. Today, the courts have carved a number of exceptions from this rule, especially where an innocent third party might be injured, as in the case of someone who defaults on child support payments. Also, as the following case holds, a beneficiary cannot use a spendthrift trust, in effect, to defraud his creditors.

Erickson v. Bank of California

97 Wash. 2d 246, 643 P.2d 670 (1982)

FACTS

George Schafer's mother created a spendthrift trust for the benefit of George and his siblings. Under the trust, when the youngest child reached 22, the trustees were to divide the remaining principal into equal shares and administer them as separate trusts. When a child reached 27, the individual trust terminated and the principal was to be distributed to the child. Six months and 6 days before his youngest sibling reached 22, George—then 27—filed his petition for bankruptcy. George's trustee in bankruptcy—the person in charge of gathering George's assets to pay his creditors—filed suit against the trustee of George's trust to attach the assets he was to receive. The trial court entered summary judgment for the trustee of George's trust. The court of appeals reversed, holding that creditors could attach the trust for necessaries.

ISSUE

Could the trustee in bankruptcy attach George's trust assets for paying creditors who supplied necessaries?

DECISION

Yes. Affirmed. The settlor intended that the trust funds would provide her children with the necessities of life. Suppliers of necessary goods and services should be able to reach the beneficiary's interest in the trust. To prohibit the bankruptcy trustee from reaching these assets would be to perpetrate a fraud on the suppliers. The Bankruptcy Act provides that all property which vests in—that is, becomes the property of—the bankrupt within 6 months after bankruptcy shall vest in the bankruptcy trustee. Schafer deliberately filed for bankruptcy 6 months and 6 days before his beneficial interest would vest, thus attempting to make his interest nontransferable.

- -

CONCLUSION

The focus of this chapter may seem to be on death, but actually it is on what one can do during one's life to plan for the consequences of death. Despite the somewhat specialized nature of the topics covered in this chapter, it is important to keep in mind that they are simply means of transferring property interests. The methodologies the chapter describes—including intestate succession—are designed to implement the wishes of the property owner as to his or her property.

Because of the availability of devices like life insurance—a topic covered in the next chapter—and co-ownership of property in joint tenancies, many people make plans for the distribution of their assets without making a will. Writing a will, however, makes good sense, since it avoids subjecting one's estate to the arbitrary rules of intestate succession. Also, if children are involved, a will can resolve what could become very difficult problems of custody.

If a large estate is involved, failing to plan for death can lead to extensive tax liabilities, even if the decedent left a valid will. Such planning requires the services of skilled professionals.

An important planning device for many people is the trust. Even individuals with more modest estates can use trusts to ensure financial stability for their survivors. But trusts have other equally important uses. Of these, the charitable trust plays a crucial role in funding many worthwhile endeavors ranging from preserving historic sites to funding hospital care for the poor.

In the next chapter, the last in this part, the focus shifts from the transfer of property to the protection of property with insurance.

A NOTE TO FUTURE CPA CANDIDATES

The CPA exam covers the administration of an estate and trusts but not particular questions as to formation and effectiveness of wills. Topics included from this chapter are tested in the business organizations section of the examination.

It is important to understand the basics about an estate. To do so, you should study Figure 29.1. If a person dies without a will the person is said to die intestate. If the deceased person has a will, the document will direct administration of the estate. Remember that joint tenant property and life insurance policies not paid to the estate are part of the estate for estate tax purposes but not subject to the will. Therefore, a provision in a will purporting to transfer the decedent's joint tenancy interest in Blackacre would not be given effect.

The person who handles the estate, if designated by the will, is called an executor (executrix if female); if not designated, an administrator (administratrix if female). In either case, the person must be approved by the court before empowered to act. The will can waive a performance bond.

The CPA exam traditionally has *heavily* emphasized trust questions in the property section of the examination. Be sure you fully understand the basics. The following are required to form an express trust:

- Trustor (settlor) with capacity
- Intent to create a trust
- Writing, if transfer of real property to the trust is involved
- Proper (valid) trust purpose
- Identified trust corpus (property)
- A trustee to hold legal title
- Beneficiary

There is no requirement that a trustee be compensated or that a successor trustee or beneficiary be named. The settlor may not revoke a trust unless such power was expressly reserved.

There are three common types of trusts covered on the exam: inter vivos (during lifetime), testamentary (effective at death), and spendthrift. The latter trust is intended to protect a beneficiary from himself and creditors by prohibiting the assignment or transfer of any interests in the trust principal.

A trustee owes fiduciary duties to act in the best interests of all beneficiaries. Unless otherwise stated in the trust, the trustee has a duty to invest the trust property so as to generate income. The trustee may separately perform accounting services for the trust. However, the trustee *cannot* borrow money or purchase property from the trust unless the trust instrument authorizes action or the beneficiaries consent.

A trust will terminate if the trust term expires, if there is an achievement of the trust purpose, or if there is a failure of the trust purpose. A trust terminates if the sole trustee and beneficiary is the same person, as there is no longer any need to separate the legal and equitable titles.

A trustee must allocate between principal and income. The simplest rule of thumb is that if an accountant would ordinarily itemize something as an expense or count it as regular income then it should be allocated to income. In contrast, if an accountant would ordinarily depreciate something as a cost or treat the income as capital gain then it should be allocated to the principal. To illustrate, interest, rent, cash dividends, and royalties are considered trust income. Trust principal includes proceeds or gains from the sale of trust property, insurance from destroyed trust property, stock splits, and stock dividends.

KEY WORDS

administrator (647)	intestate (647)
beneficiary (660)	probate court (647)
codicil (654)	revocation (667)
constructive trust (662)	settlor (660)
corpus (660)	testamentary (650)
cy pres (665)	testator (647)
decedent (646)	trust (660)
durable power of attorney (657)	trustee (660)
	will (647)
durable power of attorney for health care (657)	
executor (650)	
inter vivos trust (661)	

DISCUSSION QUESTIONS

1. What is meant by "dying intestate"? What happens to the property of a person who dies intestate?
2. What are the requirements for making a valid will?
3. What is meant by "testamentary capacity"?
4. What is the purpose of administering an estate? Who administers the estate?
5. Describe the steps in the administration of an estate.
6. What is a trust? Who are the parties to a trust?
7. Why might someone wish to establish a trust?
8. What are the requirements for forming an express trust?
9. Distinguish between an express trust and a constructive trust.
10. Describe the duties of the trustee.

CASE PROBLEMS

1. Ella Simmons died, leaving a will which was found to be defective when it was admitted for probate. Ella had designated her sister, Barbara, to receive her interest in a farm they had owned as joint tenants. Ella had also instructed that her son, Richard, not receive anything under the will. The state laws of intestate succession give Richard a right to a one-third interest in Ella's estate. Will Ella be considered to have died testate or intestate? Who is likely to prevail as to the farm? Explain.

2. In her will Emily Smith stated, "I give my Cadillac convertible to my very dear granddaughter, Leta." The residual beneficiary was Emily's gardener, Earl Long, although Emily had told Earl there would probably be very little for him, since she expected there would be very little undesignated property. Several years before her death, Emily traded the Cadillac for a Mercedes. However, Emily forgot to change her will and did not otherwise designate the taker of the Mercedes before her death. Leta has challenged the executrix's position that the Mercedes should go to Earl. If Leta challenges in court, will she prevail? Explain.

3. Jean's will left various properties and sums of money to relatives and friends. She divided the residue of her estate equally between her favorite niece and nephew. Would several substantial gifts to friends that she made in contemplation of death be subject to her will? What about a life insurance policy naming her sister as beneficiary? Explain.

4. Tom Swindle was a major stockholder of Swindle Oil, Inc. Some years before his death, Tom decided to leave all his Swindle Oil stock, then valued at around $5 million, and his residual estate, then valued at around $225,000, to his daughter, Jennifer. Tom made bequests of $50,000 for the Jane Swindle scholarship fund at the alma mater of his deceased wife, $25,000 to his church, and 1000 shares of Widget, Inc., stock, then valued at $1500, to the public library. Swindle Oil went bankrupt, and so at Tom's death he had the Widget stock, now worth $75,000, and a net of $30,000 in cash. If Jennifer does not have a right to renounce the will, will she be likely to receive the $30,000? How much, if anything, is Tom's church likely to get? Explain.

5. Jim Mills created a will, leaving all his property to his wife, Anna. Before his death, Jim and Anna discussed establishing a trust for the benefit of his nephew, Kevin, who suffered from cystic fibrosis. At Jim's instructions, his attorney prepared a codicil creating and funding a $100,000 testamentary trust for Kevin. Before it could be executed, Jim died. Kevin's parents have asked the probate court to implement the trust because of Jim's plain intention to create and fund it. How is the court likely to rule? Explain.

6. Annette's will provides for a trust upon her death. York Trust Company is named as the trustee, and the trust's terms provide for the payment of income to Annette's husband for life and for the remainder to go to her children. Do both the legal and equitable titles vest in York? Is York under an implied restriction which obligates it to obtain the beneficiary's consent if it wishes to dispose of trust assets?

7. Michael Wise, a bachelor, established a will wherein he left his entire estate to his two nephews, Samuel and Elbert Wise. The two cousins disliked each other. Elbert, the industrious cousin, was attending Victory University when the campus newspaper accidentally inserted the wrong name in a lead story: "Elbert Wise arrested for drug dealing." The paper publicly apologized and corrected its mistake in the next edition. Samuel, the mischievous cousin, gave the original article to his Uncle Michael. Angered over Elbert's apparent drug dealing, Michael executed a codicil to his will removing Elbert as a beneficiary. Michael died several days later. What legal theory would be most likely to support Elbert's challenge to the will? Does he have much chance of success? Explain.

8. Art Adams established an inter vivos trust, naming his daughter Georgia as the sole beneficiary for 15 years and as the sole remainder beneficiary of the corpus. If the trust is silent as to Art's ability to revoke the trust, could he revoke it without Georgia's consent? Can Georgia revoke the trust without Art's consent? Explain.

9. Larry Rambin properly created an inter vivos trust naming DeMello as trustee. The trust's sole asset is a fully rented office building. Rents exceed expenditures each year. The trust agreement is silent as to the allocation of items between income and principal. During the past year insurance proceeds were received as a result of a fire in the coffee shop area of the building. DeMello has allocated to principal these proceeds and the current mortgage interest payments. Correct? If the market should significantly soften so income is no longer expected to exceed expenditures for the building, and the trust is otherwise silent, would DeMello have the power to sell the building to invest in other assets? Explain.

10. In 1992, Debra Trunzler established a 10-year trust for the benefit of her daughter, Lisa. At the end of 10 years the trust principal is to be paid Lisa. Debra reserved the power to revoke the trust. She named her brother, George, trustee. George sold a trust asset, a summer lake cabin, on grounds that it "was returning no income." Lisa is very upset, as she always loved the cabin. She claims the trustee needed her approval, since she is the sole beneficiary and the trust is silent as to the trustee's power to sell trust assets. Correct? Both Debra and George have just died in an accident. There is no provision for a successor trustee. Lisa claims the trust now automatically terminates. Correct?

CHAPTER 30

Insurance

Shortly after the 1976 Olympic Games ended, NBC began promoting its television coverage of the 1980 Summer Olympics in Moscow. The network invested millions of dollars in planning and promotion for the games. But, a question occurred to someone at NBC: How valuable would the television rights to the Olympics be if the United States did not field a team? The answer was, "Not very." So NBC insured itself for the cost of its preparations for the Olympics if the United States did not participate. In 1980, when the United States withdrew from the Olympics to protest the Russian invasion of Afghanistan, the network recovered some of its investment from its insurance carrier.

NBC's precautions made excellent business sense. Almost anything which amounts to a risk, hazard, or peril can be insured against. For example, syndicates which invest in race horses for breeding buy insurance against the risk of infertility. Banks take out insurance against forged checks or negotiable instruments. However, no business can insure against failing to make a profit.

In this chapter we will focus on the most common types of insurance coverage: automobile, property, health, and life.

THE NATURE OF INSURANCE

Insurance companies *indemnify*—secure against damage or loss—the risks of individuals and businesses in return for a *premium* (money to be paid to the insurer as the consideration for insurance), usually calculated by evaluating experience with similar risks. Insurance companies will indemnify the insurance policyholder only to the extent of the financial loss suffered by the holder.

An *insurance policy* is a contract between an *insurer* (an insurance company) and an *insured* (the person or entity buying insurance). By this contract, the insured promises to pay the insurer a particular amount in exchange for the insurer's promise to cover a loss in the event of a specified occurrence.

An insurance company makes money if the revenue it receives in the form of premiums exceeds its operating costs plus the payouts on claims made on the policies it issues. For this reason, insurers must analyze the probability that a risk will occur and the probable loss which will result. Such analyses, for example, have caused auto insurers to take the lead in the fight for safer automobiles. They also result in differentiation in premiums, such as higher life insurance premiums for smokers.

Risk Transfer

The essence of insurance is *risk transfer*. A business insures itself against a peril, such as fire, which could otherwise destroy the possibility that the firm could continue its operations. The business transfers most of the risk of loss to the insurer. The insured pays the insurance company a premium equal to a proportionate part of the total predicted cost of covering such perils. This is known as *risk distribution*. For example, an insurance company sets the premium for fire insurance for a shoe store, based on its experience with similar buildings with similar operations and on the number of policyholders paying fire insurance premiums.

Thus, insurance is "risk shifting" from the insured to the insurer and "risk spreading" among the insured by the insurer.

In some instances, however, insurance is not available for a particular hazard; or even if it is available, it does not make financial sense to buy it. Suppose a shoe store is located in an area of a city which has suffered heavily from arson. The insurance premiums may be prohibitively expensive, if insurers are willing to take the risk at all.

Self-insurance

Not being able to get insurance is not the same thing, technically, as self-insurance. Self-insurers create reserves to protect themselves, and, when a loss occurs, take a casualty loss deduction against their federal income tax liability. This is an option only for corporations that are large enough to weather a major catastrophe. Goodyear, ITT, and Exxon, among others, have found it more cost-effective to self-insure than to purchase insurance from carriers.

State Regulation

For the most part, insurance is governed by state laws. Every state has its own set of laws and its own regulatory agency supervising the industry. Some states, like Massachusetts, regulate the premiums which insurers can charge for certain types of insurance. The federal Mc-Carran-Ferguson Act of 1945 exempts many aspects of insurance industry operations from the federal antitrust acts (discussed in Chapter 44) if state laws cover the activities. Some consumer advocates have criticized the Act on the grounds that it inhibits competition, which would lead to lower rates.

This chapter concentrates on the nature of insurance and on the state laws which regulate it.

THE INSURANCE CONTRACT

The insurance contract or policy specifies the perils or eventualities it covers. A property insurance policy, for instance, will specify whether or not it covers losses from flooding. The insurance contract also states the conditions that must be met before the insurance company must indemnify the insured. A common restriction in a theft policy is to specify that an insured must make a claim within a specific period or else waive coverage. The insurance contract will also specify the maximum amount of compensation for loss which the insured may receive. An automobile policy may specify a $10,000 limit for collision coverage, for example.

The common law of contracts and agency generally applies to insurance contracts, although with some variations and some different terminology. A valid insurance contract usually requires:

- Mutual assent
- Capacity
- Consideration
- Legal purpose
- Insurable interest
- Writing
- Delivery
- Notice of loss
- Proof of loss

Understanding the insurance contract requires you to remember that it is a contract. Its subject matter is unique, as are some of the terms. But, the governing principles are familiar.

Mutual Assent

Like any contract, an insurance contract requires *mutual assent*. An offer occurs when the prospective insured submits a completed application for the policy and, often, the premium. An agent will normally issue a binder, a temporary commitment by the insurance company to provide insurance. The insurance company normally reserves the right to review and approve the application before issuing a permanent policy.

Insurance companies traditionally have contended that an *agent* does not have the authority to issue a binding, permanent policy. However, courts have begun to look more closely at what is customary in the industry; in particular, identifying actions which can be inferred as being reasonably necessary for the agent to perform in carrying out his express authority. The result is a growing number of courts which recognize that an agent has authority, either implied or apparent, to bind the insurance company for property and liability coverage. In contrast, agents still are not considered to have the power to bind insurance companies on life insurance policies.

An insurance agent should be distinguished from an *insurance broker*. An insurance broker represents the insured, even though typically she is paid a commission from the insurer. Since a broker is not the insurer's agent, her job is to solicit business from those seeking to buy insurance and then to place the business with an insurance company.

Insurer's delay. If a prospective insured submits the premium with the application and the insurer unreasonably delays its decision on the application, a court will likely hold a binding contract exists. The prospective insured begins to rely upon the fact of not receiving a rejection. Had the company rejected his offer to buy promptly, he might have gained protection elsewhere.

A few states have established periods within which an insurance company must accept or reject an application. The application is accepted automatically if the insurer's delay exceeds the statutorily prescribed time. However, if the prospective insured is responsible for the delay in processing the application, as he was in the next case, the insurance company is not liable.

Atkinson v. American Agency Life Insurance Co.

165 Ga. App. 102, 299 S.E.2d 600 (1983)

FACTS

In September 1979, Atkinson took out a life insurance policy. In connection with his application, he underwent a complete medical examination. In December, he decided to replace that policy with one issued by American. The agent assured Atkinson that a policy would be issued provided that a physical showed that his health had not declined since the earlier examination. Atkinson submitted an application with a quarterly premium. The agent issued a conditional receipt, which stated that the insurance "shall be in force and effect from the date of the completed Application including any required medical examination. . . ." Atkinson then canceled his other insurance policy. Twice, the company requested him to supply the results of his physical. On Christmas, when Atkinson died, American had not received the results. His heir brought suit to recover the proceeds of the American policy. The trial court held that an insurance contract had never come into existence and granted summary judgment to American.

ISSUE

Did Atkinson's failure to supply the results of his physical prevent an insurance contract from being formed?

DECISION

Yes. Affirmed. Atkinson's heirs contended that Atkinson canceled his other policy because American assured him that the new policy would be issued. However, the agent's assurances were not that he *was* insured but that the company *would* insure him when it was satisfied that he was as healthy as he had been during the earlier physical examination. Since Atkinson did not furnish the complete medical examination, there was no insurance contract.

Capacity

Both the insured and the insurer must have capacity to contract. At common law, a minor could disaffirm a contract for insurance on the grounds of lack of capacity. However, a number of states have rejected this rule, especially with regard to automobile insurance when state law requires coverage.

An insurance company lacks capacity to enter into insurance contracts in states in which it is not licensed. All states have administrative agencies which license and regulate insurers. A company found not to be in substantial compliance with a state's regulations risks having to return the premiums it collected in that state to the policyholders. Nonetheless, it would be liable for any claims on its policies while they were in effect.

Consideration

The insured's consideration for an insurance contract is the benefit to the company of his or her promise to pay premiums when due. In exchange, the insurer promises to indemnify the insured for a loss covered by the policy.

Subrogation. In most insurance contracts— other than life insurance policies—the insured also agrees to substitute the insurance company on any claim against a third party arising out of the loss the insurer indemnified. Thus, when an insurer pays, it automatically acquires the claim and the rights of the insured. This is known as the right of *subrogation*. Subrogation simply means that when A must pay an obligation to B which C ought to have paid, A assumes B's rights to enforce the obligation against C.

Once the insurer has paid the insured, the insurer stands in the same position as the insured and may sue to enforce any claim which was available to the insured in order to recover the amount it paid. Suppose Torch Insurance Corp. issues a fire insurance policy on the True Blue Hardware Store. The store burns down as a result of faulty wiring, installed by Ed's Electric. If Torch pays the loss, Torch may sue Ed's Electric to recover what it paid True Blue. Of course, if True Blue's coverage did not fully cover its loss, True Blue may seek to recover those additional losses from Ed's Electric.

Assignment. Life insurance policies, but not any other type, may be assigned by the holder. The rationale for this rule is that the risk under a life insurance policy remains the same regardless of the beneficiary. However, if the holder of a property insurance policy on a shoe store assigned it to the owner of a fireworks factory, the risks would not be the same as those the insurer originally agreed to indemnify. Even if the insurance continued on the same piece of property, the care that different owners give the property may well differ.

Insurable Interest

The most critical requirement of an insurance contract is that the insured have an *insurable interest*, a legal right or interest capable of protection against actual loss by insurance. To be capable of protection there must be a direct relationship between the insured and the insured event, such that if the event occurs the insured would suffer an actual loss. To illustrate, a homeowner clearly has an insurable interest in her home against the loss from fire. However, the homeowner, even if an avid reader, would not likely have an insurable interest in the loss of her community's library to fire.

There are two types of insurable interest issues: timing and qualifications. As to timing, the general rule is that to recover for a loss from an insured event, the insured must have an insurable interest at the time of the loss. The exception is for life insurance, where the insurable interest must exist at the time the policy is taken out. As to qualifications, any person with a legal right or interest who can prove a loss is considered to have an insurable interest. And, there can be more than one insurable interest in the same property. For example, besides the homeowner, a lender holding a mortgage on the destroyed home would also have an insurable interest. Persons with an insurable interest include legal owners, secured (*not* unsecured) creditors, tenants, partners, stockholders, and bailees.

Life insurance. An individual always has an insurable interest in her own life, regardless of whom she names as beneficiary. A person who obtains a life insurance policy on another's life must have an insurable interest in the insured's life at the time of the insuring. For instance, Harry has an insurable interest in his wife's life. But, he could not take out a life insurance policy on someone whose name he picked out of the phone book. Harry would be gambling on that person's death.

The policyholder does not have to have an insurable interest in the insured's life at the time of death. If Harry and his wife divorce, Harry can maintain the coverage on her life, though he cannot increase it or buy a new policy. In some cases, property settlements in divorces require a spouse to purchase life insurance to assure the other spouse of continued support.

Property insurance. With property insurance, the insured's interest must exist at the time of the loss. A person has an insurable interest in property if he has both a legal interest in the property and a possibility of actual loss if the property is destroyed. Insurers will issue policies on property in which the insured does not yet have an insurable interest, but they will not pay a loss unless the insured's insurable interest has come into existence. If the interest had to exist at the time of insuring, businesses whose inventory fluctuates or builders whose risk increases as construction progresses would have to renegotiate their insurance almost every day.

More than one person can have an insurable interest in a single piece of property. For example, a homeowner and a mortgage lender each has an insurable interest in the same home. The homeowner's is in his equity; the lender's is for the amount of its loan. Similarly, a tenant and a landlord both have an insurable interest in a piece of property. Courts have held that partners and even controlling shareholders have insurable interests in their businesses.

Legal Purpose

As with any contract, one for insurance must have a legal purpose. A person may not, for instance, insure a cocaine shipment. Because murder to insurance proceeds occurs with some regularity, courts—like the one in the next case—impose on the insurer a duty to act if it has reason to suspect an applicant's motives.

- -

Lopez v. Life Insurance Company of America

406 So. 2d 1155 (Dist. Ct. App. 1981), aff'd., 443 So. 2d 947 (Fla. 1983)

FACTS   Between 1974 and 1977, Gladys Lopez bought $130,000 in life insurance policies on her husband, Jim. He signed the applications after Gladys told him they were for health insurance. During this period, the Lopez family's net worth was zero and Jim's income was $9000 per year. The monthly premiums were $622. Jim overheard his wife and her brother-in-law plotting to kill him to collect the insurance. He immediately called his insurance agent and reported what he had heard. He asked the agent to cancel any life insurance he might have. Neither the agent nor the company took any action. Several months later, Gladys and her brother-in-law kidnapped Jim, took him to a river, forced whiskey down his throat, and were about to drown him when a deputy sheriff rescued him. Jim sued the insurance company for breach of its duty of care to him. The trial court dismissed the complaint.

ISSUE Does a life insurance carrier owe a duty of care to its insured when it has notice of the beneficiary's murderous intent?

DECISION Yes. Reversed. A life insurance policy is void ab initio if the beneficiary obtained the policy intending to murder the insured. An insurer who learns of the insurance contract's illegal purpose must cancel it immediately so as not to be unjustly enriched by continued premium payments and, more important, so as not to endanger the life of the insured.

It is interesting to note that when the Florida Supreme Court affirmed this decision, one justice strongly dissented. He argued that insurers should not be burdened with the responsibility of investigating reports of threats against the insured's life.

Writing

Most states require insurance contracts to be in writing, but permit oral binders. As with all written contracts, the contracting parties—especially the insured—have an obligation to read what they are signing and not to sign if the language deviates from their understanding of the agreement.

Delivery

The common law does not require delivery of an insurance policy to the insured. However, insurers often stipulate that policies, particularly life policies, do not take effect until they are delivered to the insured. Sometimes, an intent to deliver must be established by circumstantial evidence. A court may find a *construc-*

tive delivery if the company mailed the policy to the insured or turned it over to the agent for delivery, even though no actual delivery occurred. The rationale is that the insurer did everything it intended as to delivery, and therefore the insured is entitled to coverage.

THE INSURER'S LIABILITY

An insurance policy is a contract between the insurer, the insurance company, and the insured, the policyholder. Usually, in order to trigger the insurance company's liability to pay a claim, an insured must satisfy two conditions precedent; he or she must supply the company with a notice of loss *and* a proof of loss.

Notice of Loss

All insurance policies prescribe how the insured must give the carrier notice of loss. Notice is a *condition precedent* to the insurer's obligation to pay. Failure to properly notify the insurer can mean that the insurer has no legal duty to indemnify the loss. Fire policies often require "immediate" notice—preferably before the firefighters leave—so that the insurer has a better chance to determine whether arson was involved. If immediate notice is not required, a policy usually states a specified period within which the notice must be filed.

Proof of Loss

Generally, carriers require an insured to submit satisfactory proof of his or her loss, usually within 60 days of its occurrence. A verified written statement in which the insured states his loss satisfies this requirement. Like notice of loss, submitting proof of loss on time is a condition precedent to the insurer's liability. Suppose fire destroys Hector's home. In order to collect on his policy, he must submit to his carrier an inventory listing the property destroyed and its value—generally at cost less depreciation.

THE INSURER'S DEFENSES

Violations of the notice and proof of loss requirements are an insurer's procedural defenses on its contract with the insured. However, an insurer also has substantive defenses on which to deny indemnification. These include: breach of warranties, false representations, cancellation of the policy before a loss, or lapse of the policy before a loss.

Warranties and Representations

The first two defenses relate to what the insured tells or does not tell the insurer. When a prospective insured applies for a policy, the insurer usually asks, on the application, for information relevant to the risk. For example, an auto insurer will want to know who may be driving the car, and a life insurer, the applicant's age. By law, the applicant must answer such questions candidly and honestly.

In insurance law, a *warranty* is an affirmation of fact by the insured which is either incor-

porated into the actual insurance policy or attached to it, as an application is. For example, an application for life insurance will usually ask whether the applicant is a smoker. The applicant's "yes" or "no" answer is a warranty. In determining whether to issue a policy, a carrier may consider certain of an applicant's statements but not make them part of the policy. Those statements are called *representations*.

Thus, the applicant's responses which become part of the policy are called warranties. Those which do not are called representations.

Affirmative and continuing warranties. Warranties may be either affirmative or continuing. An *affirmative warranty* is a representation that something is true at the time the policy is issued. A common property insurance warranty is the distance between the house and a fire hydrant. A *continuing warranty* relates to the existence of a fact during the course of the policy. For example, a jewelry store may state that its policy is to allow a customer to handle only one diamond ring at a time.

In order to recover on a policy, the insured must be able to prove that a warranty is *literally* true. Even a minimal deviation from the truth may permit the insurer a defense to the claim. For example, the jeweler in the last example might be denied theft coverage if she allowed the thief to handle a number of rings at once before he stole them.

At common law, an insurer could deny coverage for an untruthful statement even if it did not cause loss or death. For example, a misstatement of one's health in a life insurance application that was incorporated into the policy allowed the insurer to void the policy, even if the insured died in a shipwreck. Today, most states treat warranties made to obtain life insurance like representations.

Misrepresentations. The insured's material, false representation may excuse the insurer's performance. Materiality is the key question in determining whether an insurer may void a contract based on a misrepresentation. However, the materiality test does not require proof that the representations actually influenced the insurer. The courts generally ask whether the fact, if stated truthfully, might reasonably have influenced a carrier to accept or reject a risk or to charge a different premium. In essence, this is nothing more than the *reasonable person* standard.

Even when a misrepresentation is material, a court is more likely to permit the insurer to reduce its payment to the insured or his beneficiary than to void the policy. For instance, if a false representation on a life insurance applica-

tion relates to the insured's age, the insurer normally will pay. However, the insurer will *pro rate* the coverage, that is, the benefit paid will be the amount someone of the insured's real age would receive for the same premium amount. Suppose Ralph took out a $50,000 life insurance policy. He told the agent he was 55, although he was actually 60. A year later, Ralph died. His insurer would be liable only for the amount of insurance that his premiums would have bought had the insurer known he was 60 years old. In the next case, however, the court did not permit the survivors to recover a pro rated amount.

Mutual Benefit Life Ins. Co. v. JMR Electronics Corp.

848 F.2d 30 (2d Cir. 1988)

FACTS

JMR applied to Mutual for a $250,000 key man life insurance policy on its president, Joseph Gaon, at the nonsmoker's discount rate. Question 13(a) on the application asked, "Do you smoke cigarettes? How many a day?" Question 13(b) asked, "Did you ever smoke cigarettes?" Gaon responded, "No" to both parts. Based on these responses, Mutual issued the policy at the nonsmoker's rate. Within the period of contestability, Gaon died. A routine investigation revealed that Gaon had smoked a half pack of cigarettes per day for at least 10 years up to his death. Mutual brought suit seeking a declaration that the policy was void and an order rescinding the insurance policy. The trial court granted Mutual's motion for summary judgment and ordered JMR's premiums repaid with interest.

ISSUE

In order to warrant rescission, must an insurer prove it would not have issued the policy had it been aware of the misrepresentation?

DECISION

No. Affirmed. The New York statute states that a misrepresentation is material if "knowledge by the insurer of the facts misrepresented would have led to a refusal by the insurer to make such contract."

There is no doubt that Mutual was induced to issue the nonsmoker, discounted-premium policy to JMR precisely as a result of the misrepresentations made by Gaon concerning his smoking history. That Mutual might not have refused the risk on any terms had it known the undisclosed facts is irrelevant. Most risks are insurable at some price. The purpose of the materiality inquiry is not to permit the jury to rewrite the terms of the insurance agreement to conform to the newly disclosed facts but to make certain that the risk insured was the risk covered by the policy agreed upon. If a fact is material to the risk, the insurer may avoid liability under a policy if that fact was misrepresented . . . whether or not the parties might have agreed to some other contractual arrangement had the critical fact been disclosed. As observed by [the trial judge], a contrary result would reward the practice of misrepresenting facts critical to the underwriter's task because the unscrupulous (or merely negligent) applicant "would have everything to gain and nothing to lose" from making material misrepresentations in his application for insurance. Such a claimant could rest assured not only that he may demand full coverage should he survive the contestability period, . . . but that even in the event of a contested claim, he could be entitled to the coverage that he might have contracted for had the necessary information been accurately disclosed at the outset. New York law does not permit this anomalous result.

The incontestability clause. Commonly, life insurance policies contain an *incontestability clause*. It usually states that after a policy has been in effect for a time, often 2 years, the insurer may not assert false representation as a defense to paying on the policy. For example, the insured's description of his health would become irrelevant so long as he had made timely premium payments.

However, the incontestability clause does not affect the insurer's ability to terminate a policy for failure to pay premiums or to pro rate life insurance benefits in the case of misrepresentations of age. It also does not affect the insurer's ability to refuse to pay in the absence of an insurable interest. And the incontestability clause does not prevent an insurer from denying coverage altogether when the insured, for the purposes of obtaining life insurance, has had another person—presumably a healthier person—take the physical.

Termination of an Insurance Policy

An insurance policy's termination may result from any of a number of causes. Coverage under the policy may simply expire or lapse, as when someone buys property insurance and does not renew the policy for an additional year.

Often, the insurer has the right to cancel a policy when a condition stated in the contract occurs. These conditions change the nature, scope, or substance of the risk. An automobile insurer, for example, may cancel a policy because of an insured's numerous accidents, his failure to maintain a valid driver's license, or the sale of his car. However, an insurer usually may not cancel a life insurance policy, although it may lapse.

Forfeiture and Exclusion of Risk

An insurer may avoid paying on a policy on the grounds of forfeiture or of an exclusion of risk. A *forfeiture* results when an insured loses the right to receive insurance payments because of her intentional acts. For example, an insured forfeits her right to collect under her automobile policy if she tries to commit suicide by ramming her car into an abutment.

An *exclusion of risk* occurs when the insurer agrees to cover the applicant but expressly limits the types of risks it will cover. If a particular risk is included, then the insured or her beneficiary may not recover if that occurs. For example, life insurers often exclude coverage for suicides occurring within 2 years of the policy's issuance.

Election and Waiver

An insurer may be liable to the insured even though at one point the insurer might have been able to raise a defense to its liability. The most common reasons for liability in this instance are election and waiver.

An *election* is a voluntary choice by the insurer between two different rights or privileges. Quite often, it occurs when the insurer could have returned the premiums and avoided liability, but instead accepted the claim. Later, the insurer sought to avoid liability. In the case that follows, the court found that the insurance company had elected to cover the insured.

Dairy Land Insurance Company v. Kammerer

213 Neb. 108, 327 N.W.2d 618 (1983)

FACTS

On March 5, 1980, Auto-Owners Insurance Company issued a binder to Judith Popish covering her convertible. In her application, Popish did not reveal that Wrich was a member of her household. On March 27, while using Popish's car with her permission, Wrich had an accident. On April 10 Auto-Owners notified Popish that it was canceling her policy as of April 22 for "underwriting reasons." Auto-Owners returned a portion of Popish's premium. Later, Dairy Land—which insured the other car in the accident—filed suit for a declaratory judgment that Popish's policy provided coverage for the accident. Auto-Owners claimed that Popish's policy was void ab initio because she failed to disclose that Wrich was a member of her household. The trial court held that Popish's misrepresentation was material and entitled Auto-Owners to avoid coverage of the accident.

ISSUE

Did Auto-Owners elect to cover Wrich?

DECISION

Yes. Reversed.

> *When learning of the alleged fraud, Auto-Owners had two choices. Either it could determine that, because of the alleged fraudulent statements made to it, it wished to cancel the policy from its inception and return to Popish the entire premium, on the theory that the policy never came into existence, or it could waive the alleged fraud, keep the premium earned to date of cancellation and accept responsibility under the policy. . . . Both by its notice of cancellation and by its retention of the premium, Auto-Owners elected to recognize the existence of the policy from the date of its issuance . . . , until the date of its declared cancellation [April 22]. . . . Having made that choice, Auto-Owners acknowledged that the policy was in effect on the date of the accident [March 27]. . . .*

A *waiver* is the intentional giving up of a known right or privilege, such as the waiver of a right to a surcharge on a late premium payment. Companies can also waive their right to deny claims on the basis of late notices of loss. As in *Dairy Land*, an insurer who acts upon a late-filed claim of loss cannot seek to avoid liability later.

Thus, the common element of the election and waiver rules is that if the insured was denied compensation, it would result in an unjust hardship to him.

TYPES OF INSURANCE

A person or company can insure itself against almost any risk, peril, or hazard it might encounter. See Figure 30.1 for examples of insurance which an individual or business might obtain. This section, however, focuses on the four most common forms: auto, fire, health, and life insurance.

Auto Insurance

Until the last 20 years, the law treated automobile accidents like any other torts. Courts adjudicated liability on the basis of fault. Individuals could insure themselves against liability just as they could against other risks, but the states did not commonly require insurance. For that reason, those involved in accidents with uninsured motorists often bore the losses caused by their injuries.

The fault approach to compensating the victims of automobile accidents never worked well. By the 1960s, hundreds of thousands of accidents occurred annually, and the courts began choking on the volume of cases. At the same time, the states began changing the nature

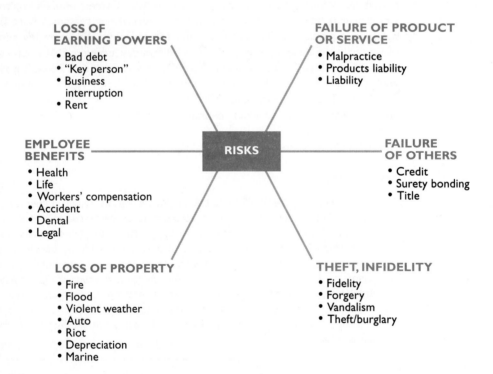

Figure 30.1 Common Business Risks and Insurance.
Besides the types of insurance discussed in this chapter, Chapter 4 and 46 discuss workers' compensation insurance, and Chapter 27 discusses title insurance. Other chapters of direct relevance to insurance questions are Chapter 34, for products liability suits; Chapter 17 and 21, for key person insurance; Chapter 20 for indemnification of corporate officers and directors; and Chapter 24, for accountants' liability for malpractice.

of automobile insurance. Many states required insurance as a condition to registering a car. Uninsured motorist coverage became a standard feature of policies. And, with the introduction of no-fault systems which at least partially eliminated negligence actions, states like Massachusetts, New Jersey, and Michigan took steps toward making automobile insurance primarily a means of compensating victims.*

The four basic types. There are four basic types of automobile insurance coverage.

Collision insurance indemnifies or reimburses the insured for property damage as a result of a collision.

Bodily injury and property damage insurance covers liability for injuries to persons or property caused by the insured's negligence. For example, Eric takes his eyes off the road to glimpse the screen of a drive-in movie. His car crosses the center line and strikes Barbara's car, injuring her and demolishing her car. Eric's insurance company would cover his liability to Barbara up to his policy limits.

Comprehensive insurance indemnifies the insured against loss of the vehicle from causes other than collision. Among the covered perils are usually fire, theft, wind storm, and vandalism. Included under most policies are normal wear and tear, gradual deterioration, and damage from freezing. If vandals spray paint all over Marsha's car, her comprehensive insurance will cover repainting it. However, insurers usually exempt personal property left in the car and audio systems which are not standard. If Cindy's car is stolen, her insurance company will pay her for the car, but not for the golf clubs she left in its trunk.

Uninsured motorist insurance is additional coverage offered under the insured's policy for situations in which the other party—assuming

that he or she is liable—either has no insurance or lacks sufficient coverage.

Here is how uninsured motorist coverage works. Suppose that Todd's truck rear-ends Ann's auto as she waits for a red light to change. Todd has no insurance, but Ann is insured. If she did not have uninsured motorist coverage, she would be covered only to the limits of her comprehensive coverage. Any losses above that would be hers to bear. Why? Presumably, Todd would not be able to pay her insurance company's subrogated claim against him, and that claim would have to be satisfied before Ann's. Uninsured motorist insurance provides extra coverage in just this circumstance.

Deductible clauses. Auto insurance is designed to cover large, unexpected losses. To avoid being swamped with small claims, insurance companies use *deductible clauses*, which specify the amount the insured must pay as a result of a loss before the insurance company becomes liable. Suppose Barb's van hits a telephone pole. Repairing the front end will cost $1750. If Barb carries a $250 deductible, her insurer will pay $1500.

In terms of costs to the insured, the lower the deductible, the higher the cost of the insurance. If Barb accepts a $250 deductible, she will pay less for her coverage than she would with a $100 deductible.

No-fault insurance statutes. Almost half the states have adopted *no-fault insurance* laws. Under them, every vehicle owner must carry insurance. Each vehicle owner looks to his or her own insurance company for the payment of damages suffered, without any consideration of who is at fault. If Bernie's car suffers $350 in damage when Evelyn runs into it, Bernie will collect that amount—less his deductible—from *his* insurance company, not Evelyn's. If Evelyn suffered personal injuries, she would collect from *her* insurer, not Bernie's. Neither driver may sue the other unless the damages exceed a dollar minimum set by statute, or, in some

---

* These developments are discussed below and in Chapter 4. Chapter 4 places the no-fault approach into the context of the defenses which often denied compensation to those who required it.

states, if a "verbal threshold" is surpassed. A verbal threshold is a statutory definition of injuries after which a tort action for damages is allowed. For example, in Minnesota, Bernie would have to exceed a $4000 threshold before he could file a tort action against Evelyn for pain and suffering, while in New York, he would have to sustain a "serious injury" to sue her. A "serious injury" is defined by statute in that state to be 90 days of disability during the 180 days following the injury. The insurance companies have no right of subrogation unless their payments exceed the statutory minimum. Figure 30.2 compares insurance based on fault with no-fault insurance.

The rationale for no-fault systems is that less time and money are consumed in settling claims arising from minor accidents because there is no subrogation or adjudication of fault.

When no-fault insurance statutes were first passed in the early 1970s, many experts felt they would become the norm for the entire country. That has not been the case. In the 1980s, only one jurisdiction, Washington, D.C., adopted a no-fault statute, while three states repealed theirs. Likewise, several attempts at federal legislation have failed. The expansion of no-fault statutes to more states currently is not anticipated.

In the next case, *Frechen v. Detroit Automobile Inter-Insurance Exchange*, a Michigan court had to determine the extent of insurance coverage for accidental bodily injury under a no-fault policy.

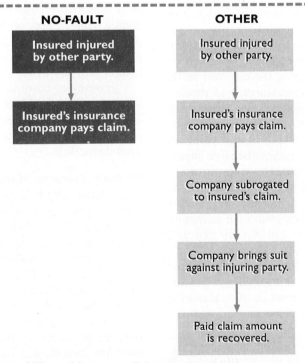

Figure 30.2 No-fault and Normal Insurance Schemes Compared.

Frechen v. Detroit Automobile Inter-Insurance Exchange

119 Mich. App. 578, 326 N.W.2d 566 (1982)

FACTS

Amelia and Martin Roesch started drinking in the afternoon. Around 12:30 A.M., they argued. Amelia stormed out of the bar, got into the car, locked the doors, and attempted to drive away. Facing a 13-mile walk home in chilly weather, Martin climbed onto the hood so that Amelia would have to stop. The car was traveling at about 2 miles per hour. Still, when Amelia hit the brakes, the car's forward inertia made Martin slide off the hood. The right tire struck him, causing severe injuries. Martin's carrier denied his claim on the grounds that Martin's injuries were "suffered or caused intentionally," which barred recovery under Michigan's no-fault statute. Martin sued his insurance carrier to recover his medical expenses. The trial court granted summary judgment to the carrier.

ISSUE

Does an unintended injury which results from an intentional act qualify as accidental bodily injury?

DECISION

Yes. Reversed. The prohibition against coverage of intentionally inflicted injuries reflects the legislature's attempt to bar recovery by people who intend to injure themselves or to commit suicide. Martin did not intend either. He was merely negligent. Negligence often involves an intentional act which falls below a recognized standard of care. Its result, a calamity, is often a foreseeable consequence, but the result is unintended. Here, Martin's injuries were the unintended result of his intentional act.

Property Insurance

Property insurance serves a host of purposes and encompasses a number of different forms. The term "fire insurance" often is used interchangeably with property insurance, although insuring against fire alone is extremely uncommon.

Coverage. "Homeowner's policies,"* which are probably the most common form of property insurance, include property, general risks, and fire coverage.

The property coverage extends to contents of the house, but valuables like antiques or jewelry must usually be covered separately. The general risks coverage includes such things as someone slipping on the sidewalk or a guest cutting his hand on a food processor. The next case reflects how far a court may go in finding that an insured is indemnified under a homeowner's policy's general risks coverage.

---

* In some states, this term includes policies issued to apartment dwellers, who do not have an insurable interest in the structure but who require insurance against damage to personal property and other risks.

State Farm Mutual Automobile Insurance Co. v. White

60 Or. App. 666, 655 P.2d 599 (1982)

FACTS   White and three others were riding in a car owned and driven by Morgan. They were traveling on an Interstate at approximately 55 miles per hour. White, who was sitting in the back seat, suddenly yelled, "Let's get crazy!", reached between the driver and the passenger in the front seat, and yanked the steering wheel. Morgan lost control of the car, which then struck the median barrier and overturned. White's insurance carriers sought a declaratory judgment that they had no responsibility to defend or pay any judgments in actions brought against White as a result of the accident. White claimed that she was covered under her homeowner's policy, which provided for personal liability coverage for negligence except for bodily injury or property damage arising out of use of a motor vehicle operated by the insured. The trial court held that White was operating the car at the time of the accident and therefore was not covered under the homeowner's policy.

ISSUE   Did White's homeowner's policy cover the injuries she caused?

DECISION   Yes. Reversed. What White did interfered with the operation of a motor vehicle. She did not operate it. She was not sitting in the driver's seat. She did not have her foot on—or even have access to—either the brake or the accelerator. Morgan controlled the car other than the steering wheel.

Under property insurance policies, the fire protection covers only what are called "hostile fires," not "friendly fires." A friendly fire occurs at a place where a fire is intended to be, like a fireplace. Thus, a person who drops his Rolex watch into his wood-burning stove would not be able to recover under his fire insurance policy. A hostile fire is one which is not intended or which has extended from a friendly fire beyond the area in which it was expected to be confined. A fire caused by lightning and one caused by an ember ejected from a fireplace are examples of hostile fires. An act of arson by a disgruntled former employee would be a hostile fire, and the employer could collect on his or her policy. If the employer committed the arson, the fire would be treated as a friendly one.

Property insurance normally covers only damage caused by the fire itself. An *extended coverage indorsement*—additional or supplemental coverage added to a basic policy—may cover smoke, water, or other fire-related damages. A property insurance policy clause, called the *insurer payout option*, permits the insurer to restore or rebuild a property.

Valued and unvalued policies. Property insurance comes in two basic forms. The first, a *valued policy*, states the covered property's value as established by appraisals. If the property is destroyed by a peril covered by the policy, the insurer must pay the insured the stated amount unless he can show mistake or fraud.

In an unvalued policy, the amount recoverable is left unstated. Instead, the policy specifies a maximum that can be recovered. An appraisal will establish what the building's value was just before its destruction by fire. If the policy maximum was set at $100,000, then the company would pay that amount in the event of an appraisal of $100,000 or more. If the building was appraised at less than $100,000, the company would pay the lesser sum.

Multiple policies. The purpose of property insurance is to indemnify the insured against actual losses. If an insured has multiple policies, no matter how much coverage they represent, he can collect a sum representing only what was actually damaged or destroyed.

If the insured has multiple policies, the amount each insurer will pay will be apportioned according to the percentage of the insured's total coverage its policy represents. Suppose Mark has two fire insurance policies on his store, which suffered $80,000 in fire damage. One of Mark's policies is for $120,000 and the other for $40,000. The amounts recoverable would be $60,000 and $20,000, respectively.

Coinsurance. In the event of a partial loss, a *coinsurance clause* may affect the recovery. A coinsurance clause reflects the insurance companies' efforts to encourage the purchase of sufficient insurance to cover the value of the property. In effect, this clause means that those who underinsure their property to avoid higher premiums have chosen a higher deductible. Thus, they share the risk with the insurance carrier.

A coinsurance clause usually provides:

- The insured must insure a minimum percentage of the property's total value—usually 80 percent.
- The value of the property will be calculated as of the time the loss occurred.
- The insurer will not be liable, in the event of a partial loss, for a greater proportion of the loss than the specified percentage *unless* the insured value equals or exceeds the stated percentage of the total value of the property.

The insurer's liability under a coinsurance clause is calculated as follows:

$$\frac{\text{Amount of policy}}{(\text{Coverage \% required}) \times (\text{property value})} \times \text{loss}$$
$$= \text{liability}$$

Assume that a building is valued at $100,000. Its owner carries $50,000 of insurance on it. It suffers a casualty loss of $8000. The carrier's liability, assuming an 80 percent clause, is

$$[(\$50,000) \div (0.80 \times \$100,000)]$$
$$\times \$8000 = \$5000$$

Thus, the insured will recover $5000. However, assume that the same property is insured for $80,000. Then

$$[(\$80,000) \div (0.80 \times \$100,000)]$$
$$\times \$8000 = \$8000$$

Here, the insured would recover the full amount of the loss.

Health and Accident Insurance

Health and accident insurance is insurance to cover the costs resulting from illness or accident. Health and accident insurance normally provides coverage for doctor bills and hospital fees plus some medicines and medical supplies. Commonly, health and accident insurance is covered in the same policy. Normally, similar coverage of medical costs is provided for both. Accident insurance often includes the payment of insurance benefits for death due to an accident and lump payments for permanent disabilities due to an accident.

Sometimes, health and accident policies provide for "income maintenance." Such coverage provides replacement of income lost as a result of the insured's inability to work. The amount of coverage and its duration—usually 2 years—is established by the policy. Many insurance companies offer income maintenance policies with an indefinite duration separate from health and accident coverage.

Some policies call for the insurer to reimburse the insured for medical costs which the insured has paid, while under other policies the insurer pays the bills directly. It is common for there to be an annual deductible amount which the insured must exceed before payment or reimbursement will begin.

AIDS and health insurance. AIDS is one of the most serious problems confronting the health insurance industry today. Indeed, the Agency for Health Care Policy and Research calculated that the lifetime medical costs of AIDS for diagnosed people in 1990, was a stunning $4.3 billion.* This translates roughly into about $75,000

to treat each person with the disease.[†] With such onerous costs involved, AIDS victims can almost never obtain health coverage if they do not already have it at the time they are seeking coverage. A notable exception is if they are fortunate enough to be in a state health insurance pool. However, what happens to a person, as in the following case, who is in the private sector and is diagnosed with AIDS *after* he starts his job?

---

* *Health Insurance Association of American Annual Report, 1990-1991* (Washington D.C.: Health Insurance Association of America, 1991).

[†] *The Costs of Treating AIDS Under Medicaid: 1986-1991* (RAND/UCLA Center of Health Care Financing Policy Studies, 1987).

McGann v. H & H Music Co.

946 F.2d 401 (5th Cir. 1991)

FACTS

John McGann was an employee of H & H Music Company in Houston. In December 1987 he was diagnosed with AIDS He subsequently began to submit claims for reimbursement under his company's health plan, issued by the plan insurer. General American. The plan contained a lifetime medical benefit amount of $1 million. Shortly after McGann informed H & H of his illness, it announced to all of its employees that effective August 1988, all lifetime medical benefits for AIDS-related claims would be limited to a $5000 lifetime maximum, under a new self-insured plan. General American would become the plan's administrator. No other such catastrophic illness was excluded. McGann sued H & H and General American, alleging that they violated Section 510 of Employee Retirement Income Security Act (ERISA), which states that it is illegal to discriminate against a participant exercising a benefit or right under an employee benefit plan. Defendant won a summary judgment at the trial level.

ISSUE

Did H & H illegally discriminate against McGann when he attempted to exercise his rights under an ERISA-qualified medical benefits plan?

DECISION

No. Affirmed. Under Section 510 of ERISA, McGann must prove that H & H specifically intended to punish him for filing for AIDS-related treatments, or that he had a right under ERISA which H & H interfered with. H & H's reduction of the maximum from $1 million to $5000, however, would apply equally to all employees at H & H who might file AIDS-related claims, not just McGann. Thus, there is no specific intent to retaliate against McGann. Moreover, under ERISA, any right for reimbursement McGann once had was lost when the health insurance plan he was covered under was terminated.

In late 1992, McGann's writ of certiorari to the U.S. Supreme Court was denied review, thus leaving the above holding intact. Predictably, the decision was greeted by a great deal of criticism, but unfortunately for many AIDS victims, McGann's cruel treatment by his employee is only too common. The law McGann attempted to use to remedy his problem. ERISA, was generally set up to protect pension plans, not health benefits. Many observers feel, however, that the Americans with Disabilities Act (ADA) would have saved McGann's coverage if it had been in effect at the time. The ADA, its regulations, and its legislative history indicate that all disabled persons must have the same access to health insurance coverage as that given to all employees. The ADA also prohibits employer discrimination against HIV carriers and those with AIDS. The language of the ADA is also significantly more expansive and protective than that of ERISA. On the other side of the argument, the ADA is very new and so has not yet been interpreted by the courts on this important issue. Thus, until there is a court case, no one can be certain whether the ADA could have worked for a person in McGann's position.

Health care costs and insurance. One of the most important and contentious issues of the 1992 presidential campaign was the issue of health care costs. The United States spends over 13 percent of its gross domestic product on health care, a figure nearly twice that of our competitors in Japan and Europe. Despite the costs, Americans have virtually the poorest access to health care in the developed world.*

---

* T. L. Greaney, "No Painless Way to Cut High Costs," *The National Law Journal*, December 21, 1992, p. 26.

Moreover, health care costs increase the expense of other types of insurance, including auto, general liability, and workers' compensation. Many experts feel that health care costs can be contained only through comprehensive and complex legislative reforms. Hence, it is quite likely that in the future, many of the medical risks and procedures now covered under health insurance policies will undergo significant change.

Life Insurance

Life insurance is actually death insurance. It provides for payment of a set amount upon the insured's death. Its purposes include protecting beneficiaries against financial losses caused by the insured's premature death and providing liquid assets to pay estate taxes and creditors. Sometimes, if there is no life insurance, personal representatives have to sell the decedent's property in order to raise sufficient cash to settle the estate. Figure 30.3 points out the differences between life insurance and property insurance, a form of indemnification insurance.

Concerning life insurance, the terminology covering those who may have a legal interest in a policy sometimes becomes confused. It is important to note that generally an owner may assign his or her interest and that a beneficiary's interest usually does not vest until the insured's death. If the beneficiary is the insured, the policy's proceeds will go to the insured's estate. So on one hand, the same person may be owner, insured, and beneficiary; on the other, a different person may assume each status. Figure 30.4 illustrates the possibilities.

Assignment. Ordinarily, an individual may change the beneficiary of a policy on his life. The insured need not obtain the permission of

	INSURABLE INTEREST NEEDED WHEN?	INDEMNI-FICATION ORIENTED?	ASSIGNABLE?	UNLIMITED INSURANCE PROCEEDS POSSIBLE?
Life insurance	Outset	No	Usually	Yes
Fire insurance	At loss	Yes	No	No

Figure 30.3 Comparison of Life and Property Insurance

the current beneficiary. An individual may also assign a life insurance policy. Upon assignment, the assignee becomes responsible for the premium payments and assumes the power to designate the beneficiary.

A designated beneficiary is considered to be a third party beneficiary. His or her right to receive the proceeds normally will not vest until the insured's death. The insured usually has the power to change beneficiaries at any time.

Multiple policies. An insured may have any number or combination of life insurance policies. Because life insurance is not indemnifica-

OWNER	INSURED	BENEFICIARY
H	H	H
H	H	W
H	W	H
H	W	W
W	H	H
W	H	W
W	W	W
W	W	H

Figure 30.4 Life Insurance Policies: Combinations of Owners, Insureds, and Beneficiaries.
These combinations are possible between husband (H) and wife (W).

tion insurance like automobile insurance, the carriers will pay all the policies on the insured's death. The principle guiding indemnification insurance is to compensate the insured for a specific loss. Life insurance is not tied to the value of the loss caused by the insured's death.

CONCLUSION

Risks are an inevitable part of one's personal and business life. Insurance cushions one against potential losses owing to common risks, such as automobile accidents, fires, theft, or tort claims. All forms of insurance in the end protect property. Even health and life insurance do so, since they protect an individual's assets or estate.

The key to insurance's viability as a means of protection is risk spreading. The insurer agrees to bear at least part of the risk, but spreads the costs of bearing it by accepting premiums from others in a similar situation. As a result, a loss suffered by one insured is shared by all those who paid premiums.

In a text in which the elements of transactions have to be separated for analysis, it is often difficult to put the elements back together for the "big picture." Insurance in particular falls victim to this dissection. Yet, insurance is an integral element of many of the transactions examined in this unit. For example, if a seller is to ship personal property to a buyer, it is often insured. Bailments should be insured. The financing of the purchase of real property, we saw, typically involves title insurance. Leased premises are often insured by both the landlord and the tenant. Finally, insurance is a crucial element in estate planning.

A NOTE TO FUTURE CPA CANDIDATES

Insurance is included in the property section of the CPA exam. The major focus is on property, fire, and casualty insurance. The exam does *not* specifically cover auto, health, or life insurance (with the exception of insurable interest applications).

The purpose of an insurance contract is to gain indemnification against negligent activity by the insured or negligent or intentional activity by a third party. To illustrate, an insured party would be indemnified for damages from arson by a disgruntled employee (a third party) but not by his own arson.

The exam covers both representations and warranties. Where an insured makes warranties which materially relate to the insurer's risk and which are integrated into the written policy, the insured will be expected to strictly comply with the warranties or risk being denied a recovery under the policy. In contrast, an insured's failure to comply with representations, oral affirmations, generally will not prevent recovery.

Questions on insurable interest focus on timing and qualification. Under the Uniform Commercial Code, an insurable interest occurs when goods are identified to a specific sales contract; for life insurance, when a policy is taken out; for property insurance, at the time of loss, not the time the policy is taken out.

A person has an insurable interest if he has both a legal interest in the property and a possibility of actual loss if the property is destroyed. Companies have an insurable interest for life insurance in key employees. Secured creditors have an insurable property interest; unsecured creditors do not. It is possible for two or more persons to have different insurable interests si-

multaneously, such as a landlord and tenant or a mortgagor and mortgagee.

Coinsurance clauses are commonly tested on the exam. There is a full illustration of the clause within this chapter. Remember, the coinsurance clause does *not* apply where there is a total loss. Also, it may seem obvious, but it does not pay the insured more than the policy coverage.

Multiple insurer situations are resolved by creating a proportion. The amount each insurer should pay is apportioned according to the percentage of the insured's total coverage an insurer's policy represents. Again, they do not pay out more than the loss.

KEY WORDS

coinsurance clause (689)
election (683)
exclusion of risk (682)
indemnification (674)
insurable interest (677)
insurance agent (675)
insurance broker (676)
insured (674)
insurer (674)
no-fault insurance (685)
premium (674)
proof of loss (680)
property insurance (687)
representation (680)
risk distribution (674)
risk transfer (674)
subrogation (677)
waiver (683)
warranty (680)

DISCUSSION QUESTIONS

1. What is the nature of insurance? What can be insured?
2. What are the elements of an insurance contract?
3. How might an insurance company be considered to have accepted an insurance application?
4. What potential defenses are available to the insurer?
5. What is meant by an insurer having made an election? A waiver?
6. What are the four major types of auto insurance coverage?

7. What is the nature of property insurance? Are multiple recoveries of insurance proceeds possible, as in life insurance?
8. What is meant by coinsurance? How does it operate?
9. What characteristics do auto, property, and health insurance share?
10. What basic types of life insurance policies are available? How do they differ?

CASE PROBLEMS

1. Carey insured his life for $25,000 and named Allen, a longtime friend, as beneficiary. The life insurance policy was a 10-year term policy. Does Allen have an insurable interest in Carey's life? If Carey assigned the policy to Allen, could Allen pay the premiums and receive the policy proceeds when Carey dies? Explain.
2. On November 1, 1984, Brady applied for a life insurance policy on her life for $50,000, naming her son as a beneficiary. She submitted a check for her first premium with the application. The application which Brady signed contained the following clause:

   The insurance policy hereby applied for shall not take effect until (1) a written or printed policy shall have been actually delivered to and accepted by the insured (Brady), while in good health, and (2) the first premium thereon is paid.

   The company issued the policy and sent it to the agent for delivery to Brady. Brady died before she received the policy. However, she was in good health when the agent received the policy. Would the policy be in effect? Explain.
3. Carl Capelan was telling a fishing story while grilling steaks on his barbecue grill. As Carl enthusiastically illustrated the length of a big fish which got away, his watch got away, falling from his arm into the fire. Carl was unable to retrieve his watch before it was destroyed. Carl's insurance policy covers hostile but not friendly fires. Would Carl's policy cover this incident? Assuming it does, what duties, if

any, would Carl have before his loss was reimbursed by his insurance company? Explain.
4. Crown Jewelry has theft insurance with American Casualty Insurance. Crown made an affirmative warranty to keep all display cases and windows clear of diamonds and other precious jewelry during closed hours. Crown has always complied. However, over one weekend, while closed, Crown placed hundreds of synthetic "diamonds" in the window under this sign: "These Gems Will Be Given Away Free to a Lucky Winner on Monday. Don't Miss It!" Orvis Herbert saw the display and broke into the store to steal the "diamonds." Once inside, Orvis realized his mistake. However, he did grab a box of Rolex watches that inadvertently had not been put in the safe. American claims that Crown breached the intent of the warranty. Crown contends that a reasonable passerby would have realized that Crown could not possibly be promising to give away hundreds of real diamonds and, besides, it was watches that were stolen. Will American prevail? Explain.
5. Carter, Wallace, and Jones were partners. Title to the partnership's office building was in Carter's name. The partnership obtained a $150,000 fire insurance policy on the building from the Amalgamated Insurance Company. The policy contained an 80 percent coinsurance clause. Subsequently, the building was totally destroyed by fire. The value of the building was $200,000 at the time the policy was issued and $160,000 at the time of the fire. Under the fire insurance policy, how much can the partnership recover? Explain.
6. On July 1, Peatross entered into a contract to sell an office building to Patterson for $500,000 on August 15. The major tenant in the office building is Siegler Insurance Company. Security National Bank presently has a mortgage lien against the building for the amount of $125,000. A fire caused extensive damage to the building on August 1. Assuming all parties listed above have a fire insurance policy with some company, which, if any, *have* an insurable interest to be able to recover? Explain.
7. David Caulkins was injured in an auto acci-

dent caused by Ellen Guerin. Caulkins had just moved to the state in which the accident occurred and in which Guerin also lives. It is a no-fault state with minimums for suit of $2000 property damage and $10,000 personal injury. Caulkins has demanded that Guerin pay his medical and auto repair bills. Caulkins's claims are both under the minimum. Guerin's attorney has told him to contact his own insurer and to stop bothering her. Caulkins does not want to file a claim with his carrier for fear his rates will go up. He asks your advice on what to do. He needs a detailed explanation.

8. Peter McClanathan, a lawyer, rented a building from Ann Godber. McClanathan secured fire insurance for the contents of the building, including his rather large law library. Godber also secured fire insurance, from the same insurer, on the building. Because of an electrical short the building was totally destroyed by fire. Three days before the fire Godber had sold the building to Tom Frakes. Godber had assigned her fire insurance policy to him as part of the sale transaction. The insurer has informed McClanathan that he cannot recover because he did not have an insurable interest. Is the insurer correct? Also, the company claims that Frakes cannot recover because he has no insurance at all. Is the insurer correct? Explain.

9. Janey Slusher purchased an office building for $200,000. Slusher secured fire insurance policies from Athena Casualty Company, for $60,000, and Erie Insurance Company, for $40,000. Each policy contained an 80 percent coinsurance clause and a provision limiting its liability to its proportion of all insurance loss. A fire has since caused $100,000 damages to the building, still valued at $200,000 at the time of the fire. How much liability, if any, does Athena have? Erie? Explain.

10. Richardson purchased a valuable, classic 1957 Chevrolet Impala convertible. Prestige Casualty Company insures such classic cars for full value but only for nongeneral driving purposes. When Richardson applied for their special collector car coverage he indicated that the car would be used only for "collector car parades, functions, and servicing." The statement was incorporated into the policy. Every Friday night during the summer, many local auto enthusiasts gather at Doogie's Drive-In and thereafter cruise the boulevard for about 3 hours each night. The cruises were unstructured and unsponsored. Some cruisers were known to "nip a Budweiser or two" during the course of the night. Richardson regularly participated in cruise night and was always a big hit with his 1957 Chevrolet. One Friday night a hit-and-run cruiser damaged Richardson's Chevrolet. Prestige has refused recovery. Has Prestige properly denied liability? Explain.

PART V PROBLEMS

The end-of-part problems serve three purposes. First, some require practical applications of legal knowledge to everyday situations. Second, they are summative, bringing together many of the issues treated individually in the chapters of a particular part. Third, the last question presents an ethical problem which, as in real life, may not have an unqualifiedly right or wrong solution. Rather, its goal is to prompt two questions: What would I do in this situation? What *should* I do in this situation?

I. A PRACTICAL PROBLEM

Becky and John are partners both in marriage and in an accounting firm. They have a 6-year-old child, Avery, and hope to have at least one more. They have agreed that if anything were to happen to either of them, Avery would remain with the survivor. If they both should die, they want John's brother, Marshall, to raise Avery. Marshall is a lawyer, and they want him to serve as their executor.

The couple owns a home in joint tenancy. Becky has a life estate in a lakefront cabin. On her death, the remainder is to go to her children, if any. If none survive her, the remainder is to go to The Nature Conservancy.

John holds 1000 shares of IBM which as a boy he inherited from his grandfather. He wants to give his alma mater, Southeastern University, 100 shares, with the remaining shares to be divided equally among his immediate family. Should none of his family survive him, he wants all the stock to go to Southeastern.

Each spouse has a $125,000 life insurance policy which names the other as beneficiary. Each has a family Bible, which they wish to go to Avery. All other property is to go to the surviving spouse or, if both are dead, to their children.

John and Becky have asked you to prepare checklists for each of them, identifying both substantive and formal matters which their lawyer should cover when he drafts their wills.

2. A SUMMATIVE PROBLEM

Irving Miller listed his country estate and the 60 acres around it for sale with Blue Star Realty. The contract gave Blue Star an exclusive listing and a 6 percent commission upon sale of the property.

Gail Dart heard from a third party that Miller's property was for sale, and immediately went to see him. Pursuant to their listing contract, Blue star had not posted a "For Sale" sign on the property, and Gail had no knowledge of its contract with Miller. Miller never told her anything about it either.

Miller showed Dart the house and grounds. She noted that the exercise room had mounted beveled glass section mirrors on one wall. Miller had installed special exercise equipment on another wall, installed two ceiling fans, and converted the closet into a tanning room. Expensive wail-to-wall carpeting covered what Miller said was a parquet floor. Outdoors, off the exercise room, Miller had built a redwood deck around a portable whirlpool.

The kitchen centered on an oak island with a grill, built-in cutting boards, and a six-burner range. The walls were covered with coordinated cabinets. The dining room featured a Louis XIV chandelier. A complex home entertainment center allowed different music to be played in every room.

Outside, Miller pointed out the extensive woodpile and the adjacent trash containers, which would remain when he left. He also showed Dart the cottage in which his Aunt Millie lived. She would, Miller assured Dart, move with him to his new estate. Miller also mentioned the bridle paths on the back of his property. Because it was muddy, they did not look at the undeveloped acreage, and in any event Dart thought the trees she could see lined a "bridal" path.

With visions of selling the building lots and keeping the house and a few acres for herself, Dart orally made an offer which Miller immediately accepted.

They agreed to close a month later. Dart had taken a business law course and decided she would do the title search and handle the closing herself. In checking the county records, she missed a scenic easement granted to the county conservation commission which restricted the undeveloped portions of Miller's property to agricultural and sylvacultural uses. At the closing, Miller's lawyer offered Dart a quitclaim deed, which she reluctantly accepted because, he said, "there's nothing wrong with the title."

The scenic easement came to light when Dart applied for a zoning variance for a proposed subdivision. Dart has also discovered that local riders have used Miller's land without his permission for 9 years. The bridle paths include a part of the land which could be developed. Worse, she hates horses.

Meanwhile, Aunt Millie did not move and has produced a 10-year lease for her cottage. She has shown no interest in being bought out.

Also, Blue Star Realty has threatened suit against Dart for the commission on the sale of Miller's estate.

Finally, Miller removed all the amenities which so impressed Dart. When he took out the wall-to-wall carpet, he ruined the parquet floor.

In despair, Dart has sought your advice as to what she can do. You have told her to see a lawyer immediately, but she has insisted that you tell her what she can expect to hear. Prepare a memorandum identifying her problems and explaining her rights.

3. A SUMMATIVE PROBLEM

Neil Erwin was appointed executor of his Uncle Walter's estate. Because his uncle had seemed to be such an organized individual, Neil expected that he would have very few problems. Unfortunately, Neil is now learning otherwise. Neil needs your advice on the problems below. Please respond to him by memo.

a. Walter had made a will leaving his farm, Willow Bend, to one granddaughter, Meg, and "my interest in Superior Oil Company" to his other granddaughter, Lindy. Prior to his death, Walter had sold Willow Bend and used the proceeds to buy another 25 percent of Superior Oil. Walter did not revise his will and Meg, now effectively disinherited, claims the 25 percent interest in Superior Oil.

b. Meg's father, John Frazier, claims that he visited Walter the day before his death and that Walter said the following: "John, I want you to be sure to tell Meg not to worry about not inheriting Willow Bend because I have drawn up a codicil for her to share Superior Oil with Lindy." Later Walter repeated this to Meg during a telephone conversation with her. Neil has found the signed codicil, but it was not witnessed or left with the will. It also was once torn in half and taped back together. Do these facts make it more likely that Meg will share in Superior Oil with Lindy?

c. Walter created an inter vivos, 10-year trust to benefit needy students at Victory University in 1987. In 1989, the student newspaper urged students to boycott Campus Exxon in protest of the *Exxon Valdez* oil spill in Alaska. Walter, the owner of the station, became angry and notified Victory University that he revoked his trust. University officials claim that since the trust was silent as to Walter's ability to revoke, he lacked legal power to do so.

d. Neil got court permission to clear an old building on one of Walter's properties to make it more saleable. The contractor hired to do the job, Preston Friedley, found a bag with $2000 in old money hidden in a wall. Walter had always rented the building and never personally occupied it. Friedley claims the money is his.

e. Walter had leased a small apartment in Chicago for his frequent business trips to that city. Neil had Walter's property removed and returned the keys to the landlord. The landlord has informed Neil that Walter's death did not terminate the lease and that the estate has the duty to either find a new tenant or continue paying the rent for the 9 months remaining on the lease.

f. Neil has been trying to sell Walter's home to settle the estate. A potential purchaser, Mark Garrett, raises and shows golden retriever dogs as an active family side business. Mark plans to add a kennel to the garage for the three to five adult dogs and six to fifteen puppies which may be on the premises at any one time. An adjacent property owner, Rita Hummingbird, has warned Neil that Mark's proposed plans would violate the subdivision rules. The plat states that "lots shall be for single-family residential purposes only" and that "no animal shall be raised, bred or kept for any purposes except household pets."

g. Walter had a small bookstore on the first floor of the Ladner Building. The first floor shops were destroyed by a fire, including the bookstore, though the building itself was saved. Neil has filed a proof of loss and proof of claim with Walter's property and fire insurance company. The building's lease agent is demanding that Neil continue making monthly payments on behalf of the estate.

h. Walter's wife had left him a life estate in her farm, Griffey Point, with the remainder to go to her son, Scott. While in possession of Griffey Point, Walter had torn down the old barn to build a tennis court. Scott has brought an action against Walter's estate claiming damages. Scott claims that the barn was still structurally sound and that his permission had not been secured.

i. Neil discovered that Walter had entered into a contract to sell a vacant piece of land on Oliver Street to Robert Levy. Levy notified Neil that he expects the estate to honor the contract, participate in the closing, have a marketable title, and deliver a warranty deed. Neil has agreed to the first three points but claims that the absence of any discussion in the contract about the type of deed means that the estate need only present a quitclaim deed. Levy disagrees.

Neil urges you to be prompt with your counsel. He is going to appear before the probate judge, Judge Stewart, in the morning.

4. AN ETHICAL PROBLEM

There are an estimated 200 conception clinics in the United States and some 2 million couples seeking reproductive assistance. Courts and legislatures have hardly begun to consider the issues, let alone set forth legal guidelines and directives.

As the new decade began, courts were struggling with the latest conflict between law, medicine, and society: frozen embryos.

An embryo is an organism in the earlier stages of its development. The frozen embryos at issue before the courts are fertilized eggs of couples who are seeking, or have obtained, a divorce after fertilization. Perhaps the most discussed case is that of Junior and Mary Sue Davis.

The Davises got married in 1980. The couple desperately wanted children but were unsuccessful in their attempts. Between 1982 and December 1988, the couple spent almost $50,000 on five unsuccessful attempts to implant an embryo in Mrs. Davis's womb. In December 1988, Mrs. Davis had nine eggs surgically removed and fertilized with sperm from Mr. Davis. Two were again implanted in Mrs. Davis's womb but, again, did not result in pregnancy. The other seven were immediately frozen so they could be implanted at a later date.

In February 1989, Mr. Davis filed for a divorce. Immediately the frozen embryos became a focus of disagreement. Mr. Davis wanted the frozen embryos to be destroyed or given to an anonymous third party, or to remain frozen forever. Mrs. Davis, however, claimed that the seven frozen embryos may represent her last opportunity to bear children and sought exclusive control of them.

The dispute over the frozen embryos raised new questions not previously addressed by law, medicine, or society.

- Are the fertilized embryos "life" or "potential for life"?
- Do the fertilized embryos themselves have any rights or privileges?
- Should Mrs. Davis be considered a pregnant woman even though the frozen embryos are in a petri dish?
- Should the embryos be considered property so they could be bought and sold?
- Should the fertilized embryos be awarded by property or custody laws in a divorce?
- What legal and social obligations, if any, would Mr. Davis have after divorce if Mrs. Davis were allowed custody, a fertilized embryo were implanted, and a child resulted? For example, would Mr. Davis have visitation rights? Would he have to provide child support for the child?
- At this point, does Mr. Davis have a right not to be a parent?
- Did the fact that Mr. Davis consented to give his sperm result in implied consent for Mrs. Davis to have an embryo implanted at a later time, whether or not they were still married?
- Should abortion laws settle the matter? Opponents of abortion claim that life starts at conception. If the courts would accept this argument, the frozen embryos would almost certainly be considered life, not property.
- What rights, if any, would Mrs. Davis have if Mr. Davis used an embryo to have a child with a different wife?

In September 1989, Tennessee Circuit Court Judge W. Dale Young ruled that the embryos are people, not property, and should go to the mother. If you had been the judge, how would you have resolved the legal, medical, and ethical issues in this case?*

---

* This problem was suggested by and adapted from material contained in: "The Rights of Frozen Embryos," *Time*, July 24, 1989, p. 63 (concerning the Yorks of Los Angeles); "Frozen Embryos: The New Frontier," *ABA Journal*, August 1989, p. 68; and "Whose Lives Are These," *Time*, October 2, 1989, p. 19

SALES

This part is about the sale of goods. "Goods" include almost anything which is movable—from bubble gum to bulldozers.

Article 2 of the Uniform Commercial Code (UCC), we saw in Part II, has replaced the common law of contracts as the law governing the sale of goods. The word "Uniform" refers to its drafters' intention that it be the law in every American jurisdiction. In fact, Article 2 has been adopted with minor variations in the District of Columbia and every state except Louisiana.*

To say that the UCC has superseded the common law is not to say that the common law is unimportant or "dead." The UCC itself rests on principles developed at common law. And, in all those areas of contracts to which the UCC does *not* apply, the common law does.

DOES ARTICLE 2
APPLY?

Since Article 2 applies only to the sale of goods, the first question to ask when presented with a contracts problem is, "Does the contract involve goods?" Article 2 defines *goods* as "all things . . . which are movable at the time of identification to the contract for sale other than the money in which the price is to be paid. . . ." [UCC §2-105(1)]. We will discuss identification in some detail in Chapter 32.

For now, focus on the phrase "all things . . . which are movable." "Movable" makes it clear that goods never include *real property*, the generic term for land and buildings. The movable requirement explains why, if you buy a condominium, the common law governs its sale to you, but Article 2 governed the sale of the lumber which went into it. Likewise, Article 2 applies whether the good is as insignificant as a paper clip or as substantial as a telecommunications satellite. Goods also include the unborn young of animals, growing crops, and other things attached to real property—like coal or timber—which the buyer or the seller can sever without injuring the land.

Sometimes, a contract involves both the sale of goods and the supplying of services. Does Article 2 apply? It does not apply if the predominant character of the transaction involves services. If you hire an architect to design your office building, you will receive goods in the form of plans. But, the predominant characteristic of the transaction is the architect's application of his or her skills to your particular needs.

Just as goods have to be distinguished from real property and services, sales must be distinguished from leases. A *lease* is a contract by which a person owning goods (the *lessor*) grants another (the *lessee*) the right to possess and use

---

* As we will see in Parts VII and VIII, the UCC supersedes other areas that the common law of contracts formerly covered. The UCC appears in Appendix I. Citations to the UCC, such as "UCC §2-201(1)," refer to the code as adopted by the American Law Institute and the National Conference on Uniform State Laws.

the goods for a specified period at a set price. Again, the test is the primary character of the contract. If a lease specifies that at its end the leasing party, the lessee, may buy the goods at a nominal price, the court may find that the transaction is essentially a sale. Many computer equipment leases have such clauses. The Code's drafters have recently proposed a new article, 2A, covering leases of goods. A summary of Article 2A can be found in the appendix to this part.

ARTICLE 2'S FUNDAMENTAL CONCEPTS

Article 2 requires a clear understanding of three terms: "merchant," "good faith," and "unconscionability."

Merchant

A *merchant* is a person who normally deals in goods of the kind involved in the transaction or who holds himself out as having knowledge or skills relating to the practices or goods involved in a particular transaction [UCC §2-104(1)]. For example, a car dealer is a merchant as to cars he sells from his lot. But, when he buys groceries for his family, he is not a merchant in those transactions. A party's merchant status often affects the rules Article 2 applies to the transaction.

Figure 31.1 tabulates where in Parts I and VI merchant status is discussed.

Good faith

Good faith means "honesty in fact" [UCC §1-201(19)]. In the case of a merchant, it means "honesty in fact and the observance of reasonable commercial standards of fair dealing in the trade" [UCC §2-103(1) (b)]. The parties cannot alter their duty of good faith by contract.

By its use of the term "good faith", the UCC expresses precisely the opposite philosophy from *caveat emptor*, "let the buyer beware." The UCC's drafters wanted to promote fair dealing and high standards in the marketplace. For that reason, good faith is the touchstone of all transactions under the UCC.

Unconscionability

Article 2's treatment of unconscionable contract provisions shows the "good faith" requirement in practice. Generally, *unconscionable* describes a contract or a clause which is so one-sided, oppressive, or unfair that it shocks a court's conscience. The UCC leaves it up to the courts to define unconscionability on a case-by-case basis. Courts may refuse to enforce contract clauses which they find to be unconscionable as a matter of law [UCC §2-302].

Usually a contract is not unconscionable unless the bargaining power of the parties is so uneven that one party can force a bargain on the other. Still, the unconscionability concept is not designed to disturb the parties' allocation of risks simply on the basis of unequal bargaining power. Rather, there must be an element of oppression or surprise. Suppose a company sold freezers door-to-door to non-English-speaking buyers. A freezer's cash price was $900, but in installments it cost $1230. Its normal retail price was between $350 and $400. A court would find that such pricing was unconscionable.

FORMING A SALES CONTRACT

An enforceable sales contract has exactly the same elements as a common law contract. There are:

- Mutual assent (offer and acceptance)

- Consideration
- Capacity
- Legality of purpose
- Writing, if subject is over $500

In Part II, we saw that the UCC is considerably less strict in its approach to mutual assent than the common law is. Even if the parties omit terms or the terms they adopt are not definite, the UCC's approach is to determine whether the parties intended to be bound and, if so, to what. Under Article 2, the courts will enforce a sales contract so long as the quantity term is present. In Chapter 31, we will explore the formation of sales contracts. For now, keep in mind that while Article 2 supersedes the common law, it is based on common law principles.

RISK OF LOSS

Between the time the parties form a sales contract and the time the goods actually change hands, there is always the possibility that the goods may be lost, damaged, or destroyed. Over the centuries, merchants devised rules governing which party bore the *risk of loss*, the legal responsibility for loss. These rules came into the common law and later, considerably modified, became part of Article 2.

While permitting the parties to allocate the risk of loss by contract, Article 2 states the rules to be applied if the parties have not agreed. These rules apply between the parties to the contract, and their application does not depend on, for example, a third party's liability or the existence of insurance. But, most important, risk of loss does not depend on which party had legal title to the goods. Instead, the UCC normally places the risk on the party best able to protect itself against the loss through insurance or other means. Chapter 32 defines the risk of loss rules.

PERFORMANCE

After the parties form a sales contract, performance is the next step.

The seller has a duty to *tender*—offer for delivery—*conforming goods*, goods which meet the contract's specifications. To make sure that the goods conform, the buyer usually has a right to inspect them before accepting them. Assume that a blacksmith orders 2000 #3 aluminum racing plates. If that is what the seller delivers, the buyer must accept them or breach the contact. *Acceptance* means taking possession of the goods coupled with an intent to own them. The buyer's payment to the seller becomes due on acceptance, unless the contract specifies otherwise.

The seller usually breaches the contract by shipping nonconforming goods. If, on inspection, the blacksmith discovers that he received 1900 #7 steel shoes, the seller has not shipped conforming goods. The buyer has the right to not accept or *reject* them without any obligation to pay for them. However, in some instances where a seller ships *nonconforming goods*, goods which do not meet the contract's specifications upon their rejection the seller has a right to substitute conforming goods. This Article 2 innovation is called the right to *cure* a defective performance.

Inspection is the critical step—both practically and legally—in the performance process because once the buyer accepts goods, he loses the right to reject them as nonconforming.

After acceptance, the buyer's remedies against the seller are limited to damages except in two instances. Only where the buyer would not have discovered the defect in the goods after a reasonable inspection or where the seller led the buyer to believe she would cure the defects does the buyer have a right to *revoke* acceptance, thereby rescinding the contract. Even when the buyer exercises a revocation of acceptance right, she retains the right to sue for damages. Performance rights under the UCC are the subject of Chapter 33.

WARRANTIES AND PRODUCT LIABILITY

A *warranty* is a guarantee or assurance. Normally, a seller of goods makes two types of warranties. First, a seller *warrants* or guarantees its title to the goods it is selling. In other words, a seller guarantees that it has the right to sell the goods. Second, a seller makes warranties of performance as to how the goods will work, what condition they are in, and what their quality is. For example, new bicycles often carry a 90-day warranty on all parts.

It is important to realize that a seller does not have to make any warranties at all. The UCC's provisions apply only when a seller chooses to make warranties. Once a seller makes warranties as to goods, Article 2 and federal and state regulations prescribe how they may be *disclaimed*—taken back—or limited by a disclaimer.

Plaintiffs often cite breaches of warranties of performance with causes of action in tort as grounds to recover damages for injuries caused by defective products. These actions, which are called *products liability suits*, can result in huge damage awards against those who manufacture or sell defective goods.

Warranties are different from other rights created by contract in that as a matter of law they extend to many third parties who suffer a physical injury as a result of a defective or hazardous product. The rationale is that a manufacturer or seller who puts a defective product on the market is better equipped to bear the cost of the injuries the product causes than those injured by it. In Chapter 34 we will examine warranties and products liability actions.

REMEDIES

Products liability suits are only one of the remedies available for breaches of sales contracts. In Chapter 35, the last chapter in this part, we will look at Article 2's approach to remedies. In some ways, the Article 2 remedies are more liberal than the common law's. For instance, specific performance is not limited to contracts involving unique goods. Still, the primary remedy—damages—is the same for both common law contract actions and Article 2 actions.

ARTICLE 2'S MAJOR CONCERNS

In sum, the five chapters in this part reflect Article 2's five principal concerns. These are:

- Have the parties formed a sales contract?
- How should the risk of loss be allocated between the parties?
- Have the parties performed their obligations?
- What warranties, if any, apply to the goods?
- What remedies are available in the event of a breach?

RELATIONSHIP TO PART II

Many, if not most, students using this textbook will have covered Part II, Contracts, prior to studying Part VI, Sales. If you did then you should remember that the primary focus of Part II was with common law contracts but that you were also introduced to a number of Sales concepts and law. As we told you then, we presented those concepts and law there because they are tested in the contracts section of the CPA exam. In Chapter 31, we reintroduce a number of the Article 2 concepts discussed in Part II to be sure you understand them from an Article 2, not common law contracts, focus.

FOR STUDENTS WHO HAVE NOT STUDIED PART II

For those students who have not yet studied Part II, Contracts, you still ought to be able to capture the concepts and understand the material. Chapter 31, Formation of Sales Contracts, is the chapter with the most overlap with the common law. Thereafter the Article 2 coverage makes very little reference to the common law or Part II. We recommend that *before* you begin reading Chapter 31, read the part opener to Part II, Contracts.

It may also be useful for you to note the following figures in Part II and refer to them while studying Chapter 31:

Figure 6.2   Demonstrates that the common law expected the parties to include all material terms, while the UCC does not.

Figure 6.3   Demonstrates that at common law if the terms were so indefinite the contract would not be enforced. Article 2 allows greater flexibility.

Figure 6.4   Shows application of firm offer rule, already discussed in this part opener.

Figure 10.3 Illustrates Statute of Frauds exceptions for Article 2. General rule, discussed earlier in this part opener, is that every contract for the sale of goods for $500 or more must be in writing to be enforceable.

Part II Appendix (at the end of Chapter 12)

> The Part II Appendix lists the major Article 2 sections discussed in Part II. The listed chapters will help you to find the material in both Parts II and VI. You may wish to turn back to Part II and read about the sections which caused you problems in Part VI.

Probably the most important concept for you to keep in mind is that common law contracts rules generally were very specific and purposefully did not leave much freedom of contract to the parties to the contract. The common law focused most on the creation of a contract, not performance. In contrast, the UCC focuses most on performance, not creation. Both the common law and the UCC provide for relief from breaches of contract.

KEY TERMS

acceptance [of performance] (703)
conforming goods (703)
cure (703)
disclaimer (704)
good (701)
good faith (702)
merchant (702)
nonconforming goods (703)

products liability (704)
rejection [of performance] (703)
revocation of acceptance [of performance] (704)
risk of loss (703)
tender (703)
unconscionability (702)
warranty (704)

Suppose you have been shopping for a Ranger Desk Computer. You received Selber Computer's quote of $2300, which you thought was too high. A few days later you find this note in your mail: "Have received 12 too many Ranger Desk Computers. Now willing to sell one to you for $1800. Accept? [Signed] David Selber, Selber Computers."

Under the common law, your acceptance of this "offer" would not result in a binding contract, since too many necessary terms are missing. What about the time of performance, the manner of payment, and the place of delivery? Even so, under the Uniform Commercial Code's (UCC) Article 2, your written response stating only "I accept" could form a binding contract.

The UCC's focus is on whether the parties intended to contract, rather than on whether parties who intended to contract covered all the details. This important shift in emphasis does not mean that a court will find a contract where an essential element, like acceptance, is missing. Rather, it alters the way a court will view the facts of a case in determining whether the parties formed a contract. When a court finds an intent to form a contract and specification of the subject matter—including quantity, it may apply the UCC's "gap fillers" to define any missing particulars.

This chapter examines how Article 2 alters the common law rules on contract formation.

CONTRACTS FOR THE SALE OF GOODS

Article 2 applies *only* to contracts for the sale of goods. The UCC defines goods as "all things . . . which are movable." Essentially, goods are items of tangible personal property, such as a boat, a horse, or a compact disc [UCC §2-105]. Article 2 does not apply to any other type of sales contracts. Therefore, the common law applies to contracts for the sale of accounting services, for the sale of land, or for the sale of a copyright.

Identifying a Contract's Nature

The determination of a contract's nature can be of critical importance to the parties to a dispute. As we have already seen in Chapter 7, the same facts can produce quite different results depending on whether the common law or the UCC applies to them. The nature of most contracts is quite clear. If, for example, you buy a corndog at a fair, you are purchasing a good. When you have a lawyer draw up a will, it is not so much the piece of paper you are paying for as the lawyer's services—the skill and time which went into drawing it up.

Some sales contracts are not so plainly of one type or another. Where there is a mix, a court will look at the transaction as a whole to determine whether Article 2 applies. It will focus on the motivation for the contract. Was it to obtain a good? Real property? A service? In the next case, the court faced this question.

Preston v. Thompson

280 S.E.2d 780 (N.C. Ct. App. 1981)

FACTS   Mrs. Preston wanted a set of dentures which would let her eat without pain. On August 15, 1978, she consulted Dr. Thompson, whom she had found by looking in the Yellow Pages for a denture specialist. Preston later claimed that Thompson told her he could make dentures which would fit to her satisfaction. Thompson denied giving her any assurances. He claimed that he fully explained the problems in treating her. In any event, Preston paid Thompson $750, the price of the treatment. She returned to his office six times for impressions and measurements. On October 20, she received her dentures. The uppers fit perfectly, but the lowers caused pain when she ate. Thompson treated her until May 1979, when she stopped the treatments. Preston brought suit under the UCC for breach of warranties of quality. The trial court granted summary judgment to Thompson.

ISSUE   Was the transaction one for the sale of goods?

DECISION   No. Affirmed. Article 2 applies to transactions between a seller and a purchaser. The essence of the transaction between a retail seller and a consumer relates to the article sold, which the seller is in the business of supplying. He is paid for the product alone. The essence of the dentist's relationship with his patient is professional services. One does not normally go to a dentist to buy items incidental to dental treatment. Preston paid for a course of dental treatment and services, not a piece of merchandise.

A similar problem arises with computer software. If a user buys software off the shelf in a computer store, the software is clearly a good. However, if software is part of a customized package, say, an accounting package for a business, a court may have to decide whether employee training, repair and service, and system upgrading were the essence of the contract as opposed to the software itself. If they were, the contract was not one for the sale of goods.

Problems in identifying a contract's nature are not limited to mixtures of goods and professional services. A lease-purchase agreement is a sales contract if it provides that at the end of the lease's term the lessee *shall* purchase the leased goods. In that instance, the contract is one for the future sale of goods. But what if the lease-purchase agreement says "may" instead of "shall"? Does the purchase price in that case make a difference? In other words, if an automobile lessee had the option to buy the leased

vehicle at $1 or at book value, would it affect the nature of the contract? Those are more difficult questions which the courts address on a case-by-case basis.

Contracts for Leases: UCC Article 2A

For the first time in 30 years, the drafters of the Uniform Commercial Code have added an article. Article 2A regulates leases of goods in a statutory structure similar to Article 2. Article 2A is designed to clear up some of the problems relating to the overlap of contracts for the sale and for the lease of goods.

In 1988, Oklahoma became the first state to adopt Article 2A. In 1990, California likewise embraced the provision. The next case will illustrate how Article 2A is influencing the manner in which a state's judiciary interprets the Uniform Commercial Code.

Cucchi v. Rollins Protective Services

574 A.2d 565 (Pa. 1990)

FACTS   The Cucchi family leased a burglar alarm system from Rollins Protective Services in 1973. In 1984, the Cucchis' home was burglarized and $36,000 was stolen. The system had been activated but did not operate properly. The Cucchis sued Rollins in 1985 for the breach of express and implied warranties. Rollins argued that the Cucchis' suit should be dismissed because the 4-year statute of limitations started to run in 1973 and so had tolled. The trial court ruled in the Cucchis' favor. On appeal to the state's intermediate appellate court, it was reversed.

ISSUE   Did the 4-year statute of limitations for the breach of express and implied warranties start to run when the alarm system was delivered in 1973?

DECISION   No. Reversed. Even though the Pennsylvania state legislature has not yet adopted UCC Article 2A on leases, it can be persuasive in deciding this case. Under Article 2A, the 4-year statute of limitations starts to run when the breach of warranty is or should be discovered. In this case, the 4-year period began in 1984 when the burglar alarm failed, and so was filed in a timely fashion in 1985.

This case brings out some interesting issues surrounding the new UCC Article 2A. First, the Pennsylvania Supreme Court indicated that it strongly supported the use of Article 2A, but stopped short of adopting it because it believed that the state legislature should do it. This judicial deference to the legislature is quite typical, since it is the job of the judicial branch to interpret, not to legislate. The court further echoed the National Conference for Commissioners on Uniform State Laws in its call for the adoption of Article 2A by the states. The National Conference had discovered that Article 2A is particularly necessary in commercial transactions because of the "exponential expansion of the number and scale of personal property lease transactions . . . involving billions of dollars annually." Article 2A was included as part of the articles on sales because of the similarity between sales and leases. However, as the court in the *Cucchi* case noted, there are significant differences between the two, such as transfer of title, incidents of ownership, taxes, and bankruptcy, which is why the court was persuaded to look to Article 2A for guidance.

Further discussion of Article 2A can be found in the appendix following the problems for the end of Part VI.

DETERMINING WHETHER A CONTRACT EXISTS

The UCC attempts to eliminate any artificial barriers to implementing the parties' intentions. It states: "A contract for sale of goods may be made in any manner sufficient to show agreement, including conduct by both parties which recognizes the existence of such a contract" [UCC §2-204(1)]. Article 2 creates a two-part test for determining whether a contract exists. First, did the parties intend to make a contract? Second, does the court have a reasonably certain basis for granting relief to a nonbreaching party [UCC §2-204(3)]?

Intent of the Parties

At common law, a contract existed if a reasonable person would recognize an intent to form one. The UCC operates on a similar principle.

Normally, courts look for signs of intent in the parties' actions and writing and in the circumstances surrounding the transaction. The court in the following case had to determine whether both parties intended to contract.

D.R. Curtis Co. v. Mason

103 Idaho 476, 649 P.2d 1232 (Ct. App. 1982)

FACTS
In April 1978, Mason telephoned the Curtis company and spoke to Bob Mai, a grain broker, about the soybean market. They then talked about Mason's spring wheat. Mason was curious about Curtis's procedure for buying a crop in the spring before a farmer knew what his harvest would be. Mai defined the terms of an agreement to purchase Mason's crop, including a quantity—9000 bushels. Mason asked to see Curtis's contract form, which Mai promised to mail him. Following the telephone conversation, Mai sold the 9000 bushels he thought he had just bought. A few weeks later, Mason received a confirmation from Curtis. Meanwhile, Mason had decided he could not deliver 9000 bushels, so he forgot about the confirmation. Later that summer Curtis representatives began to inquire about their "contract." In the course of several conversations, Mason never assented to the "contract." In late September, Mason returned the confirmation to Curtis, marked "not accepted." Curtis brought suit, but the trial court found for Mason.

ISSUE
Did the parties intend to enter into an agreement?

DECISION
No. Affirmed. During his conversation with Mai, Mason did not agree to sell his wheat. He only intended to explore the possibility of a sale. The seller must agree to sell the goods. A purchaser cannot state an agreement on its own terms and unilaterally form a contract. A confirmation does not create an enforceable contract unless a previous oral agreement exists to be confirmed, even if the confirmation contains an unconditional statement that failure to return the form would be deemed an acceptance of the contract.

Contracts by conduct. If the conduct of the parties indicates that a contract existed, but no writings exist which establish it, a court may find that a contract existed. The terms of the contract are those on which the parties' writings agree [UCC §2-207(3)]. Generally, courts imply contracts by conduct where the parties have already shipped, accepted, and paid for the goods in question before the dispute arises. Thus, the parties' actions show that they must have contracted orally. It would make no sense to permit the lack of a written contract to prevent a court from enforcing the parties' intent. However, in the next case, the court was asked to decide just how much of the parties' writings and conduct, including oral discussions, should govern their relationship in the sales contract.

American Aluminum Products Co., Inc. v. Binswinger Glass Co.

194 Ga. App. 703, 391 S.E.2d 699 (1990)

FACTS   Binswinger Glass contracted with American Aluminum Products Co. (AAPCO) to furnish metal-framed entry skylights at two office buildings. The skylights leaked, and Binswinger sued AAPCO for damages, claiming the aluminum frames did not conform to the language in the two purchase orders, which stated that the skylights would be "per plans and specs based on shop drawings to be submitted within two weeks." When the plans were disclosed, they stipulated that the skylights would be leak-free. APPCO contends that the appropriate specifications were those in the "Fischer drawings," which had been discussed in preliminary negotiations and which AAPCO argues it conformed to. Binswinger won at the trial level.

ISSUE   Was the contractual relationship between AAPCO and Binswinger governed by the purchase orders and the specifications referenced in them?

DECISION   Yes. Affirmed. Under UCC §2-207(3), "terms of the particular contract consist of those terms on which the writings of the parties agree, together with any supplementary terms incorporated under any other provisions of the [Uniform Commercial Code]." The "plans and specs" referenced to in the purchase orders constitute the terms which were agreed to. Those terms required that the skylights be watertight and leak-free. AAPCO's argument that the "Fischer drawings" governed the parties' relationship was erroneous, since they were not part of the contracts (purchase orders) and only constituted preliminary negotiations.

OFFER

Like all contracts, a sales contract requires an offer and an acceptance. Article 2 makes no essential changes to their natures.*

---

* Offers relating to auctions are discussed in Chapter 6 [UCC §2-528].

Revocation and Options

As under the common law, the offeror ordinarily has the right to revoke her offer before the offeree's acceptance. Also, a promise to keep an offer open for a period of time is not binding without consideration. Suppose that one Thursday, a classmate says to you, "I'll sell you my intermediate accounting book for

$15. You've got until Tuesday to accept." She could revoke her offer to you before Tuesday if you had not yet accepted, since you gave her no consideration for keeping the offer open. However, if you had paid her $1 to keep it open while you decided, she could not revoke her offer. This is called an irrevocable offer or an *option* contract under both the common law and the UCC.

Firm Offers

The UCC modifies the common law's option rule by not requiring consideration if a merchant makes a *firm offer*. A firm offer must be in writing and must be signed by the *merchant*, a person who normally deals in goods of the kind involved in the transaction or who holds himself out as having knowledge or skills relating to the practices or goods involved in a particular transaction [UCC §2-104(1) and the appendix to this part]. It may indicate that the offer will be kept open for a stated time *or*, if no time is stated, a court will hold that the offer remains open for a reasonable time up to 3 months [UCC §2-205]. The next case deals with the most common example of a firm offer, the "rain check."

Lowenstern v. Stop & Shop Companies, Inc.

32 U.C.C. Rep. Serv. 414 (Mass. Super. Ct., 1981)

FACTS   Lowenstern ran a small business selling records. Bradlee's, a discount chain, sold selected albums at less than Lowenstern could buy them. On February 19, Lowenstern obtained "rain checks" for four albums because the store was out of stock; these allowed him to buy the albums later at the sale price. The record department manager told him that the store would not honor rain checks for more than twenty copies of each album. On April 4, Lowenstern tried to redeem the rain checks for seventy-five copies of each album. Bradlee's refused to honor the rain checks at all. Lowenstern brought suit against Bradlee's for the 15 percent markup he would have made on the albums.

ISSUE   Was Bradlee's bound to honor the rain checks up to twenty copies per album?

DECISION   Yes. Judgment for Lowenstern. Once a customer attempts to purchase a sale item and is given a rain check, it may become a firm offer. However, the offer may limit the terms of a firm offer before it is issued. Bradlee's rain checks were firm offers, since they were made by a merchant, stated that the offer would be kept open, were in writing, and were signed by a Bradlee's employee. But, Bradlee's had told Lowenstern that the checks would not be honored for more than twenty copies and thus limited the scope of the offer.

Assume that Bradlee's did not specify an expiration date for its rain check. For record albums, a court might hold that the UCC maximum of 3 months was a reasonable period for the offer to remain open. But if the item was fresh fruit, more than a week might be unreasonable. A reasonable time varies according to the nature of the goods.

This case also raises interesting business questions as to why it was that Lowenstern could buy records cheaper from Bradlee's than he could from distributors. One reason may be the volume of records that Bradlee's purchased. A more probable reason was that Bradlee's was discounting those records below cost as price leaders to spur store traffic. Could Bradlee's limit the number of records (today, more likely cassettes or CD's) sold to any one buyer? Yes, if properly posted. Today, the small, independent music shop, like Lowenstern's, is becoming conspicuous by its absence.

Firm offers, as in the previous case, can be made only by merchants. Article 2 rules which apply to either a merchant or merchants are presented in Figure 31.1. You may wish to refer to this figure as you study the remainder of Part VI.

ACCEPTANCE

The UCC modifies the common law governing *acceptance* of an offer in two important ways. The first concerns how an offeree may accept, while the second mediates the "battle of the forms."

CONCEPT	UCC SECTION	PART II CHAPTER	PART VI CHAPTER
Merchant defined	2-104	6	Unit Overview
Merchant confirmations	2-201*	10	31
Firm offer	2-205	6	31
"Battle of the forms"	2-207*	7	31
Contract modifications	2-209*	9	31
Infringement warranty	2-312	Not covered	34
Merchantability warranty	2-314	Not covered	34
Sale on approval (or return)	2-327	Not covered	32
Risk of loss	2-509	Not covered	32
Buyer's duty/rejected goods	2-603	Not covered	33
Buyer's duty to particularize	2-605*	Not covered	33
Right to adequate assurance, grounds for reasonableness	2-209*	Not covered	33

*These sections apply *only* to situations where both the seller *and* the buyer are merchants.

Figure 31.1 Rules Relating to Merchants.
You may wish to refer to this listing of Article 2 sections covering merchants while studying the chapters in Part VI.

Reasonable Medium

The offeror may specify how the offeree may accept. The UCC does not vary that rule. What it does change are the rules which apply when the offeror does not specify a *medium of acceptance*.

Under the common law, if the offeror did not specify the medium of acceptance, the offeree had to use the same medium the offeror used to transmit the offer. If Ellen sent an order by telegram to Office Supply Co. for twenty computer stands, the common law would require the company to accept by telegram. Under the common law's "mailbox rule" (discussed in Chapter 7), an acceptance took effect on dispatch when the *offeree* used the same *medium* as the *offeror*. If the offeree used a different medium, the courts treated the acceptance as a counteroffer which the offeror could accept or reject.

Under the UCC, acceptance occurs when the offeree sends it acceptance using a reasonable medium [UCC §2-206(1)(a)]. The speed and reliability of a medium determine its reasonableness. If the offeree's medium is as speedy and reliable as the offeror's, it is reasonable. So, Office Supply Co. could respond to Ellen's offer by telex, express mail, or telegram.

"Prompt Shipment" Orders. Before Article 2's adoption, if a buyer offered to buy goods "for prompt shipment," "to be shipped immediately," or the like, the offeree could accept only by actually shipping. Under the UCC, such phrases invite *either* prompt shipment or a prompt promise to ship followed thereafter by the shipment [UCC §2-206(1)(b)].

Accommodations

Under ordinary circumstances, a shipment of *nonconforming goods*—goods which differ from those specified in the sales contract—breaches the contract and gives the buyer a basis for damages. However, this rule has an exception.

If the seller has not accepted the buyer's offer, the seller can state that he is sending nonconforming goods as an *accommodation*, as a favor, to the buyer. When this occurs, the buyer can accept the goods and form a contract or reject the shipment without liability to either seller or buyer. Suppose Office Supply Co. responds to Ellen's prompt shipment order by sending, as an accommodation, stands 8 inches longer than the ones she specified. Ellen may accept them, and thus form a contract, or reject them.

The key elements of an accommodation are the seller/offeree's lack of a prior acceptance and the notice to the buyer/offeror of the shipment's character. Had Office Supply accepted Ellen's offer and shipped nonconforming goods, it would be liable for breaching the contract.

The seller's accommodation shipment, in effect, is an offer to sell. The buyer may reject the offer or may accept it—and thereby form a conract—by taking the goods. Figure 31.2 outlines the buyer's alternatives on receiving nonconforming goods.

Accommodations benefit the buyer by encouraging the seller to ship goods immediately which he believes might satisfy the buyer. The rationale for this rule is that the buyer may be better off if the seller sends his closet conforming goods. If the goods are satisfactory, the buyer has avoided the delay of searching for an alternative source. At the same time, the UCC's requirement that the parties act in good faith protects buyers from sellers who might deliberately send nonconforming goods, hoping the buyer's urgent need will force her to accept them.

Additional or Different Terms

As with the medium of acceptance, the common law generally required the acceptance to mirror the offer's terms. The UCC looks instead for a mutual intent to contract, revealed by an agreement on the central terms. But what happens when the acceptance varies the terms

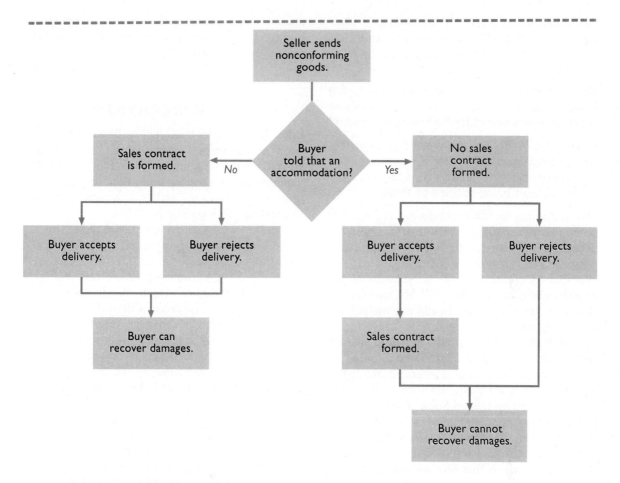

Figure 31.2 The Accommodation Rule.
If the seller has not accepted, the seller's shipment of nonconforming goods
without notifying the buyer that it is an accommodation shipment both accepts
the buyer's offer and breaches the contract.

of the offer somewhat? What happens if there is a "battle of the forms"? Is there a contract when the buyer orders on her printed form containing a page of terms and conditions favorable to her and the seller accepts with a form with terms favorable to him? If so, what are the contract's terms?

Not Between Merchants. The application of the UCC's rules concerning the inclusion of additional or different terms depends on whether a nonmerchant is a party to the transaction. If a nonmerchant is involved, the acceptance creates a contract as to the terms of the offer. The new terms are considered proposals subject to negotiation. Suppose Michael coaches his school's ski team. Plastiglass, Inc., offers to sell him 100 specially manufactured goggles for $1000. Michael responds, "I accept your offer. Deliver the goggles packed in lots of ten." Under the common law, they do not have a contract because Michael's terms did not mirror the terms of the offer. Under Article 2, Plastiglass and Michael have a contract, and Plastiglass may deliver all 100 packed together.

Between Merchants. Between merchants, different or additional terms become part of the contract unless one of the following is the case:

- The offer limits the acceptance to its terms.
- The terms materially alter the contract.
- A party objects to the terms within a reasonable time of being notified of them.

Additional or different terms do not become part of the contract if the offer limits the acceptance to its terms [UCC §2-207(2)(b)]. Suppose Plastiglass had stated in its offer, "Acceptance is conditional on acceptance of the original terms of the offer." If Michael were a merchant, their contract would not include his packaging term.

Similarly, a court would not hold that an additional term which materially altered the contract became a part of it [UCC §2-207(2)(b)]. For example, a clause in Michael's order specifies shipment by United States Postal Service. If Michael is a merchant and Plastiglass' acceptance specifies shipment by United Parcel Service, this change would not be material. Suppose, however, that Michael specified clear plastic lenses in the goggles but Plastiglass specifies tinted lenses in its acceptance. That change probably would be material.

Where clauses are within the range of trade practices, they do not affect the contract materially. For instance, a court would not invalidate a clause stating a reasonable interest rate for overdue amounts.

Additional terms do not become part of the contract if within a reasonable time the other party objects to them and the party proposing the additional terms receives the objection [UCC §2-207(2)(c)]. If Plastiglass objects to Michael's packaging term a week after it receives his order and before it ships the goggles, the term is not included. But if Plastiglass objects after Michael rejects a shipment of 100

pairs packed together, it would be too late. Figure 31.3 shows how the additional terms rules work under the UCC.

CONSIDERATION

Like the common law, Article 2 requires consideration to form a sales contract. No consideration means no contract. However, the UCC exempts from the consideration requirement firm offers, discussed earlier, and modifications to existing sales contracts.

Under the UCC, an agreement modifying a contract for the sale of goods requires good faith but needs no consideration to be binding [UCC §2-209(1)]. Suppose Baker has a long-term contract under which she is to supply bread to a hotel. The price of flour doubles, and Baker asks the hotel's management to agree to a higher price for the bread in order to cover her increased cost. The hotel agrees. Under the UCC, the hotel is bound by the modification, even though Baker provided no additional consideration.

The UCC presumes that both parties to a contact modification have acted in good faith. If this is not the case, the aggrieved party can assert the lack of good faith as a defense to performance under the new agreement. Suppose that Baker, in the last hypothetical, had demanded a higher price and threatened to stop deliveries if the hotel did not agree. If the hotel had no real alternative but to give in, a court might refuse to enforce the modification. In that event, the hotel would be excused from performing its obligations under the modification and would be entitled to a refund of any additional sums it had paid.

THE GAP FILLERS

At common law, if the parties left any terms indefinite, a court would not enforce their agreement. Under the UCC, however, the par-

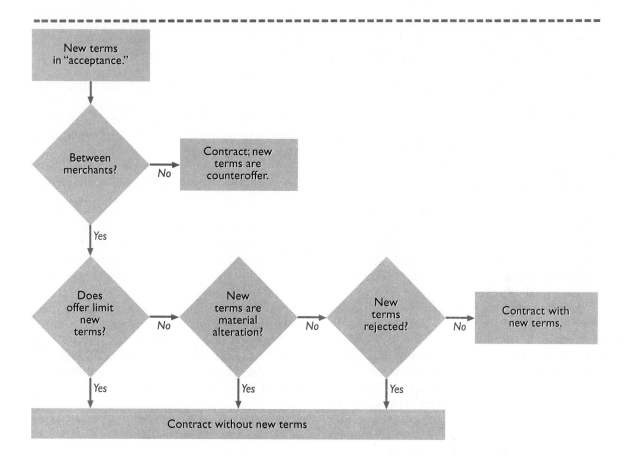

Figure 31.3 Effect of New Terms in an Acceptance Under the UCC.

ties need only agree on the quantity of the goods to be sold and sufficient terms so that a court has a reasonably certain basis for framing an appropriate remedy [UCC §2-204(3)].

The Guidelines

As discussed in Chapter 6, Article 2 provides courts with guidelines for filling gaps in terms left by the parties. These so-called gap fillers include:

- *Price*: The price is a reasonable one at the time of delivery [UCc §2-305].
- *Payment*: Payment is due at the time and place the buyer is to receive the goods [UCC §2-310].
- *Delivery*: The seller must tender all goods called for by the contract in a single delivery [UCC §2-307].
- *Place of delivery*: Delivery takes place at the seller's place of business or, if the seller has none, his residence [UCC §2-308].
- *Transportation*: Failure to agree on transportation does not affect the validity of a contract.
- *Time*: Shipment, delivery, or any other action under a contract must take place at a reasonable time [UCC §2-309(1)].

The correct application of some gap fillers requires an examination of the parties' dealings and, perhaps, some evidence concerning trade usages. The "reasonableness" standard invites the courts to appraise the facts and arrive at a fair resolution.

Quantity Terms

The courts normally will not enforce a contract without a quantity term, nor will they supply one. The rationale is that the court's purpose is not to make a contract. Without an agreed-upon quantity, the court would be doing just that. For example, an offer to sell "from one to ten #23 Acme lawnmowers for $100 each" would be unenforceable if accepted in that manner. The terms would be too indefinite. Obviously, if the quantity is not specified, neither is the price. Here that could range from $100 to $1000—a considerable difference.

As we saw in Chapter 6, output and requirements contracts are an exception to the quantity rule. An *output contract* is one in which the buyer agrees to take what the seller produces. For example, a chain of bars agrees to buy all the chips Ace Potato Chips produces each month. This is an output contract.

In a *requirements contract* the buyer agrees to purchase all it requires from the seller. Suppose that instead of agreeing to take all of Ace's output, the bar chain agreed to purchase all its potato chip needs from Ace. That would be a requirement contract.

Neither output nor requirements contracts is considered too indefinite, since the actual good faith output or requirements of a particular party provides the standard [UCC §2-206].

A requirements contract is not, therefore, just an option contract. The buyer cannot avoid buying just because someone offers a better price. The parties to a requirements contract share the risks. The seller assumes the risk of a change in the buyer's business—the buyer's risk—that makes its products less necessary. In the next case, the court had to struggle with the extreme requirements question: What happens when the buyer eliminates its requirements without purchasing anything?

Empire Gas Corp. v. American Bakeries Co.

840 F.2d 1333 (7th Cir. 1988)

FACTS   In 1979–1980, the price of gasoline rose to record levels. American Bakeries decided to convert its more than 3000 vehicles to propane, then selling at a third to half the price of gasoline. In April 1980, American contracted with Empire Gas for the purchase of 3000 propane conversion units "more or less depending upon requirements of Buyer" at $750 per unit and to "purchase propane motor fuel solely from EMPIRE GAS CORPORATION . . . as long as EMPIRE GAS CORPORATION remains in a reasonably competitive price posture with other suppliers." The contract was to last 4 years. Within days after the contract's execution, American Bakeries decided not to convert its fleet. It never gave a reason for this decision and never ordered equipment or propane from Empire. Empire brought suit seeking lost profits. A jury awarded it $3,254,963.

ISSUE   Must the buyer of goods under a requirements contract establish that it acted in good faith in reducing its purchases below its estimated requirements?

DECISION   Yes. Affirmed. The parties agreed that they had entered into a requirements contract. UCC §2-206(1) states in part:

> A term which measures the quantity by . . . the requirements of the buyer means such actual . . . requirements as may occur in good faith, except that no quantity unreasonably disproportionate to any stated estimate or in the absence of a stated estimate to any normal or otherwise comparable prior . . . requirements may be . . . demanded.

The "unreasonably disproportionate" clause explains, in part, the meaning of "good faith." By case law, it is limited to instances of disproportionately large demand, which was not the case here. The question therefore is whether American acted in good faith by demanding nothing. Had American bought from another supplier during the contract's term, clearly it would have been acting in bad faith. Equally clearly, if it had a business reason for deciding not to convert that was independent of its relationship with Empire, such as a drop in demand for its products, it would have been acting in good faith. A buyer like American cannot reduce its demand to nil and be deemed to have acted in good faith merely because it had second thoughts about the terms of the contract and wanted to get out of it. Here, American never gave any reason for its conduct. Therefore, no reasonable jury could have failed to find bad faith.

Why did American Bakeries not go through with the conversion? A probable reason has to do with a change in the comparative cost difference between gasoline and propane. The court emphasized that American Bakeries's failure to do any conversions was "unreasonably disproportionate" to the contract. What would have been the minimal conversion rate which would have allowed a court to find good faith? The court refused to speculate, instead focusing on the overall issue of good faith. Does this seem to be the best approach?

THE UCC'S STATUTE OF FRAUDS

Under both the common law and the UCC, a contract for the sale of goods for $500 or more is not enforceable unless a writing evidences the transaction. The writing must indicate that the parties have made a contract for the sale of goods, and it must be signed by the party against whom enforcement is sought or by his agent or broker.

The UCC does not specify any particular form for a written contract. The writing only needs to provide a basis for determining that a contract—as opposed to negotiations—exists. For example, car dealers commonly "put the deal together" on a scratch pad before transferring it to a form contract. Could these notes be a sale contract? Yes, if they are signed* by the party against whom enforcement of the contract is sought.

Article 2 excepts four categories of transactions from its Statute. We will examine each of these below.

Merchant Confirmation

The merchant confirmation exception covers the common situation in which merchants orally agree to a contract for $500 or more and one sends the other a signed confirmation of the

---

* As under the common law (discussed in Chapter 10), a signature does not have to be handwritten in ink. It may consist of initials or even a letterhead. All a signature does is identify the party to be charged.

transaction. A confirmation satisfies the Statute if it is sufficient to be enforced as a contract against the sender and if the recipient has reason to know of its contents.

The merchant confirmation exception applies *only* to merchants. If a merchant sends a confirmation to a nonmerchant, as in *D.R. Curtis*, above, the nonmerchant is not bound by it [UCC §2-201(2)]. The oral contract is still unenforceable.

The merchant-recipient has 10 days from receipt of the confirmation to object in writing to its terms. If the recipient does not object, the sender may enforce the confirmation as their contract. An objection must go to the essence of the contract, not to an immaterial term. While reading the next case, keep in mind that the Statute's purpose is not to protect a party who made an oral contract, but rather to protect a party who did *not*.

Simmons Oil Corp. v. Bulk Sales Corp.

498 F. Supp. 457 (D.N.J. 1980)

FACTS

On May 25, 1979, Simmons orally agreed to sell Bulk Sales 25,000 barrels of gasoline at $1.22 per gallon. The next working day, May 29, Simmons sent a confirming telex to Bulk Sales stating the terms of the contract. On May 30, Bulk Sales responded, "With reference to your telex of 5/29/79, please be advised that the payment clause is not acceptable and we suggest the substitution of a more appropriate and conventional clause." Bulk Sales then suggested two alternative methods of payment. Its telex concluded, "Please advise promptly whether this change is acceptable so that we may consider this a firm transaction." On June 1, Simmons responded, agreeing, but asked that if a particular alternative was chosen, the terms of its original telex be observed. The parties did not communicate again until June 26, when Simmons contacted Bulk Sales to learn when it would accept delivery. Bulk Sales told Simmons it did not recognize any contract. Simmons sought other buyers for its gasoline, and on July 3 sold the 25,000 gallons at the market price, 90 cents per gallon. Simmons brought suit to recover the difference between the contract price and the price at which it sold the gasoline.

ISSUE

Did Bulk Sales's May 30 telex sufficiently object to the entire transaction?

DECISION

No. Judgment for Simmons.

Although defendant argues [the May 30 telex] constitutes sufficient objection to plaintiff's May 29 telex, that argument must be rejected. The telex volunteers too much. The terms of the May 29 telex, which detailed the alleged contract, are incorporated by reference, and defendant's objection, the 'So that we may consider this a firm transaction' language not withstanding, is but a portion of the confirmation. . . .

. . . Advising on the form that an objection should take, Duesenberg and King [stated in an article]:

"The objection, if it volunteers too much, may itself amount to a satisfactory memorandum [of agreement]. The simplest advice to follow would be to send a brief, concise statement acknowledging receipt of the purported confirmation and denying

either its content or that any contract was entered. . . .Even a lone reference to price may give basis for the confirming merchant to contend that there was in truth a bargain and that oral evidence should be admitted to prove it. The [UCC's] minimization of what is required for an effective memorandum makes it exceedingly unwise to do otherwise than dispatch an unequivocal denial of all the content of the confirmation."

Specially Manufactured Goods

A seller may enforce an oral contract for specially manufactured goods which are not suitable for sale to others in the ordinary course of its business. Suppose your school's purchasing department orally ordered a custom-made auditorium curtain featuring a pattern with the school logo. If the school cancels its order after the seller makes a substantial start on the curtain, a court would enforce this agreement.

The uniqueness of the performance must indicate that some agreement existed between the parties. Still, the seller must not have received notice of the buyer's repudiation of their agreement before making either a substantial beginning on the goods' manufacture or a commitment to obtain them. Also, the circumstances of the transaction must indicate that the goods are for the particular buyer and therefore are not resaleable [UCC §2-201(3)(a)].

Admission in Legal Proceedings

The admission in legal proceedings exception to the Article 2 Statute applies when the party being sued admits in court or in a court document that he or she entered into an oral contract for the sale of goods. Then, the contract is enforceable, but not beyond the quantity of goods the party admitted was the subject of the contract [UCC §2-201(3)(b)]. Suppose a party who allegedly breached an oral agreement stated in a deposition, "I don't owe anything. When I said I'd buy your car for $3500, I didn't put it in writing." The court would have a basis for upholding the otherwise unenforceable oral contract.

The purpose of the admission exception is to prevent the use of the Statute as a sword instead of a shield. As noted earlier, the Statute is designed to protect those who do not contract, not those who wish to evade their obligations.

Part Performance

Under Article 2, part performance is another substitute for a writing. However, it only validates a contract for goods which the buyer has accepted delivery or for which the seller has accepted payment [UCC §2-201(3)(c)]. In the next case, the court was faced with a partially performed contract which the buyer sought to enforce.

Anthony v. Tidwell

560 S.W.2d 908 (Tenn. 1977)

FACTS   The Tidwells sued Anthony, claiming that they had contracted orally to buy 100 cattle from him at $500 each and had made a $1000 down payment to him. Anthony then refused to sell them the cattle. The trial court granted Anthony's motion to dismiss the complaint because the contract was unenforceable under the Statute of Frauds.

ISSUE Was any part of the contract enforceable against the seller?

DECISION Yes. Reversed. The trial court properly dismissed the complaint insofar as it sought enforcement of the entire contract. But, it erred in denying the Tidwells the opportunity of proving the partial payment and of enforcing the contract to the extent of that payment. The Tidwell's $1000 check was partial performance, which entitled them to enforce the oral contract to the extent of the payment.

PAROL EVIDENCE RULE

Article 2's *parol evidence rule* is quite similar to the common law's, which was discussed in Chapter 10. Under it, when the contracting parties intend a confirmation or a written contract to be the final expression of their agreement, that writing cannot be contradicted by evidence of any prior agreement or of a contemporaneous oral agreement [UCC §2-202]. Suppose a salesperson orally agrees to include a radio in your new car. Subsequently, you sign a written contract with the dealership stating "no radio included." In the absence of fraud or other misconduct by the salesperson, you cannot raise that omission after the sale is completed.

Consistent Additional Terms

When faced with an ambiguity in a contract, the UCC allows a court to admit evidence of consistent additional terms that the parties did not put in writing, *unless* the parties intended the writing to be the complete, exclusive statement of the contract's terms [UCC §2-202(b)]. So long as the terms of the writing are not contradicted, the fairest resolution results from admitting additional terms to clarify an ambiguity. Suppose the sales contract for the car had said simply, "Dealer to add radio." A court could admit evidence concerning the type of radio to which the contract referred.

Actions by the Parties and Usages of Trade

On occasion, a written sales contract will include language that the parties or the industry may interpret quite differently from its ordinary meaning. In those cases, a court may admit evidence to clarify otherwise clear wording. For example, a contract requires the seller to deliver "old Chicago bricks." Does that term mean old bricks from Chicago or bricks of the Old Chicago style?

Course of Dealing. A *course of dealing* is the parties' conduct over time which establishes a common basis of understanding for interpreting their writings. Suppose a contractor and a brick supplier have dealt with each other for many years. The contractor has always received old bricks from Chicago when she ordered them. The supplier would be in breach if he now sent an equivalent style [UCC §1-205].

Course of Performance. A *course of performance* is the parties' conduct during a particular contract's life. Suppose the supplier was to provide four separate deliveries of "old Chicago bricks." In the first two deliveries, the supplier provided an equivalent style, which the contractor knowingly accepted. When the third delivery of equivalent bricks arrived, the contractor rejected them. The contractor has breached her contract with the supplier. She should have objected to the first shipment [UCC §2-208(1)].

Usage of Trade. A *usage of trade* is a practice or method of dealing regularly observed in a particular place, vocation, or trade. Its use must be so regular that a party may justifiably expect that it will be observed in a particular transaction. Suppose a usage of trade among contractors permits using simulated old Chicago bricks to fulfill contracts calling for old Chicago bricks. The supplier would not breach the contract by providing them.

A usage of trade does not bind a party who is not engaged in a particular trade or does not understand it. Suppose a consumer wanted old bricks from Chicago and had not heard of the usage of trade which permitted supplying simulations. He would probably win a breach of contract action against the supplier for providing the simulations. This safeguard reflects the UCC's policy of permitting commercial parties to contract in the language of their trade, while protecting those who are not of the trade. Thus, the usage of trade rule facilitates and clarifies contracts between commercial parties. As the next case reveals, however, there are limits on what evidence of trade usages a party may introduce.

A. J. Cunningham Packing Corp. v. Florence Beef Co.

785 F.2d 348 (1st Cir. 1986)

FACTS

On December 28, 1979, Florence Beef Co. placed four orders for Australian boneless beef. The contracts required the beef to be "85% chemically lean." Listed among the conditions of sale on Cunningham's sales confirmations was:

> In the event Buyer claims product covered by this contract is less than the [specified] chemical leanness . . . , Seller has the right to arrange independent testing. Should the product test less than the guaranteed chemical leanness, Seller will allow for excessive fat content based on selling price, and Buyer will accept such as full settlement.

Testing proved the beef to be between 83.25 percent and 84.6 percent chemically lean. In accordance with the parties' prior practice, Cunningham offered to reduce the contract price according to the formula in the Meat Importers Council of America "Guidelines for the Settlement of Fat Claims." Those guidelines permitted the buyer to reject beef that was less than 80 percent chemically lean. Nonetheless, Florence rejected the four shipments. The trial court refused to admit evidence Florence offered on trade usages not consistent with the guidelines for calculating leanness, and it awarded damages to Cunningham.

ISSUE

Did the trial court abuse its discretion by refusing to admit evidence of inconsistent trade usages?

DECISION

No. Affirmed. Custom and usage are relevant to contract interpretation. A court may admit such evidence even if an ambiguity has not yet been shown. However, UCC §1-205(4) requires that a court interpret the express term of an agreement and a course of dealing or a usage of trade as consistent with one another whenever it is reasonable to do so. When such an interpretation produces an unreasonable result, the express language controls. Here, the guidelines, which the trial court admitted into evidence on the basis of trade usage and the parties' course of dealing, were reasonably consistent with the express terms of the contract.

Conflict. If there is a conflict among the various meanings of a term, the court will apply the various meanings in the following order:

- Express or plain meaning
- Course of performance
- Course of dealing
- Usage of trade

It bears repeating that a court will admit evidence as to the last three when a meaning is not express. They are admissible only to explain an ambiguity. As for the UCC's priority given conflicting terms appearing in a contract, the same ranking applies as at common law: handwritten, typewritten, and, last, printed.

CONCLUSION

This chapter has focused upon the rules concerning the creation of a contract. The basic elements required to form a common law contract apply to sales contracts, although the UCC does introduce some innovations.

In the next chapter, we will examine an area that the UCC significantly alters: the allocation of liability when the goods subject to a sales contract are lost, stolen, damaged, or destroyed. Sometimes the fault will be that of one of the parties. In that case, liability for the loss is easy to assess. However, at other times the loss is not the fault of either contracting party, as when goods in the hands of a carrier are damaged. Still, the law must assess the loss between the contracting parties.

A NOTE TO FUTURE CPA CANDIDATES

Uniform Commercial Code Article 2, Sales, is tested in the common law contracts and UCC sections of the CPA exam. The sales sections covered in this chapter and those listed in the Part II Appendix, at the end of Chapter 12, generally are covered in the contracts portion of the CPA exam.

It is important that you correctly characterize contracts on the exam. Article 2 applies to the sale of goods. Sales contracts require the same elements as the common law: mutual assent, consideration, capacity, legal objective, and, if the contract is for $500 or more, a writing. However, significantly greater flexibility is permitted under the UCC.

Two of the most tested concepts are the firm offer and "gap fillers." A firm offer requires a signed, written offer by a merchant offeror giving assurances that the offer will be held open for a stated time—if no time is stated, a reasonable time—in no case greater than 3 months. Remember, no consideration is required to have a binding firm offer and the offer*ee* need not be a merchant. For a court to utilize "gap fillers," there must exist evidence of an intent to form a sales contract and quantity terms.

The "battle of the forms" commonly has been tested on the exam. Between merchants, different or additional terms in an acceptance become part of the sales contract unless the offer limits the acceptance to its terms, the new terms materially alter the contract, or the other party objects within a reasonable time. If not between merchants, a contract results but new or different terms are considered merely proposals.

Article 2, like the common law, requires consideration to form a contract. However, remember that there are two situations where no consideration is required: a firm offer and a good faith alteration of an existing sales contract.

The UCC Statute of Frauds requires a writing by the party to be charged for sales contracts of $500 or more. One common exception, between merchants, is a written confirmation. It serves in lieu of a written contract if no objection is made within 10 days of receipt. Three other exceptions include specially manufactured goods, admission in legal proceedings, and part performance (where the buyer has accepted delivery or the seller has accepted payment).

When a dispute arises under Article 2, evidence can be introduced to clarify ambiguities. However, the parole evidence rule prohibits the introduction of evidence which varies, alters, or contradicts the sales contract. Evidence can be introduced of course of dealing (past contractual relations between the parties), course of performance (conduct of the parties during the life of the disputed contract), or usage of trade (the practice or method of dealing regularly observed in the trade).

KEY WORDS

accommodation (714)
confirmation (719)
course of dealing (722)
course of performance (722)
firm offer (712)
medium of acceptance (714)
merchant (712)
nonconforming goods (714)

output contract (718)
parol evidence rule (722)
part performance (721)
prompt shipment (714)
requirements contract (718)
Statute of Frauds (719)
usage of trade (723)

DISCUSSION QUESTIONS

1. What are the necessary elements of a sales contract under the UCC?
2. What is the test under the UCC for determining whether an agreement for the sale of goods is sufficiently definite?
3. Name three gap fillers and explain when they are applicable.
4. In what respect does Article 2 alter the common law rule as to the offeror's power to revoke?
5. Develop a fact pattern involving a firm offer.
6. Under the UCC, when does acceptance take place? Is there any way the offeror can limit that rule?
7. Explain how Article 2 alters the common law mirror image principle regarding acceptance.
8. Name two instances in which an agreement is enforceable under the UCC even absent consideration.
9. When does the Statute of Frauds apply to the sale of goods?
10. Name three exceptions to Article 2's Statute of Frauds.

CASE PROBLEMS

1. Michelle Gray wrote the Prestige Seed Company to get prices on a list of bulbs for her garden. On February 1, Prestige sends a signed response stating, "We will sell you the bulbs you listed for a total of $350 plus cost of shipment. We must have your response within 120 days." On February 10, Michelle receives a postcard from Prestige which states that their previous offer to her was being revoked "because our prices have increased." If Michelle attempts to accept Prestige's offer on February 15, will there be an enforceable sales contract? Would there be on June 15? Explain.
2. Stationery store owner John Tiner contracted to supply the public accounting firm run by Kristi Cassels with 400 reams of bonded paper at a stated price. This is the first contract between the parties. They failed to specify

where delivery was to occur, and a disagreement resulted. Citing her prior dealings with one of Tiner's close competitors, Cassels claims that she expected the paper to be delivered to her office as part of the purchase price. Alternatively, Cassels claims the contract lacked mutual assent. Tiner claims that there is no particular usage of trade in the area. If Tiner is correct, would a court be likely to find mutual assent? If so, where will the court determine delivery should have taken place?

3. Huskie Oil Company ordered thirty-five tires "for prompt shipment" from Acme Tire. Acme responded in writing, "We accept your offer. We will ship the tires you request within three working days." On the same day Huskie received this confirmation, it learned that it could buy the tires for less from United Tire. Accordingly, an official from Huskie called Acme and said, "Forget sending those tires. We asked for prompt shipment, not a letter telling us you were going to ship." Did Acme properly accept Huskie's offer? Explain.

4. Brown's Grocery ordered 100 cases of Delicious brand peas at list price from Smith Wholesalers. Because Smith had sold its entire supply of Delicious peas, it sent 100 cases of Lovely brand peas, stating clearly on the invoice that the shipment was sent only as an accommodation. Is Smith in breach of contract? Would your conclusion be the same had Smith first sent an acceptance for Delicious brand peas, but then sent the same invoice with the Lovely brand peas?

5. On Monday, Planchock, a prelaw student at Pilot University, called Snyder Computers, Inc., and ordered a Snyder Spider Computer for $1750. Payment and delivery were to occur at Snyder's store on Friday. On Tuesday, Snyder sent Planchock a confirmation, which she received at her apartment on Wednesday. A day later, Planchock found a comparable computer for less money, and she purchased it. Planchock then called Snyder and said she would not be coming in for the Spider. Snyder has brought suit against Planchock for breach of contract. Will the company prevail? Why?

Would your answer be different if the computer cost $475?

6. On October 1, Baker, a wholesaler, sent Clark, a retailer, a signed offer to sell 200 pinking shears at $9 each. The offer indicated: (1) the terms were FOB Baker's warehouse, (2) the offer must be accepted by October 10, (3) acceptance would be effective upon receipt, and (4) the terms were not to be varied by the offeree. Clark sent a telegram which arrived on October 6, accepting the offer subject to a change in the payment terms. Baker phoned Clark on October 7, rejecting the change of payment terms. Clark then indicated she would accept the October 1 offer in all respects, and expected delivery within 10 days. Baker did not accept Clark's oral acceptance of the original offer. Is there a binding contract? If so, which of Clark's terms apply? Explain.

7. In preparation for the Christmas season, Huckaby Florist Co. ordered 125 poinsettia plants from Wolcott Wholesale, Inc., for $475. Wolcott later discovered that it had accepted too many poinsettia orders. It decided to notify the florists who had ordered that it had a shortage of plants and that they would have to pay more to have their orders filled. Huckaby reluctantly agreed by telephone to pay $525 for the 125 plants. After receiving the poinsettias, Huckaby refused to pay the difference between the two prices. Wolcott claims the additional amount is due, pointing out that no consideration is required for an altered sales contract. Will Wolcott persuade a court to apply that rule in this case? If Wolcott can persuade the court, would Huckaby's defense of the lack of a writing succeed? Explain your answers.

8. For some 20 years Sawyer Supply and Tilden Corporation have had a commercial relationship. Over this period, Tilden's purchasing manager routinely ordered parts from Sawyer on condition that delivery occur within 5 working days. However, Tilden never enforced this provision. A new purchasing manager for Tilden rejects two shipments from Sawyer which arrived beyond 5 working days. Sawyer objects, stating that the deliveries were made in

Jim,

Thought you might like to see my new book.

Next time I see you, be prepared for a pop quiz! I'm working on that article on Judicial Conduct right now — your articles

uld Sawyer
poration for

vith Fisher
all of Fish-
onths. The
of increas-
ce increase
25 percent
or fuel oil.
mance on
nconscion-
its normal
y to agree
? Explain.

10. Kathy Casavant was having a garage sale in preparation for moving to Chicago. Tim Lavin was interested in purchasing a Compaq computer that she was selling, but he wanted to check her asking price with a knowledgeable friend. Kathy wrote the following: "I, Kathy Casavant, agree to sell my Compaq computer to Tim Lavin for $1200 cash. This offer expires at 5:00 P.M. today, February 24." Tim left. Tim returned at 3:30 P.M. to purchase the computer but found that Kathy had already sold it. Tim claims Kathy breached a firm offer. Kathy stated she was free to sell the computer to someone else before 5:00 P.M. Was Kathy correct? Explain.

CHAPTER 32

Risk of Loss and Title

Suppose you agreed to buy a Corvette from a Chevrolet dealer. You paid the purchase price and received the papers necessary to register and insure the car. You have to leave town for a couple of days, so you do not pick up the car from the dealer. You have registered the car, but you decide the insurance can wait. That night, the dealership burns down and your car is destroyed. Since you have the certificate of title to the car, have you lost the money you spent on it? Or, is the dealer responsible for the loss?

If the common law still governed the sale of goods, you would bear the loss because you had title to the car. The common law determined when loss shifted by who held *title*, the right to possess particular property. However, today the Uniform Commercial Code's *risk of loss* rules allocate the potential loss between the parties to a sales contract if its subject matter is lost, destroyed, or damaged before the buyer accepts the goods. And, you are in luck! An automobile dealer bears the risk of loss until it actually delivers a car to a customer.

Since the dealer had the risk of loss, can you now sue it for breach of contract? As we will see in Chapter 33, the answer to that question depends on whether it can supply you with a Corvette which fits the terms of your contract. Here, we are not concerned about breach of contract, except to note that the risk of loss rules place the risk on a breaching party.

In many cases a third party's actions or an "act of God," such as a tornado, will cause the loss. How the loss occurs, though, has no effect on the determination of whether the buyer or the seller bears the risk. Neither fault in the tort sense nor insurance coverage has any bearing on determining risk of loss. Of course, whichever party bears the loss may recover from its insurance company or a third party who caused the loss.

This emphasis on when the risk of loss shifts does not mean that identifying when title passes to the buyer is no longer important. It is critically important in determining creditors' rights, bankruptcy rights, and tax obligations. For that reason, this chapter also explores when title passes.

IDENTIFICATION

For risk of loss to shift or for title to pass, the goods which are the subject of the sales contract must exist and be identified to the sales contract [UCC §2-105(2)]. In other words, before either the risk shifts or title passes, a court must be able to determine which goods—out of all the seller's goods—were the subject matter of the contract. Goods are *identified* when they are set aside or otherwise distinguished as applying to a particular contract. The process is called *identification*.

Identification can occur either before or after formation of a sales contract. But, without identification, there can be no performance of the contract, no shift in the risk of loss, and no passage of title.

Insurable Interest

Identification of the goods means that the buyer has acquired an insurable interest in them. The buyer has an insurable interest even though the identified goods may not conform to the contract and the buyer has the option of rejecting them [UCC §2-501(1)].

Since in many cases the goods remain in the seller's control, why would a buyer—who has not taken title to the goods or paid for them—wish to insure them? The buyer may want to protect his expectations. Assume that a contractor orders ten passive solar heating systems, which it plans to incorporate into homes it is building. The contractor may wish to take out insurance against any liability she may incur to her client if the project is delayed because the units are nonconforming or damaged.

The seller, too, retains an insurable interest until title actually passes to the buyer [UCC

§2-501(2)]. But what the seller insures is quite different from what the buyer insures. The seller buys insurance for the value of the goods, not against the consequences of their loss.

Types of Goods

Existing goods. Normally, identification occurs when the contract is made if the goods already exist [UCC §2-501(1)(a)].

Usually, the seller identifies the goods, although sometimes the buyer identifies them. Until the seller actually or constructively segregates the goods, identification has not occurred. Constructive segregation might consist of designating items with particular serial numbers to the contract. For example, RCA agrees to supply Federated Department Stores with 5000 twenty-one-inch TVs. RCA can identify them to the contract by serial number without actually segregating them.

Future goods. If goods are not both existing and identified, they are termed *future goods*. For example, goods not yet manufactured are future goods. Neither title nor risk of loss can shift until after the goods come into existence and are identified. Identification of what were future goods occurs when the seller ships, marks,* or otherwise designates the goods as the subject of the contract [UCC §2-501(1)(b)]. Special rules apply to future goods like growing crops and conceived but unborn animals, but they go beyond the scope of this chapter [see UCC §2-501(1)(c)].

Substitution of goods. If the seller identified the goods to the contract, he or she may substitute goods for those identified unless and until the seller defaults, becomes insolvent, or notifies

---

* *Big Knob Volunteer Fire Co. v. Lowe & Moyer Garage, Inc.,* briefed later in this chapter, highlights the importance to the buyer of the seller's marking goods and thereby identifying them to the contract.

the buyer that the identification is final. The rationale for this rule is that most manufactured and agricultural products are *fungible,* or interchangeable. It would serve no purpose to restrict the seller's ability to substitute in such cases if the buyer has not identified the goods to the contract.

DELIVERY

In most consumer sales contracts and in many commercial contracts, the buyer takes delivery of the goods directly from the seller. Usually, when the buyer takes delivery, he assumes the risk of loss. However, the use of a *common carrier* or *carrier*—a trucking company, railroad, airline, or the like—to deliver the goods affects the point at which title and risk of loss shift. For that reason, it is important to know what type of delivery contract is involved and what the terms for delivery are.

Types of Delivery Contracts

Carrier contracts are either shipment or destination contracts. The distinction has to do with the point at which the seller's responsibility for delivery ends. The UCC regards shipment contracts as the norm.

Shipment contract. If the seller's duty is simply to make a contract for shipment with a carrier and to deliver conforming goods to that carrier, the contract is a *shipment contract*. Suppose Natalie orders fifty crates of paper from Hammermill under a shipment contract. Hammermill's responsibility ends when the carrier receives the conforming goods for shipment. At that point, the risk of loss shifts to Natalie.

Destination contract. If the seller's duty is to deliver conforming goods to a particular place, the delivery contract is a *destination contract*. Suppose their contract specifies that Hammermill must deliver the goods to Natalie at her place of business. Its responsibility for the goods does not end until the carrier delivers them to Natalie.

Delivery Terms

Over the years, merchants have developed a set of shorthand terms to indicate in part whether the contract is a shipment or a destination contract. Although they are called "delivery terms," they are also price terms, since they indicate that the seller pays the freight to a particular point.

FOB. *FOB* stands for "free on board." It means that the seller at its own expense and risk must get the goods to a certain place. Thus, FOB is *always* followed by a place designation. A contract may describe it either broadly ("FOB Los Angeles") or narrowly ("FOB buyer's plant") [UCC §2-319(1)]. FOB can indicate either a shipment or a destination contract. If a contract says, for example, "FOB seller's warehouse," it is a shipment contract, because the term indicates that the carrier will pick up the shipment there. The risk of loss, therefore, shifts at that point.

FAS and ex-ship. *FAS* ("free alongside") and *ex-ship* ("from the carrying vessel") function like "FOB" but relate only to boats. FAS indicates a shipment contract, while ex-ship indicates a destination contract. Like FOB, these two terms are always followed by a named place. For example, "FAS Portland" obligates the seller at its own expense and risk to deliver the goods alongside a named vessel or to a dock designated and provided by the buyer. At that point, the risk of loss passes to the buyer [UCC §2-319(2)]. By contrast, "ex-ship San Diego" requires the goods to be delivered from a ship which has reached San Diego, and the risk of loss shifts there [UCC §2-322].

CIF, C&F, and CF. The terms *CIF* (the cost of the goods and the insurance and freight to a

named destination) and *C&F* or *CF* (the cost of the goods and freight to the named destination indicate shipment contracts. The difference between the terms "CIF" and "C&F" is that C&F does not obligate the seller to insure the goods for the buyer's benefit [UCC §2-230]. For example, if a contract said "CIF Albuquerque," the seller would be required to pay the freight and insure the shipment to Albuquerque. The price stated in the contract would include those two items as well as the cost of the goods.

RISK OF LOSS PRESUMPTIONS

The parties to a sales contract may specify when the risk of loss passes [UCC §2-509(4)]. If they do so, their agreement controls.

When a contract does not specifically allocate risk of loss and the parties do not submit credible evidence of their intention, Article 2 supplies presumptions for a court to apply in determining when the risk shifted. A court's application of a presumption depends on the type of delivery which is to occur, who is to make the delivery, and how the delivery is to be made.

However, the shipment of nonconforming goods usually breaches a contract. Since the risk of loss generally rests on the breaching party, the shipper retains the risk regardless of the shipping term.

Delivery Term Specified

Shipment contract. In a shipment contract, the risk of loss shifts from the seller to the buyer when conforming goods are "duly delivered" to the carrier [UCC §2-509(1)(a)]. "Duly delivered" refers to the fact that in order to shift the risk of loss to the buyer, the seller must make appropriate shipping arrangements. Suppose perishable goods are involved, and a refrigerated truck is necessary. The seller cannot shift the risk of loss by shipping by dump truck.

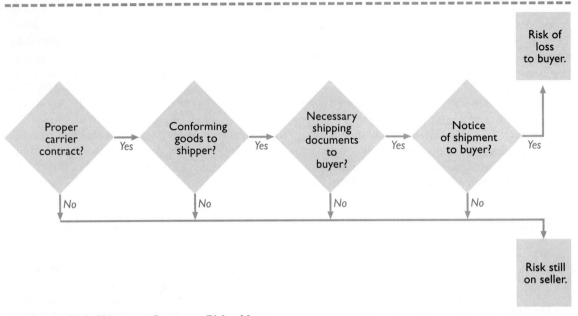

Figure 32.1 Shipment Contract: Risk of Loss.

The seller also must secure from the carrier and arrange for delivery to the buyer all the documents the buyer will need to obtain the goods from the carrier. (These documents are discussed in Chapter 38.) Finally, the seller must notify the buyer promptly of the shipment so that the buyer may know when to expect the goods [UCC §§2-503 and 2-504]. See Figure 32-1 for an outline of these requirements.

Destination contract. With a destination contract, the risk of loss does not shift to the buyer until the carrier offers or *tenders* the goods at the place designated for delivery [UCC §2-509(1)(b)].

The carrier must make the delivery at a reasonable hour. For instance, a carrier's delivery to a farmer at 2:00 A.M., would be unreasonable. By contrast, a truck farmer's 2:00 A.M. delivery to a fresh produce merchant may not be unreasonable. Also, the carrier must keep the goods available for a period reasonably necessary for the buyer to take possession. And finally, the buyer must furnish facilities rea-

sonably suited to receive the goods [UCC §2-503(1)]. Unless the contract specifies otherwise, the carrier only has to tender delivery of the goods at a loading dock. *Tender*, which can be used as either a noun or a verb, means being ready, willing, and able to perform and actually offering to perform. Figure 32-2 diagrams the shift of the risk of loss on a destination contract.

Under a destination contract, the buyer has a right to inspect the goods before accepting receipt unless the goods are sent *COD* ("cash on delivery"). If, after inspecting them, the buyer rightfully rejects the goods as nonconforming, the risk of loss remains on the seller [UCC §2-510(1)]. Inspection, acceptance, and rejection are discussed in Chapter 33.

No Delivery Term Specified

Most contracts contain at least some indication as to whether they are destination or shipment contracts. Still, courts, like the one in the next case, sometimes face a contract which has no delivery term.

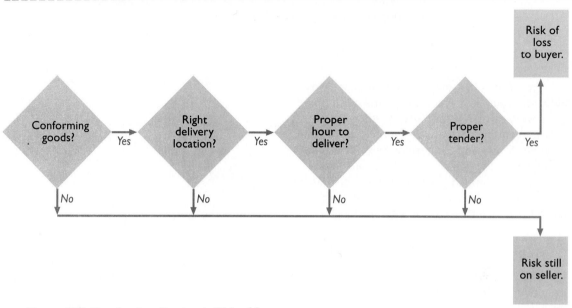

Figure 32.2 Destination Contract: Risk of Loss.

Eberhard Manufacturing Co. v. Brown

61 Mich. App. 268, 232 N.W.2d 378 (1975)

FACTS   Eberhard turned over conforming goods to a common carrier with instructions to deliver them to Brown. Their agreement did not specify who bore the risk of loss. Brown did not pay for the goods, and Eberhard brought suit to recover their price. However, a portion of the goods were lost in transit. The trial court held that theirs was a destination contract and that the risk of loss was Eberhard's as to the lost portion of the shipment.

ISSUE   Was the contract a destination contract?

DECISION   No. Reversed. The UCC regards a shipment contract as the norm and a destination contract as the variant. The seller is not obligated to deliver at a named destination and bear the risk of loss until arrival unless it agrees to do so or unless the commercial understanding of the parties' terms indicates otherwise. Brown argued that since the goods were to be shipped to his place of business, the contract required Eberhard to deliver the goods "at a particular destination." A "ship to" term, he argued, made their agreement a destination contract. But, a buyer must supply a "ship to" address whenever goods must be shipped. A "ship to" term by itself has no significance in determining whether a contract is a shipment or a destination contract for risk of loss purposes.

The case at first may seem confusing. However, the court is correct that terms of shipping for purposes of risk of loss are different from terms regarding the place goods are to be shipped. The "ship to" term here referred only to the latter, the place where the goods actually were to be shipped. A buyer who misunderstands, like Eberhard did, may unexpectedly learn they carry the risk of loss burden.

Delivery Without Carrier Shipment

If the buyer takes goods directly from the seller, the point at which the risk of loss shifts depends on whether the seller is a *merchant* as to those goods. (For a discussion of who is a *merchant*, see Chapter 31.) The buyer's merchant or non-merchant status is irrelevant [UCC §2-104].

A merchant-seller retains the risk of loss until she both tenders conforming goods and completes delivery. The merchant-seller's duty to complete delivery means that the buyer must actually receive the goods. Suppose Charlie buys a Miata from Mimi's Mazdas. He is to take delivery at 2:00 at Mimi's showroom. But, he does not arrive until 3:00. At 2:30, lightning strikes the showroom, destroying his Miata. Since delivery has not occurred, Mimi bears the risk of loss regardless of whether Charlie has paid for the goods or has taken title [UCC §2-509 (3)].

When the seller is not a merchant of goods, the risk transfers when the seller tenders. Now suppose Mimi is Charlie's next-door neighbor. He agrees to buy her Miata and promises to pick it up at 2:00. The risk of loss shifts to Charlie at 2:00 assuming Mimi is ready, willing, and able to deliver the car then [UCC §2-509(3)]. See Figure 32-3. The rationale for this distinction between sellers is that the merchant-seller can better cover the potential loss.

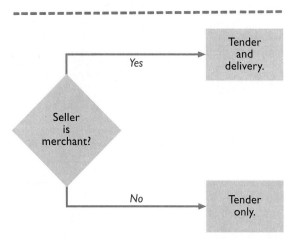

Figure 32.3 Delivery by Seller: Requirements to Shift Risk of Loss.

Delivery When Goods are Held by Another

Sometimes goods are sold without being moved. Usually, the seller has stored the goods with a third party. The seller transfers the goods by means of a *document of title*, a writing indicating ownership of goods. (Documents of title are discussed in detail in Chapter 39). Suppose X & K Importers wholesales Dutch chocolate. When it receives a shipment, X & K delivers the shipment to Abe's warehouse. Abe gives X & K a receipt in the form of a document of title for the shipment. When X & K sells the shipment, it transfers the receipt to the buyer. The buyer then can take possession of the goods, and the buyer now bears the risk of loss. When no document of title is involved, the risk passes when the holder of the goods acknowledges the buyer's right to possession [UCC §2-509(2). The law does not call for any specific form of acknowledgement.

Special Marketing Arrangements

The UCC's normal allocation of risk of loss does not apply to sales on approval and sales or returns. In a *sale on approval*, the seller guarantees the buyer the right to return conforming goods delivered primarily for the buyer's use, not for resale. A *sale or return* arrangement permits the buyer to return goods delivered primarily for resale [UCC §2-326(1)].

In a sale on approval, the seller retains the risk of loss during the approval period and bears the expense of the return. The goods remain the seller's property until the buyer accepts them. For example, a buyer make take a stereo receiver on approval for a couple of days to test its reception. By contrast, in a sale or return, the buyer simply has the option to return the goods in the event he fails to resell them. In addition, in a sale or return arrangement, the seller bears a risk of loss if the buyer's creditors seize the goods he has sold. The next case discusses this problem.

Minor v. Stevenson

227 Cal. App.3d 1613, 278 Cal.Rptr. 558 (1991)

FACTS Peter Pan Motors sold Stevenson, owner of T & S Enterprises, and a licensed car dealer, a BMW 735 iL. Later, the plaintiff, Wayne Minor, obtained a money judgment against Stevenson, and the BMW was seized under a writ of execution by the state marshall. Peter Pan Motors, which had not been paid in full, intervened, arguing that the title had not passed, since the sale was conditioned on Stevenson's payment. Minor asserted that it was a "sale or return" transaction and thus subject to his claims as a creditor. Peter Pan Motors won at trial.

ISSUE Was the sale of the BMW a "sale or return" transaction subject to the claims of Stevenson's creditors?

DECISION Yes. Reversed. Under California's version of the UCC, a "sale or return" sale occurs when three elements are present: goods are delivered to a person for sale; the person maintains a place of business for dealing in the goods; and the person operates the business under a name different from that of the person making the delivery. Also, under state law, if the sale is one of sale or return, the goods are subject to claims by the buyer's creditors. First, Stevenson bought the car for resale and, in fact, had purchased cars from Peter Pan Motors before. Second, Stevenson did maintain a business, and the BMW sported his dealership plates. Third, Stevenson sells cars, including the BMW, under the name of T & S Enterprises, not Peter Pan Motors.

PASSING OF TITLE

Title is the right to possess particular property. In determining liability for a loss, the passing of title has more importance under the common law than it does under Article 2. At common law, the allocation of loss depended on title unless the parties had agreed otherwise. Under the UCC, title is not a factor in allocating losses between the parties.

Nonetheless, the point at which title passes under a sales contract is important for potential third party purchasers of the goods, creditors, or a trustee in bankruptcy. Here, we will focus on third party purchasers. In other chapters, we will look at aspects of title as they affect secured transactions and bankruptcy.

The General Rule

The UCC permits the parties to choose when and where title to identified goods will pass [UCC §2-401(2)]. While the parties have that power, often they will not exercise it. If the parties fail to stipulate when and where title will pass, the UCC presumes that title follows possession of the goods. In fact, that is the most common situation relating to consumer goods (see Figure 32-4). For example, when you purchase lumber from a lumberyard, you receive the right to possess the goods. The lumberyard does not have to give you a title certificate, like the one for a car.

As a preventive measure, a seller usually arranges for passage of title to occur after she has been paid. That is why automobile dealers often require certified checks in payment. Still, possession and title hardly indicate that the goods have been paid for. Suppose Alan buys a watch using his Sears charge card. He has good title to the watch when he leaves the store, even though he still owes Sears for it.

Special Title Situations

Article 2 deals specifically with the passage of title and the rights of third party purchasers in certain situations.

Voidable title. Under the common law, a contract with a minor or an incompetent of certain types is voidable by the minor or the incompetent.* If a minor or an incompetent sold property, therefore, the buyer received a voidable title, since the seller could void the transaction and reclaim the goods.

The recipient of a voidable title could transfer only a voidable title to a third party purchaser. And, the person having the ability to void the title could recover the property from a third party even if the third party was a bona fide purchaser. A *bona fide* (or "good faith") *purchaser* is one who buys an item for value and without knowledge of the voidable title. Suppose under the common law a minor sold her bike to Emma's Bike Shop for $100. Emma later resold the bike for $125 to Peter, who

---

* Voidable contracts were discussed in Chapter 9.

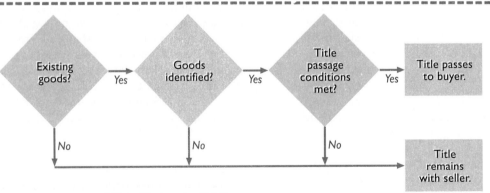

Figure 32.4 Passage of Title Under the UCC.

knew nothing of its history. The minor could void the sale to Emma and force Peter to return the bicycle, since Peter received only a voidable title from Emma.

Article 2 does not change the common law rule as it affects the parties to the immediate transaction. It still permits a person passing voidable title to void the sale. However, under Article 2, the original seller loses her right to force a third party bona fide purchaser to return property [UCC §2-403(1)]. Thus, as a bona fide purchaser, Peter could keep the bicycle. Figure 32-5 schematically compares the common law and UCC rules on voidable titles.

Stolen goods. Under Article 2, a purchaser acquires only the title that his vendor had or that his vendor had the power to transfer. For that reason, a thief cannot transfer good title to a third party, regardless of whether or not the third party is a bona fide purchaser [see UCC §2-403(1)]. If Alvin steals Becky's guitar and sells it to Donna, Donna does not take good title even though she bought it in good faith. The owner has the right to have the guitar returned.

The wronged purchaser has a cause of action against the thief or any party who took possession from the thief. Thus, Donna would have a right to get her money back if she could find the thief and was able to obtain a judgment against him. However, suppose Alvin, the thief, had sold the guitar to Ray, who then sold it to Donna. Donna could recover against either Alvin or Ray.

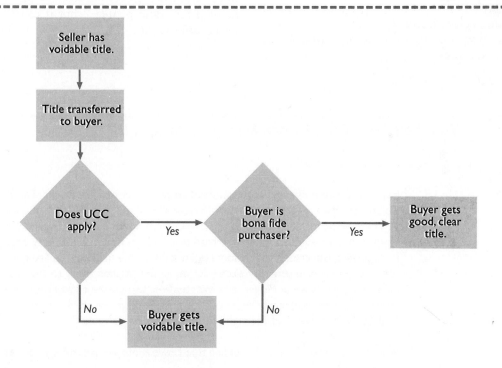

Figure 32.5 Transferring a Voidable Title.
At common law, no buyer receiving a voidable title could ever be considered to have a good title. This figure illustrates how the UCC changes that rule.

Entrustment. Entrustments are another UCC exception to the common law rule that the transferee can get only as good title as the transferor has. An *entrustment* involves giving possession—not title—of goods to a merchant who deals in goods of that kind. It gives a merchant the apparent power to transfer all rights to the goods in the ordinary course of business because the goods are of the same type as those the merchant regularly sells.

"Entrusting" in this context simply means delivery or permitting goods to remain in another's possession. The relationship between the entruster and the merchant is of no importance with respect to the passage of title. Thus, entrustments include:

- A buyer leaving goods with a merchant until she has time to pick them up
- A lawnmower owner leaving his machine with a dealer for repair
- An owner turning over antiques to a dealer for later sale

Even if the merchant obtained the good fraudulently, he has the power to transfer the entruster's rights [UCC §2-403(2) and (3)]. Suppose Edna contracts with Mickey's Watches, Inc., to have her watch cleaned. Mickey's both sells and repairs watches. Mickey sells the watch to Walt, who liked the watch when he saw it in Mickey's window. Walt would receive good title.

The UCC's drafters made a policy choice as to who bears the risk of loss in entrustments. The UCC favors the purchaser in the ordinary course of business. The entruster has a better reason to evaluate the honesty of the merchant than the purchaser does. The entruster's only recourse is against the merchant. She would have a cause of action based upon the merchant's breach of duty in selling the entrusted item. This rule seems particularly harsh when applied to "little people," but it can apply to corporations, too.

Big Knob Volunteer Fire Co. v. Lowe & Moyer Garage, Inc.

338 Pa. Super. 257, 487 A.2d 953 (1985)

FACTS Hamerly Custom Productions assembled components into fire trucks. The Big Knob Volunteer Fire Co. ordered a truck from Hamerly and paid $48,000 of the $51,000 purchase price. Hamerly ordered the chassis from Lowe & Moyer Garage, Inc., giving Lowe & Moyer a note for the purchase price. Upon delivery, Hamerly began work transforming the chassis and at some point painted the name of the fire company on the cab. However, Hamerly neither delivered the finished truck to the fire department nor paid Lowe & Moyer, and eventually it turned the chassis over to Lowe & Moyer. The fire company brought suit for possession of the truck, but the trial court held Lowe & Moyer had the right to the chassis or its value.

ISSUE Was the trial court correct in holding that Lowe & Moyer had the right to the chassis or its value?

DECISION No. Reversed. Under UCC §2-403(b), a merchant entrusted with possession of goods has "power to transfer all rights of the entruster to a buyer in the ordinary course of business." Here, Hamerly was the merchant and Lowe & Moyer the entruster. However, the UCC does not specify the moment at which a party becomes a buyer. Some courts have held that a party does not become a buyer until a sale occurs and that a sale does not occur until title passes. However, the better rule—and the one more in accord with the UCC's policy of protecting innocent purchasers—is that a party becomes a buyer in the ordinary course of business when the goods are identified to the contract. That occurred here when Hamerly painted the name of the fire company on the cab.

This case is one that pits two good faith parties against each other. Both had valid claims against Hamerly: the fire department for their considerable down payment, and Lowe & Moyer for the truck itself. Both could have protected their interests with insurance, although the fire department did not have an insurable interest until the good was identified. The stakes can be quite high when parties litigate whether identification has occurred. Had Hamerly not identified the chassis to the contract, the volunteer fire company would have lost its $48,000.

Consignments. *Consignments* involve placing goods with a merchant who has agreed to act as the seller's agent in selling them. Thus, a consignment's purpose is sale of the consigned goods. In this relationship, the seller is called the *consignor*, the merchant is called the *consignee*, and the goods are called a consignment.

Consignments differ from entrustments in that consignment carries with it the right to sell on the owner's behalf. The consignee has the power to transfer all the rights of the consignor. But, since the consigned goods belong to the consignor until sale, he bears the risk of loss until title passes.

If the consignor's goods are not conspicuously marked as his, a consignee's creditors may be able to attach them. Suppose Kristi's is an antique store. Kristi normally deals in antiques that she owns. However, Tipton asks her to handle his mother's estate on consignment. Kristi keeps Tipton's goods in a separate part of the store, but does not otherwise distinguish them as consigned goods. When Kristi's creditors attach her assets to satisfy their claims, they probably can claim Tipton's goods as well. His only recourse would to be to sue Kristi. Had Kristi posted a notice near the segregated goods stating they were on consignment, her creditors could not have attached the goods. Also, if a significant part of her business involved consignments, her creditors might not be able to attach Tipton's goods [UCC §2-326(3)].

Article 6: Bulk Transfers of Inventory

Bulk transfers of inventory are another area in which title is important. They are closely related to sales of goods under Article 2, but the subject is treated in Article 6 of the UCC.

Bulk transfers are the sale of all or a major part of a merchant's inventory not in the ordinary course of business [UCC §6-102(1)]. For instance, a retail shoe store always tries to sell as many shoes as it possibly can to individual retail customers. Therefore, the store's sale of all its casual shoes to a discounter would not be in the ordinary course of business, and so would be a bulk sale.

Enterprises subject to Article 6 are those whose principal business is the sale of merchandise from inventory, including those that manufacture what they sell. Article 6 does not apply to service businesses, like barbershops, restaurants, accounting firms, and hotels. Thus, Article 6 would not apply to a Burger King restaurant, but it would apply to a True Value hardware store [UCC §6-102(3)].

Notice requirements. Article 6's primary concern is the rights of creditors who have financed a merchant's inventory. If a merchant sells his inventory without his creditors' knowledge, the security for their loans could be seriously jeopardized. Article 6 provides notice rules with which the buyer must comply if it is to gain good title against inventory creditors. Notice permits the seller's or *transferor's* creditors to act to protect their interests.

Except in the case of an auction, a bulk transfer does not give the buyer, the *transferee*, title free of the creditors' interests in the goods unless the transferee notifies them of the transfer at least 10 days before taking possession of, or paying for, the goods [UCC §6-105]. In short, the buyer must notify the seller's creditors or risk assuming the transferor's liabilities to them. For this reason, the transferor must give the prospective transferee a signed, sworn list of all creditors with their addresses [UCC §6-104(2)]. Responsibility for the list's completeness and accuracy rests on the transferor unless the transferee knows of omissions [UCC §6-104(3)].

The notice to creditors must include who the transferee is and how the seller will allocate the proceeds from the sale. In other words, the transferee must notify the creditors whether the sale will cause the transferor's debts to them to be paid in full [UCC §6-107].

Affected transfers. Because it is the key to the application of Article 5, many court cases have turned on what a "major part" of a merchant's inventory is. In making this determination, a court compares the quantity and the value of inventory items sold to a single buyer with the total inventory. Some courts have held that a sale of as little as 5 percent of the total value of the inventory is a bulk sale *if* it is not sold in the ordinary course of business. By contrast, a transfer of a substantial part of an enterprise's production machinery is not a bulk transfer unless it is made in connection with a bulk transfer of inventory [UCC §6-102(2)].

Article 6 also applies to auction sales, but slightly differently from the way it applies to other bulk transfers. A purchaser at an auction gets good title regardless of whether the auctioneer complied with Article 6. However, in addition to the transferor, an auctioneer who knowingly sells inventory in violation of Article 6 may be personally liable to the merchant's creditors [UCC §6-108(4)].

Effect of noncompliance. The transferee's failure to give proper notice to the seller's creditors or to wait the required 10 days voids the sale, even if the buyer was a bona fide purchaser. Still, the buyer will be protected if she gave notice to all creditors on the seller's list and did not know of any omitted creditors.

A third party bona fide purchaser takes title free of any creditor claims. The rationale here is the same as in entrustments and consignments. Assume that Gordon purchases all a marina's sailboats in violation of Article 6's notice requirements. Sarah subsequently buys a sailboat from him. Sarah's title will be good against the creditors. However, a third party purchaser who knew of Gordon's noncompliance will be subject to creditor claims. If Sarah knew that Gordon's purchase was improper, she would own her sailboat subject to the rights of the marina's creditors. See Figure 32-6, which charts the workings of Article 6.

CONCLUSION

This chapter has focused on two concepts: risk of loss and passage of title. The UCC's risk of loss rules allocate potential losses between contracting parties, while the main concern of the law on the passage of title is transfers of ownership to third parties.

Who bears the risk of loss becomes important to the parties only when the goods are lost, damaged, or destroyed. If the casualty to the goods occurred following a breach, the risk of loss is assigned to the breaching party.

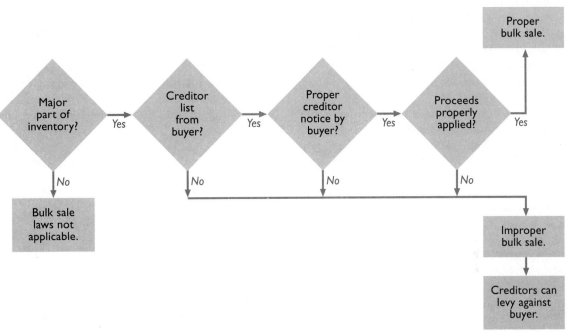

Figure 32.6 Article 6, Bulk Sale Requirements.
A transferee who fails to comply with Article 6 may find the transferor's creditors can look to him for payment.

If there is no breach, the contract between the parties may allocate a loss caused, for example, by an act of God or a third party's negligence. If the contract is silent on this point, a court will assign the risk according to the UCC rules.

Because the passage of title no longer governs the risk of loss on contracts for the sale of goods, it has less importance under the UCC than it did at common law. Nonetheless, passage of title remains a critical concept with regard to subsequent transactions with third parties.

Both risk of loss and passage of title relate to events following formation of a sales contract. Risk of loss deals primarily with casualties which occur while a party is in the process of performing its duties under the contract. Passage of title to goods is a sign that one

party has completed its performance. So, in a sense, the topics of this chapter bracket those in the next: the rights and duties of the parties relating to performance.

A NOTE TO FUTURE CPA CANDIDATES

The Article 2 sections covered here and the next three chapters are tested in the UCC portion of the CPA exam.

Identification is the process whereby goods are set aside or otherwise distinguished as applying to a particular contract. When this occurs the buyer gains an insurable interest, meaning that the buyer can obtain insurance in case of nonperformance or destruction of the goods.

Risk of loss is the most important concept to master in this chapter. Remember that the application of risk of loss rules occurs independently from issues involving title, insurance, payment by the buyer, or actions by third parties. In most factual problems on the CPA exam, the risk of loss has fallen on the party in breach of contract.

Where the parties have not specifically allocated the risk of loss, different presumptions apply depending on whether a carrier is involved. In situations not involving a carrier, a further distinction must be made as to whether the seller is a merchant. If so, risk of loss will not pass until the seller both tenders and delivers the goods. Where the seller is a nonmerchant, the seller need only tender the goods. In a shipment contract situation, "FOB: Seller's place of business," risk of loss will pass after the seller makes a proper shipment contract, delivers conforming goods to the shipper, and notifies the buyer of shipment (see Figure 32-1). In essence, the buyer has the responsibility for risk of loss once the goods leave the seller's place of business. In a destination contract, "FOB: Buyer's place of business," the seller has the responsibility for risk of loss until the shipper actually tenders the goods to the buyer at the buyer's place of business (see Figure 32-2).

Title questions generally have appeared in one of three settings: voidable title, stolen property, or entrustments. In a voidable title situation, the seller can void the contract and recover the goods(s) from the buyer. However, the seller cannot recover the goods(s) from a good faith purchaser for value who has purchased the goods from the original buyer. Stolen property is easy to remember: no one can get better title than the rightful owner. In entrustment situations (leaving the watch with the jeweler for repair), the rightful owner loses the right to recover entrusted property from a good faith purchaser.

Two other situations need to be remembered. In sale on approval situations (for buyer's usage), the risk of loss and title remain with the seller. In sale or return situations (buyer considered a purchaser), the risk of loss and title pass to the buyer when the buyer receives the goods.

Article 6 (bulk sales) questions occasionally are asked on the exam. A bulk sale is a sale not in the ordinary course of business. The transfer*ee* is required to give notice 10 days before taking possession. The failure to give proper notice or wait the required 10 days voids the sale. Bulk sale requirements are illustrated in Figure 32-6.

KEY WORDS

bona fide purchaser (736)	entrustment (738)
bulk transfer (739)	ex-ship (731)
CIF (731)	FAS (731)
consignee (739)	FOB (731)
consignment (739)	future goods (730)
consignor (739)	identification (729)
delivery term (731)	risk of loss (729)
destination contract (730)	sale on approval (735)
documents of title (734)	sale or return (735)
	shipment contract (730)
	title (729)

DISCUSSION QUESTIONS

1. When there is no breach and the seller is a merchant, when does the risk of loss pass to the buyer?
2. When there is no breach and the seller is not a merchant, when does the risk of loss pass to the buyer?
3. What is the difference between a shipment contract and a destination contract?
4. If the seller is in New York and the buyer is in Boston, what does "$5000 FOB NYC" mean?
5. What does the term "CIF" mean?
6. Which terms are delivery terms used in connection with ships? What do they mean?
7. If goods are stored in a warehouse and the

buyer intends to pick them up there, when does the risk of loss pass to the buyer?

8. What is a document of title? Who might issue one? What effect do documents of title have on the risk of loss?

9. Under the common law, risk of loss passed with title to the goods. Is risk of loss treated the same as title to the goods under the Code?

10. Leaving aside the risk of loss concept, how do the common law and the Article 2 rules on the passage of title differ?

11. What are the rights of a purchaser of consigned goods?

12. What is the principal goal of the bulk transfer laws under Article 6 of the code? How does the UCC implement that goal?

CASE PROBLEMS

1. Wexford Furniture, Inc., is in the retail furniture business and has stores located in principal cities of the United States. Its designers created a unique cocktail table. After obtaining prices and schedules, Wexford ordered 2000 tables to be made to its specifications. The tables were to be sold as part of its annual spring sales promotion. Wexford wants to know what is the earliest time at which it will have an insurable interest in the tables. Explain.

2. On June 30, Cutler entered into a contract to purchase merchandise from Perdue. The contract required that Perdue ship the goods by common carrier the following day, which it did. The shipping terms of the contract included "CIF." The shipment arrived at Cutler's business on July 2. Cutler's tax year for accounting purposes ends June 30. On that date, who bore the risk of loss for the transaction? Who held the title? Who is liable for the expenses relating to the transportation of the goods? Explain.

3. By telegram, Loesher ordered from DeFrane Corp. 10,000 yards of fabric, first-quality, 50 percent wool and 50 percent cotton. The shipping terms were FOB DeFrane's factory in Cincinnati. The goods were to be shipped to Loesher's factory in Akron. DeFrane accepted the order and packed the fabric for shipment. In the process, DeFrane discovered that half the fabric had been commingled with fabric that was 30 percent wool and 70 percent cotton. Since DeFrane did not have any more 50 percent wool fabric in stock, it decided to send the shipment to Loesher as an accommodation. The goods were shipped, and later that same day DeFrane wired Loesher, apologizing and informing Loesher of the facts. The shipment was destroyed on its way to Akron while in the hands of the carrier. Did Loesher bear the risk of loss in these circumstances? Explain.

4. Mary Ann Schmelzele of Cairo, Illinois, ordered five dining room chairs from Carolina Discount Furniture. The agreement called for the chairs to be shipped FOB: Raleigh, North Carolina. Carolina Discount arranged for Collier Transit to ship the chairs. When the Collier driver arrived to pick up the chairs, it was evident that he had been drinking heavily. The driver told the Carolina shipping clerk not to worry. He was only going 5 miles to a truck stop to sleep for the night. The shipping clerk reluctantly gave the driver the chairs and mailed the shipping documents to Mary Ann. However, the driver changed his mind and began the drive to Illinois. Before he reached North Carolina, he had an accident which destroyed the chairs. Mary Ann has received a bill from Carolina Discount for the destroyed chairs. Is she liable under the risk of loss rules of Article 2? Explain.

5. Bell Co. owned twenty engines which it deposited in a public warehouse on May 5. In return, it received a negotiable warehouse receipt in its name. Bell sold the engines to Spark Corp. On which of the following dates did the risk of loss shift to Spark?

June 11: Spark signed a contract to buy the engines from Bell for $19,000. Delivery was to be at the warehouse.
June 12: Spark paid for the engines.

June 13: Bell negotiated the warehouse receipt to Spark.

June 14: Spark received delivery of the engines at the warehouse.

Explain your answer.

6. Janet Doll, a student, bought a computer from Dick Gaar, who regularly sells computers to the public. After receiving payment in full, Gaar tendered delivery of the computer to Doll. Rather than take immediate delivery, Doll stated that she would return later that day to pick up the computer. Before Doll returned, a thief entered the store and stole the computer. Since Gaar had received payment and tendered delivery, did he bear the risk of loss? Suppose that later Joey Daniel purchased the computer from the thief for value, in good faith and without any reason to suspect the computer was stolen. Would Joey have good title to the computer? Explain your answers.

7. Barbara Haynes purchased a new 75-horsepower motor for her boat. The dealer assured Barbara that the motor would be strong enough to pull her two teenage sons when they went water skiing. However, to better assure her the dealer wrote "sale on approval for ten days" on the sales receipt. The following day Barbara put the motor on her boat and was traveling up a channel of the lake when her boat was hit by another boat negligently driven by James Pridgen. The collision severely damaged Barbara's new motor. The dealer refused to take back the motor and told Barbara she should recover her loss from Pridgen. Who had the risk of loss at the time of the accident? Would the result be different if the sale had been a sale or return transaction? Explain.

8. Carter Mitchell, 16 (a minor), advertised his 10-speed bicycle for sale in the classified ads. Howard Katz purchased the bike and immediately made needed repairs, including replacing the gearing and installing new tires. Katz then sold the bike to Frank Rogers for $100. Rogers did not know, and did not have reason to know, that Katz had purchased the bike from a minor. Shortly after buying the bike, Carter recognized it and told Rogers he wanted his bike back. Under the UCC, would Carter have a right to the return of his bike? Would the answer be different if Katz had stolen the bike? Explain.

9. Hauser Corp. transferred substantially all its inventory to Bailey. Bailey required Hauser to furnish a list of its existing creditors but did not notify them of the transfer within 30 days. However, within 30 days, Bailey in turn transferred the assets to Garrity. Garrity did not know of Bailey's failure to notify Hauser's creditors. If the transfer from Hauser to Garrity was outside the ordinary course of business, would Hauser's creditors have a claim against the property Garrity purchased? Explain.

10. Johnstone purchased all of Lomax Corporation's inventory, machinery, and fixtures. Johnstone failed to comply with the UCC's bulk transfers article. Dark, with notice of Johnstone's failure to comply, subsequently purchased some of the used machinery from Johnstone. What is the status of the machinery in Dark's hands? Explain.

Performance

Suppose Murphy contracts to buy ten sand-colored leather chairs from Office Supply Company, to be delivered by March 15. On March 5, Office Supply delivers ten black vinyl chairs, which Murphy rejects. Office Supply indicates that it will deliver the right chairs by March 15. On that day, Office Supply delivers ten crates, each marked "sand-colored leather upholstered chair." Before accepting them, Murphy opens the crates and inspects the chairs. One chair has ripped upholstery. Office Supply promises to repair the chair, so Murphy accepts all the chairs. A month passes, and Office Supply has done nothing. Murphy tells Office Supply to send someone for the damaged chair because he is revoking his acceptance of it.

This example illustrates major performance rights under the Uniform Commercial Code's (UCC) Article 2: the buyer's right to reject nonconforming goods, the seller's right to cure a defective delivery, the buyer's right to inspect goods, and the buyer's right to revoke acceptance of goods.

This array of devices is designed to assure performance. Yet, the fundamental obligations of the seller and the buyer can be stated in two sentences. A seller's duty under a sales contract is to tender conforming goods to the buyer. A buyer's duty is to take delivery, accept, and pay for conforming goods in accordance with the sales contract.

This chapter focuses solely on performance. As you read, keep in mind that in the common law of contracts, "acceptance" and "revocation" are used only in the context of contract formation. But, the UCC uses these terms in two contexts: contract formation and contract performance. This chapter assumes that the parties have an enforceable agreement. In the next two chapters, we will examine the parties' rights in the event of a breach of warranty or of the sales contract itself.

THE SELLER'S DUTIES AND RIGHTS

Generally, the seller satisfies its performance obligations by tendering delivery of conforming goods at the time and place stated in the contract. In some instances, however, a seller who delivers nonconforming goods has a right to substitute conforming goods and thereby satisfy its duty to perform.

Duty to Tender Conforming Goods

Tender and delivery. The seller must tender conforming goods to the buyer [UCC §2-503(1)]. *Tender* is the act of making the goods available to the buyer. Tender in this context may best be thought of as an offer to delivery. *Delivery*, then, is the actual change in the possession of the goods.

A proper tender requires the seller to notify the buyer in advance of the delivery, to offer the goods at a reasonable time and place, and to keep them available for the period necessary for the buyer to take possession. Usually, the contract specifies the time, place, and manner of the seller's tender. As discussed in Chapter 31, if the contract lacks one of these terms, the UCC fills the gaps.

Conforming goods. *Conforming goods* are those which fulfill the seller's obligations under the contract [UCC §2-106(2)]. Goods which do not are *nonconforming*. Suppose Silver Circle Stores orders 1000 cases of yellow tennis balls. White balls or basketballs are not conforming goods.

The *course of dealing* between the parties or *usages of trade* may affect the seller's obligations. From their past dealings, for instance, Silver Circle's purchase order, which said "1000 cases colored tennis balls," might call for yellow balls. A usage of trade might provide the same interpretation.

The perfect tender rule. In a sale involving a single delivery of goods, the buyer has a right to reject the entire shipment if any goods fail to conform [UCC §2-601]. This rule is usually stated in absolute terms and, in fact, was called at common law the *perfect tender rule*.

However, under the UCC, "perfect tender" is the wrong name for this rule—although it is still used—because a buyer must accept goods if the defects are trivial or easily correctable. To justify rejection or a revocation of acceptance, the defect must substantially impair the product's value to the buyer. So held the court in the next case.

Rozmus v. Thompson's Lincoln-Mercury Co.

209 Pa. Super. 120, 224 A.2d 782 (1966)

FACTS On Saturday, June 22, Rozmus agreed to buy a car from Thompson. He made a down payment, gave Thompson his old Chevrolet, promised to pay the balance in 5 days, and took delivery of the new car. While driving home, he noticed that smoke was coming from the exhaust and that the car made a loud banging sound. He returned the car on Monday for repair. Tuesday he retrieved the car, but the noise continued. That night he brought the car back. The dealer's vice president drove the car, confirmed the problem, and had work begun on it immediately. The problem required 15 minutes to fix. But before it could be done, Rozmus demanded another car or his old Chevrolet. When his demands were not met, he left the dealership without the new car. Forty-five days later, the car was sold to satisfy Rozmus's debt. Rozmus brought suit to recover the value of the car he traded in. The trial court found for Rozmus.

ISSUE Was Rozmus justified in revoking his acceptance of the car?

DECISION No. Reversed. The defect did not amount to a substantial impairment of the car's value. A buyer does not have the right to revoke his acceptance regardless of the nature of the defect or its effect on the goods' value.

The rationale for the UCC's approach rests on the requirement that both parties to a transaction must act in good faith and in a commercially reasonable manner. Easily remediable defects do not excuse the buyer's performance.

Perhaps a better name for the UCC approach would be the "reasonable tender" rule. For example, a furniture store would not be justified in rejecting a wood table with a slight scratch which its personnel could easily rub out.

The Right to Cure

In general, the seller has a single opportunity to tender conforming goods and satisfy its obligation under a sales contract. If the tender is not proper, the buyer may reject the goods or accept them and sue for breach of contract. However, the UCC grants a seller who is acting in good faith the right to *cure*, or the right to remedy a nonconforming tender without liability for breaching the contract in two instances: before time for performance *and* in the case of a surprise rejection. A cure consists of either substituting conforming goods or repairing defective goods.

Before time for performance. If the buyer rejects nonconforming goods before the time for the seller's performance, the seller may cure by making a conforming delivery within the time for performance. Before making the conforming delivery, the seller must notify the buyer of its intention to cure. Suppose Slideways, Inc., contracts to deliver fifty automatic slide projectors to Bob's Discount Store by June 30. On June 1, due to a shipping error, Bob's receives fifty manual projectors, which are rejected. On June 5, Slideways notifies Bob's that it will cure. To do so, Slideways must deliver fifty conforming projectors by June 30 [UCC §2-508(1)].

Giving the seller the right to cure before the time for performance cannot work to the buyer's detriment, since the buyer should receive what she contracted for at the time specified. Even if the seller intentionally, but in good faith, shipped nonconforming goods, he may cure. The UCC presumes that if the time for performance has not passed, the buyer has not been injured by an early tender of nonconforming goods.

The surprise rejection situation. The surprise rejection rule protects a seller who makes a nonconforming tender believing that the buyer will accept it, perhaps with a reduction in price. The rule permits the seller to cure even though the time for performance has passed. Of course, the seller must have acted in good faith. The seller, for instance, may not have tried to trick the buyer or to force her to take the nonconforming goods.

If the seller's belief that the buyer would accept the nonconforming tender is reasonable. the UCC's drafters thought it reasonable to allow the seller to cure. They saw granting the seller a right to cure in the surprise rejection situation as a way of encouraging a seller to attempt to meet a buyer's needs with a reasonable alternative when the conforming goods were not available.

The seller's belief that the buyer will accept the nonconforming tender may arise from prior transactions with the buyer, a usage of trade, or the particular circumstances of the transaction. For example, a conference center regularly orders light blue place mats from a restaurant supply house. The restaurant supply house has substituted medium blue mats on prior occasions when light blue was not available. If the conference center rejects a shipment of medium blue mats, the seller has a reasonable time in which to supply light blue ones.

After the rejection—even though the time for performance has passed—the seller may promptly notify the buyer of its intent to cure and do so within a reasonable time [UCC §2-508(c)]. The meanings of "promptly" and "reasonable time" depend on the circumstances of the transaction. If delivery of an order of Christmas ornaments is due on September 1, the time allowed for cure will be significantly longer than if they are to be delivered November 25.

The shaken faith doctrine. The shaken faith doctrine qualifies the seller's right to cure. A buyer who in good faith doubts the seller's ability to cure a defective tender may treat the contract as breached and not wait for the seller to cure. Goods may be so defective that the buyer loses faith in the seller's ability to repair them or cure. When goods are in this condition, the court in the next case held, the buyer is entitled to a refund of the purchase price or new—not repaired—goods.

Zabriskie Chevrolet, Inc. v. Smith

99 N.J. Super. 441, 240 A.2d 195 (Law Div. 1968)

FACTS   Mrs. Smith took delivery of a new Chevrolet from Zabriskie. After going $7/10$ mile, the car stalled at a traffic light. It stalled again 15 feet later, and each time the vehicle had to stop. About a mile later, the car could not be driven in "drive." Mrs. Smith became afraid to drive the car. She summoned her husband, who drove the car the remaining seven blocks to her home. Mr. Smith immediately notified Zabriskie that he was canceling the sale. Zabriskie picked up the car. It found that the transmission was defective and replaced it with a transmission from a vehicle in its showroom. Mr. Smith refused to take the repaired car. Zabriskie brought suit for the balance of the purchase price.

ISSUE   Did Zabriskie have a right to cure?

DECISION   No. Judgment for Smith. The right to cure it not a limitless one, controlled only by the seller's will. A cure which attempts to substitute an item not within the parties' agreement is invalid. This is particularly true where an item like a car, a major investment, loses much of its value if the owner's faith in its dependability and safety is shaken. A cure in the form of a transmission substituted by a dealer—not the factory—in a new car is not satisfactory.

Does the result in *Zabriskie Chevrolet* seem appropriate given the result in the earlier case of *Rozmus v. Thompson's Lincoln-Mercury Co.*? In other words, why does Smith get a refund and Rozmus not? Is it possible that factors other than mechanical difficulties, perhaps age or gender of the intended driver, might have influenced the judge's decision in *Zabriskie*? Should they? Might Zabriskie Chevrolet have been better off trying to satisfy its customer instead of leaving her with a now undesired car?

Figure 33-1 charts the right to cure.

BUYER'S RIGHTS AND DUTIES

When the seller tenders goods, the buyer usually may inspect them. Then, the buyer must choose between two responses: rejection and acceptance. If the goods do not conform, the buyer may reject them. When the goods conform to the sales contract (as they usually do), the buyer must accept and pay for them. Still, the goods may have defects which only time or use will reveal. In this instance, the buyer may revoke his acceptance and sue for damages.

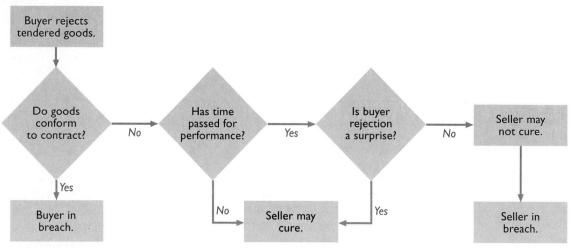

Figure 33.1 Seller's Right to Cure.

This section examines these rights and obligations.

The Right to Inspect

A buyer has the right to examine goods after delivery to determine whether they conform to the contract and, on that basis, to decide whether to accept them. The UCC terms this process *inspection*.

Normally, inspection takes place after delivery. We have already noted that *delivery* means that the buyer takes possession of the goods. Taking possession means taking control of goods as their owner. Still, until the buyer inspects the goods or waives the right to inspect them, she has not accepted them. An *acceptance* occurs only when the buyer both possesses the goods and intends to own them or fails to reject them.

The parties may agree on when, where, and how the buyer will inspect the goods. Otherwise, the buyer may inspect the goods at any reasonable time and place and in any reasonable manner [UCC §2-513]. The length of the inspection period depends on the nature of the goods. A fresh fruit and produce buyer will have a very short time in which to inspect goods because he deals in perishables. However, the manager of a computer store would have considerably longer in which to inspect a terminal. Because the buyer has taken delivery, the place of inspection usually will be his or her workplace or home.

If goods are sent *COD* "cash on delivery", the buyer must pay for them before inspecting them, unless the goods are marked "inspection allowed" or unless they are obviously nonconforming. In this case, payment does not mark acceptance. The buyer may inspect the goods and reject them after payment.

The Right to Reject

Rejection is the buyer's manifestation of an intent not to become the goods' owner. Thus, rejection is nonacceptance.

There are two types of rejection, wrongful and rightful. A wrongful rejection occurs when a buyer rejects conforming goods. The buyer is then in breach. However, suppose the buyer receives ten cases of red latex paint instead of the ten cases of red oil-based paint it ordered. The buyer may rightfully reject the nonconforming goods. If the seller does not have, or does not exercise, the right to cure, the seller is in breach.

Procedure. To be effective, a rejection must take place within a reasonable time after tender or delivery. Suppose a delivery of dresses arrived on a Friday afternoon when the buyer's staff was very busy. Delivery was accepted, and the dresses were put in a storage area until the following Monday when they could be inspected. If sending the notice of rejection closely followed the Monday inspection, a court would find the rejection to have occurred within a reasonable time.

The buyer—whether a merchant or nonmerchant—is required to notify the seller, preferably in writing, if the seller still has time to cure. The buyer must identify the particular defects on which he bases his rejection. Failure to identify any defect means that the buyer cannot cite the defect later to justify his rejection. The buyer is said to "waive the defect." Suppose the dresses in the last example all were stained and improperly seamed. The buyer would have to state these reasons for rejection. Failure to cite the stains would waive that defect.

In the next case, the buyer did not effectively reject the tendered goods.

Plateq Corp. v. Machlett Laboratories, Inc.

189 Conn. 433, 456 A.2d 786 (1983)

FACTS   Machlett placed an order with Plateq for two lead-covered, radiation-proof steel tanks to test x-ray tubes. The tanks were to be tested for radiation leaks after installation in Machlett's facility, but delivery was to take place at Plateq's plant. On October 11, Plateq had substantially completed the tanks. Machlett's engineer inspected the tanks and noted some deficiencies. Plateq promised to remedy them by the next day so that the tanks would be ready for delivery then. The engineer indicated that Plateq's proposed tender was satisfactory and told Plateq that Machlett would send a truck to pick up the goods in a day or two. Instead, Machlett sent a notice of cancellation which did not particularize the grounds for cancellation. Plateq brought suit for damages. The trial court awarded Plateq the price of the goods.

ISSUE   Did Machlett effectively reject the goods?

DECISION   No. Affirmed. Machlett accepted the tanks, primarily by signifying its willingness to take them. Therefore, Machlett could not rightfully reject the goods. Plateq was ready to tender, and would have done so but for its receipt of Machlett's notice of cancellation. That cancellation also wrongfully interfered with Plateq's contractual right to cure any postinstallation defects.

Between merchants, if a seller does not have the right to cure, she may request in writing that a merchant-buyer particularize in writing the defects in the tendered goods. A buyer's failure to respond with a complete list of defects will prevent him from relying on the unstated defects to justify rejection in a breach of contract action [UCC §2-605].

Effect of improper shipment. When a portion of a shipment consists of nonconforming goods, the buyer may reject the entire shipment. Alternatively, he may accept the conforming part while rejecting the nonconforming.

Even so, the buyer may not break up a commercial unit which comprises part of the shipment. A *commercial unit* is a unit of goods which is treated as a single whole for sale purposes. A commercial unit may be a single article, like a lawnmower; a set of articles, like a wrench set; or a quantity, like a bale or a hundredweight [UCC §2-105(6)]. Dividing a commercial unit impairs its value either in the marketplace or in use. Thus, if a buyer accepts any part of a commercial unit, he accepts the entire unit [UCC §2-606(2)]. For example, a buyer who contracts for twenty bushels of corn but accepts eighteen and a half has accepted nineteen bushels. However, by accepting nineteen bushels, the buyer does not accept twenty.

Effect of rejection. The effect of a rejection can be very important for purposes of title and risk of loss considerations. Title normally passes to the buyer at the time and place at which the seller completes the physical delivery of goods. A rejection or other refusal by the buyer to receive or retain the goods, whether or not justified, automatically reverts title of the goods to the seller [UCC §2-401(4)].

Where a rejection is justified because the tender or delivery of goods so fails to conform to the contract, the risk of loss will remain on the seller until cure or acceptance [UCC §2-510(1)]. To illustrate, the risk of loss would remain on the seller for five cartons of books which were badly water-damaged during transit.

Where the risk of loss has shifted to the buyer, an improper rejection does not revert the risk of loss to the seller. Instead, the buyer continues to bear the risk of loss. To illustrate, suppose Nike ships thirty pairs of running shoes to Al's Sporting Goods Shop via a shipment contract. Assuming a proper shipment contract has been entered into and conforming goods were shipped, the risk of loss would already be on Al's before any improper rejection. A buyer of conforming, identified goods who improperly repudiates the contract before the risk of loss has shifted to him or her will be responsible for a commercially reasonable time for any deficiencies in the seller's insurance coverage.

Buyer's duties after rejection. When the buyer rejects goods after taking delivery, the extent of the buyer's duties as to the goods depends on whether the buyer is a merchant. Nonetheless, the primary burden is on the seller to bear all costs relating to the storage, return, or resale of rejected goods.

A nonmerchant-buyer's duty is simply to exercise reasonable care toward the rejected goods [UCC §2-602(2)]. Reasonable care may require the nonmerchant, for instance, to place the goods in a public warehouse. Such an action should prevent any unnecessary loss to the seller's goods. The buyer does not have to return the goods. However, the buyer may not take any action toward them which indicates ownership, such as using the goods, selling some of them, or putting them up as collateral for a loan. A court will find that a buyer who exercises ownership powers as to rejected goods actually accepted them.

A merchant-buyer has duties toward the rejected goods beyond those of the nonmerchant. A merchant-buyer must follow any reasonable instructions from the seller as to the disposition of the goods. If the seller does not provide any instructions, the buyer must make a reasonable effort to sell them if they are perishable or threaten to decline rapidly in value [UCC §2-603(1)]. The buyer may deduct his costs from the proceeds of the sale, which of course belong to the seller.

The Duty to Accept and Pay For Conforming Goods

Acceptance occurs when, after having a reasonable opportunity to inspect the goods, a buyer either indicates that he or she will take them or fails to reject them [UCC §§2-602 and 2-606]. When the buyer accepts the goods, he or she must pay for them in the amount and manner agreed upon by the parties or, in the absence of an agreement, on delivery [UCC §2-507].

Time and manner of payment. Normally, the duty to pay arises after the time for inspection passes. The buyer may pay for goods in any medium used in the ordinary course of business, including a personal check [UCC §2-511(2)]. If the buyer reasonably expects the seller to accept a check but the seller refuses to accept it, the seller must extend the time for payment so that the buyer can raise the cash. To avoid the possibility of misunderstandings, the contract should specify the manner, time, and medium of payment.

The fact that the buyer must pay before inspection, however, does not impair any of the buyer's rights in the event of the seller's default. Thus, if Alicia's Restaurant orders china COD and the seller sends the wrong dishes, she could seek to avoid or *rescind* the transaction, or sue the seller for damages.

Breach of contract actions. Accepting goods waives only the buyer's right to reject. The buyer retains all other contractual remedies, such as a suit for damages.

To hold the seller liable, the buyer must give timely notice of the breach [UCC §2-607(3)]. In the following case, the buyer's failure to provide notice proved costly to him.

Celebrity Inc. v. Kemper

96 N.M. 508, 632 P.2d 743 (1981)

FACTS

For 5 years Celebrity sold goods to Kemper, a retailer. When shipments contained defective goods, Kemper set them aside. Celebrity's salesmen later checked the items and made an adjustment to his account. In the delivery at issue, Kemper noticed some defective items. This time, Celebrity's salesman refused to make an adjustment because the invoice specified that all returns were to be made within 5 days after receipt and only with a prior written authorization. Kemper took no further action until Celebrity threatened suit 3 months later. Then, Kemper reboxed all the remaining goods, whether defective or not, and returned them. Celebrity sued for the purchase price, but the trial court entered judgment for Kemper.

ISSUE

Was Kemper's rejection of the entire shipment valid?

DECISION

No. Reversed. Kemper failed to reject any goods which he did not bring to the salesman's attention. When a court cannot reconcile the express terms of a contract with an established course of dealing, it must give effect to the express terms [UCC §1-205(4)]. Still, Kemper was justified in following the established course of dealing until Celebrity invoked the contract's express terms. His failure to respond to the salesman's notification until threatened with suit does not accord with his obligations of good faith, diligence, reasonableness, and care. Kemper had a duty to give Celebrity a prompt, particular notice of rejection of the entire shipment.

Acceptance of nonconforming goods. For a variety of reasons, buyers often accept nonconforming goods. Perhaps the nonconformities are such that a reduced purchase price is sufficient compensation. Or, there may not be time to search out substitutes from another seller. Or, all the postrejection duties as to the goods may seem like too much bother. But, regardless of the reason, accepting nonconforming goods triggers the obligation to pay for them.

However, in two instances, a buyer who accepts nonconforming goods may revoke that acceptance. These instances are the topic of the next section.

Revocation of Acceptance

A buyer must use great care in deciding whether to accept or reject goods, since once goods are accepted, they cannot be rejected. The UCC's keying of the buyer's duty to pay to acceptance reinforces the importance of that decision. Nonetheless, in the two circumstances described below, the UCC permits a *revocation of acceptance,* which voids an acceptance [UCC §2-608]. A buyer who validly revokes acceptance is entitled to a refund of money paid for the goods. If the goods are not paid for, the buyer is freed from liability for payment.

It is critical to recognize that *revocation of acceptance has nothing to do with revoking acceptance of an offer in the formation of a sales contract*. It only affects the acceptance of goods under a sales contract.

Latent defects and promises to cure. Only when goods have hidden or *latent defects,* or when a seller fails to keep a promise to cure may the buyer revoke acceptance. Many goods—like kitchen appliances or telephone equipment—can appear conforming, but on use prove to be nonconforming. Such goods are said to have latent defects. But, even when inspection reveals goods to be nonconforming, the seller may promise to cure in order to convince the buyer to accept. If the seller fails to keep her promise, the buyer can revoke.

The buyer does not have to show that the seller acted in bad faith in order to justify revocation. The remedy's purpose is to provide relief when the buyer is surprised by a defect or disappointed in his reasonable expectation that the seller would keep her promise to cure. In the latter case, the seller's failure may be entirely innocent, as when one of her suppliers does not deliver a part.

Notice to seller. A revocation does not take effect until the buyer notifies the seller of his intention to revoke. However, the revocation must take place within a reasonable time after the buyer discovers or should have discovered the defect. Also, it must come before there is any material change in the condition of the goods which is not due solely to the defect. The revocation must apply to either the whole lot or a commercial unit included in the lot. In the next case, the buyer tried in vain to convince the court that it really did revoke its acceptance in an attempt to escape payment of a very large judgment.

Golden Needles Knitting and Glove Co., Inc. v. Dynamic Marketing

766 F.Supp. 421 (W.D.N.C. 1991)

FACTS

Golden Needles contracted to sell in May 1990 a shipment of cut-resistant surgical gloves to Dynamic Marketing in an exclusive distributorship agreement. Over $240,000 worth of gloves were then sent to the buyer. Because the gloves were considered to be a medical device, approval from the Food and Drug Administration (FDA) was necessary before they could be sold. FDA approval, however, was delayed, causing Dynamic to lose its financing. Dynamic failed to pay Golden Needles on time. Dynamic's response was to send a letter to Golden Needles in May 1990 informing it that the gloves were not marketable until there was FDA approval. In July 1990 Golden Needles sued Dynamic for payment. Dynamic argues its letter of May 1990 was sufficient notice of a revocation of acceptance under UCC §2-608(2). The trial court disagreed and granted a summary judgment to Golden Needles.

ISSUE

Was Dynamic's letter sufficient as a notice of revocation of acceptance?

DECISION

No. Affirmed. Under UCC §2-608(2), revocation of acceptance must be given in a timely fashion and must state, without equivocation, what the buyer thinks is wrong with the goods and that the buyer does not want them. Dynamic's letter of May 1990 was not sufficient in detail. Dynamic's activities subsequent to sending the letter, such as a failure to send or state an intention to return the gloves, indicated that it probably wished to keep them and continue to seek FDA approval.

It is important to note that the legal requirements for giving notice of a breach under UCC §2-607(3), discussed earlier in the *Celebrity Inc.* case, are less stringent than those for giving notice of a revocation of acceptance under UCC §2-608(2). Obviously, the revocation of acceptance is a more serious matter, since it is likely that a greater amount of time has passed and the seller is now relying on the fact that the transaction has been completed.

Impairment of value. To justify revocation, the nonconformities in the goods must substantially impair their value to the buyer. If the deviations are minor, the remedy is damages—not revocation of acceptance. Suppose Jane buys a new car. A few days later, she discovers that the front fender had been damaged and repaired before she bought the car. Her remedy probably would be damages, since a damaged fender ordinarily would not substantially impair a car's value to a buyer. By contrast, had she discovered a cracked engine block, she probably could revoke her acceptance.

In determining whether a revocation of acceptance is justified, a court evaluates the impairment of value to the particular buyer involved, not to the average buyer [UCC §2-608(1)]. The Michigan Supreme Court has even permitted a new-car buyer to revoke his acceptance because the vehicle lacked a spare tire. The buyer drove as many as 150 miles per day on Detroit freeways, often long before dawn. His fears of being stranded, the Court held, were not unreasonable and so the lack of a tire constituted a substantial impairment to him.*

Rights and duties as to the goods. A buyer who revokes an acceptance has the same rights and duties toward the goods as he would if he rejected them [UCC §2-608(3)]. By revoking, the buyer does not waive any right to recover damages for breach of contract.

---

* *Colonial Dodge, Inc. v. Miller*, 420 Mich. 452, 362 N.W. 704 (1984).

Since the buyer has the same rights and duties as to goods as he would if he had rejected them, are the seller's rights and duties the same, too? Certainly, to the extent that a buyer incurs costs due to, say, storing the nonconforming goods or purchasing replacement goods, the buyer can recover these damages, too. But, does the seller have a right to cure when the buyer revokes acceptance? The Texas Supreme Court answered that question negatively in the next case.

Gappelberg v. Landrum

555 S.W.2d 88 (Tex. 1984)

FACTS On September 5, Gappelberg bought a large-screen Advent television from Landrum's store. Gappelberg's consideration consisted of $3731.50 in cash and his old set. The Advent immediately developed serious problems, which Landrum attempted to repair. On September 26, the set stopped working. After permitting Landrum to remove the set from his home, Gappelberg demanded a refund and the return of his old set. Landrum could not return the old set because he had offered it as a prize in a store promotion. Instead, he offered Gappelberg another new Advent. Gappelberg refused the offer and brought suit. The trial court and the court of appeals held that while Gappelberg had validly revoked his acceptance. Landrum had the right to substitute the second Advent for the first.

ISSUE Does a seller have the right to cure a defective performance after a revocation of acceptance?

DECISION No. Reversed. A buyer's valid revocation of acceptance terminates any right the seller may have to cure by either repair or replacement. The UCC describes the seller's right to cure only in terms of rejection, an initial act of the buyer indicating nonacceptance. Revocation can occur only when the buyer has accepted the goods. No matter how generous the offer to cure is, the revoking buyer cannot be forced to take a product in which his faith is justifiably shaken.

Gappelberg firmly establishes an important point: the buyer's right to reject and the buyer's right to revoke are not parallel rights. Their procedures and the duties attached to them differ significantly. Figure 33-2 diagrams the revocation process.

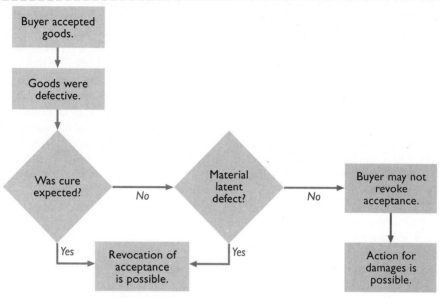

Figure 33.2 Buyer's Right to Revoke Acceptance.

MUTUAL RIGHTS OF BUYER AND SELLER

Excused Performance

Article 2 recognizes three situations in which parties to a sales contract may be excused from performance. These are a casualty to identified goods, the occurrence of conditions which require a substitution of performance, and the failure of a presupposed condition.

Casualty to identified goods. A *casualty* is a loss caused by an accident or a natural hazard. It can be either total or partial, and the UCC rules vary depending on its degree.

Assuming that neither party is at fault, the total destruction of goods identified to a contract before the risk of loss shifts voids the contract [UCC §2-613(a)]. (The identification of goods and risk of loss were discussed in the preceding chapter.) If identified goods are only partially destroyed, the buyer may demand an inspection and either void the contract or accept the goods at the contract price less their reduced value [UCC §2-613(b)]. Suppose the seller notifies the buyer that water has damaged the forty cases of computer paper the buyer had ordered. The buyer could demand to inspect the paper to determine the amount of water damage. If the damage was too great, the buyer could void the contract. If some of the paper was usable, the buyer could accept the goods at a price reduced by the value of the unusable paper.

Failure of a presupposed condition. Parties usually form contracts with certain expectations as to their ability to perform. Normally, for instance, they do not expect plague, famine, pestilence, or war to radically alter the business environment. Such expectations which are fundamental to the contract but are not routine business concerns are called *presupposed con-*

ditions. Presupposed conditions deal with events which the parties assumed would not happen and whose occurrence voids the contract.

The courts are most reluctant to void contracts on the basis of presupposed conditions which were not stipulated by the parties. The courts base their hesitance on the grounds that their role is to enforce, not make, contracts. However, the UCC does authorize courts to void contracts when the failure of an implied presupposed condition makes performance commercially impracticable [UCC §2-615].

Commercial impracticability. *Commercial impracticability* is a concept very similar to the common law's *frustration of purpose* doctrine. It is a flexible term which describes a business situation in which radically changed circumstances will cause one party a substantial and unjust loss. It does not cover situations in which a party will not make as much as it planned or will lose money on a contract because of poor business judgment.

For example, Farmer contracts with Grain Merchant to deliver 10,000 bushels of wheat at the end of the year's harvest. Unfortunately, blight destroys Farmer's entire crop. Whether Farmer's performance is excused depends first on his contract with Grain Merchant. If it specifies that the wheat was to come from Farmer's fields, Farmer would be excused. The presupposed condition was that the crop would not be wiped out.

Although the contract does not specifically say so, under the UCC, a court could find that the parties intended the existence of a crop produced on Farmer's fields to be a condition. But, if the court did not find this to be a presupposed condition, Farmer would be liable to Grain Merchant on the contract. It is important to note that the concept of commercial impracticability is not a device to save persons who fail to take such preventive law measures as inserting a clause in the contract excusing Farmer's performance in the event of a crop failure.

Under ordinary circumstances, a strike does not excuse the performance of a seller because he can obtain the goods elsewhere to meet his obligations. Like strikes, price increases are an ordinary business risk. So, too, are changes in consumer taste. Suppose a toy store orders 1000 "Happy Dolls" because every child under 6 wants one. Two weeks later, "Sad Dolls" capture the market, and "Happy Dolls" now gather dust on store shelves. A misjudgment of the market does not make performance commercially impracticable, and the toy store would still be liable on the contract.

If the failure of a presupposed condition has only partially affected the seller's ability to perform, and if the seller has a number of contracts which will not be satisfied, he must allocate his remaining production or inventory among buyers in a fair and reasonable manner [UCC §2-615(b)]. That is what the defendant-seller tried to do in the next case.

Alimenta (U.S.A.), Inc. v. Cargill, Inc.

861 F.2d 650 (11th Cir. 1988)

FACTS   In July 1980, Alimenta entered into seven contracts with Cargill under which Cargill promised to deliver to Alimenta shelled, edible peanuts. At that time, the crop still lay in the fields. A drought later that summer, whose severity the parties disputed, reduced the yield of peanuts. Cargill notified Alimenta that due to the reduced yield it would allocate deliveries among its customers. Cargill advised Alimenta that pursuant to UCC §2-615 it would receive 65 percent of the quantity for which it had contracted. Alimenta accepted its share, but it later filed suit for damages alleging Cargill had acted in bad faith in electing to proceed under UCC §2-615. After trial, a jury rendered a verdict for Cargill.

ISSUE   Was Cargill entitled to allocate under UCC §2-615?

DECISION   Yes. Affirmed. UCC §2-615 authorizes the allocation in remedy "Except so far as a seller may have assumed a greater obligation. . . ." Under Georgia law, the seller must expressly assume this greater obligation in the contract. That means the contract must include a provision to the effect that the seller will perform even though the contingencies that permit an allocation might occur. None of the contracts here contained such a clause. Therefore, Cargill was entitled to allocate if it could satisfy the jury by a preponderance of the evidence that the occurrence of the contingency was not reasonably foreseeable at the time of contracting and that the drought made performance impractical.

Substituted Performance

In very limited circumstances, the UCC permits a party to substitute an alternative means of delivery or payment for the one specified in the contract.

If the agreed manner or type of delivery becomes commercially impracticable through no fault of either party, the seller may use a reasonable substitute [UCC §2-614(1)]. Suppose a contract specifies shipment by Federal Express, but the shipper's employees go on strike. The seller could use Express Mail if the shipment would reach the buyer within a reasonable time.

Substitution of delivery modes ordinarily is not a serious problem. But, the substitution of payment media can be. This occurs in international transactions when the United States or a foreign government prohibits the use of a particular payment medium. For example, in 1983 the Mexican government prohibited its citizens from sending any money—other than Mexican pesos—out of the country. This meant that a Mexican company which had ordered goods from an American company could pay for them only with pesos, even if the contract specified U.S. dollars. As in most situations of this type, the payments in pesos were to be calculated at the official government exchange rate for dollars, not at the much less favorable open market rate.

When such a regulation is adopted, the UCC permits the seller to withdraw from wholly executory contracts. If the seller has shipped goods, it may stop the shipment. The seller need not tender delivery until the buyer has devised a way to give the seller substantially the same return as under the contract. If delivery has occurred the buyer may pay the seller in accordance with the regulation, unless it is discriminatory, oppressive, or predatory [UCC §2-614(2)].

Assurance of Performance

During the course of a contract, one party may develop legitimate concerns about the other's ability to perform his duties. As noted in Chapter 12, the concerned party, if she is acting in good faith, may demand in writing an assurance from the other party that the contract will be performed. Failure to provide such an assurance within a reasonable time, not to exceed 30 days, amounts to a repudiation of the contract [UCC §2-609].

In a dispute involving merchants, a court, like the one in the next case, will apply commercial standards in determining the reasonableness of the insecurity and the adequacy of the assurances [UCC §2-609(2)].

Clem Perrin Marine Towing, Inc. v. Panama Canal Co.

730 F.2d 186 (5th Cir. 1984)

FACTS
In 1974, Clem Perrin Marine Towing, Inc., chartered its tug to the Panama Canal Co. (PCC) for $344,880. PCC's payments were to be made in seven installments. At the end of the charter, PCC had the option to purchase the tug for $26,400. Clem Perrin agreed to provide a merchantable title if PCC exercised the option. In August 1976, PCC learned from H. J. Lopez, who had helped broker the charter, that Clem Perrin was not making the mortgage payments on the tug. On August 27, PCC wrote to Clem Perrin asking for assurance that Clem Perrin would be able to transfer merchantable title in December on the exercise of the option. The letter also noted that PCC would withhold the September 15 payment unless it received the assurance. Two days after it did not receive the September installment, Clem Perrin filed suit seeking damages for breach of contract. In December, PCC tendered the final installment along with the option payment subject to the condition that Clem Perrin furnish merchantable title. Clem Perrin did not reply. The trial court held that PCC had breached its contract with Clem Perrin.

ISSUE
Did PCC have reasonable cause in requesting assurance and, when it was not received, in withholding performance?

DECISION
Yes. Reversed. The determination of the reasonableness of a request for assurance is one of fact. Here, the trial court finding that the request was unreasonable was clearly erroneous. The standard is one of reasonable insecurity, not absolute certainty, about the performance of the other party. Faced with Clem Perrin's silence, PCC had good reason to protect itself by withholding payment.

Anticipatory Repudiation

An *anticipatory repudiation* is a party's unequivocal notice, either in words or by actions, that he or she does not intend to perform when performance is due. Thus, an anticipatory repudiation is an announcement before the time for performance that a party intends to breach the contract. (In fact, as Chapter 12 indicates, the common law refers to this as an *anticipatory breach*.) Once a party repudiates, the other party may suspend performance.

The requirement that the notice be unequivocal can create a problem for the nonbreaching party. The nonbreaching party must be certain that the other party really intends not to perform. That determination is critical because, as under the common law, a nonbreaching party has a duty to minimize or *mitigate* any damages it might suffer as a result of the breach. An anticipatory repudiation triggers that obligation. The UCC provides the non-breaching party with two alternatives when she is in doubt about the other party's intent to perform: she can test the other party's intent by asking for an assurance of performance, or she can wait a commercially reasonable time to see whether the other party changes his signals.

When the repudiation is unequivocal, the nonbreaching party may either bring a breach of contract action immediately or wait a commercially reasonable time to determine whether the other party changes his mind. The rights and duties imposed on the parties in the event of a breach of contract, including the nonbreaching party's duty to mitigate, is the subject of Chapter 35.

CONCLUSION

Most sales contracts, like most contracts generally, are performed as the parties intended. The seller properly tenders conforming goods; the buyer inspects and accepts them; and the buyer pays the seller.

When a transaction fails to follow this script, the UCC's remedial provisions become important. The key to understanding them is their goal: to see that the parties' original intent is carried out. At the same time, the UCC recognizes that perfect performance is not always possible. For that reason, sellers have the right to cure some defective performances without liability, while buyers have an obligation not to quibble about minor defects remediable by an adjustment in price.

Even so, the seller's basic obligation is to tender conforming goods at the right place and time. When the goods are nonconforming, the buyer may reject them.

The UCC's drafters intended rejection to be a buyer's most important means of protecting himself. For this reason, they emphasized

on one side the buyer's right to inspect and on the other acceptance, which triggers the buyer's duty to pay. After acceptance, the buyer still has a right to damages if the goods are nonconforming, but those damages have to be balanced against what the buyer must pay for the goods.

Acceptance requires possession of the goods by the buyer plus either an intent to own them or a failure to reject them. A buyer can revoke acceptance in only two situations: when the buyer had reason to believe the seller would cure but the seller did not, and when the product has a latent defect.

A major part of the next chapter deals with a seller's liability for latent defects. That chapter examines the law of *warranties*, or representations about the ownership and quality of goods. The seller usually makes these representations during the formation of the contract. However, liability is imposed based on an event which occurs after acceptance. For example, a dairy products manufacturer *warrants*, or guarantees, that one of its packages of cheese contains what its label say it holds. If the label says "ricotta" but out comes a roach, the manufacturer has breached his warranty. The second half of the next chapter explores the means by which the law imposes responsibility on manufacturers and sellers of defective products.

A NOTE TO FUTURE CPA CANDIDATES

Chapter 33 focuses on the various rights and duties of the seller and buyer in the performance of a sales contract. The most effective way to remember the various rules is to think of them in an actual seller-buying setting. Chapter 35 discusses remedies for breaches of contract.

The seller is to deliver goods which conform to the sales contract. If not, the seller is in breach. (Remember that in a shipment contract situation, for the seller to shift the risk of loss the seller must ship conforming goods.) The seller's right to cure, illustrated in Figure 33-1, allows the seller to correct a defective shipment of goods before being considered to be in breach of contract. Remember, the cure may be the substitution of replacement goods or the repair of the shipped goods. A buyer who has shaken faith may nullify the seller's right to cure.

The buyer has the right of inspection before acceptance. Do not confuse this right with the duty of payment. A COD ("cash on delivery") situation requires the buyer to pay for the goods without inspection but does not nullify the buyer's right to inspect the goods to determine if the goods conform to the contract. The buyer has a reasonable amount of time after receiving possession of the goods to accept or reject them. Once the buyer accepts the goods (or fails to reject them within a reasonable time) a buyer cannot later reject them. (For obvious reasons, a buyer would have more time to inspect a shipment of dresses than tomatoes.) A buyer who accepts nonconforming goods still retains the right to recover compensatory damages for breach of contract.

It is important to understand when the buyer has a right to revoke his acceptance: a cure was expected which did not occur or there exists a material latent defect (see Figure 33-2). Remember, a latent defect is one which was not apparent at the time of acceptance. For example, when a buyer properly rejects goods, the buyer will have to exercise reasonable care in holding the goods for the seller. However, if the buyer happens to be a merchant, the buyer must follow reasonable shipping instructions to return the goods to the seller (at the seller's expense and risk of loss).

It is important to understand the right to demand adequate assurances. If there exist legitimate, good faith reasons for one party to be concerned about the other party being able to perform properly, the concerned party may demand in writing an assurance that the contract will be performed. The failure to provide such an assurance within 30 days amounts to a repudiation of the contract. Likewise, the unequivocal notice of anticipatory repudiation amounts to a repudiation of the contract by that party.

KEY WORDS

acceptance (750)
anticipatory repudiation (760)
COD (750)
commercial impracticability (758)
commercial unit (752)
conforming goods (746)
cure (748)
mitigation of damages (761)
nonconforming goods (746)

perfect tender rule (747)
presupposed condition (757)
rejection (750)
revocation of acceptance (754)
shaken faith doctrine (748)
substituted performance (759)
surprise rejection rule (748)
tender (746)

DISCUSSION QUESTIONS

1. What must a seller do to perform the contract?
2. Where must the seller deliver the goods? When?
3. Explain the perfect tender rule. Under what circumstances will it not apply?
4. Explain the surprise rejection rule and the shaken faith doctrine.
5. What are the buyer's rights under a sales contract?
6. What are the buyer's obligations under a sales contract?
7. Under what circumstances may a buyer revoke an acceptance? How does this differ from rejection?
8. What are the buyer's duties after rejection?
9. Describe commercial impracticability. How does it differ from impossibility?
10. What is an anticipatory repudiation? Create an example not used in the text.

CASE PROBLEMS

1. Kent, a wholesale distributors of cameras, entered into a contract with Williams. Williams agreed to purchase 100 cameras with certain optional attachments. The contract was made on October 1 for delivery by October 15. Kent shipped the cameras on October 6, and they were delivered on October 10. The shipment did not conform to the contract in that one of the attachments was not included. Williams immediately notified Kent that he was rejecting the goods. What legal rights, if any, does Kent have? Explain.

2. Arnold's Garden Shop ordered twenty-five dark blue vinyl patio chairs, model #1190, from Easton Furniture Co. Easton was temporarily out of stock of #1190s, but decided that Arnold would probably accept #1195s, as it had in the past. Accordingly, Easton sent twenty-five #1195s, which arrived on the designated delivery date. Arnold's informed Easton that it could not accept the chairs, as they were for a customer who needed the #1190 chairs. Assuming that Easton can now locate some #1190 chairs, what rights, if any, would Easton have? Explain.

3. Cindy Brix ordered a tent to be shipped to her COD from Mountain Wood Sports. After paying the COD charges, Cindy inspected the tent. It appeared to be okay. A week later, Cindy started on a 7-day backpacking trip in Montana. During a thunderstorm on the second night, the tent's center seam pulled apart, causing a side panel to rip apart and blow away. Soaked and disgusted, Cindy junked the now useless tent, since it would only add weight to her backpack. Upon her return, Cindy sent Mountain Wood Sports a picture of the damaged tent and demanded her money back. Mountain Wood Sports claims Cindy accepted the tent when she paid the COD charges. And, Cindy cannot revoke her acceptance, since she exercised ownership of the tent by discarding it. Do you agree with Mountain Wood Sports? Discuss.

4. Mrs. Kooley purchased a new TV from Moon Radio and TV. She paid cash. Moon guaranteed 90 days' free service and replacement of any defective parts for 1 year. Two days later, Moon delivered and uncrated the set. But when Mrs. Kooley turned on the set, it did not function properly. The delivery woman told Mrs. Kooley that it was not her job to fix the set, but that a service representative would call. Mrs. Kooley unplugged the set and did not use it after the delivery woman left. A few days later the serviceperson determined that the chassis had to be removed from the cabinet to make the repair. Mrs. Kooley refused to allow this, insisting on a new set or her money back. Moon TV refused to refund the purchase price, but renewed their offer to repair the set or, if it could not be made to function properly, replace it. Who should win?

5. Kim Creghan, a writer, purchased a computer and printer from Walker Computing. Creghan had made it clear to Walker that the printer had to be able to do italics. When the printer was delivered, it was incapable of doing italics. Walker told Creghan that this was probably a problem with the connecting printer cable and that Walker would take care of it. Creghan then signed the delivery receipt. Thereafter, Creghan returned to Walker Computing three times for a different cable and had the printer inspected twice, but the problem was not rectified. After a month of frustration, Creghan told Walker that she wanted her money back or another printer. Would a court find Creghan's signing of the delivery receipt an acceptance of delivery? Under what theory should Creghan base her suit against Walker? Explain.

6. Suppose that in problem 5 Walker was unable to get the printer that Kim Creghan had ordered because the manufacturer had stopped producing it. On the day set for delivery, Walker tenders another printer at no extra cost. Walker tells Creghan that the printer, the Bates Quick Printer, costs more and is faster but is unable to do italics. If Creghan signs the delivery receipt, would she be able

to revoke her acceptance at a later time? If Creghan had simply refused the substitute printer, would Walker still have had a right to cure? Explain.

7. Thelma and Charles agreed that Charles would supply her with 250 pumpkins for her store for Halloween. In September a series of storms caused severe flooding, damaging many crops in the area of Charles's farm. Thelma called Charles and asked him if he could guarantee that she would get all 250 of her pumpkins on time. Charles said he could not at that time, but that he probably would know within several weeks if she wanted to call back. Instead of waiting, Thelma immediately ordered 250 pumpkins from Victor. When Charles attempted to deliver the 250 pumpkins on the designated delivery date, Thelma rejected them, saying that Charles had failed to give her assurance of performance in September. Was Thelma's rejection justifiable? Explain.

8. On May 1, Bush signed a contract for the sale of 5000 pounds of sugar to White Co. at 30 cents per pound. Delivery was to be made on June 10. Because of a sudden rise in sugar prices, Bush sent White a letter stating that she would not sell the sugar to White. White received the letter on May 15, at which time the market price of sugar was 40 cents per pound. Although White could have purchased sugar elsewhere in the market, it chose not to. On June 10, the market price of sugar was 50 cents per pound. White has now brought suit for breach of contract. Would Bush be likely to prevail if she raised the defense of commer-

cial impracticability? If Bush does not prevail, would White have a right to damages based upon the 50-cent-per-pound market price of sugar? Explain.

9. Harvey's Sports Shop ordered fifty sweat suit outfits (matching tops and bottoms) and twenty-five windbreakers from Lightning Sports Wear. The goods arrived COD. When Harvey's subsequently inspected the shipment they found that five windbreakers and fifteen sweat suit bottoms had defective seams. As such, Harvey's notified Lightning that they were not accepting and were returning the defective bottoms and windbreakers. Lightning claims that Harvey's waived its right of inspection and accepted the clothing when they paid for the delivery. Did Harvey's waive their right of inspection before acceptance? Can Harvey's accept the combination stated above?

10. Luglio's Pizza Shop ordered twenty tables from Carolina Furniture for its new shop location. After Carolina Furniture shipped the tables via a shipment contract, Luglio's learned that a Domino's Pizza outlet was going to be opened across the street from their new location. Fearing their inability to compete with Domino's, Luglio's canceled its lease for its new location and rejection the chairs when tendered by the carrier on grounds of commercial impracticability. Carolina Furniture claims this excuse is not justified in this case. The tables are presently in shipment back to Carolina Furniture. Is Carolina Furniture likely correct? Who presently has the title for the tables? Risk of loss? Explain.

CHAPTER 34
Warranties and Product Liability

The law of warranties and product liability defines the responsibility of businesses for products they sell. A *warranty* is a guarantee or an assurance or a representation about a product. *Product liability*, as its name implies, is the body of law describing the responsibilities of sellers and manufacturers for goods they place in commerce.

Perhaps in no area of law today do economics, ethics, and technology so often conflict as in product liability. Consider the problem faced by the developer of an innovative kidney dialysis unit. Dialysis is a crowded field. Research, development, and manufacturing costs greatly affect a product's competitiveness. So, how much testing should the company do in order to make sure that the product is safe? Should it go beyond what the federal Food & Drug Administration requires? What if the company, as well as the technology, is new and its capital will not support an extensive testing program? Do the social benefits of introducing a new technology, which can be refined as the market dictates, outweigh the possibilities of danger to individual consumers?

Manufacturers and sellers of goods must address questions such as these because juries are awarding millions of dollars in damages to injured consumers based on product liability claims. Take just one example: in 1983 a Texas jury awarded $6.8 million in compensatory and $100 million in punitive damages to a couple whose daughter died when her Mustang was struck from behind and caught fire as a result of defects in its fuel system.*

---

* An appellate court affirmed the judgment, but reduced the punitive damages to $26.4 million.

ORIGINS OF PRODUCT LIABILITY

Two hundred years ago, the questions posed above would not have arisen. Typically, buyers dealt directly with manufacturer-sellers. If a product proved defective, the buyer could sue for breach of contract or, if the product caused an injury, in tort.

Privity

As the nineteenth century progressed and mass marketing developed, one or more middlemen came to stand between the manufacturer and the ultimate consumer. However, in the 1840s and 1850s, the courts limited a manufacturer's or seller's liability almost solely to those with whom it contracted directly. The law termed those persons as being in *privity* with the manufacturer. Privity effectively limited the consumer's remedy to an action in tort or contract against the party who sold the product. Unfortunately for plaintiffs, sellers such as neighborhood markets often had considerably less resources to satisfy a judgment than did the manufacturer.

In part, the privity rule reflected the nineteenth century's prevailing social philosophy of placing as few burdens on manufacturers as possible, while leaving the consumer to guard his interest as best he could. Still, commentators and dissenting judges quickly noted the unfairness of this rule, both to the ultimate consumer and to middlemen who may have had nothing to do with the defective good's manufacture or packaging.

Nonetheless, the rule remained entrenched until 1916, when New York's highest court held, in the following case, that a consumer could sue an automobile manufacturer—as well as the dealer—in tort for the injuries caused by a defective wheel.

MacPherson v. Buick Motor Company

217 N.Y. 382, 111 N.E. 1050 (1916)

FACTS MacPherson purchased a Buick from an auto dealer which had purchased it from the Buick Motor Company. One of the car's wheels was made out of defective wood and its spokes crumbled when MacPherson was driving it. He was thrown from the car and injured. There was evidence that the defective wheel, which was not manufactured by Buick, could have been detected if Buick had exercised reasonable care. Buick defended by stating it had no duty of care except to those buyers with which it had privity. MacPherson prevailed at the trial level and at the intermediate appellate court.

ISSUE Does Buick owe MacPherson a duty of care even though he was not the immediate purchaser?

DECISION Yes. Affirmed. If a thing is in such a condition that it is reasonably foreseeable that it may injure someone when negligently made, the duty to safeguard someone from this danger should not grow out of a contract and nothing more. The manufacturer of an auto has a duty to protect those who use its product, since the very nature of an auto gives warning of probable dangers if it is constructed defectively. In this case, the car is designed to go 50 miles per hour, and if its wheels are not strong, injury is virtually a certainty. Moreover, Buick knew the car would be used by more than the buyer, since it is designed to carry three persons. The precedents set in the days of stagecoaches simply do not fit the travel of today.

Privity is virtually a dead issue today in tort actions, but as we will see at the end of this chapter, it remains important in contract and, therefore, warranty actions.

Sales and Tort Remedies

Ten years earlier, the Uniform Sales Act (1906)—the predecessor of Article 2—had introduced the concept of warranties. These warranties provide a basis for suit independent of tort remedies. Still, the tort principles discussed in Chapter 5 relating to negligence and strict liability continue to apply to a manufacturer's or seller's liability for a defective product. At the close of this chapter, we will examine them in this particular context. However, the main focus of this chapter is on Article 2's warranties.

While it is easy to confuse the two types of product liability law, you must keep their origins clearly in mind. Negligence and strict liability come from the law of torts, while warranties have a contractual nature. The plaintiff's choice of which of these theories to use against a manufacturer or seller can affect whether and what he will recover.

The Types of Article 2 Warranties

An Article 2 warranty is a guarantee or assurance about goods. Normally, a seller makes two types of warranty: warranties of title and warranties of performance.

Title and performance. The first, a *warranty of title*, guarantees the seller's right to transfer goods [UCC §2-312]. Suppose you buy, at a garage sale, a lawnmower which you later discover was stolen. You could recover from the seller if the rightful owner demands the lawnmower's return on the grounds that the seller breached his warranty of title to you.

The second type, *warranties of performance* (sometimes called guarantees), are designed to encourage honesty in transactions. They assure the buyer that the goods will conform to certain standards of performance and lead to legitimate expectations in the buyer as to how the goods should perform. For example, a Subaru should function like a well-built economy car.

Express and implied. Warranties of performance are themselves divided into two categories: express warranties and implied warranties. *Express warranties* are the guarantees which result from the parties' negotiations. They arise from a seller's actual words or actions, and they may be written or oral. If a seller tells you that a used refrigeration unit is in perfect working order, she has made an express warranty.

An express warranty may also arise from the seller's nonverbal actions, as when the seller could correct a buyer's misimpression, but does not. Suppose you said to the seller of the refrigeration unit that it did not appear to have had much use and seemed in good working condition. You may rely on your impression if the seller heard you, understood you, and did not contradict you.

Merchantability and fitness for a particular purpose. By contrast, *implied warranties* do not arise from the seller's statements. Rather, Article 2 imposes them. There are two types: implied warranties of merchantability and implied warranties of fitness for a particular purpose.

As to the first, only merchants make *warranties of merchantability*. A merchant is a person who normally deals in goods of the kind involved in the transaction or who holds himself out as having knowledge or skills relating to the practices or goods involved in a particular transaction. Merchants *warrant* or guarantee that a product is fit for the ordinary purposes for which it is sold. For example, you may reasonably expect an electric hedge clipper to trim forsythia, but not to prune a chain link fence.

The second type, *warranties of fitness for a particular purpose*, applies in those situations in which a buyer makes known to the seller the particular purpose for which she is buying the goods. Suppose Rachel is about to go on her first Colorado ski trip. She goes to a ski shop, tells the salesperson where she is going, describes her ability, and asks for recommendations as to the appropriate equipment. The shop's recommendations are warranties of fitness for a particular purpose.

In the sections which follow, we will examine each of these warranties.

WARRANTIES OF TITLE

Title is the right of ownership of property. When a buyer purchases a good, the buyer expects to receive an exclusive title to it. In other words, the buyer expects that no one else has a claim on the good unless the seller or the nature of the sale indicates otherwise. For instance, goods sold at a sheriff's sale are often subject to other claims.

The UCC protects the buyer's expectations as to title by means of the warranty of title. A warranty of title may be express, but usually it is implied. Unless the nature of the sale indicates otherwise or the seller specifically *dis-*

claims, i.e., refuses to make, the warranty, the UCC implies it.

Right to Transfer

Normally, then, in every sale of goods the seller warrants good title and the right to transfer it to the buyer. If the seller's title proves defective, the buyer has a right to recover damages from the seller [UCC §2-312(1)(a)]. Suppose Sandra accidentally sells her roommate's chair to Bill in their apartment sale. She did not have good title.

The seller also warrants that she will deliver the goods free from any *security interests* or *lien* which the buyer did not know about at the time they contracted [UCC §2-312(1)(b)]. This means that the seller warrants that she has no notice of any other interests in the property. Suppose Jane wants to sell her sailboat, which she bought with a bank loan. The bank secured its loan by taking a lien on the boat. Jack offers to buy the boat. Jane must either eliminate the bank's lien by paying off the loan before she transfers title, or provide specifically in their contract that the boat is subject to the lien.

Infringement

A merchant of the type of goods sold warrants to the buyer that the goods do not violate or *infringe* on a third person's patents, copyrights, or trademarks [UCC §2-312(3)]. As discussed in Chapter 25, patents, copyrights, and trademarks are property. If a good's design infringes on one of these property rights, the owner of the right has a claim against the goods. Assume that a clothing manufacturer sells shirts bearing the Calvin Klein logo to a store. The manufacturer impliedly warrants that she was licensed by Calvin Klein to produce the shirts. Suppose Calvin Klein obtains an injunction against the store's sale of the shirts because, in fact, the manufacturer was not authorized to place the logo on them. The manufacturer bears the responsibility for the store's loss due to the infringement claim.

A buyer who furnishes manufacturing specifications to a seller warrants that he will indemnify the seller against any infringement claim arising out of the seller's fulfillment of the specifications [UCC §2-312(3)]. Now suppose the manufacturer put the Calvin Klein logo onto the shirts after receiving assurances from the store that it was licensed to manufacture and sell such shirts. If, in fact, the store did not have a license, the responsibility for the illegal items rests with the buyer, the store. Under Article 2, this is the *only* situation in which a buyer makes a warranty.

EXPRESS WARRANTIES OF PERFORMANCE

Any seller of a good may make an express warranty. To create an express warranty, the seller does not have to use words like "warranty" or "guarantee." And, the buyer does not have to show that the seller intended to make a warranty. Rather, a seller may make express warranties in three ways: by a promise or an affirmation of fact which relates to the goods; by the seller's description of the goods; or by providing a sample or a model [UCC §2-313(1)]. A sample is an item taken from the goods to be sold, such as an apple from a bushel basket. A model, as its name suggests, is a representation of a good.

Promise or Affirmation of Fact

Any representation capable of verification—whether a promise or an affirmation of fact—becomes a warranty. The seller's statements must relate to the particular goods, must include specific representations about the characteristics of the goods, and must become part of the basis of the bargain. "Basis of the bargain" means that the statement were a factor in the buyer's decision to purchase the goods.

A seller makes an express warranty when she actively creates an expectation in the buyer about the characteristics or performance of the goods. Typically, the seller makes representations about the product in sales pitches, advertisements, or a written contract.

In order to claim that the seller made an express warranty, the buyer must show that the statements have some substance. A seller's opinions or commendations are not express warranties. Suppose the seller points to a food processor and says to the buyer, "This is a Chop Mate model 120 with twelve speeds."

Her statement is an express warranty that the machine is that particular model and that it has twelve speeds.

However, expressions of opinion, belief, judgment, or estimate by a dealer in a sales pitch are not warranties. Suppose the seller pointed to the Chop Mate and said, "This is the finest food processor on the market today." A court would find that this representation was just *puffing*, an inflated sales pitch unrelated to the characteristics of the goods. It was not a warranty. In the following case, the court had to separate representations of fact from puffing.

Crothers ex rel. Crothers v. Cohen

384 N.W. 562 (Minn. Ct. App. 1986)

FACTS

On December 22, 1980, 16-year-old Jack Crothers bought a 1970 Dodge from Maurice Boyd, a salesman employed by Norm Cohen at Norm's Auto Sales. As he and Jack listened to the engine run, Boyd represented the Dodge as being "a good runner" and as having a rebuilt carburetor. However, Boyd said nothing about an obvious defect in the accelerator linkage, which the next day caused the Dodge to crash into a tree. Jack was seriously injured. Jack's mother brought suit on his behalf. The jury specifically found that Boyd had made an express warranty to Jack on which Jack could and did rely. The court awarded Jack $165,000.

ISSUE

Did Boyd's representation amount to an express warranty?

DECISION

Yes. Affirmed. The jury did not err in finding an express warranty. Boyd stated an express affirmation, not a mere opinion, about the car's condition. His affirmation appeared to be based on facts that he, as the agent making the sale, knew. The affirmation related to the sale and was calculated to induce Jack to buy.

A buyer can recover only if the express warranty proves untrue *and* if damages can be shown. Suppose an advertisement in the paper says, "For sale. 1989 Cougar, sunroof, factory air, leather seats, AM-FM stereo, low mileage." Each word of the ad is a warranty. If the car had vinyl seats instead of leather, that would be a breach of warranty. However, the buyer must show that the leather seats were part of the basis of the bargain. If the buyer realized before buying that the seats were vinyl, he cannot show damage.

Figure 34.1 depicts the tests of an express warranty based on an affirmation of fact.

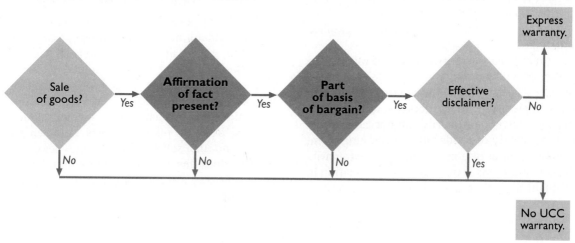

Figure 34.1 Tests for an Express Warranty Based on an Affirmation of Fact.

Description of the Goods

A description of goods which is made a part of the basis of the bargain creates an express warranty that the goods will conform to the description. A descriptive word or phrase used in a catalog or in advertising may create an express warranty. Again, the statements must relate to matters of fact and not be puffing. If a catalog says a rug is designed to avoid wear in heavy traffic areas, the buyer is entitled to rely on that description.

Sample or Model

A sample or model made part of the basis of the bargain creates an express warranty that all the goods will conform substantially to the sample or model. A *sample* is an item taken from the goods to be sold, as when a seller shows a buyer several nails from a keg. The buyer can expect all the nails from that keg to be similar in quality to what he saw. Suppose fruit is stacked in a container. The appearance of what lies on top creates an implied warranty as to the quality of the rest of the contents. They must be of equal quality to what can be seen.

A *model* is a representation of the goods to be sold. Suppose a seller shows a buyer a model demonstrating the fit of interior shutters. The buyer may expect the shutters to work the same way when the seller installs them on his windows. If not, the seller will have breached her express warranty.

IMPLIED WARRANTIES OF PERFORMANCE

Implied warranties protect the buyer's expectations concerning the performance of goods they purchase. Unlike express warranties, these warranties do not have to be specifically stated by the manufacturer or seller. Article 2 implies them unless the seller acts to eliminate them. For example, a car dealer gives an implied warranty that a vehicle is in operating condition. If the dealer does not wish to make such a warranty, she must use a disclaimer, like "as is," or state expressly that she disclaims all implied warranties.

An implied warranty is imposed by law as a matter of public policy for the protection of the people. The law implies warranties because of the complexity of many goods sold today and because buyers ordinarily cannot adequately test the quality of goods before accepting them. A manufacturer or a merchant who customarily deals in the goods is in a much better position to evaluate them than is the buyer.

Implied Warranty of Merchantability

If the seller is a merchant with respect to goods of a particular kind, Article 2 implies a warranty that the goods are merchantable [UCC §2-314(1)]. Because of their presumed expertise concerning the goods they sell, only merchants warrant merchantability. However, this warranty does not presume that a special relationship of trust or reliance exists between the buyer and the seller. Nor, as the next case reveals, does this warranty require that the seller be primarily a merchant of the type of goods in question.

Ferragamo v. Massachusetts Bay Transportation Authority

395 Mass. 581, 481 N.E.2d 477 (1985)

FACTS   The Massachusetts Bay Transportation Authority (MBTA) runs a mass transit system covering eastern Massachusetts. It offered eight 25-year-old trolley cars for sale "as is," specifically disclaiming all warranties of any type. Paul Ferragamo was the successful bidder. One of the cars had been involved in a fire which had led to the treating of forty-five firemen, several passengers, and a number of MBTA employees for exposure to polyvinyl chloride (PVC) fumes released by the burning plastics in the car. The car was covered with approximately 25 pounds of PVC compounds. The MBTA did not tell Ferragamo about the PVC. Ferragamo's 20-year-old brother, Michael, helped cut up the fire-damaged trolley. As he worked, Michael went into acute respiratory failure from which he died. Paul sued the MBTA on the grounds of negligence and a breach of its warranty of merchantability. The jury found for Paul on all counts, but the trial court ruled that the MBTA was not a merchant as to the trolley cars and issued a judgment, notwithstanding the verdict (JNOV) on the warranty claim, in favor of the MBTA.

ISSUE   Was the MBTA a merchant as to the cars?

DECISION   Yes. Reversed. A merchant is a seller who regularly deals in goods of the kind involved or who has professional status as to such goods so that it would be expected to have specialized knowledge of them [UCC §2-104]. Certainly, the MBTA's principal activity is providing mass transportation. But through its employees, it had a long-term and thorough acquaintance with the cars. While under the UCC an isolated sale does not make the seller a merchant [UCC §2-314], the MBTA sporadically sold cars for scrap.

A judgment notwithstanding the verdict (JNOV) means the judge set aside the jury's verdict and ruled the opposite way. The judge did not believe the MBTA was a merchant and therefore no implied warranty of merchantability was possible, contrary to the finding of the jury. The MBTA was found to be a merchant, since it had specialized knowledge about the trolley cars, sporadically sold cars for scrap, and should have disclosed the presence of the PVC compounds. Is this fair to the MBTA? The fact that the MBTA knew, or should have known, of the nonobvious PCV compounds undoubtedly led the courts to not recognize the MBTA's "as is" disclaimer. Does this seem proper? Does this seem fair?

Minimum standards. Article 2 does not define merchantability precisely. Rather, it states minimum standards [UCC §2-314(2)]. Thus, merchantable goods must:

- Pass without objection in the trade
- Be fit for the ordinary purposes for which such goods are used
- Be of even kind, quality, and quantity within each unit of goods and among all the units involved
- Be of fair average quality if the goods are fungible
- Be adequately contained, packaged, and labeled
- Conform to any promises or affirmations of fact made on the container or label [UCC §2-314(2)]

In sum, the purchaser has the right to expect that the goods will be fit for the ordinary purposes for which they are to be used. Further, the buyer has a right to expect that the goods will be of the quality and will perform like similar goods sold in the marketplace. Consider the following examples.

If you buy a blank video tape for your VCR, you may reasonably expect it to record without jamming.

If you purchase a fungicide for your lawn, you can reasonably expect the manufacturer to provide detailed instructions on how to use it safely.

If you receive a package from a specialty auto supply store containing replacement sheet metal for your 1965 Mustang, you may assume that it is packaged so that it will not be unreasonably dangerous to you when you open the crate.

If you purchase a six-pack of soft drinks held together by a heavy plastic carrier harness, you can reasonably expect that the harness will not fail as you carry the six-pack home.

The warranty of merchantability extends to the sale of food or drink in restaurants. Consequently, this warranty now applies to situations formerly covered solely in tort. For example, a customer ordered a glass of wine in a restaurant. The glass broke in his hand, and the resulting cuts caused a permanent injury. The court held that the restaurant breached its warranty of merchantability to the customer by not providing a container fit for the ordinary purpose for which it was to be used.*

Until recently, when something in food caused an injury to a consumer, the courts focused upon whether the item was foreign or natural to the food. If an object was foreign (like flies in soda bottles), the seller breached its warranty of merchantability. If the object was one normally and naturally found in the dish, no breach had occurred. For instance, the Supreme Judicial Court of Massachusetts held that a person born and raised in that state should expect fish chowder to contain fish bones.†

Today, courts are more likely to use the "reasonable expectation of the biter" test. It permits recovery even where a natural substance causes injury to the consumer, so long as

---

* *Shaffer v. Victoria Station, Inc.*, 91 Wash. 2d 295, 588 P.2d 233 (1978).
† *Webster v. Blue Ship Tea Room, Inc.*, 347 Mass. 421, 198 N.E.2d 309 (1964).

the biter reasonably could expect the seller to have removed the substance. As the next case shows, courts have applied the logic of this rule in areas besides food.

Flippo v. Mode O'Day Frock Shops

248 Ark. 1, 449 S.W.2d 692 (1970)

FACTS   Gladys Flippo was trying on stretch pants in a Mode O'Day Frock Shop when she suddenly felt a burning sensation on her thigh. She immediately took off the pants and shook them. A poisonous spider fell to the floor. The bite led to her hospitalization for 30 days. Flippo brought suit, alleging a breach of the warranty of merchantability. In effect, the trial court dismissed this count of her complaint.

ISSUE   Should the trial court have submitted the question of a warranty of merchantability to the jury?

DECISION   No. Affirmed.

We cannot agree [with Flippo] that the law of implied warranty of merchantability is applicable to a case of this nature. The pair of pants itself was fit for ordinary purposes for which stretch pants are used; there was nothing wrong from a manufacturing standpoint. . . . [The] spider was not a part of the product, and there is no evidence that either the manufacturer or retailer had any control of the spider, or caused it to be in the pants.

Course of dealing and customary usage. An implied warranty of merchantability may arise from the parties' course of dealing or from the customary usages in a particular trade [UCC §2-314(3)]. For example, a buyer may assume that a dealer has inspected a car before selling it to her.

Implied Warranty of Fitness For a Particular Purpose

An implied warranty of fitness for a particular purpose arises if the seller has reason to know that the buyer has a particular purpose and is relying on her to select or furnish suitable goods [UCC §2-315].

Unlike the warranty of merchantability,

this warranty does depend on a special relationship of trust between the buyer and the seller. The seller must select goods she believes are appropriate for the buyer's needs, and the buyer must rely on the seller's selection.

Let's look at an example. Roger was having trouble with mites on his prize-winning rosebushes. He took a branch to a nursery. After examining the branch, a salesperson suggested a spray to cure the mite problem. Roger bought it, took it home, and immediately used it on his bushes. The bushes died; the spray actually was harmful to rosebushes. Roger could probably recover his losses from the nursery under the particular purpose warranty. In contrast, had Roger gone to a self-serve, discount department store and secured help from a stock person, a court might find Roger's reliance unreasonable.

Figure 34.2 diagrams the tests of an implied warranty of fitness for a particular purpose.

WARRANTY DISCLAIMERS AND LIMITATIONS

A seller may disclaim, eliminate or limit, warranties associated with the goods she sells. However, her ability to do so depends on the type of warranty involved and the circumstances of the sale. Many commentators have criticized Article 2 for its various disclaimer rules and for the confusion these have caused. Figure 34.3 sorts them out. Refer to it as you study this section of the chapter.

Warranties of Title

As noted earlier, the seller must expressly disclaim warranties of title. A seller cannot disclaim warranties of title by simply stating "as is" or the like. Even if the seller states, "No warranties apply," title warranties are implied unless it is quite clear from the circumstances that they are not present, as in a sheriff's sale of unclaimed stolen property [UCC §2-312(2)].

Express Warranties

A seller may disclaim an express warranty so long as he does so in a reasonable manner. If the disclaimer is clear and conspicuous, the seller can disclaim all oral express warranties which are not included in the final contract of sale. But disclaimers are unreasonable, and therefore void, if the seller takes unreasonable advantage of his bargaining position or of the buyer's ability to understand the disclaimer or if he obscures the disclaimer's true effect.

"Unreasonable" in this context is closely related to the concept of unconscionability discussed in Chapter 32. And, the courts' power to adjust transactions is approximately the same, too. Suppose a buyer purchases a used car from

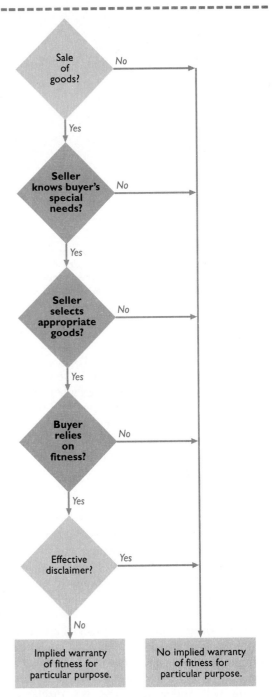

Figure 34.2 Implied Warranties of Fitness for a Particular Purpose.

	MUST SELLER BE A MERCHANT?	SELLER ACTION REQUIRED FOR WARRANTY?	ORAL DISCLAIMER EFFECTIVE?	SPECIFIC DISCLAIMER LANGUAGE REQUIRED?	"AS IS" AN EFFECTIVE DISCLAIMER?
Title (2-312)	No	No	Yes	Generally	No
Infringement (2-312(3))	No	Yes	Yes	No	Yes
Express (2-313)	No	Yes	Yes	No	No
Merchantability (2-314)	Yes	No	Yes	Generally	Yes
Fitness for particular purpose (2-315)	No	Yes	No	No	Yes

Figure 34.3 Comparison of Disclaimer Requirements.
The seller must specifically mention "title" unless the seller should realize from
the circumstances of the sale that no warranty of title is made. The seller must
mention merchantability unless it makes an "as is" type of disclaimer.

a lot with a huge sign reading, "All Cars Unconditionally guaranteed for 90 Days!" In his sales
pitch, the seller pointed to the sign when he was
asked about warranties on his cars. He did not
call the buyer's attention to the tiny print at the
bottom of the sign disclaiming all warranties of
any type. A court would find that this was an
unreasonable disclaimer.

Implied Warranties

Implied warranties, too, can be disclaimed. Although it can be more cumbersome to disclaim
an implied warranty than an express warranty,
courts are somewhat more inclined to enforce
these disclaimers.

Means of disclaiming. A disclaimer of a warranty of fitness for a particular purpose must be in
writing and be conspicuous. It must appear in
such a way that a person against whom it would
operate will notice it. Thus, the disclaimer
should be in letters which are larger than or in a
different color from those in the rest of the

document. A statement in a contract, like
"There are no warranties which extend beyond
the description on the face hereof," is sufficient
[UCC §2-316(2)].

The warranty of merchantability does not
have to be disclaimed in writing. However, if
the disclaimer is in writing, it must be conspicuous. Whether oral or written, it must mention
merchantability specifically or use an accepted
substitute for the disclaimer. "As is," "with all
faults," and similar expressions call the buyer's
attention to the exclusion of *all* implied warranties [UCC §2-316(3)(a)].

The buyer's actions, too, may eliminate implied warranties. Suppose that before entering
into the contract, the buyer examines the goods
or a sample or a model as fully as she wishes, or
refuses to study one. She waives any implied
warranties as to defects her examination should
have revealed [UCC §2-316(3)(b)].

Enforceability of disclaimers. As with disclaimers of express warranties, a court may
refuse to enforce a disclaimer of an implied

warranty which it finds was unreasonable at the time of contracting. Thus, a court may refuse to enforce a disclaimer if there was a great disparity of bargaining power between the seller and the buyer. A court is more likely to find a disclaimer unreasonable in the case of a consumer who suffers a personal injury from a product than in a case in which a consumer suffers property damage or economic loss.

Businesspeople are generally considered able to take care of their own interests. But even where disclaimers are not unreasonable, the courts do not favor them. Some courts have held that for a disclaimer to be effective, the parties must explicitly negotiate or bargain over it, and it must state specifically the qualities and characteristics being disclaimed. A disclaimer made in an invoice received after completion of a sale cannot be effective, since it was not part of the parties' bargain.

Limitations on Damages

Limitations on damages have been more successfully defended than total exclusions of warranties. The most common of these limitations attempts to exclude consequential damages for breach of a warranty. *Consequential damages* are for losses to person or property proximately resulting from a breach of warranty of a good, for example, the damage to a car when a defective tire blows out.

UCC §2-719 appears to draw a clear boundary between permissible and impermissible limitations. It states: "Limitation of consequential damages for injury to the person is prima facie unconscionable but limitation of damages where the loss is commercial is not." What this means is that a seller of a washing machine cannot limit the consequential damages resulting from personal injuries to a homeowner when the washing machine explodes. But the same seller can limit consequential damages arising out of a similar incident caused by the same defect in the same model if, say, the buyer is a laundromat and the consequential damages relate solely to loss of business.

In the following case, the South Dakota Supreme Court confronted such a limitation in a context that, as we have seen before, may or may not be commercial.

Hanson v. Funk Seeds International

373 N.W.2d 30 (S.D. 1985)

FACTS   Hanson farmed 2500 acres. In early 1980, he attended a Funk Seeds promotional meeting at which the Funk representative depicted Funk's G-4507 to be a very high yielding corn. Because of this representation, Hanson switched his order to this hybrid. The delivery receipt, signed by one of Hanson's employees, contained a limitation of warranties clause which limited warranties to an express warranty that the seeds were as described on the shipping tag and which limited damages to the price of the seed. Hanson used the seed in four fields. In one of the fields, the crop was virtually a total failure. In the other three fields and on other farms using the same hybrid, the crops were as expected. Hanson brought suit, alleging a breach of an express warranty. The trial court held the limitation was unconscionable and entered judgment for Hanson for his consequential damages.

ISSUE   Did Funk's disclaimer relieve it of liability beyond the value of the seed?

DECISION   No. Affirmed. Like most farmers, Hanson was not in a position to negotiate a more favorable warranty with the seller. Nor did he have the opportunity to test the seed before purchase. A crop failure is inevitable if the corn seed is defective. To enforce the provisions would leave Hanson without any substantial recourse for his loss, which resulted from Funk's breach.

Warranty liability for equipment like cars and tractors is often limited to repairs, correction of defects, or replacement. Such warranties usually specifically exclude any liability for consequential damages. The courts have generally enforced such limitations so long as the repair or replacement remedy remained viable. However, when a seller both fails to deliver conforming goods and does not repair or replace the equipment, a court may award consequential damages. In one case, an appellate court affirmed an award of consequential damages where the manufacturer failed to repair a tractor during the course of 3 years of repeated efforts and ultimately refused to replace it.*

CONSUMERS AND WARRANTIES

Warranties and disclaimers have aroused much debate during the past 20 years. Many courts have issued decisions in the area. Both state governments and the federal government have instituted regulations in the area. This section will give an overview of the consumer's special status with respect to warranties.

The Courts' View

The courts traditionally have felt that buyers relied less on implied warranties than on express warranties and have permitted sellers to disclaim them more readily than express warranties.

---

* *Waters v. Massey-Ferguson, Inc.*, 775 F.2d 587 (4th Cir. 1985).

The courts' view has some factual support. Studies of consumer attitudes have shown that a majority of consumers do not seriously consider the scope and availability of warranties in buying goods other than automobiles. In the early 1980s, a major appliance manufacturer found that fewer than 7 percent of its customers bought its products because of its warranties. Consumers cited various reasons for this attitude. Some said they could not understand what the warranties meant. Others believed no one fixed anything anymore. Still others said no manufacturer protected a consumer's purchase with an appropriate warranty.

Consumer advocates, like Ralph Nader, see the answer to the warranty problem as lying with the manufacturers and sellers. They cite vague warranties and manufacturers' almost routine disclaimers of implied warranties on consumer goods as a sound reason for consumer skepticism.

State Consumer Product Acts

During the 1970s, many states adopted consumer product acts which strengthen Article 2's warranties. These laws provide consumers with better warranty protection or notice of their rights or both. For example, some 20 states have passed special notice and warranty laws covering the sale of used cars. Among them, Maine and Wisconsin require a dealer to disclaim any known mechanical problems and to fix any known—but undisclosed—faults. Much of the warranty litigation going on today is occurring under state "lemon" laws.

The Magnuson-Moss Act

The federal response came in 1975 with the Magnuson-Moss Warranty—Federal Trade Commission Improvement Act. The Act affects only sellers or manufacturers who choose to provide written warranties. It does not require them. Not the least of the Act's goals is to make it clear to the consumer whether a warranty accompanies a consumer good.

The Magnuson-Moss Act applies only to consumer purchases of consumer goods. It defines consumer goods as "tangible personal property which is distributed in commerce and which is normally used for personal, family or household purposes." Thus, promises made by a health club concerning your condition after 6 weeks of its program are not subject to the Act.

Notice requirements. A seller does not have to make any warranties at all. But, assuming that a warranty exists, the Magnuson-Moss Act requires the *warrantor*, the person making the warranty, to state what type of warranty applies to the goods if they cost more than $10. If they cost more than $15, the warrantor must provide a written statement in plain English of the buyer's rights. The warrantor may adopt one of four methods for giving notice to the buyer:

- Display the text of the warranty on the product, as with a tag on a hairdryer cord.
- Place the text of the warranty close to the product, as by putting warranty cards in a holder attached to the shelf the product sits on.
- Maintain a warranty binder for consumers, as is often done at department store consumer service desks.
- Display the text on a sign near the product, such as one posted above a product display.

Full and limited warranties. The Magnuson-Moss Act divides written warranties into two types: full and limited.

A *full warranty* means that the seller will repair or replace a defective product without charge within a reasonable time after purchase. If the product cannot be repaired after repeated attempts, the consumer—at her option—is entitled to a refund or a replacement. (This is known as the "anti-lemon" provision.) Anyone owning the product—not just the original purchaser—may enforce a full warranty. The manufacturer or seller may use a warranty registration card to attempt to keep track of those to whom it has warranty obligations. However, the warrantor must notify consumers that submitting the card does not affect the warranty.

A *limited warranty* is any written warranty which falls short of a full warranty. It is quite possible to have a full warranty as to certain aspects of a product and a limited warranty for others. New cars, for example, come with a variety of limited and full warranties.

A manufacturer does not have to give any warranty at all, but if he does, he must not limit the implied warranty in such a way that the consumer is left remedyless in an unreasonably short period. Full warranties for 90 days are quite common in the small appliance industry. By contrast, a 7-day warranty period for a toaster would be unreasonable.

Remedies. The Magnuson-Moss Act encourages informal settlements of warranty disagreements. It requires commercial sellers to establish complaint handling mechanisms for consumers. A consumer must take her complaint through the informal settlement procedure before she can file a court action against a warrantor. General Motors, for instance, has established a third party arbitration program in which the car buyer may select an arbitrator from a volunteer panel maintained by the Better Business Bureau. The arbitrator's decision binds GM but not the consumer. If the consumer is dissatisfied, she may file suit against the company.

As explained in Chapter 2, both business and government are attempting to divert disputes away from the courts and into informal, less costly forums. The Magnuson-Moss Act is one of these efforts. In 1984, the Federal Trade Commission adopted a similar procedure to resolve the thousands of ''X-car'' complaints against General Motors. It is likely that we will see more such efforts in the future.

BREACH OF WARRANTY ACTIONS

Breach of warranty actions are, of course, statutory in origin, since Article 2 and its predecessor, the Uniform Sales Act, created them. They vary from the common law breach of contract action by incorporating some aspects of a common law tort action. This section examines the contract and tort elements which go into the breach of warranty action. The last section of this chapter looks at tort actions based on defective products.

Proving the Elements

In a breach of warranty suit, the plaintiff has the burden of proving:

The creation of the warranty
- Its breach
- Its causal connection to the plaintiff's injury
- The extent of the injury

It is important to note that the concept of causation in a warranty action is essentially the same as *legal cause* in a tort action, which is discussed in Chapter 4.

As already noted, a single sales transaction often gives rise to two or more warranties. For example, an express warranty might result from the use of a sample. The seller's statements about the goods may give rise to additional express warranties. At the same time, the seller may warrant the goods' merchantability or fitness for a particular purpose. A buyer may bring suit on all warranties breached by a seller.

Restrictions on Warranty Actions

Notice. In all breach of warranty actions, the nonbreaching party must give the breaching party notice of the breach within a reasonable period after he or she discovers or should have discovered it. The nonbreaching party's failure to give prompt notice can lead to the dismissal of the breach of warranty action [UCC §2-607(3)(a)].

The prompt notice requirement permits the breaching party to inspect, test, and sample the goods in order to learn the facts and preserve evidence [UCC §2-515(a)]. It also preserves the seller's right to cure a defective performance, a right which we discuss in the next chapter [UCC §2-508]. And, it may facilitate an early settlement of the dispute by raising the issue quickly.

Privity. Who can sue whom for a breach of warranty often is a question of privity. But, how privity applies depends on whether the breach caused personal injuries.

As already noted, at common law only the purchaser of a good could bring a suit alleging a breach of contract, and then only if the purchaser himself had been injured or suffered the loss. For example, suppose your neighbor borrows your lawnmower, which blows up and injures him. Under the common law, he had no contract remedy, since he did not purchase it. If you, its buyer, were injured, you could sue the seller, Viking Hardware, but not the lawnmower's manufacturer.

Under Article 2, if you were injured, you could sue Viking Hardware, the manufacturer, or both of them. The only limitation on your right to sue is that you can only recover once. If your damages are $1000, you cannot recover $1000 from each defendant.

Your neighbor's situation under Article 2 is not so clear. The UCC takes no definitive stance on his ability to sue Viking or the manufacturer. Rather, the UCC provides three alternatives for state legislatures to choose from [UCC §2-318]. Alternative A allows any person who is a member of the buyer's family or household or a guest in his home to sue if it is reasonable to expect that person to use, consume, or be affected by the goods. Your neighbor could not bring suit under alternative A. Alternative B extends the warranty to any person who may reasonably be expected to use, consume, or be affected by the goods. Your neighbor might be able to sue under alternative B. While alternatives A and B are limited to personal injuries, alternative C enlarges on alternative B by adding injuries to property as well as to persons.

About half of all American jurisdictions have adopted alternative A, the most restrictive alternative. The others have adopted either alternative B or alternative C or a rule of their own. In those states which have not adopted alternative C or a similar rule, privity applies to all claims of strictly economic injuries due to a breach of warranty. The next case illustrates how this application of privity can affect a case.

Baughn v. Honda Motor Co., Ltd.

107 Wash. 2d 127, 727 P.2d 655 (1986)

FACTS

Two 8-year-old boys were seriously injured when the Honda mini trail bike they were riding struck a truck on a public roadway. One boy was not wearing a helmet; the other's helmet came off because it had not been fastened. The boys had just run three stop signs. They did not see the truck because they were looking at the two children chasing them on another mini trail bike. In front of the operator, the Honda bore a prominent warning that stated in part:

THIS VEHICLE WAS MANUFACTURED FOR OFF-THE-ROAD USE ONLY. DO NOT OPERATE ON PUBLIC STREETS, ROADS OR HIGHWAYS.

The bike also bore a label that read, "Always Wear a Helmet." The owner's manual contained similar, prominently placed warnings. The father of one of the drivers was an experienced motorcyclist and had bought the Honda. He had instructed the children about its use. The father of the other boy had bought mini trail bikes for his children, too. He had instructed his children in their use. He had recently spanked the boy and confiscated his bike because he was riding it in the street. The fathers brought suit against Honda alleging, among other things, that Honda had breached its warranties to them. The trial court entered summary judgment in favor of Honda.

ISSUE

May a party bring a breach of warranty action against a manufacturer without also suing the dealer who sold the good?

DECISION

No. Affirmed. Contractual privity between buyer and seller is required before a plaintiff can maintain such an action. That privity was not present here because the plaintiffs sued the manufacturer but not the dealer. The privity requirement is relaxed when the manufacturer makes express representations or affirmations of fact in advertising, or otherwise, to a plaintiff. While the plaintiff does not have to rely on these representations, he must be aware of them in order to recover for their breach. Here, no such representations were made.

PRODUCTS LIABILITY

Chapter 4 introduced the tort theories of negligence and strict liability. These theories, we noted, apply to suits for damages caused by defective products. Today, when applied to cases involving personal injuries caused by manufactured goods, the traditional tort theories and the UCC's breach of warranty actions together make up what is called the law of products liability. *Products liability* law defines the liability of a commercial seller to those injured by goods it sold.

As you study the rest of this chapter, keep in mind that the same set of facts may enable a plaintiff to bring an action under theories based on warranties or negligence or strict liability, or possibly all three. Suppose Rita buys a new car. While she is traveling 65 miles per hour on an Interstate, the car's right wheel spins off. Rita may sue the car manufacturer under a breach of contract theory (violation of implied warranty of merchantability), a *negligence* theory (perhaps in design or manufacture), and a *strict liability* theory (a product in a defective condition unreasonably dangerous to the consumer). But remember: regardless of how many theories the plaintiff sues under, she is entitled to only one recovery.

Negligence

A plaintiff in a negligence case must establish the duty of care the defendant owed the plaintiff, the defendant's breach of that duty, the legal cause of the harm the plaintiff suffered, and the damages done to her. Normally, negligence involving products occurs in one of these ways:

- *Design*, such as a faulty axle on a tractor
- *Manufacture*, such as failing to secure the blade on a chain saw
- *Inspection*, such as failing to discover a faulty gas tank
- *Labeling*, such as failing to provide a warning of flammability on children's sleepwear
- *Testing*, such as failing to adequately test a drug
- *Shipping*, such as mailing a precision instrument in a paper bag

The need to prove the defendant's breach of duty makes using a negligence theory in product liability cases difficult. Suppose a new car's gas tank falls off after 3000 miles. Did the bolts shake loose during the car's transportation to the dealer? Did someone on the assembly line forget to install them? Because of these difficulties of proof, the plaintiff is more likely to choose strict liability in tort as her theory of liability. However, negligence as a theory of recovery may have been given a significant boost by the following recent California Supreme Court case regarding a rather common problem.

Strict Liability

Chapter 4's discussion of strict liability focused on dangerous animals and abnormally hazardous activities. Still, its rationale applies to the sale of defective goods. Figure 34.4 illustrates strict liability in the context of products

Mexicali Rose v. Superior Court of Alameda County

1 Cal.4th 617, 822 P.2d 1292 (1992)

FACTS   Jack Clark swallowed a 1-inch chicken bone while eating a chicken enchilada in the Mexicali Rose restaurant. Clark sued under the theories of implied warranty, strict liability, and negligence. All three theories were dismissed by the trial court and were upheld by the intermediate appellate court. The negligence claim was dismissed because of the "foreign-natural" rule, which absolves restaurants from liability when the object which injured someone is natural to that food. On appeal to the California Supreme Court, Clark argued that even though the bone was not "foreign" to the meat in the enchilada, the Mexicali Rose should have exercised reasonable care in preparing it by discovering and removing the bone.

ISSUE   Should California abandon the "foreign-natural" rule and require restaurants to exercise reasonable care when preparing food?

DECISION   Yes. Reversed. Under the strict "foreign-natural" test, natural objects in food such as bones, pits, etc., can injure a restaurant patron and the restaurant will incur no liability for negligence. This strict test should be rejected as the exclusive test for determining liability. Instead, restaurants should be required to exercise a duty of reasonable care in preparing food. In this case, Clark reasonably expected that when the Mexicali Rose prepared his enchilada, any natural substances in the food would not be of a size, shape, and/or quantity to injure him.

liability. The key difference between negligence and strict liability is that the strict liability plaintiff need not prove negligence; he or she must establish the inherent dangerousness of the product.

Any commercial seller of goods—retailer, wholesaler, or manufacturer—is liable for a good placed on the market in an unreasonably dangerous or defective condition, if this condition causes the plaintiff to be injured. The commercial nature of the seller is extremely important. You would not have a cause of action under a strict liability theory against someone who sold you an inherently unsafe hair dryer at

his garage sale. Still, you might be able to sue the manufacturer.

Privity is not required to bring an action under a strict liability theory. The plaintiff does not have to be a purchaser or even an immediate family member. In fact, the courts have broadened the classification of possible plaintiffs to include any users or consumers of a product—and bystanders, too—who are injured.

The plaintiff's case. The plaintiff must establish that the defendant is in the business of selling the product which caused the injury. Assume

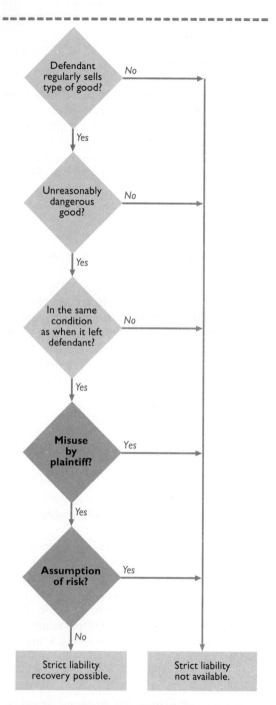

Figure 34.4 Strict Liability.

that the owner of a Chrysler dealership sells Marvin the radial saw he uses in his home workshop. When Marvin severely injures his hand with it, he would not have a cause of action under a strict liability theory against the dealer or the dealership. He might have one against the saw's manufacturer.

The product must have been sold in a defective condition and have been unreasonably dangerous to the user or consumer. The legal cause of the plaintiff's injury must be the defective condition of the product. Marvin will argue that the saw should have had an effective guard, given its dangerous nature. If the court determines that but for the absence of a guard the accident would not have happened, the manufacturer will be liable. Nonetheless, as the next case establishes, manufacturers of some inherently dangerous products will not be held liable for injuries resulting from the proper operation of their goods. In other words, a plaintiff cannot win simply by showing an injury.

Rhodes v. R. G. Industries, Inc.

173 Ga. App. 51, 325 S.E.2d 465 (1984)

FACTS	For self-protection, Mattie Hogan bought a .22-caliber pistol manufactured by R. G. Industries. She kept it hidden in the house she shared with other members of her family, five of whom were children. On May 5, 1981, several adults and children were visiting her house. Hogan's 5-year-old nephew found the pistol hidden under a chifforobe. He cocked it and put it in the basket of his 3-year-old cousin's bicycle. Later, the cousin found the gun, pulled the trigger, and fired one bullet that killed 10-year-old Kimberley Rhodes, who was seated in the next room. Kimberley's mother brought suit, alleging R. G. Industries was strictly liable because the gun was unreasonably designed and marketed to the general public. The trial court entered summary judgment in favor of R. G. Industries.
ISSUE	As a matter of law, could the manufacturer of a handgun be held liable for injuries caused when the gun performed exactly as expected?
DECISION	No. Affirmed. The U.S. Constitution guarantees the right to bear arms. The Georgia Constitution gives the legislature the power to regulate how arms are borne, but the legislature has not seen fit to ban handguns. Indeed, the enactment of licensing provisions indicates the legislature does not feel the marketing of handguns to the general public is an unreasonably dangerous activity.

The phrase "unreasonably dangerous" comes from the *Restatement (Second) of Torts*. The standard it expresses reflects a desire to balance the likelihood and gravity of potential injuries against: the utility of the product; the availability of other, safer products to meet the same need; the obviousness of the danger; public knowledge and expectation of the danger; the adequacy of instructions and warnings on safe use; and the ability to eliminate or minimize the danger without seriously impairing the product or making it unduly expensive.

Defenses

Strict liability is not a synonym for absolute liability. There are defenses to it. However, whether the seller exercised due care is not relevant in strict liability, although it is a defense to a negligence action. The seller's compliance with industry standards will not shield it when the product remains unreasonably dangerous to the public. Suppose no power saw manufacturer supplied a reflex action saw guard with its radial saws. That fact alone would not necessarily avoid liability if supplying the saw guard would have prevented the consumer's injury.

Disclaimers of liability. A disclaimer of liability generally will not work if consumers are involved. Typically courts have found that where these disclaimers are asserted against consumers, the parties did not bargain over them. Rather, the seller or manufacturer forced the disclaimer upon the consumer. A court might give effect to a disclaimer of liability when a transaction involves two businesses of relatively equal bargaining power.

While the defenses discussed below have direct relevance to strict liability actions, they also affect negligence actions.

Adequate warning of hazards. A manufacturer can insulate itself from liability for at least some known dangers by warning consumers or users. That standard is easier to state than to carry out. Consider Alcoa's problem after the decision in the next case.

Alm v. Aluminum Company of America

717 S.W.2d 588 (Tex. 1986)

FACTS During the late 1960s, Aluminum Company of America (Alcoa) marketed a system for putting aluminum caps on carbonated soft-drink bottles. In 1969, it sold a system to the Houston 7-Up Bottling Co. Seven years later, James Alm suffered a severe eye injury when the aluminum cap exploded off the top of one of the Houston Bottling 7-Up bottles. Alm brought suit against Alcoa, alleging it failed to warn of this danger. The evidence at trial showed that Alcoa had known of the problem and had mentioned in the user's manual for the system that a blow-off could occur if the bottles were not properly sealed. However, the manual did not mention the potential for causing injuries. Beginning in 1972, Alcoa developed a slide presentation, wall charts, and a technical information campaign for users of the system which did explicitly mention the hazard, but there was no evidence of what Houston 7-Up Bottling actually heard or received. The jury found Alcoa to have been grossly negligent and, in addition to the actual damages, awarded Alm $1 million in punitive damages. The trial court, however, granted Alcoa's motion for judgment notwithstanding the verdict. The court of appeals affirmed.

ISSUE Did Alcoa have a duty to warn consumers of the danger of bottle cap blow-off?

DECISION Yes. Reversed. Alcoa argued it had no duty to warn Alm because it did not manufacture or sell any component part or the final product that injured him. However, it did design, manufacture, and sell the system. In these three roles, it has a duty to exercise ordinary care. That duty requires that Alcoa inform users of hazards associated with the use of its products. Alcoa does not have a package of its own on which to place a warning. Therefore, it can avoid liability only by proving that it warned and adequately trained its intermediary so that the intermediary could pass along the warning to consumers. The adequacy of the warning and training is a question of fact to be determined by a jury.

Substantial alteration. If the good was substantially changed after it left the defendant, the plaintiff will not recover. Consider the example, discussed earlier, in which Marvin injured himself with a radial saw. Suppose the radial saw left the manufacturer with a guard, but a clerk in a hardware store removed it. The manufacturer would not be liable, though the hardware store owner might be. While that hypothetical situation represents the general rule, some courts have recently held that a manufacturer could be held liable for injuries caused by a foreseeable modification. Suppose the saw guard was so cumbersome that it was likely the end user would alter it. The manufacturer might well be liable. Suppose, however, that the alteration results in an unexpectedly dangerous situation and the user—while recognizing the danger—persists in using the altered saw. In

this instance, the manufacturer might be able to assert assumption of the risk.

Misuse. If the plaintiff misuses the product, the manufacturer may not be liable. Suppose Marvin caused the accident by altering the saw guard so that it would saw wood faster than the saw was designed to. The manufacturer probably would not be liable. Similarly, if the plaintiff used the saw to cut cast iron, the manufacturer probably would not be liable for his injury.

Misuse of the product is a difficult defense because the courts expect manufacturers to be aware of and to respond to the many ways in which their products are used. As a result, courts are quite liberal in their interpretations of what an expected use might be. In the next case, a U.S. circuit court confronted a misuse defense.

McMurray v. Deere & Co., Inc.

858 F.2d 1437 (10th Cir. 1988)

FACTS Dennis McMurray, an Oklahoma farmer, owned a 6-year-old John Deere. It was equipped with a starter safety switch to prevent it from being started while the transmission is in gear. Nonetheless, one can start the engine and thereby bypass the starter safety switch by using a technique called "hot-wiring"—placing a piece of metal between two terminals on the starter and the starter solenoid. On October 8, 1983, the starter mechanism on McMurray's tractor had malfunctioned, making it impossible to start the tractor with the key. McMurray and his helpers hot-wired the tractor several times without incident. The next day, McMurray and a friend were plowing. When they broke for lunch, the friend left a transmission lever in a position that allowed it to slip into gear when he turned the engine off. After lunch, the men hot-wired the tractor, which then lurched forward, crushing McMurray to death. McMurray's widow brought suit against Deere asserting the manufacturer's strict products liability. She alleged the tractor was defective because it could be hot-wired while in gear. Deere asserted the defense of misuse, among others. Deere produced no evidence that Mr. McMurray knew that hot-wiring the tractor could start the tractor while it was in gear. Nor did Deere show that it had warned users of its tractors of this possibility. At trial, the court denied Mrs. McMurray's request that the jury be instructed that if it found the tractor to be defective, her husband's failure to follow Deere's operating instructions would not bar recovery. Over

McMurray's objection, the court instructed the jury on the defense of misuse. The jury found for Deere.

ISSUE   Was McMurray's death caused by his use of the tractor for a purpose for which it was not intended?

DECISION   No. Reversed. It is important to distinguish misuse, which is use for an abnormal purpose, and contributory negligence, which is use for a proper purpose but in a careless manner. Oklahoma does not recognize contributory negligence as a defense in products liability actions. The defense of misuse applies to methods of using a product that the manufacturer did not intend or could not reasonably anticipate. Here, Deere intended and realized that the tractor would be used for plowing. Any carelessness in McMurray's attempt to hot-wire the tractor was only contributory negligence. This situation is entirely different from one in which, say, a farmer uses his or her tractor for an abnormal purpose, like demolishing a building.

Assumption of risk. Another possible defense is *assumption of risk*, which, as its name implies, means that the plaintiff understood the risk involved but went ahead with the activity. In the context of a product liability case, a plaintiff assumes the risk when he recognizes that a risk of injury exists as a result of the product's hazardous condition, but voluntarily uses the product anyway. In our example, if the plaintiff discovered that the saw guard was defective but continued to use the saw when a reasonable person would not have, he might not recover based on assumption of risk. We discussed assumption of risk in some detail earlier, in Chapter 4.

Contributory negligence. *Contributory negligence* was a common defense to common law negligence actions, but most jurisdictions do not recognize it as a defense to strict liability. In essence, contributory negligence barred recovery by a plaintiff whose own negligence—no matter how minor—contributed to his injuries. Today, the courts will not hold that the plaintiff contributed to his injuries if he failed to check the saw guard mechanism before using the radial saw, although that defense might have prevailed at common law.

Damages

Courts often award both *compensatory damages*, actual damages suffered, and consequential damages in strict liability cases. In addition, because strict liability cases are tort-based, not contract-based, *punitive damages* may be awarded. Punitive damages are damages awarded in situations involving a manufacturer's or seller's wanton or reckless act or disregard for the plaintiff. Punitive damages are awarded to punish the defendant and deter others from similar conduct. For example, in 1993, a Georgia jury awarded to the parents of a 17-year-old boy who was killed when his 1985 GMC pickup truck exploded some $100 million in punitive damages against General Motors Corporation.

PRODUCT LIABILITY LEGISLATION IN THE FUTURE

A major problem facing manufacturers and sellers is that state law controls in strict liability cases. Each state currently has its own laws; there is no uniform law in this area. Also, the procedural requirements for bringing product liability actions vary considerably. Some industries have obtained special legislative protection from product liability suits. The following case virtually defines the problems even the best-intentioned, piecemeal legislative approach causes.

Hyland Therapeutics v. Superior Court

175 Cal. App. 3d 287, 220 Cal. Rptr. 287 (1985)

FACTS   A 1955 state statute declared the "procurement, processing, distribution, or use of whole blood, plasma, blood products, and blood derivatives" to be "the rendition of a service . . . [not] a sale." Apparently, the legislature intended that the law would shield the blood business from product liability suits arising from the transmission of hepatitis via the exchange of blood. In 1955, no test existed for the presence of the hepatitis virus in blood products. By the 1980s, such a test did exist, as did one for AIDS.

Michele Gallagher's husband was a hemophiliac. He contracted AIDS from a blood product supplied by either Hyland Therapeutics or Miles Laboratories. He died. His intimate contact with Michele communicated the AIDS virus to her. Michele and their children brought suit against the blood manufacturers, one count of which alleged strict liability. The trial court denied the manufacturers' motions to dismiss based on the statute.

ISSUE   Did the statute require dismissal of the strict liability count?

DECISION   Yes. Reversed. The doctrine of strict liability for products applies only to commercial transfers of goods. Regardless of why the statute was passed, it defines transactions in blood products as services. Only the legislature can change the statute. Even so, the plaintiffs are not without remedies. They may show that the manufacturers were either negligently or intentionally at fault.

Another type of statute found in at least six states limits a consumer's ability to bring suit to injuries that occur within the product's anticipated useful life. The means of defining "useful life" vary widely. Some states have set presumptive limits, while others leave the question for a jury.

Many claim that the principal beneficiaries of the maze of product liability laws are lawyers. A 1984 study for the National Society of Professional Engineers showed that it costs the plaintiff 99 cents—mainly in attorney's fees—for every 59 cents in compensation in a product liability suit. No subsequent studies have reached much different conclusions.

Congress has recognized the growing problems in the products liability area. Since 1983 it has been debating a federal product liability law which would preempt state law. And, it has confronted the issue at every subsequent session without enacting any laws. Proponents of this legislation favor, among other things, requiring warning labels only for those dangers which are not obvious. For example, a user should know that glass cuts when it is broken. Also, they propose a uniform national defense of misuse of the product. They would also ban contributory negligence as a defense and would subject a manufacturer to punitive damages only once for a product defect. (Under the current system, a manufacturer can be subject to punitive damages in each product liability action.) Finally, some members of Congress have suggested that a portion of any punitive damages go to a charitable purpose rather than as a windfall to an individual plaintiff.

The Bush administration strongly opposed excessive jury awards of compensatory and punitive damages and costly legal fees in products liability cases. Former Vice President Quayle, in particular, argued for these changes, generally referred to as "tort reform." Quayle contended that tort reform was necessary for improving this country's global competitiveness. Some observers predict that the emphasis on tort reform may diminish because President Clinton was strongly supported by plaintiff's attorneys in the 1992 election.

Indeed, some legal experts feel that there may instead be a number of new, pro-consumer initiatives in the near future in products liability. One proposal being debated in Congress is the releasing of pretrial information gathered under discovery. Currently, it is customary for all such information to be sealed, at the request of the manufacturer, even if the information may be beneficial for preventing future injuries. Manufacturers obviously do not want such embarrassing information to be public or be exploited by future claimants. The proposal, which is already law in Texas, is that if the information gathered under discovery is relevant to public health and safety, it should be released.

In the coming years, some of these proposals may be adopted. Arbitration will play an increasing role in resolving product liability disputes. In addition, consumer advocates like Ralph Nader are pushing for a federal mediation law that would allow victims of personal injury claims, including products liability, to collect damages in cases too small for lawyers to take. However, it is unlikely that the number of these disputes will be reduced. The consumer orientation of commerce and production in our society makes rationalizing the system the best that can be hoped for.

CONCLUSION

In most cases, when a consumer buys a good, the item performs substantially as expected without causing any injury or loss to person or property. This chapter has been concerned with the remedies for a purchaser and other parties injured by a good.

The law of warranties often seems to students to be unrelated to the main focus of Article 2. Its similarity to the law of torts obscures the fact that the UCC's warranty sections have the same guiding principles as the rest of the sales article. The warranty provisions are designed to implement the bargain as it was made. In the interaction between sellers and buyers, sellers routinely make representations and buyers routinely develop expectations about the goods. The law of warranties is designed to give effect to the representations and to protect the expectations.

Perhaps it is an exaggeration to term the law of warranties—as some have—the acid test of a seller's good faith. Still, it is a useful concept, for a seller who disclaims warranties or who places unreasonable restrictions on those which are made tells the buyer something quite concrete about the goods.

A NOTE TO FUTURE CPA CANDIDATES

The CPA exam's coverage of products liability covers three types of actions: UCC warranty, negligence, and strict liability. It does *not* cover state and federal consumer protection legislation (such as the Magnuson-Moss Act).

CPA candidates sometimes get overwhelmed trying to learn the UCC warranties requirements shown in Figure 34-3. The key to learning the rules is to try to understand the warranties, not simply memorize them. Using personal illustrations or analogies can greatly assist this learning.

The warranty of title and warranty against infringement can be express but generally are implied. If you decide to purchase a Dallas Cowboys sweatshirt while shopping in a sporting goods store, you expect that the store is properly selling the shirts (no infringement on copyright) and that you will get good title. The UCC reflects these expectations. However, as to nonmerchant sellers, there is no implied warranty against infringement; you buy a Cowboys sweatshirt with risk of infringement at a garage sale. Because these two warranties are considered so inherent in the sale of a good, "as is" as a disclaimer is not effective.

Express warranties are any affirmation of fact. Opinions are generally not facts. Often the express warranty involves a description of goods. However, it may also involve a sample (a good drawn from the actual goods being offered for sale) or a model (a representation of the good). There are higher expectations for samples than models. Express warranties can be made or disclaimed orally or in writing. However, "as is" will not be effective to disclaim an express warranty.

The implied warranty of *merchant*ability applies only to merchants, as its name should imply. This warranty fulfills a buyer's expectation that a good will be fit for its ordinary purpose. This expectation applies to all goods, whether the goods are apple pies, microwave ovens, or cars. A merchant may orally disaffirm this warranty. However, if the warranty is in writing, the merchant must specifically mention merchantability. The warranty usually can be disaffirmed by language such as "as is."

The implied warranty of fitness for particular purpose occurs as a result of a seller matching specific goods to a stated buyer need. Here the buyer is relying on the seller's matching

action, whether the seller is a merchant or a consumer holding a garage sale. Having provided the match, the UCC requires a written disclaimer. Such disclaimer can be language such as "as is." It should be noted that the seller may be found to be making an express warranty simultaneously.

Warranty actions under the UCC are contract actions, so privity of contract is required. Third parties can recover only if members of the purchaser's family or guests in a home were injured by a product. In contrast, in a negligence or strict liability action, *not* covered by the UCC, no privity of contract is required. A negligence action may involve any facet of the sale of a product, such as negligent product design, manufacture, inspection, labelling, testing, or shipping.

For a plaintiff to recover in strict liability against a manufacturer or commercial seller, a plaintiff must prove the following:

1. The product must have been sold in a defective condition.
2. The product is unreasonably dangerous.
3. The product was not substantially altered after it left the defendant.
4. Defect caused the injury.

A defendant may raise as a defense the plaintiff's assumption of the risk (knew guard on power saw defective but used it anyway) or misuse of the product (attempted to use saw in a manner not normally used—to slice a turkey).

KEY WORDS

compensatory damages (788)	negligence (782)
contributory negligence (788)	privity (766)
	puffing (770)
disclaim (768)	punitive damages (788)
express warranty (775)	sample (771)
full warranty (779)	security interest (769)
implied warranty (768)	strict liability (783)
limited warranty (779)	warranty of fitness
model (771)	for a particular purpose (768)

warranty of merchan-
tability (768)
warranty of perform-

ance (768)
warranty of title (768)

DISCUSSION QUESTIONS

1. What kind of warranty arises when the seller affirmatively creates in the buyer expectations about the performance of goods?
2. Under Article 2, what are the requirements for an oral or written representation to be considered an express warranty?
3. What test determines whether the seller's statement is part of the basis of the bargain?
4. Give an example of "puffing" and contrast it with a statement which gives rise to an express warranty.
5. How does a model or a sample give rise to a warranty?
6. With respect to implied warranties, how relevant is the seller's intention to create the warranty?
7. What does the implied warranty of merchantability mean? How does it differ from the implied warranty of fitness for a particular purpose?
8. How do courts analyze whether a harmful substance in food constitutes a breach of an implied warranty?
9. Describe three ways in which implied warranties can be disclaimed.
10. What are two defenses which a seller has in warranty actions? Discuss each.
11. How does the Magnuson-Moss Act affect Article 2's warranty provisions?
12. What are the elements of a products liability cause of action based on a negligence theory?
13. How does strict liability in tort differ from negligence as a theory for recovery in a products liability case?

CASE PROBLEMS

1. Colossal Computer Company sold Mars Distribution Company 10 desk computers. The contract stated in bold type: "The buyer hereby purchases these computers with all faults, and all warranties are hereby expressly excluded." The computers sold have proved to be defective. Mars claims that the computers are unmerchantable. Colossal stated that it had no responsibility because of the contract disclaimer. Is Colossal right in regard to the merchantability claim? Explain.
2. Campus Store contracts with Lisa Apparel Company for Lisa to make 100 jackets specially, with the local university's mascot sewn onto the jacket. Campus Store supplies the mascot pattern and assures Lisa that the university has agreed to let it use the logo. After the store receives the jackets and places them on sale, the university brings an action against Campus Store and Lisa Apparel for trademark infringement. Assuming that a trademark infringement has occurred, has Lisa breached the implied warranty against infringement?
3. Max Elliott purchased a used van from Vango Sales Co. for $495. A clause in the written contract in boldface type provided that the van was sold "as is." Another clause provided that the contract was intended as the final expression of the parties' agreement. After driving the van for 1 week, Elliott realized that the engine was burning oil. Elliott telephoned Vango and requested a refund. Vango refused but told Elliott that it "would stand behind the engine for six months." Three weeks later, the engine exploded. Elliott claims that Vango made a warranty after the sale which is effective and not negated by the sales contract disclaimers. Vango disagrees. Would Elliott prevail in court? Explain.
4. Grand Fashions, Inc., purchased 25 dozen dresses from Lawrence Company after examining a sample made of pure silk that Lawrence Company submitted. The written confirmation Grand received contained the words "as per sample submitted to the company." Upon delivery, inspection, and testing, Grand determined that the dresses were 65 percent silk and 35 percent dacron and immediately informed Lawrence Company that it wanted to return the dresses for full credit. Lawrence Company claims that it

made no express warranties as to the percentage of silk versus dacron. Would a court be likely to uphold Lawrence's position? Explain.

5. Webster purchased a drill press for $475 from Martinson Hardware, Inc. Martinson informed Webster that they were closing out the model at a loss because it had certain deficiencies, and that it was sold "with all faults." The press has proved to be defective, and Webster wishes to rescind the purchase based upon a breach of the implied warranty of merchantability. Was Martinson's disclaimer effective? Explain. How does the Magnuson-Moss Warranty Act apply to these facts?

6. Wally, a CPA, offered to sell his chain saw to Rita, his neighbor, for $400. Rita stated that she knew nothing about chain saws but would buy the saw if it was capable of cutting down the trees in her backyard, which had an average diameter of 3 feet. Wally assured Rita that the saw "would do the job." Relying on Wally's assurance, Rita purchased the saw. Unfortunately, the saw broke under the strain of the large trees and Rita was badly injured. Rita subsequently learned that the saw was not even fit for ordinary purposes. Would Rita prevail against Wally on the basis of an implied warranty theory? On the basis of strict liability? Explain.

7. Pure Food Company packed and sold quality food products to wholesalers and fancy food retailers. One of its most popular items was "southern style" baked beans. Charleston purchased a large can of the beans from Superior Quality Grocery. Charleston's mother bit into a heaping spoonful of the beans at a family outing and fractured her jaw. The evidence revealed that the beans contained a brown stone the size of a marble. Will privity bar a lawsuit against either Pure Food or Superior Quality? Would Charleston's mother be likely to prevail in a negligence action against Superior Quality? Explain.

8. Angie White suffered an eye injury as the result of a malfunction in a power tool she had purchased from Clay Walker at Walker's garage sale. Walker had purchased the tool from Gray Hardware. The tool was manufactured by Elite Tool Company. White filed suit against Elite on the basis of strict liability. Elite had not previously been aware of the defect. Elite claims that White is precluded from suing it on the basis of strict liability because she bought the tool used. Is Elite correct? If White purchased the tool new, would Elite have a valid defense in that it followed the custom of the industry, was not negligent, and was not the direct seller to White? Explain.

9. Chuck Parks advertised his 1967 Camaro for sale in the newspaper. The advertisement stated that the car had a "totally rebuilt 327 V-8 engine." Les Schwartz did not see the newspaper ad but saw the car sitting outside Chuck's house with a for sale sign on it. Chuck said nothing to Les about the car's title or the engine. Les purchased the car and later saw the newspaper ad. Ten days later the engine blew and Les learned he had received a defective title. Chuck admits his advertisement was untrue. He claims he made no warranty of title, since he was not a merchant. Will Les be likely to prevail on the express warranty made in the newspaper advertisement? On the basis of a breach of the warranty of title? Explain.

10. Texas Supreme Court Rule 76a, approved in September 1990, prevents judges from sealing records of court settlements when secrecy might have an adverse effect on the public's health and safety. Protective orders can be issued only when the substantial interest of a litigant outweighs the public's right to know about a hazard revealed in a case. In late 1992, concern was raised that General Motors Corporation was managing to keep confidential possible design defects of the placement of its gasoline tank in certain Chevrolet and GMC pickup trucks by a series of court settlement protective orders. Does the Texas rule seem to be appropriate? Fair? Your thoughts.

The other chapters in this part have described how a sales contract is created and how it is to be performed. With this last chapter, the focus shifts to the remedies available in case of breach. The questions to be answered in this chapter are: What happens if one of the parties to a sales contract does not satisfactorily perform? What can the nonbreaching party do and not do? What can the nonbreaching party seek by way of damages or equitable remedies? What obligations still bind the nonbreaching party?

SELLER'S REMEDIES

In order to protect the seller's expectations under a sales contract, Article 2 provides remedies involving the goods, remedies involving damages, and remedies on the contract.

Remedies Involving the Goods

Seller's remedies involving the goods fall into three principal categories: withholding delivery from the buyer; stopping goods in transit; and reclaiming goods from an insolvent buyer.

Withholding delivery. The seller may withhold delivery if the buyer repudiates the contract or becomes insolvent. As discussed in Chapter 33 a nonbreaching party has the right to suspend performance on receipt of an *anticipatory repudiation*. Suppose Horace has contracted to deliver ten desks to Pegasus Equipment Company. Pegasus writes Horace that it will not accept the ordered desks, since it is overstocked with them. Pegasus has repudiated the contract, and Horace no longer has an obligation to perform.

A buyer's insolvency also permits the seller to withhold delivery unless the buyer can pay cash for the goods [UCC §2-702(1)]. If the buyer makes the cash payment, it has a right to receive the goods. Thus, if Horace learns that Pegasus is insolvent, he may demand a cash payment from Pegasus, regardless of the credit terms they had previously agreed upon.

Stopping goods in transit. If the buyer repudiates the contract or fails to make a payment, the seller can stop goods in transit only if the shipment consists of a carload, truckload, planeload, or equivalent full load. For example, Horace could stop delivery of a truckload of desks to Pegasus on its repudiation of their contract. However, he could not stop a shipment of a single desk by Consolidated Freightways. Since stopping goods in transit will impose a burden on the shipper in any case, forcing it to locate a small shipment seemed simply too great a burden to the UCC's drafters. After all, the seller could have shipped COD if he had doubts about the buyer's credit.

The "full load" restriction applies in all cases in which the seller seeks to stop goods in transit *except* when he discovers that the buyer is insolvent. If the seller learns of the buyer's insolvency while goods are in transit to the buyer, the seller may stop the goods regardless of the shipment's size [UCC §2-705].

The seller cannot stop shipment if the goods have effectively passed into the buyer's control. So, if the carrier has delivered the truckload of desks to Pegasus, Horace obviously cannot stop delivery.

If the buyer has received a negotiable document of title for the goods, the seller cannot stop the shipment. A negotiable *document of title* represents title and a right to possession of the goods. Therefore, the buyer already controls them. Similarly, if the seller has turned the goods over to a warehouseman and the warehouseman has acknowledged to the buyer that he is holding goods for the buyer, control over the goods has again passed to the buyer. Thus, if Horace tells the warehouseman to release the desks to Pegasus and the warehouseman in turn notifies Pegasus, Horace cannot stop delivery. Documents of title are examined in Chapter 39.

Finally, the seller cannot stop shipment if a carrier has reshipped the goods for the buyer. Suppose Pegasus directed the carrier to deliver the desks to one of its customers rather than to it. If the carrier is doing so, Horace cannot stop the goods in transit.

Reclaiming the goods. The seller can reclaim goods from the buyer only if the buyer received the goods on credit while she was insolvent [UCC §2-702(2)]. The seller must demand their return within 10 days after the buyer received them. However, the 10-day rule does not apply if the buyer made a written misrepresentation of solvency to the seller within the 3 months prior to delivery of the goods. So, if the buyer omitted its debts to its two largest creditors on its application to the seller for credit, the 10-day rule would not apply to the goods it subsequently bought.

A seller who elects to reclaim goods from an insolvent buyer waives any other remedy he otherwise might have against the buyer on the reclaimed goods. The seller's right to reclaim, also, is subject to the rights of bona fide purchasers. For that reason, if Pegasus sold five of Horace's desks to one of its customers in the ordinary course of its business, Horace could not recover them, nor would he have any other basis to make a claim against the third party. Pegasus, of course, would owe Horace the price of the desks.

The UCC does not place any time limit on the seller's exercise of its right to reclaim. A court probably would hold that the seller had a reasonable time in which to reclaim the goods. But as a practical matter, the seller must act immediately, since the buyer's other creditors will attach the goods to satisfy their claims.

Remedies Involving Damages

Damages is a term used to describe a court's monetary award to an injured party. The UCC does not use a single measure for the courts to use in calculating damages. Rather, the calcula-tion depends on the circumstances of the transaction and the relief the plaintiff seeks.

Regardless of which measure of damages the plaintiff seeks to have the court apply, the principle which will guide the court is that of just compensation. When the buyer breaches a sales contract, the seller has a right to be "made whole." In other words, the damage award should put the seller in no worse a position than he or she would have been in had the buyer performed.

Under the same principle, a damage award should not make the seller better off as a result of the breach. To avoid that result, a court will deduct from the damages any expenses the seller saved as a result of not having to perform. So, a seller cannot recover costs which were never incurred, like those for preparing protective packaging for a precision instrument which was never shipped. Nonetheless, the seller is entitled to the profit on the transaction, and a court will not reduce an award by this amount.

Damages following resale. If the buyer fails or refuses to perform and the seller has not delivered the goods, the seller may resell them [UCC §2-706(1)]. The seller may then sue the first buyer for the difference between the contract price plus incidental expenses and the resale price plus any expenses saved because of the first buyer's breach. That is,

Damages = (contract price + incidental expenses) − (resale price + saved expenses)

Incidental expenses include all commercially reasonable expenditures involving the goods that the seller made after the first buyer's breach. They might include charges for stopping delivery, transportation costs, or warehouse fees [UCC §2-710]. Expenses saved are those the seller avoided because of the breach [UCC §2-706].

Here is how the damage calculation works. Suppose Horace contracted to sell ten desks to Pegasus Equipment Company for $1125 including shipping costs. Pegasus breaches the contract. Horace sells the desks to Hyperion Corporation for $900. Before selling the desks to Hyperion, Horace incurred $75 in storage costs for them. Horace's damages under the formula would be:

Sales contract price: = $1125
Plus incidental costs: = + 75
                                   $1200

Less
  Resale price: $ 900
  Plus expenses saved: 125
                                        $1025

Equals
  Recoverable damages: $175

The next case makes an important point about damage computations under the UCC.

Modern Machinery v. Flathead County

202 Mont. 140, 656 P.2d 306 (1982)

FACTS

The Flathead County Commissioners called for bids for a rock crusher for the county's road department. They received three bids. Modern Machinery's $305,725 bid was the highest by over $100,000. On the road department's recommendation, the commissioners accepted Modern Machinery's bid. Three days later, an unsuccessful bidder notified the commissioners that it would sue if they accepted Modern Machinery's bid. That day, one of the commissioners instructed Modern Machinery's representative to have the order stopped. Modern Machinery asked for a letter from the commissioners canceling the order, which was not forthcoming. Modern Machinery tendered delivery, but the county refused to accept the machine. Modern Machinery then sold the crusher for $186,499.86 and brought suit for its lost profits and incidental expenses. The trial court instructed the jury that if it found that Modern Machinery was entitled to damages, "you may award any of the following: 1) Lost net profits; 2) Incidental damages such as expenses incurred in the transportation of goods after the buyer's breach." The jury awarded Modern Machinery $10,000.

ISSUE

Did the court properly instruct the jury as to the measure of damages?

DECISION

No. Remanded for rehearing on damages. The measure of damages stated in UCC §2-706 is not stated in permissive language. The UCC requires that the jury compute the damages as follows: the contract price ($305,725) plus incidental damages less the resale price ($186,499.86) and expenses saved in consequence of the county's breach. Thus, Modern Machinery's damages were far in excess of $10,000.

Private and public sales. The seller may resell the goods in either a private or a public sale, so long as the sale is commercially reasonable. *Commercially reasonable* means that every fac- et of the sale—including the method, manner, time, place, and terms—must be appropriate. If any aspect is not commercially reasonable, a court may deny the seller a *deficiency judg-*

ment, damages awarded when the resale's proceeds are less than the contract price. Had the plaintiff in the preceding case failed to resell in a commercially reasonable fashion, it would have suffered an enormous loss.

If the resale is to be private, the seller must give the first buyer reasonable notice of its intention to resell after a certain date. The notice does not have to include the time and place of the sale. Still, the notice process gives the buyer another chance to accept the goods. When time runs out, the seller may conduct a private auction or, more likely, simply negotiate the best price it can with another buyer.

The seller may choose to resell at a public sale. If so, it must give the buyer notice except where time does not permit, as when the goods are perishable or threaten to decline rapidly in value. The notice includes the place and time of the sale. The sale must be in the usual place or market for the goods if one is reasonably available. For example, a public sale of antiques should occur where they are normally sold publicly. That would not include a used car auction. The seller himself may buy the goods he is reselling.

Whether the resale is private or public, a *bona fide* purchaser takes free of any rights of the original buyer, even though the seller may fail to comply with one or more of the notice requirements.

Action for damages. A seller who decides not to resell goods may bring an action for damages against the buyer [UCC §2-708(1)]. The recoverable damages are the contract price plus incidental expenses less the market price at the time and place of tender and any expenses saved by the buyer's breach. That is,

Damages (contract price + incidental
        expenses + incidental expenses)
        − (market price + saved expenses)

The *market price* of goods is that price at which goods of the same sort are selling in the normal course of business. What the market is depends on the circumstances of the sales contract. It may be either the wholesale or the retail market. Market price becomes important in determining the seller's damages only if the market price goes down. Generally, market price relates directly to demand. If the market price goes up, the seller would simply resell the goods at a profit—for which it is not accountable to the breaching buyer [UCC §2-706(6)].

Suppose Pegasus breaches its contract with Horace to purchase ten desks for a total of $1125, including shipping costs. Horace incurs $75 in additional storage costs. The market price at the time and place for tender is $925. Horace could recover the following:

Contract price:	$1125
Plus incidental costs:	+75
	$1200
Less	
Market price:	$ 925
Plus expenses saved:	125
	$1050
Equals	
Recoverable amount:	$ 150

Action for lost profits. If damages would not make the seller whole, the seller may recover its lost profits from the buyer [UCC §2-708(2)]. *Lost profits* are those which the seller would have made from the sale plus his incidental expenses less the expenses saved as a result of the breach. Any payments the original buyer made and the proceeds from the resale are deducted from this amount. Thus,

Lost profits = (sale price − cost of goods)
        + (incidental expenses −
        saved expenses − (payments
        and/or resale proceeds)

Suppose Horace would have made a $225 profit on his sale to Pegasus. He could recover $225 plus his storage costs of $75.

An action for lost profits is appropriate when the market price has stayed the same. This remedy may seem unfair to the breaching

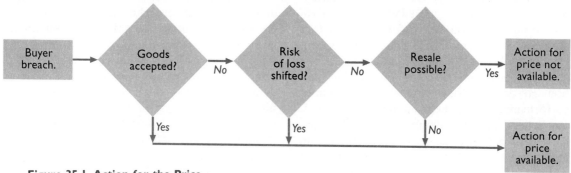

Figure 35.1 Action for the Price.
The seller may still be able to avail himself of other remedies if an action for price is not available.

buyer, since, apparently, the seller would be made whole by reselling. However, if Horace simply got his $225 profit from someone else, he would not really be whole. It has taken Horace, in effect, two sales to make one. Since the market price has remained steady, presumably so has demand. In our example, had Pegasus not breached, Horace could have made two sales and two profits. Since the resale proceeds, if any, are deducted in calculating lost profits, the seller cannot benefit from the buyer's breach.

Action for the price. If the buyer fails to pay the price due under the contract, the seller has a right to bring an action for the price plus incidental expenses. A seller may bring an action for the price only if one of the following applies:

- The buyer has accepted the goods.
- The goods were lost or destroyed after the risk of loss shifted to the buyer.
- The seller is unable to resell the goods after a reasonable attempt to do so.

The seller may have the goods when he brings the action, as when the buyer repudiates the contract. If so, he must hold them for the buyer. Suppose Pegasus wrongfully rejects the desks and returns them to Horace. He tries

unsuccessfully to resell them. He could recover the sales price plus incidental expenses from Pegasus. However, upon recovering the price, he would have to supply the desks to Pegasus. In essence, then, an action for the price in this circumstance is an action by the seller for specific performance [UCC §2-709]. Figure 35.1 diagrams an action for the price under the UCC.

Remedies as to the Contract

Chapter 33 introduced two remedies based on the contract: the right to *cure* and the right to demand assurance of performance. In this section we will examine two additional seller's rights: cancellation of the contract and identifying goods to it.

Cancellation. *Cancellation* occurs when either party to a contract puts an end to the contract because of the other party's breach [UCC §2-106(4)]. The cancelling party retains all its remedies against the breaching party.

Cancellation is a defensive maneuver. When invoked by the seller, it takes place in response to something the buyer has done or said before full performance is due. Thus, cancelling the contract, instead of demanding assurances or waiting for the buyer to change his mind, is a possible response to a buyer's *anticipatory repudiation*. Suppose Pegasus unequivocally repudiates its contract with Horace before the desks are delivered. He can cancel the contract immediately and seek damages under one of the theories described in the previous section. He does not have to wait for the time of performance to pass before filing his action.

Sellers quite commonly cancel when contracts which call for delivery of goods in installments are repudiated. Requiring the seller to continue tendering performance would not make sense.

Identification and resale. Up to this point, we have discussed the seller's remedies as if there were no question what goods were the subject of the breached contract. In other words, we have assumed—without saying so—that the goods were identified to the contract. In some cases, however, the buyer and the seller may have a binding sales contract, but the specific goods which are to pass under it have not been identified at the time of breach.

If the buyer wrongfully terminates the contract before the seller has identified the goods to the sales contract, the seller may identify goods to the contract and resell them [UCC §2-704]. The principal purpose of this section is to permit the seller to use the resale remedies which we have described above. If no goods are identified to the contract, it would be logically impossible to resell them.

When the seller is a manufacturer, the goods may not be completed at the time of the breach. In that instance, the seller may either finish manufacturing them and identify them to the contract or halt manufacturing and sell the unfinished goods for their salvage value.

If the seller decides to sell for salvage, the formula for measuring damages would be:

Damages = (contract price + incidental expenses) − (salvage price + saved expenses)

Suppose Horace is a desk manufacturer and Pegasus cancels while the desks are being constructed. Horace sells them in their unfinished condition for $350. He could recover from Pegasus the difference between the contract price ($1125 including shipping) plus his incidental expenses—which we will assume were nil—less the salvage price ($350) plus the expenses he saved as a result of the breach ($125 in shipping costs). Here, Horace would have a right to $650.

The seller must exercise reasonable commercial judgment in deciding whether to finish manufacturing the goods. In either case, it can pursue its resale remedies.

BUYER'S REMEDIES

A seller may breach by failing to tender goods; by tendering nonconforming or defective goods; or by indicating an intent not to perform.* The buyer's remedies depend on how the seller breached the contract and what type of loss the buyer incurred. And, the amount of that recovery may be limited by whether the buyer took steps to mitigate the seller's damages.

Cover

If a seller fails to tender goods in accordance with a contract, the buyer may mitigate its damages by choosing to *cover,* that is, to purchase reasonable substitutes from another source. A buyer who covers is entitled to recover from the breaching seller the difference between the

---

* UCC §2-711 contains a useful summary of the buyer's remedies. UCC §2-703 contains a similar index to the seller's remedies.

original contract price and the cover price, assuming the latter is higher than the former.

Good faith and reasonableness tests. The test of a valid cover is whether, in the context of the particular transaction, the buyer acted in good faith and in a reasonable manner. Whether hindsight may later show that the method of cover the buyer chose was not the cheapest or best is irrelevant. Suppose a paint jobber fails to deliver a specially mixed wall paint, but it is a higher grade and costs $5 more per gallon. That would be a commercially reasonable substitution.

A court will evaluate the reasonableness of a buyer's cover as of the time it was made. The decorator in the last example may have overlooked a vendor who sold cheaper paint, but if the buyer acted in good faith, the original seller would be liable. A practical test of reasonableness is whether the buyer would have done the same thing without any prospect of a successful suit against the breaching seller.

It is important to note that both merchants and nonmerchants have the right to cover. In most consumer transactions, the small quantities involved do not warrant a lawsuit to recover the difference in price.

Measures of damages. When a buyer validly covers, the measure of damages is the cover price plus any incidental expenses or consequential damages* less the contract price and any expenses saved because of the seller's breach.

However, a buyer does not have to cover. If she does not cover, her damages equal the

---

* *Consequential damages* are those losses which the breaching party had reason to know at the time of contracting would occur as a result of its breach. They arise from the nonbreaching party's particular circumstances. Consequential damages will be discussed in the next section.

difference between the market price when the buyer learned of the breach plus any incidental expenses or consequential damages and the contract price plus any expenses saved as a result of the breach (UCC §2-713).

Suppose that on May 1 Jane's Orchard agrees to sell Pathway Stores 5000 bushels of apples at $3.50 for delivery on November 1. On November 1 Jane's refuses to deliver because the market price has risen to $5.00 per bushel. Pathway would recover damages of $1.50 per bushel plus any incidental or consequential damages which covering would not have prevented.

If the buyer could cover but does not, a court will not grant specific performance. If a buyer fails to cover in an appropriate situation, a court may deny her the consequential damages she could have avoided by covering [UCC §2-715(2)]. The principle here is that of mitigation of damages: a court will not award the buyer damages she could have avoided.

Damages After Acceptance

Acceptance does not prevent the buyer from seeking damages from the seller for the nonconformities of the goods. A buyer accepts or does not revoke his acceptance of nonconforming goods when he decides he is better off with the goods than without. For instance, a business may accept beige telephone consoles though it had ordered white because it needs the new units immediately.

As noted in the last chapter, in order to impose liability on the seller, the buyer must give the seller notice of the nonconformities within a reasonable time after discovering them [UCC §2-607(3)]. Since the UCC does not define proper notice in this circumstance, the best preventive law approach is to provide a detailed notice immediately following discovery of the nonconformities. When the question of proper notice reaches the courts, they evaluate the circumstances of the transaction. In the situation in which no kind of notice is given, however, the consequences can be severe, as the next case demonstrates.

Hapag-Lloyd, A.G. v. Marine Indemnity Insurance Co. of America

576 So.2d 1330 (Fla.App. 1991)

FACTS Defective wiring was discovered by the buyer in the engine of a toploader. While waiting for a time in which to repair it, the buyer continued to use the defective toploader for 4 weeks and did not notify the seller. The defect later caused an explosion in the engine, ruining the equipment. The buyer sued the seller for breach of an express warranty. The buyer won at the trial level.

ISSUE Could the buyer, who continued to use the defective toploader and did not notify the seller, collect for breach of an express warranty?

DECISION No. Reversed. Under Florida's UCC, a buyer must notify the seller of any defect within a reasonable time or be barred from a remedy. In this case, no notice was given. If the seller had been given some notice, it could have remedied the defect and prevented the loss.

Revocation of acceptance and damages are not mutually exclusive remedies. Even though a buyer does not revoke its acceptance, it may have a right to sue for damages relating to goods it had accepted [UCC §2-714(1)]. Also, acceptance does not affect the buyer's right to sue for any other breach of contract or breach of warranty.

In fact, a buyer cannot recover for breach of a warranty unless it accepts the goods. Acceptance is a condition to a warranty cause of action. Thus, if the buyer revokes its acceptance, it cannot sue on the warranties. The measure of damages in a warranty action is the difference between the value of the goods received and the value they would have had as warranted [UCC §2-714(2)].

Incidental expenses. The buyer may recover incidental expenses resulting from the seller's breach, including those incurred in the receipt, inspection, transportation, and care of goods rightfully rejected. She may also recover any commercially reasonable charges, expenses, commissions, or the like on the purchase of substitute goods as a result of a delay or other breach [UCC §2-715(1)].

Consequential damages. A buyer may also recover *consequential damages* from the seller. These include any losses resulting from the buyer's situation which the seller had reason to know of at the time they contracted and which the buyer could not reasonably prevent by cover or other mitigating measures.

As we have seen with respect to the right to cover, a nonbreaching party may recover consequential damages when the seller fails to deliver conforming goods. A buyer can also recover them after acceptance or upon a revocation of acceptance. Suppose that at the time they contract, the buyer notifies the seller that if the specially designed machine tool he is ordering is not in his plant by a certain date, he will have to close one of his lines. The seller delivers on time, but the equipment is defective. As a result, the buyer must close the line. The seller will be liable for the damages the buyer suffers as a consequence. Consequential damages may compensate for injuries to person or property resulting from a breach of warranty [UCC §2-715(2)].

The courts historically have not favored awards of consequential damages because the losses tend to be difficult to anticipate. For that reason, they interpret the requirement of prior notice to the seller quite strictly. (This point is discussed in more detail in Chapter 12.) The parties, too, can limit consequential damages by contract, as we will see below.

Replevin

Replevin is an action brought by the buyer to recover specific goods wrongfully retained by the seller. Replevin is intended to give the buyer rights to the goods comparable to the seller's rights to the price. The buyer may use this action where goods have been identified and cover is not reasonably available [UCC §2-716(3)]. To illustrate, Cermak Produce Company orders seventy-five pumpkins from Linus Pumpkins for delivery by October 15. Because of an early frost, all pumpkin growers in the region experience major pumpkin losses. Linus

Pumpkins, which had not been destroyed by the frost, had identified the seventy-five pumpkins for Cermak but repudiates the contract to make a greater gain from selling the same pumpkins to Lucy's Produce Company. Assuming Cermak could not or would not be able to cover reasonably and could bring an action for replevin in time, Cermak would prevail. Replevin also is available to recover identified goods on the seller's insolvency where the buyer has paid part or all of the applicable price.

Specific Performance

A closely related buyer right to replevin is the buyer's right to specific performance [UCC §2-716(1)]. Specific performance under the UCC is available for unique goods, as at common law, but also "in other proper circumstances." What this means is that a court will look at the total situation which characterizes the contract. The inability to cover is strong evidence of "other proper circumstances." It is important to note that specific performance can be ordered before or after specific goods are identified to the contract. To illustrate, the comments to UCC §2-716 indicate that specific performance could be available in an output or requirements contract situation where cover from an alternative source is not reasonably possible.

In the next case, the buyer sought specific performance of a sales contract, arguing both that the good was unique and that proper circumstances existed for granting this remedy.

Klein v. Pepsico, Inc.

845 F.2d 76 (4th Cir. 1988)

FACTS   Klein contacted PepsiCo, Inc., and expressed an interest in buying a Gulfstream G-II corporate jet. After a series of offers and counteroffers, a contract apparently was formed. Negotiations later broke down and PepsiCo refused to deliver the G-II jet to Klein. Klein sued for breach of contract and requested the remedy of specific performance. The G-II jet, he contended, was unique, and the fact that he was unable to cover his loss on the later purchase of a G-III jet was a "proper circumstance" for justifying specific performance. The trial judge ruled that there was a contract and that specific performance was an appropriate remedy.

ISSUE Was it appropriate to grant the remedy of specific performance to Klein?

DECISION No. Reversed. The Virginia version of the UCC permits the buyer of goods the remedy of specific performance if the goods are unique or in other proper circumstances. Virginia's adoption of the UCC does not invalidate the equitable maxim that specific performance is not appropriate when damages are recoverable and adequate. In this case, there were twenty-one other G-II jets on the market, with three comparable to PepsiCo's jet. The fact that G-II prices rose after the breach also does not constitute proper circumstances for specific performance. Clearly, money damages would be suitable in this case.

CONTRACTUAL CONTROL OF REMEDIES

The parties may include in sales contracts remedies which the UCC does not specifically mention. Courts, however, usually regard these contractual remedies as being in addition to those provided in Article 2 unless the parties make plain their intention to exclude some of the Article 2 remedies [UCC §2-719(1)(b)].

Arbitration

As noted in Chapter 2, parties often insert a clause requiring arbitration of disputes. *Arbitration* is an arrangement whereby the parties agree to refer a dispute to an impartial third party—an *arbitrator*.

While arbitration proceedings are normally less formal than court trials, arbitrators can resolve almost any contract-related matter a court can. And, arbitration is usually a much speedier and less costly way of resolving disputes. With ever-rising legal costs and ever-lengthening court delays, contracting parties have begun relying on arbitration as a primary means of resolving disputes. For example, all three major car makers in the United States have arbitration plans which permit consumers to settle disputes outside of court.

Limitations on Consequential Damages

The parties may agree to exclude consequential damages in the event of breach so long as their exclusion is not unconscionable. A limitation on consequential damages for personal injuries resulting from the use of consumer goods is almost always unconscionable. An auto manufacturer, for example, which gives a consumer purchaser an express warranty cannot exclude consequential damages. If a wheel is defective and falls off, the consumer would have a cause of action not only for the damage to the vehicle but also for any personal injuries which resulted from the defect.

The rationale for not permitting the limitation of consequential damages for personal injuries is that the consumer is most likely to be buying for personal use. The consumer almost invariably will have less bargaining power than the seller.

Limiting consequential damages for a commercial loss usually is not unconscionable [UCC §2-719(3)]. A manufacturer, for instance, could give a nonconsumer purchaser an express warranty and exclude consequential damages. "Nonconsumer" is an extremely broad term. It includes merchants—as the UCC defines the term—every type of business entity, charitable organizations, schools, and churches. Where commercial transactions are involved, the non-consumer may have better bargaining power than a consumer and is likely to be insured against losses.

Liquidated Damages

Like the common law, the UCC permits the parties to agree at the time they contract on the amount of damages in the event of a breach. A clause in the contract which specifies the amount of damages is called a *liquidated damages* clause because it makes clear what the damages will be.*

However, the courts examine these clauses carefully because the potential for abusing them is great. A party in a superior bargaining position may insist on a liquidated damages amount which is out of all proportion to what the actual damages could be. For this reason, a court will allow the nonbreaching party to recover the stipulated amount only if it determines:

1 The amount is reasonable in view of the parties' expectations at the time of contracting.
2 The actual damages are difficult to determine in advance.
3 The parties have tailored the liquidated damages to the circumstances of the contract.

Buyers and sellers may provide for liquidated damages so long as the damages are not really a penalty [UCC §2-718]. Horace's contract with Pegasus calls for ten desks for $1000 plus shipping costs. He is aware that Pegasus has a contract to sell the ten desks. For that reason, they agree that because Pegasus will be

in breach of contract if Horace's delivery is not timely, Horace will owe Pegasus $10 damages for each day the delivery is late. A court would uphold this provision, but it would not be likely to uphold one which specified $1000 per day in liquidated damages on a $1000 contract. There, the liquidated damages clause is clearly a penalty clause.

A valid liquidated damages clause limits the claim for damages but does not bar other remedies, like specific performance or rescission.

STATUTE OF LIMITATIONS

An action for breach of a sales contract must be brought within 4 years of the time the breach occurs [UCC §2-725]. The parties may agree to reduce the limitation to as little as 1 year. However, they cannot extend it beyond 4 years.

For the purpose of determining when the limitation period on breach of warranty actions expires, the breach is assumed to have occurred when the goods were delivered to the buyer. If a contract contains a warranty which covers the goods' future performance, the statutory 4-year period begins when the buyer should have discovered the product's defect. For example, Evelyn bought a set of tires with a warranty which read, "The manufacturer will replace any tire found defective during the first 12 months or 12,000 miles, whichever comes first." The 4-year period will start at the moment within the warranty period at which Evelyn should have discovered a defect in one of the tires.

UCC §2-725(2) contains an exception to the 4-year statute for a warranty that "explicitly extends to future performance" of the product. In that instance, the cause of action does not arise until the defect is discovered. In one case, the parties stipulated that lauan siding was ordinarily supposed to last the life of the house. Since the seller represented the goods as siding, the Nebraska Supreme Court held the seller had made an express warranty that explicitly ex-

---

* The origins of this somewhat obscure term are discussed in Chapter 8, while the concept under the common law is described in Chapter 12.

tended to the siding's future performance.*
Should the court in the next case have reached
a similar result?

Moore v. Puget Sound Plywood, Inc., 214 Neb. 14,
332 N.W.2d 212 (1983). See also *Economy Housing Co.,
Inc. v. Continental Forest Products, Inc.*, 757 F.2d 200
(8th Cir. 1985).

Wilson v. Hammer Holdings, Inc.

850 F.2d 3 (1st Cir. 1988)

FACTS

In 1961, Hammer Galleries sold the Wilsons a painting titled *Femme Debout*, which it authenticated as being painted by the French artist Edouard Vuillard. Hammer stated in writing, "The authenticity of [this] picture is guaranteed." In 1985, the Wilsons had the painting examined by an expert in preparation for selling it. The expert pronounced that it was not painted by Vuillard. The Wilsons returned the painting to Hammer and filed suit seeking damages for, among other things, breach of warranty. The trial court held the Wilsons' action was barred by the statute of limitations and entered summary judgment in favor of Hammer.

ISSUE

Does a guarantee of a painting's authenticity constitute a warranty that explicitly extends to future performance?

DECISION

No. Affirmed. The trial court found the exception in UCC §2-725(2) did not apply because Hammer's warranty made no explicit reference to future performance. The Wilsons argued that a painting performs by being what the dealer represented it to be. A warranty of authenticity does not change over time. Therefore, it necessarily relates to both the present and the future condition of the artwork despite the absence of explicit language to that effect. The problem with the Wilsons' argument is that it asked the court to ignore the literal language of the statute that requires an *explicit* promise of future performance. In order to grant relief to the Wilsons, the court would have to waive the specific eligibility requirements for what is an exception to the general rule. Even if the Wilsons were to surmount this obstacle, they would still have to satisfy the UCC §2-725(2) requirement that discovery of the breach "must await the time of" future performance. Here, the Wilsons could have discovered that *Femme Debout* was a fake at any time after the time of purchase.

CONCLUSION

A primary purpose of the UCC's drafters was to streamline the law of sales and to make those buying and selling goods less slaves to detail than they were under the common law. To a large extent they succeeded. However, Article 2 remains essentially the same today as it was when it was last substantially revised in 1962, though the world has changed considerably.

Today, the courts, Congress, and state legislatures are considerably more aware of the role of consumers in sales transactions. (This will be discussed further in Chapter 45, "Consumer Protection.") In addition, Article 2's warranty and damages revisions of the common law have always been controversial and are still the subject of debate.

For these reasons, it is not surprising that some commentators believe Article 2 needs reevaluation. Some have suggested that consumer transactions be treated separately from commercial transactions, thus adopting the approach of the Magnuson-Moss Warranty Act. Others have seen a need to update the code in light of changing technologies. However, most who regularly deal with the UCC would agree with the person who said, "There's no need to revise Article 2. The same rules which govern a package going from St. Louis to New Orleans would work as well for one going from Cape Canaveral to the moon."

A NOTE TO FUTURE CPA CANDIDATES

The material in Chapter 35 has not been emphasized as much on the CPA exam as the material in the three previous chapters. However, it is still important to be aware of the basic remedies available to both the seller and buyer.

A seller's right to stop delivery occurs after a buyer's anticipatory repudiation or a buyer's insolvency, the inability to pay debts as due. Once goods are delivered the seller generally cannot get them back unless the buyer received them while insolvent.

A seller has the right to recover compensatory damages from the buyer for breach of contract. Recoverable damages include incidental costs from breach but must be reduced by expenses saved (like shipping costs). An action for lost profits is appropriate when the market price has remained the same and the seller has been denied its expected profit as a result of the breach. An action for price can be brought only if one of the following is met:

1 The buyer has accepted the goods.
2 Risk of loss shifted to the buyer before the goods were lost or destroyed.
3 The seller is unable to resell the goods after a reasonable attempt to do so.

In essence, the latter is a specific performance action.

The buyer's remedies include the right (not the requirement) to cover, to secure substitute conforming goods from another party. The additional costs to cover, less expenses saved, are recoverable from the seller. A buyer who accepts nonconforming goods has a right to compensatory damages. (Remember from Chapter 33 that a nonconformity which is not discovered until after acceptance may give the buyer the right to revoke his acceptance.) Courts are reluctant to award consequential damages unless it is very clear that the parties envisioned this possibility. Courts will almost never award punitive damages unless in a strict liability situation (a cause of action based in tort law, not the UCC).

A buyer will be successful in securing an order of specific performance if money damages would not be adequate and the goods are unique or "in other proper circumstances." The latter essentially means the buyer is unable to cover reasonably. You should remember that identification is *not* necessary for specific performance but *is* necessary for replevin, another buyer remedy.

The statute of limitations for the UCC is normally 4 years from the time the breach of contract occurs (*not* necessarily 4 years from the time of purchase). The parties can agree to reduce the statute of limitations period to just 1 year.

Figure 31.1 provides a list of Article 2 sections frequently tested on the CPA exam concerning merchant status. Those concepts discussed in Part II generally are found in the common law contracts portion of the CPA exam. The remainder generally are found in the UCC section. Remember that a merchant is anyone who normally deals in goods of the kind involved in the transaction *or* who holds himself out as having knowledge or skills relating to the practices or goods involved in a particular transaction. This means that for the purpose of the UCC, an accountant who has an active hobby buying, restoring, and selling collector cars may be considered a merchant of such cars.

KEY WORDS

cancellation (799)
commercially reason-
    able (797)
consequential dam-
    ages (801)
cover (800)

incidental ex-
    penses (796)
liquidated damages (805)
market price (798)
specific perfor-
    mance (803)

DISCUSSION QUESTIONS

1. Name five remedies available to a seller when a buyer breaches.
2. If a buyer wrongfully rejects conforming goods, what two options are available to a seller?
3. What are the requirements regarding the right of a seller to resell?
4. If the difference between the contract price and the market price would not put the seller in as good a financial position as if the contract had been performed, what alternative does he have?
5. What may a seller do if she is in the process of manufacturing the goods when the buyer breaches the contract?
6. Name three remedies available to a buyer when a seller breaches.
7. Explain the concept of cover. Is a buyer required to cover upon discovering the seller's breach? What are the implications of covering or choosing not to cover as far as damages are concerned?
8. What can a buyer do if a seller delivers non-conforming or defective goods?
9. When will a buyer have a right to specific performance?
10. When will the courts uphold the parties' agreement as to remedies? Can parties always contract to limit consequential damages in the case of a breach?
11. Are liquidated damages clauses valid? When will the courts choose not to enforce them?
12. What is the limitation on actions under Article 2? When will the period begin to run on a warranty which covers future performance?

CASE PROBLEMS

1. Sand Corp. received an order for $11,000 of assorted pottery from Gluco, Inc. The shipping terms were FOB Lime Ship Lines, seller's place of business, 2/10, net/30. Sand packed and crated the pottery for shipment, and it was loaded upon Lime's ship. While the goods were in transit to Gluco, Sand learned that Gluco was insolvent in the equity sense (unable to pay its debts in the ordinary course of business). Sand promptly wired Lime's office in Galveston, Texas, and instructed Lime to stop shipment of the goods to Gluco and to store them until further instructions. Lime complied with these instructions. Regarding the rights, duties, and liabilities of the parties, can Sand now demand cash from Gluco to complete the sale? If Gluco is prepared to pay cash, can Sand refuse? Explain.

2. Miller Publishing Company agreed to send $5500 of books on credit to Best Book Store. Miller had agreed to sell on credit only after Best furnished Miller with copies of financial statements that purportedly showed Best in good financial condition. In fact, Best had altered the financial statements and was in very poor financial condition. That became clear when Best became insolvent 15 days after receiving Miller's books. Miller wishes to recover the books from Best. Will it be successful? Explain.

3. Lawrence Grocery wrongfully rejected sixty crates of apples tendered to it by Brendler, Inc. Because the apples were beginning to age, Brendler resold the apples to another grocery store, but for $150 less than its sales contract with Lawrence. Brendler now seeks this amount less the transportation costs saved ($60) from Lawrence. Lawrence denies liability. Will Brendler prevail?

4. Milgore, the vice president of Deluxe Restaurant Chain, telephoned Specialty Restaurant Suppliers and ordered a made-to-order dishwashing unit for one of its restaurants for $12,500. Due to the specifications, the machine was not adaptable for use by other restauranteurs. Specialty constructed the

machine as agreed, but Deluxe has refused to pay for it. What remedy, if any, does Specialty have?

5. On March 11, Vizar Sales Corporation telegraphed Watson Company: "Will sell 1000 cases of coffee for $28 a case for delivery at our place of business on April 15. You may pick them up at our loading platform." Watson telegraphed its acceptance on March 12. On March 20, coffee prices rose to $30 a case. Vizar telegraphed Watson on March 21 that it repudiated the sale and would not make the delivery. The telegram was received by Watson on March 22, when the price was $32; Watson could have covered at that price, but chose not to do so. On April 15 the coffee was selling at $35 a case. Watson tendered $28,000 to Vizar and indicated it was ready to take delivery. Vizar refused to deliver. What relief, if any, is Watson entitled to? Explain.

6. Flax telephoned Sky Corp. and ordered a specially manufactured air conditioner for $1900. Subsequently, Flax realized that he miscalculated the area which was to be cooled and concluded that the air conditioner would not be acceptable. Sky had already completed work on the air conditioner and demanded payment. Sky could not resell the unit at a reasonable price. As a result, it has incurred reasonable but additional storage charges of $50. Sky Corp. had originally expected to make a profit of $350 on the sale. If Flax refuses to accept the unit and pay the $1900 and Sky Corp. brings a lawsuit, what amount, if any, is a court likely to award Sky Corp.? Explain.

7. Fenster Costume Company entered into a $25,000 contract to supply Giant Department Stores with Halloween costumes. The contract called for delivery to be completed by September 1 or $2000 a day liquidated damages would be deducted from the amount owed Fenster. Fenster's delivery occurred on September 10. Giant has tendered only $5000, and Fenster has brought a lawsuit for the remaining amount. What arguments should Fenster make? Is it likely to prevail? Explain.

8. Livingston purchased from Smits Truck Sales a truck which had serious mechanical problems. Livingston had received warranties as to future performance from Smits at the time of sale. Livingston learned of the truck's defects 8 months after the date of sale. Fifty months after the date of sale Livingston commenced an action for breach of warranty against Smits. Smits has asserted the statute of limitations as a defense since Livingston's action was not brought within 48 months of Smits's tender of delivery. Will Livingston's action be barred? Explain.

9. Amy Oakes planned to open a new restaurant, Barrister's Cafe, on July 1. She ordered a new commercial stove from Kidwell Supply for $1,800. She was promised delivery before the opening, on or before June 25. Oakes gave Kidwell a $250 deposit. On June 20, Kidwell told Oakes that the desired stove was backordered and would not be delivered before July 15. Oakes immediately canceled her order and purchased a similar stove from Chumley Supply, for $200 more. In the interim, Kidwell secured a comparable stove from another source and tendered delivery of it to Oakes on June 25. Oakes refused the stove. Was Oakes obligated to receive the stove? Would a court likely find Kidwell Supply liable for the return of her $250 deposit and $200 additional cost of cover? Explain.

10. Bell Industries entered into a contract to have Balloon Works create a special hot air balloon for them. The balloon was to have the Bell logo and be made with the Bell colors: red and black. The agreed price was $3,500. The president of Bell Industries, Harold Bell, was later seriously injured in an automobile accident. Upon reflection, he decided to have the company cancel the balloon order. Balloon Works claims they had already finished the balloon when the cancellation notice was received. Balloon Works has brought an action for the price plus $200 for advertising costs in their unsuccessful attempt to resell the balloon. Balloon Works would have made a $750 profit if there had not been a breach of contract. How much would a court likely award Balloon Works?

APPENDIX
Article 2A, Leases

Article 2A, leases, applies to the lease of goods. This appendix to Part VI is intended as a very short introduction to Article 2A. Our main goal is to help you distinguish a lease under Article 2A from a sale under Article 2 or security agreement under Article 9, discussed in Chapter 41, Security Interests in Personal Property.

As stated in Chapter 31, the purpose of Article 2A is to clear up some of the problems relating to the overlap of contracts for the sale of goods and for the lease of goods. Article 2A also attempts to distinguish between transactions which are leases and those which have lease characteristics but which are really more in the nature of a security interest governed by Article 9 of the UCC.

A "lease" is defined under Article 2A to mean "a transfer of the right to possession and use of goods for a term in return for consideration" [UCC §2A-103(j)]. Since a lease does not involve a transfer of title to the goods, a lease is *not* a sale. As such, both a sale on approval and a sale or return involve Article 2, not Article 2A, since they involve a transfer of title. A lease under Article 2A exists; it also covers any sublease.

Article 2A also does not apply to situations involving a retention or creation of a security interest [UCC §2A-103(j)]. It is necessary to consult Article 1 for the definition of a "security interest." As you will see in the examples below, a lease subject to Article 9 (is in essence a sale of a good subject to a security interest. To be considered a security interest lease subject to Article 9, not Article 2A, the following must be found:

1. The lease is not subject to termination by the lessee. This means a lessee has no ability to terminate the lease without the consent of the lessor.
2. The original term of the lease is equal to or greater than the remaining economic life of the goods. If a copier machine has an expected 4-year life, a lease for 4 or more years would be considered essentially a sale subject to a security interest.
3. The lessee is bound to renew the lease, has an option to renew the lease, or has an option to purchase the goods for no additional consideration or nominal additional consideration upon completion with the lease agreement. For example, the lessee can purchase the copier for only $1 dollar at the end of the lease.

Situations involving Article 9 are discussed in Chapter 41.

What would be an example of a lease subject to Article 2A? The comments to Article §2A-103 provide the following example involving the lease of a $1000 copier, with an estimated useful life of 36 months, for $100 a month. A lessee leases the copier machine on a month-to-month basis, with no obligation to renew beyond a month or to become the owner. If the lessee should lease the copier for the estimated useful life, the lessee will have paid $3600. Clearly the lessee has simply exercised a lease right to use the machine. An option to purchase the copier, if it exists, can be only for no additional or a nominal consideration.

Assuming a situation involving a lease of goods exists, Article 2A applies. Article 2A applies to the transactional elements of a lease. This means that it does not alter state or federal consumer protection statutes or cases. Article 2A seeks to allow significant freedom to the parties to structure their lease contract (like Article 2 seeks to allow for the sale of goods).

Article 2A closely follows Article 2. It imposes a presumption of good faith; provides relief for unconscionable conduct; recognizes firm offers; has similar risk of loss rules; provides for similar acceptance, rejection, and revocation of acceptance actions; includes the same Article 2 warranties (except no warranty of title); etc. One minor difference is that the Statute of Frauds applies to leases of $1000 or more, not $500.

The CPA exam does *not* cover Article 2A. On the CPA exam, a lease of a good is treated as a common law contract. Article 9, security interests, *is* covered on the CPA exam, but generally it does not include security lease situations.

The end-of-part problems serve three purposes. First, some require practical applications of legal knowledge to everyday situations. Second, they are summative, bringing together many of the issues treated individually in the chapters of a particular part. Third, the last question presents an ethical problem which, as in real life, may not have an unqualifiedly right or wrong solution. Rather, its goal is to prompt two questions: What would I do in this situation? What *should* I do in this situation?

1. A PRACTICAL PROBLEM

Mary Caulkins has just formed a small company, Tara Dolls. She has secured legal approval to manufacture and sell Scarlet O'Hara *Gone With the Wind* dolls.

Mary wants you to develop a very basic contract that she can use with her customers, who are mainly retail toy and hobby shops. She wants her form contract to be complete enough to protect her interests but not so thorough as to be intimidating or insulting to her customers.

Mary believes the following matters may be important to her and her customers:

- Her business is located at 1200 Main Street, Gadsen, Alabama, 35901.
- Mary has available only one doll, 22 inches tall.
- Prices are as follows:
  - 1–3 $25 each, shipping included
  - 4 or more $22, shipping included
- Mary does not want to be responsible if the dolls are damaged during transit.
- Mary plans to use Federal Express, second-day delivery service.

Mary also wants you to include any matter which you believe ought to be important to either her or her customers. Like Scarlet, Mary is not one to sit patiently, so please hurry with your answer.

2. A SUMMATIVE PROBLEM

Mary's new company, Tara Dolls, Inc., has enjoyed great success. However, success has not come without challenges. Mary has encountered a number of nagging problems which she is sure are nothing to worry about. However, just in case, she would like you to take a little time to read about them and advise her.

a. Mary has become concerned that her "satisfaction guaranteed" is being abused by retailers at Christmas time. Immediately after Christmas last year, the company received notices of return "on account of being unsatisfied" from five retailers. Mary immediately wrote to learn why they were dissatisfied. She received the following responses:

- From Kron's Toy Shop: "Two dolls were improperly glued."
- From Stoioff's Doll World: "We thought we could sell more Miss Scarlet dolls than we did."
- From DiMarzio & Fleming Toys: "Four dolls were damaged in transit. Believe guarantee overrides shipment contract terms."
- Wright's Toy Shoppe and Marvin's Dolls did not respond.

Mary decided to return money only to Kron's. In addition, Tara Dolls has dropped the "satisfaction guaranteed" warranty.

b. Tara Dolls introduced a talking Scarlet doll. Retailers were sent a cassette so they could hear what Scarlet was programmed to say. The clear, professionally developed tapes prompted many orders. Unfortunately, the layers of clothing on each Miss Scarlet doll somewhat muffled the clarity of the doll's speech. Some of Tara Doll's customers were dissatisfied with this problem and demanded their money, citing breach of warranty. Tara Dolls contends it never made any written warranty about clarity of speech.

c. Ochsner's Toy Store ordered five Miss Scarlet dolls with the green velvet dress. Because Tara Dolls were temporarily out of this doll, they notified Oshsner's that as an accommodation they were sending five of their most popular doll, Scarlet in white taffeta. The dolls were sent via a shipment contract. The dolls arrived damaged from transit and were refused by Ochsner.

d. Another customer, Dart's Doll Land, was also sent five white taffeta Scarlet dolls instead of green velvet. The order was due by, and received on, March 27. Although Dart's had accepted substituted orders in the past, it already had enough white taffeta dolls. As a result, Dart's notified Tara Dolls that they were returning the dolls and would order green dress dolls from another vendor, at $5 per doll more. Mary immediately notified Dart's that the green velvet dolls were back in stock and she was rushing five dolls to them. Dart's refused to accept these dolls and has sent Tara Dolls a bill for their additional $25 cover costs.

e. Crae Tate bought a Miss Scarlet doll from a toy store which has since gone out of business. Crae's son, Mitchell, found the doll and ate part of the dress. Mitchell got very ill and spent several days in the hospital. Tara Dolls denies responsibility, since: neither Crae nor Mitchell bought the doll from them; the Scarlet doll is clearly not food; and it fully met all industry standards in producing the Miss Scarlet dolls.

f. Another parent has brought a legal action against Tara Dolls for a similar injury. The child, Betty Schroeder, chewed on the dress while playing in the waiting room playhouse of her pediatrician. The doll was one of five different dolls provided by the doctor for children to play with while waiting to see her. Mary has responded that their Miss Scarlet doll was never marketed as a small child's doll, and neither Betty nor her parents have standing to sue Tara Dolls.

Mary is awaiting your advice. Unlike Rhett Butler's parting shot to Scarlet, Mary does care about what you have to say.

3. A SUMMATIVE PROBLEM

Blue Grass Manufacturing Company makes riding and push lawnmowers. Blue Grass has experienced some legal problems on which it needs your assistance. Please read the facts below and draft a memorandum stating your recommendations.

The Blue Grass "Colonel" riding lawnmower features a cassette deck with portable earphones and a cup holder. Blue Grass advertisements show a southern gentleman drinking a mint julep and singing along to a Frank Sinatra cassette while happily mowing his grass with "Colonel." A "Colonel" purchaser, Welby Culbertson, was reenacting the advertisement when he ran into a tree and was injured. Culbertson claims that Blue Grass is directly responsible for promoting drinking while mowing without warning of the dangers.

A purchaser of a regular gas mower, Don Savage, was operating his mower barefooted just after a rain. As Don was pushing the mower down an embankment he lost control and his right foot slid under the rear blade housing deflector shield and was badly mangled. Don has brought a legal action against Blue Grass alleging defective design of the rear shield. Blue Grass claims Don assumed the risk of injury by not wearing shoes and mowing on a wet embankment. In addition, it has produced evidence that a person wearing proper shoes would not have been injured.

Dvonch Garden Store wrote Blue Grass for a quote on five A10 mowers. On August 1, Blue Grass sent a written quote, good for 45 days, in which they agreed to sell five A10 mowers for $575 each FOB: seller's warehouse. Dvonch sent a written response on August 9, "In regard to your quote of August 1, $575 is acceptable for mowers to be sent FOB: Dvonch Garden Shop, cost of freight included. Blue Grass responded, "We are unable to process your order at your terms. Quote revoked." On September 1, Dvonch submitted an order duplicating the original Blue Grass quote, but the order was again rejected. Dvonch claims that Blue Grass has now effectively breached two different contracts.

Borst's Hardware Store ordered ten R25 mowers, payable within 10 days of delivery. Blue Grass sent a confirmation memo. Prior to shipment, an article appeared in a trade newspaper about Borst's severe cash flow problems. Borst's president acknowledged the company is at least 30 days late in paying accounts as a result of a warehouse fire but said that they hope to fully recover in the next quarter. Fearing it would not be paid, Blue Grass demanded cash at the time of delivery. Since it had customers waiting for three of the mowers, Borst's agreed. Borst's has since claimed breach of contract by Blue Grass alleging bad faith and lack of consideration for the change in terms.

The Meadows Country Club ordered by telephone four "Colonel" riding mowers painted in the club colors: Aqua and pink. Blue Grass inadvertently did not send a confirmation memo. When the mowers were tendered for delivery, the Club declined on account of unexpected financial problems and a lack of a written contract. The four aqua and pink "Colonels" were ultimately sold at a public auction for an $800 loss.

Lawn Products, Inc., ordered three "Colonels" for COD delivery. The mowers were shipped with an independent carrier. When the carrier tendered delivery, a Lawn Products employee noticed that two of the shipping crates were badly damaged. However, Lawn Products was not allowed to inspect the crates before payment. Lawn Products refused the most damaged crate. After payment, Lawn Products immediately inspected the other two mowers and notified Blue Grass that they were now rejecting the second mower damaged in transit. Blue Grass claims Lawn Products waived its rights of inspection and rejection with the COD order. In addition, Blue Grass contends that Lawn Products accepted all three mowers by accepting one mower, since the contract was not divisible.

A Blue Grass warehouse employee, Carl Ramsey, stole five "Colonels," intentionally put deep scratches into each one, and sold them to Garner's Supply. Garner knew that Blue Grass often sold defective mowers to employees at "seconds" prices rather than repaint them. Ramsey assured Garner that this was the case. Garner's publicly advertised and sold two of the mowers as factory seconds, "as is." The advertisement caught the attention of Blue Grass officials. Garner claims that he was a good faith purchaser for value and should prevail as to his three remaining mowers. As to the two mowers which it sold, Garner's claims it has no liability under the UCC to either Blue Grass or the purchasers.

Finally, Blue Grass agreed to sell twenty A10 mowers to Heseman's Garden Shop, FOB: Blue Grass loading dock #17. The mowers were ready for delivery to Heseman at the agreed upon time, place, and date. Heseman saw an old college friend on the way to the loading dock, stopped to talk, and was over an hour late in arriving at dock #17. In the interim, through no fault of Blue Grass, two mowers were run over by a negligent driver of an independent refuse truck. Heseman refused to accept or pay for those two mowers.

4. ETHICS AND THE LAW

As we have noted, the Uniform Commercial Code introduced many changes in the philosophy and substance of contract laws.

Where the common law was very particular about form, the UCC is much more relaxed. Common law judges were adamant that they did not make contracts. They would not enforce contracts made in haste without complete terms.

Some say that under UCC Article 2, modern judges make contracts for the parties. A court will enforce a sales contract if it finds that the parties intended to form a contract and the quantity term is known. The UCC's gap fillers supply missing terms which would have prevented enforcement at common law.

The UCC's critics have a strong point. Many of the gap fillers contain definitions using the words "reasonable" and its UCC variations ("seasonable," "commercially reasonable," and "unreasonable"). Indeed, they appear 95 times in Article 2, in 41 of its 102 sections.

The UCC's reliance upon "reasonable" and its variations is tied to the underlying duty of good faith. And, the flexibility gained by using the gap fillers and elastic definitions works well while relations between the contracting parties are positive.

Some legal commentators believe that the creators of the UCC created an appropriate law for commercial transactions but not for consumer sales. The ease of contract formation under Article 2, they believe, can be a trap for the unwary.

The UCC's reliance upon gap fillers, elastic definitions, and the concept of good faith can provide a facade behind which a knowledgeable party acting in bad faith can take advantage of the unsophisticated. After all, whether something is reasonable is ultimately a question of fact with the potential for an adverse jury decision. Also, the high cost of litigation often makes it difficult, if not impossible, to seek redress for bad faith by a party that is economically stronger.

As a result, consumer advocates have urged legislation which would override Article 2, like the Magnuson-Moss Warranty Act. Other examples already in place:

- Rules regarding the right to cancel for sales made in a home
- Prohibitions against false or misleading advertisements
- "Lemon" laws
- Postal regulations relating to the receipt of unsolicited products

Supporters of Article 2 believe these criticisms miss the mark. The common law's unreasonable emphasis upon form proved unworkable for the fast-paced, modern business world. The common law continues to provide even less protection for the unsophisticated than does the UCC. While Article 2 might have been made more responsive to the needs of consumers, it is, after all, primarily designed for commercial transactions. An additional comprehensive consumer sales law would add to the already existing confusion as to when Article 2 applies (sales of goods) versus when common law contract law still applies (primarily sales of services and land). When all was said and done, the less sophisticated individual would still be less sophisticated in dealing in the real world. Finally, most Article 2 contracts are fully executed to the reasonable satisfaction of both parties. As a result, UCC advocates say, "If it ain't broke, don't fix it."

You have just completed a study of Article 2 which included exposure to the Magnuson-Moss Warranty Act. You should be able to answer the questions which follow even if you have not yet studied common law contract law, found in Part II, or consumer protection legislation, found in Chapter 45.

a. Does Article 2 rely too heavily upon gap fillers, elastic definitions, and the presumption of good faith? Is your answer influenced by whether we are speaking of commercial or consumer transactions?

b. Does it seem appropriate to create a separate consumer sales law to operate in conjunction with Article 2 (covering commercial sales of goods) and the common law (covering sales of land and services)?

c. How do these issues tie into the issue of ethical behavior in contracting? Should different standards apply to different types of transactions?

VII

COMMERCIAL PAPER, CHECKS, AND DOCUMENTS OF TITLE

In Parts II and VI, we examined promises in the context of the formation and performance of contracts. Those contracts dealt primarily with the sale of services, goods, and real property.

In this part, we will again focus on promises which trigger contractual duties and liabilities. But this time, our subject covers only certain types of written promises to pay money which are assignable to other persons. They are called *negotiable instruments*. The most common of these are checks—like the ones in your checkbook—and notes—like the one you signed for your student loan.

The study of negotiable instruments differs from the study of contract law or sales law, as a problem involving a negotiable instrument is likely to require you to consider the fact pattern from two or three different perspectives. This part opener has been designed to introduce you to different perspectives by way of practical examples. Later in the chapters within this part you will learn in greater detail and application the various rules and approaches which make up the different perspectives by which one learns the law of negotiable instruments.

Chapter 39 describes other types of negotiable instruments under the Uniform Commercial Code (UCC) besides checks and notes: bills of lading (receipts issued by a carrier for goods it receives to be delivered to a third party); warehouse receipts (receipts issued by a warehouse for goods received for storage); and investment securities (corporate stocks or bonds). While there are some differences, their similarities far exceed their dissimilarities to checks and notes.

THE PARTIES AND THEIR EXPECTATIONS

On its face, your check indicates three parties are involved. When you write a check, you are the *drawer*. The check instructs your bank, called the *drawee,* to withdraw money from your account. The person to whom the check is made out and to whom the drawee is to pay the money is called the *payee.*

You may not have realized it but when you issue a check, you have—and you create—a whole series of legal expectations, rights, and duties. Your main expectation, for instance, is that the drawee will pay your check when it is presented. But what if the bank does not pay it? You have impliedly promised the payee that you stand ready to cover the amount of the check should the drawee for any reason fail to pay it.

The rationale for your duty to stand behind your checks is not hard to understand. Put yourself in a payee's position. If your paycheck bounces, you expect your employer to make it good. Thus, a check is really the drawer's promise that the payee will be paid. As we will see, a note is a direct promise of payment by the maker to the payee without the drawee's intervention.

TRANSFER AND INDORSEMENT

So long as we are dealing with the three parties to the check—the drawer, the drawee, and the payee—matters are really very simple. But with most checks, other people besides the three parties become involved. How does that happen?

Take a look at a check. Preceding the name of the payee appears "Pay to the order of" or a similar phrase. These are called *words of negotiability* and they indicate the payee may transfer or assign the check to another person. As we will see, these words alone do not make an *instrument* or written contract negotiable. Nonetheless, the presence of those words and of certain other information on the face of an instrument will quickly indicate its status.

Usually, a check is transferred by means of the payee's *indorsement*, his or her signature on the back of the check.

An indorsement, too, creates contractual rights and duties. Let's assume you cash your paycheck at a grocery store. You indorse it properly and receive cash for it. Unfortunately, your employer had insufficient funds in its account, and the check is returned, unpaid, to the grocery store. The grocery store can try to compel the drawer—your employer—to stand behind its promise to pay which the check represents. But it may also look to the check's *indorser*—you—for payment.

When you indorse a check, you impliedly *warrant* or promise that you will pay the check if it is dishonored. You cannot insist that the store look to your employer first. In fact, if the grocery collects from you, you have a right to recover from your employer.

For now, let's assume the grocery store decides to bring an action against your employer to compel payment of the check. Under the common law, as it was described in Chapter 11, a contract's assignee—the grocery—assumes precisely the same position as the assignor—you. Thus, your employer could assert any defense to payment against the grocery store that it has against you. If you falsified your time card to show more hours than you actually worked, the common law would recognize that as a valid defense to the employer's obligation. But UCC Article 3 radically alters this rule as to negotiable instruments.

DEFENSES AND NEGOTIABILITY

The UCC's change limits the defenses which a drawer can assert against certain transferees. The purpose of this change was to make negotiable instruments as freely transferable as possible.

The UCC categorizes defenses to payment of a negotiable instrument as either *real defenses* or *personal defenses*. "Real defense" might be translated best as "universal defense." Where a check is at issue, a drawer or an indorser may successfully raise a real defense—like forgery—against anyone attempting to compel payment. Thus where a drawer has a real defense, the UCC and the common law work the same way. As we will see in Chapter 37, there are only a few, carefully defined real defenses.

All other defenses are personal. A personal defense, like failure of consideration, is always good between the immediate parties to a transaction. For instance, your employee could defend your action for payment of the check by asserting that you did not put in the hours you claimed. But whether a drawer can assert a personal defense against someone else depends on that person's relationship to the check.

PROTECTED AND UNPROTECTED TRANSFEREES

By design, the UCC creates two distinct types of transferees, one of which is protected from the drawer's personal defenses and the other of which is not.

A protected transferee is one who takes a negotiable instrument in exchange for *value* (goods, services, or property) in good faith and which lacked notice of any defenses—real or personal—on the instrument. If the grocery store satisfied this test, your employer could not assert a personal defense to payment it could raise against you. Of course, your employer could then sue you for the amount it paid the grocery store on the check.

The UCC calls protected transferees of checks and notes *holders in due course*. A *holder* is a payee or transferee. "In due course" means "in the ordinary course of things." The test of protected transferee status defines when an instrument is transferred "in due course."

Limiting defenses against such transferees significantly improves transferability because it increases the chances that the holder in due course will be paid. And, that is the major reason the grocery store was willing to take your paycheck in the first place.

In fact, our system of doing business today would change drastically if protected transferee status was abolished. Huge cash transactions would become the rule instead of the exception. Transferees would insist on deep discounts to protect themselves against the possibility that the drawer might have a valid defense.

Protected transferee status is the key element which distinguishes negotiable instruments—whether we are talking about checks and notes or documents of title or investment securities—from any other type of assignable written contracts.

NEGOTIABILITY MYTHS

The emphasis on negotiability in this part sometimes leads to misconceptions about assignability in general and the value on nonnegotiable instruments. By way of a conclusion, let's look at the five most common misconceptions.

First, "If a document is not negotiable, it is not transferable." Wrong. Normally, an instrument—whether it is negotiable or not—may be transferred.

Second, "If an instrument is nonnegotiable, its holder will not be paid." False. Whether an instrument is negotiable or not has nothing to do with whether the obligor or drawer will pay it. A holder in due course will take little consideration from his status if the obligor will not pay and he lacks recourse against prior indorsers. The choice between a nonnegotiable instrument which will be paid and a negotiable instrument which will not is no choice at all.

Third, "The principles of the law of assignments do not apply to negotiable instruments." No. The general rule is that the holder of any instrument—negotiable or not—is subject to the obligor's defenses, whether the UCC would categorize them as real or personal. The UCC's exception to the rule occurs when a transferee who meets certain specific requirements acquires the instrument and with it protected status.

Fourth, "A transferee of a negotiable interest who does not have protected status cannot win an action against the drawer or obligor for payment." False. As under the common law, a transferee acquires whatever rights and duties his or her transferor had. If the transferor would have recovered from the obligor, the transferee should recover.

Fifth, "A person with protected transferee status is assured of satisfaction on the obligation." Satisfaction is never certain for anyone until the cash, goods, or securities are in hand. Perhaps baseball Hall-of-Famer Yogi Berra said it best: "The game isn't over 'til it's over."

KEY WORDS

drawee (817)
drawer (817)
holder (819)
holder in due course (819)
indorsement (818)
indorser (818)
negotiable instruments (817)

payee (817)
personal defenses (818)
real defenses (818)
value (819)
warrant (818)
words of negotiability (818)

Negotiability

This chapter introduces the concept of negotiability and shows how it applies to one type of negotiable instrument, *commercial paper*—checks, drafts, notes, and certificates of deposit. While we discuss this type of negotiable instruments only in this chapter and the next two, keep in mind that the principles of negotiability apply generally to all negotiable instruments, including documents of title and investment securities.

Commercial paper has a long history. About 800 years ago, merchants in Genoa, Florence, and Venice began to trade with one another. At that time, the three cities were really independent countries. Travel between them was not easy. Carrying money between them was positively dangerous. To solve this problem, the merchants devised a system of documents which represented money or goods and could change hands almost as freely as what they represented.

By the 1690s, when paper money first appeared in the West, notes and drafts, the principal types of commercial paper, were in common use throughout Europe. (In fact, governments got the idea for paper money from commercial paper.) These documents profoundly influenced the development of every aspect of the Western economy. Banking, for instance, gained its major impetus from the exchange of notes.

What made the commercial paper system work was a merchant's ability to examine a document and to evaluate it without having to refer to anything else. That emphasis on what the instrument itself says has made this system of exchange function even across international boundaries since the Middle Ages.

THE NECESSARY TERMS

The key to the commercial paper system is *negotiability*, or transferability. The concept of negotiability is above all one of form. By creating common expectations and shared definitions among businesspersons, adherence to form avoids uncertainty and confusion. We will deal with the concept of form throughout this chapter.

The Uniform Commercial Code (UCC) uses the word "transfer," instead of "assign," to describe how negotiable instruments change hands. The UCC uses "negotiate" to describe the usual process of transferring by which the transferee becomes a *holder*, a person in possession of a negotiable instrument. As the introduction to Part VII indicates, a *holder in due course* is a holder who has protected transferee status. He or she is protected by law from certain defenses the obligor has against the original payee.

The UCC categorizes commercial paper (Articles 3 and 4), documents of title (Article 7), and investment securities (Article 8) according to whether they are *nonnegotiable* or negotiable. Articles 3, 4, 7, and 8 apply to both negotiable and nonnegotiable instruments, but they do not deal with nontransferable contracts. Figure 36.1 illustrates the UCC's coverage schematically, while Figure 36.2 summarizes the differences between nonnegotiable and negotiable instruments.

TYPES OF COMMERCIAL PAPER

There are four types of commercial paper: notes, certificates of deposit, drafts, and checks [UCC §3-104(2)].

Promissory Notes and Certificates of Deposit

A *note*, or "promissory note," is a maker's unconditional promise to pay a certain sum on a fixed date. A *maker*, the obligor in the law of assignments, makes or *issues* the instrument. The *payee* or obligee is the party to whom the instrument is made payable. Notes are the in-

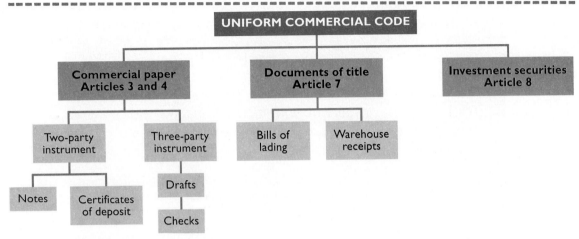

Figure 36.1 Negotiable Instruments Under the UCC.

struments most commonly used when a seller extends credit to a buyer on the purchase of goods or services [UCC §3-104(2)].

Any person may be a maker or a payee of a note. The UCC defines *person* as including a corporation, a government unit, a business, an individual, or an agent. If the instrument does not name a payee, the instrument is payable to the *bearer*, the person possessing the instru-ment [UCC §3-111(c)]. (The implications of an instrument payable to bearer are discussed later in this chapter.) Figure 36.3 illustrates a typical note.

A *certificate of deposit (CD)* is a promissory note or an acknowledgment of receipt from a bank (the maker) to a customer (the payee). A CD usually pays a fixed rate of interest and is redeemable or *payable* on a fixed date.

	NONNEGOTIABLE INSTRUMENT	NEGOTIABLE INSTRUMENT
Legal instrument?	Yes	Yes
Does type of instrument assure that it will be paid?	No	No
Can instrument be transferred to another?	Usually	Usually
Is protected transferee status possible?	No	Yes
Is instrument readily accepted in commercial trade?	Generally not	Yes

Figure 36.2 Nonnegotiable and Negotiable Instruments Compared.

December 4, 1994

Two years after date, I promise to pay to the order of
Lori Elliott TWO THOUSAND AND NO/100 DOLLARS with
interest at 8% compounded annually until fully paid.
This note arises out of the sale of a 1988 Honda Accord.

Michelle Gray
Michelle Gray

Figure 36.3 A Typical Note.
This simple promissory note contains all the elements required for negotiability.

Notes and CDs are called *two-party instruments* because only two parties are required to create them—the maker and the payee. Notes and CDs often change hands at a *discount*, or reduction, from their face value. The amount of the discount varies depending on when an instrument is due, the prevailing interest rates, the creditworthiness of the maker, and other similar factors.

Drafts and Checks

Drafts are called *three-party instruments* because three parties are required to create them. The person writing a draft, the *drawer*, issues or *draws* an instrument which unconditionally orders someone, the *drawee*, to pay a sum to the payee. Thus, the third party to a draft, the drawee, is the party to whom the payee initially looks for its payment. Figure 36.4 is a typical draft.

Checks are drafts whose drawee is a bank. A check, then, represents the drawer's order to a bank to pay a sum from the drawer's account to the payee. It is no exaggeration to say that our mercantile system operates by means of

checks. Most individuals and virtually all businesses pay and receive payments by check. Figure 36.5 is a typical check.

While drafts and checks are three-party instruments, the three parties do not all have to be different. The drawer and the drawee may be the same person or business. For instance, a bank (the drawer) draws a cashier's check upon itself (the drawee). The drawer or drawee may be the payee. Suppose Sarah writes a check to herself. She is both the drawer and the payee. Or, suppose her checking account and car loan are at the same bank, so she writes a check to her bank for her monthly car payment. The bank is both the drawee and the payee.

A draft does not have to name a payee. It may be payable to the bearer like a check drawn to "cash."

Demand and time drafts. Drafts come in two types: demand drafts and time drafts. The payee is supposed to present a *demand draft* to the drawee for payment "on sight" or on "presentment." Checks are a form of demand draft.

As a practical matter, a payee may cash or deposit a check without presenting it to the

To: Stuart Morse
       Madison, Wisconsin   July 28, 1994

Pay to the order of: Westbury Products Company $1,500.00
Fifteen hundred and no/100 dollars.
On October 9, 1995.

Pat Almdale
Pat Almdale

Figure 36.4 Draft.
A time draft is depicted.

drawer's bank. The payee's bank forwards the check to the drawee bank for payment. The Federal Reserve Board imposes specific federal depository rules, which are discussed in Chapter 39.

Time drafts are not payable until a specified date. So, they are used where the maker wants the effect of a note—that is, the instrument is payable in the future—but also wants the instrument to be paid by another party on the

WINSTON SMITH
13 St. Martins Street
Erewhon, Oceania 99999
Tel. (911) 543-2198

March 13 19 *94*   1952
                                                           1234156
                                                              013

Pay to the
Order of *Tom Parsons*   *600* $\frac{00}{100}$

— *Six hundred* —   Dollars

(VOID) **EREWHON TRUST COMPANY**
Erewhon, Oceania 99999

For *Rent*   *Winston Smith*

⑆421040471⑆ 0702⑈4205⑈4⑈ 1952

Figure 36.5 A Typical Check.
Checks are a form of draft. The name, address, and phone number on top are not legally necessary for negotiability, but without that information it is hard to cash a check anywhere except the drawee bank.

maker's account. Time drafts are especially useful when the drawee is located in a city different from the drawer.

Time drafts must be presented to the drawee for acceptance (discussed below), since they are payable at a fixed time following acceptance or "after sight." For example, a draft payable "45 days after sight" is payable 45 days after the holder presents the draft to the drawee for acceptance.

Acceptance. *Acceptance* occurs when the drawee states by means of a signed notation on the draft that it will honor the draft upon presentment for payment [UCC §3-410(1)]. Acceptance, thus, is a devise which adds an assurance to the payee that the draft will be paid when it is presented.

Consider, for example, the *certified check*. A bank certifies a check—usually by stamping it or embossing it—when it accepts the check for later payment. By certifying the check, the bank agrees to pay the check according to its terms at the time of acceptance. Either the *holder*—the person possessing a negotiable instrument—or the drawer may have a check certified. In real estate transactions, the seller quite commonly requires the purchaser's consideration to be in the form of a certified check to assure the seller that the bank will pay it.

IMPORTANCE OF NEGOTIABILITY

The part opener discussed the importance of negotiability. In brief, for commercial paper to more freely pass in trade, the UCC provides for protected holder status against personal defenses the maker or drawer may have in regard to the instrument. This protected holder status is called holder in due course. To gain this protected status requires several things, including the need for the commercial paper instrument to be negotiable. The remainder of this chapter discusses what is required to have negotiable paper.

There are two things which you should keep in the back of your mind while reading this chapter. First, the fact that an instrument is negotiable does not assure payment. Thousands of negotiable checks "bounce" every day in the United States. The fact that an instrument is nonnegotiable means that there can never be a holder in due course. For example, a nonnegotiable $10 IOU which is properly paid is preferable over a $10 negotiable check which bounces. Second, as you will see in the next chapter, holder in due course status does not prevent a maker or drawer from raising real defenses to the instrument.

NEGOTIABILITY AND FORM

Simply designating a document a note or a draft does not make it negotiable. Negotiability is strictly a matter of form. Either it exists on the instrument or it does not. To be a *negotiable instrument*, it must:

- Be written
- Be signed by the maker or drawer
- Contain an unconditional promise or order to pay a certain sum in money and no other promise, order, obligation, or power given by the maker or the drawer except those specifically authorized by the UCC
- Be payable on demand or at a definite time
- Be payable to order or bearer [UCC §3-104]

Someone looking at a document must be able to see that it satisfies these requirements. It is important to note that in the case of drafts and most negotiable notes, negotiability is determined by what appears on the face of the instrument. In these instances, what appears on the back does not affect negotiability.

The following sections examine the criteria for negotiability. As you study them, keep in mind why it is important for a check or note to be negotiable. If it is not negotiable, a subsequent transferee cannot become a holder or a holder in due course and obtain the protections of that status. Also, if presented with a non-negotiable instrument, a potential transferee may decide not to take it simply because of the difficulties in transferring it.

Writing

A negotiable instrument must be in writing. There is no such thing as an oral negotiable instrument.

The UCC defines "writing" as including printing, typewriting, or "any other intentional reduction to tangible form" [UCC §1-201(46)]. Courts have found that almost anything which has a degree of permanence and is on an easily movable substance has a tangible form. For example, newspapers sometimes carry pictures of someone writing the Internal Revenue Service a check on the shirt off his back for the taxes he owes. In theory, this form is legal. A check written on a block of ice would not have sufficient permanence, while one written on a wall would be too permanent.

Signed by the Maker or Drawer

No person is liable on an instrument unless his or her signature appears on it [UCC §3-401(1)].

A *signature* may be any name, including a trade or assumed name, or any word or mark used instead of a handwritten signature [UCC §3-401 (2)]. So, Marcia will be liable on a note she signed "X" if "X" represents her authorized signature. An agent may sign on behalf of a principal, and his or her signature will be treated as the principal's so long as it is clear that the agent is signing in a representative capacity. In the next case, a corporation attempted to avoid liability on a note by claiming that its name typed above its agents' signatures was not its signature.

First Security Bank of Brookfield v. Fastwich, Inc.

612 S.W.2d 799 (Mo. Ct. App. 1981)

FACTS   First Security Bank loaned Fastwich $10,000, evidenced by a promissory note. In the upper left corner of the note, immediately preceding the payment schedule, appeared the typewritten words, "Fastwich, Inc." In the lower right corner appeared

[typed] FASTWICH, INC.

/signed/ John J. Smith II	/s/ Carolyn Smith
/s/ Gary D. Smith	/s/ Cheryl J. Smith

The Smiths were Fastwich's officers and directors. The corporation's officers were authorized to borrow money on its behalf and to execute evidence of its indebtedness. Fastwich defaulted on the note. Fastwich claimed that it was not liable on the note because the bank failed to show that its signature was valid. The trial court entered judgment for the bank.

ISSUE   Did Fastwich's signature appear on the note?

DECISION   Yes. Affirmed. The burden of establishing a signature rests on the party claiming under it [UCC §3-307]. However, a signature is presumed to be genuine or authorized except where the action is to enforce the obligation of someone who has died or become incompetent. Until the defendant introduces evidence which would support a finding that the signature is forged or unauthorized, the plaintiff is not required to prove its authenticity. Forged or unauthorized signatures are very uncommon, and normally any evidence casting doubt on a signature is within the defendant's control. Here, the UCC permits typewritten signatures, and Fastwich did not introduce any evidence questioning the validity of its signature.

A maker's or drawer's signature does not have to appear in any particular place so long as it is on the front of the instrument. However, if its placement is ambiguous, a court will consider it an indorsement by the payee or a subsequent holder. (Indorsements are discussed in Chapter 37.) If Cheryl, as drawer, signs her bank check beneath the designated signature line instead of on it, she has signed a negotiable instrument. If the check was Steve's, and Cheryl's signature appeared below his, her signature's purpose is ambiguous.

It follows that a negotiable instrument need not be *subscribed*, that is, signed at its end. Suppose an instrument in John's handwriting read, "I, John Doe, promise to pay Mary Doe . . ." John's name in the text is an effective signature, even though he never signs at the end of the text. But, suppose the note read, "I promise to pay Mary Doe. . ." and no name was subscribed. The maker is not liable if his name does not appear anywhere on the face of a negotiable instrument.

Unconditional Promise or Order to Pay

To ensure that it may be freely bought and sold, a negotiable instrument "must contain an unconditional promise or order . . . to pay . . . , and no other promise, order, obligation or power . . . except as authorized [in the UCC]" [UCC §3-104(1)(b)].

The goal of the "unconditional promise or order to pay" requirement and the "sum certain" requirement (discussed below) is to make the value of an instrument plain on its face. Suppose that Angela wrote at the bottom of her check to a clothing store, "for blouse." That statement of consideration does not affect the check's negotiability because it does not alter the check's unconditional promise to pay [UCC §3-105(1)(b)]. In fact, most checks have a line on them for this purpose.

But, suppose Angela wrote, "Payment conditioned on blouse fitting after washing." That statement would destroy the check's negotiability because it would require a potential transferee to contact Angela to verify the blouse's fit. As a result, a potential transferee may be much less willing to acquire this check. Even if a check's negotiability is destroyed by a condition or the like, it is important to remember that a nonnegotiable instrument usually represents the issuer's or maker's enforceable contractual obligation.

The UCC *does* permit negotiable instruments to contain conditions and additional terms which either do not affect the maker's unconditional obligation or actually enhance the holder's ability to collect. These conditions and terms are discussed below.

Reference to another agreement. A negotiable instrument may refer to another agreement so long as the instrument itself is not controlled by the other document [UCC §3-105(1)(c)]. Put another way, a negotiable instrument which states all its terms on its face may refer to another agreement. For example, notes often state, "This note is secured by a mortgage between the same parties of this same date." The mortgage only secures the loan evidenced by the note. Therefore, it is not necessary to refer to the mortgage for additional or modified terms

[UCC §3-105(1)(e)]. However, suppose the note stated, "This instrument is subject to the same terms and conditions as the note signed by the same parties on January 20, 1991." Now it is nonnegotiable, because a potential holder would have to refer to another document to learn what the terms and conditions were.

Indication of a particular account, fund, or source. The UCC permits a reference to a particular account, fund, or source on a negotiable instrument only if it is an internal accounting memorandum. If a notation limits payment to a particular account, fund, or source, the limitation destroys negotiability because a potential holder has no way of knowing whether the source contains sufficient funds to pay the instrument [UCC §§3-105(1)(f) and (2)(b)]. For example, a notation, "Charge to travel account" does not restrict payment of the obligation to that account. By contrast, "Pay only from travel account" limits the source of funds available for payment and makes the instrument nonnegotiable.

Payment of commercial paper issued by government entities may be limited to particular sources, an exception to the UCC's particular fund rule. The government's taxing powers are a sufficient guarantee of payment [UCC §3-105(1)(g)].

The UCC also permits partnerships to limit the assets available to pay a negotiable instrument solely to partnership assets [UC §3-105(1)(h)]. For example, a valid clause might read, "This note is payable out of the partnership assets of the Virginia & Leonard partnership only."

Collateral. A negotiable instrument may contain a promise to maintain or protect or provide additional collateral [UCC §3-112(1)(c)]. *Collateral* is property designated as security for a loan. Such provisions obviously benefit the holder because they further assure payment. Under a clause of this type, if stock was the collateral, a holder could call for additional collateral if the stock's value declined.

A Sum Certain in Money

A negotiable instrument must state on its face the "sum certain in money" that the maker or issuer has promised to pay or ordered paid [UCC §3-104]. These four words express two requirements. First, the amount to be paid on the note must be reasonably clear from its face. And, second, the amount must be stated solely in terms of currency.

The amount requirement. In essence, the amount requirement means that the principal amount of a negotiable instrument must be clearly stated (e.g., "$60,000"). However, the note may provide for certain additions to or deductions from the principal amount which a potential transferee can calculate mechanically.

Article 3 provides that a sum is certain even though it is to be paid with one of the following:

- Stated interest or in stated installments
- Stated different rates of interest before and after default or before or after a specified date
- A stated discount or addition if paid before or after the date fixed for payment
- Exchange into a foreign currency or less exchange, whether at a fixed rate or at the current rate.
- Collection costs or attorney's fees or both on default [UCC §3-106]

These provisions do not affect the obligation to pay the instrument's face value. In fact, permitting collection costs and attorney's fees, for instance, to be calculated when they are incurred benefits the holder and enhances the instrument's value by further securing payment. Perhaps the sum certain requirement might be better stated as forbidding uncertainty as to amount where that uncertainty would work to the holder's disadvantage.

Here's what the amount requirement means in practice. Assume that a note evidences a $10,000 debt. It would be valid even if it called for 9 percent interest per annum before default and 11 percent after default. If the note specified interest at the current rate,'' it probably would be nonnegotiable, because the holder would have to determine the current rate to which the parties were referring.

The amount requirement is critical to the negotiability of notes because they typically are sold at a discount, or less than face value. Persons who buy these instruments do so because they want to make a profit. They cannot make a profit by paying the amount the maker ultimately will pay. If the sum the maker is to pay is not certain, potential transferees cannot readily calculate what to pay for a note.

The money requirement. The sum certain must be stated in terms of "money." The money need not be U.S. currency. A note payable in Swiss francs or Swedish kroners would be negotiable [UCC §3-107(2)].

The obligation must be stated purely in terms of money. An obligation stated in terms of money plus services or property, like $100 and my business law text,'' is not negotiable. The payee may know the book's value, but what about a subsequent holder who has never seen it? Remember: The goal is to eliminate valuation problems.

Payable Upon Demand or at a Definite Time

A negotiable instrument must "be payable upon demand or at a definite time" [UCC §3-104(1)(c)]. However, the UCC permits the use of mechanisms to accelerate or extend the time when a note is due and to resolve problems in dating instruments.

Prepayment and acceleration clauses. A *prepayment clause* allows the maker to pay a note earlier than its due date. An *acceleration clause* permits the holder to call for full payment before the prescribed date. The UCC permits prepayment and acceleration clauses so long as the instrument is payable on a fixed day if prepayment or acceleration does not occur.

Acceleration may occur in only two instances. First, the note may permit acceleration if a specified contingency occurs. A clause of this type might read, "Acceleration may occur upon the maker falling two months behind in installment payments." Second, acceleration may occur when the holder "deems himself to be insecure."* However, the holder may accelerate only if he believes in good faith that the prospect of payment is impaired [UCC §1-208]. Assume that the holder of a note learns that its maker is seriously considering filing for bankruptcy. The holder could accelerate in good faith. We will discuss this mechanism in more detail below.

The UCC prohibits a reference in a negotiable instrument to a separate agreement if the other agreement affects the maker or issuer's obligation to pay. However, a reference to another document to determine whether prepayment or acceleration terms apply to a note does not destroy negotiability because these clauses do not affect the maker's obligation to pay.

Extension of time by the holder. A holder always has the right to extend the time for payment, whether or not the instrument contains a clause to this effect. An extension does not impair negotiability or the value of the instrument, since the holder decides whether to grant it.

The holder must act in good faith in extending the period for payment. She may extend the time when the obligor is ready and willing to pay. Suppose Brenda holds Kyle's note. It carries an interest rate of 15 percent. On the due date, Kyle's bank is charging 10 percent for similar loans. Brenda cannot extend if, on the due date, Kyle wants to pay the note. If the rule were otherwise, by extending the note Brenda could lock Kyle into paying a higher rate of interest on the note than he would have to pay the bank. An arbitrary extension of time termi-

---

* How the holder may become insecure and the remedies Article 2 offers in this circumstance were discussed in Chapters 12 and 33.

nates the holder's right to interest during the extension.

Another important qualification of the holder's right to extend the time for payment applies to *accommodation parties* or *sureties*—parties who by cosigning agree to pay an instrument if the maker or issuer does not. An extension may discharge accommodation parties unless the holder obtains their consent to it. However, what happens if the lender is very slow to enforce the debt against the accommodation party and in the process greatly increases the amount of interest due on the note? The next distinguishes between an extension and a mere delay.

Farmers State Bank, Grafton v. Huebner

475 N.W.2d 640 (Iowa App. 1991)

FACTS Huebner and Walk, both farmers, were close friends. Walk needed to renew a loan, but the Farmers State Bank demanded additional security and an accommodation party. Huebner agreed to be the accommodation party and signed the promissory note of $41,500 at 14.5 percent interest on December 1983. From December 1983 to June 1985, Walk made small payments toward interest and principal, but by 1989 he owed over $70,620 including over $33,000 in interest. He settled with Farmers Bank by deeding his farm in lieu of foreclosure in November 1989. Farmers sued Huebner as accommodation party, and the trial court found him liable for the full amount of $70,620. Huebner, on appeal, argued that by delaying the enforcement of the note, Farmers Bank had waived its right to his guarantee of the loan.

ISSUE Does the delay in the enforcement of a promissory note discharge an accommodation party?

DECISION No. Affirmed. The general rule of law is that an agreement between the maker and the payee to extend time for payment discharges an accommodation party who has not consented. However, the holder of the note has the right to release any party or postpone the time of payment without impairing its right to enforce the obligation.

The *Farmers Bank* case illustrates a common dilemma for many lenders in the agricultural and oil-producing regions of the United States in the mid-1980s. Due to a virtual depression in these two important sectors of the economy, many farmers and small oil and gas producers could not meet their obligations. Many banks waited as long as possible by both extending loans and waiting to enforce the debt, hoping for economic conditions to improve.

Unfortunately, improvement did not come quickly enough and the billions of dollars in bad debts that accrued helped cause the now infamous failure of thousands of banks and S & L's in that decade. Today much stricter government regulations would not allow such a delay.

Extension of time by the maker or drawer. An extension of time by the maker or drawer is essentially the opposite of an acceleration clause. The UCC permits it so long as the instrument provides an ultimate time at which the instrument is due.

Contingency clauses. The UCC requires that a time instrument be payable at a certain point in the future. However, if the time for payment is contingent, the instrument is nonnegotiable [UCC §3-109(2)]. Thus, a note payable "upon Jerry Baylor's death" is nonnegotiable. The parties might accomplish their purpose—make the note payable on Baylor's death—by stating that the note is payable on, say, May 1, 2001, and including a clause accelerating the time for payment on Baylor's death. That alteration would make the note negotiable because the note would now state an ultimate date for payment.

Antedated, postdated, and undated instruments. The fact that a demand instrument is undated, antedated or postdated does not affect its negotiability [UCC §3-114]. A postdated check is negotiable, but it is not payable on demand until the stated date. For example, a check written on May 5, 1990, which is dated May 15, 1990, is not payable until May 15.

The date on an instrument is presumed to be correct [UCC §3-114(3)]. This presumption may be important in deciding whether a demand instrument has become *stale*, that is, whether too much time has passed before someone tries to cash it. Under the UCC, a check is stale after 30 days. The purpose of the staleness rule is to put a potential purchaser on notice that the instrument may be irregular. As Chapter 37 indicates, accepting a stale instrument may mean that a holder does not qualify for holder in due course status, but staleness does not relieve the maker's obligation.

The presumption that an instrument's date is correct is not absolute. For instance, people commonly put the preceding year on checks written in January. A similar mistake on a check presented for payment in July is less probable, and a bank will treat it as stale.

An undated instrument which sets no time for payment is treated as a demand instrument. But an undated time instrument payable for a fixed period "after date" is not negotiable, since the time of payment is uncertain. However, an undated instrument, if it is lost, can be negotiated years into the future, since the date put on it by a subsequent holder is presumed to be correct. That is what happened in the next case.

M.G. Sales, Inc. v. Chemical Bank

554 N.Y.S.2d 863 (A.D. 1 Dept. 1990)

FACTS   In November 1981, Gardner, as president of M.G. Sales, Inc., made out two $6000 checks drawn on the company's account at Chemical Bank. The two checks were in the form of bearer paper, since they were payable to Gardner and endorsed by him. Both checks were later lost. Neither check was dated. Gardner obtained a stop payment order that lasted for 6 months but failed to renew it. In January and February 1983, Fried found and dated both checks and cashed them at the Chemical Bank. Gardner argued that the checks could not be negotiated, and therefore his account was not liable, since he had not dated them. Chemical Bank won at the trial level.

ISSUE   Were the checks negotiable even though they were undated?

DECISION   Yes. Affirmed. The negotiability of an instrument is not affected even if it is undated, antedated, or postdated. Moreover, the date on it is presumed correct. Any fraud, such as in this case, does not affect its negotiability, but can be a defense to its payment. Although the checks looked torn and it was possible that one of the dates had been altered, it still could be assumed that the dates were correct.

Words of Negotiability

To be negotiable, an instrument must be "payable to order or to bearer" [UCC §3-104(1)(d)]. The presence of these "words of negotiability" quickly reveals that the drawer or maker intended that his or her promise to pay should extend to the initial payee and any subsequent transferees. For instance, "Pay Janet Jackson" shows an intent to limit the maker's or drawer's liability to Jackson alone, and so the instrument is not negotiable.

If an instrument lacks only words of negotiability and its terms do not forbid transfer, Article 3 still applies to it. In other words, it is transferable but nonnegotiable, which means no transferee can become a holder in due course as to it.

Payable to order. An instrument is negotiable if it states, "Pay to the order of" followed by the payee's name. These words of negotiability mean that the instrument is payable to the named payee or her transferee. Such an instrument is called *order paper* and can be either a note or a draft.

A negotiable instrument does not have to use the precise words "pay to the order" to be order paper. The following would also be acceptable:

- "Pay to Janet Jackson or her order"
- "Pay to Janet Jackson or her assigns"

The phrase "pay to the order" refers to the transferability of the instrument, not to whom it is to be paid. It means that an indorsement is necessary to negotiate the draft or note. For example, the payee line on a check reads, "Pay to the order of Felicia Chase." She must indorse the check on its back in order to cash it, whether with a bank or a storekeeper.

Payable to bearer. *Bearer paper* is a negotiable instrument which is payable to the *bearer*, the person who has physical possession of—but not necessarily legal title to—the instrument. An instrument is bearer paper when it states it is payable:

- To "bearer" or "to the order of bearer"
- To "Janet Jackson or bearer"
- To "cash" or "to the order of cash"

Almost any indication which does not designate a specific payee creates bearer paper.

Bearer paper needs on indorsement in order to be negotiated because it is not payable to a particular party. Under the UCC, a holder need only deliver the instrument to be entitled to payment. As a practical matter, however, banks often require that checks payable to bearer or to cash be indorsed by the holder. As Chapter 38 indicates, the bank wants the indorsement because it creates a separate contract between the indorser and the bank which, if the check is not paid, gives the bank a right to look to the indorser for reimbursement.

INCOMPLETE AND AMBIGUOUS INSTRUMENTS

Like any other documents, negotiable instruments can be incomplete or ambiguous. And, as with incomplete or ambiguous sales contracts, the UCC provides rules for their completion and interpretation.

Completing Instruments

An incomplete instrument cannot be enforced until it has been completed. A maker or drawer may complete the document or authorize its completion. For example, a signed check with nothing written following the words "pay to the order of" is incomplete and nonnegotiable because it is not payable to anyone, even a bearer [UCC §3-115(1)]. However, suppose that a contractor needs some special plumbing supplies. He gives an employee a signed check but leaves the payee designation blank so that the employee can insert a vendor's name when he locates the plumbing supplies. When the employee does so, the check is negotiable. (The employer also bears the risk that the employee will complete the check in an unauthorized manner, as we will see in Chapter 38.)

Rules of Interpretation

Draft or Note? A holder of a draft looks for payment first to the drawee and then to the drawer. A holder of a note looks first to the maker. If there is some doubt as to whether an instrument is a draft or a note, the holder may treat it as either [UCC §3-118(a)]. Suppose an instrument states:

> To John Doe:
> On demand I promise to pay, to the order of Julie Smith, $1000.
> /s/ Richard Roe

The instrument's holder may treat it as a draft and seek payment from Doe or as a note and seek payment from Roe.

Forms of writing. Several types of writing may appear on a single instrument, and some may conflict with others. In that case, handwritten terms control over typewritten and printed terms, while typewritten terms control over printed. So, if a note contains a typed provision calling for 12 percent interest, but someone has written in 8 percent, the handwritten figure would control.

Words and figures. Where words and figures conflict, words control over figures because generally a maker will write words with more care than figures. Only when the words are ambiguous do the figures control [UCC §3-118(c)]. If a check's dollar amount seems to say "$1000" but the written words state "Ten and no/100 dollars," the latter controls. However, if the dollar amount on the check reads "$100.50," but the written words say "One Hundred and fifty," the numbers will control, since the words are ambiguous.

Parol evidence. The law generally presumes that a written contract embodies the parties' full agreement. As discussed in Chapter 10, the purpose of the *parol evidence rule* is to bar evidence of prior or contemporaneous agreements to contradict the terms of the writing.

Often, a party contends that an agreement included a promise or condition which does not appear on the face of the negotiable instrument. Most courts, like the one in the next case, have held that parol evidence that alters the duty of the maker or drawer is not admissible.

Evenson v. Hlebechuk

305 N.W.2d 13 (N.D. 1981)

FACTS   The Hlebechuks employed Evenson to sell an apartment complex. He located a purchaser, Jacobson, who gave the Hlebechuks a down payment of $12,500. The Hlebechuks agreed to loan Jacobson $237,500 (secured by a mortgage on the complex) for 20 years, with a balloon payment due 2 years after purchase. However, Jacobson could extend payment of the balloon for an additional 2 years. When the sale was completed the Hlebechuks executed a promissory note for $12,500 to Evenson for his services. The note provided four possible times for payment: (1) the note could be paid on the due date, (2) the note could be prepaid at any time, (3) Evenson could accelerate if Jacobson rendered full performance, or (4) the Hlebechuks could extend payment for 2 years should Jacobson exercise his option to extend. Jacobson failed to make any payments and ultimately deeded the complex back to the Hlebechuks. Evenson brought suit to enforce the note. The Hlebechuks claimed that it became payable only if Jacobson made the balloon payment. The trial court entered summary judgment for Evenson.

ISSUE   Should the trial court have heard parol evidence of a condition precedent—the balloon payment—to the payment of the note?

DECISION   No. Affirmed. Parol evidence is admissible to prove a condition to the legal effectiveness of a written agreement *if* the condition does not contradict the express terms of the written agreement. Here, the condition precedent would make the unconditional promissory note unenforceable. It is so inconsistent with the note that it would have to be in writing. The note did more than just establish a definite due date, as all negotiable instruments must. It appears to cover all eventualities the parties could think of. Had they intended the balloon payment to be a condition precedent, they could easily have included it in the note.

CONCLUSION

In the last case, Evenson did not care whether the note was negotiable or not. The case gives no indication as to whether he had tried to sell the note. All Evenson was concerned about was getting paid. Had Evenson tried to sell the Hlebechuks' note, the potential transferee's primary concern also would be the likelihood of payment. Thus, the first lesson about negotiability is that it is considerably less important to all concerned than the likelihood of payment.

The second lesson is that negotiability is primarily the concern of the transferee. The rules we have examined in this chapter are designed to identify the instrument's character for the transferee. As a practical matter, if you approach a negotiable instruments problem from the perspective of what assurances of transferability a transferee would want, you will not go far wrong.

The third lesson is one which will become clearer in the next chapter. Although commercial paper is often referred to as a "cash substitute," notes and drafts demand a level of sophistication and an attention to detail which cash does not. They are cash substitutes only for those with sufficient knowledge of the law to protect themselves as drawer, maker, payee, or transferee.

In the next chapter, we will examine holders in due course, the transferees who take instruments free of most of the obligor's defenses to the underlying obligation. As you read that chapter, keep in mind the fourth major lesson of negotiability: Being free of an obligor's contractual defenses is important primarily when the obligor wishes to assert them and one transferee wants to negotiate the instrument to another.

A NOTE TO FUTURE CPA CANDIDATES

The 1990 amendments to Articles 3 and 4 were not being tested on the CPA exam at the time of the Fourth Edition. The appendix at the end of this chapter sets forth the most significant of the minor changes should they be included on the exam in future years. Documents of title are now tested, if at all, in association with bailments in the property section of the CPA exam.

It is important for you to understand the significance of an instrument being negotiable: it permits there to be a holder with protected status, a holder in due course. You should be familiar with Figure 36-2, which compares non-negotiable and negotiable instruments.

Article 3 covers four types of commercial paper: drafts (including trade acceptances), checks, notes, and certificates of deposits. Drafts and checks are three-party instruments which have a drawer, drawee, and payee. (For an instrument to qualify as a check it must be payable on demand.) Promissory notes and certificates of deposits are two-party instruments which have a maker and payee.

To be negotiable, an instrument must:

- *Be in writing.* Remember that the writing must have a "tangible form" with a "degree of permanence."
- *Be signed by the maker or drawer.* An "X" would suffice if with intent as a signature. A signature can occur anywhere on the face of the instrument.
- *Contain an unconditional promise or order to pay.* The instrument may make reference to the transaction "payment on mortgage" but cannot be subject to the terms of another instrument, "subject to mortgage terms."
- *Be a sum certain payable only in money.* Money can be any country's official currency. Sum certain must be ascertainable from

the face of the instrument. The providing for security, different rates of interest, collection costs, attorney fees, etc., in case of default is acceptable. Likewise, a discount for early payment is also permissible.

- *Be payable on demand or at a definite time.* Checks must be demand instruments. A time instrument subject to acceleration is still negotiable if prospects for payment is impaired or upon a specified contingency. Thus, a note payable "when the Chicago Cubs win the pennant" would not be negotiable. The fact that a check is antedated or postdated does not destroy negotiability. Undated prevents negotiability only if a date is needed to know when a time instrument is payable.
- *Words of negotiability.* This is very important. An instrument must be "payable to the order of." It is bearer paper if no payee is named, order paper if named. A note which simply states "pay to Mike Clauretie" would not be negotiable. If properly made out to "A and B," it requires the indorsement of both A and B. If to "A or B," it can be negotiated with either A or B. If payable to "A or bearer," it is considered bearer paper.

Where there is ambiguity, a holder may treat an instrument as either a draft or a note. Remember, words control over figures.

KEY WORDS

acceleration clause (830)
bearer paper (833)
certificate of deposit (823)
check (824)
commercial paper (822)
draft (824)
drawee (824)
drawer (824)
maker (822)
negotiable instrument (826)

note (822)
order paper (833)
payee (822)
prepayment clause (830)
signature (827)
three-party instrument (824)
two-party instrument (824)

DISCUSSION QUESTIONS

1. What is the major objective of Article 3?
2. What are the types of commercial paper?
3. Who are the parties to a note? To a draft?
4. What liability does a drawer have on a draft?
5. What are the two types of drafts?
6. Why is form stressed as the test for negotiability?
7. What are the formal requirements for negotiability?
8. What are the differences between bearer paper and order paper?
9. Describe the principal types of clauses in an instrument which destroy negotiability. Give an example of each.
10. How does the parol evidence rule interact with the "unconditional promise to pay" requirement?

CASE PROBLEMS

1. Explain why the instrument below is or is not negotiable.

```
PAY THROUGH TEXAS COMMERCE BANK NATIONAL ASSOCIATION HOUSTON, TEXAS

DRAFT No. 043757                          DATE   1/31/94              35-60
                                                                     1130
PAY  TWO HUNDRED SIXTEEN AND 58/100         DOLLARS $   216.58

     VALUE RECEIVED                    IN PAYMENT OF
     NO 84-4914 L* C 048501                 FULL AND FINAL SETTLEMENT
                                            OF YOUR CLAIM
PAY TO
THE      Arnold Ziffel
ORDER OF Haney Farm
         Hooterville, Erewhon 99999

ACCEPTED BY:                  SIGNED: David K. Moore

CLAIM NO.  DOCKET NO.  INCIDENT DATE  STATE  TYPE   VEHICLE NO.        EMPLOYEE
2876541    87-2345     11/13/93       LA     PDT                  □ RN □ RL □ NN □ NL
TO                            AFFILIATE/DEPT.  REGION/DIVISION  DISTRICT      STATION NO.
   INTERNATIONAL              MARKETING        CORS / S         DALLAS CORS   51004CO
   WIDGET CORPORATION
   HOUSTON, TEXAS

⑈O 2800 2049⑈:   148⑈3 18 20  8⑈
```

2. Is the following instrument negotiable? What type of instrument is it? Explain.

```
$700.00          Provo, Utah      June 1, 1993

    Thirty days after date I promise to pay to the
    order of
                    Cash

                Seven hundred        Dollars
    at              Boise, Idaho

    Value received with interest at the rate of ten
    percent per annum.
    This instrument is secured by a conditional
    sales contract.
    No. 20   Due July 1, 1995    Len Bowie
```

3. Analyze the following instrument and determine whether it is negotiable.

```
I, Margaret Dunlop, hereby promise to pay
to the order of Caldwell Motors five thousand
dollars ($5000) upon the receipt of the final
distribution from the estate of my deceased
uncle, Carlton Dunlop. This negotiable
instrument is given by me as the down payment
on my purchase of a 1994 Lincoln Continental.

                    Margaret Dunlop
                    Margaret Dunlop
```

4. Is the following instrument negotiable? What type of instrument is it? Explain.

April 1, 1994

Pay to the order of
Donald Kent, fifteen days after date, $100.00

One hundred and no/100 _____ Dollars

Union Corp.
Ridgefield, Connecticut   *Dale Cox*

re: Down payment on auto purchase

5. Analyze the instrument below to determine whether it is negotiable.

April 2, 1994

Charles Noreen
21 West 21st Street
St. Louis, Missouri

I, Charles Noreen, do hereby promise to pay to Roger Smith, Two Thousand Dollars ($2000) one year from date, with 8% interest upon due presentment.

FOR: Payment for used IBM typewriters.

Charles Noreen

6. Is the following instrument negotiable? What type of instrument is it? Explain.

No. 1625

FAIR FOOD WHOLESALERS, INC.
22 Woodrow Wilson Hayes Lane
Columbus, Ohio

Jan. 10, 1994

On demand the undersigned promises to pay to
Bearer $1,200.00

Twelve hundred & no/100's   Dollars

Fair Food Wholesalers, Inc.

By ___*James Duff*___
James Duff, President

For: _____

7. On July 1, 1990, Martin Hayes signed a promissory note which was made payable to the order of Jones Fabricating, Inc., for $10,000, plus 12 percent interest, payable 90 days from date. On the front of the note, above his signature, Hayes wrote: "Subject to satisfactory delivery of goods purchased this date. Delivery to be made no later than July 31, 1990." Is the note negotiable? Explain.

8. The instrument below was received by Best Realtors from Ted Green in connection with Green's purchase of land located in Rye, New York. The note was given for the balance due on the purchase and was secured by a first mortgage on the land. Is it negotiable? What type of instrument is it? Explain.

$90,000.00   Rye, N.Y.
                             May 1, 1993

For value received, six years after date, I promise to pay to the order of Best Realtors NINETY THOUSAND and 00/100 DOLLARS with interest at 16% compounded annually until fully paid. This instrument arises out of the sale of land located in N.Y. and the law of N.Y. is to be applied to any question which may arise. It is secured by a first mortgage on the land conveyed. It is further agreed that :
1. Purchaser will pay the costs of collection including attorney's fees upon default.
2. Purchaser may repay the amount outstanding on any anniversary date of this note.

___*Ted Green*___
Ted Green

9. Camille Ellis inherited a large amount of IBM stock and some cash from her Uncle Rick. She decided to purchase a small farm, Blackacre, from Deborah Tomasek. Ellis paid Tomasek $75,000 down and gave her a $75,000 note at 9 percent interest, due in 5 years. Ellis's note made reference to the purchase of Blackacre, stated that the note was secured by Blackacre and 100 shares of IBM stock, and reserved to Ellis the right to pay the note when due in cash or in IBM stock of equal value at that time. A question has arisen

as to whether the note is negotiable. Is it? Explain.

10. Rick Thompson agreed to purchase an antique grandfather clock from Karen Kierbow. Karen has received in the mail a deposit payable to her name. However, Karen is unsure whether the instrument is intended to be a draft or a note. The instrument states a bank's name, First Security Bank, but has no checking account number. In addition, Karen is unsure about the amount of the deposit, as Rick's figures stated $75 but his written words stated $80. Do the problems above prevent the instrument from being negotiable? Does the UCC permit Karen to treat it as a check for $80? Explain.

CHAPTER APPENDIX: 1990 UCC AMENDMENTS

The Part Opener mentioned the fact that Articles 3 and 4 were amended in 1990 but not integrated into the text because not adopted by the CPA exam at the time of the Fourth Edition. The most significant changes affecting this chapter and the other three in this part include the following:

- Article 3 now recognizes only two categories of negotiable instruments: promissory notes and drafts. A check is simply a particular kind of draft. (Chapter 36)
- A check no longer needs specific words of negotiability. Stated another way, "Pay to Roland Kidwell" is negotiable if a check, nonnegotiable if not. (Chapter 36)
- Commercial paper providing for floating or variable interest is negotiable even if the current rate cannot be determined from the face of the instrument. (Chapter 36)
- The requirement of good faith has been expanded to require the taker to have observed reasonable standards of fair dealing. (Chapter 37)
- The amendments integrate the FTC's holder in due course rule for consumer negotiable instruments. (Chapter 37)
- A check signed "without recourse" does *not* alter the indorser's warranty liabilities. (Chapter 38)
- An *anomalous indorsement* is where a person indorses the instrument as an accommodation party (acting like a surety). (Chapter 38)
- An indorser's liability is extended from seven days to 30 days. (Chapter 38)
- A new three-year statute of limitations now applies to most Article 3 and 4 situations. (Chapter 38)
- Article 4A, a new article, applies to fund transfers. This article was established to primarily deal with electronic fund transfers. (Chapter 39)

You may wish to refer back to this appendix at the conclusion of your study of Part VII.

Although the drafters of the Uniform Commercial Code (UCC) intended negotiable instruments to be like money, they are not money. *Negotiating* or transferring them is more complicated than handing someone a ten-dollar bill. However, the drafters did try to keep the process simple. That is why they emphasized the form of the instrument rather than the parties' intent.

The last chapter examined the nature of a negotiable instrument and identified the key persons who have rights in the negotiation process. This chapter turns to the process itself—how negotiable instruments change hands and who finally pays them or suffers the loss when they are not paid—and to transferees who are granted protected transferee status—holders in due course.

It is important to keep in mind that what you are studying in this chapter is a series of contracts. The negotiable instrument itself is a contract, and each time it is sold and bought, its seller and buyer contract. Each contract in this chain creates rights and duties. Articles 3 and 4 do not deal with any of the underlying obligations which might lead to a negotiable instrument's changing hands. Rather, these Articles focus on the rights and liabilities of the parties as to the instrument itself.

NEGOTIATION

Both negotiable and nonnegotiable instruments may be assigned, but only negotiable instruments may be negotiated. *Negotiation* is the transfer of an instrument in such form that the transferee becomes a holder. The term refers to transactions involving a negotiable instrument after its issuance and before its presentment for payment. The *issuance* of a negotiable instrument is its first *delivery*—change of possession—to a holder. (For now, think of a holder as a possessor of an instrument.)

The principal distinction between assignment and negotiation is that only transferees by negotiation have the possibility of being entitled to protected transferee status. In other words, only transferees whose transferors are holders can become holders in due course.

A *holder in due course* ordinarily is a holder who purchased an instrument for value, in good faith, and without notice that the instrument is overdue or has been dishonored, or of any adverse claims against or defenses to the instrument. Each element of this definition will be discussed below.

Consideration Not Required

The transfer of a negotiable instrument to a holder does not require an exchange of consideration. A check may be a gift to the payee, but that does not affect his or her status as a holder and, therefore, its negotiability.

Bearer and Order Paper

The way in which an instrument is negotiated depends on whether it is bearer or order paper. *Bearer paper*, it will be recalled, is commercial paper which is payable to the person who has physical possession of it. Any new possessor becomes a holder on delivery [UCC §3-202(1)]. Even a thief can be a holder of bearer paper. Suppose Steve leaves a check made out to cash on his desk while he goes to lunch. Fred walks by, sees it, and steals it. Fred is now a holder. If Fred negotiates it at the college store to pay for some T-shirts, the store becomes a holder in due course.

Order paper is commercial paper which is payable to the order of a named payee. The negotiation of order paper requires both delivery and an *indorsement*, a signature, usually on the back of an instrument. Now suppose Steve's check was made payable to the order of Susan Gray. She would have to *indorse*—sign—it and deliver it in order to negotiate it. If Fred stole it off Steve's desk, he could not be a

TYPE OF PAPER	INDORSEMENT REQUIRED?	DELIVERY REQUIRED?
Bearer paper:		
• On its face, or	No	Yes
• Blank indorsement		
Order paper:		
• On its face, or	Yes	Yes
• Special indorsement		

Figure 37.1 Requirements for Negotiation.

holder and his transferee could not become a holder in due course. Why? A *holder* is one who is in possession of an instrument drawn, issued, or indorsed to him or to his order or to bearer or in blank [UCC §1-201(20)]. The check is made out to Susan, so Fred does not meet any of these conditions. Since he is not a holder, his transferee cannot be one, either. Figure 37.1 compares bearer and order paper.

An instrument made payable to joint payees, like "Susan Gray and Michael Manson," must be indorsed by both. An instrument payable to alternative payees, like "Susan Gray or Michael Manson," only needs an indorsement by one or the other. But, what about a check payable to the order of "Susan Gray/Michael Manson"? The court in the following case dealt with that question.

Ryland Group, Inc. v. Gwinnett County Bank

151 Ga. App. 148, 259 S.E.2d 152 (1979)

FACTS   [The Ryland Group] brought suit against . . . Gwinnett County Bank and Jack Harper to recover on certain checks drawn on [Harper's] account at the bank and allegedly paid without proper indorsement. The checks were made payable to "Jack Harper/Plymart" in some instances, and to "Jack Harper/Lowes Doravil" in others. [The Ryland Group's] contention is that the diagonal slash, or "virgule" symbol, between the names on the payee line of the checks signified joint payees requiring indorsement by both parties whereas the bank paid the checks with only Harper's indorsement. This appeal is from the grant of summary judgment to the bank and denial of summary judgment to The Ryland Group.

ISSUE   Does a virgule between the names of the payees on a check require joint indorsements?

DECISION   No. Judgment affirmed.

[The Ryland Group conceded in its brief] that the symbol (/), a slash or diagonal line, had been defined to mean alternative construction. . . . Thus, the bank's payment of the checks with only Harper's indorsement was not only proper but was required. . . .

During oral argument of this case, [the Ryland Groups' counsel] was asked by the court why the maker of the checks did not write the word "and" between the names of the payees if that was its intention. Counsel's reply was that the checks were written by computer. The court makes no suggestion about changing computers, but it does bring to mind the following: "To err is human but to really foul things up requires a computer."

Classification of Indorsements

When an instrument is created it is either negotiable or nonnegotiable and either bearer or order paper. If an instrument is nonnegotiable on the front of the instrument, no subsequent indorsement on the back of the instrument, can cause the instrument to become negotiable. In contrast, it is possible by indorsement to change a negotiable instrument to nonnegotiable and back again. It is also possible by indorsement to change an instrument from order to bearer paper and the reverse. In other words, once an instrument has been negotiated, the last indorsement determines whether the instrument is bearer or order paper and whether it can still be negotiated. The various types of indorsements are discussed next.

Blank and special indorsements. All indorsements are either blank or special.

A *blank indorsement* is one in which the person indorsing the instrument, the *indorser,* does not make the instrument payable to a specific person or party, the *indorsee.* A blank indorsement turns order paper into bearer paper. Assume that a check is payable to the order of Michael Manson. Michael indorses it:

/s/Michael Manson

and negotiates it to Susan Gray. Susan can negotiate Michael's check by delivery only. But, a thief could negotiate it, too, since negotiation of bearer paper does not require a valid indorsement by the holder. If the thief negotiated it to a person who qualified as a holder in due course, neither the maker nor a previous holder could avoid paying the check on the grounds of theft. For that reason, it is never advisable to indorse in blank.

A *special indorsement* always names a specific person as indorsee. Any specially indorsed instrument becomes payable to the order of the special indorsee, and it may be negotiated only by the indorsee's signature. Thus, a special indorsement turns bearer paper into order paper. Assume that Michael's check is payable to cash. He writes on its back:

Pay Susan Gray
/s/ Michael Manson

and gives it to Susan. His is a special indorsement, and in order to negotiate the check, Susan will have to indorse and deliver it.

A holder may convert a blank indorsement into a special indorsement simply by writing over the indorser's signature any contract consistent with the character of the indorsement to her [UCC §3-204(3)]. If Michael indorses a check to Susan in blank, she may write above Michael's signature, "Pay Susan Gray."

Nonrestrictive and restrictive indorsements. All indorsements are either nonrestrictive or restrictive. Blank and special indorsements by themselves are *nonrestrictive indorsements* because they do not limit the indorsee's ability to negotiate the instrument. A *restrictive indorsement* attempts to limit the indorsee in some manner [UCC §3-205]. One may be found in conjunction with either a blank or a special indorsement. However, the restriction cannot prevent the instrument's transfer or negotiation [UCC §3-206]. The rationale for this apparent contradiction—that an indorsement can restrict transfer and yet not restrict it—will become apparent from the description of the four types of restrictive indorsements recognized in Article 3.

1. *Conditional.* A conditional indorsement

states a condition which must occur before the indorsee may negotiate the instrument. For instance,

Pay Susan Gray
If she has not found
a job by July 4, 1994
/s/Michael Manson

is both a conditional and a special indorsement. If this language appeared on the front of the instrument, it would destroy negotiability because the instrument would no longer state an unconditional promise to pay. In an indorsement, it does not affect negotiability because the face of the instrument determines negotiability. Conditional indorsements are not common.

2. *Transfer Prohibition.* Some indorsements are intended to limit further transfer or negotiation to a specific indorsee. However, transfer prohibitions are treated as if they were nonrestrictive indorsements. Again, if this restriction appeared on the face of the instrument, it would destroy the instrument's negotiability because the instrument would no longer be payable to order or bearer. In an indorsement, it cannot make the instrument nonnegotiable. For example,

Pay Susan Gray only
/s/Michael Manson

seems to restrict transfer to Susan Gray. Nonetheless, Susan could negotiate the instrument to anyone she pleased.

3. *For Deposit or Collection.* Quite routinely, a holder will indorse a check "For deposit only" or "For collection" and negotiate the check to a bank. By using those restrictions, the holder instructs a bank to apply the proceeds from the check to his or her account.

The UCC requires the bank to pay the check in accordance with such an indorsement. If it does not, the bank loses its holder in due course status as to the amount not properly credited to the depositor. Since the restrictive indorsement affects only the contract between the indorser and the indorsee bank, giving effect to the indorsement does not affect the instrument's negotiability. In fact, the UCC provides that banks which subsequently take the check should treat the indorsement as nonrestrictive [UCC §3-206(3)]. Assume that a $200 check bears the following indorsement:

For deposit only
/s/Michael Manson

Michael's bank credits his account for only $100 and forwards the check to the drawee bank for collection. The bank is only a holder in due course as to the $100 it credited to Michael's account. It remains subject to any claims or defenses on the check up to $100. As the next case points out, "For deposit only" places another burden on the depository bank.

4. *In Trust Indorsement.* An *in trust indorsement* indicates that an instrument "is for the benefit or use of the indorser or another party" [UCC §3-205]. For example,

Pay Susan Gray
For account of T. J. Golden, minor
/s/Michael Manson

is an in trust indorsement. An in trust restriction binds only the first taker after the indorser. Thus, Susan's indorsee would have to make sure than she applied the funds to Robert's account [UCC §3-206(4)].

Spielman v. Manufacturers Hanover Trust Co.

90 A.D.2d 499, 454 N.Y.S.2d 753 (N.Y. App. Div. 1982)

FACTS The attorney for the trustees of the Production Workers Union Local 148 Welfare Fund told the trustees that a lawsuit against the fund could be settled for $16,500. The trustees gave him a check drawn to the order of the law firm representing the plaintiff. The check was deposited in Chemical Bank and accepted by the fund's bank, Manufacturers Hanover Trust Co. Later, the trustees learned that their attorney's representations were false. Also, he had forged the payee law firm's indorsement on the check. Above it appeared "Pay to special acct # 012-043478," and beneath it, "FOR DEPOSIT ONLY SPECIAL ACCT # 012-043478." Chemical credited the proceeds to the attorney's account bearing that number. The payee law firm did not have an account at Chemical. The trustees sued Chemical to recover the value of the check. The trial court granted summary judgment in favor of the trustees.

ISSUE Was Chemical liable for failing to pay on the check in accordance with its restrictive indorsement?

DECISION Yes. Affirmed. The clear indication of both directions—to pay and to deposit—was to deposit the check in an account identified by a number. However, Chemical should have noticed that the payee law firm did not have an account with it. Absent a contrary indication in the indorsement, the words "For deposit only" mean for deposit into the account of the payee-indorser, not into that of the person presenting the instrument for negotiation.

Qualified and unqualified indorsements. A *qualified indorsement* indicates that an indorser assumes no liability under the usual indorsement contract, which is discussed below. For example, a qualified indorsement might read:

Pay to Susan Gray
Without Recourse
/s/Michael Manson

Recourse is the right of a subsequent indorser to recover from a prior indorser in the event the instrument is *dishonored,* that is, not accepted or not paid. An *unqualified indorsement,* which is the normal type, does not disclaim liability under the indorser's contract, which is discussed below. With the exception of the "without recourse" example, all of the examples above are unqualified indorsements.

Figure 37.2 charts the different types of indorsements.

Form of Indorsements

Indorsements normally appear on the back of an instrument, but Article 3 does not require them to appear there. What the UCC does require is that an indorsement be written either by the holder or on the holder's behalf. Also, it must be either on the instrument or on a paper so firmly attached to the instrument as to become a part of it. [UCC §3-202(2)]. Paper-clipping an indorsement to a negotiable instrument will not do, but stapling will.

The name of an instrument's payee or indorsee may be wrong or misspelled without affecting negotiability. The holder may indorse

INDORSEMENT	IN BLANK	SPECIAL	RESTRICTIVE	NONRESTRICTIVE	QUALIFIED	UNQUALIFIED
|s| Michael Manson	X			X		X
Pay Susan Gray |s| Michael Manson		X		X		X
Pay Susan Gray only |s| Michael Manson		X	X			X
For deposit only |s| Michael Manson	X		X			X
Pay Susan Gray for account of T.J. Golden |s| Michael Manson		X	X			X
To Susan Gray, without recourse |s| Michael Manson		X		X	X	

Figure 37.2 Comparison of Indorsements.
This figure characterizes the various types of indorsements commonly found on the back of negotiable instruments.

in the name given in the instrument or in his own name or both. Suppose Susan Gray is a check's payee, but her name appears as "Grey." She could indorse "Susan Grey." The transferee, particularly one who gives value, may require indorsements in both names, thus insuring negotiability by eliminating any question as to the indorsement [UCC §3-203].

Location of Indorsements

In 1988, the Federal Reserve Board issued regulations specifying where indorsements may be placed on checks. Before the regulations took effect, indorsers—including depository and collecting banks—could indorse a check in any manner anywhere on its back. As a result, the status of indorsers was often confusing and the check-clearing process was slowed.

Now, the back of a check is divided into three sections. Nonbanks are to indorse checks only on the reverse in the 1.5 inches from the trailing edge—on a personal check, the edge

where the maker's name and address are printed. The depository bank, the bank that first receives the check, uses the next 1.5 inches. The remaining 3 inches are reserved for subsequent collecting banks—banks involved in clearing the check back to the drawer's bank.

Failure to follow the Fed's requirements does not affect a check's negotiability. However, it may cause a check to be returned and a deposit to be reversed, if required information is obscured.

PREREQUISITES FOR HOLDER IN DUE COURSE STATUS

As noted earlier, the UCC defines a holder in due course as:

- A holder
- Who purchases an instrument for value
- In good faith
- Without notice that the instrument is over-due or has been dishonored or of any de-

fenses to or adverse claims against the instrument [UCC §3-302]

The following sections examine these prerequisites to holder in due course status.

Holder

A holder in due course must, first of all, be a holder. A *holder* is a person who possesses a negotiable instrument drawn, issued, or indorsed to him or his order or to bearer or in blank [UCC §1-201(20)].

Becoming a holder. Rightful possession of a negotiable instrument results from its being drawn, issued, or negotiated to the holder. *Drawn* means written. *Issued* refers to the first delivery of commercial paper to a holder [UCC §3-102(1)(a)]. When Blake writes a check to Georgia and hands it to her, he has issued it. Georgia may now seek payment or transfer it to another.

But, note the use of the word "possession" in the definition of holder. A person does not have to own an instrument in order to be its holder. For example, an agent or a trustee in possession of an instrument may be a holder when acting on behalf of a principal or a trust which actually owns the instrument.

Rights of a holder. A person who has a negotiable instrument does not have a right to payment on it unless he or she is a holder. A holder has the right to transfer, negotiate, collect, or sue to enforce payment of a negotiable instrument he or she possesses. The next case shows what a holder must prove in order to convince a court to enforce the contract represented by a negotiable instrument.

Leopold v. Halleck

106 Ill. App. 3d 386, 436 N.E.2d 29 (1982)

FACTS Leopold brought suit to recover on a negotiable instrument payable to his order and signed by Halleck. At trial, Leopold produced the note and introduced it as Plaintiff's Exhibit No. 1. Leopold then called Halleck as a witness. Halleck admitted that the signature on the note was his. Leopold moved the note into evidence, rested his case, and moved for a directed verdict. Halleck did not introduce any evidence. But, in response to Leopold's motion, Halleck also moved for a directed verdict. The trial court granted Halleck's motion on the grounds that Leopold had failed to prove Halleck's liability.

ISSUE Did Leopold have to establish anything more than the existence of the note and the validity of Halleck's signature to prove Halleck's liability?

DECISION No. Reversed. Leopold had shifted the burden of proof to Halleck. "When signatures are admitted or established, production of the instrument entitles a holder to recover on it unless the defendant establishes a defense" [UCC §3-307(2)]. The holder only has to prove his status as a holder, the note's negotiability, or any other requirement after the defendant presents some evidence that the holder or the instrument does not satisfy a particular mandatory requirement.

For Value

To become a holder in due course, a holder must give value for the negotiable instrument [UCC §3-303]. A holder who acquires the instrument for free or as a gift does not give value. The UCC does not succinctly define value. Rather, it includes a number of examples of what it may be or what may affect it. While often similar, value is *not* simply contract law consideration. To illustrate, a promise to perform an act in the future constitutes consideration but would *not* qualify as the giving of value. Once the promise is performed, however, value will have been given. Suppose, Rick writes a check to the Chicago Bears for two season tickets. The Bears will have given value for Rick's check when they send the tickets to him.

Antecedent debt. Another major difference from contract law consideration is the UCC's treatment of **antecedent debt,** past consideration. Under the UCC [UCC §3-303(2)], antecedent debt qualifies as value. To illustrate, assume LaShonda purchases a television set at Sears using her Sears credit card. The following month LaShonda sends Sears a monthly payment of $30 towards her bill. Sears gives no new consideration to support LaShonda's payment of $30. However, Sears has previously given consideration to LaShonda, the television set, so they will be considered to be acquiring her check for value. Of course, Sears must still meet the other requirements to become a holder in due course.

Discounts. The UCC does *not* require that a holder exchange equal value in acquiring a negotiable instrument. It is a common business practice for negotiable notes, primarily notes, to be sold at a **discount,** an amount less than the face value of the instrument. For example, used-car dealers and furniture dealers often sell goods to consumers on credit by way of a negotiable note and then discount the note, sell it for less than face value, to a finance company. Upon notice by the finance company to the consumer, the consumer thereafter must make monthly payments to the finance company.

A holder who acquires a negotiable instrument for a discount and becomes a holder in due course can enforce the instrument for the full face value of the instrument. Suppose Marsha gives Sam a $1000 note. Sam negotiates it, sells it, to Raymond for $850. As Figure 37.3 illustrates, Raymond becomes a holder in due course for the note's full value of $1000. What if Raymond had instead given $500, or $100 or even $10? In all three cases Raymond will have given value for purposes of the UCC. However, an excessive discount can raise questions about the purchaser's good faith and about whether he likely knew that something was wrong with the instrument.

Security interests. A holder takes an instrument for value to the extent that she acquires a security interest in it. Under the UCC, a *security interest* is an interest in personal property or fixtures which secures payment or performance of an obligation. For example, in Figure 37.4, assume that John gives Helen a note for $1000. Helen puts up the note as collateral to secure a $750 loan from Central Loan Company. Central Loan would become a holder in due course only up to $750 [UCC §3-303(a)].

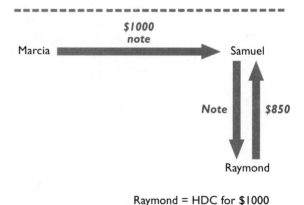

Figure 37.3 Giving of Value I.
A discounted note.

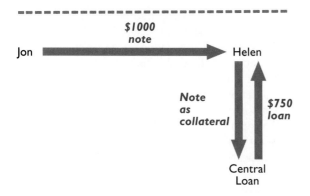

Central Loan = HDC for $750

Figure 37.4 Giving of Value II.
A note as collateral.

Account balance	= $ 500
Paycheck deposit	= 1500
New balance	$2000
Less cleared check	− 1000
New balance	$1000

Bank = HDC for $500 (by FIFO analysis)

Figure 37.5 Giving of Value III.
A bank deposit.

Bank deposits. A bank's acceptance of a check for deposit does not mean that the bank has given value. Assume that Peg deposits all of her $1500 paycheck. She has not yet received value, even though the bank gives her a receipt and credit her account. Only as she begins writing checks or withdrawing money from the account does the bank give value. Thus, if she had the bank pay her $100 in cash and deposited the remainder, the bank became a holder in due course to the extent of $100 of her $1500 check.

With active accounts, this rule could pose a problem in determining when the bank gives value for a particular check. To avoid that difficulty, the UCC adopts the first-in, first-out (FIFO) method. Suppose Peg already had $500 in her bank account when she made her $1500 deposit. When a $1000 check she wrote to Rod clears her account, she will have a balance of $1000. As Figure 37.5 shows, her bank would now be a holder in due course to the extent of the $500 they had given on her paycheck [UCC §4-208(2)].

Good Faith

Good faith means "honesty in fact in the conduct or transaction concerned" [UCC §1-201(19)].

The UCC's test of good faith is subjective. The criteria for evaluating good faith are what the holder actually believed, understood, and knew at the time she took the instrument. The courts look to the circumstances of the transfer in making these determinations. For example, a bank would not be acting in good faith if it failed to question a check whose amount and signature lines showed signs of erasures. The bank's conduct relates directly to the transaction—the negotiation of the check to it. By contrast, as the next case implies, the bank has no obligation to ask a holder whether he or she gave good consideration for a check.

Chemical Bank v. Haskell

51 N.Y.2d 85, 432 N.Y.2d 478, 411 N.E.2d 1339 (1980)

FACTS In 1972 Haskell and others became involved in a limited partnership, Quarry Square Associates, which was developing an apartment complex. Stanndco Developer's, Inc., and David Quigley were the general partners. The limited partners made capital contributions by executing notes. In 1973, Quigley approached Chemical Bank to borrow money, using the notes as collateral. Chemical declined, but offered to buy the notes. Quigley, acting as Quarry's general partner, indorsed the notes to Quarry as an individual and then indorsed the notes to the bank. The bank drew a check for $274,390 to the order of Stanndco. The check did not indicate that Stanndco was to handle the funds as Quarry's general partner. Ten months later, the general partners filed for bankruptcy. Chemical then sued the limited partners on the notes. The limited partners asserted that the bank did not purchase the notes in good faith and should have been on notice of irregularities in the transaction. The trial court found for the bank, but the intermediate appellate court reversed.

ISSUE

Were the irregularities in the transaction sufficient to cast doubt on Chemical's good faith?

DECISION

No. Reversed. The test of a holder's good faith is not whether a reasonable banker in Chemical's position would have inquired about Stanndco's performance of its partnership duties, but whether Chemical actually knew of a breach of Stanndco's duties. If Chemical did not have actual knowledge which would prevent a commercially honest individual from taking the instruments, it acted in good faith. Chemical was not bound to be alert for circumstances which would cause suspicion. It had no obligation as a purchaser of negotiable paper to investigate its transferor's financial position or the progress of the construction project. Also, Stanndco had at least apparent authority to negotiate the notes. Thus, Chemical was a holder in due course.

"Good faith" does not mean "good business judgment." For instance, a holder may acquire a note issued by a business widely known to be virtually bankrupt. That reveals poor business judgment, but not necessarily a lack of good faith. Still, if a reasonable person would have inquired about the instrument, a court may have difficulty accepting an assertion of good faith.

Lack of Notice

Logically, when a holder who is acting in good faith takes an instrument, he or she cannot have notice that there is something wrong with it or that the issuer or a prior holder has a defense to,

or claim against, it. For that reason, the UCC defines a holder in due course as a person who takes an instrument without notice of such facts. In this section, we will examine what a holder in due course may not know about when the instrument is negotiated to him or her. But first, we must turn to what the UCC defines as notice.

As the next case indicates, a person has notice of a fact when he or she:

- Has actual knowledge of it
- Has received notification of it
- Had reason to know that it exists based on all the facts and circumstances known at the time in question [UCC §1-201(25)]

Indyk v. Habib Bank Ltd.

694 F.2d 54 (2d Cir. 1982)

FACTS
On February 4, 1980, the Indyks contracted to sell Munroe Contract Corporation to Dome Investment Company for $1 million. Dome made a $157,765 down payment. At the closing 2 days later, the Indyks received, as payment of the balance, a cashier's check drawn on the Habib Bank and signed by its assistant vice president. The check was postdated June 4, 1980. At the closing, the Indyks may have been aware that Dome then lacked the funds to complete the transaction. The Indyks presented the check June 4, but the bank refused to pay. The Indyks brought suit against the bank. The bank claimed that the check was issued without either authority or consideration and that the postdating of the check put the Indyks on notice that the transaction was irregular. The trial court found for the Indyks.

ISSUE
Did the fact the check was postdated deny the Indyks holder in due course status?

DECISION
No. Affirmed. The postdating alone was not sufficient to give the Indyks notice that the bank had a defense on the instrument. Banks normally do not postdate cashier's checks, but the Indyks had no reason to know this. The fact that the Indyks might have been aware of Dome's lack of funds does not necessarily mean they knew that Dome had not given Habib consideration for the check. Dome might well have paid for it with a note or other noncash consideration.

Notice that the instrument is overdue. Notice that a negotiable instrument is overdue prevents a purchaser from becoming a holder in due course [UCC §3-304(3)]. A purchaser is presumed to have notice of what the instrument reveals on its face. So, if a note's due date is November 1, 1993 and it is November 3, 1993, the purchaser is on notice.

Demand instruments are considered overdue if the purchaser knows that he has taken the instrument after a demand for payment has been made. Suppose Skip attempts to cash a check, but the bank refuses to pay it because of insufficient funds. If Skip negotiates the check to Mary, who knows that he attempted to cash it, she cannot become a holder in due course. The same rule applies if a purchaser knows that a previous holder has accelerated an instrument's time for payment, since that usually means that the issuer has defaulted [UCC §3-304(3)].

A purchaser of a demand instrument is also on notice if more than a reasonable time has passed since its issuance. For example, a reasonable time for presenting a check to a drawee for payment is 30 days [UC §3-503(2)(a)]. Even though the check may be honored subsequently, the purchaser is not a holder in due course.

Notice of discharge. Since a *discharge* is a release from or termination of a party's contractual obligation, notice of discharge prevents a purchaser from becoming a holder in due course as to any discharged party. However, a purchaser may become a holder in due course so long as not all the parties to the instrument have been discharged. Discharge is discussed in Chapter 38.

Notice of dishonor. If the purchaser has notice that the instrument's drawee or issuer has refused to accept or pay it, he or she cannot become a holder in due course as to it. In this case, the drawee or issuer is said to *dishonor* the instrument by refusing to accept or pay it. This topic, too, will be discussed in Chapter 38.

Notice of a defense or claim. A holder in due course may not have notice of a defense against, or a claim to, the instrument at the time he or she takes it. [UCC §3-302(1)(c)].

Where the holder did not receive actual notice of a claim or defense, the courts look to the circumstances of the transaction for evidence of notice. The face of an instrument itself may give notice of a possible defense or claim. A defective or highly irregular instrument should cause a potential transferee to inquire as to its terms, validity, or ownership. An incomplete instrument, like a check lacking the drawer's signature, is highly irregular. So, too, is a note which bears visible evidence of a material alteration, such as changes in the amount, the due date, the interest rate, or the payee's name [UCC §3-304(1)(a)].

However, even actual knowledge of a defect does not always prevent a purchaser of a negotiable instrument from becoming a holder in due course. Suppose a purchaser knows that an instrument was incomplete when drawn. Unless she knows that it was improperly completed, she takes it as a holder in due course [UCC §3-304(4)]. Also, knowledge that an instrument is antedated or postdated alone does not affect holder in due course status.

As the definition of notice indicates, knowledge of a defense or claim may come from a source other than the instrument itself. Where an issuer has a defense on the underlying obligation, the face of the instrument will rarely reveal it. Notice has to come from another source, such as the issuer or the transferor.

Absence of Direct Dealing

The preceding sections traced the elements of the definition of a holder in due course contained in UCC §3-302. There is, however, another element of this status: the holder in due course is only protected from the defenses on the obligation of those with whom he or she has not dealt directly [UCC §3-305(2)].

The effect of the absence of direct dealing requirement is clearest when a payee is a holder in due course. Practically, holder in due course status is of little benefit in this situation because the payee either has notice of the maker or drawer's defenses or has dealt directly with the maker or drawer. The next case is a typical payee as holder in due course case.

Bank One v. Myers

14 Ohio App. 3d 196 (1984)

FACTS   Louella Myers bought a mobile home with the proceeds of a mortgage loan she obtained from Bank One. She signed a promissory note payable to Bank One. Thereafter, she sued the seller and the manufacturer based on a breach of warranty. She then defaulted on the note. The bank repossessed the mobile home, sold it, and brought suit against Myers for the deficiency. Myers attempted to assert her breach of warranty defense, which ordinarily could not be raised against a holder in due course. Since both parties agreed that Bank One was a holder in due course, the trial court granted summary judgment to the bank.

ISSUE

Could Myers assert her breach of warranty defense against the bank?

DECISION

Yes. Reversed. A holder in due course only takes an instrument free from certain defenses which may be asserted by a party to the instrument with whom the holder in due course has not dealt [UCC §3-305(2)]. Here, the bank had dealt with Myers.

DEFENSES AND HOLDERS IN DUE COURSE

The UCC categorizes defenses on negotiable instruments as either real or personal defenses. A *real defense* is one of the limited number of contractual defenses on the instrument which the UCC permits an issuer or prior holder to assert against any holder—including holders in due course. All other defenses are termed *personal defenses* because the UCC effectively limits them to actions between parties who actually dealt with one another. Thus, the rule is that any defenses which are not real defenses are personal defenses.

It is because of the fear of a real defense subsequently being raised that many would-be holders in due course, such as convenience stores or banks, refuse to accept two-party checks.

The next sections discuss some of the variations involving real defenses.

Real Defenses

Only real defenses defeat the interests of a holder in due course. They are:

- Incapacity, duress, or illegality of the transaction which voids the party's obligation
- Infancy, to the extent that it is a defense in a common law contract action
- A misrepresentation which induced the party to sign the instrument with neither the knowledge nor the opportunity to obtain knowledge of its character or terms
- Discharge of the maker or drawer in bankruptcy proceedings
- Notice of any other party's discharge
- A material alteration, but only to the extent of the alteration
- An unauthorized signature [UCC §3-305]

The previous section contrasted a number of the real defenses with personal defenses. This section will emphasize only some of the important variations.

Incapacity, duress, and illegality. Article 3 limits a party's ability to assert the defenses of incapacity, duress, and illegality to those situations in which they would void the contract. In the next case, the maker of a note asserted the defense of illegality of contract against a holder in due course.

Wilson v. Steele

211 Cal.App.3d 1053, 259 Cal.Rptr. 851 (Cal.App. 1989)

FACTS

Williams was granted a power of attorney from her mother. She entered into a contract to remodel her mother's house with Michael Jackson & Associates, an unlicensed contractor. A promissory note, secured by a deed of trust, was executed in favor of Home Budget Improvement Service, a company owned by Jackson, as payment for the work. Home Budget later sold the note to Ken and Ron Steele. Williams disappeared and Jackson never finished the job. Williams's mother had died after the note had been executed. Her estate, through the administrator, Wilson, sought to nullify the note, arguing it was illegal and void, since Jackson was not a licensed contractor. Wilson won at the trial level.

ISSUE   Is Jackson's status as an unlicensed contractor a defense which can be asserted against a holder in due course?

DECISION   Yes. Reversed. The California UCC provides that a holder in due course does not take free of the defense of illegality of contract which renders the underlying obligation a nullity. California's Business and Professions Code states that only licensed contractors can maintain an action in court for the collection of money in the performance of a construction contract. Thus, the contract between Williams and Jackson's company was void and the defense of illegality of contract can be asserted against the Steeles, as holders in due course.

Real fraud. The UCC's misrepresentation defense should not be confused with the common law defense of innocent misrepresentation. Rather, the UCC's misrepresentation defense more closely resembles the common law's *fraud in the execution* or "real fraud" defense, described in Chapter 9. In essence, the issuer cannot have had an opportunity to know what he or she was signing. The existence of this defense depends on a careful factual examination, which might include the issuer's ability to read and write, mental capacity, the opportunity to learn of the fraud, and the like. The court in *FDIC v. Turner* referred to this defense, but the plaintiffs did not establish it.

Material alterations and unauthorized signatures. A material alteration is one which significantly affects the terms or nature of the instrument. However, a material alteration is a real defense only to the extent of the alteration. For example, a note's original amount, $3000, is altered to read "$30,000." The maker has a real defense as to the $27,000 attributable to the alteration, but the maker remains liable for the $3000.

"Unauthorized signatures" describes two situations: outright forgeries and instances in which an agent exceeds his or her authority. Generally, only forgeries are real defenses, and then only if the alleged issuer's negligence did not play a key role in the forgery. The rules on unauthorized signatures are discussed in detail in Chapter 38. In the following case, a guarantor of an issuer of a note was a competent, well-educated person, but the extent of the debt and the persons he became obligated to had been significantly altered by an unscrupulous banker.

FDIC v. Turner

869 F.2d 270 (6th Cir. 1989)

FACTS   Milton Turner was maker on a number of promissory notes held by the United American Bank in Knoxville (UAB-Knoxville). Jake Butcher, as its president and CEO, informed Turner that the bank was about to be audited and he needed Turner to execute a continuing guaranty to place in the loan files for one of Turner's firms. Turner signed it and left blank the place for the debtor and for the amount he would guarantee. Later the blanks were filled in by an unknown person. Lovell Road Properties, a limited partnership owned partly by Butcher, was inserted as the maker. A figure of $2,141,270.91 appeared as the amount guaranteed. The UAB-Knoxville name on the printed form was obliterated with correction fluid and replaced with City and County Bank of Knox County (CCB-Knox County), which was owned by C. H. Butcher, Jake's brother. Turner had no ownership interest in Lovell Road Properties or knowledge of the changes. In 1983, CCB-Knox County was declared insolvent by Tennessee, and later the FDIC was named receiver of CCB-Knox County's notes and obligations. The Federal Deposit Insurance Corporation (FDIC) sued Turner as a guarantor of the Lovell Road Properties, and sought collection of the debt. Turner argued the guaranty was void on the basis of the real defense of fraud in the factum or execution. The FDIC prevailed at the trial level.

ISSUE   Was Turner's obligation as guarantor of the Lovell Road Properties void on the basis of fraud in the execution?

DECISION   Yes. Reversed. Real fraud, for which a holder in due course is susceptible, would be a misrepresentation that the maker or guarantor has neither knowledge of or a reasonable opportunity to obtain knowledge of the essential terms. In this case it must be determined if Turner, in light of his age, his education, his confidence in making the obligation with Butcher, and the apparent necessity for acting quickly, had a reasonable opportunity to learn of the essential terms of the note he guaranteed. Turner was unaware of the essential terms and signed based on misrepresentations of who was the maker and the holding bank. Moreover, Butcher, as Turner's banker, was authorized and trusted to fill in the blanks with the appropriate information. Turner then did so at Butcher's urgence to secure Turner's own debts.

In the 1980s, thousands of savings and loan institutions (S & L's) and banks failed due to crooked bank officers like Jake Butcher. The U.S. government, which insures an individual's deposits up to $100,000, subsequently took over the operations of these institutions through the FDIC, for banks, and the Resolute Trust Company (RTC), for failed S & L's. In the *Turner* case, an issue was raised about whether the FDIC can be a holder in due course. The courts in these kinds of cases have consistently ruled that the FDIC (as well as the RTC) acquires the same rights as a holder in due course. The reasoning for this stance is partially one of public policy. The FDIC must do everything it can to protect bank depositors. In taking over and enforcing a failed lending institution's obligations,

the FDIC needs to be a holder in due course to achieve that goal efficiently. Unfortunately for American taxpayers, who will eventually pay hundreds of billions of dollars for all the deceit and mismanagement of lending institutions in the so-called greed decade (the 1980s), even a holder in due course could not collect after such blatant fraud.

Jake Butcher was eventually sentenced to 20 years in prison for the millions of dollars he and his brother swindled, but he was released in May 1992 after serving only 6 years and 8 months. Like more of the S & L and bank officers in the 1980s, Butcher was a highly respected man who twice ran for the governorship of Tennessee and owned a two-state, billion-dollar banking empire. Although Butcher is out of prison, his life will not be comfortable. He has millions of dollars in tax debts and civil judgments. Moreover, because the money was acquired through fraud and false pretenses, the judgments were not discharged when Butcher petitioned for bankruptcy. A discussion of nondischargeable debts is provided in Chapter 43 on Bankruptcy.

Personal Defenses

Any defense not classified as a real defense is a personal defense. Two keys help distinguish personal from real defenses. First, the underlying obligation must be void, not voidable, to give rise to a real defense. Second, neither failure nor lack of consideration is ever a real defense.

Duress. Normally, duress is a personal defense. For instance, the high-pressure tactics of an unscrupulous salesperson rarely give rise to a real defense. Rather, the duress must be of the degree produced by a gun pointed at the head in order to become a real defense [UCC §3-305].

Incapacity. Incapacity by reason of age or mental condition is a personal defense to the extent that the law declares the underlying contracts to be voidable rather than void. The classic example here is of a person who is insane but who has not been declared incompetent by a court. That person's obligations are voidable. Obligations entered into after a declaration of incompetency are void, and then incompetency becomes a real defense [UCC §3-305(2)(b)].

Illegality. The illegality of the underlying obligation is a personal defense unless the law declares the contract to be void, not voidable.

Fraud in the inducement. Fraud in the inducement is a personal defense, but, as discussed below, fraud in the execution is a real defense. For instance, a maker may be induced to sign a note on a representation that the obligation is voidable. However, as the next case shows, if a later holder does not have notice of that representation, he becomes a holder in due course [UCC §3-304(1)(b)].

Favors v. Yaffe

605 S.W.2d 342 (Tex. Civ. App. 1980)

FACTS
In 1971 the Favors bought some land in Arizona after a salesman said that the seller, Cochise College Park, Inc., would refund their money if, after inspecting the property, they wished to back out. The Favors executed a mortgage and a promissory note to Cochise. Cochise gave then a written "Money Back Guarantee And Exchange Privilege." Three months later, the Favors inspected the property and demanded their money back. Cochise offered to extend the guarantee and to try to resell their tract, sharing the profit with the Favors. They agreed. Unknown to the Favors, Cochise had sold their note to Yaffe 12 days after they executed it. Yaffe had no knowledge of the money-back guarantee or the representations relating to it. Cochise went bankrupt, and the Favors then stopped making payments on the note. Yaffe brought suite on the note. The trial court entered judgment for him.

ISSUE
Did Yaffe take the instrument subject to the Favors' defense of fraud in the inducement?

DECISION

No. Affirmed. A holder in due course takes the instrument free from all claims and defenses of a party to the instrument with whom he has not dealt except, among others, that a misrepresentation induced the maker to sign the instrument without knowledge of, or an opportunity to discover, its character or its essential terms [UCC §3-305]. This is the only type of representation defense that makers can assert against a holder in due course with whom they have not dealt.

Many of the saddest cases decided under Article 3 involved persons who were fraudulently induced to sign negotiable instruments. The cases often involved the elderly or the ill-educated, who bought goods or contracted for home repairs without carefully reading what they were signing. They later found that what they had bought was not as represented and, worse, that they had to pay for it because the instrument had passed to a holder in due course. Rules adopted by the Federal Trade Commission in 1976 resolved this problem by essentially eliminating holder in due course status as to consumer credit transactions. These regulations are discussed at the end of this chapter.

Failure of consideration. Knowledge that a negotiable instrument was issued in exchange for a promise of later performance does not prevent someone from becoming a holder in due course, even if there was a later failure of consideration. Assume that Georgia Products gave Wedding Dress, Inc, a note for $1000 as a deposit on its order. Wedding Dress's transferee can become a holder in due course, even though she knows that performance is not yet due. However, if the purchaser knew at the time of the transaction that Wedding Dress's performance was overdue, that fact indicated a failure of consideration. Without such knowledge, the transferee is a holder in due course, and Georgia Products could not raise its failure of consideration defense in an action on the note.

Lack of consideration. Lack of consideration is also a personal defense. Suppose a father issued

a note payable to his son. The son's consideration was love and affection, which, as we saw in Chapter 8, is not good consideration. Nonetheless, the father could not raise the defense of lack of consideration against a holder in due course with whom he had not dealt.

Breach of contract. Breach of contract is, of course, a valid defense between the original contracting parties, but it is not available to the issuer if the instrument has passed to a holder in due course.

Discharge other than in bankruptcy. All discharges other than those by a bankruptcy court constitute personal defenses. For that reason, an issuer who pays a negotiable instrument must be sure to take it out of circulation or cancel it or both. Otherwise, the issuer may have to pay it twice [UCC §3-601 and 602].

Unauthorized completion of an incomplete instrument. The UCC does not protect issuers who sign instruments leaving blank the payee's name or the amount or both. In those cases in which a court might allow a defense that the completion was unauthorized, it would be only a personal defense.

Nondelivery of bearer instrument. As Chapter 38 indicates, *delivery* of a negotiable instrument by the issuer is a voluntary transfer of possession. If a bearer instrument is stolen before delivery, the defense of nondelivery is available only against a holder, not against a holder in due course.

THE SHELTER RULE

As we have seen, the general rule of assignment law applies to the transfer of a negotiable instrument. That is, in brief, a transferee generally takes an instrument with the same rights and liabilities as his or her transferor had. What distinguishes Article 3 from the common law is that in certain situations a type of transferee—a holder in due course—can have rights the transferor did not have. In particular, the transferee may not be subject to personal defenses to which the transferor was vulnerable.

When the transferor is a holder in due course, a transferee who does not qualify independently may secure the same protection as if he or she were a holder in due course. Called the *shelter rule,* this result follows from the general rule of assignment law. Here is how it works. Suppose a holder in due course gives her son a note as a gift. The son's failure to give value would disqualify him from becoming a holder in due course if his mother were not a holder in due course. Since he received the note from a holder in due course, he assumes that status.

The shelter rule has two important limitations. A transferee may not take advantage of it if:

> He or she has been a party to any fraud or illegality affecting the instrument, or
> He or she had notice of a defense or claim against the instrument as its prior holder.

These limitations prevent a person from "laundering" a negotiable instrument by passing it through a holder in due course.

The restrictions on the shelter rule do not apply to a party who knows of a possible defense but is not a party to the conduct giving rise to it. Suppose Allan gives Bobby a $3500 check to buy a 5-year-old Mustang. Bobby knows the car has major mechanical problems, but he does not tell Allan. Bobby transfers the check to Carla, a holder in due course. Carla in turn transfers the note to Daryl, a friend of

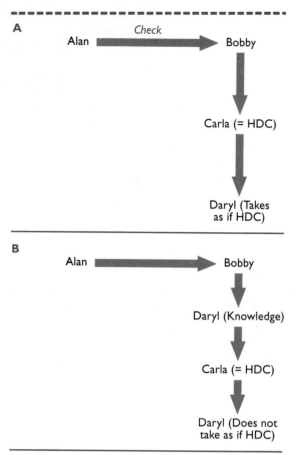

Figure 37.6 Shelter Rule Illustrated.
Note in *b* that a transferee who was a party to a fraud or misconduct or a previous holder with knowledge cannot take *as if* a holder in due course.

Bobby's who knows of his misrepresentation. This knowledge prevents Daryl from being a holder in due course. However, the shelter rule allows Daryl to take the check as if he was a holder in due course. Allan's personal defenses are cut off against Daryl. Had Daryl been a co-owner of the car or a prior holder of the instrument, he would not have been able to benefit from the shelter rule. Figure 37.6 illustrates this example.

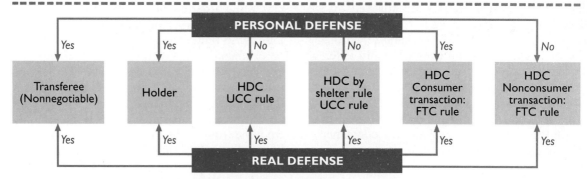

Figure 37.7 Ability to Raise Defenses Against Transferees.
This figure diagrams when a holder may be subject to a maker or issuer's personal and real defenses.

THE FTC'S HOLDER IN DUE COURSE RULE

In 1976, the Federal Trade Commission (FTC) issued a rule which effectively abolished the holder in due course concept as applied to consumer credit contracts. The rule covers any sale or lease of goods or services to consumers, but not to real estate transactions.

The general rules on the assignment of contracts—which allow both personal and real defenses to be raised against a subsequent holder—apply to consumer credit contracts. For example, Leslie purchased a sailboat from Shark's Marina on credit. Shark sold the note to Mariners Bank. Under the UCC, Mariners would be a holder in due course, and Leslie would not be able to assert any of her personal defenses against it. However, under the FTC rule, she would establish a personal defense, such as the boat's unseaworthiness, as a defense on the note.

The FTC adopted this rule because it found that many merchants were selling goods or services to consumers on credit and then, without performing their obligations fully, negotiating the notes to a holder in due course. Since the UCC is a state law, the FTC could not amend it. So, the UCC does not reflect the FTC's changes [see UCC §3-302]. Under the FTC's regulation, states can preempt the federal rule by adopting a stricter statute. Some states have adopted such statutes.

Under the FTC's rule, merchants must insert a clause into their consumer credit contracts which preserves the customer's right to assert his defenses on the contract against any subsequent holders. The clause, which must appear in boldface 10-point type, states:

NOTICE
ANY HOLDER OF THIS CONSUMER CREDIT CONTRACT IS SUBJECT TO ALL CLAIMS AND DEFENSES THE DEBTOR COULD ASSERT AGAINST THE SELLER OF GOODS OR SERVICES OBTAINED WITH THE PROCEEDS HEREOF, RECOVERY HEREUNDER BY THE DEBTOR SHALL NOT EXCEED AMOUNTS PAID BY THE DEBTOR HEREUNDER.

The FTC's holder in due course rule does not apply to sales of more than $25,000 or to consumer purchases on credit cards. Persons who buy goods or services which cost more than $25,000 are presumed not to need the FTC's protection.

Figure 37.7 summarizes the ability to assert defenses against a holder in due course.

Credit card purchases are covered by the federal Fair Credit Billing Act. Under that Act, if a consumer purchases merchandise worth $50 or more on a card and lives within 10 miles of where the goods were purchased, the consumer may suspend payment by making a good faith effort to return the item and asking for a refund or replacement. Until the consumer's dispute with the merchant is resolved, the consumer is not obligated to pay the credit card company.

CONCLUSION

This chapter has focused on how a transferee of a negotiable instrument can gain the protected transferee status called holder in due course. The qualifications are simply stated. A holder in due course must acquire an instrument in good faith, for value, and without any notice of any defect, or by taking from another transferee who had holder in due course status.

The principal importance of holder in due course status is that it cuts off the issuer's and others' personal defenses on the instrument. If no one offers a defense to payment, holder in due course status is irrelevant because the holder has a right to payment. The only remaining concern is payment—a principal topic of the next chapter. But, the next chapter's focus is considerably broader than that. It also explores the liabilities created by the series of contracts which may make up the negotiation process.

A NOTE TO FUTURE CPA CANDIDATES

Questions involving negotiation and holder in due course status almost always appear on the CPA exam. It is imperative that you understand how commercial paper is negotiated and know how a holder can become a holder in due course or take as if a holder in due course by the shelter rule.

Figure 37.1 illustrates the requirements for negotiation. Bearer paper requires only deliv-ery, while order paper requires proper indorse-ment and delivery. On the CPA exam it is not unusual to find a note or check with a series of indorsements. To be sure that proper negotia-tion has occurred, it is necessary to track the instrument from the point of being drawn through the indorsements. Remember, whether an instrument is negotiable is determined only from the front of the instrument. A nonnegotia-ble instrument cannot be made negotiable. In contrast, you must review both sides of an in-strument to determine whether an instrument is presently order or bearer paper and this status can change back and forth.

The CPA exam assumes that you are able to characterize different indorsements. As such, you should try covering up the shaded portions of Figure 37.2 to see if you can proper-ly characterize the six illustrated indorsements. Candidates sometimes become confused and think an indorsement in blank means there was no indorsement. This is, of course, not true. In blank means that there is an indorsement. Thereafter the instrument is bearer paper.

As mentioned previously, it is critical that you know the requirements for someone to be-come a holder in due course. The UCC requires that the person:

- *Be a holder*. Remember that a person cannot become a holder if there is a missing or im-proper necessary indorsement.
- *Give value*. Unlike consideration in common law contracts situations, a promise to per-form is *not* value and antecedent debt *is* val-ue. (An example of the latter is making a monthly payment to Sears for an earlier pur-chased and financed refrigerator.) It is criti-cal that you understand Figures 37.3, 37.4, and 37.5 involving value. Be careful not to confuse good faith with value. A $10 bill would be value for a $1000 note, but if a defense were later raised a court could be expected to closely scrutinize the exchange in regard to good faith.
- *Good faith*. Good faith is a subjective test which protects an honest, stupid person.

However, there are limits to what a court will believe.

- *Lack of notice.* This is tied closely to good faith. A person who knows or should know (overdue instrument) a defense has notice.

The CPA exam often includes a question involving the shelter rule, illustrated in Figure 37.6. Remember that a person who knows of a defense when he takes the instrument cannot qualify as a holder in due course. However, under assignment law the assignee takes the same rights as his assignor had, so if the assignor was a holder in due course the assignee will be. The only exception to the shelter rule is that a previous party cannot launder the instrument to later take as a holder in due course.

The ultimate purpose of determining whether an instrument is negotiable, whether negotiation has properly occurred, and whether a party has become a holder in due course is to determine whether a maker or drawer can prevail as to a *personal* defense. You should understand that a maker or drawer will always prevail as to *real* defenses, including:

- Discharge of the maker in bankruptcy
- Infancy, to the extent that it is a defense to a simple contract
- Unauthorized or forged necessary signature
- The extent of a material alteration

The most common personal defenses covered on the exam are:

- Breach of contract (including nonperformance of a condition precedent)
- Failure of consideration
- Fraud in the inducement

The CPA exam does *not* cover the FTC's holder in due course rule.

KEY WORDS

blank indorsement (843)
discharge (851)
good faith (849)
holder (842)
holder in due course (841)
indorsement (841)
notice (850)
personal defense (853)
qualified indorsement (845)
real defense (853)
restrictive indorsement (843)
shelter rule (858)
special indorsement (843)

DISCUSSION QUESTIONS

1. Define the principal types of indorsements and give an example of each.
2. Who is a holder? Why might this status be important to a transferee?
3. What are the requirements to become a holder in due course?
4. Although a payee is a holder, a payee will seldom qualify as a holder in due course. Why?
5. What is an "antecedent debt"? Will satisfaction of an antecedent debt constitute the giving of value under Article 3's definition of a holder in due course?
6. To what extent does a bank become a holder in due course of checks deposited in a customer's account?
7. Will taking a negotiable instrument at a discount prevent a holder from becoming a holder in due course? If not, to what extent is such a person a holder in due course?
8. Does the knowledge that an incomplete instrument has been completed always bar someone from becoming a holder in due course? If not, when does it?
9. What is the shelter rule and how does it affect transferees of negotiable instruments?
10. What distinguished real from personal defenses? What are real defenses under the UCC?
11. How does the FTC's rule on holders in due course affect Article 3's coverage? Why did the FTC consider the rule necessary?

CASE PROBLEMS

1. Tommy Phillips issued a check payable to Jere Hatcher for $75. Jere indorsed the check:

Pay to Bob Alberts Only
Without Recourse
Jere Hatcher

Bob's last name is actually spelled "Aalberts." What type of indorsement has Hatcher made? How should Aalberts indorse the check? Explain.

2. John Daly received a check which was originally made payable to the order of one of his customers, Al Pine. The following indorsement was written on the bank of the check:

    How would the indorsement on this check be classified? What is the legal effect of the indorsement? Explain.

Al Pine, without recourse, for collection only

3. Georgia purchased a used computer from Vic for $1000, $250 in cash and $750 in the form of a negotiable promissory note due in 2 months. Fearing that Georgia would discover that the computer was defective, Vic immediately transferred the note to Tom Isaacs in exchange for discharge of a $400 debt. When the note came due, Tom attempted unsuccessfully to collect from Georgia, who by then had discovered that the computer was worthless. Tom has sued Georgia. Has Tom paid sufficient consideration to qualify as a holder in due course? Under the UCC, will Tom prevail as to the entire amount of the note, $750? Explain.

4. Baylor borrowed $2000 from Commercial Bank. The debt was evidenced by a negotiable note payable to bearer due September 1, 1994. Baylor paid the note on August 10, and the bank gave it to him. However, the note bore no indication that it had been paid or cancelled. On his way home, Baylor lost the note. Laura Selber found it and promptly sold it to Ralph Tyler. Assuming Tyler meets the crite-

ria of a holder in due course, does he have a right to the full $2000 on or before September 1, 1994?

5. Pam Trimble wrote a check for $35 to Ken Bangston for a dresser he was selling at his garage sale. Bangston cleverly raised the amount of the check from $35 to $85, indorsed it, and gave it to his hunting club toward his past dues. The club manager took the check in good faith and did not know of the check's alteration. In the interim, Pam discovered termites in the dresser, returned it to Bangston, and stopped payment on her check. In an action by the hunting club on her check to Bangston, what should be the result? Explain.

6. Marlin ordered merchandise from Plant, to be delivered the following day. He gave Plant a check payable to her order drawn on his account in First Bank. They agreed that the check would not be cashed unless delivery was received and accepted. The goods were not delivered, and Marlin notified Plant that he was exercising his right to rescind. Plant negotiated the check for full value to Rose, who took it in good faith and without notice of any defense. Rose then negotiated it for full value to Quirk, who knew of Plant's breach of the agreement. Marlin has stopped payment on the check and refuses to pay it. Would Marlin have a valid defense in a suit by Quirk for the amount of the check? Explain.

7. Troy fraudulently induced Carl to make a negotiable instrument payable to this order in exchange for goods he never intended to deliver. Troy negotiated the note to Gordon, who took with notice of the fraud. Gordon, in turn, negotiated it to Wagner, a holder in due course. Wagner presented it to Carol for payment but she refused to honor it. Wagner contacted Gordon, who agreed to reacquire the instrument by negotiation from Wagner. Can Gordon successfully assert the right of his prior transferee, Wagner, as a result of the repurchase? Explain.

8. Way's Used Cars sold Jenny Parker what turned out to be a lemon. Jenny paid Way $1000 cash and gave Way a note for $4000. Way sold the note to Central Bank for $3700.

Central Bank regularly purchases notes from Way. The bank was without notice of Jenny's complaints against Way. Will Jenny prevail under Article 3? Under the FTC modification of the holder in due course rule? Explain.

9. On January 9. Nancy Adger wrote a note to Wiley Drabant for $750, due on July 30. The note was given by Adger in exchange for a sign which Drabant was to make by March 1 for her new office. On February 1, Drabant borrowed $500 for 90 days from American Bank, putting up as collateral Adger's note. Drabant never delivered the sign to Adger and defaulted on the note to American Bank. In an action by American Bank against Adger, what is Adger's liability, if any, to the bank? Explain.

10. Olivia Perot wrote a check to Mary Sweeney for $350 for a pedigreed puppy. Mary cashed the check at First Bank, taking $50 in cash and depositing the remainder. The deposit brought Mary's checking account up to $425. Olivia subsequently learned that her puppy lacked papers. She returned the dog to Mary and stopped payment on her check. At the time First Bank learned of Olivia's defense, Mary had written three checks, worth a total of $150, against the $425. To what extent, if at all, is First Bank a holder in due course as to Olivia? Explain.

CHAPTER 38

Payment and the Liabilities of the Parties

The entire system of commercial paper rests on one belief: that when an instrument is presented for payment, it will be paid and the liabilities associated with it discharged. The system could not work if payment were not the rule. Indeed, only 1 percent of the 47 billion checks Americans write annually bounce. Still, that is 470 *million* bouncing checks.*

This chapter describes how payment is made, and the many ways liabilities are discharged. The check collection process is discussed in the following chapter. You may wish to refer to Figure 39.1 to begin to visualize this process.

DISCHARGE

Payment *discharges*—terminates or releases— a contractual obligation. However, an obligation evidenced by commercial paper, like any other contract, may be discharged in a number of ways besides payment. If the instrument has been negotiated, payment or discharge has the effect of releasing other contractual obligations which grew out of its negotiation. These potential liabilities—which are normally triggered only if the obligation is not paid—are discussed in the following sections. This section focuses on what usually happens to the obligations represented by negotiable instruments.

Payment and Tender of Payment

The most common way in which liability is discharged is through payment. The *payor's* (the party paying the instrument) contract is to pay the holder. Payment discharges the payor even if she has notice of a third party's adverse claim. Except in cases of theft or of a restrictive indorsement, the drafters of the UCC saw no reason to inconvenience the payor because of a

---

* "Not All Endorse the Changes," *USA Today*, Sept. 1, 1988, p. B1.

dispute between other parties to the instrument, unless they indemnified her or served her with an appropriate court order. However, a payor who pays in bad faith or who pays in a manner not consistent with the terms of a restrictive indorsement is not relieved of liability and could be forced to pay the same amount again [UCC §3-603].

A person who indicates that he or she is ready, willing, and able to perform obligations under a contract is said to *tender* performance. "Tender" may be used as either a verb or a noun. A tender of performance is an indication of a willingness and ability to perform [UCC §3-604(3)].

A payor who tenders payment which the holder refuses to accept is discharged as to all subsequent liability for interest, costs, or attorney's fees [UCC §3-604(1)]. Assume that the maker of a $10,000 note tenders the total principal and interest due to the holder, but the holder refuses to accept it. The maker is still liable for the full amount due the holder, but no more interest accrues, no penalty charges attach, and no attorney's fees for collecting the note will be granted.

If the holder refuses tender, any party having recourse against the person tendering performance is completely discharged. In effect, the holder waives his rights against them by not taking the payment when it is available.

Renunciation and Cancellation

A negotiable instrument represents a contract. For that reason, any action which would discharge a simple contract may discharge liability under a negotiable instrument. A simple agreement will do. For example, if the maker agrees to paint the holder's house in return for a release from liability, the agreement discharges the maker.

A holder may, even without consideration, discharge any party to the instrument by renunciation or cancellation [UCC §3-605(1)]. A *re-*

nunciation requires either a writing signed and delivered to the party to be discharged or the surrender of the instrument to that party. A *cancellation* usually consists of drawing a line through or striking a person's signature or of mutilating or destroying the instrument. Dis-

charge of a particular party—like a prior indorser—does not affect the holder's title where the holder retains it. But, what happens when a note is cancelled in error? That was the question in the next case.

Gover v. Home and City Savings Bank

574 So.2d 307 (Fla. App. 1 Dist. 1991)

FACTS   Gover's mortgage was accidentally canceled due to a clerical error by an employee at Home and City Savings Bank (HCSB). Gover received the canceled note, release of the mortgage, and title to the collateral. Gover subsequently stopped making payments on the note and HCSB repossessed the collateral. HCSB, in a motion for summary judgment, argued that the note and mortgage were still valid because the cancellation was unintentional. HCSB won at the trial level.

ISSUE   Was the unintentional and mistaken cancellation of the promissory note invalid?

DECISION   Yes. Affirmed. A cancellation or renunciation of an instrument is not effective if it is done unintentionally or is caused by mistake. Gover argues that under the plain meaning of the Florida UCC a holder can cancel an instrument even without consideration "[b]y renouncing his rights by a writing signed and delivered or by surrender of the instrument to the party to be discharged." This argument is erroneous, since such an effect cannot occur without the intent of the lender to discharge the debtor.

Impairment of Recourse or Collateral

When the holder agrees not to sue any person again whom another party to the instrument has a right of recourse, the holder discharges that party's obligations on the instrument. However, the discharge affects not only that party but also all subsequent indorsers.

The same rule applies if the holder impairs the *collateral* for the instrument. If a maker gives his payee a car as collateral for his note and the payee wrecks it, that action discharges the subsequent indorsers but not the maker [UCC §3-606(1)]. This subject will be discussed in considerable detail in Part VIII.

GENERAL PRINCIPLES OF LIABILITY

In the context of Article 3, "liability" refers primarily to responsibility for paying the instrument. The first principle guiding the determination of liability is, "No person is liable on an instrument unless his signature appears thereon" [UCC §3-401(1)]. However, that does not mean that a person's handwritten signature must appear. The UCC's definition of signature, discussed in Chapter 36, allows many different indications of responsibility as a person's signature—including some not actually made by the issuer.

Signature by Authorized Representative

An authorized representative may place a person's signature on a negotiable instrument [UCC §3-403]. This happens commonly in principal-agent relationships, including those between corporate officers and their corporations.

Generally, an agent can bind her principal so long as the agent has *express, implied,* or *apparent* authority to sign his name. Also, the agent must sign her principal's name. Suppose Debbie Kent is an agent for Triangle, Inc. Debbie purchased some inventory for Triangle's business and issued the supplier. Viking Company, a note signed:

Triangle, Inc.
by Debbie Kent, Agent

Triangle would be liable on the instrument, since its name appears on it [UCC §3-403]. However, Debbie would not be liable on the note; her agency status is clear from her signature.

An agent who signs in an agency capacity but does not list her principal will have sole legal responsibility, as to subsequent takers from the payee, for the negotiable instrument she executes. Between the immediate parties, however, either the agent of the payee may introduce parol evidence to establish the principal's identity. Now suppose that Debbie simply signed the note to Viking:

by Debbie Kent, Agent

In later litigation over the note, either Debbie or Viking could introduce parol evidence to establish that Triangle was Debbie's principal and therefore was liable on it. But as between a bank to which Viking negotiated the note—or any other subsequent holder—and Debbie, only she would be liable on it.

In the next case, a Minnesota appellate court had to determine whether an agency relationship existed.

Greyhound Lines, Inc. v. First State Bank

366 N.W.2d 354 (Minn. Ct. App. 1985)

FACTS Greyhound brought suit against the First State Bank of Rollingstone, seeking payment of a check the bank had allegedly accepted. The bank did not dispute the facts stated in the affidavit (attached to Greyhound's motion for summary judgment) of Lou Hodnik, a Greyhound supervisor. B. C. Dahl was a commission agent for Greyhound. To settle his account, he presented Hodnik with a check payable to Greyhound for $9730.44 drawn on—and bearing the printed name and logo of—the First State Bank of Rollingstone. Hodnik could not accept the check without confirmation that the account contained funds to cover the check. Dahl returned with the check signed by Duane Klein, the bank's vice president. Hodnik knew Klein and his position at the bank. He called Klein. Klein assured him that the funds were in the account and that he understood he signed the check for the bank. On presentation, the bank dishonored the check because the account had insufficient funds. The trial court entered summary judgment against the bank.

ISSUE Was parol evidence—Hodnik's affidavit—admissible to establish that Klein signed as the bank's agent?

DECISION Yes. Affirmed. A bank's printed name and logo on a check are sufficient to name it as principal of an agent to determine whether the agent signs on behalf of the principal. Here, the signature did not indicate a representative capacity. As between the immediate parties to the negotiation of a check, the plaintiff may establish the principal's liability by an examination of both the face of the instrument and the circumstances surrounding the signature.

Transferee's Right to an Indorsement

Any transfer of order paper for value gives the transferee the specifically enforceable right to have the transferor's unqualified indorsement. If, for example, Michelle cashes a check made out to her but forgets to indorse it, the bank can require her to indorse it [UCC §3-201].

Unauthorized Signatures

In general, an unauthorized or forged signature will not function as that of the person whose name is signed [UCC §3-404(1)]. It follows that no one who takes order paper as a result of an unauthorized or forged indorsement can become a holder.

Negotiation is the process by which a transferee becomes a holder. Negotiation of order paper takes place by indorsement, but an indorsement is effective only if it is authorized. For that reason, a person who takes an order instrument from a forger normally cannot become a holder, since the indorsement to the transferee would not be authorized. An unauthorized indorsement operates as the signature of the person whose name is signed only if that person either is estopped from denying its validity or ratifies it.

A *ratification* is an act by which a principal indorses an unauthorized action taken by an agent which otherwise would not have bound the principal. An unauthorized signature may be ratified. If it is, the ratifying party becomes liable to the holder, and the signer's liability is discharged. However, the signer may be liable to the ratifying party [UCC §3-404(2)]. Assume that Dotty ratifies Sol's forgery of a check he stole from her. She would be liable to the person holding the check. Her ratification, however, would have no impact on Sol's criminal prosecution or on his civil liability to her.

Negligence Inviting Forgery

Generally, makers and drawers cannot raise the defense of an unauthorized signature if their negligence allows or invites forgery [UCC §3-404 Comment 4]. For example, suppose that an employer's check imprinting machine which has signing capability always sits unlocked on the bookkeeper's desk. If an employee writes an unauthorized check with it, the employer will be liable. Similarly, a maker or drawer who signs a check but negligently leaves open the payee line or the amount of the instrument will be liable on it.

The UCC identifies specific situations in which forgery is not an effective defense to liability on an instrument. These situations are best thought of as amplifications of the negligence rule.

Imposters. Where an imposter causes a drawer or maker to issue an instrument to him in another's name, then negotiates it to a holder in due course, the drawer or maker is liable. Assume that Al overhears Ed say that he is going to Microworks to pick up a check. Al gets to Microworks first, tells the bookkeeper he is Ed, and takes the check. He forges Ed's indorsement and transfers the check to Robin, a holder in due course. In an action on the check, Robin would prevail because Microworks did not use due care to identify Ed as the check's recipient [UCC §3-405(1)(a)].

Faithless agents. An issuer is liable to a holder in due course on an instrument if an agent supplies a payee's name for payment but intends the payee to have no interest in the instrument when it is issued. Assume that Greta manages Walter's store. She submits a payroll voucher for Polly. Walter makes out a check to Polly and hands it to Greta to give Polly. Greta forges Polly's indorsement and negotiates the check to a holder in due course. The holder in due course will prevail in an action against Walter on the check. The burden of verifying whether an employee gets her check belongs on the employer. More importantly, the employer has the responsibility to hire faithful agents [UCC §3-405(1)(c)].

Fictitious payees. An issuer is also liable to a holder in due course when the person signing on its behalf intends the payee to have no interest in the instrument. The pattern of these cases rarely varies. Usually, a manager has authority to write paychecks. She issues them to nonexistent or *fictitious* payees, forges the indorsements, and cashes them. A holder in due course will prevail, since the employer should have had either better accounting controls or a more trustworthy employee writing checks [UCC §3-405(1)(b)].

PRIMARY CONTRACTUAL LIABILITY

A holder looks for payment first to those with primary contractual liability, then to those with secondary contractual liability, and finally to those who made warranties on transfer or presentment of an instrument. We will examine secondary and warranty liability in the following sections.

Primary contractual liability results from an implied unconditional promise by the maker of a note or the *acceptor* of a draft (usually the drawee) to pay the instrument upon its presentment for payment. On a two-party instrument, the maker alone is primarily liable for payment. However, on a three-party instrument, neither the drawer nor the drawee is primarily liable unless the drawee pays or *accepts*—promises to pay—the draft.

Presentment

A *presentment* is a demand for payment or acceptance made upon the issuer, maker, acceptor, drawee, or other payor on behalf of the holder [UCC §3-504(1)]. The holder of a note or an accepted draft has merely to present it for payment to impose primary liability on the maker or acceptor—the drawee, usually.

Upon presentment, a maker or acceptor may *dishonor*—refuse to pay or accept—the instrument and raise a defense to payment, such as a material alteration. The drawer promises to pay only if the payee presents the draft to the drawee and the drawee does not pay or accept it. Suppose Kerry writes a check to Wagner Clothing Store on his personal checking account. If his bank refuses to pay the check because of insufficient funds, he will be responsible for paying the check.

Acceptance

A check or a draft does not assign particular funds in the drawee's hands for its payment. However, a holder is assured of payment by an *acceptance*, a drawee's signed promise to honor a draft when it is presented in the future [UCC §3-410(1)]. In fact, the drawee has no obligation to pay the holder unless it accepts the draft [UCC §3-409].

Either the drawer or the payee may seek acceptance of the draft. An acceptance is limited to the terms of the instrument at the time of acceptance. If a draft is for $30,000 when it is accepted, the drawee is not bound to pay $300,000 if the draft has been altered to that amount when it is presented for payment.

Effect of drawee's acceptance or payment. If any party is going to be primarily liable on a draft, it is going to be the drawee, but only if it accepts or pays the draft. If the drawee dishonors the draft, the holder must look to the drawer, who is secondarily liable.

Acceptance is not payment and is not incorporated into payment. If a bank pays a draft on presentment, the bank has assumed the liability that the instrument represents. Since it has paid the draft, obviously, it has not accepted the draft for future payment.

Certification of checks. If the draft is a check, acceptance is called *certification*, and the accepted draft is called a *certified check*. When a bank certifies a check, it transfers the money necessary to pay it from the drawer's account to a special reserve. However, a bank is under no obligation to certify a check, even when an account contains sufficient funds to cover it [UCC §3-411(2)].

If the holder has the check certified, the certification discharges the liability of the drawer and of all previous indorsers [UCC §3-411(1)]. Suppose Jane uses an uncertified check to buy a car. The dealer takes the check to her bank and has it certified. The bank has now assumed all liability for the check. By contrast, if the drawer has the check certified, she remains secondarily liable on it.

Once a bank has certified a check, it may not object that the drawer's signature is forged. A bank has the responsibility of knowing what its drawer's signature looks like.

Acceptance varying a draft. If the drawee offers to accept a draft in a way which varies the terms of the draft as presented, the holder may refuse the acceptance and treat the draft as dishonored. Suppose the drawee attempts to accept only a part of the amount of the draft. The holder may treat this offer as a refusal to pay the entire amount [UCC §3-412(1)].

Acceptance by estoppel. In unusual situations, a court may hold that a drawee is estopped from denying acceptance even though it never physically noted its acceptance on the draft. In these cases, the drawee generally did something which caused the holder to reasonably believe that the drawee had accepted the draft. To permit the drawee to refuse payment would injure the holder, who relied on the drawee's representation. That is the reasoning in the case which follows.

- -

Carroll v. Twin City Pontiac Used Cars, Inc.

397 So. 2d 42 (La. Ct. App. 1981)

FACTS   Carroll agreed to buy a 1976 Buick from Twin City. He then obtained First National Bank's commitment for a $3200 auto loan. Carroll returned to Twin City, where a salesman confirmed the commitment in a telephone conversation with First National's president. Twin City then sold Carroll the Buick for $4045, of which $845 was the trade-in value of his 1970 Chrysler. Carroll's draft on First National Bank represented the $3200 balance. Twin City sent the draft to First National for payment. Meanwhile, Twin City sold the Chrysler for $200. First National held the draft for 2 or 3 weeks and then refused to pay it. As a result, Carroll and Twin City rescinded the sale. Carroll sued Twin City for damages, and Twin City in turn sued the bank. The trial court found for Carroll against Twin City and for Twin City against the bank. In each case it awarded $200, the Chrysler's value.

ISSUE   Was First National liable for its failure to honor the draft?

DECISION   Yes. Affirmed. A bank is not liable on a draft unless it accepts or pays it. However, nothing in Article 3 affects "any liability in contract, tort or otherwise, arising from any . . . representation which is not an acceptance" [UCC §3-409(2)]. Twin City's claim is not on the draft itself, but for damages as a result of First National's breach of its promise to honor the draft.

SECONDARY CONTRACTUAL LIABILITY

Secondary contractual liability is conditional. Every drawer and indorser is secondarily liable on instruments she issues or indorses. The drawer promises to pay the instrument if the drawee does not. An indorser promises to pay the instrument if the maker or the drawee does not pay it.

Drawer's Liability

A drawer promises to pay a draft personally only if a holder makes a timely or *due presentment* to the drawee for payment or acceptance and the draft is dishonored [UCC §3-413(2) and 3-507(1)(a)].

"Due presentment" varies, depending on the type of instrument involved. The UCC presumes that a check should be presented for payment within 30 days of its issuance [UCC §3-503(2)(a)].* Other negotiable instruments must be presented within a reasonable time. Failure to present within the period for presentment does not discharge the drawer's liability. However, it may affect the transferee's holder in due course status, since it signals that the instrument is overdue.

---

* The 30-day period for due presentment should not be confused with the period during which a drawee bank may pay the check. A bank is under no obligation to its customer—the drawer—to pay a check which is presented more than 6 months after its date, though the bank may charge a customer's account for payment after that if the check is paid in good faith [UCC §4-404].

The Indorser's Contract

An unqualified indorsement represents the indorser's contractual promise that upon notice of dishonor he or she will pay the instrument according to its terms at the time of the indorsement. For an indorser to be liable on a dishonored negotiable instrument, a subsequent indorser or holder must notify the indorser of dishonor:

- Within 7 days of the indorser's indorsement, *and*
- In accordance with the midnight notice rules covering a holder giving notice of dishonor

The next two sections discuss the "downstream" liability of indorsers and transferors and the "upstream" notice of dishonor rules for a holder seeking to impose secondary liability.

Indorser liability. The indorser's contract is enforceable by his or her transferee or by any later indorser who pays the instrument after dishonor [UCC §3-414(1)]. An indorser's contract is enforceable only if all of the following took place:

- Within 7 days after the indorsement, the holder presented the instrument for payment or initiated bank collection.
- The instrument was dishonored.
- Notice of the dishonor was given to the indorser in a timely fashion.
- The indorsement was not qualified.

Like a drawer, an indorser does not expect to

pay personally, and in fact obligations on in-dorser contracts are rarely invoked.

To hold an indorser of an uncertified check liable, the holder must present the check for payment or initiate bank collection within 7 days after the indorsement [UCC §3-503(2)(b)]. Except in some very limited circumstances, failure to present a check within this period results in the indorser's discharge, regardless of whether the delay injured the indorser [UCC §3-502(1)(a)].

Only those who actually indorse a negotiable instrument make an indorser's contract. A person who transfers an instrument to another without indorsement does not promise to pay the instrument upon dishonor. Assume that Betsy Nettleton received a check from Vaughn Westway. If Vaughn did not indorse it, he is not liable to Betsy on an indorser's contract. However, he may have warranty liability.

Notice of dishonor. A notice of dishonor does not have to be in any particular form and may be oral or written [UCC §3-508(3)].

Under the so-called midnight deadline rule, a bank must provide notice of dishonor to the indorser before midnight on the next banking day after it has either dishonored an instrument or received notice itself. Anyone other than a bank must give notice of dishonor before midnight of the third business day following the dishonor or receipt of notice of the dishonor [UCC §3-508(2)]. Failure to give notice within the applicable period results in the indorser's discharge.

INDORSER "DOWNSTREAM" LIABILITY	7 DAYS AFTER INDORSEMENT

Holder "Upstream" notice requirements

• Holder = bank: by midnight	Next business day
• Holder ≠ bank: by midnight	Third business day

Figure 38.1 Check Indorsement Notice Rules.

Suppose John Frazier indorses and negotiates a check on December 1. Six days after his indorsement, the check is dishonored. A subsequent holder, Neil Erwin, gives John notice by midnight the second business day after dishonor. Neil will have met the upstream notice requirement, but John will not be liable because his 7-day downstream liability period has lapsed. Thus, the combination of the downstream liability limit and the upstream notice requirement imposes significant barriers to triggering an indorser's secondary liability. See Figure 38.1.

Written notice of dishonor is effective when sent, even if the indorser does not receive it or receives it after the time for dishonor has passed [UCC §3-508(4)]. A court will excuse a delay in providing notice of dishonor only in extraordinary circumstances, as the next case illustrates.

First Wyoming Bank v. Cabinet Craft Distributors, Inc.

624 P.2d 227 (Wyo. 1981)

FACTS Quality Kitchens delivered a $10,000 check drawn on First Wyoming Bank of Sheridan to its payee, Cabinet Craft. On May 6, Cabinet Craft deposited the check in the Security Bank of Billings, Montana. Security Bank credited Cabinet Craft's account and started the check through the bank collection system. On May 22, First

Wyoming received the check and sent it by courier to a computer center in Billings for processing. Normally, the courier waited for the checks to be processed and returned them to Sheridan. However, when the courier reached Billings, he discovered that flooding had closed the main road to Sheridan. Although there was an alternative route available, the checks were placed on a Western Airlines flight the next morning, May 23. They did not arrive until May 25, when First Wyoming dishonored the check because of insufficient funds in Quality Kitchens' account. Cabinet Craft brought suit against First Wyoming for the amount of the check. The trial court found for Cabinet Craft.

ISSUE

Did First Wyoming have an excuse for failing to dishonor the check in a timely fashion?

DECISION

No. Affirmed. UCC §4-108(2) excuses delay by a bank if it is caused by "interruption of communication facilities, suspension of payments by another bank, war, emergency conditions or other circumstances beyond the control of the bank provided it exercises such diligence as the circumstances require." The burden of proving diligence rests on the bank. Here, it offered no evidence that it attempted to trace the checks when they failed to arrive. Also, the bank had an alternative to using Western Airlines: its courier could have taken the less direct route back to Sheridan.

Order of indorser liability. Unless they otherwise agree indorsers are liable to one another in the order in which they indorse, which is presumed to be the order in which their signatures appear on the instrument" [UCC §3-414(2)]. If a prior indorser reacquires an instrument, the intervening indorsers' contracts are automatically discharged as to the reacquiring indorser [UCC §3-208]. A qualified indorsement, of course, disclaims the indorser's normal promise to pay the instrument under the indorsement contract [UCC §3-414 Comment 1].

Supplying a necessary indorsement. A *depository bank*—the bank at which the check is deposited for payment—may supply its customer's necessary indorsement. Commonly, banks stamp checks lacking an indorsement:

Credited to the account of the within named payee.
Absence of indorsement guaranteed.

In effect, the bank supplies the indorsement.

However, if the check bears a *legend*—a notation—to the effect that the payee's indorsement is required, the bank may not supply it [UCC §4-205(1)].

WARRANTY LIABILITY

A *warranty* is a guarantee or assurance as to something's quality or nature. A person who transfers an instrument for consideration or presents an instrument for acceptance or payment makes warranties as to his or her title and the validity of the instrument. These warranties may provide a remedy for dishonor for someone taking a negotiable instrument where there is no indorser's contract or where it has expired. However, these warranties are quite limited in scope.

Transfer Warranties

A person who transfers a negotiable instrument for consideration makes transfer warranties to

| PARTY | CONTRACT LIABILITY | | | TRANSFER WARRANTY LIABILITY | |
	PRIMARY	SECONDARY	NONE	TO ALL SUBSEQUENT TRANSFEREES	TO NEXT SUBSEQUENT TRANSFEREE ONLY
Maker	X				
Acceptor (drawer who accepts draft)	X				
Drawer		X			
Drawee			X		
Indorser (except by qualified indorsement)		X		X	
Indorser by qualified indorsement			X	X*	
Transferor, not an indorser			X		X†

*Qualified indorser states that he *knows* of no defects.
†Liable if consideration is received from transferee.

Figure 38.2 Liability on Commercial Paper.

the transferee and, if the transfer is by indorsement, to subsequent holders. Transfer warranties are not made to a maker, acceptor, or drawee [UCC §3-417(2)]. A transferor makes the following warranties:

- The transferor has good title or the transfer is authorized.
- All signatures are genuine or authorized.
- The instrument has not been materially altered.
- The transferor has no knowledge of any insolvency proceeding involving the maker, acceptor, or drawer or an unaccepted instrument.
- No defense of any party is good against the transferor [UCC §3-417(2)].

When holders transfer instruments by means of qualified or "without recourse" indorsements, they warrant that they have no knowledge of a defense which would be good against them rather than that no defenses are good against them [UCC §3-417(3)]. All other transfer warranties apply. Thus, a qualified indorsement carries with it a warranty of good title.

Figure 38.2 tabulates the liabilities on commercial paper.

Warranties of Presentment

All prior transferors and the person who presents an instrument for payment or acceptance make three warranties to a person who accepts or pays it in good faith. First, they warrant either their good title or their authority to receive payment of the instrument [UCC §3-417(1)]. For example, if the instrument is a check, a person presenting it for payment impliedly warrants to the bank that no indorsement is forged.

Second, they warrant that they have no

knowledge that the signature of the maker or drawer is unauthorized. However, a holder in due course acting in good faith does not give this warranty, since a maker is presumed to know his signature and a drawee bank, its customer's.

Third, they warrant that the instrument has not been materially altered. Again, the holder in due course is exempted, and for similar reasons.

OTHER CONTRACTUAL RELATIONSHIPS

The obligations which arise in three other contractual relationships involving negotiable instruments are worth noting. These are the drawee's obligations to third parties and to the drawer, the drawer's duties to the drawee, and the responsibilities of an accommodation party.

Drawee Liability to Third Parties and Drawer

A drawee may refuse to pay a draft without liability to a third party holder even if the drawer has sufficient funds in the account to cover the check. As a practical matter, a drawee bank usually will pay because its failure to honor a draft may breach its contract with the drawer. However, no third party can force the drawee to pay unless it has accepted the draft.

The drawer can require a bank which pays a check with a forged indorsement or drawer's signature to restore the money to his account. In the following case, the plaintiff tried to take advantage of the drawee's liability for paying a forged instrument.

McIsaac v. Bank of New York

74 A.D.2d 717, 425 N.Y.S.2d 678 (App. Div. 1980)

FACTS   Dr. McIsaac ordered a surgical camera from Optical Associates Sales, Inc. A check dated July 21, 1978, accompanied the order. The check was indorsed "Ophthalmic Instrument Sales, Inc." and cashed. Optical and Ophthalmic engaged in a single business at the same location, were owned and operated by the same people, and used joint Yellow Pages advertising and telephone listings. McIsaac knew this from an earlier transaction. On August 6, McIsaac received his account statement and canceled checks, including the check to Optical Associates. He did not notify the bank of any irregularity until February 16, 1979. In the interim, Optical had notified him that its "financial embarrassment" prevented it from filling his order. McIsaac brought suit against the bank for wrongfully paying the check. The trial court found for McIsaac.

ISSUE   Did the bank wrongfully pay the check to Ophthalmic?

DECISION   No. Reversed.

A drawee bank stands in a debtor-credit relationship to its customer and may make payment on checks drawn against its customer's account only as directed by the drawer. However, a drawer may be precluded from recovering on an improperly paid check where the proceeds . . . actually reached the person intended to receive them. . . .

The facts reveal that any loss suffered by the plaintiff is not due to any wrongful act on the part of the bank. On the contrary, any loss is due to the insolvency of the payee. The proceeds of the check did in fact reach the entity intended which precludes the drawee from recovering against the bank.

Drawer's Duty to Drawee

The court in *McIsaac* also held that a bank customer has a duty to examine his statements and checks immediately after receiving them. He should look carefully for alterations to the face of his checks. However, he has no duty to evaluate the payee's or any other indorser's signature. Chapter 39 will discuss the drawer's duty to examine his checks.

Accommodation Party's Contract

In credit situations involving borrowers with less established credit records, often the borrower must have a cosigner in order to receive a loan. For example, new college graduates often must secure a cosigner, often a parent, on a note to purchase a new car. In effect, a cosigner lends his creditworthiness. A cosigner under Article 3 is called an *accommodation party*. An accommodation party agrees to pay the instrument should the maker or issuer fail to do so [UCC §3-415(1)].*

So long as value is given for the instrument, the accommodating party will be liable in the capacity in which he signed. For example, if Jack signs as an accommodation maker, he will be liable to a holder as a comaker. An accommodation drawer or indorser has secondary liability similar to that of any drawer or indorser. An accommodation party may not defend against a third party holder by claiming that he received no consideration for lending his name to the accommodated party. His consideration is that the accommodated party received, say, the loan she wanted. The next case illustrates how this rule works in practice.

---

* Chapter 40 discusses sureties and guarantors in detail.

Armstrong v. Armstrong

714 F.Supp. 451 (D. Colo. 1989)

FACTS   Dick and Bob Armstrong were general partners in a limited partnership. To establish a line of credit at the Minnequa Bank, Bob, Dick, and their wives agreed to guarantee the notes of the partnership. A few years later, one of the notes came due and was not paid. Bob's widow, Rogene, purchased the note to settle her obligation and sued Dick and his wife Jean, as guarantors. Dick and Jean argued that they did not receive consideration for being guarantors on the note. In a motion for summary judgment at the trial level, Rogene prevailed.

ISSUE   Was the guaranty agreement unenforceable because the guarantors purportedly failed to receive consideration?

DECISION   No. Affirmed. After the execution of an agreement guaranteeing a loan which is relied upon by the lender, the guarantor's agreement is enforceable. When the guarantors signed the guaranty agreement, the instrument began: "For valuable consideration, the undersigned . . . jointly and severally unconditionally guarantee and promise to pay. . . ." Thus, the fact that the bank relied upon the agreement to make the loan in question indicates that there was no failure of consideration, since both parties received whatever they had bargained for.

REVISION OF ARTICLES 3 AND 4

Articles 3 and 4 were developed almost 40 years ago. Since then, banking technology and services, and the demands on them, have changed radically. For example, 40 years ago there were no ATM machines. It was not considered unreasonable for a check from a distant city to take 7 days to clear. Variable-rate negotiable notes were something business finance classes contemplated but never expected to become commonplace.

The National Conference of Commissioners on Uniform State Laws and the American Law Institute are currently engaged in a thorough review of both Articles 3 and 4. Revised Articles 3 and 4 are expected to be available for state adoption sometime during 1990. A new article, Article 4A, became available in late 1989. It applies to wholesale or commercial electronic fund transfers.

What will the revised Articles 3 and 4 include? Variable-rate notes will be specifically recognized. The scope of Article 4 will be broadened to include savings and loans, and credit unions. Electronic check collection will be recognized. And, refusal of cashier checks will be made more difficult.

mercial paper changes hands are not exceptions to these rules.

The obligations evidenced by commercial paper are satisfied by payment. When that occurs, normally all other contractual liabilities associated with the instrument's transfers are discharged. Article 3's rules on liability—like holder in due course status—become important only in the rare instances in which performance does not occur.

The levels of liability reflect a holder's reasonable expectation of who should be liable on the instrument. At the same time, Article 3 stringently restricts the liability for paying the instrument of those most remote from its issuance.

The goals reflected in the Code's ordering of liability are the same as those expressed in the holder in due course concept. The drafters wished to make identification of liability as mechanical and fair as possible, while placing the lightest possible restrictions on the free flow of commercial paper.

The principles of negotiability examined in Chapters 36 through 38 also apply to documents of title and investment securities, which are the topics of the next chapter.

CONCLUSION

Every contract creates rights and obligations. And in most instances, the parties perform their reciprocal duties. The contracts by which com-

A NOTE TO FUTURE CPA CANDIDATES

The CPA exam focus in this chapter is on the liabilities, defenses, and rights of parties to commercial paper and discharge. You should

be sure to understand Figure 38.2, as it provides an important overview of both contract and warranty liability under Article 3.

In regard to contract liability, no one is primarily liable on a draft or check at the time of issue. Certification of a check by the holder, securing the bank's acceptance of the check, will release any prior indorsers and the drawer. (In contrast, a drawer securing certification will remain secondarily liable.) The UCC presumes a check will be presented within 30 days of issuance. The failure to do so does not release the drawer but may affect the ability of the holder to establish holder in due course status.

An indorser, *merely by the act of indorsement* (without regard to consideration), agrees to pay the instrument if it is not paid when properly presented for payment. (Obviously, a person who transfers an instrument without indorsing it can have *no* indorser liability.) As Figure 38.1 illustrates, an indorser's "downstream" contract liability is only for 7 days. To hold an indorser liable, a holder must give prompt notice of nonpayment: if a bank, by the next business day; otherwise, by the third business day. An excused delay in presentment may extend the time for notice.

A person who transfers a negotiable instrument *for consideration* makes transfer warranties to the transferee, and *if the transfer is by indorsement*, to subsequent holders. The warranties include the following:

- Good title or authorized transfer
- All signatures are genuine or authorized
- No defense of any party against instrument

A qualified indorsement, "without recourse," eliminates the indorser liability (and alters the warranty liability to read, in effect: the transferor knows of no defense(s) good against the instrument).

In regard to forged signatures, a person whose signature was forged is generally not liable on the instrument. (However, remember that the forged signature of a drawer or maker potentially makes the forger liable in that capac-

ity.) An exception may occur, however, for negligence inviting forgery. For a drawer, this may consist of easy access to a check-imprinting machine, which invites forgery. There are three common exceptions to the rule that a forged indorsement cannot transfer title:

- *Face-to-face imposters*—(where a maker or drawer of a negotiable instrument, in a face-to-face situation, voluntarily transfers it to an unknowing imposter).
- *Faithless agents*—where manager supplies a payee's name for payment but intends the payee to have no interest in the instrument when it is issued
- *Fictitious payees*—where an agent with the authority to issue checks issues a check to a nonexistent or fictitious payee, forges the indorsement, and cashes the check

Candidates on the CPA exam sometimes struggle with a question because what seems to be a good faith party is about to end up with liability. Do not shy away from this result; it is often the case.

KEY WORDS

acceptance (869)	primary contractual
accommodation	liability (869)
party (876)	renunciation (865)
cancellation (865)	secondary contractual
depository bank (873)	liability (871)
discharge (865)	tender (865)
dishonor (869)	unauthorized signa-
presentment (869)	ture (868)
	warranty liability (873)

DISCUSSION QUESTIONS

1. What rights does a transferor acquire from her transferee?
2. What is meant by: "No person is liable on an instrument unless his signature appears thereon"?

3. What is the general rule concerning forged indorsements? What were the policy reasons behind the UCC drafters' decision to create special rules covering forgeries involving employers and their agents?
4. What is primary liability? Secondary liability?
5. What steps must a holder take in order to hold a drawer liable?
6. What steps must a holder take in order to hold an indorser liable?
7. What is the contractual liability of a transferor of a negotiable instrument who does not indorse? Who indorses "without recourse"?
8. What is an accommodation party? What liability does an accommodation party have?
9. What are the warranties of presentment?
10. What are the transferor's warranties?

CASE PROBLEMS

1. Maxwell is a holder of a check which was originally payable to the order of Clark and has the following indorsements on its back:

Clark

Pay to the order of White

Smithers

Without recourse

White

Dobbling

The bank refuses to pay the check. Assuming that time limits are not an issue, what recourse, if any, does Maxwell have against prior transferors of the check? What liability, if any, does White have on the instrument? Explain.

2. Elizabeth Stephens received a check payable to her for $300. Elizabeth negotiated the check by special indorsement to Clay Sandefur. Sandefur transferred the check for value, without indorsement, to Rick Thompson. When Thompson realized the indorsement was missing, he returned the check to Sandefur. Sandefur indorsed the check "Without recourse, Clay Sandefur." Thompson immediately objected and demanded an unqualified indorsement but Sandefur refused. Since then the drawer has stopped payment and raised a defense of which neither Sandefur nor Thompson had previously known. What liability, if any, does Sandefur have to Thompson? Explain.

3. An otherwise valid negotiable bearer note is signed with the forged signature of Darby. Archer, who believed he knew Darby's signature, bought the note in good faith from Harding, the forger. Archer transferred the note without indorsement to Barker, in partial payment of a debt. Barker then sold the note to Chase for 80 percent of its face amount and delivered it without indorsement. When Chase presented the note for payment at maturity, Darby refused to honor it, pleading forgery. Chase gave proper notice of dishonor to Archer and Barker. What liability, if any, do Archer and Barker have? Explain.

4. Bloom signed a check drawn on United Trust Co. payable to Duval's order. Mask stole the check from Bloom, forged Duval's signature on its back, and cashed it at the Corner Check Cashing Company. Corner deposited it with its bank, Town National Bank. Town National proceeded to collect on the check from United. Assuming that none of the parties mentioned was negligent, who will bear the loss if the amount cannot be recovered from Mask? Why?

5. Grad agreed to lend $500 to Paterson on a time note. Prior to delivery of the executed note to Paterson, Keller indorsed the note in blank as an accommodation for payee Paterson. Paterson negotiated the note to Meade by special indorsement. Meade negotiated it to Knight, a holder in due course. The note was not paid when due. Sketch the back of the note and the indorsements. What potential liability, if any, does Keller have to Knight? Explain.

6. Bob Kelly is an agent for Godwin Enterprises. Kelly negotiated for the purchase of ten com-

puters from Hamilton Computers. To pay for the computers Kelly gave Hamilton a negotiable note for $2400 payable 6 months from the date of the note. Kelly signed the note, "Bob Kelly, Agent." A memo line on the note said "Godwin computers" but there was no other reference to Godwin Enterprises. The note was negotiated to a holder in due course, Hank Henry. The note was not paid when due. Henry has brought suit against Godwin Enterprises for payment. Godwin denies liability. Correct? Explain.

7. Hawkins, the assistant to the controller of a general partnership, told the controller that the firm owned Samual $500. Samuel did not exist. Relying on Hawkins's statement, the controller signed the firm's name to a check to Samuel's order. Hawkins indorsed the check "Henry Samuel" and cashed it at a liquor store. The controller learned of the fraud and had payment stopped on the check before the liquor store had cashed the check. The liquor store has brought suit on the check against the partnership for the amount of the check. Is the liquor store likely to prevail? Explain.

8. Davidson bore a remarkable physical resemblance to Ford, one of the town's most prominent citizens. He presented himself one day at the Friendly Finance Company, represented himself as Ford, and requested a loan of $500. The manager mistakenly, but honestly, believed Davidson was Ford. Being anxious to please so prominent a citizen, the manager gave Davidson a $500 check payable to Ford's order. Davidson cashed it at Robbins' Supply, Inc., which took it in the ordinary course of business. Will Robbins ultimately prevail against Friendly? Explain.

9. Wynelle Leeth owned and operated Wyn's Deli. Wynelle's office was next to the deli's public restrooms. One day, Wynelle sent an employee to her office to get some change. In a hurry, the employee forgot to close and re-lock the office door. A customer about to use a restroom looked in and noticed the deli check-writing machine sitting on Wynelle's desk next to a book of blank deli checks. The customer slipped into the office, ran off five checks for $100 each, and left. Wynelle stopped payment on the five checks when she realized they were missing. The customer negotiated the five checks to five different holders in due course who now all claim full payment. Will they prevail against Wynelle? Explain.

10. Manhal Shukayr gave a check for $200 to Betty Naughton for a bike she was selling. After taking delivery, Manhal discovered that the bike's frame was cracked, and he stopped payment on his check. Naughton negotiated the check on April 1 to Roy Produce. On April 4, Roy Produce negotiated the check to Sandra Carson. On April 9, Carson negotiated the note to Jo Rose. On April 11, Rose presented the check to Shukayr's bank and learned payment had been stopped. Jo wishes to recover from one of the prior transferors, all of whom made in blank indorsements. To what extent, if any, is it important whether Jo or any of the indorsers is a holder in due course? Assuming Jo gives notice on April 13, which indorsers, if any, will have liability? Explain.

CHAPTER 39

Banking, Documents of Title, and Investment Securities

In the last three chapters we focused on commercial paper and its transfer under Article 3 of the Uniform Commercial Code (UCC). This chapter initially focuses upon the bank collection process and then turns to the banking relationship between the drawer and drawee. Thereafter, this chapter examines the transfer of two other types of negotiable instruments, documents of title and investment securities.

THE CHECK COLLECTION PROCESS

UCC Article 4 covers relationships between banks and between banks and their customers and the check collection process. The *check collection process* includes the transactions between banks from the time a check is deposited until the check is paid by the drawee bank.

The check collection processes involve some unique terminology. What is more important is that you understand the basic collection process. To help you do so, Figure 39.1 illustrates what would happen if Peggy French, in Dallas, were to send a $500 check to Tucker Supply, in Chicago, for an exercise bicycle. While Tucker Supply could go to Peggy's bank in Dallas to cash the check, the practical reality is that they will simply deposit her check in their bank account with their Chicago bank. Since the Chicago bank is in a different region of the country than Peggy's, the Chicago bank will send the check through the Federal Reserve System. Ultimately the check will be presented against funds in Peggy's Dallas bank account. Within a month Peggy will most likely get the canceled check with her monthly statement. In the meantime, Tucker Products will separately ship the exercise bicycle to Peggy.

The simple transaction illustrated in Figure 39.1 involves four different articles of the UCC:

- Article 2 for the underlying sales agreement
- Article 3, the $500 check
- Article 4, the check collection process
- Article 7, shipping documents

The remainder of this chapter focuses on Articles 4 and 7. We will come back to Figure 39.1 to discuss what would happen if the exercise bicycle proved to be defective when delivered and Peggy stops payment on her $500 check. (Peggy may find stopping payment on her check to be a more expedient way to deal with her problem with Tucker Supply than to rely only on Article 2 remedies.) We will also discuss how long Tucker supply must wait for Peggy's check "to clear" before they can begin writing checks against this deposit.

Bank Collection Issues

Earlier chapters presented discussions on a number of matters that affect the bank collection process. These include:

- Warranties of presentment made by the depositor. (Other warranties exist in the collection process, but they exceed the scope of this text.)
- Indorsements purporting to limit further negotiation, which would preclude the use of intermediary banks.
- Notice requirements for a check not paid when presented for payment.

Three major matters, however, remain to be discussed.

Stop payment orders. A check represents the drawer's order to their bank to pay a sum from the drawer's account to the payee. A *stop payment order* is an instruction by the drawer to the drawee bank not to pay a particular check. To illustrate, if Peggy French sought to stop payment on her $250 check to Tucker Supply, Figure 39.1, she would contact her bank, Republic Bank of Dallas.

A stop payment order may be oral or written. If it is oral, it is valid for only 14 days. If it is written, it is valid for 6 months and may be renewed for an additional 6 months. In either

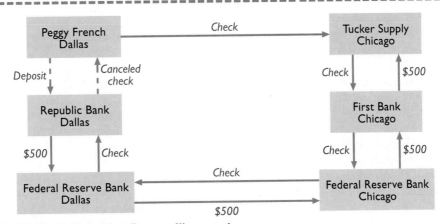

Figure 39.1 The Bank Collection Process Illustrated.
This diagram of the text hypothetical uses the parties' names.

case, the order must be received at such time and in such manner as to afford the bank a reasonable opportunity to act on it prior to any action by the bank [UCC §4-403]. To illustrate, assume Peggy calls her bank to order a stop payment on a check given to a caterer for a delivered wedding cake which proves to be spoiled. Republic Bank, with some 100 branches, receives her call at 10:00 A.M. At 10:30, the caterer cashes the check at one of Republic Bank's branches in Plano. Republic Bank would probably not have liability for failure to follow the stop payment order. A contrary ruling might be expected if the check was cashed in the Plano branch the following day.

Many bank customers believe that if they give proper and timely notice to their bank to stop payment on a check that the bank will be responsible for the check if it fails to do so. In many situations, this will not be true.

The customer has the burden of establishing loss resulting from the payment of an item contrary to a binding stop payment order [UCC §4-403(3)]. If Peggy's notice was timely then the bank would be responsible for crediting her account for the amount of her check to the caterer because she had a bona fide personal defense, failure of consideration. However, if the caterer had negotiated the check to a holder in due course and this party had deposited the check for payment then Peggy would not have prevailed with her personal defense. In this situation her bank would not have liability having paid out over a stop payment order

Missing indorsements. A *depository bank*, the bank at which the check is deposited, can supply a missing indorsement for the original payee on the front of the check unless the check contains the words "payee indorsement required" or the like [UCC §4-205]. In our hypothetical illustrated in Figure 39.1, First Bank of Chicago could supply Tucker Supply's missing indorsement so that the check can pass through the collection process. However, a depository bank cannot supply the necessary indorsement for a special indorsement on the back of the check.

Usually, a depository bank supplies a missing indorsement by stamping the back of the check with "indorsement guaranteed" or similar language to signify that the depository bank claims to have the right to transfer the check for collection. If the bank lacks this right, a drawer could require that his or her account be re-credited.

Final payment. The drawee's bank, sometimes called the *payor bank*, and a *collecting bank*, any bank which a check passes after deposit until paid, generally give only provisional credit for a check on the day it is received. A provisional credit is an appropriate mechanism here, since the customer made a deposit, but the bank may learn that it should not have the credit. When Tucker Supply deposits its check from Peggy French, Tucker Supply's bank will provisionally credit his account, pending the completion of the collection process.

If the bank wishes to revoke the provisional credit because the drawer's account contains insufficient funds or for another valid reason, the bank must dishonor the check by midnight of the next business day [UCC §4-213]. If the bank does not dishonor the check within that period, payment is final.

Federal Depository Rules

In 1988, the Federal Reserve Board imposed new regulations that required banks, savings institutions, and credit unions to clear checks deposited in checking accounts faster. Before the Fed took action, banks waited as much as 1 week to credit the deposit of a local check and 2 weeks for an out-of-town check.

Under the new rules, the bank must give its customer access to deposited funds within:

- One day for electronically deposited checks or cashier's or government checks
- Three days for local checks
- Seven days for nonlocal checks

Thus, the proceeds from a local check deposited on Monday must be available to the depositor by Thursday. In this context, a local check is one drawn in one institution and deposited in another institution with the same Federal Reserve check-processing region. (There are forty-eight regions.)

The "$100 tomorrow" provision of the regulations requires banks to permit up to $100 in credits against a check the day after its deposit to cover outstanding checks presented for payment.

A bank may delay crediting a check to an account if it has good grounds to do so and it notifies its customer. Good grounds include: a reasonable suspicion that the check may be no good: repeated overdrafts by the customer within the last 6 months; or more than $5000 is deposited in 1 day.

THE PAYOR BANK AND ITS CUSTOMER: THEIR RELATIONSHIP

Earlier chapters of this part covered a number of topics that apply to the particular relationship between banks and their customers. These include:

- Stop payment orders
- Certification of checks
- Effect of a drawer's forged signature
- Effect of a forged indorsement
- Warranties of presentment

The drawer-customer and the drawee-payor bank establish their contractual relationship when the customer opens a checking account with the bank. In part, they have an agency-principal relationship, since the drawer appoints the bank as an agent to collect and pay checks.

Basic Duties of the Customer

The customer's basic duties are simple. First, the customer must keep sufficient money in a checking account to cover written checks so that checks do not bounce. Suppose Kim, while at the bookstore, finds that her books for the term are going to cost more than she planned. She cannot face returning to the long lines after she has more cash in her account. So she decides to write a check for more than her account balance, intending to cover the check before it clears. She forgets to do so. She has breached her duty to the bank and, more important, may face criminal charges filed by the bookstore.

The customer also has a duty to use reasonable care in examining returned canceled checks to discover his or her unauthorized signature or any alteration of an item. The duty of reasonable care includes the duty to examine promptly, as we saw in the last chapter. Upon finding a forgery or a material alteration, the customer must promptly notify the bank [UCC §4-406(1)]. The effects of a customer's failure to examine canceled checks or to notify the bank will be discussed later in the chapter.

The Payor's Duties: Payment of Checks

In general terms, the duty a payor bank owes to its customer is to pay checks drawn properly upon the account. In the next case, the question appears to be whether the bank paid a check that was properly drawn. But, is it?

Spec-Cast, Inc. v. First Natl. Bk. & Tr. Co. of Rockford

128 Ill. 2d 167, 538 N.E.2d 543 (1989)

FACTS   On February 9, 1983, Jackson agreed to loan Lundquist $20,000 to finance his failing used car business. He gave Lundquist an unsigned check for $20,000 payable to Richard's Auto Sales. The next day, Lundquist gave Jackson a $20,000 unsecured note that recited, in part, that it was for "value received." The same day, Jackson deposited $20,000 in his checking account. On February 11, the bank paid the unsigned check. When his canceled checks arrived in March, Jackson realized the bank had paid the unsigned check. On March 15, Jackson met with the bank, which told him it could do nothing, since it had paid the check. In May, Lundquist made an interest payment to Jackson of $589, which proved to be the last payment made on the note. On June 1, 1984, Lundquist and Richard's Auto Sales filed for bankruptcy. The $20,000 note was listed as a debt. Jackson received nothing in the bankruptcy proceedings. Jackson brought suit against the bank seeking reimbursement of the $20,000. At trial, a bank officer testified that the bank had not followed its normal procedure with unsigned checks, which was to obtain authorization to pay it. The trial court held that Jackson had ratified the bank's payment, and entered judgment for the bank.

ISSUE   Under UCC §3-401(1), are any defenses available to a bank that pays an unsigned check?

DECISION   Yes. Affirmed. Under UCC §3-401(1), a bank is bound by the deposit agreement and may not legally pay out funds except upon the approval and signature it has been instructed are necessary. Here, the bank failed to exercise reasonable care when it paid the check. However, the bank is not precluded from raising a defense. UCC §1-103 expressly permits defenses available under the Code to be supplemented by common law defenses, unless the Code specifically displaces them. UCC §3-401(1) does not displace the common law defenses. In this instance, the bank could raise the common law defense of ratification. The trial court correctly held that Jackson received the benefit of the payment of the check when he received the $20,000 promissory note from Lundquist. He would not have been entitled to Lundquist's note had the bank not paid the check. Thus, Jackson ratified the bank's payment when he accepted the note and an interest payment on it. Though Jackson initially objected to payment of the check, he ultimately accepted its payment and looked to the payee for satisfaction.

As discussed in the last chapter, a check does not operate as an immediate assignment of funds [UCC §3-409], and the drawee has secondary liability on the instrument. Therefore, the bank has no duty to a presenter of a check drawn upon the customer's account to pay the check even if the account holds sufficient funds. That duty runs to the customer only.

While a bank owes to a customer a number of duties under the checking account agreement, the UCC, and bank governmental regulations, the focus here is on the six basic duties of a bank.

Insufficient funds. If a customer's account lacks sufficient funds to cover a presented check, the bank can charge the account even though the charge creates an overdraft. The official comments on UCC §4-401 state, "the draft authorizes the payment . . . and carries an implied promise to reimburse the drawee." Without an agreement to the contrary, however, a bank has no obligation to honor an overdraft. A refusal to honor a check because of insufficient funds is not a wrongful dishonor.

Wrongful dishonor. A payor bank is liable to its customer for damages proximately caused by a wrongful dishonor [UCC §4-402]. Such damages normally consist of compensation for "bounced check" charges the customer incurred with the payee, but they could include damages for an arrest or a criminal prosecution of the customer or other consequential damages.

Stale checks. A bank also has the duty to consider stale checks drawn on a customer's account. A *stale check* is one which is presented more than 6 months after the date on its face.

Under UCC §4-404, a bank is not obligated to pay an uncertified stale check of a customer. However, the bank may choose in good faith to honor such a check. The official comments indicate that it is usual banking practice for a bank to consult the drawer about the stale check, though a bank is under no legal obligation to do so. Banks commonly honor checks drawn early in January even when they bear the prior year's date. Putting January 12, 1993 instead of January 12, 1994 on a check will usually not affect its acceptance by a bank.

Customer's death. A bank also has the duty to consider payment when it knows of the customer's death. The death of a customer does not revoke the authority of the bank to accept, pay, or collect until the bank knows of the death and has reasonable opportunity to act on the information. Yet even with knowledge the bank may continue to pay or certify checks drawn by the drawer for a 10-day period after the drawer's death "unless ordered to stop payment by a person claiming an interest in the account" [UCC §4-405(2)]. Such a person may be a surviving relative, creditor, executor, or the like.

Privacy. The federal Right to Privacy Act (FRPA) prevents administrative agencies or law enforcement federal officials from gaining access through a bank to information relating to a customer's account without complying with specified procedures. In general, the customer must be given advance notice and an opportunity to be heard, and the customer must grant permission.

Congress intended that FRPA would limit access to private information for nonessential reasons. However, FRPA contains specific exceptions to the customer notice and consent requirements. Under certain situations a bank must turn over customer information upon being served with a proper search warrant. These situations include:

- A danger of physical injury to a person
- A threat of serious property damage
- A person's fight to avoid prosecution
- Access authorized under the Internal Revenue Code

Consumer activists have praised Congress for its goals in enacting FRPA, but they have criticized the Act's exceptions as too broad and too liberally interpreted in favor of administrative agencies and law enforcement officials.

The Payor's Duties: Forged and Altered Checks

The previous chapter examined a drawer's liability for a forged or altered check. Here, the focus is on the drawee-drawer relationship rather than the drawee-holder or holder in due course relationship.

Forged signature of the drawer. In general, a customer is not liable for a check drawn on his or her account with a forged drawer's signature [UCC §3-401(1)]. If the drawee-payor bank charges such a check to the customer's account, the account must be recredited. The drawee has a signature card for the account, and the law expects the bank to recognize the drawer's signature. The validity of this assumption is open to question. Branch banking, bank mergers, and interstate banking have vastly complicated signature recognition, but the duty remains the same.

As we saw in the last chapter, this rule has its exceptions. If the customer bears primary responsibility for the forged signature, the payor will not be liable. This occurs in two situa-

tions in which the bank exercised ordinary care in paying the check:

- The customer fails to adequately control access to a check writing machine.
- The customer fails to inspect his or her monthly statements and checks promptly and with reasonable care or fails to notify promptly the payor of forged signatures.

In the latter case, the customer's negligence costs him or her the right to have the account recredited regardless of the drawee's negligence or lack thereof. One year is considered the maximum time for reporting a forged drawer's signature [UCC §4-406(4)].

A series of forgeries by the same person cuts the reasonable period down to a maximum of 14 days following receipt of the statement. Thereafter, the customer bears the loss because the drawer could have kept the bank from running up losses [UCC §4-406(2)(b)].

Forged indorsements. As with a forged drawer's signature, a forged necessary indorsement gives the drawer a right to have his or her account recredited. Suppose Herb writes a check to Virginia Humphrey. Nancy steals it and forges Virginia's signature. Herb has the right to have his account recredited. The examination and notice rules are the same for forged indorsements except that the drawer has a maximum of 3 years to report forged indorsements [UCC §4-406(4)]. Some have criticized this rule because the drawee usually does not have signature cards for the indorsers.

Altered check. The drawee has a duty to examine the amount of a check for apparent alterations. Normally, the drawee must recredit the customer's account for the amount of an alteration. Suppose Herb writes a check for $7. A clever forger alters the check to read $700. Herb is liable for only $7.

This rule, too, has its exception. Where the customer's negligence substantially contributes to the alteration, the drawee will not be liable.

The drawer must notify the drawee of an altered check within 1 year.

ELECTRONIC BANKING

During the 1980s, banking changed dramatically with the advent of automated teller machines (ATMs). An ATM is a computer terminal to which a customer gains access through a plastic card, similar in appearance to a credit card, and an access code. Regional and national ATM networks evolved that today permit holders of an ATM card to gain access to accounts from almost anywhere in the country.

Since 1984, a closely related electronic funds use has appeared: point-of-sales debit cards. A debit card permits the holder to pay directly for goods or services from a checking account with a special ATM card. A customer inserts a debit card into a terminal and enters his or her code and the amount of the purchase. The store's account is immediately credited, and the buyer's checking account debited, in the amount of the purchase. Monthly debit card usage has soared nationally from some 50,000 transactions a month in 1984 to well over 10 million today. Today, in many metropolitan areas, one can buy McNuggets at McDonald's, fruit at Kroger's, and gas at Exxon with a debit card.

Many legal problems have accompanied the advent of ATM and debit cards. For instance, how is liability to be allocated when a customer loses an ATM card? Practical problems surround the illegal or improper entry into ATM systems.

The courts have struggled to characterize ATM transactions. The trend appears to be to treat cash withdrawals from an ATM machine in a way similar to cashing a check. The UCC still has not recognized ATM or debit card activities.

In 1978, Congress passed the Electronic Funds Transfer Act. The Act specifies the information and terms ATM and debit card issu-ers must communicate to consumers. ATM customer agreements have become quite similar in scope to checking account agreements, although they are signed separately by a banking customer. It is likely that the Act will be amended during the 1990s to reflect developments in this expanding technology.

DOCUMENTS OF TITLE

UCC Article 7 applies to just one type of bailment: a bailment which is evidenced by a document of title. A *document of title* is a bailment receipt addressed to or issued by a bailee. A *bailee*, for Article 7 purposes, is a "person who by a warehouse receipt, bill of lading or other document of title acknowledges possession of goods and contracts to deliver them" [UCC §7-102(1)(a)]. Here, we will concern ourselves with just the two major types of bailees who issue documents of title: warehousemen and common carriers.

A document of title represents personal property which the *bailor* has either sorted or shipped. Besides being a receipt, it also states the storage or shipment contract. A document of title is evidence that the person holding it is entitled to receive, possess, direct, and dispose of the document and the goods it covers. It must cover goods in the bailee's possession which either are specifically identified in the document or are *fungible* portions of an identified mass, like a quantity of stored grain [UCC §1-201(15)].

Negotiability

Documents of title may be either nonnegotiable or negotiable. As under Article 3, the negotiability of documents of title is a matter of form. Any document which does not contain words of negotiability is nonnegotiable, and Article 7 does not apply to it.

Nonnegotiable documents of title are transferred under the contract law of assignments, which is discussed in Chapter 11. It is important to note that warehousemen can issue nonnegotiable warehouse receipts and common carriers can issue nonnegotiable bills of lading. Nonnegotiable instruments are transferred subject to all defenses that are valid against the transferor. In this chapter we will discuss only negotiable bills of lading and warehouse receipts.

A document of title is negotiable if it says that the goods are to be delivered "to the order of" a named person or "to bearer."

Documents of title are negotiated like commercial paper. If it is an order document, a document of title is negotiated by indorsement and delivery. If it is a bearer document, it is negotiated by delivery alone. In general, the transferee of a document of title takes it subject to any defenses applicable to the transferor [UCC §7-504(1)]. However, Article 7 grants certain transferees protected status similar to that of holders in due course.

Holder by Due Negotiation

A *holder by due negotiation* takes a document of title free of the maker's personal defenses. To qualify as a holder by due negotiation, a holder must:

- Purchase a negotiable document of title
- in good faith
- without notice of any defense against or claim to it
- for value
- in the regular course of business or financing or in settlement or payment of a money obligation [UCC §8-302].

The tests for the first four qualifications are the same as those for a holder in due course. For example, as with a holder in due course, failure of consideration is no defense against a holder by due negotiation. Suppose Pontz Corporation gives Baxter, Inc., a check for 1000 widgets which are to be shipped by EFG Truckers. Baxter delivers the widgets to EFG and receives a negotiable bill of lading, which it forwards to Pontz. Pontz immediately sells the bill of lading to a holder by due negotiation. When Pontz's check bounces, Baxter cannot stop the shipment and retrieve the goods. EFG would be liable to the holder by due negotiation if it stopped the shipment.

The only difference between applying the first four criteria to a holder in due course and applying them to a holder by due negotiation is that payment of an *antecedent debt* does not constitute value for a document of title [UCC §7-501(4)]. Here is what this means in practice. Suppose Willard issues Sarah a negotiable note for $500. Sarah transfers the note to Peter to satisfy an existing debt of $425. Under Article 3, Peter has given value to Sarah and qualifies as a holder in due course. However, if Sarah had transferred a negotiable document of title to Peter, he would not qualify as a holder by due negotiation.

Regular course of business. The fifth qualification for holder by due negotiation status is unique to Article 7. A document of title's transfer must be in the regular course of business. To qualify, it must satisfy two criteria.

First, the transferor of the negotiable document of title must be either someone who owns the goods represented by the instrument or someone who normally deals with such documents. Because nonspecialists rarely deal in documents of title which do not represent their own goods, the UCC's drafters believed that "no commercial purpose is served by allowing a tramp or a professor to 'duly negotiate' an order bill of lading for hides or cotton"* which do not belong to him.

Thus, Article 7 limits qualified transferors —other than the goods' owner—to those who regularly trade or transfer negotiable documents of title, such as a bank, a carrier, or a distributor. If the transferor does not meet these criteria, the transferee may be denied holder by due negotiation status.

---

* UCC §7-501 Comment 1.

The second criterion for a transfer in the regular course of business is whether the transaction is a normal one for the transferor and for the particular type of instrument involved. If not, the transferee is on notice that he or she must inquire further about the document and the transferor's right to negotiate it. For instance, a person who trades in grain warehouse receipts would not be expected to be the transferor of a warehouse receipt for Xerox copiers. There may be nothing wrong with the transaction, but the transferee must inquire or forego holder by due negotiation status. Similarly, the transferee must inquire if the document is stale, or if the price of the document is well below the market, or if a term has obviously been altered.

The rationale for the regular course of business requirement is that documents of title are negotiated through specific channels accepted by the trade. The UCC's goal is free transferability within these channels, not the creation of a new, general market.

Rights. A holder who takes a document by due negotiation acquires title to the document itself and to the goods which the document represents. She may enforce the issuer's obligation to hold or deliver the goods according to the terms of the document, free of any defense or claim except those arising under the document's terms or under Article 7 [UCC §7-502(1)(d)].

Like the holder in due course, the holder by due negotiation takes the document free of some defenses. The holder by due negotiation has a right to the goods even though: the bailee has surrendered the goods to someone else; the previous negotiation amounted to a breach of duty; or a prior holder lost possession of the document as a result of misrepresentation, fraud, accident, mistake, duress, loss, theft, conversion, or a prior transfer of either the goods or the document.

Shelter rule. Article 7 contains a shelter rule similar to that in Article 3. It permits the transferee of a holder by due negotiation to acquire

the same status without paying value for the document.

The transferee may not acquire holder by due negotiation status under the shelter rule if he was a party to fraud in the issuance of the document or if he had notice of any defect or defense while a prior holder [UCC §7-504(1)]. Assume that Rodger purchases a document of title, but because it was not in his ordinary course of business, he did not qualify as a holder by due negotiation. Later, Rodger reacquires the document from a holder by due negotiation. He would then have holder by due negotiation status. But if, in the interim, Rodger had learned of a defect or defense, he would not qualify as a holder by due negotiation.

Transferor Warranties

Like an indorser of commercial paper, a transferor of a negotiable document of title warrants all the following to her transferee:

- The document is genuine.
- She has no knowledge of any fact which would impair its validity or worth.
- The transfer is rightful.
- The transfer is fully effective [UCC §7-507].

If the transferee lacks title, for example, the new holder takes the goods subject to the true owner's title and any liens on the property at the time of transfer [UCC §7-503]. The transferor, therefore, would be liable to her transferee on her warranty of title.

Banks or other intermediaries involved in the collection process for a document of title do not warrant its genuineness or effectiveness. They warrant only their good faith and their authority to act. For example, a bank would warrant it has agency authority to pass a bill of lading to a buyer of goods when the buyer pays it the purchase price.

Stolen documents and goods. The holder of a negotiable document of title has a duty to see that it does not improperly enter the stream of commerce. In other words, he must protect the document against theft.

If goods are stolen and then transferred for a negotiable document of title, that document—even if negotiated to a holder by due negotiation—does not give its holder good title. Suppose Eddie steals a truckload of corn from Nick. Eddie transfers possession to ABC Elevators in exchange for a negotiable warehouse receipt. Eventually, the receipt is transferred to Pam in the ordinary course of business. Although it may have been duly negotiated to her, Nick would prevail in an action to recover the corn. Now suppose it was Nick who stored the corn, and Eddie stole the receipt from him. If Pam ultimately took the document by due negotiation, she would prevail against Nick because he had a duty to protect the receipt from theft.

Warehousemen

A *warehouseman* is "a person engaged in the business of storing goods for hire" [UCC §7-102(1)(h)]. All warehousemen are bailees, but, of course, not all bailees are warehousemen.

Warehouse Receipt. A warehouseman acknowledges receiving property for storage by issuing a written *warehouse receipt* which names the bailor and states the terms of the contract for storage [UCC §7-201(1)]. Suppose Helen received a negotiable warehouse receipt for some furniture she stored in Perkins's warehouse. She could negotiate it to Gil by indorsement and delivery if it is an order receipt or by delivery alone if it is a bearer receipt. Upon negotiation, Gil takes title to the receipt and to the goods it represents. To secure the bailed goods, Gil must surrender the receipt to Perkins.

Liability. A warehouseman is liable for misdelivery of or damage to the bailed goods if this is caused by his failure to exercise the care a reasonably careful person would exercise under similar circumstances. However, unless he agrees otherwise, the warehouseman is not liable for damages which he could *not* have avoided by the exercise of reasonable care [UCC §7-204(1)]. The next case shows how this standard applies in practice.

Fugate v. Brockway, Inc.

937 F.2d 960 (4th Cir. 1991)

FACTS   Brockway manufactured glass bottles for Miller Brewing Company. Fugate was an independent warehouseman who contracted with Brockway to store the bottles. Brockway provided Fugate with a handbook for handling the bottles, including detailed instructions for preventing pest control problems. Fugate was diligent about inspecting and exterminating the warehouse for insects. Later, Miller Brewing discovered cockroaches in some of its bottles from Fugate's warehouse. An inspection revealed that there were thousands of them which could not be seen under the concrete slabs. The pesticide forced them up from their nesting areas. Brockway argued that Fugate failed to exercise due care required of a warehouseman. At the trial level, Fugate prevailed.

ISSUE   Was Fugate liable for damages for failing to exercise the due care required of a warehouseman?

DECISION   Yes. Reversed. A warehouseman is liable for damages for failure to exercise the due care a reasonably prudent person would under similar circumstances. Due to the nature of the goods being stored, it was imperative that Fugate exercise an even more rigorous program for preventing insect encroachment. Thus, Fugate was liable even though the infestation was not readily detectable.

A related, important issue raised in the *Fugate* case was whether Brockway was contributorily negligent. Brockway, like Fugate, was also accused of failing to inspect properly the warehouse before contracting to store the bottles there, and consequently was partially culpable for the insect problem. The court, however, made it clear that Brockway did not have to adhere to as demanding a standard of due care as Fugate, the warehouseman. In fact, the court asserted that Brockway needed to have "definite knowledge" of the problem and then fail to act upon it in order for it to be contributorily negligent. Since the warehouseman is more aware of its own facilities and can better control how it manages the goods, its standard of due care clearly should be greater.

A warehouseman can limit its liability for damage or loss if it both:

- Gives the bailor the opportunity—for a higher fee—to store property *without* a limitation on its liability and
- Identifies the limitation on each item or unit of measurement [UCC §7-204(2)]

Courts often hold void blanket limitations on liability. Even where such limitations are not void, the warehouseman's ability to limit his exposure is restricted. Usually, the limitation appears on the receipt in terms like "Maximum liability $1000." That alone, however, will not insulate the warehouse from liability. It must bring the limitation directly to the bailor's attention.

Warehouse lien. A warehouse has a *possessory lien* against a bailor's goods for any unpaid storage charges. A possessory lien gives the warehouseman a security interest in the bailed goods to the extent of his charges. The warehouseman's security interest takes priority over that of the warehouse receipt's holder to the extent of the charges.

The warehouse lien automatically attaches to the goods. Its amount depends on the nature of the receipt issued for the goods. If the receipt is nonnegotiable, the lien is for the usual charges for storing goods of the same type. If the receipt is negotiable, the lien against a holder by due negotiation is limited to the amount of the storage charges stated on the document or, if none is stated, to the reasonable value of storing the specific goods.

Unlike the other possessory liens, such as the artisan's lien, a warehouse lien on stored goods can include the charges due for merchandise previously returned to the bailor. However, in order to assert this lien, the warehouseman must put a notation to that effect on the receipt [UCC §§7-209 and 7-210].

Common Carriers

A *common carrier* is usually a corporation licensed by the government to provide transportation services to the public. With certain exceptions, a common carrier must serve all, though it does not have to carry every type of property or serve every possible destination. By contrast, a *private carrier* operates under a contract with a particular consignor and may choose whom to serve and where. This chapter deals only with common carriers.

Bills of lading. A *bill of lading* is a document evidencing the carrier's receipt of goods for shipment and stating the terms of the transportation contract.* Only a person engaged in the business of shipping or forwarding goods may issue a bill of lading.

The contract for transportation between a *consignor*—a bailor who is having the goods shipped—and a common carrier creates a *mutual benefit bailment*. Its purpose is the delivery of the property to a *consignee*—the person to whom or to whose order the bill of lading promises delivery—in exchange for compensation to the carrier [UCC §7-102(1)]. Suppose Tucker agrees to sell twenty desks to Utility Supply Co., to be shipped by TRS Transit Systems. Tucker is the consignor and bailor, TRS is the bailee, and Utility Supply Co. is the consignee.

Duty to accept goods. Generally, a carrier must accept all goods consigned to it. However, it need not accept goods for storage or shipment for which it does not have room. Nor does it have to accept goods for which it does not have appropriate means of transportation. A carrier does not have to take a shipment of ice cream if it lacks freezer trucks. However, the carrier must provide proper facilities for transporting goods it accepts.

Parol evidence rule. A bill of lading is a written contract. However, the *parol evidence rule* applies only to the contractual aspect of the bill, not to evidence of receipt. Thus, if Interstate Barge's bill indicates that it received twenty drill presses for shipment, the consignor may introduce parol evidence to show that it delivered twenty-five presses to Interstate's dock. The consignor has the burden of proof. Suppose that when Interstate unloads the barge, the presses do not match the description on the bill. Interstate may use parol evidence to contradict

the description. However, now the burden of proof rests on Interstate.

A good faith purchaser of the bill may rely on the bill's description of the goods unless something on the face of the bill puts him on notice that he may not so rely. In other words, a carrier is bound by the description on the bill. Suppose the NOP Railroad issues a negotiable bill of lading whose description states: "1 car load, 200 cases Napa Valley wine." The railroad is bound by that description. However, the railroad would not be bound if the bill said: "1 car load, 200 cases—value, contents, and quantity unknown. Consignor says Napa Valley wine."

Duties as to delivery. The common carrier must attempt to follow the consignor's instructions on routing and manner of shipment as stated in the bill of lading. However, adverse weather, shortages of equipment, government regulations, or other intervening factors may compel the carrier to use a substitute means of delivery.

How delivery is made depends on whether the bill is negotiable or not. If the consignor ships under a negotiable bill of lading, the carrier must deliver the goods only to the bill's holder in exchange for the bill. If the bill is nonnegotiable, the carrier simply delivers the goods to the consignee. The difference in treatment is due to the fact that a negotiable bill represents not only a shipping contract but also title to goods. A nonnegotiable bill is just a shipping contract; title to the goods passes by another means.

Possessory lien. A carrier's duty to deliver goods is conditioned upon payment of the applicable shipping and related charges. If these are not paid, the carrier may refuse to deliver the goods, even to a holder by due negotiation. Like a warehouseman, a carrier has a possessory lien in the goods it accepts for consignment for the amount of its charges. It may sell the goods if, ultimately, it is not paid.

A carrier's lien may also include charges

---

* Technically, bills of lading are used only for ground or marine transport. We will use the term to include *airbills,* which are bills of lading for air transport [UCC §1-201].

for preserving perishable goods. The lien may apply to goods consigned by a person not authorized to contract with the carrier, provided the carrier did not know of the consignor's lack of authority [UCC §7-307(2)]. Thus, the lien is valid even against the real owner of stolen goods. The UCC grants this protection to common carriers alone, since, by law, they are required to accept goods presented for shipment.

Stopping delivery. Once a carrier has issued a negotiable bill of lading and taken possession of the goods, the goods cannot be stopped in transit or recovered, except by the holder of the negotiable bill of lading. The reason for this rule is that the negotiable bill constitutes title, and only the owner of goods may stop goods in transit [UCC §7-504].

Under Article 2, a seller who discovers after the delivery of goods to a carrier that the buyer of the goods is insolvent may stop delivery without breaching the sales contract [UCC §2-705], but only if the bill of lading is nonnegotiable. Because a nonnegotiable bill of lading is simply a shipping contract, the seller can modify it. However, if the stoppage proves wrongful and the shipper is held liable by the consignee, the consignor must indemnify the carrier. In practice, many carriers simply ignore stop orders and complete shipment in accordance with the directions on the bill.

Trade acceptances. Often a seller of goods will be in one city, say Dallas, while the buyer is in another, say Houston. Under the sales contract, goods are to be shipped by a particular carrier, say EFG Transport Co., with payment to the seller occurring before the buyer receives the goods. Commonly, the seller has a third party, usually a bank, in the buyer's city hold the bill of lading until the buyer pays the purchase price or transportation costs, or both. Upon payment, the bank transfers the bill of lading to the buyer, who then surrenders it to the carrier in exchange for the goods. Using normal banking channels, the bank sends the

money paid by the Houston buyer to the seller's bank.

In order to facilitate this type of transaction, the seller is likely to use a *trade acceptance*—a form of draft governed by Article 3—with a negotiable bill of lading. With a trade acceptance, the seller is the drawer, the buyer is the drawee, and the bank holding the bill is the payee. The trade acceptance makes clear to the payee precisely what is to be paid to release the bill of lading.

Figure 39.2 illustrates a typical transaction involving a trade acceptance. It is important to recognize that there are three contracts involved. First, the negotiable bill of lading is a shipment contract which also serves as title to the goods. Second, there is, of course, the underlying sales contract, which determines the rights and obligations of the parties in accordance with Article 2. And third, there is the trade acceptance, which is the means of payment for the goods.

INVESTMENT SECURITIES

Investment securities, such as stocks and bonds, are the principal means used by corporations to finance their operations. In Part IV, the discussion of securities centered on their role in financing the corporation and on federal regulation of their issuance and sale to the public. Article 8 and this chapter are concerned with the execution of these transactions, not their purposes. Under Article 8, *investment securities* are negotiable instruments issued by a corporation which evidence ownership interests or debt obligations. The term includes, for example, stock and corporate bonds.

The themes of Articles 3, 4, and 7 are closely paralleled in Article 8, and so, despite their very different subject matter, they are often studied together. For instance, Article 8's bona fide purchasers enjoy a protected status similar to that of holders in due course and holders by due negotiation.

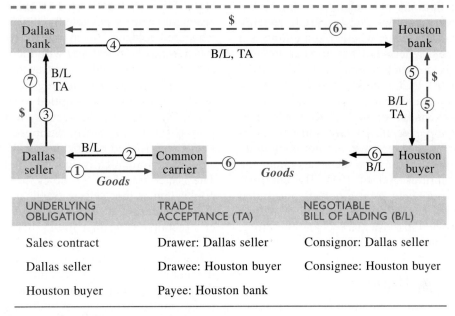

Figure 39.2 How a Trade Acceptance Works.
The circled numbers indicate the usual order of events in a transaction involving
a trade acceptance. The dotted lines indicate actions initiated by, or on behalf of,
the buyer.

Article 8 has a very limited scope. It does not in any way affect the federal and state laws concerning reporting requirements or the anti-fraud provisions relating to the issuing and trading of securities. Nor does it amend state corporation statutes by defining the nature of the rights that flow from ownership of these negotiable instruments.* Rather, Article 8 describes the mechanics of transferring investment securities after their issuance.

Characteristics of Securities

Article 8 defines *securities* as shares, participations, or other interests in an issuer's property or enterprise, or obligations of the issuer, which are:

- Represented by an instrument† issued in bearer or registered form
- Of a type commonly bought and sold in securities markets or of a type commonly recognized as a medium for investment
- Either one of a class or series or by its terms divisible into a class or series of shares, participations, interests, or obligations [UCC §8-102(1)].

---

* The UCC divides securities into two types, uncertificated and certificated. Uncertificated securities were added to Article 8 when, because of greatly increasing stock exchange volume, some believed that securities would eventually be issued without certificates. At present these are quite rare, and we will not discuss them.

---

† These topics are discussed in Chapters 19, 21, and 23.

The definitions of "securities" under the federal securities laws and the UCC roughly correspond. However, whether something is a security under federal law has no bearing upon whether it is an Article 8 security [UCC §8-102].

Under the UCC, the key test is whether a security is of a type commonly traded on a securities exchange or market. For example, most *limited partnership* interests are not Article 8 securities because they are not commonly traded. However, they are securities under the federal Securities Act of 1933. By contrast, stock in *closely held corporations* is not traded on securities exchanges. Still, it is of a type normally traded in those markets and therefore, it is within the Article 8 definition.

Negotiation

As you have seen, negotiation is the transfer of a negotiable instrument from one holder to another after issuance. Article 8's requirements for the negotiation of investment securities parallel already familiar aspects of earlier articles. However, in one critical area, Article 8 is unique. Article 8's distinction between bearer and registered securities is not parallel to Article 3 and 7's bearer and order instruments.

Bearer and registered forms. Investment securities are issued in either bearer or registered form. A security is in *bearer* form if on its face it indicates that it is payable to the bearer [UCC §8-102(1)(e)]. Normally, the only securities issued in bearer form are bonds, and even these are becoming uncommon.

A security in *registered* form specifies the person entitled to hold it or the right it repre-

sents [UCC §8-102(1)(d)]. For example, an investment security payable to "Sheila Davis, or registered assigns" is in registered form. Its transfer may be registered with the issuer and a new certificate issued in the transferee's name.

Generally, if an issuer registers a security to a person who is not entitled to it, the issuer will have to reissue the security to the rightful person [UCC §8-404(2)]. Suppose John finds Sheila's registered certificate for 1000 shares of stock and fraudulently indorses it to himself. The issuer transfers the stock to John on its books, and he then sells it. Sheila is entitled to a duplicate certificate from the issuer. The issuer's recourse is against John [UCC §8-311].

A certificate retains its original character as a registered or bearer certificate, regardless of the indorsement's form. By contrast, under Article 3, order paper becomes bearer paper if it is made out to bearer or is indorsed in blank. Thus, if Sheila indorses her registered certificate in blank, it remains in registered form.

Transfer. Transfer of an investment security—whatever its form—requires delivery. If the investment is in registered form, it also requires an indorsement. A transferor may indorse the security itself or use a *stock power*, a separate transfer document attached to a security [UCC §8-308(1)]. An indorsement without actual delivery will not transfer the certificate.

If the transferor has completed delivery, a purchaser has a specifically enforceable right to have any necessary indorsement supplied. In the next case, an action to compel a transferor to indorse, the transferor completed delivery in a unique fashion.

Schultz v. Schultz

31 UCC Rptg. Serv. 1442 (Mo. Ct. App. 1981)

FACTS   The Schultz family owned a closely held corporation. Jack gave his brother, Sol, four shares in the company. Shortly thereafter, Jack learned that Sol had sold one of the four shares to outsiders to finance a vacation in Hawaii. Greatly upset by this, Jack confronted Sol. They had a heated discussion. The next day, Sol went to Jack's house, where they resumed their argument. Sol told Jack, "Here's your stock. Shove them up your. . . ." He threw the stock on Jack's desk and ran out of the house. The certificates, which were in registered form, were not indorsed. The trial court held that Sol transferred the stock to Jack.

ISSUE   Did Sol's actions constitute delivery of the certificates?

DECISION   Yes. Affirmed. Sol contended that his failure to indorse showed that he never intended to give the shares to Jack. However, in view of Sol's delivery of the shares to Jack and the language he used, he did intend to transfer ownership to his brother. While the UCC speaks in terms of a "purchase" of securities, the term includes gratuitous transfers [UCC §1-201(32)]. So, when Sol delivered the unindorsed securities, the transfer was complete. Jack has a specifically enforceable right to Sol's indorsement [UCC §8-307].

Warranties. A transferor of an investment security makes warranties to the transferee [UCC §8-306]. These include:

- The transfer is effective and rightful.
- The security is genuine.
- The security has not been altered.
- The transferor knows of no fact which might impair the security's validity.

Bona fide purchasers. The common law of assignments applies to the transfer of investment securities, just as it does to the transfer of other negotiable instruments. Upon delivery of an investment security, a transferee acquires the same rights in the instrument as his transferor had. However, he is also subject to the same defenses. This means, for example, that a defense of failure of consideration could be raised against a holder [UCC §8-301(1)].

However, like Articles 3 and 7, Article 8 excepts certain transferees from the full application of the law of assignments. A good faith or *bona fide purchaser* acquires securities free of certain types of adverse claims. A bona fide purchaser must:

- Take delivery of either a security in bearer form or a security in registered form issued to him or indorsed to him or in blank
- Give value for the security in good faith and without notice of any adverse claims

The tests for the second prong of the bona fide purchaser test are similar to those for a holder in due course under Article 3. Thus, a person who knows that the transferor acquired the certificates fraudulently cannot become a bona fide purchaser. Similarly, a purchaser who is offered 1000 shares of IBM at $1 per share may give value for them, but she has notice of a probable defect or defense, since IBM has not sold at that price in the last 50 years.

Shelter rule. Like Articles 3 and 7, Article 8 has a shelter rule. Under it, a bona fide purchaser's transferee—whether by negotiation or gift—assumes the transferor's rights. However, the new holder may not be a party to any actions leading to an adverse claim or have had notice of an adverse claim or defense while a prior holder. In the next case, creditors of a bankrupt corporation tried to invoke the shelter rule to the disadvantage of two of its officers.

In re Ralph A. Veon, Inc.

12 Bankr. 186 (Bankr. W.D. Pa. 1981)

FACTS

Ralph A. Veon, Inc., applied for a strip mining license from the Pennsylvania Department of Environmental Resources. The department required it to post a $200,000 security bond for the mining operation. Because Veon had financial troubles, no bonding company would write the bond. Two Veon officers bought $200,000 in bearer bonds and delivered them to the state on Veon's behalf as security for the mining permit. Both the corporation's president (by letter) and its board of directors (by resolution) acknowledged that the bonds belonged to the two officers, not Veon. Veon filed for bankruptcy, and shortly thereafter, the Department denied the license application. The Department released the bonds to Veon's trustee in bankruptcy. The creditors claimed that the bonds should be considered corporate assets for the purpose of satisfying their claims.

ISSUE

Was the company a bona fide purchaser of the bonds from its officers?

DECISION

No. Judgment for the officers. The creditors claimed that Veon acquired the rights of a bona fide purchaser under the shelter rule, since its transferors, the two officers, were bona fide purchasers. The officers, however, intended Veon to acquire a possessory interest in the bonds only for a limited purpose and time. They created a bailment relationship, which is exempt from the shelter rule [UCC §8-301(3)]. A valid transfer requires a delivery with an intent to change ownership. Here, neither the officers nor Veon intended to change the bonds' ownership.

Statute of Frauds. In order to be enforceable under Article 8, a contract for the sale of securities must:

- Be in writing
- Specify the quantity and price of the securities
- Be signed by the party against whom enforcement is sought or his authorized agent

Essentially, Article 8's Statute of Frauds parallels Article 2's relating to the sale of goods.*

---
* Compare UCC §2-201 with UCC §8-319. Article 2's Statute is discussed in Chapter 31.

For example, a confirmation of a securities transaction which would be enforceable against the sender binds the party to whom it is sent if she fails to send a written objection to its contents within 10 days after its receipt. The major procedural difference between the two is that a contract for investment securities must specify both the quantity and the price, while quantity is the essential term under Article 2.

Sometimes, the sale of securities may be made orally between trusting parties. What happens if, in reliance of the sale, one of the parties suffers an injustice? The next case examines how a court wrestled with the problem.

Medesco, Inc., v. LNS International, Inc.

762 F.Supp. 920 (D.Utah 1991)

FACTS
Medesco, Inc., through its CEO, Faulkner, orally promised to sell 39,000 shares of common stock to Soeng Ting of LNS in exchange for $139,000 in working capital. The agreement was put in writing but never signed by LNS. LNS did, however, send Medesco, Inc., $7500 to attend a trade fair. Faulkner, reasonably expecting to receive the balance, prepared and made displays for the fair, made customer contacts, and promised to ship products to customers. LNS never sent more money. In a motion for summary judgment, LNS argued the agreement was oral and so therefore barred under the statute of frauds regarding the sale of securities. Medesco, Inc., argues that LNS should be estopped from denying that there was an oral contract.

ISSUE
Are there any material issues of fact which may be raised in determining whether LNS can be estopped from asserting that it has the Statute of Frauds as a defense?

DECISION
Yes. Motion denied. If there are allegations of material fact which may be sufficient for establishing that promissory estoppel should prevent the raising of the defense of Statute of Frauds, then the motion for summary judgment should be denied. The doctrine of promissory estoppel supplements the Statute of Frauds. Thus, a party can be estopped from using the Statute of Frauds defense in the sale of securities if justice can be averted only by the enforcement of one of the party's promise. In this case, Medesco, Inc., relied on LNS's promise to buy the stock. LNS could reasonably foresee Medesco's reliance on the promise of the sale. Hence, it would now be unjust to not permit Medesco to find that no contract, even an oral one, exists.

CONCLUSION

Unlike commercial paper, documents of title and investment securities are rarely encountered by business law students. Checks come into their lives far more often than bills of lading.

Conceptually, Articles 7 and 8 pose problems because both may place greater emphasis on the underlying transaction than does Article 3. For example, negotiable bills of lading and negotiable warehouse receipts may have a direct effect on the original sales contract. Title passes with the bill of lading, while risk of loss passes with the warehouse receipt.

Nonetheless, the common themes of Article 3, 7, and 8 are far more significant than the variations. Negotiability, protected transferees, rights in the instrument separate from the underlying obligation, and the shelter rule are just some of the similarities.

Operationally, the provisions of Articles 7 and 8 closely parallel those of Article 3. When in doubt as to how the law applies to, say, a warehouse receipt's negotiability, the best rule is to apply the Article 3 solution. For example, the concept of the holder in due course is paralleled in both Articles 7 and 8. Figure 39.3 illustrates the basic interrelationships among the three Articles.

ARTICLE	III	VII	VII	VIII
Topic	Negotiable instruments	Warehouse receipts	Bills of lading	Investment securities
Subject coverage	Money paper	Storage receipt	Shipping receipt	Investment paper
Is protected holder status possible?	Yes; holder in due course	Yes; holder by due negotiation	Yes; holder by due negotiation	Yes; bona fide purchaser
Is assignment law applicable if not above?	Yes	Yes	Yes	Yes
Does shelter rule exist?	Yes	Yes	Yes	Yes
Does antecedent debt constitute value?	Yes	No	No	No
Is form particularly important?	Yes	No	No	No
Implied transferor warranty states what?	No defects in title	No known defects in title	No known defects in title	No known defects in title

Figure 39.3 UCC Comparison Chart.
This chart compares the key aspects of the three negotiable instruments examined in this chapter with those of commercial paper.

A NOTE TO FUTURE CPA CANDIDATES

Banking, documents of title, and investment securities are all covered on the CPA exam. The latter two topics are often contrasted with commercial paper, illustrated in Figure 39.3. You should be sure you understand this figure. Federal depository rules, electronic banking matters, and the processes shown in Figures 39.1 and 39.3 are *not* tested on the exam.

Banking questions generally deal with the customer-bank relationship. When a check is written there is no primary party. A payee cannot force a drawee to pay a check. Only the drawer can bring an action against the drawee for wrongfully dishonoring a check. A drawee is not obligated to pay a stale check, a check more than 6 months old.

The other commonly tested matter between a bank and customer are the rules regarding stop payment orders. An oral stop payment notice is good for only 14 days, a written notice for 6 months. Remember that the bank must have a reasonable opportunity to act on the order. For a bank to have liability for wrongfully paying out over a stop payment order, the customer must be able to prove how he suffered a loss. Often on the CPA exam the customer has only a personal defense which would not be effective against a holder in due course. As such, the bank has no liability.

Most of the concepts applicable to documents of title and investment securities are identical to those of commercial paper, although sometimes with different names of terms. For example, instead of holder in due course, Article 7 uses the term "holder by due negotiation" and Article 8 refers to "bona fide purchaser.'' The shelter rule applies to all three articles. Articles 7 and 8 substantially differ from Article 3 in the following ways:

- Protected shelter status can occur only in a business setting.
- Antecedent value does not constitute value.
- The implied transferor warranty states that no known defects in title exist.

In regard to negotiable warehouse receipts, a seller does *not* warrant to the purchaser that the warehouseman will honor the document. A warehouse receipt will still be negotiable even though it contains a contractual limitation on the warehouseman's liability. A warehouse receipt cannot qualify as both a negotiable warehouse receipt and negotiable commercial paper, as the latter can be payable only in money (not money or stored goods).

As to bills of lading, a negotiable bill of lading represents title to the goods. The carrier must deliver the goods only to a party holding the negotiable bill of lading. In contrast, if the bill of lading is nonnegotiable, the carrier should deliver the goods to the consignee of the bill of lading (the person to whom the goods are shipped). In either case, a carrier can collect storage or transportation expenses from the purchaser of the bill of lading and can limit liability on the goods they carry.

As to negotiable investment securities, any restrictions on their transfer must be written on the face of the securities, not be part of a contract. Investment securities need not be publicly traded. Registering the transfer of the stock certificates is not a requirement to become a bona fide purchaser. A transferor of a stock certificate warrants that the certificate is genuine and has not been materially altered.

KEY WORDS

bailee (888)
bailor (888)
bill of lading (893)
bona fide pur-
 chaser (897
check collection pro-
 cess (882)
collecting bank (884)
common carrier (892)
consignee (892)
consignor (893)
depositary bank (883)
documents of title (888)
holder by due negotia-
 tion (889)
investment secu-
 rity (894)
payor bank (884)
shelter rule (897)
stop payment
 order (882)
trade acceptance (894)
warehouseman (891)
warehouse receipt (891)

DISCUSSION QUESTIONS

1. Describe the bank collection process that would apply to a check that was drawn on a Chicago bank, mailed to a New York City catalog company, and deposited in the company's bank. (Both cities have Federal Reserve Banks.)
2. What requirements must be met if a stop payment order is to be binding upon the payor bank? Who may stop payment on a check?
3. What is the general rule regarding a forged signature of a drawer or an indorser? Describe the customer's duty to review canceled checks.
4. A customer has insufficient funds to cover a check presented to the payor bank for collection. What may the bank do?
5. What are the two types of documents of title? How are they negotiated?
6. What are the requirements for becoming a holder by due negotiation? How do they differ from those for becoming a holder in due course?
7. For the purpose of becoming a holder by due negotiation, does satisfaction of an antecedent debt constitute the giving of value?
8. For the purpose of becoming a holder by due negotiation, what is a transfer in the regular course of business?
9. What is an investment security? How does Article 8 differ from the federal Securities Acts?
10. What is meant by a bona fide purchaser? How does a bona fide purchaser resemble a holder in due course?

CASE PROBLEMS

1. Stuart Morse sent a check for $60 to Crazy Al's Camera Shop for five cartons of video-tapes. Crazy Al's sent only three cartons, worth $36. Stuart instructed his bank to stop payment on his check. Although the bank received his instructions in a timely and appropriate manner, it inadvertently paid the check. Stuart claims that the bank owes him the full $60. The bank claims it need recredit Stuart's account for only $24. Is the bank correct? Explain.

2. A thief broke into Rebecca Dutton's apartment and stole a number of items, including some blank checks. Rebecca did not discover the theft of the checks. The thief forged six checks over a period of 3 months. Rebecca failed to discover the forged checks. She hates numbers and always gets confused trying to balance her checking account. Now, in a effort to determine why Rebecca bounced so many checks, Rebecca's best friend has balanced her account and discovered the forgeries. Rebecca claims that the bank had no right to pay the forged checks. Is she correct? Must the bank recredit her account because of its failure to discover the forged drawer's signature on her checks? Explain.

3. Howard Corporation purchased the following instrument in good faith and for value from Luft Manufacturing, Inc. Crandall indorsed

---

July 2, 1993

McHugh Wholesalers, Inc.
Pullman, Washington

Pay to the order of Luft Manufacturing, Inc., one thousand seven hundred dollars ($1700) three months after acceptance.

Peter Crandall, Pres.
Peter Crandall, President
Luft Manufacturing, Inc.

Accepted *July 12, 1993*
McHugh Wholesalers, Inc.

By *Charles Towne, President*

---

the instrument on the back in his capacity as president of Luft when it was transferred to Howard on July 15, 1993. Is this instrument negotiable under either Article 7 or Article 8? What is Howard's status? Explain.

4. Boyd Corporation owned 100 cases of canned fish and stored them in a public warehouse. It asked for and received from the bailee a negotiable warehouse receipt payable to bearer. It sold the document for cash in the ordinary course of business to Payton Corporation. Boyd delivered the document and indorsed it:

Deliver to order of Payton Corporation
/s/Boyd Corp.

A thief then stole the document and forged Payton's signature. The thief sold and delivered the document to Slate Corporation, which bought it for cash in good faith and in the ordinary course of business. Has Boyd duly negotiated the warehouse receipt to Payton? Does Payton have legal title to the warehouse receipt? Explain.

5. Packard, a new warehouseman, is uncertain about his potential liabilities under the Uniform Commercial Code. Packard wishes you to answer the following questions for him:
   a. "Will I be treated as an insurer?"
   b. "Will I be liable for the nonreceipt or misdescription of the goods stored, even to a good faith purchaser for value of a warehouse receipt?"
   c. "Can I limit my liability with respect to loss or damage to goods while they are in my possession?"
   d. "Can I be held liable for damages which could have been avoided through the exercise of due care?"

6. Stella runs a new common carrier and is uncertain about various aspects of negotiable bills of lading. She wants you to answer the following questions for her:
   a. Is a negotiable bill of lading a type of commercial paper as defined by the UCC?
   b. If prompt notice is given to the carrier in possession of the goods, does a loss to the owner result if the negotiable bill of lading is lost or stolen?

c. Does a negotiable bill of lading give the rightful possessor the ownership of the goods?

7. Dwight Corporation purchased the following instrument from John Q. Billings in good faith:

No. 7200   ***REGISTERED*** $10,000
Magnum Cum Laude Corporation

Ten year 14% Debenture, Due May 15, 2000

Magnum Cum Laude Corporation, a Delaware Corporation, for value received, hereby promises to pay the sum of TEN THOUSAND DOLLARS ($10,000) TO JOHN Q. BILLINGS, or registered assigns, at the principal office or agency of the Corporation in Wilmington, Delaware.

On the reverse side of the instrument, the following appeared:

For value received
The undersigned sells, assigns, and transfers
To DWIGHT CORPORATION
/s/JOHN Q. BILLINGS

Billings' signature was guaranteed by Capital Trust Company. Magnum's 14 percent debentures are listed on the Pacific Coast Exchange. What kind of instrument is this? Is it negotiable? Explain.

8. Nina, an investor, has purchased a certificate representing 500 shares of common stock of the Sims Corporation from a former clerk of the corporation. It was the clerk's duty to prepare stock certificates from a supply of blanks for signature of the corporate secretary. The clerk forged the corporate secretary's signature on a bearer certificate and delivered the certificate for value to Nina. She did not have notice of the forgery, and now demands a reissued certificate from the corporation in her own name. The corporation claims that it has no liability to reissue a certificate in Nina's name and that the investor's bearer certificate is null and void. Is the corporation correct? Explain.

9. Howard Poarch has a checking account at Fidelity Bank of Denver. Howard forgot to note in his checkbook a withdrawal of $50 which he made at an ATM machine. A check payable to Mary Musser for $80 was presented to Fidelity Bank. At the time of presentment. Howard had only $70 in his account. The bank honored the check, charged Howard's account $15 for insufficient funds, and sent him a request to cover his account immediately. Howard deposited a Social Security check for $150 to cover the negative $25 balance. Fidelity Bank refused to let Howard draw upon the remainder of the funds for 3 days. Did the bank operate properly in both cases? Explain.

10. Seven Victory University students were arrested for blocking entry to the ROTC buildings. The students were peacefully protesting ROTC's recruitment policies. They used expensive placards that were very critical of the university administration. The administration asked the county prosecutor to secure search warrants to review the checking accounts of the seven students to try to determine how their protest was funded. The review was done without notice to the students on the grounds of a "potential threat of serious property damage to Victory University buildings."
The lawyers for the students have learned of this and filed a protest under the Federal Right to Privacy Act. Is a court likely to side with the students? Explain.

The end-of-part problems serve three purposes. First some require practical application of legal knowledge to everyday situations. Second, they are summative, bringing together many of the issues treated individually in the chapters of a particular part. Third, the last question presents an ethical problem which, as in real life, may not have an unqualifiedly right or wrong solution. Rather, its goal is to prompt two questions: What would I do in this situation? What *should* I do in this situation?

1. A PRACTICAL PROBLEM

Assume that you are the treasurer of Castina Industries, Inc. The board has authorized you to create and sign negotiable notes on Castina's behalf. Castina's purchasing agent, Jane Austin, has just given you the terms of an agreement she made with Petro Products, Inc., to buy $25,000 of chemicals for Castina's Santa Fe plant. The parties have agreed to the provisions below but are willing to have you modify them to the extent necessary to guarantee the note's negotiability. Austin has asked that you write her a brief memorandum on any changes you make, which should accompany the completed, executed note.

- The note shall be dated March 1, 1994, and shall be payable when Specter Corp. purchases a new #10 Castina boring machine or on September 1, 1994, whichever occurs first.
- On the due date, Castina will owe the principal amount ($25,000) plus interest at 12 percent per annum from the date of the note.
- The note is to include a clause giving Petro the right to accelerate if it should in good faith feel insecure as to Castina's ability to pay the note when due.
- The note is to include a clause stating Petro's right to reasonable attorneys' fees and court costs for collection on the note in the event Castina defaults.
- The note is to be conditioned on the satisfactory condition of the chemicals on their arrival at the Santa Fe plant and for 30 days thereafter, and on their being grade AA or better.

In drafting the note, be sure to prepare it in proper form, but do not worry about it looking printed. Negotiable notes can be handwritten on a yellow pad.

2. A SUMMATIVE PROBLEM

The Caddo County judges have learned that you have just completed studying commercial paper in your business law course and wish for you to advise them on a number of pending cases involving commercial paper. *You should assume only the UCC applies, not the federal "FTC rule."*

a. Case 94-49. *Britt v. Backofen.* Greg Backofen purchased a sailboat from Gray's Marina for $3200. Backofen paid Gray's $1600 down and gave them two $800 notes, one for $800 payable "10 days after receipt of my federal income tax refund." Gray's Marina transferred this note to Tommy Britt as payment for his having painted the marina showroom. Britt's bill to Gray's had been $550. Immediately after taking possession of the boat, Backofen found that there was a serious latent defect. Backofen got his income tax refund on March 27 but has refused to pay Britt. Britt has brought suit claiming to be a holder in due course owed $800. Recommendation? Explain.

b. 94-59. *Spillman v. Backofen.* In regard to Backofen's second $800 note to Gray's Marina, payable on May 1 of this year, Gray's negotiated the note to

Dawn Hines for $650. Hines had no knowledge of Backofen's complaint against Gray's Marina until told by Justin Spillman. Spillman told Hines that he was at the marina and heard the marina proprietor, Michelle Gray, say to someone that "Backofen ought to get an unpleasant surprise by the time he passes Buzzard's Island." Hines told Spillman he could have the apparently worthless note, as she was going back to Gray's to get back her $650. On May 1, Spillman was refused payment by Backofen. Spillman has brought suit to collect the $800. Recommendation? Explain?

c. Case 94-67. *Centenary College v. Romero.* Shawna Romero received a $250 check drawn by Kennon Hensley to Derrick Steele as partial payment for a car. The check was in the form of bearer paper when received by Romero. Romero, a holder in due course, indorsed the check in blank and gave it to her cousin, Kim Sexton. Kim contributed the check to the alumni fund of her college alma mater, Centenary College. When Centenary put the check through for collection it was rejected on account of insufficient funds. The college gave notice to Romero 6 days after her indorsement, 3 days after learning the check was not paid. Romero claims she has no liability on the check because she was a holder in due course, received no consideration when she transferred it to Sexton, and the college gave no consideration when it acquired the note. Recommendation? Explain.

d. Case 94-71. *Blakeny's Garage v. Fairbanks.* Josh Fairbanks left his checkbook in plain view in his unlocked car while at the YMCA. A passerby, Al Parr, spotted and took the checkbook. Parr took his car to Blakeny's Garage and claimed to be Fairbanks. Parr paid the $350 repair bill by signing Fairbank's name and completing one of his blank checks. Blakeny's deposited the check in their checking account but the check was returned on account of insufficient funds. The garage claims they are holders in due course who should prevail against Fairbanks on account of his negligence leading to the forgery. Fairbanks claims the garage's only recourse on the check would be against Parr. Recommendation? Explain.

e. 94-74. *Straub v. ABC Transit.* Blakeny's Garage ordered a $1200 rebuilt Chevrolet engine from Brennan's Automart. Brennan's shipped the engine via ABC Carriers and sent the negotiable bill of lading to Blakeny's. Blakeny's indorsed the bill and had it in the office area ready to be given to ABC Transit. A customer, Glenn Gleason, stole it and subsequently sold it to Barry Straub, an accountant who as a hobby is restoring a 1967 Corvette. Gleason told Straub that he had ordered the engine for a 1966 Chevrolet Malibu convertible he was restoring but rising costs had caused him to change his mind. Straub said he understood rising restoration costs and did not probe for a further explanation or verification. ABC Transit refused to turn the engine over the Straub. Straub claims he has a right to the engine as a holder by due negotiation. ABC Transit and Blakeny's Garage disagree. Recommendation? Explain.

f. Case 94-80. *Van Vugt v. Gaslin.* Melissa Gaslin received her paycheck from Garfield's, a restaurant where she worked. She indorsed the check in blank and was on the way to her bank when Melvin McKinney managed to steal it from her purse. McKinney subsequently negotiated the check to Matt Van Vugt, a holder in due course. Gaslin told Garfield's that her check had been stolen and they stopped payment on it. When the check was not paid, Van Vugt brought an action against Gaslin on her indorsement. Gaslin claims Van Vugt has no cause of action because McKinney, a thief, stole her check. Recommendation? Explain.

3. A SUMMATIVE
PROBLEM

Quick Shop, Inc., operates Quick Shop Convenience Stores throughout the Midwest. Recently, the comptroller's office has been swamped with commercial paper problems. As the person who has studied Articles 3 and 4 most recently, you have been asked to sort them out. You are to provide a one-paragraph explanation for each of your answers.

a. The Geneva, Illinois, store manager sent in a week's payroll to the accounting department. Steve Persinger's name appeared on it. He was listed as having worked 25 hours at a rate of $3.50 per hour. The check was cut and returned to the store manager for distribution. Persinger does not exist. The store manager kept the check, forged an indorsement to herself, and then indorsed it to her landlord as part of the next month's rent. Can the landlord force Quick Shop to pay the check?

b. A Cincinnati Quick Shop has a problem with a stolen check. It cashed a check issued by Mary Kerrick to the Reverend Gregory Smith. The check bears Smith's indorsement to Quick Shop and, under it, verification that the store manager looked at two pieces of identification before accepting the check. Unfortunately, Evan Massey, a notorious pickpocket and forger, had stolen Smith's wallet and bore enough resemblance to the picture on Smith's driver's license to fool the store manager. In the meantime, Kerrick had stopped payment on the check. Can Quick Shop collect from Kerrick?

c. At Quick Shop's Appleton, Wisconsin, store, Jeff Rutter used an $80 check to pay for beach party supplies. Jeff was a regular customer and often paid by check. This check, however, was issued by David Marske to Karen Rutter, Jeff's aunt, who had indorsed it in blank. The bank has returned the check to Quick Shop because of Marske's stop payment order. Marske claims that Jeff stole the indorsed check from his aunt and raised the amount from $30 to $80. Marske denies any liability on the instrument. What, if anything, can Quick Shop collect from Marske?

d. The Ames, Iowa, outlet took a $50 check with Stuart Morse issued to Louise French for ten used record albums. She indorsed it in blank—but qualified her indorsement—and negotiated the check to Janet Lynch. Hours later, Morse called French and demanded his check back. The records were unplayable. French tried to reach Lynch, but Lynch was at Quick Shop negotiating the check—without indorsement—for four cases of beer. Morse's bank dishonored the check, and Quick Shop within the appropriate time limits notified Lynch of the dishonor. What is Lynch's contract and warranty liability to Quick Shop?

e. Quick Shop purchased some new milk cases for its Freeport, Illinois, distribution center. The manufacturer, Dairy Systems, Inc., used a trade acceptance, naming Quick Shop as the drawee. Dairy Systems gave the $30,000 trade acceptance to Polestar bank in satisfaction of a $22,000 note. Polestar presented the instrument to Quick Shop for acceptance. Before it was presented for payment, however, Quick Shop's testing revealed that the cooling system was defective and unrepairable. Is Quick Shop liable to Polestar Bank on the trade acceptance?

4. ETHICS AND THE LAW

The concept of the holder in due course was devised to permit the free flow of commercial paper. It accomplished this goal by protecting from many of the maker's defenses a good faith purchaser for value who lacked notice of any defenses to or defects in the instrument. Article 3 explicitly chooses to protect the interests of such transferees rather than those of makers.

After years of consumer complaints, the Federal Trade Commission (FTC) effectively reversed that choice where consumer notes are concerned. Too many consumers had signed negotiable notes in exchange for goods or services, only to find that what they got was not what they had expected and that their notes had been sold to a holder in due course—usually a commercial lender.

Today, a commercial lender buying such notes is on notice that it cannot become a holder in due course. The consumer may raise any defense to payment on the note that would be available against the original payee.

The FTC's rule has had both good and bad effects. To the good is the caution commercial lenders now show in taking negotiable notes from businesses not known for their good customer relations. Health clubs, door-to-door appliance sales operations, and retailers specializing in low-income customers have felt the effects of the FTC rule.

To the bad is the difficulty those businesses which do not engage in shoddy practices now have in selling consumer notes at a reasonable discount. These businesses face an unpleasant choice. They may either act as lenders themselves or recover the increased discount by raising the overall price of the goods or services they sell. For consumers, the bottom line is the same: increased prices.

Citing these costs to consumers, many businesses and commercial lenders are lobbying the FTC for an outright repeal of its holder in due course regulations. They also argue that Article 3's emphasis was correct and should never have been tampered with. Finally, they argue that the business climate has changed and that the types of abuses that existed before the FTC regulation would not reappear. Awareness of business ethics has increased to such a point that the FTC should not legislate them. In any event, a consumer should always have the option of waiving the protection of the FTC rule.

To what extent is the FTC's holder in due course rule a legislation of ethics? If it is, should federal regulatory agencies be adopting regulations?

Would a rule which permitted a consumer's knowing, uncoerced waiver of the protections of the FTC at once accomplish the rule's goals and restore some flexibility to commercial transactions involving consumer notes?

Since both ultimately involve human beings, is there any moral justification for distinguishing between the treatment of consumers and businesses in this context?

Karen, a 21-year-old junior, needs a car to get to school and to her job. She finds a suitable car for $3000, which Franklin National Bank agrees to loan her. As a condition of making the loan, Franklin asks Karen to have someone cosign the promissory note. Her father agrees to act as her *surety*, a person who promises to pay an obligation in the event of the default of the principal debtor.

As a condition of the loan, Karen must also give Franklin National the right—in the event that she violates her obligations under their loan agreement—to take the car and sell it to satisfy her obligation, without suing her first for breach of contract. When the bank receives a security interest, it becomes a *secured creditor*. The car is the *collateral*, property which secures an obligation.

Most credit extended for small purchases of personal property or services is *unsecured*. If Karen charges her books on her MasterCard, MasterCard does not have a security interest in them.

Loans to purchase services or personal property are not the only type of secured credit arrangement. Every day, people borrow using their real estate to secure their obligations. Suppose the combination of what Karen can earn and borrow is not sufficient to pay for school. her father takes out a mortgage loan from Franklin National. A *mortgage* is a security interest in real property which the debtor—the *mortgagor*—gives to the creditor—the *mortgagee*—to secure an obligation.

A secured creditor has a distinctly better chance than an unsecured creditor to recover at least a portion of a debt, because a secured creditor can liquidate the collateral without the lengthy delay of a breach of contract action. In essence, that right continues even if the debtor files bankruptcy. Suppose Karen's father cannot pay his debts as they come due. He files for bankruptcy. Franklin National Bank will have first claim on his house or the proceeds from its sale because of its security interest. After Franklin is paid, any proceeds which remain will probably go to other creditors.

This part describes the means by which creditors attempt to assure themselves of a debtor's performance and the effectiveness of those assurances in bankruptcy proceedings.

SAFEGUARDING LOANS

Creditors have three principal means of safeguarding their loans: suretyships, security interests in personal property, and security interests in real property.

Laws governing credit transactions

The laws discussed in this part apply, generally, to all creditors, whether commercial or noncommercial. A mortgagee, for instance, may be anyone; savings and loans and banks are not the only entities that can make mortgage loans. In practice, this means that all lenders have the same methods available to them for ensuring that their security interests are effective against both the debtor and any third parties who might claim an interest in the property.

For the most part, the common laws governs suretyships and security interests in real property. The common law also covers certain types of security interests in personal property, though today the methods created by Article 9 of the Uniform Commercial Code (UCC) predominate. These are all matters of state law. Bankruptcy, however, is a matter of federal law and is administered by the U.S. Bankruptcy Courts.

Creditors must pay close attention to some other state and federal laws governing credit transactions. For example, the rate of interest may not exceed the limit imposed by the state's *usury* law. Also, as Chapter 37 indicated with respect to holders in due course, federal and state consumer protection laws and regulations have an enormous impact on how consumer credit transactions are conducted. Chapter 45 discusses consumer credit transactions.

Suretyship

A *suretyship* is a promise to the creditor by a third party—a surety—to answer for the debt of the person to whom the money is lent—the *principal debtor*—upon her failure to pay. A surety may be paid—compensated—or unpaid—uncompensated. Bonding companies, which for a fee agree to make good, say, an embezzlement by a bank teller should this occur, are examples of compensated sureties. A common example of an unpaid surety is the parent who cosigns her son's student loans.

When the principal debtor fails to pay the debt when due, the surety becomes liable. The creditor need not make further demands on the principal debtor before demanding payment from the surety. The surety's obligations, it is important to note, continue even if the principal debtor enters bankruptcy. In fact, one of the principal reasons a lender requires a surety is to protect itself against the principal debtor's bankruptcy.

Chapter 40 examines the surety and his obligations.

Protecting security interests

Much of Chapters 41 and 42 centers on one question: How can a creditor prevent a third party from gaining an interest in collateral which would limit or destroy the value of the creditor's security interest? Put another way, how can the creditor make the security interest binding on third parties?

A moment's reflection reveals how very important this question is. Suppose a bank has a lien on a 1993 Mustang. Ford sold tens of thousands of similar cars. The bank's security interest is virtually worthless without a mechanism which prevents a third party from buying one Mustang and avoiding the bank's security interest or prevents another creditor from claiming a superior security interest. At the same time, such a mechanism must satisfy the debtor's trustee in bankruptcy of the validity of the security interest.

The main solution to this problem is called *recording,* that is, making security interests a matter of public record. Depending on the nature of the collateral and the type of interest, the appropriate public records are maintained either in the courthouse for the country where the personalty or realty is located or in the office of the secretary of state for the state where the personalty is.

When security interests are properly recorded, third parties have what is called constructive notice. *Constructive notice* simply means that the law treats a person as having notice of what is on the public record.

The principle at work here is simply this: A third party with notice cannot defeat the interest of the secured creditor in most circumstances. But the public records are not the only sources of notice. The third party may learn of the security interest in any number of ways. Regardless of how that knowledge comes, it is *actual notice*.

Possession of property by a third party is a form of actual notice. If property is in the hands of another, the potential buyer or creditor is on notice that the party holding it may have a security, ownership, or possessory interest in it. Suppose Tammy wants to buy Arlen's stock in IBM Corporation. Arlen executes a bill of sale for the stock and tells Tammy his stockbroker is holding it for him. Tammy is on notice that the broker may have an interest superior to hers in the stock.

Voluntary and involuntary security interests

Voluntary security interests require an agreement and an exchange of value. Under Article 9, for example, a *security agreement* between the creditor and the debtor creates the lien, and the extension of credit is exchanged for the promise to repay. Chapter 41 discusses voluntary security interests in personal property.

A mortgage is also a voluntary lien. The mortgage may apply to property the mortgagor already owns or to property the mortgagor buys with the borrowed money. *Remember*: A bank does not give mortgages; it receives them. Mortgages are a principal topic of Chapter 42.

As discussed in Chapters 25 and 41, involuntary liens on personal property are called *artisan's* or *mechanic's liens*. Such liens arise when a repair person or contractor does work on personal property and the owner does not pay for it. The lien covers the costs of the parts and the services. It remains in effect so long as the repair person or contractor retains the property.

Unless the applicable state statute provides otherwise, an artisan's or mechanic's lien takes precedence over all other ownership and security interests. Suppose Lillian bought a used Toyota with money she borrowed from the bank. She gave the bank a security interest in the car which the bank recorded. Some months later, Bob's Garage puts a new transmission in the Toyota. If Lillian does not pay for the repairs and Bob does not return the car to her, he has an effective mechanic's lien on the car. His interest in the car would be superior both to Lillian's and to the bank's.

Involuntary liens also apply to real property. The most common of these are the mechanic's liens and materialman's. These liens apply to property to which the lien holder has contributed value without receiving the compensation due him or her. Unlike involuntary liens on personal property, these liens must be recorded to be effective.

Involuntary liens place economic pressure on the debtor. Without the availability of a mechanic's lien, a contractor would be at a severe disadvantage should a homeowner decline to pay. The contractor could not recover the value of his work simply by removing the materials. Chapter 42 discusses involuntary liens on real property.

BANKRUPTCY

No matter how well secured creditors are, bankruptcy of a debtor can affect them adversely. When deciding whether to grant a loan, creditors always consider the possibility of the debtor's bankruptcy. It is this possibility which often determines the interest charged and the security demanded.

Bankruptcies may be either voluntary or involuntary. In an involuntary bankruptcy, creditors force the debtor into bankruptcy. In either case, the test of bankruptcy is whether the debtor is paying his debts as they come due, *not* whether the debtor's liabilities exceed his assets.

Some debts are not dischargeable in bankruptcy; that is, declaring bankruptcy does not relieve the debtor's obligation to pay. On the other hand, some of the bankrupt's property is exempt from creditor claims. Depending on whether the debts are secured or unsecured, the creditors have very different rights. These rights are one of the main topics covered in Chapter 43.

CONCLUSION

Voluntary security interests are normally ancillary to the main purpose of the contract. The security interest binds the debtor and the creditor from the time of execution. But the creditor usually is less concerned about binding the debtor than about binding third parties. The key to binding them is notice.

Surety interests also have to be executed and, where required, recorded precisely according to the law. This is one area of the law where the courts rarely give creditors the benefit of the doubt.

At the same time, this area of the law is also one which is designed to give the secured creditor quick satisfaction. The procedures for obtaining payment from a surety and liquidating collateral are designed to speed money into the creditor's hands. Even the bankruptcy preferences work to this end.

KEY WORDS

actual notice (910)
artisan's lien (911)
collateral (909)
constructive notice (910)
mechanic's lien (911)
mortgage (909)
mortgagee (909)
mortgagor (909)

principal debtor (910)
recording (910)
secured creditor (909)
security agreement (911)
surety (909)
suretyship (910)
unsecured (909)
usury (910)

Suretyship

TDH Corporation needs a $100,000 loan to finance a new production line. TDH has three shareholder-officers, Tom, Dick, and Harriet. Their capital contributions consisted, respectively, of management experience, technical expertise, and financial resources. A bank has committed itself to make the loan, but it requires that Harriet promise to repay the loan personally should TDH default. When the officers execute the promissory note on behalf of the corporation, each signs as a TDH officer. Harriet signs again as an individual.

The relationship between Harriet and the bank is called a suretyship. A *suretyship* is a contractual relationship resulting from the unconditional promise of the *surety* (Harriet) to be answerable to the *creditor* (the bank) for the obligation of the *principal debtor* (TDH) should it default. Figure 40.1 diagrams this contractual relationship.

A surety becomes liable to the creditor when the principal debtor fails to perform. The creditor does not have to try to secure performance from the principal debtor first. The creditor may go directly to the surety. If TDH Corp. fails to meet a loan payment, the bank may turn immediately to Harriet for the $100,000.

Suppose the bank asked for more security for its loan than Harriet's suretyship agreement. It insisted that the production line serve as *collateral*, property designated as security for a loan. If TDH defaults, the bank now has three alternatives: compel the principal debtor to pay, demand payment from the surety, or obtain a court order to either claim or sell the collateral. Unfortunately for Harriet, the bank does not have to look to the collateral first. But should Harriet pay the loan, she would assume the bank's rights in the collateral. Figure 40.2 illustrates the creditor's and the surety's options on the principal debtor's default.

The bank has yet another option for securing its loan to TDH. It could ask that all three shareholder-officers sign the note as cosureties. If they do so and TDH defaults, the bank may seek payment from any one or combination of them.

This chapter explores the nature of suretyships and the surety's rights and duties. The next two chapters discuss collateral.

CREATION OF THE SURETY RELATIONSHIP

Suretyship agreements are among the most common business contracts. Their purposes range from securing loans to securing performance of construction contracts to securing an appearance in court.

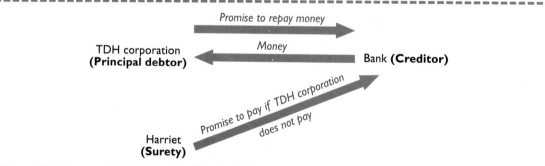

Figure 40.1 Suretyship Relationship Illustrated.

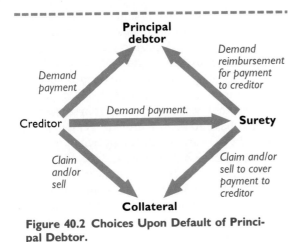

Figure 40.2 Choices Upon Default of Principal Debtor.

Purposes

Loans. Suretyships, as noted above, commonly secure loans. If you have a student loan, your parents may well have cosigned it as sureties. Lenders also particularly want sureties for small and start-up businesses.

In some instances, a surety relationship arises when the purchaser of a home assumes an existing mortgage obligation. The buyer assuming the loan becomes the principal debtor, and the seller—the original buyer—becomes the surety. The surety in this instance can, of course, try to obtain a novation of the original loan and thereby obtain his release. Chapter 42 discusses the assumption of mortgages in more detail.

Performance bonds. Suretyship contracts are sometimes called *performance bonds*. These suretyship contracts often involve construction projects, particularly on public projects. The builder must find a surety to stand behind its promise to fulfill the construction contract. The surety bond generally will be secured from a surety company in business to accept such risks. For businesses without a proven record of successful work and/or financial strength, it can be difficult gaining a surety bond, especially at an affordable rate.

Here is how a construction performance bond works. Suppose Acme Construction Corp. obtains a contract to build a new jail for Suffolk County. Its contract with the country will require that Acme obtain a performance bond in a certain amount so that if the corporation defaults, the county could collect on the bond and complete the building. Any subcontractors would have similar requirements for surety bonding. As a result of the weak economy, many prime contractors no longer are willing to act as sureties for subcontractors.

Employers often demand a type of performance bond called a *fidelity bond* from employees who handle large sums of valuable property. These bonds serve as insurance against embezzlement, theft, or destruction of property. Normally, fidelity bonds are written by commercial surety companies.

Bail bonds. Finally, bail bonds are a form of suretyship agreement. A *bail bond* is a device designed to ensure that a criminal defendant will appear for trial. The bond enables prisoners to be released pending their trial. Failing to appear for trial causes forfeiture of the bond.

This chapter's primary concern lies with suretyships which secure loans.

Consideration

The law does not require independent consideration for a guaranty signed at the same time as the principal agreement. In other words, the consideration given to the surety by the creditor for the suretyship contract is the creditor's agreement to lend money to the principal debtor. Without the suretyship the lender would not make the loan. Therefore, the surety's consideration is the lender's agreement to extend credit. In the TDH example, Harriet is bound by her promise to the bank because the bank made the loan only after she made her promise.

Quite routinely, lenders agree to a lower

interest rate if the borrower provides a surety. The lower rate is consideration. Suppose, however, the bank did not demand that Harriet act as a surety for TDH. TDH defaults, and the bank threatens to attach the company's assets unless TDH provides a surety on an extension of the obligation. The bank's extension of time to TDH is consideration for the promise of the company's surety.

Notice

As of March 1, 1985, the Federal Trade Commission (FTC) required lenders to provide the following written notice to prospective sureties.

> *You are being asked to guarantee this debt. Think carefully before you do. If the borrower doesn't pay the debt, you will have to. Be sure you can afford to pay if you have to, and that you want to accept this responsibility.*
>
> *You may have to pay up to the full amount of the debt if the borrower does not pay. You may also have to pay late fees or collection costs, which increase this amount.*
>
> *The creditor can collect his debt from you without first trying to collect from the borrower. The creditor can use the same collection methods against you that can be used against the borrower, such as suing you, garnishing your wages, etc. If this debt is ever in default, the fact may become a part of your credit record.*
>
> *This notice is not the contract that makes you liable for the debt.*

Under the FTC rule, the lender must give this notice to sureties before they can become obligated on the debt. As we will see, the notice accurately summarizes the surety's obligations.

The Statute of Frauds

The suretyship clause of the Statute of Frauds requires that a suretyship contract be in writing to be enforceable. Any signed writing—including the loan agreement—which contains the surety's promise satisfies the Statute.

The *lending object rule* exempts a surety agreement from the Statute of Frauds if the surety's primary reason, or leading object, for agreeing to stand behind a debt is a benefit to her. In other words, a suretyship agreement does not have to be in writing if its main goal is to benefit the surety, not the principal debtor.*

Suppose Bob's Builders, Inc., agrees to build a house for Jill. Bob falls behind in his payments to the lumberyard, which then notifies Jill it will not provide any more supplies. Jill orally promises to pay the lumberyard for all supplies delivered to her home in the future if Bob does not pay for them. Later, Jill may not cite the Statute to avoid paying the lumberyard. Her leading object was not to aid Bob's Builders but to have her home built. The same logic exempts from the Statute a promise by a corporation's sole shareholder to guarantee the corporation's debt.

THE CREDITOR'S RIGHTS AND DUTIES

Essentially, the creditor has one right: to be paid. All other rights are subsidiary to that one. The creditor has very few duties, and these relate primarily to preserving collateral for the surety.

Right to Payment

By the principal debtor. The creditor has a right to receive from the principal debtor the performance of a valid, legally enforceable contract. The creditor also has the right to have the debtor tender payment at the time and place fixed by their agreement. The creditor's failure to accept a proper tender relieves the principal debtor of any future interest liability but not of his obligation on the principal and the interest to the date of the rejection.

---

* Chapter 10 discusses the suretyship clause and the leading object rule.

By the surety. Upon the default of the principal debtor, the creditor has a right to the surety's performance. The creditor need not proceed against the collateral of the principal debtor before seeking satisfaction from the surety. However, as discussed below, the creditor's right to performance or payment is subject to any defenses the surety can raise either on his own behalf or on behalf of the principal debtor.

By the guarantor. *Guarantors*, sometimes called guarantors of payment, function quite similarly to sureties. Guarantors promise to pay if the principal debtor does not, but the guarantor conditions the promise on the creditor's reasonable diligence in seeking payment from the principal debtor. The creditor may show a good faith effort by logs of telephone calls, copies of letters, and the like. Also, a guarantor might condition payment on the creditor's seeking to satisfy the debt from any collateral in his possession.

In the next case, the defendant sought to be treated as a guarantor rather than as a surety in a last-ditch attempt to evade liability.

General Motors Acceptance Corp. v. Daniels

303 Md. 254, 492 A.2d 1306 (1985)

FACTS   John Daniels agreed to buy a used car from a dealer. Because of his poor credit rating, John asked his brother, Seymoure, to cosign the installment sales contract. Seymoure signed on the "buyer" line, while John signed on the "cobuyer" line. The dealer assigned the contract to General Motors Acceptance Corporation (GMAC). A year later, GMAC declared the loan in default and repossessed the car in a "total loss" condition. John could not be located, so GMAC brought suit against Seymoure. The trial court held that Seymoure was a guarantor and that GMAC had to bring suit first against John before it could proceed against Seymour. An appellate court affirmed the judgment.

ISSUE   Is a person who signs an installment sales contract for the purpose of lending his credit to the purchaser a guarantor of the contract?

DECISION   No. Reversed. A contract of guaranty is collateral to and independent of the main contract. Thus, the guarantor is not a party to the original obligation. A guarantor essentially insures the principal's ability to pay by agreeing to pay the damages upon notice of the principal's default. A surety, however, simply promises to do the same thing that the principal undertakes. As here, the joint execution of a contract by the principal and another excludes the idea of a guaranty and points to a suretyship.

By the guarantor of collection. A *guarantor of collection* adds conditions to those guarantors normally require. A guarantor of collection does not agree to pay the principal debtor's obligation unless all the following occur:

- The creditor notifies the principal debtor that the debt is due.
- The creditor seeks payment from the debtor, including bringing a lawsuit.

STATUS	ABLE TO RECOVER DIRECTLY FROM THE SURETY/ GUARANTOR?	REQUIRED TO FIRST ATTEMPT RECOVERY FROM DEBTOR?	
		BY DEMAND ON DEBTOR?	BY ATTEMPT BY LAWSUIT?
Surety	Yes	No	No
Guarantor (of payment)	No	Yes	No
Guarantor (of collection)	No	Yes	Yes

Figure 40.3 Comparison of Surety Versus Guarantor Status.
A guarantor is like a surety with the exception that not liable without first specific action by the creditor to collect from the debtor.

- The creditor's judgment against the debtor remains unsatisfied.

Thus a surety makes an unconditional promise to the creditor, while a guarantor—of payment or collection—makes a conditional one. Other than the differences outlined above, a surety and a guarantor have essentially the same rights and obligations. For that reason, what is said of sureties in the balance of this chapter applies equally to guarantors. Figure 40-3 compares collection requirements.

Duty to Preserve Collateral

Upon payment of the debt, the creditor must turn over to the person who paid it any collateral which secured the debt. The creditor has a duty to both the debtor and the surety to preserve any collateral. Failure to do so may reduce the obligation of the principal debtor—and therefore of the surety. Suppose a creditor accidentally destroys a $10,000 painting which the principal debtor provided as collateral for a $50,000 loan. The loss reduces the debt to $40,000.

The principal debtor has a right to any excess the creditor receives from the collateral's sale to satisfy the debt. Suppose, in the previous example, that after reducing her obligation to $8000, the principal debtor defaults. The creditor then sells her painting for $10,000. The principal debtor is entitled to the remaining $2000.

THE SURETY'S DEFENSES

Sureties may raise the contractual—but not personal—defenses of the principal debtor against the creditor. The surety may also raise his own contractual and personal defenses. It is important to note, however, that "personal defenses" in this context does not mean the same thing as "personal defenses" as to negotiable instruments.

The Principal Debtor's Defenses

The surety may assert any of the contractual defenses of the principal debtor against the creditor. These include the creditor's material breach of the primary contract, failure of consideration, or lack of assent due to the creditor's coercion. If because of a contractual defense the creditor could not recover against the principal debtor, the creditor may not recover from the surety.

However, the surety may not assert the personal defenses of the principal debtor, such as lack of capacity, insolvency, or discharge in bankruptcy. These are normal business considerations which prompt a creditor to demand a surety, especially for new businesses or minors borrowing to purchase automobiles.

Discharge of the Principal Debtor's Obligation

If the obligation of the principal debtor has been discharged, the creditor may not recover from the surety. Also, if the principal debtor has properly tendered payment which the creditor refused to accept, the surety's obligation is discharged. Suppose the principal debtor tenders payment to Middle Bank, her creditor. The bank refuses the tender because it mistakenly believes the payment is subject to a delinquency charge. The surety of the principal debtor is discharged.

Alteration of the Principal Debtor's Contract

Alteration of the obligations of the principal debtor without the surety's consent releases the surety. Some common examples of alterations include:

- Extensions of time for payment
- Release of the principal debtor
- Return of collateral supplied to the creditor (but only to the extent of the collateral's value)
- Failure to notify the surety of an act or a development which materially increases his risk

Suppose a bank teller embezzles $5000. He is caught but makes restitution and promises never to steal again. The bank retains him and does not tell its bonding company about the theft. Later, the teller disappears with $400,000. The bonding company will not be liable. In the next case, a bank tried to protect itself at the sureties' expense.

Watseka First National Bank v. Ruda

175 Ill. App. 3d 753, 531 N.E.2d 28 (1988)

FACTS   The Rudas owned 1000 acres of farmland. Their son-in-law, Ken Ward, farmed it and paid rent to them. Ward financed his operations primarily through Watseka First National Bank. In May 1983, the Rudas guaranteed two notes in the amount of $246,000 signed by Ward. The notes were due on March 27, 1984. Although Ward's cash flow position was questionable, the bank had agreed to loan the money with the Ruda's guaranty. The notes contained identical clauses allowing the bank to accelerate when "the holder deems itself insecure." On October 21, the bank met with Ward and Mr. Ruda. The bank notified them that the notes were to be accelerated and that Ward should begin selling assets in order to avoid foreclosure. The grounds cited for the bank's action were its discovery of a prior lien on the property and of a one quarter interest in the crop then being harvested held by a partner of Ward's. (Later, the bank would also cite the decline in the Ruda's net worth due to declining land values.) However, the bank's records showed it had known of both the lien and the partnership interest well before it had made the loan. In any case, Ward immediately began selling equipment, cattle, and grain and turning the proceeds over to the bank. Ward's attempt to secure other financing failed, and the bank accelerated the notes. In 1984, the Rudas sold their farm, which reduced their net worth from $2,000,000 to $1,000,000. The bank brought suit against Ward and the Rudas for the balance due on the notes. Ward declared bankruptcy and the bank proceeded against the Rudas. The trial court held that the bank had "no basis for accelerating the maturity date on the notes" but entered judgment for $186,322.97 in favor of the bank.

ISSUE

Did the bank materially alter the terms of Ward's obligation without the Rudas's consent?

DECISION

Yes. Reversed. UCC §1-208 provides that a party accelerating payment may "do so only if he in good faith believes that the prospect of payment . . . is impaired." Here, the bank had no reasonable basis for such a belief. It could not advance as a good faith reason for acceleration the same facts that were the basis for requiring a guarantor in the first place. The failure to deal with the Rudas in good faith releases them from liability as sureties.

Looking at the case at bar through the prism of applicable case law, it is obvious that the terms of the principal obligation were materially changed . . . when the bank chose to accelerate the due date of the principal obligation. Because of the Bank's acceleration . . . , the Ward's became unexpectedly indebted to such an extent that their only recourse was bankruptcy. If the Bank had not accelerated . . . , the Wards might have been able to reduce the principal debt with income received between the time of the acceleration and the time the notes would otherwise have matured. Additionally, the Bank's acceleration and other conduct hampered the Ward's ability to obtain refinancing. Had they refinanced, the Wards might have been able to meet their obligations without financial assistance from their guarantors. . . .

The success of the alteration defense often depends on whether the surety is compensated or uncompensated. If the surety is not compensated and does not consent to the alteration, like the Rudas, he is likely to be released totally. If the surety is compensated, the release will extend only to the additional risk.

Lack of Assent

The surety's ability to assert the lack of assent defenses—for example, undue influence, coercion, and fraud—may depend on whether the principal debtor or the creditor solicited the surety.

If the principal debtor solicits the surety, the surety may not raise the lack of assent defenses against the creditor, because the surety should have checked his client's credit history. Also, in such cases, the law simply favors the creditor over the surety if the creditor, in good faith, has relied upon the suretyship.

If the creditor solicited the surety's participation, the surety may raise the lack of assent defenses. Suppose State Bank convinces Surety Company to act as a surety for Grocery Company. If the bank misrepresents Grocery's past defaults, Surety has a defense on its obligation.

Nonetheless, a surety may assert his or her lack of capacity at the time of entering into the suretyship, the illegality or unconscionability of the surety contract or its purpose, or the creditor's lack of good faith.

Most suretyship or guaranty agreements now contain "boilerplate" language, that is, wording that is standard and consistently repeated in the printed forms, that creates an ongoing obligation to secure future advances made to the principal debtor. Moreover, the surety's or guarantor's liability extends to new obligations even without their permission. These are referred to as "continuing guaranty"

agreements. Courts generally rule that such language is not unconscionable, since a person, including a surety, is presumed to understand what he signs.* However, is it unconscionable to extend a suretyship obligation to the heirs of the surety if the agreement's boilerplate language provides for such liability? The next case discusses that issue.

---

* *Carney v. Central National Bank*, 450 N.E. 1034 (Ind. Ct. App. 1983).

Commercial National Bank v. Pipe Sales of Shreveport, Inc.

600 So.2d 130 (La.App. 1992)

FACTS Byram and George Palmer signed a "Continuing Guaranty" in favor of Commercial National Bank (CNB) for the debts of Pipe Sales. Two years later, George died. Two promissory notes, executed 14 months after George's death, were not paid. The Continuing Guaranty agreement contained boilerplate language which provided that CNB "may extend any obligation of the debtor one or more times . . . without notice or consent." The agreement also contained the statement that "I hereby bind myself, my heirs and assigns." George's heirs argued that CNB had knowledge of his death and that the agreement does not extend without their consent. CNB prevailed at the trial level in a motion for summary judgment.

ISSUE Are there genuine issues of fact to deny a summary judgment over whether the surety's liability extends to his heirs in a continuing guaranty agreement?

DECISION Yes. Reversed. A surety's obligation under a continuing guaranty agreement ends as to future transactions by the death of the surety, provided the creditor had knowledge. CNB's argument that George Palmer's heirs are bound is ambiguous and so cannot act as a waiver of the general rule that the obligation ends at the surety's death. Thus, there are issues of fact which must be disposed of, such as CNB's knowledge of Palmer's death, before the heirs' liability can be determined.

Statutes of Limitations and Set-offs

The surety may assert that the statute of limitations has run on her obligation. For the surety, the key date is when her obligation—not that of the principal debtor—arises. In other words,

for the surety the statute of limitations begins running when the principal debtor defaults, thereby giving the creditor the right to look to the surety for performance.

As we will see below, the statute of limitations on the surety's claim against the principal debtor for reimbursement only begins to run when the surety pays the creditor. Therefore, the dates on which the statute runs on the surety's and the principal debtor's obligation may be different.

A surety has a right of set-off as to the creditor's debts to the surety. Suppose the creditor owes the surety $300 on a separate transaction and the principal debtor fails to pay the creditor $1000 on a note on which the surety is obligated. The surety may deduct the $300 from that obligation and pay the creditor $700.

THE SURETY'S RIGHTS AGAINST THE PRINCIPAL DEBTOR

If the surety pays the obligation of the principal debtor, the principal debtor has a duty to reimburse the surety. While the surety has a number of remedies against the principal debtor, it must be kept in mind that these remedies are only as good as the debtor's credit or collateral.

Exoneration

Exoneration is a court order obtained by the surety directing the principal debtor to pay the creditor so that the surety will not have to pay. It is usually not a satisfactory remedy for the surety because if the principal debtor could pay, she probably would have done so. Also, the surety must pay legal expense and court costs in order to obtain the order. And, perhaps

most important, even if the defaulting debtor could pay, the creditor can recover from the surety without waiting for the surety to obtain exoneration.

Indemnification

The principal debtor must *indemnify* the surety for his expenses in paying the debt so long as the surety pays in good faith and does not know of a valid defense to that debt. Suppose a surety must pay a creditor $5000. The surety now has a right to recover that amount plus his incidental costs from the principal debtor. If the rule were otherwise, a principal debtor would have no reason even to consider payment.

In certain instances the law does not permit indemnification, as when the principal debtor is discharged in bankruptcy. The law presumes the surety understands that the potential for bankruptcy of the principal debtor is a major reason why the creditor wants a surety. Also, as Chapter 43 indicates, the philosophy behind the Bankruptcy Code is that the debtor should get a fresh financial start.

Subrogation

A surety who pays the obligation of the principal debtor "steps into the shoes of the creditor" and assumes whatever rights against the principal debtor the creditor has. This is called *subrogation*. In the following case, a surety sought reimbursement from a principal debtor who was himself a surety.

United States v. Frisk

675 F.2d 1079 (9th Cir. 1982)

FACTS   On October 26, 1970, Jerome Frisk received a $1000 student loan from the Bank of America under the Federal Insured Student Loan Program (FISLP). His father, Richard, cosigned the note. The first monthly installment was due on July 25, 1973. The Frisks made no payments. On March 28, 1974, the federal government paid the bank on the note under its insurance contract. On March 18, 1980, the government filed suit on the note against Richard. He claimed the 6-year statute of limitations had run because the government was a subrogated assignee of the bank and the cause of action arose when Jerome defaulted. The trail court entered judgment for the government.

ISSUE

Was the federal government a surety?

DECISION

Yes. Affirmed. While the FISLP subrogates the government to the lender's rights and entitles the government to an assignment of the note, it does not limit the government to the rights of an assignee. Where a surety enters into a contract of suretyship with the consent of the principal debtor—here, the Frisks—and pays the principal's obligation, the law implies the principal's promise to reimburse the surety. Upon payment of the debt, the surety has a right of action against the principal for reimbursement of the amount paid plus interest. Under the FISLP the government promises to pay the borrower's debt tot he insured lender in the event that the borrower defaults. When Jerome applied for the loan which Richard cosigned, they consented to the government's suretyship. As a surety, the government's cause of action arose on March 28, 1974, the date it paid the lender.

THE PRINCIPAL DEBTOR'S DEFENSES AGAINST THE SURETY

Normally, the principal debtor must pay the surety if the surety has paid the obligation to the creditor. However, the principal debtor has several defenses against the surety. These include:

- Bankruptcy of the principal debtor
- The surety's payment of the debt after receiving notice of a proper defense
- Satisfaction to the extent that the principal debtor made payments which the creditor received
- Expiration of the statute of limitations on the obligation of the principal debtor

- Failure to assert a valid defense

The principal debtor has the burden of fully advising the surety of his defenses. Of course, as a practical matter, most sureties ask the principal debtor if any reason exists for not paying the debt. A surety who knows that the principal debtor has a defense to the obligation, but who pays the debt anyway, may not recover the payment from the principal debtor. After all, the principal debtor would not have had to pay the alleged creditor. Also, as noted above, the principal debtor must indemnify the surety so long as the surety acts in good faith and does not know of a valid defense against the obligation.

THE COSURETIES' RIGHTS AND DUTIES

A *cosurety* is one of two or more persons who serve as sureties for the same debt and for the same creditor. While becoming a cosurety requires the same principal debtor and the same debt, knowledge of the existence of the other

While the surety assumes the creditor's rights in the collateral upon payment, she also assumes the creditor's duties. These duties, which are discussed above, include preserving the collateral and, upon its liquidation, paying any excess proceeds to the debtor.

surety or sureties is not necessary. Gloria and Edith each might agree independently to act as a surety for Archie's loan. Still, they are cosureties.

Cosureties do not have to enter into suretyship agreements at the same time that the debt was incurred or simultaneously with one another. In fact, it is quite common for lenders to ask for additional sureties when they extend the time for payment of a loan to a company in financial difficulties.

Right of Contribution

A cosurety who pays the principal debtor's obligation has a right of *contribution* from his cosureties. This right permits the person who paid to demand that the cosureties reimburse him for their shares of the debt. He does not have to seek reimbursement from the principal debtor before looking to his cosureties. However, as the next case proves, not all who appear to be cosureties are.

Gigliotti v. Gigliotti

35 Conn. Supp. 672, 406 A.2d 614 (Super. Ct. 1979)

FACTS
Paul and Valerie were divorced. While they were married, Paul's brother, Vito, applied for a loan for his real estate business. The bank agreed to make the loan if Paul would cosign the note and pledge stock he and Valerie owned. Valerie cosigned the note at Paul's request, believing he was the principal borrower. The bank had not requested her signature, nor had she agreed to be Vito's surety. When the note became past due, Paul paid it and brought suit against Valerie for her share. The trial court held that Paul was Vito's surety while Valerie was Paul's and entered judgment for Valerie.

ISSUE
Was Valerie a cosurety?

DECISION
No. Affirmed. Actions for contributions are based on the principal that each cosurety should contribute proportionally to discharge the common obligation. However, where the obligation of one person is primary and that of another is secondary, the person with the primary obligation has no right of contribution. Valerie signed the note believing her husband to be the principal borrower. A cosurety who signs an obligation at the request of another surety and for his benefit is not liable for a contribution.

Also, a cosurety has a right of subrogation upon payment and may take possession of any collateral. Suppose a cosurety pays a note for the principal debtor which is secured by a lien on the debtor's car. The cosurety steps into the creditor's shoes and can execute on the lien. If the proceeds from the sale are insufficient, he may seek contributions from the other cosureties.

Calculating the contribution. Normally, cosureties share their obligation equally, although they may agree to do otherwise. Suppose Al, Bonnie, and Carol are cosureties on a $10,000 note. When the debtor defaults, $8000 remains due. Al agreed to be a surety for $5000, Bonnie for $3000, and Carol for $2000. The proportional shares for the $8000 balance would be:

$$\text{Al} \qquad \frac{\$5000}{\$10000} \times \$8000 = \$4000$$

$$\text{Bonnie} \quad \frac{\$3000}{\$10000} \times \$8000 = \$2400$$

$$\text{Carol} \quad \frac{\$2000}{\$10000} \times \$8000 = \$1600$$

If Al pays the entire $8000, Bonnie must contribute $2400 and Carol $1600.

Release of a Cosurety

Release of one cosurety reduces the remaining cosureties' obligations proportionally. Suppose that before default the creditor released Carol from her obligation. Al and Bonnie would be released to the extent of Carol's obligation. Thus, Carol's absence would reduce the total obligation by $1600—her share of the $8000. The remaining cosureties would owe:

$$\text{Al} \qquad \frac{\$5000}{\$8000} \times \$6400 = \$4000$$

$$\text{Bonnie} \quad \frac{\$3000}{\$8000} \times \$6400 = \$2400$$

That is how the formula works when a cosurety's full obligation is discharged. However, what happens if a cosurety is insolvent? Should their proportion of the cosureties' obligations be calculated or should they be excluded? The following case wrestles with that issue.

Harris v. Handmacher

185 Ill.App.3d 1023, 542 N.E.2d 77 (Ill.App. 1989)

FACTS Abner Harris, Philip and Betty Handmacher, and Irving and Sandra Waxman were cosureties for the principal debtor, Handmacher Company, Inc., on promissory notes executed in favor of Continental Illinois National Bank. The Handmacher Company later went into bankruptcy and had an outstanding debt of over $2 million. The trial court later determined the proportionate share of the debt among the cosureties. It was rule that the Handmachers had paid their proportionate share, but the Waxmans still owed about $68,000. Harris, meanwhile, had his security deposit of over $250,000 seized by the bankruptcy court. As depositor, he argued that the Waxmans were insolvent and so their proportion of the debt should not be included in the calculations. If they were excluded then the solvent Handmachers would have to pay more, which would constitute a greater reimbursement to Harris for the loss of his deposit. In a motion for summary judgment at the trial level, the court ruled that insolvent cosureties should not have their proportion of the debt included in the calculation, but denied the motion, since there were genuine facts in dispute concerning the Waxmans' insolvency.

ISSUE Are there issues of genuine fact which must be resolved in determining whether the cosurety is insolvent and should therefore be excluded in calculating proportionate shares?

DECISION Yes. Affirmed. If one or more cosureties is required to pay part or all of the debt, the remaining cosureties are liable to contribute their proportionate share. However, insolvent cosureties are excluded in calculating the proportions due to the inequity that would result to the creditor. There are still genuine issues of facts, since the Waxmans' affidavit did not contain enough information to determine whether they were insolvent.

CONCLUSION

Commercial lending practices often require that the borrower obtain a surety to provide the lender with greater security against default. For a lender, a surety makes good business sense. By contrast, persons who agree to be uncompensated sureties often find they displayed poor business judgment.

A person asked to be a surety should carefully analyze the risks and his or her ability to pay the entire debt. *Remember*: The creditor need not attempt collection from the principal debtor but can go straight to the surety for payment or performance. In addition, if the obligation of the principal debtor is discharged in bankruptcy, the creditor certainly will look to the surety to cover the debt. Thomas Jefferson died broke, in part because he was an uncompensated surety for large loans made to his friends.

A NOTE TO FUTURE CPA CANDIDATES

Suretyship is a part of the debtor-creditor relationships portion of the CPA exam. Suretyship questions also sometimes appear in the common law contract portion of the examination in regard to the Statute of Frauds (the "S" of "MY LEGS") or in regard to consideration.

It is important that you be able to conceptualize a suretyship relationship. Develop a basic scenario that you can visualize and remember. For example, perhaps you are purchasing a new car and the lender is requesting that you have a surety, a cosigner, on the note. It is common to find uncompensated sureties on the exam. It is seldom a defense, since consideration will otherwise be present in the problem.

You need to know the basic rights and duties of the parties. The creditor's most important right is to receive payment. If not paid when due, the surety can require either the debtor or the surety to pay. Remember that the surety has no legal right to force the creditor first to go against the debtor and/or any collateral securing the loan.

A surety can assert any *contractual, not personal,* defense which the principal debtor could have successfully raised. Contractual defenses may include lack of mutual assent, lack of consideration, fraud, etc. Personal defenses which may *not* be raised include lack of capacity, insolvency, discharge in bankruptcy, or death. (Personal defenses are reasons that a creditor generally will want a surety.)

A surety may also raise his own contractual defenses to performance. However, remember two things. First, consideration need not directly flow to the surety. Second, a surety cannot raise as a defense that he entered into a surety relationship because of fraudulent representations of the principal debtor *unless* the creditor can be shown to have been aware.

A creditor's release of the debtor will also release the surety *unless* the creditor specifically reserves its rights against the surety. (If so, the surety could still recover from the principal debtor.) An uncompensated surety is discharged with any change in contract. A compensated surety will be released to the extent there is a materially increased risk (for example, to the extent of the value of released collateral).

A surety who pays a creditor is subrogated to the rights the creditor had versus the principal debtor, including rights to collateral. The surety may also seek reimbursement.

You may encounter a guarantor or guarantor of collection on the exam. To recover against a guarantor, the creditor must be able to show reasonable diligence in seeking payment from the principal debtor. To recover against a guarantor of collection, the creditor must show that she attempted to enforce the promissory note but failed.

You can count on a cosurety problem. As a result, you should be sure you understand the illustrative example in this chapter involving Al, Bonnie, and Carol. Remember that cosureties may be potentially liable for different amounts of the debt and need not have become cosureties at the same time. A release of a cosurety will proportionately release the remaining cosurety(ies).

KEY WORDS

collateral (914)
contribution (924)
cosurety (923)
creditor (914)
guarantor (917)
guarantor of collection (917)

indemnification (922)
leading object rule (916)
principal debtor (914)
subrogation (922)
surety (914)
suretyship (914)

DISCUSSION QUESTIONS

1. Identify the parties to a suretyship contract.
2. Provide several common examples of a surety relationship.
3. What conditions, if any, apply to the obligation of a surety to pay? Of a guarantor? Of a guarantor of collection?
4. Need the surety receive consideration to become a surety? Need he or she receive compensation? Explain.
5. Explain what is meant by the leading object rule.
6. What are the basic rights of the creditor?
7. What are the basic rights of the surety?
8. What are the basic defenses of the surety?
9. What is a cosurety? What is required to have a cosuretyship situation?
10. What are the basic rights and duties of the principal debtor?

CASE PROBLEMS

1. Dustin is a very cautious lender. When approached by Lanier regarding a $2000 loan, Dustin demanded not only an acceptable surety but also collateral equal to 50 percent of the loan. Lanier obtained King Surety Company as his surety and gave Dustin rare coins worth $1000 as collateral. One week before the loan's due date, Lanier assured Dustin he would have no difficulty in making payment. He persuaded Dustin to return the coins, since they had increased in value and he had a prospective buyer. What is the legal effect of the release of collateral on King Surety? Explain.
2. Watt contacted Republic Bank for a business loan. Republic refused to make the loan unless Watt could provide adequate security or an acceptable surety. Watt asked Regis, one of his trade customers, to act as surety on the loan. In order to induce Regis to sign, Watt made certain fraudulent representations and submitted a materially false financial statement. Watt is now insolvent, and Republic seeks to hold Regis liable. Will Republic prevail against Regis? Explain.
3. Maxwell was the head cashier of Amalgamated Merchants Bank. Excelsior Surety Company bonded Maxwell for $200,000. An internal audit revealed that Maxwell had embezzled $1000. Maxwell persuaded the bank not to report him and promised to pay the money back within 10 days. The bank agreed and informed neither the police nor Excelsior of the theft. Maxwell shortly thereafter embezzled $75,000 and fled. Excelsior refuses to pay. Is Excelsior liable? Explain.

4. Clark is a surety on a $100,000 obligation Thompson owes to Owens. The debt is secured by a $50,000 mortgage on Thompson's factory. Thompson goes bankrupt, and Clark satisfies the debt. Is Clark entitled to make a claim in the bankruptcy proceeding? Could Clark recover against Thompson if Thompson has already completed bankruptcy proceedings and been discharged? Explain.

5. Samp conducts the following transactions. Explain which, if any, establish Samp as a surety:
   a. Samp says: "Ship goods to my son and I will pay for them.
   b. Samp guarantees a debt of a corporation he controls.
   c. Samp sells an office building to Park, and, as part of the consideration, Park assumes Samp's mortgage on the property.

6. Simpson and Thomas made separate suretyship contracts with Allan to guarantee repayment of Allan's $12,000 loan to Parker. Simpson's guarantee was for $12,000, and Thomas's guarantee was for $8000. Parker defaults, and Simpson pays Allan. Thomas believes no cosuretyship relationship exists between Simpson and himself because their contracts were separate, so he refuses to contribute. What, if anything, may Simpson recover from Thomas? Explain.

7. Vintage Car Sales both financed and sold used cars. Kelly McCullar, a minor, agreed to purchase a used Mustang convertible from Vintage. Vintage demanded as a condition of the sale that Kelly find a surety for the $10,000 loan. Kelly talked her friend Mary Musser and her boyfriend, Howard, into signing as cosureties. Both Mary and Howard had recently come of age. Vintage released Mary several weeks later when her parents learned of the agreement and complained vehemently to Vintage. Kelly has defaulted. vintage has demanded that Howard pay them $9400, the amount still owed. Howard claims that as a cosurety he was never liable for more than $5000. In the alternative, Howard contends that the release of Mary reduced his potential liability to $5000. Is he correct on either ground? Explain.

8. West promised to make Noll a loan of $180,000 if Noll obtained sureties to secure the loan. Noll entered into an agreement with Carr, Gray, and Pine, who would act as cosureties on his loan from West. The agreement between Noll and the cosureties provided that compensation would be paid to each cosurety. It further indicated that the maximum liability of each cosurety would be as follows: Carr $180,000, Gray $60,000, and Pine $120,000. West accepted the commitment of the sureties and made the loan to Noll. After paying nine installments totaling $90,000, Noll defaulted. Gray's debts (including his surety obligation to West on the Noll loan) were discharged in bankruptcy. Subsequently, Carr paid the entire debt outstanding of $90,000. What amount, if any, may Carr recover from Gray? From Pine? Explain.

CHAPTER 41

Security Interests in Personal Property

Selling goods on credit is an integral part of the operations of most nonretail businesses. The seller cannot do without credit sales, yet he must be realistic about the prospect of customers who do not pay. The problem is how to remain competitive by extending credit while protecting oneself.

The principal solution lies in careful evaluations of credit risks. Once the creditor has decided to extend credit, the law permits the use of some safeguards. Besides suretyships, the creditor can demand a *security interest* or lien —the terms are roughly synonymous—in property belonging to a debtor. This chapter examines secured transactions in which the debtor voluntarily gives the creditor a security interest on personal property to ensure repayment. However, as we will see, Article 9 of the Uniform Commercial Code (UCC) uses the term ''security interest'' in a sense which is somewhat different from its meaning under the common law.

Security interests in a debtor's property have two important practical consequences for a secured party—who is *always* a creditor. First, if the debtor defaults, the creditor can take the property subject to the security interest without the necessity of a breach of contract action. Thus, the lien significantly improves the likelihood of timely repayment. Second, should the debtor file for bankruptcy, a creditor's security interest remains valid. The creditor will still receive what the collateral will bring.

The somewhat detailed rules you will study in this chapter sometimes obscure the true role in commerce of security interests in personal property. Security interests play an auxiliary role. Few people contract just to get a security interest. A security interest merely reduces a creditor's risks somewhat on the underlying contract.

PRE-UCC SECURITY METHODS

This chapter focuses on Article 9 of the Uniform Commercial Code (UCC). However, some techniques commonly used today to provide security for credit transactions existed before Article 9 was adopted in 1962. An understanding of these techniques will place Article 9 in the proper perspective.

Pledges

In a *pledge*, the debtor gives the creditor actual possession of the debtor's personal property to hold as security. Rightful possession of the debtor's property puts other creditors on notice of the creditor's security interest in the property.

Pledges commonly take either of two forms. The distinction between the two types of pledges rests on whether the borrower's property is paid for. In the first type, the borrower purchases the pledged item on a time payment plan, but the property remains with the seller until it is fully paid for. For example, an item placed on layaway with a department store does not belong to the buyer until it is paid for. In the second type of pledge, the borrower pledges property he or she already owns to secure a loan. For example, a borrower may pledge a stereo system to a pawn shop to secure a loan. The second form of pledge is far more commonly used today than the first.

The drawback to pledges is that the borrower may need the pledged property. Borrowing to buy manufacturing equipment makes little sense if the lender retains possession until the borrower pays for it. Pledging requires that the lender become a bailee and, therefore, that the lender use due care to protect and preserve the pledged property. This may pose no difficulty with stock certificates, but it may be impossible if the lender does not have facilities, say, to store heavy industrial equipment.

Conditional Sales Contracts

In a *conditional sales contract*, the buyer takes possession of the goods but the seller retains title until the buyer completes payment. Thus, the condition is payment. Today, this device is used more commonly in the purchase of real estate.

Field Warehouse Contracts

In a *field warehouse contract*, the borrower gives inventory goods to a creditor as collateral. However, unlike the case with a pledge, the borrower retains the inventory on his or her premises. But the goods are kept segregated and under the lender's control. For instance, the borrower may designate a warehouse—or a physically separate portion of one—for this purpose. The creditor places the *field warehouseman*, who is either his agent or an independent contractor, in charge of the property. As the borrower repays the creditor, the field warehouseman releases inventory to the borrower.

A third party purchaser can never defeat the creditor's interest in personalty under a field warehouse contract so long as the creditor controls the collateral. As with a pledge, the borrower cannot transfer actual possession until he pays the lender.

Field warehousing is not commonly used because of the cost of maintaining the warehouses and because many inventory items simply are not appropriate for such arrangements. This device works best for inventory which moves slowly, like oil-well rigging equipment, farm implements, livestock, and road construction equipment. Article 9 provides alternatives to the lender which offer many similar protections without the costs of field warehousing.

Chattel Mortgages

A *chattel mortgage* is a document by which the debtor gives the creditor a security interest in personal property. The borrower retains possession of the collateral, but the chattel mortgage specifically gives the lender a lien on the goods. To *perfect* a chattel mortgage, and thus make it binding on third parties, the lender files it in the courthouse of the county where the goods are located. The principle behind this system is that citizens have *constructive notice* of what is on the public record. Therefore, it is fair to give a lender who has recorded a lien a better claim on the goods than third parties who have not recorded their claims. Article 9 adopts the chattel mortgage procedure.

Essentially, a chattel mortgage is what Article 9 refers to as a *security agreement*. Like the common law chattel mortgage system, Article 9, too, centers on notice to third parties as the key to a valid security interest.

OVERVIEW OF ARTICLE 9

Article 9 defines the creditor's protection against those who buy from, or extend credit to, the debtor [UCC §9-101 Comment].* The sections which follow focus on the transactions covered by Article 9; who the *secured party*—the party that is to have the security interest—must consider in designing the interest; how the parties create the interest; how the security interest takes effect; and what happens in the event of the debtor's default.

Transactions Covered

Article 9 covers any transaction in which the parties intend to create a security interest in personal property or in *fixtures*, personal property attached to real property [UCC §9-102(1)].

Personal property in this context includes goods of almost every type. The following are additional items of personalty in which a lender may have a security interest:

- *Chattel paper*: combined promissory notes and security agreements—used commonly in retail consumer credit sales
- *Negotiable instruments* and *documents of title*

---

* There is more deviation among the states on Article 9 than on any other UCC article. Originally promulgated in 1962, Article 9 was substantially revised in 1972. Some states have not adopted the 1972 changes. Most have, and this chapter covers Article 9 as amended.

- *Accounts*: the UCC term for accounts receivable
- *Intangible property*: a patent, copyright, or trademark are examples

Article 9 excludes certain transactions from its coverage, primarily because other laws regulate the security interests arising from them [UCC §9-104]. Among these are:

- An assignment of an employee's claim for wages or other compensation
- An assignment as collateral of a claim under an insurance policy
- A real estate mortgage
- A landlord's lien
- A sale of accounts as part of the sale of the entire business

Classification of Goods

The type of goods used as collateral determines how the secured party should perfect its security interest. Article 9 classifies goods into four categories.

Consumer goods are those bought primarily for personal, family, or household purposes [UCC §9-109(1)]. *Inventory* consists of goods held for sale in the ordinary course of business [UCC §9-109(4)]. *Equipment* consists of goods primarily used in business—including farming or a profession—which are neither inventory nor farm products [UCC §9-109(2)].

The fourth classification, *farm products*, includes crops and livestock and the products of crops and livestock, as well as supplies used or produced in farming so long as they are in the hands of a debtor engaging in farming operations. In the next case, if the bank could have convinced a bankruptcy court that chickens were equipment and eggs were inventory, it would have been a secured creditor and recovered considerably more of its loan than it did.

In re K. L. Smith Enterprises, Ltd.

2 Bankr. 280 (Bankr. D. Colo. 1980)

FACTS In Smith's unique method of housing hens and collecting eggs, the chickens resided in "egg production units," large circular structures containing four concentric circles of caged hens, ten tiers high. The circles revolved through the building, passing stations for feeding, watering, egg collection, and manure removal. In 1976, Smith borrowed $2.4 million from the United Bank of Denver. Smith executed two security agreements which gave the bank a security interest in all its inventory and equipment. Three years later, shortly before it filed for bankruptcy, Smith concluded three large sales: two involved eggs, and one involved laying hens. United Bank claimed a security interest in the proceeds from those transactions.

ISSUE Are chickens "equipment" and eggs "inventory"?

DECISION No. The bank asserted that where the sole business is the production of eggs, the eggs cease being farm products and become inventory. However, the Official Comment to UCC §9-109 states:

> *Products of crops or livestock, even though they remain in the possession of a person engaged in farming operations, lose their status as farm products if they are subjected*

to a manufacturing process. What is and what is not a manufacturing operation is not determined by this Article. At one end of the scale some processes are so closely connected with farming—such as pasteurizing milk or boiling sap to produce maple syrup or maple sugar—that they would not rank as manufacturing. On the other hand an extensive canning operation would be manufacturing. The line is one for the courts to draw. After farm products have been subjected to a manufacturing operation, they become inventory if held for sale.

Packaging eggs in cartons is not a manufacturing process like a canning operation. And if eggs are products of "livestock," the hens must be "livestock."

United Bank should have included farm products and livestock in its security agreement. But its chicken and egg argument contains an important lesson. Under Article 9, the debtor's use determines the nature of personal property. Smith sold its farm products—eggs—to Safeway Stores. In Safeway's hands, the eggs became inventory. When a shopper bought a dozen eggs at his local Safeway, the eggs became consumer goods. Clearly, when Gertrude Stein wrote, "A rose is a rose is a rose," she did not have Article 9 in mind.

Potential Competitors of the Secured Party

Normally, a creditor will not lend money unless he or she believes the borrower will be able to repay it with interest. A creditor who acquires a security interest in the borrower's property is better protected because the creditor can have the property sold to cover the money owed by the borrower. The problem is that other creditors may want the property liquidated to satisfy their claims. Figure 41.1 illustrates potential competing parties, who include:

- *The debtor*: This is the person who owes payment or other performance of the secured obligation, whether or not he or she owns or has rights in the collateral [UCC §9-105].
- *Unsecured creditors*: These are creditors of the debtor who are owed payment or other performance but who lack security interests in particular property.

- *Lien creditors*: These are creditors who have secured a lien against the debtor's property as a result of services or a court judgment.
- *Other secured creditors*: The creditor may have given a security interest in the same collateral to another creditor, as well.
- *The trustee in bankruptcy*: The trustee in bankruptcy reviews all claims of secured party status and has the power, where appropriate, to treat a secured creditor as an unsecured creditor.
- *Transferees of the collateral*: The transferee of collateral may be a purchaser, the recipient of a gift, or an heir of the debtor's estate.

The Approach of Article 9

Article 9 is easier to understand if you keep in mind three basic things.

- Article 9 applies to situations where a debtor puts up *personal property* collateral to secure a loan. To illustrate, Tanya purchases a new Camaro and puts the car up as collateral to secure her note with GMAC.
- *Attachment* is the *process* whereby a creditor gains legal rights in the collateral against the debtor. If Tanya fails to make her car payments to GMAC she will lose the Camaro to them.
- *Perfection* is the *process* whereby a creditor gains rights in the collateral as against third parties. If perfected, GMAC will have rights in the Camaro over possible other creditors and the trustee in bankruptcy.

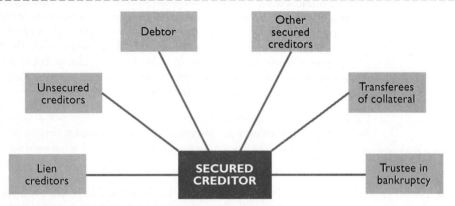

Figure 41.1 Parties Competing with a Secured Creditor.
A security interest may be an ancillary matter in a transaction, but for the creditor it is an important one. As this figure reveals, the secured creditor has many potential competitors for the asset securing the obligation.

Figure 41.2 provides an overview of attachment and perfection. The sections which follow will better define and explain the processes applicable to the terms. For now, understand that for a creditor to be best protected there needs to be *both* attachment and perfection.

ATTACHMENT

Attachment is the process by which the creditor creates a security interest and gains a secured interest in property of the debtor. In other words, attachment brings the security interest

	ATTACHMENT	PERFECTION
Purpose	Rights against debtor.	Rights against third parties.
Requirements	Security agreement* *and* Creditor gives value *and* Debtor has rights in collateral.	Attachment.
Methods of perfection.		Automatic (PMSI in consumer goods) or Possession or Filing finance statement.

*Need not be in writing if creditor retains possession of collateral.

Figure 41.2 Creation and Perfection of a Security Interest.

into effect between the creditor and the debtor. Once attachment occurs, the secured party need not do anything further. No form of public notice is required to achieve and/or maintain the security interest as to the debtor.

Attachment occurs when:

- The secured party gives value.
- The debtor has rights in the collateral.
- The debtor executes a written security agreement, unless the creditor has possession of the collateral.

Until *all* the above are completed—the order does not matter—the creditor does not have a secured interest and is an unsecured creditor. Other creditors or a trustee in bankruptcy can challenge a party's assertion of a secured interest. Thus, a creditor that considers itself secured may discover it is unsecured if it does not follow the steps discussed in this section.

Value

The secured party must give value before a security interest can attach. *Value* consists of any consideration sufficient to support a simple common law contract—including a binding commitment to extend credit, whether or not the credit is drawn—plus antecedent debt [UCC §1-201(44)].

The effect of antecedent debt is best illustrated by hypotheticals. Suppose that on May 1, Liberty Bank makes a binding commitment to extend a $3 million line of credit to Willow Widgets. On May 10, Willow Widgets borrows $150,000 from Liberty Bank. Liberty Bank first gave value on May 1.

Now suppose that also on May 1 Willow Widgets enters into a contract to deliver 1000 widgets to Delta Manufacturing, Inc., on credit. After delivery Delta fails to pay as provided by the credit terms. On June 15, Delta gives Willow Widgets a security interest in the widgets it has not paid for. Willow will be considered to have given value on June 15 even though Delta already owed it for the widgets.

Rights in the Collateral

The debtor must have rights in the collateral, but he does not have to own it free from all other interests [UCC §9-202]. Suppose Tom bought a new tractor from a John Deere dealer for $35,000. He paid $15,000 in cash and gave the dealer a $20,000 note which was secured by a purchase money security interest (discussed later in this chapter) in the tractor. Tom may later use his equity in the tractor as security for a $5000 loan from Household Finance. The Household Finance lien on the tractor would stand second to the dealer's lien, but the security interest of Household Finance may be perfected against the interests of others.

The Security Agreement

Under UCC §9-203(a), a secured party must obtain a *security agreement*, an agreement that creates a security interest. The agreement must be in writing unless the secured party is in possession of the collateral. A secured party could have a security agreement, for example, if it was a department store selling a coat on layaway, or a creditor to whom the debtor has pledged 100 shares of IBM, or a creditor that has established a field warehouse.

To be valid, a written security agreement must:

- Be signed by the debtor (the secured party is not required to sign).
- Show that the debtor is giving the secured party an interest in the collateral.
- Contain a description that reasonably identifies the collateral.

Article 9 does permit generic descriptions of collateral, such as "all inventory stored in the Little Rock warehouse" or "all #20 widgets stored in the Decatur plant" [UCC§9-203(1)(a)].

Common Security Provisions

Often, a secured creditor wants a security interest not only in present collateral but also in:

- Future advances
- After-acquired property
- Proceeds

Future advances. As previously discussed, businesses often secure a commitment from a lender for a line of credit that they may draw on over time. The lender may structure the security agreement so that its security interest applies to each borrowing under the line of credit. Thus, a *future advance* is money that is borrowed after the original security interest has attached and that is covered by the original security agreement. Each time the business draws against its line of credit, the lender is said to give new value. However, the lender also gave value in granting the line of credit. So either rationale works.

After-acquired property. *After-acquired property* is property that does not exist or that the debtor has not acquired at the time the security agreement is executed.

Quite commonly, nonconsumer debtors give secured creditors rights in future inventory or soon-to-be-acquired equipment. Such an arrangement results in a *floating lien*, a lien which is released as to inventory being sold and attaches to inventory being acquired. For example, the description "all #14 ball bearings stored in the Sunnyvale Warehouse, now or hereafter acquired" in a security agreement gives the secured creditor a security interest in newly acquired goods, a shipment of #14 ball bearings, without having to file again.

Floating liens have two major limitations. First, the security interest does not attach until the debtor gains a legal interest in the goods. Second, while the original secured party can gain a security interest in subsequently acquired goods, the priority of this interest may be subject to the interest of the lender, whether a seller or a third party, who actually financed the purchase. Later in this chapter, we discuss this interest, which is known as a purchase money security interest (PMSI).

However, a creditor cannot take a security interest in a consumer's after-acquired property unless the debtor acquires rights in the property within 10 days after the secured party gives value or the creditor provides additional value for it [UCC 9-204(2)]. In other words, after 10 days, the creditor will have to lend the consumer the money which made the additional purchases possible if it is to hold a security interest in the after-acquired property.

Thus, the UCC after-acquired property rule makes provision for the differences in sophistication between commercial purchasers and consumers. An after-acquired property clause in a consumer financing agreement might otherwise become a trap for the unwary. A consumer probably would not realize that an after-acquired property clause in a security agreement covering kitchen appliances, for example, would also give a creditor a lien on the television the consumer might buy in 6 months.

Proceeds. *Proceeds* include whatever the sale, exchange, collection, or other disposition of collateral generates [UCC §9-306(1)]. Suppose a bank has a right to the proceeds of inventory it finances for a car dealer. The dealer sells a new car from inventory the bank financed in exchange for cash, a trade-in, a note, and a security interest. The bank has a right to all the dealer received.

A security agreement automatically covers the secured party's right to the proceeds even if it does not contain an explicit statement to that effect. If proceeds were not covered, the secured party would lose its security if the debtor sold the collateral and then became insolvent.

Creditors also have a right of temporary perfection in proceeds for 10 days after their receipt by the debtor [UCC §9-306(3)(c)]. Suppose the car dealer receives a promissory note in exchange for a car whose purchase he financed through a bank. The bank has a temporary perfection in the promissory note.

From a practical standpoint, the creditor's right to proceeds offers little protection. The car dealer could cut off the bank's interest by transferring the note to a holder in due course. For that reason, an after-acquired property clause covering inventory generally gives better protection, since inventory is tangible and identifiable.

PERFECTION

For the most part, attachment affects only the debtor and the creditor. Without perfection, the security interest usually does not affect the persons about whom the creditor is most concerned: those who may have a competing claim on the goods.

"Perfection" is also a term not to be taken literally. *Perfection* describes the process by which the creditor's security interest becomes invulnerable to competing claims on the goods.

Perfection can occur in any one of three ways. First, rightful possession of collateral perfects the creditor's interest in it. Of course, that is the principle behind pledges and field warehouse arrangements. Second, placing the interest on the appropriate public record—in other words, "recording" it—perfects the creditor's interest.

Third, in certain situations perfection occurs automatically upon attachment. Generally, automatic perfection relates to *purchase money security interests (PMSIs)* in consumer goods. A PMSI in consumer goods arises where a creditor or the seller lends money specifically for the purchase of the goods involved [UCC §9-302(1)], for example, if a bank finances the purchase or a new boat. Figure 41.3 illustrates the three ways of perfection.

Automatic Perfection

A PMSI in consumer goods is perfected as soon as it attaches, without recording or possession [UCC §9-302(1)(d)]. Suppose Debby buys on

SECURED PROPERTY	ATTACHMENT ALONE		ATTACHMENT PLUS POSSESSION		ATTACHMENT PLUS FILING	
	PERMITTED	REQUIRED	PERMITTED	REQUIRED	PERMITTED	REQUIRED
Consumer goods	X		X		X	
Negotiable instruments				X		
Securities				X		
Money				X		
Accounts						X
General intangibles						X
Documents			X		X	
Chattel paper			X		X	
Nonconsumer goods			X		X	

Figure 41.3 Methods of Perfection Under Article 9.

credit a refrigerator for her home from Montgomery Ward. The fact that Debby charges the refrigerator on her personal Montgomery Ward credit card does not alone give Montgomery Ward a security interest. She *must* also execute a security agreement. Montgomery Ward perfects its security interest when Debby signs the security agreement and the company gives her value—the refrigerator.

A PMSI holder prevails against all third parties except a third party purchaser who can show he bought without knowledge of the security interest, for value, and for his personal, family, or household use [UCC §9-307(2)]. Suppose Debby sells the refrigerator to a stranger, Tony, for $400, and he moves it into the kitchen of his home. Tony's purchase probably defeats Montgomery Ward's security interest, even though the interest had been perfected.

As we will see, the PMSI holder can protect itself against third parties by recording.

Article 9 does not recognize a PMSI in consumer goods for the financing of motor vehicles or fixtures, or goods attached to real estate [UCC §302(1)(d)]. For example, the seller of a built-in oven could not rely upon automatic perfection, but the seller of a countertop microwave oven could.

Possession

Possession provides notice of the existence of a security interest to third parties. Either the secured party of his agent may have possession. The very fact that another person has rightful possession of the collateral at least raises a question about that person's interest in it. Suppose Merrill Lynch requires that Bob pledge his 500 shares of IBM stock as collateral for his account. When the brokerage takes possession of the stock, it perfects its security interest. Its interest remains perfected so long as it holds the stock.

Security interests in certain types of personal property can be perfected *only* by possession [UCC §9-304(1)]. These include:

- Negotiable instruments and documents of title
- Securities
- Cash

It should be fairly obvious why possession is required. A U.S. currency bill, like a $10 bill, has a serial number on it. However, commerce simply could not function if a person or business were charged with checking courthouse financing statement records on each bill tendered for exchange or payment. Similar problems would exist with negotiable instruments, documents of title, and most securities.

By contrast, a debtor usually cannot transfer by delivery claims represented by accounts and general intangibles. Therefore, the secured party would not hold anything a third party would have reason to inquire about. Thus, for accounts and general intangibles, possession is not a permissible means of perfection [UCC §9-305].

For most creditors, possession is an unsatisfactory means of perfection. For them, the answer is to leave the debtor in possession and to place their interests on public record by recording a financing statement.

Filing Under Article 9

The most common means of perfecting a security interest under Article 9 is *recording*, the filing of a document relating to property interests—in this instance, a financing statement or its equivalent—with the state or county office that maintains the appropriate public record of such interests.

The nature of the financing statement. A *financing statement* must contain:

- The names of the debtor and the secured party
- An address of the secured party from which information concerning the security interest may be obtained
- A mailing address for the debtor

Uniform Commercial Code — FINANCING STATEMENT — Form UCC-1

IMPORTANT — Read instructions on back before filling out form

This FINANCING STATEMENT is presented to a filing officer for filing pursuant to the Uniform Commercial Code.

4. ☐ Filed for record in the real estate records.	5. ☐ Debtor is a Transmitting Utility.	6. No. of Additional Sheets Presented:
1. Debtor(s) (Last Name First) and address(es)	2. Secured Party(ies) and address(es)	3. For Filing Officer (Date, Time, Number, and Filing Office)
Sage, Samual L. d.b.a. S&S Stores 1798 East 59th Place Miami, FL 33101	Computer Credit Corp. 88771 West Flagler Ext. Miami, FL 33109	

7. This financing statement covers the following types (or items) of property:

One (1) Viewtron mini computer system, consisting of a CPU (s/n 71908) and six terminals (s/n T2098 through T2103, inclusive) together with Viewtron inventory and wordprocessing software and related manuals and templates.

☐ Products of Collateral are also covered.

Whichever is Applicable (See Instruction Number 9)	Samuel L. Sage, d.b.a. S&S Stores *Samuel L. Sage* Signature(s) of Debtor (Or Assignor)	Computer Credit, Corp. *R.D. Cardell, pres.* Signature(s) of Secured Party (Or Assignee)

Debtor Copy
STANDARD FORM — UNIFORM COMMERCIAL CODE — FORM UCC-1   Rev. Jan. 1980   *Forms may be purchased from Hobbs & Warren, Inc. Boston, Mass. 02101*

Figure 41.4 A Financing Statement.
While a financing statement summarizes a security agreement, it must fully and accurately describe the collateral.

- The debtor's signature
- A statement indicating the types or describing the items of collateral [UCC §9-402(1)].

Figure 41.4 is a completed financing statement.

Adequacy of notice. A creditor may record a security agreement instead of a financing statement if the agreement satisfies all the requirements of a financing statement. However, the reverse does *not* work: a financing statement cannot be substituted for a security agreement, because a financing statement does not grant a security interest.

The description of collateral in a financing statement is generally much briefer, less detailed, and more generic than the description in a security agreement. It is sufficient so long as a reasonably careful third party could understand it. A financing statement covering all television sets in the State Street warehouse of Star Stereo need not list serial numbers or even brand names. ''All television sets'' will do.

Courts often test the adequacy of the financing statement by asking whether a reasonably diligent third party searching the public records would have found the filing. But, Kansas law, which the court in the next case applied, sets a higher standard.

Pearson v. Salina Coffee House, Inc.

831 F.2d 1531 (10th Cir. 1987)

FACTS Salina Coffee House (SCH) sold furnishings and kitchen equipment to Hilton Inn. It filed financing statements using that name, which was signed by the Inn's manager. However, "Hilton Inn" was a trade name. The debtor's legal name was Beacon Realty Investment Company of Salina. Beacon Realty filed for bankruptcy. Only then did SCH learn of its existence. The trustee in bankruptcy filed a complaint in the bankruptcy court challenging the validity of SCH's liens. The trustee claimed that the SCH's security interest was unperfected because the financing statement failed to list the entity's legal name. The bankruptcy court ruled that it was inequitable to penalize SCH for failing to file in the name of an entity it did not know existed, and entered judgment for SCH. The district court reversed.

ISSUE Were the financing statements filed by Salina effective to protect its security interest?

DECISION No. District court judgment affirmed. UCC §9-402(7) states:

> *A financing statement sufficiently shows the name of the debtor if it gives the individual, partnership or corporate name of the debtor, whether or not it adds other trade names or the names of partners.*

The UCC Official Comments on this section indicate that the filing in a trade name alone is not sufficient. The Kansas Comments expressly reject filing under a trade name alone because UCC §9-402(7) requires indexing under the entity's legal name. This rigid requirement furthers the objectives of the UCC's recording system for secured transactions. It assures notice to subsequent creditors in a manner designed to make them aware of any earlier security interests in the collateral superior to theirs. SCH's approach would require after-the-fact judicial inquiries to determine which creditors knew of the debtor's legal name. This would defeat the simplicity of the UCC's system. And, it does not seem too much to ask that a creditor find out the legal name of its debtor.

Time of filing. A financing statement can be filed before or after attachment, even though it is not effective as to third parties until the security interest attaches. Thus, before the security interest attaches, the parties must have a valid security agreement, the creditor must have given value, and the debtor must have rights in the collateral. Suppose City National Bank agrees to finance Al's new sailboat. City National could file Al's signed financing statement before or after loaning him the money, but its interest is not perfected until Al obtains an interest in the boat.

A creditor often will file a financing statement before actually lending money in order to assure itself of protection when it does give value. Since order of recording normally determines the priority of security interests, the creditor wants to make sure another creditor does not have an opportunity to file or a good faith purchaser does not have a chance to buy the goods without notice. As will be seen below, creditors must file a financing statement before giving value for a PMSI in inventory.

Place of filing. State law determines where financing statements are filed. Most states have adopted what is called a "local/central" filing system. For farm products, farm equipment, and consumer goods, creditors file financing statements "locally," that is, in the country where the debtor resides or the goods are lo-

cated. For crops or fixtures, creditors file in the county where the land is located. In all other cases, they file "centrally," that is, with the state.

Continuation statements. A financing statement is valid for 5 years. A creditor can file an unlimited number of *continuation statements* which renew the financing statement—and therefore its security interest—for an additional 5 years. The next case illustrates what happens when a creditor fails to file a continuation statement properly.

Kubota Tractor Corp. v. Citizens & Southern National Bank

198 Ga. App. 830, 403 S.E.2d 218 (Ga. App. 1991)

FACTS On September 11, 1978, Kubota Tractor filed a security agreement perfecting a security interest between itself and Harvey's, Inc., a dealer in farm equipment. On August 12, 1983, a month before the 5 years would expire on its security agreement, Kubota filed a document with the handwritten caption "Amendment" which contained modifications to the September 11, 1978, financing statement, including a broad after-acquired property clause. On March 2, 1984, Kubota filed a document expressly identified as a continuation statement of the September 11, 1978, agreement. Harvey's, Inc., later could not satisfy its obligations to Kubota and another creditor, Citizens & Southern National Bank. Citizens Bank prevailed in its motion for summary judgment when it argued that Kubota lost its security interest by not extending its continuation statement within 5 years.

ISSUE Did the trial court err by ruling that Kubota's security interest against Harvey's lapsed when it failed to file a continuation statement within 5 years?

DECISION No. Affirmed. A continuation statement is effective for 5 years after filing. Kubota's March 11, 1984, continuation statement was not filed in a timely manner. Kubota's argument that its continuation statement filed on August 12, 1983, was effective, since it was within the 5-year period, was erroneous. A valid continuation statement cannot include an amendment to the original financing statement, nor can it add more collateral without originally having an after-acquired property clause. The August 12, 1983, continuation statement also did not adequately identify the original statement by file number or expressly state that the original statement is still effective.

Termination of filing. A *termination statement* is a document placed on the public record which states that a party no longer claims a security interest under a financing statement which is referenced by file number [UCC §9-404]. A debtor who has fulfilled the obligation for which a security interest was given has a right to have the secured party file a termination statement. Suppose Townsend Furniture files a financing statement covering the living room suite it sold Lorne Seidman on credit. When he makes the final payment, Lorne has a right to have the financing statement covering his furniture terminated.

A financing statement automatically *lapses* —fails or loses effect—5 years after filing. No termination statement need be filed for a financing statement that has lapsed. As previously discussed, for the financing statement to continue in effect, the secured party must file a continuation statement.

PREVENTIVE LAW MEASURES

The previous two sections spelled out the requirements to gain attachment and perfection. To lessen the possibility of later legal problems, a creditor should heed the following advice in regard to security agreements and/or financing statements:

- Do not underestimate the truth of Murphy's Law ("What ever can go wrong, will go wrong"). Be protected.
- Be sure to provide the debtor's exact legal name. Many debtors operate or control a number of small companies.
- If you are dealing with a PMSI situation, be sure you understand and note whether the debtor is acquiring and financing the goods as an individual or an agent of a business. If the former, note further whether it is for a consumer or business purpose. If the latter, be sure the agent is an authorized person to sign on behalf of the debtor.

- While generic descriptions are permitted, be as specific and accurate in describing the collateral as you can.
- If possible, make your firm the "loss payee" on the debtor's insurance policy covering the collateral. This will assure that the debtor does not receive and spend insurance proceeds intended to cover collateral which has been lost, stolen, or destroyed.
- If in doubt as to whether to file a financing statement, file one.

The above points do not assure against possible loss by the creditor. However, a secured creditor who follows the pointers is less likely to find itself at the end of the bankruptcy line with the debtor's unsecured creditors, a place where 10 to 15 cents on the dollar is a fortunate recovery.

PRIORITY RULES

The UCC establishes rules for determining which secured party will prevail when two or more have claims on the same collateral. The general rule is that the first to file wins. The major exceptions to that rule involve PMSI perfections and temporary perfections.

The General Rule

Between two creditors with unperfected security interests, the first to perfect—by filing or possession—generally prevails. The Official Comments for UCC §9-312 describe this approach as "a race of diligence among creditors."* Whether the first creditor to perfect has notice of competing interests at the time she perfects her own interest has no bearing on the validity of her interest. Suppose Commonwealth Trust and First Bank lend money to

---

* Chapter 27 discussed the states' varying philosophies on priorities of interests. The fact that a state has adopted Article 9 indicates nothing about its law as to recording other interests in property.

Rochester's Clothing Store and both take a secured interest in Rochester's existing inventory. If Commonwealth Trust files first, its interest is superior to that of First Bank even though it has knowledge of the unfiled security interest of First Bank.

PMSI Perfection

Quite routinely, a prospective lender finds that a debtor is seeking a loan, say, to buy new inventory, and that an existing creditor already holds a perfected security interest under a floating lien in after-acquired inventory. Clearly, the second lender would not be so interested in making the loan, since the first creditor would have priority. Article 9 contains special rules for creditors with a PMSI interest to facilitate the extension of credit in these circumstances.

Filing a PMSI in consumer goods. As discussed earlier, a PMSI in consumer goods is perfected by attachment alone. Attachment alone provides protection to the secured party against:

- The debtor
- Other creditors
- The trustee in bankruptcy

However, attachment alone does *not* protect the creditor against a buyer of the collateral who purchases without knowledge of the security interest, for value and for his own personal, family, or household purposes [UCC §9-307(2)]. Protection against third party purchasers requires that the creditor file a financing statement.

A secured party has a 10-day temporary perfection from the date of delivery on the consumer goods to the debtor in which to perfect its security interest against third party purchasers. In other words, if the secured party files a financing statement within the grace period, perfection is retroactive to the delivery date. For example, on April 15 Alex bought on

TYPES OF GOODS	DEBTOR	OTHER CREDITORS	TRUSTEE IN BANK-RUPTCY	THIRD PARTY PURCHASER
Consumer goods:				
• Attachment alone	Yes	Yes	Yes	No
• Filing within 10 days	Yes	Yes	Yes	Yes
Equipment or farm products:				
• Attachment alone	Yes	No	No	No
• Filing within 10 days	Yes	Yes	Yes	Yes
• Filing beyond 10 days	Yes	Maybe	No	Maybe
Inventory:				
• Attachment alone	Yes	No	No	No
• Notice, filed before possession	Yes	Yes	Yes	No
• Otherwise	Yes	Maybe	No	No

Yes = method effective against party
No = method not effective against party
Maybe = protected only as to filing subsequently and/or third party purchasers

Figure 41.5 Protection Under PMSIs.
This table assumes that attachment has taken place.

credit new furnishings for his house from Circle Furniture. He signed a security agreement that day. He took delivery on May 1, and Circle Furniture filed the financing statement on May 8. In effect, Circle perfected its interest on May 1.

If the value of the goods is relatively small, the creditor may choose to forego the expense of preparing and filing a financing statement and to gamble that the debtor will not find a good faith purchaser. Really, this is not much of a gamble, since the creditor is fully protected against the debtor's bankruptcy, other creditors, and a bad faith third party purchaser. Figure 41.5 tabulates the protection afforded a creditor with a PMSI interest that is properly filed.

PMSIs in equipment and farm goods. Unlike the case of a creditor with a PMSI in consumer goods, attachment alone for a creditor with a PMSI in equipment or farm products does not provide protection against any third parties or a trustee in bankruptcy. However, the recording of a financing statement within 10 days of delivery of the equipment or farm products will secure the desired protection. For this reason, bankruptcy courts, like the one in the next case, often have to determine when the debtor took possession of goods.

In re Badger Aluminum Extrusion Corp.

7 Bankr. 251 (Bankr. S.D.N.Y. 1980)

FACTS   National Bank of North America (NBNA) held a perfected security interest in all of Badger's existing and after-acquired machinery and equipment. On July 28, 1977, Badger purchased a diesel generator set from Montgomery Leasing Corp. under a conditional sales contract. Within a few days, Montgomery assigned the contract to Long Island Trust Company (LIT). LIT perfected its security interest on August 16. Badger received the bare generator on July 29. The delivery of the rest of the set continued until October 17. Badger's trustee in bankruptcy petitioned the court to determine which bank held a secured interest in the generator set.

ISSUE   Did Badger possess the generator set on July 29?

DECISION   No. Judgment for LIT. Possession in this context means physical control of the collateral. Badger did not possess the generator set before the time it received the last of the component parts.

As Figure 41.5 illustrates, failure to comply with the 10-day rule means that the trustee in bankruptcy can defeat the PMSI interest and that the results of the race to record will alone determine the priority among other creditors. Suppose Atlas Manufacturing has a PMSI in equipment purchased by Texas Oil, Inc. Atlas delivers pipe to Texas Oil on May 1. First Bank lends money to Texas oil for other purposes but on May 5 files a financing statement covering the Texas Oil "pipe equipment." On May 12, Atlas files its financing statement. The security interest of First Bank will have priority. Had Atlas filed within 10 days, say, on May 8, it would have held the senior security interest.

PMSIs in inventory goods. Article 9 recognizes that if a second creditor provides the money used to purchase new inventory, that creditor must be allowed a superseding priority. Thus, Article 9 also recognizes a PMSI in inventory goods.

To perfect a PMSI for inventory goods, the secured party must take two steps in addition to recording. The secured party must:

1 Provide notice to any other creditor on file whose financing statement covers inventory
2 Record its financing statement before the debtor receives possession of the goods

The filing-before-delivery requirement precludes the 10-day grace period applicable to noninventory goods.

A buyer from inventory in the ordinary course of the debtor's business takes title free of any security interest even if the buyer knows of the interest [UCC §9-307(1)]. Suppose a sign in a car dealership window says that World Finance Company has financed all the dealership's inventory. Even so, a buyer would take her car free of the World Finance interest. This rule is necessary in order to maintain a free flow of commerce. The secured party has alternative methods of protecting itself, such as pledging or field warehousing, and it has a right to the proceeds from the sale.

The rule that a third party purchaser from inventory takes title free of any security interests has three major exceptions. First, a buyer in the ordinary course of business would not include a *bulk sale* purchaser.* If Arnie's Auto Liquidators buys a dealership's entire inventory, the purchase is not in the ordinary course of business. Arnie would take ownership subject to any outstanding security interests. Second, the buyer must be giving new value, not

---

* Bulk sales of inventory are discussed in Chapter 32.

receiving goods in payment for an earlier debt. Finally, this rule does not apply to someone who buys farm products from a person engaged in farming operations [UCC §9-307(2)].

Secured parties that lend for inventory and comply with the PMSI perfection rules noted above prevail against earlier perfected secured creditors. *In re Badger Aluminum Extrusion Corp.*, above, is an example of this rule at work. Where a negotiable document of title is involved, the party holding the document prevails.

Temporary Perfection

In certain instances, Article 9 permits temporary perfection of a security interest when actual perfection has not taken place. We have already seen how temporary perfection works for PMSI interests in non-inventory. Other than that, the two most common situations involve negotiable instruments and movement of collateral.

The UCC does not provide a temporary perfection for a PMSI in inventory. Thus, the rules described above supply solely to PMSIs in non-inventory goods.

Negotiable instruments. A creditor secured by an interest in a negotiable instrument has 21 days to file a financing statement or take possession. Suppose that on January 18 Bank Two lent $100,000 to Ace Department Store to finance inventory acquisition. The bank took a security interest in a negotiable bill of lading payable to Ace's order. Ace, however, retained the bill of lading. The bank must take possession of the bill by February 8 to retain its perfected interest.

A secured party that gives up negotiable documents held as collateral so that the debtor may sell the goods remains protected for 21 days. Suppose that on March 10 Bank Two releases the bill to Ace so that Ace could obtain the goods to sell in its store. The bank would have a continued perfected interest in the proceeds from the bill until April 1.

Movement of collateral. Security interests in collateral—except cars—moved from one state to another are temporarily perfected for 4 months. Suppose Ace moved stereos from its Miami warehouse to its San Antonio store. The holder of the security interest in those goods would have 4 months to perfect its interest in Texas from the time the stereo crossed the Texas state line.

DEFAULT AND FORECLOSURE

Taking Possession of Collateral

Upon the debtor's default, the secured party has the right to keep the collateral, if she has it, and to sell it [UCC §9-504]. If not, the creditor has the right to take possession of the collateral. If the debtor does not turn it over voluntarily, the creditor may use self-help, so long as she does not breach the peace.

Physical violence used on the debtor certainly is a breach of the peace. Also, the courts do not permit the secured party to enter the debtor's home or business without permission. However, the creditor can break into a car sitting in the debtor's driveway.

The debtor or someone with his authority must consent to the repossession; otherwise, the courts require the use of legal processes. Although courts have held that children lack the capacity to consent, many courts, like the federal court in the next case, have taken an extremely broad view of what amounts to consent.

Williams v. Ford Motor Credit Company

674 F.2d 717 (8th Cir. 1982)

FACTS   When Cathy and David Williams were divorced, the court ordered David to make payments to Ford Motor Credit Company on their Mustang, which the court granted to Cathy. David failed to make the payments. One morning at 4:30, a wrecker pulled into Cathy's driveway, hooked up her car, and started to tow it away. To no avail, she pleaded with the two men in the wrecker, explaining that she had been trying to make up the late payments. She also told them that the car contained personal property which did not belong to her. One of the men retrieved those items from the car, handed them to her, and drove off with the car in tow. Neither man made any threats toward her, nor did they do anything which caused her to fear physical harm. Cathy brought suit for damages against the repossession company and Ford Motor Credit Company. The injury awarded her $5000 in damages, but the trial court entered judgment notwithstanding the verdict in favor of Ford and the repossession company.

ISSUE   Did a breach of the peace occur in the process of the repossession?

DECISION   No. Affirmed. Cathy did not object to the repossession. Had she done so, a breach would have occurred. Nor did the repossession involve any incident which might tend to provoke violence. Therefore, it was lawful.

Sale of Collateral

The secured party may sell, lease, or otherwise dispose of the collateral in its current condition or following any commercially reasonable preparation [UCC §9-504(1). However, the creditor does not have a completely free hand as to what happens to the collateral.

Public or private sale. The UCC permits either a public or a private sale of the collateral. The UCC does not define the term ''public sale,'' though the official comments say it means an auction [UCC §2-706 Comment 4]. In practice, the term has come to include both oral bidding and sealed bids. The secured party has a right to bid on the collateral, and the debtor must receive any surplus [UCC §9-504(2)].

If the sale is private, the secured party has no right to bid unless the collateral is of a type sold in a recognized market or subject to widely distributed standard price quotations [UCC §9-504(3)]. So if the collateral consists of stocks in companies listed on the New York Stock Exchange, the creditor may purchase them at the market price. But if the collateral is a used car, the National Automobile Dealer Association ''Bluebook'' would not provide a satisfactory value because the prices of individual cars can vary greatly from the prices listed in the book. Again, any surplus must be turned over to the debtor.

It is important to note that saying the creditor may bid on the collateral does not imply that if the creditor is the high bidder, it will pay for the goods. Rather, the creditor gains the right to the collateral for the amount bid. Suppose the creditor has a security interest in 100 personal computers to cover a $40,000 debt. After default, the creditor has them sold at a public sale. The creditor makes the top bid, $25,000. This means that $25,000 is the value of the collateral, and the creditor may now seek a *deficiency judgment* for the remaining $15,000. In short, as with any top bid in a sale of the collateral, the creditor's top bid establishes the collateral's value and determines what the debtor still owes.

Timing and notice of sale. The UCC does not specify when the sale must occur. It only says that the sale must take place within a ''commercially reasonable time'' [UCC §2-706(2)]. This means, for example, that perishables must be sold much faster than, say, steel garbage pails.

The creditor may sell on short notice or without any notice to the debtor if the collateral is perishable, threatens to decline quickly in value—like Christmas trees the week before Christmas—or is of a type customarily sold on a recognized market [UCC §9-504(3)]. Normally, if the sale is public, the creditor must provide reasonable notice to the debtor of its time and place. If the sale is private, the creditor must notify the debtor of the time after which the sale will occur. The debtor may waive notice of the sale.

Retaining Collateral

A secured party may propose that he keep the collateral as his own in exchange for discharging the obligation and abandoning any right to a deficiency judgment [UCC §9-505 Comment 1]. If he does not receive a written objection within 21 days, he may keep the goods. Thus, the secured party cannot retain consumer collateral if either the consumer objects or the 60 percent rule applies. The rationale for the 60 percent rule is that consumers may not be as wise as they should be about objecting to the retention of collateral. When at least 60 percent of the loan has been paid, a consumer may do better in a sale. But if the debtor objects to the proposal, the secured party must sell the collateral.

This rule does not apply to consumer goods where the debtor has paid 60 percent or more of the cash price on a PMSI in consumer goods or 60 percent of the loan on a non-PMSI in consumer goods. The idea is to prevent a sale of the consumer's collateral which would probably bring less than the actual loan amount to the debtor. The creditor having a right to resell the goods of the consumer debtor must dispose of them within 90 days, or the debtor may recover them in an action for *conversion*.

Failure to Follow the Collateral Rules

Failure to observe the law on disposing of collateral can cause the secured party to be liable to the debtor for damages or to lose its right to a deficiency judgment [UCC §9-507]. If the debtor learns about it in time, he can obtain an injunction against the improper sale by the secured party. In the next case, the creditor failed to observe the collateral rules and consequently had the burden of proving that it was still entitled to a deficiency judgment.

Bank of Chapmanville v. Workman

406 S. E. 2d 58 (W. Va. 1991)

FACTS   The Workmans bought a mobile home and financed it with a loan from the Bank of Chapmanville. Five years later, they defaulted. The Workmans received a "notice of right to cure default," and "final demand letter," and after no response, the bank placed a "notice of public sale" in the local newspaper. There were no bidders at the public sale, so the bank bought the home for $10,614. There was no appraisal, but a guidebook was consulted to determine price. Several months later the mobile home was sold for $13,000. The bank subsequently sued the Workmans for a deficiency of $7873.25, which represented the difference between what the bank paid at the public sale and the remainder owed on the note. The Workmans defended against the deficiency, arguing that the mobile home was not sold in a "commercially reasonable" manner. The bank prevailed in a directed verdict.

ISSUE   Were there reasonable doubts to infer that the trial court erred in directing a verdict in favor of the bank for the deficiency?

DECISION   Yes. Reversed and remanded. Collateral can be sold at public or private proceedings, but every aspect of the disposition, such as the method, manner, time, place, and terms, must be commercially reasonable. In this case, the bank failed to (1) list the specific address of the mobile home; (2) list a telephone number for inquiries; (3) and mention any opportunities to inspect the home before sale.

In the *Workman* case, the West Virginia Supreme Court also wrestled with how to treat a creditor and its rights to a deficiency judgment when it fails to sell the collateral in a commercially reasonable manner. Presently, the states are divided on whether to apply one of the following three rules: (1) an "absolute bar" to the recovery of the deficiency; (2) a "set-off" to the amount of the deficiency by the damages incurred by the debtor; and (3) the "rebuttable presumption" rule. Under the last approach, there is a presumption that the fair market value of the collateral equals the debt. The creditor must then bear the burden of proving what the collateral is worth. The collateral must, however, be less than the balance of the debt for a deficiency to arise. On remand in *Workman*, the Bank of Chapmanville had to prove that the mobile home had a fair market value of less than $18,487.25, which is the balance left on the note. Since the bank was able to sell it in a subsequent private sale for $13,000, it appears that the Workmans will likely still owe a deficiency.

The West Virginia Supreme Court contended that the "rebuttable presumption" rule is the fairest middle ground between the interests of creditors and debtors. The "absolute bar" rule favors the debtor too much, since a creditor's right to the deficiency is totally lost if it fails to see the collateral in a commercially reasonable manner. Furthermore, it is sometimes difficult for creditors to observe and understand all the sometimes trivial and technical requirements under the law, as well as knowing what is reasonable under the circumstances. The "set off" rule, on the other hand, can be overly partial to creditors, since it is argued that debtors usually are not in a position to prove what actual damages are in order to set off that amount against the deficiency.

The above issue is of major importance to both creditors and debtors. Normally, personal property, like autos, trailers, etc., depreciate in value faster than the notes can be paid down, creating negative equity. Consequently, lenders must be able to pursue debtors for deficiencies, since their collateral has diminished in value. Debtors, however, have suffered the loss of a valuable piece of property, and now must further contend with a sometimes large deficiency judgment. The size of the deficiency often can mean the difference between going bankrupt or not.

CONCLUSION

Secured transactions result when a party lending money or extending credit wishes to have more than the debtor's word to rely on for payment of the debt. Even so, a security interest rarely guarantees full repayment of the obligation. But it does minimize the potential loss.

A debtor gives a creditor a secured interest in his property by means of a security agreement. Once the debtor signs the security agreement—unless the creditor has actual possession of the collateral, the debtor has an interest in the collateral, and the creditor has given value to the debtor—then the security interest attaches to the property.

Except in the case of a PMSI in consumer goods, attachment alone does not bind third parties. Article 9 allows the creditor to perfect by possessing personalty or by placing a financing statement on the public record. While the rules of perfection are fairly simple, the ramifications of noncompliance are potentially drastic.

A NOTE TO FUTURE CPA CANDIDATES

Security interests in personal property generally constitute one-third of the UCC questions on the CPA exam. Given the fact that the UCC section generally constitutes 25 percent of the total exam, it is important that you work to master this chapter.

Four basic concepts are emphasized on the exam:

- Attachment of security agreements
- Perfection of security interests
- Priorities between creditors
- Rights of creditors, debtors, and third parties

To understand Article 9 you need to be able to visualize the processes applicable to security interests.

Article 9 deals with secured debt involving personal property, *not* secured debt involving real property or unsecured debt. To illustrate, your purchasing a new set of tires with your

Sears credit card results in unsecured debt. Sears has no rights to the return of the tires if you should ultimately fail to pay for them.

If you should wish to charge a greater amount, perhaps to purchase a new refrigerator and stove for your first house, Sears may wish to retain a security interest in the appliances. A security agreement is the debtor giving the creditor a security interest in the goods, the appliances. Since the purchaser of appliances will assume possession of the appliances, the security agreement would have to be in writing. The security agreement will attach, become effective, when the:

- Security agreement is signed by the debtor
- Creditor has given value (credit for the debtor to purchase the appliances)
- Debtor has rights in the collateral (the appliances)

Ordinarily attachment does not result in perfection, rights against third parties. However, if a purchase money security interest (PMSI) in consumer goods is involved, as there would be with our Sears example, then perfection will occur upon attachment. (The exam sometimes speaks of automatic perfection upon attachment.) In all other situations, the creditor must retain possession of the collateral or file a financing statement to gain perfection against third parties. It is important that you know and understand Figure 41.2. Note that filing a financing statement is *not* required for attachment.

On the CPA exam you are expected to know the various methods of perfection under Article 9. Figure 41.3 provides this information. However, it is best simply to remember that there are three types of collateral commonly tested on the exam which can be perfected only by possession: negotiable instruments, securities, and money. A field warehouse is an effective form of possession but often not practical as a result of costs.

PMSIs are almost always covered on the CPA exam. You need to know Figure 41.5. To resolve a PMSI question correctly you must correctly characterize the goods involved *in relation to the purchaser/debtor* as being consumer goods, equipment, farm products, or inventory. In regard to our previous example involving Sears, Sears would have to file a financing statement to be protected against third party purchasers of the collateral. Remember, they are still protected as to the debtor and the trustee in bankruptcy.

For PMSIs involving equipment or inventory, attachment and the filing of a financing statement must both occur. There are three additional important points to remember. First, a creditor can *never* gain perfection against third parties for inventory (*even if the third party knows of the security interest*). Second, for PMSIs in consumer goods or equipment, filing by the tenth day relates back to the first day. Third, for inventory, the PMSI creditor must provide notice to already filed creditors *and* file the financing statement *before* giving the debtor-buyer possession. If not, the PMSI creditor will/not perfected as to third parties.

Some miscellaneous matters to note:

- It is quite common for there to be more than one secured creditor for the same collateral.
- Only the debtor need sign a security agreement or financing statement.
- A recorded financing statement is constructive notice. You are presumed to know it.
- Ordinarily, security interests have priority based on the order of filing. The exception is a proper PMSI.
- A creditor can purchase the collateral at a private sale *provided that* the sale is conducted in a commercially reasonable manner. A good faith purchaser for value prevails whether the sale is public or private.
- A "true consignment" occurs when an agent sells the goods for the owner, as is often true for art galleries. The owner of the collateral is protected if it is known that the art gallery operates by true consignment or financing statement filed.

- A properly perfected secured creditor is protected for up to four months if the debtor moves the collateral to another state.

KEY WORDS

after-acquired property (936)	perfection (937)
attachment (934)	pledge (930)
chattel mortgage (931)	proceeds (936)
continuation statement (941)	purchase money security interests (PMSIs) (937)
field warehouse contract (931)	recording (938)
financing statement (938)	security agreement (931)
	security interest (930)
	termination statement (942)

DISCUSSION QUESTIONS

1. What is the purpose of a security interest in personal property?
2. What is a pledge? A chattel mortgage? Were the concepts behind either device carried over into Article 9?
3. What types of transactions are covered by Article 9?
4. How are goods classified under Article 9? Why is it important to know how goods are classified?
5. Who are the potential competitors to a secured party for the value represented by collateral?
6. What is the purpose of a security agreement? What is necessary for a security agreement to attach?
7. What is the purpose of an after-acquired property clause in a security agreement?
8. How is a security interest perfected?
9. What is the rule for a temporary perfection of PMSIs in noninventory goods?
10. What are the rights of a secured party as to the collateral after the debtor defaults?

CASE PROBLEMS

1. Henk Boat Sales secured financing for its annual spring boat sale from American Bank. American agreed to the loan, however, only if Henk agreed to a field warehouse arrangement for the boats purchased for the sale. Henk agreed. By accident, the bank failed to have Henk sign the written security agreement that it had prepared and did not file a financing statement. American Bank properly established the field warehouse. Later, Henk borrowed money from Walls Bank and gave them a security interest in "all inventory." Walls filed its financing statement. If a dispute should arise as to the boats covered by the warehouse agreement, which would prevail? Explain.

2. On May 2, Commercial Bank agreed to loan Tyler Corporation $50,000. Tyler signed a security agreement and financing statement covering its existing equipment. On May 4, Commercial filed the financing statement. On May 7, State Bank loaned Tyler $60,000. State had notified Commercial on May 5 of its intention to make the loan. Tyler signed a security agreement and financing statement covering the same equipment. On May 8, State filed the financing statement. On May 10, Commercial loaned Tyler $50,000. If Tyler defaults on both loans, who will have the priority security interest in the equipment? Explain.

3. Fogel purchased a TV set for $900 from Hamilton Appliance Store. Hamilton took a promissory note signed by Fogel and a security interest for the $800 balance due on the set. Hamilton's policy was not to file a financing statement until the purchaser defaulted. Fogel obtained a loan of $500 from Reliable Finance, which took and recorded a security interest in the set. A month later, Fogel defaulted on several loans and one of his creditors, Harp, obtained a judgment against Fogel, which was properly recorded. After making several payments, Fogel defaulted on a payment due to Hamilton, which then recorded its financing statement after Reliable's filing and the entry of the Harp judgment. The following week, Fogel sold the set for $300 to Mobray at a garage sale.

Which of the parties has the priority claim to the set? Explain.

4. Clearview Manufacturing, Inc., sells golf equipment to wholesale distributors, who sell to retailers, who in turn sell to golfers. In most instances, the equipment is sold on credit with a security interest in the goods taken by each of the respective sellers. Which parties, if any, would qualify as purchase money secured parties? Which parties, if any, would normally have to file or have possession of the goods to perfect their security interests? Explain.

5. The Gordon Manufacturing Company manufactures lathes. It sold on credit twenty-five general-use lathes to Hardware City, a large retail outlet. Hardware City sold one of the lathes to Johnson for use in his home repair business, reserving a security interest for the unpaid balance. However, Hardware City did not file a financing statement. Johnson's creditors are asserting rights against the lathe. Describe what type of goods the lathe was to each party to the transaction. Must Gordon and Hardware City file to perfect their security interest? Explain.

6. On June 3, Southern Finance loaned Lee Corp. $20,000 to purchase four computers for use in its trucking business. Lee contemporaneously executed a promissory note and security agreement. On June 7, Lee purchased the computers with the $20,000, obtaining possession that same day. One June 10, Mort, a judgment creditor of Lee, levied on the computers. When, if ever, did the Southern Finance security interest attach? If Southern Finance files a financing statement on June 11, which of the parties will have a priority security interest in the computers? Explain.

7. Merchant's Bank finances Bates Buick's inventory. To secure a loan, Bates has given Merchant's a properly executed security agreement on its present and future inventory and in the proceeds from the sale of inventory. Bates sold a new Riviera from its inventory to Warren, for which Warren paid with a $6000 certified check and the trade-in on his used Toronado. As compared with the other Bates Buick creditors, what rights, if any, does Merchant's Bank have as to the Toronado and the certified check? Explain.

8. Perdue Marina sold a boat to Herb Wright on an installment contract. Wright had paid 70 percent of the purchase price but then failed to make subsequent payments. Hank Perdue, the marina proprietor, confiscated the boat while Herb had it tied to a public dock. Hank immediately contracted to sell the boat to a friend, Powers McGuire. Herb claims that the seizure of the boat was improper and that Hank has no legal right to go through with the sale to Powers. Is Herb correct about the seizure? About the planned sale? Explain.

CHAPTER 42

Security Interests in Real Property

Tom and Angie had saved enough money for a down payment on a house. They found what they wanted, a 10-year-old house being sold by its original owner. The big selling points were the seller's offer to finance the purchase himself and a newly expanded kitchen which opened onto a new patio. Tom and Angie quickly agreed to the seller's terms. Relying on the seller and the seller's real estate agent, Tom and Angie bought the house without consulting a lawyer of their own. The terms required that they give the seller a down payment, a promissory note for the balance of the purchase price, and a *mortgage*,* a voluntary security interest in real property.

A few months passed. Then, Tom and Angie received a shock in the form of a notice that the contractor who had done the kitchen and patio work was seeking a court order to have their house sold. The seller had not paid the contractor $10,000 for the work, and the contractor had placed a *mechanic's lien*—an involuntary security interest in property for the value of improvements—on the house before they bought it.

Now, Tom and Angie went to a lawyer. They discovered that none of their agreements with the seller mentioned responsibility for mechanic's liens, which meant they would have to pay the lien. Worse, the seller had sold their note and transferred the mortgage to a holder in due course and disappeared, so they could not recover from the seller.

Tom and Angie learned a very expensive lesson which they could have avoided by applying preventive law principles. Having a lawyer review real estate sales contracts and the deed and do a *title search* is considerably cheaper than paying off liens.

This chapter examines how voluntary and involuntary liens are created, how liens are perfected against third parties, what rights the creditor obtains by having a lien, and what defenses, if any, the property owner can raise against the lien.

THE NATURE OF LIENS

In the context of real property, the terms "lien" and "security interest" are synonyms. Both describe devices which use a debtor's interest in land as security for the repayment of a debt.

Effects on the Use of Land

Liens generally do not affect the way a property owner uses or "enjoys" land. Rather, they affect either the right to continue to own the property or the ability to sell it freely.

A lien may allow the lienholder to force an involuntary sale of the land in order to satisfy the debt it secures. Suppose a homeowner defaults on his mortgage. The bank may sell the property to satisfy the debt. This process is called *foreclosure of a mortgage.*

Commonly, however, liens remain passive interests in real property for many years. A homeowner with a 30-year mortgage, for instance, has a lien on his property until he pays the loan it secures. So long as he makes the monthly mortgage payments on time and does not violate any of the loan's other conditions, the lien's effect will be passive.

Properly recorded liens, like a mortgage, affect the ability to sell real property. Liens "run with the property," meaning a purchaser buys property subject to the liens on it unless they are *released* or discharged. Buyers are reluctant to assume responsibility for existing liens and usually insist on a title free of such *encumbrances.*

---

* The word "mortgage" was formed in the fourteenth century by joining the French words for "dead" and "pledge." The reason for this odd mix was that the property interest of the person pledging the realty as security for a loan "died" upon default. As noted below, today the mortgagee's *right of redemption* gives the mortgagee the capability to retain the property after default.

	INTERESTS		IF BUYER/BORROWER DEFAULTS			
	BUYER'S INTEREST	LENDER'S INTEREST	COURT APPROVAL TO SELL?	STRICT FORFEITURE?	EQUITABLE REDEMPTION RIGHTS?	RIGHT OF REDEMPTION RIGHTS?
Mortgage	Legal title	Lien	Yes	No	Yes	Varies**
Second mortgage	Legal title	Second lien	Yes	No	Yes	Varies**
Deed of trust	Grantor (title reverts back)	Trust beneficiary	No	No	No*	No
Purchase money mortgage	Legal title	Lien	Yes	No	Yes	Varies**
Land contracts (common law)	Equitable title	Legal title	No	Yes	No	No

*Right of reinstatement.
**Varies from state-to-state.

Figure 42.1 Comparison of Real Estate Financing Methods.

Voluntary and Involuntary Liens

Liens can be either voluntary or involuntary. *Voluntary liens* are ones which the holder of a property interest grants to another, usually in exchange for credit or services. Almost all home buyers, for instance, purchase their homes with borrowed money. Most lenders require that the purchaser give the lender a mortgage on the property equal to the amount borrowed.

Involuntary liens, like the mechanic's lien, arise when a statute permits a creditor to secure a debt by means of a security interest in the debtor's property.

MORTGAGES AND SIMILAR DEVICES

Mortgage loans are by far the most common real estate financing devices. However, there are a number of alternatives, such as land contracts or deeds of trust. As you study this section, refer to Figure 42.1, which compares the various financing methods.

The Mortgage Transaction

A *mortgage* is an interest in the borrower's land which she gives her creditor to secure her debt. The borrower is the *mortgagor*, the person giving the mortgage. The lender is the *mortgagee*, the party receiving the mortgage. Suppose Alicia wants to buy a town house. She will be the mortgagor, since she will give a mortgage on the property to her lender, the mortgagee.

Usually, the mortgagor gives the mortgagee this interest in the property as a condition of the loan. The mortgagor's signed promissory note

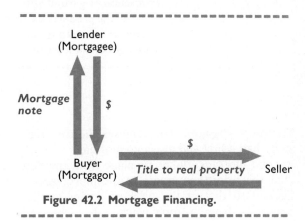

Figure 42.2 Mortgage Financing.

for the amount borrowed plus interest evidences the loan. Figure 42.2 illustrates the usual home mortgage transaction. Sometimes, as in the next case, one party has a reason to disguise the true nature of a transaction.

James v. Ragin

432 F. Supp. 887 (W.D.N.C. 1977)

FACTS   In 1973 the Jameses bought a house. Ragin acted as their real estate agent. Not long afterward, the Jameses defaulted on their two mortgages and could not arrange additional financing. They approached Ragin, who offered them a "take it or leave it" deal: the Jameses would sell the property to Ragin; they would rent it from him for 6 months; and after paying rent for 6 months, they would repurchase their home. The original "sale price" to Ragin was $22,457.21, the sum of the two mortgages on the property. That amount was between $1500 and $4500 less than the property's fair market value. The repurchase price was $23,457.21, and the Jameses' monthly rent was $254.10. Ragin's net was to be $1600 over 6 months on a loan of $6165.40, a return of more than 50 percent. The Jameses actually rented from May 28, 1974, until October 31, 1975. Then, citing the Federal Truth in Lending Act, 15 U.S.C. §§1601 *et seq.*, they attempted to rescind the transaction, claiming that the transaction was not a sale but was, in effect, a mortgage loan and that therefore Ragin was required to provide them in advance with a statement of the cost of financing.

ISSUE   Was the agreement, in effect, a mortgage?

DECISION   Yes. Judgment for the Jameses. The intent of the parties determines whether a conveyance with an option to repurchase represents a true sale or a loan and security interest. The court must consider whether (1) the transaction created a debtor-creditor relationship, (2) the transferor remained in possession of the premises, (3) the transferor was under duress and hard-pressed for money, (4) the transaction originated with a loan application, and (5) the purported sale price was less than the property's worth. Here, the arrangement clearly was not a sale with an option to repurchase but was a loan with a security interest—which required a statement of the cost of financing.

Second mortgages. The Jameses' house originally had a first and a second mortgage on it. A *second mortgage* takes its name from the fact that the priority it grants to the mortgagor is second to that of the primary lender on the proceeds from a foreclosure sale. "Second mortgage" is also a generic term for any mortgage after the first.

Often, people seek a second mortgage when a bank loan will not cover the real property's full purchase price. First-time buyers, in particular, may have to borrow the balance from another lender. Suppose Alicia can borrow $60,000 of the $75,000 purchase price of a town house from Central Savings & Loan but still needs $5000. Her parents agree to lend it to her, secured by a second mortgage. If Alicia should fail to pay both Central Savings & Loan and her parents, Central would have first rights to the proceeds of the foreclosure sale.

Formal Requirements

Statute of Frauds. Mortgages transfer interest in real property. Therefore, the *Statute of Frauds* requires that mortgages be in writing and be signed by the mortgagor. Mortgagees must be named, but they need not sign. Also, mortgages must describe the property and clearly create a lien interest granted to the mortgagee. Finally, mortgages must be delivered to, and accepted by, the mortgagee.

Recording. A properly recorded mortgage serves as a notice of a legal interest and binds third parties, even one who fails to discover it. Third parties are said to have *constructive notice* of the mortgage because it is in the public records.

For recording purposes, the law treats mortgages in much the same way as it treats deeds. Like a deed, a mortgage binds the immediate parties without recording. In other words, failing to record the mortgage does not affect the rights and duties of the mortgagor and mortgagee. However, the unrecorded mortgage is of no legal effect to good faith purchases for value without notice of it.

Only a foolish mortgagee would fail to record to a mortgage, since that would allow a third party with a subsequent mortgage to take priority in the event of a foreclosure and sale of the property. That means the later mortgagee would have first claim on the proceeds for the satisfaction of its claim, while the earlier one could look only to see what was left. Just how that might happen depends on the state's recording statute.

As Figure 27.5 illustrates, recording statutes fall into three categories. A *race* statute, as its name implies, awards priority to the first mortgage recorded, regardless of whether that mortgagee had notice of an earlier, unrecorded mortgage. A *notice* statute awards priority to the later mortgage if the mortgagee did not have notice of the earlier, unrecorded mortgage—regardless of whether the later mortgagee records. A *race-notice* gives priority to the later mortgage if it is the first one recorded and the mortgagee does not have notice of the earlier, unrecorded mortgage.

The holder of an unrecorded mortgage has no claim on a subsequent good faith purchaser of the property. Because the mortgage is unrecorded, the interest has not attached to the land. Suppose Central Savings & Loan makes the $60,000 mortgage loan to Alicia but fails to record the mortgage. A good faith purchaser for value who did not know of Central's mortgage would take ownership of Alicia's town house free of Central's lien. Of course, Alicia would still be liable on her promissory note to Central, but Central would have lost its security interest in the town house.

To avoid the possibility of intervention by another creditor or a good faith purchaser, a commercial mortgagee normally insists that the deed and the mortgage be recorded at the same time. For the same reason, the lender will insist that all liens on the property be satisfied before the time when title passes, the *closing*.

Deeds of Trust

A *deed of trust* is similar to a mortgage in that the borrower puts up her property as collateral to ensure payment of the borrowed amount. A deed of trust results from a three party transaction following the closing. The grantor, the purchaser of the property, creates the trust by transferring the property to a trustee who holds the property for the benefit of the beneficiary—the lender.

Legal ownership remains with the trustee

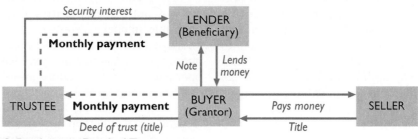

Figure 42.3 Parties to a Deed of Trust.

until the purchaser-grantor completes payment of the loan. The trustee acts as a conduit, receiving payments from the grantor and giving them to the beneficiary. When the grantor pays off the loan, the trustee reconveys the property. Figure 42.3 illustrates the process.

To the lender, a deed of trust is a particularly attractive arrangement because the trustee can be given the power to sell the property relatively quickly in the event of default without any involvement by the courts. The potential for abuse of this power explains why some states do not permit the use of deeds of trust, since all that is generally required in a power of sale is notice to the grantor, often in the form of a certified letter, and publication of the proposed date of the sale.

Seller Financing

Because buyers often have trouble accumulating a 20 to 30 percent down payment, and meeting the high interest rates commercial lenders require, sellers often assume part of the financing for the home purchaser. Generally, this financing takes either of two forms: a purchase money mortgage or a land contract.

Purchase money mortgages. With a *purchase money mortgage*, a seller conveys title to the buyer but take a mortgage for the money which the seller has yet to receive from the buyer. For example, Alicia sells her town house to Andy for $100,000. Andy puts down $15,000 of his own money, borrows $70,000 from First Bank, and gives Alicia a purchase money mortgage for $15,000.

If the seller finances only part of the purchase price and a commercial lender finances the greater share, the seller's mortgage generally will be subordinate to that of the commercial lender. Where the seller finances the entire purchase price, of course, the seller has the first lien on the property. In either case, the seller's rights of foreclosure and the buyer's right of *redemption*—the right to avoid the sale by paying the amount due, plus penalties—are those of a normal mortgage relationship. (The right of redemption is discussed below.)

Land contracts. Land contracts permit buyers to defer commercial financing in the hope that interest rats will drop or their financial condition will improve. A *land contract* is a contract to buy real property under which the seller finances part or all of the purchase price. However, the seller retains *legal title* until the buyer pays the final installment. The buyer has *equitable title*, which means that he has the right to have the legal title conveyed to him when he pays in full. Suppose Alicia sells her town house to Andy for $100,000, using a land contract. Andy pays $15,000 down, and Alicia finances the balance. Alicia holds the legal title and Andy the equitable.

The parties set a time in the land contract

for full payment, commonly 3 to 5 years after the time of contracting. Until then, the buyer makes periodic installment payments of about the same amount as he would be paying on a mortgage for a similar loan. The amount due at the termination of the land contract—the remainder of the principal—is called a *balloon payment*. In our example, at the end of 3 years, Andy would have to pay Alicia $85,000 less any principal he paid over the 3 years.

Failing to record a land contract can have consequences similar to those which can result from failing to record a mortgage. Recording the land contract prevents conveyance to a good faith third party purchaser. If a land contract is *not* on record, a good faith purchaser takes the property free of the interest it represents. Also, the buyer's equitable interest gives him a lien of the seller's property which is in the priority of its filing. For example, Andy's land contract would rank below the mortgage of Central Savings and Loan. His lien's amount would equal the down payment plus any principal he had paid. If the land contract is not recorded, it is treated—with regard to third parties—as if it did not exist.

Historically, land contracts had a serious drawback for the buyer. Under the common law, failing to make installments or other breaches resulted in *strict forfeiture*, meaning the purchaser lost everything he had paid on the contract. Strick forfeiture often resulted in an unjustly enriched seller. Unscrupulous sellers waited for buyers to stumble into relatively minor breaches and then sought an order of forfeiture.

Most states have modified the strict forfeiture rule. Commonly, if the buyer has paid the seller for a number of years or has paid a certain percentage of the sale price—often 20 to 25 percent—the buyer is no longer subject to strict forfeiture and is treated like a mortgagor.

Financing Laws

Normally, four laws apply to the financing of residential real estate: the state usury law, the federal Truth-in Lending Act, the Equal Credit Opportunity Act, and the federal Real Estate Settlement Procedures Act.

State *usury* laws limit the interest rate which a lender may legally charge. The federal Truth-in-Lending Act requires that a lender fully disclose the cost of credit so that consumers can compare the cost of financing offered by lenders and shop for advantageous credit terms. The lender must provide the consumer with a statement of full cost of the borrowing, including the finance charge and the annual percentage rate. The Act, however, applies only to loans to natural persons for nonbusiness purposes. The Truth-in-Lending Act is discussed in more detail in Chapter 45.

The federal Real Estate Settlement Procedures Act (RESPA) and the Truth-in-Lending Act have similar goals. RESPA applies where a lender—other than the seller—takes a purchase money mortgage to secure the loan. The most common type of mortgage, a *purchase money mortgage*, is one in which the lender supplies the money needed to purchase the real estate in return for a mortgage on that real estate securing the loan. RESPA applies to federally chartered savings and loans and to savings and loans or banks insured by, respectively, the Federal Savings and Loan Insurance Corporation (FSLIC) or the Federal Deposit Insurance Corporation (FDIC).

When a borrower applies for a mortgage loan, RESPA requires that the lender provide a good faith estimate of the loan settlement charges. These include:

- Lender administrative costs (e.g., credit report charges, inspection fees, and document preparation costs)
- Attorneys' fees
- Title insurance premiums
- Points (i.e., the percentage of the loan added as a service charge)
- Surveyors' fees
- Transfer and recording fees

Before the closing, the lend may correct estimates which have changed because of fluctuating market costs or good faith erors. However, lenders in some states, do owe a duty to those seeking loans to exercise good faith and fair dealing when handling loan applications. Lenders have also been sued for negligence for failing to complete paperwork within certain time frames resulting in the borrower having to pay a higher interest rate; they have also been sued for miscalculating how much a borrower can qualify for.*

The Equal Credit Opportunity Act (ECOA) was created to prevent lenders from discriminating in their loan practices on the basis of gender, marital status, race, religion, national origin, age, or receipt of public assistance. Recently, lenders in Atlanta and other cities have been accused of "redlining" their loans, which, if true, is a violation of ECOA. Redlining is the practice of not making mortgage loans for the purchase of homes in predetermined areas. These neighborhoods, often predominately minority in composition, are perceived as being too risky. ECOA outlaws such stereotyping of neighborhoods, and requires that loan decisions be made individually based on the prospective borrowers' creditworthiness. ECOA will be discussed in more detail in Chapter 45 on consumer protection.

THE RIGHTS AND DUTIES OF THE PARTIES TO A MORTGAGE

The mortgage primarily determines the rights and duties of the parties to it. State annd federal laws often have some impact, such as on the interest rate charged, a mortgagor's ability to assume a government-insured mortgage, and the requirements for foreclosure.

Although the mortgagor grants the mortgage to the mortgagee, its terms will strongly favor the mortgagee. After all, a commercial mortgagee generally prepared the mortgage and

the accompanying note. And the mortgagor needs the mortgagee's money more than the mortgagee needs the mortgagor's business. The creditor's natural leverage in these transactions has led many states to enact legislation to protect the mortgagor.

The Mortgagor

Right to possession. The mortgagor's primary right is to retain possession of the real property subject to the mortgage so long as she makes timely payments. The mortgagor's rights after *default*—failure to make timely payments—are discussed below.

Right to prepay. A mortgagor has the right to prepay at any time before the note comes due without a penalty such as added interest. The mortgagor's right does not depend on any action of the mortgagee, including prior approval. Suppose Alicia has a 30-year mortgage. She may prepay it in, say, the tenth year, and Central Savings must release its lien.

Mortgagors most commonly prepay because they have sold the property. The new buyer provides the money to prepay the seller's mortgage. In practice, the proceeds from the buyer's mortgage go to prepay the seller's mortgage.

Right to assign. Before the 1970s, most mortgages were "assumable," meaning a third party—with the lender's approval—could assume the mortgagor's primary obligation for the remainder of its term. The party assuming the mortgage took on joint liability with the original mortgagor.

After an assumption, the seller-mortgagor remains liable unless the mortgagee agrees to a novation. A *novation* is an agreement between the parties to the original agreement to substitute the performance of a third party for that of one of the original parties and to release that original party's obligation. The mortgage lien remains against the property. Suppose Alicia

---

* *Jacques v. First National Bank of Maryland*, 515 A.2d 756 (Md. 1986).

sells her town house to Kyle. Kyle agrees to assume her obligation to Central Savings & Loan. Kyle will be liable to Central Savings and to Alicia for the mortgage payments. Should he fail to make the payments, Central could require that Alicia make them. Thus, if there is not a novation, the original mortgagor must be careful about whom she permits to assume the mortgage. A wise seller will demand a large cash payment from a buyer assuming a mortgage so that the buyer will have too much equity in the property to stop paying the mortgage.

During the 1970s and early 1980s, lenders suffered because their fixed interest, long-term mortgages locked them into rates of return considerably below the market. To make sure history does not repeat itself, virtually all mortgages today contain prohibitions against assumption in the form of a *due-on-sale* clause. Under this clause, the entire balance of the debt becomes due and payable if the borrower conveys title to the mortgaged property to another without the lender's permission. Only loans insured by the Federal Housing Administration (FHA) or the Veterans Administration (VA) commonly permit assumption.

Now, however, even VA and FHA loans which were originated in the late 1980s cannot be freely assumed, as they were in the past. During the slump in real estate experienced in that decade, particularly in the oil and agricultural regions of the country, some unscrupulous buyers assumed FHA and VA loans from sellers anxious to sell their homes, while never being required to submit to a credit check. These "buyers" then leased out the houses, never intending to pay on the assumed note. The lenders then proceeded to foreclose on the property, which often took months. After receiving sometimes a considerable amount of money in rents for months from a large number of homes, the buyers would then disappear. This criminal practice, known as "equity skimming," was one of the prime reasons why the rules governing the assumability of FHA and VA loans became more restrictive. Moreover, just like Alicia, who was liable as the seller for Kyle's failure to make payments in the above example, the persons who sold to equity skimmers were similarly left personally liable on the notes. However, unlike Kyle, they usually could not be found. Now, unfortunately, many honest people with credit blemishes often caused by unemployment, divorce, etc. can no longer assume these more recent VA and FHA loans as they once could. The law now requires a credit check.

A buyer can purchase property without having the mortgage released. This is called "taking subject to" a mortgage. As with a mortgage assumption, the buyer makes the mortgage payments. But the buyer who takes subject to a mortgage is not personally liable on the promissory note whose payment the mortgage secures. Of course, the property remains subject to foreclosure if the payments are not made. The terms of many mortgages forbid "subject to" sales of the mortgaged property.

The Mortgagee

Right to payment. The mortgagee's principal right is to receive the mortgage payments in accordance with its terms. Normally, the amount of the principal and at least the initial interest rate are stated in the note and the financing statement. These documents will also state the total amount—principal plus interest—which will be paid if the mortgage runs its full term.

Quite normally, the lender will require the mortgagor to make additional payments—at least temporarily—to cover real estate taxes and property insurance. Many mortgages also include premiums for credit life insurance policies, which pay the mortgage in the event of the mortgagor's death.

Right to vary interest rates. Today, mortgages are classified according to whether their rates of interest are fixed for their term or are variable. Until about 1980, fixed rate mortgages were the rule. The variable rate mortgage was the lenders' major response to the interest rate fluctuations of the 1970s and early 1980s.

A variable rate mortgage usually requires that the lender adjust the interest rate at fixed intervals according to the prevailing rate at the time. Usually, however, the adjustment may not exceed 3 percent in either direction. Suppose Alicia's variable rate mortgage is at 9 percent for the first 3 years. At the end of that period, the Central Savings & Loan must adjust it to the currently prevailing mortgage rate. However, the adjustment may not exceed 3 percent. If the mortgage rate in 3 years is 13 percent, Central may increase Alicia's rate to only 12 percent.

Right to assign. The mortgagee usually has the right to assign the mortgage to another creditor. Banks quite commonly sell their mortgage loans. The assignment has no effect on the mortgagor, since all that is being assigned is the right to payment. However, upon notice, the mortgagor may have to pay the new holder instead of the original mortgagor.

Right to accelerate payment. Most mortgages contain an *acceleration clause*, which permits the mortgagee to demand paymment of the entire debt upon the mortgagor's failure to make scheduled payments or upon another material breach.

A *material breach* is a significant one. Thus, besides failing to make prompt payments, examples of material breaches which would justify acceleration include:

- Failing to keep the property in good repair (i.e., impairing the collateral)
- Selling to a third party who is taking subject to the mortgage
- Allowing the property insurance to lapse
- Neglecting to pay property taxes and assessments

Right to foreclose. If the acceleration is proper and the mortgagor cannot pay the full amount, the mortgagee may begin foreclosure proceedings. A foreclosure clause permits the mortgagee to secure a court order allowing it to sell the property subject to the mortgage. Still, as the next case indicates, the mortgagee cannot foreclose for trivial breaches.

Karas v. Wasserman

91 A.D.2d 812, 458 N.Y.S.2d 280 (App. Div. 1982)

FACTS   In 1976 the Wassermans puchased a bungalow colony using a $125,000 mortgage loan from Karas. Five years later, Karas brought a foreclosure action. The mortgage provided for acceleration of the entire principal balance upon any of a number of kinds of defaults. Karas grounded her complaint on the Wassermans' failures: (1) to furnish her on demand with a statement of the amount due on the mortgage and of any offsets or defenses the Wassermans had against that amount; (2) to provide her with receipts showing payment of all taxes, assessments, and insurance premiums; and (3) to make prompt mortgage payments.

When Karas moved for summary judgment, the Wassermans responded with an affidavit stating that they had made all payments required under the mortgage and had actually overpaid by more than $500. They admitted the other defaults. The trial court denied summary judgment and Karas appealed.

ISSUE   Did the Wassermans' admission of the two defaults entitle Karas to summary judgment?

DECISION   No. Affirmed. The Wassermans' affidavit raised issues of fact which required a trial. Further, acceleration clauses in mortgages are not strictly enforced regardless of the circumstances and nature of the default. In order to prevent unconscionable conduct by a mortgagee, the court may deny foreclosure in the case of a minor default. If the Wassermans established that they had made all the payments required by the mortgage, the trial court could deny foreclosure. If, before filing suit, Karas had never complained of the Wassermans' pattern of not provided receipts, she would be estopped from foreclosing on that ground.

Foreclosure actions must comply both with the terms of the mortgage and with state law. While procedures vary from state to state, essentially the following occurs. The mortgagee files suit, alleging the mortgagor is in arrears or in breach of the mortgage. If the mortgagee proves her case, the court will instruct the sheriff to conduct an auction of the property. If the proceeds of the sale exceed the cost of the sale plus the total amount owed to the mortgagee, the excess belongs to the mortgagor—if there are no other lienholders.

Suppose Alicia continued to own her town house but fell behind in her payments. Central Savings & Loan had her town house sold in a sheriff's sale. If the sale brought $70,000 and the administrative costs and first mortgage obligation totaled $63,000, Central would receive its $63,000. The other lienholders—according to their priority—would take the sums owed to them out of the sale's proceeds. Thus, the holders of Alicia's second mortgage, her parents, would receive their $5000, and Alicia would be entitled to the remaining $2000.

Right to a deficiency judgment. If the sale brought only $60,000, however, Central Saving & Loan could seek the balance it was owed in an action for a *deficiency judgment*. But, it should be noted that Central would now be an unsecured creditor in seeking to collect this debt, since the collateral is now exhausted.

Deficiency judgments have become very important since the early 1980s. Starting in the oil-producing areas and the midwestern agricultural regions of the country, that decade was marked by a severe recession which caused a deflationary spiral of raw material prices, wages, and real property. Eventually, the recession and the consequential collapse in real estate prices spread throughout most of the United States, particularly the Northeast. Indeed, by the early 1990s, the once booming Southern California housing market was the scene of plunging values of as much as 35 percent. When prices collapse quickly and drastically, many property owners experience "negative equity." This means the value of their homes is less than the mortgage note securing it. Moreover, the loss of value caused by recession is often accompanied by a loss of a job. When this happens some owners may simply deed their property back to the lender (if the lender will take it), let the house go to a foreclosure, or even abandon it. If a foreclosure occurs, most homes in a distressed market do not sell for the amount of the mortgage note, since usually the only bidder is the lender. This difference, as Alicia experienced above, then becomes a debt a borrower still must pay in the form of a deficiency judgment. Unfortunately, because these debts often are substantial, due to low bids and administrative and attorneys' fees, the property owner often must file for bankruptcy to discharge the deficiency judgment.

Because of the potential abuse to home-owners caused by deficiency judgments, the states have laws which limit the amount a deficiency can be. Moreover, at least six states have antideficiency statutes, which prohibit deficiency judgments on a person's homesteaded property or farm.* Many mortgagors attempt to avoid foreclosure and deficiency judgments by negotiating workouts with the mortgagees. Workouts are discussed below.

Obviously, the impact of foreclosure on a person's real property can be financially severe, as discussed above. However, there are second chances for distressed borrowers, like Alicia, to regain their property: redemption.

Redemption: The Mortgagor's Final Right

Once the mortgagee declares the mortgagor to be in default and seeks to foreclose, the mortgagor usually has two chances to avoid losing her property.

Between the time of the default and the foreclosure sale, the mortgagor may exercise her *equity of redemption*. Here, "redemption" describes the mortgagor's ability after default to pay all the principal, interest, and penalties due to date in order to reinstate the loan or to secure the return of the property.

---

* R. Aalberts and T. M. Clauretie, "The Impact of Legal Costs in the Default-Foreclosure Process of Residential Mortgages," *American Business Law Journal*, 25 (Winter 1988), p. 575.

During this period of equitable redemption, which varies among the states from several months to almost a year, the mortgagor may attempt a *loan workout* with the mortgagee. Workouts can include a deed in lieu of foreclosure (deeding the property to the mortgagee to forgive the debt), an extension of the period of loan repayment and amortization, a reduction of the loan principal, a temporary deferment of loan payments, and added security given to the mortgagee, such as a surety or pledging of other assets. Mortgagees are sometimes quite receptive to a workout, since generally they do not like to accumulate a large inventory of real property, which they must then manage and market. As discussed above, the mortgagee often is the only bidder of property in a foreclosure, particularly in a distressed market.

The mortgagor may also have a *right of redemption*. Created by statute in about half the states, this right permits the mortgagor to redeem the property after the judicial sale by paying the amount of the sale price plus a statutory interest rate. Normally, the mortgagor must exercise this right within 1 year. Failure to redeem within the prescribed period means the purchaser gains good title against the mortgagor.

A second mortgage holder also has a right of redemption, since, following foreclosure by the first mortgage holder, the second mortgage holder loses the right to foreclose. Before the foreclosure sale, the junior secured parties can pay off the first mortgage themselves. As the second mortgage holder in the next case found, redemption often is the only way to protect its interest.

National Credit Union Share Insurance Fund v. University Developers

335 N.W.2d 559 (N.D. 1983)

FACTS   On January 15, 1980, University Developers gave a second mortgage on the Village Resubdivision to National Credit Union Share Insurance Fund in the amount of

$976,992.65. The mortgage was made subject to the a first mortgage of $425,000 held by the Jamestown Community Co-op Credit Union. On February 17, 1981, National filed an action to foreclose its mortgage. Jamestown filed a similar action. On February 8, 1982, the trial court ordered foreclosure on Jamestown's first mortgage. At a sheriff's sale, Jamestown bought the Village Resubdivision. The proceeds satisfied only Jamestown's mortgage and some related costs. On October 14, 1982, the trial court awarded summary judgment to National, foreclosing its mortgage.

ISSUE   Could National foreclose on its second mortgage after Jamestown had foreclosed on its first mortgage?

DECISION   No. Reversed. Jamestown's foreclosure extinguished National's right to foreclose. National was left to its right of redemption.

The grantor in a deed of trust, like a mortgagor, has a period of time *before* the property is sold in which he can exercise his *right of reinstatement*. This right is very similar to a mortgagor's equity of redemption. However, he lacks a right of redemption *after* the property has been sold. For that reason, when the trustee of a deed of trust executes her power of sale, the buyer receives good title immediately.

Military personnel are, in certain circumstances, also given protections from foreclosure on their homes. *The Soldiers and Sailors Relief Act* provides that mortgagors in active military service be given special notice if there is a default of their mortgage, and it allows the courts to delay foreclosure actions against those mortgagors. As was witnessed in the Persian Gulf War in 1990–1991, many reservists who were called up suffered economically, since their military pay often was less than their civilian salaries.

INVOLUNTARY LIENS

When a mortgagor grants a mortgage, she voluntarily creates a lien on her property. By contrast, involuntary liens result from an action by a third party and do not require the consent or approval of the property owner. The sections which follow examine the six principal types of involuntary liens. However, it should be noted that state statutes govern the creation of these liens, so they vary somewhat from state to state.

Mechanic's Lien

A *mechanic's lien* secures payment for contractors and others who supply services, labor, or materials which enhance the value or condition of another's real property. Services or products incorporated into real property cannot be retained or reclaimed if the property owner unjustifiably refuses to pay.

The permanent improvement requirement. Mechanic's liens are available only to those who make permanent improvements to property. An *improvement* includes erection, repair, alteration, or demolition. Thus, a contractor who paints an entire house or a plumber who installs a new bathroom has a right to a mechanic's lien. But improvements made by a window washer are temporary. Still, courts have given the term "permanent improvement" a very broad reading. For example, surveyors may claim a mechanic's lien even though their stakes disappear in the process of constructing a building. Architects' and engineers' services also qualify.

Landowner's consent. Generally, the landowner must have knowledge of, and give consent to, the improvements. An owner's authorized agent may give consent.

Disputes often arise as to a tenant's author-ity to bind the landlord for the expense of improvements. That authority frequently depends on the tenant's duty to keep the premises in good repair. Under most repair and maintenance covenants, the leasehold property would not be subject to a mechanic's lien for major improvements authorized by a tenant without the landlord's consent. In the next case, however, the landlord was liable.

Thirteenth Street Corp. v. A-1 Plumbing & Heating Co., Inc.

640 P.2d 1130 (Colo. 1982)

FACTS   Thirteenth Street Corp. owned a building which Kenyon-Megill, Inc., leased. Under the lease, the tenant could not make any improvements or alterations costing more than $250 without written consent from Thirteenth Street. If Kenyon-Megill made improvements, it had to require that all contractors and subcontractors waive their rights to file mechanic's liens against Thirteenth Street. In mid-1974, Kenyon-Megill received oral consent to remodel the building. During the renovation, the president of Thirteenth Street toured the building. Kenyon-Megill did not obtain waivers from any of the contractors or subcontractors. Kenyon-Megill became insolvent before completing the remodeling. Nine plaintiffs brought suit against Thirteenth Street to determine the validity of their mechanic's liens. The trial court found that all the improvements were permanent and entered judgment in favor of the lienholders.

ISSUE   Were the liens valid against Thirteenth Street?

DECISION   Yes. Affirmed. A landlord who authorized the tenant's improvements may be subject to a mechanic's lien if it knows contractors are providing materials and services for the improvements but it does not post notices that its interest will not be subject to a lien. Thirteenth Street had orally authorized the improvements, and it had actual notice that the building was undergoing extensive alterations.

Perfection and enforcement. Normally, a contractor does not require court approval to file a mechanic's lien against the property where he provided services. In order to *perfect* a mechanic's lien, the contractor must simply give the property owner notice that the lien will be filed and record it properly.

Once filed, a mechanic's lien causes a de-fect in the title. An owner wishing to sell his property usually will have to remove the lien before a prospective purchaser will pay the purchase price. In this sense, it is a "passive" lien. But mechanic's liens do not remain passive. Most states require that the lienholder bring an action to enforce the lien within 2 years; otherwise, the lienholder will lose the lien interest.

The lineholder may force a public sale of the property if its owner fails to satisfy the debt.

Time for filing and retroactivity. Usually, the party claiming the lien must record it within 3 months after completing the work. Just what "completion" means is often an issue for the courts. Suppose a contractor finishes building Justin's garage on March 1. On March 15 the contractor returns to modify the garage door so that it will work correctly. Was the garage completed on March 1 or March 15? Most jurisdictions would say March 15.

Mechanic's liens are usually retroactive to the time when the work justifying the lien began. If the contractor began work on Justin's garage on February 15, a mechanic's lien filed May 1 will apply retroactively to February 15, assuming the state has a 3-month filing period (Figure 42.4).

Because of the combination of the lien's retroactive effect and the postcompletion filing period, a mechanic's lien can appear unexpectedly. Of course, this is a problem only for a good faith lender or purchaser who may not realize a mechanic's lien could be filed. Before agreeing to make a mortgage loan or to purchase real property, a person should inspect carefully for new construction or repairs. If there are signs of new work, the borrower or seller should be required to demonstrate that the work is paid for.

Subcontractor's rights. In about half the states, a landowner must pay only the amount of the contract. Under these statutes, known as the "New York Rule," a subcontractor who is not paid by the general contractor cannot protect herself by placing a lien directly on the home she worked on. However, in the remaining states, which follow the "Pennsylvania Rule," a subcontractor who is not paid can file a lien directly on the property. This has sometimes resulted in the landowner paying *more* than she owed under the contract, since she may have already paid the general and then must later pay some or all of the subcontractors to remove their mechanics' liens.

To prevent a homeowner from paying in excess of the contract, states following the Pennsylvania Rule provide legal protections. Some of these statutes require that the general contractor furnish the property owner with waivers or statements from the subcontractors showing that they have been paid, before the property owner is required to pay the contractor. Also in these states, subcontractors must give timely notice of any outstanding claims they may have or they lose their rights to file liens directly. If these requirements are not complied with, a subcontractor's remedy is only against the general contractor. However, a property owner should always be vigilant and protect herself by only hiring reputable, licensed general contractors who guarantee that

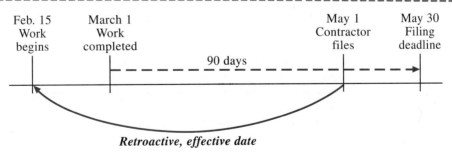

Retroactive, effective date

Figure 42.4 Mechanic's Lien.

their subcontractors and material suppliers will be paid. Property owners also should carefully read and pay attention to any paperwork they receive to make sure they are given notice of any of the above problems.

Materialman's Lien

A *materialman's lien* is a lien granted to a supplier whose goods are permanently incorporated into another's land or property. For example, the lumber company which supplied the wood for Justin's garage could have a lien against the property for the value of the lumber used in the garage. When the materialman is paid, the lien would be removed.

The materialman's lien works like the mechanic's lien, and it has the same rationale for its existence. But who has the favored lien interest: the creditor who has lent money to the person having the building built, the materialman, or the "mechanic"? The next case deals with a creditor-materialman dispute.

People's Bank & Trust Co. v. L. & T. Developers, Inc.

434 So. 2d 669 (Miss. 1983)

FACTS Bruce Homes, Inc. purchased three house lots. Bruce negotiated three construction loans secured by deeds of trust to the Bank of Mississippi and the People's Bank. Unrelated debts were pressing, and Bruce diverted $50,500 of the funds the banks lent on the three houses. Meanwhile, the Wickes Corporation provided over $7000 in materials and supplies. It filed a materialman's lien. The banks later foreclosed on Bruce. The trial court found that the lenders had not exercised reasonable diligence to ensure that the monies advanced were used in construction on the three tracts, and it awarded first priority to Wickes.

ISSUE Between a construction lender and a materialman, should the materialman have priority?

DECISION Yes. Affirmed.

A materialman, a mechanic or other similar parties . . . typically furnish the supplies, materials or services which are indispensable to the successful prosecution of the construction project. That these potential [lienholders] render their services and perform their work, generally on credit, is to everyone's benefit, including the construction lender. For as these parties give value, the value of the construction lender's collateral is enhanced.

If, as here, the materialmen are not paid, quite likely the construction lender will be unjustly enriched at their expense. . . .

We emphasize the ease with which the construction lender may protect itself. Construction lenders may make advances in the form of drafts or checks payable directly to materialmen or payable to materialmen and the builder jointly. Such a practice, of course, would render the present fiasco impossible. . . .

Attachment Lien

An unsecured creditor obtains an *attachment lien* against specific real property to serve as collateral in the event it wins a lawsuit against the debtor. Suppose XYZ Finance Company files suit against Sandra on a $4000 note and simultaneously places an attachment lien on her home in case it wins. If Sandra wins the lawsuit, XYZ must remove the lien immediately. If XYZ wins and Sandra does not pay the judgment, XYZ can petition the court to have the property sold at a sheriff's sale.

Attachment liens were quite common until a generation or two ago. Today, courts severely restrict their use. Some state's statutes governing attachment liens, for example, have been found to violate due process rights under the Constituion, since the property owner cannot sell or mortgage his property, sometimes for years. Typically, due process requires that prospective debtors be given adequate notice and a fair hearing before an attachment lien is placed on their real property because of the potential for abuse such as the following case discusses.

Connecticut v. Doehr

115 L.Ed 2d 1 (1991)

FACTS

Brian Doehr allegedly beat up John DiGiovanni, breaking his wrist and severely damaging his eye. DiGiovanni submitted an application for attaching Doehr's home in the amount of $75,000 and then sued him for assault and battery. Several days later the sheriff attached a lien on Doehr's property. Under Connecticut law, Doehr had no right to notice or a hearing prior to the lien attaching to his home as long as DiGiovanni could show "probable cause" that his claim was valid. After attachment, Doehr would then have the right to an adversary hearing and judicial review to remove the lien and receive double damages if no probable cause existed. Doehr filed suit against DiGiovanni claiming that Connecticut's law violated the due process clause under the Fourteenth Amendment. Summary judgment was granted to DiGiovanni. On appeal the judgment was reversed.

ISSUE

Did Connecticut's statute allowing the prejudgment attachment of real estate without prior notice and a hearing violate the due process clause?

DECISION

Yes. Affirmed. The prejudgment attachment of real estate without any prior notice and hearing violates the due process clause of the Fourteenth Amendment if there is no showing of exceptional or exigent circumstances and without the posting of a bond. In this case, there was little likelihood that Doehr was about to transfer or mortgage his property in a way that would deprive DiGiovanni of later satisfying his judgment. Connecticut's interest in protecting the rights of plaintiffs is minimal compared to the risk of a person mistakenly being stripped of his property.

Judgment Lien

A *judgment lien* results when a party awarded damages files the court's judgment against the real estate of the losing party in the county where the land is located. Assume XYZ Finance wins a judgment against Sandra. She owns a house in Tyler County and a farm in Polk County. XYZ should file judgment liens in both counties. Filing in one county or the other will affect only the property located in the county of filing.

A judgment lien applies to *all* the defendant's real property located in the county where the lien is filed. By contrast, an attachment lien applies only to specified real estate. A judgment lien may be filed by the winning party in every county where the judgment debtor may have property. The lien applies to property the debtor currently owns as well as to land she may acquire for up to 10 years.

Judgment liens can trap the unwary. Because they are not filed against a particular piece of property, a prospective purchaser must check the judgment lien record which is maintained separately from the mortgage and title records.

Execution Lien

An *execution lien*, or a *writ of execution*, is a notice, usually filed by the sheriff, that a particular piece of real property is to be sold at a public sale to settle an unpaid judgment. While other liens may function—temporarily, at least —as a passive means of pressuring a debtor, an execution lien signals definite action. Suppose Dick owns three parcels in Middlesex County. A judgment lien filed in the Middlesex County Courthouse would apply to all three. However, an execution lien filed by the Middlesex County Sheriff would apply only to the particular parcel listed in the lien.

The sheriff's sale generally takes place in the same manner as a mortgage foreclosure sale. Some states even grant the judgment debtor redemption rights.

Figure 42.5 compares attachment, judgment, and execution liens.

Tax Lien

A *tax lien* comes into existence when a government unit places a lien on specific real property because of its owner's failure to pay taxes.

Real property taxes. A real propert taxing unit does not have to file a lien. Rather, it need only give public notice by way of a delinquent tax report, which usually is both published in a local newspaper and recorded in the courthouse. If the owner does not pay the back taxes, the sheriff will sell the property at a public sale.

A property owner is charged with knowing whether he has paid his property taxes and with reading the published delinquent tax report. Nonetheless, the taxing entity will provide notice to the delinquent taxpayer before the sale. Some states grant redemption rights following a tax sale.

Other taxes. With all other tax liens, the government unit must file a tax delinquency notice in the courthouse of the county where the delinquent taxpayer owns real property. This notice results in a lien being placed against the taxpayer's property in that county. Suppose Janet owes the Internal Revenue Service $6000. The IRS may file a tax delinquency notice in her county which, in effect, gives the IRS a $6000 lien against her home.

Tax liens, too, are satisfied by the proceeds from a sheriff's sale. Notice requirements, redemption rights, and the like, vary by jurisdiction.

Maintenance fees and assessments lien. In recent years, particularly in high growth and retirement areas of the Sunbelt, multiunit housing has become very popular. Multiunit housing is appealing for a number of reasons: it is often less expensive, easier to keep up, and the own-

	ATTACHMENT LIEN	JUDGMENT LIEN	EXECUTION LIEN
Acquired before a court case?	Yes	No	No
Need to file against particular real property?	Yes	No	Yes
Need to file in county where land is located?	Yes	Yes	Yes
Applies to property acquired in the future?	No	Yes	No
Is filing a result of securing a court judgment?	No	Yes	Yes
Does lien indicate that a public sale is pending?	No	No	Yes

Figure 42.5 Comparison of Judicial Liens.

ers have access to shared amenities, such as swimming pools and tennis courts. Examples of multiunit housing include condominiums, town houses, time-sharing interests, and planned unit developments (PUDs). Multiunit housing typically is governed by a "declaration of covenants, conditions and restrictions" (CCRs) and bylaws which contain the rights and responsibilities of the unit owners, as well as maintenance fees and assessments. If the fees and assessments are not paid, the multiunit association has the authority under the CCRs to enforce the obligation by placing a lien on the individual's unit and then can execute on it in a foreclosure proceeding. Moreover, as the next case indicates, these fees and assessments have priority over any mortgages the owner may later place on his property.

American Holidays v. Foxtail Owners

821 P.2d 577 (Wyo. 1991)

FACTS
Condoshare Jackson Limited Partnership recorded a "Declaration of Condominium" for the Foxtail Condominium Project in January 1981. The Declaration empowered the Project to levy assessments against the shared interest of all the condominium owners, and stated that the payments would be secured by a lien. In September 1984, Ed and Clara Meier executed a note and mortgage secured by their Foxtail condominium in favor of The Time Store, Inc., which recorded it in March 1985. It was later assigned to the American Holidays, Inc. In December 1985 the Meiers defaulted on the mortgage. They also failed to pay their association fees. In October 1989 the Association filed a lien for unpaid dues. The Association then filed a

complaint to foreclose and claimed it had priority over American Holidays. The Association prevailed in a motion for summary judgment.

ISSUE   Does the Association's assessment lien have priority over the mortgage even though the mortgage was recorded before the lien matured?

DECISION   Yes. Affirmed. Any legal instrument creating an interest in land which is recorded first constitutes notice and takes priority over any later interest. In this case, the Declaration of Condominium for the Foxtail Condominium Project was recorded before American Holiday's mortgage. Thus, it takes priority as a lien on the Meiers's condominium.

CONCLUSION

Security interests can affect both residential and nonresidential realty. Where the owner voluntarily gives the interest to secure credit, the lien is generally passive. So long as the mortgagor continues to make payments on time and does not otherwise violate the mortgage note provisions, the mortgagee will have no basis for foreclosure. In this circumstance, the restrictions on the mortgagor's ability to sell the property are minimal *if* the price to be paid exceeds the value of the security interests. The mortgagor always has the right to prepay the mortgage note.

A holder of an involuntary lien has no greater rights than a mortgagee. But an involuntary lien can pose greater problems than a voluntary lien for the property owner, since the lien indicates the strong possibility of litigation over the property.

Like any security interest, an interest in real property is designed to ensure that a creditor can salvage something if the debtor defaults. The next chapter, Bankruptcy, makes clear why it is so important to the creditor to make certain the lien is filed at the earliest possible moment and in the proper form. To do otherwise may cost the creditor secured status and significantly reduce the chances of recovering anything.

A NOTE TO FUTURE CPA CANDIDATES

Security interests in real property are tested as a part of the property section of the CPA exam. The four major areas covered on the exam are the characteristics of the security interests, recording requirements, priorities between mortgagees, and rights and obligations in foreclosure.

The CPA exam traditionally tests on mortgages, second mortgages, and purchase money mortgages. These three types of mortgages are compared in Figure 42.1. Note that all three have the same characteristics: if the buyer defaults there is the need for court approval to sell the property, strict forfeiture is not available, and the mortgagor has redemption rights.

It is important to know the requirements of a mortgage. To be enforceable a mortgage must:

- Be in writing and signed by the mortgag*or*
- Include a description of the debt and land involved
- Include a granting of a security interest in the real property from the mortgagor to the mortgagee
- Be delivered by the mortgagor to the mortgagee

A mortgage need *not*:

- Be signed by the mortgagee
- Contain the actual amount of the underlying debt and interest
- Be recorded by the mortgagee

It should be added, however, that a mortgage ordinarily does include mention of the underlying debt and interest and *should* be recorded in order to be effective against subsequent third parties gaining an interest in the property.

It is important for you to refer to Figure 27.5 to make sure you understand the three types of recording statutes: race, race-notice, and notice. Often these recording requirements are asked in a mortgage, not a deed, setting.

A properly recorded first mortgage has priority over all subsequent mortgages on the property, called second mortgages. If both mortgages are foreclosed, the first mortgage must be satisfied before any second mortgages receive proceeds of the sale. Default on a second mortgage does not result in a default in the first mortgage.

A mortgage can be assigned unless prohibited by the terms of the mortgage. A person who assumes the mortgage becomes personally liable to the mortgagee. A person buying subject to the mortgage is *not* personally liable for the mortgage but may lose the property if foreclosure occurs.

If property is foreclosed, a mortgagor may assert the equitable right of redemption before the judicial sale by paying off the mortgage with any applicable penalties. After the property is foreclosed the mortgagor again has an opportunity to pay off the mortgage, with applicable penalties, within a statutory time limit and regain the property. The mortgagor who does not redeem the property has the right to any proceeds above the amount owed for the mortgage, with applicable penalties.

KEY WORDS

constructive notice (957)
deed of trust (957)
execution lien (970)
foreclosure (954)
involuntary lien (965)
judgment lien (970)
land contract (958)
loan workout (964)
materialman's lien (968)
mortgage (955)
mortgagee (955)
mortgagor (955)
purchase money mortgage (958)
redemption (958)
right of reinstatement (965)
second mortgage (956)
Soldiers and Sailors Relief Act (965)
tax lien (970)
voluntary lien (955)
writ of execution (970)

DISCUSSION QUESTIONS

1. What is a lien? How can a lien arise?
2. How is a mortgage created?
3. Why should a mortgage be recorded?
4. What are the basic rights and duties of a mortgagor?
5. What are the basic rights and duties of a mortgagee?
6. Compare a deed of trust, a purchase money mortgage, and a land contract to a mortgage in regard to possession of title; right to foreclose, and right to redeem.
7. When does a creditor have a right to a deficiency judgement?
8. What is required to be able to file a mechanic's lien? When can it be filed?
9. What is a materialman's lien? Does it take priority over a mechanic's lien?
10. The Mississippi Supreme Court in *People's Bank & Trust Co. v. L & T Developers, Inc.*, made a number of suggestions about how a bank could protect itself against a debtor who fails to pay its suppliers and subcontractors. How realistic are those suggestions?

CASE PROBLEMS

1. On June 1, 1987, Byrd Corporation purchased a high rise from Slade Corp. for $375,000. The building was encumbered by a mortgage and note dated May 1, 1980, executed by Slade. The mortgagee, Fale Bank, had duly recorded the mortgage. Byrd acquired the property sub-

ject to Fale's mortgage (whose outstanding balance was $300,000) and, in addition, gave a mortgage on the building to Foxx Finance to secure a non-purchase money promissory note for $50,000. Before making any payments on either loan, Byrd defaulted. The building was properly sold at a foreclosure sale for $280,000. Slade claims it has no liability for the deficiency, since it was automatically released upon Byrd's acquisition. Is this correct? What amount is Fale entitled to receive out of the proceeds: What amount is Foxx entitled to receive? Explain.

2. Moch sold her farm to Watkins and took back a purchase money mortgage which she failed to record. A subsequent mortgagee recorded his mortgage but admits he had heard there was a prior mortgage. Watkins gave the farm to a friend, who took it without knowledge of either mortgage and who claims title clear of both mortgages. Will the friend prevail? Explain.

3. Peters defaulted on a purchase money mortgage held by Fairmont Realty. Over several months, Fairmont's attempts to obtain payment were futile, and the mortgage payments are several months in arrears. Consequently, Fairmont foreclosed on the mortgage. Does Peters have the right to remain in possession as long as his equity in the property exceeds the amount of the debt? What rights of redemption, if any, does Peters have? Explain.

4. Gray owned a warehouse free of any encumbrances. Gray borrowed $30,000 from Harp Finance and executed a promissory note secured by a mortgage on the warehouse. The state within which the warehouse was located had a race-notice recording statute. Harp did not record its mortgage. Thereafter, Gray applied for a loan with King Bank, supplying King with certified financial statements which disclosed Harp's mortgage. After reviewing the financial statements, King approved Gray's loan for $25,000 taking an executed promissory note secured by a mortgage on the warehouse. King promptly recorded its mortgage. Will King's mortgage be superior? Would the result be the same if the jurisdiction had a pure race recording statute? Explain.

5. Watts gave a mortgage on a vacant lot to Fast to secure payment of a note. Fast assigned the note and mortgage to Beal, who paid 85 percent of the note's face value. Neither Fast nor Beal recorded the mortgage. Subsequently, Fast assigned the same note and mortgage to Rusk, who paid 75 percent of the note's face value and who had no notice of the prior assignment to Beal. Rusk promptly recorded the mortgage and the assignment. Watts has made no payments on the note. The jurisdiction has a notice-type recording statute. Under the circumstances, is Rusk entitled to the full face amount of the Watts note? Explain.

6. Brendler sold his house to Austin by land contract for $75,000. Under the terms of the sale, Austin was to pay $10,000 at the outset, make monthly payments of $600 for 3 years, and then pay the remainder in a balloon payment. A mortgage to Central Bank remains on the house. Brendler accepted Austin's payments but defaulted on the mortgage. Central Bank has begun foreclosure proceedings. Will the Brendler-Austin land contract, which Austin properly recorded, prevent Central Bank from foreclosing? If Austin pays off Brendler on the house, would Austin still have to satisfy Central Bank for the months in which he paid Brendler? Explain.

7. Chuck Hawkinson gave a first mortgage on his home to Valley Bank and a second mortgage to Jim Laird. Hawkinson's employer went out of business and he was unable to maintain payments on either note. At the time of default, Hawkinson owed Valley Bank $75,000 and Laird $15,000. Valley Bank foreclosed and sold the home at a foreclosure sale to Donna Watson for $70,000. The state statute provides a 2-year right of redemption. The market value for houses like Chuck's in his neighborhood is between $80,000 and $90,000. Why is Watson likely to have gotten the house at such a discount? Could Laird redeem the property? If so, why might he consider this? Explain.

8. Grover Corporation finished modernizing a kitchen for Mary Potter on April 1. On April 10, Phillip Eason agreed to purchase Mary's home. Mary told Phillip that her brother had

done the recent work and that it was all paid for, showing Phillip what appeared to be a receipt from her brother. Eason purchased the home on May 1. On May 5, Grover filed a mechanic's lien on the property. Eason claims that the mechanic's lien is not effective, since it was not recorded before his purchase, and that he had purchased the property in good faith and for value. Do you agree? Explain.

CHAPTER 43

Bankruptcy

The goal of the Federal Bankruptcy Code is to provide the debtor with a fresh start. For the consumer, the most important aspects of the fresh start are the Code's provision for adequate property for a return to normal life and the discharge of his debts with a release from creditor collection efforts.* For a business in financial straits, bankruptcy can mean relief and a chance to reorganize.

A fresh start will do the debtor little good if it is not accompanied by sound financial planning, but that aspect of bankruptcy exceeds the scope of this book. Here, the focus is on bankruptcy's effects on creditors.

Generally, creditors assume the risk that their debtors may go bankrupt. Through reserves against bad debts and devices such as security interests, creditors attempt to protect themselves. In the end, society bears the costs, as creditors spread their costs among their customers.

Until the 1970s, this societal cost had increased only gradually with the number of bankruptcy cases filed. In 1978, Congress enacted the Bankruptcy Reform Act, which made the process significantly less burdensome and costly to debtors. Unfortunately, bankruptcy reform immediately preceded two major recessions, and filings began overwhelming the courts. In 1983, over 400,000 bankruptcy cases were filed, a number far exceeding the total of all other federal cases combined. Even that statistic understates the true effect, since bankruptcy cases often generate more litigation. For just one type of example, look at the cases in Chapter 40 involving creditors and the sureties of their bankrupt debtors.

Some commentators viewed this flood of bankruptcies as an abuse of the system, particularly by those trying to avoid consumer credit or student loan obligations. In 1984, Congress reacted to these criticisms with the Bankruptcy Amendments and Federal Judgeship Act, which

redressed the balance in favor of creditors. But, the 1984 Act did not stem the flood. The number of annual new bankruptcy filings have continued to increase each year since 1984, but the rate of increase began to decline in 1992. In that year, 977,478 new bankruptcy cases were filed, 72,725 involving businesses, representing a 6.4 percent increase in filings over 1991.

This chapter examines the three principal types of bankruptcy proceedings. Each is referred to by its chapter in the Bankruptcy Code: straight bankruptcy (Chapter 7); reorganization (Chapter 11); and regular income plans (Chapter 13). Chapter 7 is the most common proceeding. Also, most of the concepts and procedural approaches found in Chapter 7 carry over to proceedings under Chapters 11 and 13. For these reasons, this chapter focuses on Chapter 7.

This chapter takes a transactional approach to the bankruptcy laws; that is, it looks at a Chapter 7 proceeding from the initial filing to the debtor's final discharge. First, however, let us examine some alternatives to bankruptcy and the courts which actually oversee the process.

ALTERNATIVES TO BANKRUPTCY

Bankruptcy is not the only method of dealing with a debtor's financial failure. This section examines the three most common alternatives to bankruptcy.

Composition and Extension Agreements

In a *composition agreement*, each participating creditor agrees to take a percentage of what the debtor owes to him or her in exchange for the other creditors' agreement to do likewise and for the debtor's promise to pay according to a schedule. Unlike the other bankruptcy alternatives discussed below, a composition agree-

---

* 5 *Collier on Bankruptcy*, §1325.01 (15th ed., 1982).

ment leaves the debtor's affairs in his or her hands.

A creditor has a choice as to payment. A creditor may choose a lump sum payment which is less than the amount owed. Alternatively, a creditor may elect to receive an amount paid in increments over the period of the agreement which would be greater than the amount he or she would receive in a lump sum settlement. Creditors agree to these arrangements rather than risk a still greater loss from a worsening of the debtor's financial condition or bankruptcy.

By contrast, in an *extension agreement*, the creditors agree to extend the time for payment by the debtor but do not agree to take less than what is owed. Otherwise, extension agreements and composition agreements are indistinguishable.

State, not federal, laws govern composition agreements. Under the common law, a composition agreement did not bind nonparticipating creditors. Now, however, under some statutes, a composition agreement does bind them if a majority of the creditors agree to one.

A creditor may not withdraw from a composition agreement. Debts included in it are not discharged until the debtor completes performance. A debtor's breach while the agreement is executory revives the original debts to the extent that the debtor has not paid them.

Creditors' Committee

Under a *creditors' committee* arrangement, the debtor transfers control of his or her business and financial affairs to a group, or committee, of creditors. For all practical purposes, the committee acts as a custodian and makes the debtor's business and financial decisions. However, a dissenting creditor—one who does not agree to formation of the creditors' committee —can nullify it by forcing the debtor into involuntary bankruptcy.

Assignment for the Benefit of Creditors

Under an *assignment for the benefit of creditors*, the debtor voluntarily assigns all of his or her assets to a *trustee*, or custodian, to manage for the creditors' benefit. As with a creditors' committee, the debtor gives up control of his or her business and financial affairs. Again, a dissenting creditor may force the debtor into involuntary bankruptcy.

Figure 43.1 compares the three principal alternatives to bankruptcy.

THE BANKRUPTCY COURTS

The U.S. Constitution, Article 1 §8(4), empowers Congress to establish "uniform laws on bankruptcies throughout the United States."

	RECEIVER OR TRUSTEE UTILIZED?	BASIS FOR INVOLUNTARY BANKRUPTCY?	MUST DEBTOR AGREE?	DEBTOR CHOOSES TRUSTEE?	COURT APPROVAL REQUIRED?
Composition or extension agreements	No	No	Yes	Not applicable	No
Creditors' committees	Yes	Yes	Yes	Probably not	No
Assignments for the benefit of creditors	Yes	Yes	Yes	Yes	No

Figure 43.1 Comparison of Nonbankruptcy Actions.

For that reason, bankruptcy proceedings are governed by federal law and supervised by federal courts.

Under the 1978 Act

From a purely legal standpoint, the most controversial change of the Bankruptcy Reform Act of 1978 affected who supervised bankruptcy proceedings. For generations, the U.S. district courts had jurisdiction over these proceedings, but they assigned day-to-day management to a *referee*, a person appointed by the court. The referee oversaw, for instance, the organization of the debtor's assets and any distributions to creditors. The district court heard appeals from the referee's actions and had the ultimate power to decide legal and factual questions.

The 1978 Act created bankruptcy courts with judges who had the power to decide not only bankruptcy cases but also related cases—such as breach of contract actions—transferred to them from district courts or state courts when the debtor went into bankruptcy.

This arrangement was flawed because bankruptcy judges were not to be full-fledged federal judges. The bankruptcy judges were to be appointed by the President and confirmed by the Senate—as Article 3 of the Constitution required in regard to other federal judges—but their terms were only 14 years, not life. If the bankruptcy judges were to decide cases which, but for the bankruptcy proceedings, would be under the jurisdiction of a district court, the bankruptcy court judges had to meet the Article 3 requirements. Adopting this reasoning, in 1982 the Supreme Court declared the delegation of powers to the bankruptcy judges to be unconstitutional.*

Under the 1984 Amendments

For more than 2 years, Congress struggled to resolve—in one act—the objections of both

---

* *Northern Pipeline Construction Co. v. Marathon Pipe Line Co.*, 458 U.S. 50 (1982).

creditors and the Supreme Court to the 1978 Act. The result, the 1984 Amendments, made bankruptcy judges appointees of the U.S. courts of appeals and limited their terms to 14 years.

The 1984 Amendments also narrowed the jurisdiction of the bankruptcy courts to "core proceedings." A precise definition of "core proceedings" has yet to emerge from litigation. However, it is safe to assume that the proceedings described below will be included in the jurisdiction of the bankruptcy courts.

Each federal judicial district has a bankruptcy court. A proceeding is usually begun in the district in which the bankrupt resides or in which the bankrupt's principal place of business is located.

STRAIGHT BANKRUPTCY UNDER CHAPTER 7

The goals of a Chapter 7 proceeding vary, depending on whether the debtor is a business or an individual.

Partnerships or corporations which enter into Chapter 7 do so to bring their business to a complete end. Thus, the goal in Chapter 7 proceedings is simply to generate the maximum payout to creditors. It is not to provide a discharge and a new start.

With individuals, the goals are somewhat different. The individual's assets—less just enough to keep the debtor going—are distributed to the creditors in an equitable fashion. But paying the creditors is also the means to another end: a fresh start for the debtor. Usually at the end of the bankruptcy proceeding, the bankrupt's debts are discharged.

This section focuses on the individual in Chapter 7. While the goals are different for businesses, the procedures, except as noted, are the same. It is important to note that Steps 1 through 6 in the Chapter 7 procedure outlined below are also present in the procedures for Chapters 11 and 13.

Step 1: Filing

A Chapter 7 proceeding may be voluntary or involuntary, depending on whether it is instituted by a debtor or by creditors.

Voluntary bankruptcy. A bankruptcy is voluntary when the debtor initiates the proceeding. Normally, the debtor is incapable of paying debts as they come due, but the Bankruptcy Code has no such requirement for voluntary bankruptcy.

Given the Code's less drastic alternatives under Chapters 11 and 13, it is extremely rare for a debtor who is not broke to file under Chapter 7. In fact, the 1984 Amendments require that individuals filing under Chapter 7 sign a statement expressing that they understand the differences between the relief offered under Chapter 7 and that under Chapter 13, they know they can file under either Chapter, and they have elected Chapter 7. Debtors' attorneys must attach signed statements to the effect that they have advised their clients of these facts. Both statements are filed with the bankruptcy court.

To initiate a Chapter 7 proceeding, the debtor files a petition and pays a filing fee. Accompanying the petition is a *statement of affairs*, which provides background personal financial material, including the debtor's occupation and income, tax return data, bank account data, property held by third parties, and a list of property transfers and extraordinary gifts made within the preceding year. Eventually, the debtor must submit a *schedule of assets and liabilities*, which identifies all the debtor's property and its fair market value, as well as creditors and the amount owed to each.

Involuntary bankruptcy. When a court grants the creditors' petition to force a debtor into Chapter 7, the bankruptcy is involuntary. The creditors must establish three criteria, which are discussed below.

1 The debtor is unable to pay his debts as they come due.

2 The debtor has had at least $5000 of unsecured credit extended to him.

3 The required number of unsecured creditors has filed against the debtor, *or* the debtor has transferred his property to a custodian (e.g., a creditor's committee or a trustee).

Insolvency in the equity sense. In order to force the debtor into involuntary bankruptcy, the creditors must show that the debtor cannot pay his debts as they come due. This is known as "insolvency in the equity sense." Equity in this context means "fairness," particularly toward creditors. "Equity" here does not refer to an excess of liabilities over assets, although that *is* another definition of insolvency. A debtor may have more assets than liabilities and yet be unable to pay his debts as they come due—something which is unfair to creditors.

The distinction between these two definitions of insolvency is an extremely important one. The second definition, which is referred to as "insolvency in the bankruptcy sense," is a key test for determining whether a debtor has made improper dispositions of assets before entering bankruptcy. (This topic is discussed below.) But insolvency in the bankruptcy sense is *not the test for involuntary bankruptcy!*

More than $5000 in unsecured credit. The amount of unsecured credit extended to the debtor must exceed $5000. Unsecured credit is credit whose repayment is not ensured—in part, at least—by a lien on particular assets belonging to the debtor. A personal loan usually falls into this category.

As applied to the amount criterion, the test of a debtor's ability to pay reflects his present capacity, not his past record or future promise. Isolated instances of nonpayment are not sufficient. Suppose that one month Kyle has a $7000 VISA bill. If he forgets to mail a check for the minimum payment, VISA could not force him into involuntary bankruptcy.

The 1984 Amendments exclude from the $5000 minimum any amounts allegedly due a creditor petitioning for involuntary bankruptcy which are the subject of a good faith dispute between the debtor and the creditor.

Necessary number of unsecured creditors. The number of unsecured creditors required to force a debtor into involuntary bankruptcy varies according to the number of unsecured creditors he has. With eleven or fewer unsecured creditors, one can begin an involuntary bankruptcy proceeding. With twelve or more, three are needed. Secured creditors do not count presumably because they are protected by their collateral.

The debtor's assignment of his assets to a custodian is an alternative ground for involuntary bankruptcy. Usually, an unsecured creditor seeking involuntary bankruptcy on this ground feels the custodial arrangement is not to its advantage.

Petitions for involuntary bankruptcy are not granted automatically. A debtor who succeeds in having a petition dismissed can potentially recover court costs, attorneys' fees, compensatory damages, and, if filed in bad faith, punitive damages.

Step 2: Establishing Administration of the Debtor's Estate

Automatic stay. The filing of a bankruptcy petition automatically *stays*—suspends—the creditors' collection efforts.

Under the 1978 Act, an order for relief automatically stayed any legal proceedings against the debtor. The automatic stay provision not only halted cases already filed but also kept plaintiffs from filing their claims anywhere except in the bankruptcy court. For instance, one of Manville Corporation's reasons for filing for bankruptcy (albeit under Chapter 11) in 1983 was to stay hundreds of asbestos-related personal injury cases in which it was, or was about to be, a defendant.

The breadth of this provision gave the bankruptcy courts jurisdiction over actions which otherwise could not be brought in federal courts. This provision in part led to the Supreme Court declaration that the bankruptcy courts did not meet constitutional standards. The 1984 Amendments considerably narrowed the jurisdiction of the bankruptcy court by eliminating their ability to hear what would otherwise be state court proceedings, unless the parties agreed to submit the dispute to the bankruptcy court.

Order for relief. A bankruptcy judge formally begins a Chapter 7 proceeding by accepting the filing of the bankruptcy petition and issuing an *order of relief.*

In a proceeding involving an individual, however, the bankruptcy judge has the option, under the 1984 Amendments, to dismiss the petition if granting relief would result in a "substantial abuse" of the provisions of Chapter 7. Congress reasoned that bankruptcy is a privilege, not a right. Even where fraud is *not* present, the circumstances may dictate that a discharge in bankruptcy would not be fair to the creditors.

Before this change in the Code, a star football player for the Dallas Cowboys filed for bankruptcy after his player contract had expired. Several days after filing for bankruptcy he signed a new, large multiyear contract. A bankruptcy judge today might find this evidence of "substantial abuse." The next case illustrates why.

In re Kelly

841 F.2d 908 (9th Cir. 1988)

FACTS   The Zolgs sold their Tucson home to the Kellys. Later, the Kellys sued the Zolgs and the realtor for fraud, breach of contract, and several other grounds arising out of the transaction. An Arizona Superior Court found for the defendants and awarded them

$16,369.90 in attorneys' fees and costs. The Arizona Court of Appeals affirmed and awarded the defendants an additional $5610.73 in attorneys' fees. The state supreme court declined to review. Shortly thereafter, the Kellys filed a petition for relief under Chapter 7 in the bankruptcy court. The petition listed $181,350 in assets, $147,000 in debt secured by mortgages against their home, and $25,000 in unsecured debt arising out of the lawsuit.* Before filing for bankruptcy, the Kellys paid off all their unsecured creditors, consolidating some of that debt into a secured line of credit with a bank. Shortly after filing, Mr. Kelly sold his one-third interest in his law firm for the nominal sum of $100. The Kellys admitted in the course of a creditors' examination that their income exceeded their expenses by $440 per month. The court found that half their $500 per month for "recreation" was excessive. On its own motion, the bankruptcy court determined that the bulk of the Kellys' debts were "primarily consumer debts" and that granting relief would be a substantial abuse of the Code because they could easily pay off their debts. The Kellys sought reconsideration from the court, which affirmed its earlier decision. The Kellys then appealed to the Bankruptcy Review Panel, which reversed on the grounds that the debts were not primarily consumer debts.

ISSUE

Would granting the Kellys' petition amount to a substantial abuse of the Bankruptcy Code?

DECISION

Yes. Bankruptcy court judgment reinstated. The 1984 Amendments to Chapter 7 of the Bankruptcy Code contain the following provision:

> . . . [The] court, on its own motion . . . , may dismiss a case filed by an individual debtor . . . whose debts are primarily consumer debts if it finds that the granting of relief would be a substantial abuse of the provisions of this chapter.

A mortgage debt is clearly a consumer debt, since it serves a family or household purpose. The debt arising out of the state court suit also served a household purpose, since it arose out of the purchase of the Kellys' home. Therefore, the first prerequisite to dismissal is satisfied. Granting the petition would abuse Chapter 7 because with little effort the Kellys could pay their debts as they came due. The ability to pay alone—without a showing of fraud or the like—is sufficient grounds to dismiss the petition.

---

* The difference is attributable to postjudgment interest.

In re Kelly should prompt thoughts about the merits of the Kellys' original claims and abuse of the judicial process. It probably will not surprise you to learn that attorney Kelly represented his wife and himself at least in their appeal to the Ninth Circuit.

The interim trustee and the creditors' committee. After issuing the order, the court must appoint a neutral party, called the *interim trustee*, to begin handling the debtor's estate. (What makes up an estate is discussed in Step 4. For now, assume that the estate includes all the debtor's property.) Normally, the most important task of the interim trustee is to prepare for the first meeting of the bankrupt's creditors, called the *creditors' committee* meeting.

The creditors' committee reviews the documentation the debtor supplies, probes for possible omissions of assets or liabilities, and interviews the debtor under oath about his financial condition. The committee also decides whether to elect another person as the permanent trustee. If the committee does not elect someone else, the interim trustee becomes the permanent trustee.

Step 3: Protecting the Debtor's Assets

The trustee represents and administers the debtor's estate. She is charged with investigating, gathering, preserving, converting, and accounting for the debtor's assets. As trustee, she can sue and be sued on the estate's behalf. She also identifies the creditors and notifies them of the proceedings. In large part, the balance of this section describes the trustee's role.

The trustee attempts to maximize the size of the debtor's bankruptcy estate by pruning costs and gathering assets. While she clearly has responsibilities to the creditors in marshaling the assets, she also has a duty to the debtor to act in good faith.

Review of contracts. The trustee reviews all the debtor's contracts. Those contracts not specifically retained are automatically canceled after 60 days. The trustee will cancel those executory or partially executed contracts which she regards as unfavorable to the debtor.

The trustee's ability to cancel a contract does not mean that the cancelations are not breaches of contracts. They are. However, claims for damages resulting from these breaches generally become unsecured debts and receive bottom priority among debts to be paid. Suppose the debtor leased his store from Murphy. The trustee cancels the lease, which has 3 months to run. The debtor's estate owes Murphy 3 months' rent. However, if the estate lacks sufficient assets to satisfy all the unsecured creditors—a near certainty—Murphy will recover, at most, a fraction of the rent he is due.

Security interests. The Bankruptcy Code requires that the court honor security interests. Nonetheless, the trustee must make certain security interests were properly obtained and perfected.

When dealing with alleged security interests, the trustee assumes the role of a hypothetical unsecured creditor. Her goal is to eliminate claims which have a higher priority than the bottom-priority claims of unsecured creditors. She may challenge any security interest which did not attach, attached too late, or was not perfected. Suppose Horton Industries sells inventory to Beckwell Corp. on credit. Horton records its purchase money security interest (PMSI) 12 days after delivery but before any other creditor. Its failure to file within 10 days, as the UCC requires, may defeat its security interest, and Horton would become an unsecured creditor.

Turnover of assets. The trustee also searches out all the debtor's property held by third parties in order to bolster the debtor's estate. For example, if James lent office furniture to Linda, James's trustee would attempt to recover it. In the following case, the debtor's motives for transferring property were fraudulent.

In re Kaiser

722 F.2d 1580 (2d Cir. 1983)

FACTS   In October 1978, Kaiser purchased a home in Miami in his wife's name for $295,000, of which he paid $50,000 in cash. A mortgage was given by "Gerald Kaiser and Joan Kaiser, his wife" to cover the balance. At that time, Kaiser's liabilities amounted to $494,901.32, most of which remained when he filed his Chapter 7 petition in February 1981. Kaiser made the monthly mortgage payments and paid for maintenance and improvements to the house—his home—out of his corporation's accounts. His wife earned no income from 1960 through 1981, had no investments, and held no other significant assets in her name. In his petition, Kaiser failed to mention the Miami house or any of the payments he had made on it. His trustee asked the bankruptcy court to include the house in Kaiser's bankruptcy estate on the ground that putting the house in his wife's name amounted to a fraudulent transfer of assets. The bankruptcy court granted this relief, and the district court affirmed.

ISSUE   Did Kaiser's purchasing the property in his wife's name indicate a scheme to defraud creditors?

DECISION   Yes. Affirmed. Debtors who intend to shield their assets from creditor attack while continuing to benefit from the assets rarely announce their fraudulent purpose. For that reason, the courts have developed "badges of fraud" from which they infer intent. These include: (1) the lack or inadequacy of consideration; (2) the family relationship between the parties; (3) the retention of possession, benefit, or use of the property; (4) the transferor's financial condition before and after the transfer; (5) the existence of a pattern of conduct after the onset of financial difficulties; and (6) the general chronology of the events or transactions in question. Here, Kaiser's activities bore a more-than-adequate number of badges of fraud.

Step 4: Assembling and Liquidating the Debtor's Assets

The trustee's task is to locate, assemble, and liquidate the debtor's assets so that the creditors may be paid. As *Kaiser* indicates, this can be no small job.

The range of assets. Initially, all the assets the debtor possesses at the time of filing are in-cluded in the debtor's bankruptcy estate. The trustee presumes that any property held in the debtor's name is property within the bankruptcy estate unless it can be shown otherwise. But in the case which follows, the trustee reached too far to include property within the estate.

In re Sommer

28 Bankr. 95 (Bankr. D.Colo. 1983)

FACTS   Sommer and his wife filed for bankruptcy. Listed in the Statement of Financial Affairs under "Property Held for Another Person" was a 1956 Jaguar allegedly owned by their son, Gregory. The trustee sought an order turning over a 50 percent interest in the car for inclusion in the Sommers' bankruptcy estate. The car was purchased on August 8, 1977, for $7007.70 in the form of a cashier's check drawn on funds from Gregory's passbook account. Gregory was then a minor. Solely because of the voidable nature of contracts with minors, the dealer had required that Mr. Sommer be a joint contracting party. Gregory never intended his father to have any interest in the car. Sommer never used the Jaguar either as transportation or as security for a loan and never claimed it as an asset. The car was in storage with Sommer's goods, but Gregory contributed to the storage costs.

ISSUE   Did Sommer have a one-half interest in the Jaguar which should be turned over to the trustee in bankruptcy?

DECISION   No. If the debtor does not have a right to possess or use the property at the beginning of the case, the trustee cannot acquire those rights through a turnover action.

After identifying the debtor's assets, the trustee's mission is to convert the debtor's assets to cash so that she can pay the creditors. However, the trustee must segregate from the rest of the estate *exempted assets*, which the creditor will be allowed to keep, and *secured assets*, whose proceeds the trustee must apply to specific obligations. What happens to these assets is discussed below.

Postfiling assets, such as wages the debtor receives after filing, do not become part of the bankruptcy estate. However, proceeds from an inheritance, a property settlement in a divorce or separation, or a life insurance policy are included if the debtor receives them within 180 days after the petition is filed.

Ordinarily, the debtor's bankruptcy estate does not include assets which the debtor transferred or sold before filing. However, as *Kaiser* showed, the law permits the trustee to recover improperly transferred assets such as preferential transfers to creditors or fraudulent conveyances.

Preferential transfers. The trustee may void certain preferential transfers of property made within the year preceding filing. *Preferential transfers*, or *preferences*, are prefiling transfers to a creditor for *antecedent*—already existing—debts, which allow the creditor to receive more than he or she would receive in a Chapter 7 proceeding. For example, a debtor may pay an unsecured debt he owes to his sister just before filing because he knows she will get little or nothing from his bankruptcy estate. That payment is an improper preference.

The key test here is whether, at the time of the transfer, the debtor was "insolvent in the bankruptcy sense," that is, his liabilities exceeded his assets. The Bankruptcy Code presumes insolvency in the 90 days preceding the filing. Either the debtor or the creditor receiving payment may rebut the presumption. For instance, 80 days before filing, Neil paid off his long-standing MasterCard balance. His other unsecured creditors will receive 10 percent of what they are due, but with this payment included, MasterCard will receive 100 percent.

The trustee's concern is with improper or unfair preferences. If Neil became insolvent in the bankruptcy sense when his printing shop burned down 40 days before filing, the trustee probably would permit the preference to MasterCard. Even if Neil could not rebut the presumption of insolvency, the trustee might allow the payment to stand if, as here, it was an ordinary debt.*

In the next case, a trustee had to struggle to establish the exact day in which a transfer occurred to prove that it was improper.

---

* The 1978 Act did not allow the trustee to void a transfer made in the ordinary course of business within 45 days after the debt was incurred. That meant, for example, that Neil's $1000 payment to Ink Spots, Inc., for his monthly ink shipment was not a preference. Such payments still are not improper preferences, but the 1984 Amendments did eliminate the 45-day reference. Congress believed the ordinary debt exception covered the situation.

Barnhill v. Johnson

112 S.Ct. 1386 (1992)

FACTS   The debtors, all individuals in a partnership, delivered a check personally to Barnhill, one of their creditors, on November 18. Barnhill endorsed it and the drawee bank honored the check on November 20, which was exactly 90 days before the debtors filed for bankruptcy. Johnson, the trustee in bankruptcy, sought to recover the money from Barnhill claiming that it was a preferential transfer since it occurred within 90 days of filing for bankruptcy. Barnhill argued the transfer took place on November 18 when he received it, which was 92 days before the filing. The Bankruptcy Court sided with Barnhill. The Federal District Court affirmed. The Court of Appeals reversed.

ISSUE   Is the transfer of a check for purposes of determining whether there is a preferential transfer deemed to occur when the bank honored the check?

DECISION   Yes. Affirmed. Under the Bankruptcy Code a transfer is "every mode, . . . absolute or conditional, . . . of disposing of . . . property or . . . an interest in property." In this case, an unconditional transfer did not occur until November 20. From the time Barnhill received the check until the bank honored it, he did not own the funds. However, when the bank honored the check, it was the same as if the money was handed to Barnhill.

The trustee may set aside preferential transfers made within a year before filing to an *insider*—a person, partnership, or corporation closely associated with the debtor. Figure 43.2

	TIME PRIOR TO FILING OF BANKRUPTCY	MUST DEBTOR HAVE BEEN INSOLVENT?	IS DEBTOR PRESUMED INSOLVENT?	UNEQUAL CREDITOR PAYMENTS REQUIRED?	DOES RULE APPLY TO INSIDERS?	DOES RULE APPLY TO NONINSIDERS?
90-day preference rule	90 days	Yes	Yes	Yes	Yes	Yes
Insider preference rule	90 days to 1 year	Yes	Yes*	Yes	Yes	No

*Under the 1978 Act the answer was no.

Figure 43.2 Preference Rules Compared.

compares the 90-day and the insider preference rules.

A substantially contemporaneous exchange between the creditor and the debtor in which the debtor receives new value is not a preferential transfer. Suppose Neil bought a new binding machine for his printing operation 89 days before filing. The seller required payment within 30 days, and Neil made the payment on time. The trustee could not void this preference.

The 1984 Amendments introduced an exemption from the preference rules. A creditor may retain what would be an improper preference if it amounted to less than $600 and if the debtor is an individual with primarily consumer debts. The rationale for this exemption is purely practical. Such sums are almost impossible to retrieve and are not so large that they seriously damage the rights of other creditors.

Fraudulent transfers. The Bankruptcy Code permits the trustee to void fraudulent transactions made within 1 year of the petition's filing. These transactions fall into one of two categories: intentional or constructive frauds.

An *intentional fraud* occurs when the debtor conveys property intending to hinder, delay, or defraud any creditor. The trustee may void the transaction regardless of whether the debtor was insolvent when it took place. For example, debtors often anticipate bankruptcy and begin to dispose of assets at minimal prices or to give them to friends and relatives. Another common practice is for debtors to inflate the sums owed to friends or relatives in order to diminish the amounts payable to business creditors.

By contrast, *constructive fraud* does not require an intent to defraud. The law treats certain transactions as if they were fraudulent —even though the debtor did not intend to defraud—because this is the only way to be just to all the creditors. Usually in such cases, the conveyance results in the debtor's receiving less than a reasonably equivalent value. In order to void a transaction of this type, the trustee must show one of the following:

- The debtor was insolvent or became insolvent as a result of the transaction.
- The debtor was engaged in business or was about to engage in business and was severely undercapitalized.
- The debtor knew he was running up debts beyond his capacity to repay them.

Step 5: Determining the Debts

The debtor must submit the names of all her creditors at the time she files for bankruptcy. When the creditors' committee meets, the debtor will be questioned under oath about other possible creditors. The trustee also checks state and county records for any perfected security interests.*

Failure to schedule. Since only *scheduled* or listed, debts are discharged, it is clearly in the debtor's interest to schedule all of them. That is why the debtor, a surety, or a trustee may submit a debt on behalf of a creditor who has not scheduled it.

The debtor's failure to list a creditor means liability to that creditor continues even after discharge in bankruptcy. Suppose Harvey's Homes, Inc., owes Valley Lumber Company $3700. Harvey's does not list Valley as an unsecured creditor, and Valley does not learn of the bankruptcy proceeding. Harvey's debt to Valley is nondischargeable. It does the debtor no conceivable good to omit a creditor from his schedule. Thus, Harvey will want to make sure his debt to Valley Lumber is listed.

Failure to file. The trustee notifies all creditors whom the debtor lists of the bankruptcy proceeding and of the necessity for filing their claims within 6 months after the initial date set for the first meeting of the creditors. A creditor that receives notice of the proceeding but either fails to file or files late loses its rights to recover from the debtor.

A secured creditor need not file to be scheduled for the secured portion of its debt. However, if part of the creditor's debt is unsecured, the creditor must file for that portion. Suppose the debtor owes Last Bank $5000, $3000 of which is secured by a lien on the debtor's snowmobile. Last Bank would have to file for the unsecured $2000.

Debts "deemed allowed." A claim of an unsecured debt is presumed to be proper and will

be *deemed allowed* unless another creditor or the trustee makes a proper objection to it. If a creditor no longer has the right to sue the debtor on an obligation, the creditor may not assert the obligation in the bankruptcy proceeding. So one creditor may contest another's claim on the grounds that the statute of limitations has run on the claim.

Step 6: Segregating the Debtor's Exemptions

In order to give the discharged debtor a fresh start, the Bankruptcy Code allows the debtor to segregate certain of his property which will not be subject to creditor claims. The Bankruptcy Reform Act of 1978 permits the debtor to elect between his state's and the federal personal and household *exemptions*, segregated property, in determining which property he may keep.

The Act permits the states to enact legislation prescribing more restrictive state exemptions and prohibiting debtors within that state from taking advantage of the federal exemptions. Under the 1984 Amendments, if a husband and wife file jointly and if they have a choice, they must agree on whether to use the federal or state exemptions. If they cannot agree, the federal exemptions apply.

More than twenty-five states have enacted exemption lists. They vary widely, but the federal list shows what they are like. For instance, it exempts:

- Household goods, furnishings, and clothing used personally by the debtor or his family up to a total of $4000 in value
- Jewelry up to $500 in value
- Trade tools, professional books, and the like, up to $750 in value
- One vehicle up to $1200 in value
- Real property or additional personal property (possibly cash) up to $3750 in value

It is important to note that the exempted assets are simply ones the debtor is allowed to keep. If the debtor is completely wiped out, he or she may have little or nothing to keep.

---

* Creditors who have failed to comply with the filing requirements described in Chapters 41 and 42 are considered unsecured.

Step 7: Distributing Assets to Secured Creditors

The trustee pays the lien of a secured creditor up to the collateral's liquidation value—that is, what the collateral is, or can be, sold for. If the property's value is greater than the lien, the excess goes to the unsecured creditors. If the collateral's value is less than the lien's, the trustee must provide the secured creditor with either the secured property or its cash equivalent.* Suppose Ameribank has a $90,000 lien on the debtor's $110,000 crane. Shortly before filing for bankruptcy, the debtor wrecks the crane, reducing its value to $10,000. The trustee will give Ameribank either the crane or $10,000. As to the balance, the bank becomes an unsecured creditor. To avoid this situation, creditors normally insist that their collateral be fully insured and that they have a lien on the insurance proceeds.

Step 8: Distributing Assets to Unsecured Creditors

After segregating the debtor's exemptions and satisfying the claims of the secured creditors, the trustee prepares a *distribution schedule*. It categorizes unsecured creditors within the seven priorities of payout specified by the Bankruptcy Code.

The trustee may pay *all* creditors within a specific priority before paying any of those in the next priority. Think of paying creditors within their priorities as being like filling seven glasses from one pitcher. The trustee fills the first glass before putting anything into the second; some glasses toward the end may remain

empty. The priorities represented by the empty glasses are called *unfunded priorities*. Creditors in unfunded priorities—like the sixth and seventh glass in the above example—get nothing, and the debtor owes them nothing after discharge.† Figure 43.3 illustrates the order in which priorities are paid.

If the trustee's "pitcher" runs out while she is filling a "glass," she pays the creditors in that priority on a pro rata basis. Suppose the total claims of creditors in the fifth priority are $10,000, but only $5000 remains. Each creditor would get 50 cents on each dollar owed by the debtor.

The paragraphs which follow examine each of the seven priorities of payout set forth in the Bankruptcy Code. Keep in mind that these priorities apply to *both* business and personal bankruptcies.

Priority 1: administrative expenses. Administrative expenses are the expenses associated with handling the debtor's bankruptcy proceeding. Generally, they include:

- Trustee's fee
- Trustee's expenses
- Accountant's fee
- Appraisers' fee
- Attorneys' fees

The trustee recommends the amounts of the administrative expenses and fees. These recommendations are reviewed by the bankruptcy court and approved, if they are reasonable. The trustee, if qualified, may provide professional services, such as legal or accounting services, with the court's approval.

Priority 2: interval claims. *Interval claims* are unsecured debts arising in the ordinary course of the debtor's business between the filing of the bankruptcy petition and the order for relief.

Interval claims receive a high priority be-

---

* One side effect of the 1978 Act was a 33 percent drop between 1979 and 1982 in the average number of unsecured loans. Put another way, the number of secured loans increased significantly, and their average amount decreased. As Chapter 41 indicates, it costs money to attach and perfect security interests. Many expect unsecured loans to increase as a result of the 1984 Amendments and, consequently, the societal cost of secured loans to drop.

† Taxes and a few other debts are nondischargeable. Nondischargeable debts are discussed below.

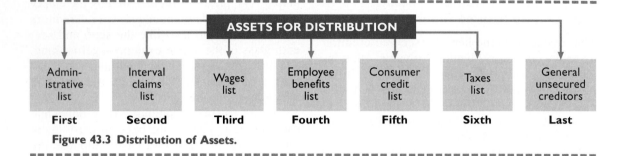

Figure 43.3 Distribution of Assets.

cause, otherwise, creditors might cut the debtor off simply as a result of the filing of the petition. If the bankruptcy court rejected the petition but the creditors had stopped dealing with the debtor, the debtor might be forced into insolvency when he need not have been. Actually, at this point the debtor is a decent risk, since there will usually be enough assets to pay creditors in the second priority, although perhaps tardily.

Priority 3: wage list. The wage list contains the wages owed to the debtor's employees within 90 days preceding the debtor's filing for bankruptcy or the termination of its business, whichever occurred first. Under the Bankruptcy Code, no employee may receive more than $2000 in this priority. Any amount due above $2000 becomes a general debt obligation under Priority 7. The $2000 limit is designed to protect the common worker rather than executives and policymakers, who presumably had some control over the business's fate.

In calculating what is due an employee, the trustee includes vacation pay, sick pay, and severance pay. Taxes paid by the employer on the employee's behalf—like withheld federal income taxes—fall into priority 3.

Priority 4: employees benefits list. Employee benefits essentially are payments owed on behalf of the employees to their pension funds. The employer's obligation must have arisen within 180 days of bankruptcy or the end of its business, whichever occurred first. The maximum allocation under Priority 4 is $2000 per employee *minus* what the employee received under Priority 3. Any excess falls under Priority 7. Suppose Dialogue Corporation went bankrupt. Martha, an employee, received $1700 under Priority 3. Dialogue also owes her pension fund a $1000 contribution on her behalf. Of that, $300 would fall under Priority 4 and $700 under Priority 7.

Priority 5: consumer credit list. The consumer credit list itemizes deposits for the purchase or lease of goods or services made with the debtor before the filing of bankruptcy. Here, the maximum claim is $900 per purchaser if the deposit was on something for personal or family use. Suppose Paula paid a $400 security deposit to her landlord, who then went bankrupt. Her claim would fall under Priority 5.

Priority 6: tax list. Any tax not already paid under a higher priority falls into Priority 6. As discussed below, if not enough remains in the bankruptcy estate to pay the taxes, the debtor remains liable for them after discharge.

Priority 7: general debt obligations. General debt obligations are those unsecured debts "deemed allowed" by the trustee. Creditors in this last priority have little hope of receiving full payment for their unsecured claims. Most creditors not secured as to part or all of a debt find themselves in this priority.

Step 9: Nondischargeable Debts

Normally, the rule in bankruptcy proceedings is, "What you got is what you get!" However, certain types of debts are not dischargeable and continue to be the debtor's responsibility after he or she receives a discharge in bankrupty. *Nondischargeable debts* include:

- Taxes
- Fines and penalties imposed by the government
- Embezzled funds which have not been repaid
- Alimony, maintenance, and child support
- Credit card purchases above $1000 made within 20 days before filing
- Judgments resulting from the operation of a motor vehicle while intoxicated
- Debts incurred by means of the debtor's false pretenses, false representations, or fraud
- Judgments in nonnegligence tort actions
- Educational loans

The last three categories require some clarification.

False pretenses, false representations, and fraud. Debts resulting from the debtor's false pretenses, false representations, or fraud are not dischargeable. Before the Bankruptcy Reform Act, a court could deny a debtor discharge in bankruptcy because of a fraudulent transaction. Now, such a debtor *may* be discharged but not as to the questionable debts. Determining when an activity becomes fraudulent may pose a difficult question of fact for the bankruptcy court, but in the next case, the issue became what the creditor—not the debtor—had done.

In re Ward

857 F.2d 1082 (6th Cir. 1988)

FACTS In a Ward's Chapter 7 proceeding, Manufacturers Hanover Trust Company (MHT) sought to exempt from discharge Ward's indebtedness on a Mastercard. MHT claimed Ward obtained the card by making false representations. Ward received the card after completing an application. MHT sent Ward the application as part of a nationwide direct mail promotion to enroll new customers in its retail consumer credit business. In May 1985, he received the card with a preapproved credit limit of $2000. By June 5, he had run his account up to $2200. MHT admitted that it had not requested a financial statement from Ward, nor did it check his financial responsibility. A check would have revealed Ward's indebtedness on at least 12 credit accounts, an embezzlement conviction, and a restitution order arising out of the conviction amounting to $250,000. In short, as the bankruptcy court held, Ward was hopelessly insolvent. MHT's normal practice was to order a credit bureau report, but it could produce no evidence that it had done so in Ward's case. MHT alleged that Ward's indebtedness to it was nondischargeable because he obtained the money by false representations that he was financially responsible and would repay MHT. Ward responded that MHT, by failing to investigate his financial responsibility, assumed the risk of nonpayment. The bankruptcy court agreed with Ward and held the MHT indebtedness to be dischargeable. The District Court affirmed.

ISSUE   Did MHT reasonably rely on Ward's representations about his financial condition?

DECISION   No. Affirmed. To except a debt from discharge, the creditor must prove: the debtor obtained money through a material misrepresentation that at the time the debtor knew was false or made with recklessness as to its truth; the debtor intended to deceive; and the creditor reasonably relied upon the false representation and that reliance was the proximate cause of its loss. The bankruptcy court correctly held that MHT did not reasonably rely on Ward's false representations because it failed to verify Ward's credit or to investigate the truth of what he said.

Creditors sometimes try to qualify for a false representation exemption by telling borrowers not to answer questions on credit applications honestly. Then, the creditor can complain in a bankruptcy proceeding of intentional omissions. If this ploy is proved, the creditor will lose its claim for an exemption. But it is often difficult to show that the creditor told the debtor, for instance, not to list his mortgage. A borrower should always answer questions on a credit application accurately and take the chance of not receiving credit.

Nonnegligence tort judgments. Tort obligations resulting from the debtor's negligence are dischargeable. Suppose Stella carelessly pulls out of a parking lot and her car rams into Fred's van. The bankruptcy court will discharge her debt arising from Fred's $25,000 judgment against her. However, if the debtor's liability is based on intentional or grossly negligent conduct, the debts will not be discharged. Suppose Stella' car rammed into Fred's van when she exited the parking lot at 50 miles per hour. She then slugged Fred for getting in her way. A court based its $250,000 award on its findings that her conduct was grossly negligent as to the crash and intentional as to the punch. Her liability would be nondischargeable in bankruptcy.

Educational loans. A debtor cannot discharge educational loans which come due within 5 years of filing bankruptcy, unless his inability to discharge these loans would impose an undue hardship on him or his dependents. Congress wanted to prevent students from securing a discharge immediately after graduation. Many young doctors, it was believed, had filed for bankruptcy so that they could enjoy the full profits of their labors. However, as in the next case, if former students act in good faith, the bankruptcy court may discharge their student loans.

In re Carter

29 Bankr. 228 (Bankr. N.D. Ohio 1983)

FACTS   Kenneth and Phoebe Carter filed under Chapter 7. They scheduled Kent State University as an unsecured creditor for $10,700 in student loans. Phoebe received a bachelor's degree in early childhood education and a master's degree in child guidance. Kenneth was a political science major but did not receive a degree. At the time of filing, Kenneth worked at a youth development center, and Phoebe worked in a program for mentally retarded adults. Both received less than $6 per hour. Neither job required a degree. Phoebe could not locate work in her field because she had no teaching experience and was overqualified. Kent State admitted that its placement bureau could not locate more suitable or higher-paying jobs than the ones the Carters held. The Carters alleged the repayment of the student loans would be an undue hardship on them and their four children. The budget which the Carters submitted to the court made no provision for dental, medical, or related expenses. Just maintaining their minimal standard of living would require $78 per month more than their income.

ISSUE   Would not discharging the student loans be an undue hardship on the Carters?

DECISION   Yes. In determining whether repaying a student loan would create an undue hardship, courts look not only at present income but also at anticipated future income. Here, it is highly unlikely that Kenneth would ever obtain a position where he would be able to use the education he received as a political science major. While Phoebe had a marketable skill, it did not appear she would soon be able to obtain a teaching position. A university has an obligation to see that its students receive some guidance when they choose majors. This should include a discussion of the probable job market in that major following graduation.

Step 10: Discharge

The Bankruptcy Code expresses a liberal policy toward discharges. A debtor may be denied a discharge only if he or she intentionally hides assets, destroys property, makes false representations to the trustee or creditors' committee, refuses to obey a lawful order of the court, or the like. In one case, a doctor mired himself and others in real estate speculations. By the time he declared bankruptcy, his debts had amounted to $19 million. Just before filing his petition, he converted virtually all his assets—about $70,000—into exempt property. He was denied discharge.*

As we have seen already, the court does have the power to deny discharge as to certain transactions. Still, even where one or more such transactions occur, the Code's policy is to grant discharge. If the court grants discharge,

the debtor will not be able to file for bankruptcy again for 6 years.

REORGANIZATION UNDER CHAPTER 11

Chapter 11 protects debtors from creditors while they attempt to reorganize their finances. In a Chapter 11 proceeding, all parties aim to preserve the debtor's assets so that it can continue in business and ultimately pay the creditors more than they would receive after a Chapter 7 liquidation.

Chapter 11 is available to anyone who could file under Chapter 7, except stock or commodity brokers, insurance companies, banks, and savings and loans. Generally, however, businesses take advantage of it, since individuals have a similar remedy under Chapter 13. Foster Grant, Continental Airlines, Texaco, and Schwinn Corp. are just four examples of corporations which filed Chapter 11 proceedings.

---

* *Norwest Bank Nebraska, N.A. v. Tveten*, 848 F.2d 871 (8th Cir. 1988).

Filing and Administration

Like a Chapter 7 proceeding, a Chapter 11 proceeding may be voluntary or involuntary. If it is involuntary, the petition must satisfy the same criteria as an involuntary Chapter 7 proceeding. Either the debtor or any other *party in interest* —that is, an unsecured creditor—may request the court to convert a Chapter 11 proceeding into a Chapter 7 proceeding. As in a Chapter 7 case, the creditors meet.

Debtor in possession. Chapter 11 presumes the debtor will remain in possession of its assets during reorganization. In these situations, the debtor is referred to as a *debtor in possession*. As such, the debtor has rights and powers similar to those of a Chapter 7 trustee and performs many of the same functions. The rationale for this arrangement is that the debtor knows the business best, and if it is acting in good faith, has a vested interest in nurturing the business back to health. However, the bankruptcy court may appoint an examiner, when necessary, to conduct investigations into the debtor's business affairs.

Appointment of trustee. The bankruptcy court will appoint a trustee only if such an appointment is in the interests of the creditors or equity security holders or for cause. Appropriate causes include fraud, dishonesty, incompetence, or gross mismanagement of the debtor's affairs. Even when the court has cause, as it did with A. H. Robins Manufacturing Co. (maker of the Dalkon Shield), the court will be most reluctant to remove the managers who know the business.

The court may terminate the trustee's appointment and return the debtor to possession at any time before it confirms the plan for reorganization of the debtor. For instance, when charges of dishonesty against a debt prove unfounded, the court may withdraw the appointment.

Reorganization Plan

Within 120 days after the court grants an order for relief, the debtor may file a *reorganization plan* for the court's approval. If the debtor does not file one within 120 days or if the court does not approve the debtor's plan within 180 days, any of the creditors may file one. The court's approval will depend on whether the plan shows good faith in allocating resources, contains a process for the creditors to follow in voting on the plan, and shows that the plan is likely to succeed without the need for further financial reorganization.

Contents of plan. A reorganization plan must divide ownership interests and debts into classes, specify how each class will be treated, and ensure the same treatment for all claims within a particular class.

The treatment of executory contracts often provokes controversy. The plan will provide for their assumption, rejection, or assignment. As is true of a Chapter 7 proceeding, rejection of an executory contract will likely result in a claim for damages for breach of contract. Still, economic reality may justify rejection. For example, a plan may call for the debtor to terminate a lease of 35,000 square feet of store space because the reorganized business will require only 10,000 square feet.

Confirmation of plan. To bind the creditors, the bankruptcy court must confirm the plan after due notice to the creditors and a hearing. Essentially, the court will approve the plan if:

- The plan is presented in good faith and in accordance with the bankruptcy code.
- The plan's provisions are reasonable and feasible. (In other words, the plan is likely to succeed without the need for further reorganization or the likelihood of straight bankruptcy.)
- Either each priority of creditors or shareholders has approved the plan or the class's interest is not impaired by the plan.

As a practical matter, the creditors often strongly dispute their treatment. When the court confirms a plan over the objections of one or more classes of creditors or shareholders, the result is referred to as a "cramdown." "Cramdown" is a singularly apt term. Manville Corporation's reorganization plan called for the establishment of a $2.6 billion trust fund to compensate asbestos victims. The money would come from cash, bonds, and up to 20 percent of the company's annual profits for nearly 30 years. Manville replaced its 24 million shares of stock with a new issue of 48 million shares, half of which went to the trust. Manville's pre-organization stockholders were to receive one new share for every eight shares they previously held.*

* "Humbled but Raring to Go," *Time*, Nov. 21, 1988, p. 113.

Effect of confirmation. When approved, the reorganization plan becomes a contract between the debtor and its creditors. The court will set a time by which the debtor is to complete the plan. The debtor's discharge depends on its good faith efforts to perform its obligations under the plan.

Failure to obtain the court's approval of a plan may cause a Chapter 11 proceeding to be turned into a Chapter 7 proceeding. On the other hand, can a nonbusiness individual in the midst of a Chapter 7 proceeding convert it into a Chapter 11 proceeding, which is traditionally used only by businesses? The next case discusses that issue.

Toibb v. Radloff

111 S.Ct. 2197 (1991)

FACTS Sheldon Toibb was employed for 2 years for the Independence Electric Corporation (IEC), a company he helped to organize. He owned 25 percent of its stock. Toibb was later terminated from IEC. Unable to find work and heavily in debt, he filed for Chapter 7 bankruptcy. He listed his IEC shares of stock as nonexempt assets and listed their value as unknown. Later IEC offered Toibb $25,000 for the stock. To save some of his stock, he decided to convert his bankruptcy to Chapter 11 and filed a plan to reorganize his debts. On its own motion, the Bankruptcy Court dismissed his Chapter 11 petition, since he was not engaged in a business. The Bankruptcy Court's decision was upheld by the district court and court of appeals.

ISSUE Can Toibb, as an individual, nonbusiness debtor, reorganize under Chapter 11?

DECISION Yes. Reversed. Under the Bankruptcy Code, to qualify as a debtor under Chapter 11, it states that "Only a person that may be a debtor under Chapter 7 of this title, except a stockbroker or a commodity broker, and a railroad may be a debtor under Chapter 11 of this title." To be a debtor under Chapter 7, the Code states that: "A person may be a debtor under Chapter 7 of this title only if such person is not—(1) a railroad; (2) a domestic insurance company, bank . . . ; or (3) a foreign insurance company, bank, . . . engaged in such business in the United States." Even though the structure and legislative history of Chapter 11 makes it appear that it is primarily intended for business debtors, there is no expressed business requirement.

While Toibb's victory now permits individual, nonbusiness debtors to reorganize under Chapter 11, very few individuals are expected to follow Toibb's bankruptcy route. Because Chapter 11 actions are generally much more complex and lengthier, the administrative and legal costs tend to be significantly greater than a Chapter 7 liquidation. Chapter 11 will appeal to those individuals with both large amounts of assets and debts who want to pay their debts over time and who were previously precluded from Chapter 13, discussed next, because of too much debt. For individuals with relatively few assets, Chatper 7 will continue to be chosen because the liberal personal exemption categories shield many assets and it is the quickest, least costly means of getting in and out of bankruptcy.

REGULAR INCOME PLANS UNDER CHAPTER 13

Chapter 13 is designed for individuals with regular income. These proceedings are reorganization plans for individuals or sole proprietors who wish to pay their creditors but want to avoid the normal collection remedies. As with Chapters 7 and 11, filing a proceeding under Chapter 13 stays all collection proceedings. Additionally, it stays any involuntary bankruptcy actions under Chapter 7. For a more complete comparison of the three types of bankruptcy proceedings, see Figure 43.4.

Qualifications

Chapter 13 proceedings are purely voluntary. The debtor's unsecured debts may not exceed

-----

	CHAPTER 7	CHAPTER 11	CHAPTER 13
Goal = immediate discharge of payment?	Yes	No	No
Involuntary action possible?	Yes	Yes	No
Test = "ability to pay debts as they come due"?	Yes	Yes	Yes
Debtor = individual?	Yes	Yes	Yes
Debtor = sole proprietor?	Yes	Yes	Yes
Debtor = partnership?	Yes	Yes	No
Debtor = corporation?	Yes	Yes	No
Matter of federal law?	Yes	Yes	Yes

Figure 43.4 Comparison of Bankruptcy Under Chapters 7, 11, and 13.

$100,000, his secured debts $350,000. The person filing must have a regular income which is sufficiently stable and regular to enable the debtor to make payments under his plan. Thus, a laid-off manager whose unemployment benefits have run out would not qualify under Chapter 13.

Some debtors favor Chapter 13, since less stigma attaches to it than to straight bankruptcy. They may also prefer it if close friends or family members have acted as their sureties. Almost certainly, a creditor will take action against a surety if the debtor files under Chapter 7. But a debtor's plan can provide that debts involving sureties will be paid in full, although possibly with an extension of time. The secured creditors may be willing to take this assurance, thus sparing the debtor's sureties.

A debtor may file a Chapter 13 petition even if he or she has been discharged under Chapter 7 within the past 6 years. One advantage of Chapter 13 proceedings over Chapter 7 is that no trustee takes the debtor's assets. Instead, for example, the debtor may continue to run his or her unincorporated business. Under Chapter 7, such a venture would be terminated.

The Repayment Plan

As under Chapter 7, the debtor is required to meet with a creditors' committee to review his financial condition. Then, within 10 days of the filing of the order for relief, the debtor is required to present a repayment plan. Debtors often require extensions of time in order to prepare the plan, which under Chapter 13 only they can submit.

A Chapter 13 plan is a combination of a composition plan and an extension plan. The debtor pays the unsecured creditors something less than the full amount (composition) and over a longer period of time than originally agreed upon (extension).

Court review. Once the repayment plan is submitted, the Bankruptcy Court reviews the plan to determine whether all unsecured creditors will receive as much as they would in a Chapter 7 proceeding and whether the debtor proposed the plan in good faith. The plan also must demonstrate that the position of the secured creditors is ensured. Finally, the court must find that the debtor is likely to be able to complete the plan. Failure to gain the court's approval may force the debtor to convert his Chapter 13 case into a Chapter 7 case.

If the plan is approved, the court will appoint a trustee to act on the debtor's behalf. The trustee receives the debtor's income and makes scheduled payments to creditors. Normally, the debtor has 3 years to complete the plan, although the court may allow a 2-year extension. Completion of the plan discharges all debts which were part of the plan. Failure to complete it probably will lead to a Chapter 7 proceeding.

The 1984 Amendments require that a debtor begin payments into the plan within 30 days of its filing with the court. The debtor cannot wait for the court's approval. Congress reasoned that the debtor will have to start making payments at some point, and it might as well be sooner instead of later.

The good faith requirement. Before the Bankruptcy Reform Act of 1978, the debtor had to receive not only court approval for the repayment plan but also a collective vote of approval from both secured and unsecured creditors. This rule prevented a plan which was unfair to the creditors from being submitted and approved.

The 1978 Act altered this requirement so that the debtor needs collective approval from the secured creditors only. This change compels bankruptcy judges to place greater weight on the requirement that debtors act in good faith. Figure 43.5 lists the factors a court may consider in determining good faith. In the next case, the court applied those factors.

Good faith means different things in different contexts, as we have seen. Here's a checklist for Chapter 13 devised by the Bankruptcy Court for the Southern Dictrict of Georgia and widely cited by other courts. It also applies to Chapters 11 and 12.

---

a. The amount of the debtor's income from all sources
b. The debtor's regular and recurring living expenses
c. The amount of the attorneys' fee to be awarded in the case and to be paid by the debtor
d. The probable duration of the plan
e. The debtor's motivations and sincerity in seeking relief
f. The debtor's ability to earn and the likelihood of future increases or reductions in earning
g. Special situations, such as large medical expenses or unusual care required for a family member
h. How often the debtor has sought relief under the Bankruptcy Act
i. The circumstances under which the debtor contracted the debts and how he or she has dealt with the creditors
j. Whether the amount of percentage of payment the debtor offers is consistent with the purpose and spirit of the Act or would amount to a mockery of honest, hardworking, well-intended debtors who pay a higher percentage of their claims
k. The burden administration of the plan will place on a trustee
l. The rehabilitative provisions of the Bankruptcy Reform Act that are to be construed liberally in favor of the debtor

---

Source: Matter of Kull, 12 Bankr. 654, 659 (S.D. Ga. 1981), *aff'd sub nom. In re Kitchens,* 702 F. 2d 885 (11th Cir. 1983).

Figure 43.5 A List of Factors a Court May Consider in Determining Good Faith.

In re Doersam

849 F.2d 237 (6th Cir. 1988)

FACTS   Doersam borrowed $10,000 from a bank to finance her graduate education at the University of Dayton. She also cosigned a $5000 student loan for her daughter. Both her and her daughter's loans were guaranteed by the Ohio Student Loan Commission. She worked as a systems analyst at NCR Corporation at an annual salary of $24,000 per year. The job required a masters degree. On November 6, 1985, about 6 weeks before her graduation, she filed a petition and plan under Chapter 13. The plan proposed payment of 19 percent of her unsecured debt to creditors at a rate of $375 per month over 36 months. Doersam's total unsecured debt was $18,418.55, 81 percent of which represented her student loans. She did not list the Ohio Student Loan Commission as a creditor. Her schedules listed rent at $300 per month and food at $400. She listed her 23-year-old daughter and 1-year-old granddaughter as dependents, even though the daughter had a low-paying job. After finally learning of

Doersam's proceeding, the Commission filed objections to the confirmation of her plan. The bankruptcy court chose not to deal with the "elusive bad faith issue," but found no hardship that would prevent Doersam from satisfying her student loan debts. On appeal, the district court affirmed, holding that Doersam's plan had been filed in bad faith.

ISSUE   Did Doersam's conduct indicate that she had filed her plan in good faith?

DECISION   No. Affirmed. The mere fact that a debtor attempts to discharge a debt— guaranteed student loans—that would be nondischargeable under Chapter 7 is not alone sufficient to justify a finding that the plan was not proposed in good faith. However, the structure of these loans is of relevance to the determination of good faith. These loans do not require repayment until after graduation. When a debtor accepts a student loan and then before its maturity attempts to extinguish it in bankruptcy without ever making a payment, it stretches credulity to say the debtor made an honest effort to pay these debts as the Bankruptcy Code requires. More-over, listing her working daughter and a grandchild for whom Doersam is not legally responsible, and the food budget of $400 per month based on these listings, further indicated the plan was not filed in good faith.

OTHER BANKRUPTCY PROCEEDINGS

Besides Chapters 7, 11, and 13, there are two other substantive chapters: Chapter 9, dealing with adjustments of debts of a municipality, and Chapter 12, dealing with reorganization of farming operations.

Chapter 9

Chapter 9 is a very limited, seldom used remedy. The most likely filer under Chapter 9 would be an entity like a mosquito control district or an unincorporated village.

The power of a bankruptcy court in Chapter 9 proceedings is severely limited. Unless the debtor or the plan provides otherwise, the court cannot interfere with the debtor's:

- Political or governmental powers
- Property or revenues
- Use of enjoyment of any income-producing property

Chapter 12

Essentially, Chapter 12 is a cross between Chapters 11 and 13. It is primarily designed to protect family farming operations. Before Chapter 12 entered the Code in 1986, it was difficult to structure relief for a farmer under Chapter 13 because a farmer does not have regular, monthly income. Therefore, Chapter 12 is geared toward annual, rather than monthly, income.

Under Chapter 12, the qualifications for a family farmer are:

- An individual's aggregate income must not exceed $1.5 million
- More than 50 percent of the individual's gross income must come from farming, and
- At least 80% of the farmer's debt must arise from his or her farming operations.

In the next case, the court faced a question quite similar to that in *Frigaliment Importing Co. v. B.N.S. International Sales Corp.*, briefed in Chapter 10.

In re McNeal

848 F.2d 170 (11th Cir. 1988)

FACTS

On March 3, 1987, McNeal filed a petition for voluntary bankruptcy under Chapter 12. During 1986, McNeal earned $17,394.12 as a deputy sheriff of Jeff Davis County, Georgia. In addition, he received $23,563 in what he referred to as "income from farming." Of this, $8860 came from cleaning chicken coops owned by other farmers and selling the manure for fertilizer, and $1670 from "machine work" in the chicken house operation. The Federal Land Bank moved to dismiss McNeal's petition on the grounds that he did not qualify as a family farmer. The bankruptcy court denied the motion but the district court reversed, dismissing the petition.

ISSUE

Is a chicken coop cleaning service a farming operation?

DECISION

No. District court judgment affirmed. Chapter 12 of the Bankruptcy Code provides in part: a "family farmer" is

> *an individual . . . engaged in a farming operation . . . , and such individual . . . [must] receive from such farming operation more than 50 percent of such individual's . . . gross income for the taxable year preceding the taxable year in which the case . . . was filed.*

Because of this provision, the characterization of the chicken house cleaning income disposes of this case. Chapter 12 makes special provisions for farmers based on the cyclical nature of farming. A drought or a year of low prices which make a farmer temporarily unable to pay the bills should not consign him or her to involuntary bankruptcy. This rationale is informed by the concept of farming's risks. McNeal's chicken house operations had nothing to do with the traditional risks of farming, especially since they were in McNeal's words "cash up front" operations. As for the sale of the manure, this activity did not relate to McNeal's farming operations but those of others. The mere purchase and sale of farm by-products does not make a "farming operation."

FUTURE BANKRUPTCY LEGISLATION

Congress has continued to debate what should be the national policy and law in regard to bankruptcy. The major stakeholders in bankruptcy actions—bondholders, consumers, creditors, stockholders, and unions—all agree that the bankruptcy system is overburdened, that administrative costs have become too great, and that in too many Chapter 11 cases the company's remaining assets get drained in futile efforts to save the company. The identified "culprits" include too many consumers with no moral values, entrenched managers being allowed to remain in control in Chapter 11 cases and, of course, lawyers. What the stakeholders cannot agree on is how to make the bankruptcy system be more efficient, fair, and effective.

Chapter 11, established with the 1978 Act,

has come under criticism that too often it is used to:

- Stiff creditors, enrich lawyers, and protect bad managers
- Cut wages and renege on employee health care and pension plans
- Simply prolong the inevitable—failure

Numerous studies point out the excessive extensions of time granted to businesses in Chapter 11 to present for approval reorganization plans. The result—further escalation in administrative costs and the draining of corporate assets.

Some legal commentators are now recommending to Congress that Chapter 11 be eliminated. Instead, they would leave a company's fate up to its creditors, who could choose to either raise capital to pay off debtholders or take the company into liquidation (termination). Others respond that such drastic action is not required.

It appears that Congress will consider compromise measures involving Chapter 11 proceedings, perhaps to limit existing management's control of the reorganization plan and/or restricting which companies can reorganize rather than liquidate. If so, bankrupty courts would have to evaluate the concerns of all interested parties in a hearing to decide whether a company ought to be allowed to reorganize or should immediately be liquidated. In addition, it is likely that Congress will consider measures to try to force bankruptcy courts to better adhere to realistic reorganization plan timetables. Expedited, prepackaged Chapter 11 reorganizations are also likely to be explored.

Some small-business advocates are calling on Congress to consider a new Bankruptcy Code chapter for small businesses: Chapter 10. Chapter 10 would provide a fast-track bankruptcy process for small businesses who cannot afford the high administrative costs and time-consuming practices associated with Chapter 11 proceedings. Others contend that small-business owners would be better served by Congress changing the debt ceiling limits and providing greater flexibility for Chapter 13 actions.

The Clinton administration has indicated that it will carefully evaluate the bankruptcy laws to try to identify reasoned solutions acceptable to all major stakeholders. This is an important, appropriate goal. Still, a knowledgeable betting person would probably be more inclined to bet on the Chicago Cubs playing in another World Series (they last appeared, and lost, in 1945), before major stakeholders in bankruptcy ever arrive at a consensus agreement on bankruptcy law changes.

CONCLUSION

Eighty years elapsed between the last two major revisions of the Federal Bankruptcy Code. In a society which depends so much on credit, it is hardly surprising that the debate was vigorous before, during, and after the enactment of the Bankruptcy Reform Act of 1978.

While it is possible that the 1978 Act went too far in liberalizing the availability of bankruptcy, and while it is true that some have abused the system, most who claim bankruptcy protection needed it. A 1983 study of 753 cases in the northeast showed that the average bankrupt consumer had debts of $17,432, gross assets of $4200, and an income of approximately $13,000. (In 1980 the national median family income was $21,000.)

The 1984 Amendments went far—perhaps too far—toward addressing creditors' complaints about the 1978 Act. Already, many commentators have harshly criticized the core proceedings test for bankruptcy court jurisdiction and the substantial abuse test for determining the acceptability of Chapter 7 filing.

Abuses and all, the bankruptcy system works. Considering that it replaced debtors' prisons—an eighteenth-century remedy for insolvency—our bankruptcy laws keep people working and repaying.

A NOTE TO FUTURE CPA CANDIDATES

Bankruptcy is part of the debtor-creditor relationships section on the exam (which also includes suretyship). The CPA candidate is expected to know the Chapter 7 requirements for bankruptcy and the basic steps in the bankruptcy process, and about preferential transfers, competing claims, discharge, and debts not discharged by bankruptcy. In addition, general awareness of Chapter 11 and 13 is expected.

To file a voluntary petition in bankruptcy a debtor need only state the existence of debts. The law does *not* require the debtor to prove he is:

- Bankrupt in the equity sense (cannot pay debts as due)
- Bankrupt in the bankruptcy sense (liabilities exceed assets)

To file an involuntary petition in bankruptcy, the following must be proved:

- The debtor is bankrupt in the equity sense.
- There is $5000 or more of *un*secured debt (*not* dependent on the number of unsecured creditors).
- The required minimum number of unsecured creditors exists (three or more unsecured creditors if there are twelve or more unsecured creditors in total, otherwise one sufficient), or the debtor transferred property to a custodian.

The filing of a bankruptcy petition automatically stays (suspends) creditor collection efforts, including lawsuits, of unsecured and secured creditors. If issuing an order for relief would result in "substantial abuse" the petition will be dismissed. Otherwise, the petition will be granted, an order for relief will be entered, and an interim trustee in bankruptcy will be appointed to meet with the creditors. The creditors may (*not* must) elect a permanent trustee and/or establish a creditor's committee.

It is important for you to understand the function of the bankruptcy trustee: to sort out competing creditor claims, to assemble assets, to review actions by the debtor, and to oversee the bankruptcy estate. Income or proceeds received by the debtor after an order for relief is entered will *not* be part of the bankrupt estate unless received within 180 days of the filing of the petition from inheritance, a property settlement in a divorce or separation, or a life insurance policy. A trustee may perform another role for a fee, such as also being the income tax preparer, if authorized and if the fees are approved by the court.

It is importannt for you to know and understand the preference rules illustrated in Figure 43.2. A contemporaneous exchange (one for new value) is acceptable (*not* voidable).

Individual debtors under Chapter 7 are permitted exemptions, meaning that they can retain certain assets after bankruptcy. Secured creditors have a right to the *value* of their secured collateral or the equivalent amount in money. (Any amount owed above the value of the collateral is considered unsecured debt). Once these two steps are completed, the estate distributes assets to unsecured creditors as illustrated in Figure 43.3. Remember, all claims of a priority class are paid before any claims of the next priority class and that an employee claimant can receive a maximum of $2000 for Steps 3 and 4 (wages and benefits).

Once all claims which can be paid are paid, the court generally issues a discharge in bankruptcy to the debtor. (Although partnerships and corporations can use Chapter 7, they are not given discharges.) Some debts are nondischargeable, including nonlisted debt, government fines, taxes and penalties, embezzled funds, alimony, maintenance and child support, debts incurred by means of false pretenses, most educational loans and nonnegligence tort judgments.

Chapter 11, reorganization, is available to individuals, partnerships, and corporations. (It is *not* available to banks, insurance companies, or savings and loan institutions.) A trustee often is appointed but does *not* have to be appointed. The debtor often is allowed to remain in possession and management of a company during bankruptcy. A creditor's committee, if established, must consist of some unsecured creditors. A debtor is given 120 days to offer a reorganization plan (which must include coverage of all administrative expenses).

KEY WORDS

assignment for the benefit of creditors (978)	distribution (989)
	exemption (988)
	extension agree-
Chapter 7 (979)	ment (978)
Chapter 11 (993)	insider (986)
Chapter 13 (996)	insolvency (980)
composition agree-	interim trustee (982)
ment (977)	interval claims (989)
creditors' commit-	nondischargeable
tee (978)	debt (991)
debtor in posses-	order for relief (981)
sion (994)	preference (985)
deemed allowed (988)	

DISCUSSION QUESTIONS

1. Describe some of the alternatives to bankruptcy for a debtor who is having trouble paying his debts as they come due.
2. Distinguish between a voluntary bankruptcy case and an involuntary one. Which types of bankruptcy proceedings can be involuntary?
3. Distinguish between insolvency in the equity sense and insolvency in the bankruptcy sense. Which is the test to initiate an involuntary bankruptcy proceeding?
4. Briefly describe the roles of the trustee and the creditors' committee.
5. What are the rules regarding improper preferences?
6. What are the rules regarding fraudulent conveyances?

7. Describe how a secured creditor must be treated. What happens if the creditor's claim exceeds the value of the collateral?
8. What is meant by "the debtor's exemptions"? What determines whether the debtor may elect between the state and federal exemptions?
9. Will nondischargeable debts prevent the debtor from receiving a discharge in bankruptcy? How do they affect a Chapter 13 proceeding?
10. Contrast the purposes of Chapter 11 and 13 with those of Chapter 7.

CASE PROBLEMS

1. The unsecured creditors of Kalmback Printers are considering entering into a composition agreement to help the printing company become more stable. For the agreement to be workable, the creditors will have to agree to accept only 60 cents on the dollar. A major creditor, Virgil Lacy, is doubtful that the printing company can recover. Under the law applicable to composition agreements, is it necessary that all unsecured creditors participate in the agreement? Suppose that after paying half of the scheduled debts, the printer filed for bankruptcy. Will the creditors be permitted to file a claim for the full portion of what was to be forgiven? Explain.
2. Karen Denton has filed for bankruptcy under Chapter 7. Luther Boston was named interim trustee. At the first meeting of the creditors' committee Boston was selected as trustee. Being a CPA, Boston asked and received permission from the bankruptcy court to prepare Denton's tax returns for the past year. Secured creditors have complained about Boston's meticulous review of and lack of appropriate respect for their claims of security interests. Unsecured creditors feel that Boston should not be allowed to recover a separate fee for his tax preparer services. Do the secured creditors have a strong basis for their objection? Do the unsecured? Explain.
3. John Barry, doing business as John Barry Fashions, is worried that his creditors might file an involuntary bankruptcy proceeding against him. His net worth is $8000 ($108,000 assets —

$100,000 liabilities). However, his cash flow is negative and he has been hard-pressed to meet current obligations as they mature. He is, in fact, some $12,500 in arrears in payments to his creditors on bills submitted during the past 2 months. In what way is Barry insolvent? Can Barry prevent an involuntary bankruptcy proceeding? Explain.

4. Valley Finance Company lent Michelle $8000 to purchase a Mazda. Just prior to bankruptcy, Michelle accidentally wrecked the car. The car is now worth $1000, and there was no insurance on it. Valley Finance claims it has a secured claim and priority to the extent of $6000, the amount that Michelle owed at the time when the order for relief was made. The trustee claims that Valley's priority is limited to $1000. Who is correct? If the trustee is correct, what rights, if any, does Valley have to the remaining $5000? Explain.

5. Sonoma, Inc., filed a petition for Chapter 7 bankruptcy. Five months before filing bankruptcy, the board of directors of Sonoma voted to repay a $25,000 note owed to the company president's father, Joe Lambright. The note was 6 months overdue when paid. In addition, Sonoma paid a distributor, Aaron Manufacturing, $75,000 for new inventory just 7 days before filing for bankruptcy. Both payments have come under attack by creditors. The company president, Tanya Rich, has offered proof that the corporation was solvent when the loan was made by her father to the corporation. Assuming the president is correct, would the bankruptcy court be likely to find the loan repayment to be a voidable preferential transfer? The payment to Aaron Manufacturing? Explain.

6. Dick Byrne filed for bankruptcy under Chapter 7 on July 1. A review of past transactions by Byrne showed that on March 27 he had received a $10,000 settlement of an accident claim. Although he then was some $20,000 past due to a number of creditors, Byrne used the money to purchase a new power boat immediately. In addition, just 45 days prior to his filing bankruptcy he paid $750 to American Express to cover past due charge debts. Would Byrne's purchase of the Mustang be considered an improper preferential payment? Would the payment to American Express be considered an improper payment? Explain.

7. Ted Dolson has filed a voluntary petition in bankruptcy. His assets are listed as $4200, his liabilities $18,750. His creditors include (1) three employees, each of whom wages of $100 per week have not been paid for 6 weeks; (2) the U.S. government, which claims $6900 in back income and social security taxes; (3) his former wife, who wants $3000 in back alimony; and (4) his suppliers, who want $7050 for goods purchased on open accounts. Which debts, if any, are not dischargeable in bankruptcy? If sufficient assets existed, what would be the order of payout on these claims?

8. Hard Times, Inc., is insolvent. Its liabilities exceed its assets by $13 million. Hard Times is owned by its president, Waters, and members of his family. Waters, whose assets are estimated at less than $1 million, guaranteed the loans of the corporation. A consortium of banks is Hard Times's principal creditor, having loaned it $8 million, the bulk of which is unsecured. The banks decided to seek reorganization of Hard Times, and Waters has agreed to cooperate. No request has been made by the creditors for the appointment of a trustee. What is the role of Hard Times likely to be in the reorganization? The creditors' committee has asked the bankruptcy court for authorization to file the sole plan of reorganization of Hard Times. Hard Times has objected. Is Hard Times likely to prevail? Explain.

The end-of-part problems serve three purposes. First, some require practical applications of legal knowledge to everyday situations. Second, they are summative, bringing together many of the issues treated individually in the chapters of a particular part. Third, the last question presents an ethical problem which, as in real life, may not have an unqualifiedly right or wrong solution. Rather, its goal is to prompt two questions: What would I do in this situation? What *should* I do in this situation?

I. A PRACTICAL PROBLEM

On September 1, Fall River Restaurant Supplies, Inc., sold Gail Bliss a new meat slicer. Bliss paid $250 down and is financing combined principal and interest of $1150 over 30 months. Fall River Restaurant Supplies is located in the Mills Shopping Center, 1502 Commonwealth Ave., Fall River, Massachusetts 02722. Bliss's business address is Gail's Deli, Dover Way, Fall River, Massachusetts 02726. She is the sole proprietor of her business and also teaches criminal justice at New Bedford State College.

Her new machine, Razor Sharpe's Model 610, serial number 977C3534, is made entirely of unpainted stainless steel. She is also purchasing an extra blade and a 12-month extended warranty in addition to the 24-month parts and service warranty which comes with the machine. Bliss plans to take delivery of the slicer on September 2, at which time she will execute a note which includes a security agreement and a financing statement.

Figure 41.4 is a financing statement. Using the facts given above, draft appropriate language for each of its numbered paragraphs.

2. A SUMMATIVE PROBLEM

Peter Daniel is a well-known financial advisor. However, Daniel is concerned that some of his clients may be more in need of a lawyer than a financial advisor. Daniel would like your assistance in sorting out his problems.

a. Pam Beacher purchased and financed a Miata roadster from Classic Car Sales. Pam's friend Jacqueline Martinez, agreed to be the surety on Pam's note. Soon after the purchase, Pam moved to Oregon. Several months later, Classic informed Jacqueline that Pam had just returned the Miata. Classic demanded that Jacqueline, as surety, immediately pay the $700 difference still owed on the note. Having misplaced Pam's address, Jacqueline concluded that Pam must not have been able to find a new job; she paid the $700. The next day she received a letter from Pam in which Pam stated that she had returned the car because of a continuing disagreement about a defect with the car. Jacqueline wishes to know whether she has a right to indemnification.

b. Alice Frazier purchased a home on a land contract from James Ballengee. Their contract calls for Frazier to make monthly payments and a final balloon payment in 5 years. Ballangee agreed to continue to make his monthly mortgage payments to Sklar Finance Company. Ballengee's mortgage with Sklar prohibits assumption. Alice wishes to know what financial obligations, if any, she may have to Sklar Finance Company. In addition, she is concerned about what legal rights she may have if Sklar should foreclose on the property, if Ballengee fails to make monthly payments, or if they accelerate the payment.

c. Steve Tilley decided to expand his bookstore. Steve's inventory is valued at $60,000. On May 1, Steve signed a security agreement and financing statement with Commercial Bank for his inventory as a part of an application to borrow $20,000. Commercial Bank filed a financing statement on May 3. On May 5, the bank informed Steve that they had approved his request and had available a $20,000 line of credit. On May 10, Steve borrowed $3000 against the line of credit. Because of questions concerning another loan Steve secured about the same time, Steve needs to know when Commercial Bank's interest was perfected.

d. Leah Alban purchased a town house 12 years ago when she was a graduate student at Victory University. She sold the town house on a loan assumption to Debra Byers. Since then, the town house has been sold by loan assumption by Byers to Arnold Stroebel; by Stroebel to Annie Mitchell; and by Mitchell to Ron Page. The mortgagee, Victory Savings, never granted a novation or release on the mortgage. Page has filed for bankruptcy. The town house was sold for less than the remaining balance on the mortgage. Victory Savings has demanded that Alban now pay this amount. Alban wants to know the following: If she pays, will she have a right of contribution from Byers and Stroebel? In the alternative, would she be considered a secured creditor, Page's?

e. Bob DeBerg's Porsche dealership financed and sold a Porsche Carrera to Kevin Long, a pro basketball player. The car was put up as collateral. Although Long's assets appear to be greater than his liabilities, he has fallen further and further behind in payments to all his creditors, including DeBerg. Long paid $45,000 cash down but only $600 on the $35,000 note since then. On his application for financing with DeBerg, Long failed to list very high alimony and child support payments that he owed to his ex-wives. Long has threatened to file for bankruptcy if creditors push him too far. Long may sign a big contract in a few months. However, DeBerg is now sufficiently disgusted that he wants to either repossess and keep the car or try to find two other creditors and force Long into bankruptcy (although he fears losing money with this option). DeBerg wants to know his rights under Article 9.

f. Assuming the same facts as in item *e*, what are DeBerg's rights under the Bankruptcy Code?

g. Dottie Gross and Helena Daidone agreed to be sureties for Dottie's sister, Fran. Fran borrowed $32,000 from National Bank to purchase inventory and equipment for her new gourmet shop. Fran gave National a PMSI interest in the inventory and equipment which they properly filed. The gourmet shop failed to raise sufficient dough and fell into bankruptcy. National Bank has brought an action against Helena for the $29,000 still due it. Helena cannot understand how she could be sued for $29,000, since a cosurety should be liable for only half, $14,500. She is confused and wants to learn about her rights and duties.

h. McSwain Farms financed and sold a riding horse, Sir Grady, to Art Sample. Art found that the bumps and jostling of horseback riding were more than he anticipated and sold Sir Grady to Peter Rotolo. Art had to file for bankruptcy while still owing McSwain for Sir Grady. The farm is unsure of its legal status in Art's bankruptcy case. Ideally, McSwain would like to retrieve Sir Grady from Rotolo. McSwain wants to know its options.

3. A SUMMATIVE PROBLEM

You have been appointed to serve as the bankruptcy trustee for the Carter Corporation in an involuntary Chapter 7 proceeding. The following situations demand your immediate attention. You must determine the rights of the bankruptcy estate. Of course, the bankruptcy court will review your determinations, so you must explain the rationales for each of your conclusions.

a. Alpha Corp. financed the sale of equipment to Carter. Alpha received a security agreement and a financing statement from Carter. Alpha filed the financing statement 12 days after Carter took possession. No other creditor had a security interest in Carter's equipment at that point. Alpha now claims a security interest in the equipment in the amount Carter still owes: $25,000.

b. Beta, Inc., sold 1000 widgets to Carter on credit. The widgets went into inventory. Beta received a security agreement and a financing statement from Carter. Because State Bank had already filed a financing statement covering after-acquired inventory, Beta notified State Bank and filed its financing statement before it delivered the widgets to Carter. State Bank now claims that it has a security interest in the widgets and that its interest takes priority over Beta's interest because Beta was second in time and had notice of its interest.

c. Gamma, Inc., is a surety on a $60,000 note which Delta Corp. issued to Carter. Delta is in bankruptcy, too. Gamma claims it is not liable on its suretyship contract because Delta misrepresented its financial position to Gamma's officers to induce Gamma to act as surety. Gamma also claims it would not be equitable to require Delta to pay, since both the obligor and the obligee are now bankrupt and Gamma's right of subrogation against Delta is essentially worthless.

d. With money borrowed from First Bancorp, Carter had bought five trucks from Epsilon Truck Sales. First Bancorp filed its financing statement within 10 days of the date Carter took possession. In Epsilon's showroom, a large banner read, "All of Epsilon's truck inventory is subject to Prarie Bank's inventory lien." Epsilon has defaulted on its obligation to Prarie Bank, so Prarie Bank has filed a claim against Carter's five trucks. Of course, so has First Bancorp.

e. Four months before it went into bankruptcy, Carter paid off two separate $20,000 loans to major shareholders. One of the creditors paid was Betsy Barry, the CEO's mother. Barry did not know anything about the company's financial straits, nor did she know that other creditors were not being paid. She has already donated the $20,000 she received to her alma mater. The other creditor who received $20,000 was Lillian Cobb, a Carter officer. Cobb was aware of Carter's financial condition, but because of her daughter's critical illness, she had to have the money.

f. Before Carter entered Chapter 7, its warehouse burned down. Unfortunately, one of the bills Carter had not paid was its property insurance premium, so it was uninsured. There were two mortgages on the destroyed warehouse. On the first, Carter owes $100,000; on the second, $25,000. The site is now worth $30,000. The second mortgage holder has claimed to be secured to the extent of $6000.

g. Sigma Construction completed a small office building for Carter on April 1. Three weeks after construction ended, Carter applied for a second mortgage on the building from Century Bank. A Carter officer had orally assured the Century loan officer that Carter had paid all the construction costs. The mortgage was properly executed and recorded. On June 24, Sigma filed a mechanic's lien against the building. The state in which the building is located requires that mechanic's liens be filed within 90 days. Century Bank claims that it has a priority on the building and that the obligation due it is nondischargeable.

4. LAW AND ETHICS

The following item appeared in *The Wall Street Journal.*

> *. . . Consider an effort by a mortgage insurance company to counsel homeowners who had fallen behind in their mortgage payments.*
>
> *The insurer, Investors Mortgage Insurance, initiated the counselling program a few years ago in Southern California and Ohio. Counsellors, who were paid only when a homeowner caught up on overdue payments, advised homeowners on how to straighten out their finances to avoid foreclosure.*
>
> *The results were sharply different. Out of 547 problem mortgages in Ohio and several nearby states, the counsellor was able to develop ways for 27% of the homeowners to catch up on their payments.*
>
> *In contrast, the loan counsellor in California quit in frustration after only 5% of referrals could be convinced it was worth their effort to cure the defaults. An Investors Mortgage official says many of the owners wouldn't even talk to the loan counsellor while others reasoned that the cost of getting current in their payments exceeded their equity in the home. James Aylward, president of Investors Mortgage, attributes Midwestern success and California failure to a different "buyer morality" in each area.**

a. Is Mr. Aylward correct? Do ethical considerations apply to mortgage defaults at all? If the costs of becoming current—late charges, penalties, and the like—exceed the mortgagor's equity, should morality or a cold business appraisal control the mortgagor's actions?

b. Does the traditional ethical view that a person must make every effort to meet his or her obligations apply when the obligation is to a large, impersonal equity like a bank? Should the obligation to pay be relative; that is, should it depend on how critical the debtor's default would be to the creditor's solvency?

c. Does the ready availability of bankruptcy affect the moral obligation to repay? Since the debtor can essentially walk away from most debts upon discharge, has the bankruptcy remedy eroded traditional morality? Would the reinstitution of debtors' prison spur private morality in the right direction?

d. Given the economic dislocations—like recessions, depressions, and panics—our nation regularly suffers, do you think our ancestors were any better about paying their debts than we are today?

---

* R. Guenther, "Real Estate: 'Buyer Morality' . . . Syndicators Get a Break . . . Home Controls," *The Wall Street Journal*, Mar. 20, 1985, p. 33, col. 1

THE LEGAL ENVIRONMENT OF BUSINESS

The title of this part, "The Legal Environment of Business," in most instances is used to mean "government regulation." More specifically, it is applied to business's relations with *administrative agencies*.

When used in that sense, it is too narrow, because the word "environment" takes in *all* the factors that affect a business's habitat. Thus, properly understood, the legal environment includes every area—from civil procedure to secured transactions—examined in this book.

Yet, the phrase "legal environment" is appropriate as a metaphor for government regulation. It reveals the importance of government regulation as a complex barometer of the societal pressures on business. Government regulation also gauges where the pressures come from.

GOVERNMENT REGULATION

A regulation tends to be the product of many forces. Our system of government institutionalizes negotiation, compromise, and accommodation, and so it is rare for a particular interest group—whether a consumer group, a manufacturing association, or some other such group—to dictate a regulation. As Chapter 3 demonstrated, federal and state statutes have designed the *quasi-legislative* process to expose issues to as many points of view as possible.

This part describes how a number of administrative agencies—principally the Federal Trade Commission (FTC), the National Labor Relations Board (NLRB), and the U.S. Environmental Protection Agency (EPA)—carry out the functions Congress assigned them. It presumes some familiarity with the history and procedural law described in Chapter 3.

Many political and legal historians subscribe to the idea that American constitutional law reflects primarily the working out of economic relationships within our society. Indeed, a working knowledge of history is particularly important to an understanding of government regulation. The structure within which government and business now coexist seems quite mad unless one understands that it evolved in response to particular economic and political phenomena. The Interstate Commerce Commission and state public utilities commissions were the first administrative agencies. They appeared in the 1870s and 1880s, when the railroads became so vital to American commerce that they effectively controlled transportation and could, through their power to set rates, strangle an entire region.

ANTITRUST LAW

The FTC was the next great administrative agency to appear. Overall, its purpose is to maintain a competitive and fair marketplace. One of its principal subfunctions is to ensure that business combinations such as those which characterized the last two decades of the nineteenth century and the first decade of the twentieth century do not appear again.

Today, we have become accustomed to bigness in business. But being big is not the same as controlling a market. Consider what the following companies have in common:

Atlantic Richfield	Standard Oil of California	Mobil
Buckeye Pipeline	Standard Oil of Indiana	Penzoil
Conoco	Borne Chemical	Sohio
Marathon Oil	Cheesebrough-Pond	Washington Oil
Trans Union	Exxon	

These fourteen companies were part of the Standard Oil Trust, which by 1880 refined 95 percent of the nation's oil.*

In Chapter 21, we discussed *voting trusts*, in which shareholders assign their right to vote their stock to a trustee, who usually votes the stock as he wishes. John D. Rockefeller chose this device to control all aspects of the oil business, from extraction to consumer marketing. He had to use a voting trust because until the 1880s state laws did not permit one corporation to own shares in another or the residents of one state to own stock in a corporation incorporated in another state. Rockefeller purchased corporations using dummy shareholders who assigned their voting rights to the unincorporated trust. Thus, he was able to control the entire industry.

The Standard Oil Trust was not unique. By 1890 approximately 100 trusts controlled industries as widely separated as whiskey, sugar, tobacco, cattle feed, beef, nails, bicycles, electric appliances, copper, linseed oil, and envelopes.†
Trusts touched virtually every significant aspect of life in the United States.

In 1890, Congress enacted the Sherman Antitrust Act. It allowed the Attorney General of the United States, who heads the Department of Justice, to seek relief against businesses and individuals who engaged in practices aimed at restraining trade or monopolizing an industry. A *monopoly* is the power to control prices and exclude competition.

Also in the 1890s, almost all states amended their corporation laws to permit both corporations and out-of-state investors to own shares. The monopolists quickly turned their trusts into corporations.‡

Nonetheless, the term "antitrust" survived. Today, as Chapter 44 demonstrates, it describes a series of laws which seek to preserve, protect, and promote a competitive, free market. Thus, a better name would be the procompetition laws.

CONSUMER PROTECTION

The FTC's responsibilities for policing the marketplace extend well beyond the antitrust laws. These other responsibilities, which are quite varied, are often lumped together under the heading "consumer protection."

Federal consumer protection laws have always been controversial. Many people take the position that such regulation belongs at the state level. And in fact, many states have quite extensive consumer protection regulations. Others

---

* M. Moskowitz et al., *Everybody's Business* (San Francisco: Harper & Row, 1980), pp. 500–501.

† M. Josephson, *The Robber Barons* (New York: Harcourt Brace Jovanovich, 1934, 1962), p. 381.

‡ Freidman, *A History of American Law* (New York: Simon & Schuster, 1973), pp. 405–408.

contend that private litigation under tort, sales, or contract law resolves consumer disputes more effectively than new remedies—whether federal or state.

To a degree, these arguments are a response to a changing philosophy of government regulation. Since 1914, the FTC has regulated unfair and deceptive trade practices. The agency, not individuals, has taken the lead in challenging false advertising and sharp dealing affecting the public marketplace. While the FTC's enforcement ardor varied according to the President's philosophy, business became accustomed to its policing of the marketplace.

The consumer movement of the 1960s and 1970s demanded something different: statutes granting individual consumers new protections and remedies, primarily relating to lending and sales practices and consumer product safety.* Today, the public generally supports the current consumer legislation. However, two questions persist in the minds of many businesspeople:

- Does the average consumer understand the rights that consumer legislation confers? If not, is the consumer any better off?
- Are consumer protection laws cost effective? Is the increased cost of goods and services to the public as a whole worth the benefits conferred on the few wronged consumers?

The debate on these points shows no signs of abating. Chapter 45 explores its cause.

EMPLOYMENT
LAW

"Employment law," like "consumer protection," is a term which encompasses a broad range of legislation. Such laws fall into three categories.

First, employee benefit laws seek to protect workers' physical and financial well-being. Under the common law, workers could not sue either their employers or their fellow employees for damages suffered in on-the-job accidents. Thus, the employer's obligation to injured employees was purely moral.

With the industrialization of America, the number of injured employees increased to such an extent that family and private charity could not meet the demand for help. By the 1930s every state had developed a workers' compensation program which paid benefits to workers injured in employment-related accidents. These programs are administered by state agencies.

Second, labor laws regulate the relationship between unions and employers and between unions and their members. With industrialization and the growth of large businesses came labor unions. From the 1880s through the 1930s, bitter strikes for union recognition plagued the railroad, steel, coal, copper, and automobile industries. The Great Depression of the 1930s made labor peace a necessity. Starting in 1932, Congress began enacting the pieces of what is now the National Labor Relations Act. In 1935, Congress created the National Labor Relations Board to oversee this complex field.

Third, antidiscrimination laws are designed to prevent or remedy employment practices which discriminate against individuals on account of their race, color, gender, or religion. The first of these statutes, the federal Civil Rights Act of 1964, came about as a result of discrimination against blacks, not only in

---

* Consumer product safety issues are within the jurisdiction of the Consumer Product Safety Commission, which is discussed in Chapter 45.

employment but in all areas of American social and economic life. Federal enforcement of antidiscrimination laws lies primarily with the Equal Employment Opportunity Commission. Virtually all states have employment antidiscrimination laws and commissions, like the Ohio Civil Rights Commission, which enforce them.

Chapter 46 explores all three types of employment laws.

ENVIRONMENTAL
REGULATION

We began this introduction by noting the apparent misuse of the word "environment" in the phrase "legal environment of business." The word is also apparently misused in Chapter 47, since "environmental" describes a host of laws designed to prevent degradation of our natural surroundings.

Environmental regulation really began in the early 1900s with not very effective attempts to clean up water supplies. As the century progressed, it became increasingly clear that by-products of our way of life were profoundly and negatively affecting our habitat. So, beginning in the mid-1960s, environmental laws began sprouting at every level, regulating everything from air and water pollution to nuclear waste.

Environmental law reflects the character of modern society in ways that no other area of law does. It often affects projects that have significant economic impact, sometimes even those of national importance. It involves an interplay between highly sophisticated, technically competent government agencies and business. And, it reflects public concern about the quality of life in the United States.

Nothing better illustrates the relationship between environmental laws and our society than the goals Congress set for the nation in the National Environmental Policy Act (NEPA):*

> *(1) [to] fulfill the responsibilities of each generation as trustee of the environment for succeeding generations;*
>
> *(2) [to] assure for all Americans safe, healthful, productive, and esthetically and culturally pleasing surroundings;*
>
> *(3) [to] attain the widest range of beneficial uses of the environment without degradation, risk to health or safety, or other undesirable and unintended consequences;*
>
> *(4) [to] preserve important historic, cultural, and natural aspects of our national heritage, and maintain, wherever possible, an environment which supports diversity and variety of individual choice;*
>
> *(5) [to] achieve a balance between population and resource use which will permit high standards of living and a wide sharing of life's amenities; and*
>
> *(6) [to] enhance the quality of renewable resources and approach the maximum attainable recycling of depletable resources.*

Read literally, these goals imply that everything from student loan funding to food stamp appropriations is environmental legislation. The word "environment" takes in all of humankind's surroundings, so such a reading is not wrong.

---

* 42 U.S.C. §4331(b).

NEPA has profoundly changed the manner in which both government and business view projects which affect the human environment. NEPA and state laws which have followed its philosophy now compel the many federal, state, and local agencies to review such projects very broadly, taking into account not only their economic and social effects, but also their consequences for the human habitat. Thus, the use of the word "environmental" to describe these laws is appropriate.

Chapter 47 examines how federal and state environmental laws are administered.

INTERNATIONAL
LAW

Since the mid-1970s, the flood tide of imports and the ebb tide of American exports have dominated the economic news. First came the surge in Japanese consumer electronics and then its sudden erosion of the very foundation of our economy: steel, autos, and heavy equipment. The mainstay of our exports—cereal grains—suffered heavy losses as foreign demand dropped. Even our banks—supposedly the most sophisticated in the world—found themselves teetering on the edge of ruin as Third World borrowers stretched out their repayment schedules or reneged on their promises altogether.

Why we have found ourselves in this horrible predicament has as many explanations as there are commentators. However, it seems beyond argument that we, as a nation, did not realize until it was too late that our economic survival required that we compete in world markets. The dramatic improvements over the last 100 years in transportation and communications have made the world much smaller.

Competing in world markets requires an understanding of the rules that make international transactions possible. It also requires a cultural sensitivity, that is, an awareness that we are *not* all alike under the skin. And, indeed, the differences in legal systems reflect our varied cultures. Chapter 48 introduces you to the process of transacting business outside the United States.

CONCLUSION

Chapters 44 through 48 illustrate the ways in which society has attempted to cope with the profound changes in physical, social, and economic life which have occurred since the Industrial Revolution hit this country full force in the 1840s.

As responses to these massively complex problems, they are inadequate. And, though administrative agencies were meant to be nonpolitical instruments carrying our national policy, government regulation of business has proved to be intensely controversial. A politician's attitude toward business was judged by his or her regulatory philosophy.

The Reagan-Bush years are often cited as a period of tremendous reduction in the federal government's regulation of business. In some industries, such as the air carrier industry, this is obvious and true. However, for most businesses the impact of federal regulation grew with new requirements in regards to such things as sexual harassment, disabled workers and clean air quality. President Clinton is attempting to exercise a cautious approach to further regulation but some problems, such as the rights of the Spotted Owl versus lumber cutters, continue to foster even more federal regulations.

There are many business and political commentators who believe that business deregulation has gone too far. These commentators point to the ruins of ruthless competition in our deregulated economy: failed banks, savings and loans, airlines, etc. In addition, they cite the hostile takeover craze of the 1980s which were possible because of relaxed regulation which has caused thousands of workers to lose their jobs and/or pensions. However, given the reality of an ever increasingly global economy, it may not be possible for the United States to revert back to a significantly more regulated economy even if politicians sought to do so.

KEY WORDS

antitrust (1009)
consumer protection (1010)
Equal Employment Opportunity
   Commission (EEOC) (1012)
Federal Trade Commission
   (FTC) (1009)

monopoly (1010)
National Environmental Policy
   Act (NEPA) (1012)
voting trusts (1010)

CHAPTER 44
Antitrust

Why does Du Pont no longer own 23 percent of General Motors? Why did seven independent regional telephone companies replace AT&T as the provider of local telephone service? Acting under the antitrust laws, courts ordered both Du Pont and AT&T to divest themselves of these interests and assets.

From its inception in the 1890s, antitrust law has been politically controversial. Enforcement tends to reflect the views of the national administration about the marketplace and the dangers large economic organizations pose to society. It is no small irony of the Reagan-Bush era that its leaders preached the virtues of small businesses and entrepreneurs while they presided over a massive consolidation among the nation's largest businesses.

Some have defended this consolidation in the name of competitiveness. Presumably, efficiencies achieved by concentrating particular businesses in a few hands will make the nation better able to compete against the Japanese and others who are not fettered by restrictive antitrust laws. Indeed, under the so-called keiretsu system in Japan, firms in that nation openly and legally cooperate by exchanging technological information, capitalizing each other, and favoring other keiretsu members in business dealings over outsiders including, of course, American businesses. Moreover, until very recently, Japan's "dango" system had for years excluded foreign construction firms from competing there because prior consultation among local bidders on public works projects was allowed.

Sceptics see consolidation as a means of obtaining market control in order to raise prices. They point to the deregulation of the airline industry which, after a number of new lines came and were absorbed, consolidated into a few major carriers.

It will probably not be long before the verdict comes in. Competition from the Pacific rim countries, the new European Community (after 1992), and the new capitalist countries in Eastern Europe is putting our businesses to the test. Soon we will know whether size and consolidation benefit us in world commerce. It will probably be somewhat longer before a judgment is reached on the domestic social costs and benefits.

Some prominent members of the Clinton administration have advocated more cooperation between labor, industry, and the government in order to better compete in a highly competitive global market. Such support will likely continue a trend toward the relaxation of the exchange of technological information and other cooperative ventures, such as research consortiums, begun in 1984 by the passage of the National Cooperative Research Act. This Act will be discussed later in this chapter. Indeed there has been ample evidence of the benefits of cooperation among competitors. In 1992, for example, the U.S. regained the lead in the world in the production of computer chips. The main reason was joint research in an effort known as Semiconductor Manufacturing Technology or Sematech. This consortium, between competitors IBM, AT&T, and Intel, was funded 50/50 by these companies and the Department of Defense. It was noted in subsequent government reports that one of the primary reasons for the success was improved communication between the competitors. Other joint research currently underway includes the Big Three auto dealers to develop safer and more fuel efficient cars, a consortium of the Big Three and 14 major oil companies to produce cleaner gasoline to comply with the Clean Air Act of 1990, and joint research among the Big Three, the Department of Energy and the Electric Power Research Institute to build a better vehicle battery. It should be emphasized, however, that most cooperative efforts between competitors is still illegal under antitrust laws and that some government supervision is required to comply with the National Cooperative Research Act.

THE SCOPE OF FEDERAL ANTITRUST LAW

As the introduction to this part suggests, a better name for the antitrust laws today might be the procompetition laws. This chapter focuses on four federal statutes: the Sherman Act; the Clayton Act; the Robinson-Patman Act; and the Federal Trade Commission Act. The Robinson-Patman Act actually amends the Clayton Act §2. Still, courts refer to the two acts as if they were separate, and so will we. Virtually all states have antitrust laws, too. However, these laws are beyond the scope of this chapter.

The four federal statutes overlap in many respects. Nonetheless, it is easier to look at each statute individually—as we will—rather than looking at all four thematically.

The Antitrust Suit

The Federal Trade Commission or the Attorney General of the United States may bring a civil antitrust action. Also, any private individual or other entity who is injured by activities which violate the antitrust laws may seek an injunction or damages. As will become clear, antitrust suits are extremely expensive to prosecute, but the statutes provide an incentive for private plaintiffs: *treble* (triple) damages.

A business activity violates the antitrust laws if it constitutes an illegal restraint of trade. In determining whether such a restraint exists, the courts apply one of two standards after the plaintiff has made a *prima facie case* that the defendant's actions amounted to activities prohibited by statute.* These standards, which the Supreme Court has developed in antitrust cases, determine what defenses the defendant may present.

---

* Of course, if the plaintiff fails to establish a prima facie case, the court will grant the defendant's motion for a directed verdict in its favor.

The per se standard. The first standard, the *per se* standard, is quite simple. "Per se" is a Latin phrase meaning "by itself" or "alone." When the phrase is used to describe a violation, it means that the plaintiff does not have to prove anything beyond the fact of the forbidden conduct in order to prevail.

In the antitrust context, the Supreme Court first determined in the 1927 case of *U.S. v. Trenton Potteries** that certain conduct amounts to a per se violation of the statutes. If the plaintiff establishes that the forbidden conduct took place, the defendant has no mitigating defenses. For example, an agreement between two supposed competitors to fix the price for their goods is a per se violation of the antitrust laws. A defendant's only defense when a plaintiff has alleged a per se violation is proof that the offense never occurred.

The courts view a per se violation as having such an injurious effect on competition that the defendant can produce no counterbalancing justification. Thus, a defendant to whose conduct the per se standard applied could not defend on the grounds that a price-fixing agreement actually lowered consumer costs.

The rule of reason standard. Where it applies, the *rule of reason* standard permits the defendant to prove that the activity was not sufficiently unreasonable to amount to an antitrust violation. In other words, the defendant may rebut a prima facie case by introducing mitigating evidence. For example, under the Robinson-Patman Act, it is a violation for a supplier to charge one wholesale customer a higher price than it charges another. But, if the supplier can show that it cost more to produce the items for Company A than it did for Company B, the supplier can avoid liability.

Starting in 1911, in *Standard Oil of New Jersey v. U.S.†,* the Supreme Court has applied

---

* *U.S. v. Trenton Potteries,* 273 U.S. 392 (1927).
† *Standard Oil of New Jersey v. U.S.,* 221 U.S. 1 (1911).

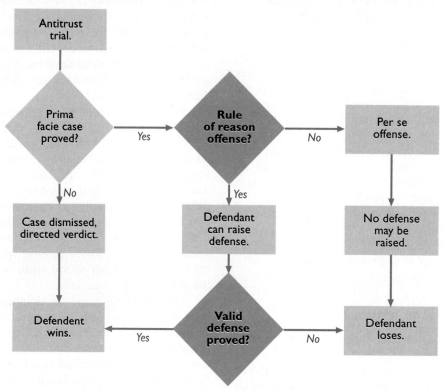

Figure 44.1 Comparison of the Rule of Reason and the Per Se Standards.
In essence, where the per se standard applies, a defendant faced with a prima facie case which it cannot rebut has no defense.

Court has applied a rule of reason approach to conduct alleged to violate the antitrust laws until experience—meaning a series of cases—reveals that this conduct is anticompetitive in virtually all circumstances. Then, the Court will apply the per se standard. Figure 44.1 compares the two standards.

THE SHERMAN ACT §1: RESTRAINT OF TRADE

The Sherman Act §1 prohibits any contract, combination, or conspiracy to restrain trade or commerce. Since a business cannot contract, combine, or conspire with itself, a §1 violation always requires two or more parties, each of which is capable of independent action. The Supreme Court has held, for instance, that a subsidiary corporation is incapable of conspiring with a parent.

Because of its breadth, §1 needs to be interpreted reasonably by both plaintiffs and the courts. Almost any contract restrains trade in one way or another. If a store features Levis, it might not buy Wranglers. There is nothing wrong with that. Sherman Act enforcement centers on conduct which severely and wrongfully limits competition. These wrongs—each of which is discussed below—include price fixing, resale price maintenance, allocation of markets between competitors, boycotts, and tying arrangements.*

Price Fixing

Price fixing can have no goal other than the elimination of competition. After all, our system rests on the assumption that the market sets the price. For that reason the per se standard applies to price-fixing cases.

Price fixing falls into two categories: vertical and horizontal. *Vertical price fixing* describes a situation in which a seller sets the price at which the buyer may resell the seller's goods. Vertical price fixing is discussed under the heading "resale price maintenance."

Agreement between competitors. *Horizontal price fixing* is price fixing between competitors. Simply put, competitors may not meet to discuss and set prices.

The most obvious type of price fixing occurs when competitors actually discuss and agree on prices. For example, just before Braniff International went bankrupt in 1982, its president taped a phone conversation he had with the president of American Airlines. Braniff's president wanted advice on how to avoid bankruptcy.

> Braniff: *Do you have a suggestion for me?*
> American: *Yes, I have a suggestion for you. Raise your [deleted] fares 20 percent. I'll raise mine the next morning.*
> Braniff: *Robert, we. . . .*
> American: *You'll make more money and I will, too.*
> Braniff: *We can't talk about pricing.*
> American: *Oh [deleted], Howard. We can talk about any [deleted] thing we want to talk about.*

Braniff and American did not agree to fix their fares. Nonetheless, the Department of Justice filed suit against American, charging solicitation to fix prices. The case was later dropped.

In 1992, nine airlines settled a class-action lawsuit alleging price fixing for domestic air travel fares between January 1, 1988, to June 30, 1992.* The airlines have contributed a total of $450 million in airline coupons and cash. It is estimated that 10 million claims ultimately will be processed.

Usually, the evidence of price fixing is circumstantial. *Circumstantial evidence* is evidence based not on actual personal knowledge but on facts from which a conclusion may be drawn. Suppose four chief executive officers are talking about a widget their companies sell for between $1.85 and $1.90.

> Universal Widget: *You guys do what you want about pricing, but we plan to up the price to $2.00 per widget.*
> Global Widget: *I don't know how you got that figure, but $2.00 happens to be our optimum price, too.*
> Galactic Widget: *I don't know whether we'll sell ours for $2.00, but I know we can't sell them for anything less than $2.00.*

World Wide Widget's president does not join in the discussion, which then ends. The next day all four companies raise their prices to $2.00. A court would find that their conduct amounted to price fixing. The lesson here is that price-fixing conspirators do not have to use the language of contract in order to violate the law. Their "agreement" can be considerably more vague.

Price leadership. *Price leadership* is at the extreme edge of agreements to fix prices. The term describes the situation in which a particular industry has a leader whose pricing strongly influences that of other companies in the industry.

Most courts have held that price leadership

---

* Tying arrangements are discussed in connection with the Clayton Act §3.

* Airlines involved in the settlement were American, Continental, Delta, Midway, Northwest, Pan American, TWA, United, and USAir.

does not amount to price fixing. For example, airlines and car rental agencies often announce special fares for designated periods. The end dates seem designed to encourage competitors to halt their special rates at approximately the same time. So long as a competitor simply meets competition by following a price leader, it will not violate the Sherman Act §1.

The counterargument to price leadership is *conscious parallelism,* an argument by an antitrust plaintiff that, though an overt agreement among the defendants is unprovable, the circumstantial evidence of action by competitors in the same market is so closely paralleled that it points to the likelihood of an agreement.

When one Boston–New York air shuttle raises its ticket prices and the other immediately raises its fares to the same level, exploring the location of the line between price leadership and conscious parallelism would seem worthwhile.

Keep in mind that conscious parallelism is not illegal as long as the pricing decision is made by competitors independently of each other. The following case discusses whether there really was a pricing agreement or simply conscious parallelism among twenty-one Japanese electronics firms competing in the highly competitive U.S. market.

Matsushita Electric Industrial Co. v. Zenith Radio Corp.

475 U.S. 574 (1986)

FACTS

Zenith and other U.S. television manufacturers sued Matsushita and twenty other Japanese T.V. makers for conspiring, since 1953, to set artificially low prices in the American market. The allegations were that the Japanese companies were able to sell the T.V.s at up to a 25 percent loss in the United States because they had a virtual monopoly in their own market due to import tariffs and other favorable government policies. It was further alleged that once the U.S. manufacturers were driven out of the market due to the "predatory pricing," prices would rise to reflect the Japanese monopoly. Matsushita won on a summary judgment at the trial level. The court of appeals reversed.

ISSUE

Was there a sufficient amount of evidence of a conspiracy to fix prices by Matsushita and the others to create a genuine issue for trial?

DECISION

No. Reversed. In order to prove a conspiracy to use predatory pricing to drive out the competition under the Sherman Antitrust Act, the court must speculate about a number of factors. Among the evidence the court will look at is whether the conspirators possessed the ability and the motivation to maintain an agreement and to forego profits for several decades as an investment in the future. First, to maintain a conspiracy to fix prices for years is immensely more difficult than if a manufacturer does it alone, due to the tendency by competitors to cheat on each other. The prospects for attaining a monopoly must also be favorable. In this case, two decades after the alleged conspiracy, the Japanese companies are not close to having a monopoly. In fact, Zenith and RCA control 40 percent of the market. Last, the fact that the companies are enjoying profits in the Japanese market does not prove they are conspiring in this country to forego profits here.

The past two decades have indeed been a period of great economic anxiety over Japanese competition. As the plaintiffs demonstrated in the above case, there is a strong perception that they are not competing fairly in this country. Whether this was true of the Japanese or was simply making them a scapegoat for our economic woes, "Japanese bashing" was in vogue in the 1980s, even among some leaders of Congress. In the early part of the 1990s, with Japan struggling with its own recession and seeking also to restructure its economy in the wake of profound global economic and political changes, a new trade relationship between Japan and the United States may be on the horizon.

Fees set by trade or professional associations. Until the mid-1970s, trade and professional organizations representing lawyers, doctors, engineers, and others commonly established minimum fee schedules. These professionals defended fee schedules on the ground that set fees maintain high-quality service by avoiding price cutting.

In a series of cases beginning in 1975, the Supreme Court rejected the argument that minimum fee schedules are reasonable restraints on trade.

The medical and legal professions have tried repeatedly to convince Congress to exempt them from the antitrust statutes. But unlike organized labor, whose collective bargaining agreements are exempt, these professions have not convinced Congress to extend this protection to them.

Resale Price Maintenance

Resale price maintenance, a form of vertical price fixing, is a per se violation of §1. The term describes a situation in which the seller will sell

---

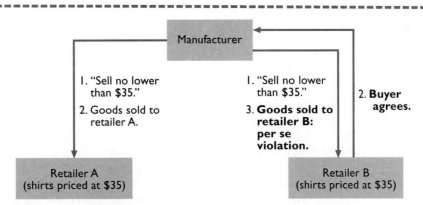

Figure 44.2 Resale Price Maintenance.
Resale price maintenance requires concerted action. Here, the sale to Retailer B is a per se violation, since Retailer B made a return promise to maintain the price. The manufacturer did not violate the law as to Retailer A, since there was no return promise.

only to a buyer who agrees not to sell the goods for less—or, conceivably, more—than a specified price. The buyer's return promise to maintain the price is the violation. Suppose Unlimited Clothing Corp. wants to ensure that its Ostrich logo sport shirts are always associated with high quality. For that reason, retailers must promise not to sell the shirts for less than $35 per shirt as a condition of Unlimited's permission to market the shirt. Requiring this promise is a per se violation.

A seller is not powerless to enforce the price structure it wants. *All* it cannot do is extract the return promise. If the seller expresses its pricing policy to the buyer but does not demand the buyer's promise to observe it, the seller may do as it wishes. If the retailer sells the shirts for less than $35, Unlimited may stop supplying them.

A strong argument can be made that the law here stresses form over substance. The effect on the marketplace seems the same under both scenarios. See Figure 44.2. The next case discusses a new variation on a seller's refusal to sell to a retailer.

Business Electronics Corp. v. Sharp Electronics Corp.

485 U.S. 717 (1988)

FACTS   Sharp Electronics Corp., a manufacturer, supplied both Business Electronics Corp., and Hartwell, both retailers in Houston, with calculators for resale. Sharp had a "suggested retail price" policy but did not obligate its customers to sell at those prices. Business Electronics sold the Sharp calculators at a discount, well below Sharp's suggested retail price, while Hartwell did not. Hartwell, fearful of the competition, lodged several complaints to Sharp threatening to stop selling its calculators if it did not stop supplying Business Electronics. Sharp complied. At the trial level, Business Electronics won. The court of appeals reversed.

ISSUE   Was the agreement between Sharp Electronics and Hartwell, which resulted in Sharp refusing to supply Business Electronics, a form of resale price maintenance that is illegal per se?

DECISION   No. Affirmed. Since 1911, resale price maintenance has been illegal per se. However, not all vertical agreements are necessarily illegal per se unless they demonstrate a pernicious effect on competition and are lacking in redeeming value. Vertical restraints which would be per se illegal are those in which there is an agreement on price. Some vertical non-price agreements have shown the capability of stimulating positive economic benefits even if they do allow dealers to raise prices. These benefits may include a greater profit for hiring and training more employees, providing better customer services, and the discouraging of "free-riders," who benefit but do not pay for their competitors' advertising and promotions. Thus, non-price vertical restraints should be scrutinized under the "rule of reason" to weigh both the positive and negative effects of the agreement before determining its legality.

In the wake of the *Business Electronics* case, many small businesses engaged in discounting were greatly alarmed. Indeed, a number of smaller discounters blamed their bankruptcies on fallout from this case, claiming that they were no longer able to buy inventory from their normal suppliers because of complaints from larger, more powerful competitors. Other small discounters sought a different market niche by going into full-service activities and upped their prices to pay for it.* As a result of pressure from small-business interests and some consumer groups, Congress attempted to overrule the decision legislatively in 1988 by proposing the Retail Competitive Enforcement Act, but it failed. Obviously, discounting is not dead, and in fact it is now flourishing. One reason is that the large, powerful discounters like Wal-Mart and K-Mart were never affected by this decision, since there are no retail competitors who could pressure a supplier not to deal with them.

Market Allocation

The franchise system in the United States is based on the concept that the franchise purchaser buys an exclusive territory in which to operate.† This is called a *territorial market allocation*. Thus, when someone buys a Wendy's franchise, Wendy's will not sell to someone else who could put a restaurant across the street from the first.

If given a broad reading, the Sherman Act §1 would make franchising illegal. In effect, a franchise is an agreement to eliminate other competitors in that particular chain. Therefore, some argue, the chain's restaurants can maintain higher prices than they could if they had a competitor across the street. The contrary argument is that a McDonald's is a greater price threat than another Wendy's.

The standard applied to market allocations

---

* R. Aalberts and E. Day, "Is Discounting Destined for Difficult Times?" *Business*, vol. 39, 1989, p. 27.
† For a discussion of franchises, see Chapter 22.

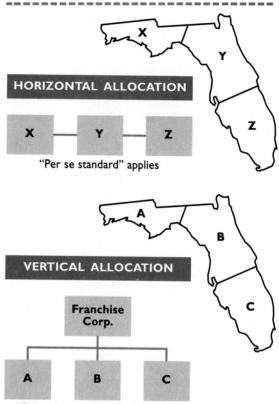

Figure 44.3 Market Allocation.
While the actual territories covered by the agreements are identical, the standard that applies differs depending on whether the allocation is horizontal or vertical.

depends on whether they are horizontal or vertical. Horizontal refers to dividing markets between competitors, while vertical refers to allocations within a single entity. See Figure 44.3.

The per se test applies to horizontal territorial market allocations because these are agreements between competitors to allocate market areas. In essence, horizontal market allocations are covenants not to compete that are illegal, as we noted in Chapter 9. Vertical allocations, however, seem less burdensome to trade, and if they are reasonable—as many franchise arrangements are—they do not violate the antitrust laws.

Boycotts

A seller can choose unilaterally not to sell its product to a buyer, and vice versa. However, an agreement between two or more businesses not to deal with another is called a *joint boycott* and is a per se violation. See Figure 44-4. The key here is the agreement. Suppose Orange, Grape, and Plum manufacture personal computers. Discount City sells personal computers as loss leaders. The manufacturers agree not to sell their computers to Discount City so that they can keep their prices up. The three companies have committed a per se violation.

The target of a boycott has a cause of action under the Sherman Act §1. If the boycott is effective, the boycotted firm will suffer an economic loss. But are there others who suffer real injuries from boycotts? The Supreme Court faced that question in the next case.

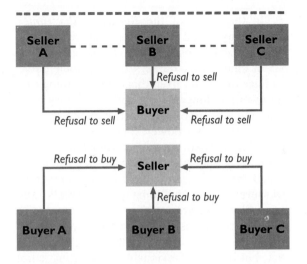

Figure 44.4 Group Boycotts.
A group boycott may result from either an agreement not to sell or an agreement not to buy. In either case, the per se standard applies.

Blue Shield of Virginia v. McCready

457 U.S. 465 (1982)

FACTS	McCready's employer provided her with health insurance under a Blue Shield plan. The plan covered the cost of outpatient treatment for mental disorders only if a psychiatrist or a psychologist under a physician's supervision provided the treatment. McCready required psychotherapy and chose to be treated by a clinical psychologist not under a physician's supervision. Blue Shield refused to reimburse her costs. McCready filed suit, alleging that Blue Shield and the Neuropsychiatric Society of Virginia had conspired to boycott clinical psychologists. The trial court dismissed, holding that McCready was not a segment of the market competitively endangered by the boycott. That segment included only psychologists, so she could not prove an injury. The court of appeals reversed.
ISSUE	Did McCready suffer an injury for which the antitrust laws provided a remedy?
DECISION	Yes. Affirmed. The Clayton Act §4 provides a treble damages remedy to any person injured by reason of anything forbidden in the antitrust laws, including the Sherman

Act §1. Just because the boycott was aimed at psychologists does not mean that McCready did not suffer an injury as a result of it. Harm to her and those like her not only was foreseeable, it was a necessary step in effecting the boycott. Therefore, her injury was of a type covered by the Clayton Act §4.

THE SHERMAN ACT §2: MONOPOLIES

Committing a Sherman Act §1 violation always requires more than one party. However, normally only one party commits a Sherman Act §2 violation.

The Sherman Act §2 describes three separate violations: acquiring a monopoly wrongfully; attempting to monopolize (an activity falling short of a monopoly); and conspiracy to monopolize (an effort by two or more to monopolize). Attempt and conspiracy require proof that the defendants specifically intended to monopolize, so these offenses are difficult to prove and consequently seldom alleged. For that reason, we will discuss only the violation of acquiring a monopoly wrongfully.

Legal Monopolies

Some monopolies are legal. Exceptions to the laws discussed in this chapter permit some arrangements which would otherwise be in violation. For instance, Congress exempted major league baseball from the antitrust laws. The government even grants monopolies, as to electric companies or water companies or cable television companies.

Simply have the power to control prices or exclude competition is not an antitrust violation. Thus, a company which develops a patent may have a legal monopoly. Suppose Beaufort Tooling Company patents a tundra drilling bit whose durability surpasses that of any similar bit on the market. Its 90 percent market share would not be a §2 violation. (Remember: As Chapter 25 notes, a patent is a legal monopoly).

Similarly, a monopoly that is thrust upon a company is not a violation. A company which has persisted in manufacturing hand-crank telephone systems might be in this category.

Illegal Monopolies

Having illegal monopoly power is a rule of reason offense. To prove a monopoly case, the plaintiff must show that the defendant has the power to control prices or to exclude competition within a particular line of commerce in a particular part of the country. The plaintiff does not have to show a specific intent to monopolize. Rather, the evidence focuses on defining the product market and the affected geographical market.

The law does not prescribe a percentage of the market which a monopoly defendant must control. However, the higher the percentage, the more likely the court is to find a monopoly.

Product market. Calculating relative market share requires, first, a definition of the product market. In other words, what are the product's competitors?

In determining what products make up a market, a court must examine the interchangeability of other products with the one in question. Interchangeable products are products that buyers would substitute if the price of the product in question went up while the other products' prices stayed constant. Suppose the prices of orange and white tennis balls are the same. If the price of orange tennis balls then went up 40 percent, but the price of white tennis balls remained the same, tennis players would buy more white balls. But, if the price of beer went up by 40 percent, demand for milk would not be affected.

Geographic market. In general, a product's geographical market is the area in which the defendant allegedly has the monopoly. A monopoly may be considerably less than national in scope. For instance, a court found that Wisconsin, Illinois, and Michigan constituted a market in a monopoly case involving beer. So long as the area sufficiently affects interstate commerce, a court will accept the plaintiff's description of it. In a case involving grocery stores, the Supreme Court accepted Los Angeles as an appropriately defined market.

Predatory Pricing

You may recall in the *Matsushita* case, discussed earlier, a conspiracy to engage in predatory pricing was discussed but was dismissed because the court felt that, among other reasons, it was virtually impossible for twenty-one competitors to do so without eventual cheating. With that many competitors, it is much more likely that similar prices among so many is almost always the result of conscious parallelism. More often, predatory pricing is successfully accomplished when there are only a few competitors in a well-defined market. The market in the next case was defined by statute: the United States Tax Court!

National Reporting Co. v. Alderson Reporting Co., Inc.

567 F. Supp. 1011 (E.D.Mo. 1983)

FACTS
In 1974, the U.S. Tax Court consisted of fourteen judges who heard cases throughout the country. The court contracted for court reporting services on a national basis. In 1974, the court specified the use of a sophisticated recording device to improve the quality of transcripts. As a result, only National bid. Its competitors, led by Alderson, attempted unsuccessfully to convince Congress to alter the Tax Court's bidding specifications. Alderson then began negotiations to buy out National, but these broke down in 1979 when Alderson pleaded guilty to criminal antitrust charges. In 1980, Alderson successfully bid $1.27 per manuscript page, although its actual costs exceeded $4 per page. As a result, National went out of business. In 1981, Alderson submitted a bid about three times higher. The Tax Court awarded the contract to a higher bidder because Alderson had given it poor service. National sued Alderson for damages, alleging that its 1980 bid was predatory and anticompetitive.

ISSUE
Did Alderson use anticompetitive pricing to gain its monopoly?

DECISION
Yes. Judgment for National. A violation of the Sherman Act §2 consists of (1) possession of monopoly power in the relevant market, and (2) the willfull acquisition of that power, as distinguished from growth or development as a consequence of a superior product, business skills, or historical accident. The Tax Court's system gave the successful bidder a natural monopoly power. Businesses are entitled to compete vigorously and fairly for a market which can support only one supplier. Still, the normal competitive rules govern the struggle to be the sole survivor. And bidding below cost is a severely anticompetitive tactic which violates the Sherman Act.

Research Consortiums

Congress has long tried to encourage research and technological development in the United States so that U.S. companies would make stronger competitors in the world marketplace. In 1984, it passed the National Cooperative Research Act, which relaxes antitrust restrictions on competing firms that wish to form joint research and development ventures—commonly called "research consortiums." Before, joint activities of this sort at least potentially subjected the participants to liability for a per se violation.

The Act requires that firms wishing to develop a research consortium must provide the FTC and the Justice Department with advance notice of the consortium's proposed research and licensing activities. This requirement has now been repealed, however, suggesting that Congress feels advancing competitiveness in a cutthroat global economy overrides some antitrust policy considerations. Research consortiums are subject to only single (not treble) damages. In certain situations, if a research consortium is challenged under §1 of the Sherman Act and it prevails, the consortium recovers attorney's fees.

As discussed earlier in this chapter, Sematech, a combination of IBM, AT&T, and Intel, was one of the first consortiums to successfully take advantage of the Act. Since then, the Big Three car makers, major oil companies, along with some government agencies, have combined their efforts to improve gasoline, make cars safer and to develop a workable car battery.

THE CLAYTON ACT §3: TYING, RECIPROCAL DEALING, AND EXCLUSIVE DEALING ARRANGEMENTS

The Clayton Act of 1914 both expands on the Sherman Act and eases the plaintiff's burden in proving antitrust violations. It targets conduct that threatens to lessen competition substan-tially or to create a monopoly if left unchecked. By contrast, the Sherman Act concentrates on the results of anticompetitive conduct. It deals more with eliminating existing monopolies than with preventing them. In one way, though, the scope of Clayton Act is more limited than that of the Sherman Act. The Clayton Act applied to the sale of goods, wares, or commodities, but not to the sale of services.

The Clayton Act §3 defines three violations: tying arrangements, reciprocal dealing arrangements, and exclusive dealing arrangements. They have a common prerequisite: the arrangement must involve a "not insubstantial" amount of interstate activity. While the courts make this determination on a case-by-case basis, a fair rule of thumb is that $500,000 must be involved. The practical effect of the "not insubstantial" requirement is that while the per se standard applies to all §3 violations, a defendant may avoid liability by demonstrating the practice's minimal effect on interstate commerce.

Tying Arrangements

A tying arrangement occurs when a seller agrees to sell a product or item (the *tying product*) only if the buyer agrees to buy an accompanying item (the *tied product*). In other words, buyers must take something they would not ordinarily buy from this vendor in order to get something they really want. Suppose the manufacturer of a highly advanced plain paper copier also requires buyers to purchase a year's supply of ordinary plain paper from it in order to buy the machine. The copier is the tying product; the paper is the tied. See Figure 44.5.

Relationship between products. A tying arrangement is a per se violation if the seller has sufficient market power that buyers will purchase the tying product whether or not they have to buy the tied product. It is a situation which can arise only where few or no alternatives to the tying product are available. If the buyer has a choice—even one involving some inconvenience or a somewhat different product—there is no antitrust violation.

$$\text{Required purchase} = \boxed{\text{Tying product}} + \boxed{\text{Tied product}}$$

Figure 44.5 A Tying Arrangement.
The key elements here are the seller's attempt to control the tying product's market and the tied product's ready availability elsewhere. Note that a reciprocal dealing arrangement is essentially the reverse of a tying agreement. The buyer's power is the key to the violation.

Sellers sometimes argue that they must require buyers to purchase the tied product because the tying product's proper functioning depends on the tied product's quality. Or, they claim that it would be impractical to separate the products. Fifty years ago, IBM voided the warranty of its punch card machines if users did not buy IBM cards. Poor quality cards might jam, it argued, causing customers to fault the machine itself. IBM controlled the punch card machine market, but there was nothing unique about its punch cards. The Supreme Court held that the two products were not inseparably tied together. IBM could set punch card standards for its machines, but it could not require the use of IBM cards as a condition of its warranty.*

Today, banks and credit unions vehemently continue to protest a more recent sales practice of the "Big Three" automakers to spur sluggish new-car sales by offering consumers a choice of a rebate or cut-rate financing. The commercial lenders contend they cannot possibly match the "Big Three's" new car rates, often as low as 2.9 percent. As a result, their percentage of the car loan market has declined significantly over the past 10 years. So far, their claim of an illegal tie-in arrangement has gone unrecognized by Congress or the courts.

Full-line forcing. A common variation on tying agreements is *full-line forcing*. In this arrange-

---

* *International Business Machines Corp. v. United States,* 298 U.S. 131 (1936).

ment, the buyer must take the seller's entire product line in order to get the products it wants. Suppose a department store wants to carry Blaire Clothing's very popular women's apparel. But Blaire agrees to sell to the store only if it also purchases Blaire's new line of children's clothing. This is a clear Clayton Act §3 violation.

Choice of remedies. The Sherman Act §1 and the Clayton Act §3 prohibit tying arrangements. A violation of the Clayton Act is a violation of the Sherman Act. However, as noted earlier, the Clayton Act affects only goods, wares, or commodities, while the Sherman Act extends to services as well. But the Clayton Act can be used to check a potential tying arrangement at its birth.

Reciprocal Dealing Arrangements

Reciprocal dealing arrangements are essentially the reverse of tying arrangements. Here, the buyer has such economic power that he can require the seller to purchase something from him as a condition of his purchase from the seller. For example, suppose that Mamouth Motors told Gasket Co., a small supplier, that it would buy gaskets from Gasket Co. only if Gasket Co. used Mamouth Motors vehicles exclusively. Mamouth would abuse its market power by insisting on this arrangement. Of course, Gasket Co. might consider it smart business to buy or lease Mamouth products in the future. Only an agreement to do so offends the Clayton Act.

Reciprocal dealing arrangements are per se violations. The courts reason that the smaller company, the seller, may need the sale too much to insist that it take place without the return obligation. By forcing the seller to buy from the buyer, the buyer removes the seller from the marketplace as to those goods.

Exclusive Dealing Arrangements

Exclusive dealing arrangements are either *requirements* or *output contracts*. As noted in

Chapter 31, a requirements contract is one in which a company agrees to purchase all it needs of a product from one supplier. Mamouth Motors, for instance, might agree to buy all the windshields it will need, if any, from Victor Glass Company. Mamouth cannot purchase windshields from any other seller. However, Victor may continue to sell glass to any other purchaser.

An output contract is one in which a company agrees to buy all the production of another company. Thus, Mamouth might agree to buy all the output of Delta Axle Corporation, if there is any. Mamouth may still buy axles from other vendors, but Delta, if it produces any axles, must sell them to Mamouth. What would make these arrangements illegal under the Clayton Act §3 is, again, the presence of a return promise not to deal with others.

This rule has two notable exceptions. First, the per se standard normally applies only to contracts exceeding $500,000. Second, the courts generally permit utilities and natural resource companies to enter into long-term contracts of this type without being in violation of the law. These companies need the certainty of supply and demand, respectively, in order to meet customer needs and to plan.

THE CLAYTON ACT §7: MERGERS

A merger results when one company acquires another and the acquired company ceases to exist independently. There are three basic types of mergers. *Vertical mergers* involve contracting parties in a supply chain. For example, if True Value Hardware bought back one of its franchises, it would be a vertical merger.

Because they effectively remove a seller from the market, *horizontal mergers* receive the government's most careful scrutiny. *Conglomerate mergers* involve companies that are not in the same line of commerce. As in General Motors' acquisition of Electronic Data Systems (EDS), the companies involved are often in quite different fields.

The Clayton Act §7 restricts mergers and acquisitions which might lessen competition or lead to a monopoly. It does not apply, as the Sherman Act §2 does, to monopolies which have grown of their own accord. However, the Clayton Act §7 includes the lesser violation of a tendency to create a monopoly. The government tends to use the Clayton Act instead of the Sherman Act's antimonopoly provision wherever possible because it is easier to prove a Clayton Act violation. In addition, states and private parties may seek to prevent or undo mergers as a remedy under §7.

Social and Political Considerations

Although mergers are common at all levels of business, their pace among the largest corporations accelerated rapidly in the 1980s. In 1976, the average merger involved corporations with combined assets of $9 million. By 1986, the figure had passed $50 million and was growing every year. Many commentators have criticized this "merger mania" because the dollars spent acquiring existing plant or reserves do not go into new capital development and research.

During the 1980s the business world witnessed many mergers of well-known, blue-chip corporations. Corporations such as RJR acquired Nabisco, General Motors bought Hughes Tool and Electronic Data Systems, Sony created a communications giant when it took over Columbia Pictures, and Chevron purchased Gulf Oil.

While mergers can be extremely complicated for the participants, for the Department of Justice and the FTC they can pose highly complex questions which mix economics, law, finance, and politics.

Because it is easier to prevent a proposed merger than to order divestiture of an acquired company, a 1976 law requires premerger notification to the FTC and the Justice Department. If the government objects, it notifies an acquiring company that it will challenge the acquisition if it proceeds. One 1989 merger involved two firms with combined annual revenues of more than $10 billion and market value of $18 billion: Time and Warner Communications. Within weeks after Time and Warner announced their engagement, Paramount Communications (a conglomerate that became famous as Gulf + Western Industries) bid $175 a share for Time. The Department of Justice announced that it needed to review the impact of Paramount's offer. That alone caused Paramount to withdraw, and the Time-Warner merger proceeded.

Market Analysis

The question here is whether a merger violates the Clayton Act's prohibition of mergers or acquisitions that will probably lessen competition or tend to create a monopoly. Determining the answer requires an analysis of product and geographic markets similar to that required under the Sherman Act §2 and consideration of some other factors, as well.

The potential entrant doctrine. The *potential entrant doctrine* applies to a type of merger which some argue is a fourth distinct category. This type, called a *product extension merger*, occurs when a corporation purchases a company not in an identical market but in one close enough so that products of the acquired company extend the acquiring company's product line.

The potential entrant doctrine comes into play when the acquired company is in a market characterized by a small number of competitors and the acquiring company is one which could enter the acquired company's market on its own. For example, when Ford Motor Company originally decided to enter the spark plug business, it did so by acquiring Autolite. Autolite and Champion (a GM subsidiary) accounted for 65 percent of all spark plug sales, although Champion had 50 percent of all sales. The government forced Ford to *divest*—sell off—Autolite, because at the time of the merger Ford itself was a potential entrant into the spark plug manufacturing market.

The key here is that the threat of entry keeps the market competitive.* That was one of the Supreme Courts points in the following case, perhaps the most famous potential entrant case.

---

* *Ford Motor Co. v. United States*, 405 U.S. 562 (1972).

FTC v. Procter & Gamble Company

386 U.S. 568 (1967)

FACTS   In 1957, Procter & Gamble was the nation's leading producer of packaged detergents, with 54.4 percent of the market. That year, it acquired Clorox Chemical Company, the only national manufacturer of household liquid bleach. Clorox held 48.8 percent of its market, with the balance going to a number of regional brands. Before acquiring Clorox, Procter & Gamble had considered diversifying its product lines related to its basic detergent-soap-cleanser business. Liquid bleach had been a distinct possibility. Procter & Gamble's dominant position in its basic business, its unique ability to compete directly with Clorox, and its huge advertising budget led the FTC to order Procter & Gamble to divest itself of Clorox. However, the Court of Appeals reversed.

ISSUE   Did Procter's acquisition of Clorox limit potential competition in the liquid bleach market?

DECISION   Yes. FTC order reinstated.

> The Commission . . . found that the acquisition of Clorox by Procter eliminated Procter as a potential competitor. . . . Procter was engaged in a vigorous program of diversifying into product lines closely related to its basic products. Liquid bleach was a natural avenue of diversification since it is complementary to Procter's products, is sold to the same customers through the same channels, and is advertised and merchandised in the same manner. Procter had substantial advantages in advertising and sales promotion which . . . are vital to the success of liquid bleach. . . . Procter had considered the possibility of independently entering but decided against it because the acquisition of Clorox would enable Procter to capture a more commanding share of the market.
>
> It is clear that the existence of Procter at the edge of the industry exerted considerable influence on the market. First, the market behavior of the liquid bleach industry was influenced by each firm's predictions of the market behavior of its competitors, actual and potential. Second, the barriers to entry by a firm of Procter's size and with its advantages were not significant. There is no indication that the barriers were so high that the price Procter would have to charge would be above the price that would maximize the profits of the existing firms. Third, the number of potential entrants was not so large that the elimination of one would be insignificant. Few firms would have the temerity to challenge a firm as solidly entrenched as Clorox. Fourth, Procter was found by the Commission to be the most likely entrant. . . .

Ultimately both Ford and Procter & Gamble began competing directly with their former acquisitions. Procter & Gamble—15 years lat- ... , and Ford established its Motorcraft line of spark plugs. And, in 1988 Clorox invaded Procter & Gamble's detergent market. However, Clorox found the costs of this market too great and pulled the plug on Clorox detergent in 1991.

The failing company doctrine. When a company is failing and cannot attract an acquirer whose ownership would not diminish competition, in order to save jobs and investments the government will allow a merger which it otherwise would have challenged.

There are significant arguments against the failing company doctrine. For example, when Chrysler seemed on the brink of bankruptcy in the late 1970s, the federal government authorized it to seek a merger with GM or Ford. Neither wanted Chrysler, so the government guaranteed Chrysler's bank loans in exchange for stock. With Chrysler's recovery in the early 1980s, competition in the auto industry benefited from the bailout as it would not have done from a merger. Ironically, Chrysler took advantage of the failing company doctrine to acquire American Motors Corporation (AMC) in 1988. All Chrysler wanted was AMC's Jeep line and therefore it shut down AMC's aging Kenosha, Wisconsin, plant. AMC is now just a footnote to automotive history.

In another area, newspapers, Congress has permitted two newspapers to merge in all but name in order to avoid one-newspaper towns. One of the most controversial involves Detroit's two newspapers, which once were fearsome competitors. Within months of the merger, advertising charges soared while, media critics claimed, the quality of the reporting declined. The jury is still out on the benefits of that law.

A larger philosophical problem bothers critics of efforts to save failing businesses. It would seem that if the free market mechanism is really to work, companies which cannot compete should be allowed to fail. But failures of the magnitude of Chrysler's have social—and therefore political—impacts which outweigh the purely economic.

Merger guidelines. In order to facilitate market analyses by potential merger participants, the Department of Justice periodically issues guidelines that indicate when the government is likely to question a consolidation. The guidelines tend to vary according to the President's views on mergers.

In 1984, guidelines were issued which were designed to promote efficiency and to factor in the effect of foreign competition and world markets on the merging companies. In 1992, a new five-step test was issued to determine whether a merger has anticompetitive effects. The revised guidelines stress a more realistic analysis of a particular market if a merger were to occur, including an analysis of potential "uncommitted entrants," the probable pricing impact, and the potential benefit to consumers versus the anticompetitive effects. However, the guidelines still focus on the so-called Herfindahl-Hirschman Index (HHI) for determining whether a horizontal merger should be attacked.

The HHI is derived by squaring the market shares of all the firms in the relevant product market. The result is that when there are many firms in a less concentrated market, the HHI will be low and the Justice Department will not intervene to deter the merger. In a highly concentrated market of just a few firms, however, a proposed merger would trigger a high HHI and a Justice Department action to prevent merger. It was for the latter reason that in 1992 the Justice Department pressured Gillette not to acquire Wilkinson Sword's U.S. shaving business. (Gillette was permitted to acquire their overseas shaving business.)

THE CLAYTON ACT §8: INTERLOCKING DIRECTORATES

The Clayton Act §8 prohibits interlocking boards of directors. Interlocking directorates occur when a person is a member of the boards of two or more corporations at the same time *if*: the corporations engage in similar product markets, and the aggregate capital of both corporations is $1 million or more. Banks, banking associations, and common carriers are exempted from §8's control because they are closely regulated.

There is no §8 violation when the corporations do not compete. For example, a member of the board of directors of Golden Nugget Casinos could serve on GE's board. However, if she served on Ramada Inns' board, she would violate §8, since Ramada owns casinos. The rationale for §8 is that a director can easily obtain information from one company and give it to another, a patently unfair trade practice.*

THE ROBINSON-PATMAN ACT: PRICE DISCRIMINATION

A common misconception is that a seller of goods—whether a manufacturer, a distributor, or a retailer—can sell to anyone at any price without fear of government interference. A party *can* sell or not sell to whomever it pleases. However, if a commercial seller—other than a retailer—sells at one price to one buyer, the presumption is that the seller cannot legally sell the same product at a different price to another buyer. See Figure 44.6.

That is the rule established by the Robinson-Patman Act, which is actually §2 of the Clayton Act. The Robinson-Patman Act makes it a violation to knowingly give or receive a different price from that which applies to sales to others. Without that protection, Congress believed, "little businesses" could not compete with, say, Sears, K-Mart, and Wal-Mart.

---

* Of course, as Chapter 20 points out, a director who fails to give her company her utmost loyalty breaches her fiduciary duty to that company and may be liable to it in damages.

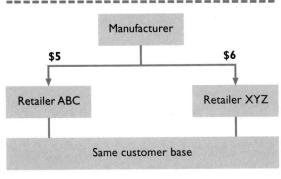

Figure 44.6 Price Discrimination.

Proving a Civil Violation

In order to establish a *price discrimination* case, the plaintiff must show two or more actual sales in interstate commerce closely related in time. The goods must be of like grade and quality, but sold at different prices to the same customer base. The sales must be of goods for resale, since the Clayton Act does not apply to sales of services or to sales by retailers or private parties.

The plaintiff must establish that the prices in the transactions were in fact different. For example, if a plaintiff could show that a manufacturer of garden tools charged Sears one price for a hoe and an independent family-owned hardware store another, it might state a cause of action. Also, the price discrimination must substantially lessen competition or tend to create a monopoly. The Robinson-Patman Act forbids unequal treatment of different customers in comparable transactions only when there is an actual or potential effect on competition.

There has been much debate about the "like grade and quality" requirements. Suppose Izod sells to two merchants sport shirts that are identical except that the shirts sold to the first merchant bear Izod's alligator emblem, while those sold to the second lack the emblem. Can Izod charge the two merchants different prices? In the following case, the Supreme Court held that a label does not differentiate products for the purpose of determining grade and quality.

FTC v. The Borden Company

383 U.S. 637 (1966)

FACTS   Borden sold evaporated milk under the Borden name, a nationally advertised brand. At the same time, it marketed evaporated milk under various private brand names owned by its customers. The private brand milk was physically identical to the Borden brand milk. However, Borden wholesaled the private brands at lower prices than the Borden brand. The FTC found the Borden's and the private label milk to be of like grade and quality, and held that the price differential was discriminatory. It issued Borden a cease and desist order, which the court of appeals set aside.

ISSUE   Are identical products sold in different packaging of like grade and quality for the purposes of the Robinson-Patman Act?

DECISION   Yes. Nothing in the Robinson-Patman Act indicates that grade—as distinguished from quality—is to be determined not by the characteristics of the product itself, but rather by consumer preferences, brand acceptability, or what customers think of it and are willing to pay for it. The economic factors relating to the private brands and Borden's national advertising are not considered under the "like grade and quality" test.

_____

Does *Borden* really answer the question about Izod? Could it not be argued that the alligator is a vanity factor which should be allowed to justify higher prices? The Supreme Court has not answered those questions. But the decision of the Court of Appeals on remand in *Borden* seems to clarify matters.* That court found no violation of the Robinson-Patman Act because milk buyers could purchase for resale either Borden's brand or the private label brands or both. So there was no competitive advantage or disadvantage associated with the price difference, and therefore there was no injury.

The presumption seems to be that when a company like Ralph Lauren sells for resale clothes with its logo on them, it may not discriminate between buyers. But if it sells two identical lines, one bearing its polo player and the other not, Ralph Lauren can charge different prices for the two lines. It simply cannot charge different prices to buyers of the same line. However, a seller does have defenses in price discrimination cases.

Defenses

The rule of reason standard applies to alleged violations of the Robinson-Patman Act. Thus, faced with a prima facie showing of a violation, the defendant may present defenses, the more common of which are discussed in the following paragraphs.

Cost Justification. The seller may justify a price difference if it can show that there are actual cost savings due to the method of production used, the quantities ordered, or the functions assumed by the buyer. For example, NAPA,

the auto parts stores, may receive a functional discount, since it saves sellers distribution costs. Sellers deliver orders to a NAPA warehouse, and NAPA distributes the goods to individual stores.

However, beware. A quantity discount in and of itself is not justified. The seller must be able to document actual savings. Thus, NAPA is not entitled to a discount simply because it places a much larger order than the corner gas station. For this reason, twelve retail service station owners were awarded $1.35 million against Texaco on grounds they were charged higher rates for gasoline than were two wholesale distributors. Texaco was unable to prove that the discounts to the wholesalers were related to actual cost savings.*

The Robinson-Patman Act does not forbid discrimination in sales at retail. It applies only to sales for resale. Thus, a retail office supply catalog can offer substantial discounts based on quantity.

Change in market conditions or marketability. A change in market conditions related to a product may justify different prices to different sellers. For instance, Santa Claus outfits are worth more before Christmas than after Christmas.

Changes in the product's marketability also warrant price differentials. Ripe apples, for example, are worth more than overripe apples. Water-damaged books are worth significantly less than those in mint condition.

Meeting competition. A seller may meet—but not beat—a price available to one of its customers from a competitor. Suppose Southern Com-

---

* *FTC v. The Borden Co.*, 381 F.2d 175 (5th Cir. 1967).

* *Texaco, Inc. v. Hasbrouck*, 110 S. Ct. 2535 (1990).

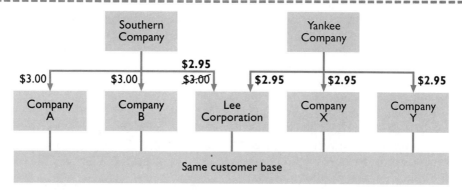

Figure 44.7 Meeting Competition: a Legal Arrangement.
The **$2.95** price from Southern to Lee is *legal*, since Southern is meeting a competitor's price to one of its customers, Lee.

pany has been selling towels to Lee Corporation for $3 each. Yankee Company quotes Lee $2.95 each for a similar grade and quality towel. Southern could match Yankee's $2.95 price. See Figure 44.7.

The customer receiving the price break must originally be the seller's. Suppose Lee demands a $2.95 price from Southern, since its competitor, Grant Corp., is receiving the towels at $2.95 from Yankee. In this case, Southern

would not be meeting a price of its own competitor, Yankee Company, so a price reduction would be illegal. See Figure 44.8.

In Figures 44.7 and 44.8, note that both Southern and Yankee have the same base of potential customers. The Robinson-Patman Act requires that the price discrimination affect the same customer base. If the customer bases are different, there can be no price discrimination. Suppose Southern sells only to customers along

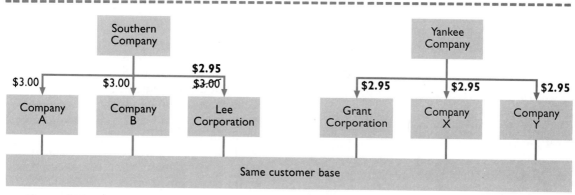

Figure 44.8 Meeting Competition: an Illegal Arrangement.
The **$2.95** price from Southern to Lee is illegal, since Southern is not meeting a competitor's price.

the Gulf Coast, while Yankee markets its towels only in Maine, New Hampshire, and Vermont. Their customer bases are different, and therefore Southern cannot violate the Robinson-Patman Act by beating Yankee's prices.

A seller who does not know the actual price offered its customer is protected if it beats the competitor's price while acting in good faith. Suppose Lee tells Southern it will switch to Yankee unless Southern lowers its price. Southern lowers its price to $2.92 in good faith, not knowing Yankee's price. Southern has not violated the law, nor has Lee. A number of commentators have criticized this result, since Lee knows the price and has figured out how to receive a still lower price.

Levels of Competition

Price discrimination can occur at various levels of competition.

Primary line discrimination. *Primary line discrimination* occurs when the seller's competitor challenges the seller's granting of different prices. For example, if Southern Company sells its towels to Lee for $2.95 and to all other customers at $3, it has no defense if Yankee Company brings suit complaining of price discrimination.

In order to receive damages or to justify an injunction, the competitor must show that the price discrimination caused actual damage. The simple difference in price will not justify a recovery.

Secondary line discrimination. *Secondary line discrimination* involves competition between the customers of sellers. In order to prevail, the customer only has to show potential injury from the practice. Suppose Mega Corp. sues Southern because it must pay $3 for the towels that Lee buys for $2.95. Mega would win against Southern Company without showing any actual competitive injury. Just showing the price differential is enough, although to prevail, the

price discrimination must occur over a discernible period of time. Put another way, the victim of secondary line discrimination does not have to wait until it suffers an actual loss to sue. However, before it can collect treble damages, Mega Corp. must prove actual damages.

ANTITRUST LAW EXCEPTIONS AND EXEMPTIONS

Over the years, there have developed many judicial exceptions and statutory exemptions to the antitrust laws. Perhaps the most famous judicial exception is the 1922 Supreme Court ruling which found that professional baseball is "an amusement," not a business dependent on interstate trade for its viability. However, professional baseball's antitrust immunity status has lately come under close scrutiny by Congress.

Examples of other exceptions or exemptions include the following:

- The liability insurance industry has enjoyed exemption since passage of the McCarran-Ferguson Act in 1945.
- In 1990, television industry officials were granted an exemption to discuss development of guidelines to limit the depiction of violence on television.
- As previously discussed, companies that gain market prominence because of their own patent(s) are exempt.
- Certain regulated industries, such as banking, utilities, and railroad, enjoy different levels of exemptions.
- Legitimate activities involving organized labor, discussed in Chapter 46, have been exempt since 1932.
- Various trade activities involving foreign laws and/or governments are exempt as a result of various treaties.

Because of mounting consumer criticism, Congress and the courts may become more restrictive in regard to exceptions and exemptions.

THE FEDERAL TRADE COMMISSION ACT §5: UNFAIR OR DECEPTIVE PRACTICES

The Federal Trade Commission (FTC), which was created the same year the Clayton Act was enacted, shares civil enforcement of the Clayton Act with the Attorney General. The FTC also has exclusive jurisdiction to enforce the Federal Trade Commission Act (1914).

The FTC Act gives the FTC concurrent civil jurisdiction with the Department of Justice to enforce the Sherman and Clayton Acts. However, its principal antitrust enforcement tool is §5 of the FTC Act, which charges it to prevent "(1) unfair methods of competition in commerce, and (2) unfair or deceptive acts or practices in commerce."

The FTC Act empowers the FTC to prosecute anticompetitive acts and practices which, if left unchecked, might ripen into antitrust violations. Also, the FTC's authority to eliminate deceptive acts and practices gives it an even broader focus than the Clayton Act. While this authority is sometimes used against antitrust violators, its principal impact is in the protection of consumers.

A number of commentators have criticized §5's vagueness. But, Congress purposely never defined either clause. It intended to grant the FTC broad power to check anticompetitive activity which fell short of a Sherman or Clayton Act violation but still adversely affected trade. Of course, any violation of the Sherman and Clayton Acts is also an FTC Act violation. So, the FTC often brings suit under all three acts.

The FTC's principal means of enforcement is the *cease and desist order*—which is like an injunction—against a particular anticompetitive practice. Normally, before issuing the order, the FTC tries to reach an agreement with the offending business on the order's contents. If they agree, the order has virtually the same effect as a consent decree. If agreement proves impossible, the FTC issues the order. Should the business not comply, the FTC may seek enforcement of its order by a U.S. Court of Appeals.

The breadth of §5 permits it to be used against not only antitrust violations but also other predatory practices, such as deceptive advertising. We will have more to say about this aspect of the FTC Act in Chapter 45.

FTC §5 currently is making a comeback as an enforcement tool of antitrust law. Due to its already discussed vagueness, and hence flexibility, §5 is being used in a variety of imaginative ways. In late 1992, for example, the FTC used §5 to attach an *invitation* by one competitor to fix prices with another. Such an action might not be sufficient to trigger the Sherman Act.

PROSECUTING AN ANTITRUST VIOLATION

The Antitrust Civil Suit

Anyone injured by antitrust activity can bring a civil action. Thus, the potential plaintiffs are:

- The U.S. Attorney General
- The Federal Trade Commission
- State attorneys general
- Competitors
- Customers
- Consumers

Even foreign countries can bring an antitrust suit, as India did against Pfizer, Inc., in 1984. Private litigation constitutes 90 percent of antitrust action.*

Civil actions based on violations of the federal antitrust laws must be brought in a U.S. District Court. Relief can take a number of forms: an injunction, a seizure of property, treble damages, special orders, and a consent decree. Each of these is discussed below.

---

* "Antitrust Shift Eyed with Doubt," *National Law Journal*, March 9, 1992, p. 36.

Injunctions. A court may issue an injunction forbidding a party to engage in activity which violates the antitrust laws. For example, a court could enjoin competitors who agreed to fix prices from doing so.

Seizure of goods. A court may order a federal marshal to seize goods moving in interstate commerce if they are being used to implement an anticompetitive practice. This remedy has not been used often. It would apply, say, to goods shipped under an agreement among competitors to divide a particular geographical market among them. However, even if a court ordered goods seized, it would not bar the company from interstate commerce. The company still has a right to do business which does not violate the antitrust laws.

Treble damages. The antitrust laws' damage remedy is uniquely punitive. A successful plaintiff receives three times its actual damages as well as its legal costs, including attorney's fees. A plaintiff who proves $500,000 in actual damages would automatically be awarded $1.5 million plus her attorney's fees.

In order to establish a case for treble damages, the plaintiff must show a violation of the antitrust laws, *proximate cause* (a connection between her and the alleged antitrust activity), and damages. Thus a successful plaintiff who did not establish an actual injury could conceivably receive no damages, even if she proved her case.

Some have criticized the treble damage mechanism as an invitation to sue, since the rewards of winning can be so great. Some have even called plaintiffs' attorneys specializing in antitrust suits "bounty hunters." These comments make it sound as if treble damage awards are an everyday occurrence. They are not. Antitrust cases require extensive, detailed preparation and can last years. For example, the Attorney General filed suit against IBM in 1969 and dropped the suit in 1982 just as it was going to trial.

Special orders. In addition to money damages or an injunction, a court may issue a special order requiring a defendant to take a specific action.

The most common special order is *divestiture,* which requires a corporation to sell or liquidate particular subsidiaries or assets. For example, Pabst acquired Blatz beer and later was required to divest itself of Blatz. G. Heileman & Co., another large brewer, bought Blatz.

The beer industry is one where the Department of Justice has meddled for years without success. With the 1989 merger of Coors and Stroh's, the market shares of the top four brewers were:

Anheuser-Busch	40.4%
Miller's	20.7
Coors	19.7
Heileman	7.8*

Consent decrees. When the parties to an antitrust suit agree to settle before the court passes on the case's merits a *consent decree* is often the result. A consent decree is entered as the judgment of the court, so it requires the court's approval.

The key element of virtually all consent decrees is that the defendant does not admit any wrongdoing, although he agrees to some remedial action. Perhaps the most famous consent decree was that in which AT&T agreed to divest itself of its regional telephone companies, two of which are now called Pacific Telesis and NYNEX.

For a defendant, a consent decree can make good sense. First, it is a negotiated settlement. The defendant may have reason to believe it can strike a better deal with the plaintiff than it will get from a jury or a judge. Second, as noted above, the defendant usually does not admit any fault. Thus, unlike a judgment in a civil or criminal case, a consent decree cannot be cited in a later case as a finding of a violation

---

* "Coors May Take a Gulp of a Gulp of a Rival Brew," *Business Week,* August 21, 1989, p. 70.

of the antitrust laws. In other words, a consent decree lacks any precedential value.

Criminal Sanctions

The Sherman and Robinson-Patman Acts provide for criminal penalties. The Department of Justice may seek either fines or prison sentences for violations. The fines may reach $350,000 for individuals and $10 million for corporations. A court may sentence an individual antitrust defendant to prison for up to 3 years.

Quite often, antitrust criminal defendants will plead *nolo contendere*, or "no contest." While pleading nolo contendere subjects a defendant to criminal penalties, unlike a guilty plea it cannot be used as evidence of wrongdoing in any other criminal or civil action.

The advantage to a defendant of pleading nolo contendere is that it usually avoids the humiliation and cost of a trial. Often, too, both prosecutors and courts are willing to consider lighter penalties in exchange for avoiding a trial. Despite its advantages, pleading nolo contendere can have costs for the defendant beyond the criminal penalties, as the next case reveals.

Bar Association of Greater Cleveland v. Bogomolny

10 Ohio St. 3d 110, 461 N.E.2d 1294 (1984)

FACTS

[The business defendants] named in the indictment were First National Supermarkets, Inc., [doing business as (*d.b.a.*)] Pick-N-Pay Supermarkets, Fisher Foods, Inc., d.b.a. Fazio's, and the Association of Stop-N-Shop Super Markets. The individuals named in the indictment were four chief officers of these corporations, including [Bogomolny] who was Chairman, President, and Chief Executive Officer of First National Supermarkets, Inc.

The defendants were charged with trying to fix, raise, stabilize, and maintain the advertised prices and everyday shelf prices of grocery products and the advertised prices of some meat items sold in Cuyahoga County, thereby unreasonably restraining trade. . . .

Bogomolny, an attorney, pleaded nolo contendere to two violations of the Sherman Act, and the U.S. District Court found him guilty. The Bar Association sought to have him disbarred for violating the Code of Professional Responsibility, which forbids conduct involving moral turpitude, dishonesty, fraud, deceit, or misrepresentation.

Bogomolny asserted that his plea of nolo contendere did not admit the prosecution's factual allegations and that a violation of the Sherman Act was not in itself prohibited conduct. For that reason he contended that the violations did not involve moral turpitude. The Board of Commissioners on Grievances and Discipline of the Bar ordered Bogomolny suspended indefinitely from the practice of law.

ISSUE

Are violations of the Sherman Act also breaches of an attorney's professional code of responsibility?

DECISION

Yes. Recommendation adopted.

Under the facts presented, a finding of guilty on two counts of violating the Sherman

Act constitutes misconduct. . . . The fact that the respondent entered a plea of nolo contendere to the allegations makes it no less a violation under the Disciplinary Rules.

CONCLUSION

Regardless of their philosophy concerning antitrust laws, all agree that the antitrust laws are difficult to apply, that political considerations probably affect enforcement considerations all too often, that many breaches of the antitrust laws go unpunished, and that the antitrust laws need to consider the broader world marketplace and not focus simply on the American marketplace. Even so, by restricting monopolies and by minimizing restraints on trade, the antitrust laws have succeeded in their goal of increasing competition.

Nonetheless, the Reagan-Bush administrations, reflecting the hands-off philosophy of business regulation, filed almost no antitrust cases, civil or criminal, other than for price fixing, and made every effort to settle those it inherited from earlier administrations.

The Reagan-Bush administrations also advocated—without success—an end to the prohibitions against resale price maintenance and tying arrangements, and a change in the standard applied to horizontal market allocations from per se to rule of reason.

These changes, the Reagan-Bush administrations argued, reflected the desires of business for antitrust deregulation. However, it became clear early on that virtually the only businesses that were actively in favor of antitrust deregulation were those that were defendants in antitrust suits. Public opinion polls have consistently shown that a clear majority of businesspeople—and of the public—favor continued antitrust enforcement.

This difference of opinion reflects a continuation of a 200-year debate in this country about business's proper size and role in society. The Jeffersonian/Populist view that big is per se bad has repeatedly clashed with the Hamiltonian view that business should be left unfettered to define its own relationship to society. The debate isn't ever likely to be fully settled.

A NOTE TO FUTURE CPA CANDIDATES

The CPA exam no longer directly tests on antitrust law. However, restraints of trade, also discussed in Chapter 9, are sometimes asked in a common law contracts setting. Remember, there are only two situations where restraints of trade are possible:

- Contracts between an employer and employee to prevent a knowledgeable ex-employee from competing with her previous employer for a period of time and distance
- The sale of a business where the seller is prohibited from establishing or operating a competing business for a period of time and within a specified distance.

Contracts between competitors to not compete with each other are illegal.

KEY WORDS

boycott (1024)
cease and desist order (1037)
exclusive dealing arrangement (1028)
full-line forcing (1028)
horizontal market allocation (1023)
per se violation (1017)
price discrimination (1032)

price fixing (1019)
reciprocal dealing arrangement (1028)
resale price maintenance (1021)
rule of reason (1017)
treble damages (1038)
tying arrangement (1027)
vertical market allocation (1023)

DISCUSSION QUESTIONS

1. What are the primary purposes of the antitrust laws?
2. What are the primary antitrust acts?
3. Who may bring an antitrust suit?
4. What is meant by treble damages? What other remedies besides treble damages are available?
5. Distinguish between the rule of reason and the per se standard. Who created them?
6. Distinguish the test used for a monopoly violation from the test used for a merger violation.
7. Give the elements of the following Sherman Act violations: price fixing, resale price maintenance, group boycott, reciprocal dealing arrangements, and tying contracts.
8. Give the elements of the following Clayton Act violations: tying contracts, exclusive dealing arrangements, and interlocking directorates.
9. What is the purpose of the Robinson-Patman Act? What are the primary defenses under the Act?
10. What is the purpose of the Federal Trade Commission Act? What is the principal criticism of its application to antitrust violations?

CASE PROBLEMS

1. Loop Corp. made a major breakthrough in the development of a micropencil. Loop has patented the product and is seeking to maximize its profit potential. Loop has achieved a monopoly by selling the product at whatever price the traffic will bear. In a civil monopoly action brought against Loop by the Justice Department, what is the likely outcome?
2. Alpha, Beta, and Gamma own competing Greek fast food restaurants in Erewhon. They decide that the city would be better served with souvlaki if they divided it into exclusive territories. The state attorney general has brought an antitrust action against them, claiming that their agreement is illegal. Is the

attorney general an appropriate plaintiff? What is the likely outcome?

3. Grubar is a troublesome appliance price-cutter. The other retail appliance dealers dislike Grubar's price-cutting, and he is equally unpopular with the national appliance manufacturers. Grubar's appliance sales constitute less than 0.01 percent of the market. The marketplace has an abundance of retailers, and competition is vigorous. The manufacturers and the retailers jointly decided to boycott Grubar, thereby significantly limiting the availability of appliances to him, and thus hoping to drive him out of business. Grubar has commenced legal action against the various parties on the basis of a violation of the Sherman Act. He is seeking injunctive relief and damages. The defendants argue that Grubar's market share precludes him from being able to rely upon federal antitrust laws for relief. Are they correct? Is Grubar likely to recover treble damages? Explain.
4. Viking Discount Stores sold Becker Company's watches below cost to lure customers into the store. When Viking refused to stop this practice, Becker stopped selling to it. Viking somehow obtained Becker's watches from another source. Becker was able to put pressure on Viking by convincing two other companies, Polar Shirt and Sharpie Razor, to cease dealing with Viking. Viking claims that both Becker actions constitute antitrust violations. What is the likely result of Viking's suit against Becker? Explain.
5. Mason Corp. manufactures and sells various interrelated products. It is almost the only maker of one of the items. This unique product is in great demand and is sold throughout the United States. Mason realized the importance of this product and decided to capitalize on the situation by requiring all buyers to take at least two other Mason products if they want this product. Is the company's plan legal? Explain your answer.
6. Olympus Sailing Works merged with American Sail Co. Together the two companies control 65 percent of the sailboat market in three states. The federal government has brought a

merger action under the Clayton Act §7. American claims that if the product market is considered to be all boats sold in the three states, its share is only 14 percent. If you were the judge, would you include speedboats, party barge boats, small fishing boats, and rowboats in American's product market? What tests would you use in making your evaluation of each type of boat?

7. Premier Manufacturing Company is a major manufacturer of garden hose. Premier sells 5/8-inch garden hose in 25-foot lengths to Mounds Garden Center in Moline, Illinois, for $3.25 each in lots of 100. Lately Mounds has been losing a number of sales to the Lilac Garden Center, just across the Mississippi River, in Iowa. Lilac also sells Premier garden hoses but has recorded tremendous sales of an equivalent hose from a new manufacturer, Dingo Rubber Company. Dingo is selling its hose to Lilac for $2.95 per hose in lots of 100. Because of its limited distribution capabilities, Dingo will not fill orders from potential buyers east of the Mississippi River. Premier is considering Mound's demand for a similar $2.95 price but is unwilling to provide a similar reduction for other area retailers. Assuming that Dingo's pricing is not illegal, would Premier violate the Robinson-Patman Act if it agreed to Mound's demand? Could Premier match the Dingo price for Lilac? Explain.

8. Boggle Toys, Inc., sells toys to Gem Stores, a large department store chain, and to Fantastic Discounts, a major toy warehouse store. Both receive prices below those Boggle offers to other retailers in the market area. Boggle's pricing policy toward Gem is based solely on the fact that Gem is a new customer. Boggle offered the low prices in order to gain Gem's business, and thereby soak up its own surplus production capacity. Fantastic's lower prices are the result of Boggle's efforts to meet a competitor's prices on similar goods. Has Boggle violated the Robinson-Patman Act as to Gem? As to Fantastic? Explain.

9. Real Issues. Today's business periodicals continue to be full of stories concerning the collapse of General Motors and IBM. How-

ever, it was not too many years ago that stories questioned how much longer the Department of Justice could wait before breaking up the two giant companies. In fact, GM took a number of actions in the early 1960s not to become more competitive but to better shield the corporation from possible government divestiture action. Today, GM is reversing many of these actions in an attempt to regain competitiveness. Today, many business commentators contend that Microsoft, a $1.7 billion company which dominates the computer software industry, ought to be prosecuted for monopoly power for its popular product, Windows. Some contend that the United States should be pleased to have such a dominant world-class company and do nothing to jeopardize Microsoft's success. Still others contend that in an ever-changing global marketplace, Microsoft should simply be left alone, that it will eventually lose dominance just like GM or IBM. What makes the most sense to you? Explain.

10. Real Issues. In 1992, Congress renewed debate about professional baseball's antitrust immunity after an announced sale and move of the San Francisco Giants to St. Petersburg was ultimately denied by major league baseball owners "in the best interests of professional baseball." Many members of the Senate's antitrust subcommittee stated they found it difficult to accept that baseball is not a business when professional baseball, basketball, and hockey all are subject to the antitrust laws. Many baseball old-timers contend that today's $40 million plus baseball players no longer play the game for the love of the game but for the greed of money. To them, the exorbitant salaries and resulting high ticket prices have made professional baseball games less and less accessible to the average fan. Professional baseball counters by saying that baseball continues to be an "amusement," our national pasttime. If you were a member of the Senate antitrust subcommittee, how would you vote in regard to baseball's antitrust immunity: amusement or business?

Consumer Protection

Anna recently got a divorce. In addition to the $1250 per month she earns, she receives $500 per month in alimony and child support from her ex-husband.

Anna needs furniture for her new apartment. Fred's Fabulous Furniture Fair, Inc., offers new living room suites for "no money down and 12 months to pay with approved credit." Anna picked out the suite she liked and applied for credit, listing both her salary and what she received from her ex-husband. Five days later, she received a letter from Fred's, saying only that it had rejected her credit application. Anna has repeatedly requested that Fred's tell her why it rejected her application, but the store has refused.

Until 1970, Anna's experience was all too common. Women in general and divorced women in particular had an extremely difficult time obtaining credit. Often, creditors refused to include alimony and child support payments in a woman's income. Also, women and men alike had no right to learn why they had not received credit. Completely erroneous information could ruin individual's credit ratings, but they had no recourse.

Today, consumers have a right to know why creditors reject their applications. They have a right to correct erroneous data. And, women have a right to be treated equally when they apply for credit. As recently as 20 years ago, many of these rights, which are taken for granted today, were inconceivable. This chapter explores the federal statutes which brought about these and other changes in consumer protection laws.

THE NATURE OF CONSUMER PROTECTION LAWS

A *consumer* is a natural person—as opposed to a legal person, like a corporation—who engages in transactions involving money, property, or services primarily for personal, family, and household purposes. Put another way, all individuals are consumers unless they enter into a transaction for a business purpose.

The consumer protection statutes discussed in this chapter, for the most part, are less than 20 years old. Like the securities acts, their primary goal is to ensure that the consumer has sufficient facts on which to base a rational decision. Except for outrageous abuses, the law does not try to insulate consumers from the consequences of their choices. As the U.S. Supreme Court said of the Truth-in-Lending Act, the consumer protection laws mark the shift from the nineteenth-century philosophy of "let the buyer beware" to one of "let the seller inform."*

Consumer protection laws, some argue, respond to the disparity in bargaining power and the distance between individuals and vendors in a society based on mass consumption. Until about 130 years ago, business entities were small, local in scope, and usually unincorporated. If someone owned a buggy which proved defective, he could return it directly to the person who made it for repair. Today a General Motors car may have traveled 3000 miles to your dealer. The chances are that you will never deal directly with GM, much less with any of the assembly line workers who actually built your car.

This explanation of consumer protection laws has some validity but is entirely too simple. Consumer protection laws cut across virtually every area in which individuals do business. Consider for a moment a few areas covered elsewhere in this book that have strong consumer protection aspects: securities regulation, antitrust laws, the bankruptcy code, the FTC's holder in due course regulations, and the Magnuson-Moss Warranty Act.

The ways in which consumers' rights are enforced under these statutes and those consid-

---

* *Mourning v. Family Publications Services, Inc.* 411 U.S. 356 (1973).

ered in this chapter vary. Many are enforced through administrative proceedings. Some may, either initially or ultimately, be enforced through lawsuits filed by consumers. State or federal agencies, such as a district attorney's office or the Federal Trade Commission, enforce others.

This chapter surveys what is formally called consumer protection legislation. Because of the variety of these laws at every level of government—from the town to the federal—this chapter emphasizes the federal consumer laws. But before looking at particular laws, some background is in order.

NONFEDERAL SOURCES OF CONSUMER PROTECTION

While the focus of the media's coverage of consumer protection regulations is always Washington, D.C., much—if not most—of the action is centered in the states. And, this is how it has always been.

The Common Law and the UCC

At the end of the nineteenth century, the buyer had the task of ferreting out the flaws in products and the pitfalls in transactions before contracting. The common law thus favored the strong over the weak in any consumer transaction. Even so, the common law did offer consumers some protection in the most extreme cases. For instance, the courts voided contracts made under duress, undue influence, or coercion.

Protections such as these were not sufficient, however. Neither the Uniform Sales Act nor the Uniform Commercial Code—which modified the common law—specifically protected the consumer. However, the UCC's emphasis on good faith did significantly reduce the unfairness that had developed in the common law. Still, other remedies were necessary.

State Regulation

In the United States, perhaps the earliest forms of consumer protection legislation were state laws regulating usury and weights and measures. *Usury* laws set the maximum rates of interest lenders could charge borrowers.

Weights and measures laws mandate the use of accurate means of weighing and measuring in trade or business. These laws were particularly important in an agarian society and remain so in our society, which relies, for instance, on accurate readings from gas pumps. Today, in every state, a state or local agency checks weighing and measuring devices used in trade.

Consumer protection is not an area in which federal regulators are always ahead of the states. During the 1970s, most states enacted laws specifically regulating consumer transactions. These laws complemented and often expanded on the federal regulatory efforts. For instance, in the mid-1970s a number of states began regulating used car sales. Turned-back odometers and concealed defects were particular targets. The FTC did not adopt regulations in this area until 1983. In the next case, New York had a unique statute specifically dealing with a troublesome service industry.

Faer v. Vertical Fitness & Racquet Club, Ltd.

119 Misc. 2d 295, 462 N.Y.S. 784 (Civ. Ct. 1983)

FACTS   On March 2, 1981, Faer joined the Vertical Fitness & Racquet Club. Before Faer joined, the club's program director told him that the club would soon have eight racquetball courts, a large gym with exercise equipment, a restaurant, and a large swimming pool. Faer had said that he intended to play racquetball twice a week, use exercise equipment three times a week, swim regularly, and use the restaurant to entertain clients. During the term of Faer's membership, only two courts were available during the winter, one small gym with limited exercise equipment was open, the restaurant opened in December, and there was no large pool. Since he could rarely use the facilities because of the heavy demand for them, Faer brought suit for the return of his $864 membership fee.

ISSUE

Was Faer entitled to a refund of his membership fee?

DECISION

Yes. Judgment for Faer. New York's General Business Law §626 provides that a health club's direct or indirect misrepresentation of its size, location, facilities, or equipment is an unfair and deceptive trade practice and is unlawful. Here, the club misrepresented the extent, location, size, and availability of its facilities to Faer.

The states' power to regulate consumer transactions comes from their police powers. As noted in Chapter 3, the states' police powers are extremely broad. Federal agencies like the FTC have the power to regulate in the same areas. However, unless the federal regulations preempt the state, the stricter of the regulations governs. For example, an FTC regulation permits a consumer purchasing goods or services valued at $25 or more from a door-to-door vendor to rescind the transaction within 3 days. If a state law permitted rescission of any transaction involving $10 or more, it would govern in that state.

Where the improper activity of a wrongdoer is occurring across a number of states, it is not uncommon for the attorneys general of the states to work together for a common settlement. In 1992, Sears, after making a $8 million settlement in California, entered into an agreement with the attorneys general of forty-one states to implement a program to standardize automobile repair practices which included the elimination of commissions and sales quotas. The states had alleged that because of the commission and sales quotas for its auto repair salespersons, Sears repair shops sometimes persuaded customers to have unneeded auto repairs. Unfortunately, this practice is still felt to be fairly common in the auto repair industry.

State consumer protection laws have proved popular and effective, although their range and their enforcement mechanisms vary enormously. The federal statutes examined below reflect the same regulatory philosophy as the states'.

THE FTC ACT: UNFAIR OR DECEPTIVE ACTS OR PRACTICES

The Federal Trade Commission has two main responsibilities: to prevent "(1) unfair methods of competition in commerce and (2) unfair or deceptive acts or practices in commerce" [Federal Trade Commission Act §5]. At noted in the previous chapter, the FTC's change to prevent "unfair methods of competition" describes its role in preventing antitrust violations. This chapter will focus on unfair or deceptive acts or practices.

Unfair acts and practices are those which wrong or take advantage of a consumer. The next case, a state case construing a statute similar to §5, presents a fairly typical example of an unfair act.

Sherwood v. Bellevue Dodge, Inc.

35 Wash. App. 741, 669 P.2d 1258 (1983)

FACTS	The Sherwoods bought a car on credit from Bellevue Dodge. They filled out and signed all the appropriate documents, including a promissory note. In connection with the note, the Sherwoods granted Bellevue Dodge a security interest in the car, which it never perfected. In order to repossess a vehicle, Washington statutes require the dealer to have a perfected security interest. When the Sherwoods got behind in their payments on the note. Bellevue directed a towing company to retrieve the car at Mrs. Sherwood's place of work. Although Mrs. Sherwood begged the tow truck operators not to take the car, they did. This occurred in full view of her coworkers. One week later, a court ordered Bellevue to return the car. The Sherwoods brought suit for damages under Washington's Consumer Protection Act. The trial court found for the Sherwoods.*
ISSUE	Is repossessing a car without a valid security interest a violation of Washington's Consumer Protection Act?
DECISION	Yes. Judgment affirmed. A Consumer Protection Act violation consists of unfair or deceptive conduct within the sphere of trade or commerce which has an impact on the public interest. The public interest requirement is satisfied by a violation of another statute which proximately causes damage to persons meant to be protected by that statute.

---

* Perfection of security interests in personal property is discussed in Chapter 41. For the manner in which a car may be repossessed, see *Williams v. Ford Motor Credit Co.*, 674 F.2d 717 (8th Cir. 1982), also in Chapter 41.

Deceptive acts and practices are sales techniques or representations which have the tendency or the capacity to mislead consumers. For example, under pressure from the FTC, Sears agreed not to advertise at a low price plain white washers which its stores did not have in stock. Customers arrived at Sears stores looking for the advertised washers. After telling the customers that the washers were out of stock, salespeople would convince them to buy more expensive machines. This sales technique is called a "bait and switch."

The FTC directs its enforcement efforts toward keeping consumers from becoming confused, coerced, or deceived by business promotions or overenthusiastic salespeople. The FTC Act permits the agency to seek a cease and desist order before a consumer suffers an actual injury. Also, if the FTC identifies an advertisement containing a falsehood, the advertisement is presumed to be deceiving to consumers. The FTC's efforts to control misleading advertising focus on product pricing, representations as to the product, product demonstrations, and product comparisons. We will examine each of these below.

Pricing

The FTC requires that advertised sale price savings in fact exist. Consumers tend to think of themselves as bargain hunters. So, if two merchants sell an identical blue blazer at the same price, the one who advertises "$50 off!" stands a considerably better chance of making a sale than the merchant who does not. Such statements make it easier for consumers to convince themselves that they should buy and buy now.

Advertised savings should be from the price which the seller normally charges for the item. If the "sale" price is the everyday price, it cannot be a sale price. In many cases, the everyday price will be the "suggested retail price," a nonbinding figure placed on the item by the manufacturer. However, if the suggested retail price is not the price the seller usually charges and if the seller's competition also does not use the suggested retail price, it is not an appropriate gauge for cost savings.

Suppose a tennis shop regularly sells Wilson Championship brand tennis balls at $2.75 per can. The shop cannot advertise a "Memorial Day special sale—$2.75 per can." Nor, in this situation, can the tennis shop advertise "25 cents off" if the suggested retail price is $3.00 per can.

In some instances, the manner of pricing can be misleading. Mary Carter Paints used to advertise that the consumer always got 2 gallons for every gallon purchased. However, a consumer could not buy just 1 gallon of Mary Carter paint. In essence the buyer was buying 2 gallons of paint for the advertised price.

Representations

The FTC regulates the types of representation that companies may make about products. For example, FTC guidelines state that a product is not new after it has been on the market for 6 months. Thus, Coca-Cola Co. had to remove "New!" from its cans of reformulated Coca-Cola, so the product is now called "Coke" and the original is known as "Coke Classic."

Substantiation. A seller must be able to substantiate any claims made about the product.

False statements about a product's performance, durability, quality, or character may lead to FTC intervention. At one time, for example, Listerine claimed in its advertising that it could prevent and cure colds and sore throats. Listerine could substantiate these claims and had to change and qualify its advertising.

Endorsements. Some celebrities, such as Murphy Brown's Candace Bergen who advertises for Sprint have made second careers of product endorsements. The FTC requires that an advertiser have a reasonable basis for the performance claims contained in testimonials, even if the testimonial reflects the endorser's honestly held views. Generally, a celebrity may not endorse a product he does not actually use. The FTC challenged Olympic champion Bruce Jenner's endorsement of Wheaties, but General Mills and Jenner prevailed by proving the endorsement's validity. A celebrity is not bound forever to one product in a market. Several sports figures who endorsed Miller Lite later switched to Budweiser Light.*

The actual use rule exempts a celebrity who obviously could not endorse based on personal use. Some years ago, for instance, former all-pro quarterback Joe Namath endorsed pantyhose on TV. By contrast, a representation by a supposed expert who is simply an actor is a potential violation. If Bill Cosby endorsed prescription drugs as a television doctor, the advertisement would be deceptive.

Demonstrations. The FTC prohibits deceptive demonstrations. Any demonstration must show what the consumer may rightfully expect. Citing this ground, the FTC challenged Campbell Soup's technique of placing clear marbles in its

---

* Other agencies regulate endorsements as well. The reason Miller Lite used retired athletes for its advertisements from 1980 through 1987 was a U.S. Treasury (Bureau of Alcohol, Tobacco and Firearms) regulation forbidding the use of active athletes for such ads. The Food and Drug Administration also regulates advertising.

soup to make it appear thicker and frothier on television.

Product comparisons. The FTC encourages product comparisons as a means of educating the public. A product comparison must be made under equal conditions. In a Pepsi challenge, the Pepsi cannot be chilled and the Coke unchilled. If prices are compared, they must be for similar products.

A product comparison may not simply disparage to attack the competition. Suppose that testing on laboratory rats shows that consuming a pound a day of a preservative commonly used in minute quantities in jelly statistically increases the chances of getting cancer of the nose. Nat's Natural Jellies may not run an ad presenting its preservative-using competitors' labels as tombstones.

The Lanham Act has been amended to prohibit advertisers from misrepresenting the qualities or characteristics of "another person's goods, services, or commercial activities." Before, the Lanham Act only prohibited an advertiser from misrepresenting his or her own product.

Under the amendments, accuracy does not afford total protection against liability if the true statement gives a false impression. For example, Lysol contended that Glade is 97 percent water and gas. It is. But, the remaining 3 percent is what traditionally makes up an air spray product. So, now both what an advertiser literally says and the actual message communicated to an audience will be evaluated. And, since the Lanham Act is a federal law, advertisers can expect more consistency in decisions on product comparison issues.

Enforcement

Most deceptive advertising complaints do not result in litigation. Rather, the advertiser and the FTC enter into a *consent decree* in which the advertiser agrees to stop doing something which it does not admit was wrong in the first place.

If the parties do not agree to a consent decree, the FTC may issue a cease and desist order to the advertiser to suspend false or misleading advertisements. Failure to comply with such an order can result in fines of up to $10,000 per day. Also, the FTC can require corrective advertising—as it did in the case of Listerine—informing the public that a claim was incorrect.

Large retailers in particular often claim that they are at a disadvantage because the FTC monitors their advertising closely, while small, independent businesses are not subject to such scrutiny. A small retailer normally does not have to worry about the FTC's supervision because the FTC cannot possibly monitor all businesses. Since many state consumer protection agencies do monitor small enterprises, the validity of this complaint depends largely on how active a particular state is in consumer protection.

Advertising is not the only area in which large, multioutlet retailers feel they are subject to greater supervision than their smaller competitors. Their complaints also extend to supervision of their credit practices.

THE CONSUMER CREDIT PROTECTION ACT

Almost all consumers borrow money at some point. For the average person, borrowing from a commercial lender often causes extreme anxiety. The process is intimidating. Loan applications are not uniform, and often require details which require effort to track down. And, there are so many variables to consider. What is the effect of a fixed interest rate versus a variable rate? What are the consequences of a single, double, or triple default? What about prepayment of the loan?* Finally, the actual loan

---

* These topics are discussed in Chapter 1 and 2.

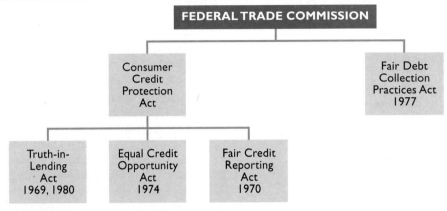

Figure 45.1 Federal Consumer Credit Legislation.

forms contain paragraphs of tiny print, often in a language which only resembles English.

To make matters worse, the borrower is constantly reminded that the lender has the upper hand. The lender has the money the borrower needs. In part, though, the lender's power comes from the consumer's lack of discipline. Borrowers often decide to make a major purchase, put down a deposit, and then look for financing. What they should do is reverse the process: identify the financing options open to them and then buy.

No legislation can force consumers to do what they ought to do or to educate themselves when they do not choose to learn. Recognizing that fact, Congress chose instead to make the conditions of credit clearer for those who choose to pay attention to them and to ensure that creditors make decisions on credit applications without regard to race or gender.

Congress initially focused on enabling consumers to shop for credit. The result was the Truth-in-Lending Act of 1969. In 1970, the Fair Credit Reporting Act gave consumers a series of remedies aimed at correcting inaccurate credit records. In 1974, Congress addressed the problem of access to credit by women and minorities in the Equal Credit Opportunity Act. The Truth-in-Lending Simplification and Re-

form Act of 1980 tuned up the 1969 Act. We will discuss each of these statutes, which collectively are referred to as the Consumer Credit Protection Act.

We shall also discuss the Fair Debt Collection Practices Act of 1978, which attempted to remedy the legendary abuses in consumer lenders' collection practices. Figure 45.1 diagrams the FTC's enabling acts relating to credit.

The Truth-in-Lending Act

The Truth-in-Lending Act requires lenders to inform consumers of the cost of credit. In theory, this information enable borrowers to shop for the lender with the most competitive rates.

The lack of uniformity among consumer lenders in stating terms and costs was a major target of the Truth-in-Lending Act. A borrower attempting to compare costs at different institutions often faced the proverbial ''apples and oranges'' comparison. Some lenders, for instance, expressed their interest rates on an annual basis, while others quoted a monthly basis, which might seem lower than the annual but was in fact higher. Congress hoped that simpler, clearer loan information would make the process of securing credit less intimidating.

Thus, the Truth-in-Lending Act is a disclosure act, not an act which regulates costs. It requires lenders to disclose the cost of credit in a uniform manner—as an annual percentage rate. Unlike a usury law, it does not limit the amount the creditor may charge for its money.

Consumer loan restriction. The Truth-in-Lending Act applies to lenders who make mortgage loans and consumer loans of less than $25,000. Consumers who can raise more than $25,000, Congress thought, should be able to protect themselves. However, there is no upper limit on the act's application to mortgage loans to individuals.

The lender must be in the business of regularly extending credit for which it imposes a finance charge. Thus, the Act does not apply just to banks and savings and loans. It also covers retail stores which regularly finance purchases.

A lender cannot hide finance charges in order to avoid being subject to the Act. Under *Regulation Z,* the Federal Reserve Board regulation which implements the law, if the consumer is to make four or more installment

---

DISCLOSURES REQUIRED UNDER FEDERAL AND STATE LAW

ANNUAL PERCENTAGE RATE The cost of my credit as a yearly rate.	FINANCE CHARGE The dollar amount the credit will cost me.	AMOUNT FINANCED The amount of credit provided to me or on my behalf.	TOTAL OF PAYMENTS The amount I will have paid after I have made all payments as scheduled.
_____%	$_____	$_____	$_____

My Payment Schedule will be:

No of Payments	Amount of Payments	When Payments are Due

PROPERTY INSURANCE: (Check and complete if applicable)
☐ I am required to purchase property insurance from a company of my choice that is acceptable to you. I understand such insurance is not available through the Bank.

INSURANCE
Credit life and credit disability insurance are not required to obtain credit, and is not available through the Bank.

SECURITY I an giving a security interest in:
☐ A motor vehicle

New or Used	Make	Year	Model	Type	Vehicle I.D. Number

☐ Other _____

Describe

Collateral securing other loans with the Bank may also secure this loan.

Filing Fees $_____

Non-filing insurance $_____

LATE PAYMENT
If a payment is more than 10 days late, a charge of $5.00 or 5% of the late payment(s), whichever is less, will become immediately due and payable to the Bank.

PREPAYMENT
If I pay this Note early I may be entitled to a refund of part of the finance charge.

I understand that the rest of this Note contains additional information about nonpayment, default, any required repayment in full before the schedule date and prepayment refunds.

Figure 45.2 A Disclosure Statement.
This disclosure statement satisfies federal truth-in-lending requirements. It should be noted that it is only part of a promissory note which may also contain a security agreement.

payments, a finance charge is imputed when none is stated. Suppose Sara buys a dining room suite from Friendly Freddie's Furniture. The terms are $1200, payable in twelve equal installments "with no finance charges." If the current imposed interest rate under Registration Z is 10 percent, $120 of the price would be treated as a finance charge.

The imputed interest formula came into existence in recognition of the fact that no business can afford to lend money for an extended period without charging for it. While it is a rigid standard and the actual hidden rate could be much higher, it has encouraged compliance with the Act.

The Act also applies to advertised financing rates. However, only the FTC can sue a lender to compel it to take out advertising to correct misstatements.

Lender's duties. Before the credit agreement is signed, the lender must give the borrower a statement—sometimes called a disclosure form or financing statement—which lists all financ-

ing costs and any service fees for making the loan. The finance cost must reflect the costs of the loan, meaning the application and process charges as well as the actual interest. For instance, mortgage lenders often charge a loan origination fee which includes the cost of title insurance for the lender. The lender must explain this and state the charge. See Figure 45.2, a typical disclosure statement.

Recent federal legislation requires credit card issuers to disclose to applicants and cardholders the annual interest rate, the monthly fee, the grace period (if any), and any other terms of this nature. This information is to be presented in a chart to be designed by the Federal Reserve Board that will facilitate consumer comparisons of credit cards.

Right to rescind. When the borrower puts up his home as security for a second mortgage, he has the right to rescind the credit transaction within 3 business days. In some instances, the right to rescind continues for a much longer period, as it did in the following case.

Steele v. Ford Motor Credit Co.

783 F.2d 1016 (11th Cir. 1986)

FACTS

On March 26, 1981, Steele borrowed $3000 from Ford for 36 months. The interest on the loan for its full term was $945. Three months later, Steele took out another loan from Ford, this one secured by a second mortgage on his house. Part of the proceeds from the second loan went to pay off the first. Because of this refinancing, Steele paid only $195.81 in retained interest on the original loan. That figure, however, should have been about $24 lower. Eventually, Steele defaulted on the second loan, and Ford filed suit to foreclose on its mortgage. That prompted Steele to file this suit to rescind the second loan on the ground that Ford had materially understated its cost. The trial court entered summary judgment for Ford.

ISSUE

Does an understatement of the cost of a loan have to be material in order to warrant rescission?

DECISION

No. Judgment reversed. Any understatement of a finance charge is material because any understatement would be of some significance to the consumer. This holding assumes the disclosure of the finance charge to be more important than the other disclosures required by the Act. It is. The finance charge is the total cost of the loan to the borrower. Other factors may be relevant to consumers shopping for a loan, but the finance charge is likely to be of prime importance.

This right to rescind does not apply to first mortgages. Congress recognized that consumers understood the nature of first mortgages as liens against the property. Rather, this right was designed to protect consumers against slick sales practices by home improvement contractors who convinced consumers to sign notes they did not realize were second mortgages. In the same vein, the Act provides that when a builder is to have a second mortgage, she must wait 3 days before beginning to work unless the homeowner has an emergency which threatens the property or life.

Penalties. The Truth-in-Lending Act provides both criminal and civil penalties. Criminal penalties may include up to 1 year in prison or a $5000 fine or both for each violation.

In a civil action by a consumer against a lender, the consumer may claim his actual damages, his attorney's fees, and a penalty up to twice the finance charge. The amount of the penalty may be no less than $100 and no more than $1000 per violation.

The Truth-in-Lending Reform Act of 1980 provides a lender with a defense. If the lender notifies the borrower of a correction to the financing statement within 15 days of learning of the error and before the consumer has made a complaint to the FTC, the lender will not be liable. After all, the primary purpose of the Truth-in-Lending Act is to ensure that consumers have accurate information, not to penalize lenders who act in good faith. In the next case, the lender asserted another statutory defense: a good faith clerical error.

Reliable Finance Co. v. Jenkins

7 Ohio Misc. 2d 24, 454 N.E. 2d 993 (Muni. Ct. 1982)

FACTS

In December 1972, Jenkins borrowed $1999.83 from Reliable Finance Co. to purchase a 1968 Buick. She received a "Disclosure Statement of Loan" which purported to list all the information the Truth-in-Lending Act required. The total of all payments due Reliable was $2639.16, with the last payment to be made in January 1975. By August 1980, when she stopped making payments, Jenkins had paid $1916.69. In December 1980, Reliable sued Jenkins for $1034.5, the balance due on the loan plus late charges. Jenkins claimed that the Disclosure Statement omitted a $54.37 charge for credit life insurance and sought the penalty prescribed under the Act. Reliance claimed that its secretaries customarily checked to see that all boxes on the Statement were filled in, but it admitted that they received no training as to the substance of the disclosures and made no independent computations.

ISSUE

Was Reliable's error made in good faith?

DECISION   No. Judgment for Jenkins. A lender can escape liability by showing that a violation of the Truth-in-Lending Act was unintentional and resulted from a good faith error, notwithstanding procedures designed to avoid such errors. In short, the lender must show that it has a reasonable rechecking procedure. Here, the error was easy to commit, but it also was of a type that could easily be caught with an inexpensive screening procedure. Reliable had a duty to check the figures and correct errors, and it did not satisfy this duty. The $1000 penalty and Jenkins's attorney's fee offset Reliable's claim completely.

Credit card and ATM card liability. The Truth-in-Lending Act also limits consumer liability for the use of a credit card by an unauthorized person to $50. There are hundreds of millions of cards outstanding and 73 million of them are lost or stolen each year. Congress determined that the risk of loss should not fall on the consumer. The credit card companies were regarded as having the capacity to protect and insure themselves against loss.*

The Fair Credit Billing Act applies to credit cards. It requires statements of credit terms and of all related charges.

Many credit cards also serve as automatic teller machine (ATM) cards, although many banks use a separate card. ATM cards allow the user to deposit and withdraw funds and to receive cash advances. ATMs were exotic only a decade ago, but by the mid-1980s over $260 billion was processed through them each year.

The Federal Reserve Board's Regulation E

governs liability for the unauthorized use of ATM cards. The consumer's liability is limited to $50 if the consumer notifies the issuer within 2 days of the card's loss. If the cardholder reports the loss within 60 days of the card's loss, his or her liability is limited to $500. A consumer who does not notify the issuer within 60 days will be liable for the entire loss. These liability restrictions apply even if the consumer was negligent, as when a consumer tapes his or her personal identification number on the back of the card.

The Equal Credit Opportunity Act

Being aware of the finance charges on a loan does an individual little good if a lender will not lend to her for reasons that have nothing to do with her creditworthiness. The Equal Credit Opportunity Act (ECOA) outlaws discrimination in evaluating and granting credit because of race, color, gender, age, religion, marital status, or national origin. The next case deals with a lender who made its decisions to extend credit based on race.

---

* For an ironic example of why Congress allocated liability in this fashion, see *In re Ward;* 857 F. 2d 1082 (6th Cir. 1988), briefed in Chapter 43.

United States v. American Future Systems, Inc.

571 F. Supp. 551 (E.D. Pa. 1983)

FACTS   American Future Systems (AFS) sold china, crystal, cookware, and tableware on credit. AFS aimed its sales efforts at white females in 4-year colleges who were beyond their freshman year. AFS extended credit to persons in this group regardless of age, prior credit history, or other normal indicia of creditworthiness. The goods they bought on credit were shipped to them immediately. All others—including black females and freshmen—received their goods after they had made three consecutive payments. These persons were not told that they received different credit terms than the target market. AFS discriminated between the two groups on the basis of data it had developed that indicated that minority-group members had a significantly greater default rate. The government sought to enjoin AFS from violating the ECOA.

ISSUE   Was AFS justified in offering the two groups different terms?

DECISION   No. Injunction issued. AFS's categorization had nothing to do with individual credit-worthiness, since few of its customers had credit histories. It resulted from a conscious marketing decision to maximize profits by excluding or severely restricting the socially disadvantaged from its credit. Under the ECOA, each credit applicant must be able to assume that a lender will extend equal credit opportunities on the terms given all other persons in the same position, based on the individual credit application, unless she is given a good faith explanation for her different treatment.

AFS's discrimination on the basis of race violated the ECOA despite AFS's attempt to justify it on the basis of experience. A similar practice by banks, called redlining, was a principal target of the ECOA's drafters. The term "redlining" refers to the practice of making red marks on a city map to indicate neighborhoods dominated by minorities. Banks regarded mortgage loans made to individuals on properties in redlined areas as high risk, and would not accept applications for mortgage loans on properties in these neighborhoods.

The ECOA makes redlining illegal. Today lenders must consider applications regardless of the property's location. Of course, the lender may refuse to make the loan if the value of the property does not justify the risk of lending. Thus, the only difference under the ECOA may be that the lender must review the application. The response—"no"—may well be the same.

Prohibitions relating to gender and marital status. Historically, women—especially divorced and young single women—found it difficult to borrow. For example, in calculating a woman's ability to repay, lenders often would not consider alimony as income. Also, they would discount the loan rating of a single woman between 18 and 35, assuming that she would sooner or later leave the workplace to bear children. Under the Equal Credit Opportunity Act it is now illegal to:

- Ask a woman whether she is married unless she wants her husband to be able to take advantage of her credit status
- Ask a woman what her child-bearing plans are
- Ask a woman what method of birth control she uses, if any
- Discount a woman's loan rating because she is in her child-bearing years
- Report a credit transaction solely in the husband's name when a joint account exists

Under the Federal Reserve Board regulations, the ECOA applied to personal loans, not business loans. Women argued that they were discriminated against as proprietors because they were regularly required to have their husbands cosign for loans, while the reverse was not true. Women's groups pushed to prohibit creditors from asking applicants to disclose their marital status for business loans. Some twenty states—but not the Fed—banned marital status questions.

Finally, in response to these complaints, Congress enacted the Women's Business Ownership Act of 1988. It extends the ECOA prohibition against discrimination to applicants for business credit. Now, small business commercial loan applicants, female and male alike, have a right to an *adverse action notice*—a written statement of reasons for any denial of credit.

Calculating the applicant's income. A lender must tell potential borrowers that they need not list alimony, child support, or maintenance payments as income on credit applicants. In practice, this means that if Mary receives alimony and child support from her ex-husband but would rather establish personal credit based on her own employment, she does not have to list the money she receives from him.

Should a credit applicant choose to list alimony and the like, the creditor must treat these as income regardless of whether the Internal Revenue Code treats them as such. This provision eliminates the possibility of a creditor basing a lending decision on the applicant's federal income tax return, which would show a lower income figure. Instead, the creditor must perform a separate evaluation based on figures the applicant supplies.

While the creditor must treat alimony and child support payments as income, it may ask whether they are up to date and how long they will continue. For example, the Family Court may have awarded Mary temporary alimony and child support, but if her ex-husband makes payments irregularly—or only after being threatened by her lawyer—a lender may consider this in making a credit decision.

Another problem working mothers faced before the ECOA was enacted was that credi-

tors discounted or ignored earnings from part-time employment. The ECOA requires that such earnings be treated as income.

Denial of credit. In order to minimize the possibility that a decision not to lend might be made for improper reasons, a lender must give specific reasons to a consumer who is denied credit. For example, a person who is denied credit because she is new to a community has a right to know that this is the reason her loan application was turned down.

The Fair Credit Reporting Act

If the lender's reason for denying credit is based on invalid information in a credit report, the Fair Credit Reporting Act permits the consumer to challenge the denial and the correct any errors of fact or analysis. The Act covers credit report made on an individual in connection with:

- Consumer credit for personal, family, or household purposes
- Hiring or retention in employment
- The purchase of insurance

Until the Fair Credit Reporting Act was passed, individuals generally had no way of finding out what was in credit report or of correction information in them. Someone could apply for a mortgage and be turned down because of a report that she failed to repay a $200 student loan—even though that report was completely wrong. Worse, she had no right to learn the basis for her rejection from the lender. If the report was prepared by a private company, not the lender, she had no legal remedy to compel the company to correct its records. Such misinformation could affect her credit rating permanently.

How big a problem is this? According to *Business Week,* a credit bureau trade association estimates that only ¹/₁₀ of 1 percent of the 500 million credit reports issued annually contain an error.* But, that translates into 500,000 erroneous reports each year.

Consumer's rights. Today, if a lender rejects a consumer's credit application, the consumer must be told whether it was because of an adverse credit report. If it was, she has a right to know the source of that report. She also has a right to learn what the report says, if she requests it within 60 days of the rejection of her credit application. She has a right to have the report corrected if it contains erroneous information. If, however, she disputes something in the report and the dispute cannot be resolved, she has a right to have a paragraph added giving her version.

A consumer has a right to have most adverse information purged after 7 years, including successfully completing a Chapter 13 bankruptcy action. The unsuccessful completion of a Chapter 13 action or discharge by a Chapter 7 action cannot be purged for 10 years. The purpose of the expungement provision is to cease to penalize consumers who have learned their lessons and have established good credit habits. This is especially beneficial for many new college graduates who may take several years to establish good credit habits.

Duties of reporting agencies and their clients. The Fair Credit Reporting Act covers both agencies which report credit data and those who use that information in lending decisions.

The reporting agencies are responsible for the information they assemble, interpret, and then supply to clients. Thus, a credit bureau obviously is covered by the Act. However, the Act exempts those who simply provide factual data on transactions. American Express, for example, is exempt when it reports whether a cardholder pays his bills each month.

The Act also applies to those businesses which use reports to decide whether to grant credit to a consumer. These businesses have a duty to disclose why a consumer is denied credit.

Investigative reports. The Act requires that a consumer to be told that she will be subject to a consumer investigative report on her credit. She must consent to this report. Prospective employers and life insurance companies often commission these reports in order to evaluate the consumer's lifestyle, morals, character, and the life. The Act attempts to reduce the possibility of error by requiring the investigative agency to use reasonable procedures. Thus, an investigator who goes to only one neighbor to discuss the subject of a report probably violates the law, particularly if the neighbor slanders the subject, and the investigator does not bother to check the tale.

Enforcement. Enforcement of the Fair Credit Reporting Act begins with consumers making a formal complaint. A point of interest: The number of complaints per year declined from around 4000 complaints per year in the late 1970s to around 2000 in 1992. The Act provides both civil and criminal penalties for violations. The FTC enforces the Act civilly under the "unfair and deceptive acts of practices" clause of the FTCA.

The Act can also be enforced by means of direct consumer suits against the lender or the credit reporting agency. The consumer suit is more common than FTC action. In a direct suit, if the plaintiff can show willful noncompliance with the Act, she will receive her actual damages as well as punitive damages, if appropriate. If the noncompliance is not willful, the plaintiff must prove negligence in order to recover her actual damages. Punitive damages are not awarded in cases in which the violation was not willful.

Criminal liability under the Fair Credit Reporting Act is quite limited. A federal criminal

---

* "When You Don't Get Credit Where Credit Is Due," *Business Week,* October 2, 1989, p. 116.

action is possible against a person who uses false pretenses to gain credit information. Suppose Vera wonders about her fiance's financial status. She pretends he has filed a credit application with a store where she works in order to obtain a credit report on him. She could be prosecuted under the Act.

Due to the potentially serious effects of erroneous credit reporting on people's lives, Congress has seriously considered imposing greater regulatory oversight on credit-reporting agencies. In reaction to these threats, companies such as TRW are attempting to reform their systems internally to be more responsive to consumer complaints.

The Fair Debt Collection Practices Act

Abusive debt collection practices, like harassing phone calls, physical threats, or embarrassing confrontations in the presence of neighbors are not common. However, they do occur. In 1978 Congress was sufficiently upset by consumers' horror stories to pass the Fair Debt Collection Practices Act. This Act applies only to consumer debts.

A bill collection agency can send neither letters with return addresses indicating it is a bill collector nor postcards, since these might embarrass a debtor.

Consumer debt collection agencies. The Act applies *only* to consumer debt collection agencies and law firms in the business of collecting debts for others. It does not apply to firms collecting their own accounts. Thus, while a debt collection firm is covered, Marshall Field or the May Company would not be. Congress believed that firms collecting their own debts are less likely to engage in unfair practices, since they will want to retain their customers. Some writers have questioned this rationale, arguing that the difference in coverage reflects the retailers' greater political influence.

The rationale for exemptions does not bear much examination. If a debt collection practice is an evil, it should be wrong for all who collect debts. This criticism is especially telling, since the Act also exempts government units collecting overdue taxes and bills.

Abusive practices. The Act defines a number of practices as abusive. These include threats of injury to property, person, or possessions and the use of obscene language. If an agency threatens arrest or a lawsuit, it must have that remedy available to it in the particular situation. Otherwise, such threats are improper. Also, a bill collector cannot represent himself as an attorney when he is not. In fact, he must state his status and role.

Telephoning debtors between 9:00 at night and 8:00 in the morning or at work is an abusive practice. Even if an agency observes this prohibition, it may commit an abusive practice if it calls the debtor too often. The law leaves the determination of how many calls are too many up to the debtor. When the debtor feels that the calls have become an intrusion, she may write the credit collection agency asking that they cease. Once it has received this notice, the agency can *only* deal with her attorney—if the debtor directs them to her attorney—or sue her.

Remedies. A consumer subjected to an abusive credit collection practice may sue the bill collector in tort for her actual damages suffered, including those for *invasion of privacy* or the *intentional infliction of emotional distress*. For example, a credit collection agency threatened to call members of an elderly woman's church to tell them she was an unchristian cheat. That act amounted to the intentional infliction of emotional distress.

The FTC, an individual consumer acting alone, or a class of consumers may enforce the Act. They may seek actual damages, statutory damages (not exceeding $1000), attorneys' fees, and court costs. In a class action, the Act limits statutory damages to $500,000 or 1 percent of the net worth of the debt collector—plus actual damages, attorneys' fees, and costs.

CONSUMER PRODUCT SAFETY ACT

In 1967, Ralph Nader published *Unsafe at Any Speed,* an indictment of GM's first compact car, the Corvair. GM's reaction to the book—it tried first to discredit, then to persecute, Nader—created an enormous consumer demand for a mechanism that would make manufacturers act responsibly with regard to the safety of the products they put into commerce. This pressure led Congress to enact the Consumer Product Safety Act in 1972. The Act created the Consumer Product Safety Commission (CPSC). This five-member board's duty is to protect the public from unreasonable risks of harm resulting from dangerous or potentially dangerous consumer products.

The Consumer Product Safety Commission

Manufacturers and distributors fought the Act, claiming that the red tape associated with a new federal agency would significantly increase the cost of their goods. Further, they argued, they were extremely sensitive to the potential loss of consumer goodwill as a result of defective products. Also, consumers had adequate remedies for safety problems in the sales, contract, and tort remedies. And finally, the market mechanism—of which these remedies were a part—would winnow out unsatisfactory products more economically than a new agency. These arguments are now being made in favor of abolishing the CPSC.

However, in its short life, the CPSC has forced sellers to repair, replace, or refund the purchase price of over 300 million potentially hazardous goods. And, the CPSC estimates it has prevented more than 1 million injuries per year. Still, the CPSC estimates that well over 100,000 children per year must go to hospital emergency rooms for injuries sustained from children's toys. Nonetheless, its budget and staff have been drastically cut since 1981.

Product standards. The Commission monitors and evaluates product information so that it can educate the public on safety problems. Thus, besides issuing regulations banning flammable children's sleepwear, the Commission started a public awareness campaign so that consumers could identify dangerous sleepwear purchased before the ban.

The Commission also used product information to develop regulations setting uniform product safety standards for lawnmowers, toys, workshop electrical tools, lead paint, and the like. For example, the CPSC has attempted to establish uniform standards for the 70 million bicycles in the United States today. One regulation made wheel reflectors mandatory on new bicycles so that motorists can see them more easily at night.

Businesses manufacturing or selling items that are covered by the Commission's regulations must submit data, test results, and information on customer experience to show their compliance. Because of the dangers inherent in some types of products, a manufacturer may be required to establish compliance with CPSC regulations before a new product may be sold to the public. For example, suppose Grass Corporation has just entered the business of manufacturing power lawnmowers. Grass would have to show that its mowers comply with the Commission's safety requirements before putting them into stores.

Notification of safety problems. A manufacturer who learns of safety problems with its products as a result of consumer use must promptly report that experiential information to the Commission. So, if Grass Corp. learns that one of its models is subject to fires from a leaky gas line, it must notify the CPSC immediately so that it can inform the public of the danger, if necessary. If Grass does not do so voluntarily, the Commission may suspend sales of that model.

Enforcement

Civil and administrative. Either consumers or the Commission may enforce the Act through civil actions. A consumer can sue for damages caused by a manufacturer's noncompliance with safety standards. The Act also provides for attorneys' fees in such cases.

Where appropriate, the CPSC may seek an injunction against the distribution of a product pending the commission's determination of the product's compliance with CPSC standards. In the next case, the court had to determine what the CPSC must prove in order to obtain an injunction.

United States v. Sun & Sand Imports Ltd., Inc.

564 F. Supp. 1402 (S.D.N.Y. 1983), aff'd, F.2d 184 (2d Cir. 1984)

FACTS Sun & Sand imported "Footsies" and "Nectarines," garments for infants and toddlers. The garments have attached feet and cover the entire body except the head and hands. The CPSC's enforcement division instituted an administrative proceeding which would lead to an administrative determination as to their compliance with the flammability standard for infant sleepwear. It also filed this suit to enjoin their sale pending determination of their compliance. Sun & Sand admitted that the garments were made of flammable material. But, it contended that the two products were not marketed as sleepwear, and so the standard did not apply. The CPSC introduced evidence that Sun & Sand's efforts to market the garments exclusively as playwear were ineffective, that stores frequently mingled Footsies and Nectarines with garments intended for sleep, and that the products were indistinguishable from common children's sleepwear.

ISSUE Had the CPSC raised a serious question as to whether the two products were sleepwear under its regulations?

DECISION Yes. Injunction granted. In order to obtain an injunction in these circumstances, the CPSC must prove, as it did, that questions about a product's compliance with its regulations raise such significant issues that its distribution should be enjoined until the agency has made a determination. The CPSC does not have to prove that its enforcement division's position will prevail ultimately.

The Commission may seek a court order to seize or ban the sale of a product because of the safety hazards it poses. Bans can have far-reaching effects. The Commission has adopted a regulation which forbids the export to another country of hazardous products recalled in this country. Violators may be subject to civil penalties of up to $500,000.

Criminal. The Department of Justice has jurisdiction to enforce the criminal sanctions of the Act. These can result in fines of up to $50,000 or imprisonment of up to 1 year, or both.

OTHER FEDERAL LAWS PROTECTING CONSUMERS

At the beginning of the chapter, we illustrated the breadth of federal consumer protection laws by listing some that we had covered in earlier chapters. Some other that are not covered anywhere in this book deserve at least a mention.

The various acts administered by the Food & Drug Administration (FDA) regulate the purity and safety of food products and prescription and nonprescription drugs. The FDA requires proof of testing for drugs, as well as proper labeling. It also directs recalls when a product under its supervision poses a health hazard.

The FDA enforces the rules of food labeling. To illustrate, the FDA specifically regulates the usage of the following words: Fresh, light/lite, low-fat, low-calorie, no cholesterol, lean, reduced and natural. In 1991, the FDA, in two separate actions, got Procter & Gamble to agree to drop "Fresh" from the name of "Citrus Hill Fresh Choice" orange juice, since its orange juice is made from concentrate, and "no cholesterol" from their Crisco Corn Oil label.*

The Environmental Protection Agency (EPA) tests the fuel efficiency of each year's car models. Some consider all of EPA's regulatory responsibilities to have a consumer protection aspect.

The National Highway Traffic Safety Administration (NHTSA) oversees automobile safety issues, including recalls for safety reasons. In 1983 alone, there were recalls of 110 domestic models and 30 imported models, involving 6 million cars.

These agencies are just the prominent examples. Any others, like the Department of Labor, have extensive consumer responsibilities.

There are many more federal statutes which are designed to protect the health and safety of the consumer. For example, a number of federal statutes specifically regulate the marketing of products, including warnings, information and restrictions concerning hazardous toys, cigarette smoking and smokeless tobacco, meat, poultry, eggs, furs, flammable fabrics, insecticides, fungicides, rodenticides and collectables.

As a finale to our discussion of consumer protection laws, the federal protection of trademarks deserves note.* While the trademark laws may seem to protect primarily a business interest, the next case shows that they have a significant role in assuring the consumer that she receives what she thinks she is buying.

---

* "Procter & Gamble: On a Short Leash," *Business Week,* July 21, 1991, p. 76.

* Chapter 25 discusses the enforcement of trademarks in more detail.

LaCoste Alligator, S.A. v. Bluestein's Men's Wear, Inc.

569 F. Supp. 491 (D.S.C. 1983)

FACTS   LaCoste owns various U.S. trademarks, including "LACOSTE," "IZOD," and a depiction of an alligator. Floyd ran a flea market. He admitted that he bought a lot of shirts which resembled LaCoste's and then purchased 10,000 alligator logos which he believed had originally belonged to LaCoste. He personally sewed many of these on the shirts and sold them at his flea market. LaCoste brought suit, seeking seizure of the counterfeit goods, an injunction against Floyd, and triple damages.

ISSUE   Were Floyd's actions likely to create confusion in the public's mind between his shirts and LaCoste's?

DECISION   Yes. Judgment for LaCoste. Floyd clearly intended that the public should take his fakes to be real LaCoste's. Although a showing of an actual intent to confuse or mislead the public is not required, Floyd did so intend.

CONCLUSION

Congress and the state legislatures enacted consumer protection laws to curb improper and unethical business practices, to give consumers greater leverage in their disputes with businesses, and to ensure that consumers have enough information to choose intelligently from among competing products.

Today's consumer has good reason to be more confident that a product advertisement will be forthright, that he will be able to understand the commitment he makes when he borrows money, and that the product he buys will be free of unreasonable risks of injury. This assurance improves the quality of life for the consumer, his family, and his friends.

However, consumer protection laws are unlikely to be expanded in the near future. Many businesses are still resisting statutes that are already on the books, contending that the balance has shifted too far in favor of the consumer. It is now the consumer, they contend, who has the upper hand and who does not necessarily act honorably or in good faith. A debtor's new power to free himself of debt collection efforts simply by requesting this freedom seems to many businesspeople simply the most blatant of many examples.

Also, the costs of consumer protection lead to higher prices for services and products. Especially in times of recession, businesspersons feel that the costs of government safety specifications outweigh their benefits. The reduction in demand caused by higher prices in turn causes a reduction in the work force and ultimately leads to a further diminution in the consumer's ability to purchase goods. In other words, the cost of consumer protection is a real cost.

While there can be little question that the consumer protection laws have cleaned up the marketplace, they have disappointed many of their advocates. They seen to have added another layer of litigation to the traditional remedies. Until consumer advocates and manufacturers can reach agreement on the scope of remedies and the means of enforcing them, the costs of consumer protection are likely to remain higher than they would be in an ideal world. Yet, in an era when 6 million cars must be recalled in a single year, the need for consumer protection regulations is plain.

A NOTE TO FUTURE CPA CANDIDATES

The CPA exam does not test the material in this chapter. Candidates should *not* mix or substitute material in this chapter with common law contract questions or answers.

KEY WORDS

bait and switch (1047)   redlining (1055)
consent decree (1049)   Regulation Z (1051)
consumer (1044)   usury (1045)

DISCUSSION QUESTIONS

1. "Consumer protection laws have their origins in the common law of contracts." Is that statement correct?
2. With the advent of federal consumer protection laws, what role do state consumer protection laws play?
3. What is meant by the phrase "deceptive acts or practices"?
4. What are the principal federal rules governing advertising, and who enforces them?
5. What is the main purpose of the federal Truth-in-Lending Act? When does the federal law apply?
6. What is the purpose of the Fair Credit Reporting Act, and when does it apply?
7. What is the purpose of the Fair Debt Collection Practices Act, and when does it apply?
8. What is the purpose of the Consumer product Safety Commission? Why might it be controversial?
9. What are some examples of federal agencies other than the FTC and the CPSC that are involved in consumer protection?
10. Are the consumer protection laws cost-effective? What are the arguments for returning to a "let the buyer beware" philosophy?

CASE PROBLEMS

1. New Wave Waterbed Manufacturers sells its waterbeds in factory outlets. New Wave pays Mickey Santos, an Olympic champion, to endorse its $225 Dreamer model in a television commercial. Although he sleeps on a board, Santos tells the public, "I can't get a good night's sleep unless I'm on my Dreamer." Once the ads start running, New Wave withholds shipments of Dreamers to its stores, telling its sales force to steer customers to the $325 Golden Dreamer. What problems might New Wave encounter as a result of this sales campaign?
2. In one of its advertisements, the Baxter Chair Company says, "If you've got a bad back, you're going to love our Gentleman's Chair. Experience has proved that its special support is just the thing for aching backs." The experience cited is four letters Baxter has received from satisfied users during the 3 years the chair has been on the market. Baxter has just received a letter from the FTC questioning the ad. If the FTC decides to take formal action against Baxter, what is the probable outcome?
3. National Motors Co. advertises that its sub-compact sedan, the Squirt, sells for $350 less and gets 6 more miles per gallon than a competitor's Spring XL. While this is true, the Squirt is National's base model, while the Spring XL is the top of the competitor's line. The Sprint base model gets the same gas mileage and sells for $200 less than the Squirt. The FTC determines that National's ads are highly persuasive to the public and issues a cease the desist order. Are National's ads in violation of FTC regulations?
4. Caulkins Men's Store decided to capitalize on the popularity of the Hill & Stream shirt by placing a logo similar to Hill & Stream's carp on some shirts it purchased from Hong Kong. H&S Manufacturing Corporation, the carp logo's trademark holder, has sought an injunction against Caulkin's sale of the shirts. Caulkins plans to defend on the grounds that it makes no representation that these are shirts made by H&S. What is the likely result?
5. Cefalu Appliance financed the sale of new kitchen appliances to Helen Wetter. Helen had problems with the appliances—they did not work properly—and suspended her monthly payments while she attempted to get satisfaction. Cefalu has turned Wetter's account over to Enoch's Collection Services. Enoch called Wetter several times to discuss the matter but each time she rudely told him to send Cefalu to fix her problems and hung up. Getting no positive results, Enoch called Wetter's employer and Victory University, where Wetter is working part-time on an MBA degree. He told them of her "bad debts and unprofessional conduct." Wetter is furious and contends that Enoch has broken the law. Is a court likely to agree? Explain.
6. Linda and Gerry Wilson applied for a first

mortgage with First Federal Savings & Loan. The loan officer told them that their loan would be at 13 percent, but failed to give them any other particulars on the costs until the closing. Two months after the closing, the Wilsons hired Hoefer Roofing to put on a new roof. The Wilsons agreed to give Hoefer a second mortgage on their home securing their payment. Two days after signing the second mortgage agreement, Gerry decided to cancel the agreement because he had just been laid off. Hoefer refuses to consent to the cancelation. Has either company violated the Truth-in-Lending Act? If so, how?

7. Gloria Stivak sought a used-car loan from General Finance Company. The loan officer, Mr. Murphy, asked Ms. Stivak what her personal plans might be during the period of the loan. Ms. Stivak, an attorney, felt that the question prompted responses from female applicants concerning their marriage and child-bearing plans. She filed a complaint against General Finance. General Finance has defended on the grounds that it asks all applicants the same question. What is the probable result under the Equal Credit Opportunity Act? Explain.

8. The Consumer Product Safety Commission has received a number of complaints about the Victory 3000 ten-speed bicycle. The chain slips persistently. This condition has caused riders to lose control, and some have received serious injuries. Victory claims that the bike owners' improper maintenance caused the problem. The CPSC has determined that the level of maintenance required to keep the bike on the road far exceeds that of any equivalent nonracing ten-speed and is well beyond the level expected by consumers. What remedies might the CPSC seek?

9. Real Issues. Several years ago Volvo featured a television advertisement wherein a "monster truck" was shown in a car-flattening event crushing some twenty cars except for three used Volvos. The point of the advertisement was that Volvos are built with greater strength to protect the driver and passenger in case of an accident. Unfortunately, it was later learned that the three Volvos had survived the truck stomping because they had been modified with steel-reinforced roofs. The State of Texas filed suit claiming false and deceptive advertising. Volvo explained that its advertising agency was showing a reenactment of a "monster truck" event sponsored by the Arthritis Foundation of Vermont where after repeated passes by a "monster truck" a used Volvo station wagon remained largely intact and uncrushed while the cars surrounding it were crushed. Volvo stated that they did not know of the modifications until after the complaint was filed. Given the above facts, how would you have advised Volvo to respond to the complaint by the State of Texas? Explain.

10. Real Issues. As discussed in the chapter, the Fair Credit Reporting Act requires after 10 years a deletion of the fact that a person unsuccessfully completed a Chapter 13 bankruptcy action or was involved in a Chapter 7 action. Many creditors argue that this provision provides unwarranted consumer protection in that it prevents a creditor from learning important past behavior which might occur again. They argue that the expunged information should remain a permanent part of a consumer's record. They contend that a consumer who has established and maintained a good credit record will face very little, if any, adverse effects. In contrast, creditors stand to lose a great deal, especially when they are working with persons who have been involved in bankruptcy a couple of times over an extended period of time. Consumer rights advocates generally disagree. They contend that 10 years is a sufficient time to judge the creditworthiness of an applicant for credit. Your thoughts?

Nostalgia for simpler times conceals the reality of working life in the past. For Americans, this self-deception holds particularly true for the nineteenth century.

For all save the very wealthy, work under conditions that are almost unimaginable today consumed 10 to 14 hours 6 days a week. Help wanted ads often closed with lines like ''Irish need not apply.'' Ten-year-olds worked at extremely hazardous jobs in mines and mills. Employers could prevent labor unions from organizing their employees. Levels of pay were often below what it cost to subsist. Employees injured on the job lacked any remedy against their employers and bore the cost of the injury themselves. When, because of age, employees could no longer work, with very few exceptions they had to support themselves from their savings or induce family members to care for them.

Gradually, in the late nineteenth century, Congress and the state legislatures began to address these issues. Today, statutes cover virtually every aspect of employment, from hiring to employee benefits during retirement. These statutes passed by Congress under its commerce clause powers, modified or abolished the common law governing employment contracts between employers and employees and that governing injuries suffered by employees on the job. However, they also created rights never contemplated by the common law, such as the right to an equal opportunity for employment.

This chapter provides an overview of these statutes. We have divided them into those that affect employment discrimination, labor unions and their activities, employee benefits, and employee safety.*

---

* We have examined other aspects of the relationship between employer and employee in Chapter 4, Torts, and Chapters 13–15, Agency and Employment. So strictly speaking, this chapter covers the law relating to employment, promotion, discharge, wages, benefits, and workplace conditions.

FEDERAL EMPLOYMENT DISCRIMINATION LAWS

Until the 1960s, laws covering employment discrimination virtually did not exist. The first comprehensive legislation was the federal Civil Rights Act of 1964. That law is often referred to as ''Title VII,'' a reference to the part of the act that prohibits employment discrimination. Most states followed with similar laws. Since 1964, Congress has passed several other laws attacking discrimination in employment. This section examines the more important federal antidiscrimination laws.

Some students believe discrimination suits are relics from the 1970s, that they are things of the past. Not so. Just ask Pan Am, which settled an age discrimination case brought by pilots for $17.2 million; or AT&T, which settled a pregnancy discrimination case for $10 million; or Honda, which settled a race and sex discrimination case for $6 million; or State Farm, which settled a sex discrimination case that cost the company more than $50 million; or General Motors, which settled a race discrimination case for $10 million. Those are just a sampling of the larger judgments from 1987 through 1989.

Just how pervasive is racial discrimination in the 1990s? In 1990, the Urban Institute conducted an empirical study of employment discrimination involving 476 sets of paired applicants in Chicago and Washington, D.C. The black applicants experienced discriminatory treatment about three times more than did the white job seekers. Moreover, the white applicant progressed in the hiring process over the black counterpart 20 percent of the time, while the black applicant advanced over the white counterpart in 7 percent of the cases studied.

Similarly, a 1992 poll conducted by the *National Law Journal* disclosed that 78 percent of adult Americans believe that ''some, most or all'' employers practice some kind of discrimination, while 25 percent have actually experienced it.*

Businesspeople must make themselves aware of the antidiscrimination laws. Nondiscrimination is the law, and employees—and the plaintiffs bar—know it. Indeed, employment discrimination litigation has skyrocketed a stunning 2000 percent from 1970 to 1990! This explosion of litigation has been accompanied by huge judgments and expensive and time-consuming class-action suits. Such companies as State Farm Insurance, Eveleth Taconite Company, and Shoney's restaurants have been targets of such suits. State Farm ultimately ended up settling its sex discrimination suit in 1992 for a record $157 million. Shoney's, by late 1992, was still fighting a class-action lawsuit involving all black employees who worked at Shoney's and Captain D's restaurants in twenty states from 1988 to 1991. That amounts to 75,000 employees!

The Civil Rights Act of 1964

The Civil Rights Act of 1964 was the first comprehensive federal assault on employment discrimination. The Act created the Equal Employment Opportunity Commission (EEOC) to enforce its provisions.

Coverage of Title VII. The Civil Rights Act forbids discrimination based upon race, color, national origin, sex, or religion. These are called "suspect" *criteria*, or standards, and the Act specifically forbids any form of discrimination in hiring, promotion, retention, transfer, retirement, or the like based on one or more of the criteria.

The Act covers any employer with fifteen or more employees, including state and local governments. (State antidiscrimination laws generally cover employers with fewer employ-

ees.) It also covers unions and employment agencies, both of which can affect who gets hired.

Aggrieved employees must seek relief under a state law, if one exists. If they do not gain relief at the state level, then they can pursue a federal remedy through the EEOC. For example, Mary works for Hitech, Inc., in Massachusetts. She believes that Hitech did not promote her because of her gender. She must bring her complaint of employment discrimination first to the Massachusetts Commission Against Discrimination. If she does not obtain relief there, she may file a complaint with the EEOC.

In order to prove a violation of Title VII, employees must show that an employer failed to hire, retain, or promote them on the basis of one of the forbidden criteria—race, color, national origin, gender, or religion. Violations involve two practices: different treatment of individuals based on any of the suspect criteria or particular impact of an employment practice on a racial, ethnic, gender, or religious group. Needless to say, the two practices often overlap.

Different treatment of individuals. To prove a case of differing treatment of an individual on account of race, creed, color, gender, religion, or national origin, the plaintiff must show that the different treatment was intentional, that the employer purposefully discriminated. The plaintiff may establish discrimination by means of *circumstantial evidence*—evidence based not on actual personal knowledge but on facts from which a conclusion can be drawn.

The ability to use circumstantial evidence is an important advantage for plaintiffs, because nowadays employers rarely discriminate overtly, much less document their wrongdoing. For instance, a plaintiff might show that the percentage of minority workers in an employer's factory is far smaller than the percentage of eligible minority workers in the area surround-

---

* R. Sanborn, "Bias Law Booms," *The National Law Journal*, July 27, 1992, p. 1.

ing the plant. Or an employee in a promotion discrimination case might show that an employer has comparatively few minority workers in leadership positions within the company. For example, Major League baseball owners have been highly criticized for the lack of minority positions in the management of major league baseball clubs.

Finally, an employee may show that the employer allowed such discriminatory working conditions to exist that the employee had to resign. Courts have awarded damages when an employer permits racial or sexual harassment by fellow employees to occur openly within the workplace.

Establishing a prima facie case requires the plaintiff to prove that he or she belongs to a group protected by the act. The plaintiff must then show that he or she applied for a job for which the employer was seeking applicants, and that, though he or she was qualified for the job, the employer did not offer it. And that the job remained open while the employer kept searching.

Once the plaintiff has established a prima facie case, the burden shifts to the employer to prove that it had a legitimate, nondiscriminatory reason for not hiring, promoting, or retaining the plaintiff. Of course, the plaintiff may introduce evidence to rebut the defendant's explanation.

Testers. Since proving discrimination can be, as seen above, very difficult, the EEOC and private civil rights groups have begun to use "testers" to investigate employment discrimination. Testers are hired to apply for jobs they do not intend to accept for the singular aim of uncovering discrimination. Frequently they are undergraduate or graduate students (often law students) who enjoy being paid while developing job interviewing skills at the same time. Typically, one black and one white "applicant" are carefully matched and instructed to perform in a comparable manner at the application and interview. There have been a number of cases

that have been prosecuted based on tester evidence. In 1990, the NAACP filed a suit against Lord & Taylor department stores in Miami when a black female tester with significant work experience was turned down for a job for which a white female tester, with less experience, was hired later that same day.* Likewise, in 1992, Brooks Brothers in Boston was sued after the white applicant was told the position was available and he could apply, but the black applicant was told an hour later it was filled. Brooks Brothers is defending on the premise that there was no harm suffered, since the testers were not really job seekers.† In April, 1993 Brooks Brothers settled the case. As part of the settlement, the company admitted no wrongdoing, but agreed to institute minority outreach and affirmative action programs in three of its stores; plus make payments to a state trust fund for equal employment rights.‡ Not surprisingly, testing has been criticized, since it is argued that "controlling" the appearance and behavior of two people in two situations simply cannot be done. Some personnel managers, alerted to testing, are now instructed to note and substantiate all differences among applicants in a checklist.

Employment practices. Certain employment practices seem neutral on the surface but actually have markedly different impacts on groups protected by the Civil Rights Act. A plaintiff may demonstrate that standards, requirements, or tests for employment or promotion lack a substantial relationship to the *actual* requirements of the job. Courts have found the following criteria to bear a questionable relationship to particular jobs.

---

* J. Wymer, III, and D. Sudbury, "Employment Discrimination 'Testers'—Will Your Hiring Practices Pass?" *Employee Relations Law Journal*, 17, Spring 1992.
† J. Pereira, "Boston Case May Spur Job-Bias," *Wall Street Journal*, November 27, 1992, p. 12A.
‡ R. Suskind, Brooks Bros. settles Job-Bias Suit; Inquiry Used Controversial 'Tests,' *Wall Street Journal*, April 23, 1993, p. B6.

- Arrest (as opposed to conviction) record
- Education, unless relevant to the position
- Applicant's debts or assets
- Photograph with resume
- Name of applicant's pastor or religious leader
- Marital status
- Birthplace
- Dependents
- Credit standing
- Applicant's maiden name

Many of these items appear neutral, but courts have determined that employers may not inquire into them because they cut against blacks in employment decisions. Blacks, for instance, are generally arrested on charges which lack legal merit more often than whites. Thus, their arrest—as opposed to conviction—records may not reflect actual criminal conduct. The courts have also forbidden employers to ask about the highest educational level achieved unless it is related to the job. A higher percentage of blacks than of white lacks a high school diploma.

In proving a case of discrimination based on a hiring practice, a plaintiff must show that the practice results in a racial imbalance and lacks a legitimate business justification. For example, a company's requirement that its maintenance workers have high school diplomas would have a disparate impact on blacks and hispanics, whose graduation rates are lower than whites. The requirement, which must be shown by the employer to be job-related, probably could not be justified because it would require the company to establish a correlation between a high school diploma and the skills required to do the job.

For a brief period, from 1989 to 1991, the burden of proving that an employer's apparently race-neutral hiring practices had a disparate impact on protected groups like minorities, was shifted from the defendant-employer to the plaintiff-employee. This came about after a Supreme Court ruling in the case of *Wards Cove*

*Packing Co. v. Antonio.** The new approach essentially eliminated this manner of proving discrimination under Title VII, because of the difficulty and expense to the plaintiff. The Civil Rights Act of 1991, discussed later in this chapter, placed the burden back on the employer-defendant to prove that a hiring policy was job-related. This provision of the 1991 Act resurrected the pre-1989 approach, which had been previously established by a Supreme Court decision.†

The repudiation of the *Wards Cove* decision under the 1991 Act was surrounded by controversy. Many businesses felt that placing the burden of proof on the defendant forces the business to adopt hiring "quotas." Put another way, in order for businesses to avoid being sued, some claim they must hire a number of minorities and women to make it look like their policies do not have a disparate impact on these groups.

Bona fide occupational qualifications. An employer may discriminate in hiring on the basis of national origin, gender, or religion when one of these is a *bona fide occupational qualification* (BFOQ). There is no such thing as a BFOQ which justifies race or color discrimination, however. A theater company could insist that applicants to play Juliet in *Romeo and Juliet* be female. Still, the company could not reject a black Juliet because of its white Romeo or because its audience would prefer a white Juliet.

Courts look upon the BFOQ defense with great skepticism. In fact, the Supreme Court has described it as "an extremely narrow exception to the general prohibition of discrimination."‡ The employer must show that a business necessity justifies the BFOQ. Customer preference alone, as the next case shows, will not help the employer.

* *Wards Cove Packing Co. v. Antonio*, 109 S.Ct. 2115 (1989)
† *Griggs v. Duke Power Company*, 401 U.S. 424 (1971).
‡ *Dothard v. Rawlinson*, 433 U.S. 321, 334 (1977).

Diaz v. Pan American World Airways, Inc.

442 F.2d 385 (5th Cir. 1971)

FACTS   Celio Diaz applied for a flight attendant's position with Pan Am. The airline rejected him because it restricted that position to females. Pan Am's passengers overwhelmingly preferred to be served by females. Also, a psychiatrist testified that females better attended to the special psychological needs of airline passengers. Diaz filed charges of sexual discrimination with the Equal Employment Opportunity Commission (EEOC). When the Commission failed to resolve the matter, Diaz brought suit. The trial court found for Pan Am.

ISSUE   For the job of flight attendant, was being a female a BFOQ reasonably necessary to the normal operation of Pan Am's business?

DECISION   No. Reversed. The Civil Rights Act requires a court to apply a business necessity test, not a business convenience test. Discrimination based on gender is valid only when not hiring members of one gender exclusively would undermine the essence of the business operation. An airline's primary function is transporting passengers safely. No one suggested that male stewards would jeopardize or even reduce the airline's ability to provide safe transportation. Pan Am could consider an individual's ability to perform the job's nonmechanical functions. However, because those aspects of the job are not reasonably necessary to the normal operation of Pan Am's business, Pan Am could not exclude all males simply because most males could not perform them adequately.

Under the BFOQ exception, a French restaurant may hire only French natives. Similarly, a Roman Catholic church may hire only Catholics. The next case is perhaps the most extreme example of a religious BFOQ.

Kern v. Dynalectron Corp.

577 F. Supp. 1196 (N.D. Tex 1983)

FACTS   Kern, a helicopter pilot, applied for a job with Dynalectron. Under a contract with the Saudi Arabian government, Dynalectron was recruiting pilots to fly patrol missions along the pilgrimage route to Mecca. Because such flights entered the holy area around Mecca, and since Saudi law specifies beheading as the penalty for a non-Muslim entering this area, a condition of employment was that the pilots be Muslims. Kern understood this condition when he applied for and accepted the job. However, after formally converting from Baptist to Muslim, he changed his mind. Dynalectron offered him another position which would become available in 4 months. Kern declined that position and demanded that he be given another position immediately. The company refused. He brought suit, alleging religious discrimination in employment.

ISSUE

Was being a Muslim a legitimate BFOQ for Dynalectron's pilots flying into Mecca?

DECISION

Yes. Judgment for Dynalectron. Kern established a prima facie case of religious discrimination. But, Dynalectron's business is to provide helicopter pilots. The essence of its business would be undermined by the beheading of its non-Muslim pilots. Dynalectron had a reasonable basis for believing that all non-Muslims would be unsafe in this position. Therefore, Dynalectron's discrimination against non-Muslims generally and Kern specifically was lawful, since an applicant's religion was a qualification reasonably related to the employer's business.

Gender discrimination. The original draft of the Civil Rights Act of 1964 did not cover gender discrimination. The day before the Act passed, a Congressman attempting to ensure the legislation's defeat offered an amendment adding the provision. The Act's proponents willingly accepted the amendment, and, as a result, treatment of women in the workplace profoundly changed.

Height, weight, lifting, and similar requirements are objective tests that may have a discriminatory effect. Recent U.S. Supreme Court decisions have made clear that employers who rely heavily on subjective evaluations and criteria must also review their procedures for discriminatory effects. Academic tenure decisions* and partnership evaluations in law and accounting† firms will require careful scrutiny. Now, in disparate-treatment cases where a plaintiff can show that gender was a motivating factor in her not being promoted, the burden of proof shifts to the defendant-employer to show by a preponderance of the evidence that it denied the promotion for other reasons.

Title VII forbids employers to classify or advertise jobs by gender unless a person's gender relates directly to job performance. Job classifications based on gender are not warranted simply because the work may be dangerous, physically demanding, or dirty. Instead, an employer must establish work-related physical tests to screen applicants of both genders. A court, for instance, required New York City to modify its physical tests for firefighter applicants on the grounds that they favored men but bore no relation to a person's ability to perform as a firefighter. The armed forces recently expanded the positions available to women in combat, in particular in regards to air combat pilots. As the following case shows, an employer has the burden of showing that it cannot find employees of one gender who possess the job-related capabilities of the other before it limits applicants to those of one gender.

* *University of Pennsylvania v. Equal Employment Opportunity Com'n*, Case 493 U.S. 182 (1990).
† *Price Waterhouse v. Hopkins*, 490 U.S. 228 (1989).

Weeks v. Southern Bell Telephone & Telegraph Co.

408 F.2d 228 (5th Cir. 1969)

FACTS   Southern Bell denied Mrs. Weeks's bid for the job of switchman because of her gender, not because she lacked any other qualifications. The job went to the only bidder for the job, a man with less seniority than Mrs. Weeks. Southern Bell regarded the position as one requiring "strenuous activity" for which women were not qualified. Primarily, this activity consisted of occasionally lifting objects weighing between 30 and 40 pounds. Mrs. Weeks filed a complaint with the EEOC. When the matter could not be resolved there, she filed suit. The trial court found for Southern Bell.

ISSUE   Could only men perform the duties required of a switchman?

DECISION   No. Reversed. The burden of proof was on Southern Bell to demonstrate that the switchman's position fits within the BFOQ exception. Southern Bell introduced no evidence that the switchman's duties were so strenuous that all, or substantially all, women would be unable to perform them. Southern Bell assumed, on the basis of a stereotyped characterization, that few or no women could safely lift 30 pounds, whereas all men could. The Civil Rights Act rejects just this type of romantic paternalism.

The courts have taken a skeptical view of height or weight requirements which prevent the employment of women. For example, many women have successfully challenged police department rules which imposed unreasonable height restrictions on applicants.

Another effect of Title VII's prohibition against gender discrimination is the demise of state laws which protected women in the workplace. Many of these laws arose from the treatment of women in the late nineteenth and early twentieth centuries. Such laws, for instance, required longer breaks for women working on assembly lines than for men. More recently, the Supreme Court ruled in 1991* that employers could not refuse to hire or terminate women in their childbearing years even if the job required being exposed to toxic materials or radiation.

---
* *International Union v. Johnson Controls*, 111 S.Ct. 1196 (1991).

This was true even if it could result in the firm's liability for birth defects, miscarriages, or infertility. Today, the combination of prohibitions against gender discrimination and better regulation of the workplace and work day (discussed below) have made these statutes either unconstitutional—because the federal laws have preempted them—or unnecessary.

Sexual harassment. Probably no form of discrimination has received more publicity in recent years than sexual harassment. A growing awareness and a strong reaction to the practice reached a new high after the 1991 Supreme Court confirmation hearings of Clarence Thomas, who, ironically as former head of the EEOC, allegedly sexually harassed his associate, Anita Hill. Since that episode, serious sexual harassment charges have been directed against the Navy in the Tailhook sex scandal, and against several lawmakers, most notably

Senator Packwood of Oregon. Indeed, since the Thomas-Hill hearings, the EEOC has reported a dramatic increase in such claims, and over 81 percent of Fortune 500 companies now provide sexual harassment sensitivity training for their employees.

Sexual harassment takes many forms. Of course, the easiest violations to define—although not necessarily to prove—are the "quid pro quo" cases. Here, the employee is offered a promotion, raise, or other job benefit in exchange for sexual favors.

Sexual harassment may occur where the environment created by the employer leads to toleration of sexual innuendo in conversations or actions, the treatment of individuals like sex objects, and the like. In the following case, the Supreme Court unanimously upheld the plaintiff's right to maintain a sexual harassment suit, called a hostile environment case, under Title VII where the plaintiff suffers no economic loss.

Meritor Savings Bank v. Vinson

106 S. Ct. 2399 (1986)

FACTS   In 1974, Meritor Savings Bank hired Mechelle Vinson as a teller trainee. During Vinson's 90-day training period her supervisor, Sidney Taylor, acted as a father figure. His actions included lending Vinson money for an apartment. At the end of Vinson's probationary period, Taylor took her out to dinner and afterward suggested they have sexual relations. Vinson at first refused, but Taylor persisted. Fearing the loss of her job, she complied. Vinson estimated that she had had intercourse with Taylor forty to fifty times between 1975 and 1977, during and after banking hours in various parts of the building, including the vault. In addition, Vinson claimed that on several occasions Taylor assaulted and raped her. Vinson was fired for reasons unrelated to her harassment claim. Vinson brought suit against the bank under Title VII, alleging the bank permitted the existence of a hostile or offensive work environment that led to her sexual harassment. The bank had no knowledge of the harassment. The district court held for the bank, but the court of appeals reversed.

ISSUE   When a claim is based on the existence of a hostile work environment resulting in sexual harassment, is the claim actionable under Title VII where the sexual relationship was voluntary?

DECISION   Yes. Court of appeals affirmed. The fact that sex-related conduct was voluntary, in the sense that the victim was not forced to participate against her will, is not a defense to a sexual harassment claim. The "correct inquiry is whether [the employee] by her conduct indicated that the alleged sexual advances were unwelcome, not whether her participation in sexual intercourse was voluntary." Thus, the plaintiff could establish a claim of sexual harassment by alleging that she voluntarily entered into an unwelcome sexual act or relationship which, in turn, created a hostile working environment. Nonetheless, when the case is retried, the trial court may admit evidence relating to the plaintiff's supposedly provocative dress and her frequent conversations about her sexual exploits.

The Court failed to clarify the standard of liability imposed on an employer for acts of its supervisors of which it had no actual knowledge. A concurring opinion signed by four members of the Court called for the imposition of strict liability for sexual harassment by a supervisor regardless of the employer's knowledge of the harassment. The Court's opinion suggests that a properly structured internal complaint and review process, coupled with a sexual harassment policy, might prevent an employer from being liable under Title VII.

One of the most important legal developments since the *Meritor Savings* case has been the adoption of several courts of an objective standard called the "reasonable victim standard." Since women are almost always the victims of sexual harassment, it has more commonly been called a "reasonable woman's standard." Sexual harassment is very difficult to define, particularly between the viewpoints of a man and a woman. This standard is used to gauge whether the purported sexual harassment would be perceived as such by a reasonable woman in a similar situation, since sexual harassment does not arise until it is deemed as "unwelcomed" by the victim. This is very similar to the reasonable person standard applied in tort law. It has been argued that by adopting a reasonable woman's point of view, a woman would be protected from offensive behavior that a man might not necessarily sense. Likewise, it would protect men from the hypersensitive woman. So far, the federal Ninth Circuit* and a district court in Florida† have adopted the view. In 1993, the federal Eighth Circuit similarly embraced the standard.‡

The reasonable woman approach has had its detractors. For instance, some fear that businesses will overreact to such an ambiguous definition and decline to hire women. Others point to the fact that it stifles constitutionally protected speech, since a person will not be sure whether his actions are unwelcomed or not and is therefore forced to yield to the new rules of "political correctness." Finally, there is concern that a reasonableness standard will spread to other Title VII classifications, with businesses having to grapple with such evasive behavioral determinations as the "reasonable African-American" standard, or the "reasonable Buddhist" standard.

Another related issue that could have broad legal and ethical ramifications in the future is the sexual harassment of employees by third parties, such as a company's vendors or customers. It is thought that many women are being subjected to it but do not report it for fear of being perceived as unable to handle the job. In a case tried in Las Vegas in early 1993, a female blackjack dealer failed in her suit against the Las Vegas Hilton for not protecting her after she complained about alleged verbal sexual harassment from gamblers at her table. The trial judge had formally ruled that the Hilton would have a duty to protect her if such harassment did exist. The jury, however, felt that several customer remarks and leering did not amount to sexual harassment. The implications of this case to restaurants, truck stops, casinos, and many other such establishments could be significant.

Religious discrimination. An employer must accommodate the religious beliefs and needs of its employees except where an accommodation imposes an undue hardship on the conduct of the employer's business. Where reasonably possible, employees' schedules should allow them to observe their religious beliefs while carrying out their jobs. If, for instance, an employee's faith celebrates its holy day on Saturday, the employer must make every reasonable

---

* *Ellison v. Brady*, 934 F.2d 872 (9th Cir. 1991).

† *Robinson v. Jacksonville Shipyards, Inc.*, 760 F.Supp. 1486 (N.D. Fla 1991).

‡ *Burns v. MacGregor*, Electronics Industries, 989 F. 2d 959 (8th Cir. 1993).

effort to accommodate its observance by the employee. An employee need not be a member of the religious group before being employed.

An employer has met its obligations when it demonstrates that it has offered a reasonable accommodation to the employee. The employer does not have to show how each of the employee's possible alternative accommodation ideas would result in undue hardship for the employer. The extent of undue hardship on the employer's business is at issue only where the employer claims that it is unable to offer any reasonable accommodation without such hardships.

Affirmative action. In the early cases after enactment of Title VII courts commonly found it necessary to order an *affirmative action program*—a plan designed to prevent discrimination from continuing—as a remedy to eradicate the effect of years of discrimination, most commonly against blacks or women. In establishing an affirmative action program for an employer, the court would generally consider a large volume of statistical information in an attempt to formulate appropriate goals for the employer, a timetable for implementation, and a yardstick of some sort for measurement of an employer's effort and success. For example, a court might require that an employer accept one black applicant for every three white applicants for an apprenticeship program until the level of black employees reached a certain level.

As the courts began ordering affirmative action programs, many employers, after reviewing their employment practices, elected to establish affirmative action programs to meet the expectations of Title VII. As affirmative action programs—both voluntary and involuntary—spread, a reaction set in among those most adversely affected by the programs: commonly, white males. These workers have complained that they are the victims of reverse discrimination, especially where the workers

gaining favorable treatment were not themselves ever subjected to discrimination by the employer. In essence, the courts have upheld affirmative action programs that state goals—as opposed to firm quotas—to address an imbalance in employment.

Starting in 1981, the Justice Department argued that the civil rights laws offer relief not to groups but only to specific individuals who can prove that they were victims of racial bias. Hiring goals and timetables were therefore quotas and constituted reverse discrimination.

In 1986 and 1987, the Supreme Court rejected this position in a series of cases. As a result, race-conscious plans implemented pursuant to solid evidence of past discrimination will be upheld, so long as they are not permanent or overly rigid, are tailored to meet some rational measures of compliance (i.e., the percentage of minorities in a relevant labor pool or community), and do not cause innocent persons to lose existing property interests (e.g., jobs, apartments, and the like). However, the next case will discuss what happens to an employer who, in the interests of diversifying its workplace without a specific plan or court order, discriminates against a white male.

It is interesting to note that reverse discrimination cases have been on the rise in recent years. Discrimination against white males is generally illegal, unless there is a valid affirmative action plan or court order allowing it, as discussed above. Unfortunately for employers, this puts them in a squeeze between the interests of diversifying their work force and thwarting suits from minorities and women, and threats of reverse discrimination suits by white males who are feeling similarly frustrated in finding jobs.

The Civil Rights Act of 1991

The Civil Rights Act of 1991 is an amendment to six other civil rights acts. These include the Civil Rights Act of 1964, as well as the Age

----

Arenson v. Southern University Law Center

911 F.2d 1124 (5th Cir. 1990)

FACTS   Southern University of Louisiana was once required by law to be all black and today is still predominately black. Its law school, however, is about 40 percent white with a slight majority of black professors. The plaintiff, Arenson, a white male, was hired as a non-tenure track, visiting professor in 1985. His contract was renewed for the 1985–1986 academic year. In February 1986, Arenson requested that he be granted a tenure track position for the following year, but was refused because of a depressed budget. At the same time, the law school hired Evelyn Wilson, a black female, to a tenure track position as a writing instructor. After Wilson was hired, Arenson made several more requests, which were all denied. There was evidence at the trail that the Chair of the Tenure and Promotion Committee had stated that maintaining a racial balance was important and that there were "too many white law professors" at Southern. Arenson sued under the Civil Rights Act of 1964 for race discrimination and was awarded $65,000 in damages at the trial level. However, the trail judge overturned the jury's verdict in a judgment notwithstanding the verdict (JNOV).

ISSUE   Was there sufficient evidence from which a reasonable jury could find that Southern Law School was engaged in illegal employment discrimination?

DECISION   Yes. Reversed. To prove race discrimination a plaintiff must show that he belongs to a racial minority; that he applied and was qualified; that he was rejected despite his qualifications; and that after the rejection the position remained open and the employer continued to seek applicants. Once this "prima facie" case is established, the burden shifts to the defendant to rebut the presumption of illegal discrimination. One could conclude that Arenson was denied the position for discriminatory reasons. The fact that Ms. Wilson had less experience than Arenson, plus faculty comments about maintaining a black majority on the faculty, is sufficient evidence to allow the jury's determination about the facts to stand.

Discrimination in Employment Act (ADEA) and the Americans with Disabilities Act (ADA), which are both discussed later. Its passage ended several years of intense debate between the Bush administration, which had vetoed a comparable bill in 1990, and civil rights groups. Probably its most publicized effect has been the reversal of the *Wards Cove* case, reviewed earlier. However, the 1991 Act similarly reversed several other controversial Supreme court decisions disfavored by civil rights groups.

One of the 1991 Act's most important provisions concerns damages. Before the Act, only race and ethnic discrimination could result in punitive and compensatory damages, such as pain and suffering. Now victims of *intentional* discrimination based on gender, religion, and disability can also be awarded such damages.

The foregoing damages do have their limitations, based on the size of the business, as stated below:

Number of Employees	Upper Limit of Compensatory and Punitive Damages
0–14	No damages
15–100	$50,000
101–200	$100,000
201–500	$200,000
Over 500	$300,000

Many observers see these monetary limitations as a fair balance between the cost of doing business and awarding the victims of discrimination. One of the greatest criticisms is that intentional discrimination based on race and ethnic classifications is still unlimited under the old Reconstruction Era Civil Rights Act of 1866, while gender discrimination, for example, is now capped. To some, this implies that race discrimination is more objectionable than gender discrimination.

Several other aspects of the 1991 Act deserve mention. First, a jury trial can now be requested for a complaint under the Act. Second, a common practice known as race-norming of tests, decried by many as reverse discrimination, is now illegal. Race-norming is an adjustment to test scores, such as civil service tests, made to benefit minorities and create more diversity in the workplace. Race-norming sometimes resulted in a minority applicant getting a job with a lower score than a white applicant. The rejection of race-norming was part of the compromise with former President Bush for signing the Act. Finally, the 1991 Act applies the Civil Rights Act of 1964 extraterritorially. This means an American company operating overseas must abide by that Act, unless its compliance would conflict with the laws of the country in which it is operating. Thus, if a company in Saudi Arabia rejects a woman applicant because the job would require her to drive

there, there would be no violation, as women are not allowed to drive in that country.

Glass ceiling initiative. The so-called glass ceiling is a metaphor often used to illustrate the fact that women and minorities are underrepresented at management levels in the United States. As part of the Civil Rights Act of 1991, a Glass Ceiling Commission was established to study why this occurs and to offer recommendations to open more opportunities for women and minorities at management levels. To reward industries who advance these goals, the Act set up a National Award for Diversity and Excellence in American Executive Management.

The Equal Pay Act

The federal Equal Pay Act of 1963 requires employers to pay employees, regardless of gender, the same amount for substantially equal work under similar working conditions. The Act applies only to discrimination by gender. It does not apply, for instance, to a situation in which an employer pays black employees less than white employees for the same work, regardless of gender.

Substantially equal work means that the work the employer requires of two employees is essentially the same for most of their working hours. Occasional lifting of heavy items, for instance, may not justify a higher wage if the items could be lifted in smaller quantities or with mechanical assistance. However, the Equal Pay Act does not forbid wage discrimination if it is due to seniority, merit, or piece rates. If the courts find an equal pay violation, they will always raise the lower wage to the greater wage.

A persistent Equal Pay Act issue is whether job descriptions, required under the law, reflect an objective appraisal of what the job really requires. Inflated job descriptions, for example, have been used as a subterfuge by employers to justify paying a man more than a woman.

Comparable worth. Even with the Equal Pay Act and Title VII, women's wages in 1993 were still estimated to be less than 70 percent of what men earn on average. Still, that figure represents an improvement over 1973's 57 percent.

The slowness with which this gap is closing has led some groups to suggest the concept of *comparable worth* as a means of equalizing men's and women's wages. The concept calls for paying the same sum for jobs that require similar amounts of skill and effort. If implemented, comparable worth would require that jobs be studied and point values be assigned for the skills, effort, and responsibility each requires. Some advocates of comparable worth believe that these evaluations should be conducted nationwide. Others have called for a company-by-company approach.

Opponents have argued that there is no way to compare, for example, the "worth" of a secretary with that of a truck driver. Also, increasing women's wages without equivalent increases in productivity could rekindle inflation. Finally, comparable worth might price women out of the market and so actually reduce female employment.

If the experience of Great Britain and Australia are any guide, the concept of comparable worth may have merit. In Australia, during the decade following enactment of a comparable worth statute, women's wages have increased from 65 percent of men's to 80 percent. Some thirty states either have adopted comparable worth in evaluating state jobs or are actively considering doing so.

One place comparable worth has made little headway is the federal courts. Generally, they have refused to find comparable worth to be an integral component of either the Equal Pay Act or Title VII. Congress, too, has shown no inclination to adopt comparable worth.

The Pregnancy Discrimination Act

The federal Pregnancy Discrimination Act of 1979, which amended Title VII, forbids employers to discriminate on the basis of pregnancy or the fact of having given birth.

Employers may not force a women to stop working if she is still capable of performing her job adequately, nor may employers set a fixed time that a woman must be away from work after giving birth. Unmarried women receive the same protection as married women.

Employers also are not permitted to deny sick leave for an abortion if they allow sick leave for childbirth. However, an employer need not pay for a voluntary abortion. Finally, employers may not exclude coverage for pregnancy and childbirth from an employee health care policy if the employer offers comprehensive medical coverage to male employees.

The Supreme Court neither imposed maternity leave requirements across the country nor required that states enact maternity leave statutes. The Court held only that states would not violate federal law if they choose to enact such laws. The rights of women who give birth have been greatly expanded by the passage of the Family and Medical Leave Act in early 1993. This Act will be discussed in detail later in the chapter.

The Age Discrimination in Employment Act

The Age Discrimination in Employment Act of 1967 prohibits discrimination based upon age against employees over 40 years old. The Act covers only employers with twenty or more employees. However, an employer may discriminate on the basis of age in those situations in which most older employees could not perform the required duties. The next case illustrates an employer's right in this area.

Forcing employees into early retirement, except for an inability to do assigned work, can result in liability for age discrimination. Indeed,

Usery v. Tamiami Trail Tours, Inc.

531 F.2d 224 (5th Cir. 1976)

FACTS

Tamiami refused to hire two applicants, aged 43 and 57, as bus drivers solely because of their ages. The rejected applicants brought suit under the Age Discrimination in Employment Act. Tamiami's policy, based on safety considerations, was not to hire anyone over 40 as a driver. The ability to operate a bus safely declines with age, but no medical or psychological test can distinguish the effects of the aging process on individuals' ability to perform a bus driver's duties safely. Also, Tamiami's drivers fell into two categories, depending on seniority. Drivers with little seniority had to be available for trips on as little as 24-hour notice—sometimes across the country. Drivers remained in this extremely stressful category for from 7 to 12 years. After that, they took regularly scheduled routes which were significantly less stressful. The trial court held that Tamiami had established a BFOQ defense to the charge of age discrimination.

ISSUE

Would voiding Tamiami's policy result in an increased risk of harm to its passengers?

DECISION

Yes. Affirmed. Tamiami's business was the safe transportation of bus passengers. If all or substantially all members of a class do not qualify or if there is no practical way to reliably differentiate the qualified applicants in a class from the unqualified, the BFOQ exception permits class discrimination. It was enough for Tamiami to show that elimination of the hiring policy might jeopardize the life of one or more passengers.

since the massive downsizing of the American work force in the 1980s and the recession of the early 1990s, age discrimination has become one of the most frequently litigated areas of employment discrimination law. Moreover, many claimants are successful when careless managers speak of hiring "new blood" or of telling workers that they are "slowing down." And the litigious trend is not likely to abate as the work force ages. It is estimated, for instance, that by the year 2000, the number of persons 35 and older will increase by 70 million, and that by 2030, 30 percent of the population will be 55 or older.*

---

* R. Aalberts and E. Kelly, "Waivers Under the ADEA: An Analysis of the Age Discrimination in Employment Waiver Protection Act of 1989," *Labor Law Journal*, December 1989, p. 737.

One common means of downsizing has been for companies to offer their older workers an "exit incentive program." This means that the worker receives pension plan credits and cash bonuses to retire in exchange for signing a waiver releasing all rights she may have to sue for age and all other kinds of discrimination under the law. There has been extensive criticism of these waivers, since many feel they are signed under duress due to the unequal bargaining power between the older worker and the employer. Proponents claim that it is merely an exercise of the freedom to contract and that the waivers are a fair way to retire workers as well as preventing litigation.

Condemnation of the waivers resulted in the passage of the Older Workers Benefit Protection Act of 1990 (OWBPA). The OWBPA gives terminated workers the following protections which must accompany the waiver.

- Workers must receive some compensation above their normal benefits and severance pay.
- Waivers must be in plain English, refer to the ADEA, and suggest that workers see a lawyer.
- Workers must have 21 days to sign the waivers, or 45 days if it is due to a mass layoff or buyout incentive, and 7 days to change their mind after signing it.
- If workers are victims of a mass layoff, they must be given the names and ages of everyone else affected by the cutback, including those not fired.

An amendment to the Age Discrimination in Employment Act that took effect January 1, 1987, abolished mandatory retirement at age 70 for employees of companies with twenty or more employees. Thirteen states—including California, New York, and Florida—had already outlawed a mandatory retirement age. However, the Act still allows mandatory retirement at age 70 for high-level executives who receive generous pension plans from their employer. The Act provides up to 7 years for state and local law enforcement officials and firefighters, as well as university professors, to be guaranteed the benefits of the law.

The effect of the abolition of mandatory retirement is unclear. The average retirement age, now 63, has been falling for 25 years. In 1986, of 19.1 million Americans age 70, only 1.1 million worked.* Nonetheless, businesses opposed the change on the basis that it will force companies to remove some workers who might otherwise be "carried" until retirement to avoid unpleasant separations. Also, without the ability to plan personnel actions based upon mandatory retirements, some employers may have to cope with bad morale among employees whose futures appear blocked. Finally, business expects an increase in employment discrimination suits, as management must terminate workers who refuse to retire.

The results of a 1992 study by researchers at Penn State, however, might eventually change employers' minds. The study found that the job fitness of police, firefighters, and prison officers is not affected by age.* Presently, persons in positions like these and in transportation, as discussed in the *Usery* case above, are exempt from protections under age discrimination laws because of safety considerations.

The Rehabilitation Act of 1973

The Rehabilitation Act of 1973 requires every employer doing $2500 or more business with the federal government each year to take affirmative steps to employ disabled workers. Primary contractors with the government must impose the same requirement on their subcontractors. Employers covered by the Act must make "reasonable accommodations" to the disabled, such as wheelchair ramps, special restroom facilities, and reserved parking areas.

The Act applies only to personal service contracts. The federal government considers building a highway to be a personal service, but selling or leasing a building is not.

To benefit from the Act, employees must be capable or performing a given job with reasonable accommodations for their disabilities. Drug users and alcoholics are not protected if their addictions impair their work.

The Americans with Disabilities Act of 1990

The Americans with Disabilities Act (ADA) of 1990 is considered by many to be the most far-reaching and significant civil rights law since the 1964 Act. In fact, many of the protections accorded women and minorities in the 1964 Act

---

* "Mandatory Retirement Gets Put Out to Pasture," *Business Week*, November 3, 1986, p. 31.

* *Wall Street Journal*, January 5, 1993, p. 1.

are now in place for the disabled. In addition, the ADA greatly expands much of what was covered under the Rehabilitation Act of 1973. The ADA is comprised of five titles. Title III, discussed in Chapter 28 on the Relationship between Landlord and Tenant, covers accessibility of the disabled in public accommodations. Title I regulates employment practices, including hiring, promotions, and terminations. As of July, 1992, Title I applied to all private businesses with twenty-five or more employees. By July 1994, businesses with fifteen or more employees will be similarly covered. The importance of the ADA is underscored by the fact that there are an estimated 43 million Americans who fall under one or more of the following three definitions of "disabled."

- A physical or mental impairment that substantially limits one or more of the major life activities of an individual
- A record of such an impairment
- Being regarded as having such an impairment

The ADA, its interpretive regulations, and its legislative history refer to both general and specific types of physical and mental disabilities. The general language of the law is intentional to allow for future interpretations of particular disabilities. Specific listings include cerebral palsy, multiple sclerosis, cancer, heart disease, as well as HIV infection and AIDS. Recovering alcoholics and drug addicts are likewise protected under the Act, although the ADA allows drug testing to confirm a former user's abstinence. The ADA also specifically excludes certain conditions including: environmental and cultural deprivations, such as a prison record; certain sexual disorders, like transsexualism and pedophilia; and personality traits, like a quick temper and poor judgment. Major life functions include walking, talking, working, seeing, breathing, and learning. Thus, if a former cancer victim can perform all the major life functions, he would not be disabled under the first definition. However, if an em-

ployer does not hire the person because of his history of cancer, or the employer perceives him as still being disabled because of stereotypes about the disease, the cancer victim would still fall under the second or third definition of disabled.

Before the passage of the ADA, if a disabled person was not covered under the Rehabilitation Act of 1973 or state disability laws, an employer could legally discriminate, and often did. Indeed, in Senate hearings prior to its passage, two-thirds of disabled Americans between the ages of 16 and 64 were not working, yet 66 percent of those unemployed, or 8.2 million in absolute terms, wanted a job. Now, after the ADA, if a person is deemed disabled under one or more of these definitions, an employer must ponder a number of factors.

The applicant's qualifications. The ADA states that a qualified person is "an individual who, with or without reasonable accommodation, can perform the "essential functions" of the employment position. . . ." Because of a lack of guidance in the law, it is difficult to know what exactly the essential functions of a job are. Thus, its interpretation will likely become one of the most litigious areas of the ADA, since courts will be called upon to determine what essential functions are on a case-by-case basis. The regulations state that an employer's judgment, written job descriptions, information from advertising and the interview, and terms of a collective bargaining agreement may, among other things, be used to define the term. One thing is certain, however: the determination of whether an applicant can perform the essential functions of a job cannot be derived from a physical or mental exam taken *before* an offer is tendered. However, if a postoffer physical or mental exam uncovers the fact that the new hire is seeking a job which he plainly cannot do because of a serious physical or mental problem, he would not be qualified for the job. The reason for disallowing preoffer physical or mental exams is so that if a newly hired worker is later rejected, the employer would have the burden or proving why the disabled person is not qualified and why a "reasonable accommodation" is not possible.

Reasonable accommodation. If the disabled applicant is judged to be unqualified, an employer still must make a reasonable accommodation for the employee in his employment practices. Thus, the reasonable accommodation requirement would apply to hiring, as well as to promotions and terminations. The following are specific examples of reasonable accommodations as stated in the regulations and legislative history:

- Increased accessibility to facilities (e.g., ramps for wheelchairs, reading facilities for the blind)
- Acquisition or modification of equipment (e.g., special computer systems, audio recorders, mechanical page turners, etc.)
- Qualified readers and interpreters (e.g., reader for blind employee, interpreter for deaf employee)
- Modifications of exams, training materials, or policies (e.g., these must be "disability-neutral" to not exclude the disabled)
- Flexibility of work schedule (e.g., early leave to catch special bus for wheelchair-bound employee, part-time schedule for employee suffering from stress)
- Job restructuring (e.g., if job is best suited for a disabled person, he should get it, although segregation of disabled is discouraged; does *not* require "bumping" of nondisabled employee)

Undue hardship. Clearly, the cost of these accommodations may not be reasonable for some businesses. The legislative history of the ADA emphasizes that compliance should not result in business failures. Therefore, if a business can demonstrate that a reasonable accommodation would cause financial and other inordinate problems, the "undue burden" defense would exempt its implementation. For example, if a

nightclub with dim lights is asked to make the lights brighter for a visually impaired waiter, this would be an undue burden, since it might ruin the club's desired atmosphere. Precedent from the Rehabilitation Act, which will likely be persuasive when applied to the ADA, indicates that the undue burden defense will not be easy to satisfy, especially for large companies with resources.*

There is no doubt that ADA compliance is going to cost money. In particular, there will almost certainly be a great deal of litigation as the often vague law is interpreted on a case-by-case basis by the courts. In March, 1993, the first ADA trial of a Title I employment discrimination suit occurred. The plaintiff, a victim of brain cancer, was awarded $572,000 by the jury. The award was ultimately reduced due to the caps imposed by the 1991 Civil Rights Act. The amount of the award, plus the fact that the EEOC prosecuted the case with uncharacteristic dispatch, illustrates the potential effects of the ADA.†

Title I of the ADA is, as mentioned, enforced by the EEOC, but private enforcement already has been initiated by civil rights groups representing the disabled. And, as discussed above, punitive and compensatory damages, capped by a firm's size, can be awarded under the Civil Rights Act of 1991, for intentional discrimination against the disabled. Proponents feel that society will be the ultimate beneficiary as businesses hire the generally competent disabled worker who will no longer be dependent on others.

Emerging Employment Discrimination Issues

While it would be comforting to think that legislation has addressed all possible discriminatory

---

* R. Aalberts and D. Hardigree, "Risk Management Implications of the ADA: Employment Issues," *The CPCU Journal*, 45, September 1992, p. 156.

† R. Samborn, "First ADA Jury Verdict Big Loss for Employer," *The National Law Journal*, vol. 15, March 29, 1993, p. 17.

bases in employment, it would not be realistic. In fact, some major new issues are emerging.

Sexual orientation and workplace rights. The highly contentious issue of gay rights has recently come into the forefront in the wake of the "family values" debates of the 1992 presidential election. Presently, there is no federal civil rights act outlawing workplace discrimination based on sexual orientation. However, the states of Connecticut, Hawaii, Massachusetts, Minnesota, New Jersey, Wisconsin, and the District of Columbia, as well as a number of cities, have such protections. Wisconsin's is the most extensive, disallowing exemptions for religious organizations or a BFOQ as a defense.*

The explosiveness of the issue has become intense and widespread. In 1992, Colorado voters approved an amendment to its constitution that prohibits legal claims of discrimination by gays and rescinded existing antidiscriminatory laws in three of that states' cities. This resulted in a boycott initiative of that state as a tourist destination. In Oregon, the voters rejected a constitutional amendment that would have required teaching children in schools that homosexuality is "abnormal, wrong, unnatural and perverse." Clearly, these developments will continue to fuel much controversy, hindering the chances of more state or federal legislation in the workplace and elsewhere. Indeed, the foregoing public reaction and the initial stiff resistance that greeted President Clinton's announcement that gays would no longer be discriminated against in the military, may influence how these issues will be handled.

In early 1993, the Hawaiian Supreme Court issued a ruling that may have a profound effect on gay rights for the entire U.S. The court held that Hawaii's statute outlawing same-sex marriages was unconstitutional unless a state court, on remand, can justify it by a "compelling state interest." In the past, it has been virtually impossible for state courts to bear the burden of proving that such an interest exists. Thus, it is likely that homosexual marriages will soon be legally recognized in Hawaii.

The implications of this decision is momentous. Spouses of such marriages will be entitled to the civil rights and obligations of a legally sanctioned marriage contract such as inheritance, alimony, survivorship rights for social security and workers compensation benefits, and health insurance, to mention a few. Moreover, if upheld, a same-sex marriage in Hawaii might be recognized in all the other states under the "full faith and credit" clause of the U.S. Constitution, discussed in Chapter 1.

Smoking in the workplace. In the 1980s, smoking in the workplace rapidly declined from an acceptable behavior to a greatly restricted one. By 1992, twenty-two states and the District of Columbia had passed laws regulating smoking in the private sector, while 34 percent of employers now totally ban smoking from the workplace.* In early 1993, the EPA issued a controversial report on passive smoke that may be the catalyst in furthering the total prohibition of workplace smoking. For the first time, that agency concluded that passive smoke is a dangerous carcinogen, in a league with asbestos and radon, that annually causes 3000 lung cancer deaths, and 150,000 to 300,000 cases of bronchitis and pneumonia in children. The study further revealed the dangerous reach of passive smoke by pointing out that while only 26 percent of the population actually smokes, 63 percent has nicotine in its blood. For employers, some legal experts feel the report will greatly increase workers' compensation claims for those who have contact with coworkers and customers who smoke. Customers who experience respiratory problems from smoke in bars, restaurants, and other such facilities may also

---

* Howard Simon and Erin Daly, "Sexual Orientation in Workplace Rights: A Potential Landmine for Employers?" *The Employee Relations Law Journal*, Vol. 18, Summer 1992, p. 39.

* E. Felsenthal, "EPA Report Sparks Antismoking Plans," *Wall Street Journal*, January 7, 1993, p. B1.

sue those businesses. As a consequence, businesses may now have to ban smoking entirely to prevent expensive lawsuits.

Some studies have also concluded that there is a significant probability that workers who smoke suffer a higher rate of absenteeism, sickness, and death, and increase the cost of health insurance.* Some companies have responded by refusing to hire people who smoke or, in some extreme cases, terminating smokers who smoke at all, even off the job. Such extreme measures against smokers have met with significant opposition. By 1992, twenty states had enacted smokers' rights laws which forbid private employers from discriminating against smokers in hiring as well as prohibiting employers from taking action against workers who smoke away from the workplace. Some of these statutes go even further, such as those in Colorado, Nevada, and North Dakota, forbidding general discrimination against those who engage in *any* lawful activity off the job.†

Other issues. Several other issues generally lumped into the employment discrimination category remain on various legislative agendas. These include: universal health insurance; treating compulsive gambling as a disease, and the argument that obesity is a disability.

LABOR LAW

The term "labor law" sounds like a synonym for employment law. Actually, it refers to the body of law that governs the relationships among labor unions, their members, and employers.

Until the 1930s, the American Labor movement faced tremendous obstacles in its efforts to organize workers because the law effectively

took the side of the employers. In the 1930s, Congress enacted laws that legalized and protected unions' right to organize. As noted in Chapter 43, the federal legislation in this area has preempted state law for the most part.

Unions have been in decline for more than a generation. In 1945, 35 percent of the work force was organized; in 1980, 23 percent. Today unions represent under 16.1 percent.* This decline is in part attributable to the movement away from manufacturing jobs, a traditional rich source for union membership. Also, distrust of unions is widespread. In 1989, Nissan defeated a union organizing attempt in Tennessee because of this. Another reason for the decline of American unions lies in the laws described in the preceding section, which offer workers protection in their jobs that their grandparents probably never had. More sensitive employers, who have implemented better management processes (including grievance rights) also have reduced the demand for unions. Often cited examples of companies of this type are Federal Express and IBM.

Today, the National Labor Relations Board (NLRB) oversees labor relations in the private sector, with some notable exceptions. These include railroads, airline workers, independent contractors, supervisors, managers, and domestic and agricultural workers. In addition, since the NLRB regulates only those businesses which affect interstate commerce, it sometimes chooses not to exercise its jurisdiction if the firm is deemed to be too small. It also enforces four acts which are collectively known as the National Labor Relations Act. This section examines those four acts. Figure 46.1 tabulates the main labor laws.

The Norris-LaGuardia Act

The Norris-LaGuardia Act of 1932 is significant primarily for its prohibition against the use of state or federal injunctions to halt labor dis-

---

* R. Aalberts, "Not Having a Smoking Policy Is Risky Business, *Business Forum*, 14, Summer 1989, p. 16.
† D. Vaughn, "Smoking in the Workplace: A Management Perspective," *Employee Relations Law Journal*, 18, Summer 1992, p. 133.

* *Wall Street Journal*, May 5, 1992, p. A1.

NORRIS-LAGUARDIA ACT (1932)	WAGNER ACT (1935)	TAFT-HARTLEY ACT (1947)	LANDRUM-GRIFFIN ACT (1959)
• Limited federal injunctions in labor disputes	• NLRB created • Organized labor election process established • Employer can be forced to recognize and bargain with union as a result of union election • Employer unfair labor practices established	• Created union unfair labor practices • Established employer "free speech" rights in elections • Permits state "right-to-work" laws	• Established internal union rights for members • Further restrained certain organized labor secondary activities

Figure 46.1 Major Legislation Affecting Organized Labor.

putes. Employers had used injunctions to prevent employee solicitation for union membership, picketing, or strikes. The federal courts may not issue an injunction to prevent these activities if a labor dispute is involved.

The Act does permit state injunctions to the extent necessary to maintain law and order. For example, an employer may not obtain an injunction from a federal court to prohibit labor pickets from picketing on public property. A state court, however, may issue an injunction reducing the number of pickets at a plant gate, establishing an entry way to the employer's premises for those crossing the picket line, or prohibiting picketing violence.

The Norris-LaGuardia Act also outlaws "yellow dog contracts," which require employees as a condition of employment to agree never to join a union. As a matter of policy, the Act establishes that employees are free to organize and bargain collectively without employer interference. However, the Act places no legal duty on the employer to bargain with its employees.

The Wagner Act

Labor leaders have referred to the Wagner Act of 1935 as the Magna Carta of labor. It required a private employer to recognize and bargain with a union which represented its employees. It also created the NLRB to enforce federal labor laws.

Duty to recognize and bargain. An employer has a legal duty to recognize and bargain with a union which represents the majority of employees within a bargaining unit. A *bargaining unit* is a grouping of nonmanagement employees with similar interests and working conditions. A place of business may contain more than one bargaining unit. A grocery store may have a meat cutter's union and a retail clerk's union representing appropriate groups of its employees.

An employer need not volunteer to recognize a union even if the union claims to represent a majority of employees. The employer may insist that the union verify its majority status through a representation election conducted by the NLRB. To gain an election, the union must produce for the NLRB authorization cards signed by at least 30 percent of the employees within the bargaining unit. An authorization card gives the union authority to represent an employee or to have the union seek an election, or both.

To win an election, the union must receive a majority of the votes cast. Suppose a bargaining unit has one hundred employees. Forty-six vote for Union A and forty-five vote for no union. Union A wins the election. Suppose, instead, that the election involves two unions. Union A gets thirty-four votes and Union B gets twenty-two votes, while the remaining thirty-one votes go for no union. The NLRB will stage a runoff between the two top choices. Here, Union B would be eliminated.

Unfair labor practices by employers. The Wagner Act describes a number of actions which, if committed by the employer, constitute violations of the law, termed *unfair labor practices*. Examples of unfair labor practices include refusing to bargain in good faith with a recognized union and discriminating against employees because of their union affiliation or support.

The NLRB may respond to an unfair labor practice by fining the employer, by ordering the employer to cease the practice, or by issuing other remedial orders. An employer, for instance, may fire an employee because of persistent tardiness. However, if that excuse conceals the real reason for the firing—that the employee is a union organizer—the NLRB probably will order the employee reinstated.

It is also an unfair labor practice for an employer to dominate or interfere with labor organizations. This unfair labor practice may eventually be modified by what transpires in a case called *Electromation*,* which is named after the company involved, a small electrical

parts maker in Indiana. In the 1980s, Electromation, Inc., decided to experiment with "quality circles" and other employee participation programs to improve their product and to be more competitive. The quality circles also dealt with labor problems like absenteeism and pay scales for skilled workers. Soon after, the teamsters filed a complaint with the NLRB, claiming that these quality circles were shams, designed to undermine legitimate unions. The NLRB ultimately ruled against Electromation's setup in a narrowly written opinion, but the issue will not be cleared up until the current appeals, to be heard by the Federal Seventh Circuit in 1993, are exhausted.

Some observers feel certain kinds of quality circles will be permitted in the future, depending on the issues discussed. Thus, such topics as efficiency, quality, productivity, and conservation of supplies, material, and equipment would probably be legal, while discussions about wages, grievances, work schedules, and other traditional union issues would have to be left out of quality circle deliberations. Proponents feel that quality circles, used in Japan and some European nations, could make American business more competitive. By 1993, at least one proposal was in Congress to amend the NLRA to permit quality circles.†

A common employer unfair labor practice involves union elections. If the company either promises to provide new benefits or takes away existing benefits during the union election campaign, it commits an unfair labor practice. So held the Supreme Court in the next case.

---

* *Electromation, Inc.*, 309 NLRB 163 (December 16, 1992).

† D. Fortney and S. Ranalli, "How *Electromation* Affects Employees," *The National Law Journal*, February 15, 1993, p. 20.

NLRB v. Exchange Parts Co.

375 U.S. 405 (1964)

FACTS   The boilermaker's union sought to organize the workers at Exchange Parts Company. Two weeks before the representation election. Exchange Parts announced two new employee vacation benefits in a letter urging its employees to reject the union. The NLRB found that the purpose of the announcement was to induce the employees to reject the union and that this constituted an unfair labor practice. The Court of Appeals reversed, since the company put the benefits into effect without any hint that they would be withdrawn if its employees voted for the union.

ISSUE   Did Exchange Parts unlawfully interfere with the union election?

DECISION   Yes. Reversed.

> *The National Labor Relations Act establishes the right of employees to organize for mutual aid without employer interference. It prohibits not only threats and promises but also behavior favorable to employees which is undertaken to influence their choice for or against unionization.*
>
> *The danger inherent in well-timed increases in benefits is the suggestion of a fist inside the velvet glove. Employees are not likely to miss the inference that the source of benefits now conferred is also the source from which future benefits must flow and which dry up if it is not obliged. The absence of conditions of threats relating to particular benefits would be of controlling significance only if it could be presumed that no question of additional. benefits or renegotiation of existing benefits would arise in the future. Of course no such presumption in tenable.*

During an election campaign, an employer may state that it favors one union rather than another. However, it may not provide active assistance to one union to help it win an election against another union.

The Taft-Hartley Act

Organized labor sometimes refers to the Taft-Hartley Act of 1947 as the "Slave Labor Law." The act defines actions which constitute unfair labor practices by unions. In addition, it guarantees an employer's right to "free speech" in union representational elections and authorizes states to pass so-called right to work laws, which permit employees not to join a union even though it represents the employee's bargaining unit.

Unfair labor practices by unions. The Taft-Hartley Act defines three main types of unfair union labor practices. First, a union may not institute a *secondary boycott*. A secondary boycott involves picketing or striking an employer who is not a party to the original labor dispute. Suppose the steelworkers go on strike at U.S.

Steel. The union may not place pickets at General Motors' plants just because U.S. Steel sells steel to General Motors.

Second, a refusal by a union to bargain in good faith constitutes an unfair labor practice. A union, for instance, may not issue a set of demands and then refuse to discuss alternatives with management.

Third, a union may not coerce an employee into joining. For example, a union organizer cannot make personal threats against employees to induce them to sign authorization cards.

Regulation of union representation elections. The Wagner Act forbids management promises, threats, or false accusations during election campaigns. However, under the Taft-Hartley Act's "free speech" provision, an employer may say whatever it wishes during the campaign so long as it does not engage in the forbidden conduct. An employer might, for instance, properly say that it would prefer its employees to vote for no union. But the employer may not threaten to fire anyone for favoring a union shop.

Like an employer, a union may not make

any threats or false accusations during an election campaign. However, it may make promises concerning the performance the employees may expect from it. A union might state that it expects to gain higher wages and job security assurances from the employer.

Violations of these rules may lead the NLRB to order a new election if the losing party can trace its loss to the other party's illegal acts.

Another category of election abuse, misrepresentation, has proved nettlesome for the NLRB. The NLRB has vacillated on the issue of whether employer or union misrepresentations just prior to an election warranted a new election. In 1962, the NLRB held that it would order a new election if a party's misrepresentation "involved a substantial departure from the truth at a time which prevents the other party . . . from making an effective reply." In 1977, the NLRB reversed itself. In 1978, the NLRB reversed itself again, holding that it would review election misrepresentations. Just 4 years later, the NLRB reversed itself yet again in the following case.

In re Midland National Life Ins. Co.

263 N.L.R.B. 24 (1982)

FACTS

The United Food and Commercial Workers Union attempted to organize Midland's employees. The union lost the first representation election, but, because of irregularities and coercion, the NLRB ordered a second election. On the day before the second election, Midland included in its employees' pay envelopes a document that seriously misrepresented the union's organizing activities and the national union's financial affairs. The second election resulted in a tie vote. An NLRB hearing officer recommended that a third election be held.

ISSUE

Should the NLRB order a new election?

DECISION

No. Reversed.

The ill effects of the [Hollywood Ceramics (1962)] rule include extensive analysis of campaign propaganda, restriction of free speech, variance in application as between the Board and the courts, increasing litigation, and a resulting decrease in the finality of election results.

In sharp contrast to the Hollywood Ceramics standard, Shopping Kart [(1977)] "draws a clear line between what is and what is not objectionable." Thus, "elections will be set aside not on the basis of the substance of the representation, but the deceptive manner in which it was made. As long as the campaign material is what it purports to be, i.e., mere propaganda of a particular party, the Board would leave the task of evaluating its contents solely to the employees." Where due to forgery, no voter would recognize the propaganda "for what it is," Board intervention is warranted. [The Board readopted the Shopping Kart standard.]. . .

We appreciate that today's decision is likely to cause concern. . . . We take [this step] because of our emphatic belief that the Shopping Kart rule is the most appropriate accommodation of all the interests here involved. . . .Unlike its predecessor, it is a clear, realistic rule of easy application which lends itself to definite, predictable, and speedy results. It removes impediments to free speech by permitting parties to speak without fear that inadvertent errors will provide the basis for endless delay or overturned elections. . . .

. . . As is obvious from today's decision, the policy views of the Board have changed. We cannot permit earlier decisions to endure forever if, in our view, their effects are deleterious and hinder the goals of the Act. . . .

As *Midland* indicates, if one of the parties uses forged documents which the voter cannot recognize for the propaganda it is, the NLRB will order a new election based on this misrepresentation. In one forged document, the NLRB appeared to recommend that employees reject a union.

Right to work laws. Under one of the most controversial of the Taft-Hartley Act provisions, states may choose to enact a so-called right to work law. In a right to work state, an employee may choose not to belong to his or her bargaining unit's recognized union. The employee remains covered by the collective bargaining agreement negotiated by the union and receives the same wage as union members, but need not pay union dues. Approximately twenty states, primarily in the South and West, have right to work laws.

In "union shop" states, by contrast, an employee must pay union dues and initiation fees to the recognized union, usually within 30 days of its selection, or be terminated by the employer. An employer may not agree with the union to discriminate in any other way against an employee who is not a union member. An employer may not, for example, discharge an employee who does not pay a union fine or assessment, since the law treats these as internal union matters.

But, note: the law does not require the employee in a union shop state to join the union. Nonmembers' dues and initiation payments compensate the union for negotiating on their behalf.

A worker in *any* state may refuse to join a union. The advantage to not joining is that the employee is not bound by a union order not to cross a picket line. The disadvantage is that the employee gives up all rights to vote on union officers or on collective bargaining agreements.

An employer need not ever agree to a union shop arrangement, even if the employer is located in a union shop state. "Right to work" means that the employee has the right to choose whether to belong to a union or not. An employer always has the right to grant that right to its employees.

The Landrum-Griffin Act

In the mid- and late 1950s, union corruption—particularly in the teamsters' and dock workers' unions—dominated the news. The Landrum-Griffin Act of 1959 attempted to reduce internal union corruption by guaranteeing union members certain rights. Among these are the following:

- The right to vote in union elections
- The right to speak at union meetings
- The right to receive union financial reports
- The right to receive treatment equal to that of other members

From that list, it is easy to deduce the conditions which led to the Landrum-Griffin Act. However, most unions then and now extended those rights to their members.

One other aspect of the Landrum-Griffin Act bears noting. It also expands restrictions on unions' actions against persons not primarily involved in a labor dispute.

The Future of Labor Law

The Landrum-Griffin Act became law at a time when the power of unions seemed to be ever-increasing. Ironically, organized labor had probably reached the height of its influence. Union membership figures have changed little since then, and the percentage of the work force that is unionized has declined.

Corruption and organizing issues have become less important to organized labor than simple survival. The nation's work patterns have shifted away from the heavy industries and crafts that provided significant union membership in the past. In fact, in the 1992 presidential election, Clinton, the Democrat, most actively sought the support of the strongest arm of organized labor today—the American Federation of Teachers. Many younger workers tend to believe that unions have no relevance to their concerns today.

The unions' traditional identification with the Democratic Party has not helped them. The Democrats have controlled the presidency—and therefore the power to appoint NLRB members—for only 4 years since 1968 and only 12 years since 1952.

Labor law will continue to be important to the more than 12 million union workers and to the millions of nonunionized employees in union shop companies. However, labor law is unlikely to ever regain the central position in employment law that it held before 1970. Instead, the focus has shifted to laws which affect all workers, union and nonunion.

Despite the gloomy outlook for unions, the following subsections reveal that unions have, in recent years, scored a number of small victories. There is also a fair chance that their future may brighten under President Clinton and the Democratic majority in Congress.

The Worker Adjustment and Retraining Notification Act. In 1989, The Worker Adjustment and Retraining Notification Act (WARN) was passed. WARN requires employers with 100 or more workers to give workers who are going to be laid off 60 days' notice. Local governments must also be informed, since the layoffs will adversely affect the area economy.

Worker replacement. In the aftermath of such embittered strikes as the air traffic control strike of 1981 and the 5-month-long strike by Caterpillar workers in Peoria, Illinois, in 1992, the issue of an employer's right to hire permanent replacements has resurfaced as an important issue. This issue affects only workers on "economic strikes," since the law entitles those on so-called unfair labor practice strikes their jobs back. Because most workers on economic strikes are normally reinstated (air traffic controllers were an exception) the employers' right to replace them is more of a threat than a reality. However, in the 1986 TWA strike,* flight attendants and other replacements who crossed the picket lines of striking workers were not later "bumped" by those returning strikers with seniority. This is obviously a strong disincentive for veteran workers to strike in the future, since they may lose valuable seniority rights. In response, to the ominous power yielded by employers, organized labor is aggressively lobbying Congress for laws to limit the hiring of replacements. So far, only Minnesota has such limitations. However, there is visible support for this law within the Clinton administration and in Congress.

EMPLOYEE BENEFIT LAWS

The primary purpose of employee benefit laws is to assure workers a basic minimum existence while they are working, when they are unemployed, and following retirement.

The Fair Labor Standards Act

The Fair Labor Standards Act of 1938 established that employers must pay their workers a

---

* *TWA v. Independent Federation of Flight Attendants,* 489 U.S. 426 (1989).

minimum wage and observe a standard work-week. Since then, Congress has amended these provisions many times. But the other important provisions of the Act, dealing with the employment of children, have remained relatively unchanged.

Minimum wage and standard workweek. Initially, Congress mandated a minimum wage of 25 cents per hour for a standard workweek for 44 hours. In 1985, the federal minimum wage was $3.35 per hour and the standard workweek was 40 hours. In computing the minimum wage, the employer may include piece rates, commissions, salary, or bonuses. The Act does not cover all employees. For instance, seasonal employees and management are not covered by the minimum wage provisions.

The Fair Labor Standards Act introduced the concept of "time-and-a-half" for overtime. This means that an employer must pay a minimum of one and a half times a worker's hourly rate for every hour in excess of the standard workweek that the worker labors. The law does not require overtime pay for work in excess of 8 hours on any given day. For example, if Jonathan works 12 hours for 3 working days and 2 hours on a fourth, he has no right to overtime pay.

In 1989, with the workweek at 40 hours, Congress enacted a new minimum wage. It established a two-tier structure effective in 1990. A "training wage" set below the minimum was meant to encourage employers to hire younger unemployables and train them. The training wage is to last only 6 months, at which time the regular minimum wage takes effect. In 1991, the training wage was scheduled at $3.61 per hour and the regular minimum at $4.25.*

There are a number of businesses exempted from the minimum wage and overtime provisions. These include managerial and professional employees, certain enterprises which gross under $500,000 year, and most farm and casual workers, like baby-sitters.

The overtime requirement to pay time-and-a-half after 40 hours also has its exceptions.

Under Labor Department regulations, workers covered under the Fair Labor Standards Act whose hours fluctuate from week to week can be paid on a consistent salary basis instead of by the hour, if their employer chooses to do so. Although the consistency of receiving a foreseeable rate of pay may look attractive, the worker who exceeds 40 hours a week does not by law have to receive what he might have earned under an hourly pay scheme.† In a 1975 case, for example, it was legal for an employee of a small drugstore to work 12 hours a day, 7 days a week, and receive no overtime pay at all.‡ This "loophole," negatively referred to by workers in various parts of the country as "Chinese" overtime or the fluctuating workweek, has become more prevalent, since the advent of the recession and a surplus of workers for blue collar jobs. With studies showing that workers are becoming increasingly more concerned and distressed about their weakening unions, vanishing jobs, and low pay, such compensation schemes may only add to workplace hostilities.

Child labor. The Fair Labor Standards Act imposed severe restriction on the use of child labor in manufacturing, mining, and other hazardous industries. It virtually bans employment of children 13 years of age and under. It also imposes restrictions on the hours and types of jobs that those between the ages of 13 and 18 may work. For example, it restricts—but does not totally prohibit—employment of 16- and 17-year-olds in hazardous industries. However, it imposes no restrictions on employers using minors between these ages in nonhazardous work. By contrast, 14- and 15-year-olds may be employed only in certain specified nonhazardous jobs.

---

* States are free to establish minimum wages so long as they exceed the federal minimum wage.
† C. Martin and J. Newman, "The FLSA Overtime Provisions: A New Controversy?" *Compensation and Benefits Review*, 24, 1992 p. 60.
‡ *Rau v. Darlings Drug Store, Inc.*, 388 F.Supp. 877 (W.D. Pa. 1975).

The Family and Medical Leave Act

The first major legislative act signed by President Clinton was the Family and Medical Leave Act. The Act, applicable to employers with fifty or more employees, grants workers up to 12 weeks of unpaid leave for the birth or adoption of a child or a serious illness in the family. To illustrate, John and Becky are about to adopt a daughter, Emily. John works for IBM, while Becky is a dental assistant for a sole practitioner dentist. Emily's employer would not be covered by the Act. However, IBM obviously would be, so John would be eligible to take up to 12 weeks of unpaid leave to care for Emily. John's employer, IBM, is required to hold his job and to continue health care benefits for him, if any, that he otherwise would have received.

To be eligible for the unpaid leave, a worker has to have worked at least 25 hours a week for 12 months. The Act defines a "serious health problem" as a problem that would keep employees from performing their jobs. While the Act is presently vague, it is expected that new regulations will provide greater guidance. Employers are permitted to require up to three medical opinions and certifications on the need for leave for either the worker or a family member.

An employer is permitted to substitute a worker's accrued paid leave as part of the 12-week period. The employer may also recoup any health care premiums paid on behalf of a worker who chooses not to return to work. An employer can deny unpaid leave to salaried employees within the highest-paid 10 percent of its work force, if permitting such a worker to take the leave would create "substantial and grievous injury" to the business operations.

There is concern that because of the Act some employers will discriminate against women of child-bearing years out of fear that they will be without their services for 12 weeks while they care for a newborn baby. Only time will tell whether this concern is justified.

Unemployment Insurance

Employers are required to pay both state and federal unemployment taxes to compensate workers who lose their jobs through no fault of their own *and* cannot find suitable substitute employment. Under the Federal Unemployment Tax Act (FUTA), an employer is entitled to a credit for state unemployed taxes and a business expense deduction when making its federal tax payment. The payment is made to the Internal Revenue Service (IRS).

An employer's rate of tax is dependent on its record of claims. For example, fast food restaurants often have fairly high rates of claims. An employer with a good claims record may be entitled to an additional federal credit. An employer may not elect to self-insure.

Unemployment compensation is not the same as welfare. An employee need not be in financial need in order to receive benefits. The only requirement is that the employee have worked a certain number of weeks before being laid off, and be ready, able, and willing to take similar employment. If, for instance, Dora, a soap opera queen, is "killed off" in a script, she may collect even though the show made her independently wealthy.

Certain categories of employees do not qualify for unemployment compensation. These include family workers in small family-owned businesses and agricultural employees on small farms.

The Social Security Act

The Social Security Act of 1935 sought to protect workers when they were either unemployed or unable to work. It was this Act which prompted the states to enact the unemployment compensation programs just discussed.

However, the program most people associate with this act is the Social Security system, which provides retirement, disability, and Medicare benefits. The Act requires the employer to deduct the employee's contribution to the system and to match it on a dollar-for-dollar basis. Should the employer fail to make the deduction, it is liable for the employee's share, too. A self-employed person must pay the full assessment against her *net* profit from employment. Net profit results after business expenses are subtracted from business income.

FICA is assessed against an employee's wages. A common question of both employers and employees is what constitutes "wages." Wages include all compensation for employment, including commissions, bonuses, vacation pay, non-cash compensation, tips if greater than $20, and severance allowances. Wages do *not* include travel reimbursement, employer-paid employee medical and health benefits, or retirement payments. For self-employed persons, wages do not include interest or case dividends.

An employer has the responsibility to withhold and pay Social Security for employees, not for independent contractors. Regulations require an employer to withhold Social Security if an employee earns more than $50 per quarter, no matter how frequently the employee works. It is widely acknowledged that this regulation is frequently not followed, especially in situations involving domestic help. To illustrate, the IRS estimates that 1.5 million households annually fail to report income of domestic workers, resulting in some $2 billion in estimated lost taxes. This issue became front page news when it was disclosed early in the Clinton administration that Commerce Secretary Ron Brown and Attorney-General designate Zoë Baird had failed to report income and make FICA deductions for a regular domestic worker in their homes.

The Employee Retirement Income Security Act

Even with annual cost of living adjustments, Social Security benefits offer retirees only a minimum subsistence. In fact, Congress never intended Social Security to be the principal or sole source of retirement income. Instead, retirees were supposed to look to private pension plans and their own savings. However, as a result of quirks, bankruptcies, and outright fraud, many employees lost pension benefits even though they had paid into programs for many years.

To remedy that situation, Congress enacted the Employee Retirement Income Security Act (ERISA) in 1974. ERISA does not require an employer to provide a pension plan for its employees. Rather, it offers greater protection to employees who are covered by such plans.

Under the Act, employers annually place their pension contributions on behalf of their employees into a pension trust. The trust must be independent of the employer. It may be a union-established pension trust such as the Teamsters' Central States Pension Fund.

In perhaps its most important section, ERISA sets forth rules governing *vesting*— when employees have a right to receive the employer's contribution in addition to their own. It also establishes the Pension Benefit Guaranty Corporation, which insures pension benefits just as the Federal Deposit Insurance Corporation insures savings deposits in national banks. Unfortunately, many observers feel that the Pension Benefit Guaranty Corporation is on the verge of insolvency, which may require a multi-billion-dollar bailout. And, like the S & L fiasco, it will be financed by the taxpayers.

One misconception about ERISA is that it fully protects so-called welfare benefits such as health benefits. As the *McGann* case, discussed in Chapter 30 (on insurance) will attest to, it generally does not. In *McGann*, the employer did not violate ERISA when it reduced the health insurance coverage of an employee with AIDS from $1 million to $5,000. However, it is likely that the ADA may provide protection from such actions in the future.

EMPLOYEE SAFETY LAWS

As noted earlier, the common law prevented employees from recovering from their employers for injuries suffered on the job. Beginning with New York in 1910, the states enacted workers' compensation systems which replaced the common law. The effect of these statutes on tort law is discussed in Chapter 4.

Workers' Compensation Statutes

Every state has a workers' compensation statute. However, these statutes vary from state to state. Generally, they provide benefits for employees who are accidentally injured on the job or who develop an occupationally related disease. Usually, a commission establishes and awards benefits to employees for injuries up to and including death. The benefits are paid from a fund into which employers pay according to the number of past claims against them.

Injuries on the job. The state commissions give the employee the benefit of the doubt as to whether the injury or illness resulted from activity "on the job." For instance, employees have recovered when they suffered injuries kicking a vending machine, or while playing softball for an employer-sponsored softball team. Some have even recovered for injuries received at a company picnic.

Employee negligence and employer defenses. An employee will receive workers' compensation benefits even though he or she was negligent. Even if an employer instructs its employees not to do something, and an employee ignores the instruction and is injured as a result, the employee will recover. Suppose that Mark's supervisor repeatedly told him not to drive his forklift faster than 10 mph around a corner in the warehouse. If Mark breaks a leg when he flips over the forklift while going 20 mph, he probably will recover. An employee will not be allowed to recover for injuries suffered as a result of alcoholic consumption or intentional, self-inflicted action.

As noted in Chapter 4, the effect of the adoption of workers' compensation laws was to eliminate the employers' common law defenses of assumption of the risk and contributory negligence. These laws also revoked another common law doctrine, the Fellow Servant Rule, which denied recovery to employees if they were injured because of the negligence of their fellow employees. The theory at common law was that employees could best look after their own welfare.

In some instances, an employee can sue in tort for injuries suffered on the job. One instance is when the employer injures a worker intentionally or as the result of reckless disregard for the worker's safety. A worker may also be able to sue in tort under a so-called third party suit. Suppose that Gustafson, an employee of Cook Industries, was injured by a robot on an assembly line that had just been fixed by Whiteside, a repairwoman for Vermillion Robot Repair. If it could be proved that Whiteside was negligent in repairing the robot, Gustafson could recover from Cook Industries, under workers' compensation, and also recover more generous tort damages from Whiteside and Vermillion. However, Gustafson will have to reimburse the workers' compensation carrier to the extent that this recovery duplicates his earlier compensation from it.

The benefit system. Under workers' compensation statutes, workers receive benefits according to a schedule that sets amounts for types of injuries and diseases. Workers' compensation claim expenses have nearly tripled since 1980, to over $70 *billion* a year in 1993. As a result, employers are increasingly looking to the states to take dramatic action to slash the perceived runaway costs of workers' compensation.

Some states permit large employers to insure themselves or to use a private insurance carrier. From the workers' standpoint, the recovery system is essentially the same. An employer who does not contribute to a state system and has not received permission from the state to obtain other coverage may be subject to liability in excess of that established under the state's workers' compensation laws.

The Occupational Safety and Health Act

The Occupational Safety and Health Act (1970) created the Occupational Safety and Health Administration (OSHA). OSHA establishes federal health and safety standards for the workplace, and enforces them. In addition, about half the states have their own OSHAs enforcing health and safety rules that must be at least as tough, or more stringent, than the federal OSHA's provision.

Regulations. Since its creation, both employers and employees have found much to criticize about OSHA. While employees and labor unions have complained that OSHA has not issued safety standards quickly enough and enforced them rigorously enough, employers contend that it has issued overly detailed and picky rules. At one point, OSHA took the position that an employer's costs in meeting a given safety standard were not relevant in the consideration of whether or not to adopt the standard. As the following case indicates, the courts disagreed.

American Petroleum Institute v. OSHA

581 F.2d 493 (5th Cir. 1978)

FACTS
Benzene has long been recognized as a toxic substance capable of producing severe health problems, including death. Between 1946 and 1971, the government's recommended threshold limit for benzene exposure declined from 100 parts per million (ppm) to 10 ppm. Several studies had shown that exposure to benzene at levels in excess of 10 ppm resulted in increased levels of leukemia. However, no one had studied levels below 10 ppm. In 1977, OSHA issued a standard limiting occupational exposure to benzene to 1 ppm per 8-hour day. Several producers and users of benzene challenged the 1977 regulation, claiming that OSHA had not shown that the reduction was necessary to provide healthful places of employment.

ISSUE
Had OSHA established a link between the regulation and an improvement in health conditions?

DECISION
No. The regulation was invalid. OSHA must show that a hazard exists and that its regulation will reduce the risk from it. No standard should impose added costs or inconvenience without a reasonable assurance that it will reduce the frequency or severity of illnesses. Although OSHA does not have to conduct an elaborate cost-benefit analysis, it does have to determine whether the benefits expected from the standard bear a reasonable relationship to its costs. While OSHA had studied the costs of the new standard—$500 million—it had not determined whether that expenditure would actually improve worker health. OSHA merely assumed that benefits from the reduction might be appreciable. It could not point to evidence documenting a leukemia risk at 10 ppm, even though that had been the exposure level for 6 years before OSHA issued the new standard.

In recent years, OSHA has streamlined its regulations. It has placed greater emphasis on health rules rather than safety rules. And, it has implemented self-monitoring and reporting systems in many industries in which historically there have been few violations.

Enforcement. Businesses found OSHA's enforcement techniques no less controversial than its approach to regulation. In its first years, OSHA took the position that its inspectors did not require search warrants in order to conduct on-site safety inspections. However, in *Marshall v. Barlow's, Inc.* (excerpted in Chapter 5, Criminal Law), the Supreme Court held that an inspector must produce a search warrant if the employer refuses to admit the inspector to the job site voluntarily. OSHA uses a combination of fines and remedial orders to enforce its regulations.

CONCLUSION

The law of the workplace is, and will remain, one of the most dynamic areas of business law. Labor law may be receding in importance, but as America's population ages, Social Security and pension laws will become even more controversial than they are already. As more and more women and minorities enter the workplace with increasingly high ambitions, antidiscrimination and work environment laws will continue to evolve.

The improvements in working conditions and in the national standard of living brought about by the statutes we have discussed are one of the genuine bright spots in the history of government regulation. It simply cannot be argued that the country would have been better off without these laws. That is not to say that no abuses exist. The news media often report abuses of both the workers' compensation and antidiscrimination statutes. But these relatively uncommon examples are more examples of devious ingenuity than of rot in the regulatory structure.

After 12 years of relative inaction under the Reagan-Bush administrations, some observers feel that OSHA may be revitalized. New OSHA regulations on ergonomics, video display terminal hazards, and cancer-causing agents are expected to expand. In addition, the requirement under the former administration of a cost-benefit analysis for all proposed regulations may be relaxed. The cost-benefit approach, which places a premium on the regulatory costs to business, sometimes resulted in OSHA as well as some environmental initiatives from ever becoming law.*

A NOTE TO FUTURE CPA CANDIDATES

Beginning in 1994, the CPA exam tests all major subject areas of Chapter 46 except for Labor Law. Some areas, such as the FLSA, OSHA, and ERISA, are rather straight-forward. To be prepared for them you should understand their basic objectives, coverage, and application. The other areas of coverage tend to be more involved.

Employment discrimination law primarily focuses on Title VII: race, color, religion, gender, and national origin. It is important to understand that sexual harassment generally is found in two different situations: "quid pro quo" or hostile work environment. In either case, it is the noncensensual aspect which causes liability. Candidates should also understand the discrimination laws applicable to age and disability. Remember that age discrimination laws apply to persons over forty. The Equal Employment Opportunity Commission is charged with enforcing employment discrimination laws.

---

* E. Gellhorn, "Clinton Will Change Regulatory Climate," *The National Law Journal*, November 23, 1992, p. 17.

Social Security questions traditionally focus on coverage and benefits. The Federal Insurance Contributions Act (FICA) imposes tax liability against employers, employees, and self-employed individuals. An employer is required to match her employee's contribution on a dollar-for-dollar basis and pay both to the federal government. Under FICA, wages, commissions, bonuses, and fees are considered employment income. (Employee reimbursement matters, such as travel reimbursement, are *not* considered employment income; nor would such things as interest received or cash dividends.) Self-employment tax is assessed against a person's *net* profit from employment.

Unemployment insurance questions traditionally focus on sources of funding. The purpose of the Federal Unemployment Tax Act (FUTA) is to compensate workers who lose their jobs through no fault of their own *and* cannot find substitute employment. Taxes payable under FUTA are deductible by the employer as a business expense. FUTA payments are payable to the IRS.

Workers' compensation questions traditionally focus on the basis for employee recovery. All states have workers' compensation statutes. The statutes are intended to compensate workers who suffer injury or disease during the course of employment *regardless of negligence*. What this means is that so long as the employee is not injured as the result of intentional self-inflicted action or alcoholic consumption, the employee can recover. The fact that the employee may have been negligent, grossly negligent, did not follow specific safety instructions, or was injured by a fellow worker will not be a bar to compensation. In turn for this no-fault compensation, an employee is generally prohibited from also directly recovering against the employer (unless he was injured as a result of an intentional employer act). An injured employee may recover against a third party who causes the workplace injury (although the employee may have to reimburse the workers' compensation carrier).

KEY WORDS

Americans with Disabilities Act (ADA) (1080)
bargaining unit (1085)
bona fide occupational qualifications (BFOQ) (1069)
comparable worth (1078)
Employee Retirement Income Security Act (ERISA) (1093)

Occupational Safety and Health Administration (OSHA) (1094)
secondary boycott (1087)
Social Security (1092)
unemployment insurance (1092)
unfair labor practice (1086)
workers' compensation (1093)

DISCUSSION QUESTIONS

1. Why was there a need for employment legislation? Provide five examples of different employment laws.
2. What types of discrimination does Title VII cover? Which federal agency has jurisdiction over Title VII matters?
3. What conduct may result in a finding of sexual harassment?
4. Where must a person file an employment discrimination charge? What will be the test to determine whether employment discrimination has occurred?
5. What is the primary purposes of the Americans with Disabilities Act?
6. What is required to establish a violation of the Equal Pay Act? Is the comparable worth doctrine equivalent to this statute?
7. The Age Discrimination in Employment Act covers employees of what ages? What aspects of employment does the law cover?
8. What is an unfair labor practice? Which government agency oversees enforcement of the National Labor Relations Act?
9. What is meant by a "right to work" state? Does a union in a right to work place of employment still have a duty to represent non-union workers in the bargaining unit?
10. Why does organized labor sometimes refer to the Taft-Hartley Act as the "Slave Labor Law"? What was the primary purpose of the Landrum-Griffin Act?

CASE PROBLEMS

1. Don Bell, who is black, applied for a maintenance position with Coastal Supply Company. Bell had been a maintenance worker for 12 years at a local college. His employment record was good. Coastal rejected Bell because he tested positive for AIDS—although he is asymptomatic—and because he lacks a high school degree. Coastal cannot prove a direct correlation between the high school degree and performance of maintenance duties but believes that it should be free under the law to seek the best qualified work force that it can hire. Coastal has no federal contracts and employs only thirty-five persons. Bell claims illegal discrimination. Is he correct as to AIDS? As to his lack of a high school degree? Explain.

2. Humphrey Tool Company modified its apprenticeship training program to allocate 50 percent of the positions to minority applicants. Humphrey's president said that the voluntary change was thought necessary, as minority workers make up 12 percent of the company work force and 44 percent of the area work force. The plan would be in effect "indefinitely." Mark LeBarron, a white applicant, brought an action challenging the plan, alleging that he was denied admission to the program, that his qualifications were greater than those of many of the minority applicants who were admitted, and that the plan violates Title VII, since it constitutes reverse discrimination. What are the basic requirements to justify this type of affirmative action program? Is LeBarron likely to prevail? Explain.

3. The Chicago Stars professional baseball team released Roger Dodger, a 37-year-old outfielder, because they wanted to retain a younger ballplayer. Assuming that Dodger could prove that he was equal to or better than the younger player, would he prevail in an action brought under the Age Discrimination in Employment Act? What difference, if any, would it make if Dodger were 5 years older? Explain.

4. Gail Dart, an aerobics instructor at Champion's Health Spa, is 3 months pregnant with her second child. The Spa has told Gail that she will have to cease instructing classes after her seventh month because it would be unhealthy for the baby and not in keeping with the in-shape look the Spa requires of its instructors. Gail worked well for another spa through the eighth month of her first pregnancy. Gail has notified Champion's that she will challenge their decision. Under what Act should Gail make her challenge? Will Gail prevail? Explain.

5. Ed, Dottie, Helena, and Fran all work on the assembly line at Jaguar Manufacturing Company. Ed is paid $6.25 per hour, while the women are paid $5.75. The only difference in their jobs is that Ed has to lift and connect a rather heavy control box to a junction box above the assembly line cable in the morning and remove it at night. The women feel they should get the same rate of pay as Ed, since it takes him no longer than 30 seconds twice a day to do that which makes his job different from theirs. Jaguar contends that the jobs obviously do not involve substantially equal work, since the women admit that none of them can do the required lifting. Are the women likely to prevail? Explain.

6. Studs Merkle was the accountant for Smolinski Produce Company. His normal workweek was Monday through Friday. Studs was involved in a serious automobile accident but somehow survived unhurt. The accident occurred in front of the Fifth Day Evangelical Church, a church which worships and takes a day of rest on Fridays. Feeling that God was directing him to this new church, Studs immediately joined. After using all his vacation days on the following eight consecutive Fridays, Studs told the company manager that he wanted to be allowed to work Saturdays instead of Fridays. The manager rejected the claim on the basis that Friday is the busiest day for the company, even though it is also open on Saturday mornings. Studs was fired when he was absent on the following Friday. If Studs brings an action under Title VII, alleging a failure to accommodate his religion, what issues are likely to be explored by the court? Explain.

7. The Assemblers Union is trying to organize

the plant employees of Vassar Manufacturing Company. Ten employees go to Charles Vassar, the company president, and tell him that the employees would undoubtedly vote against the union if he would assure them that the plant would finally be air-conditioned and wages raised to the level of Vassar's competitors. Said one employee, "We encouraged the union to solicit here to put pressure on you, but we sure as heck do not need to be paying union dues if you are agreeable to these demands." Vassar told the employees that he would agree, as he certainly did not favor having the union recognized as their representative. The union lost the election and has challenged Vassar's actions. Vassar claims that his actions were protected by the Taft-Hartley Act's "free speech" provision. Would the NLRB agree? What is the Board likely to order? Explain.

8. A group of eleven employees of Walker Wells Bakery Company, which has a total of sixteen workers, went into the office of the general manager and demanded that the company recognize and begin bargaining with their union, the Brotherhood of Dough Raisers. The general manager refused and vowed never to recognize the union unless it won an election. Three of the five employees who did not attend the meeting have told management that if the union should gain recognition, they would want nothing to do with it under their right to be nonunion workers in a right to work state. Since more than 50 percent of the employees have indicated their desire for the union to represent them, must the employer recognize the union? If the union is ultimately recognized, would the three employees have a right to represent themselves in such matters as pay, benefits, etc.? Explain.

9. Real Issues. As a result of the increased awareness and response to sexual harassment, a new reality of the workplace is that there can be a fine line between courtship and court. For example, Mary may enjoy repeated teasing with some sexual innuendo from Greg but be very upset by similar action from Bud, especially if Bud is a supervisor. Assuming Bud "meant no harm," Bud may be very upset to be charged with sexual harassment. Assuming such an action went to court, a court would focus not on Bud's intention but on the effect of his actions from Mary's perspective. As a result, many men claim the law has gone too far, especially since it can be highly subjective and therefore ambiguous what may or may not be considered to be sexual harassment by another person. What are your thoughts? Explain.

10. Real Issues. When the Supreme Court ruled in 1991 that employers could not refuse or terminate women in their child-bearing years even if the job required being exposed to toxic materials or radiation, it caused major discussion and disagreement. Employers claimed they were in a "Catch-22" situation, since they would violate the law by attempting to block women from such work but if they hired such women they risked potential liability for birth defects, miscarriages, or infertility. Many women's rights advocates rebutted by saying that too often an employer's supposed concern for women is simply a smokescreen to be able to conduct business "as usual," without women. Some commentators have suggested a middle-ground approach: allow a neutral panel of experts to evaluate probable risk. If the risk of toxicity is present, an employer would be exempted from the requirement to hire women for that job. What is your opinion of this compromise? Explain.

CHAPTER 47

Protection of the Environment

THE ORIGINS OF ENVIRONMENTAL LEGISLATION

Thirty years ago, most people thought of environmental laws in terms of controlling specific types of pollution. The National Environmental Policy Act, enacted in 1969, and the legislation which followed it reflect a dramatic change in the way in which humans look at their surroundings. To understand what has changed and why, some history is in order.

The Role of the Mosquito

For thousands of years, malaria and yellow fever annually afflicted millions of people. Until 1900, few suspected that the mosquito transmitted both diseases. Once the culprit was identified, governments around the world began draining swamps and spreading oil on standing water to prevent mosquito larvae from hatching. These efforts controlled mosquito-borne diseases where they were applied.

During World War II, Americans fought on Pacific islands where no one had tried to control the mosquito. But in the 1930s chemists had discovered a chemical which eradicated mosquitos and similar pests—DDT. The armed forces used it heavily during the war, and afterward DDT became a common household chemical. During mosquito season, towns sprayed it across broad areas, not worrying about its contact with animals or humans.

By the late 1950s, the mosquito was under control in the United States, but many species of birds—particularly those which fed on fish and small animals—were dying out. And, scientists were discovering DDT in many organisms, including humans. When policymakers dealt with the mosquito issue, they had not factored in the eradication effort's effects on other life forms.

The Silent Spring

The public first became widely aware of DDT's effects through Rachel Carson's best seller, *The Silent Spring* (1962). Through it, the public came to understand that one change in the environment triggers others, often unintended. Wiping out mosquitos had an enormous cost among other life forms. Carson's evidence convinced many that before anyone undertook a project affecting the environment, its consequences should be analyzed. This recognition led directly to environmental legislation. Between 1967 and 1979, it dominated the agendas of Congress and the state legislatures. It has reemerged at the top of the Congressional calendar in the wake of the *Exxon Valdez* disaster in 1989, and it was a key issue in the 1992 presidential campaign.

Environmental legislation is not a single convenient body of laws, like the Uniform Commercial Code. Rather than cataloging the dozens of environmental statutes, we have chosen in this chapter to demonstrate how these laws work by examining how some of them affect the mining of coal and its use as a fuel. The situations examined below are hypothetical, and the state laws cited are composites. And, of necessity, we will address only selected aspects of a few environmental laws.

A MINING OPERATION

Suppose United Coal Company owns the right to mine coal on 1000 acres of land in the state of Belmont. The seams it owns are relatively close to the surface, so it uses surface-mining or strip-mining techniques. Using heavy earth-moving equipment and explosives, the miners strip the soil, clay, and rock above the coal. The coal is then extracted using bulldozers and large power shovels. Strip mining can cause air pollution and damage from blasting, but its most serious potential environmental consequence is water pollution.

The material removed to expose the coal is called *overburden.* The overburden is pushed aside into *spoil,* or waste, piles. During the mining operations—and afterward—the spoil piles are highly erodable and can lead to stream siltation. Also, rainwater and *groundwater*— water below the land's surface—usually accumulate in the pit. When coal contains high levels of sulfur, as it does in eastern states, water running off the coal and the spoil piles can lead to concentrations of sulfuric acid in streams that are sufficient to destroy aquatic life.

United plans to take coal from the pit by truck to an existing barge terminal on the Zenith River. The most direct route to the terminal would require construction of a dirt road across pastureland owned by the U.S. Department of the Interior's Bureau of Land Management. United would need an *easement* from the Bureau to build the road. United anticipates that the roadbed will have to handle up to 120 trips per day by heavy coal trucks.

The road will end at a state highway, not far from the town of Wigan, population 965. The coal trucks will pass through Wigan to reach the terminal. United could use a less direct route that does not go through either federal land or Wigan, but it would add as much as 10 miles to each trip.

United Coal has planned this project for several years. During that time, it has consulted with many federal, state, and local officials. Representatives of the company have also met with citizens groups ranging from chambers of commerce to environmental groups. The scientific, social, and political information thus developed helped shape the company's plans. The company is now ready to begin implementing its plan, but in order to do so it needs a variety of easements, permits, and licenses from federal and state authorities. United would probably apply for many of these licenses at approximately the same time. However, for the purposes of our analysis we will treat the phases separately.

National Environmental Policy Act

In order to construct the road, United Coal needs an easement from the Bureau of Land Management (BLM). After United and BLM discussed terms and conditions informally, United made a formal proposal to purchase the easement. Because BLM was at least willing to consider the proposal, the National Environmental Policy Act came into play.

The National Environmental Policy Act (NEPA) embodies the lessons of *The Silent Spring.* It requires an interdisciplinary examination of the potential environmental effects of the actions of federal agencies. NEPA's purpose is "to promote efforts which will prevent or eliminate damage to the environment." The means Congress chose were procedural.

Impact on decision making. NEPA affects only *how* federal administrators make decisions. It applies solely to agencies in the executive branch of government, not to Congress or the courts. Congress does not have to prepare an environmental impact statement when it considers legislation, and courts do not have to prepare them before they issue decisions.

NEPA does not state a single substantive goal, like the reduction of carbon monoxide emissions from automobiles. Such goals appear in legislation that addresses specific environmental problems. Thus, the key word in NEPA's title is "policy." NEPA requires all federal agencies to conform their regulatory programs to ensure compliance with NEPA's purposes and goals. This means that agencies must inject environmental considerations into their decision-making processes.

Environmental impact statements. NEPA is also an environmental full disclosure law. A federal agency like the Bureau of Land Management must prepare a detailed evaluation of the consequences of any of its actions which significantly affect the quality of the environment.

Before acting on United Coal's proposal, BLM will examine it to determine whether it would have significant environmental consequences. This study, an *environmental assessment,* determines whether a full-scale consideration of environmental issues—an *environmental impact statement (EIS)*—is required. Both these documents describe the overall impact of a proposed federal action on the environment, and discuss alternatives to that action and their consequences. The agency with primary responsibility for the decision must prepare the environmental assessment and EIS.

Before BLM decides whether it will prepare an EIS, it must give the public notice of the proposed action (granting United Coal the easement) and an opportunity to submit facts which might affect the agency's decision regarding preparation of an environmental impact statement. Usually, the public's input takes the form of written comments on a draft environmental assessment that suggests areas of environmental concern, such as the effect of truck traffic on the town of Wigan. If the project will not have a significant effect on the environment, the assessment will satisfy NEPA. However, if there is any real question about the action's effects, BLM must prepare an environmental impact statement.

If BLM determines that is must prepare an EIS for United Coal's easement, it will authorize studies of the area to be affected by the proposed easement. The studies in this case will include its effect on traffic on connecting roads. BLM will circulate the draft to other concerned federal, state, and local agencies as well as to members of the public. BLM will invite comments on the draft. Once the comment period passes, the agency prepares a final EIS, which usually responds to the comments.

The final EIS will recommend a course of action on the proposal and discuss alternatives to it—including not granting the easement. The recommended action and the alternatives are based on a systematic balancing of environmental and other considerations.

An environmental impact statement "cannot be found wanting simply because the agency failed to include every alternative . . . conceivable by the mind of man."* If the agency does not review all the realistic alternatives, it is up to the public to raise them during the comment process. In this case, for instance, BLM should consider other routes to the terminal which might minimize Wigan's traffic problems. However, it need not consider obviously unrealistic alternatives, such as transporting coal to the barges by helicopter.

NEPA does *not* require an agency to elevate environmental concerns over other legitimate considerations in selecting its course of action. NEPA demands only a hard look at environmental issues and a good faith, objective assessment of the consequences of an agency's actions. Other statutes express a national policy in favor of the orderly exploitation of natural resources. So, if BLM decides that the national interest in encouraging the development of domestic coal reserves outweighs the road's negative environmental effects, it may grant the easement. However, it is quite likely that BLM will condition the easement, for example, by restricting United's use of the road to certain hours to limit the traffic effects on Wigan.

The Federal Action Requirement. NEPA applies only to major federal actions. The next case illustrates how a court determines what a major federal action is.

---

* *Vermont Yankee Nuclear Power Corp. v. Natural Resources Defense Council Inc.,* 435 U.S. 519, 551 (1978). Another aspect of this case in briefed in Chapter 3.

National Organization for the Reform of Marijuana Laws v. Drug Enforcement Administration

545 F. Supp. 981 (D.D.C 1982)

FACTS

In 1981, the Florida Department of Law Enforcement (FDLE), with the assistance of the U.S. Drug Enforcement Administration (DEA), identified more than 100 marijuana fields. FDLE planned to spray paraquat, a herbicide, on some of the fields. DEA provided assistance to FDLE, including training in, and financing for, aerial surveying. DEA also shared technical information on herbicides. In 1982, DEA budgeted $60,000 to assist marijuana law enforcement in Florida, but none was to be used for spraying, nor were DEA personnel involved in the actual spraying. DEA's environmental assessment concluded that the spraying would not have a significant effect on the environment and that DEA's involvement did not require an EIS. The plaintiff challenged DEA's decision not to prepare an EIS.

ISSUE

Was DEA's involvement in the spraying program major federal action?

DECISION

No. Judgment for DEA. The distinguishing feature of federal involvement is the agency's ability to influence or control the outcome. The EIS process is supposed to inform the decision maker. To warrant an EIS, the DEA administrator would have needed authority to exercise discretion over the outcome. If federal funding is not present, the courts have been reluctant to impose the NEPA requirements. However, even without federal funding, courts have found federal action when agencies issue permits, approve plans, or give other "go ahead" signals. Here, none of these NEPA triggers were present. DEA provides the program's impetus and technical expertise. But, the state officials determine which fields to spray and then carry out the eradication.

Even where no funding is involved, as the court in the last case indicated, an agency's overt action to further a project may trigger NEPA's requirements. BLM's granting of the easement to United Coal would further the project. Even so, whether BLM must prepare an EIS will depend on whether granting the easement will significantly affect the environment. The agency makes that determination on the basis of a subjective analysis of the road's impacts.

Significant effect on the environment. The federal action must have the potential to cause significant environmental effects. There must be a reasonably close causal relationship between the change in the physical environment and the effect.

If BLM grants the easement, United will construct the road. Among the road's potential effects—which BLM must consider in determining whether or not to prepare an EIS—are erosion as a result of initial construction, construction noise and dust, disturbance of habitat through which the road will pass, and potential pollution from road surface runoff. In the next case, the court examined other factors which an agency might consider when the action involves constructing a road.

Foundation for North American Wild Sheep v. Department of Agriculture

681 F.2d 1172 (9th Cir. 1982)

FACTS

Curtis owned a mine in California's San Gabriel mountains. To reach it, he had to use one of two roads that passed through the Angeles National Forest. One crossed the upper reaches of two canyons, while the other was on the floor of the canyons. The upper road, built in 1933, was used continuously until 1969, when it washed out. In 1978, Curtis proposed to the National Forest Service that it allow him to reconstruct the upper road, because the lower required more than twenty stream crossings and was subject to severe flooding. Curtis proposed to clear the road of vegetation, widen it to 12 feet, and repair washed-out areas. However, the upper road passed directly through an area occupied by a herd of Desert Bighorn sheep. The Bighorn population had declined by 97 percent in 100 years, and both federal and state laws gave the species special protection. The Forest Service did an environmental assessment in which it examined four alternatives. Despite strong objections to the assessment's thoroughness and studies indicating that contact with humans affected the animals' ability to reproduce, the Forest Service decided not to do an EIS. It granted Curtis permission to reconstruct the road, but imposed a number of conditions on the road's use to mitigate its effects on the sheep. The Foundation brought suit, seeking to compel the Forest Service to prepare an EIS. The trial court found for the Service.

ISSUE

Was allowing Curtis to reconstruct the road an action that significantly affected the quality of the human environment?

DECISION

Yes. Reversed. The standard to be applied is whether the proposed project may significantly degrade some human environmental factor. That does not mean the agency must determine that a significant effect will in fact occur. If substantial questions are raised as to whether a project *may* have a significant effect, an EIS must be prepared. Here, the assessment's conclusion that reopening the road would not have a significant effect on the environment was unreasonable. The mitigation measures required of Curtis indicated the potential severity of the impact.

Judicial review. Under NEPA, judicial review of agency decisions is quite limited. NEPA requires an agency to consider the environmental consequences of its actions before acting. In practice, this means the agency must develop a *record,* which a federal court can review, documenting its environmental appraisal.* Here,

this consists of reports generated by agency specialists, comments by other government agencies and private individuals and groups on the proposed project's environmental effects, the environmental assessment and the EIS, and the agency's decision.

---

* This chapter deals only with agency review under the environmental statutes. State or federal administrative

procedures acts—depending on the reviewing agency—also apply to these reviews. These acts are discussed in Chapter 3.

A court may not substitute its evaluation of the record for the agency's. It simply reviews the adequacy—not the outcome—of the agency's evaluation of environmental issues, as evidenced by the administrative record. Under NEPA, an agency is free to choose the most environmentally damaging course of action so long as it has factored the consequences into its decision. Suppose that United Coal's road would cause serious soil erosion problems. BLM considered that fact, but concluded that it should grant the easement for the road's construction. A court reviewing that decision might disagree with it. But, so long as BLM openly considered the environmental impacts and its decision is consistent with the agency's duties, the court must not disturb its decision.

If a court finds that an agency did not comply with NEPA, it can require the agency to prepare an EIS or to cure defects in one it has prepared. Since the agency may not act until it has considered the proposed action's environmental consequences, a court's order to cure a defect in the agency's NEPA considerations effectively forces the agency to reconsider its decision.

Thus, in our hypothetical, the Bureau of Land Management's action on United Coal's proposal will survive court scrutiny under NEPA if the agency:

- Considers all the reasonable possible environmental consequences of the road
- Considers reasonable alternatives to its actions
- Ensures that the public has an opportunity to provide input for its decision
- Makes certain that its action on United Coal's proposal is in accordance with BLM's governing statutes

But NEPA is only one of the statutes which apply to United's proposed mine. Others have a direct impact on how the actual mining is carried out.

THE SURFACE MINING CONTROL & RECLAMATION ACT OF 1977

In 1937, West Virginia enacted the first strip-mining control legislation. But 1976, thirty-three states had such laws. However, these statutes were far from uniform, and enforcement was erratic. Some states, for example, did not regulate noise and dust from mines. The absence of regulation and sometimes less than enthusiastic enforcement left individuals to fight environmental degradation and property damage on a case-by-case basis, usually under the common law action of *nuisance*.* Individuals were at a great disadvantage in these suits, since they had less financial and emotional reserves than the companies.

The inadequacies of state regulation led Congress to enact the Surface Mining Control & Reclamation Act of 1977 (SMCRA). The Act comprehensively regulates surface mine development, operation, and reclamation, primarily through a state-administered *permit*—license—program. The SMCRA also requires the Department of the Interior to develop a regulatory program for mining on lands owned by the federal government.

Congress did not intend the SMCRA to preempt state regulation. Rather, SMCRA establishes minimum national standards for surface mining and state regulation programs. State programs need not be identical to the program established for federal lands. However, a state program may be no less effective than the federal minimum standards.

Federal-state administration. The SMCRA created the Office of Surface Mining within the U.S. Department of the Interior, which developed a permanent regulatory program for surface-mining operations. That program

---

* The law of nuisance is discussed in Chapter 27.

incorporates the environmental performance standards stated in the Act. For example, the Act requires the mining company to:

- Stabilize spoil piles to prevent erosion
- Avoid toxic mine drainage
- Regrade the land using extracted materials
- Replace topsoil in the reclamation process
- Restore the mined area to a condition in which the uses before mining can be supported

In the late 1970s and early 1980s, all states in which surface mining takes place amended their laws and regulations to conform with the federal Act's minimum standards. Belmont, the hypothetical state in which United Coal operates, was among them. Belmont and the other surface-mining states also submitted administrative programs to the Office of Surface Mining for its approval, which they received.

The Office of Surface Mining offers technical assistance to the states and periodically evaluates state programs. Once a state has an approved program in place, the federal government exercises enforcement powers only when state enforcement is lax. The Office may enforce permit conditions directly and, if necessary, take over the entire state permit-issuing process. However, Congress intended direct intervention in state regulatory programs to be an extraordinary remedy.

The application process. It would be inaccurate to say that United's first step is to apply for a permit to mine on its land. By the time United applies for the permit, it will have done an enormous amount of planning concerning how it will go about the mining.

Not the least of the reasons for this planning is the level of detail the application requires. A typical application requires the following information:

- Maps showing the location of all features of the mining operation

- A timetable for mining and reclamation
- A premining water quality analysis
- A program for monitoring water quality during mining
- A coal refuse disposal plan
- A program for controlling erosion
- A plan for the use of explosives
- An air pollution control plan
- A plan for revegetation
- A plan for postmining land use

A completed application can run to hundreds of pages. Once it is filed, the state agency begins its review.

With its application, United Coal must submit copies of advertisements which will appear in the classified section of local newspapers notifying the public of its application for a permit. The company will mail notices to residents of property adjacent to the mining area. The notices will invite the public to submit comments either in writing or at a public hearing.

Under the SMCRA program, the state issues the permits to mine. Belmont's Bureau of Reclamation will determine whether United Coal may mine in certain areas, how long it may conduct its operation, and what conditions it must meet during mining. The Bureau also will determine whether United's techniques for avoiding environmental degradation are sufficient and whether its proposed reclamation plan meets the state's criteria.

After considering the application and any comments on it, the Bureau will either issue a permit (for not more than 5 years) or deny the application. If it grants the permit, it will not necessarily accept all of United's proposal. The bureau may impose restrictions on the mining operation. For example, if United's blasting plan does not sufficiently minimize danger to adjacent residences, the Bureau can limit the size of the charges United can use.

United will also have to post a *performance bond* to guarantee the reclamation of each acre of land it affects in its mining operation.* The amount of the bond will vary depending on the Bureau's appraisal of the difficulty of reclaiming the site. If United's reclamation efforts are not successful, the state will order part or all of the bond forfeited and do the reclamation itself.

Postpermit supervision. Like every other state with a qualified SMCRA program, Belmont has a team of surface-mining inspectors who monitor operations and reclamation. Violations of Belmont's surface-mining law and regulations carry both civil and criminal penalties. If an inspector were to note that United Coal allowed polluted water to escape into a nearby stream, the state could seek an *injunction* ordering United to halt the runoff and seek criminal penalties for violating its surface-mining law.

Postpermit supervision does not end with the mining. United must reclaim the land to its approximate original contour and its original condition—including vegetation. The Bureau of Surface Mining will retain jurisdiction over the site for at least 2 years to ensure that the reclamation is successful. At the end of that period, if the reclamation is successful, it will release United's reclamation bond.

One-stop Permitting

For many years, a major complaint about environmental regulation was that it required a project proponent, like United, to seek permits from a number of different agencies which could have quite different approaches to the application process. This multiplied the paperwork and hearings. Some states still take this approach. However, other states, like Pennsylvania and Belmont, have a unified or "one-stop" permit system. In Pennsylvania, a single application serves for the following permits:

- The Surface Mining Conservation & Reclamation Act

- The Clean Streams Law
- The Air Pollution Control Act
- The Coal Refuse Disposal Control Act
- The Dam Safety & Encroachment Act
- The Solid Waste Management Act
- The Clean Water Act (NPDES Permit)

The agencies that are specifically charged with enforcing these acts review each surface-mining application for the elements within their jurisdiction. United will have to obtain separately any federal, state, or local permits that are not covered by the unified program. As we will see later in this chapter, states which have adopted versions of NEPA can have a somewhat different one-stop permit process.

The Clean Water Act

NPDES permits. The objective of the federal Clean Water Act* is to restore and maintain the chemical, physical, and biological integrity of the nation's waters. It requires that operators of *point sources* (defined in the case below) of pollutants discharged into navigable waters obtain a National Pollutant Discharge Elimination System (NPDES) permit. In this context, the term *navigable waters* is completely misleading. It means:

> [Any] waterway within the United States
> . . . , including normally dry arroyos,
> through which water may flow, where such
> water will ultimately end up in public waters
> such as a river or stream, tributary to a riv-
> er or stream, lake, reservoir, bay, gulf, sea
> or ocean either within or adjacent to the
> United States.†

Keep this definition in mind as you read the next case, in which a court struggles with the definition of "point source."

---

* See *In re Ralph A. Veon, Inc.*, 12 Bankr. 186 (W.D. Pa. 1981), briefed in Chapter 39, which involves a bond of this type.

* The Clean Water Act is also called the Federal Water Pollution Control Act.
† *Leslie Salt Co. v. Froehlke*, 578 F.2d 742, 755 (9th Cir. 1978).

Sierra Club v. Abston Construction Co., Inc.

620 F.2d 41 (5th Cir. 1980)

FACTS   At times, rainwater runoff or water draining from Abston's strip mine carried silt or sulfuric acid deposits into a stream. Occasionally, Abston tried to halt the runoff by constructing sediment basins designed to catch the water before it reached the creek. The company's efforts were not always successful. The Sierra Club brought suit under the Clean Water Act, claiming that Abston's activities created point sources of pollutants. The trial court found for Abston.

ISSUE   Did Abston create point sources of pollutants?

DECISION   Yes. Reversed.

The parties do not dispute the ultimate fact that these pollutants appeared in the creek due to excess rainfall. Nor is there any disagreement the activities would be prohibited if the pollutants had been pumped directly into the waterways. The parties differ only on the legal responsibility of the miners for controlling the runoff. . . .

The plaintiff may prevail . . . only if the miners have violated some effluent limitations under the Act. . . . Those limitations . . . apply only to 'point sources' of pollutants [which the Act defines as:]

. . . "Any discernible, confined and discrete conveyancy, including but not limited to any pipe, ditch, channel, tunnel, conduit, well, discrete fissure, container, rolling stock, . . . or vessel or other floating craft, from which pollutants are or may be discharged. . . ."

The court held that pollution that resulted solely from the effects of rainfall carried by gravity into streams did not come from a point source.

[However, gravity] flow, resulting in a discharge into a navigable body of water, may be part of a point source discharge if the miner at least initially collected or channeled the water and other materials. A point source may also be present where miners design spoil piles from discarded overburden such that, during periods of precipitation erosion of spoil pile walls results in discharges into a navigable body of water by means of ditches, gulleys and similar conveyances, even if the miners have done nothing beyond the mere collection of rock and other materials. . . . Nothing in the Act relieves miners from liabilities simply because the operators did not actually construct those conveyances, so long as they are reasonably likely to be the means by which pollutants are ultimately deposited into a navigable body of water.

The NPDES regulatory scheme is similar to that of SMCRA. A state may issue NPDES permits if the U.S. Environmental Protection Agency (EPA) approves its NPDES program. However, EPA has the power to play a far greater role in the issuance of NPDES permits than the Department of the Interior has with respect to surface mining permits. If the EPA objects to a proposed permit, the state must modify it. If the state does not modify the permit and issue it, the EPA may issue it as modified.

Belmont has an approved program and issues NPDES permits as a part of its SMCRA permitting process. United's NPDES permit will specify the condition the water must be in when it leaves the site. United must use the best available demonstrated control technology to meet limitations on *effluent*—something which flows out—but the choice of the specific control techniques is left to United. United will have to specify those techniques in its strip-mine permit application. Like permits issued under the SMCRA, NPDES permits are issued for not more than 5 years.

However, what would happen if Belmont's EPA-approved program was less stringent than that of an adjacent state's approved program? Could the adjacent state undo Belmont's program and force it to upgrade its program if a facility in Belmont was polluting its water? The following case addresses that issue.

Arkansas v. Oklahoma

112 S.Ct 1046 (1992)

FACTS A sewage treatment plan in Fayetteville, Arkansas, obtained an EPA-approved permit under the National Pollution Discharge Elimination System (NPDES). Under the permit, the plant was allowed to release up to 6.1 million gallons a day into a stream in northwest Arkansas, which eventually runs into the Illinois River in Oklahoma. The EPA permitted the amount of discharge after examining the effects on streams and rivers in both states. The state of Oklahoma challenged the permit, stating that this level of pollution violated that state's water quality standards. An administrative law judge (ALJ) ruled in favor of Arkansas, stating that the discharge does not violate the Clean Water Act, since it would not have an "undue impact" on Oklahoma's water quality. The EPA upheld the ALJ's ruling. The circuit court of appeals overruled the EPA's decision and concluded that a state may intervene and bar the EPA-issued permit if its water quality standards are violated.

ISSUE Is the EPA, in carrying out its functions under the Clean Water Act, vested with the authority to determine whether a permit should be issued?

DECISION Yes. Reversed. The EPA, under the Clean Water Act, has broad authority to establish conditions for issuing NPDES permits. When the EPA issued the permit to the Fayetteville facility, it was a reasonable exercise of its statutory discretion, which Oklahoma cannot legally challenge. Since the EPA correctly observed the Clean Water Act, the court of appeals must defer to the EPA's interpretation of its own regulations. The court also cannot substitute its own factual findings for those of that agency.

This case strongly reaffirms the EPA's role in supervising and carrying out environmental policy in this country. Although there is a sharing of power between the states and the EPA, that agency's reasonable determinations of what the law means when applied to specific environmental problems will be decisive. However, the case also underscores the highly contentious political implications of interstate environmental issues. Currently, the government of Nevada is fighting federal efforts to make it the national disposal site for the nation's entire nuclear waste. In view of the significant power of the federal government in matters of interstate commerce, a small state with just over 1 million people will almost certainly lose that battle. Such controversies are likely to remain unsettled.

The Noise Control Act

The Noise Control Act of 1972 regulates noise emissions from products sold in interstate commerce. The Act empowers the EPA to develop noise emission standards for certain products, such as portable air compressors and heavy-duty trucks—both of which United Coal will use—to prevent a patchwork of state regulations which would impede the free flow of goods.

The Act, however, recognizes the states' primary interest in noise control. Nothing in it restricts a state's ability to limit working hours and the places in which noisy activity can take place. For example, Belmont can regulate the passage of trucks through Wigan's residential areas to between 7 A.M. and 7 P.M.

AN ELECTRIC GENERATING FACILITY

United Coal's principal domestic customer is the Franklin Electric Company. Franklin operates power plants throughout Oceania, another hypothetical state.

Imported oil was cheap from the 1940s through the 1960s, so Franklin constructed a number of oil-fired generating plants. However, when the price of imported oil increased five-fold in the 1970s and the supplies seemed uncertain, Franklin decided to convert some of its

facilities from oil to coal, including one in Port City.

Most coal in this country reaches its ultimate consumer by rail or barge. United Coal will truck the coal to a barge-loading facility on the Zenith River. The Zenith River empties into the ocean near Port City. Port City does not have sufficient coal-loading facilities to handle the volume that Franklin anticipates. Franklin has offered to buy from the state a waterfront site that is currently occupied by a warehouse to use as an unloading and storage facility for the coal it will receive from United. While this facility and the converted power plant will require permits already familiar from United's mining operation, like an NPDES permit, it also will require clearance under a number of other statutes, including some designed specially to protect the marine environment.

The State Environment Policy Act

Oceania has its own version of NEPA, which requires an environmental report for each major state action. Its "little NEPA" has much the same procedural requirements as the federal act.

Oceania's Department of Public Works (DPW), which owns the warehouse site, would have to prepare an environmental report on the proposed action: the development of the site sold to Franklin into a coal-unloading and -storage facility. As under NEPA, DPW would be considered the lead agency for the project because its acceptance or rejection of Franklin's proposal will determine whether any other agency will have to act on the project. As the lead agency, DPW has the responsibility for preparing the environmental report, with input from the public and from other agencies which must pass on the project. DPW would have to consider, for example, the impact on the harbor water of construction of new piers to handle the coal barges. Thus, DPW's report would also serve as Oceania's Division of Waterways' report on Franklin's application to construct piers in tidal waters belonging to the state.

The Coastal Zone Management Act

The federal Coastal Zone Management Act is a planning act designed to preserve, protect, develop, and restore the resources of the nation's coastal zone. The Act encourages all coastal states—including those along the Great Lakes —to prepare programs outlining long-range conservation and development programs for their coastal zones.

Not the least of the Act's goals was to convince states to inventory their coastal resources and to begin to prioritize areas for development or conservation. However, a coastal zone management program is not a super-zoning plan. Rather, it is a flexible statement of priorities and concerns to be factored into decisions affecting the coastal zone.

Like NEPA, the Coastal Zone Management Act (CZMA does not require a state to give preferences to environmental considerations. On the contrary, it encourages the use of harbor facilities for maritime commerce. Oceania's coastal zone management plan designates the section of Port City in which Franklin's proposed plant will be located for heavy industrial development.

CZMA's key incentive for states to participate in the Program is that federal agencies, permittees, and licensees must show that their proposed developments comply with the state's program. An applicant for a federal permit, for example, must obtain from the state a certification of consistency with the state's plan. A federal agency may not approve a project which lacks such a certification except upon a finding that it is consistent with the CZMA's purposes or that it is necessary for national security.

Oceania and Port City may be eligible for funds from the Coastal Energy Impact Fund to reduce the effects caused by Franklin's development. Congress created this fund to help overcome local objections to projects such as power plants and offshore drilling for oil and gas.

The Clean Water Act

NPDES permit. If any of Franklin Electric's operations at its coal-loading facility will result in discharges into the harbor waters, then an NPDES permit will be required. For instance, the area of the plant site in which coal is stored will be a point source. Coal plants usually maintain a 60-day supply—a veritable mountain of coal. Water running off the coal creates a pollution problem similar to the one United Coal faced in its mining operation.

Coal plants generally have greater water requirements than oil plants because they require water for cooling coal ash. Thus, Franklin Electric's converted plant may require a new NPDES permit. Of course, hydroelectric plants also require vast quantities of water. They, too, have an effect on aquatic life, which led to the next case.

National Wildlife Federation v. Consumers Power Co.

862 F.2d 580 (6th Cir. 1988)

FACTS   Consumers Power owns 51 percent of the Ludington Hydroelectric facility, one of the world's largest pumped storage facilities. More than 20 billion gallons of water may pass between its man-made reservoir and Lake Michigan. The facility generates power by drawing water from the lake into its reservoir and then letting the water from the reservoir flow through its turbines into Lake Michigan. Fish and other aquatic organisms are carried through the system ("entrained") when water is drawn from the lake. A substantial quantity of these are destroyed in the process. The Ludington facility did not have an NPDES permit that covered the discharge of entrained fish (alive and dead) into Lake Michigan. The National Wildlife Federation brought suit seeking, in part, an order compelling Consumers to apply for an NPDES permit covering the entrained fish. The trial court entered partial summary judgment in favor of National Wildlife.

ISSUE

Did the entrained fish constitute an addition of pollutants to the navigable waters of the United States?

DECISION

No. Reversed. The Clean Water Act defines the term "discharge of pollutants" as "any addition of any pollutant to navigable waters from any point source." "Pollutant" includes "biological materials," which live fish or the remains of dead ones are. EPA regulates seafood processors who process fish taken from the sea and then release the remains into the water. EPA classifies fish remains in that instance as pollutants. And here, the district court held that an "addition" occurs because the Ludington facility's turbines created the pollutant. But, the facility, unlike seafood processors, never removes the fish from the waters of the United States.

> To be sure, the manipulation of water by the Ludington facility's turbine changes the form of the pollutant from live fish to a mixture of live and dead fish in the process of generating electricity. However, this does not mean that the Ludington facility "adds" a pollutant to Lake Michigan. . . . [The facility] does not create the fish which become entrained in the process of generating electricity. If the district court decision were upheld, a [NPDES] permit would be required even for a dam which released alive all fish passing through it from and into waters of the United States, since the CWA does not distinguish between living and dead "biological materials."

Dredge and fill permits. The channel leading to Franklin's proposed facility will have to be dredged and the *spoil*—in the context of dredging, bottom sediments—disposed of. Under the Clean Water Act, the U.S. Army Corps of Engineers regulates all construction in navigable waterways. Here, navigable means something a boat can use, not the NPDES definition. However, the Corps' dredge and fill responsibilities do *not* fall under NEPA's defense-related activities exemption.

Two separate permits are involved. The dredge permit covers only the removal of the spoil. A separate permit is required to dispose of the dredged material, since it often contains high concentrations of toxic heavy metals, like arsenic and chromium, from generations of unregulated waste disposal.

Wetlands protection. Franklin must also be concerned whether their activities destroy wetlands. In the past, it was never a problem for landowners simply to fill in wetland areas they owned such as swamps, small ponds, etc., in order to develop their land. In recent years, however, it was discovered that wetlands, crucial for plant and animal habitats, water quality, and flood control, were being destroyed at an alarming rate. Indeed, the EPA estimated that half the wetland acreage in the lower forty-eight states had already been destroyed. In response, the Clean Water Act provided that anyone wishing to discharge "dredged or fill material" into "navigable waters" must first secure a permit from the U.S. Army Corps of Engineers. The EPA can, however, legally block the Corps from issuing the permits if it wishes. The penalty for violating this provision of the Clean Water Act can be severe. In 1990 a father and son in Florida were sentenced to a 21-month prison sentence for dumping unpolluted sand on their property, even though they had the permission of state officials.*

One of the greatest controversies surrounding the protection of wetlands is how to define a wetland. In 1987 the Corp of Engineers promulgated regulations designed to create a workable definition. Under the Corps of Engineers' approach, wetlands generally are visible swamps, marshes, bogs, and such. However, in 1989, in response to criticism that the definition was too lax, the Bush administration issued the much stricter 1989 Manual. Under the 1989 Manual a wetland, as long as it supports some animal or plant life, does not have to be permanently wet. Thus, a desert arroyo is a wetland if it is wet 7 days a year. Areas dry at the surface all year long are considered wetlands if there is water as low as 18 inches below the surface. Indeed, about half of Vermont, 40 percent of Maryland's Eastern Shore, and much of Houston's suburbs would have to be protected under the 1989 Manual!†

In the waning days of the Bush administration, a compromise was struck between the 1989 and 1987 definitions of wetlands. It will be up to the Clinton administration to decide what wetland policy will be implemented in the future.

The so-called "property rights" movement, discussed in Chapter 27 on real property, was catalyzed in part by the wetlands controversy. Landowners who are denied permits and so cannot develop their land are now arguing that this rejection is tantamount to a "regulatory taking" that requires "just compensation" under the Fifth Amendment to the Constitution. Under the rationale of the 1992 *Lucas* case, presented in Chapter 27, it is quite possible that if the government wishes to deprive a landowner of the opportunity to develop her land for economic gain, it may have to pay dearly for the luxury of having a well-protected environment.

The Endangered Species Act

The dredging required alongside Franklin Electric's pier is minimal. However, in performing its environmental assessment to determine whether NEPA requires an EIS for the project, the Corps learns that Beentoun bivalves populate the area to be dredged. Beentoun bivalves are a species of clam which appears on the Endangered Species List. This discovery will force the Corps to prepare an EIS and will trigger a painstaking review of the shellfish's *habitat,* a site where an organism normally lives or grows.

The Endangered Species Act requires federal agencies to ensure that any action they authorize, fund, or carry out is not likely to jeopardize the continued existence of any endangered or threatened species, or result in the destruction or adverse modification of habitats critical to its survival.

The Department of the Interior has primary responsibility for enforcing the Endangered Species Act. The Department must use the best scientific and commercial data available in designating endangered species and critical habitats. As to critical habitats, the Department must also weigh the designation's negative economic impact, if any. Where it outweighs the benefits of preservation, the Department may not designate an area unless not designating a habitat will result in a species' extinction.

The Act does not require that a species be preserved in the site in which it is found. However, species often are finely attuned to their

---

* "A Judge's Lament," *Wall Street Journal,* April 8, 1993, p. A 14.
† R. Blessen, "Wetlands Policy Still Unsettled," *The National Law Journal,* February 15, 1993, p. 26.

specific habitat, and moving them is impossible. If that should be true here, either the Corps will deny the permit, or the Corps or Franklin Electric can appeal to a special Cabinet-level tribunal for an exemption from the Act.

The Resource Conservation and Recovery Act

The federal Resource Conversation and Recovery Act (RCRA) establishes minimum national standards for identification, transportation, treatment, storage, and disposal of hazardous waste. While the EPA maintains its own program, the states can administer equivalent programs with the EPA's approval.

Hazardous waste. The RCRA defines hazardous waste as:

> a solid waste, or combination of solid wastes, which because of its quantity, concentration, or physical, chemical, or infectious characteristics may—
>> cause, or significantly contribute to an increase in mortality or an increase in serious irreversible, or incapacitating reversible, illness; or pose a substantial present or potential hazard to human health or the environment when improperly treated, stored, transported, or disposed of, or otherwise managed.

The Act leaves the specific identification of these wastes to the EPA.

Suppose the warehouse which Franklin Electric will tear down to build its new facility contains several transformers, devices which change electricity from a higher voltage to a lower voltage or vice versa. The transformers contain oil treated with polychlorinated biphenyls (PCBs). Because PCBs have a very high ignition temperature, transformer makers used them to reduce the likelihood of fire if a transformer ruptured. However, PCBs are highly toxic and, if they escape into water or soil, extremely difficult to remove.

Transportation and disposal. The EPA has identified PCBs as a hazardous waste. Because of the cost of removing and disposing of the oil, responsibility for the oil will figure significantly in Franklin's negotiations with Oceania's DPW.

Suppose Franklin initiates the removal of the transformers. It then becomes subject to RCRA's regulations covering generators of hazardous waste. Before Franklin can have the transformers removed, it must obtain an EPA identification number for the shipment. It must then prepare a *manifest*—a document containing a list of the shipment's contents, and its origin, destination, and carrier—describing the waste and designating the facility with which Franklin contracted to handle the waste. Each container must be marked as to its contents and source.

If Franklin contracts with a hauler to move the oil, the transporter must have an EPA license to receive hazardous waste. The transporter may not accept the shipment until Franklin supplies it with the manifest. The EPA or a state hazardous waste management agency must also license the facility which will ultimately treat, store, or dispose of the PCB-laden oil.

When in operation, a coal-fired electric generating station produces hundreds of tons of ash waste annually. These wastes are specifically excluded from coverage under the RCRA. Many states require coal ash to be deposited in licensed landfill facilities. However, Franklin need not throw away the material. Coal ash has many industrial uses. It is used in manufacturing concrete blocks and as a base for road construction. These uses are exempt from the licensing requirements.

The Comprehensive Environmental Response, Compensation, and Liability Act

Suppose the waste hauler to whom Franklin consigned the PCB-laden oil took it to Clean Environment Inc., a licensed facility for the disposal of such waste. Clean Environment accepts the waste, but instead of disposing of it, the company just buries the drums in its landfill. Some time passes. Clean Environment sells its now capped landfill for a housing development and promptly goes out of business. Mike Malasuerte, the developer, hits oil—Franklin's, to be precise—when he excavates his first cellar hole. Who is responsible for cleaning up the mess left by Clean Environment?

Responsible parties. The Comprehensive Environmental Response, Compensation, and Liability Act of 1980 and the Superfund Amendments and Reauthorization Act (SARA) of 1986, which we will collectively refer to as

"CERCLA," imposes liability for cleaning up hazardous wastes on:

- The current owner or operator of the waste disposal facility
- The person who owned or operated the facility at the time hazardous wastes were disposed there
- The person who arranged for the disposal of the waste
- The person who accepted the waste for transportation or disposal

In short, everyone from Franklin to Malasuerte is a potentially responsible person under CERCLA. The next case illustrates how far CERCLA liability can extend.

Smith Land & Improvement Corp. v. Celotex Corp.

851 F.2d 86 (3d Cir. 1988)

FACTS   Philip Carey Co. put a large pile of industrial waste, including asbestos, on a tract of land it owned. In 1963, it sold the land to Smith's predecessor corporation. Before the sale, Smith's predecessor had inspected the property five times and knew how Carey had used the property. Through a series of transactions beginning in 1967, Carey's interests ended up as parts of Celotex and Rapid-American Corp. In 1984, the U.S. EPA notified Smith that if Smith did not alleviate the asbestos hazard on its land, the EPA would perform the work and then seek reimbursement. Smith corrected the condition to the EPA's satisfaction at a cost of $218,945.44. When Celotex and Rapid-American declined to accept responsibility for the cleanup costs, Smith brought suit seeking reimbursement. The district court entered summary judgment for both defendants holding that the doctrine of *caveat emptor* barred Smith's claim. It held that the purchase price reflected the possibility of environmental risks.

ISSUE   Under CERCLA, are successor corporations to a facility operator responsible for contributing to or reimbursing the costs of an EPA-mandated cleanup?

DECISION   Yes. Reversed. The expenses of hazardous waste cleanups

can be borne by two sources: the entities which had a specific role in the production of continuation of the hazardous condition, or the taxpayers through federal funds. CERCLA leaves no doubt that Congress intended the burden to fall on the latter only when the responsible parties lacked the wherewithal to meet their obligations. Congressional intent supports the conclusion that, when choosing between the taxpayers or a successor corporation, the successor should bear the cost. Benefits from the use of the pollutant as well as savings resulting from the failure to use non-hazardous disposal methods insured to the original corporation, its successors and their respective stockholders and accrued only indirectly, if at all, to the general public.

Doctrines such as *caveat emptor* and "clean hands" have no place in CERCLA cases because they could bar relief regardless of the blameworthiness of a party. However, CERCLA expressly conditions the amount of contribution on the application of equitable considerations. Thus, if the tract's purchase price was reduced to allow for environmental problems. Smith should not be entitled to double compensation.

Imposing liability on corporations that had no contact with the site of a facility for 25 years may seen drastic. However, the intent of CERCLA is to hold as many parties strictly liable for environmental cleanup as possible, with some very limited exceptions. The policy behind CERCLA, as the above case attests to, is not to apportion the liability equitably among all those responsible, but to defray the costs as much as possible from the American taxpayer. Consequently, any responsible party can be held "jointly and severally" liable. What this means is that any of the parties involved in our problem—the seller, the buyer, the lender, the waste hauler, and the electric generating facility—could all together or individually be held liable for the *full* amount of the cleanup. The government will simply go after the party that has the "deepest pocket." However, buyers of land with toxic wastes, like Mike Malasuerte, and the lenders which finance such purchases, like the Port City Bank, are usually unaware of the waste. Despite their lack of awareness, how would these parties fare under CERCLA?

Responsible parties: buyers and lenders. Buyers, like Mike Malasuerte, who claim to have no knowledge of the PCB-laden oil, as well as lenders who foreclose and take the property back, do have to worry about liability under CERCLA. What then are the chances that Mike Malasuerte will be found liable for the

cleanup? First, to diminish his liability exposure, Mike should have tried to protect himself contractually before he bought the land. He should have demanded that the seller, Clean Environment, Inc., insert a "hold harmless" clause in the purchase agreement. Such a clause would state that the seller will indemnify Mike if there are any future hazardous waste cleanup costs. Of course, this provision was not agreed to by the government, so Mike still might have had to pay for the cleanup. And his chances of being indemnified would only be as good as Clean Environment's assets might permit him to recover.

Even without a "hold harmless" clause, Mike Malasuerte could, as a purchaser, also assert the *innocent third party defense*. This defense, created in 1986 under SARA, might exonerate Mike if he can demonstrate that he neither knew nor could reasonably have known about the PCB-laden oil when he bought the land. To satisfy this defense, Mike would have to conduct appropriate inquiries concerning previous owners and uses of the land in line with customary real estate practices. Put another way, Mike must exercise "environmental due diligence." At the very least, he should have executed a title search to determine who the previous owners were, inspected the site carefully, and interviewed both the people who worked there and those who live in the area. Unfortunately for Mike, he did none of these things. The fact that Mike willingly purchased the land from a licensed facility of waste demonstrates that he was less than diligent.

Suppose also that Mike Malasuerte had received financing for his housing development from the Port City Bank. Before the PCB-laden oil is discovered, however, Mike goes bankrupt. Port City Bank forecloses on the property and is, as commonly occurs, the only party to bid on Mike's property at the foreclosure sale. Unfortunately for Port City Bank, it could also end up paying for the cleanup, since it is now the owner. However, as a lender, Port City Bank can argue that the property was simply a means of securing the loan and that, as a bank it was only acting to protect its security interest.

Fortunately for Port City Bank, it may also have a defense known as the *security interest exemption*. Prior to 1992, as a result of the highly controversial *U.S v. Fleet Factors Corp.** case, lenders were very vulnerable for paying cleanup costs for hazardous wastes on property they had seized when executing their security interests. To incur cleanup liability under the rule in *Fleet Factors*, it only had to be proved that the lender's involvement with managing the facility was sufficiently broad to create an inference that it could affect hazardous waste disposal, if it chose to.

However, under new EPA regulations promulgated in April 1992,† Port City Bank will *not* be liable for a clean-up under CERCLA if it complies with several requirements. First, Port City Bank must sell the property in a "reasonably expeditious manner," under commercially acceptable means, such as advertising it, listing it with a broker, etc. Second, the Bank cannot outbid, reject, or fail to act within 90 days after receiving a "bona fide firm offer of fair consideration." Finally, it must be determined whether the Port City Bank had exercised too much control over Mike's property development activities before the foreclosure. If it had, it could not claim the defense and would be liable for

the cleanup. However, Port City Bank is permitted to operate the development *after* foreclosure without jeopardizing the lose of the exemption.

If Port City is accused of having exercised too much control over Malasuerte's property *prior* to its foreclosure and seizure, the new EPA rules also provide guidance by categorically providing examples of management activity which a lender can participate in and still *not* incur the liability of cleanup costs. These are:

- any and all actions before the security interest (mortgage, deed of trust) was created
- periodically monitoring and inspecting the property
- ongoing involvement in response to an inspection
- requiring the borrower to clean up any contamination
- requiring the borrower to comply with the laws
- restructuring the loan documents
- requiring the payment of more rent or interest
- exercising any right the lender has under law or under any warranties, covenants, conditions or promises of the borrower
- providing specific or general financial or administrative advice, suggestions, and even control

Clearly, both Mike's and Port City Bank's problems could have been avoided if they had obtained a thorough environmental assessment or audit of the property before buying and financing it. Of course, had Mike known of the PCB-laden oil, he would not have bought the property, nor would Port City Bank have financed it. However, Port City Bank also had a second chance to avoid liability by refusing to bid on the property at foreclosure. Buying property that contains toxic wastes at a foreclosure is clearly not a good option for a lender even though it may have the security interest exemption. The lender will only have to sell the land

---

* *United States v. Fleet Factors Corp.*, 901 F.2d 1550 (11th Cir. 1990).
† 57 *Fed. Reg.* 18344 (April 29. 1992).

later to recoup its loses. Obviously the market for environmentally suspect property is dismal at best, since the exemption cannot be assigned to Port City's buyer. A buyer who is aware of the waste will in effect be purchasing the legal obligation to pay for a costly environmental cleanup and so would have to factor in that cost before making an offer on the land. Thus, had Port City known before the foreclosure about the PCB-laden oil, it may have been economically wiser not to bid on it at all.

Other responsible parties. There may be even *more* responsible parties to an environmental cleanup under CERCLA. The above are only the more common targets. Suppose that Clean Environment, Inc., a sprawling company with facilities in several states, sold one of its licensed facilities to Sanitary Waste Co. In this case, known as an asset acquisition, Sanitary Waste would be liable for future government actions particular only to the Clean Environment, Inc., site which it purchased. But if Sanitary Waste purchased *all* of Clean Environment's stock in a merger, it would be responsible for any of the disposals and cleanups that Clean Environment, Inc., would be responsible for, even those that occurred years ago. This greater liability in the second instance is known as *successor liability*. The *Smith Land & Improvement* case, discussed above, is a poignant example of how strict successor liability can be.

Finally, if Clean Environment, Inc., decides to lease its facilities, instead of selling them, to Sanitary Waste, both of them would be liable, even if Sanitary Waste, as a tenant, creates the waste problem. However, would Sanitary Waste, as a tenant, be responsible for a cleanup created by its lessor, Clean Environment? It could be responsible, unless it can show that when it leased the premises, it was an innocent third party lessee. To prove its innocence, Sanitary Waste would be required to show that it diligently attempted to discover whether there was an environmental problem. In fairness to tenants, particularly on shorter-term leases, the EPA does not sue them if the lessor can be found.

Insurance coverage. If Mike Malasuerte, or any of the other parties, are found to be liable under CERCLA, would their insurance cover their losses? This is currently one of the greatest legal controversies concerning environmental liability, since billions of dollars are at stake. Since 1986, all comprehensive general liability (CGL) policies, held by most businesses, have specifically excluded the cost of pollution cleanup. The legal fight centers around pre-1986 policies and the interpretation of the specific words "sudden and accidental" contained in those policies. The insurance industry argues any cleanups occurring before 1986 are covered by CGL policies only if the pollution was discharged instantaneously and was unintended. Courts in a number of states, including California, Iowa, Massachusetts, Minnesota, North Carolina, Washington, and Wisconsin* have ruled that the words have a much broader meaning and have required the insurers to pay for the cleanups, even though the accident may have been accidental and occurred slowly over a period of time. Courts in Maine and New Hampshire, on the other hand, have sided with the insurers.

Superfund. The concept most closely associated with CERCLA is the Hazardous Substances Superfund. The $8.5 billion in the fund comes from a variety of taxes and was to be spent by the end of 1991. In 1990, another $8.5 billion was authorized for cleanup for 1990 to 1994. However, some estimates are that an additional $100 billion will be necessary to cleanup the more than 679 priority sites over the next 50 years. As it was noted in the Smith Land & Improvement Corp. case Congress intended these funds to be drawn upon only when a responsible party could not be identified. The Superfund is woefully underfunded.

---

* *Just v. Reclamation Ltd.*, 456 N.W.2d (Wis. 1990).

Hazardous substances and pollutants under CERCLA. The Act's definition of "hazardous substance" and "pollutant or contaminant" give some idea of the magnitude of CERCLA's impact. Hazardous substances include *any* hazardous or toxic substance identified under other federal environmental statutes as well as substances EPA so classifies. Some substances are excluded: petroleum and natural gas, nuclear by-products, engine exhausts, and normal applications of field fertilizer, among others.

CERCLA also authorizes the EPA to respond when a "pollutant or contaminant" poses an immediate or substantial danger to the environment. In essence. pollutants or contaminants are any substances not classified as "hazardous" that may pose a threat to the environment.

The breadth of CERCLA's coverage and the extent of the liability to which responsible persons may be subject have drastically changed the ground rules for businesses like Franklin Electric and United Coal. Those changes are permanent.

The Clean Air Act of 1970

The federal Clean Air Act of 1970 requires the EPA to establish National Ambient Air Quality Standards (NAAQS) for various types of pollutants. There are two types of standards. Primary standards define the margin necessary to protect public health. Secondary standards define the margin necessary to protect the public welfare, such as the public's interest in visibility and in preventing damage to living organisms. NAAQS standards exist for the pollutants associated with burning coal. These pollutants include sulfur dioxide, particulates (e.g., ash), and nitrogen oxides.

State implementation plans. The Clean Air Act, like the Clean Water Act and the SMCRA, provides for state implementation of national goals. States that wish to manage their own programs adopt plans called *state implementa-*

tion plans (SIPs) which outline how they will meet the NAAQS requirements and other provisions of the Clean Air Act. The EPA approves these plans. States may set stricter ambient air standards than the EPA's. While the states oversee enforcement of their SIPs, the EPA also can enforce them. SIPs have the force of federal law, unlike state NPDES and SMCRA regulations.

Prevention of significant deterioration. If Port City has attained the NAAQS standard for the pollutants which the plant will emit, then the plant is subject to Prevention of Significant Deterioration (PSD) regulations. If Port City has not attained NAAQS levels, then Franklin Electric's plant will be subject to the Nonattainment regulations. With respect to both the PSD and Nonattainment regulations, the state may establish standards that are more stringent than the federal government's baseline.

The PSD regulations apply to major emitting facilities, including newly constructed and modified sources of air pollutants which have the potential to emit more than 250 tons of any regulated air pollutant per year. Franklin Electric's coal-fired plant will emit more than 250 tons per year of the pollutants noted above. Each major emitting facility must undergo a detailed preconstruction review and obtain a permit from Oceania's Division of Air Quality before it begins construction. The Division will not license the plant if its emissions will violate NAAQS standards or if it will cause pollution levels to rise above levels established for the region.

New Source Performance Standards. Franklin Electric must ensure that it does not exceed the New Source Performance Standards (NSPS) for power plants by using the best available control technology for the pollutants which the new plant will emit in significant amounts. The best available control technology is determined on a case-by-case basis. The Oceania Division of Air Quality will take into consideration energy, environmental, economic, and other costs associated with the technology. Technology does not necessarily mean machinery. It may mean modifying production processes, hours of work, or other procedures. In Franklin Electric's permit application, it must describe what control technology it intends to use to meet these requirements.

Emissions in a nonattainment area. Emissions from a new facility in a nonattainment area either cannot exceed specified increments stated in the SIP or, when added to all other sources of emissions in the air quality control region, must produce lower total emissions than before the source became operational. That means that a new source must somehow produce an overall reduction in emissions in the region equal to or greater than the emissions that result from its operation.

A proposed source in a nonattainment area must meet the lowest achievable emission rate, the most stringent emission limitation the SIP contains. It is either the lowest emission rate achievable or the lowest rate actually achieved by a similar type of facility. Even if Franklin can satisfy these criteria, it must also show, if it wants to build a plant in a nonattainment area, that all other sources of air pollution it owns within Oceania meet applicable emission limitations.

Oceania must have an EPA-approved SIP for the nonattainment area. If it does not, it may not approve any new or modified facilities within the area.

Bubble concept. The inability to expand industry in nonattainment areas can obviously stunt any future economic growth in Oceania. However, under the *bubble concept*, there may be a chance for attracting new plants. Under the bubble concept, the EPA considers all facilities that comprise an industrial complex as a single source of pollution under an imaginary bubble. If all the emissions from Franklin and other polluters fall below the amount permitted under the state-approved SIP plan for that area, then an additional facility could be added. This is true even if the Franklin plant by itself does not attain the lowest emission rate achievable by a similar type of facility. Likewise, if Franklin installed new pollution control devices to lower its emissions in the bubble, it could add a new facility or, in some instances, sell its "pollution permit rights" to other firms which are struggling to meet the standards in the nonattainment area.

The Clean Air Act of 1990

The Clean Air Act of 1970 was amended in 1990 to respond to four areas of concern: ambient air quality, reduction of ozone and carbon dioxide, toxic pollutants, and acid rain. This amendment is of concern to Port City and Oceania, since they must now comply with the new requirements.

New ambient air standards. The state of Oceania, which manages its own plan or SIP, must now issue a new one to conform to the EPA's new NAAQS for major air pollutants. The new SIP will specify for Oceania the nonattainment areas, attainment areas, and those areas which cannot be categorized for each of the pollutants. The new SIPs must also show how Oceania is going to implement, monitor, and enforce its plan. The EPA can reject Oceania's plan and thrust another plan on it if it disapproves.

Reduction of ozone and carbon dioxide. Under the 1990 Act, ninety-six cities were found to have not complied with ozone and carbon dioxide levels, from car exhaust. If Port City, for example, is one of the ninety-six cities deemed to have a "moderate" problem, it has until 1996 to comply. Those with "serious" problems, like Baton Rouge, Lousiana, or "severe" problems like Houston, Texas, will have until 1999 and 2005, respectively. These cities will have to submit plans which call for tougher vehicle emissions inspections, more car pooling, and other such measures. The 1990 Act also calls for new tailpipe emission standards for all cars by 1995 and tougher standards for 2004 and 2007 model cars. Alternative fuels, like natural gas, will be required to be used more, particularly in the smoggiest cities and by those who own fleets of cars. Natural gas is being touted more and more for its clean burning attributes and because of the fact that the United States has plentiful amounts of it, while accessible oil reserves are dwindling.

Toxic pollutants. Any companies in Oceania which emit one or more of the ninety-one EPA-defined toxic substances must reduce their emissions substantially. Under the 1990 Act, the EPA will set "minimum emission rates" (MER) for each of these pollutants. By 2000, the standards for how much of these pollutants can be legally emitted will be very strict.

Acid rain. Franklin Electric Plant, as stated earlier, generates its electricity from coal. Coal and oil burning emits sulfur dioxide and nitrous oxides, which are the two main ingredients in acid rain. When these pollutants return to the earth in rain and snow, they kill vegetation and seriously harm the ecosystem. The 1990 Act requires that Franklin reduce its emissions of these two pollutants to one-half its 1990 levels by 2000. However, if Franklin's emissions are cleaner than the law allows, it can sell its rights to emit more to a utility or to other coal- or oil-burning plants which cannot meet the standards.

Other State and Local Permits

Franklin will have to obtain other permits that are more or less directly related to environmental concerns. For example, if it plans to discharge industrial wastes into Port City's sewer system, it will have to obtain an industrial discharge permit. It will also have to obtain sewer

and water connection permits from the city's Water & Sewer Commission.

This chapter has emphasized the process for obtaining environmental permits. Remember, however, that Franklin Electric will have to obtain many state and local permits that are unrelated to environmental concerns. For example, it will have to obtain a building permit from the city's building department, which enforces Oceania's building code. Also, the Port City Fire Department must certify that the facility has sufficient fire exits, fire extinguishers, and the like.

The Future of Environmental Laws

The Bush administration was viewed as being hostile to environmental laws by requiring the Office of Management and Budget and the President's Council on Competitiveness, headed by Vice President Quayle, to oversee new regulations. The result was that environmental laws, seen by these groups as being too expensive and burdensome on business, were modified or eliminated. However, the Bush administration can be partially credited for passing the Clean Air Act of 1990.

Some observers feel that the Clinton administration will be more pro-environment, especially because of Vice President Gore's unabashed position as an environmentalist. In particular, the Clinton administration is likely to embrace natural gas and clean coal technology, intensify efforts to prevent air and water pollution, protect forests and wetlands, and reduce the use of toxic chemicals. The 1990 Clean Air Act also is likely to be vigorously enforced. Furthermore, we may see the imposition of a carbon dioxide tax, which would spur the development of alternative fuels and energy. Finally, the 1992 Biodiversity Treaty, previously signed by all major nations but the United States, was finally signed in mid-1993 by a more supportive Clinton administration. That Treaty is meant to preserve species of plants and animals which are currently being destroyed at an alarming rate.*

Indeed, everyone wishes to live in a healthy environment. But at what cost are these laws acceptable, if they cause unemployment and other structural problems in the economy? One thing is certain: the struggle between environmental goals and economic well-being will continue to be at the center of American public policy debates.

CONCLUSION

Environmental laws reflect the public's increasing concern about the availability of natural resources and their allocation. Without question, these laws have succeeded, for example, in restoring many streams to the point where people can swim and fish in them. Still, they remain controversial, particularly among those who believe that only the marketplace should allocate resources. To them, the public should decide the tolerable level of environmental degradation by demonstrating how much they are willing to pay for the goods produced by polluting industries, like aluminum and steel. This argument has attracted little support among the public, which has consistently supported vigorous enforcement of the environmental laws.

A NOTE TO FUTURE CPA CANDIDATES

Beginning in 1994, the CPA exam has included environmental law topics. Candidates should be familiar with the major environmental laws, especially CERCLA. The candidate should understand the possibilities of lender and/or previous owner liability under CERCLA. The candidate should also understand the purpose

---

* E. Gellhorn, "Clinton Administration Will Change Regulatory Climate," *The National Law Journal,* November 23, 1991, p. 18.

and basic usage of environmental impact statements.

KEY WORDS

bubble concept (1121)
CERCLA (1115)
effluent (1110)
environmental impact
    statement
    (EIS) (1102)
groundwater (1102)
habitat (1114)
innocent (1117)
navigable waters (1108)
NEPA (1102)
point source (1108)
record (1105)
spoil (1113)
third party de-
    fense (1117)

DISCUSSION QUESTIONS

1. Give examples of some of the goals set forth in the National Environment Policy Act (NEPA). Are the Act's goals directed solely at pollution?
2. What is the purpose of NEPA? To whom does it apply? Does it address specific environmental problems?
3. What is an environmental impact statement (EIS)? What is its purpose? What alternatives must be evaluated?
4. What is the applicable standard for judicial review of an agency decision under NEPA? What if the court's judgment differs from the agency's?
5. Given the creation of federal minimum standards for such things as air, water, and noise pollution, what is the states' role in the administration of environmental matters?
6. What is one-stop permitting and how does it work?
7. What are the primary goals of the Clean Water Act?
8. What are the primary goals of the Clean Air Acts of 1970 and 1990?
9. What are the primary goals of the Resource Conservation & Recovery Act?
10. What is the primary goals of CERCLA? What are the distinctive aspect of liability under CERCLA?

CASE PROBLEMS

1. GAG Construction Company, a private contractor, is erecting a building under a contract with a federal agency. GAG claims that its construction activities do not constitute federal action, so that it is not subject to an environmental evaluation under NEPA. Citizens to Preserve Nature has challenged the lack of an environmental impact statement for the project. Is one necessary? Assuming that it is, what remedy might the group secure?

2. The federal Department of Transportation has decided to build portions of an interstate across Cross Lake instead of going around the lake. The lake provides recreation and drinking water to the adjacent city. The cost of going over the water was considered to be much less than that of securing land clearances, even though the bridge will be at least 2 miles long. A citizen's group. Coalition to Preserve Cross Lake, has protested because the EIS does not evaluate potential damage to the lake from vehicle accidents on the bridge. What is the likely outcome?

3. A federal agency is developing an EIS for a pending project. Concerned citizens have objected that the agency is considering only those alternatives that it has the power to implement and not the alternative of no action at all. The agency's response is that the requirement that it consider all reasonable alternatives applies only to decisions it might make. Since Congress budgeted money for the project, no action is not an alternative. Is the agency correct? Explain.

4. The state has charged Fort Swampie, a Marine base, with violating EPA-approved state regulations regarding effluent discharges into navigable waters. The base commander claims that state pollution laws are not applicable to federal government actions, but only to state or private party actions. The commander also claims that the Clean Water Act does not apply, since the river is too clogged to be navigable. Is the commander correct? Explain.

5. Hammer 'n Anvil, Inc., is a foundry. It is installing a new processing line which is so loud that federal safety regulations require all workers within 100 yards to wear protective ear coverings to prevent deafness. The state legislature has passed a law which restricts the use of machinery creating noises at this level to the period between 8:00 A.M. and 7:00 P.M. Would the statute conflict with the federal Noise Control Act? What would your answer be if the statute prohibited use of foundry lines generating noise at those levels within the state?

6. The state of Emergency has an approved Coastal Zone Management Program. It calls for the development of marine-related industries in the East Bay section of Harbor Town. Engulf & Devour, a conglomerate, bought a pier from a shipping company and has applied to the U.S. Army Corps of Engineers for a permit to construct a marina adjacent to the pier. The marina will serve a 1000-unit hotel-condominium complex the company plans to build on the pier itself. If the state opposes the development, what rights does it have under the Coastal Zone Management Act? Does the Act allow the Corps to issue the permit if the state objects? Could the state legitimately use any other land use controls to block the project? If so, what are they?

7. National Ashcan wants to locate its new steel mill in Pulaskiville. For the last 10 years, Pulaskiville has ranked among the ten cities in the country with the dirtiest air. Assuming that it is in a nonattainment region, what regulations under the Clean Air Acts of 1970 and 1990 would apply to the mill's construction? Do those regulations provide for consideration of the plant's positive economic impact on the area if it is built? If they do not, should an agency be permitted to weigh economic benefits against the impact of poor air quality on public health?

8. Morse Plating Company is a silver-plating firm. Part of the silver-plating process results in discharge water containing pollutants which are harmful if swallowed by animals. Morse discharges this water into a small stream which runs past the factory and flows into another stream which ultimately flows into the Odessa River. Neither the streams

nor the river is navigable. The cost of developing a contained water treatment system would be prohibitive to Morse, as it has a plant with older equipment and limited available space. Morse is concerned that if it should be forced to treat the water, it may have to lay off its seventy-five workers in an area already economically depressed. What act, in any, would apply to the discussed situation? Assuming that Morse would be found in violation of this act, do you believe that the law should contain exception for companies in situations like this? Explain.

9. Real Issues. In 1992, the Supreme Court ruled in two different cases that states cannot prevent the entry of garbage and hazardous materials from other states by imposing either special fees or absolute prohibitions. The Court ruled that, absent a showing of a unique danger, prohibitions against out-of-state waste violates interstate commerce. A state is allowed to impose uniform fees on disposal of these materials without discriminating on the point of origin. The decisions have been criticized by many environmental advocates on three grounds:

a. For allowing major municipalities and states effectively to export their waste and garbage elsewhere without incentive to become a catalyst in the protection of the environment
b. For underappreciating the risk of shipped waste escaping en route
c. That the destination state in left with the potential long-term risks and costs to their environment

As such, these advocates argue that if a state cannot totally bar such shipments they ought to be able to levy a tax even if the shipped waste will move through their state to another state. Such a state right might require a limitation to the interstate commerce clause of the United States Constitution. What position would you take if such a constitutional amendment were to be proposed? Explain.

10. Probably no U.S. endangered species is better known than the northern spotted owl. During the 1992 presidential campaign, while in the Pacific Northwest, President Bush stated, "It is time that we worried not only about endangered species, but about endangered jobs" (*Business Week,* October 19, 1993, p. 108). One direct cost to consumers has been an increase in the price of wood products. To illustrate, environmental regulations in the Pacific Northwest helped contribute to a 41 percent increase in the price of wood of an average new house, a $3000 increase, from 1992 to 1993 (*USA Today,* February 3, 1993, p. B1). Environmentalists agree that the economic impact of environmental rules applies unevenly to different industries and regions. However, they also point to strong economic pluses: The Pacific Northwest has become more popular to nontimber industries, has benefited from an increase in tourism, has preserved jobs in fishing, has created a new environmental services industry which employs people, and has improved timber lands productivity (*Business Week,* October 19, 1993, p. 109). Vice President Al Gore, not so kindly called "Ozone Man" by President Bush during the 1992 campaign, strongly contends that a proper balance can be found which both protects important ecosystems and helps fosters jobs. If you were a member of Congress considering the impact of environmental regulations, what would be your primary concern? Explain.

International Transactions

Jane Acosta owns and operates a small company in the suburbs of St. Louis. The company makes tennis rackets, selling them to department stores and sporting goods stores, which in turn sell the rackets to consumers. Jane recently went to Brazil, where she found a new material to use in making racket grips. Her company also received a large order for tennis rackets from a chain of sporting goods stores in Mexico. On Jane's desk is a letter from an Australian businessman proposing a contract naming him as the exclusive Australian distributor of Acosta tennis rackets. Finally, Jane is negotiating a contract with a Czech tennis player for an endorsement of Acosta rackets.

Jane Acosta's company, like an increasing number of American businesses, is operating in an international legal environment. In order to manage her business effectively, she needs to know whether the United States has import restrictions or tariffs on goods from Brazil; whether Mexican law imposes restrictions or tariffs on tennis rackets shipped from the United States; whether exclusive distributorships are legal in Australia; and whether Czech law allows individuals to enter into contracts abroad. For all her company's business transactions, Jane will want to minimize the possibility of litigation in unfamiliar settings.

The purpose of this chapter is to introduce you to the international legal environment of business so that when you encounter business law issues within an international setting, you will be able to recognize legal issues, evaluate business options, and make effective business decisions.

THE NATURE OF THE INTERNATIONAL LEGAL ENVIRONMENT

The international legal environment of business consists of a mixture of several different kinds of law, including the internal laws of different countries, "private international law," and "public international law." A country's internal law, for example, is its law governing contracts, torts, or property. *Private international law* is the law in each country that determines how that country's legal system will resolve disputes between parties from different nations. For example, in a contract dispute between a French business and a Nigerian citizen, will a French court apply its law or Nigerian law? If the Nigerian citizen obtains a judgment in a Nigerian court, will French courts enforce the judgment in France? *Public international law* refers to the law of nations. This law is often found in treaties, such as the General Agreement on Tariffs and Trade (GATT). It may also be established by multinational organizations, such as the United Nations.

Major Legal Traditions

Each country in the world has its own legal system, but many countries share legal traditions. A *legal tradition* refers in part to the kinds of legal institutions a country might have, such as courts, parliaments, or commissions. More important, countries sharing the same legal tradition tend to have similar attitudes about the nature and sources of law and about the role of law in society.

The common law tradition. As discussed in Chapter 1, the United States is a common law country. The common law tradition originated in medieval England and spread to the United States, Canada, Australia, and other countries that are now or formerly were members of the British Empire. Although specific rules of law vary widely among the common law countries, each country shares a tradition formed primarily by judges focusing on individual disputes. The primary source of law in common law countries is case law precedent, although judges also interpret statutes and use custom to resolve legal disputes.

The civil law tradition. The civil law tradition originated more than 2000 years ago, during the time of the Roman Empire. Starting in the early nineteenth century, most of the civil law countries enacted comprehensive civil law codes, the most significant of which was the Napoleonic Code of France. As Napoleon conquered other European countries, he introduced French legal institutions and his civil code. Later, the civil code and the civil law tradition were introduced in the countries colonized by the European powers.* Today, the civil law tradition prevails in most of Western Europe, Central and South America, and many countries in Asia and Africa.

In contrast to the judge-made law emphasized in the common law tradition, the sources of law in civil law countries are statutes, regulations, and the customary practices in the society. Statutes prevail over regulations, but in the absence of a contrary statute or regulation, custom is considered to be an acceptable source of law. The function of a judge in a civil law country is to interpret the sources of law. Judicial decisions are not law, and precedents are not considered to be sources of law.

The socialist legal tradition. The newest of the major legal traditions is the socialist, which began with the Russian revolution in 1917. With the collapse in the late 1980s of the Soviet Union and the Eastern European satellite countries it once controlled, the socialist legal tradition has far fewer adherents today. Those nations remaining include the Peoples Republic of China, North Korea, Vietnam, Laos, and Cuba.

In the socialist tradition, the sole source of law is the legislature, which reflects the will of the people. Unlike the law in common law and civil law countries, the purpose of law in socialist systems is to create the conditions for a new social order. In the new social order, law itself will ultimately become unnecessary and will disappear.

Religious legal traditions. Many countries base their legal systems on religious laws and principles. For example, Hinduism has had a major impact on the laws of India, as has Judaism on the laws of Israel, and Confucianism on the laws of China and Japan. Legal systems based on the laws of Islam have become increasingly influencing legal systems in Africa and Asia.

The principles of Islamic law are very different from those of any of the other major legal traditions. In the Islamic legal tradition, law is revealed by God and cannot be changed. The function of legal institutions is to enforce the divine law. Kings or legislatures may establish administrative regulations but not new law. The function of judges in Islamic systems is to apply the law to specific cases, not to develop or define the law. To find the law, a judge looks to the *Quran*, the sacred book of Islam, as it has been interpreted by Islamic religious scholars.

Mixed traditions. Very few countries have legal systems reflecting only one legal tradition. Historical patterns of colonialism, economic development, and world trade have led to the blending of different traditions. The Japanese legal system, for example, mixes:

- The Confucian tradition of ordered hierarchy and filial obligation
- The civil law tradition, especially the German Civil Code
- The common law tradition, especially American law

These traditions took root in the Japanese legal environment at different points in Japanese history, and they have blended to influence the way Japanese people and businesses view the role of law and legal institutions.

---

* The Napoleonic Code is a major source of the law in Louisiana, which was once a French colony, and in Puerto Rico, which was once a Spanish colony. In Canada, the province of Quebec follows the civil law tradition as part of its heritage.

Multinational Organizations and Agreements

In addition to being aware of the ways people in different countries view law and their own legal systems, the businessperson should be familiar with the role that international organizations and multinational agreements assume in the conduct of business. Although many different organizations and agreements affect international business transactions, the most significant are the United Nations, the European Economic Community, and the General Agreement on Tariffs and Trade.

The United Nations. The United Nations is an international political organization with many different functions. Of interest to persons doing business in an international environment is the United Nations Commission on International Trade Law (UNCITRAL). UNCITRAL has developed the Convention on the International Sale of Goods (CISG), a treaty regulating the international sale of goods. In the United States, the CISG has replaced Article 2 of the Uniform Commercial Code for some contracts for the sale of goods.

The European Community. The European Community (EC), or Common Market, was established to promote political and economic unity and strength in European member countries. Currently, Belgium, Denmark, France, Greece, Ireland, Italy, Luxembourg, the Netherlands, Portugal, Spain, the United Kingdom, and Germany belong to the EC. Eight nations—Austria, the Czech Republic, Finland, Hungary, Norway, Poland, Sweden, and Switzerland—have recently applied for membership. And three nations—Turkey, Malta, and Cyprus—have been seeking membership for a period of time, but with no success as of 1993. In the case of Turkey, a potentially important entrant, its economic and human rights policies have been a source of apprehension for the democratic nations of the EC.

The EC has its own legislative, executive, and judicial institutions. By joining the EC, a member country gives up some of its authority to regulate trade and competitive business practices in its own country. When EC law conflicts with the laws of a member country, EC law prevails. A citizen of a member country can sue in the courts of his own country, but the judge must apply any relevant EC law.

On January 1, 1993, new regulations officially went into effect for creating the free movement of money, goods, and labor throughout the EC. In the quest of the ultimate goal of establishing a single economic system, the European Commission, one of the EC's governing bodies, has been designing uniform regulations for product safety, packaging of products and a minimum wage for workers. Moreover, an agreement to establish a single currency, called European currency unit (ECU), was ratified in a treaty in November, 1991 in Maastricht, the Netherlands. It is scheduled to be in circulation by the end of this decade and will be used by the EC's 340 million consumers. Two potentially formidable hurdles remain, however, before the Maastricht goes into effect. After approval by Danish voters in a May, 1993 referendum, the treaty must still be ratified by the British Parliament and by Germany's Constitutional Court.

The integration of the nations of the EC has required individual nations to subordinate their economic and sometimes even their unique cultural characteristics in the interests of uniformity. To accomplish this goal, the EC is requiring its members to change some internal laws so that they are consistent with the laws of the other member countries. In other areas, the EC is removing trade barriers using the legal principle of *reciprocity*. Suppose that a product meets content standards in Germany, but would not meet French standards. Reciprocity requires the German government to accept the French standards. In return, its product content standards would be accepted in France. The next case illustrates how reciprocity works in the EC.

Rewe-Zentral A.G. v. Bundesmonopolverwaltung fur Branntwein [Cassis de Dijon]

1973 3 C.M.L.R. 494 (E. Comm. Ct. J.)

FACTS

Rewe imported goods into West Germany. It applied to the Bundesmonopolver-waltung fur Branntwein (Federal Monopoly Administration for Spirits) for an import permit for Cassis de Dijon, a French liqeur. Rewe's application was refused, because German law required an alcohol content of at least 25 percent for liqueurs, and the alcohol content of Cassis de Dijon was only 15 to 20 percent. Rewe sued in a German court to overturn the minimum alcohol content regulation. The German court referred issues of European Community law to the Court of Justice of the European Communities for a preliminary ruling.

ISSUE

Does the German regulation restrain trade among member countries in violation of EC law?

DECISION

Yes. Although the German government argued that restrictions on the alcohol content of beverages are necessary to protect consumers and to protect public health, the court did not find the government's argument convincing. It found no purpose in the "general public interest" that could outweigh the need for free movement of goods among members of the EC. As to alcholic beverages, the court found "no valid reason, why, provided that they have been lawfully produced and marketed in one of the member-States, alcoholic beverages should not be intro-duced into any other member-State. . ."

The foregoing case illustrates the strong EC goal of eradicating barriers to the free move-ment of goods even if it is at the expense of local traditions and economic standards. How-ever, occasionally a country's promotion of its provincial customs and heritage can also hinder the free movement of goods and even labor. A notable case in point involved a Dutch citizen who was rejected in the late 1980s for a college teaching position in Ireland. She was not quali-fied under Irish law because she did not know how to speak the official language of Ireland, Gaelic. She argued that since English was the language used in education, business, and most other matters in Ireland, the Irish language re-quirement, spoken by only a third of the coun-try, was essentially an unreasonable and illegal barrier to the free movement of workers within the EC. The EC's judicial body, the European Court of Justice, ruled that the language re-quirement met a recognized EC aim of preserv-ing both cultural richness and a linguistic heritage and that Ireland's language require-ment was strictly necessary in achieving that aim. The Court further declared that by meeting this test, Ireland did not illegally infringe on the fundamental freedom workers have to move among the various EC countries.*

The general agreement on tariffs and trade. The General Agreement on Tariffs and Trade

---

* *Groener v. Minister of Education,* 1990 56 C.M.L.R. 401.

(GATT) is a multinational agreement that provides a framework for the growth of international trade and the reduction of tariffs among member countries. The GATT is a major source of international trade law. Approximately 100 countries now subscribe to the GATT, while a number of other countries claim to follow the GATT without having formally adopted it. Members of the GATT participate in periodic "rounds" of diplomatic discussions aimed at the further lowering of barriers to worldwide trade. The United States has never formally ratified the GATT by a two-thirds vote of the Senate, but the GATT was adopted by an executive order of the President.

The latest round of GATT talks were held in Uruguay. The issues advanced there in the early 1990s included the bolstering of patent and copyright protection, slashing subsidies to farmers, eliminating quotas that restrict imports, and liberalizing rules governing international banking and telecommunications. GATT policies, such as those mentioned above, often are very controversial, since they can greatly alter the structure of a nation's domestic farms and industries. Thus in 1992, when former President Bush aggressively encouraged the GATT goal (as well as U.S. trade policy) of decreasing subsidiaries to French farmers in order to increase U.S. agricultural exports to that nation, the news was greeted with boycotts and violent riots in Paris and other French cities. Indeed, French and other European farmers, as well as Japanese rice farmers, are among the most subsidized and protected businesspersons in the world. However, multinational agreements such as those proposed by GATT and other legal and economic pressures may soon signal an end to those long-standing policies of protectionism. A more specific treatment of GATT and tariffs appears later in this chapter.

INTERNATIONAL CONTRACTS

Suppose Acosta, Inc., wants to enter into a contract to sell its tennis rackets to Deu-tschsport, A.G., a chain of sporting goods stores in Germany. What kinds of problems should Acosta anticipate in the negotiation and performance of the contract? How can Acosta be certain that it will be paid for the goods? What happens if the buyer breaches the agreement?

Contracts between businesses from different countries pose risks not found in domestic agreements. For example, an Iowa business doesn't usually have to negotiate with the aid of a translator when selling goods to a Montana buyer, and a New York buyer doesn't worry about a revolution in Georgia that will prevent shipment of goods under a contract. These problems, and others, do occur in international transactions.

Contract Negotiation and Drafting

Language barriers. Contract problems can arise when the buyer and seller cannot communicate in the same language. The *Frigaliment* case, briefed in Chapter 10, is one example of the problems encountered when buyers and sellers speak different languages. When the parties to a contract must negotiate and draft agreements in more than one language, they should carefully specify which version of any final agreement will be the official contract document. Otherwise, translation errors could change the substantive rights of the parties.

A second language problem results from the different meanings some commercial terms have in different legal systems. For example, you saw in Chapter 32 that the commercial term "FOB" is used to define the seller's delivery obligation and risk of loss with respect to goods. Under UCC §2-319, if the contract states that the sale of goods takes place "FOB seller's warehouse," the seller's obligation is to deliver the goods to a common carrier at the warehouse. In the commercial law of most other countries, however, "FOB seller's warehouse" requires that the seller actually load the goods aboard the carrier before delivery is complete.

In most countries, "FOB seller's warehouse" is equivalent to the term "FOB vessel" under UCC §2-319.

Capacity. Another problem that sometimes arises in the course of negotiating a contract is the legal status of the foreign party to the contract. In many socialist countries, the state, through state-run trading companies, enters into contracts with foreign businesses. The *Ocean Tramp Tankers* case, briefed later in this chapter, involves a Soviet state trading company as a defendant. If the state-run trading company breaches its contract, the foreign business may have trouble getting relief in the government's courts and may face claims that the government is immune from lawsuits in other courts.

Even where the foreign entity is privately owned, its legal status may be uncertain. In the United States, a seller dealing with a corporation knows that the firm's liability on the contract is limited. An American seller dealing with a German buyer will probably not know what to expect of a German *Aktiengesellschaft* (A.G.), a large public corporation, or *Gesellschaft mit beschrankter Haftung* (G.m.b.H.), a close corporation. The early involvement of an attorney knowledgeable in the business law of foreign countries may prevent substantial financial losses in the event of a breach of contract.

Legality. Another problem found in international contracts that is rarely encountered in domestic transactions is the legality of the subject matter. As you read in Chapter 9, contracts violating statutes are generally not enforceable. The internal laws and public policies of the countries of both parties may affect the legality of their contract. In addition, most countries have import and export regulations which can be violated by the contracting parties. For example, an American business contracting to buy Cuban cigars would violate the Trading with the Enemy Act and be subject to criminal penalties.

Currency fluctuations and controls. The value of many currencies, including the dollar, fluctuates from day to day. The parties involved in a contract should allocate the risk of rising or falling currency values by specifying how and when the price of goods will be paid. For example, if the value of the dollar falls relative to the German mark, Acosta rackets will cost less for a German company to buy. Acosta's contract with the German buyer should state whether the purchase price is payable in dollars or marks, and the time when payment is due.

Currency controls may make payment for goods difficult, if not impossible. Some countries may require that local companies pay in local currency only, not in dollars. Other countries limit the amount of money their businesses can hold in currencies other than their own. The seller should probably not rely on the buyer's representations about currency laws, but should seek the advice of its own lawyers.

In some countries, currency controls may force buyers and sellers of products to be more creative in negotiating payment terms. One practice, known as *countertrade*, involves paying for goods with other goods, or creating offsetting contracts allowing foreign companies to take their profits out of the country. For example, Pepsico sells soft drinks in Poland. It uses the proceeds from those sales to purchase chairs from Polish manufacturers. Pepsico then exports the chairs to the United States, where it uses them in its Pizza Hut restaurants. A carefully negotiated countertrade agreement allows the seller to bring its profits home, and helps the foreign country build its own economy.

War and frustration. As Chapters 12 and 33 indicate, a court may excuse the performance of contractual obligations when the performance becomes impossible, commercially impracticable, or frustrated. International settings provide risks for contract performance not often found in purely domestic transactions. Although most legal systems recognize the concept of excuses for performance, the requirements are not always the same as those found in UCC §2-615. The law in different countries varies considerably. Egypt's closing of the Suez Canal in 1956 led to a flood of litigation in English and other courts, because ships traveling between Europe and Asia had to make a long and expensive detour around the continent of Africa. In the next case, the court had to determine whether such rerouting constituted frustration.

Ocean Tramp Tankers Corp. v. V/O Sovfracht (the *Eugenia*)

[1964] 1 All E.R. 161 (C.A. 1963)

FACTS

Sovfracht, a Russian state trading corporation, chartered the ship *Eugenia* to carry iron and steel from the Black Sea to India. Agents for the parties negotiated a charter contract in London. At the time of the negotiations, the Egyptian government had just seized the Suez Canal. In response, the United Kingdom and France were building up their military forces in the area. The parties knew there was a risk that the canal would be closed, but they were unable to agree on contractual language allocating that risk. They contracted without expressly covering the possible closing of the canal.

Shortly after entering the Suez Canal on her way to India, the *Eugenia* became trapped when English planes attacked Egyptian targets and Egyptian forces blockaded the canal. A northbound exit was cleared 2 months later, but no efforts were made to clear a southbound exit. The *Eugenia* left the canal, went round the Cape of Good Hope to India, and delivered her cargo. The *Eugenia's* owner claimed that the contract required payment for the time the ship was trapped in the canal, while the charterer claimed frustration.

ISSUE

Did the closing of the Suez Canal so alter the obligations of the parties that the contract was frustrated?

DECISION

No. To find frustration, the court must determine that it would be "positively unjust" to hold the parties to their contract. The closing of the canal did not bring about a "fundamentally different situation" than that contemplated by the parties. The charter was for the voyage, not a particular route; the cargo was not affected by the delay: and the trip around the Cape of Good Hope merely made the voyage more expensive and longer.

Letters of Credit

A *letter of credit* is a bank's written promise to pay a sum of money on behalf of its customer when a third party makes a proper demand for payment [UCC §5-103(1)(a)]. Two kinds of letters of credit are commonly used in international transactions. One is the documentary letter of credit. The second is the standby letter of credit.

Within the United States, UCC Article 5 governs the use of letters of credit. In international transactions, however, letters of credit are usually controlled by the Uniform Customs and Practice for Documentary Credits (UCP), a document published by the International Chamber of Commerce. The UCP is not actually a law; it is a restatement of the customs and practices of the international banking community. Alabama, Arizona, Missouri, and New York have amended Article 5 of the UCC to provide that parties may choose to have their letters of credit governed by the UCP rather than by Article 5 of the UCC.

Documentary letters of credit. Some contracts for the sale of goods require that the buyer obtain a *documentary letter of credit*. This contract provision requires that the buyer obtain a promise from its bank to pay the seller when the seller presents the proper documents to the buyer's bank. The documentary letter of credit is a method of payment for goods that reduces the seller's risk that the goods will be shipped but not paid for.

The bank issues a letter of credit by stating in a signed writing that it will honor demands for payment made in compliance with certain conditions [UCC §5-103(1)(a)]. The conditions are usually the presentment of documents in a particular form. The buyer and seller determine in their original contract the amount of the credit and the number and form of documents required for payment.

By issuing a letter of credit, the buyer's bank agrees to examine any presented documents with care to be sure they comply on their face with the specifications of the letter of credit. The bank is not responsible for falsifications or for determining whether the underlying contract between buyer and seller has actually been performed [UCC §5-109]. When the bank receives the proper documents in proper form, it must pay on the letter of credit [UCC §5-114].

In some instances, the seller may not be satisfied receiving a letter of credit from the buyer's bank in a foreign country. The seller may require that the buyer's letter of credit be confirmed by another bank, usually one in the seller's place of business. The seller's bank, in confirming the letter of credit, promises that it will honor the original letter of credit issued by the buyer's bank [UCC §5-103(1)(f)]. To be paid, the seller just has to present the correct documents, in correct form, to the confirming bank.

Suppose Acosta, Inc., agrees to sell 5000 tennis rackets to Deutschsport for $100,000. Acosta requires that Deutschsport obtain a confirmed letter of credit for $100,000. The terms of the letter require that Acosta submit an invoice, packing list, shipper's export declaration, and bill of lading to show that the goods have been shipped. If Deutschsport wants to be sure that the shipped goods conform to the contract, it can require an inspection by an independent third party and require an inspection certificate as a document Acosta will need to present to obtain payment.

Deutschsport will ask its local bank to issue a letter of credit in favor of Acosta. The German bank will then advise the confirming bank in St. Louis that it has opened a letter of credit in Acosta's favor, stating the terms of the letter of credit. The St. Louis bank then sends Acosta a confirmed letter of credit, promising to pay Acosta upon presentation of the documents specified in the letter of credit.

When Acosta receives the confirmed letter of credit from its bank, it will ship the goods, making sure to obtain all the documents required for payment. Acosta will then take the required documents to its bank, which will examine them carefully. If the documents comply with the terms of the letter of credit, the bank will pay Acosta and then forward the documents to the German bank with a demand for payment. The German bank will reimburse the St. Louis bank, and it will inform Deutschsport that the documents have arrived and that payment is due. (See Figure 48.1.)

The advantage of using letters of credit is that the risk of loss to the seller and the banks is

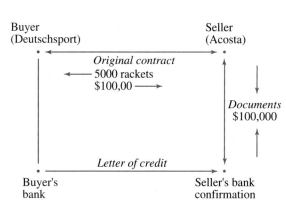

Buyer
(Deutschsport)

Seller
(Acosta)

Original contract
← 5000 rackets
$100,00 →

Documents
$100,000

Letter of credit

Buyer's
bank

Seller's bank
confirmation

Figure 48.1 Documentary letters of credit.

minimized. The buyer's bank knows its customer, and it can either extend credit or set aside funds from the customer's account to ensure its payment. The seller deals with a local bank upon shipment of the goods and does not have to wait for payment. The seller's bank knows the reputation and standing of the buyer's bank, and it has access to methods within the banking community of ensuring payment from the buyer's bank.

Standby letters of credit. A *standby letter of credit* is a guarantee for the performance of a contract. It protects the buyer from losses in the event the seller breaches the agreement. The buyer using a standby letter of credit will require that the seller obtain a promise from a bank which guarantees that the bank will pay the amount of the credit if the seller breaches the contract.

As for documentary letter of credit, the bank's obligation to pay when the proper demand is made is independent of the buyer's and seller's contract. Because the bank does not verify that a breach occurred, the buyer and seller must agree on what will constitute a breach of contract and on the way that the buyer will demand payment. If a demand is made in the proper form, the bank will almost always have to pay the buyer, even if the seller really did not breach the contract. In the next case, the plaintiff learned some hard lessons about the pitfalls of using standby letters of credit.

Recon/Optical, Inc. v. Government of Israel

816 F.2d 854 (2d Cir. 1987)

FACTS   Recon/Optical contracted to provide an aerial reconnaissance system for the Israeli Air Force. The contract provided that all disputes would be settled by arbitration. The contract also provided that work would continue on the project pending an arbitrator's decision. A contradictory provision allowed either party to terminate performance in the event of a "material breach" of the agreement. Israel required Recon to obtain a standby letter of credit, which was payable upon Israel's certification to the bank that it was "entitled" to payment because of Recon's failure to deliver contract items or due to any "other material breach" by Recon. As work progressed under the contract, Recon submitted contract modifications, which the Israeli Air Force representative orally accepted. Israel denied the authority of the representative to make changes and refused to pay Recon. Recon submitted the dispute to arbitration, but terminated performance, claiming a material breach by Israel. Israel claimed Recon breached and demanded $21.5 million under the standby letter of credit. Recon sued in federal district court to enjoin payments; it lost, and appealed to the Second Circuit.

ISSUE   Was Israel's demand for payment under the letter of credit fraudulent? Should the court have issued an injunction against payment?

DECISION   No. No. Judgment of the district court affirmed. Fraud results from "first causing the default, then attempting to reap the benefit of the guarantee." Although the parties disagree about who breached the contract, Israel is pursuing the remedy of arbitration provided in the contract. It did not prevent Recon from performing. Israel's claim for payment is consistent with what the parties bargained for in their contract.

Dispute Resolution

While it is important for managers to practice preventive law in all kinds of business dealings, preventive law is especially important in the international context. Chapter 2 discussed the American procedures for dispute resolution. The manager who fails to plan in advance for the possibility of contract problems invites lawsuits in unfriendly forums applying unfamiliar rules of law. An American manager might well be uncomfortable with the idea of a trial before a judge in a socialist legal system, for example.

The time for practicing preventive law in an international contract is during contract negotiation and drafting. Once the parties to a contract disagree over the meaning of the contract, it will be difficult to obtain an agreement on how to resolve problems without litigation. Three kinds of contract provisions are often used to plan for the possibility of disputes: choice-of-forum, binding arbitration, and choice-of-law clauses.

Choice of forum. Often, courts in more than one country will have jurisdiction over a contract dispute. For example, an American company contracts with a Greek shipping company to deliver goods to a port in France, where the goods will then be shipped by land to the buyer in Switzerland. If the goods are damaged in transit, the courts of four countries could have jurisdiction over the subsequent litigation.

Parties to international contracts generally can agree to have a particular court decide disputes arising from the contract. By inserting a *choice-of-forum clause* in their contract, the parties choose the place for dispute resolution. For example, the parties to a contract could specify that all disputes will be tried by the court in Marseilles, France. Some courts have been reluctant to give effect to choice-of-forum clauses, especially when they will thus not be able to hear a dispute involving a local party. These courts are especially reluctant to enforce a choice-of-forum clause when the parties choose a country that has no connection to the contract and agree to submit themselves to the jurisdiction of that country's courts. English courts, for example, have long been used as a neutral forum for the resolution of international contract disputes. The next case shows the attitude of the U.S. Supreme Court toward choice-of-forum clauses in international contracts.

International commercial arbitration. An alternative to choosing a forum for litigation is for the parties to agree to submit their disputes to binding arbitration. Usually, arbitration clauses specify the place of arbitration, the number of arbitrators, and the rules for resolving the dispute. The American Arbitration Association,

---

M/S *Bremen* v. Zapata Off-Shore Company

407 U.S. 1 (1972)

FACTS	Zapata, an American corporation, contracted with Unterweser, a German corporation, to have one of Zapata's oil-drilling rigs towed from Louisiana to a point off the coast of Italy where Zapata would use the rig to drill for oil. The contract stated, "Any dispute arising must be treated before the London Court of Justice." As Unterweser's tug, the M/S *Bremen,* towed the rig through international waters in the Gulf of Mexico, a severe storm damaged the oil rig. The rig was towed to Tampa, Florida, where Zapata filed suit in the federal district court, alleging negligent towing and breach of contract. The court took jurisdiction of the dispute despite Unterweser's motion to dismiss based on the choice-of-forum clause. The court of appeals affirmed.
ISSUE	Should the court give effect to the parties' agreement to raise all disputes in the London Court of Justice?
DECISION	Yes. Reversed. The court should enforce the forum clause unless Zapata can show that enforcement would be unreasonable or unjust, or that the clause was invalid by reason of fraud or overreaching. The choice of London as a forum was "made in arm's-length negotiation by experienced and sophisticated businessmen and absent some compelling and countervailing reason it should be honored by the parties and enforced by the courts."

---

the International Chamber of Commerce, and the London Court of Arbitration are some of the private organizations with rules for the conduct of commercial arbitration. UNCITRAL has also developed arbitration procedures that have gained wide acceptance in business. The same problems that have applied to choice-of-forum clauses have also applied to arbitration provisions, although arbitration is gaining wide acceptance by courts in many different countries.

Choice of law. Even when parties to an international contract include a choice-of-forum clause or an arbitration clause, the substantive rules of law will vary among legal systems. Many international contracts contain *choice-of-law*

clauses, which specify the country or state whose law will govern the rights and duties of the parties.

Generally, most countries allow parties to a contract to choose the law they wish to apply to their relationship, as long as their choice of law bears some relationship to the transaction. UCC §1-105(1), for example, allows parties to a transaction governed by the Code to choose the law they wish to govern their contract, so long as the transaction "bears a reasonable relation" to the chosen law.

When parties fail to choose the law they wish to have apply to their contract, a court or an arbitrator will choose the law most closely connected with the contract. Parties choosing a forum generally use the laws of the forum country to determine their obligations under the contract.

The Convention on the International Sale of Goods

As mentioned earlier, the United Nations Commission on International Trade (UNCITRAL) supervised the development of the Convention on the International Sale of Goods (CISG). This code was created in 1966 by a highly respected staff of lawyers from every region of the world, representing countries which use the common law, civil law, and socialist law systems. As of the early 1990s, about thirty countries, including the United States, were signatories. For American businesspersons, CISG is applicable only when three conditions exist:

- The contract must be for the commercial sale of goods.
- The contract must be between parties that have their principal places of business in different countries.
- The places of business must be in countries that have agreed to CISG.

Thus, if an American businessperson agrees to sell tennis balls to a buyer who has her principal place of business in Austria, which has also agreed to the Convention, the provisions of the CISG would apply if a dispute should later arise. In a broader sense, this means that UCC Article 2, which governs the sale of goods in this country, has now been replaced in controlling many of the international commercial transactions that Americans engage in today.

The 101 articles of CISG, much like the analogous UCC Article 2, regulate most facets of a contract of sale. This includes extensive provisions regarding the forming of the sales contract, warranties, remedies, and nonperformance. However, unlike the UCC, which was derived from the common law, CISG borrows heavily from the French civil law and its code.

Some experts have noted that the CISG appears to be simpler to understand and more precisely written than similar UCC provisions. This is likely to be due (at least in part) to the civil law's tradition of relying on legislatively written codes designed to react prescriptively to very specific legal problems, as opposed to the common law tradition of a court reacting to problems after their arise.

TARIFFS AND OTHER TRADE BARRIERS

The close of the 1980s and the beginning of the 1990s saw rapid change in economies around the world. While socialist nations such as Poland and Germany experienced the most dramatic political and economic changes, the economic structure of nations all over the globe underwent substantial alterations. In many cases, the result of economic change has been a new search for foreign trading partners. Newly opened economies offer new opportunities for traders, yet those opportunities exist in very unstable label environments. The laws regulating imports and exports will change in each country as that nation's political and economic needs change.

The economic changes of the past decade will accelerate worldwide efforts to reduce barriers to free world trade. The member nations of the European Community and the General Agreement on Tariffs and Trade are currently engaged in multilateral efforts to reduce impediments to free trade. Recent bilateral trade treaties, such as the Canada–United States Free Trade Agreement, will also reduce barriers to a truly international marketplace.

Virtually every country in the world regulates the movement of goods across its borders. A business shipping goods across national borders needs to be aware of three major kinds of regulation: tariffs, nontariff barriers to trade, and export controls.

Tariffs

A *tariff* is a tax placed on imported goods by the destination country. This tax is sometimes called a "duty" or a "customs duty." Governments use tariffs primarily to protect domestic industries from foreign competition. However, economists have debated for many years whether the benefits for protectionism are outweighed by the harmful effects of allowing inefficient industries to remain in the marketplace. Governments may also impose tariffs for revenue-raising purposes, and in some cases they use tariffs to attempt to control the volume of imports in relation to exports (the balance of trade).

The function of the GATT. As you learned in the first section of this chapter, the General Agreement on Tariffs and Trade (GATT) is the most important multilateral regulatory agreement concerning tariffs. The purpose of the GATT is to promote free trade and to reduce tariffs around the world. The GATT promotes the nondiscriminatory reduction of tariffs through the use of most-favored-nation status for all members. A second function of the GATT is to allow member countries to protect their own economies against unfair foreign competition by imposing antidumping measures and duties to counteract export subsidies by other countries. The United States and many other countries apply both of these principles in order to regulate the market for imported goods.

Most-favored-nation status. The concept of most-favored-nation status is designed to promote world trade without discrimination. A *most-favored-nation* will be charged a tariff on its goods at least as low as that charged on the same kind of goods from any other nation. For example, if an American buyer imports German cameras, the most-favored-nation status of Germany would mean that the tariff on those cameras would be at least as low as the tariff on similar cameras imported from other countries.

Countries agreeing to the GATT agree to give each other most-favored-nation status. Because so many countries are members of the GATT, every reduction a country makes in its tariffs affects most of its trading partners. Non-GATT countries may also be granted most-favored-nation status. Most socialist countries did not sign the GATT, but many have been granted most-favored-nation status by the United States and other trading partners. In some instances, most-favored-nation status has been granted or withheld for nontrade reasons. The loss of most-favored-nation status means that higher tariff rates may be charged on imported goods. For example, in 1982, Poland lost its most-favored-nation status with the United States, after its government declared martial law. In 1987, the United States restored most-favored-nation status to Poland after its government enacted a series of reforms.

Antidumping In recent years, many American industries have charged that foreign products have been dumped in the American market. *Dumping* takes place when a product is sold in an export market at a price below that charged for the equivalent product in the home market. A foreign producer may dump goods in order to gain market share in a foreign country or to use excess capacity at home.

The U.S. government has enacted antidumping legislation, following the principles of the GATT. The antidumping legislation provides that when a foreign product is sold in the United States for less than it is sold in its country of origin, and such sales harm an existing or developing American industry, then the tariff on the dumped goods will be increased by the difference between the foreign market value and the comparable price of the goods in the American market.

Export subsidies and countervailing duties.
Many countries, including the United States, aid domestic businesses by providing tax reductions and incentives, subsidizing financing, and government grants. The GATT recognizes that while there are many valid social and economic reasons to assist domestic industries, government subsidies of exports can distort competition in other countries. The GATT allows countries to impose special duties, known as *countervailing duties*, to offset the amount of any unfair export subsidies. In the Trade Agreements Act of 1979, Congress provided that if an American industry is harmed by unfair export subsidies granted to foreign competitors, a countervailing duty equal to the amount of the subsidy will be imposed on the goods. The Act also encourages the resolution of trade disputes through diplomatic, rather than judicial, channels.

An example of the process for resolving allegations of unfair subsidies is the complaints filed in 1982 by several American steel manufacturers, alleging that seven EEC countries provided unfair export subsidies for steel products and seeking countervailing duties on the import of those products. While the steel companies presented their case in the federal courts and administrative agencies, the secretary of commerce negotiated with the countries charged in the complaint. Just hours before countervailing duties were scheduled to go into effect, the EC agreed to limit imports to the American market. The American producers then agreed to withdraw their complaints.

Canada–United States free trade. In 1988, Canada and the United States entered into the Canada–United States Free Trade Agreement. The Free Trade Agreement, a bilateral treaty, provides for the elimination of all tariffs on goods trading between Canada and the United States by 1998. It also substantially reduces other barriers to the free movement of goods, services, and people, and to investment between the two countries. One of the most innovative portions of the treaty provides for the two countries to submit disputes over allegations of dumping and unfair trade subsidies to a binational panel for resolution. The dispute resolution provisions will replace litigation in American and Canadian courts over trade practices involving firms for both countries. Some experts are critical of the Free Trade Agreement, saying that it violates the spirit of multilateral cooperation in trade and undermines the GATT. Other experts defend the treaty, saying that it will create a free trade zone similar in many ways to the EC.

The North American Free Trade Association. Since the late 1980s, the United States, Canada, and Mexico have been hammering out details for the creation of the so-called North American Free Trade Association (NAFTA), designed to create a free trade zone between the three nations. In late 1992, the leaders of the three countries signed the treaty. If it becomes a reality, the North American Free Trade Association (NAFTA) would rival, if not surpass, the EC in size and economic clout. Indeed, the three nations now possess about 360 million consumers and a massive $6 trillion market.

The passage of NAFTA, as of mid-1993, was still clouded by controversy and doubt. Organized labor and environmental groups in the United States lobbied for side agreements with Mexico to ensure that it will have labor and environmental laws in place similar to those in this country. Moreover, a federal judge ruled in mid-1993 that an environmental impact statement must be prepared to evaluate the treaties potential effects on the environment. This, if upheld on appeal, could take years and would likely kill the treaty. Labor is also very fearful, and perhaps rightly so, of losing thousands of jobs to Mexico. Although some groups in Mexico oppose NAFTA, particularly those which desire to retain the heavy government control of the past, it appears that the majority of citizens of that country are anxious for the treaty to go into effect. Many Mexicans envision an acceleration of new business and industry movement into Mexico as greatly enriching their country. Some economists also predict that numerous foreign businesses, from East Asia in particular, will move into Mexico to take advantage of that country's location as a staging area for entering the U.S. market. Others intend to reap the rewards of a Mexican labor pool that is now cheaper than many of the Asian powerhouses such as Singapore, Hong Kong, South Korea, and Taiwan.

NAFTA also enjoys considerable support in this country. Proponents contend that once the treaty is ratified that the United States will be more globally competitive, since it will be in the heart of perhaps the richest and largest free trade market in the world. Ultimately, NAFTA could also produce thousands of new jobs in the United States due to greater exports to both Canada and Mexico. Small and medium-sized companies might also profit greatly since, unlike bigger companies, they often do not have the means to dodge the high trade barriers that Mexico is only now in the process of removing. Multinational companies, already doing business in these countries, similarly foresee great potential for business expansion if NAFTA is passed. A case in point is Procter & Gamble. In its first quarterly 1993 report to its shareholders, it claimed the nearly $100 million in exports and 1,500 domestic jobs that now exist because of exports to Mexico, would double provided the treaty is ratified.

NAFTA's chances of passage are enhanced by the fact that it is subject to the so-called *fast-track procedure*. The fast-track system was created in 1974 and subsequently given added clout in the 1988 Omnibus Trade and Competitiveness Act, discussed later in this chapter. It was devised mainly because foreign heads of state in the past were reluctant to sign a treaty with a U.S. president for fear of having it later rejected or revised by Congress. Now, once Congress approves the fast-track procedure on a prospec-

tive treaty, and it has been signed by the leaders of the countries involved, Congress has up to 8 months to vote all or nothing, without amendments, on its ratification.*

Nontariff Barriers

In addition to paying duties on goods moved across borders, a business may encounter a variety of nontariff barriers to trade. One example of a nontariff barrier would be an import quota on automobiles. The United States has numerous statutes and regulations that act as barriers to international trade, including safety and environmental standards for imported products, protections for the American holders of trademarks, bans on imported goods from countries such as North Vietnam and Cuba, and requirements that government agencies "buy American" in many circumstances. Many other countries also have nontariff trade barriers in forms similar to those found in the United States. In addition, a country will sometimes impose import bans in order to regulate the flow of money out of the country. In 1981, for example, Syria banned imports of air conditioners, perfume, cosmetics, cigarettes, and peanuts in order to conserve hard currency.

Unfair Trade Practices

In recent years, American companies in a variety of industries have challenged the international trade practices of competitors. In 1988, Congress enacted the Omnibus Trade and Competitiveness Act to strengthen the competitive position of American firms in the global marketplace. The most controversial provision of the law, known as "Super 301," empowers the United States Trade Representative to identify countries engaging in unfair trade practices, ne-

---

* "U.S., Canada and Mexico Initial North American Free Trade Agreement, *U.S. Department of State Dispatch*, Vol. 3, No. 41, October 12, 1992, p. 765.

gotiate for the elimination of those practices, and if the negotiations fail, to retaliate against those countries.

One of the main areas of concern for American businesses is the protection of patent, copyright, and trademark rights from traders seeking to import counterfeit goods or other products that diminish the value of the rights. The 1988 trade law prohibits the importation of goods that infringe on U.S. patents, trademarks, copyrights, or protected computer chip designs. Under Super 301 the U.S. Trade Representative may also identify countries with unfair policies toward patent, copyright, and trademark rights for negotiation or retaliation. As of 1989, twenty-five countries, including Brazil, Mexico, South Korea, and China, were on the "watch list" for possible future action.

Export Controls

A business wishing to export goods to another country will need to be aware of export controls or limitations which may apply to the goods. In the United States, the Export Administration Act regulates the flow of goods and technology to other countries. The Act requires every exporter to obtain an export license. Most licenses are general licenses and are obtained by filling out an export declaration at the Post Office or some other point of shipment. The Commerce Department must validate the export license if the export of goods or technology would interfere with the foreign policy or national security interests of the United States.

The United States is a member of the Coordinating Committee for Multilateral Export Controls (COCOM), a group composed of representatives of all the NATO countries (except Iceland), and Japan. The 1988 trade law placed much of the authority to control exports in the hands of COCOM, and made easier exports to COCOM member countries. The trade law also allows import and government procurement

bans of up to 5 years against companies exporting goods or technology in violation of COCOM rules. These new penalties were in response to an incident in which Toshiba, a Japanese business, sold sophisticated machine parts to the Soviet Union in violation of Japanese export control laws.

THE MULTINATIONAL ENTERPRISE

Ford, McDonald's, Volkswagen, Mitsubishi, and Nestlé are names familiar to customers around the world. Almost everyone can name at least a few of the giant multinational corporations dominating world markets for goods and services. As means of transportation and communication improve, national boundaries no longer define the limits of business activity.

Despite the prominence of the largest multinational corporations, however, multinational business enterprises take many different forms and raise many interesting issues of law and business ethics. The material that follows will introduce you to some of the different ways of doing business in a multinational setting and to some of the legal and ethical problems raised by multinational business enterprises.

Forms of Organization

An American business may organize its operations as a sole proprietorship, partnership, limited partnership, or corporation. A business operating in more than one country will need to develop the organizational style that is best suited to the business's legal, financial, managerial, and marketing needs. There are many different ways to structure a multinational enterprise, ranging from direct selling to formal parent-subsidiary structures. The choice of legal form reflects the business decision of whether simply to sell in international markets or to establish operations abroad. Each kind of organization raises different risks and legal concerns.

Direct sales. The simplest way for a company to do business abroad is to enter into contracts to sell its goods or services to foreign customers. As discussed earlier, however, international contracts have special problems not found in purely domestic contracts. Also, a company selling goods overseas may encounter both tariff and nontariff barriers to trade.

A company selling goods overseas may sometimes want to engage a foreign representative to help the company find customers for its products. An agency agreement may be subject to the internal laws of the country of the foreign representative. The law of agency varies greatly in different countries. For example, agency law in Germany, Belgium, France, and much of Latin America makes terminating an agency relationship difficult, even if the principal has good cause. The manager who fails to plan for differences in the law of agency in different countries may find her company sued in a foreign court for wrongfully terminating an agency relationship or may be unable to terminate an agency relationship with an incompetent agent.

Foreign distributorships. Another method of selling goods in foreign countries is selling through a foreign distributor. In contrast to an agent in an agency relationship, the foreign distributor actually purchases the goods from the manufacturer, and then resells them to customers in the foreign country. Some distributorship agreements provide for exclusive territories for the distributor. Particularly in EC countries, exclusive distributorship agreements may violate antitrust law, as the next case, decided by the Court of Justice of the European Communities, shows.

Consten and Grundig v. Commission of the EEC

1966 E. Comm. Ct. J. Rep. 299

FACTS   Grundig, a German manufacturer of televisions, radios, and similar equipment, entered into a contract with Consten, a French company. Consten became the distributor of Grundig products in France and, in return, agreed not to sell any Grundig products outside France. Grundig agreed not to sell its products to any other company in France and agreed to restrict its other distributors from selling Grundig products in France.

ISSUE   Does the exclusive distributorship agreement violate EC antitrust law?

DECISION   Yes. EC law forbids agreements affecting trade between member states that "are designed to prevent, restrict, or distort competition" within the EC, or which have that effect. The Consten-Grundig agreement aims to create separate, isolated national markets. Such an agreement is contrary to the purposes of the EC and distorts competition within the EC.

Licensing agreements. Another method of doing business in an international environment is the use of licensing agreements. Licensing agreements are often used to exercise intellectual property rights, such as patents and trademarks, in a multinational setting. For example, an American company has a patent for an antiarthritis drug. It can sell its knowledge of how to make the drug to an Italian company. The licensing agreement between the two companies would grant to the Italian company the right to make and sell the drug in Italy using the patent of the American company. The American company would receive a fee based on the amount of drugs manufactured or sold.

The success of a licensing agreement depends on several factors. One consideration is how well the internal law of the foreign country protects patents, trademarks, and copyrights. There are several multinational treaties regulating patents and trademarks, but the law varies among different countries. Also, the licensor must be aware of the antitrust implications of the licensing agreement. One of the most important factors in the success of licensing agreements is the skill of the foreign company. If, in our example, the Italian company produces a poor-quality product, the reputation of the American company will be injured, because it's name often will be on the product.

One form of licensing agreement increasingly used as a structure for international business is the franchise. Many of the reasons discussed in Chapter 22 favoring franchising as a way to organize a business apply to international as well as domestic businesses. In addition, franchising can be an attractive way for a company to explore unfamiliar markets while making only a small investment of its own funds.

Subsidiaries. A business may way to maintain greater control over the manufacturing and marketing of its products than is possible using distribution and licensing agreements, but it may find tariff or other obstacles to direct selling. It may choose to establish a branch office abroad, but foreign businesses often find restrictions on the establishment of operations, as well as disadvantages in tax and legal treatment of foreign corporations. Most of the larger multinational corporations organize subsidiary corporations in the countries in which they do business. The parent company maintains some level of managerial control, yet it has the flexibility that is needed to adapt to different business conditions in different countries. Most subsidiaries are organized under the internal corporate law of the foreign country, providing some level of limited liability and, sometimes, favorable tax treatment in the host country.

In the same way that American corporations use "Inc." after their names to indicate their corporate status, businesses in other countries use different abbreviations to indicate their corporate status. For example, the letters "S.A.," for *Société Anonyme*, indicate corporate status in French-speaking countries.

Subsidiaries are often wholly owned by the parent corporation. In some situations, however, the parent will own a majority, or sometimes just a minority, of the stock in the subsidiary, with the remainder of the stock held by investors from the subsidiary's country. The amount of ownership interest will reflect the need the parent corporation has for controlling the activities of the subsidiary. Additionally, many countries, especially developing countries, require substantial local investment, management, or control of the board of directors.

The use of foreign subsidiaries will not always protect the parent corporation from liability for acts occurring abroad. For example, Union Carbide, a Delaware corporation, owns 51 percent of Union Carbide India, Ltd. (UCI), a company organized under Indian law. The remaining 49 percent of UCI's stock is owned by Indian nationals. The majority of the directors of UCI are Indian nationals, as are most of the employees at UCI's thirteen plants in India.

On December 2, 1984, a cloud of poisonous gas escaped from the UCI plant in Bhopal, killing thousands of people and injuring hundreds of thousands more. The government of India has sued Union Carbide on behalf of the accident victims, alleging that the American parent company is responsible for the accident. In 1989, a settlement agreement obligating Union Carbide to pay $470 million was still under review by Indian courts.

Joint ventures. Another form of direct investment in a foreign country is the joint venture, a project entered into by two or more companies. As you read in Chapter 16, joint ventures resemble partnerships. In the international context, two or more companies, often from different countries, either work together in partnership to accomplish a project or form a new business entity. As with subsidiaries, the choice of this form of business organization may be the result of laws restricting foreign investment. The choice may also reflect the ability of each venturer to bring different business skills to the project.

One significant problem created by the use of joint ventures, as well as subsidiaries, is legal prohibitions on ownership by foreign companies. Many nations insist that majority ownership be held by a domestic entity or, in the case of some socialist countries, the government. Others will not allow ownership interests in certain strategic industries. The United States, for example, limits foreign ownership of certain defense industries. Many others restrict how much a foreign company can own of that nation's telecommunications and utilities industries.

Since the collapse of the communist system in Eastern Europe, joint ventures are becoming a common means of investing in the former Soviet sphere. Today, joint ventures between American companies and companies in Hungary, Russia, Latvia, the Ukraine, and other countries manufacture food, light bulbs, energy, soft drinks, and many other goods and services.

Special Problems of Multinational Enterprises

No matter how a multinational enterprise organizes its business activities, it will encounter cultural, political, and economic differences between its headquarters country and the countries in which it does business. As multinational businesses grow larger and more successful in the global marketplace, they may become the target for hostility toward foreign investment and may sometimes find their property seized by foreign governments. They will also operate in legal environments whose regulation of safety, the environment, and competitive practices is less than that of their headquarters country. The material that follows will focus on American-based multinational enterprises.

Expropriation and nationalization. When a company invests directly in a foreign country, by opening a branch office, building a factory, or establishing a subsidiary or joint venture, one of the most significant risks it will face is the risk that its property will be seized by the government. Every government has the right to take private property as part of its sovereign power. In the United States, under the Fifth Amendment to the Constitution, the government may take private property, as long as it takes the property for a public purpose and compensates the owner.

Expropriation occurs when a government seizes foreign-owned private property. Expropriations that do not provide fair compensation result in the confiscation of foreign-owned property and violate the principles of public international law. Some expropriations may also involve the *nationalization* of the private property, meaning that the government itself becomes the owner of the property. Expropriation and nationalization occur in industrialized as well as developing nations. Canada, England, Chile, Venezuela, India, Saudi Arabia, Iran, Cuba, and many other countries have taken foreign-owned private property in the past.

For the multinational enterprise, the problem becomes one of how to minimize the risks of expropriation or nationalization of business operations abroad. The United States has treaties with some foreign countries to protect the interests of American companies against expropriation. In addition, private insurance is available against the risks of expropriation. American companies doing business in developing countries may be able to obtain insurance from the Overseas Private Investment Corporation (OPIC), a federal agency under the control of the State Department. The U.S. Department of Commerce, often through its local offices, is also a source of knowledge and assistance for those businesses which wish to export their goods and services. Finally, some larger multinational organizations employ specialists in analyzing and monitoring the political environment of the countries where the multinational does business.

If a foreign country seizes property and fails to provide just compensation for the taking, an American business will have difficulty getting relief from courts. Foreign courts will probably be unsympathetic to the American claim, and, assuming jurisdictional problems can be solved, American courts will often apply the doctrine of *sovereign immunity* or the *act-of-state* doctrine to deny the claim of the American business.

The doctrine of sovereign immunity exists in many countries around the world. It makes the government of a foreign country immune from lawsuits even when a local court has proper jurisdiction. Sovereign immunity poses special problems when the foreign government acts in purely commercial matters and then claims immunity from suit. For example, many socialist countries trade with the United States using government-owned and -operated trading companies. The doctrine of sovereign immunity, applied broadly, would prevent a local business from obtaining damages for a breach of a contract for the sale of goods.

The United States has restricted the scope of sovereign immunity in American courts by the adoption of the Foreign Sovereign Immunities Act of 1976. The Act provides procedures for obtaining jurisdiction of foreign governments in American courts, provides that commercial activities of foreign governments are not entitled to immunity, and provides that a commercial property in the United States belonging to a foreign government such as its bank accounts, may be used to satisfy judgments against the government.

In the following case, an American citizen attempted to obtain jurisdiction over a foreign government by arguing that his injuries were the result of commercial activities conducted in the United States.

Saudi Arabia v. Nelson

113 S. Ct. 1471 (1993)

FACTS   Scott Nelson was recruited by the Hospital Corporation of America (HCA) to work as a monitoring systems engineer in a hospital in Saudi Arabia. While on the job, Nelson detected safety defects in the hospital's oxygen and nitrous oxide lines that posed a fire hazard. After reporting the problem repeatedly, Nelson was arrested by the Saudi government. He alleged the police "shackled, tortured and beat" him and deprived him of food for 4 days, and that he was forced to endure an overcrowded, rat-infested cell, and received fresh air and exercise only once a week. His wife was also informed that she could secure his release only in exchange for sexual favors. After 39 days Nelson was finally released at the behest of his U.S. senator. Nelson later sued the Saudi government in a federal district court for a number of intentional torts, including battery, wrongful arrest, false imprisonment, and infliction of mental distress. The court dismissed the suit for lack of subject matter jurisdiction under the Foreign Sovereign Immunities Act of 1976, which immunizes foreign governments from actions initiated in U.S. courts. The court of appeals overruled the district court, ruling that the "commercial activities" exception applies, since Nelson was recruited and hired in the United States.

ISSUE

Did the fact that Nelson was recruited and hired in the United States entitle him to sue Saudi Arabia under the Foreign Sovereign Immunities Act?

DECISION

No. Reversed. Under the Foreign Sovereign Immunities Act, a foreign nation is "presumptively immune" from being sued in U.S. courts. One exception can arise in a case "in which the action is based upon a commercial activity carried on in the United States by the foreign state." The torts committed by the Saudi government do not constitute a "commercial activity." For a nation to conduct a commercial activity, it must exercise those commercial activities that a private citizen might. On the other hand, those powers that are uniquely engaged in by a government would not qualify under the exception. In this case, the torture committed by the Saudi government was an "abuse of the power of the police" and so is "peculiarly sovereign in nature."

The interstate commerce clause of the U.S. Constitution has been interpreted quite liberally to allow federal regulation of many matters which ordinarily may not be associated with interstate commerce. To illustrate, in *Wickard v. Filburn*, discussed in Chapter 3, the U.S. Supreme Court found that a farmer growing wheat for his own use was still engaged in interstate commerce. Title VII of the Civil Rights Act of 1964, discussed in Chapter 46, applies to all employers with fifteen or more employees, on the basis that this number of employees has an effect on interstate commerce. In this case, the Supreme Court chose to construe the Foreign Sovereign Immunities Act strictly. Does this result seem fair to Nelson? Should it matter for purposes of considering issues of jurisdiction that a possible federal court judgment might prove difficult, if not impossible, to enforce against a refusing foreign nation?

Another bar to the recovery of compensation for expropriated property has been the act-of-state doctrine. In the United States, the doctrine is still under development by the courts and by Congress. It is generally agreed that the purpose of the doctrine is to avoid having American courts determine the legality of the laws of foreign governments in their own countries. There is some disagreement as to whether the act-of-state doctrine applies to all internal laws of foreign countries or only to laws affecting public, not commercial, purposes. The act-of-state doctrine was a key issue in determining the outcome of the next case.

Banco Nacional de Cuba v. Sabbatino

376 U.S. 398 (1964)

FACTS
To retaliate for a reduction in the import quota of sugar from Cuba to the United States, the Cuban government nationalized many companies in which Americans held interests. A sugar broker in New York had a contract to purchase a boatload of sugar from one of the newly nationalized companies. To obtain the sugar, the broker entered into a new agreement to buy the boatload from the Cuban government. When the broker received the money from the sale of the sugar to its customers, it paid the sugar company in New York, instead of the Cuban government. Banco Nacional, the agent of the Cuban government, sued to stop Sabbatino, the receiver of the New York assets of the sugar company, from disposing of the proceeds of the sale. The broker defended its actions on the ground that the Cuban expropriation violated international law.

ISSUE
Does the act-of-state doctrine prevent the court from deciding whether the Cuban expropriation violated international law?

DECISION
Yes. Although the courts have the power to judge the validity of foreign laws, the Constitution gives the power to conduct foreign relations to the executive and legislative branches of government. In the courts, a piecemeal approach to the problem of foreign expropriations could interfere with the foreign policy objectives of the executive branch and with diplomatic efforts to resolve the problems caused by the expropriation.

After *Sabbatino*, Congress passed a law designed specifically to overrule the result reached by the Supreme Court. As a result, on remand to the lower courts, Banco Nacional lost the case. Despite the congressional action, the act-of-state doctrine remains a substantial barrier to compensation for the expropriation of property.

Legal and ethical standards for business conduct. American firms doing business in foreign countries often encounter different standards for business conduct. In some countries, bribes paid to foreign officials may help an American company win contracts. In other countries, gift giving is an accepted part of any business relationship and is perceived to be unrelated to bribery. For American businesses, the *Foreign Corrupt Practices Act of 1977 (FCPA)* regulates business conduct that might be interpreted in American culture as bribery. The FCPA has two major provisions. First, it requires that companies maintain adequate accounting systems and records so that illegal or questionable payments will come to the attention of top management and the Securities and Exchange Commission. Second, the FCPA prohibits the payment of money or gifts to a foreign official, or to someone who will act as a conduit to a foreign official, for the purpose of influencing the acts or decisions of the foreign official. The antibribery provisions of the FCPA have been quite controversial. Many American companies claim that the FCPA prevents them from competing in an international environment where bribes or even gifts are an accepted method of influencing the decisions of foreign governments.

The Foreign Corrupt Practices Act does, as discussed in Chapter 5 on criminal law, exempt "grease" payments. These are disbursements made to lower ministerial officers, who have no discretionary powers, in exchange for performing routine governmental actions. Examples of grease payments include money paid for obtaining permits and licenses, processing governmental papers, providing police protection, and supplying water or power. The argument for allowing these kinds of exceptions is that it is customery in some countries to make these payments; otherwise the services might not be performed.

A second problem faced by American businesses operating abroad, especially in underdeveloped nations, is whether the foreign subsidiaries of American businesses should be required to meet American regulatory requirements or less stringent foreign requirements. For example, is Union Carbide responsible for meeting American safety and environmental standards in its subsidiary's plant in Bhopal, India? Those who argue for this requirement believe that American multinationals have the expertise and the money to meet more stringent American requirements and that failure to do so is a form of exploitation of less developed nations. Those who argue against requiring the companies to meet American standards argue that foreign governments are capable of enacting laws and regulations to meet the needs of their own countries.

One of the most difficult questions American businesses face is whether to do business in countries whose political systems are repugnant to American law and social values. For example, American businesses sometimes have subsidiaries in South Africa. There, the system of legalized segregation known as apartheid keeps blacks from participating as citizens in their own country and subjects blacks to arrest, im-

prisonment, and abuse without recourse to law. American multinational enterprises have been a force for reform in South Africa, and American attitudes favoring equal opportunity and opposing segregation and racism have led to improved standards of living for black employees in American-owned companies. Indeed, as of 1993, the current South African government was working hard to dismantle apartheid in the face of extraordinary obstacles. Yet critics of the American presence in South Africa contend that doing business there, in any form and with even the best of intentions, implies acceptance of apartheid and support of the South African government. As Chapter 21 discussed, the decision to do business in South Africa or in other repressive countries may lead to shareholder resolutions against the company's policy. In some instances, a decision to do business in a repressive country may result in pension funds and other large investors excluding the company's stock from their investment portfolios.

CONCLUSION

Businesses operate in an international environment under many different circumstances. A business may buy products from a foreign supplier or sell products to foreign customers. Increasing numbers of businesses are establishing operations in other countries, opening branch offices, organizing subsidiaries under foreign corporation laws, and creating joint ventures with businesses from other countries.

A manager needs to be aware of the legal environment in other countries in order to do business effectively. Different countries perceive the role of law in society in very different ways. Substantive rules of law and procedures for litigation will vary from country to country, and a large body of law regulating exports and imports exists in almost every country.

Although the material in this chapter is only an introduction to the international legal environment, it will provide you with information you can use to minimize the risks of doing business in the global marketplace. The material should also serve as a reminder that the American legal system is just one perspective on the role of law in business. Managing effectively in an international environment requires a global outlook and respect for other forms of law for business.

A NOTE TO FUTURE CPA CANDIDATES

The CPA exam does not include a separate section covering international law. However, today's public accountant is likely to encounter many international issues discussed in this chapter, especially international letters of credit and dispute resolution clauses.

The Foreign Corrupt Practices Act, a part of the Securities Exchange Act of 1934, is sometimes covered in the Securities section of the exam. As discussed in Chapter 24, the Act prohibits any U.S. corporation—whether registered under the Securities Act or not—from bribing foreign officials to obtain business. The Act also requries that any corporation registered under the 1934 Act establish internal accounting controls so that it can maintain accountability for the control of its assets, whether the company engages in international trade or not. Failure to keep the required records is a criminal offense.

KEY WORDS

act of state (1151)
countertrade (1137)
countervailing duties (1145)
documentary letter of credit (1139)
dumping (1144)
expropriation (1150)
fast-track procedure (1146)
most-favored nation (1144)
nationalization (1150)
reciprocity (1134)
sovereign immunity (1151)
standby letter of credit (1140)
tariff (1144)

DISCUSSION QUESTIONS

1. Where do judges find the law when they resolve disputes in common law, civil law, socialist law, and Islamic law countries?
2. How is the EC using the law to eliminate trade barriers among its member countries?
3. Explain the purposes of the GATT and how it works toward its goals.
4. Explain the differences between documentary letters of credit and standby letters of credit.
5. What are the differences between choice-of-forum clauses and choice-of-law clauses in international contracts?
6. Explain most-favored-nation status. Why can many nations have the status at the same time?
7. What does the American government do when it determines that foreign goods have been dumped on the American market or finds that exports from foreign countries have been unfairly subsidized?
8. List the major ways of doing business in foreign countries. Which methods require investment and which methods are buyer-seller relationships?
9. Why would a business need to establish subsidiaries in foreign countries instead of just entering into contracts with suppliers and customers?
10. What is the difference between expropriation and nationalization?

CASE PROBLEMS

1. Grady Co., an American brewery, bought 1000 tons of hops from Brauer, a German grower. The terms of sale were "FOB Hamburg." Brauer delivered the hops to the shipper at the port in Hamburg, and the shipper stored them in a warehouse pending the arrival of a ship to take the hops to America. Before the goods could be loaded on board the ship, the warehouse burned, destroying the hops. Who bears the risk of loss? Describe what the parties should have done to avoid this problem.

2. A Russian company hired a German ship to take a cargo of turpentine from Russia to England. The contract required that all claims and disputes resulting from the shipment must be judged in Russia in accordance with the Russian Merchant Shipping Code. While the ship was in transit, the cargo was sold to English buyers. When the boat was unloaded in England, 3 tons of turpentine were missing, and remainder was contaminated with linseed oil, which had been carried on an earlier voyage. The English buyers sued the German owners in Londen. Must the dispute be heard in Russia? Explain.

3. While visiting in Europe from the United States, Cecil Ramey entered into a contract to purchase a Jaguar convertible for personal usage from Jaguar Auto, Ltd., an automobile dealership. The dealership agreed to ship the car to the United States from London. Ramey, a business law professor, had specified in the sales agreement that any dispute would be resolved by the UCC. The car was damaged in shipment and a dispute has arisen as to responsibility for the loss. Assuming the Convention on the International Sale of Goods has been ratified by the European country where the sale took place, would it apply to this transaction? Explain.

4. Alberto-Culver, an American corporation, makes toiletries and hair-care products. It purchased three businesses from Scherk, a German citizen. The contract provided that all disputes would be arbitrated in Paris, but that Illinois law would control the rights of the parties. Alberto-Culver sued Scherk for breach of contract, misrepresentation, and securities fraud under §10(b) of the Securities Act of 1934. It claimed that the policies of the Securities Act required that an American court, not a foreign arbitrator, hear the case. Should the federal court dismiss the Alberto-Culver complaint? Explain.

5. Leninland is a socialist country whose state trading company recently began exporting golf carts to the United States. The price in the United States is far below that charged by American golf cart makers, and it is even less than the price Leninland charges buyers in its own country. The American Golf Cart Association (AGCA) filed a complaint with the U.S. government, charging that the carts were being dumped in the American market in violation of U.S. law. The U.S. government agreed, and now needs to calculate proper antidumping duties. Leninland argues that the duty should be the difference between the U.S. price and the Leninland price. AGCA argues that because Leninland has a state-controlled economy, the Leninland price is not a fair market value. AGCA wants the duty to be the difference between the U.S. price and the price of similar goods in a free-market country, such as Canada. What is the best way to calculate the antidumping duty? Explain.

6. Downs Co., an American make of computer chips, has been approached by Schlegel, A.G., a German electronics company. Schlegel offers to purchase substantial numbers of computer chips from Downs and resell them in Western European countries. It also proposes to provide warranty and repair service through its European locations. Schlegel would also like assurances from Downs that Downs will not sell to other companies in Europe. Does this proposed agreement violate any European or American laws? Explain.

7. Cole, Inc., an American mining company, recently discovered a large amount of gold in one of its mines in the small, impoverished country of Despare. Shortly afterward, a new government came to power in Despare, vowing to redistribute the wealth to all the people and send the Americans home. When the mine managers came to work the next morning, they found several hundred Desparean soldiers operating the mine and were told to leave the mine, and the country, at once. The Desparean government has offered compensation in Desparados, the worthless local currency. Cole, Inc., knows that the Desparean government has several million dollars in deposits in U.S. banks. Can Cole sue for damages or for compensation in dollars? Explain.

8. Nestlé is a Swiss-based multinational corporation making many different food products, including coffee, instant formula, and chocolate. Nestlé marketed powdered infant formula in underdeveloped countries, using many of the techniques it used in more developed nations. However, the powdered formula was often mixed with contaminated water by mothers who could not read the instructions on the packaging. Many infant deaths were attributed to using the powdered formula instead of breast feeding. In the early 1980s consumer and church groups boycotted Nestlé products in an attempt to make Nestlé limit its business operations in underdeveloped nations. Nestlé ultimately changed its business practices, agreeing to conform to a World Health Organization code for marketing infant formula. What restrictions do you think should be placed on the competitive practices of multinational organizations operating in underdeveloped nations? Is this an appropriate subject for international agreements? Explain.

9. Real Issues. Tariffs and trade barriers often are discussed in regard to U.S. trade with Japan, especially concerning the automobile industry. One example of an American trade duty is a 25 percent surcharge on light trucks and vans. This duty has allowed the U.S. "Big 3" automakers to gain and retain a significant sales advantage in these major market segments. Detroit is concerned that if the surcharge were reduced or eliminated, the Japanese would quickly gain sales at the cost of more American autoworkers. Should the United States be expected to reduce or eliminate the 25 percent surcharge? Should such action be dependent on the Japanese first or simultaneously eliminating further tariffs and trade barriers to U.S. products? Explain.

10. Real Issues. With the fall of the U.S.S.R., many businesses and businesspersons from the United States have gone to Russia seeking to develop trade opportunities and/or partnerships. Since the Russian government formerly entered into all contracts on behalf of the Russian people and businesses, few new Russian "capitalists" were prepared to negotiate effectively with western businesses and businesspersons. Some of the American companies and individuals took advantage of this situation to impose dispute resolution clauses involving various state laws. For example, one known contract for the sale of used copier machines from the United States provided that all disputes be resolved under the law of Arkansas. Since few, if any, Russian law libraries include Arkansas state law, the Russian businessperson in this case was left without practical remedies when the U.S. company breached the sales contract. As a result of such "deals" the Russian government has begun to discuss possible nonrecognition of such clauses where the contract was created and/or was to be performed substantially in Russia. Does this seem like a reasonable action for the Russian government to consider? What potential legal problems, if any, might exist if all countries chose to do this? Explain.

The end-of-part problems serve three purposes. First, some require practical applications of legal knowledge to everyday situations. Second, they are summative, bringing together many of the issues treated individually in the chapters of a particular part. Third, the last question presents an ethical problem which, as in real life, may not have an unqualified right or wrong solution. Rather, its goal is to prompt two questions: What would I do in this situation? What *should* I do in this situation?

1. A PRACTICAL PROBLEM

Personnel experts continually struggle to create job application forms which give hiring officers the information they need without violating state or federal anti-discrimination laws. For that reason, you are less than thrilled when your new boss tells you to draft such a form. (She has made your task somewhat easier by telling you to leave the layout to the printer. You are just to formulate the questions and to explain any variations between the company's hiring goals and your form.)

Here is what you know about your employer and its needs. Vickie's Ltd. is a traditional women's apparel store catering to a wealthy clientele. The application form is to be used for applicants for full-time sales positions. Vickie's feels that it must know the legal maximum about it employees so that the store will never be embarrassed by later disclosures of previous criminal activity, questionable social habits, bad credit, or unacceptable sexual practices. Its customers prefer salespersons to be female, between 30 and 50, neat but not particularly attractive, polite, and knowledgeable about fashion. The store would like to accommodate its customers' preferences.

2. A SUMMATIVE PROBLEM

Abbington Stores operate two department stores in Megalopolis, a city of over 3 million. Its customers tend to be fashion-conscious trend setters to whom price is not a major concern. Among young businesspersons, an Abbington credit card is a sign of having arrived.

a. Ginger Reilly is divorced and has a 5-year-old son who lives with her. Her ex-husband makes his child support and property settlement installment payments promptly. Reilly applied for a credit card at Abbington's new Shreve Square store. The form asked for personal employment income and/or the applicant's spouse's income. It provided no space for any other income. Reilly decided that Abbington did not consider her ex-husband's payments to be income and did not include them. Abbington rejected her application and, because its "credit reviews are a private matter," has refused to tell her why.

b. Shortly after Abbington opened its Shreve Square store, Dan Porter, an officer of Fashion Circle Stores, approached Abbington's management. Fashion Circle operated similar stores in a nearby—but smaller—city, Metropolis. Porter's proposition was simply this: if Abbington would not open any stores in Metropolis, Fashion Circle would not open any stores in Megalopolis. Abbington had no interest in any sort of expansion, but liked the idea of not having competition from Fashion Circle. So, over a drink, an Abbington officer told Porter, "Look. We're not so naive about the law as to actually agree to what you proposed. But, if you hear about a new store coming into Metropolis, I can tell you it won't be ours."

c. Andy Hardy had observed the many beautiful women who patronize Abbington's cosmetic counters. One morning he noticed a help wanted ad which read in part:

COSMETIC SALESPERSON
Wanted. A woman with an eye to taste.
No previous experience or training necessary.
Apply: Personnel Manager, Abbington's North End.

Andy thought this position would be an ideal way to meet women. But when he applied for the job, the personnel manager told him it was reserved for a woman, since both Abbington's and the industry's surveys indicated that customers of both genders overwhelmingly preferred female cosmetics salespersons. Nonetheless, Abbington offered him an identical position in the sporting goods department—an offer Andy refused.

d. Wally Thomas, a 24-year-old, 6-foot 4-inch black man, was hired by Abbington to work in its stockroom. Soon after Wally began, some women coworkers learned that Wally was once arrested for aggravated rape. The women told management that they were scared to have Wally in their area and would quit if he were retained. Management investigated and found the rumor to be true. However, management also learned that the case was dropped by the district attorney before it ever went to trial. Wally's coworkers remained adamant against his retention, however, as they felt his lack of a trial was more the result of the efforts of a noted civil rights lawyer than of Wally's innocence. Being unable to otherwise appease the group of workers, Abbington fired Wally for his failure to report the arrest during the application process and because of the disruptive effect of his presence. Wally has filed a race discrimination charge against Abbington.

e. The manager of the Shreve Square store saw a lodge brother examining a $900 garden tractor. The manager told his lodge brother that he would sell the tractor to him at a special price, $670. The lodge brother quickly accepted. Another customer overheard the conversation and demanded the same price. The manager refused, saying it was a special deal for a special friend. The other customer has filed a complaint with the Federal Trade Commission.

f. Nutty Nicky's is a discount store. It sells top-of-the-line Apollo televisions for less than Abbington's and four other local stores. Nicky has gained notoriety from her television ads, in which she apparently smashes five Apollo TVs bearing the names of her competitors and the prices at which they sell Apollos. In the same ad, Nicky promises to give the right to smash one of her Apollos to the first customer who can produce proof that one of her five competitors is selling Apollos for less than she is. Even though Abbington and Nicky's other victims will lose money of the arrangement, they have agreed to rotate a special sale on Apollos which will undercut Nicky's advertising.

g. Mike Jackson applied for a position in the men's department at the Shreve Square store. Mike suffered extensive burn damage to his face and upper body several years ago in a freak accident at a high school pep rally. Although he has had extensive plastic surgery, Mike's face is still badly marred. However, he is not otherwise disabled or affected by the fire. Although otherwise qualified, Mike was denied the sales position because the store was concerned that customers might feel uncomfortable with his appearance. He was offered an equal-paying stockroom position but he refused it. Mike has now filed a lawsuit demanding he be hired in the sales position.

Analyze Abbington's liability in the circumstances described in each of the preceding paragraphs. Explain your answers.

3. A SUMMATIVE PROBLEM

The new president of Champion Products, Inc., has heard that the company faces a number of potential lawsuits. She is concerned. She has asked for your informed opinion about the following problems.

a. While on his break, an employee, Russell Jackson, lit a cigarette on one of the company's loading docks. The docks were a no-smoking area. Gasoline fumes ignited, and he was burned horribly. Jackson has filed a workers' compensation claim.

b. A YMCA (open to both men and women) is nearby the company sales offices. Many Champion employees, including Karen Najdowski, change at the Y and then go running on an adjacent park running course. During the summer, Karen began wearing only aerobic fitness tops, not T-shirts. (Such tops, essentially sport bras, were commonly worn by younger female runners and aerobic class participants at the Y.) Tom Bartecki, a coworker who regularly saw Karen running at noon, began making personal remarks to her at work concerning her "sexy appearance" and "shapely body." Karen told coworkers that Tom's comments were harmless, as he was simply "an old couch potato having a little fun." However, another coworker, Stephanie Berg, repeatedly complained to their area supervisor about having to listen to this unwelcomed banter. Stephanie was told to "lighten up," as it clearly did not involve her. Stephanie has now filed a complaint with the EEOC alleging a hostile working environment.

c. After Stephanie filed her complaint with the EEOC, Champion issued a new employee policy requiring all workers to be "appropriately dressed throughout the day on all business days." Karen's supervisor called her in and told her the company expected her to wear a T-shirt on her noontime runs. Karen initially complied but soon reverted to wearing aerobic fitness tops when her male coworkers were not required to wear T-shirts while running. After three warnings, Champion fired Karen. Karen has filed a gender discrimination suit with the EEOC.

d. Cindy Argianas, a factory worker, was severely injured when struck by a forklift truck driven by a coworker. An independent analysis found that the forklift truck was manufactured and sold with a defective steering mechanism. Because Cindy had completed her workday and was walking to the employee parking lot when struck, she contends that she is not restricted by workers' compensation and can directly sue both Champion and the forklift truck manufacturer.

e. Federal regulations require that orange juice be 100 percent pure or be labeled "orange drink." Champion's marketing department has produced a new advertising slogan for their refrigerated orange drink: "the all-natural choice for healthy consumers." In addition, they have developed a bright new carton with abstract orange and green stripes. A consumer advocate, Sam Tuma, has challenged the slogan for improperly implying that the orange drink is actually orange juice.

f. Champion's expert division wants to take advantage of the opening of the new markets in eastern Europe. It entered into a distribution contract with a Romanian distributor who agreed to distribute Champion's breakfast cereals throughout eastern Europe. The contract's choice-of-forum clause provides that all disputes will be tried by a court in Bonn, West Germany. Champion's new president wants to know whether this means West German law will be used to settle disputes.

g. Some department stores have begun to give deep discounts on Champion's ''Monticello'' line of premium men's shirts. Champion has notified these stores that it will cease selling the shirts to any retailer found selling them below $30. Champion has set up an 800 number so sellers of Monticello shirts can easily report violations of the $30 directive. Champion has already acted upon one complaint, from Livesay's Men Store, to verify and suspend sales to B. Haynes, Ltd., one of Livesay's competitors. B. Haynes, Ltd., claims that Champion's actions violated the antitrust laws.

4. AN ETHICAL PROBLEM

Since their inception following the enactment of the Civil Rights Act of 1964, affirmative action programs have been highly controversial. Most business leaders admit that some form of program was necessary because of entrenched resistance to employing and promoting women and minorities, and to paying them comparably to white males. Affirmative action programs give those groups which historically have suffered from employment discrimination a chance to achieve the financial rewards and status they would have received in the absence of discrimination.

Until 1981, the federal government actively promoted such programs. Then, the U.S. Department of Justice began to take the position that affirmative action programs lead to ''reverse discrimination'' against while males. In other words, by attempting to redress earlier discrimination against women and minorities, affirmative action programs caused actual discrimination.

Advocates of this change in federal policy claim that Title VII was meant to provide a remedy for specific acts of discrimination, not to create programs to remedy generations of discrimination. Also, the current generations of women and minority-group members have not suffered the discrimination that earlier generations did.

Those who favor continuation of the plans contend that they are working but still need more time. They acknowledge that the percentage of blacks in the work force has risen by 50 percent and there has been a fivefold increase in the number of black managers in the past 25 years. However, they point to the fact that 97 percent of the senior executives of the largest U.S. companies are white, only 5 percent of all managers in the United States are black, and only 5 percent of all professionals are black.*

These statistics do not begin to compare inequities of compensation. Women are quick to point out that they continue to face hiring hurdles, glass ceilings, and unfair compensation when compared to men. Most black and women leaders say that their primary goal is equality of opportunity. Affirmative action is seen as a critical linkage to this goal.

---

* ''Race in the Workplace: Is Affirmative Action Working?'', *Business Week*, July 8, 1991, p. 50.

The debate over affirmative action can be heated when the economy is strong and expanding. During times when the economy is stagnant or declining, with a significant number of employers downsizing their work force, the debate can become truly intense. The reality of massive layoffs at once dominant companies like General Motors and IBM has shattered the career dreams of many middle-aged, middle-level managers, most often white male. Even at relatively healthy companies, many more middle-aged white men will personally witness an increasing percentage of women and blacks rising to positions once "owned" by white men. The ultimate legal weapon for many of these middle-aged white men may be the Age Discrimination in Employment Act. For the employer caught in the middle, the prospects of balance and harmony in the workplace may appear fleeting.

Is the fate of affirmative action programs a question of law or of ethics, or both? Assuming that the question has an ethical dimension, define it. Assuming that the proponents of affirmative action are correct, is there a point at which affirmative action programs should stop? Can you devise a mechanism which does not involve numerical quotas for ensuring that minorities and women are hired by employers who historically have discriminated against them?

Appendixes

Uniform Commercial Code*

ARTICLE 1: GENERAL PROVISIONS

Part 1: Short Title, Construction, Application and Subject Matter of the Act

§1-101. Short Title. This act shall be known and may be cited as Uniform Commercial Code.

§1-102. Purposes; Rules of Construction; Variation by Agreement.

(1) This Act shall be liberally construed and applied to promote its underlying purposes and policies.

(2) Underlying purposes and policies of this Act are

(a) to simplify, clarify and modernize the law governing commercial transactions;

(b) to permit the continued expansion of commercial practices through custom, usage and agreement of the parties;

(c) to make uniform the law among the various jurisdictions.

(3) The effect of provisions of this Act may be varied by agreement, except as otherwise provided in this Act and except that the obligations of good faith, diligence, reasonableness and care prescribed by this Act may not be disclaimed by agreement but the parties may by agreement determine the standards by which the performance of such obligations is to be measured if such standards are not manifestly unreasonable.

(4) The presence in certain provisions of this Act of the words "unless otherwise agreed" or words of similar import does not imply that the effect of other provisions may not be varied by agreement under subsection (3).

(5) In this Act unless the context otherwise requires

(a) words in the singular number include the plural, and in the plural include the singular;

(b) words of the masculine gender include the feminine and the neuter, and when the sense so indicates words of the neuter gender may refer to any gender.

§1-103. Supplementary General Principles of Law Applicable. Unless displaced by the particular provisions of this Act, the principles of law and equity, including the law merchant and the law relative to capacity to contract, principal and agent, estoppel, fraud, misrepresentation, duress, coercion, mistake, bankruptcy, or other validating or invalidating cause shall supplement its provisions.

§1-104. Construction Against Implicity Repeal. This Act being a general act intended as a unified coverage of its subject matter, no part of it shall be deemed to be impliedly repealed by subsequent legislation if such construction can reasonably be avoided.

§1-105. Territorial Application of the Act; Parties' Power to Choose Applicable Law.

(1) Except as provided hereafter in this section, when a transaction bears a reasonable relation to this state and also to another state or nation the parties may agree that the law either of this state or of such other state or nation shall govern their rights and duties. Failing such agreement this Act applies to transactions bearing an appropriate relation to this state.

(2) Where one of the following provisions of this Act specifies the applicable law, that provision governs and a contrary agreement is effective only to the extent permitted by the law (including the conflict of laws rules) so specified:

Rights of creditors against sold goods. Section 2-402.

Applicability of the Article on Bank Deposits and Collections. Section 4-102.

---

*Copyright 1978 by The American Law Institute and the National Conference of Commissioners on Uniform State Laws. Reprinted with permission of the Permanent Editorial Board for the Uniform Commercial Code. The 1972 version of Article 9 and the 1977 version of Article 8 appear in this appendix.

Bulk transfers subject to the Article on Bulk Transfers. Section 6-102.

Applicability of the Article on Investment Securities. Section 8-106.

Perfection provisions of the Article on Secured Transactions. Section 9-103.

§1-106. Remedies to Be Liberally Administered.

(1) The remedies provided by this Act shall be liberally administered to the end that the aggrieved party may be put in as good a position as if the other party had fully performed but neither consequential or special nor penal damages may be had except as specifically provided in this Act or by other rule of law.

(2) Any right or obligation declared by this Act is enforceable by action unless the provision declaring it specifies a different and limited effect.

§1-107. Waiver or Renunciation of Claim or Right After Breach.
Any claim or right arising out of an alleged breach can be discharged in whole or in part without consideration by a written waiver or renunciation signed and delivered by the aggrieved party.

§1-108. Severability.
If any provision or clause of this Act or application thereof to any person or circumstances is held invalid, such invalidity shall not affect other provisions or applications of the Act which can be given effect without the invalid provision or application, and to this end the provisions of this Act are declared to be severable.

§1-109. Section Captions.
Section captions are parts of this Act.

Part 2: General Definitions and Principles of Interpretation

§1-201. General Definitions.
Subject to additional definitions contained in the subsequent Articles of this Act which are applicable to specific Articles or Parts thereof, and unless the context otherwise requires, in this Act.

(1) "Action" in the sense of a judicial proceeding includes recoupment, counterclaim, set-off, suit in equity and any other proceedings in which rights are determined.

(2) "Aggrieved party" means a party entitled to resort to a remedy.

(3) "Agreement" means the bargain of the parties in fact as found in their language or by implication from other circumstances including course of dealing or usage of trade or course of performance as provided in this Act, (Section 1-205 and 2-208). Whether an agreement has legal consequences is determined by the provisions of this Act, if applicable; otherwise by the law of contracts (Section 1-103). (Compare "Contract".)

(4) "Bank" means any person engaged in the business of banking.

(5) "Bearer" means the person in possession of an instrument, document of title, or certificated security payable to bearer or indorsed in blank.

(6) "Bill of lading" means a document evidencing the receipt of goods for shipment issued by a person engaged in the business of transporting or forwarding goods, and includes an airbill. "Airbill" means a document serving for air transportation as a bill of lading does for marine or rail transportation, and includes an air consignment note or air waybill.

(7) "Branch" includes a separately incorporated foreign branch of a bank.

(8) "Burden of establishing" a fact means the burden of persuading the triers of fact that the existence of the fact is more probable than its non-existence.

(9) "Buyer in ordinary course of business" means a person who in good faith and without knowledge that the sale to him is in violation of the ownership rights or security interest of a third party in the goods buys in ordinary course from a person in the business of selling goods of that kind but does not include a pawnbroker. All persons who sell minerals or the like (including oil and gas) at wellhead or minehead shall be deemed to be persons in the business of selling goods of that kind. "Buying" may be for cash or by exchange of other property or on secured or unsecured credit and includes receiving goods or documents of title under a pre-existing contract for sale but does not include a transfer in bulk or as security for or in total or partial satisfaction of a money debt.

(10) "Conspicuous": A term or clause is conspicuous when it is so written that a reasonable person against whom it is to operate ought to have noticed it. A printed heading in capitals (as: NON-NEGOTIABLE BILL OF LADING) is conspicuous. Language in the body of a form is "conspicuous" if it is in larger or other contrasting type or color. But in a telegram any stated term is "conspicuous". Whether a term or clause is "conspicuous" or not is for decision by the court.

(11) "Contract" means the total legal obligation

which results from the parties' agreement as affected by this Act and any other applicable rules of law. (Compare "Agreement".)

(**12**) "Creditor" includes a general creditor, a secured creditor, a lien creditor and any representative of creditors, including an assignee for the benefit of creditors, a trustee in bankruptcy, a receiver in equity and an executor or adminsitrator of an insolvent debtor's or assignor's estate.

(**13**) "Defendant" includes a person in the position of defendant in a cross-action or counterclaim.

(**14**) "Delivery" with respect to instruments, documents of title, chattel paper, or certificated securities means voluntary transfer of possession.

(**15**) "Document of title" includes bill of lading, dock warrant, dock receipt, warehouse receipt or order for the delivery of goods, and also any other document which in the regular course of business or financing is treated as adequately evidencing that the person in possession of it is entitled to receive, hold and dispose of the document and the goods it covers. To be a document of title a document must purport to be issued by or addressed to a bailee and purport to cover goods in the bailee's possession which are either identified or are fungible portions of an identified mass.

(**16**) "Fault" means wrongful act, omission or breach.

(**17**) "Fungible" with respect to goods or securities means goods or securities of which any unit is, by nature or usage of trade, the equivalent of any other like unit. Goods which are not fungible shall be deemed fungible for the purposes of this Act to the extent that under a particular agreement or document unlike units are treated as equivalents.

(**18**) "Genuine" means free of forgery or counterfeiting.

(**19**) "Good faith" means honesty in fact in the conduct or transaction concerned.

(**20**) "Holder" means a person who is in possession of a document of title or a certificated instrument or an investment security drawn, issued or indorsed to him or to his order or to bearer or in blank.

(**21**) To "honor" is to pay or to accept and pay, or where a credit so engages to purchase or discount a draft complying with the terms of the credit.

(**22**) "Insolvency proceedings" includes any assignment for the benefit of creditors or other proceedings intended to liquidate or rehabilitate the estate of the person involved.

(**23**) A person is "insolvent" who either has ceased to pay his debts in the ordinary course of business or cannot pay his debts as they become due or is insolvent within the meaning of the federal bankruptcy law.

(**24**) "Money" means a medium of exchange authorized or adopted by a domestic or foreign government as part of its currency.

(**25**) A person has "notice" of a fact when

(**a**) he has actual knowledge of it; or

(**b**) he has received a notice or notification of it; or

(**c**) from all the facts and circumstances known to him at the time in question he has reason to know that it exists.

A person "knows" or has "knowledge" of a fact when he has actual knowledge of it. "Discover" or "learn" or a word or phrase of similar import refers to knowledge rather than to reason to know. The time and circumstances under which a notice or notification may cease to be effective are not determined by this Act.

(**26**) A person "notifies" or "gives" a notice or notification to another by taking such steps as may be reasonably required to inform the other in ordinary course whether or not such other actually comes to know of it. A person "receives" a notice or notification when

(**a**) it comes to his attention; or

(**b**) it is duly delivered at the place of business through which the contract was made or at any other place held out by him as the place for receipt of such communications.

(**27**) Notice, knowledge or a notice or notification received by an organization is effective for a particular transaction from the time when it is brought to the attention of the individual conducting that transaction, and in any event from the time when it would have been brought to his attention if the organization had exercised due diligence. An organization exercises due diligence if it maintains reasonable routines for communicating significant information to the person conducting the transaction and there is reasonable compliance with the routines. Due diligence does not require an individual acting for the organization to communicate information unless such communication is part of his regular duties or unless he has reason to know of the transaction and that the transaction would be materially affected by the information.

(**28**) "Organization" includes a corporation, government or governmental subdivision or agency, business trust, estate, trust, partnership or association, two or more persons having a joint or common interest, or any other legal or commercial entity.

(**29**) "Party", as distinct from "third party", means a person who has engaged in a transaction or made an agreement within this Act.

(**30**) "Person" includes an individual or an organization (See Section 1-102).

(**31**) "Presumption" or "presumed" means that the trier of fact must find the existence of the fact presumed unless and until evidence is introduced which would support a finding of its non-existence.

(**32**) "Purchase" includes taking by sale, discount, negotiation, mortgage, pledge, lien, issue or re-issue, gift or any other voluntary transaction creating an interest in property.

(**33**) "Purchaser" means a person who takes by purchase.

(**34**) "Remedy" means any remedial right to which an aggrieved party is entitled with or without resort to a tribunal.

(**35**) "Representative" includes as agent, an officer of a corporation or association, and a trustee, executor or administrator of an estate, or any other person empowered to act for another.

(**36**) "Rights" includes remedies.

(**37**) "Security interest" means an interest in personal property or fixtures which secures payment or performance of an obligation. The retention or reservation of title by a seller of goods notwithstanding shipment or delivery to the buyer (Section 2-401) is limited in effect to a reservation of a "security interest". The term also includes any interest of a buyer of accounts or chattel paper, which is subject to Article 9. The special property interest of a buyer of goods on identification of such goods to a contract for sale under Section 2-401 is not a "security interest", but a buyer may also acquire a "security interest" by complying with Article 9. Unless a lease or consignment is intended as security, reservation of title thereunder is not a "security interest" but a consignment is in any event subject to the provisions on consignment sales (Section 2-326). Whether a lease is intended as security is to be determined by the facts of each case; however, (a) the inclusion of an option to purchase does not itself make the lease one intended for security, and (b) an agreement that upon compliance with the terms of the lease the lessee shall become or has the option to become the owner of the property for no additional consideration or for a nominal consideration does make the lease one intended for security.

(**38**) "Send" in connection with any writing or notice means to deposit in the mail or deliver for transmission by any other usual means of communication with postage or cost of transmission provided for and properly addressed and in the case of an instrument to an address specified thereon or otherwise agreed, or if there by none to any address reasonable under the circumstances. The receipt of any writing or notice within the time at which it would have arrived if properly sent has the effect of a proper sending.

(**39**) "Signed" includes any symbol executed or adopted by a party with present intention to authenticate a writing.

(**40**) "Surety" includes guarantor.

(**41**) "Telegram" includes a message transmitted by radio, teletype, cable, any mechanical method of transmission, or the like.

(**42**) "Term" means that portion of an agreement which relates to a particular matter.

(**43**) "Unauthorized" signature or indorsement means one made without actual, implied or apparent authority and includes a forgery.

(**44**) "Value". Except as otherwise provided with respect to negotiable instruments and bank collections (Sections 3-303, 4-208 and 4-209) a person gives "value" for rights if he acquires them

   (**a**) in return for a binding commitment to extend credit or for the extension of immediately available credit whether or not drawn upon and whether or not a chargeback is provided for in the event of difficulties in collection; or

   (**b**) as security for or in total or partial satisfaction of a pre-existing claim; or

   (**c**) by accepting delivery pursuant to a pre-existing contract for purchase; or

   (**d**) generally, in return for any consideration sufficient to support a simple contract.

(**45**) "Warehouse receipt" means a receipt issued by a person engaged in the business of storing goods for hire.

(**46**) "Written" or "writing" includes printing, typewriting or any other intentional reduction to tangible form. As amended 1962 and 1972.

§1-201. General Definitions *(1977 Amendments).*

Subject to additional definitions contained in the

subsequent Articles of this Act which are applicable to specific Articles or Parts thereof, and unless the context otherwise requires, in the Act:

* * *

(5) "Bearer" means the person in possession of an instrument, document of title, or certificated security payable to bearer or indorsed in blank.

* * *

(14) "Delivery" with respect to instruments, documents of title, chattel paper, or certificated securities means voluntary transfer of possession.

* * *

(20) "Holder" means a person who is in possession of a document of title or an instrument or a certificated investment security drawn, issued or indorsed to him or his order or to bearer or in blank.

* * *

§1-202. Prima Facie Evidence by Third Party Documents. A document in due form purporting to be a bill of lading, policy or certificate of insurance, official weigher's or inspector's certificate, consular invoice or any other document authorized or required by the contract to be issued by a third party shall be prima facie evidence of its own authenticity and genuineness and of the facts stated in the document by the third party.

§1-203. Obligation of Good Faith. Every contract or duty within this Act imposes an obligation of good faith in its performance or enforcement.

§1-204. Time; Reasonable Time; "Seasonably".

(1) Whenever this Act requires any action to be taken within a reasonable time, any time which is not manifestly unreasonable may be fixed by agreement.

(2) What is a reasonable time for taking any action depends on the nature, purpose and circumstances of such action.

(3) An action is taken "seasonably" when it is taken at or within the time agreed or if no time is agreed at or within a reasonable time.

§1-205. Course of Dealing and Usage of Trade.

(1) A course of dealing is a sequence of previous conduct between the parties to a particular transaction which is fairly to be regarded as establishing a common basis of understanding for interpreting their expressions and other conduct.

(2) A usage of trade is any practice or method of dealing having such regularity of observance in a place, vocation or trade as to justify an expectation that it will be observed with respect to the transaction in question. The existence and scope of such a usage

are to be proved as facts. If it is established that such a usage is embodied in a written trade code or similar writing the interpretation of the writing is for the court.

(3) A course of dealing between parties and any usage of trade in the vocation or trade in which they are engaged or of which they are or should be aware give particular meaning to and supplement or qualify terms of an agreement.

(4) The express terms of an agreement and an applicable course of dealing or usage of trade shall be construed wherever reasonable as consistent with each other; but when such construction is unreasonable express terms control both course of dealing and usage of trade and course of dealing controls usage of trade.

(5) An applicable usage of trade in the place where any part of performance is to occur shall be used in interpreting the agreement as to that part of the performance.

(6) Evidence of a relevant usage of trade offered by one party is not admissible unless and until he has given the other party such notice as the court finds sufficient to prevent unfair surprise to the latter.

§1-206. Statute of Frauds for Kinds of Personal Property Not Otherwise Covered.

(1) Except in the cases described in subsection (2) of this section a contract for the sale of personal property is not enforceable by way of action or defense beyond five thousand dollars in amount or value of remedy unless there is some writing which indicates that a contract for sale has been made between the parties at a defined or stated price, reasonably identifies the subject matter, and is signed by the party against whom enforcement is sought or by his authorized agent.

(2) Subsection (1) of this section does not apply to contracts for the sale of goods (Section 2-201) nor of securities (Section 8-319) nor to security agreements (Section 9-203).

§1-207. Performance or Acceptance Under Reservation of Rights. A party who with explicit reservation of rights performs or promises performance or assents to performance in a manner demanded or offered by the other party does not thereby prejudice the rights reserved. Such words as "without prejudice", "under protest" or the like are sufficient.

§1-208. Option to Accelerate at Will. A term providing that one party or his successor in interest may accelerate payment or performance or require collateral or additional collateral "at will" or "when he deems himself insecure" or in words of similar import shall be construed to mean that he shall have power to do so only if he in good faith believes that the prospect of payment or performance is impaired. The burden of establishing lack of good faith is on the party against whom the power has been exercised.

§1-209. Subordinated Obligations. An obligation may be issued as subordinated to payment of another obligation of the person obligated, or a creditor may subordinate his right to payment of an obligation by agreement with either the person obligated or another creditor of the person obligated. Such a subordination does not create a security interest as against either the common debtor or a subordinated creditor. This section shall be construed as declaring the law as it existed prior to the enactment of this section and not as modifying it. Added 1966.

Note: *This new section is proposed as an optional provision to make it clear that a subordination agreement does not create a security interest unless so intended.*

ARTICLE 2: SALES

Part 1: Short Title, General Construction and Subject Matter

§2-101. Short Title. This Article shall be known and may be cited as Uniform Commercial Code—Sales.

§2-102. Scope; Certain Security and Other Transactions Excluded From This Article. Unless the context otherwise requires, this Article applies to transactions in goods; it does not apply to any transaction which although in the form of an unconditional contract to sell or present sale is intended to operate only as a security transaction nor does this Article impair or repeal any statute regulating sales to consumers, farmers or other specified classes of buyers.

§2-103. Definitions and Index of Definitions.

(1) In this Article unless the context otherwise requires

(a) "Buyer" means a person who buys or contracts to buy goods.

(b) "Good faith" in the case of a merchant means honesty in fact and the observance of reasonable commercial standards of fair dealing in the trade.

(c) "Receipt" of goods means taking physical possession of them.

(d) "Seller" means a person who sells or contracts to sell goods.

(2) Other definitions applying to this Article or to specified Parts thereof, and the sections in which they appear are:

"Acceptance". Section 2-606.
"Banker's credit". Section 2-325.
"Between merchants". Section 2-104.
"Cancellation". Section 2-106(4).
"Commercial unit". Section 2-105.
"Confirmed credit". Section 2-325.
"Conforming to contract". Section 2-106.
"Contract for sale". Section 2-106.
"Cover". Section 2-712.
"Entrusting". Section 2-403.
"Financing agency". Section 2-104.
"Future goods". Section 2-105.
"Goods". Section 2-105.
"Identification". Section 2-501.
"Installment contract". Section 2-612.
"Letter of Credit". Section 2-325.
"Lot". Section 2-105.
"Merchant". Section 2-104.
"Overseas". Section 2-323.
"Person in position of seller". Section 2-707.
"Present sale". Section 2-106.
"Sale". Section 2-106.
"Sale on approval". Section 2-326.
"Sale or return". Section 2-326.
"Termination". Section 2-106.

(3) The following definitions in other Articles apply to this Article:

"Check". Section 3-104.
"Consignee". Section 7-102.
"Consignor". Section 7-102.
"Consumer goods". Section 9-109.
"Dishonor". Section 3-507.
"Draft". Section 3-104.

(4) In addition Article 1 contains general definitions and principles of construction and interpretation applicable throughout this article.

§2-104. Definitions: "Merchant"; "Between Merchants"; "Financing Agency".

(1) "Merchant" means a person who deals in goods of the kind or otherwise by his occupation holds himself out as having knowledge or skill peculiar to the practices or goods involved in the transaction or to whom such knowledge or skill may be attributed by

his employment of an agent or broker or other intermediary who by his occupation holds himself out as having such knowledge or skill.

(**2**) "Financing agency" means a bank, finance company or other person who in the ordinary course of business makes advances against goods or documents of title or who by arrangement with either the seller or the buyer intervenes in ordinary course to make or collect payment due or claimed under the contract for sale, as by purchasing or paying the seller's draft or making advances against it or by merely taking it for collection whether or not documents of title accompany the draft. "Financing agency" includes also a bank or other person who similarly intervenes between persons who are in the position of seller and buyer in respect of the goods (Section 2-707).

(**3**) "Between merchants" means in any transaction with respect to which both parties are chargeable with the knowledge or skill of merchants.

§2-105. Definitions: Transferability; "Goods"; "Future" Goods; "Lot"; "Commercial Unit".

(**1**) "Goods" means all things (including specially manufactured goods) which are movable at the time of identification to the contract for sale other than the money in which the price is to be paid, investment securities (Article 8) and things in action. "Goods" also includes the unborn young of animals and growing crops and other identified things attached to realty as described in the section on goods to be severed from realty (Section 2-107).

(**2**) Goods must be both existing and identified before any interest in them can pass. Goods which are not both existing and identified are "future" goods. A purported present sale of future goods or of any interest therein operates as a contract to sell.

(**3**) There may be a sale of a part interest in existing identified goods.

(**4**) An undivided share in an identified bulk of fungible goods is sufficiently identified to be sold although the quantity of the bulk is not determined. Any agreed proportion of such a bulk or any quantity thereof agreed upon by number, weight or other measure may to the extent of the seller's interest in the bulk be sold to the buyer who then becomes an owner in common.

(**5**) "Lot" means a parcel or a single article which is the subject matter of a separate sale or delivery, whether or not it is sufficient to perform the contract.

(**6**) "Commercial unit" means such a unit of goods as by commercial usage is a single whole for purposes of sale and division of which materially impairs its character or value on the market or in use. A commercial unit may be a single article (as a machine) or a set of articles (as a suite of furniture or an assortment of sizes) or a quantity (as a bale, gross, or carload) or any other unit treated in use or in the relevant market as a single whole.

§2-106. Definitions: "Contract"; "Agreement"; "Contract for Sale"; "Sale"; "Present Sale"; "Conforming" to Contract; "Termination"; "Cancellation".

(**1**) In this Article unless the context otherwise requires "contract" and "agreement" are limited to those relating to the present or future sale of goods. "Contract for sale" includes both a present sale of goods and a contract to sell goods at a future time. A "sale" consists in the passing of title from the seller to the buyer for a price (Section 2-401). A "present sale" means a sale which is accomplished by the making of the contract.

(**2**) Goods or conduct including any part of a performance are "conforming" or conform to the contract when they are in accordance with the obligations under the contract.

(**3**) "Termination" occurs when either party pursuant to a power created by agreement or law puts an end to the contract otherwise than for its breach. On "termination" all obligations which are still executory on both sides are discharged but any right based on prior breach or performance survives.

(**4**) "Cancellation" occurs when either party puts an end to the contract for breach by the other and its effect is the same as that of "termination" except that the cancelling party also retains any remedy for breach of the whole contract or any unperformed balance.

§2-107. Goods to Be Severed From Realty: Recording.

(**1**) A contract for the sale of minerals or the like (including oil and gas) or a structure or its materials to be removed from realty is a contract for the sale of goods within this Article if they are to be severed by the seller but until severance a purported present sale thereof which is not effective as a transfer of an interest in land is effective only as a contract to sell.

(**2**) A contract for the sale apart from the land of growing crops or other things attached to realty and capable of severance without material harm thereto but not described in subsection (1) or of timber to be cut is a contract for the sale of goods within this Article whether the subject matter is to be severed by the buyer or by the seller even though it forms part of the realty at the time of contracting, and the parties can by identification effect a present sale before severance.

(3) The provisions of this section are subject to any third party rights provided by the law relating to realty records, and the contract for sale may be executed and recorded as a document transferring an interest in land and shall then constitute notice to third parties of the buyer's rights under the contract for sale.

Part 2: Form, Formation and Readjustment of Contract

§2-201. Formal Requirements; Statute of Frauds.

(1) Except as otherwise provided in this section a contract for the sale of goods for the price of $500 or more is not enforceable by way of action or defense unless there is some writing sufficient to indicate that a contract for sale has been made between the parties and signed by the party against whom enforcement is sought or by his authorized agent or broker. A writing is not insufficient because it omits or incorrectly states a term agreed upon but the contract is not enforceable under this paragraph beyond the quantity of goods shown in such writing.

(2) Between merchants if within a reasonable time a writing in confirmation of the contract and sufficient against the sender is received and the party receiving it has reason to know its contents, it satisfies the requirements of subsection (1) against such party unless written notice of objection to its contents is given within 10 days after it is received.

(3) A contract which does not satisfy the requirements of subsection (1) but which is valid in other respects is enforceable

(a) if the goods are to be specially manufactured for the buyer and are not suitable for sale to others in the ordinary course of the seller's business and the seller, before notice of repudiation is received and under circumstances which reasonably indicate that the goods are for the buyer, has made either a substantial beginning of their manufacture of commitments for their procurement; or

(b) if the party against whom enforcement is sought admits in his pleading, testimony or otherwise in court that a contract for sale was made, but the contract is not enforceable under this provision beyond the quantity of goods admitted; or

(c) with respect to goods for which payment has been made and accepted or which have been received and accepted (Sec. 2-606.)

§2-202. Final Written Expression: Parol or Extrinsic Evidence. Terms with respect to which the confirmatory memoranda of the parties agree or which are otherwise set forth in a writing intended by the parties as a final expression of their agreement with respect to such terms as are included therein may not be contradicted by evidence of any prior agreement or of a contemporaneous oral agreement but may be explained or supplemented

(a) by course of dealing or usage of trade (Section 1-205) or by course of performance (Section 2-208); and

(b) by evidence of consistent additional terms unless the court finds the writing to have been intended also as a complete and exclusive statement of the terms of the agreement.

§2-203. Seals Inoperative. The affixing of a seal to a writing evidencing a contract for sale or an offer to buy or sell goods does not constitute the writing a sealed instrument and the law with respect to sealed instruments does not apply to such a contract or offer.

§2-204. Formation in General.

(1) A contract for sale of goods may be made in any manner sufficient to show agreement, including conduct by both parties which recognizes the existence of such a contract.

(2) An agreement sufficient to constitute a contract for sale may be found even though the moment of its making is undetermined.

(3) Even though one or more terms are left open a contract for sale does not fail for indefiniteness if the parties have intended to make a contract and there is a reasonably certain basis for giving an appropriate remedy.

§2-205. Firm Offers. An offer by a merchant to buy or sell goods in a signed writing which by its terms gives assurance that it will be held open is not revocable, for lack of consideration, during the time stated or if no time is stated for a reasonable time, but in no event may such period of irrevocability exceed three months; but any such term of assurance on a form supplied by the offeree must be separately signed by the offeror.

§2-206. Offer and Acceptance in Formation of Contract.

(1) Unless otherwise unambiguously indicated by the language or circumstances

(a) an offer to make a contract shall be construed as inviting acceptance in any manner and by any medium reasonable in the circumstances;

(b) an order or other offer to buy goods for prompt or current shipment shall be construed as inviting acceptance either by a prompt promise to ship or by the prompt or current shipment of conforming or nonconforming goods, but such a shipment of nonconforming goods does not constitute an acceptance if the seller seasonably notifies the buyer that the shipment is offered only as an accommodation to the buyer.

(2) Where the beginning of a requested performance is a reasonable mode of acceptance an offeror who is not notified of acceptance within a reasonable time may treat the offer as having lapsed before acceptance.

§2-207. Additional Terms in Acceptance or Confirmation.

(1) A definite and seasonable expression of acceptance or a written confirmation which is sent within a reasonable time operates as an acceptance even though it states terms additional to or different from those offered or agreed upon, unless acceptance is expressly made conditional on assent to the additional or different terms.

(2) The additional terms are to be construed as proposals for addition to the contract. Between merchants such terms become part of the contract unless:

(a) the offer expressly limits acceptance to the terms of the offer;

(b) they materially alter it; or

(c) notification of objection to them has already been given or is given within a reasonable time after notice of them is received.

(3) Conduct by both parties which recognizes the existence of a contract is sufficient to establish a contract for sale although the writings of the parties do not otherwise establish a contract. In such case the terms of the particular contract consist of those terms on which the writings of the parties agree, together with any supplementary terms incorporated under any other provisions of this Act.

§2-208. Course of Performance or Practical Construction.

(1) Where the contract for sale involves repeated occasions for performance by either party with knowledge of the nature of the performance and opportunity for objection to it by the other, any course of performance accepted or acquiesced in without objection shall be relevant to determine the meaning of the agreement.

(2) The express terms of the agreement and any such course of performance, as well as any course of dealing and usage of trade, shall be construed whenever reasonable as consistent with each other; but when such construction is unreasonable, express terms shall control course of performance and course of performance shall control both course of dealing and usage of trade (Section 1-205).

(3) Subject to the provisions of the next section on modification and waiver, such course of performance shall be relevant to show a waiver or modification of any term inconsistent with such course of performance.

§2-209. Modification, Rescission and Waiver.

(1) An agreement modifying a contract within this Article needs no consideration to be binding.

(2) A signed agreement which excludes modification or rescission except by a signed writing cannot be otherwise modified or rescinded, but except as between merchants such a requirement on a form supplied by the merchant must be separately signed by the other party.

(3) The requirements of the statute of frauds section of this Article (Section 2-201) must be satisfied if the contract as modified is within its provisions.

(4) Although an attempt at modification or rescission does not satisfy the requirements of subsection (2) or (3) it can operate as a waiver.

(5) A party who has made a waiver affecting an executory portion of the contract may retract the waiver by reasonable notification received by the other party that strict performance will be required of any term waived, unless the retraction would be unjust in view of a material change of position in reliance on the waiver.

§2-210. Delegation of Performance; Assignment of Rights.

(1) A party may perform his duty through a delegate unless otherwise agreed or unless the other party has a substantial interest in having his original promisor perform or control the acts required by the con-

tract. No delegation of performance relieves the party delegating of any duty to perform or any liability for breach.

(**2**) Unless otherwise agreed all rights of either seller or buyer can be assigned except where the assignment would materially change the duty of the other party, or increase materially the burden or risk imposed on him by his contract, or impair materially his chance of obtaining return performance. A right to damages for breach of the whole contract or a right arising out of the assignor's due performance of his entire obligation can be assigned despite agreement otherwise.

(**3**) Unless the circumstances indicate the contrary a prohibition of assignment of "the contract" is to be construed as barring only the delegation to the assignee of the assignor's performance.

(**4**) An assignment of "the contract" or of "all my rights under the contract" or an assignment in similar general terms is an assignment of rights and unless the language or the circumstances (as in an assignment for security) indicate the contrary, it is a delegation of performance of the duties of the assignor and its acceptance by the assignee constitutes a promise by him to perform those duties. This promise is enforceable by either the assignor or the other party to the original contract.

(**5**) The other party may treat any assignment which delegates performance as creating reasonable grounds for insecurity and may without prejudice to his rights against the assignor demand assurances from the assignee (Section 2-609).

Part 3: General Obligation and Construction of Contract

§2-301. General Obligations of Parties. The obligation of the seller is to transfer and deliver and that of the buyer is to accept and pay in accordance with the contract.

§2-302. Unconscionable Contract or Clause.

(**1**) If the court as a matter of law finds the contract or any clause of the contract to have been unconscionable at the time it was made the court may refuse to enforce the contract, or it may enforce the remainder of the contract without the unconscionable clause, or it may so limit the application of any unconscionable clause as to avoid any unconscionable result.

(**2**) When it is claimed or appears to the court that the contract or any clause thereof may be unconscionable the parties shall be afforded a reasonable oppor-

tunity to present evidence as to its commercial setting, purpose and effect to aid the court in making the determination.

§2-303. Allocation or Division of Risks. Where this Article allocates a risk or a burden as between the parties "unless otherwise agreed", the agreement may not only shift the allocation but may also divide the risk or burden.

§2-304. Price Payable in Money, Goods, Realty, or Otherwise.

(**1**) The price can be made payable in money or otherwise. If it is payable in whole or in part in goods each party is a seller of the goods which he is to transfer.

(**2**) Even though all or part of the price is payable in an interest in realty the transfer of the goods and the seller's obligations with reference to them are subject to this Article, but not the transfer of the interest in realty or the transferor's obligations in connection therewith.

§2-305. Open Price Term.

(**1**) The parties if they so intend can conclude a contract for sale even though the price is not settled. In such a case the price is a reasonable price at the time for delivery if

(**a**) nothing is said as to price; or

(**b**) the price is left to be agreed by the parties and they fail to agree; or

(**c**) the price is to be fixed in terms of some agreed market or other standard as set or recorded by a third person or agency and it is not so set or recorded.

(**2**) A price to be fixed by the seller or by the buyer means a price for him to fix in good faith.

(**3**) When a price left to be fixed otherwise than by agreement of the parties fails to be fixed through fault of one party the other may at his option treat the contract as cancelled or himself fix a reasonable price.

(**4**) Where, however, the parties intend not to be bound unless the price be fixed or agreed and it is not fixed or agreed there is no contract. In such a case the buyer must return any goods already received or if unable so to do must pay their reasonable value at the time of delivery and the seller must return any portion of the price paid on account.

§2-306. Output, Requirements and Exclusive Dealings.

(**1**) A term which measures the quantity by the output of the seller or the requirements of the buyer means such actual output or requirements as may occur in good faith, except that no quantity unreasonably disproportionate to any stated estimate or in the absence of a stated estimate to any normal or otherwise comparable prior output or requirements may be tendered or demanded.

(2) A lawful agreement by either the seller or the buyer for exclusive dealing in the kind of goods concerned imposes unless otherwise agreed an obligation by the seller to use best efforts to supply the goods and by the buyer to use best efforts to promote their sale.

§2-307. Delivery in Single Lot or Several Lots. Unless otherwise agreed all goods called for by a contract for sale must be tendered in a single delivery and payment is due only on such tender but where the circumstances give either party the right to make or demand delivery in lots the price if it can be apportioned may be demanded for each lot.

§2-308. Absence of Specified Place for Delivery. Unless otherwise agreed

(a) the place for delivery of goods is the seller's place of business or if he has none his residence; but

(b) in a contract for sale of identified goods which to the knowledge of the parties at the time of contracting are in some other place, that place is the place for their delivery; and

(c) documents of title may be delivered through customary banking channels.

§2-309. Absence of Specific Time Provisions; Notice of Termination.

(1) The time for shipment or delivery or any other action under a contract if not provided in this Article or agreed upon shall be a reasonable time.

(2) Where the contract provides for successive performances but is indefinite in duration it is valid for a reasonable time but unless otherwise agreed may be terminated at any time by either party.

(3) Termination of a contract by one party except on the happening of an agreed event requires that reasonable notification be received by the other party and in agreement dispensing with notification is invalid if its operation would be unconscionable.

§2-310. Open Time for Payment or Running of Credit; Authority to Ship Under Reservation. Unless otherwise agreed

(a) payment is due at the time and place at which the buyer is to receive the goods even though the place of shipment is the place of delivery; and

(b) if the seller is authorized to send the goods he may ship them under reservation, and may tender the documents of title, but the buyer may inspect the goods after their arrival before payment is due unless such inspection is inconsistent with the terms of the contract (Section 2-513); and

(c) if delivery is authorized and made by way of documents of title otherwise than by subsection (b) then payment is due at the time and place at which the buyer is to receive the documents regardless of where the goods are to be received; and

(d) where the seller is required or authorized to ship the goods on credit the credit period runs from the time of shipment but post-dating the invoice or delaying its dispatch will correspondingly delay the starting of the credit period.

§2-311. Options and Cooperation Respecting Performance.

(1) An agreement for sale which is otherwise sufficiently definite (subsection (3) of Section 2-204) to be a contract is not made invalid by the fact that it leaves particulars of performance to be specified by one of the parties. Any such specification must be made in good faith and within limits set by commercial reasonableness.

(2) Unless otherwise agreed specifications relating to assortment of the goods are at the buyer's option and except as otherwise provided in subsections (1) (c) and (3) of Section 2-319 specifications or arrangements relating to shipment are at the seller's options.

(3) Where such specifications would materially affect the other party's performance but is not seasonably made or where one party's cooperation is necessary to the agreed performance of the other but is not seasonably forthcoming, the other party

(a) is excused for any resulting delay in his own performance; and

(b) may also either proceed to perform in any reasonable manner or after the time for a material part of his own performance treat the failure to specify or to cooperate as a breach by failure to deliver or accept the goods.

§2-312. Warranty of Title and Against Infringement; Buyer's Obligation Against Infringement.

(1) Subject to subsection (2) there is in a contract for sale a warranty by the seller that

(a) the title conveyed shall be good, and its transfer rightful; and

(b) the goods shall be delivered free from any security interest or other lien or encumbrance of which the buyer at the time of contracting has no knowledge.

(2) A warranty under subsection (2) will be excluded or modified only by specific language or by circumstances which give the buyer reason to know that the person selling does not claim title in himself or that he is purporting to sell only such right or title as he or a third person may have.

(3) Unless otherwise agreed a seller who is a merchant regularly dealing in goods of the kind warrants that the goods shall be delivered free of the rightful claim of any third person by way of infringement or the like but a buyer who furnishes specifications to the seller must hold the seller harmless against any such claim which arises out of compliance with the specifications.

§2-313. Express Warranties by Affirmation, Promise, Description, Sample.

(1) Express warranties by the seller are created as follows:

(a) Any affirmation of fact or promise made by the seller to the buyer which relates to the goods and becomes part of the basis of the bargain creates an express warranty that the goods shall conform to the affirmation or promise.

(b) Any description of the goods which is made part of the basis of the bargain creates an express warranty that the goods shall conform to the description.

(c) Any sample or model which is made part of the basis of the bargain creates an express warranty that the whole of the goods shall conform to the sample or model.

(2) It is not necessary to the creation of an express warranty that the seller use formal words such as "warrant" or "guarantee" or that he have a specific intention to make a warranty, but an affirmation merely of the value of the goods or a statement purporting to be merely the seller's opinion or commendation of the goods does not create a warranty.

§2-314. Implied Warranty: Merchantability; Usage of Trade.

(1) Unless excluded or modified (Section 2-316), a warranty that the goods shall be merchantable is implied in a contract for their sale if the seller is a merchant with respect to goods of that kind. Under this section the serving for value of food or drink to be consumed either on the premises or elsewhere is a sale.

(2) Goods to be merchantable must be at least such as

(a) pass without objection in the trade under the contract description; and

(b) in the case of fungible goods, are of fair average quality within the description; and

(c) are fit for the ordinary purposes for which such goods are used; and

(d) run, within the variations permitted by the agreement, of even kind, quality and quantity within each unit and among all units involved; and

(e) are adequately contained, packaged, and labeled as the agreement may require; and

(f) conform to the promises or affirmations of fact made or the container or label if any.

(3) Unless excluded or modified (Section 2-316) other implied warranties may arise from course of dealing or usage of trade.

§2-315. Implied Warranty: Fitness for Particular Purpose.

Where the seller at the time of contracting has reason to know any particular purpose for which the goods are required and that the buyer is relying on the seller's skill or judgment to select or furnish suitable goods, there is unless excluded or modified under the next section an implied warranty that the goods shall be fit for such purpose.

§2-316. Exclusion or Modification of Warranties.

(1) Words or conduct relevant to the creation of an express warranty and words or conduct tending to negate or limit warranty shall be construed wherever reasonable as consistent with each other; but subject to the provisions of this Article on parol or extrinsic evidence (Section 2-202) negation or limitation is inoperative to the extent that such construction is unreasonable.

(2) Subject to subsection (3), to exclude or modify the implied warranty of merchantability or any part of it the language must mention merchantability and in case of a writing must be conspicuous, and to exclude or modify any implied warranty of fitness the exclusion must be by a writing and conspicuous. Language to exclude all implied warranties of fitness is sufficient if it states, for example, that "There are no warranties which extend beyond the description on the face hereof."

(3) Notwithstanding subsection (2)

(a) unless the circumstances indicate otherwise, all implied warranties are excluded by expressions like "as is", "with all faults" or other language which in common understanding calls the buyer's attention to the exclusion of warranties and makes plain that there is no implied warranty; and

(b) when the buyer before entering into the contract has examined the goods or the sample or model as fully as he desired or has refused to examine the goods there is no implied warranty with regard to defects which an examination ought in the circumstances to have revealed to him; and

(c) an implied warranty can also be excluded or modified by course of dealing or course of performance or usage of trade.

(4) Remedies for breach of warranty can be limited in accordance with the provisions of this Article on liquidation or limitation of damages and on contractual modification of remedy (Sections 2-718 and 2-719).

§2-317. Cumulation and Conflict of Warranties Express or Implied. Warranties whether express or implied shall be construed as consistent with each other and as cumulative but if such construction is unreasonable the intention of the parties shall determine which warranty is dominant. In ascertaining that intention the following rules apply:

(a) Exact or technical specifications displace an inconsistent sample or model or general language of description.

(b) A sample from an existing bulk displaces inconsistent general language of description.

(c) Express warranties displace inconsistent implied warranties other than an implied warranty of fitness for a particular purpose.

§2-318. Third Party Beneficiaries of Warranties Express or Implied.

Note: *If this Act is introduced in the Congress of the United States this section should be omitted. (States to select one alternative.)*

Alternative A—A seller's warranty whether express or implied extends to any natural person who is in the family or household of his buyer or who is a guest in his home if it is reasonable to expect that such person may use, consume or be affected by the goods and who is injured in person by breach of the warranty. A seller may not exclude or limit the operation of this section.

Alternative B—A seller's warranty whether express or implied extends to any natural person who may reasonably be expected to use, consume or be affected by the goods and who is injured in person by breach of the warranty. A seller may not exclude or limit the operation of this section.

Alternative C—A seller's warranty whether express or implied extends to any person who may reasonably be expected to use, consume or be affected by the goods and who is injured by breach of the warranty. A seller may not exclude or limit the operation of this section with respect to injury to the person of an individual to whom the warranty extends. As amended 1966.

§2-319. F.O.B. and F.A.S. Terms.

(1) Unless otherwise agreed the term F.O.B. (which means "free on board") at a named place, even though used only in connection with the stated price, is a delivery term under which

(a) when the term is F.O.B. the place of shipment, the seller must at that place ship the goods in the manner provided in this Article (Section 2-504) and bear the expense and risk of putting them into the possession of the carrier; or

(b) when the term is F.O.B. the place of destination, the seller must at his own expense and risk transport the goods to that place and there tender delivery of them in the manner provided in this Article (Section 2-503);

(c) when under either (a) or (b) the term is also F.O.B. vessel, car or other vehicle, the seller must in addition at his own expense and risk load the goods on board. If the term is F.O.B. vessel the buyer must name the vessel and in an appropriate case the seller must comply with the provisions of this Article on the form of bill of lading (Section 2-323).

(2) Unless otherwise agreed the term F.A.S. vessel (which means "free alongside") at a named port, even though used only in connection with the stated price, is a delivery term under which the seller must

(a) at his own expense and risk deliver the goods alongside the vessel in the manner usual in that port or on a dock designated and provided by the buyer; and

(b) obtain and tender a receipt for the goods in exchange for which the carrier is under a duty to issue a bill of lading.

(3) Unless otherwise agreed in any case falling

within subsection (1) (a) or (c) or subsection (2) the buyer must seasonably give any needed instructions for making delivery, including when the term is F.A.S. or F.O.B. the loading berth of the vessel and in an appropriate case its name and sailing date. The seller may treat the failure of needed instructions as a failure of cooperation under this Article (Section 2-311). He may also at his option move the goods in any reasonable manner preparatory to delivery or shipment.

(4) Under the term F.O.B. vessel or F.A.S. unless otherwise agreed the buyer must make payment against tender of the required documents and the seller may not tender nor the buyer demand delivery of the goods in substitution for the documents.

§2-320. C.I.F. and C.&F. Terms.

(1) The term C.I.F. means that the price includes in a lump sum the cost of the goods and the insurance and freight to the named destination. The term C.&F. or C.F. means that the price so includes cost and freight to the named destination.

(2) Unless otherwise agreed and even though used only in connection wtih the stated price and destination, the term C.I.F. destination or its equivalent requires the seller at his own expense and risk to

 (a) put the goods into the possession of a carrier at the port for shipment and obtain a negotiable bill or bills of lading covering the entire transportation to the named destination; and

 (b) load the goods and obtain a receipt from the carrier (which may be contained in the bill of lading) showing that the freight has been paid or provided for; and

 (c) obtain a policy or certificate of insurance, including any war risk insurance, of a kind and on terms then current at the port of shipment in the usual amount, in the currency of the contract, shown to cover the same goods covered by the bill of lading and providing for payment of loss to the order of the buyer or for the account of whom it may concern; but the seller may add to the price the amount of the premium for any such war risk insurance; and

 (d) prepare an invoice of the goods and procure any other documents required to effect shipment or to comply with the contract; and

 (e) forward and tender with commercial promptness all the documents in due form and with any indorsement necessary to perfect the buyer's rights.

(3) Unless otherwise agreed the term C.&F. or its equivalent has the same effect and imposes upon the seller the same obligations and risks as a C.I.F. term except the obligation as to insurance.

(4) Under the term C.I.F. or C.&F. unless otherwise agreed the buyer must make payment against tender of the required documents and the seller may not tender nor the buyer demand delivery of the goods in substitution for the documents.

§2-321. C.I.F. or C.&F.: "Net Landed Weights"; "Payment on Arrival"; Warranty of Condition on Arrival. Under a contract containing a term C.I.F. or C.&F.

(1) Where the price is based on or is to be adjusted according to "net landed weights", "delivered weights", "out turn" quantity or quality or the like, unless otherwise agreed the seller must reasonably estimate the price. The payment due on tender of the documents called for by the contract is the amount so estimated, but after final adjustment of the price a settlement must be made with commercial promptness.

(2) An agreement described in subsection (1) or any warranty of quality or condition of the goods on arrival places upon the seller the risk of ordinary deterioration, shrinkage and the like in transportation but has no effect on the place or time of identification to the contract for sale or delivery or on the passing of the risk of loss.

(3) Unless otherwise agreed where the contract provides for payment on or after arrival of the goods the seller must before payment allow such preliminary inspection as is feasible; but if the goods are lost delivery of the documents and payment are due when the goods should have arrived.

§2-322. Delivery "Ex-Ship".

(1) Unless otherwise agreed a term for delivery of goods "ex-ship" (which means from the carrying vessel) or in equivalent language is not restricted to a particular ship and requires delivery from a ship which has reached a place at the named port of destination where goods of the kind are usually discharged.

(2) Under such a term unless otherwise agreed

 (a) the seller must discharge all liens arising out of the carriage and furnish the buyer with a direction which puts the carrier under a duty to deliver the goods; and

 (b) the risk of loss does not pass to the buyer until the goods leave the ship's tackle or are otherwise properly unloaded.

§2-323. Form of Bill of Lading Required in Overseas Shipment; "Overseas".

(1) Where the contract contemplates overseas shipment and contains a term C.I.F. or C.&F. or F.O.B. vessel the seller unless otherwise agreed must obtain a negotiable bill of lading stating that the goods have been loaded on board or, in the case of a term C.I.F. or C.&F., received for shipment.

(2) Where in a case within subsection (1) a bill of lading has been issued in a set of parts, unless otherwise agreed if the documents are not to be sent from abroad the buyer may demand tender of the full set; otherwise only one part of the bill of lading need be tendered. Even if the agreement expressly requires a full set

(a) due tender of a single part is acceptable within the provisions of this Article on cure of improper delivery (subsection (1) of Section 2-508); and

(b) even though the full set is demanded, if the documents are sent from abroad the person tendering an incomplete set may nevertheless require payment upon furnishing an indemnity which the buyer in good faith deems adequate.

(3) A shipment by water or by air on a contract contemplating such shipment is "overseas" insofar as by usage of trade or agreement it is subject to the commercial, financing or shipping practices characteristic of international deep water commerce.

§2-324. "No Arrival, No Sale" Term. Under a term "no arrival, no sale" or terms of like meaning, unless otherwise agreed,

(a) the seller must properly ship conforming goods and if they arrive by any means he must tender them on arrival but he assumes no obligation that the goods will arrive unless he has caused the nonarrival; and

(b) where without fault of the seller the goods are in part lost or have so deteriorated as no longer to conform to the contract or arrive after the contract time, the buyer may proceed as if there had been casualty to identified goods (Section 2-613).

§2-325. "Letter of Credit" Term; "Confirmed Credit".

(1) Failure of the buyer seasonably to furnish an agreed letter of credit is a breach of the contract for sale.

(2) The delivery to seller of a proper letter of credit suspends the buyer's obligation to pay. If the letter of credit is dishonored, the seller may on seasonable notification to the buyer require payment directly from him.

(3) Unless otherwise agreed the term "letter of credit" or "banker's credit" in a contract for sale means an irrevocable credit issued by a financing agency of good repute and, where the shipment is overseas, of good international repute. The term "confirmed credit" means that the credit must also carry the direct obligation of such an agency which does business in the seller's financial market.

§2-326. Sale on Approval and Sale or Return; Consignment Sales and Rights of Creditors.

(1) Unless otherwise agreed, if delivered goods may be returned by the buyer even though they conform to the contract, the transaction is

(a) a "sale on approval" if the goods are delivered primarily for use, and

(b) a "sale or return" if the goods are delivered primarily for resale.

(2) Except as provided in subsection (3), goods held on approval are not subject to the claims of the buyer's creditors until acceptance; goods held on sale or return are subject to such claims while in the buyer's possession.

(3) Where goods are delivered to a person for sale and such person maintains a place of business at which he deals in goods of the kind involved, under a name other than the name of the person making delivery, then with respect to claims of creditors of the person conducting the business the goods are deemed to be on sale or return. The provisions of this subsection are applicable even though an agreement purports to reserve title to the person making delivery until payment or resale or uses such words as "on consignment" or "on memorandum". However, this subsection is not applicable if the person making delivery

(a) complies with an applicable law providing for a consignor's interest or the like to be evidenced by a sign, or

(b) establishes that the person conducting the business is generally known by his creditors to be substantially engaged in selling the goods of others, or

(c) complies with the filing provisions of the Article on Secured Transactions (Article 9).

(4) Any "or return" term of a contract for sale is to be treated as a separate contract for sale within the statute of frauds section of this Article (Section 2-201) and as contradicting the sale aspect of the con-

tract within the provisions of this Article on parol or extrinsic evidence (Section 2-202).

§2-327. Special Incidents of Sale on Approval and Sale or Return.

(1) Under a sale on approval unless otherwise agreed

(a) although the goods are identified to the contract the risk of loss and the title do not pass to the buyer until acceptance; and

(b) use of the goods consistent with the purpose of trial is not acceptance but failure seasonably to notify the seller of election to return the goods is acceptance, and if the goods conform to the contract acceptance of any part is acceptance of the whole; and

(c) after due notification of election to return, the return is at the seller's risk and expense but a merchant buyer must follow any reasonable instructions.

(2) Under a sale or return unless otherwise agreed

(a) the option to return extends to the whole or any commercial unit of the goods while in substantially their original condition, but must be exercised seasonably; and

(b) the return is at the buyer's risk and expense.

§2-328. Sale by Auction.

(1) In a sale by auction if goods are put up in lots each lot is the subject of a separate sale.

(2) A sale by auction is complete when the auctioneer so announces by the fall of the hammer or in other customary manner. Where a bid is made while the hammer is falling in acceptance of a prior bid the auctioneer may in his discretion reopen the bidding or declare the goods sold under the bid on which the hammer was falling.

(3) Such a sale is with reserve unless the goods are in explicit terms put up without reserve. In an auction with reserve, the auctioneer may withdraw the goods at any time until he announces completion of the sale. In an auction without reserve, after the auctioneer calls for bids on an article or lot, that article or lot cannot be withdrawn unless no bid is made within a reasonable time. In either case a bidder may retract his bid until the auctioneer's announcement of completion of the sale, but a bidder's retraction does not revive any previous bid.

(4) If the auctioneer knowingly receives a bid on the seller's behalf or the seller makes or procures such a bid, and notice has not been given that liberty for such bidding is reserved, the buyer may at his option avoid the sale or take the goods at the price of the last good faith bid prior to the completion of the sale. This subsection shall not apply to any bid at a forced sale.

Part 4: Title, Creditors and Good Faith Purchasers

§2-401. Passing of Title; Reservation for Security; Limited Application of This Section.   Each provision of this Article with regard to the rights, obligations and remedies of the seller, the buyer, purchasers or other third parties applies irrespective of title to the goods except where the provision refers to such title. Insofar as situations are not covered by the other provisions of this Article and matters concerning title become material the following rules apply:

(1) Title to goods cannot pass under a contract for sale prior to their identification to the contract (Section 2-501), and unless otherwise explicitly agreed the buyer acquires by their identification a special property as limited by this Act. Any retention or reservation by the seller of the title (property) in goods shipped or delivered to the buyer is limited in effect to a reservation of a security interest. Subject to these provisions and to the provisions of the Article on Secured Transactions (Article 9), title to goods passes from the seller to the buyer in any manner and on any conditions explicitly agreed on by the parties.

(2) Unless otherwise explicitly agreed title passes to the buyer at the time and place at which the seller completes his performances with reference to the physical delivery of the goods, despite any reservation of a security interest and even though a document of title is to be delivered at a different time or place; and in particular and despite any reservation of a security interest by the bill of lading

(a) if the contract requires or authorizes the seller to send the goods to the buyer but does not require him to deliver them at destination, title passes to the buyer at the time and place of shipment; but

(b) if the contract requires delivery at destination, title passes on tender there.

(3) Unless otherwise explicitly agreed where delivery is to be made without moving the goods.

(a) if the seller is to deliver a document of title, title passes at the time when and the place where he delivers such documents; or

(b) if the goods are at the time of contracting

already identified and no documents are to be delivered, title passes at the time and place of contracting.

(4) A rejection or other refusal by the buyer to receive or retain the goods, whether or not justified, or a justified revocation of acceptance revests title to the goods in the seller. Such revesting occurs by operation of law and is not a "sale".

§2-402. Rights of Seller's Creditors Against Sold Goods.

(1) Except as provided in subsections (2) and (3), rights of unsecured creditors of the seller with respect to goods which have been identified to a contract for sale are subject to the buyer's rights to recover the goods under this Article (Section 2-502 and 2-716).

(2) A creditor of the seller may treat a sale or an identification of goods to a contract for sale as void if as against him a retention of possession by the seller is fraudulent under any rule of law of the state where the goods are situated, except that retention of possession in good faith and current course of trade by a merchant-seller for a commercially reasonable time after a sale or identification is not fraudulent.

(3) Nothing in this Article shall be deemed to impair the rights of creditors of the seller

    (a) under the provisions of the Article on Secured Transactions (Article 9); or

    (b) where identification to the contract or delivery is made not in current course of trade but in satisfaction of or as security for a pre-existing claim for money, security or the like and is made under circumstances which under any rule of law of the state where the goods are situated would apart from this Article constitute the transaction a fraudulent transfer or voidable preference.

§2-403. Power to Transfer; Good Faith Purchase of Goods; "Entrusting".

(1) A purchaser of goods acquires all title which his transferor had or had power to transfer except that a purchaser of a limited interest acquires rights only to the extent of the interest purchased. A person with voidable title has power to transfer a good title to a good faith purchaser for value. When goods have been delivered under a transaction of purchase the purchaser had such power even though

    (a) the transferor was deceived as to the identity of the purchaser, or

    (b) the delivery was in exchange for a check which is later dishonored, or

    (c) it was agreed that the transaction was to be a "cash sale", or

    (d) the delivery was procured through fraud punishable as larcenous under the criminal law.

(2) Any entrusting of possession of goods to a merchant who deals in goods of that kind gives him power to transfer all rights of the entruster to a buyer in ordinary course of business.

(3) "Entrusting" includes any delivery and any acquiescence in retention of possession regardless of any condition expressed between the parties to the delivery or acquiescence and regardless of whether the procurement of the entrusting or the possessor's disposition of the goods have been such as to be larcenous under the criminal law.

(4) The rights of other purchasers of goods and of lien creditors are governed by the Articles on Secured Transactions (Article 9), Bulk Transfers (Article 6) and Documents of Title (Article 7).

Part 5: Performance

§2-501. Insurable Interest in Goods; Manner of Identification of Goods.

(1) The buyer obtains a special property and an insurable interest in goods by identification of existing goods as goods to which the contract refers even though the goods so identified are non-conforming and he has an option to return or reject them. Such identification can be made at any time and in any manner explicitly agreed to by the parties. In the absence of explicit agreement identification occurs

    (a) when the contract is made if it is for the sale of goods already existing and identified;

    (b) if the contract is for the sale of future goods other than those described in paragraph (c), when goods are shipped, marked or otherwise designated by the seller as goods to which the contract refers;

    (c) when the crops are planted or otherwise become growing crops or the young are conceived if the contract is for the sale of unborn young to be born within twelves months after contracting or for the sale of crops to be harvested within twelve months or the next normal harvest season after contracting whichever is longer.

(2) The seller retains an insurable interest in goods so long as title to or any security interest in the goods remains in him and where the identification is by the seller alone he may until default or insolvency or notification to the buyer that the identification is final substitute other goods for those identified.

(3) Nothing in this section impairs any insurable interest recognized under any other statute or rule of law.

§2-502. Buyer's Right to Goods on Seller's Insolvency.

(1) Subject to subsection (2) and even though the goods have not been shipped a buyer who has paid a part or all of the price of goods in which he has a special property under the provisions of the immediately preceding section may on making and keeping good a tender of any unpaid portion of their price recover them from the seller if the seller becomes insolvent within ten days after receipt of the first installment on their price.

(2) If the identification creating his special property has been made by the buyer he acquires the right to recover the goods only if they conform to the contract for sale.

§2-503. Manner of Seller's Tender of Delivery.

(1) Tender of delivery requires that the seller put and hold conforming goods at the buyer's disposition and give the buyer any notification reasonably necessary to enable him to take delivery. The manner, time and place for tender are determined by the agreement and this Article, and in particular

    (a) tender must be at a reasonable hour, and if it is of goods they must be kept available for the period reasonably necessary to enable the buyer to take possession; but

    (b) unless otherwise agreed the buyer must furnish facilities reasonably suited to the receipt of the goods.

(2) Where the case is within the next section respecting shipment tender requires that the seller comply with its provisions.

(3) Where the seller is required to deliver at a particular destination tender requires that he comply with subsection (1) and also in any appropriate case tender documents as described in subsections (4) and (5) of this section.

(4) Where goods are in the possession of a bailee and are to be delivered without being moved

    (a) tender requires that the seller either tender a negotiable document of title covering such goods or procure acknowledgement by the bailee of the buyer's right to possession of the goods; but

    (b) tender to the buyer of a non-negotiable document of title or of a written direction to the bailee to deliver is sufficient tender unless the buyer seasonably objects, and receipt by the bailee of notification of the buyer's rights fixes those rights as against the bailee and all third persons; but risk of loss of the goods and of any failure by the bailee to honor the non-negotiable document of title or to obey the direction remains on the seller until the buyer has had a reasonable time to present the document or direction, and a refusal by the bailee to honor the document or to obey the direction defeats the tender.

(5) Where the contract requires the seller to deliver documents

    (a) he must tender all such documents in correct form, except as provided in this Article with respect to bills of lading in a set (subsection (2) of Section 2-323); and

    (b) tender through customary banking channels is sufficient and dishonor of a draft accompanying the documents constitutes non-acceptance or rejection.

§2-504. Shipment by Seller.

Where the seller is required or authorized to send the goods to the buyer and the contract does not require him to deliver them at a particular destination, then unless otherwise agreed he must

    (a) put the goods in the possession of such a carrier and make such a contract for their transportation as may be reasonable having regard to the nature of the goods and other circumstances of the case; and

    (b) obtain and promptly deliver or tender in due form any document necessary to enable the buyer to obtain possession of the goods or otherwise required by the agreement or by usage of trade; and

    (c) promptly notify the buyer of the shipment.

Failure to notify the buyer under paragraph (c) or to make a proper contract under paragraph (a) is a ground for rejection only if material delay or loss ensues.

§2-505. Seller's Shipment under Reservation.

(1) Where the seller has identified goods to the contract by or before shipment:

    (a) his procurement of a negotiable bill of lading to his own order or otherwise reserves in him a security interest in the goods. His procurement of the bill to the order of a financing agency or of the buyer indicates in addition only the seller's expectation of transferring that interest to the person named.

(b) a non-negotiable bill of lading to himself or his nominee reserves possession of the goods as security but except in a case of conditional delivery (subsection (2) of Section 2-507) a non-negotiable bill of lading naming the buyer as consignee reserves no security interest even though the seller retains possession of the bill of lading.

(2) When shipment by the seller with reservation of a security interest is in violation of the contract for sale it constitutes an improper contract for transportation within the preceding section but impairs neither the rights given to the buyer by shipment and identification of the goods, to the contract nor the seller's powers as a holder of a negotiable document.

§2-506. Rights of Financing Agency.

(1) A financing agency by paying or purchasing for value a draft which relates to a shipment of goods acquires to the extent of the payment or purchase and in addition to its own rights under the draft and any document of title securing it any rights of the shipper in the goods including the right to stop delivery and the shipper's right to have the draft honored by the buyer.

(2) The right to reimbursement of a financing agency which has in good faith honored or purchased the draft under commitment to or authority from the buyer is not impaired by subsequent discovery of defects with reference to any relevant document which was apparently regular on its face.

§2-507. Effect of Seller's Tender; Delivery on Condition.

(1) Tender of delivery is a condition to the buyer's duty to accept the goods and, unless otherwise agreed, to his duty to pay for them. Tender entitles the seller to acceptance of the goods and to payment according to the contract.

(2) Where payment is due and demanded on the delivery to the buyer of goods or documents of title, his right as against the seller to retain or dispose of them is conditional upon his making the payment due.

§2-508. Cure by Seller of Improper Tender or Delivery; Replacement.

(1) Where any tender or delivery by the seller is rejected because non-conforming and the time for performance has not yet expired, the seller may seasonably notify the buyer of his intention to cure and may then within the contract time make a conforming delivery.

(2) Where the buyer rejects a non-conforming tender which the seller had reasonable grounds to believe would be acceptable with or without money allowance the seller may if he seasonably notifies the buyer have a further reasonable time to substitute a conforming tender.

§2-509. Risk of Loss in the Absence of Breach.

(1) Where the contract requires or authorizes the seller to ship the goods by carrier

(a) if it does not require him to deliver them at a particular destination, the risk of loss passes to the buyer when the goods are duly delivered to the carrier even though the shipment is under reservation (Section 2-505); but

(b) if it does require him to deliver them at a particular destination and the goods are there duly tendered while in the possession of the carrier, the risk of loss passes to the buyer when the goods are there duly so tendered as to enable the buyer to take delivery.

(2) Where the goods are held by a bailee to be delivered without being moved, the risk of loss passes to the buyer

(a) on his receipt of a negotiable document of title covering the goods; or

(b) on acknowledgement by the bailee of the buyer's right to possession of the goods; or

(c) after his receipt of a non-negotiable document of title or other written direction to deliver as provided in subsection (4) (b) of Section 2-503.

(3) In any case not within subsection (1) or (2), the risk of loss passes to the buyer on his receipt of the goods if the seller is a merchant; otherwise the risk passes to the buyer on tender of delivery.

(4) The provisions of this section are subject to contrary agreement of the parties and to the provisions of this Article on sale on approval (Section 2-327) and on effect of breach on risk of loss (Section 2-510).

§2-510. Effect of Breach on Risk of Loss.

(1) Where a tender or delivery of goods so fails to conform to the contract as to give a right of rejection the risk of their loss remains on the seller until cure or acceptance.

(2) Where the buyer rightfully revokes acceptance he may to the extent of any deficiency in his effective insurance coverage treat the risk of loss as having rested on the seller from the beginning.

(3) Where the buyer as to conforming goods already identified to the contract for sale repudiates or is otherwise in breach before risk of their loss has passed to him, the seller may to the extent of any deficiency in his effective insurance coverage treat the risk of loss as resting on the buyer for a commercially reasonable time.

§2-511. Tender of Payment by Buyer; Payment by Check.

(1) Unless otherwise agreed tender of payment is a condition to the seller's duty to tender and complete any delivery.

(2) Tender of payment is sufficient when made by any means or in any manner current in the ordinary course of business unless the seller demands payment in legal tender and gives any extension of time reasonably necessary to procure it.

(3) Subject to the provisions of this Act on the effect of an instrument of an obligation (Section 3-802), payment by check is conditional and is defeated as between the parties by dishonor of the check on due presentment.

§2-512. Payment by Buyer Before Inspection.

(1) Where the contract requires payment before inspection non-conformity of the goods does not excuse the buyer from so making payment unless

(a) the non-conformity appears without inspection; or

(b) despite tender of the required documents the circumstances would justify injunction against honor under the provisions of this Act (Section 5-114).

(2) Payment pursuant to subsection (1) does not constitute an acceptance of goods or impair the buyer's right to inspect or any of his remedies.

§2-513. Buyer's Right to Inspection of Goods.

(1) Unless otherwise agreed and subject to subsection (3), where goods are tendered or delivered or identified to the contract for sale, the buyer has a right before payment or acceptance to inspect them at any reasonable place and time and in any reasonable manner. When the seller is required or authorized to send the goods to the buyer, the inspection may be after their arrival.

(2) Expenses of inspection must be borne by the buyer but may be recovered from the seller if the goods do not conform and are rejected.

(3) Unless otherwise agreed and subject to the provisions of this Article on C.I.F. contracts (subsection (3) of Section 3-221), the buyer is not entitled to inspect the goods before payment of the price when the contract provides

(a) for delivery "C.O.D." or on other like terms; or

(b) for payment against documents of title, except where such payment is due only after the goods are to become available for inspection.

(4) A place or method of inspection fixed by the parties is presumed to be exclusive but unless otherwise expressly agreed it does not postpone identification or shift the place for delivery or for passing the risk of loss. If compliance becomes impossible, inspection shall be as provided in this section unless the place or method fixed was clearly intended as an indispensable condition failure of which avoids the contract.

§2-514. When Documents Deliverable on Acceptance; When on Payment. Unless otherwise agreed documents against which a draft is drawn are to be delivered to the drawee on acceptance of the draft if it is payable more than three days after presentment; otherwise, only on payment.

§2-515. Preserving Evidence of Goods in Dispute. In furtherance of the adjustment of any claim or dispute

(a) either party on reasonable notification to the other and for the purpose of ascertaining the facts and preserving evidence has the right to inspect, test and sample the goods including such of them as may be in the possession or control of the other; and

(b) the parties may agree to a third party inspection or survey to determine the conformity or condition of the goods and may agree that the findings shall be binding upon them in any subsequent litigation or adjustment.

Part 6: Breach, Repudiation and Excuse

§2-601. Buyer's Rights on Improper Delivery. Subject to the provisions of this Article on breach in installment contracts (Section 2-612) and unless otherwise agreed under the sections on contractual limitations of remedy (Sections 2-718 and 2-719), if the goods or the tender of delivery fail in any respect to conform to the contract, the buyer may

(a) reject the whole; or

(b) accept the whole; or

(c) accept any commercial unit or units and reject the rest.

§2-602. Manner and Effect of Rightful Rejection.

(1) Rejection of goods must be within a reasonable time after their delivery or tender. It is ineffective unless the buyer seasonably notifies the seller.

(2) Subject to the provisions of the two following sections on rejected goods (Section 2-603 and 2-604).

    (a) after rejection any exercise of ownership by the buyer with respect to any commercial unit is wrongful as against the seller; and

    (b) if the buyer has before rejection taken physical possession of goods in which he does not have a security interest under the provisions of this Article (subsection (3) of Section 2-711), he is under a duty after rejection to hold them with reasonable care at the seller's disposition for a time sufficient to permit the seller to remove them; but

    (c) the buyer has no further obligations with regard to goods rightfully rejected.

(3) The seller's rights with respect to goods wrongfully rejected are governed by the provisions of this Article on Seller's remedies in general (Section 2-703).

§2-603. Merchant Buyer's Duties as to Rightfully Rejected Goods.

(1) Subject to any security interest in the buyer (subsection (3) of Section 2-711), when the seller has no agent or place of business at the market of rejection a merchant buyer is under a duty after rejection of goods in his possession or control to follow any reasonable instructions received from the seller with respect to the goods and in the absence of such instructions to make reasonable efforts to sell them for the seller's account if they are perishable or threaten to decline in value speedily. Instructions are not reasonable if on demand indemnity for expenses is not forthcoming.

(2) When the buyer sells goods under subsection (1), he is entitled to reimbursement from the seller or out of the proceeds for reasonable expenses of caring for and selling them, and if the expenses include no selling commission then to such commission as is usual in the trade or if there is none to a reasonable sum not exceeding ten per cent on the gross proceeds.

(3) In complying with this section the buyer is held only to good faith and good faith conduct hereunder is neither acceptance nor conversion nor the basis of an action for damages.

§2-604. Buyer's Options as to Salvage of Rightfully Rejected Goods. Subject to the provisions of the immediately preceding section on perishables if the seller gives no instructions within a reasonable time after notification of rejection the buyer may store the rejected goods for the seller's account or reship them to him or resell them for the seller's account with reimbursement as provided in the preceding section. Such action is not acceptance or conversion.

§2-605. Waiver of Buyer's Objections by Failure to Particularize.

(1) The buyer's failure to state in connection with rejection a particular defect which is ascertainable by reasonable inspection precludes him from relying on the unstated defect to justify rejection or to establish breach

    (a) where the seller could have cured it if stated seasonably; or

    (b) between merchants when the seller has after rejection made a request in writing for a full and final written statement of all defects on which the buyer proposes to rely.

(2) Payment against documents made without reservation of rights precludes recovery of the payment for defects apparent on the face of the documents.

§2-606. What Constitutes Acceptance of Goods.

(1) Acceptance of goods occurs when the buyer

    (a) after a reasonable opportunity to inspect the goods signifies to the seller that the goods are conforming or that he will take or retain them in spite of their nonconformity; or

    (b) fails to make an effective rejection (subsection (1) of Section 2-602), but such acceptance does not occur until the buyer has had a reasonable opportunity to inspect them; or

    (c) does any act inconsistent with the seller's ownership; but if such act is wrongful as against the seller it is an acceptance only if ratified by him.

(2) Acceptance of a part of any commercial unit is acceptance of that entire unit.

§2-607. Effect of Acceptance; Notice of Breach; Burden of Establishing Breach After Acceptance; Notice of Claim or Litigation to Person Answerable Over.

(1) The buyer must pay at the contract rate for any goods accepted.

(2) Acceptance of goods by the buyer precludes rejection of the goods accepted and if made with knowledge of a nonconformity cannot be revoked because of

it unless the acceptance was on the reasonable assumption that the non-conformity would be seasonably cured but acceptance does not of itself impair any other remedy provided by this Article for non-conformity.

(3) Where a tender has been accepted

(a) the buyer must within a reasonable time after he discovers or should have discovered any breach notify the seller of breach or be barred from any remedy; and

(b) if the claim is one for infringement or the like (subsection (3) of Section 2-312) and the buyer is sued as a result of such a breach he must so notify the seller within a reasonable time after he receives notice of the litigation or be barred from any remedy over for liability established by the litigation.

(4) The burden is on the buyer to establish any breach with respect to the goods accepted.

(5) Where the buyer is sued for breach of a warranty or other obligation for which his seller is answerable over

(a) he may give his seller written notice of the litigation. If the notice states that the seller may come in and defend and that if the seller does not do so he will be bound in any action against him by his buyer by any determination of fact common to the two litigations, then unless the seller after seasonable receipt of the notice does come in and defend he is so bound.

(b) if the claim is one for infringement or the like (subsection (3) of Section 2-312) the original seller may demand in writing that his buyer turn over to him control of the litigation including settlement or else be barred from any remedy over and if he also agrees to bear all expense and to satisfy any adverse judgment, then unless the buyer after seasonable receipt of the demand does turn over control the buyer is so barred.

(6) The provisions of subsection (3), (4) and (5) apply to any obligation of a buyer to hold the seller harmless against infringement or the like (subsection (3) of Section 2-312).

§2-608. Revocation of Acceptance in Whole or in Part.

(1) The buyer may revoke his acceptance of a lot or commercial unit whose non-conformity substantially impairs its value to him if he has accepted it

(a) on the reasonable assumption that its non-

conformity would be cured and it has not been seasonably cured; or

(b) without discovery of such non-conformity if his acceptance was reasonably induced either by the difficulty of discovery before acceptance or by the seller's assurances.

(2) Revocation of acceptance must occur within a reasonable time after the buyer discovers or should have discovered the ground for it and before any substantial change in condition of the goods which is not caused by their own defects. It is not effective until the buyer notifies the seller of it.

(3) A buyer who so revokes has the same rights and duties with regard to the goods involved as if he had rejected them.

§2-609. Right to Adequate Assurance of Performance.

(1) A contract for sale imposes an obligation on each party that the other's expectation of receiving due performance will not be impaired. When reasonable grounds for insecurity arise with respect to the performance of either party the other may in writing demand adequate assurance of due performance and until he receives such assurance may if commercially reasonable suspend any performance for which he has not already received the agreed return.

(2) Between merchants the reasonableness of grounds for insecurity and the adequacy of any assurance offered shall be determined according to commercial standards.

(3) Acceptance of any improper delivery or payment does not prejudice the aggrieved party's right to demand adequate assurance of future performance.

(4) After receipt of a justified demand failure to provide within a reasonable time not exceeding thirty days such assurance of due performance as is adequate under the circumstances of the particular case is a repudiation of the contract.

§2-610. Anticipatory Repudiation. When either party repudiates the contract with respect to a performance not yet due the loss of which will substantially impair the value of the contract to the other, the aggrieved party may

(a) for a commercially reasonable time await performance by the repudiating party; or

(b) resort to any remedy for breach (Section 2-703 or Section 2-711), even though he has notified the repudiating party that he would await the latter's performance and has urged retraction; and

(c) in either case suspend his own performance or proceed in accordance with the provisions of this Article on the seller's right to identify goods to the contract notwithstanding breach or to salvage unfinished goods (Section 2704).

§2-611. **Retraction of Anticipatory Repudiation.**

(1) Until the repudiating party's next performance is due he can retract his repudiation unless the aggrieved party has since the repudiation cancelled or materially changed his position or otherwise indicated that he considers the repudiation final.

(2) Retraction may be by any method which clearly indicates to the aggrieved party that the repudiating party intends to perform, but must include any assurance justifiably demanded under the provisions of this Article (Section 2-609).

(3) Retraction reinstates the repudiating party's rights under the contract with due excuse and allowance to the aggrieved party for any delay occasioned by the repudiation.

§2-612. **"Installment Contract"; Breach.**

(1) An "installment contract" is one which requires or authorizes the delivery of goods in separate lots to be separately accepted, even though the contract contains a clause "each delivery is a separate contract" or its equivalent.

(2) The buyer may reject any installment which is nonconforming if the non-conformity substantially impairs the value of that installment and cannot be cured or if the non-conformity is a defect in the required documents, but if the non-conformity does not fall within subsection (3) and the seller gives adequate assurance of its cure the buyer must accept that installment.

(3) Whenever non-conformity or default with respect to one or more installments substantially impairs the value of the whole contract there is a breach of the whole. But the aggrieved party reinstates the contract if he accepts a non-conforming installment without seasonably notifying of cancellation or if he brings an action with respect only to past installments or demands performance as to future installments.

§2-613. **Casualty to Identified Goods.** Where the contract requires for its performance goods identified when the contract is made, and the goods suffer casualty without fault of either party before the risk of loss passes to the buyer, or in a proper case under a "no arrival, no sale" term (Section 2-324) then

(a) if the loss is total the contract is avoided; and

(b) if the loss is partial or the goods have so deteriorated as no longer to conform to the contract the buyer may nevertheless demand inspection and at his option either treat the contract as avoided or accept the goods with due allowance from the contract price for the deterioration or the deficiency in quantity but without further right against the seller.

§2-614. **Substituted Performance.**

(1) Where without fault of either party the agreed berthing, loading, or unloading facilities fail or an agreed type of carrier becomes unavilable or the agreed manner of delivery otherwise becomes commercially impracticable but a commercially reasonable substitute is available, such substitute performance must be tendered and accepted.

(2) If the agreed means or manner of payment fails because of domestic or foreign governmental regulation, the seller may withhold or stop delivery unless the buyer provides a means or manner of payment which is commercially a substantial equivalent. If delivery has already been taken, payment by the means or in the manner provided by the regulation discharges the buyer's obligation unless the regulation is discriminatory, oppressive or predatory.

§2-615. **Excuse by Failure of Presupposed Conditions.** Except so far as a seller may have assumed a greater obligation and subject to the preceding section on substituted performance:

(a) Delay in delivery or non-delivery in whole or in part by a seller who complies with paragraphs (b) and (c) is not a breach of his duty under a contract for sale if performance as agreed has been made impracticable by the occurrence of a contingency the non-occurrence of which was a basic assumption on which the contract was made or by compliance in good faith with any applicable foreign or domestic governmental regulation or order whether or not it later proves to be invalid.

(b) Where the causes mentioned in paragraph (a) affect only a part of the seller's capacity to perform, he must allocate production and deliveries among his customers but may at his option include regular customers not then under contract as well as his own requirements for further manufacture. He may so allocate in any manner which is fair and reasonable.

(c) The seller must notify the buyer seasonably that there will be delay or non-delivery and, when allocation is required under paragraph (b), of the estimated quota thus made available for the buyer.

§2-616. Procedure on Notice Claiming Excuse.

(**1**) When the buyer receives notification of a material or indefinite delay or an allocation justified under the preceding section he may by written notification to the seller as to any delivery concerned, and where the prospective deficiency substantially impairs the value of the whole contract under the provisions of this Article relating to breach of installment contracts (Section 2-612), then also as to the whole,

> (**a**) terminate and thereby discharge any unexecuted portion of the contract; or
>
> (**b**) modify the contract by agreeing to take his available quota in substitution.

(**2**) If after receipt of such notification from the seller the buyer fails so to modify the contract within a reasonable time not exceeding thirty days the contract lapses with respect to any deliveries affected.

(**3**) The provisions of this section may not be negated by agreement except in so far as the seller has assumed a greater obligation under the preceding section.

Part 7: Remedies

§2-701. Remedies for Breach of Collateral Contracts Not Impaired.   Remedies for breach of any obligation or promise collateral or ancillary to a contract for sale are not impaired by the provisions of this Article.

§2-702. Seller's on Discovery of Buyer's Insolvency.

(**1**) Where the seller discovers the buyer to be insolvent he may refuse delivery except for cash including payment for all goods theretofore delivered under the contract, and stop delivery under this Article (Section 2-705).

(**2**) Where the seller discovers that the buyer has received goods on credit while insolvent he may reclaim the goods upon demand made within ten days after the receipt, but if misrepresentation of solvency has been made to the particular seller in writing within three months before delivery the ten day limitation does not apply. Except as provided in this subsection the seller may not base a right to reclaim goods on the buyer's fraudulent or innocent misrepresentation of solvency or of intent to pay.

(**3**) The seller's right to reclaim under subsection (2) is subject to the rights of a buyer in ordinary course or other good faith purchaser under this Article (Section 2-403). Successful reclamation of goods excludes all other remedies with respect to them. As amended 1966.

§2-703. Seller's Remedies in General.   Where the buyer wrongfully rejects or revokes acceptance of goods, or fails to make a payment due on or before delivery or repudiates with respect to a part or the whole, then with respect to any goods directly affected and, if the breach is of the whole contract (Section 2-612), then also with respect to the whole undelivered balance the aggrieved seller may

> (**a**) withhold delivery of such goods;
>
> (**b**) stop delivery by any bailee as hereafter provided (Section 2-705);
>
> (**c**) proceed under the next section respecting goods still unidentified to the contract;
>
> (**d**) resell and recover damages as hereafter provided (Section 2-706);
>
> (**e**) recover damages for non-acceptance (Section 2-708) or in a proper case the price (Section 2-709);
>
> (**f**) cancel.

§2-704. Seller's Right to Identify Goods to the Contract Notwithstanding Breach or to Salvage Unfinished Goods.

(**1**) An aggrieved seller under the preceding section may

> (**a**) identify to the contract conforming goods not already identified if at the time he learned of the breach they are in his possession or control;
>
> (**b**) treat as the subject of resale goods which have demonstrably been intended for the particular contract even though those goods are unfinished

(**2**) Where the goods are unfinished an aggrieved seller may in the exercise of reasonable commercial judgment for the purposes of avoiding loss and of effective realization either complete the manufacture and wholly identify the goods to the contract or cease manufacture and resell for scrap or salvage value or proceed in any other reasonable manner.

§2-705. Seller's Stoppage of Delivery in Transit or Otherwise.

(**1**) The seller may stop delivery of goods in the possession of a carrier or other bailee when he discovers the buyer to be insolvent (Section 2-702) and may stop delivery of carload, truckload, planeload or larger shipments of express or freight when the buyer repudiates or fails to make a payment due before delivery or if for any other reason the seller has a right to withhold or reclaim the goods.

(**2**) As against such buyer the seller may stop delivery until

(**a**) receipt of the goods by the buyer; or

(**b**) acknowledgement to the buyer or by any bailee of the goods except a carrier that the bailee holds the goods for the buyer; or

(**c**) such acknowledgement to the buyer by a carrier by reshipment or as warehouseman; or

(**d**) negotiation to the buyer of any negotiable document of title covering the goods.

(**3**) (**a**) To stop delivery the seller must so notify as to enable the bailee by reasonable diligence to prevent delivery of the goods.

(**b**) After such notification the bailee must hold and deliver the goods according to the directions of the seller but the seller is liable to the bailee for any ensuing charges or damages.

(**c**) If a negotiable document of title has been issued for goods the bailee is not obliged to obey a notification to stop until surrender of the document.

(**d**) A carrier who has issued a non-negotiable bill of lading is not obliged to obey a notification to stop received from a person other than the consignor.

§2-706. Seller's Resale Including Contract for Resale.

(**1**) Under the conditions stated in Section 2-703 on seller's remedies, the seller may resell the goods concerned or the undelivered balance thereof. Where the resale is made in good faith and in a commercially reasonable manner the seller may recover the difference between the resale price and the contract price together with any incidental damages allowed under the provisions of this Article (Section 2-710), but less expenses saved in consequence of the buyer's breach.

(**2**) Except as otherwise provided in subsection (3) or unless otherwise agreed resale may be at public or private sale including sale by way of one or more contracts to sell or of identification to an existing contract of the seller. Sale may be as a unit or in parcels and at any time and place and on any terms but every aspect of the sale including the method, manner, time, place and terms must be commercially reasonable. The resale must be reasonably identified as referring to the broken contract, but it is not necessary that the goods be in existence or that any or all of

them have been identified to the contract before the breach.

(**3**) Where the resale is at private sale the seller must give the buyer reasonable notification of his intention to resell.

(**4**) Where the resale is at public sale

(**a**) Only identified goods can be sold except where there is a recognized market for a public sale of futures in goods of the kind; and

(**b**) it must be made at a usual place or market for public sale if one is reasonably available and except in the case of goods which are perishable or threaten to decline in value speedily the seller must give the buyer reasonable notice of the time and place of the resale; and

(**c**) if the goods are not to be within the view of those attending the sale the notification of sale must state the place where the goods are located and provide for their reasonable inspection by prospective bidders; and

(**d**) the seller may buy.

(**5**) A purchaser who buys in good faith at a resale takes the goods free of any rights of the original buyer even though the seller fails to comply with one or more of the requirements of this section.

(**6**) The seller is not accountable to the buyer for any profit made on any resale. A person in the position of a seller (Section 2-707) or a buyer who has rightfully rejected or justifiably revoked acceptance must account for any excess over the amount of his security interest, as hereinafter defined (subsection (3) of Section 2-711).

§2-707. "Person in the Position of a Seller".

(**1**) A "person in the position of a seller" includes as against a principal an agent who has paid or become responsible for the price of goods on behalf of his principal or anyone who otherwise holds a security interest or other right in goods similar to that of a seller.

(**2**) A person in the position of a seller may as provided in this Article withhold or stop delivery (Section 2-705) and resell (Section 2-706) and recover incidental damages (Section 2-710).

§2-708. Seller's Damages for Non-acceptance or Repudiation.

(**1**) Subject to subsection (2) and to the provisions of this Article with respect to proof of market price (Section 2-723), the measure of damages for non-acceptance or repudiation by the buyer is the difference between the market price at the time and place for tender and the unpaid contract price together with any incidental damages provided in this Article (Section 2-710), but less expenses saved in consequence of the buyer's breach.

(2) If the measure of damages provided in subsection (1) is inadequate to put the seller in as good a position as performance would have done then the measure of damages is the profit (including reasonable overhead) which the seller would have made from full performance by the buyer, together with any incidental damages provided in this Article (Section 2-710), due allowance for costs reasonably incurred and due credit for payments or proceeds of resale.

§2-709. Action for the Price.

(1) When the buyer fails to pay the price as it becomes due the seller may recover, together with any incidental damages under the next section, the price

(a) of goods accepted or of conforming goods lost or damaged within a commercially reasonable time after risk of their loss has passed to the buyer; and

(b) of goods identified to the contract if the seller is unable after reasonable effort to resell them at a reasonable price or the circumstances reasonably indicate that such effort will be unavailing.

(2) Where the seller sues for the price he must hold for the buyer any goods which have been identified to the contract and are still in his control except that if resale becomes possible he may resell them at any time prior to the collection of the judgment. The net proceeds of any such resale must be credited to the buyer and payment of the judgment entitles him to any goods not resold.

(3) After the buyer has wrongfully rejected or revoked acceptance of the goods has failed to make a payment due or has repudiated (Section 2-610), a seller who is held not entitled to the price under this section shall nevertheless be awarded damages for non-acceptance under the preceding section.

§2-710. Seller's Incidental Damages. Incidental damages to an aggrieved seller include any commercially reasonable charges, expenses or commissions incurred in stopping delivery, in the transportation, care and custody of goods after the buyer's breach, in connection with return or resale of the goods or otherwise resulting from the breach.

§2-711. Buyer's Remedies in General; Buyer's Security Interest in Rejected Goods.

(1) When the seller fails to make delivery or repudiates or the buyer rightfully rejects or justifiably revokes acceptance then with respect to any goods involved, and with respect to the whole if the breach goes to the whole contract (Section 2-612), the buyer may cancel and whether or not he has done so may in addition to recovering so much of the price as has been paid

(a) "cover" and have damages under the next section as to all the goods affected whether or not they have been identified to the contract; or

(b) recover damages for non-delivery as provided in this Article (Section 2-713).

(2) Where the seller fails to deliver or repudiates the buyer may also

(a) if the goods have been identified recover them as provided in this Article (Section 2-502); or

(b) in a proper case obtain specific performance or replevy the goods as provided in this Article (Section 2-716).

(3) On rightful rejection or justifiable revocation of acceptance a buyer has a security interest in goods in his possession or control for any payments made on their price and any expenses reasonably incurred in their inspection, receipt, transportation, care and custody and may hold such goods and resell them in like manner as an aggrieved seller (Section 2-706).

§2-712. "Cover"; Buyer's Procurement of Substitute Goods.

(1) After a breach within the preceding section the buyer may "cover" by making in good faith and without unreasonable delay any reasonable purchase of or contract to purchase goods in substitution for those due from the seller.

(2) The buyer may recover from the seller as damages the difference between the cost of cover and the contract price together with any incidental or consequential damages as hereinafter defined (Section 2-715), but less expenses saved in consequence of the seller's breach.

(3) Failure of the buyer to effect cover within this section does not ban him from any other remedy.

§2-713. Buyer's Damages for Non-Delivery or Repudiation.

(1) Subject to the provisions of this Article with respect to proof of market price (Section 2-723), the measure of damages for non-delivery or repudiation by the seller is the difference between the market price at the time when the buyer learned of the breach and the contract price together with any incidental

and consequential damages provided in this Article (Section 2-715), but less expenses saved in consequence of the seller's breach.

(**2**) Market price is to be determined as of the place for tender or, in cases of rejection after arrival or revocation of acceptance as of the place of arrival.

§2-714. Buyer's Damages for Breach in Regard to Accepted Goods.

(**1**) Where the buyer has accepted goods and given notification (subsection (3) Section 2-607) he may recover as damages for any non-conformity of tender the loss resulting in the ordinary course of events from the seller's breach as determined in any manner which is reasonable.

(**2**) The measure of damages for breach of warranty is the difference at the time and place of acceptance between the value of the goods accepted and the value they would have had if they had been as warranted, unless special circumstances show proximate damages of a different amount.

(**3**) In a proper case any incidental and consequential damages under the next section may also be recovered.

§2-715. Buyer's Incidental and Consequential Damages.

(**1**) Incidental damages resulting from the seller's breach include expenses reasonably incurred in inspection, receipt, transportation and care and custody of goods rightfully rejected, any commercially reasonable charges, expenses or commissions in connection with effecting cover and any other reasonable expense incident to the delay or other breach.

(**2**) Consequential damages resulting from the seller's breach include

(**a**) any loss resulting from general or particular requirements and needs of which the seller at the time of contracting had reason to know and which could not reasonably be prevented by cover or otherwise; and

(**b**) injury to person or property proximately resulting from any breach of warranty.

§2-716. Buyer's Right to Specific Performance or Replevin.

(**1**) Specific performance may be decreed where the goods are unique or in other proper circumstances.

(**2**) The decree for specific performance may include such terms and conditions as to payment of the price, damages, or other relief as the court may deem just.

(**3**) The buyer has a right of replevin for goods identified to the contract if after reasonable effort he is unable to effect cover for such goods or the circumstances reasonably indicate that such effort will be unavailing or if the goods have been shipped under reservation and satisfaction of the security interest in them has been made or tendered.

§2-717. Deduction of Damages From the Price.
The buyer on notifying the seller of his intention to do so may deduct all or any part of the damages resulting from any breach of the contact from any part of the price still due under the same contract.

§2-718. Liquidation or Limitation of Damages; Deposits.

(**1**) Damages for breach by either party may be liquidated in the agreement but only at an amount which is reasonable in the light of the anticipated or actual harm caused by the breach, the difficulties of proof of loss, and the inconvenience or nonfeasibility of otherwise obtaining an adequate remedy. A term fixing unreasonably large liquidated damages is void as a penalty.

(**2**) Where the seller justifiably withholds delivery of goods because of the buyer's breach, the buyer is entitled to restitution of any amount by which the sum of his payments exceeds

(**a**) the amount to which the seller is entitled by virtue of terms liquidating the seller's damages in accordance with subsection (1), or

(**b**) in the absence of such terms, twenty per cent of the value of the total performance for which the buyer is obligated under the contract or $500, whichever is smaller.

(**3**) The buyer's right to restitution under subsection (2) is subject to offset to the extent that the seller establishes

(**a**) a right to recover damages under the provisions of this Article other than subsection (1), and

(**b**) the amount or value of any benefits received by the buyer directly or indirectly by reason of the contract.

(**4**) Where a seller has received payment in goods their reasonable value or the proceeds of their resale shall be treated as payments for the purposes of subsection (2); but if the seller has notice of the buyer's breach before reselling goods received in part performance, his resale is subject to the conditions laid down in this Article on resale by an aggrieved seller (Section 2-706).

§2-719. Contractual Modification or Limitation of Remedy.

(1) Subject to the provisions of subsections (2) and (3) of this section and of the preceding section on liquidation and limitation of damages,

    (a) the agreement may provide for remedies in addition to or in substitution for those provided in this Article and may limit or alter the measure of damages recoverable under his Article, as by limiting the buyer's remedies to return of the goods and repayment of the price or to repair and replacement of non-conforming goods or parts; and

    (b) resort to a remedy as provided is optional unless the remedy is expressly agreed to be exclusive, in which case it is the sole remedy.

(2) Where circumstances cause an exclusive or limited remedy to fail of its essential purpose, remedy may be had as provided in this Act.

(3) Consequential damages may be limited or excluded unless the limitation or exclusion is unconscionable. Limitation of consequential damages for injury to the person in the case of consumer goods is prima facie unconscionable but limitation of damages where the loss is commercial is not.

§2-720. Effect of "Cancellation" or "Rescission" on Claims for Antecedent Breach.

Unless the contrary intention clearly appears, expressions of "cancellation" or "rescission" of the contract or the like shall not be construed as a renunciation or discharge of any claim in damages for an antecedent breach.

§2-721. Remedies for Fraud.

Remedies for material misrepresentation or fraud include all remedies available under this Article for non-fraudulent breach. Neither rescission or a claim for rescission of the contract for sale nor rejection or return of the goods shall bar or be deemed inconsistent with a claim for damage or other remedy.

§2-722. Who Can Sue Third Parties for Injury to Goods.

Where a third party so deals with goods which have been identified to a contract for sale as to cause actionable injury to a party to that contract

    (a) right of action against the third party is in either party to the contract for sale who has title to or a security interest or a special property or an insurable interest in the goods; and if the goods have been destroyed or converted a right of action is also in the party who either bore the risk of loss under the contract for sale

or has since the injury assumed that risk as against the other;

    (b) if at the time of the injury the party plaintiff did not bear the risk of loss as against the other party to the contract for sale and there is no arrangement between them for disposition of the recovery, his suit or settlement is, subject to his own interest, as a fiduciary for the other party to the contract;

    (c) either party may with the consent of the other sue for the benefit of whom it may concern.

§2-723. Proof of Market Price: Time and Place.

(1) If an action based on anticipatory repudiation comes to trial before the time for performance with respect to some or all of the goods, any damages based on market price (Section 2-708 or Section 2-713) shall be determined according to the price of such goods prevailing at the time when the aggrieved party learned of the repudiation.

(2) If evidence of a price prevailing at the times or places described in this Article is not readily available the price prevailing within any reasonable time before or after the time described or at any other place which in commercial judgment or under usage of trade would serve as a reasonable substitute for the one described may be used, making any proper allowance for the cost of transporting the goods to or from such other place.

(3) Evidence of a relevant price prevailing at a time or place other than the one described in this Article offered by one party is not admissible unless and until he has given the other party such notice as the court finds sufficient to prevent unfair surprise.

§2-724. Admissibility of Market Quotations.

Whenever the prevailing price or value of any goods regularly bought and sold in any established commodity market is in issue, reports in official publication or trade journals or in newspapers or periodicals of general circulation published as the reports of such market shall be admissible in evidence. The circumstances of the preparation of such a report may be shown to affect its weight but not its admissibility.

§2-725. Statute of Limitations in Contracts for Sale.

(1) An action for breach of any contract for sale must be commenced within four years after the cause of action has accrued. By the original agreement the parties may reduce the period of limitation to not less than one year but may not extend it.

(2) A cause of action accrues when the breach occurs, regardless of the aggrieved party's lack of knowledge of the breach. A breach of warranty occurs when tender of delivery is made, except that where a warranty explicitly extends to future performance of the goods and discovery of the breach must await the time of such performance the cause of action accrues when the breach is or should have been discovered.

(3) Where an action commenced within the time limited by subsection (1) is so terminated as to leave available a remedy by another action for the same breach such other action may be commenced after the expiration of the time limited and within six months after the termination of the first action unless the termination resulted from voluntary discontinuance or from dismissal for failure or neglect to prosecute.

(4) This section does not alter the law on tolling of the statute of limitations nor does it apply to causes of action which have accrued before this Act becomes effective.

ARTICLE 3: COMMERCIAL PAPER

Part 1: Short Title, Form and Interpretation
§3-101. **Short Title.** This Article shall be known and may be cited as Uniform Commercial Code—Commercial Paper.

§3-102. **Definitions and Index of Definitions.**

(1) In this Article unless the context otherwise requires

(a) "Issue" means the first delivery of an instrument to a holder or a remitter.

(b) An "order" is a direction to pay and must be more than an authorization or request. It must identify the person to pay with reasonable certainty. It may be addressed to one or more such persons jointly or in the alternative but not in succession.

(c) A "promise" is an undertaking to pay and must be more than an acknowledgment of an obligation.

(d) "Secondary party" means a drawer or endorser.

(e) "Instrument" means a negotiable instrument.

(2) Other definitions applying to this Article and the sections in which they appear are:

"Acceptance". Section 3-410.

"Accommodation party". Section 3-415.

"Alteration". Section 3-407.

"Certificate of deposit". Section 3-104.

"Certification". Section 3-411.

"Check". Section 3-104.

"Definite time". Section 3-109.

"Dishonor". Section 3-507.

"Draft". Section 3-104.

"Holder in due course". Section 3-202.

"Negotiation". Section 3-202.

"Note". Section 3-104.

"Notice of dishonor". Section 3-508.

"On demand". Section 3-108.

"Presentment". Section 3-504.

"Protest". Section 3-509.

"Restrictive Indorsement". Section 3-205.

"Signature". Section 3-401.

(3) The following definitions in other Articles apply to this Article:

"Account". Section 4-104.

"Banking Day". Section 4-104.

"Clearing house". Section 4-104.

"Collecting bank". Section 4-105.

"Customer". Section 4-104.

"Depositary Bank". Section 4-105.

"Documentary Draft". Section 4-104.

"Intermediary Bank". Section 4-105.

"Item". Section 4-104.

"Midnight deadline". Section 4-104.

"Payor bank". Section 4-105.

(4) In addition Article 1 contains general definitions and principles of construction and interpretation applicable throughout this Article.

§3-103. **Limitations on Scope of Article.**

(1) This Article does not apply to money, documents of title or investment securities.

(2) The provisions of this Article are subject to the provisions of the Article on Bank Deposits and Collections (Article 4) and Secured Transactions (Article 9).

§3-104. **Form of Negotiable Instruments; "Draft"; "Check"; "Certificate of Deposit"; "Note".**

(1) Any writing to be a negotiable instrument within this Article must

(a) be signed by the maker or drawer; and

(b) contain an unconditional promise or order to pay a sum certain in money and no other promise, order, obligation or power given by the maker or drawer except as authorized by this Article; and

(c) be payable on demand or at a definite time; and

(d) be payable to order or to bearer.

(2) A writing which complies with the requirements of this section is

(a) a "draft" ("bill of exchange") if it is an order;

(b) a "check" if it is a draft drawn on a bank and payable on demand;

(c) a "certificate of deposit" if it is an acknowledgement by a bank of receipt of money with an engagement to repay it;

(d) a "note" if it is a promise other than a certificate of deposit.

(3) As used in other Articles in this Act, and as the context may require, the terms "draft", "check", "certificate of deposit" and "note" may refer to instruments which are not negotiable within this Article as well as to instruments which are so negotiable.

§3-105. When Promise or Order Unconditional.

(1) A promise or order otherwise unconditional is not made conditional by the fact that the instrument

(a) is subject to implied or constructive conditions; or

(b) states its consideration, whether performed or promised, or the transaction which gave rise to the instrument, or that the promise or order is made or the instrument matures in accordance with or "as per" such transaction; or

(c) refers to or states that it arises out of a separate agreement or refers to a separate agreement for rights as to prepayment or acceleration; or

(d) states that is drawn under a letter of credit; or

(e) states that it is secured, whether by mortgage, reservation of title or otherwise; or

(f) indicates a particular account to be debited or any other fund or source from which reimbursement is expected; or

(g) is limited to payment out of a particular fund or the proceeds of a particular source, if the instrument is issued by a government or governmental agency or unit; or

(h) is limited to payment out of the entire assets of a partnership, unincorporated association, trust or estate by or on behalf of which the instrument is issued.

(2) A promise or order is not unconditional if the instrument

(a) states that it is subject to or governed by any other agreement; or

(b) states that it is to be paid only out of a particular fund or source except as provided in this section. As amended 1962.

§3-106. Sum Certain.

(1) The sum payable is a sum certain even though it is to be paid

(a) with stated interest or by stated installments; or

(b) with stated different rates of interest before and after default or a specified date; or

(c) with a stated discount or addition if paid before or after the date fixed for payment; or

(d) with exchange or less exchange; whether at a fixed rate or at the current rate; or

(e) with cost of collection or an attorney's fee or both upon default.

(2) Nothing in this section shall validate any term which is otherwise illegal.

§3-107. Money.

(1) An instrument is payable in money if the medium of exchange in which it is payable is money at the time the instrument is made. An instrument payable in "currency" or "current funds" is payable in money.

(2) A promise or order to pay a sum stated in a foreign currency is for a sum certain in money and, unless a different medium of payment is specified in the instrument, may be satisfied by payment of that number of dollars which the stated foreign currency will purchase at the buying sight rate for that currency on the day on which the instrument is payable or, if payable on demand, on the day of demand. If such an instrument specifies a foreign currency as the medium of payment the instrument is payable in that currency.

§3-108. Payable on Demand.   Instruments payable on demand include those payable at sight or on presentation and those in which no time for payment is stated.

§3-109. Definite Time.

(1) An instrument is payable at a definite time if by its terms it is payable

(a) on or before a stated date or at a fixed period after a stated date; or

(b) at a fixed period after sight; or

(c) at a definite time subject to any acceleration; or

(d) at a definite time subject to extension at the option of the holder, or to extension to a further definite time at the option of the maker or acceptor or automatically upon or after a specified act or event.

(2) An instrument which by its terms is otherwise payable only upon an act or event uncertain as to time of occurrence is not payable at a definite time even though the act or event has occurred.

§3-110. Payable to Order.

(1) An instrument is payable to order when by its terms it is payable to the order or assigns of any person therein specified with reasonable certainty, or to him or his order, or when it is conspicuously designated on its face as "exchange" or the like and names a payee. It may be payable to the order of

(a) the maker or drawer; or

(b) the drawee; or

(c) a payee who is not maker, drawer or drawee; or

(d) two or more payees together or in the alternative; or

(e) an estate, trust or fund, in which case it is payable to the order of the representative of such estate, trust or fund or his successors; or

(f) an office, or an officer by his title as such in which case it is payable to the principal but the incumbent of the office or his successors may act as if he or they were the holder; or

(g) a partnership or unincorporated association, in which case it is payable to the partnership or association and may be indorsed or transferred by any person thereto authorized.

(2) An instrument not payable to order is not made so payable by such words as "payable upon return of this instrument properly indorsed."

(3) An instrument made payable both to order and to bearer is payable to order unless the bearer words are handwritten or typewritten.

§3-111. Payable to Bearer.

An instrument is payable to bearer when by its terms it is payable to

(a) bearer or the order of bearer; or

(b) a specified person or bearer; or

(c) "cash" or the order of "cash", or any other indication which does not purport to designate a specific payee.

§3-112. Terms and Omissions Not Affecting Negotiability.

(1) The negotiability of an instrument is not affected by

(a) the omission of a statement of any consideration or of the place where the instrument is drawn or payable; or

(b) a statement that collateral has been given to secure obligation either on the instrument or otherwise of an obligor on the instrument or that in case of default on those obligations the holder may realize on or dispose of the collateral; or

(c) a promise or power to maintain or protect collateral or to give additional collateral; or

(d) a term authorizing a confession of judgment on the instrument if it is not paid when due; or

(e) a term purporting to waive the benefit of any law intended for the advantage or protection of any obligor; or

(f) a term in a draft providing that the payee by indorsing or cashing it acknowledges full satisfaction of an obligation of the drawer; or

(g) a statement in a draft drawn in a set of parts (Section 3-801) to the effect that the order is effective only if no other part has been honored.

(2) Nothing in this section shall validate any term which is otherwise illegal. As amended 1962.

§3-113. Seal.

An instrument otherwise negotiable is within this Article even though it is under a seal.

§3-114. Date, Antedating, Postdating.

(1) The negotiability of an instrument is not affected by the fact that it is undated, antedated or postdated.

(2) Where an instrument is antedated or postdated the time when it is payable is determined by the stated date if the instrument is payable on demand or at a fixed period after date.

(3) Where the instrument or any signature thereon is dated, the date is presumed to be correct.

§3-115. Incomplete Instruments.

(1) When a paper whose contents at the time of signing show that it is intended to become an instrument is signed while still incomplete in any necessary respect it cannot be enforced until completed, but when it is completed in accordance with authority given it is effective as completed.

(2) If the completion is unauthorized the rules as to material alteration apply (Section 3-407), even though the paper was not delivered by the maker or drawer, but the burden of establishing that any completion is unauthorized is on the party so asserting.

§3-116. Instruments Payable to Two or More Persons.   An instrument payable to the order of two or more persons

(a) if in the alternative is payable to any one of them and may be negotiated, discharged or enforced by any one of them who has possession of it;

(b) if not in the alternative is payable to all of them and may be negotiated, discharged or enforced only by all of them.

§3-117. Instruments Payable With Words of Description.   An instrument made payable to a named person with the addition of words describing him

(a) as agent or officer of a specified person is payable to his principal but the agent or officer may act as if he were the holder;

(b) as any other fiduciary for a specified person or purpose is payable to the payee and may be negotiated, discharged or enforced by him;

(c) in any other manner is payable to the payee unconditionally and the additional words are without effect on subsequent parties.

§3-118. Ambiguous Terms and Rules of Construction.   The following rules apply to every instrument:

(a) Where there is doubt whether the instrument is a draft or a note the holder may treat it as either. A draft drawn on the drawer is effective as a note.

(b) Handwritten terms control typewritten and printed terms, and typewritten control printed.

(c) Words control figures except that if the words are ambiguous figures control.

(d) Unless otherwise specified a provision for interest means interest at the judgment rate at the place of payment from the date of the instrument, or if it is undated from the date of issue.

(e) Unless the instrument otherwise specifies two or more persons who sign as maker, acceptor or drawer or indorser and as a part of the same transaction are jointly and severally lia-

ble even though the instrument contains such words as "I promise to pay."

(f) Unless otherwise specified consent to extension authorizes a single extension for not longer than the original period. A consent to extension, expressed in the instrument, is binding on secondary parties and accommodation makers. A holder may not exercise his option to extend an instrument over the objection of a maker or acceptor or other party who in accordance with Section 3-604 tenders full payment when the instrument is due.

§3-119. Other Writings Affecting Instrument.

(1) As between the obligor and his immediate obligee or any transferee the terms of an instrument may be modified or affected by any other written agreement executed as a part of the same transaction, except that a holder in due course is not affected by any limitation of his rights arising out of the separate written agreement if he had no notice of the limitation when he took the instrument.

(2) A separate agreement does not affect the negotiability of an instrument.

§3-120. Instruments "Payable Through" Bank.   An instrument which states that is is "payable through" a bank or the like designates that bank as a collecting bank to make presentment but does not of itself authorize the bank to pay the instrument.

§3-121. Instruments Payable at Bank.

Note: *If this Act is introduced in the Congress of the United States this section should be omitted. (States to select either alternative.)*

Alternative A—A note or acceptance which states that is is payable at a bank is the equivalent of a draft drawn on the bank payable when it falls due out of any funds of the maker or acceptor in current account or otherwise available for such payment.

Alternative B—A note or acceptance which states that it is payable at a bank is not of itself an order or authorization to the bank to pay it.

§3-122. Accrual of Cause of Action.

(1) A cause of action against a maker or an acceptor accrues

(a) in the case of a time instrument on the day after maturity;

(b) in the case of a demand instrument upon its date or, if no date is stated, on the date of issue.

(2) A cause of action against the obligor of a demand or time certificate of deposit accrues upon demand, but demand on a time certificate may not be made until on or after the date of maturity.

(3) A cause of action against a drawer of a draft or an indorser of any instrument accrues upon demand following dishonor of the instrument. Notice of dishonor is a demand.

(4) Unless an instrument provides otherwise, interest runs at the rate provided by law for a judgment

    (a) in the case of a maker, acceptor or other primary obligor of a demand instrument, from the date of demand;

    (b) in all other cases from the date of accrual of the cause of action. As amended 1962.

Part 2: Transfer and Negotiation
§3-201. **Transfer: Right to Indorsement.**

(1) Transfer of an instrument vests in the transferee such rights as the transferor has therein, except that a transferee who has himself been a party to any fraud or illegality affecting the instrument or who as a prior holder had notice of a defense or claim against it cannot improve his position by taking from a later holder in due course.

(2) A transfer of a security interest in an instrument vests the foregoing rights in the transferee to the extent of the interest transferred.

(3) Unless otherwise agreed any transfer for value of an instrument not then payable to bearer gives the transferee the specifically enforceable right to have the unqualified indorsement of the transferor. Negotiation takes effect only when the indorsement is made and until that time there is no presumption that the transferee is the owner.

§3-202. **Negotiation.**

(1) Negotiation is the transfer of an instrument in such form that the transferee becomes a holder. If the instrument is payable to order it is negotiated by delivery with any necessary indorsement; if payable to bearer it is negotiated by delivery.

(2) An indorsement must be written by or on behalf of the holder and on the instrument or on a paper so firmly affixed thereto as to become a part thereof.

(3) An indorsement is effective for negotiation only when it conveys the entire instrument or any unpaid residue. If it purports to be of less it operates only as a partial assignment.

(4) Words of assignment, condition, waiver, guaranty, limitation or disclaimer of liability and the like accompanying in indorsement do not affect its character as an indorsement.

§3-203. **Wrong or Misspelled Name.** Where an instrument is made payable to a person under a misspelled name or one other than his own he may indorse in that name or his own or both, but signature in both names may be required by a person paying or giving value for the instrument.

§3-204. **Special Indorsement; Blank Indorsement.**

(1) A special indorsement specifies the person to whom or to whose order it makes the instrument payable. Any instrument specially indorsed becomes payable to the order of the special indorsee and may be further negotiated only by his indorsement.

(2) An indorsement in blank specifies no particular indorsee and may consist of a mere signature. An instrument payable to order and indorsed in blank becomes payable to bearer and may be negotiated by delivery alone until specially indorsed.

(3) The holder may convert a blank indorsement into a special indorsement by writing over the signature of the indorser in blank any contract consistent with the character of the indorsement.

§3-205. **Restrictive Indorsements.** An indorsement is restrictive which either

    (a) is conditional; or

    (b) purports to prohibit further transfer of the instrument; or

    (c) includes the words "for collection", "for deposit", "pay any bank", or like terms signifying a purpose of deposit or collection; or

    (d) otherwise states that it is for the benefit or use of the indorser or of another person.

§3-206. **Effect of Restrictive Indorsement.**

(1) No restrictive indorsement prevents further transfer or negotiation of the instrument.

(2) An intermediary bank, or a payor bank which is not the depositary bank, is neither given notice nor otherwise affected by a restrictive indorsement of any person except the bank's immediate transferor or the person presenting for payment.

(3) Except for an intermediary bank, any transferee under an indorsement which is conditional or includes the words "for collection", for deposit", "pay any bank", or like terms (subparagraphs (a) and (c) of Section 3-205) must pay or apply any value given

by him for or on the security of the instrument consistently with the indorsement and to the extent that he does so he becomes a holder for value. In addition such transferee is a holder in due course if he otherwise complies with the requirements of Section 3-302 on what constitutes a holder in due course.

(**4**) The first taker under an indorsement for the benefit of the indorser or another person (subparagraph (d) of Section 3-205) must pay or apply any value given by him for or on the security of the instrument consistently with the indorsement and to the extent that he does so he becomes a holder for value. In addition such taker is a holder in due course if he otherwise complies with the requirements of Section 3-302 on what constitutes a holder in due course. A later holder for value is neither given notice nor otherwise affected by such restrictive indorsement unless he has knowledge that a fiduciary or other person has negotiated the instrument in any transaction for his own benefit or otherwise in breach of duty (subsection (2) of Section 3-304).

§3-207. Negotiation Effective Although It May Be Rescinded.

(**1**) Negotiation is effective to transfer the instrument although the negotiation is

    (**a**) made by an infant, a corporation exceeding its powers, or any other person without capacity; or

    (**b**) obtained by fraud, duress or mistake of any kind; or

    (**c**) part of an illegal transaction; or

    (**d**) made in breach of duty.

(**2**) Except as against a subsequent holder in due course such negotiation is in an appropriate case subject to rescission, the declaration of a constructive trust or any other remedy permitted by law.

§3-208. Reacquisition.

Where an instrument is returned to or reacquired by a prior party he may cancel any indorsement which is not necessary to his title and reissue or further negotiate the instrument, but any intervening party is discharged as against the reacquiring party and subsequent holders not in due course and if his indorsement has been cancelled is discharged as against subsequent holders in due course as well.

Part 3: Rights of a Holder

§3-301. Rights of a Holder.

The holder of an instrument whether or not he is the owner may transfer or negotiate it and, except as otherwise provided in Section 3-603 on payment or satisfaction, discharge it or enforce payment in his own name.

§3-302. Holder in Due Course.

(**1**) A holder in due course is a holder who takes the instrument

    (**a**) for value; and

    (**b**) in good faith; and

    (**c**) without notice that it is overdue or has been dishonored or of any defense against or claim to it on the part of any person.

(**2**) A payee may be a holder in due course.

(**3**) A holder does not become a holder in due course of an instrument

    (**a**) by purchase of it at judicial sale or by taking it under legal process; or

    (**b**) by acquiring it in taking over an estate; or

    (**c**) by purchasing it as part of a bulk transaction not in regular course of business of the transferor.

(**4**) A purchaser of a limited interest can be a holder in due course only to the extent of the interest purchased.

§3-303. Taking for Value.

A holder takes the instrument for value

    (**a**) to the extent that the agreed consideration has been performed or that he acquires a security interest in or a lien on the instrument otherwise than by legal process; or

    (**b**) when he takes the instrument in payment of or as security for an antecedent claim against any person whether or not the claim is due; or

    (**c**) when he gives a negotiable instrument for it or makes an irrevocable commitment to a third person.

§3-304. Notice to Purchaser.

(**1**) The purchaser has notice of a claim or defense if

    (**a**) the instrument is so incomplete, bears such visible evidence of forgery or alteration, or is otherwise so irregular as to call into question its validity, terms or ownership or to create an ambiguity as to the party to pay; or

    (**b**) the purchaser has notice that the obligation of any party is voidable in whole or in part, or that all parties have been discharged.

(**2**) The purchaser has notice of a claim against the instrument when he has knowledge that a fiduciary has negotiated the instrument in payment of or as security for his own debt or in any transaction for his own benefit or otherwise in breach of duty.

(**3**) The purchaser has notice that an instrument is overdue if he has reason to know

    (**a**) that any part of the principal amount is overdue or that there is an uncured default in payment of another instrument of the same series; or

    (**b**) that acceleration of the instrument has been made; or

    (**c**) that he is taking a demand instrument after demand has been made or more than a reasonable length of time after its issue. A reasonable time for a check drawn and payable within the states and territories of the United States and the District of Columbia is presumed to be thirty days.

(**4**) Knowledge of the following facts does not of itself give the purchaser notice of a defense or claim

    (**a**) that the instrument is antedated or postdated;

    (**b**) that it was issued or negotiated in return for an executory promise or accompanied by a separate agreement, unless the purchaser has notice that a defense or claim has arisen from the terms thereof;

    (**c**) that any party has signed for accommodation;

    (**d**) that an incomplete instrument has been completed, unless the purchaser has notice of any improper completion;

    (**e**) that any person negotiating the instrument is or was a fiduciary;

    (**f**) that there has been default in payment of interest on the instrument or in payment of any other instrument, except one of the same series.

(**5**) The filing or recording of a document does not of itself constitute notice within the provisions of this Article to a person who would otherwise be a holder in due course.

(**6**) To be effective notice must be received at such time and in such manner as to give a reasonable opportunity to act on it.

§3-305. Rights of a Holder in Due Course. To the extent that a holder is a holder in due course he takes the instrument free from

(**1**) all claims to it on the part of any person; and

(**2**) all defenses of any party to the instrument with whom the holder has not dealt except

    (**a**) infancy, to the extent that it is a defense to a simple contract; and

    (**b**) such other incapacity, or duress, or illegality of the transaction, as renders the obligation of the party a nullity; and

    (**c**) such misrepresentation as has induced the party to sign the instrument with neither knowledge nor reasonable opportunity to obtain knowledge of its character or its essential terms; and

    (**d**) discharge in insolvency proceedings; and

    (**e**) any other discharge of which the holder has notice when he takes the instrument.

§3-306. Rights of One Not Holder in Due Course. Unless he has the rights of a holder in due course any person takes the instrument subject to

    (**a**) all valid claims to it on the part of any person; and

    (**b**) all defenses of any party which would be available in an action on a simple contract; and

    (**c**) the defenses of want or failure of consideration, non-performance of any condition precedent, non-delivery, or delivery for a special purpose (Section 3-408); and

    (**d**) the defense that he or a person through whom he holds the instrument acquired it by theft, or that payment or satisfaction to such holder would be inconsistent with the terms of a restrictive indorsement. The claim of any third person to the instrument is not otherwise available as a defense to any party liable thereon unless the third person himself defends the action for such party.

§3-307. Burden of Establishing Signatures, Defenses and Due Course.

(**1**) Unless specifically denied in the pleading each signature on an instrument is admitted. When the effectiveness of a signature is put in issue

    (**a**) the burden of establishing it is on the party claiming under the signature; but

    (**b**) the signature is presumed to be genuine or authorized except where the action is to enforce the obligation of a purported signer who has died or become incompetent before proof is required.

(**2**) When signatures are admitted or established, production of the instrument entitles a holder to recover on it unless the defendant establishes a defense.

(**3**) After it is shown that a defense exists a person claiming the rights of a holder in due course has the burden of establishing that he or some person under whom he claims is in all respects a holder in due course.

Part 4: Liability of Parties

§3-401. Signature.

(1) No person is liable on an instrument unless his signature appears thereon.

(2) A signature is made by use of any name, including any trade or assumed name, upon an instrument, or by any word or mark used in lieu of a written signature.

§3-402. Signature in Ambiguous Capacity.
Unless the instrument clearly indicates that a signature is made in some other capacity it is an indorsement.

§3-403. Signature by Authorized Representative.

(1) A signature may be made by an agent or other representative, and his authority to make it may be established as in other cases of representation. No particular form of appointment is necessary to establish such authority.

(2) An authorized representative who signs his own name to an instrument

(a) is personally obligated if the instrument neither names the person represented nor shows that the representative signed in a representative capacity;

(b) except as otherwise established between the immediate parties, is personally obligated if the instrument names the person represented but does not show that the representative signed in a representative capacity, or if the instrument does not name the person represented but does show that the representative signed in a representative capacity.

(3) Except as otherwise established the name of an organization preceded or followed by the name and office of an authorized individual is a signature made in a representative capacity.

§3-404. Unauthorized Signatures.

(1) Any unauthorized signature is wholly inoperative as that of the person whose name is signed unless he ratifies it or is precluded from denying it; but it operates as the signature of the unauthorized signer in favor of any person who in good faith pays the instrument or takes it for value.

(2) Any unauthorized signature may be ratified for all purposes of this Article. Such ratification does not of itself affect any rights of the person ratifying against the actual signer.

§3-405. Impostors; Signature in Name of Payee.

(1) An indorsement by any person in the name of a named payee is effective if

(a) an impostor by use of the mails or otherwise has induced the maker or drawer to issue the instrument to him or his confederate in the name of the payee; or

(b) a person signing as or on behalf of a maker or drawer intends the payee to have no interest in the instrument; or

(c) an agent or employee of the maker or drawer has supplied him with the name of the payee intending the latter to have no such interest.

(2) Nothing in this section shall affect the criminal or civil liability of the person so indorsing.

§3-406. Negligence Contributing to Alteration or Unauthorized Signature.
Any person who by his negligence substantially contributes to a material alteration of the instrument or to the making of an unauthorized signature is precluded from asserting the alteration or lack of authority against a holder in due course or against a drawee or other payor who pays the instrument in good faith and in accordance with the reasonable commercial standards of the drawee's or payor's business.

§3-407. Alteration.

(1) Any alteration of an instrument is material which changes the contract of any party thereto in any respect, including any such change in

(a) the number or relations of the parties; or

(b) an incomplete instrument, by completing it otherwise than is authorized; or

(c) the writing as signed, by adding to it or by removing any part of it.

(2) As against any person other than a subsequent holder in due course

(a) alteration by the holder which is both fraudulent and material discharges any party whose contract is thereby changed unless that party assents or is precluded from asserting the defense;

(b) no other alteration discharges any party and the instrument may be enforced according to its original tenor, or as to incomplete instruments according to the authority given.

(3) A subsequent holder in due course may in all

cases enforce the instrument according to its original tenor, and when an incomplete instrument has been completed, he may enforce it as completed.

§3-408. Consideration. Want or failure of consideration is a defense as against any person not having the rights of a holder in due course. (Section 3-305), except that no consideration is necessary for an instrument or obligation thereon given in payment of or as security for an antecedent obligation of any kind. Nothing in this section shall be taken to displace any statute outside this Act under which a promise is enforceable notwithstanding lack or failure of consideration. Partial failure of consideration is a defense pro tanto whether or not the failure is in an ascertained or liquidated amount.

§3-409. Draft Not as Assignment.

(1) A check or other draft does not of itself operate as an assignment of any funds in the hands of the drawee available for its payment, and the drawee is not liable on the instrument until he accepts it.

(2) Nothing in this section shall affect any liability in contract, tort or otherwise arising from any letter of credit or other obligation or representation which is not an acceptance.

§3-410. Definition and Operation of Acceptance.

(1) Acceptance is the drawee's signed engagement to honor the draft as presented. It must be written on the draft, and may consist of his signature alone. It becomes operative when completed by delivery or notification.

(2) A draft may be accepted although it has not been signed by the drawer or is otherwise incomplete or is overdue or has been dishonored.

(3) Where the draft is payable at a fixed period after sight and the acceptor fails to date his acceptance the holder may complete it by supplying a date in good faith.

§3-411. Certification of a Check.

(1) Certification of a check is acceptance. Where a holder procures certification the drawer and all prior indorsers are discharged.

(2) Unless otherwise agreed, a bank has no obligation to certify a check.

(3) A bank may certify a check before returning it for lack of proper indorsement. If it does so the drawer is discharged.

§3-412. Acceptance Varying Draft.

(1) Where the drawee's proffered acceptance in any manner varies the draft as presented the holder may refuse the acceptance and treat the draft as dishonored in which case the drawee is entitled to have his acceptance cancelled.

(2) The terms of the draft are not varied by an acceptance to pay at any particular bank or place in the United States, unless the acceptance states that the draft is to be paid only at such bank or place.

(3) Where the holder assents to an acceptance varying the terms of the draft each drawer and indorser who does not affirmatively assent is discharged. As amended 1962.

§3-413. Contract of Maker, Drawer and Acceptor.

(1) The maker or acceptor engages that he will pay the instrument according to its tenor at the time of his engagement or as completed pursuant to Section 3-115 on incomplete instruments.

(2) The drawer engages that upon dishonor of the draft and any necessary notice of dishonor or protest he will pay the amount of the draft to the holder or to any indorser who takes it up. The drawer may disclaim this liability by drawing without recourse.

(3) By making, drawing or accepting the party admits against all subsequent parties including the drawee the existence of the payee and his then capacity to indorse.

§3-414. Contract of Indorser; Order of Liability.

(1) Unless the indorsement otherwise specifies (as by such words as "without recourse") every indorser engages that upon dishonor and any necessary notice of dishonor and protest he will pay the instrument according to its tenor at the time of his indorsement to the holder or to any subsequent indorser who takes it up, even though the indorser who takes it up was not obligated to do so.

(2) Unless they otherwise agree indorsers are liable to one another in the order in which they indorse, which is presumed to be the order in which their signatures appear on the instrument.

§3-415. Contract of Accommodation Party.

(1) An accommodation party is one who signs the instrument in any capacity for the purpose of lending his name to another party to it.

(2) When the instrument has been taken for value before it is due the accommodation party is liable in the capacity in which he has signed even though the taker knows of the accommodation.

(3) As against a holder in due course and without notice of the accommodation oral proof of the accom-

modation is not admissible to give the accommodation party the benefit of discharges dependent on his character as such. In other cases the accommodation character may be shown by oral proof.

(**4**) An indorsement which shows that it is not in the chain of title is notice of its accommodation character.

(**5**) An accommodation party is not liable to the party accommodated, and if he pays the instrument has a right of recourse on the instrument against such party.

§3-416. Contract of Guarantor.

(**1**) "Payment guaranteed" or equivalent words added to a signature mean that the signer engages that if the instrument is not paid when due he will pay it according to its tenor without resort by the holder to any other party.

(**2**) "Collection guaranteed" or equivalent words added to a signature mean that the signer engages that if the instrument is not paid when due he will pay it according to its tenor, but only after the holder has reduced his claim against the maker or acceptor to judgment and execution has been returned unsatisfied, or after the maker or acceptor has become insolvent or it is otherwise apparent that it is useless to proceed against him.

(**3**) Words of guaranty which do not otherwise specify guarantee payment.

(**4**) No words of guaranty added to the signature of a sole maker or acceptor affect his liability on the instrument. Such words added to the signature of one of two or more makers or acceptors create a presumption that the signature is for the accommodation of the others.

(**5**) When words of guaranty are used presentment, notice of dishonor and protest are not necessary to charge the user.

(**6**) Any guaranty written on the insrument is enforcible notwithstanding any statute of frauds.

§3-417. Warranties on Presentment and Transfer.

(**1**) Any person who obtains payment or acceptance and any prior transferor warrants to a person who in good faith pays or accepts that

(**a**) he has a good title to the instrument or is authorized to obtain payment or acceptance on behalf of one who has a good title; and

(**b**) he has no knowledge that the signature of the maker or drawer is unauthorized, except that this warranty is not given by a holder in due course acting in good faith

(**i**) to a maker with respect to the maker's own signature; or

(**ii**) to a drawer with respect to the drawer's own signature, whether or not the drawer is also the drawee; or

(**iii**) to an acceptor of a draft if the holder in due course took the draft after the acceptance or obtained the acceptance without knowledge that the drawer's signature was unauthorized; and

(**c**) the instrument has not been materially altered, except that this warranty is not given by a holder in due course acting in good faith

(**i**) to the maker of a note; or

(**ii**) to the drawer of a draft whether or not the drawer is also the drawee; or

(**iii**) to the acceptor of a draft with respect to an alteration made prior to the acceptance if the holder in due course took the draft after the acceptance, even though the acceptance provided "payable as originally drawn" or equivalent terms; or

(**iv**) to the acceptor of a draft with respect to an alteration made after the acceptance.

(**2**) Any person who transfers an instrument and receives consideration warrants to his transferee and if the transfer is by indorsement to any subsequent holder who takes the instrument in good faith that

(**a**) he has a good title to the instrument or is authorized to obtain payment or acceptance on behalf of one who has a good title and the transfer is otherwise rightful; and

(**b**) all signatures are genuine or authorized; and

(**c**) the instrument has not been materially altered; and

(**d**) no defense of any party is good against him; and

(**e**) he has no knowledge of any insolvency proceeding instituted with respect to the maker or acceptor or the drawer of an unaccepted instrument.

(**3**) By transferring "without recourse" the transfer limits the obligation stated in subsection (2) (d) to a warranty that he has no knowledge of such a defense.

(**4**) A selling agent or broker who does not disclose the fact that he is acting only as such gives the warranties provided in this section, but if he makes such disclosure warrants only his good faith and authority.

§3-418. Finality of Payment of Acceptance.   Except for recovery of bank payments as pro-

vided in the Article on Bank Deposits and Collections (Article 4) and except for liability for breach of warranty on presentment under the preceding section, payment or acceptance of any instrument is final in favor of a holder in due course, or a person who has in good faith changed his position in reliance on the payment.

§3-419. Conversion of Instrument; Innocent Representative.

(1) An instrument is converted when

(a) a drawee to whom it is delivered for payment refuses on demand either to pay or to return it; or

(b) any person to whom it is delivered for payment refuses on demand either to pay or to return it; or

(c) it is paid on a forged indorsement.

(2) In an action against a drawee under subsection (1) the measure of the drawee's liability is the face amount of the instrument. In any other action under subsection (1) the measure of liability is presumed to be the face amount of the instrument.

(3) Subject to the provisions of this Act concerning restrictive indorsements a representative, including a depositary or collecting bank, who has in good faith and in accordance with the reasonable commercial standards applicable to the business of such representative dealt with an instrument or its proceeds on behalf of one who was not the true owner is not liable in conversion or otherwise to the true owner beyond the amount of any proceeds remaining in his hands.

(4) An intermediary bank or payor bank which is not a depositary bank is not liable in conversion solely by reason of the fact that proceeds of an item indorsed restrictively (Sections 3-205 and 3-206) are not paid or applied consistently with the restrictive indorsement of an indorser other than its immediate transferor.

Part 5: Presentment, Notice of Dishonor and Protest

§3-501. When Presentment, Notice of Dishonor, and Protest Necessary or Permissible.

(1) Unless excused (Section 3-511) presentment is necessary to charge secondary parties as follows:

(a) presentment for acceptance is necessary to charge the drawer and indorsers of a draft where the draft so provides, or is payable elsewhere than at the residence or place of business of the drawee, or its date of payment depends upon such presentment. The holder may at his option present for acceptance any other draft payable at a stated date;

(b) presentment for payment is necessary to charge any indorser;

(c) in the case of any drawer, the acceptor of a draft payable at a bank or the maker of a note payable at a bank, presentment for payment is necessary, but failure to make presentment discharges such drawer, acceptor or maker only as stated in Section 3-502(1)(b).

(2) Unless excused (Section 3-511)

(a) notice of any dishonor is necessary to charge any indorser;

(b) in the case of any drawer, the acceptor of a draft payable at a bank or the maker of a note payable at a bank, notice of any dishonor is necessary, but failure to give such notice discharges such drawer, acceptor or maker only as as stated in Section 3-502(1)(b).

(3) Unless excused (Section 3-511) protest of any dishonor is necessary to charge the drawer and indorsers of any draft which on its face appears to be drawn or payable outside of the states, territories, dependencies and possessions of the United States, the District of Columbia and the commonwealth of Puerto Rico. The holder may at his option make protest of any dishonor of any other instrument and in the case of a foreign draft may on insolvency of the acceptor before maturity make protest for better security.

(4) Notwithstanding any provision of this section, neither presentment nor notice of dishonor nor protest is necessary to charge an indorser who has indorsed an instrument after maturity. As amended 1966.

§3-502. Unexcused Delay; Discharge.

(1) Where without excuse any necessary presentment or notice of dishonor is delayed beyond the time when it is due

(a) any indorser is discharged; and

(b) any drawer or the acceptor of a draft payable at a bank or the maker of a note payable at a bank who because the drawee or payor bank becomes insolvent during the delay is deprived of funds maintained with the drawee or payor bank to cover the instrument may discharge his liability by written assignment to the holder of his rights against the drawee or payor bank in respect of such funds, but such drawer, acceptor or maker is not otherwise discharged.

(2) Where without excuse a necessary protest is

delayed beyond the time when it is due any drawer or indorser is discharged.

§3-503. Time of Presentment.

(1) Unless a different time is expressed in the instrument the time for any presentment is determined as follows:

(a) where an instrument is payable at or a fixed period after a stated date any presentment for acceptance must be made on or before the date it is payable;

(b) where an instrument is payable after sight it must either be presented for acceptance or negotiated within a reasonable time after date or issue whichever is later;

(c) where an instrument shows the date on which it is payable presentment for payment is due on that date;

(d) where an instrument is accelerated presentment for payment is due within a reasonable time after the acceleration;

(e) with respect to the liability of any secondary party presentment for acceptance or payment of any other instrument is due within a reasonable time after such party becomes liable thereon.

(2) A reasonable time for presentment is determined by the nature of the instrument, any usage of banking or trade and the facts of the particular case. In the case of an uncertified check which is drawn and payable within the United States and which is not a draft drawn by a bank the following are presumed to be reasonable periods within which to present for payment or to initiate bank collection:

(a) with respect to the liability of the drawer, thirty days after date or issue whichever is later; and

(b) with respect to the liability of an indorser, seven days after his indorsement.

(3) Where any presentment is due on a day which is not a full business day for either the person making presentment or the party to pay or accept, presentment is due on the next following day which is a full business day for both parties.

(4) Presentment to be sufficient must be made at a reasonable hour, and if at a bank during its banking day.

§3-504. How Presentment Made.

(1) Presentment is a demand for acceptance or payment made upon the maker, acceptor, drawee or other payor by or on behalf of the holder.

(2) Presentment may be made

(a) by mail, in which event the time of presentment is determined by the time of receipt of the mail; or

(b) through a clearing house; or

(c) at the place of acceptance or payment specified in the instrument or if there be none at the place of business or residence of the party to accept or pay. If neither the party to accept or pay nor anyone authorized to act for him is present or accessible at such place presentment is excused.

(3) It may be made

(a) to any one of two or more makers, acceptors, drawees or other payor; or

(b) to any person who has authority to make or refuse the acceptance or payment.

(4) A draft accepted or a note made payable at a bank in the United States must be presented at such bank.

(5) In the cases described in Section 4-210 presentment may be made in the manner and with the result stated in that section. As amended 1962.

§3-505. Rights of Party to Whom Presentment Is Made.

(1) The party to whom presentment is made may without dishonor require

(a) exhibition of the instrument; and

(b) reasonable identification of the person making presentment and evidence of his authority to make it if made for another; and

(c) that the instrument be produced for acceptance or payment at a place specified in it, or if there be none at any place reasonable in the circumstances; and

(d) a signed receipt on the instrument for any partial or full payment and its surrender upon full payment.

(2) Failure to comply with any such requirement invalidates the presentment but the person presenting has a reasonable time in which to comply and the time for acceptance or payment runs from the time of compliance.

§3-506. Time Allowed For Acceptance or Payment.

(1) Acceptance may be deferred without dishonor until the close of the next business day following presentment. The holder may also in a good faith effort to obtain acceptance and without either dishonor of the instrument or discharge of secondary parties allow postponement of acceptance for an additional business day.

(2) Except as a longer time is allowed in the case of documentary drafts drawn under a letter of credit, and unless an earlier time is agreed to by the party to pay, payment of an instrument may be deferred without dishonor pending reasonable examination to determine whether it is properly payable, but payment must be made in any event before the close of business on the day of presentment.

§3-507. Dishonor: Holder's Right of Recourse; Term Allowing Re-Presentment.

(1) An instrument is dishonored when

    (a) a necessary or optional presentment is duly made and due acceptance or payment is refused or cannot be obtained within the prescribed time or in case of bank collections the instrument is seasonably returned by the midnight deadline (Section 4-301); or

    (b) presentment is excused and the instrument is not duly accepted or paid.

(2) Subject to any necessary notice of dishonor and protest, the holder has upon dishonor an immediate right of recourse against the drawers and indorsers.

(3) Return of an instrument for lack of proper indorsement is not dishonor.

(4) A term in a draft or an indorsement thereof allowing a stated time for re-presentment in the event of any dishonor of the draft by nonacceptance if a time draft or by nonpayment if a sight draft gives the holder as against any secondary party bound by the term an option to waive the dishonor without affecting the liability of the secondary party and he may present again up to the end of the stated time.

§3-508. Notice of Dishonor.

(1) Notice of dishonor may be given to any person who may be liable on the instrument by or on behalf of the holder or any party who has himself received notice, or any other party who can be compelled to pay the instrument. In addition an agent or bank in whose hands the instrument is dishonored may give notice to his principal or customer or to another agent or bank from which the instrument was received.

(2) Any necessary notice must be given by a bank before its midnight deadline and by any other person before midnight of the third business day after dishonor or receipt of notice of dishonor.

(3) Notice may be given in any reasonable manner. It may be oral or written and in any terms which identify the instrument and state that it has been dishonored. A misdescription which does not mislead the party notified does not vitiate the notice. Sending the instrument bearing a stamp, ticket or writing stating that acceptance or payment has been refused or sending a notice of debit with respect to the instrument is sufficient.

(4) Written notice is given when sent although it is not received.

(5) Notice to one partner is notice to each although the firm has been dissolved.

(6) When any party is in insolvency proceedings instituted after the issue of the instrument notice may be given either to the party or to the representative of his estate.

(7) When any party is dead or incompetent notice may be sent to his last known address or given to his personal representative.

(8) Notice operates for the benefit of all parties who have rights on the instrument against the party notified.

§3-509. Protest; Noting for Protest.

(1) A protest is a certificate of dishonor made under the hand and seal of a United States consul or vice consul or a notary public or other person authorized to certify dishonor by the law of the place where dishonor occurs. It may be made upon information satisfactory to such person.

(2) The protest must identify the instrument and certify either that due presentment has been made or the reason why it is excused and that the instrument has been dishonored by nonacceptance or nonpayment.

(3) The protest may also certify that notice of dishonor has been given to all parties or to specified parties.

(4) Subject to subsection (5) any necessary protest is due by the time that notice of dishonor is due.

(5) If, before protest is due, an instrument has been noted for protest by the officer to make protest, the protest may be made at any time thereafter as of the date of the noting.

§3-510. Evidence of Dishonor and Notice of Dishonor. The following are admissible as evidence and create a presumption of dishonor and of any notice of dishonor therein shown:

    (a) a document regular in form as provided in the preceding section which purports to be a protest;

    (b) the purported stamp or writing of the drawee, payor bank or presenting bank on the instrument or accompanying it stating that acceptance or payment has been refused for reasons consistent with dishonor;

    (c) any book or record of the drawee, payor

bank, or any collecting bank kept in the usual course of business which shows dishonor, even though there is no evidence of who made the entry.

§3-511. Waived or Excused Presentment, Protest or Notice of Dishonor or Delay Therein.

(1) Delay in presentment, protest or notice of dishonor is excused when the party is without notice that it is due or when the delay is caused by circumstances beyond his control and he exercises reasonable diligence after the cause of the delay ceases to operate.

(2) Presentment or notice or protest as the case may be is entirely excused when

    (a) the party to be charged has waived it expressly or by implication either before or after it is due; or

    (b) such party has himself dishonored the instrument or has countermanded payment or otherwise has no reason to expect or right to require that the instrument be accepted or paid; or

    (c) by reasonable diligence the presentment or protest cannot be made or the notice given.

(3) Presentment is also entirely excused when

    (a) the maker, acceptor or drawee of any instrument except a documentary draft is dead or in insolvency proceedings instituted after the issue of the instrument; or

    (b) acceptance or payment is refused but not for want of proper presentment.

(4) Where a draft has been dishonored by nonacceptance a later presentment for payment and any notice of dishonor and protest for nonpayment are excused unless in the meantime the instrument has been accepted.

(5) A waiver of protest is also a waiver of presentment and of notice of dishonor even though protest is not required.

(6) Where a waiver of presentment or notice of protest is embodied in the instrument itself it is binding upon all parties; but where it is written above the signature of an indorser it binds him only.

Part 6: Discharge
§3-601. Discharge of Parties.

(1) The extent of the discharge of any party from liability on an instrument is governed by the sections on

    (a) payment or satisfaction (Section 3-603); or

    (b) tender of payment (Section 3-604); or

    (c) cancellation or renunciation (Section 3-605); or

    (d) impairment of right of recourse or of collateral (Section 3-606); or

    (e) reacquisition of the instrument by a prior party (Section 3-208); or

    (f) fraudulent and material alteration (Section 3-407); or

    (g) certification of a check (Section 3-411); or

    (h) acceptance varying a draft (Section 3-412); or

    (i) unexcused delay in presentment or notice of dishonor or protest (Section 3-502).

(2) Any party is also discharged from his liability on an instrument to another party by any other act or agreement with such party which would discharge his simple contract for the payment of money.

(3) The liability of all parties is discharged when any party who has himself no right of action or recourse on the instrument

    (a) reacquires the instruments in his own right; or

    (b) is discharged under any provision of this Article, except as otherwise provided with respect to discharge for impairment of recourse or of collateral (Section 3-606).

§3-602. Effect of Discharge Against Holder in Due Course.   No discharge of any party provided by this Article is effective against a subsequent holder in due course unless he has notice thereof when he takes the instrument.

§3-603. Payment or Satisfaction.

(1) The liability of any party is discharged to the extent of his payment or satisfaction to the holder even though it is made with knowledge of a claim of another person to the instrument unless prior to such payment or satisfaction the person making the claim either supplies indemnity deemed adequate by the party seeking the discharge or enjoins payment or satisfaction by order of a court of competent jurisdiction in an action in which the adverse claimant and the holder are parties. This subsection does not, however, result in the discharge of the liability

    (a) of a party who in bad faith pays or satisfies a holder who acquired the instrument by theft or who (unless having the rights of a holder in due course) holds through one who so acquired it; or

    (b) of a party (other than an intermediary

bank or a payor bank which is not a depository bank) who pays or satisfies the holder of an instrument which has been restrictively indorsed in a manner not consistent with the terms of such restrictive indorsement.

(2) Payment or satisfaction may be made with the consent of the holder by any person including a stranger to the instrument. Surrender of the instrument to such a person gives him the rights of a transferee (Section 3-201).

§3-604. Tender of Payment.

(1) Any party making tender of full payment to a holder when or after it is due is discharged to the extent of all subsequent liability for interest, costs and attorney's fees.

(2) The holder's refusal of such tender wholly discharges any party who has a right of recourse against the party making the tender.

(3) Where the maker or acceptor of an instrument payable otherwise than on demand is able and ready to pay at every place of payment specified in the instrument when it is due, it is equivalent to tender.

§3-605. Cancellation and Renunciation.

(1) The holder of an instrument may even without consideration discharge any party

(a) in any manner apparent on the face of the instrument or the indorsement, as by intentionally cancelling the instrument or the party's signature by destruction or mutilation, or by striking out the party's signature; or

(b) by renouncing his rights by a writing signed and delivered or by surrender of the instrument to the party to be discharged.

(2) Neither cancellation or renunciation without surrender of the instrument affects the title thereto.

§3-606. Impairment of Recourse or of Collateral.

(1) The holder discharges any party to the instrument to the extent that without such party's consent the holder

(a) without express reservation of rights releases or agrees not to sue any person against whom the party has to the knowledge of the holder a right of recourse or agrees to suspend the right to enforce against such person the instrument or collateral or otherwise discharges such person, except that failure or delay in effecting any required presentment, protest or notice of dishonor with respect to any such person does not discharge any party as to whom

presentment, protest or notice of dishonor is effective or unnecessary; or

(b) unjustifiably impairs any collateral for the instrument given by or on behalf of the party or any person against whom he has a right of recourse.

(2) By express reservation of rights against a party with a right of recourse the holder preserves

(a) all his rights against such party as of the time when the instrument was originally due; and

(b) the right of the party to pay the instrument as of that time; and

(c) all rights of such party to recourse against others.

Part 7: Advice of International Sight Draft

§3-701. Letter of Advice of International Sight Draft.

(1) A "letter of advice" is a drawer's communication to the drawee that a described draft has been drawn.

(2) Unless otherwise agreed when a bank receives from another bank a letter of advice of an international sight draft the drawee bank may immediately debit the drawer's account and stop the running of interest pro tanto. Such a debit and any resulting credit to any account covering outstanding drafts leaves in the drawer full power to stop payment or otherwise dispose of the amount and creates no trust or interest in favor of the holder.

(3) Unless otherwise agreed and except where a draft is drawn under a credit issued by the drawee, the drawee of an international sight draft owes the drawer no duty to pay an unadvised draft but if it does so and the draft is genuine, may appropriately debit the drawer's account.

Part 8: Miscellaneous

§3-801. Drafts in a Set.

(1) Where a draft is drawn in a set of parts, each of which is numbered and expressed to be an order only if no other part has been honored, the whole of the parts constitutes one draft but a taker of any part may become a holder in due course of the draft.

(2) Any person who negotiates, indorses or accepts a single part of a draft drawn in a set thereby becomes liable to any holder in due course of that part as if it were the whole set, but as between different holders in due course to whom different parts have been ne-

gotiated the holder whose title first accrues has all rights to the draft and its proceeds.

(3) As against the drawee the first presented part of a draft drawn in a set is the part entitled to payment, or if a time draft to acceptance and payment. Acceptance of any subsequently presented part renders the drawee liable thereon under subsection (2). With respect both to a holder and to the drawer payment of a subsequently presented part of a draft payable at sight has the same effect as payment of a check notwithstanding an effective stop order (Section 4-407).

(4) Except as otherwise provided in this section, where any part of a draft in a set is discharged by payment or otherwise the whole draft is discharged.

§3-802. Effect of Instrument on Obligation for Which It Is Given.

(1) Unless otherwise agreed where an instrument is taken for an underlying obligation

> (a) the obligation is pro tanto discharged if a bank is drawer, maker or acceptor of the instrument and there is no recourse on the instrument against the underlying obligor; and
>
> (b) in any other case the obligation is suspended pro tanto until the instrument is due or if it is payable on demand until its presentment. If the instrument is dishonored action may be maintained on either the instrument or the obligation; discharge of the underlying obligor on the instrument also discharges him on the obligation.

(2) The taking in good faith of a check which is not postdated does not of itself so extend the time on the original obligation as to discharge a surety.

§3-803. Notice to Third Party. Where a defendant is sued for breach of an obligation for which a third person is answerable over under this Article he may give the third person written notice of the litigation, and the person notified may then give similar notice to any other person who is answerable over to him under this Article. If the notice states that the person notified may come in and defend and that if the person notified does not do so he will in any action against him by the person giving the notice be bound by any determination of fact common to the two litigations, then unless after seasonable receipt of the notice the person notified does come in and defend he is so bound.

§3-804. Lost, Destroyed or Stolen Instruments. The owner of an instrument which is lost, whether by destruction, theft or otherwise, may maintain an action in his own name and recover from any party liable thereon upon due proof of his ownership, the facts which prevent his production of the instrument and its terms. The court may require security indemnifying the defendant against loss by reason of further claims on the instrument.

§3-805. Instruments Not Payable to Order or to Bearer. This Article applies to any instrument whose terms do not preclude transfer and which is otherwise negotiable within this Article but which is not payable to order or to bearer, except that there can be no holder in due course of such an instrument.

ARTICLE 4: BANK DEPOSITS AND COLLECTIONS

Part 1: General Provisions and Definitions

§4-101. Short Title. This Article shall be known and may be cited as Uniform Commercial Code— Bank Deposits and Collections.

§4-102. Applicability.

(1) To the extent that items within this Article are also within the scope of Articles 3 and 8, they are subject to the provisions of those Articles. In the event of conflict the provisions of this Article govern those of Article 3, but the provisions of Article 8 govern those of this Article.

(2) The liability of a bank for action or non-action with respect to any item handled by it for purposes of presentment, payment or collection is governed by the law of the place where the bank is located. In the case of action or non-action by or at a branch or separate office of a bank, its liability is governed by the law of the place where the branch or separate office is located.

§4-103. Variation by Agreement; Measure of Damages; Certain Action Constituting Ordinary Care.

(1) The effect of the provisions of this Article may be varied by agreement except that no agreement can disclaim a bank's responsibility for its own lack of good faith or failure to exercise ordinary care or can limit the measure of damages for such lack or failure; but the parties may by agreement determine the standards by which such responsibility is to be measured if such standards are not manifestly unreasonable.

(2) Federal Reserve regulations and operating letters, clearing house rules, and the like, have the effect

of agreements under subsection (1), whether or not specifically assented to by all parties interested in items handled.

(3) Action or non-action approved by this Article or pursuant to Federal Reserve regulations or operating letters constitutes the exercise of ordinary care and, in the absence of special instructions, action or non-action consistent with clearing house rules and the like or with a general banking usage not disapproved by this Article, prima facie constitutes the exercise of ordinary care.

(4) The specification or approval of certain procedures by this Article does not constitute disapproval of other procedures which may be reasonable under the circumstances.

(5) The measure of damages for failure to exercise ordinary care in handling an item is the amount of the item reduced by an amount which could not have been realized by the use of ordinary care, and where there is bad faith it includes other damages, if any, suffered by the party as a proximate consequence.

§4-104. **Definitions and Index of Definitions.**

(1) In this Article unless the context otherwise requires

(a) "Account" means any account with a bank and includes a checking, time, interest or savings account;

(b) "Afternoon" means the period of a day between noon and midnight;

(c) "Banking day" means that part of any day on which a bank is open to the public for carrying on substantially all of its banking functions;

(d) "Clearing house" means any association of banks or other payors regularly clearing items;

(e) "Customer" means any person having an account with a bank or for whom a bank has agreed to collect items and includes a bank carrying an account with another bank;

(f) "Documentary draft" means any negotiable or nonnegotiable draft with accompanying documents, securities or other papers to be delivered against honor of the draft;

(g) "Item" means any instrument for the payment of money even though it is not negotiable but does not include money;

(h) "Midnight deadline" with respect to a bank is midnight on its next banking day following the banking day on which it receives the relevant item or notice or from which the time for taking action commences to run, whichever is later;

(i) "Properly payable" includes the availability of funds for payment at the time of decision to pay or dishonor;

(j) "Settle" means to pay in cash, by clearing house settlement, in a charge or credit or by remittance, or otherwise as instructed. A settlement may be either provisional or final;

(k) "Suspends payments" with respect to a bank means that it has been closed by order of the supervisory authorities, that a public officer has been appointed to take it over or that it ceases or refuses to make payments in the ordinary course of business.

(2) Other definitions applying to this Article and the sections in which they appear are:

"Collecting bank". Section 4-105.

"Depositary bank". Section 4-105.

"Intermediary bank". Section 4-105.

"Payor bank". Section 4-105.

"Presenting bank". Section 4-105.

"Remitting bank". Section 4-105.

(3) The following definitions in other Articles apply to this Article:

"Acceptance". Section 3-410.

"Certificate of deposit". Section 3-104.

"Certification". Section 3-411.

"Check". Section 3-104.

"Draft". Section 3-104.

"Holder in due course". Section 3-302.

"Notice of dishonor". Section 3-508.

"Presentment". Section 3-504.

"Protest". Section 3-509.

"Secondary party". Section 3-102.

(4) In addition Article 1 contains general definitions and principles of construction and interpretation applicable throughout this Article.

§4-105. **"Depositary Bank"; "Intermediary Bank"; "Collecting Bank"; "Payor Bank"; "Presenting Bank"; "Remitting Bank".** In this Article unless the context otherwise requires:

(a) "Depositary bank" means the first bank to which an item is transferred for collection even though it is also the payor bank;

(b) "Payor bank" means a bank by which an item is payable as drawn or accepted;

(c) "Intermediary bank" means any bank to which an item is transferred in course of collection except the depositary or payor bank;

(**d**) "Collecting bank" means any bank handling the item for collection except the payor bank;

(**e**) "Presenting bank" means any bank presenting an item except a payor bank;

(**f**) "Remitting bank" means any payor or intermediary bank remitting for an item.

§4-106. Separate Office of a Bank. A branch or separate office of a bank [maintaining its own deposit ledgers] is a separate bank for the purpose of computing the time within which and determining the place at or to which action may be taken or notices or orders shall be given under this Article and under Article 3. As amended 1962.

Note: *The brackets are to make it optional with the several states whether to require a branch to maintain its own deposit ledgers in order to be considered to be a separate bank for certain purposes under Article 4. In some states "maintaining its own deposit ledgers" is a satisfactory test. In others branch banking practices are such that this test would not be suitable.*

§4-107. Time of Receipt of Items.

(**1**) For the purpose of allowing time to process items, prove balances and make the necessary entries on its books to determine its position for the day, a bank may fix an afternoon hour of 2 P.M. or later as a cut-off hour for the handling of money and items and the making of entries on its books.

(**2**) Any item or deposit of money received on any day after a cut-off hour so fixed or after the close of the banking day may be treated as being received at the opening of the next banking day.

§4-108. Delays.

(**1**) Unless otherwise instructed, a collecting bank in a good faith effort to secure payment may, in the case of specific items and with or without the approval of any person involved, waive, modify or extend time limits imposed or permitted by this Act for a period not in excess of an additional banking day without discharge of secondary parties and without liability to its transferor or any prior party.

(**2**) Delay by a collecting bank or payor bank beyond time limits prescribed or permitted by this Act or by instructions is excused if caused by interruption of communication facilities, suspension of payments by another bank, war, emergency conditions or other circumstances beyond the control of the bank provided it exercises such diligence as the circumstances require.

§4-109. Process of Posting. The "process of posting" means that usual procedure followed by a payor bank in determining to pay an item and in re-

cording the payment including one or more of the following or other steps as determined by the bank:

(**a**) verification of any signature;

(**b**) ascertaining that sufficient funds are available;

(**c**) affixing a "paid" or other stamp;

(**d**) entering a charge or entry to a customer's account;

(**e**) correcting or reversing an entry or erroneous action with respect to the item. Added 1962.

Part 2: Collection of Items: Depositary and Collecting Banks

§4-201. Presumption and Duration of Agency Status of Collecting Banks and Provisional Status of Credits; Applicability of Article; Item Indorsed "Pay Any Bank".

(**1**) Unless a contrary intent clearly appears and prior to the time that a settlement given by a collecting bank for an item is or becomes final (subsection (3) of Section 4-211 and Sections 4-212 and 4-213) the bank is an agent or sub-agent of the owner of the item and any settlement given for the item is provisional. This provision applies regardless of the form of indorsement or lack of indorsement and even though credit given for the item is subject to immediate withdrawal as of right or is in fact withdrawn; but the continuance of ownership of an item by its owner and any rights of the owner to proceeds of the item are subject to rights of a collecting bank such as those resulting from outstanding advances on the item and valid rights of setoff. When an item is handled by banks for purposes of presentment, payment and collection, the relevant provisions of this Article apply even though action of parties clearly establishes that a particular bank has purchased the item and is the owner of it.

(**2**) After an item has been indorsed with the words "pay any bank" or the like, only a bank may acquire the rights of a holder

(**a**) until the item has been returned to the customer initiating collection; or

(**b**) until the item has been specially indorsed by a bank to a person who is not a bank.

§4-202. Responsibility for Collection; When Action Seasonable.

(**1**) A collecting bank must use ordinary care in

(**a**) presenting an item or sending it for presentment; and

(**b**) sending notice of dishonor on non-payment or returning an item other than a documentary draft to the bank's transferor [or directly to the depositary bank under subsection (2) of Section 4-212] (*see note to Section* 4-212) after learning that the item has not been paid or accepted, as the case may be; and

(**c**) settling for an item when the bank receives final settlement; and

(**d**) making or providing for any necessary protest; and

(**e**) notifying its transferor of any loss or delay in transit within a reasonable time after discovery thereof.

(**2**) A collecting bank taking proper action before its midnight deadline following receipt of an item, notice or payment acts seasonally; taking proper action within a reasonably longer time may be seasonable but the bank has the burden of so establishing.

(**3**) Subject to subsection (1)(a), a bank is not liable for the insolvency, neglect, misconduct, mistake or default of another bank or person or for loss or destruction of an item in transit or in the possession of others.

§4-203. Effect of Instructions. Subject to the provision of Article 3 concerning conversion of instruments (Section 3-419) and the provisions of both Article 3 and this Article concerning restrictive indorsements only a collecting bank's transferor can give instructions which affect the bank or constitute notice to it and a collecting bank is not liable to prior parties for any action taken pursuant to such instructions or in accordance with any agreement with its transferor.

§4-204. Methods of Sending and Presenting; Sending Direct to Payor Bank.

(**1**) A collecting bank must send items by reasonably prompt method taking into consideration any relevant instructions, the nature of the item, the number of such items on hand, and the cost of collection involved and the method generally used by it or others to present such items.

(**2**) A collecting bank may send

(**a**) any item direct to the payor bank;

(**b**) any item direct to any non-bank payor if authorized by its transferor; and

(**c**) any item other than documentary drafts to any non-bank payor, if authorized by Federal Reserve regulation or operating letter, clearing house rule or the like.

(**3**) Presentment may be made by a presenting bank at a place where the payor bank has requested that presentment be made. As amended 1962.

§4-205. Supplying Missing Indorsement; No Notice from Prior Indorsement.

(**1**) A depositary bank which has taken an item for collection may supply any indorsement of the customer which is necessary to title unless the item contains the words "payee's indorsement required" or the like. In the absence of such a requirement a statement placed on the item by the depositary bank to the effect that the item was deposited by a customer or credited to his account is effective as the customer's indorsement.

(**2**) An intermediary bank, or payor bank which is not a depositary bank, is neither given notice nor otherwise affected by a restrictive indorsement of any person except the bank's immediate transferor.

§4-206. Transfer Between Banks. Any agreed method which identifies the transferor bank is sufficient for the item's further transfer to another bank.

§4-207. Warranties of Customer and Collecting Bank on Transfer or Presentment of Items; Time for Claims.

(**1**) Each customer or collecting bank who obtains payment or acceptance of an item and each prior customer and collecting bank warrants to the payor bank or other payor who in good faith pays or accepts the item that

(**a**) he has a good title to the item or is authorized to obtain payment or acceptance on behalf of one who has a good title; and

(**b**) he has no knowledge that the signature of the maker or drawer is unauthorized, except that this warranty is not given by any customer or collecting bank that is a holder in due course and acts in good faith

(**i**) to a maker with respect to the maker's own signature; or

(**ii**) to a drawer with respect to the drawer's own signature, whether or not the drawer is also the drawee; or

(**iii**) to an acceptor of an item if the holder in due course took the item after the acceptance or obtained the acceptance without knowledge that the drawer's signature was unauthorized; and

(**c**) the item has not been materially altered, except that this warranty is not given by any customer or collecting bank that is a holder in due course and acts in good faith

(**i**) to the maker of a note; or

(**ii**) to the drawer of a draft whether or not the drawer is also the drawee; or

(iii) to the acceptor of an item with respect to an alteration made prior to the acceptance if the holder in due course took the item after the acceptance, even though the acceptance provided "payable as originally drawn" or equivalent terms; or

(iv) to the acceptor of an item with respect to an alteration made after the acceptance.

(2) Each customer and collecting bank who transfers an item and receives a settlement or other consideration for it warrants to his transferee and to any subsequent collecting bank who takes the item in good faith that

(a) he has a good title to the item or is authorized to obtain payment or acceptance on behalf of one who has a good title and the transfer is otherwise rightful; and

(b) all signatures are genuine or authorized; and

(c) the item has not been materially altered; and

(d) no defense of any party is good against him; and

(e) he has no knowledge of any insolvency proceeding instituted with respect to the maker or acceptor or the drawer of an unaccepted item.

In addition each customer and collecting bank so transferring an item and receiving a settlement or other consideration engages that upon dishonor and any necessary notice of dishonor and protest he will take up the item.

(3) The warranties and the engagement to honor set forth in the two preceding subsections arise notwithstanding the absence of indorsement or words of guaranty or warranty in the transfer or presentment and collecting bank remains liable for their breach despite remittance to its transferor. Damages for breach of such warranties or engagement to honor shall not exceed the consideration received by the customer or collecting bank responsible plus finance charges and expenses related to the item, if any.

(4) Unless a claim for breach of warranty under this section is made within a reasonable time after the person claiming learns the breach, the person liable is discharged to the extent of any loss caused by the delay in making claim.

§4-208. Security Interest of Collecting Bank in Items, Accompanying Documents and Proceeds.

(1) A bank has a security interest in an item and any accompanying documents or the proceeds of either

(a) in case of an item deposited in an account to the extent to which credit given for the item has been withdrawn or applied;

(b) in case of an item for which it has given credit available for withdrawal as of right, to the extent of the credit given whether or not the credit is drawn upon and whether or not there is a right of charge-back; or

(c) if it makes an advance on or against the item.

(2) When credit which has been given for several items received at one time or pursuant to a single agreement is withdrawn or applied in part the security interest remains upon all the items, any accompanying documents or the proceeds of either. For the purpose of this section, credits first given are first withdrawn.

(3) Receipt by a collecting bank of a final settlement for an item is a realization on its security interest in the item, accompanying documents and proceeds. To the extent and so long as the bank does not receive final settlement for the item or give up possession of the item or accompanying documents for purposes other than collection, the security interest continues and is subject to the provisions of Article 9 except that

(a) no security agreement is necessary to make the security interest enforceable (subsection (1) (b) of Section 9-203); and

(b) no filing is required to perfect the security interest; and

(c) the security interest has priority over conflicting perfected security interests in the item, accompanying documents or proceeds.

§4-209. When Bank Gives Value for Purposes of Holder in Due Course.   For purposes of determining its status as a holder in due course, the bank has given value to the extent that it has a security interest in an item provided that the bank otherwise complies with the requirements of Section 3-302 on what constitutes a holder in due course.

§4-210. Presentment by Notice of Item Not Payable by, Through or at a Bank; Liability of Secondary Parties.

(1) Unless otherwise instructed, a collecting bank may present an item not payable by, through or at a bank by sending to the party to accept or pay a written notice that the bank holds the item for acceptance

or payment. The notice must be sent in time to be received on or before the day when presentment is due and the bank must meet any requirement of the party to accept or pay under Section 3-505 by the close of the bank's next banking day after it knows of the requirement.

(**2**) Where presentment is made by notice and neither honor nor request for compliance with a requirement under Section 3-505 is received by the close of business on the day after maturity or in the case of demand items by the close of business on the third banking day after notice was sent, the presenting bank may treat the item as dishonored and charge any secondary party by sending him notice of the facts.

§4-211. Media of Remittance; Provisional and Final Settlement in Remittance Cases.

(**1**) A collecting bank may take in settlement of an item

(**a**) a check of the remitting bank or of another bank on any bank except the remitting bank; or

(**b**) a cashier's check or similar primary obligation of a remitting bank which is a member of or clears through a member of the same clearing house or group as the collecting bank; or

(**c**) appropriate authority to charge an account of the remitting bank or of another bank with the collecting bank; or

(**d**) if the item is drawn upon or payable by a person other than a bank, a cashier's check, certified check or other bank check or obligation.

(**2**) If before its midnight deadline the collecting bank properly dishonors a remittance check or authorization to charge on itself or presents or forwards for collection a remittance instrument of or on another bank which is of a kind approved by subsection (1) or has not been authorized by it, the collecting bank is not liable to prior parties in the event of the dishonor of such check, instrument or authorization.

(**3**) A settlement for an item by means of a remittance instrument or authorization to charge is or becomes a final settlement as to both the person making and the person receiving the settlement

(**a**) if the remittance instrument or authorization to charge is of a kind approved by subsection (1) or has not been authorized by the person receiving the settlement and in either case

the person receiving the settlement acts seasonably before its midnight deadline in presenting, forwarding for collection or paying the instrument or authorization,—at the time the remittance instrument or authorization is finally paid by the payor by which it is payable;

(**b**) if the person receiving the settlement has authorized remittance by a non-bank check or obligation or by a cashier's check or similar primary obligation of or a check upon the payor or other remitting bank which is not of a kind approved by subsection (1)(b),—at the time of the receipt of such remittance check or obligation; or

(**c**) if in a case not covered by sub-paragraphs (a) or (b) the person receiving the settlement fails to seasonably present, forward for collection, pay or return a remittance instrument or authorization to it to charge before its midnight deadline,—at such midnight deadline.

§4-212. Right of Charge-Back or Refund.

(**1**) If a collecting bank has made provisional settlement with its customer for an item and itself fails by reason of dishonor, suspension of payments by a bank or otherwise to receive a settlement for the item which is or becomes final, the bank may revoke the settlement given by it, charge back the amount of any credit given for the item to its customer's account or obtain refund from its customer whether or not it is able to return the items if by its midnight deadline or within a longer reasonable time after it learns the facts it returns the item or sends notification of the facts. These rights to revoke, charge-back and obtain refund terminate if and when a settlement for the item received by the bank is or becomes final (subsection (3) of Section 4-211 and subsections (2) and (3) of Section 4-213).

[(**2**) Within the time and manner prescribed by this section and Section 4-301, an intermediary or payor bank, as the case may be, may return an unpaid item directly to the depositary bank and may send for collection a draft on the depositary bank and obtain reimbursement. In such case, if the depositary bank has received provisional settlement for the item, it must reimburse the bank drawing the draft and any provisional credits for the item between banks shall become and remain final.]

Note: *Direct returns is recognized as an innovation that is not yet established bank practice, and therefore, Paragraph 2 has been bracketed. Some lawyers* *have doubts whether it should be included in legislation or left to development by agreement.*

(**3**) A depositary bank which is also the payor may charge-back the amount of an item to its customer's account or obtain refund in accordance with the section governing return of an item received by a payor bank for credit on its books. (Section 4-301).

(**4**) The right to charge-back is not affected by

    (**a**) prior use of the credit given for the item; or

    (**b**) failure by any bank to exercise ordinary care with respect to the item but any bank so failing remains liable.

(**5**) A failure to charge-back or claim refund does not affect other rights of the bank against the customer or any other party.

(**6**) If credit is given in dollars as the equivalent of the value of an item payable in a foreign currency the dollar amount of any charge-back or refund shall be calculated on the basis of the buying sight rate for the foreign currency prevailing on the day when the person entitled to the charge-back or refund learns that it will not receive payment in ordinary course.

§4-213. Final Payment of Item by Payor Bank: When Provisional Debits and Credits Become Final; When Certain Credits Become Available for Withdrawal.

(**1**) An item is finally paid by a payor bank when the bank has done any of the following, whichever happens first:

    (**a**) paid the item in cash; or

    (**b**) settled for the item without reserving a right to revoke the settlement and without having such right under statute, clearing house rule or agreement; or

    (**c**) completed the process of posting the item to the indicated account of the drawer, maker or other person to be charged therewith; or

    (**d**) made a provisional settlement for the item and failed to revoke the settlement in the time and manner permitted by statute, clearing house rule or agreement.

Upon a final payment under subparagraphs (b), (c) or (d) the payor bank shall be accountable for the amount of the item.

(**2**) If provisional settlement for an item between the presenting and payor banks is made through a clearing house or by debits or credits in an account between them, then to the extent that provisional debits or credits for the item are entered in accounts between the presenting and payor banks or between

the presenting and successive prior collecting banks seriatim, they become final upon final payment of the item by the payor bank.

(**3**) If a collecting bank receives a settlement for an item which is or becomes final (subsection (3) of Section 4-211, subsection (2) of Section 4-213) the bank is accountable to its customer for the amount of the item and any provisional credit given for the item in an account with its customer becomes final.

(**4**) Subject to any right of the bank to apply the credit to an obligation of the customer, credit given by a bank for an item in an account with its customer becomes available for withdrawal as of right

    (**a**) in any case where the bank has received a provisional settlement for the item—when such settlement becomes final and the bank has had a reasonable time to learn that the settlement is final;

    (**b**) in any case where the bank is both a depositary bank and a payor bank and the item is finally paid,—at the opening of the bank's second banking day following receipt of the item.

(**5**) A deposit of money in a bank is final when made but, subject to any right of the bank to apply the deposit to an obligation of the customer, the deposit becomes available for withdrawal as of right at the opening of the bank's next banking day following receipt of the deposit.

§4-214. Insolvency and Preference.

(**1**) Any item in or coming into the possession of a payor or collecting bank which suspends payment and which item is not finally paid shall be returned by the receiver, trustee or agent in charge of the closed bank to the presenting bank or the closed bank's customer.

(**2**) If a payor bank finally pays an item and suspends payments without making a settlement for the item with its customer or the presenting bank which settlement is or becomes final, the owner of the item has a preferred claim against the payor bank.

(**3**) If a payor bank gives or a collecting bank gives or receives a provisional settlement for an item and thereafter suspends payments, the suspension does not prevent or interfere with the settlement becoming final if such finality occurs automatically upon the lapse of certain time or the happening of certain events (subsection (3) of Section 4-211, subsections (1)(d), (2) and (3) of Section 4-213).

(**4**) If a collecting bank receives from subsequent

parties settlement for an item which settlement is or becomes final and suspends payments without making a settlement for the item with its customer which is or becomes final, the owner of the item has a preferred claim against such collecting bank.

Part 3: Collection of Items: Payor Banks
§4-301. Deferred Posting; Recovery of Payment by Return of Items; Time of Dishonor.

(**1**) Where an authorized settlement for a demand item (other than a documentary draft) received by a payor bank otherwise than for immediate payment over the counter has been made before midnight of the banking day of receipt the payor bank may revoke the settlement and recover any payment if before it has made final payment (subsection (1) of Section 4-213) and before its midnight deadline it

> (**a**) returns the item; or

> (**b**) sends written notice of dishonor or nonpayment if the item is held for protest or is otherwise unavailable for return.

(**2**) If a demand item is received by a payor bank for credit on its books it may return such item or send notice of dishonor and may revoke any credit given or recover the amount thereof withdrawn by its customer, if it acts within the time limit and in the manner specified in the preceding subsection.

(**3**) Unless previous notice of dishonor has been sent an item is dishonored at the time when for purposes of dishonor it is returned or notice sent in accordance with this section.

(**4**) An item is returned:

> (**a**) as to an item received through a clearing house, when it is delivered to the presenting or last collecting bank or to the clearing house or is sent or delivered in accordance with its rules; or

> (**b**) in all other cases, when it is sent or delivered to the bank's customer or transferor or pursuant to his instructions.

§4-302. Payor Bank's Responsibility for Late Return of Item.
In the absence of a valid defense such as breach of a presentment warranty (subsection (1) of Section 4-207), settlement effected or the like, if an item is presented on and received by a payor bank the bank is accountable for the amount of

> (**a**) a demand item other than a documentary draft whether properly payable or not if the bank, in any case where it is not also the depositary bank, retains the item beyond midnight of the banking day of receipt without settling for it or, regardless of whether it is also the depositary bank, does not pay or return the item or send notice of dishonor until after its midnight deadline; or

> (**b**) any other properly payable item unless within the time allowed for acceptance or payment of that item the bank either accepts or pays the item or returns it and accompanying documents.

§4-303. When Items Subject to Notice, Stop-Order, Legal Process or Setoff; Order in Which Items May be Charged or Certified.

(**1**) Any knowledge, notice or stop-order received by, legal process served upon or setoff exercised by a payor bank, whether or not effective under other rules of law to terminate, suspend or modify the bank's right or duty to pay an item or to charge its customer's account for the item, comes too late to so terminate, suspend or modify such right or duty if the knowledge, notice, stop-order or legal process is received or served and a reasonable time for the bank to act thereon expires or the setoff is exercised after the bank has done any of the following:

> (**a**) accepted or certified the item;

> (**b**) paid the item in cash;

> (**c**) settled for the item without reserving a right to revoke the settlement and without having such right under statute, clearing house rule or agreement;

> (**d**) completed the process of posting the item to the indicated account of the drawer, maker or other person to be charged therewith or otherwise has evidenced by examination of such indicated account and by action its decision to pay the item; or

> (**e**) become accountable for the amount of the item under subsection (1)(d) of Section 4-213 and Section 4-302 dealing with the payor bank's responsibility for late return of items.

(**2**) Subject to the provisions of subsection (1) items may be accepted, paid, certified or charged to the indicated account of its customer in any order convenient to the bank.

Part 4: Relationship between Payor Bank and Its Customer
§4-401. When Bank May Charge Customer's Account.

(**1**) As against its customer, a bank may charge

against his account any item which is otherwise properly payable from that account even though the charge creates an overdraft.

(2) A bank which in good faith makes payment to a holder may charge the indicated account of its customer according to

(a) the original tenor of his altered item; or

(b) the tenor of his completed item, even though the bank knows the item has been completed unless the bank has notice that the completion was improper.

§4-402. **Bank's Liability to Customer for Wrongful Dishonor.** A payor bank is liable to its customer for damages proximately caused by the wrongful dishonor of an item. When the dishonor occurs through mistake liability is limited to actual damages proved. If so proximately caused and proved damages may include damages for an arrest or prosecution of the customer or other consequential damages. Whether any consequential damages are proximately caused by the wrongful dishonor is a question of fact to be determined in each case.

§4-403. **Customer's Right to Stop Payment; Burden of Proof of Loss.**

(1) A customer may by order to his bank stop payment of any item payable for his account but the order must be received at such time and in such manner as to afford the bank a reasonable opportunity to act on it prior to any action by the bank with respect to the item described in Section 4-303.

(2) An oral order is binding upon the bank only for fourteen calendar days unless confirmed in writing within that period. A written order is effective for only six months unless renewed in writing.

(3) The burden of establishing the fact and amount of loss resulting from the payment of an item contrary to a binding stop payment order is on the customer.

§4-404. **Bank Not Obligated to Pay Check More Than Six Months Old.** A bank is under no obligation to a customer having a checking account to pay a check, other than a certified check, which is presented more than six months after its date, but it may charge its customer's account for a payment made thereafter in good faith.

§4-405. **Death or Incompetence of Customer.**

(1) A payor or collecting bank's authority to accept, pay or collect an item or to account for proceeds of its collection if otherwise effective is not rendered ineffective by incompetence of a customer of either bank existing at the time the item is issued or its collection is undertaken if the bank does not know of an adjudication of incompetence. Neither death nor incompetence of a customer revokes such authority to accept, pay, collect or account until the bank knows of the fact of death or of an adjudication of incompetence and has reasonable opportunity to act on it.

(2) Even with knowledge a bank may for 10 days after the date of death pay or certify checks drawn on or prior to that date unless ordered to stop payment by a person claiming an interest in the account.

§4-406. **Customer's Duty to Discover and Report Unauthorized Signature or Alteration.**

(1) When a bank sends to its customer a statement of account accompanied by items paid in good faith in support of the debit entries or holds the statement and items pursuant to a request or instructions of its customer or otherwise in a reasonable manner makes the statement and items available to the customer, the customer must exercise reasonable care and promptness to examine the statement and items to discover his unauthorized signature or any alteration on an item and must notify the bank promptly after discovery thereof.

(2) If the bank establishes that the customer failed with respect to an item to comply with the duties imposed on the customer by subsection (1) the customer is precluded from asserting against the bank

(a) his unauthorized signature or any alteration on the item if the bank also establishes that it suffered a loss by reason of such failure; and

(b) an unauthorized signature or alteration by the same wrongdoer on any other item paid in good faith by the bank after the first item and statement was available to the customer for a reasonable period not exceeding fourteen calendar days and before the bank receives notification from the customer of any such unauthorized signature or alteration.

(3) The preclusion under subsection (2) does not apply if the customer establishes lack of ordinary care on the part of the bank in paying the item(s).

(4) Without regard to care or lack of care of either the customer or the bank a customer who does not within one year from the time the statement and items are made available to the customer (subsection (1) discover and report his unauthorized signature or any alteration on the face or back of the item or does not within 3 years from that time discover and report

any unauthorized indorsement is precluded from asserting against the bank such unauthorized signature or indorsement or such alteration.

(5) If under this section a payor bank has a valid defense against a claim of a customer upon or resulting from payment of an item and waives or fails upon request to assert the defense the bank may not assert against any collecting bank or other prior party presenting or transferring the item a claim based upon the unauthorized signature or alteration giving rise to the customer's claim.

§4-407. Payor Bank's Right to Subrogation on Improper Payment. If a payor bank has paid an item over the stop payment order of the drawer or maker or otherwise under circumstances giving a basis for objection by the drawer or maker, to prevent unjust enrichment and only to the extent necessary to prevent loss to the bank by reason of its payment of the item, the payor bank shall be subrogated to the rights

> **(a)** of any holder in due course on the item against the drawer or maker; and
> **(b)** of the payee or any other holder of the item against the drawer or maker either on the item or under the transaction out of which the item arose; and
> **(c)** of the drawer or maker against the payee or any other holder of the item with respect to the transaction out of which the item arose.

Part 5: Collection of Documentary Drafts
§4-501. Handling of Documentary Drafts; Duty to Send for Presentment and to Notify Customer of Dishonor. A bank which takes a documentary draft for collection must present or send the draft and accompanying documents for presentment and upon learning that the draft has not been paid or accepted in due course must seasonably notify its customer of such fact even though it may have discounted or bought the draft or extended credit available for withdrawal as of right.

§4-502. Presentment of "On Arrival" Drafts. When a draft or the relevant instructions require presentment "on arrival", "when goods arrive" or the like, the collecting bank need not present until in its judgment a reasonable time for arrival of the goods has expired. Refusal to pay or accept because the goods have not arrived is not dishonor; the bank must notify its transferor of such refusal but

need not present the draft again until it is instructed to do so or learns of the arrival of the goods.

§4-503. Responsibility of Presenting Bank for Documents and Goods; Report of Reasons for Dishonor; Referee in Case of Need. Unless otherwise instructed and except as provided in Article 5 a bank presenting a documentary draft

> **(a)** must deliver the documents to the drawee on acceptance of the draft if it is payable more than three days after presentment; otherwise, only on payment; and
> **(b)** upon dishonor, either in the case of presentment for acceptance or presentment for payment, may seek and follow instructions from any referee in case of need designated in the draft or if the presenting bank does not choose to utilize his services it must use diligence and good faith to ascertain the reason for dishonor, must notify its transferor of the dishonor and of the results of its effort to ascertain the reasons therefor and must request instructions.

But the presenting bank is under no obligation with respect to goods represented by the documents except to follow any reasonable instructions seasonably received; it has a right to reimbursement for any expense incurred in following instructions and to prepayment of or indemnity for such expenses.

§4-504. Privilege of Presenting Bank to Deal with Goods; Security Interest for Expenses.

(1) A presenting bank which, following the dishonor of a documentary draft, has seasonably requested instructions but does not receive them within a reasonable time may store, sell, or otherwise deal with the goods in any reasonable manner.

(2) For its reasonable expenses incurred by action under subsection (1) the presenting bank has a lien upon the goods or their proceeds, which may be foreclosed in the same manner as an unpaid seller's lien.

ARTICLE 5: LETTERS OF CREDIT

§5-101. Short Title. This Article shall be known and may be cited as Uniform Commercial Code—Letters of Credit.

§5-102. Scope.

(1) This Article applies

> **(a)** to a credit issued by a bank if the credit requires a documentary draft or a documentary demand for payment; and

(b) to a credit issued by a person other than a bank if the credit requires that the draft or demand for payment be accompanied by a document of title; and

(c) to a credit issued by a bank or other person if the credit is not within subparagraphs (a) or (b) but conspicuously states that it is a letter of credit or is conspicuously so entitled.

(2) Unless the engagement meets the requirements of subsection (1), this Article does not apply to engagements to make advances or to honor drafts or demands for payment, to authorities to pay or purchase, to guarantees or to general agreements.

(3) This Article deals with some but not all of the rules and concepts of letters of credit as such rules or concepts have developed prior to this act or may hereafter develop. The fact that this Article states a rule does not by itself require, imply or negate application of the same or a converse rule to a situation not provided for or to a person not specified by this Article.

§5-103. Definitions.

(1) In this Article unless the context otherwise requires

(a) "Credit" or "letter of credit" means an engagement by a bank or other person made at the request of a customer and of a kind within the scope of this Article (Section 5-102) that the issuer will honor drafts or other demands for payment upon compliance with the conditions specified in the credit. A credit may be either revocable or irrevocable. The engagement may be either an agreement to honor or a statement that the bank or other person is authorized to honor.

(b) A "documentary draft" or a "documentary demand for payment" is one, honor of which is conditioned upon the presentation of a document or documents. "Document" means any paper including document of title, security, invoice, certificate, notice of default and the like.

(c) An "issuer" is a bank or other person issuing a credit.

(d) A "beneficiary" of a credit is a person who is entitled under its terms to draw or demand payment.

(e) An "advising bank" is a bank which gives notification of the issuance of a credit by another bank.

(f) A "confirming bank" is a bank which engages either that it will itself honor a credit already issued by another bank or that such a credit will be honored by the issuer or a third bank.

(g) A "customer" is a buyer or other person who causes an issuer to issue a credit. The term also includes a bank which procures issuance or confirmation on behalf of that bank's customer.

(2) Other definitions applying to this Article and the sections in which they appear are:

"Notation of Credit". Section 5-108.

"Presenter". Section 5-112(3).

(3) Definitions in other Articles applying to this Article and the sections in which they appear are:

"Accept" or "Acceptance". Section 3-410.

"Contract for sale". Section 2-106.

"Draft". Section 3-104.

"Holder in due course". Section 3-302.

"Midnight deadline". Section 4-104.

"Security". Section 8-102.

(4) In addition, Article 1 contains general definitions and principles of construction and interpretation applicable throughout this Article.

§5-104. Formal Requirements; Signing.

(1) Except as otherwise required in subsection (1)(c) Section 5-102 on scope, no particular form of phrasing is required for a credit. A credit must be in writing and signed by the issuer and a confirmation must be in writing and signed by the confirming bank. A modification of the terms of a credit or confirmation must be signed by the issuer or confirming bank.

(2) A telegram may be a sufficient signed writing if it identifies its sender by an authorized authentication. The authentication may be in code and the authorized naming of the issuer in an advice of credit is a sufficient signing.

§5-105. Consideration.
No consideration is necessary to establish a credit or to enlarge or otherwise modify its terms.

§5-106. Time and Effect of Establishment of Credit.

(1) Unless otherwise agreed a credit is established

(a) as regards the customer as soon as a letter of credit is sent to him or the letter of credit or an authorized written advice of its issuance is sent to the beneficiary; and

(b) as regards the beneficiary when he receives a letter of credit or an authorized written advice of its issuance.

(2) Unless otherwise agreed once an irrevocable

credit is established as regards the customer it can be modified or revoked only with the consent of the customer and once it is established as regards the beneficiary it can be modified or revoked only with his consent.

(3) Unless otherwise agreed after a revocable credit is established it may be modified or revoked by the issuer without notice to or consent from the customer or beneficiary.

(4) Notwithstanding any modification or revocation of a revocable credit any person authorized to honor or negotiate under the terms of the original credit is entitled to reimbursement for or honor of any draft or demand for payment duly honored or negotiated before receipt of notice of the modification or revocation and the issuer in turn is entitled to reimbursement from its customer.

§5-107. Advice of Credit; Confirmation; Error in Statement of Terms.

(1) Unless otherwise specified an advising bank by advising a credit issued by another bank does not assume any obligation to honor drafts drawn or demands for payment made under the credit but it does assume obligation for the accuracy of its own statement.

(2) A confirming bank by confirming a credit becomes directly obligated on the credit to the extent of its confirmation as though it were its issuer and acquires the rights of an issuer.

(3) Even though an advising bank incorrectly advises the terms of a credit it has been authorized to advise, the credit is established as against the issuer to the extent of its original terms.

(4) Unless otherwise specified the customer bears as against the issuer all risks of transmission and reasonable translation or interpretation of any message relating to a credit.

§5-108. "Notation Credit"; Exhaustion of Credit.

(1) A credit which specifies that any person purchasing or paying drafts drawn or demands for payment made under it must note the amount of the draft or demand on the letter or advice of credit is a "notation credit".

(2) Under a notation credit

(a) a person paying the beneficiary or purchasing a draft or demand for payment from him acquires a right to honor only if the appropriate notation is made and by transferring or forwarding for honor the documents under the credit such a person warrants to the issuer that the notation has been made; and

(b) unless the credit or a signed statement that an appropriate notation has been made accompanies the draft or demand for payment the issuer may delay honor until evidence of notation has been procured which is satisfactory to it but its obligation and that of its customer continue for a reasonable time not exceeding thirty days to obtain such evidence.

(3) If the credit is not a notation credit

(a) the issuer may honor complying drafts or demands for payment presented to it in the order in which they are presented and is discharged pro tanto by honor of any such draft or demand;

(b) as between competing good faith purchasers of complying drafts or demands the person first purchasing has priority over a subsequent purchaser even though the later purchased draft or demand has been first honored.

§5-109. Issuer's Obligation to Its Customer.

(1) An issuer's obligation to its customer includes good faith and observance of any general banking usage but unless otherwise agreed does not include liability or responsibility

(a) for performance of the underlying contract for sale or other transaction between the customer and the beneficiary; or

(b) fcr any act or omission of any person other than itself or its own branch or for loss or destruction of a draft, demand or document in transit or in the possession of others; or

(c) based on knowledge or lack of knowledge of any usage of any particular trade.

(2) An issuer must examine documents with care so as to ascertain that on their face they appear to comply with the terms of the credit but unless otherwise agreed assumes no liability or responsibility for the genuineness, falsification or effect of any document which appears on such examination to be regular on its face.

(3) A non-bank issuer is not bound by any banking usage of which it has no knowledge.

§5-110. Availability of Credit in Portions; Presenter's Reservation of Lien or Claim.

(1) Unless otherwise specified a credit may be used in portions in the discretion of the beneficiary.

(2) Unless otherwise specified a person by presenting a documentary draft or demand for payment

under a credit relinquishes upon its honor all claims to the documents and a person by transferring such draft or demand or causing such presentment authorizes such relinquishment. An explicit reservation of claim makes the draft or demand non-complying.

§5-111. Warranties on Transfer and Presentment.

(1) Unless otherwise agreed the beneficiary by transferring or presenting a documentary draft or demand for payment warrants to all interested parties that the necessary conditions of the credit have been complied with. This is in addition to any warranties arising under Articles 3, 4, 7 and 8.

(2) Unless otherwise agreed a negotiating, advising, confirming, collecting or issuing bank presenting or transferring a draft or demand for payment under a credit warrants only the matters warranted by a collecting bank under Article 4 and any such bank transferring a document warrants only the matters warranted by an intermediary under Articles 7 and 8.

§5-112. Time Allowed for Honor or Rejection; Withholding Honor or Rejection by Consent; "Presenter".

(1) A bank to which a documentary draft or demand for payment is presented under a credit may without dishonor of the draft, demand or credit

(a) defer honor until the close of the third banking day following receipt of the documents; and

(b) further defer honor if the presenter has expressly or impliedly consented thereto. Failure to honor within the time here specified constitutes dishonor of the draft or demand and of the credit [except as otherwise provided in subsection (4) of Section 5-114 on conditional payment].

Note: *The bracketed language in the last sentence of subsection (1) should be included only if the optional provisions of Section 5-114(4) and (5) are included.*

(2) Upon dishonor the bank may unless otherwise instructed fulfill its duty to return the draft or demand and the documents by holding them at the disposal of the presenter and sending him an advice to that effect.

(3) "Presenter" means any person presenting a draft or demand for payment for honor under a credit even though that person is a confirming bank or other correspondent which is acting under an issuer's authorization.

§5-113. Indemnities.

(1) A bank seeking to obtain (whether for itself or another) honor, negotiation or reimbursement under a credit may give an indemnity to induce such honor, negotiation or reimbursement.

(2) An indemnity agreement inducing honor, negotiation or reimbursement

(a) unless otherwise explicitly agreed applies to defects in the documents but not in the goods, and

(b) unless a longer time is explicitly agreed expires at the end of ten business days following receipt of the documents by the ultimate customer unless notice of objection is sent before such expiration date. The ultimate customer may send notice of objection to the person from whom he received the documents and any bank receiving such notice is under a duty to send notice to its transferor before its midnight deadline.

§5-114. Issuer's Duty and Privilege to Honor; Right to Reimbursement.

(1) An issuer must honor a draft or demand for payment which complies with the terms of the relevant credit regardless of whether the goods or documents conform to the underlying contract for sale or other contract between the customer and the beneficiary. The issuer is not excused from honor of such a draft or demand by reason of an additional general term that all documents must be satisfactory to the issuer, but an issuer may require that specified documents must be satisfactory to it.

(2) Unless otherwise agreed when documents appear on their face to comply with the terms of a credit but a required document does not in fact conform to the warranties made on negotiation or transfer of a document of title (Section 7-507) or of a certificated security (Section 8-306) or is forged or fraudulent or there is fraud in the transaction

(a) the issuer must honor the draft or demand for payment if honor is demanded by a negotiating bank or other holder of the draft or demand which has taken the draft or demand under the credit and under circumstances which would make it a holder in due course (Section 3-302) and in an appropriate case would make it a person to whom a document of title has been duly negotiated (Section 7-502) or a bona fide purchaser of a certificated security (Section 8-302); and

(b) in all other cases as against its customer, an issuer acting in good faith may honor the draft or demand for payment despite notification from the customer of fraud, forgery or other defect not apparent on the face of the documents but a court of appropriate jurisdiction may enjoin such honor.

(3) Unless otherwise agreed an issuer which has duly honored a draft or demand for payment is entitled to immediate reimbursement of any payment made under the credit and to be put in effectively available funds not later than the day before maturity of any acceptance made under the credit.

[(4) When a credit provides for payment by the issuer on receipt of notice that the required documents are in the possession of a correspondent or other agent of the issuer

(a) any payment made on receipt of such notice is conditional; and

(b) the issuer may reject documents which do not comply with the credit if it does so within three banking days following its receipt of the documents; and

(c) in the event of such rejection, the issuer is entitled by charge back or otherwise to return to the payment made.]

[(5) In the case covered by subsection (4) failure to reject documents within the time specified in subparagraph (b) constitutes acceptance of the documents and makes the payment final in favor of the beneficiary.]

Note: *Subsections (4) and (5) are bracketed as optional. If they are included the bracketed language in the last sentence of Section 5-112(1) should also be included.*

§**5-115. Remedy for Improper Dishonor or Anticipatory Repudiation.**

(1) When an issuer wrongfully dishonors a draft or demand for payment presented under a credit the person entitled to honor has with respect to any documents the rights of a person in the position of a seller (Section 2-707) and may recover from the issuer the face amount of the draft or demand together with incidental damages under Section 2-710 on seller's incidental damages and interest but less any amount realized by resale or other use or disposition of the

subject matter of the transaction. In the event no resale or other utilization is made the documents, goods or other subject matter involved in the transaction must be turned over to the issuer on payment of judgment.

(2) When an issuer wrongfully cancels or otherwise repudiates a credit before presentment of a draft or demand for payment drawn under it the beneficiary has the rights of a seller after anticipatory repudiation by the buyer under Section 2-610 if he learns of the repudiation in time reasonably to avoid procurement of the required documents. Otherwise the beneficiary has an immediate right of action for wrongful dishonor.

§**5-116. Transfer and Assignment.**

(1) The right to draw under a credit can be transferred or assigned only when credit is expressly designated as transferable or assignable.

(2) Even though the credit specifically states that it is nontransferable or nonassignable the beneficiary may before performance of the conditions of the credit assign his right to proceeds. Such an assignment is an assignment of an account under Article 9 on Secured Transactions and is governed by that Article except that

(a) the assignment is ineffective until the letter of credit or advice of credit is delivered to the assignee which delivery constitutes perfection of the security interest under Article 9; and

(b) the issuer may honor drafts or demands for payment drawn under the credit until it receives a notification of the assignment signed by the beneficiary which reasonably identifies the credit involved in the assignment and contains a request to pay the assignee; and

(c) after what reasonably appears to be such a notification has been received the issuer may without dishonor refuse to accept or pay even to a person otherwise entitled to honor until the letter of credit or advice of credit is exhibited to the issuer.

(3) Except where the beneficiary has effectively assigned his right to draw or his right to proceeds, nothing in this section limits his right to transfer or negotiate drafts or demands drawn under the credit.

§**5-117. Insolvency of Bank Holding Funds for Documentary Credit.**

(1) Where an issuer or an advising or confirming bank or a bank which has for a customer procured is-

suance of a credit by another bank becomes insolvent before final payment under the credit and the credit is one to which this Article is made applicable by paragraphs (a) or (b) of Section 5-102(1) on scope, the receipt or allocation of funds or collateral to secure or meet obligations under the credit shall have the following results:

(**a**) to the extent of any funds or collateral turned over after or before the insolvency as indemnity against or specifically for the purpose of payment of drafts or demands for payments drawn under the designated credit, the drafts or demands are entitled to payment in preference over depositors or other general creditors of the issuer or bank; and

(**b**) on expiration of the credit or surrender of the beneficiary's rights under it unused any person who has given such funds or collateral is similarly entitled to return thereof; and

(**c**) a charge to a general or current account with a bank if specifically consented to for the purpose of indemnity against or payment of drafts or demands for payment drawn under the designated credit falls under the same rules as if the funds had been drawn out in cash and then turned over with specific instructions.

(**2**) After honor or reimbursement under this section the customer or other person for whose account the insolvent bank has acted is entitled to receive the documents involved.

ARTICLE 6: BULK TRANSFERS

§6-101. Short Title. This Article shall be known and may be cited as Uniform Commercial Code—Bulk Transfers.

§6-102. "Bulk Transfers"; Transfers of Equipment; Enterprises Subject to This Article; Bulk Transfers Subject to This Article.

(**1**) A "bulk transfer" is any transfer in bulk and not in the ordinary course of the transferor's business or a major part of the materials, supplies, merchandise or other inventory (Section 9-109) of an enterprise subject to this Article.

(**2**) A transfer of a substantial part of the equipment (Section 9-109) of such an enterprise is a bulk transfer if it is made in connection with a bulk transfer of inventory, but not otherwise.

(**3**) The enterprises subject to this Article are all those whose principal business is the sale of merchandise from stock, including those who manufacture what they sell.

(**4**) Except as limited by the following section all bulk transfers of goods located within this state are subject to this Article.

§6-103. Transfers Excepted From This Article. The following transfers are not subject to this Article:

(**1**) Those made to give security for the performance of an obligation;

(**2**) General assignments for the benefit of all the creditors of the transferor, and subsequent transfers by the assignee thereunder;

(**3**) Transfers in settlement or realization of a lien or other security interests;

(**4**) Sales by executors, administrators, receivers, trustees in bankruptcy, or any public officer under judicial process;

(**5**) Sales made in the course of judicial or administrative proceedings for the dissolution or reorganization of a corporation and of which notice is sent to the creditors of the corporation pursuant to order of the court or administrative agency;

(**6**) Transfers to a person maintaining a known place of business in this State who becomes bound to pay the debts of the transferor in full and gives public notice of that fact, and who is solvent after becoming so bound;

(**7**) A transfer to a new business enterprise organized to take over and continue the business, if public notice of the transaction is given and the new enterprise assumes the debts of the transferor and he receives nothing from the transaction except an interest in the new enterprise junior to the claims of creditors;

(**8**) Transfers of property which is exempt from execution. Public notice under subsection (6) or subsection (7) may be given by publishing once a week for two consecutive weeks in a newspaper of general circulation where the transferor had its principal place of business in this State an advertisement including the names and addresses of the transferor and transferee and the effective date of the transfer.

§6-104. Schedule of Property, List of Creditors.

(**1**) Except as provided with respect to auction sales (Section 6-108), a bulk transfer subject to this Article is ineffective against any creditor of the transferor unless:

(a) the transferee requires the transferor to furnish a list of his existing creditors prepared as stated in this section; and

(b) the parties prepare a schedule of the property transferred sufficient to identify it; and

(c) the transferee preserves the list and schedule for six months next following the transfer and permits inspection of either or both and copying therefrom at all reasonable hours by any creditor of the transferor, or files the list and schedule in (a public office to be here identified).

(2) The list of creditors must be signed and sworn to or affirmed by the transferor or his agent. It must contain the names and business addresses of all creditors of the transferor, with the amounts when known, and also the names of all persons who are known to the transferor to assert claims against him even though such claims are disputed. If the transferor is the obligor of an outstanding issue of bonds, debentures or the like as to which there is an indenture trustee, the list of creditors need include only the name and address of the indenture trustee and the aggregate outstanding principal amount of the issue.

(3) Responsibility for the completeness and accuracy of the list of creditors rests on the transferor, and the transfer is not rendered ineffective by errors or omissions therein unless the transferee is shown to have had knowledge.

§6-105. Notice to Creditors. In addition to the requirements of the preceding section, any bulk transfer subject to this Article except one made by auction sale (Section 6-108) is ineffective against any creditor of the transferor unless at least ten days before he takes possession of the goods or pays for them, whichever happens first, the transferee gives notice of the transfer in the manner and to the persons hereafter provided (Section 6-107).

§6-106. Application of the Proceeds. In addition to the requirements of the two preceding sections:

(1) Upon every bulk transfer subject to this Article for which new consideration becomes payable except those made by sale at auction it is the duty of the transferee to assure that such consideration is applied so far as necessary to pay those debts of the transferor which are either shown on the list furnished by the transferor (Section 6-104) or filed in writing in the place stated in the notice (Section 6-

107) within thirty days after the mailing of such notice. This duty of the transferee runs to all the holders of such debts, and may be enforced by any of them for the benefit of all.

(2) If any of said debts are in dispute the necessary sum may be withheld from distribution until the dispute is settled or adjudicated.

[(3) If the consideration payable is not enough to pay all of the said debts in full distribution shall be made pro rata.]

Note: *This section is bracketed to indicate division of opinion as to whether or not it is a wise provision, and to suggest that this is a point on which State enactments may differ without serious damage to the principle of uniformity.*

In any State where this section is omitted, the following parts of sections, also bracketed in the text, should also be omitted, namely:

Section 6-107(2)(e).

    6-108(3)(c).

    6-109(2).

In any State where this section is enacted, these other provisions should be also.

Optional Subsection (4)

[(4) The transferee may within ten days after he takes possession of the goods pay the consideration into the (specify court) in the county where the transferor had its principal place of business in this state and thereafter may discharge his duty under this section by giving notice by registered or certified mail to all the persons to whom the duty runs that the consideration has been paid into that court and that they should file their claims there. On motion of any interested party, the court may order the distribution of the consideration to the persons entitled to it.]

Note: *Optional subsection (4) is recommended for those states which do not have a general statute providing for payment of money into court.*

§6-107. The Notice.

(1) The notice to creditors (Section 6-105) shall state:

(a) that a bulk transfer is about to be made; and

(b) the names and business addresses of the transferor and transferee, and all other business names and addresses used by the transferor within three years last past so far as known to the transferee; and

(c) whether or not all the debts of the transferor are to be paid in full as they fall due as a result of the transaction, and if so, the address to which creditors should send their bills.

(2) If the debts of the transferor are not to be paid in full as they fall due or if the transferee is in doubt on that point then the notice shall state further:

(a) the location and general description of the property to be transferred and the estimated total of the transferor's debts;

(b) the address where the schedule of property and list of creditors (Section 6-104) may be inspected;

(c) whether the transfer is to pay existing debts and if so the amount of such debts and to whom owing;

(d) whether the transfer is for new consideration and if so the amount of such consideration and the time and place of payment; [and]

[(e) if for new consideration the time and place where creditors of the transferor are to file their claims.]

(3) The notice in any case shall be delivered personally or sent by registered or certified mail to all the persons shown on the list of creditors furnished by the transferor (Section 6-104) and to all other persons who are known to the transferee to hold or assert claims against the transferor.

Note: *The words in brackets are optional. See Note under §6-106.*

§6-108. Auction Sales; "Auctioneer".

(1) A bulk transfer is subject to this Article even though it is by sale at auction, but only in the manner and with the results stated in this section.

(2) The transferor shall furnish a list of his creditors and assist in the preparation of a schedule of the property to be sold, both prepared as before stated (Section 6-104).

(3) The person or persons other than the transferor who direct, control or are responsible for the auction are collectively called the "auctioneer". The auctioneer shall:

(a) receive and retain the list of creditors and prepare and retain the schedule of property for the period stated in this Article (Section 6-104);

(b) give notice of the auction personally or by registered or certified mail at least ten days before it occurs to all persons shown on the list of creditors and to all other persons who are known to him to hold or assert claims against the transferor; [and]

[(c) assure that the net proceeds of the auction are applied as provided in this Article (Section 6-106).]

(4) Failure of the auctioneer to perform any of these duties does not affect the validity of the sale or the title of the purchasers, but if the auctioneer knows that the auction constitutes a bulk transfer such failure renders the auctioneer liable to the creditors of the transferor as a class for the sums owing to them from the transferor up to but not exceeding the net proceeds of the auction. If the auctioneer consists of several persons their liability is joint and several.

Note: *The words in brackets are optional. See Note under §6-106.*

§6-109. What Creditors Protected; [Credit for Payment to Particular Creditors].

(1) The creditors of the transferor mentioned in this Article are those holding claims based on transactions or events occurring before the bulk transfer, but creditors who become such after notice to creditors is given (Sections 6-105 and 6-107) are not entitled to notice.

[(2) Against the aggregate obligation imposed by the provisions of this Article concerning the application of the proceeds (Section 6-106 and subsection (3) (c) of 6-108) the transferee or auctioneer is entitled to credit for sums paid to particular creditors of the transferor, not exceeding the sums believed in good faith at the time of the payment to be properly payable to such creditors.]

Note: *The words in brackets are optional. See Note under §6-106.*

§6-110. Subsequent Transfers.
When the title of a transferee to property is subject to a defect by reason of his noncompliance with the requirements of this Article, then:

(1) a purchaser of any of such property from such transferee who pays no value or who takes with notice of such noncompliance takes subject to such defect, but

(2) a purchaser for value in good faith and without such notice takes free of such defect.

§6-111. Limitation of Actions and Levies.
No action under this Article shall be brought nor levy made more than six months after the date on which the transferee took possession of the goods unless the transfer has been concealed. If the transfer has been

concealed, actions may be brought or levies made within six months after its discovery.

ARTICLE 7: WAREHOUSE RECEIPTS, BILLS OF LADING AND OTHER DOCUMENTS OF TITLE

Part 1: General

§7-101. Short Title.   This Article shall be known and may be cited as uniform Commercial Code—Documents of Title.

§7-102. Definitions and Index of Definitions.

(**1**) In this Article, unless the context otherwise requires:

(**a**) "Bailee" means the person who by a warehouse receipt, bill of lading or other document of title acknowledges possession of goods and contracts to deliver them.

(**b**) "Consignee" means the person named in a bill to whom or to whose order the bill promises delivery.

(**c**) "Consignor" means the person named in a bill as the person from whom the goods have been received for shipment.

(**d**) "Delivery order" means a written order to deliver goods directed to a warehouseman, carrier or other person who in the ordinary course of business issues warehouse receipts or bills of lading.

(**e**) "Document" means document of title as defined in the general definitions in Article 1 (Section 1-201).

(**f**) "Goods" means all things which are treated as movable for the purposes of a contract of storage or transportation.

(**g**) "Issuer" means a bailee who issues a document except that in relation to an unaccepted delivery order it means the person who orders the possessor of goods to deliver. Issuer includes any person for whom an agent or employee purports to act in issuing a document if the agent or employee has real or apparent authority to issue documents, notwithstanding that the issuer received no goods or that the goods were misdescribed or that in any other respect the agent or employee violated his instructions.

(**h**) "Warehouseman" is a person engaged in the busines of storing goods for hire.

(**2**) Other definitions applying to this Article or to specified Parts thereof, and the sections in which they appear are:

"Duly negotiate". Section 7-501.

"Person entitled under the document". Section 7-403(4).

(**3**) Definitions in other Articles applying to this Article and the sections in which they appear are:

"Contract for sale". Section 2-106.

"Overseas". Section 2-323.

"Receipt" of goods. Section 2-103.

(**4**) In addition Article 1 contains general definitions and principles of construction and interpretation applicable throughout this Article.

§7-103. Relation of Article to Treaty, Statute, Tariff, Classification or Regulation.   To the extent that any treaty or statute of the United States, regulatory statute of this State or tariff, classification or regulation filed or issued pursuant thereto is applicable, the provisions of this Article are subject thereto.

§7-104. Negotiable and Non-Negotiable Warehouse Receipt, Bill of Lading Or Other Document of Title.

(**1**) A warehouse receipt, bill of lading or other document of title is negotiable

(**a**) if by its terms the goods are to be delivered to bearer or to the order of a named person; or

(**b**) where recognized in overseas trade, if it runs to a named person or assigns.

(**2**) Any other document is non-negotiable. A bill of lading in which it is stated that the goods are consigned to a named person is not made negotiable by a provision that the goods are to be delivered only against a written order signed by the same or another named person.

§7-105. Construction Against Negative Implication.   The omission from either Part 2 or Part 3 of this Article of a provision corresponding to a provision made in the other Part does not imply that a correspondnig rule of law is not applicable.

Part 2: Warehouse Receipts: Special Provisions

§7-201. Who May Issue a Warehouse Receipt; Storage Under Government Bond.

(**1**) A warehouse receipt may be issued by any warehouseman.

(**2**) Where goods including distilled spirits and agricultural commodities are stored under a statute requiring a bond against withdrawal or a license for the issuance of receipts in the nature of warehouse receipts, a receipt issued for the goods has like effect as a warehouse receipt even though issued by a person who is the owner of the goods and is not a warehouseman.

§7-202. **Form of Warehouse Receipt; Essential Terms; Optional Terms.**

(1) A warehouse receipt need not be in any particular form.

(2) Unless a warehouse receipt embodies within its written or printed terms each of the following, the warehouseman is liable for damages caused by the omission to a person injured thereby:

(a) the location of the warehouse where the goods are stored;

(b) the date of issue of the receipt;

(c) the consecutive number of the receipt;

(d) a statement whether the goods received will be delivered to the bearer, to a specified person, or to a specified person or his order;

(e) the rate of storage and handling charges, except that where goods are stored under a field warehousing arrangement a statement of that fact is sufficient on non-negotiable receipt;

(f) a description of the goods or of the packages containing them:

(g) the signature of the warehouseman, which may be made by his authorized agent;

(h) if the receipt is issued for goods of which the warehouseman is owner, either solely or jointly or in common with others, the fact of such ownership; and

(i) a statement of the amount of advances made and of liabilities incurred for which the warehouseman claims a lien or security interest (Section 7-209). If the precise amount of such advances made or of such liabilities incurred is, at the time of the issue of the receipt, unknown to the warehouseman or to his agent who issues it, a statement of the fact that advances have been made or liabilities incurred and the purpose thereof is sufficient.

(3) A warehouseman may insert in his receipt any other terms which are not contrary to the provisions of this Act and do not impair his obligation of delivery (Section 7-403) or his duty of care (Section 7-204). Any contrary provisions shall be ineffective.

§7-203. **Liability for Non-Receipt or Misdescription.** A party to or purchaser for value in good faith of a document of title other than a bill of lading relying in either case upon the description therein of the goods may recover from the issuer damages caused by the non-receipt or misdescription of the goods, except to the extent that the document conspicuously indicates that the issuer does not know whether any part or all of the goods in fact were received or conform to the description, as where the description is in terms of marks or labels or kind, quantity or condition, or the receipt or description is qualified by "contents, condition and quality unknown," "said to contain" or the like, if such indication be true, or the party or purchaser otherwise has notice.

§7-204. **Duty of Care; Contractual Limitation of Warehouseman's Liability.**

(1) A warehouseman is liable for damages for loss of or injury to the goods caused by his failure to exercise such care in regard to them as a reasonably careful man would exercise under like circumstances but unless otherwise agreed he is not liable for damages which could not have been avoided by the exercise of such care.

(2) Damages may be limited by a term in the warehouse receipt or storage agreement limiting the amount of liability in case of loss or damage, and setting forth a specific liability per article or item, or value per unit of weight, beyond which the warehouseman shall not be liable; provided, however, that such liability may on written request of the bailor at the time of signing such storage agreement or within a reasonable time after receipt of the warehouse receipt be increased on part or all of the goods thereunder, in which event increased rates may be charged based on such increased valuation, but that no such increase shall be permitted contrary to a lawful limitation of liability contained in the warehouseman's tariff, if any. No such limitation is effective with respect to the warehouseman's liability for conversion to his own use.

(3) Reasonable provisions as to the time and manner of presenting claims and instituting actions based on the bailment may be included in the warehouse receipt or tariff.

(4) This section does not impair or repeal . . .

Note: *Insert in subsection (4) a reference to any statute which imposes a higher responsibility upon the* *warehouseman or invalidates contractual limitations which would be permissible under this Article.*

§7-205. Title Under Warehouse Receipt Defeated in Certain Cases. A buyer in the ordinary course of business of fungible goods sold and delivered by a warehouseman who is also in the business of buying and selling such goods takes free of any claim under a warehouse receipt even though it has been duly negotiated.

§7-206. Termination of Storage at Warehouseman's Option.

(1) A warehouseman may on notifying the person on whose account the goods are held and any other person known to claim an interest in the goods require payment of any charges and removal of the goods from the warehouse at the termination of the period of storage fixed by the document, or, if no period is fixed, within a stated period not less than thirty days after the notification. If the goods are not removed before the date specified in the notification, the warehouseman may sell them in accordance with the provisions of the section on enforcement of a warehouseman's lien (Section 7-210).

(2) If a warehouseman in good faith believes that the goods are about to deteriorate or decline in value to less than the amount of his lien within the time prescribed in subsection (1) for notification, advertisement and sale, the warehouseman may specify in the notification any reasonable shorter time for removal of the goods and in case the goods are not removed, may sell them at public sale held not less than one week after a single advertisement or posting.

(3) If as result of a quality or condition of the goods of which the warehouseman had no notice at the time of deposit the goods are a hazard to other property or to the warehouse or to persons, the warehouseman may sell the goods at public or private sale without advertisement on reasonable notification to all persons known to claim an interest in the goods. If the warehouseman after a reasonable effort is unable to sell the goods he may dispose of them in any lawful manner and shall incur no liability by reason of such disposition.

(4) The warehouseman must deliver the goods to any person entitled to them under this Article upon due demand made at any time prior to sale or other disposition under this section.

(5) The warehouseman may satisfy his lien from the proceeds of any sale or disposition under this sec-

tion but must hold the balance for delivery on the demand of any person to whom he would have been bound to deliver the goods.

§7-207. Goods Must Be Kept Separate; Fungible Goods.

(1) Unless the warehouse receipt otherwise provides, a warehouseman must keep separate the goods covered by each receipt so as to permit at all times identification and delivery of those goods except that different lots of fungible goods may be commingled.

(2) Fungible goods so commingled are owned in common by the persons entitled thereto and the warehouseman is severally liable to each owner for that owner's share. Where because of overissue a mass of fungible goods is insufficient to meet all the receipts which the warehouseman has issued against it, the persons entitled include all holders to whom overissued receipts have been duly negotiated.

§7-208. Altered Warehouse Receipts. Where a blank in a negotiable warehouse receipt has been filled in without authority, a purchaser for value and without notice of the want of authority may treat the insertion as authorized. Any other unauthorized alteration leaves any receipt enforceable against the issuer according to its original tenor.

§7-209. Lien of Warehouseman.

(1) A warehouseman has a lien against the bailor on the goods covered by a warehouse receipt or on the proceeds thereof in his possession for charges for storage or transportation (including demurrage and terminal charges), insurance, labor, or charges present or future in relation to the goods, and for expenses necessary for preservation of the goods or reasonably incurred in their sale pursuant to law. If the person on whose account the goods are held is liable for like charges or expenses in relation to other goods whenever deposited and it is stated in the receipt that a lien is claimed for charges and expenses in relation to other goods, the warehouseman also has a lien against him for such charges and expenses whether or not the other goods have been delivered by the warehouseman. But against a person to whom a negotiable warehouse receipt is duly negotiated a warehouseman's lien is limited to charges in an amount or at a rate specified on the receipt or if no charges are so specified then to a reasonable charge for storage of the goods covered by the receipt subsequent to the date of the receipt.

(2) The warehouseman may also reserve a security

interest against the bailor for a maximum amount specified on the receipt for charges other than those specified in subsection (1), such as for money advanced and interest. Such a security interest is governed by the Article on Secured Transactions (Article 9).

(3) (a) A warehouseman's lien for charges and expenses under subsection (1) or a security interest under subsection (2) is also effective against any person who so entrusted the bailor with possession of the goods that a pledge of them by him to a good faith purchaser for value would have been valid but is not effective against a person as to whom the document confers no right in the goods covered by it under Section 7-503.

(b) A warehouseman's lien on household goods for charges and expenses in relation to the goods under subsection (1) is also effective against all persons if the depositor was the legal possessor of the goods at the time of deposit. "Household goods" means furniture, furnishings and personal effects used by the depositor in a dwelling.

(4) A warehouseman loses his lien on any goods which he voluntarily delivers or which he unjustifiably refuses to deliver. (As amended in 1966.)

§7-210. Enforcement of Warehouseman's Lien.

(1) Except as provided in subsection (2), a warehouseman's lien may be enforced by public or private sale of the goods in block or in parcels, at any time or place and on any terms which are commercially reasonable, after notifying all persons known to claim an interest in the goods. Such notification must include a statement of the amount due, the nature of the proposed sale and the time and place of any public sale. The fact that a better price could have been obtained by a sale at a different time or in a different method from that selected by the warehouseman is not of itself sufficient to establish that the sale was not made in a commercially reasonable manner. If the warehouseman either sells the goods in the usual manner in any recognized market therefor, or if he sells at the price current in such market at the time of his sale, or if he has otherwise sold in conformity with commercially reasonable practices among dealers in the type of goods sold, he has sold in a commercially reasonable manner. A sale of more goods than apparently necessary to be offered to insure satisfaction of the obligation is not commercially reasonable except in cases covered by the preceding sentence.

(2) A warehouseman's lien on goods other than goods stored by a merchant in the course of his business may be enforced only as follows:

(a) All persons known to claim an interest in the goods must be notified.

(b) The notification must be delivered in person or sent by registered or certified letter to the last known address of any person to be notified.

(c) The notification must include an itemized statement of the claim, a description of the goods subject to the lien, a demand for payment within a specified time not less than ten days after receipt of the notification, and a conspicuous statement that unless the claim is paid within that time the goods will be advertised for sale and sold by auction at a specified time and place.

(d) The sale must conform to the terms of the notification.

(e) The sale must be held at the nearest suitable place to that where the goods are held or stored.

(f) After the expiration of the time given in the notification, an advertisement of the sale must be published once a week for two weeks consecutively in a newspaper of general circulation where the sale is to be held. The advertisement must include a description of the good, the name of the person on whose account they are being held, and the time and place of the sale. The sale must take place at least fifteen days after the first publication. If there is no newspaper of general circulation where the sale is to be held, the advertisement must be posted at least ten days before the sale in not less than six conspicuous places in the neighborhood of the proposed sale.

(3) Before any sale pursuant to this section any person claiming a right in the goods may pay the amount necessary to satisfy the lien and the reasonable expenses incurred under this section. In that event the goods must not be sold, but must be retained by the warehouseman subject to the terms of the receipt and this Article.

(4) The warehouseman may buy at any public sale pursuant to this section.

(5) A purchaser in good faith of goods sold to enforce a warehouseman's lien takes the goods free of any rights of persons against whom the lien was valid, despite noncompliance by the warehouseman with the requirements of this section.

(6) The warehouseman may satisfy his lien from the proceeds of any sale pursuant to this section but must hold the balance, if any, for delivery on demand to any person to whom he would have been bound to deliver the goods.

(7) The rights provided by this section shall be in addition to all other rights allowed by law to a creditor against his debtor.

(8) Where a lien is on goods stored by a merchant in the course of his business the lien may be enforced in accordance with either subsection (1) or (2).

(9) The warehouseman is liable for damages caused by failure to comply with the requirements for sale under this section and in case of willful violation is liable for conversion. As amended in 1962.

Part 3: Bills of Lading: Special Provisions
§7-301. Liability for Non-Receipt or Misdescription; "Said to Contain"; "Shipper's Load and Count"; Improper Handling.

(1) A consignee of a non-negotiable bill who has given value in good faith or a holder to whom a negotiable bill has been duly negotiated relying in either case upon the description therein of the goods, or upon the date therein shown, may recover from the issuer damages caused by the misdating of the bill or the non-receipt or misdescription of the goods, except to the extent that the document indicates that the issuer does not know whether any part or all of the goods in fact were received or conform to the description, as where the description is in terms of marks or labels or kind, quantity, or condition or the receipt or description is qualified by "contents or condition of contents of packages unknown", "said to contain", "shipper's weight, load and count" or the like, if such indication be true.

(2) When goods are loaded by an issuer who is a common carrier, the issuer must count the packages of goods if package freight and ascertain the kind and quantity if bulk freight. In such cases "shipper's weight, load and count" or other words indicating that the description was made by the shipper are ineffective except as to freight concealed by packages.

(3) When bulk freight is loaded by a shipper who makes available to the issuer adequate facilities for weighing such freight, an issuer who is a common carrier must ascertain the kind and quantity within a reasonable time after receiving the written request of the shipper to do so. In such cases "shipper's weight" or other words of like purport are ineffective.

(4) The issuer may by inserting in the bill the words "shipper's weight, load and count" or other words of like purport indicate that the goods were loaded by the shipper; and if such statement be true the issuer shall not be liable for damages caused by the improper loading. But their omission does not imply liability for such damages.

(5) The shipper shall be deemed to have guaranteed to the issuer the accuracy at the time of shipment of the description, marks, labels, number, kind, quantity, condition and weight, as furnished by him; and the shipper shall indemnify the issuer against damage caused by inaccuracies in such particulars. The right of the issuer to such indemnity shall in no way limit his responsibility and liability under the contract of carriage to any person other than the shipper.

§7-302. Through Bills of Lading and Similar Documents.

(1) The issuer of a through bill of lading or other document embodying an undertaking to be performed in part by persons acting as its agents or by connecting carriers is liable to anyone entitled to recover on the document for any breach by such other persons or by a connecting carrier of its obligation under the document but to the extent that the bill covers an undertaking to be performed overseas or in territory not contiguous to the continental United States or an undertaking including matters other than transportation this liability may be varied by agreement of the parties.

(2) Where goods covered by a through bill of lading or other document embodying an undertaking to be performed in part by persons other than the issuer are received by any such person, he is subject with respect to his own performance while the goods are in his possession to the obligation of the issuer. His obligation is discharged by delivery of the goods to another such person pursuant to the document, and does not include liability for breach by any other such persons or by the issuer.

(3) The issuer of such through bill of lading or

other document shall be entitled to recover from the connecting carrier or such other person in possession of the goods when the breach of the obligation under the document occurred, the amount it may be required to pay to anyone entitled to recover on the document therefor, as may be evidenced by any receipt, judgment, or transcript thereof, and the amount of any expense reasonably incurred by it in defending any action brought by anyone entitled to recover on the document therefor.

§7-303. Diversion; Reconsignment; Change of Instructions.

(1) Unless the bill of lading otherwise provides, the carrier may deliver the goods to a person or destination other than that stated in the bill or may otherwise dispose of the goods on instructions from

(a) the holder of a negotiable bill; or

(b) the consignor on a non-negotiable bill notwithstanding contrary instructions from the consignee; or

(c) the consignee on a non-negotiable bill in the absence of contrary instructions from the consignor, if the goods have arrived at the billed destination or if the consignee is in possession of the bill; or

(d) the consignee on a non-negotiable bill if he is entitled as against the consignor to dispose of them.

(2) Unless such instructions are noted on a negotiable bill of lading, a person to whom the bill is duly negotiated can hold the bailee according to the original terms.

§7-304. Bills of Lading in a Set.

(1) Except where customary in overseas transportation, a bill of lading must not be issued in a set of parts. The issuer is liable for damages caused by violation of this subsection.

(2) Where a bill of lading is lawfully drawn in a set of parts, each of which is numbered and expressed to be valid only if the goods have not been delivered against any other part, the whole of the parts constitute one bill.

(3) Where a bill of lading is lawfully issued in a set of parts and different parts are negotiated to different persons, the title of the holder to whom the first due negotiation is made prevails as to both the document and the goods even though any later holder may have received the goods from the carrier in good faith and discharged the carrier's obligation by surrender of his part.

(4) Any person who negotiates or transfers a single part of a bill of lading drawn in a set is liable to holders of that part as if it were the whole set.

(5) The bailee is obliged to deliver in accordance with Part 4 of this Article against the first presented part of a bill of lading lawfully drawn in a set. Such delivery discharges the bailee's obligation on the whole bill.

§7-305. Destination Bills.

(1) Instead of issuing a bill of lading to the consignor at the place of shipment a carrier may at the request of the consignor procure the bill to be issued at destination or at any other place designated in the request.

(2) Upon request of anyone entitled as against the carrier to control the goods while in transit and on surrender of any outstanding bill of lading or other receipt covering such goods, the issuer may procure a substitute bill to be issued at any place designated in the request.

§7-306. Altered Bills of Lading. An unauthorized alteration or filling in of a blank in a bill of lading leaves the bill enforceable according to its original tenor.

§7-307. Lien of Carrier.

(1) A carrier has a lien on the goods covered by a bill of lading for charges subsequent to the date of its receipt of the goods for storage or transportation (including demurrage and terminal charges) and for expenses necessary for preservation of the goods incident to their transportation or reasonably incurred in their sale pursuant to law. But against a purchaser for value of a negotiable bill of lading a carrier's lien is limited to charges stated in the bill or the applicable tariffs, or if no charges are stated then to a reasonable charge.

(2) A lien for charges and expenses under subsection (1) on goods which the carrier was required by law to receive for transportation is effective against the consignor or any person entitled to the goods unless the carrier had notice that the consignor lacked authority to subject the goods to such charges and expenses. Any other lien under subsection (1) is effective against the consignor and any person who permitted the bailor to have control or possession of the goods unless the carrier had notice that the bailor lacked such authority.

(3) A carrier loses his lien on any goods which he voluntarily delivers or which he unjustifiably refuses to deliver.

§7-308. Enforcement of Carrier's Lien.

(1) A carrier's lien may be enforced by public or private sale of the goods, in block or in parcels, at any time or place and on any terms which are commercially reasonable, after notifying all persons known to claim an interest in the goods. Such notification must include a statement of the amount due, the nature of the proposed sale and the time and place of any public sale. The fact that a better price could have been obtained by a sale at a different time or in a different method from that selected by the carrier is not of itself sufficient to establish that the sale was not made in a commercially reasonable manner. If the carrier either sells the goods in the usual manner in any recognized market therefor or if he sells at the price current in such market at the time of his sale or if he has otherwise sold in conformity with commercially reasonable practices among dealers in the type of goods sold he has sold in a commercially reasonable manner. A sale of more goods than apparently necessary to be offered to ensure satisfaction of the obligation is not commercially reasonable except in cases covered by the preceding sentence.

(2) Before any sale pursuant to this section any person claiming a right in the goods may pay the amount necessary to satisfy the lien and the reasonable expenses incurred under this section. In that event the goods must not be sold, but must be retained by the carrier subject to the terms of the bill and this Article.

(3) The carrier may buy at any public sale pursuant to this section.

(4) A purchaser in good faith of goods sold to enforce a carrier's lien takes the goods free of any rights of persons against whom the lien was valid, despite noncompliance by the carrier with the requirements of this section.

(5) The carrier may satisfy his lien from the proceeds of any sale pursuant to this section but must hold the balance, if any, for delivery on demand to any person to whom he would have been bound to deliver the goods.

(6) The rights provided by this section shall be in addition to all other rights allowed by law to a creditor against his debtor.

(7) A carrier's lien may be enforced in accordance with either subsection (1) or the procedure set forth in subsection (2) of Section 7-210.

(8) The carrier is liable for damages caused by failure to comply with the requirements for sale under this section and in case of willful violation is liable for conversion.

§7-309. Duty of Care; Contractual Limitation of Carrier's Liability.

(1) A carrier who issues a bill of lading whether negotiable or non-negotiable must exercise the degree of care in relation to the goods which a reasonably careful man would exercise under like circumstances. This subsection does not repeal or change any law or rule of law which imposes liability upon a common carrier for damages not caused by its negligence.

(2) Damages may be limited by a provision that the carrier's liability shall not exceed a value stated in the document if the carrier's rates are dependent upon value and the consignor by the carrier's tariff is afforded an opportunity to declare a higher value or a value as lawfully provided in the tariff, or where no tariff is filed he is otherwise advised of such opportunity; but no such limitation is effective with respect to the carrier's liability for conversion to its own use.

(3) Reasonable provisions as to the time and manner of presenting claims and instituting actions based on the shipment may be included in a bill of lading or tariff.

Part 4: Warehouse Receipts and Bills of Lading: General Obligations

§7-401. Irregularities in Issue of Receipt or Bill or Conduct of Issuer. The obligations imposed by this Article on an issuer apply to a document of title regardless of the fact that

(a) the document may not comply with the requirements of this Article or of any other law or regulation regarding its issue, form or content; or

(b) the issuer may have violated laws regulating the conduct of his business; or

(c) the goods covered by the document were owned by the bailee at the time the document was issued; or

(d) the person issuing the document does not come within the definition of warehouseman if it purports to be a warehouse receipt.

§7-402. Duplicate Receipt or Bill; Overissue. Neither a duplicate nor any other document of title purporting to cover goods already represented by an outstanding document of the same issuer confers any right in the goods, except as provided in the case of bills in a set, overissue of documents for fungible goods and substitutes for lost, stolen or destroyed documents. But the issuer is liable for damages caused by his overissue or failure to identify a duplicate document as such by conspicuous notation on its face.

§7-403. Obligation of Warehouseman or Carrier to Deliver; Excuse.

(1) The bailee must deliver the goods to a person entitled under the document who complies with subsections (2) and (3), unless and to the extent that the bailee establishes any of the following:

(a) delivery of the goods to a person whose receipt was rightful as against the claimant;

(b) damage to or delay, loss or destruction of the goods for which the bailee is not liable [, but the burden of establishing negligence in such cases is on the person entitled under the document];

Note: *The brackets in (1)(b) indicate that State enactments may differ on this point without serious damage to the principle of uniformity.*

(c) previous sale or other disposition of the goods in lawful enforcement of a lien or on warehouseman's lawful termination of storage;

(d) the exercise by a seller of his right to stop delivery pursuant to the provisions of the Article on Sales (Section 2-705);

(e) a diversion, reconsignment or other disposition pursuant to the provisions of this Article (Section 7-303) or tariff regulating such right;

(f) release, satisfaction or any other fact affording a personal defense against the claimant;

(g) any other lawful excuse.

(2) A person claiming goods covered by a document of title must satisfy the bailee's lien where the bailee so requests or where the bailee is prohibited by law from delivering the goods until the charges are paid.

(3) Unless the person claiming is one against whom the document confers no right under Sec. 7-503(1), he must surrender for cancellation or notation of partial deliveries any outstanding negotiable document covering the goods, and the bailee must cancel the document or conspicuously note the partial delivery thereon or be liable to any person to whom the document is duly negotiated.

(4) "Person entitled under the document" means holder in the case of a negotiable document, or the person to whom delivery is to be made by the terms of or pursuant to written instructions under a nonnegotiable document.

§7-404. No Liability for Good Faith Delivery Pursuant to Receipt or Bill.

A bailee who in good faith including observance of reasonable commercial standards has received goods and delivered or otherwise disposed of them according to the terms of the document of title or pursuant to this Article is not liable therefor. This rule applies even though the person from whom he received the goods had no authority to procure the document or to dispose of the goods and even though the person to whom he delivered the goods had no authority to receive them.

Part 5: Warehouse Receipts and Bills of Lading: Negotiation and Transfer

§7-501. Form of Negotiation and Requirements of "Due Negotiation".

(1) A negotiable document of title running to the order of a named person is negotiated by his indorsement and delivery. After his indorsement in blank or to bearer any person can negotiate it by delivery alone.

(2) (a) A negotiable document of title is also negotiated by delivery alone when by its original terms it runs to bearer.

(b) When a document running to the order of a named person is delivered to him the effect is the same as if the document had been negotiated.

(3) Negotiation of a negotiable document of title after it has been indorsed to a specified person requires indorsement by the special indorsee as well as delivery.

(4) A negotiable document of title is "duly negotiated" when it is negotiated in the manner stated in this section to a holder who purchases it in good faith without notice of any defense against or claim to it on the part of any person and for value, unless it is established that the negotiation is not in the regular course of business or financing or involves receiving the document in settlement or payment of a money obligation.

(5) Indorsement of a non-negotiable document neither makes it negotiable nor adds to the transferee's rights.

(6) The naming in a negotiable bill of a person to be notified of the arrival of the goods does not limit the negotiability of the bill nor constitute notice to a

purchaser thereof of any interest of such person in the goods.

§7-502. Rights Acquired by Due Negotiation.

(**1**) Subject to the following section and to the provisions of Section 7-205 on fungible goods, a holder to whom a negotiable document of title has been duly negotiated acquires thereby:

(**a**) title to the document;

(**b**) title to the goods;

(**c**) all rights accruing under the law of agency or estoppel, including rights to goods delivered to the bailee after the document was issued; and

(**d**) the direct obligation of the issuer to hold or deliver the goods according to the terms of the document free of any defense or claim by him except those arising under the terms of the document or under this Article. In the case of a delivery order the bailee's obligation accrues only upon acceptance and the obligation acquired by the holder is that the issuer and any indorser will procure the acceptance of the bailee.

(**2**) Subject to the following section, title and rights so acquired are not defeated by any stoppage of the goods represented by the document or by surrender of such goods by the bailee, and are not impaired even though the negotiation or any prior negotiation constituted a breach of duty or even though any person has been deprived of possession of the document by misrepresentation, fraud, accident, mistake, duress, loss, theft or conversion, or even though a previous sale or other transfer of the goods or document has been made to a third person.

§7-503. Document of Title to Goods Defeated in Certain Cases.

(**1**) A document of title confers no right in goods against a person who before issuance of the document has a legal interest or a perfected security interest in them and who neither

(**a**) delivered or entrusted them or any document of title covering them to the bailor or his nominee with actual or apparent authority to ship, store or sell or with power to obtain delivery under this Article (Section 7-403) or with power of disposition under this Act (Sections 2-403 and 9-307) or other statute or rule of law; nor

(**b**) acquiesced in the procurement by the bailor or his nominee of any document of title.

(**2**) Title to goods based upon an unaccepted delivery order is subject to the rights of anyone to whom a negotiable warehouse receipt or bill of lading covering the goods has been duly negotiated. Such a title may be defeated under the next section to the same extent as the rights of the issuer or a transferee from the issuer.

(**3**) Title to goods based upon a bill of lading issued to a freight forwarder is subject to the rights of anyone to whom a bill issued by the freight forwarder is duly negotiated; but delivery by the carrier in accordance with Part 4 of this Article pursuant to its own bill of lading discharges the carrier's obligation to deliver.

§7-504. Rights Acquired in the Absence of Due Negotiation; Effect of Diversion; Seller's Stoppage of Delivery.

(**1**) A transferee of a document, whether negotiable or nonnegotiable, to whom the document has been delivered but not duly negotiated, acquires the title and rights which his transferor had or had actual authority to convey.

(**2**) In the case of a nonnegotiable document, until but not after the bailee receives notification of the transfer, the rights of the transferee may be defeated

(**a**) by those creditors of the transferor who could treat the sale as void under Section 2-402; or

(**b**) by a buyer from the transferor in ordinary course of business if the bailee has delivered the goods to the buyer or received notification of his rights; or

(**c**) as against the bailee by good faith dealings of the bailee with the transferor.

(**3**) A diversion or other change of shipping instructions by the consignor in a non-negotiable bill of lading which causes the bailee not to deliver to the consignee defeats the consignee's title to the goods if they have been delivered to a buyer in ordinary course of business and in any event defeats the consignee's rights against the bailee.

(**4**) Delivery pursuant to a non-negotiable document may be stopped by a seller under Section 2-705, and subject to the requirement of due notification there provided. A bailee honoring the seller's instructions is entitled to be indemnified by the seller against any resulting loss or expense.

§7-505. Indorser Not a Guarantor for Other Parties.
The indorsement of a document of title issued by a bailee does not make the indorser liable for any default by the bailee or by previous indorsers.

§7-506. Delivery Without Indorsement: Right to Compel Indorsement. The transferee of a negotiable document of title has a specifically enforceable right to have his transferor supply any necessary indorsement but the transfer becomes a negotiation only as of the time the indorsement is supplied.

§7-507. Warranties on Negotiation or Transfer of Receipt or Bill. Where a person negotiates or transfers a document of title for value otherwise than as a mere intermediary under the next following section, then unless otherwise agreed he warrants to his immediate purchaser only in addition to any warranty made in selling the goods

>   **(a)** that the document is genuine; and
>   **(b)** that he has no knowledge of any fact which would impair its validity or worth; and
>   **(c)** that his negotiation or transfer is rightful and fully effective with respect to the title to the document and the goods it represents.

§7-508. Warranties of Collecting Bank as to Documents. A collecting bank or other intermediary known to be entrusted with documents on behalf of another or with collection of a draft or other claim against delivery of documents warrants by such delivery of the documents only its own good faith and authority. This rule applies even though the intermediary has purchased or made advances against the claim or draft to be collected.

§7-509. Receipt or Bill: When Adequate Compliance With Commercial Contract. The question whether a document is adequate to fulfill the obligations of a contract for sale or the conditions of a credit is governed by the Articles on Sales (Article 2) and on Letters of Credit (Article 5).

Part 6: Warehouse Receipts and Bills of Lading: Miscellaneous Provisions
§7-601. Lost and Missing Documents.

(1) If a document has been lost, stolen or destroyed, a court may order delivery of the goods or issuance of a substitute document and the bailee may without liability to any person comply with such order. If the document was negotiable the claimant must post security approved by the court to indemnify any person who may suffer loss as a result of nonsurrender of the document. If the document was not negotiable, such security may be required at the discretion of the court. The court may also in its discretion order payment of the bailee's reasonable costs and counsel fees.

(2) A bailee who without court order delivers goods to a person claiming under a missing negotiable document is liable to any person injured thereby, and if the delivery is not in good faith becomes liable for conversion. Delivery in good faith is not conversion if made in accordance with a filed classification or tariff or, where no classification or tariff is filed, if the claimant posts security with the bailee in an amount as least double the value of the goods at the time of posting to indemnify any person injured by the delivery who files a notice of claim within one year after the delivery.

§7-602. Attachment of Goods Covered by a Negotiable Document. Except where the document was originally issued upon delivery of the goods by a person who has no power to dispose of them, no lien attaches by virtue of any judicial process to goods in the possession of a bailee for which a negotiable document of title is outstanding unless the document be first surrendered to the bailee or its negotiation enjoined, and the bailee shall not be compelled to deliver the goods pursuant to process until the document is surrendered to him or impounded by the court. One who purchases the document for value without notice of the process or injunction takes free of the lien imposed by judicial process.

§7-603. Conflicting Claims; Interpleader. If more than one person claims title or possession of the goods, the bailee is excused from delivery until he has had a reasonable time to ascertain the validity of the adverse claims or to bring an action to compel all claimants to interplead and may compel such interpleader, either in defending an action for nondelivery of the goods, or by original action, whichever is appropriate.

ARTICLE 8: INVESTMENT SECURITIES

Part 1: Short Title and General Matters
§8-101. Short Title. This Article shall be known and may be cited as Uniform Commercial Code—Investment Securities.

§8-102. Definitions and Index of Definitions.

(1) In this Article, unless the context otherwise requires:

>   **(a)** A "certificated security" is a share, participation, or other interest in property of or an enterprise of the issuer or an obligation of the issuer which is

(**i**) represented by an instrument issued in bearer or registered form:

(**ii**) of a type commonly dealt in on securities exchanges or markets or commonly recognized in any area in which it is issued or dealt in as a medium for investment; and

(**iii**) either one of a class or series or by its terms divisible into a class or series of shares, participations, interest, or obligations.

(**b**) An "uncertificated security" is a share, participation, or other interest in property or an enterprise of the issuer or an obligation of the issuer which is

(**i**) not represented by an instrument and the transfer of which is registered upon books maintained for that purpose by or on behalf of the issuer;

(**ii**) of a type commonly dealt in on securities exchanges or markets; and

(**iii**) either one of a class or series or by its terms divisible into a class or series of shares, participations, interests, or obligations.

(**c**) A "security" is either a certificated or an uncertificated security. If a security is certificated, the terms "security" and "certificated security" may mean either the intangible interest, the instrument representing that interest, or both, as the context requires. A writing that is a certificated security is governed by this Article and not by Article 3, even though it also meets the requirements of that Article. This Article does not apply to money. If a certificated security has been retained by or surrendered to the issuer or its transfer agent for reasons other than registration of transfer, other temporary purpose, payment, exchange, or acquisition by the issuer, that security shall be treated as an uncertificated security for purposes of this Article.

(**d**) A certificated security is in "registered form" if

(**i**) it specifies a person entitled to the security or the rights it represents, and

(**ii**) its transfer may be registered upon books maintained for that purpose by or on behalf of the issuer, or the security so states.

(**e**) A certificated security is in "bearer form" if it runs to bearer according to its terms and not by reason of any indorsement.

(**2**) A "subsequent purchaser" is a person who takes other than by original issue.

(**3**) A "clearing corporation" is a corporation registered as a "clearing agency" under the federal securities laws or a corporation:

(**a**) at least 90 percent of whose capital stock is held by or for one or more organizations, none of which other than a national securities exchange or association, holds in excess of 20 percent of the capital stock of the corporation, and each of which is

(**i**) subject to supervision or regulation pursuant to the provisions of federal or state banking laws or state insurance laws,

(**ii**) a broker or dealer or investment company registered under the federal securities laws, or

(**iii**) a national securities exchange or association registered under the federal securities laws; and

(**b**) any remaining capital stock of which is held by individuals who have purchased at or prior to the time of their taking office as directors of the corporation and who have purchased only so much of the capital stock as is necessary to permit them to qualify as directors.

(**4**) A "custodian bank" is a bank or trust company that is supervised and examined by state or federal authority having supervision over banks and is acting as custodian for a clearing corporation.

(**5**) Other definitions applying to this Article or to specified Parts thereof and the sections in which they appear are:

"Adverse claim".	Section 8-302.
"Bona fide purchaser".	Section 8-302.
"Broker".	Section 8-303.
"Debtor".	Section 9-105.
"Financial intermediary".	Section 8-313.
"Guarantee of the signature".	Section 8-402.
"Initial transaction statement".	Section 8-408.
"Instruction".	Section 8-308.
"Intermediary Bank".	Section 4-105.
"Issuer".	Section 8-201.
"Overissue".	Section 8-104.
"Secured Party".	Section 9-105.
"Security Agreement".	Section 9-105.

(**6**) In addition Article 1 contains general definitions and principles of construction and interpretation applicable throughout this Article.

§8-103. Issuer's Lien. A lien upon a security in favor of an issuer thereof is valid against a purchaser only if:

>(a) the security is certificated and the right of the issuer to the lien is noted conspicuously thereon; or

>(b) the security is uncertificated and a notation of the right of the issuer to the lien is contained in the initial transaction statement sent to the purchaser or, if his interest is transferred to him other than by registration of transfer, pledge, or release, the initial transaction statement sent to the registered owner or the registered pledgee.

§8-104. Effect of Overissue; "Overissue".

(1) The provisions of this Article which validate a security or compel its issue or reissue do not apply to the extent that validation, issue, or reissue would result in overissue; but if:

>(a) an identical security which does not constitute an overissue is reasonably available for purchase, the person entitled to issue or validation may compel the issuer to purchase the security for him and either to deliver a certificated security or to register the transfer of an uncertificated security to him, against surrender of any certificated security he holds; or

>(b) a security is not so available for purchase, the person entitled to issue or validation may recover from the issuer the price he or the last purchaser for value paid for it with interest from the date of his demand.

(2) "Overissue" means the issue of securities in excess of the amount the issuer has corporate power to issue.

§8-105. Certificated Securities Negotiable; Statements and Instructions Not Negotiable; Presumptions.

(1) Certificated securities governed by this Article are negotiable instruments.

(2) Statements (Section 8-408), notices, or the like, sent by the issuer of uncertificated securities and instructions (Section 8-308) are neither negotiable instruments nor certificated securities.

(3) In any action on a security:

>(a) unless specifically denied in the pleadings, each signature on a certificated security, in a necessary indorsement, on an initial transaction statement, or on an instruction, is admitted;

>(b) if the effectiveness of a signature is put in issue, the burden of establishing it is on the party claiming under the signature, but the signature is presumed to be genuine or authorized;

>(c) if signatures on a certificated security are admitted or established, production of the security entitles a holder to recover on it unless the defendant establishes a defense or a defect going to the validity of the security;

>(d) if signatures on an initial transaction statement are admitted or established, the facts stated in the statement are presumed to be true as of the time of its issuance; and

>(e) after it is shown that a defense or defect exists, the plaintiff has the burden of establishing that he or some person under whom he claims is a person against whom the defense or defect is ineffective (Section 8-202).

§8-106. Applicability. The law (including the conflict of law rules) of the jurisdiction of organization of the issuer governs the validity of a security, the effectiveness of registration by the issuer, and the rights and duties of the issuer with respect to:

>(a) registration of transfer of a certificated security;

>(b) registration of transfer, pledge, or release of an uncertificated security; and

>(c) sending of statements of uncertificated securities.

§8-107. Securities Transferable; Action for Price.

(1) Unless otherwise agreed and subject to any applicable law or regulation respecting short sales, a person obligated to transfer securities may transfer any certificated security of the specified issue in bearer form or registered in the name of the transferee, or indorsed to him or in blank, or he may transfer an equivalent uncertificated security to the transferee or a person designated by the transferee.

(2) If the buyer fails to pay the price as it comes due under a contract of sale, the seller may recover the price of:

>(a) certificated securities accepted by the buyer:

>(b) uncertificated securities that have been

transferred to the buyer or a person designated by the buyer; and

(**c**) other securities if efforts at their resale would be unduly burdensome or if there is no readily available market for their resale.

§8-108. Registration of Pledge and Release of Uncertificated Securities. A security interest in an uncertificated security may be evidenced by the registration of pledge to the secured party or a person designated by him. There can be no more than one registered pledge of an uncertificated security at any time. The registered owner of an uncertificated security is the person in whose name the security is registered, even if the security is subject to a registered pledge. The rights of a registered pledgee of an uncertificated security under this Article are terminated by the registration of release.

Part 2: Issue—Issuer
§8-201. "Issuer".

(**1**) With respect to obligations on or defenses to a security, "issuer" includes a person who:

(**a**) places or authorizes the placing of his name on a certificated security (otherwise than as authenticating trustee, registrar, transfer agent, or the like) to evidence that it represents a share, participation, or other interest in his property or in an enterprise, or to evidence his duty to perform an obligation represented by the certificated security;

(**b**) creates shares, participations or other interests in his property or in an enterprise or undertakes obligations, which shares, participations, interests, or obligations are uncertificated securities;

(**c**) directly or indirectly creates fractional interests in his rights or property, which fractional interests are represented by certificated securities; or

(**d**) becomes responsible for or in place of any other person described as an issuer in this section.

(**2**) With respect to obligations on or defenses to a security, a guarantor is an issuer to the extent of his guaranty, whether or not his obligation is noted on a certificated security or on statements of uncertificated securities sent pursuant to Section 8-408.

(**3**) With respect to registration of transfer, pledge, or release (Parts 4 of this Article), "issuer" means a person on whose behalf transfer books are maintained.

§8-202. Issuer's Responsibility and Defenses; Notice of Defect or Defense.

(**1**) Even against a purchaser for value and without notice, the terms of a security include:

(**a**) if the security is certificated, those stated on the security;

(**b**) if the security is uncertificated, those contained in the initial transaction statement sent to such purchaser, or if his interest is transferred to him other than by registration of transfer, pledge, or release, the initial transaction statement sent to the registered owner or registered pledgee; and

(**c**) those made part of the security by reference, on the certificated security or in the initial transaction statement, to another instrument, indenture, or document or to a constitution, statute, ordinance, rule, regulation, order or the like, to the extent that the terms referred to do not conflict with the terms stated on the certificated security or contained in the statement. A reference under this paragraph does not of itself charge a purchaser for value with notice of a defect going to the validity of the security, even though the certificated security or statement expressly states that a person accepting it admits notice.

(**2**) A certificated security in the hands of a purchaser for value or an uncertificated security as to which an initial transaction statement has been sent to a purchaser for value, other than a security issued by a government or governmental agency or unit, even though issued with a defect going to its validity, is valid with respect to the purchaser if he is without notice of the particular defect unless the defect involves a violation of constitutional provisions, in which case the security is valid with respect to a subsequent purchaser for value and without notice of the defect. This subsection applies to an issuer that is a government or governmental agency or unit only if either there has been substantial compliance with the legal requirements governing the issue or the issuer has received a substantial consideration for the issue as a whole or for the particular security and a stated purpose of the issue is one for which the issuer has power to borrow money or issue the security.

(**3**) Except as provided in the case of certain unauthorized signature (Section 8-205), lack of genuineness of a certificated security or an initial transaction statement is a complete defense even against a purchaser for value and without notice.

(**4**) All other defenses of the issuer of a certificated or uncertificated security, including nondelivery and conditional delivery of a certificated security, are ineffective against a purchaser for value who has taken without notice of the particular defense.

(**5**) Nothing in this section shall be construed to affect the right of a party to a "when, as and if issued" or a "when distributed" contract to cancel the contract in the event of a material change in the character of the security that is the subject of the contract or in the plan or arrangement pursuant to which the security is to be issued or distributed.

§8-203. **Staleness as Notice of Defects or Defenses.**

(**1**) After an act or event creating a right to immediate performance of the principal obligation represented by a certificated security or that sets a date on or after which the security is to be presented or surrendered for redemption or exchange, a purchaser is charged with notice of any defect in its issue or defense of the issuer if:

(**a**) the act or event is one requiring the payment of money, the delivery of certificated securities, the registration of transfer or uncertificated securities, or any of these on presentation or surrender of the certificated security, the funds or securities are available on the date set for payment or exchange, and he takes the security more than one year after that date; and

(**b**) the act or event is not covered by paragraph (a) and he takes the security more than 2 years after the date set for surrender or presentation or the date on which performance became due.

(**2**) A call that has been revoked is not within subsection (1).

§8-204. **Effect of Issuer's Restrictions on Transfer.** A restriction on transfer of a security imposed by the issuer, even though otherwise lawful, is ineffective against any person without actual knowledge of it unless:

(**a**) the security is certificated and the restriction is noted conspicuously thereon; or

(**b**) the security is uncertificated and a notation of the restriction is contained in the initial transaction statement sent to the person or, if his interest is transferred to him other than by registration of transfer, pledge, or release, the initial transaction statement sent to the registered owner or the registered pledgee.

§8-205. **Effect of Unauthorized Signature on Certificated Security or Initial Transaction Statement.** An unauthorized signature placed on a certificated security prior to or in the course of issue or placed on an initial transaction statement is ineffective, but the signature is effective in favor of a purchaser for value of the certificated security or a purchaser for value of an uncertificated security to whom such initial transaction statement has been sent, if the purchaser is without notice of the lack of authority and the signing has been done by:

(**a**) an authenticating trustee, registrar, transfer agent, or other person entrusted by the issuer with the signing of the security, of similar securities, or of initial transaction statements or the immediate preparation for signing of any of them; or

(**b**) an employee of the issuer, or of any of the foregoing, entrusted with responsible handling of the security or initial transaction statement.

§8-206. **Completion or Alteration of Certificated Security or Initial Transaction Statement.**

(**1**) If a certificated security contains the signatures necessary to its issue or transfer but is incomplete in any other respect:

(**a**) any person may complete it by filling in the blanks as authorized; and

(**b**) even though the blanks are incorrectly filled in, the security as completed is enforceable by a purchaser who took it for value and without notice of the incorrectness.

(**2**) A complete certificated security that has been improperly altered, even though fraudulently, remains enforceable, but only according to its original terms.

(**3**) If an initial transaction statement contains the signatures necessary to its validity, but is incomplete in any other respect:

(**a**) any person may complete it by filling in the blanks as authorized; and

(**b**) even though the blanks are incorrectly filled in, the statement as completed is effective in favor of the person to whom it is sent if he purchased the security referred to therein for value and without notice of the incorrectness.

(4) A complete initial transaction statement that has been improperly altered, even though fraudulently, is effective in favor of a purchaser to whom it has been sent, but only according to its original terms.

§8-207. **Rights and Duties of Issuer With Respect to Registered Owners and Registered Pledgees.**

(1) Prior to due presentment for registration of transfer of a certificated security in registered form, the issuer or indenture trustee may treat the registered owner as the person exclusively entitled to vote, to receive notifications, and otherwise to exercise all the rights and powers of an owner.

(2) Subject to the provisions of subsections (3), (4), and (6), the issuer or indenture trustee may treat the registered owner of an uncertificated security as the person exclusively entitled to vote, to receive notifications, and otherwise to exercise all the rights and powers of an owner.

(3) The registered owner of an uncertificated security that is subject to a registered pledge is not entitled to registration of transfer prior to the due presentment to the issuer of a release instruction. The exercise of conversion rights with respect to a convertible uncertificated security is a transfer within the meaning of this section.

(4) Upon due presentment of a transfer instruction from the registered pledgee of an uncertificated security, the issuer shall:

(a) register the transfer of the security to the new owner free of pledge, if the instruction specifies a new owner (who may be the registered pledgee) and does not specify a pledgee;

(b) register the transfer of the security to the new owner subject to the interest of the existing pledgee, if the instruction specifies a new owner and the existing pledgee; or

(c) register the release of the security from the existing pledge and register the pledge of the security to the other pledgee, if the instruction specifies the existing owner and another pledgee.

(5) Continuity of perfection of a security interest is not broken by registration of transfer under subsection (4)(b) or by registration of release and pledge under subsection (4)(c), if the security interest is assigned.

(6) If an uncertificated security is subject to a registered pledge:

(a) any uncertificated securities issued in exchange for or distributed with respect to the pledged security shall be registered subject to the pledge;

(b) any certificated securities issued in exchange for or distributed with respect to the pledged security shall be delivered to the registered pledgee; and

(c) any money paid in exchange for or in redemption of part or all of the security shall be paid to the registered pledgee.

(7) Nothing in this Article shall be construed to affect the liability of the registered owner of a security for calls, assessments, or the like.

§8-208. **Effect of Signature of Authenticating Trustee, Registrar, or Transfer Agent.**

(1) A person placing his signature upon a certificated security or an initial transaction statement as authenticating trustee, registrar, transfer agent, or the like, warrants to a purchaser for value of the certificated security or a purchaser for value of an uncertificated security to whom the initial transaction statement has been sent, if the purchaser is without notice of the particular defect, that:

(a) the certificated security or initial transaction statement is genuine;

(b) his own participation in the issue or registration of the transfer, pledge, or release of the security is within his capacity and within the scope of the authority received by him from the issuer; and

(c) he has reasonable grounds to believe that the security is in the form and within the amount of the issuer is authorized to issue.

(2) Unless otherwise agreed, a person by so placing his signature does not assume responsibility for the validity of the security in other respects.

Part 3: Transfer
§8-301. **Rights Acquired by Purchaser.**

(1) Upon transfer of a security to a purchaser (Section 8-313), the purchaser acquires the rights in the security which his transferor had or had actual authority to convey unless the purchaser's rights are limited by Section 8-302(4).

(2) A transferee of a limited interest acquires rights only to the extent of the interest transferred. The creation or release of a security interest in a security is the transfer of a limited interest in that security.

§8-302. "Bona Fide Purchaser"; "Adverse Claim"; Title Acquired by Bona Fide Purchaser.

(1) A "bona fide purchaser" is a purchaser for value in good faith and without notice of any adverse claim:

(a) who takes delivery of a certificated security in bearer form or in registered form, issued or indorsed to him or in blank;

(b) to whom the transfer, pledge or release of an uncertificated security is registered on the books of the issuer; or

(c) to whom a security is transferred under the provisions of paragraph (c) (d) (i), or (g) of Section 8-313(1).

(2) "Adverse claim" includes a claim that a transfer was or would be wrongful or that a particular adverse person is the owner of or has an interest in the security.

(3) A bona fide purchaser in addition to acquiring the rights of a purchaser (Section 8-301) also acquires his interest in the security free of any adverse claim.

(4) Notwithstanding Section 8-301(1), the transferee of a particular certificated security who has been a party to any fraud or illegality affecting the security, or who as a prior holder of that certificated security had notice of an adverse claim, cannot improve his position by taking from a bona fide purchaser.

§8-303. "Broker".

"Broker" means a person engaged for all or part of his time in the business of buying and selling securities, who in the transaction concerned acts for, buys a security from, or sells a security to, a customer. Nothing in this Article determines the capacity in which a person acts for purposes of any other statute or rule to which the person is subject.

§8-304. Notice to Purchaser of Adverse Claims.

(1) A purchaser (including a broker for the seller or buyer, but excluding an intermediary bank) of a certificated security is charged with notice of adverse claims if:

(a) the security, whether in bearer or registered from, has been indorsed "for collection" or "for surrender" or for some other purpose not involving transfer; or

(b) the security is in bearer form and has on it an unambiguous statement that it is the property of a person other than the transferor. The mere writing of a name on a security is not such a statement.

(2) A purchaser (including a broker for the seller or buyer, but excluding an intermediary bank) to whom the transfer, pledge, or release of an uncertificated security is registered is charged with notice of adverse claims as to which the issuer has a duty under Section 8-403(4) at the time of registration and which are noted in the initial transaction statement sent to the purchaser or, if his interest is transferred to him other than by registration of transfer, pledge, or release, the initial transaction statement sent to the registered owner or the registered pledge.

(3) The fact that the purchaser (including a broker for the seller or buyer) of a certificated or uncertificated security has notice that the security is held for a third person or is registered in the name of or indorsed by a fiduciary foes not create a duty of inqury into the rightfulness of the transfer or constitute constructive notice of adverse claims. However, if the purchaser (excluding an intermediary bank) has knowledge that the proceeds are being used or the transaction is for the individual benefit of the fiduciary or otherwise in breach of duty, the purchaser is charged with notice of adverse claims.

§8-305. Staleness as Notice of Adverse Claims.

An act or event that creates a right to immediate performance of the principal obligation represented by a certificated security or sets a date on or after which a certificated security is to be presented or surrendered for redemption or exchange does not itself constitute any notice of adverse claims except in the case of a transfer:

(a) after one year from any date set for presentment or surrender for redemption or exchange; or

(b) after 6 months from any date set for payment of money against presentation or surrender of the security if funds are available for payment on that date.

§8-306. Warranties on Presentment and Transfer of Certificated Securities; Warranties of Originators of Instructions.

(1) A person who presents a certificated security for registration of transfer or for payment or exchange warrants to the issuer that he is entitled to the registration, payment, or exchange. But, a purchaser for value and without notice of adverse claims who receives a new, reissued, or re-registered certificated security on registration of transfer or receives an initial transaction statement confirming the registration of transfer of an equivalent uncertificated security to him warrants only that he has no knowledge of any unauthorized signature (Section 8-311) in a necessary indorsement.

(**2**) A person by transferring a certificated security to a purchaser for value warrants only that:

(**a**) his transfer is effective and rightful;

(**b**) the security is genuine and has not been materially altered; and

(**c**) he knows of no fact which might impair the validity of the security.

(**3**) If a certificated security is delivered by an intermediary known to be entrusted with delivery of the security on behalf of another or with collection of a draft or claim against delivery, the intermediary by delivery warrants only his own good faith and authority, even though he has purchased or made advances against the claim to be collected against the delivery.

(**4**) A pledgee or other holder for security who redelivers a certificated security received, or after payment and on order of the debtor delivers that security to a third person makes only the warranties of an intermediary under subsection (3).

(**5**) A person who originates an instruction warrants to the issuer that:

(**a**) he is an appropriate person to originate the instruction; and

(**b**) at the time the instruction is presented to the issuer he will be entitled to the registration of transfer, pledge, or release.

(**6**) A person who originates an instruction warrants to any person specially guaranteeing his signature (subsection 8-312(3)) that:

(**a**) he is an appropriate person to originate the instruction; and

(**b**) at the time the instruction is presented to the issuer

(**i**) he will be entitled to the registration of transfer, pledge, or release; and

(**ii**) the transfer, pledge, or release requested in the instruction will be registered by the issuer free from all liens, security interests, restrictions, and claims other than those specified in the instruction.

(**7**) A person who originates an instruction warrants to a purchaser for value and to any person guaranteeing the instruction (Section 8-312(6)) that:

(**a**) he is an appropriate person to originate the instruction;

(**b**) the uncertificated security referred to therein is valid; and

(**c**) at the time the instruction is presented to the issuer

(**i**) the transferor will be entitled to the registration of transfer, pledge, or release;

(**ii**) the transfer, pledge, or release requested in the instruction will be registered by the issuer free from all liens, security interests, restrictions, and claims other than those specified in the instruction; and

(**iii**) the requested transfer, pledge, or release will be rightful.

(**8**) If a secured party is the registered pledgee or the registered owner of an uncertificated security, a person who originates an instruction of release or transfer to the debtor or, after payment and on order of the debtor, a transfer instruction to a third person, warrants to the debtor or the third person only that he is an appropriate person to originate the instruction and at the time of instruction is presented to the issuer, the transferor will be entitled to the registration of release or transfer. If a transfer instruction to a third person who is a purchaser for value is originated on order of the debtor, the debtor makes to the purchaser the warranties of paragraphs (b), (c)(ii) and (c)(iii) of subsection (7).

(**9**) A person who transfers an uncertificated security to a purchaser for value and does not originate an instruction in connection with the transfer warrants only that:

(**a**) his transfer is effective and rightful; and

(**b**) the uncertificated security is valid.

(**10**) A broker gives to his customer and to the issuer and a purchaser the applicable warranties provided in this section and has the rights and privileges of a purchaser under this section. The warranties of and in favor of the broker acting as an agent are in addition to applicable warranties given by and in favor of his customer.

§8-307. Effect of Delivery Without Indorsement; Right to Compel Indorsement. If a certificated security in registered form has been delivered to a purchaser without a necessary indorsement he may become a bona fide purchaser only as of the time the indorsement is supplied; but against the transferor, the transfer is complete upon delivery and the purchaser has a specifically enforceable right to have any necessary indorsement supplied.

§8-308. Indorsements; Instructions.

(**1**) An indorsement of a certificated security in

registered form is made when an appropriate person signs on it or on a separate document an assignment or transfer of the security or a power to assign or transfer it or his signature is written without more upon the back of the security.

(**2**) An indorsement may be in blank or special. An indorsement in blank includes an indorsement to bearer. A special indorsement specifies to whom the security is to be transferred, or who has power to transfer it. A holder may convert a blank indorsement into a special indorsement.

(**3**) An indorsement purporting to be only of part of a certificated security representing units intended by the issuer to be separately transferable is effective to the extent of the indorsement.

(**4**) An "instruction" is an order to the issuer of an uncertificated security requesting that the transfer, pledge, or release from pledge of the uncertificated security specified therein be registered.

(**5**) An instruction originated by an appropriate person is:

(**a**) a writing signed by an appropriate person; or

(**b**) a communication to the issuer in any form agreed upon in a writing signed by the issuer and an appropriate person.

If an instruction has been originated by an appropriate person but is incomplete in any other respect, any person may complete it as authorized and the issuer may rely on it as completed even though it has been completed incorrectly.

(**6**) "An appropriate person" in subsection (1) means the person specified by the certificated security or by special indorsement to be entitled to the security.

(**7**) "An appropriate person" in subsection (5) means:

(**a**) for an instruction to transfer or pledge an uncertificated security which is then not subject to a registered pledge, the registered owner; or

(**b**) for an instruction to transfer or release an uncertificated security which is then subject to a registered pledge, the registered pledgee.

(**8**) In addition to the persons designated in subsections (6) and (7), "an appropriate person" in subsections (1) and (5) includes:

(**a**) if the person designated is described as a fiduciary but is no longer serving in the described capacity, either that person or his successor;

(**b**) if the persons designated are described as more than one person as fiduciaries and one or more are no longer serving in the described capacity, the remaining fiduciary or fiduciaries, whether or not a successor has been appointed or qualified;

(**c**) if the person designated is an individual and is without capacity to act by virtue of death, incompetence, infancy, or otherwise his executor, administrator, guardian, or like fiduciary;

(**d**) if the persons designated are described as more than one person as tenants by the entirety or with right of survivorship and by reason of death all cannot sign the survivor or survivors;

(**e**) a person having power to sign under applicable law or controlling instrument; and

(**f**) to the extent that the person designated or any of the foregoing persons may act through an agent, his authorized agent.

(**9**) Unless otherwise agreed, the indorser of a certificated security by his indorsement or the originator of an instruction by his origination assumes no obligation that the security will be honored by the issuer but only the obligations provided in Section 8-306.

(**10**) Whether the person signing is appropriate is determined as of the date of signing and an indorsement made by or an instruction originated by him does not become unauthorized for the purposes of this Article by virtue of any subsequent change of circumstances.

(**11**) Failure of a fiduciary to comply with a controlling instrument or with the law of the state having jurisdiction of the fiduciary relationship, including any law requiring the fiduciary to obtain court approval of the transfer, pledge, or release, does not render his indorsement or an instruction originated by him unauthorized for the purposes of this Article.

§8-309. Effect of Indorsement Without Delivery.   An indorsement of a certificated security, whether special or in blank, does not constitute a transfer until delivery of the certificated security on which it appears or, if the indorsement is on a separate document, until delivery of both the document and the certificated security.

§8-310. Indorsement of Certificated Security in Bearer Form.   An indorsement of a certificated security in bearer form may give notice of adverse claims (Section 8-304) but does not otherwise affect any right to registration the holder possesses.

§8-311. Effect of Unauthorized Indorsement or Instruction. Unless the owner, or pledgee has ratified an unauthorized indorsement or instruction or is otherwise precluded from asserting its ineffectiveness:

(a) he may assert its ineffectiveness against the issuer or any purchaser, other than a purchaser for value and without notice of adverse claims, who has in good faith received a new, reissued, or re-registered certificated security on registration of transfer or received an initial transaction statement confirming the registration of transfer, pledge, or release of an equivalent uncertificated security to him; and

(b) an issuer who registers the transfer of a certificated security upon the unauthorized indorsement or who registers the transfer, pledge, or release of an uncertificated security upon the unauthorized instruction is subject to liability for improper registration (Section 8-104).

§8-312. Effect of Guaranteeing Signature, Indorsement or Instruction.

(1) Any person guaranteeing a signature of an indorser of a certificated security warrants that at the time of signing:

(a) the signature was genuine;

(b) the signer was an appropriate person to indorse (Section 8-308); and

(c) the signer had legal capacity to sign.

(2) Any person guaranteeing a signature of the originator of an instruction warrants that at the time of signing:

(a) the signature was genuine;

(b) the signer was an appropriate person to originate the instruction (Section 8-308) if the person specified in the instruction as the registered owner or registered pledgee of the uncertificated security was, in fact, the registered owner or registered pledgee of such security, as to which fact the signature guarantor makes no warranty;

(c) the signer had legal capacity to sign; and

(d) the taxpayer identification number, if any, appearing on the instruction as that of the registered owner or registered pledgee was the taxpayer identification number of the signer or of the owner or pledgee for whom the signer was acting.

(3) Any person specially guaranteeing the signature of the originator of an instruction makes not only the warranties of a signature guarantor (subsection (2)) but also warrants that at the time the instruction is presented to the issuer:

(a) the person specified in the instruction as the registered owner or registered pledgee of the uncertificated security will be the registered owner or registered pledgee; and

(b) the transfer, pledge, or release of the uncertificated security requested in the instruction will be registered by the issuer free from all liens, security interests, restrictions, and claims other than those specified in the instruction.

(4) The guarantor under subsections (1) and (2) or the special guarantor under subsection (3) does not otherwise warrant the rightfulness of the particular transfer, pledge, or release.

(5) Any person guaranteeing an indorsement of a certificated security makes not only the warranties of a signature guarantor under subsection (1) but also warrants the rightfulness of the particular transfer in all respects.

(6) Any person guaranteeing an instruction requesting the transfer, pledge, or release of an uncertificated security makes not only the warranties of a special signature guarantor under subsection (3) but also warrants the rightfulness of the particular transfer, pledge, or release in all respects.

(7) No issuer may require a special guarantee of signature (subsection (3)), a guarantee of indorsement (subsection (5)), or a guarantee of instruction (subsection (6)) as a condition to registration of transfer, pledge, or release.

(8) The foregoing warranties are made to any person taking or dealing with the security in reliance on the guarantee, and the guarantor is liable to the person for any loss resulting from breach of the warranties.

§8-313. When Transfer to Purchaser Occurs: Financial Intermediary as Bona Fide Purchaser; "Financial Intermediary".

(1) Transfer of a security or a limited interest (including a security interest) therein to a purchaser occurs only:

(a) at the time he or a person designated by him acquires possession of a certificated security;

(b) at the time the transfer, pledge, or release of an uncertificated security is registered to him or a person designated by him;

(c) at the time his financial intermediary acquires possession of a certificated security specially indorsed to or issued in the name of the purchaser;

(**d**) at the time a financial intermediary, not a clearing corporation, sends him confirmation of the purchase and also by book entry or otherwise identifies as belonging to the purchaser

(**i**) a specific certificated security in the financial intermediary's possession;

(**ii**) a quantity of securities that constitute or are part of a fungible bulk of certificated securities in the financial intermediary's possession or of uncertificated securities registered in the name of the financial intermediary; or

(**iii**) a quantity of securities that constitute or are part of a fungible bulk of securities shown on the account of the financial intermediary on the books of another financial intermediary;

(**e**) with respect to an identified certificated security to be delivered while still in the possession of a third person, not a financial intermediary, at the time that person acknowledges that he holds for the purchaser;

(**f**) with respect to a specific uncertificated security the pledge or transfer of which has been registered to a third person, not a financial intermediary, at the time that person acknowledges that he holds for the purchaser;

(**g**) at the time appropriate entries to the account of the purchaser or a person designated by him on the books of a clearing corporation are made under Section 8-320;

(**h**) with respect to the transfer of a security interest where the debtor has signed a security agreement containing a description of the security, at the time a written notification, which, in the case of the creation of the security interest, is signed by the debtor (which may be a copy of the security agreement) or which, in the case of the release or assignment of the security interest created pursuant to this paragraph, is signed by the secured party, is received by

(**i**) a financial intermediary on whose books the interest of the transferor in the security appears:

(**ii**) a third person, not a financial intermediary, in possession of the security, if it is certificated;

(**iii**) a third person, not a financial intermediary, who is the registered owner of the security, if it is uncertificated and not subject to a registered pledge; or

(**iv**) a third person, not a financial intermediary, who is the registered pledgee of the security, if it is uncertificated and subject to a registered pledge;

(**i**) with respect to the transfer of a security interest where the transferor has signed a security agreement containing a description of the security, at the time new value is given by the secured party; or

(**j**) with respect to the transfer of a security interest where the secured party is a financial intermediary and the security has already been transferred to the financial intermediary under paragraphs (a), (b), (c), (d), or (g), at the time the transferor has signed a security agreement containing a description of the security and value is given by the secured party.

(**2**) The purchaser is the owner of a security held for him by a financial intermediary, but cannot be a bona fide purchaser of a security so held except in the circumstances specified in paragraphs (c), (d)(i), and (g) of subsection (1). If a security so held is part of a fungible bulk, as in the circumstances specified in paragraphs (d)(ii) and (d)(iii) of subsection (1), the purchaser is the owner of a proportionate property interest in the fungible bulk.

(**3**) Notice of an adverse claim received by the financial intermediary or by the purchaser after the financial intermediary takes delivery of a certificated security as a holder for value or after the transfer, pledge, or release of an uncertificated security has been registered free of the claim to a financial intermediary who has given value is not effective either as to the financial intermediary or as to the purchaser. However, as between the financial intermediary and the purchaser the purchaser may demand transfer of an equivalent security as to which no notice of adverse claim has been received.

(**4**) A "financial intermediary" is a bank, broker, clearing corporation or other person (or the nominee of any of them) which in the ordinary course of its business maintains security accounts for its customers and is acting in that capacity. A financial intermediary may have a security interest in securities held in account for its customer.

§8-314. Duty to Transfer, When Completed.

(**1**) Unless otherwise agreed, if a sale of a security is made on an exchange or otherwise through brokers:

(**a**) the selling customer fulfills his duty to transfer at the time he:

(**i**) places a certificated security in the possession of the selling broker or of a person designated by the broker;

(**ii**) causes an uncertificated security to be registered in the name of the selling broker or a person designated by the broker;

(**iii**) if requested, causes an acknowledgment to be made to the selling broker that a certificated or uncertificated security is held for the broker; or

(**iv**) places in the possession of the selling broker or of a person designated by the broker a transfer instruction for an uncertificated security, providing the issuer does not refuse to register the requested transfer if the instruction is presented to the issuer for registration within 30 days thereafter; and

(**b**) the selling broker, including a correspondent broker acting for a selling customer, fulfills his duty to transfer at the time he:

(**i**) places a certificated security in the possession of the buying broker or a person designated by the buying broker;

(**ii**) causes an uncertificated security to be registered in the name of the buying broker or a person designated by the buying broker;

(**iii**) places in the possession of the buying broker or of a person designated by the buying broker a transfer instruction for an uncertificated security, providing the issuer does not refuse to register the requested transfer if the instruction is presented to the issuer for registration within 30 days thereafter; or

(**iv**) effects clearance of the sale in accordance with the rules of the exchange on which the transaction took place.

(**2**) Except as provided in this section and unless otherwise agreed, a transferor's duty to transfer a security under a contract of purchase is not fulfilled until he:

(**a**) places a certificated security in form to be negotiated by the purchaser in the possession of the purchaser or of a person designated by the purchaser;

(**b**) causes an uncertificated security to be registered in the name of the purchaser or a person designated by the purchaser; or

(**c**) if the purchaser requests, causes an acknowledgment to be made to the purchaser that certificated or uncertificated security is held for the purchaser.

(**3**) Unless made on an exchange, a sale to a broker purchasing for his own account is within subsection (2) and not within subsection (1).

§8-315. Action Against Transferee Based Upon Wrongful Transfer.

(**1**) Any person against whom the transfer of a security is wrongful for any reason, including his incapacity, as against anyone except a bona fide purchaser, may:

(**a**) reclaim possession of the certificated security wrongfully transferred;

(**b**) obtain possession of any new certificated security representing all or part of the same rights:

(**c**) compel the origination of an instruction to transfer to him or a person designated by him an uncertificated security constituting all or part of the same rights; or

(**d**) have damages.

(**2**) If the transfer is wrongful because of an unauthorized indorsement of a certificated security, the owner may also reclaim or obtain possession of the security or a new certificated security, even from a bona fide purchaser, if the ineffectiveness of the purported indorsement can be asserted against him under the provisions of this Article on unauthorized indorsements (Section 8-311).

(**3**) The right to obtain or reclaim possession of a certificated security or to compel the origination of a transfer instruction may be specifically enforced and the transfer of a certificated or uncertificated security enjoined and a certificated security impounded pending the litigation.

§8-316. Purchaser's Right to Requisites for Registration of Transfer, Pledge, or Release on Books. Unless otherwise agreed, the transferor of a certificated security or the transferor, pledgor, or pledgee of an uncertificated security on due demand must supply his purchaser with any proof of his authority to transfer, pledge, or release or with any other requisite necessary to obtain registration of the transfer, pledge, or release of the security; but if the transfer, pledge, or release is not for value, a transferor, pledgor, or pledgee need not do so unless the purchaser furnishes the necessary expenses. Failure within a reasonable time to comply with a demand made gives the purchaser the right to reject or rescind the transfer, pledge, or release.

§8-317. Creditors' Rights.

(**1**) Subject to the exceptions in subsections (3) and (4), no attachment or levy upon a certificated security or any share or other interest represented thereby which is outstanding is valid until the security is actually seized by the officer making the attachment or levy, but a certificated security which has been surrendered to the issuer may be reached by a creditor by legal process at the issuer's chief executive office in the United States.

(**2**) An uncertificated security registered in the name of the debtor may not be reached by a creditor except by legal process at the issuer's chief executive office in the United States.

(**3**) The interest of a debtor in a certificated security that is in the possession of a secured party not a financial intermediary or in an uncertificated security registered in the name of a secured party not a financial intermediary (or in the name of a nominee of the secured party) may be reached by a creditor by legal process upon the secured party.

(**4**) The interest of a debtor in a certificated security that is in the possession of or registered in the name of a financial intermediary or in an uncertificated security registered in the name of a financial intermediary may be reached by a creditor by legal process upon the financial intermediary on whose books the interest of the debtor appears.

(**5**) Unless otherwise provided by law, a creditor's lien upon the interest of a debtor in a security obtained pursuant to subsection (3) or (4) is not a restraint on the transfer of the security, free of the lien, to a third party for new value; but in the event of a transfer, the lien applies to the proceeds of the transfer in the hands of the secured party or financial intermediary, subject to any claims having priority.

(**6**) A creditor whose debtor is the owner of a security is entitled to aid from courts of appropriate jurisdiction, by injunction of otherwise, in reaching the security or in satisfying the claim by means allowed at law or in equity in regard to property that cannot readily be reached by ordinary legal process.

§8-318. No Conversion by Good Faith Conduct. An agent or bailee who in good faith (including the observance of reasonable commercial standards if he is in the business of buying, selling, or otherwise dealing with securities) has received certificated securities and sold, pledged, or delivered them or has sold or caused the transfer or pledge of uncertificated securities over which he had control according to the instructions of his principal, is not liable for conversion or for participation in breach of fiduciary duty although the principal had no right so to deal with the securities.

§8-319 Statute of Frauds. A contract for the sale of securities is not enforceable by way of action or defense unless:

(**a**) there is some writing signed by the party against whom enforcement is sought or by his authorized agent or broker, sufficient to indicate that a contract has been made for sale of a stated quantity of described securities at a defined or stated price;

(**b**) delivery of a certificated security or transfer instruction has been accepted, or transfer of an uncertificated security has been registered and the transferee has failed to send written objection to the issuer within 10 days after receipt of the initial transaction statement confirming the registration, or payment has been made, but the contract is enforceable under this provision only to the extent the delivery, registration, or payment;

(**c**) within a reasonable time a writing in confirmation of the sale or purchase and sufficient against the sender under paragraph (a) has been received by the party against whom enforcement is sought and he has failed to send written objection to its contents within 10 days after its receipt; or

(**d**) the party against whom enforcement is sought admits in his pleading, testimony, or otherwise in court that a contract was made for the sale of a stated quantity of described securities at a defined or stated price.

§8-320. Transfer or Pledge Within Central Depository System.

(**1**) In addition to other methods, a transfer, pledge, or release of a security or any interest therein may be effected by the making of appropriate entries on the books of a clearing corporation reducing the account of the transferor, pledgor, or pledgee and increasing the account of the transferee, pledgee, or pledgor by the amount of the obligation, or the number of shares or rights transferred, pledged, or released, if the security is shown on the account of a transferor, pledgor, or pledgee on the books of the clearing corporation; is subject to the control of the clearing corporation; and

    (**a**) if certificated,

        (**i**) is in the custody of the clearing corporation, another clearing corporation, a custodian bank or a nominee of any of them; and

        (**ii**) is in bearer form or indorsed in blank by an appropriate person or registered in the name of the clearing corporation, a custodian bank, or a nominee of any of them; or

    (**b**) if uncertificated, is registered in the name of the clearing corporation, another clearing corporation, a custodian bank, or a nominee of any of them.

(**2**) Under this section entries may be made with respect to like securities or interests therein as a part of a fungible bulk and may refer merely to a quantity of a particular security without reference to the name of the registered owner, certificate or bond number, or the like, and, in appropriate cases, may be on a net basis taking into account other transfers, pledges or releases of the same security.

(**3**) A transfer under this section is effective (Section 8-313) and the purchaser acquires the rights of the transferor (Section 8-301). A pledge or release under this section is the transfer of a limited interest. If a pledge or the creation of a security interest is intended, the security interest is perfected at the time when both value is given by the pledgee and the appropriate entries are made (Section 8-321). A transferee or pledgee under this section may be a bona fide purchaser (Section 8-302).

(**4**) A transfer or pledge under this section is not a registration of transfer under Part 4.

(**5**) That entries made on the books of the clearing corporaton as provided in subsection (1) are not appropriate does not affect the validity or effect of the entries or the liabilities or obligations of the clearing corporation to any person adversely affected thereby.

§8-321. Enforceability, Attachment, Perfection, and Termination of Security Interests.

(**1**) A security interest in a security is enforceable and can attach only if it is transferred to the secured part or a person designated by him pursuant to a provision of Section 8-313(1).

(**2**) A security interest so transferred pursuant to agreement by a transferor who has rights in the security to a transferee who has given value is a perfected security interest, but a security interest that has been transferred soley under paragraph (i) of Section 8-313(1) becomes unperfected after 21 days unless, within that time, the requirements for transfer under any other provision of Section 8-313(1) are satisfied.

(**3**) A security interest in a security is subject to the provisions of Article 9, but:

    (**a**) no filing is required to perfect the security interest; and

    (**b**) no written security agreement signed by the debtor is necessary to make the security interest enforceable, except as otherwise provided in paragraph (h), (i), or (j) of Section 8-313(1).

The secured party has the rights and duties provided under Section 9-207, to the extent that they are applicable, whether or not the security is certificated, and, if certificated, whether or not it is in his possession.

(**4**) Unless otherwise agreed, a security interest in a security is terminated by transfer to the debtor or a person designated by him pursuant to a provision of Section 8-313(1). If a security is thus transferred, the security interest, if not terminated, becomes unperfected unless the security is certificated and is delivered to the debtor for the purpose of ulitmate sale or exchange or presentation, collection, renewal, or registration of transfer. In that case, the security interest becomes unperfected after 21 days unless, within that time, the security (or securities for which it has been exchanged) is transferred to the secured party, or a person designated by him pursuant to a provision of Section 8-313(1).

Part 4: Registration

§8-401. Duty of Issuer to Register Transfer, Pledge, or Release.

(**1**) If a certificated security in registered form is presented to the issuer with a request to register transfer or an instruction is presented to the issuer with a request to register transfer, pledge, or release, the issuer shall register the transfer, pledge, or release as requested if:

    (**a**) the security is indorsed or the instruction was originated by the appropriate person or persons (Section 8-308);

    (**b**) reasonable assurance is given that those indorsements or instructions are genuine and effective (Section 8-402);

(c) the issuer has no duty as to adverse claims or has discharged the duty (Section 8-403);

(d) any applicable law relating to the collection of taxes has been complied with; and

(e) the transfer, pledge, or release is in fact rightful or is to a bona fide purchaser.

(2) If an issuer is under a duty to register a transfer, pledge, or release of a security, the issuer is also liable to the person presenting a certificated security or an instruction for registration or his principal for loss resulting from any unreasonable delay in registration or from failure or refusal to register the transfer, pledge, or release.

§8-402. Assurance that Indorsements and Instructions Are Effective.

(1) The issuer may require the following assurance that each necessary indorsement of a certificated security or each instruction (Section 8-308) is genuine and effective:

(a) in all cases, a guarantee of the signature (Section 8-312(1) or (2)) of the person indorsing a certificated security or originating an instruction including, in the case of an instruction, a warranty of the taxpayer identification number or, in the absence thereof, other reasonable assurance of identity:

(b) if the indorsement is made or the instruction is originated by an agent, appropriate assurance of authority to sign;

(c) if the indorsement is made or the instruction is originated by a fiduciary, appropriate evidence of appointment or incumbency;

(d) if there is more than one fiduciary, reasonable assurance that all who are required to sign have done so; and

(e) if the indorsement is made or the instruction is originated by a person not covered by any of the foregoing, assurance appropriate to the case corresponding as nearly as may be to the foregoing.

(2) A "guarantee of the signature" in subsection (1) means a guarantee signed by or on behalf of a person reasonably believed by the issuer to be responsible. The issuer may adopt standards with respect to responsibility if they are not manifestly unreasonable.

(3) "Appropriate evidence of appointment or incumbency" in subsection (1) means:

(a) in the case of a fiduciary appointed or qualified by a court, a certificate issued by or under the direction or supervision of that court or an officer thereof and dated within 60 days before the date of presentation for transfer, pledge, or release; or

(b) in any other case, a copy of a document showing the appointment or a certificate issued by or on behalf of a person reasonably believed by the issuer to be responsible or, in the absence of that document or certificate, other evidence reasonably deemed by the issuer to be appropriate. The issuer may adopt standards with respect to the evidence if they are not manifestly unreasonable. The issuer is not charged with notice of the contents of any document obtained pursuant to this paragraph (b) except to the extent that the contents relate directly to the appointment or incumbency.

(4) The issuer may elect to require reasonable assurance beyond that specified in this section, but if it does so and, for a purpose other than that specified in subsection (3)(b), both requires and obtains a copy of a will, trust, indenture, articles of co-partnership, bylaws, or other controlling instrument, it is charged with notice of all matters contained therein affecting the transfer, pledge, or release.

§8-403. Issuer's Duty as to Adverse Claims.

(1) An issuer to whom a certificated security is presented for registration shall inquire into adverse claims if;

(a) a written notification of an adverse claim is received at a time and in a manner affording the issuer a reasonable opportunity to act on it prior to the issuance of a new, reissued, or reregistered certificated security, and the notification identifies the claimant, the registered owner, and the issue of which the security is a part, and provides an address for communications directed to the claimant; or

(b) the issuer is charged with notice of an adverse claim from a controlling instrument it has elected to require under Section 8-402(4).

(2) The issuer may discharge any duty of inquiry by any reasonable or certified mail at the address furnished by him or, if there be no such address, at his residence or regular place of business that the certificated security has been presented for registration of transfer by a named person, and that the transfer will be registered unless within 30 days from the date of mailing the notification, either:

(a) an appropriate restraining order, injunction, or other process issues from a court of competent jurisdiction; or

(b) there is filed with the issuer an indemnity bond, sufficient in the issuer's judgment to protect the issuer and any transfer agent, registrar, or other agent of the issuer involved from any loss it or they may suffer by complying with the adverse claim.

(3) Unless an issuer is charged with notice of an adverse claim from a controlling instrument which it has elected to require under Section 8-402(4) or receives notification of an adverse claim under subsection (1), if a certificated security presented for registration is indorsed by the appropriate person or persons the issuer is under no duty to inquire into adverse claims. In particular:

(a) an issuer registering a certificated security in the name of a person who is a fiduciary or who is described as a fiduciary is not bound to inquire into the existence, extent, or correct description of the fiduciary relationship; and thereafter the issuer may assume without inquiry that the newly registered owner continues to be the fiduciary until the issuer receives written notice that the fiduciary is no longer acting as such with respect to the particular security;

(b) an issuer registering transfer on an indorsement by a fiduciary is not bound to inquire whether the transfer is made in compliance with a controlling instrument or with the law of the state having jurisdiction of the fiduciary relationship, including any law requiring the fiduciary to obtain court approval of the transfer; and

(c) the issuer is not charged with notice of the contents of any court record or file or other recorded or unrecorded document even though the document is in its possession and even though the transfer is made on the indorsement of a fiduciary to the fiduciary himself or to his nominee.

(4) An issuer is under no duty as to adverse claims with respect to an uncertificated security except:

(a) claims embodied in a restraining order, injunction, or other legal process served upon the issuer if the process was served at a time and in a manner affording the issuer a reasonable opportunity to act on it in accordance with the requirements of subsection (5);

(b) claims of which the issuer has received a written notification from the registered owner or the registered pledgee if the notification was received at a time and in a manner affording the issuer a reasonable opportunity to act on it in accordance with the requirements of subsection (5);

(c) claims (including restrictions on transfer not imposed by the issuer) to which the registration of transfer to the present registered owner was subject and were so noted in the initial transaction statement sent to him; and

(d) claims as to which an issuer is charged with notice from the controlling instrument it has elected to require under Section 8-402(4).

(5) If the issuer of an uncertificated security is under a duty as to an adverse claim, he discharges that duty by:

(a) including a notation of the claim in any statements sent with respect to the security under Sections 8-408(3), (6), and (7); and

(b) refusing to register the transfer or pledge of the security unless the nature of the claim does not preclude transfer or pledge subject thereto.

(6) If the transfer or pledge of the security is registered subject to an adverse claim, a notation of the claim must be included in the initial transaction statement and all subsequent statements sent to the transferee and pledgee under Section 8-408.

(7) Notwithstanding subsections (4) and (5), if an uncertificated security was subject to a registered pledge at the time the issuer first came under a duty as to a particular adverse claim, the issuer has no duty as to that claim if transfer of the security is requested by the registered pledgee or an appropriate person acting for the registered pledgee unless:

(a) the claim was embodied in legal process which expressly provides otherwise;

(b) the claim was asserted in a written notification from the registered pledgee;

(c) the claim was one as to which the issuer was charged with notice from a controlling instrument it required under Section 8-402(4) in connection with the pledgee's request for transfer; or

(d) the transfer requested is to the registered owner.

§8-404. Liability and Non-Liability for Registration.

(1) Except as provided in any law relating to the

collection of taxes, the issuer is not liable to the owner, pledgee, or any other person suffering loss as a result of the registration of a transfer, pledge, or release of a security if:

(**a**) there were on or with a certificated security the necessary indorsements or the issuer had received an instruction originated by an appropriate person (Section 8-308); and

(**b**) the issuer had no duty as to adverse claims or has discharged the duty (Section 8-403).

(**2**) If an issuer has registered a transfer of a certificated security to a person not entitled to it, the issuer on demand shall deliver a like security to the true owner unless:

(**a**) the registration was pursuant to subsection (1);

(**b**) the owner is precluded from asserting any claim for registering the transfer under Section 8-405(1); or

(**c**) the delivery would result in overissue, in which case the issuer's liability is governed by Section 8-104.

(**3**) If an issuer has improperly registered a transfer, pledge, or release of an uncertificated security, the issuer on demand from the injured party shall restore the records as to the injured party to the condition that would have obtained if the improper registration had not been made unless:

(**a**) the registration was pursuant to subsection (1); or

(**b**) the registration would result in overissue, in which case the issuer's liability is governed by Section 8-104.

§8-405. Lost, Destroyed, and Stolen Certificated Securities.

(**1**) If a certificated security has been lost, apparently destroyed, or wrongfully taken, and the owner fails to notify the issuer of that fact within a reasonable time after he has notice of it and the issuer registers a transfer of the security before receiving notification, the owner is precluded from asserting against the issuer any claim for registering the transfer under Section 8-404 or any claim to a new security under this section.

(**2**) If the owner of a certificated security claims that the security has been lost, destroyed, or wrongfully taken, the issuer shall issue a new certificated security or, at the option of the issuer, an equivalent uncertificated security in place of the original security if the owner:

(**a**) so requests before the issuer has notice that the security has been acquired by a bona fide purchaser;

(**b**) files with the issuer a sufficient indemnity bond; and

(**c**) satisfies any other reasonable requirements imposed by the issuer.

(**3**) If, after the issue of a new certificated or uncertificated security, a bona fide purchaser of the original certificated security presents it for registration of transfer, the issuer shall register the transfer unless registration would result in overissue, in which event the issuer's liability is governed by Section 8-104. In addition to any rights on the indemnity bond, the issuer may recover the new certificated security from the person to whom it was issued or any person taking under him except a bona fide purchaser or may cancel the uncertificated security unless a bona fide purchaser or any person taking under a bona fide purchaser is then the registered owner or registered pledgee thereof.

§8-406. Duty of Authenticating Trustee, Transfer Agent, or Registrar.

(**1**) If a person acts as authenticating trustee, transfer agent, registrar, or other agent for an issuer in the registration of transfers of its certificated securities or in the registration of transfers, pledges, and releases of its uncertificated securities, in the issue of new securities, or in the cancellation of surrendered securities:

(**a**) he is under a duty to the issuer to exercise good faith and due diligence in performing his functions; and

(**b**) with regard to the particular functions he performs, he has the same obligation to the holder or owner of a certificated security or to the owner or pledgee of an uncertificated security and has the same rights and privileges as the issuer has in regard to those functions.

(**2**) Notice to an authenticating trustee, transfer agent, registrar or other agent is notice to the issuer with respect to the functions performed by the agent.

§8-407. Exchangeability of Securities.

(**1**) No issuer is subject to the requirements of this section unless it regularly maintains a system for issuing the class of securities involved under which both certificated and uncertificated securities are regularly issued to the category of owners, which includes the person in whose name the new security is to be registered.

(**2**) Upon surrender of a certificated security with all necessary indorsements and presentation of a written request by the person surrendering the security, the issuer, if he has no duty as to adverse claims or has discharged the duty (Section 8-403), shall issue to the person or a person designated by him an equivalent uncertificated security subject to all liens, restrictions, and claims that were noted on the certificated security.

(**3**) Upon receipt of a transfer instruction originated by an appropriate person who so requests, the issuer of an uncertificated security shall cancel the uncertificated security and issue an equivalent certificated security on which must be noted conspicuously any liens and restrictions of the issuer and any adverse claims (as to which the issuer has a duty under Section 8-403(4)) to which the uncertificated security was subject. The certificated security shall be registered in the name of and delivered to:

(**a**) the registered owner, if the uncertificated security was not subject to a registered pledge; or

(**b**) the registered pledgee, if the uncertificated security was subject to a registered pledge.

§8-408. Statements of Uncertificated Securities.

(**1**) Within 2 business days after the transfer of an uncertificated security has been registered, the issuer shall send to the new registered owner and, if the security has been transferred subject to a registered pledge, to the registered pledgee a written statement containing:

(**a**) a description of the issue of which the uncertificated security is a part;

(**b**) the number of shares or units transferred;

(**c**) the name and address and any taxpayer identification number of the new registered owner and, if the security has been transferred subject to a registered pledge, the name and address and any taxpayer identification number of the registered pledgee;

(**d**) a notation of any liens and restrictions of the issuer and any adverse claims (as to which the issuer has a duty under Section 8-403(4)) to which the uncertificated security is or may be subject at the time of registration or a statement that there are none of those liens, restrictions, or adverse claims; and

(**e**) the date the transfer was registered.

(**2**) Within 2 business days after the pledge of an uncertificated security has been registered, the issuer shall send to the registered owner and the registered pledgee a written statement containing:

(**a**) a description of the issue of which the uncertificated security is a part;

(**b**) the number of shares or units pledged;

(**c**) the name and address and any taxpayer identification number of the registered owner and the registered pledgee;

(**d**) a notation of any liens and restrictions of the issuer and any adverse claims (as to which the issuer has a duty under Section 8-403(4)) to which the uncertificated security is or may be subject at the time of registration or a statement that there are none of those liens, restrictions or adverse claims; and

(**e**) the date the pledge was registered.

(**3**) Within 2 business days after the release from pledge of an uncertificated security has been registered, the issuer shall send to the registered owner and the pledgee whose interest was released a written statement containing:

(**a**) a description of the issue of which the uncertificated security is a part;

(**b**) the number of shares or units released from pledge;

(**c**) the name and address and any taxpayer identification number of the registered owner and the pledgee whose interest was released;

(**d**) a notation of any liens and restrictions of the issuer and any adverse claims (as to which the issuer has a duty under Section 8-403(4)) to which the uncertificated security is or may be subject at the time of registration or a statement that there are none of those liens, restrictions or adverse claims; and

(**e**) the date the release was registered.

(**4**) An "initial transaction statement" is the statement sent to:

(**a**) the new registered owner and, if applicable, to the registered pledgee pursuant to subsection (1);

(**b**) the registered pledgee pursuant to subsection (2); or

(**c**) the registered owner pursuant to subsection (3).

Each initial transaction statement shall be signed by or on behalf of the issuer and must be identified as "Initial Transaction Statement."

(**5**) Within 2 business days after the transfer of an

uncertificated security has been registered, the issuer shall send to the former registered owner and the former registered pledgee, if any, a written statement containing:

> (a) a description of the issue of which the uncertificated security is a part;
> (b) the number of shares or units transferred;
> (c) the name and address and any taxpayer identification number of the former registered owner and of any former registered pledgee; and
> (d) the date the transfer was registered.

(6) At periodic intervals no less frequent than annually and at any time upon the reasonable written request of the registered owner, the issuer shall send to the registered owner of each uncertificated security a dated written statement containing:

> (a) a description of the issue of which the uncertificated security is a part;
> (b) the name and address and any taxpayer identification number of the registered owner;
> (c) the number of shares or units of the uncertificated security registered in the name of the registered owner on the date of the statement;
> (d) the name and address and any taxpayer identification number of any registered pledgee and the number of shares or units subject to the pledge; and
> (e) a notation of any liens and restrictions of the issuer and any adverse claims (as to which the issuer has a duty under Section 8-403(4)) to which the uncertificated security is or may be subject or a statement that there are none of those liens, restrictions, or adverse claims.

(7) At periodic intervals no less frequent than annually and at any time upon the reasonable written request of the registered pledgee, the issuer shall send to the registered pledgee of each uncertificated security a dated written statement containing:

> (a) a description of the issue of which uncertificated security is a part;
> (b) the name and address and any taxpayer identification number of the registered owner;
> (c) the name and address and any taxpayer identification number of the registered pledgee;
> (d) the number of shares or units subject to the pledge; and
> (e) a notation of any liens and restrictions of the issuer and any adverse claims (as to which the issuer has a duty under Section 8-403(4)) to which the uncertificated security is or may

be subject or a statement that there are none of those liens, restrictions, or adverse claims.

(8) If the issuer sends the statements described in subsections (6) and (7) at periodic intervals no less frequent than quarterly, the issuer is not obliged to send additional statements upon request unless the owner or pledgee requesting them pays to the issuer the reasonable cost of furnishing them.

(9) Each statement sent pursuant to this section must bear a conspicuous legend reading substantially as follows: "This statement is merely a record of the rights of the addressee as of the time of its issuance. Delivery of this statement, of itself, confers no rights on the recipient. This statement is neither a negotiable instrument nor a security."

ARTICLE 9: SECURED TRANSACTIONS; SALES OF ACCOUNTS AND CHATTEL PAPER

Part 1: Short Title, Applicability and Definitions

§9-101. Short Title.   This Article shall be known and may be cited as Uniform Commercial Code—Secured Transactions.

§9-102. Policy and Subject Matter of Article.

(1) Except as otherwise provided in Section 9-104 on excluded transactions, this Article applies:

> (a) to any transaction (regardless of its form) which is intended to create a security interest in personal property or fixtures including goods, documents, instruments, general intangibles, chattel paper or accounts; and also
> (b) to any sale of accounts or chattel paper.

(2) This Article applies to security interests created by contract including pledge, assignment, chattel mortgage, chattel trust, trust deed, factor's lien, equipment trust, conditional sale, trust receipt, other lien or title retention contract and lease or consignment intended as security. This Article does not apply to statutory liens except as provided in Section 9-310.

(3) The application of this Article to a security interest in a secured obligation is not affected by the fact that the obligation is itself secured by a transaction or interest to which this Article does not apply.

Note: *The adoption of this Article should be accompanied by the repeal of existing statutes dealing with conditional sales, trust receipts, factor's liens where* *the factor is given a nonpossessory lien, chattel mortgages, crop mortgages, mortgages on railroad equipment, assignment of accounts and generally statutes regulating security interests in personal property.*

Where the state has a retail installment selling act or small load act, that legislation should be carefully examined to determine what changes in those acts are needed to conform them to this Article. This Article primarily sets out rules defining rights of a secured party against persons dealing with the debtor; it does not prescribe regulations and controls which may be necessary to curb abuses arising in the small loan business or in the financing of consumer purchases on credit. Accordingly there is no intention to repeal existing regulatory acts in those fields by enactment or re-enactment of Article 9. See Section 9-203(4) and the Note thereto.

§9-103. Perfection of Security Interests in Multiple State Transactions.

(1) Documents, instruments and ordinary goods.

(a) This subsection applies to documents and instruments and to goods other than those covered by a certificate of title described in subsection (2), mobile goods described in subsection (3), and minerals described in subsection (5).

(b) Except as otherwise provided in this subsection, perfection and the effect of perfection or non-perfection of a security interest in collateral are governed by the law of the jurisdiction which the collateral is when the last event occurs on which is based the assertion that the security interest is perfected or unperfected.

(c) If the parties to a transaction creating a purchase money security interest in goods in one jurisdiction understand at the time that the security interest attaches that the goods will be kept in another jurisdiction, then the law of the other jurisdiction governs the perfection and the effect of perfection or non-perfection of the security interest from the time it attaches until thirty days after the debtor receives possession of the goods and thereafter if the goods are taken to the other jurisdiction before the end of the thirty-day period.

(d) When collateral is brought into and kept in this state while subject to a security interest perfected under the law of the jurisdiction from which the collateral was removed, the security interest remains perfected, but if action is required by Part 3 of this Article to perfect the security interest,

(i) if the action is not taken before the expiration of the period of perfection in the other jurisdiction or the end of four months after the collateral is brought into this state, whichever period first expires, the security interest becomes unperfected at the end of that period and is thereafter deemed to have been unperfected as against a person who became a purchaser after removal;

(ii) if the action is taken before the expiration of the period specified in subparagraph (i), the security interest continues perfected thereafter;

(iii) for the purpose of priority over a buyer of consumer goods (subsection (2) of Section 9-307), the period of the effectiveness of a filing in the jurisdiction from which the collateral is removed is governed by the rules with respect to perfection in subparagraphs (i) and (ii).

(2) Certificate of title.

(a) This subsection applies to goods covered by a certificate of title issued under a statute of this state or of another jurisdiction under the law of which indication of a security interest on the certificate is required as a condition of perfection.

(b) Except as otherwise provided in this subsection, perfection and the effect of perfection or non-perfection of the security interest are governed by the law (including the conflict of laws rules) of the jurisdiction issuing the certificate until four months after the goods are removed from that jurisdiction and thereafter until the goods are registered in another jurisdiction, but in any event not beyond surrender of the certificate. After the expiration of that period, the goods are not covered by the certificate of title within the meaning of this section.

(c) Except with respect to the rights of a buyer described in the next paragraph, a security interest, perfected in another jurisdiction otherwise than by notation on a certificate of title, in goods brought into this state and thereafter covered by a certificate of title issued by this state is subject to the rules stated in paragraph (d) of subsection (1).

(d) If goods are brought into this state while a

security interest therein is perfected in any manner under the law of the jurisdiction from which the goods are removed and a certificate of title is issued by this state and the certificate does not show that the goods are subject to the security interest or that they may be subject to security interests not shown on the certificate, the security interest is subordinate to the rights of a buyer of the goods who is not in the business of selling goods of that kind to the extent that he gives value and receives delivery of the goods after issuance of the certificate and without knowledge of the security interest.

(3) Accounts, general intangibles and mobile goods.

(a) This subsection applies to accounts (other than an account described in subsection (5) on minerals) and general intangibles and to goods which are mobile and which are of a type normally used in more than one jurisdiction, such as motor vehicles, trailers, rolling stock, airplanes, shipping containers, road building and construction machinery and commercial harvesting machinery and the like, if the goods are equipment or inventory leased or held for lease by the debtor to others, and are not covered by a certificate of title described in subsection (2).

(b) The law (including the conflict of laws rules) of the jurisdiction in which the debtor is located governs the perfection and the effect of perfection or non-perfection of the security interest.

(c) If, however, the debtor is located in a jurisdiction which is not a part of the United States, and which does not provide for perfection of the security interest by filing or recording in that jurisdiction, the law of the jurisdiction in the United States in which the debtor has its major executive office in the United States governs the perfection and the effect of perfection or non-perfection of the security interest through filing. In the alternative, if the debtor is located in a jurisdiction which is not a part of the United States or Canada and the collateral is accounts or general intangibles for money due or to become due, the security interest may be perfected by notification to the account debtor. As used in this paragraph, "United States" includes its territories and possessions and the Commonwealth of Puerto Rico.

(d) A debtor shall be deemed located at his place of business if he has one, at his chief executive office if he has more than one place of business, otherwise at his residence. If, however, the debtor is a foreign air carrier under the Federal Aviation Act of 1958, as amended, it shall be deemed located at the designated office of the agent upon whom service of process may be made on behalf of the foreign air carrier.

(e) A security interest perfected under the law of the jurisdiction of the location of the debtor is perfected until the expiration of four months after a change of the debtor's location to another jurisdiction, or until perfection would have ceased by the law of the first jurisdiction, whichever period first expires. Unless perfected in the new jurisdiction before the end of that period, it becomes unperfected thereafter and is deemed to have been unperfected as against a person who became a purchaser after the change.

(4) Chattel paper. The rules stated for goods in subsection (1) apply to a possessory security interest in chattel paper. The rules stated for accounts in subsection (3) apply to a non-possessory security interest in chattel paper, but the security interest may not be perfected by notification to the account debtor.

(5) Minerals. Perfection and the effect of perfection or non-perfection of a security interest which is created by a debtor who has an interest in minerals or the like (including oil and gas) before extraction and which attaches thereto as extracted, or which attaches to an account resulting from the sale thereof at the wellhead or minehead are governed by the law (including the conflict of laws rules) of the jurisdiction wherein the wellhead or minehead is located.

§9-103. Perfection of Security Interests in Multiple State Transactions (*1977 Amendments*).

* * *

(3) Accounts, general intangibles and mobile goods.

(a) This subsection applies to accounts (other than an account described in subsection (5) on minerals) and general intangibles (other than uncertificated securities) and to goods.

* * *

(6) Uncertificated securities. The law (including the conflict of laws rules) of the jurisdiction or organization of the issuer governs the perfection and the

effect of perfection or non-perfection of a security interest in uncertificated securities.

§9-104. Transactions Excluded From Article. This Article does not apply

(**a**) to a security interest subject to any statute of the United States to the extent that such statute governs the rights of parties to and third parties affected by transactions in particular types of property; or

(**b**) to a landlord's lien; or

(**c**) to a lien given by statute or other rule of law for services or materials except as provided in Section 9-310 on priority of such liens; or

(**d**) to a transfer of a claim of wages, salary or other compensation of an employee; or

(**e**) to a transfer by a government or governmental subdivision or agency; or

(**f**) to a sale of accounts, or chattel paper as part of a sale of the business out of which they arose, or an assignment of accounts or chattel paper which is for the purpose of collection only, or a transfer of a right to payment under a contract to an assignee who is also to do the performance under the contract or a transfer of a single account to an assignee in whole or partial satisfaction of a preexisting indebtedness; or

(**g**) to a transfer of an interest in or claim in or under any policy of insurance, except as provided with respect to proceeds (Section 9-306) and priorities in proceeds (Section 9-312); or

(**h**) to a right represented by a judgment (other than a judgment taken on a right to payment which was collateral); or

(**i**) to any right of set-off; or

(**j**) except to the extent that provision is made for fixtures in Section 9-313, to the creation or transfer of an interest in or lien on real estate, including a lease or rents thereunder; or

(**k**) to a transfer in whole or in part of any claim arising out of tort; or

(**l**) to a transfer of an interest in any deposit account (subsection (1) of Section 9-105), except as provided with respect to proceeds (Section 9-306) and priorities in proceeds (Section 9-312).

§9-105. Definitions and Index of Definitions.

(**1**) In this Article unless the context otherwise requires:

(**a**) "Account debtor" means the person who is obligated on an account, chattel paper or general intangible;

(**b**) "Chattel paper" means a writing or writings which evidence both a monetary obligation and a security interest in or a lease of specific goods, but a charter or other contract involving the use or hire of a vessel is not chattel paper. When a transaction is evidenced both by such a security agreement or a lease and by an instrument or a series of instruments, the group of writings taken together constitutes chattel paper;

(**c**) "Collateral" means the property subject to a security interest, and includes accounts and chattel paper which have been sold;

(**d**) "Debtor" means the person who owes payment or other performance of the obligation secured, whether or not he owns or has rights in the collateral, and includes the seller of accounts or chattel paper. Where the debtor and the owner of the collateral are not the same person, the term "debtor" means the owner of the collateral in any provision of the Article dealing with the collateral, the obligor in any provision dealing with the obligation, and may include both where the context so requires;

(**e**) "Deposit account" means a demand, time savings, passbook or like account maintained with a bank, savings and loan association, credit union or like organization, other than an account evidenced by a certificate of deposit;

(**f**) "Document" means document of title as defined in the general definitions of Article 1 (Section 1-201), and a receipt of the kind described in subsection (2) of Section 7-201;

(**g**) "Encumbrance" includes real estate mortgages and other liens on real estate and all other rights in real estate that are not ownership interests.

(**h**) "Goods" includes all things which are movable at the time the security interest attaches or which are fixtures (Section 9-313), but does not include money, documents, instruments, accounts, chattel paper, general intangibles, or minerals or the like (including oil and gas) before extraction. "Goods" also includes standing timber which is to be cut and removed under a conveyance or contract for sale, the unborn young of animals, and growing crops.

(i) "Instrument" means a negotiable instrument (defined in Section 3-104), or a security (defined in Section 8-102) or any other writing which evidences a right to the payment of money and is not itself a security agreement or lease and is of a type which is in ordinary course of business transferred by delivery with any necessary indorsement or assignment;

(j) "Mortgage" means a consensual interest created by a real estate mortgage, a trust deed on real estate, or the like;

(k) An advance is made "pursuant to commitment" if the secured party has bound himself to make it, whether or not a subsequent event of default or other event not within his control has relieved or may relieve him from his obligation.

(l) "Security agreement" means an agreement which creates or provides for a security interest;

(m) "Secured party" means a lender, seller or other person in whose favor there is a security interest, including a person to whom accounts or chattel paper have been sold. When the holders of obligations issued under an indenture of trust, equipment trust agreement or the like are represented by a trustee or other person, the representative is the secured party;

(n) "Transmitting utility" means any person primarily engaged in the railroad, street railway or trolley bus business, the electric or electronics communications transmission business, the transmission of goods by pipeline, or the transmission or the production and transmission of electricity, steam, gas or water, or the provision of sewer service.

(2) Other definitions applying to this Article and the sections in which they appear are:

"Account". Section 9-106.
"Attach". Section 9-203.
"Construction mortgage". Section 9-313(1).
"Consumer goods". Section 9-109(1).
"Equipment". Section 9-109(2).
"Farm products". Section 9-109(3).
"Fixture". Section 9-313.
"Fixture filing". Section 9-313.
"General intangibles". Section 9-106.
"Inventory". Section 9-109(4).
"Lien creditor". Section 9-301(3).
"Proceeds". Section 9-306(1).

"Purchase money security interest". Section 9-107.
"United States". Section 9-103.

(3) The following definitions in other articles apply to this Article:

"Check". Section 3-104.
"Contract for sale". Section 2-106.
"Holder in due course". Section 3-302.
"Note". Section 3-104.
"Sale". Section 2-106.

(4) In addition Article 1 contains general definitions and principles of construction and interpretation throughout this Article.

§9-105. Definitions and Index of Definitions *(1977 Amendments).*

(1) In this Article unless the context otherwise requires:

* * *

(i) "Instrument" means a negotiable instrument (defined in Section 3-104), or a certificated security (defined in Section 8-102) or . . .

* * *

§9-106. Definitions: "Account"; "General Intangibles". "Account" means any right to payment for goods sold or leased or for services rendered which is not evidenced by an instrument or chattel paper, whether or not it has been earned by performance. "General intangibles" means any personal property (including things in action) other than goods, accounts, chattel paper, documents, instruments, and money. All rights to payment earned or unearned under a charter or other contract involving the use or hire of a vessel and all rights incident to the charter or contract are accounts.

§9-107. Definitions: "Purchase Money Security Interest". A security interest is a "purchase money security interest" to the extent that it is

(a) taken or retained by the seller of the collateral to secure all or part of its price;

(b) taken by a person who by making advances or incurring an obligation gives value to enable the debtor to acquire rights in or the use of collateral if such value is in fact so used.

§9-108. When After-Acquired Collateral Not Security for Antecedent Debt. Where a secured party makes an advance, incurs an obligation, releases a perfected security interest, or otherwise gives new value which is to be secured in whole or in part by after-acquired property his security interest in the after-acquired collateral shall be deemed to be taken for new value and not as security for an antecedent debt if the debtor acquires his rights in such collateral either in the ordinary course of his business or under a contract of purchase made pursuant to the security agreement within a reasonable time after new value is given.

§9-109. Classification of Goods; "Consumer Goods"; "Equipment"; "Farm Products"; "Inventory". Goods are

(1) "consumer goods" if they are used or bought for use primarily for personal, family or household purposes;

(2) "equipment" if they are used or bought for use primarily in business (including farming or a profession) or by a debtor who is a non-profit organization or a governmental subdivision or agency or if the goods are not included in the definitions of inventory, farm products or consumer goods;

(3) "farm products" if they are crops or livestock or supplies used or produced in farming operations or if they are products of crops or livestock in their unmanufactured states (such as ginned cotton, wool-clip, maple syrup, milk and eggs), and if they are in the possession of a debtor engaged in raising, fattening, grazing or other farming operations. If goods are farm products they are neither equipment nor inventory;

(4) "inventory" if they are held by a person who holds them for sale or lease or to be furnished under contracts of service or if he has so furnished them, or if they are raw materials, work in process or materials used or consumed in a business. Inventory of a person is not to be classified as his equipment.

§9-110. Sufficiency of Description. For the purposes of this Article any description of personal property or real estate is sufficient whether or not it is specific if it reasonably identifies what is described.

§9-111. Applicability of Bulk Transfer Laws. The creation of a security interest is not a bulk transfer under Article 6 (see Section 6-103).

§9-112. Where Collateral Is Not Owned by Debtor. Unless otherwise agreed, when a secured party knows that collateral is owned by a person who is not the debtor, the owner of the collateral is entitled to receive from the secured party any surplus under Section 9-502(2) or under Section 9-504(1), and is not liable for the debt or for any deficiency after resale, and he has the same right as the debtor

(a) to receive statements under Section 9-208;

(b) to receive notice of and to object to a secured party's proposal to retain the collateral

in satisfaction of the indebtedness under Section 9-505;

(c) to redeem the collateral under Section 9-506;

(d) to obtain injunctive or other relief under Section 9-507(1); and

(e) to recover losses caused to him under Section 9-208(2).

§9-113. Security Interests Arising Under Article on Sales. A security interest arising solely under the Article on Sales (Article 2) is subject to the provisions of this Article except that to the extent that and so long as the debtor does not have or does not lawfully obtain possession of the goods

(a) no security agreement is necessary to make the security interest enforceable; and

(b) no filing is required to perfect the security interest; and

(c) the rights of the secured party on default by the debtor are governed by the Article on Sales (Article 2).

§9-114. Consignment.

(1) A person who delivers goods under a consignment which is not a security interest and who would be required to file under this Article by paragraph (3)(c) of Section 2-326 has priority over a secured party who is or becomes a creditor of the consignee and who would have a perfected security interest in the goods if they were the property of the consignee, and also has priority with respect to identifiable cash proceeds received on or before delivery of the goods to a buyer, if

(a) the consignor complies with the filing provision of the Article on Sales with respect to consignments (paragraph (3)(c) of Section 2-326) before the consignee receives possession of the goods; and

(b) the consignor gives notification in writing to the holder of the security interest if the holder has filed a financing statement covering the same types of goods before the date of the filing made by the consignor; and

(c) the holder of the security interest receives the notification within five years before the consignee receives possession of the goods; and

(d) the notification states that the consignor expects to deliver goods on consignment to the consignee, describing the goods by item or type.

(2) In the case of a consignment which is not a security interest and in which the requirements of the

preceding subsection have not been met, a person who delivers goods to another is subordinate to a person who would have a perfected security interest in the goods if they were the property of the debtor.

Part 2: Validity of Security Agreement and Rights of Parties Thereto

§9-201. General Validity of Security Agreement. Except as otherwise provided by this Act a security agreement is effective according to its terms between the parties, against purchasers of the collateral and against creditors. Nothing in this Article validates any charge or practice illegal under any statute or regulation thereunder governing usury, small loans, retail installment sales, or the like, or extends the application of any such statute or regulation to any transaction not otherwise subject thereto.

§9-202. Title to Collateral Immaterial. Each provision of this Article with regard to rights, obligations and remedies applies whether title to collateral is in the secured party or in the debtor.

§9-203. Attachment and Enforceability of Security Interest; Proceeds; Formal Requisites.

(**1**) Subject to the provisions of Section 4-208 on the security interest of a collecting bank and Section 9-113 on a security interest arising under the Article on Sales, a security interest is not enforceable against the debtor or third parties with respect to the collateral and does not attach unless

    (**a**) the collateral is in the possession of the secured party pursuant to agreement, or the debtor has signed a security agreement which contains a description of the collateral and in addition, when the security interest covers crops growing or to be grown or timber to be cut, a description of the land concerned; and

    (**b**) value has been given; and

    (**c**) the debtor has rights in the collateral.

(**2**) A security interest attaches when it becomes enforceable against the debtor with respect to the collateral. Attachment occurs as soon as all of the events specified in subsection (1) have taken place unless explicit agreement postpones the time of attaching.

(**3**) Unless otherwise agreed a security agreement gives the secured party the rights to proceeds provided by Section 9-306.

(**4**) A transaction, although subject to this Article, is also subject to . . . . *, and in the case of conflict between the provisions of this Article and any such statute, the provisions of such statute control. Failure to comply with any applicable statute has only the effect which is specfied therein.

Note: *At * in subsection (4) insert reference to any local statute regulating small loans, retail installment sales and the like.*

The foregoing subsection (4) is designed to make it clear that certain transactions, although subject to this Article, must also comply with other applicable legislation.

This Article is designed to regulate all the "security" aspects of transactions within its scope. There is, however, much regulatory legislation, particularly in the consumer field, which supplements this Article and should not be repealed by its enactment. Examples are small loan acts, retail installment selling acts and the like. Such acts may provide for licensing and rate regulation and many prescribe particular forms of contract. Such provisions should remain in force despite the enactment of this Article. On the other hand if a retail installment selling act contains provisions of filing, rights on default, etc., such provisions should be repealed as inconsistent with this Article except that inconsistent provisions as to deficiencies, penalties, etc., in the Uniform Consumer Credit Code and other recent related legislation should remain because those statutes were drafted after the substantial enactment of the Article and with the intention of modifying certain provisions of this Article as to consumer credit.

§9-203. Attachment and Enforceability of Security Interest; Proceeds; Formal Requisites (1977 Amendments).

(**1**) Subject to the provisions of Section 4-208 on the security interest of a collecting bank, Section 8-321 on security interests in securities and Section 9-113 on a security interest arising under the Article on Sales, a security interest is not enforceable against the debtor or third parties with respect to the collateral and does not attach unless:

    (**a**) the collateral is in the possession of the secured party pursuant to agreement, or the debtor has signed a security agreement which contains a description of the collateral and in addition, when the security interest covers crops growing or to be grown or timber to be cut, a description of the land concerned;

    (**b**) value has been given; and

    (**c**) the debtor has rights in the collateral.

* * *

§9-204. After-Acquired Property; Future Advances.

(**1**) Except as provided in subsection (2), a security

agreement may provide that any or all obligations covered by the security agreement are to be secured by after-acquired collateral.

(2) No security interest attaches under an after-acquired property clause to consumer goods other than accessions (Section 9-314) when given as additional security unless the debtor acquires rights in them within ten days after the secured party gives value.

(3) Obligations covered by a security agreement may include future advances or other value whether or not the advances or value are given pursuant to commitment (subsection (1) of Section 9-105).

§9-205. Use or Disposition of Collateral Without Accounting Permissible. A security interest is not invalid or fraudulent against creditors by reason of liberty in the debtor to use, commingle or dispose of all or part of the collateral (including returned or repossessed goods) or to collect or compromise accounts or chattel paper, or to accept the return of goods or make repossessions, or to use, commingle or dispose of proceeds, or by reason of the failure of the secured party to require the debtor to account for proceeds or replace collateral. This section does not relax the requirements of possession where perfection of a security interest depends upon possession of the collateral by the secured party or by a bailee.

§9-206. Agreement Not to Assert Defenses Against Assignee; Modification of Sales Warranties Where Security Agreement Exists.

(1) Subject to any statute or decision which establishes a different rule for buyers or lessees of consumer goods, an agreement by a buyer or lessee that he will not assert against an assignee any claim or defense which he may have against the seller or lessor is enforceable by an assignee who takes his assignment for value, in good faith and without notice of a claim or defense, except as to defenses of a type which may be asserted against a holder in due course of a negotiable instrument under the Article on Commercial Paper (Article 3). A buyer who as part of one transaction signs both a negotiable instrument and a security agreement makes such an agreement.

(2) When a seller retains a purchase money security interest in goods the Article of Sales (Article 2) governs the sale and any disclaimer, limitation or modification of the seller's warranties. Amended in 1962.

§9-207. Rights and Duties When Collateral is in Secured Party's Possession.

(1) A secured party must use reasonable care in the custody and preservation of collateral in his pos-

session. In the case of an instrument or chattel paper reasonable care includes taking necessary steps to preserve rights against prior parties unless otherwise agreed.

(2) Unless otherwise agreed, when collateral is in the secured party's possession

(a) reasonable expenses (including the cost of any insurance and payment of taxes or other charges) incurred in the custody, preservation, use or operation of the collateral are chargeable to the debtor and are secured by the collateral;

(b) the risk of accidental loss or damage is on the debtor to the extent of any deficiency in any effective insurance coverage;

(c) the secured party may hold as additional security any increase or profits (except money) received from the collateral, but money so received, unless remitted to the debtor, shall be applied in reduction of the secured obligation;

(d) the secured party must keep the collateral identifiable but fungible collateral may be commingled;

(e) the secured party may repledge the collateral upon terms which do not impair the debtor's right to redeem it.

(3) A secured party is liable for any loss caused by his failure to meet any obligation imposed by the preceding subsections but does not lose his security interest.

(4) A secured party may use or operate the collateral for the purpose of preserving the collateral or its value or pursuant to the order of a court of appropriate jurisdiction or, except in the case of consumer goods, in the manner and to the extent provided in the security agreement.

§9-208. Request for Statement of Account or List of Collateral.

(1) A debtor may sign a statement indicating what he believes to be the aggregate amount of unpaid indebtedness as of a specified date and may send it to the secured party with a request that the statement be approved or corrected and returned to the debtor. When the security agreement or any other record kept by the secured party identifies the collateral a debtor may similarly request the secured party to approve or correct a list of the collateral.

(2) The secured party must comply with such a request within two weeks after receipt by sending a written correction or approval. If the secured party claims a security interest in all of a particular type of collateral owned by the debtor he may indicate that

fact in his reply and need not approve or correct an itemized list of such collateral. If the secured party without reasonable excuse fails to comply he is liable for any loss caused to the debtor thereby; and if the debtor has properly included in his request a good faith statement of the obligation or a list of the collateral or both, the secured party may claim a security interest only as shown in the statement against persons misled by his failure to comply. If he no longer has an interest in the obligation or collateral at the time the request is received he must disclose the name and address of any successor in interest known to him and he is liable for any loss caused to the debtor as a result of failure to disclose. A successor in interest is not subject to this section until a request is received by him.

(**3**) A debtor is entitled to such a statement once every six months without charge. The secured party may require payment of a charge not exceeding $10 for each additional statement furnished.

Part 3: Rights of Third Parties; Perfected and Unperfected Security Interests; Rules of Priority

§9-301. Persons Who Take Priority Over Unperfected Security Interests; Right of "Lien Creditor".

(**1**) Except as otherwise provided in subsection (2), an unperfected security interest is subordinate to the rights of

(**a**) persons entitled to priority under Section 9-312;

(**b**) a person who becomes a lien creditor before the security interest is perfected;

(**c**) in the case of goods, instruments, documents, and chattel paper, a person who is not a secured party and who is a transferee in bulk or other buyer not in ordinary course of business, or is a buyer of farm products in ordinary course of business, to the extent that he gives value and receives delivery of the collateral without knowledge of the security interest and before it is perfected;

(**d**) in the case of accounts and general intangibles, a person who is not a secured party and who is a transferee to the extent that he gives value without knowledge of the security interest and before it is perfected.

(**2**) If the secured party files with respect to a purchase money security interest before or within ten days after the debtor receives possession of the collateral, he takes priority over the rights of a transferee in bulk or of a lien creditor which arise between the time the security interest attaches and the time of filing.

(**3**) A "lien creditor" means a creditor who had acquired a lien on the property involved by attachment, levy or the like and includes an assignee for benefit of creditors from the time of assignment, and a trustee in bankruptcy from the date of the filing of the petition or a receiver in equity from the time of appointment.

(**4**) A person who becomes a lien creditor while a security interest is perfected takes subject to the security interest only to the extent that it secures advances made before he becomes a lien creditor or within 45 days thereafter or made without knowledge of the lien or pursuant to a commitment entered into without knowledge of the lien.

§9-302. When Filing Is Required to Perfect Security Interest; Security Interests to Which Filing Provisions of This Article Do Not Apply.

(**1**) A financing statement must be filed to perfect all security interests except the following:

(**a**) a security interest in collateral in possession of the secured party under Section 9-305;

(**b**) a security interest temporarily perfected in instruments or documents without delivery under Section 9-304 or in proceeds for a 10 day period under Section 9-306;

(**c**) a security interest created by an assignment of a beneficial interest in a trust or a decedent's estate;

(**d**) a purchase money security interest in consumer goods; but filing is required for a motor vehicle required to be registered; and fixture filing is required for priority over conflicting interests in fixtures to the extent provided in Section 9-313;

(**e**) an assignment of accounts which does not alone or in conjunction with other assignments to the same assignee transfer a significant part of the outstanding accounts of the assignor;

(**f**) a security interest of a collecting bank (Section 4-208) or arising under the Article on Sales (see Section 9-113) or covered in subsection (3) of this section;

(**g**) an assignment for the benefit of all the creditors of the transferor, and subsequent transfers by the assignee thereunder.

(2) If a secured party assigns a perfected security interest, no filing under this Article is required in order to continue the perfected status of the security interest against creditors of and transferees from the original debtor.

(3) The filing of a financing statement otherwise required by this Article is not necessary or effective to perfect a security interest in property subject to

(**a**) a statute or treaty of the United States which provides for a national or international registration or a national or international certificate of title or which specifies a place of filing different from that specified in this Article for filing of the security interest; or

(**b**) the following statutes of this state: [[list any certificate of title statute covering automobiles, trailers, mobile homes, boats, farm tractors, or the like, and any central filing statute*.]]; but during any period in which collateral is inventory held for sale by a person who is in the business of selling goods of that kind, the filing provisions of this Article (Part 4) apply to a security interest in that collateral created by him as debtor; or

(**c**) a certificate of title statute of another jurisdiction under the law of which indication of a security interest on the certificate is required as a condition of perfection (subsection (2) of Section 9-103).

(4) Compliance with a statute or treaty described in subsection (3) is equivalent to the filing of a financing statement under this Article, and a security interest in property subject to the statute or treaty can be perfected only by compliance therewith except as provided in Section 9-103 on multiple state transactions. Duration and renewal of perfection of a security interest perfected by compliance with the statute or treaty are governed by the provisions of the statute or treaty; in other respects the security interest is subject to this Article.

§9-302. When Filing is Required to Perfect Security Interest; Security Interests to Which Filing Provisions of This Article Do Not Apply (*1977 Amendments*).

(1) A financing statement must be filed to perfect all security interests[s] except the following:

* * *

(**f**) a security interest of a collecting bank (Section 4-208) or in securities (Section 8-321) or arising under the Article on Sales (see Section

9-113) or covered in subsection (3) of this section;

* * *

§9-303. When Security Interest Is Perfected; Continuity of Perfection.

(1) A security interest is perfected when it has attached and when all of the applicable steps required for perfection have been taken. Such steps are specified in Section 9-304, 9-305 and 9-306. If such steps are taken before the security interest attaches, it is perfected at the time when it attaches.

*Note: *It is recommended that the provisions of certificate of title acts for perfection of security interests by notation on the certificates should be amended to exclude coverage of inventory held for sale.*

(2) If a security interest is originally perfected in any way permitted under this Article and is subsequently perfected in some other way under this Article, without an intermediate period when it was unperfected, the security interest shall be deemed to be perfected continuously for the purposes of this Article.

§9-304. Perfection of Security Interest in Instruments, Documents, and Goods Covered by Documents; Perfection by Permissive Filing; Temporary Perfection Without Filing or Transfer of Possession.

(1) A security interest in chattel paper or negotiable documents may be perfected by filing. A security interest in money or instruments (other than instruments which constitute part of chattel paper) can be perfected only by the secured party's taking possession, except as provided in subsections (4) and (5) of this section and subsections (2) and (3) of Section 9-306 on proceeds.

(2) During the period that goods are in the possession of the issuer of a negotiable document therefor, a security interest in the goods is perfected by perfecting a security interest in the document, and any security interest in the goods otherwise perfected during such period is subject thereto.

(3) A security interest in goods in the possession of a bailee other than one who has issued a negotiable document therefor is perfected by issuance of a document in the name of the secured party or by the bailee's receipt of notification of the secured party's interest or by filing as to the goods.

(4) A security interest in instruments or negotiable documents is perfected without filing or the taking of possession for a period of 21 days from the time it attaches to the extent that it arises for new value given under a written security agreement.

(**5**) A security interest remains perfected for a period of 21 days without filing where a secured party having a perfected security interest in an instrument, a negotiable document or goods in possession of a bailee other than one who has issued a negotiable document therefor

    (**a**) makes available to the debtor the goods or documents representing the goods for the purpose of ultimate sale or exchange or for the purpose of loading, unloading, storing, shipping, transshipping, manufacturing, processing or otherwise dealing with them in a manner preliminary to their sale or exchange, but priority between conflicting security interests in the goods is subject to subsection (3) of Section 9-312; or

    (**b**) delivers the instrument to the debtor for the purpose of ultimate sale or exchange or of presentation, collection, renewal or registration of transfer.

(**6**) After the 21 day period in subsections (4) and (5) perfection depends upon compliance with applicable provisions of this Article.

§9-304. Perfection of Security Interest in Instruments, Documents, and Goods, Covered by Documents; Perfection by Permissive Filing; Temporary Perfection Without Filing or Transfer of Possession *(1977 Amendments)*.

(**1**) A security interest in chattel paper or negotiable documents may be perfected by filing. A security interest in money or instruments (other than certificated securities or instruments which constitute part of chattel paper) can be perfected only by the secured party's taking possession, except as provided in subsections (4) and (5) of this section and subsections (2) and (3) of Section 9-306 on proceeds.

* * *

(**4**) A security interest in instruments (other than certificated securities) or negotiable documents is perfected without filing or the taking of possession for a period of 21 days from the time it attaches to the extent that it arises for new value given under a written security agreement.

(**5**) A security interest remains perfected for a period of 21 days without filing where a secured party having a perfected security interest in an instrument (other than a certificated security), a negotiable document or goods in possession of a bailee other than one who has issued a negotiable document therefor:

* * *

    (**b**) delivers the instrument to the debtor for the purpose of ultimate sale or exchange or of presentation, collection, renewal, or registration of transfer.

(**6**) After the 21 day period in subsection (4) and (5) perfection depends upon compliance with applicable provisions of this Article.

§9-305. When Possession by Secured Party Perfects Security Interest Without Filing.

A security interest in letters of credit and advices of credit (subsection (2)(a) of Section 5-116), goods, instruments, money, negotiable documents or chattel paper may be perfected by the secured party's taking possession of the collateral. If such collateral other than goods covered by a negotiable document is held by a bailee, the secured party is deemed to have possession from the time the bailee receives notification of the secured party's interest. A security interest is perfected by possession from the time possession is taken without relation back and continues only so long as possession is retained, unless otherwise specified in this Article. The security interest may be otherwise perfected as provided in this Article before or after the period of possession by the secured party.

§9-305. When Possession by Secured Party Perfects Security Interest Without Filing *(1977 Amendments)*.

A security interest in letters of credit and advices of credit (subsection (2)(a) of Section 5-116), goods, instruments (other than certificated securities), money, negotiable documents, or chattel paper may be perfected by the secured party's taking possession of the collateral. If such collateral other than goods covered by a negotiable document is held by a bailee, the secured party is deemed to have possession from the time the bailee receives notification of the secured party's interest. A security interest is perfected by possession from the time possession is taken without relation back and continues only so long as possession is retained, unless otherwise specified in this Article. The security interest may be otherwise perfected as provided in this Article before or after the period of possession by the secured party.

§9-306. "Proceeds"; Secured Party's Rights on Disposition of Collateral.

(**1**) "Proceeds" includes whatever is received upon the sale, exchange, collection or other disposition of collateral or proceeds. Insurance payable by reason of loss or damage to the collateral is proceeds, except to the extent that it is payable to a person other than a party to the security agreement. Money, checks, deposit accounts, and the like are "cash proceeds". All other proceeds are "non-cash proceeds".

(2) Except where this Article otherwise provides, a security interest continues in collateral notwithstanding sale, exchange or other disposition thereof unless the disposition was authorized by the secured party in the security agreement or otherwise, and also continues in any identifiable proceeds including collections received by the debtor.

(3) The security interest in proceeds is a continuously perfected security interest if the interest in the original collateral was perfected but it ceases to be a perfected security interest and becomes unperfected ten days after receipt of the proceeds by the debtor unless

(a) a filed financing statement covers the original collateral and the proceeds are collateral in which a security interest may be perfected by filing in the office or offices where the financing statement has been filed and, if the proceeds are acquired with cash proceeds, the description of collateral in the financing statement indicates the types of property constituting the proceeds; or

(b) a filed financing statement covers the original collateral and the proceeds are identifiable cash proceeds; or

(c) the security interest in the proceeds is perfected before the expiration of the ten day period.

Except as provided in this section, a security interest in proceeds can be perfected only by the methods or under the circumstances permitted in this Article for original collateral of the same type.

(4) In the event of insolvency proceedings instituted by or against a debtor, a secured party with a perfected security interest in proceeds has a perfected security interest only in the following proceeds:

(a) in identifiable non-cash proceeds and in separate deposit accounts containing only proceeds;

(b) in identifiable cash proceeds in the form of money which is neither commingled with other money nor deposited in a deposit account prior to the insolvency proceedings;

(c) in identifiable cash proceeds in the form of checks and the like which are not deposited in a deposit account prior to the insolvency proceedings; and

(d) in all cash and deposit accounts of the debtor in which proceeds have been commingled with other funds, but the perfected security interest under this paragraph (d) is

(i) subject to any right of set-off; and

(ii) limited to an amount not greater than the amount of any cash proceeds received by the debtor within ten days before the institution of the insolvency proceedings less the sum of (I) the payments to the secured party on account of cash proceeds received by the debtor during such period and (II) the cash proceeds received by the debtor during such period to which the secured party is entitled under paragraphs (a) through (c) of this subsection (4).

(5) If a sale of goods results in an account or chattel paper which is transferred by the seller to a secured party, and if the goods are returned to or are repossessed by the seller or the secured party, the following rules determine priorities:

(a) If the goods were collateral at the time of sale, for an indebtedness of the seller which is still unpaid, the original security interest attaches again to the goods and continues as a perfected security interest if it was perfected at the time when the goods were sold. If the security interest was originally perfected by a filing which is still effective, nothing further is required to continue the perfected status; in any other case, the secured party must take possession of the returned or repossessed goods or must file.

(b) An unpaid transferee of the chattel paper has a security interest in the goods against the transferor. Such security interest is prior to a security interest asserted under paragraph (a) to the extent that the transferee of the chattel paper was entitled to priority under Section 9-308.

(c) An unpaid transferee of the account has a security interest in the goods against the transferor. Such security interest is subordinate to a security interest asserted under paragraph (a).

(d) A security interest of an unpaid transferee

asserted under paragraph (b) or (c) must be perfected for protection against creditors of the transferor and purchasers of the returned or repossessed goods.

§9-307. Protection of Buyers of Goods.

(1) A buyer in ordinary course of business (subsection (9) of Section 1-201) other than a person buying farm products from a person engaged in farming operations takes free of a security interest created by his seller even though the security interest is perfected and even though the buyer knows of its existence.

(2) In the case of consumer goods a buyer takes free of a security interest even though perfected if he buys without knowledge of the security interest, for value and for his own personal, family or household purposes unless prior to the purchase the secured party has filed a financing statement covering such goods.

(3) A buyer other than a buyer in ordinary course of business (subsection (1) of this section) takes free of a security interest to the extent that it secures future advances made after the secured party acquires knowledge of the purchase, or more than 45 days after the purchase, whichever first occurs, unless made pursuant to a commitment entered into without knowledge of the purchase and before the expiration of the 45 day period.

§9-308. Purchase of Chattel Paper and Instruments.

A purchaser of chattel paper or an instrument who gives new value and takes possession of it in the ordinary course of his business has priority over a security interest in the chattel paper or instrument.

(a) which is perfected under Section 9-304 (permissive filing and temporary perfection) or under Section 9-306 (perfection as to proceeds) if he acts without knowledge that the specific paper or instrument is subject to a security interest; or

(b) which is claimed merely as proceeds of inventory subject to a security interest (Section 9-306) even though he knows that the specific paper or instrument is subject to the security interest.

§9-309. Protection of Purchasers of Instruments and Documents.

Nothing in this Article limits the rights of a holder in due course of a negotiable instrument (Section 3-302) or a holder to whom a negotiable document of title has been duly negotiated (Section 7-501) or a bona fide purchaser of a se-

curity (Section 8-301) and such holders or purchasers take priority over an earlier security interest even though perfected. Filing under this Article does not constitute notice of the security interest to such holders or purchasers.

§9-309. Protection of Purchasers of Instruments, Documents and Securities (1977 Amendments).

Nothing in this Article limits the rights of a holder in due course of a negotiable instrument (Section 3-302) or a holder to whom negotiable document of title has been duly negotiated (Section 7-501) or a bona fide purchaser of a security (Section [8-301] 8-302) and such holders or purchasers take priority over an earlier security interest even though perfected. Filing under this Article does not constitute notice of the security interest to such holders or purchasers.

§9-310. Priority of Certain Liens Arising by Operation of Law.

When a person in the ordinary course of his business furnishes services or materials with respect to goods subject to a security interest, a lien upon goods in the possession of such person given by statute or rule of law for such materials or services takes priority over a perfected security interest unless the lien is statutory and the statute expressly provides otherwise.

§9-311. Alienability of Debtor's Rights: Judicial Process.

The debtor's rights in collateral may be voluntarily or involuntarily transferred (by way of sale, creation of a security interest, attachment, levy, garnishment or other judicial process) notwithstanding a provision in the security agreement prohibiting any transfer or making the transfer constitute a default.

§9-312. Priorities Among Conflicting Security Interests in the Same Collateral.

(1) The rules of priority stated in other sections of this Part and in the following sections shall govern when applicable: Section 4-208 with respect to the security interests of collecting banks in items being collected, accompanying documents and proceeds; Section 9-103 on security interests related to other jurisdictions; Section 9-114 on consignments.

(2) A perfected security interest in crops for new value given to enable the debtor to produce the crops during the production season and given not more than three months before the crops become growing crops by planting or otherwise takes priority over an earlier perfected security interest to the extent that such earlier interest secures obligations due more

than six months before the crops become growing crops by planting or otherwise, even though the person giving new value had knowledge of the earlier security interest.

(**3**) A perfected purchase money security interest in inventory has priority over a conflicting security interest in the same inventory and also has priority in identifiable cash proceeds received on or before the delivery of the inventory to a buyer if

(**a**) the purchase money security interest is perfected at the time the debtor receives possession of the inventory; and

(**b**) the purchase money secured party gives notification in writing to the holder of the conflicting security interest if the holder had filed a financing statement covering the same types of inventory (i) before the date of the filing made by the purchase money secured party, or (ii) before the beginning of the 21 day period where the purchase money security interest is temporarily perfected without filing or possession (subsection (5) of Section 9-304); and

(**c**) the holder of the conflicting security interest receives the notification within five years before the debtor receives possession of the inventory; and

(**d**) the notification states that the person giving the notice has or expects to acquire a purchase money security interest in inventory of the debtor, describing such inventory by item or type.

(**4**) A purchase money security interest in collateral other than inventory has priority over a conflicting security interest in the same collateral or its proceeds if the purchase money security interest is perfected at the time the debtor receives possession of the collateral or within ten days thereafter.

(**5**) In all cases not governed by other rules stated in this section (including cases of purchase money security interests which do not qualify for the special priorities set forth in subsections (3) and (4) of this section), priority between conflicting security interests in the same collateral shall be determined according to the following rules:

(**a**) Conflicting security interests rank according to priority in time of filing or perfection. Priority dates from the time a filing is first made covering the collateral or the time the security interest is first perfected, whichever is earlier, provided that there is no period there-

after when there is neither filing nor perfection.

(**b**) So long as conflicting security interests are unperfected, the first to attach has priority.

(**6**) For the purposes of subsection (5) a date of filing or perfection as to collateral is also a date of filing or perfection as to proceeds.

(**7**) If future advances are made while a security interest is perfected by filing or the taking of possession, the security interest has the same priority for the purposes of subsection (5) with respect to the future advances as it does with respect to the first advance. If a commitment is made before or while the security interest is so perfected, the security interest has the same priority with respect to advances made pursuant thereto. In other cases a perfected security interest has priority from the date the advance is made.

§9-312. Priorities Among Conflicting Security Interests in the Same Collateral (*1977 Amendments*).

(**7**) If future advances are made while a security interest is perfected by filing, the taking of possession, or under Section 8-321 on securities, the security interest has the same priority for the purposes of subsection (5) with respect to the future advances as it does with respect to the first advance. If a commitment is made before or while the security interest is so perfected, the security interest has the same priority with respect to advances made pursuant thereto. In other cases a perfected security interest has priority from the date the advance is made.

* * *

§9-313. Priority of Security Interests in Fixtures.

(**1**) In this section and in the provisions of Part 4 of this Article referring to fixture filing, unless the context otherwise requires

(**a**) goods are "fixtures" when they become so related to particular real estate that an interest in them arises under real estate law

(**b**) a "fixture filing" is the filing in the office where a mortgage on the real estate would be filed or recorded of a financing statement covering goods which are or are to become fixtures and conforming to the requirements of subsection (5) of Section 9-402

(**c**) a mortgage is a "construction mortgage" to the extent that it secures an obligation incurred for the construction of an improvement on land including the acquisition cost of the land, if the recorded writing so indicates.

(2) A security interest under this Article may be created in goods which are fixtures or may continue in goods which become fixtures, but no security interest exists under this Article in ordinary building materials incorporated into an improvement on land.

(3) This Article does not prevent creation of an encumbrance upon fixture pursuant to real estate law.

(4) A perfected security interest in fixtures has priority over the conflicting interest of an encumbrancer or owner of the real estate where

(a) the security interest is a purchase money security interest, the interest of the encumbrancer or owner arises before the goods become fixtures, the security interest is perfected by a fixture filing before the goods become fixtures or within ten days thereafter, and the debtor has an interest of record in the real estate or is in possession of the real estate; or

(b) the security interest is perfected by a fixture filing before the interest of the encumbrancer or owner is of record, the security interest has priority over any conflicting interest of a predecessor in title of the encumbrancer or owner, and the debtor has an interest of record in the real estate or is in possession of the real estate; or

(c) the fixtures are readily removable factory or office machines or readily removable replacements of domestic appliances which are consumer goods, and before the goods become fixtures the security interest is perfected by any method permitted by this Article; or

(d) the conflicting interest is a lien on the real estate obtained by legal or equitable proceedings after the security interest was perfected by any method permitted by this Article.

(5) A security interest in fixtures, whether or not perfected, has priority over the conflicting interest of an encumbrancer or owner of the real estate where

(a) the encumbrancer or owner has consented in writing to the security interest or has disclaimed an interest in the goods as fixtures; or (b) the debtor has a right to remove the goods as against the encumbrancer or owner. If the debtor's right terminates, the priority of the security interest continues for a reasonable time.

(6) Notwithstanding paragraph (a) of subsection (4) but otherwise subject to subsections (4) and (5), a security interest in fixtures is subordinate to a construction mortgage recorded before the goods become fixtures if the goods become fixtures before the completion of the construction. To the extent that it is given to refinance a construction mortgage, a mortgage has this priority to the same extent as the construction mortgage.

(7) In cases not within the preceding subsections, a security interest in fixtures is subordinate to the conflicting interest of an encumbrancer or owner of the related real estate who is not the debtor.

(8) When the secured party has priority over all owners and encumbrancers of the real estate, he may, on default, subject to the provisions of Part 5, remove his collateral from the real estate but he must reimburse any encumbrancer or owner of the real estate who is not the debtor and who has not otherwise agreed for the cost of repair of any physical injury, but not for any diminution in value of the real estate caused by the absence of the goods removed or by any necessity of replacing them. A person entitled to reimbursement may refuse permission to remove until the secured party gives adequate security for the performance of this obligation.

§9-314. Accessions.

(1) A security interest in goods which attaches before they are installed in or affixed to other goods takes priority as to the goods installed or affixed (called in this section "accessions") over the claims of all persons to the whole except as stated in subsection (3) and subject to Section 9-315(1).

(2) A security interest which attaches to goods after they become part of a whole is valid against all persons subsequently acquiring interests in the whole except as stated in subsection (3) but is invalid against any person with an interest in the whole at the time the security interest attaches to the goods who has not in writing consented to the security interest or disclaimed an interest in the goods as part of the whole.

(3) The security interests described in subsections (1) and (2) do not take priority over

(a) a subsequent purchaser for value of any interest in the whole; or

(b) a creditor with a lien on the whole subsequently obtained by judicial proceedings; or

(c) a creditor with a prior perfected security interest in the whole to the extent that he makes subsequent advances

if the subsequent purchase is made, the lien by judicial proceedings obtained or the subsequent advance under the prior perfected security interest is made or contracted for without knowledge of the security interest and before it is perfected. A purchaser of the whole at a fore-closure sale other than the holder of a perfected security interest purchasing at his own foreclo-sure sale is a subsequent purchaser within this section.

(**4**) When under subsections (1) or (2) and (3) a secured party has an interest in accessions which has priority over the claims of all persons who have interests in the whole, he may on default subject to the provisions of Part 5 remove his collateral from the whole but he must reimburse any encumbrancer or owner of the whole who is not the debtor and who has not otherwise agreed for the cost of repair of any physical injury but not for any diminution in value of the whole caused by the absence of the goods removed or by any necessity for replacing them. A person entitled to reimbursement may refuse permission to remove until the secured party gives adequate security for the performance of this obligation.

§9-315. Priority When Goods are Commingled or Processed.

(**1**) If a security interest in goods was perfected and subsequently the goods or a part thereof have become part of a product or mass, the security interest continues in the product or mass if

(**a**) the goods are so manufactured, processed, assembled or commingled that their identity is lost in the product or mass; or

(**b**) a financing statement covering the original goods also covers the product into which the goods have been manufactured, processed or assembled. In a case to which paragraph (b) applies, no separate security interest in that part of the original goods which has been manufactured, processed or assembled into the product may be claimed under Section 9-314.

(**2**) When under subsection (1) more than one security interest attaches to the product or mass, they rank equally according to the ratio that the cost of the goods to which each interest originally attached bears to the cost of the total product or mass.

§9-316. Priority Subject to Subordination.
Nothing in this Article prevents subordination by agreement by any person entitled to priority.

§9-317. Secured Party Not Obligated On Contract of Debtor.
The mere existence of a security interest or authority given to the debtor to dispose of or use collateral does not impose contract or tort liability upon the secured party for the debtor's acts or omissions.

§9-318. Defenses Against Assignee; Modification of Contract After Notification of Assignment; Term Prohibiting Assignment Ineffective; Identification and Proof of Assignment.

(**1**) Unless an account debtor has made an enforceable agreement not to assert defenses or claims arising out of a sale as provided in Section 9-206 the rights of an assignee are subject to

(**a**) all the terms of the contract between the account debtor and assignor and any defense or claim arising therefrom; and

(**b**) any other defense or claim of the account debtor against the assignor which accures before the account debtor receives notification of the assignment.

(**2**) So far as the right to payment or a part thereof under an assigned contract has not been fully earned by performance, and notwithstanding notification of the assignment, any modification of or substitution for the contract made in good faith and in accordance with reasonable commercial standards is effective against an assignee unless the account debtor has otherwise agreed but the assignee acquires corresponding rights under the modified or substituted contract. The assignment may provide that such modification or substitution is a breach by the assignor.

(**3**) The account debtor is authorized to pay the assignor until the account debtor receives notification that the amount due or to become due has been assigned and that payment is to be made to the assignee. A notification which does not reasonably identify the rights assigned is ineffective. If requested by the account debtor, the assignee must seasonably furnish reasonable proof that the assignment has been made and unless he does so the account debtor may pay the assignor.

(**4**) A term in any contract between an account debtor and an assignor is ineffective if it prohibits assignment of an account or prohibits creation of a security interest in a general intangible for money due or to become due or requires the account debtor's consent to such assignment or security interest.

Part 4: Filing

§9-401. Place of Filing; Erroneous Filing; Removal of Collateral.

First Alternative Subsection (1)

(**1**) The proper place to file in order to perfect a security interest is as follows:

(**a**) when the collateral is timber to be cut or is

minerals or the like (including oil and gas) or accounts subject to subsection (5) of Section 9-103, or when the financing statement is filed as a fixture filing (Section 9-313) and the collateral is goods which are or are to become fixtures, then in the office where a mortgage on the real estate would be filed or recorded;

(b) in all other cases, in the office of the [[Secretary of State]]

Second Alternative Subsection (1)

(1) The proper place to file in order to perfect a security interest is as follows:

(a) when the collateral is equipment used in farming operations, or farm products, or accounts or general intangibles arising from or relating to the sale of farm products by a farmer, or consumer goods, then in the office of the . . . . in the county of the debtor's residence or if the debtor is not a resident of this state then in the office of the . . . . in the county where the goods are kept, and in addition when the collateral is crops growing or to be grown in the office of the . . . . in the county where the land is located;

(b) when the collateral is timber to be cut or is minerals or the like (including oil and gas) or accounts subject to subsection (5) of Section 9-103, or when the financing statement is filed as a fixture filing (Section 9-313) and the collateral is goods which are or are to become fixtures, then in the office where a mortgage on the real estate would be filed or recorded;

(c) in all other cases, in the office of the . . . . . .

Third Alternative Subsection (1)

(1) The proper place to file in order to perfect a security interest is as follows:

(a) when the collateral is equipment used in farming operations, or farm products, or accounts or general intangibles arising from or relating to the sale of farm products by a farmer, or consumer goods, then in the office of the . . . . . . in the county of the debtor's residence or if the debtor is not a resident of this state then in the office of the . . . . . . in the county where the goods are kept, and in addition when the collateral is crops growing or to be grown in the office of . . . . . . in the county where the land is located;

(b) when the collateral is timber to be cut or is minerals or the like (including oil and gas) or

accounts subject to subsection (5) of Section 9-103, or when the financing statement is filed as a fixture filing (Section 9-313) and the collateral is goods which are or are to become fixtures, then in the office where a mortgage on the real estate would be filed or recorded;

(c) in all other cases, in the office of the . . . . . and in addition, if the debtor has a place of business in only one county of this state, also in the office of . . . . . . of such county, or, if the debtor has no place of business in this state, but resides in the state, also in the office of . . . . . . of the county in which he resides.

Note: *One of the three alternatives should be selected as subsection (1).*

(2) A filing which is made in good faith in an improper place or not in all of the places required by this section is nevertheless effective with regard to any collateral as to which the filing complied with the requirements of this Article and is also effective with regard to collateral covered by the financing statement against any person who has knowledge of the contents of such financing statement.

(3) A filing which is made in the proper place in this state continues effective even though the debtor's residence or place of business or the location of the collateral or its use, whichever controlled the original filing, is thereafter changed.

Note: *Language in double brackets is Alternative Subsection (3).*

[[(3) A filing which is made in the proper county continues effective for four months after a change to another county of the debtor's residence or place of business or the location of the collateral, whichever controlled the original filing. It becomes ineffective thereafter unless a copy of the financing statement signed by the secured party is filed in the new county within said period. The security interest may also be perfected in the new county after the expiration of the four-month period; in such case perfected dates from the time of perfection in the new county. A change in the use of the collateral does not impair the effectivness of the original filing.]]

(4) The rules stated in Section 9-103 determine whether filing is necessary in this state.

(5) Notwithstanding the preceding subsections, and subject to subsection (3) of Section 9-302, the proper place to file in order to perfect a security interest in collateral, including the fixtures, of a transmit-

ting utility is the office of the [[Secretary of State]]. This filing constitutes a fixture filing (Section 9-313) as to the collateral described therein which is or is to become fixtures.

(**6**) For the purposes of this section, the residence of an organization is its place of business if it has one or its chief executive officer if it has more than one place of business.

Note: *Subsection (6) should be used only if the state chooses the Second or Third Alternative Subsection (1).*

§9-402. Formal Requisites of Financing Statement; Amendments; Mortgage as Financing Statement.

(**1**) A financing statement is sufficient if it gives the names of the debtor and the secured party, is signed by the debtor, gives an address of the secured party from which information concerning the security interest may be obtained, gives a mailing address of the debtor and contains a statement indicating the types, or describing the items, of collateral. A financing statement may be filed before a security agreement is made or a security interest otherwise attaches. When the financing statement covers crops growing or to be grown, the statement must also contain a description of the real estate concerned. When the financing statement covers timber to be cut or covers minerals or the like (including oil and gas) or accounts subject to subsection (5) of Section 9-103, or when the financing statement is filed as a fixture filing (Section 9-313) and the collateral is goods which are or are to become fixtures, the statement must also comply with subsection (5). A copy of the security agreement is sufficient as a financing statement if it contains the above information and is signed by the debtor. A carbon, photographic or other reproduction of a security agreement or a financing statement is sufficient as a financing statement if the security agreement so provides or if the original has been filed in this state.

(**2**) A financing statement which otherwise complies with subsection (1) is sufficient when it is signed by the secured party instead of the debtor if it is filed to perfect a security interest in

(**a**) collateral already subject to security interest in another jurisdiction when it is brought into this state, or when the debtor's location is changed to this state. Such a financing statement must state that the collateral was brought into this state or that the debtor's lo-

cation was changed to this state under such circumstances; or

(**b**) proceeds under Section 9-306 if the security interest in the original collateral was perfected. Such a financing statement must describe the original collateral; or

(**c**) collateral as to which the filing has lapsed; or

(**d**) collateral acquired after a change of name, identity or corporate structure of the debtor (subsection (7)).

(**3**) A form substantially as follows is sufficient to comply with subsection (1):

Name of Debtor (or assignor) . . . .
Address . . . .
Name of secured party (or assignee) . . . .
Address . . . .

1. This financing statement covers the following types (or items) of property:
(Describe) . . . .
2. (If collateral is crops) The above described crops are growing or are to be grown on:
(Describe Real Estate) . . . .
3. (If applicable) The above goods are to become fixtures on (Describe Real Estate) . . . . . and this financing statement is to be filed [[for record]] in the real estate records. (If the debtor does not have an interest of record)
The name of a record owner is . . . .
4. (If products of collateral are claimed) Products of the collateral are also covered.

(use whichever is applicable)

. . . .
Signature of Debtor (or Assignor)

. . . .
Signature of Secured Party
(or Assignee)

(**4**) A financing statement may be amended by filing a writing signed by both the debtor and the secured party. An amendment does not extend the period of effectiveness of a financing statement. If any amendment adds collateral, it is effective as to the added collateral only from the filing date of the amendment. In this Article, unless the context otherwise requires, the term "financing statement" means the original financing statement and any amendments.

(**5**) A financing statement covering timber to be cut or covering minerals or the like (including oil and gas) or accounts subject to subsection (5) of Section 9-103, or a financing statement filed as a fixture filing (Section 9-313) where the debtor is not a transmitting utility, must show that it covers this type of collateral, must recite that it is to be filed [[for record]] in the real estate records, and the financing statement must contain a description of the real estate [[sufficient if it were contained in a mortgage of the real estate to give constructive notice of the mortgage under the law of this state]]. If the debtor does not have an interest of record in the real estate, the financing statement must show the name of a record owner.

(6) A mortgage is effective as a financing statement filed as a fixture filing from the date of its recording if (a) the goods are described in the mortgage by item or type, (b) the goods are or are to become fixtures related to the real estate described in the mortgage, (c) the mortgage complies with the requirements for a financing statement in this section other than a recital that it is to be filed in the real estate records, and (d) the mortgage is duly recorded. No fee with reference to the financing statement is required other than the regular recording and satisfaction fees with respect to the mortgage.

(7) A financing statement sufficiently shows the name of the debtor if it gives the individual, partnership or corporate name of the debtor, whether or not it adds other trade names or the names of partners. Where the debtor so changes his name or in the case of an organization name, identity or corporate structure that a filed financing statement becomes seriously misleading, the filing is not effective to perfect a security interest in collateral acquired by the debtor more than four months after the change, unless a new appropriate financing statement is filed before the expiration of that time. A filed financing statement remains effective with respect to collateral transferred by the debtor even though the secured party knows of or consents to the transfer.

(8) A financing statement substantially complying with the requirements of this section is effective even though it contains minor errors which are not seriously misleading.

Note: *Language in double brackets is optional.*

Note: *Where the state has any special recording system for real estate other than the usual grantor-grantee index (as, for instance, a tract system or a title registration or Torrens system) local adaptations of*

subsection (5) and Section 9-403(7) may be necessary. See Mass. Gen. Laws Chapter 106, Section 9-409.

§9-403. What Constitutes Filing; Duration of Filing; Effect of Lapsed Filing; Duties of Filing Officer.

(1) Presentation for filing of a financing statement and tender of the filing fee or acceptance of the statement by the filing officer constitutes filing under this Article.

(2) Except as provided in subsection (6) a filed financing statement is effective for a period of five years from the date of filing. The effectiveness of a filed financing statement lapses on the expiration of the five year period unless a continuation statement is filed prior to the lapse. If a security interest perfected by filing exists at the time insolvency proceedings are commenced by or against the debtor, the security interest remains perfected until termination of the insolvency proceedings and thereafter for a period of sixty days or until expiration of the five year period, whichever occurs later. Upon lapse the security interest becomes unperfected, unless it is perfected without filing. If the security interest becomes unperfected upon lapse, it is deemed to have been unperfected as against a person who became a purchaser or lien creditor before lapse.

(3) A continuation statement may be filed by the secured party within six months prior to the expiration of the five year period specified in subsection (2). Any such continuation statement must be signed by the secured party, identify the original statement by file number and state that the original statement is still effective. A continuation statement signed by a person other than the secured party of record must be accompanied by a separate written statement of assignment signed by the secured party of record and complying with subsection (2) of Section 9-405, including payment of the required fee. Upon timely filing of the continuation statement, the effectiveness of the original statement is continued for five years after the last date to which the filing was effective whereupon it lapses in the same manner as provided in subsection (2) unless another continuation statement is filed prior to such lapse. Succeeding continuation statements may be filed in the same manner to continue the effectiveness of the original statement. Unless a statute on disposition of public records provides otherwise, the filing officer may remove a lapsed statement from the files and destroy it immediately if

he has retained a microfilm or other photographic records, or in other cases after one year after the lapse. The filing officer shall so arrange matters by physical annexation of financing statements to continuation statements or other related filings, or by other means, that if he physically destroys the financing statements of a period more than five years past, those which have been continued by a continuation statement or which are still effective under subsection (6) shall be retained.

(**4**) Except as provided in subsection (7) a filing officer shall mark each statement with a file number and with the date and hour of filing and shall hold the statement or a microfilm or other photographic copy thereof for public inspection. In addition the filing officer shall index the statements according to the name of the debtor and shall note in the index the file number and the address of the debtor given in the statement.

(**5**) The uniform fee for filing and indexing and for the stamping a copy furnished by the secured party to show the date and place of filing for an original financing statement or for a continuation statement shall be $ . . . . if the statement is in the standard form prescribed by the . . . . . and otherwise shall be $ . . . . plus in each case, if the financing statement is subject to subsection (5) of Section 9-402, $ . . . . The uniform fee for each name more than one required to be indexed shall be $ . . . . The secured party may at his option show a trade name for any person and an extra uniform indexing fee of $ . . . . shall be paid with respect thereto.

(**6**) If the debtor is a transmitting utility (subsection (5) of Section 9-401) and a filed financing statement so states, it is effective until a termination statement is filed. A real estate mortgage which is effective as a fixture filing under subsection (6) of Section 9-402 remains effective as a fixture filing until the mortgage is released or satisfied or recorded or its effectiveness otherwise terminates as to the real estate.

(**7**) When a financing statement covers timber to be cut or covers minerals or the like (including oil and gas) or accounts subject to subsection (5) of Section 9-103, or is filed as a fixture filing, [[it shall be filed for record and]] the filing officer shall index it under the names of the debtor and any owner of record shown on the financing statement in the same fashion as if they were the mortgagors in a mortgage of the real estate described, and, to the extent that the law of this state provides for indexing of mortgages under the name of the mortgagee, under the name of the secured party as if he were the mortgagee, thereunder, or where indexing is by description in the same fashion as if the financing statement were a mortgage of the real estate described.

Note: *In states in which writings will not appear in the real estate records and indices unless actually recorded the bracketed language in subsection (7) should be used.*

§9-404. Termination Statement.

(**1**) If a financing statement covering consumer goods is filed on or after . . . . , then within one month or within ten days following written demand by the debtor after there is no outstanding secured obligation and no commitment to make advances, incur obligations or otherwise give value, the secured party must file with each filing officer with whom the financing statement was filed, a termination statement to the effect that he no longer claims a security interest under the financing statement, which shall be identified by file number. In other cases whenever there is no outstanding secured obligation and no commitment to make advances, incur obligations or otherwise give value, the secured party must on written demand by the debtor send the debtor, for each filing officer with whom the financing statement was filed, a termination statement to the effect that no longer claims a security interest under the financing statement, which shall by identified by file number. A termination statement signed by a person other than the secured party of record must be accompanied by a separate written statement of assignment signed by the secured party of record complying with subsection (2) of Section 9-405, including payment of the required fee. If the affected secured party fails to file such a termination statement as required by this subsection, or to send such a termination statement within ten days after proper demand therefor he shall be liable to the debtor for one hundred dollars, and in addition for any loss caused to the debtor by such failure.

(**2**) On presentation to the filing officer of such a termination statement he must note it in the index. If he has received the termination statement in duplicate, he shall return one copy of the termination statement to the secured party stamped to show the time of receipt thereof. If the filing officer has a microfilm or other photographic record of the financing statement, and of any related continuation statement, statement of assignment and statement of release, he may remove the originals from the files at any time after receipt of the termination statement, or if he has no such record, he may remove them from the files at any time after one year after receipt of the termination statement.

(3) If the termination statement is in the standard form prescribed by the . . . . . , the uniform fee for filing and indexing the termination statement shall be $. . . , and otherwise shall be $. . . . . . . plus in each case an additional fee of $. . . . . . . for each name more than one against which the termination statement is required to be indexed.

Note: *The date to be inserted should be the effective date of the revised Article 9.*

§9-405. Assignment of Security Interest; Duties of Filing Officer Fees.

(1) A financing statement may disclose an assignment of a security interest in the collateral described in the financing statement by indication in the financing statement of the name and address of the assignee or by an assignment itself or a copy thereof on the face or back of the statement. On presentation to the filing officer of such a financing statement the filing officer shall mark the same as provided in Section 9-403(4). The uniform fee for filing, indexing and furnishing filing data for a financing statement so indicating as assignment shall be $. . . . . . . if the statement is in the standard form prescribed by the . . . . and otherwise shall be $. . . . . . . plus in each case an additional fee of $. . . . . for each name more than one against which the financing statement is required to be indexed.

(2) A secured party may assign of record all or part of his rights under a financing statement by the filing in the place where the original financing statement was filed of a separate written statement of assignment signed by the secured party of record and setting forth the name of the secured party of record and the debtor, the file number and the date of filing of the financing statement and the name and address of the assignee and containing a description of the collateral assigned. A copy of the assignment is sufficient as a separate statement if it complies with the preceding sentence. On presentation to the filing officer of such a separate statement, the filing officer shall mark such separate statement with the date and hour of the filing. He shall note the assignment on the index of the financing statement, or in the case of a fixture filing, or a filing covering timber to be cut, or covering minerals or the like (including oil and gas) or accounts subject to subsection (5) of Section 9-103, he shall index the assignment under the name of the assignor as grantor and, to the extent that the law of this state provides for indexing the assignment of a mortgage under the name of the assignee, he shall index the assignment of the financing statement under the name of the assignee. The uniform fee for filing, indexing and furnishing filing data about such a separate statement of assignment shall be $ . . . . . if the statement is in the standard form prescribed by the . . . . . and otherwise shall be $ . . . . , plus in each case an additional fee of $ . . . . for each name more than one against which the statement of assignment is required to be indexed. Notwithstanding the provisions of this subsection, an assignment of record of a security interest in a fixture contained in a mortgage effective as a fixture filing (subsection (6) of Section 9-402) may be made only by an assignment of the mortgage in the manner provided by the law of this state other than this Act.

(3) After the disclosure or filing of an assignment under this section, the assignee is the secured party of record.

§9-406. Release of Collateral; Duties of Filing Officer; Fees.
A secured party of record may be his signed statement release all or a part of any collateral described in a filed financing statement. The statement of release is sufficient if it contains a description of the collateral being released, the name and address of the debtor, the name and address of the secured party, and the file number of the financing statement. A statement of release signed by a person other than the secured party of record must be accompanied by a separate written statement of assignment signed by the secured party of record and complying with subsection (2) of Section 9-405, including payment of the required fee. Upon presentation of such a statement of release to the filing officer he shall mark the statement with the hour and date of filing and shall note the same upon the margin of the index of the filing of the financing statement. The uniform fee for filing and noting such a statement of release shall be $ . . . . if the statement is in the standard form prescribed by the . . . . . and otherwise shall be $ . . . , plus in each case an additional fee of $ . . . . for each name more than one against which the statement of release is required to be indexed.

[[**§9-407. Information From Filing Officer.**]]

[[(**1**) If the person filing any financing statement, termination statement, statement of assignment, or statement of release, furnishes the filing officer a copy thereof, the filing officer shall upon request note upon the copy the file number and date and hour of the filing of the original and deliver or send the copy to such person.

[[(**2**) Upon request of any person, the filing officer shall issue his certificate showing whether there is on file on the date and hour stated therein, any presently effective financing statement naming a particular debtor and any statement of assignment thereof and if there is, giving the date and hour of filing of each such statement and the names and addresses of each secured party therein. The uniform fee for such a certificate shall be $ . . . . if the request for the certificate is in the standard form prescribed by the [[Secretary of State]] and otherwise shall be $. . . . . . . Upon request the filing officer shall furnish a copy of any filed statement or statement of assignment for a uniform fee of $ . . . . per page.]]

Note: *This section is proposed as an optional provision to require filing officers to furnish certificates. Local law and practices should be consulted with regard to the advisability of adoption.*

§9-408. Financing Statements Covering Consigned or Leased Goods.   A consignor or lessor of goods may file a financing statement using the terms "consignor," "consignee," "lessor," "lessee" or the like instead of the terms specified in Section 9-402. The provisions of this Part shall apply as appropriate to such a financing statement but its filing shall not of itself be a factor in determining whether or not the consignment or lease is intended as security (Section 1-201(37)). However, if it is determined for other reasons that the consignment or lease is so intended, a security interest of the consignor or lessor which attaches to the consigned or leased goods is perfected by such filing.

Part 5: Default

§9-501. Default; Procedure When Security Agreement Covers Both Real and Personal Property.

(**1**) When a debtor is in default under a security agreement, a secured party has the rights and remedies provided in this Part and except as limited by subsection (3) those provided in the security agreement. He may reduce his claim to judgment, foreclose

or otherwise enforce the security interest by any available judicial procedure. If the collateral is documents the secured party may proceed either as to the documents or as to the goods covered thereby. A secured party in possession has the rights, remedies and duties provided in Section 9-207. The rights and remedies referred to in this subsection are cumulative.

(**2**) After default, the debtor has the rights and remedies provided in this Part, those provided in the security agreement and those provided in Section 9-207.

(**3**) To the extent that they give rights to the debtor and impose duties on the secured party, the rules stated in the subsections referred to below may not be waived or varied except as provided with respect to compulsory disposition of collateral (subsection (3) of Section 9-504 and Section 9-505) and with respect to redemption of collateral (Section 9-506) but the parties may by agreement determine the standards by which the fulfillment of these rights and duties is to be measured if such standards are not manifestly unreasonable:

> (**a**) subsection (2) Section 9-502 and subsection (2) of Section 9-504 insofar as they require accounting for surplus proceeds of collateral;
> (**b**) subsection (3) of Section 9-504 and subsection (1) of Section 9-505 which deal with disposition of collateral;
> (**c**) subsection (2) of Section 9-505 which deals with acceptance of collateral as discharge of obligation;
> (**d**) Section 9-506 which deals with redemption of collateral; and
> (**e**) subsection (1) of Section 9-507 which deals with the secured party's liability for failure to comply with this Part.

(**4**) If the security agreement covers both real and personal property, the secured party may proceed under this Part as to the personal property or he may proceed as to both the real and the personal property in accordance with his rights and remedies in respect of the real property in which case the provisions of this Part do not apply.

(**5**) When a secured party has reduced his claim to judgment the lien of any levy which may be made upon his collateral by virtue of any execution based upon the judgment shall relate back to the date of the perfection of the security interest in such collateral. A judicial sale, pursuant to such execution, is a foreclosure of the security interest by judicial procedure within the meaning of this section, and the secured party may purchase at the sale and thereafter hold the collateral free of any other requirements of this Article.

§9-502. Collection Rights of Secured Party.

(1) When so agreed and in any event on default the secured party is entitled to notify an account debtor or the obligor on an instrument to make payment to him whether or not the assignor was theretofore making collections on the collateral, and also to take control of any proceeds to which he is entitled under Section 9-306.

(2) A secured party who by agreement is entitled to charge back uncollected collateral or otherwise to full or limited recourse against the debtor and who undertakes to collect from the account debtors or obligors must proceed in a commercially reasonable manner and may deduct his reasonable expenses of realization from the collections. If the security agreement secures an indebtedness, the secured party must account to the debtor for any surplus, and unless otherwise agreed, the debtor is liable for any deficiency. But, if the underlying transaction was a sale of accounts or chattel paper, the debtor is entitled to any surplus or is liable for any deficiency only if the security agreement so provides.

§9-503. Secured Party's Right to Take Possession After Default.
Unless otherwise agreed a secured party has on default the right to take possession of the collateral. In taking possession a secured party may proceed without judicial process if this can be done without breach of the peace or may proceed by action. If the security agreement so provides the secured party may require the debtor to assemble the collateral and make it available to the secured party at a place to be designated by the secured party which is reasonably convenient to both parties. Without removal a secured party may render equipment unusable, and may dispose of collateral on the debtor's premises under Section 9-504.

§9-504. Secured Party's Right to Dispose of Collateral After Default; Effect of Disposition.

(1) A secured party after default may sell, lease or otherwise dispose of any or all of the collateral in its then condition or following any commercially reasonable preparation or processing. Any sale of goods is subject to the Article on Sales (Article 2). The proceeds of disposition shall be applied in the order following to

    (a) the reasonable expenses of retaking, holding, preparing for sale or lease, selling, leasing and the like and, to the extent provided for in the agreement and not prohibited by law, the reasonable attorneys' fees and legal expenses incurred by the secured party;

    (b) the satisfaction of indebtedness secured by the security interest under which the disposition is made;

    (c) the satisfaction of indebtedness secured by any subordinate security interest in the collateral if written notification of demand therefor is received before distribution of the proceeds if completed. If requested by the secured party, the holder of a subordinate security interest must seasonably furnish reasonable proof of his interest, and unless he does so, the secured party need not comply with his demand.

(2) If the security interest secures an indebtedness, the secured party must account to the debtor for any surplus, and, unless otherwise agreed, the debtor is liable for any deficiency. But if the underlying transaction was a sale of accounts, or chattel paper, the debtor is entitled to any surplus or is liable for any deficiency only if the security agreement so provides.

(3) Disposition of the collateral may be by public or private proceedings and may be made by way of one or more contracts. Sale or other disposition may be as a unit or in parcels and at any time and place and on any terms but every aspect of the disposition including the method, manner, time, place and terms must be commercially reasonable. Unless collateral is perishable or threatens to decline speedily in value or is of a type customarily sold on a recognized market, reasonable notification of the time and place of any public sale or reasonable notification of the time after which any private sale or other intended disposition is to be made shall be sent by the secured party to the debtor, if he has not signed after default a statement renouncing or modifying his right to notification of sale. In the case of consumer goods no other notification need be sent. In other cases notification shall be sent to any other secured party from whom the secured party has received (before sending his notification to the debtor or before the debtor's renunciation of his rights) written notice of a claim of an interest in the collateral. The secured party may buy at any public sale and if the collateral is of a type which is the subject of widely distributed standard price quotations he may buy at private sale.

(4) When collateral is disposed of by a secured party after default, the disposition transfers to a purchaser for value all of the debtor's rights therein, discharges the security interest under which it is made and any security interest of lien subordinate thereto. The purchaser takes free of all such rights and interests even though the secured party fails to comply with the requirements of this Part or of any judicial proceedings

   (a) in the case of a public sale, if the purchaser has no knowledge of any defects in the sale and if he does not buy in collusion with the secured party, other bidders or the person conducting the sale; or

   (b) in any other case, if the purchaser acts in good faith.

(5) A person who is liable to a secured party under a guaranty, indorsement, repurchase agreement or the like and who receives a transfer of collateral from the secured party or is subrogated to his rights has thereafter the rights and duties of the secured party. Such a transfer of collateral is not a sale or disposition of the collateral under this Article.

§9-505. Compulsory Disposition of Collateral; Acceptance of the Collateral as Discharge of Obligation.

(1) If the debtor has paid sixty per cent of the cash price in the case of a purchase money security interest in consumer goods or sixty per cent of the loan in the case of another security interest in consumer goods and has not signed after default a statement renouncing or modifying his rights under this Part a secured party who has taken possession of collateral must dispose of it under Section 9-504 and if he fails to do so within ninety days after he takes possession the debtor at his option may recover in conversion or under Section 9-507(1) on secured party's liability.

(2) In any other case involving consumer goods or any other collateral a secured party in possession may, after default, propose to retain the collateral in satisfaction of the obligation. Written notice of such proposal shall be sent to the debtor if he has not signed after default a statement renouncing or modifying his rights under this subsection. In the case of consumer goods no other notice need be given. In other cases notice shall be sent to any other secured party from whom the secured party has received (before sending his notice to the debtor or before the debtor's renunciation of his rights) written notice of a claim of an interest in the collateral. If the secured party receives objection in writing from a person entitled to receive notification within twenty-one days after the notice was sent, the secured party must dispose of the collateral under Section 9-504. In the absence of such written objection the secured party may retain the collateral in satisfaction of the debtor's obligation.

§9-506. Debtor's Right to Redeem Collateral. At any time before the secured party has disposed of collateral or entered into a contract for its disposition under Section 9-504 or before the obligation has been discharged under Section 9-505(2) the debtor or any other secured party may unless otherwise agreed in writing after default redeem the collateral by tendering fulfillment of all obligations secured by the collateral as well as the expenses reasonably incurred by the secured party in retaking, holding and preparing the collateral for disposition, in arranging for the sale, and to the extent provided in the agreement and not prohibited by law, his reasonable attorneys' fees and legal expenses.

§9-507. Secured Party's Liability for Failure to Comply With This Part.

(1) If it is established that the secured party is not proceeding in accordance with the provisions of this Part disposition may be ordered or restrained on appropriate terms and conditions. If the disposition has occurred the debtor or any person entitled to notification or whose security interest has been made known to the secured party prior to the disposition has a right to recover from the secured party any loss caused by a failure to comply with the provisions of this Part. If the collateral is consumer goods, the debtor has a right to recover in any event an amount not less than the credit service charge plus ten per cent of the principal amount of the debt or the time price differential plus 10 per cent of the cash price.

(2) The fact that a better price could have been obtained by a sale at a different time or in a different method from that selected by the secured party is not of itself sufficient to establish that the sale was not made in a commercially reasonable manner. If the secured party either sells the collateral in the usual manner in any recognized market therefor or if he sells at the price current in such market at the time of his sale or if he has otherwise sold in conformity with reasonable commercial practices among dealers in the type of property sold he has sold in commercially reasonable manner. The principles stated in the two preceding sentences with respect to sales also

apply as may be appropriate to other types of disposition. A disposition which has been approved in any judicial proceeding or by any bona fide creditors' committee or representative of creditors shall conclusively be deemed to be commercially reasonable, but this sentence does not indicate that any such approval must be obtained in any case nor does it indicate that any disposition not so approved is not commercially reasonable.

ARTICLE 10: EFFECTIVE DATE AND REPEALER

[omitted]

ARTICLE 11: EFFECTIVE DATE AND TRANSITION PROVISIONS

[omitted]

Uniform Partnership Act

Part I Preliminary Provisions

§1. Name of Act. This act may be cited as Uniform Partnership Act.

§2. Definition of Terms. In this act, "Court" includes every court and judge having jurisdiction in the case.

"Business" includes every trade, occupation, or profession.

"Person" includes individuals, partnerships, corporations, and other associations.

"Bankrupt" includes bankrupt under the Federal Bankruptcy Act or insolvent under any state insolvent act.

"Conveyance" includes every assignment, lease, mortgage, or encumbrance.

"Real property" includes land and any interest or estate in land.

§3. Interpretation of Knowledge and Notice.

(1) A person has "knowledge" of a fact within the meaning of this act not only when he has actual knowledge thereof, but also when he has knowledge of such other facts as in the circumstances shows bad faith.

(2) A person has "notice" of a fact within the meaning of this act when the person who claims the benefit of the notice:

(a) States the fact to such person, or

(b) Delivers through the mail, or by other means of communication, a written statement of the fact to such person or to a proper person at his place of business or residence.

§4. Rules of Construction.

(1) The rule that statutes in derogation of the common law are to be strictly construed shall have no application to this act.

(2) The law of estoppel shall apply under this act.

(3) The law of agency shall apply under this act.

(4) This act shall be so interpreted and construed as to effect its general purpose to make uniform the law of those states which enact it.

(5) This act shall not be construed so as to impair the obligations of any contract existing when the act goes into effect, nor to affect any action or proceedings begun or right accrued before this act takes effect.

§5. Rules for Cases Not Provided for in This Act. In any case not provided for in this act the rules of law and equity, including the law merchant, shall govern.

Part II Nature of Partnership

§6. Partnership Defined.

(1) A partnership is an association of two or more persons to carry on as co-owners a business for profit.

(2) But any association formed under any other statute of this state, or any statute adopted by authority, other than the authority of this state, is not a partnership under this act, unless such association would have been a partnership in this state prior to the adoption of this act; but this act shall apply to limited partnerships except in so far as the statutes relating to such partnerships are inconsistent herewith.

§7. Rules for Determining the Existence of a Partnership. In determining whether a partnership exists, these rules shall apply:

(1) Except as provided by section 16 persons who are not partners as to each other are not partners as to third persons.

(2) Joint tenancy, tenancy in common, tenancy by the entireties, joint property, common property, or part ownership does not of itself establish a partnership, whether such co-owners do or do not share any profits made by the use of the property.

(3) The sharing of gross returns does not of itself establish a partnership, whether or not the persons sharing them have a joint or common right or interest in any property from which the returns are derived.

(4) The receipt by a person of a share of the profits of a business is prima facie evidence that he is a partner in the business, but no such inference shall be drawn if such profits were received in payment:

(a) As a debt by installments or otherwise,

(b) As wages of an employee or rent to a landlord,

(c) As an annuity to a widow or representative of a deceased partner,

(d) As interest on a loan, though the amount of payment vary with the profits of the business,

(e) As the consideration for the sale of a good-will of a business or other property by installments or otherwise.

§8. Partnership Property.

(1) All property originally brought into the partnership stock or subsequently acquired by purchase or otherwise on account of the partnership, is partnership property.

(2) Unless the contrary intention appears, property acquired with partnership funds is partnership property.

(3) Any estate in real property may be acquired in the partnership name. Title so acquired can be conveyed only in the partnership name.

(4) A conveyance to a partnership in the partnership name, though without words of inheritance, passes the entire estate of the grantor unless a contrary intent appears.

Part III   Relations of Partners to Persons Dealing with the Partnership

§9.   Partner Agent of Partnership as to Partnership Business.

(1) Every partner is an agent of the partnership for the purpose of its business, and the act of every partner, including the execution in the partnership name of any instrument, for apparently carrying on in the usual way the business of the partnership of which he is a member binds the partnership, unless the partner so acting has in fact no authority to act for the partnership in the particular matter, and the person with whom he is dealing has knowledge of the fact that he has no such authority.

(2) An act of a partner which is not apparently for the carrying on of the business of the partnership in the usual way does not bind the partnership unless authorized by the other partners.

(3) Unless authorized by the other partners or unless they have abandoned the business, one or more but less than all the partners have no authority to:

   (a) Assign the partnership property in trust for creditors or on the assignee's promise to pay the debts of the partnership,

(b) Dispose of the good-will of the business,

(c) Do any other act which would make it impossible to carry on the ordinary business of a partnership,

(d) Confess a judgment,

(e) Submit a partnership claim or liability to arbitration or reference.

(4) No act of a partner in contravention of a restriction on authority shall bind the partnership to persons having knowledge of the restriction.

§10.   Conveyance of Real Property of the Partnership.

(1) Where title to real property is in the partnership name, any partner may convey title to such property by a conveyance executed in the partnership name; but the partnership may recover such property unless the partner's act binds the partnership under the provisions of paragraph (1) of section 9, or unless such property has been conveyed by the grantee or a person claiming through such grantee to a holder for value without knowledge that the partner in making the conveyance, has exceeded his authority.

(2) Where title to real property is in the name of the partnership, a conveyance executed by a partner, in his own name, passes the equitable interest of the partnership, provided the act is one within the authority of the partner under the provisions of paragraph (1) of section 9.

(3) Where title to real property is in the name of one or more but not all the partners, and the record does not disclose the right of the partnership, the partners in whose name the title stands may convey title to such property, but the partnership may recover such property if the partner's act does not bind the partnership under the provisions of paragraph (1) of section 9, unless the purchaser or his assignee, is a holder for value, without knowledge.

(4) Where the title to real property is in the name of one or more or all the partners, or in a third person in trust for the partnership, a conveyance executed by a partner in the partnership name, or in his own name, passes the equitable interest of the partnership, provided the act is one within the authority of the partner under the provisions of paragraph (1) of section 9.

(5) Where the title to real property is in the names of all the partners a conveyance executed by all the partners passes all their rights in such property.

§11. Partnership Bound by Admission of Partner.   An admission or representation made by any

partner concerning partnership affairs within the scope of his authority as conferred by this act is evidence against the partnership.

§12. Partnership Charged with Knowledge of or Notice to Partner. Notice to any partner of any matter relating to partnership affairs, and the knowledge of the partner acting in the particular matter, acquired while a partner or then present to his mind, and the knowledge of any other partner who reasonably could and should have communicated it to the acting partner, operate as notice to or knowledge of the partnership, except in the case of a fraud on the partnership committed by or with the consent of that partner.

§13. Partnership Bound by Partner's Wrongful Act. Where, by any wrongful act or omission of any partner acting in the ordinary course of the business of the partnership or with the authority of his co-partners, loss or injury is caused to any person, not being a partner in the partnership, or any penalty is incurred, the partnership is liable therefor to the same extent as the partner so acting or omitting to act.

§14. Partnership Bound by Partner's Breach of Trust. The partnership is bound to make good the loss:

(a) Where one partner acting within the scope of his apparent authority receives money or property of a third person and misapplies it; and

(b) Where the partnership in the course of its business receives money or property of a third person and the money or property so received is misapplied by any partner while it is in the custody of the partnership.

§15. Nature of Partner's Liability. All partners are liable

(a) Jointly and severally for everything chargeable to the partnership under sections 13 and 14.

(b) Jointly for all other debts and obligations of the partnership; but any partner may enter into a separate obligation to perform a partnership contract.

§16. Partner by Estoppel.

(1) When a person, by words spoken or written or by conduct, represents himself, or consents to another representing him to any one, as a partner in an existing partnership or with one or more persons not actual partners, he is liable to any such person to whom such representation has been made, who has, on the faith of such representation, given credit to the actual or apparent partnership, and if he has made such representation or consented to its being made in a public manner he is liable to such person, whether the representation has or has not been made or communicated to such person so giving credit by or with the knowledge of the apparent partner making the representation or consenting to its being made.

(a) When a partnership liability results, he is liable as though he were an actual member of the partnership.

(b) When no partnership liability results, he is liable jointly with the other persons, if any, so consenting to the contract or representation as to incur liability, otherwise separately.

(2) When a person has been thus represented to be a partner in an existing partnership, or with one or more persons not actual partners, he is an agent of the persons consenting to such representation to bind them to the same extent and in the same manner as though he were a partner in fact, with respect to persons who rely upon the representation. Where all the members of the existing partnership consent to the representation, a partnership act or obligation results; but in all other cases it is the joint act or obligation of the person acting and the persons consenting to the representation.

§17. Liability of Incoming Partner. A person admitted as a partner into an exisiting partnership is liable for all the obligations of the partnership arising before his admission as though he had been a partner when such obligations were incurred, except that this liability shall be satisfied only out of partnership property.

Part IV Relations of Partners to One Another

§18. Rules Determining Rights and Duties of Partners. The rights and duties of the partners in relation to the partnership shall be determined, subject to any agreement between them, by the following rules:

(a) Each partner shall be repaid his contributions, whether by way of capital or advances to the partnership property and share equally in the profits and surplus remaining after all liabilities, including those to partners, are satisfied; and must contribute towards the losses, whether of capital or otherwise, sustained by the partnership according to his share in the profits.

(b) The partnership must indemnify every partner in respect of payments made and personal liabilities reasonably incurred by him in the ordinary and proper conduct of its business, or for the preservation of its business or property.

(c) A partner, who in aid of the partnership makes any payment or advance beyond the amount of capital which he agreed to contribute, shall be paid interest from the date of the payment.

(d) A partner shall receive interest on the capital contributed by him only from the date when repayment should be made.

(e) All partners have equal rights in the management and conduct of the partnership business.

(f) No partner is entitled to remuneration for acting in the partnership business, except that a surviving partner is entitled to reasonable compensation for his services in winding up the partnership affairs.

(g) No person can become a member of a partnership without the consent of all the partners.

(h) Any difference arising as to ordinary matters connected with the partnership business may be decided by a majority of the partners; but no act in contravention of any agreement between the partners may be done rightfully without the consent of all the partners.

§19. Partnership Books. The partnership books shall be kept, subject to any agreement between the partners, at the principal place of business of the partnership, and every partner shall at all times have access to and may inspect and copy any of them.

§20. Duty of Partners to Render Information. Partners shall render on demand true and full information of all things affecting the partnership to any partner or the legal representative of any deceased partner or partner under legal disability.

§21. Partner Accountable as a Fiduciary.

(1) Every partner must account to the partnership for any benefit, and hold as trustee for it any profits derived by him without the consent of the other partners from any transaction connected with the formation, conduct, or liquidation of the partnership or from any use by him of its property.

(2) This section applies also to the representatives of a deceased partner engaged in the liquidation of the affairs of the partnership as the personal representatives of the last surviving partner.

§22. Right to an Account. Any partner shall have the right to a formal account as to partnership affairs:

(a) If he is wrongfully excluded from the partnership business or possession of its property by his co-partners,

(b) If the right exists under the terms of any agreement,

(c) As provided by section 21.

(d) Whenever other circumstances render it just and reasonable.

§23. Continuation of Partnership beyond Fixed Term.

(1) When a partnership for a fixed term or particular undertaking is continued after the termination of such term or particular undertaking without any express agreement, the rights and duties of the partners remain the same as they were at such termination, so far as is consistent with a partnership at will.

(2) A continuation of the business by the partners or such of them as habitually acted therein during the term, without any settlement or liquidation of the partnership affairs, is prima facie evidence of a continuation of the partnership.

Part V   Property Rights of a Partner

§24. Extent of Property Rights of a Partner. The property rights of a partner are (1) his rights in specific partnership property, (2) his interest in the partnership, and (3) his right to participate in the management.

§25. Nature of a Partner's Right in Specific Partnership Property.

(1) A partner is co-owner with his partners of specific partnership property holding as a tenant in partnership.

(2) The incidents of this tenancy are such that:

(a) A partner, subject to the provisions of this act and to any agreement between the partners, has an equal right with his partners to possess specific partnership property for partnership purposes; but he has no right to possess such property for any other purpose without the consent of his partners.

(b) A partner's right in specific partnership

property is not assignable except in connection with the assignment of rights of all the partners in the same property.

(c) A partner's right in specific partnership property is not subject to attachment or execution, except on a claim against the partnership. When partnership property is attached for a partnership debt the partners, or any of them, or the representatives of a deceased partner, cannot claim any right under the homestead or exemption laws.

(d) On the death of a partner his right in specific partnership property vests in the surviving partner or partners, except where the deceased was the last surviving partner, when his right in such property vests in his legal representative. Such surviving partner or partners, or the legal representative of the last surviving partner, has no right to possess the partnership property for any but a partnership purpose.

(e) A partner's right in specific partnership property is not subject to dower, curtesy, or allowances to widows, heirs, or next of kin.

§26. Nature of Partner's Interest in the Partnership. A partner's interest in the partnership is his share of the profits and surplus, and the same is personal property.

§27. Assignment of Partner's Interest.

(1) A conveyance by a partner of his interest in the partnership does not of itself dissolve the partnership, nor, as against the other partners in the absence of agreement, entitle the assignee, during the continuance of the partnership, to interfere in the management or administration of the partnership business or affairs, or to require any information or account of partnership transactions, or to inspect the partnership books; but it merely entitles the assignee to receive in accordance with his contract the profits to which the assigning partner would otherwise be entitled.

(2) In case of a dissolution of the partnership, the assignee is entitled to receive his assignor's interest and may require an account from the date only of the last account agreed to by all the partners.

§28. Partner's Interest Subject to Charging Order.

(1) On due application to a competent court by any judgment creditor of a partner, the court which entered the judgment, order, or decree, or any other court, may charge the interest of the debtor partner with payment of the unsatisfied amount of such judgment debt with interest thereon; and may then or later appoint a receiver of his share of the profits, and of any other money due or to fall due to him in respect of the partnership, and make all other orders, directions, accounts, and inquiries which the debtor partner might have made, or which the circumstances of the case may require.

(2) The interest charged may be redeemed at any time before foreclosure, or in case of a sale being directed by the court may be purchased without thereby causing a dissolution:

    (a) With separate property, by any one or more of the partners, or

    (b) With partnership property, by any one or more of the partners with the consent of all the partners whose interests are not so charged or sold.

(3) Nothing in this act shall be held to deprive a partner of his right, if any, under the exemption laws, as regards his interest in the partnership.

Part VI Dissolution and Winding Up

§29. Dissolution Defined. The dissolution of a partnership is the change in the relation of the partners caused by any partner ceasing to be associated in the carrying on as distinguished from the winding up of the business.

§30. Partnership not Terminated by Dissolution. On dissolution the partnership is not terminated, but continues until the winding up of the partnership affairs is completed.

§31. Causes of Dissolution. Dissolution is caused:

(1) Without violation of the agreement between the partners,

    (a) By the termination of the definite term or particular undertaking specified in the agreement,

    (b) By the express will of any partner when no definite term or particular undertaking is specified,

    (c) By the express will of all the partners who have not assigned their interests or suffered them to be charged for their separate debts, either before or after the termination of any specified term or particular undertaking,

    (d) By the expulsion of any partner from the

business bona fide in accordance with such a power conferred by the agreement between the partners;

(**2**) In contravention of the agreement between the partners, where the circumstances do not permit a dissolution under any other provision of this section, by the express will of any partner at any time;

(**3**) By any event which makes it unlawful for the business of the partnership to be carried on or for the members to carry it on in partnership;

(**4**) By the death of any partner;

(**5**) By the bankruptcy of any partner or the partnership;

(**6**) By decree of court under section 32.

§32. Dissolution by Decree of Court.

(**1**) On application by or for a partner the court shall decree a dissolution whenever:

    (**a**) A partner has been declared a lunatic in any judicial proceeding or is shown to be of unsound mind,

    (**b**) A partner becomes in any other way incapable of performing his part of the partnership contract,

    (**c**) A partner has been guilty of such conduct as tends to affect prejudicially the carrying on of the business,

    (**d**) A partner willfully or persistently commits a breach of the partnership agreement, or otherwise so conducts himself in matters relating to the partnership business that it is not reasonably practicable to carry on the business in partnership with him,

    (**e**) The business of the partnership can only be carried on at a loss,

    (**f**) Other circumstances render a dissolution equitable.

(**2**) On the application of the purchaser of a partner's interest under sections 27 or 28:

    (**a**) After the termination of the specified term or particular undertaking,

    (**b**) At any time if the partnership was a partnership at will when the interest was assigned or when the charging order was issued.

§33. General Effect of Dissolution on Authority of Partner. Except so far as may be necessary to wind up partnership affairs or to complete transactions begun but not then finished, dissolution terminates all authority of any partner to act for the partnership,

(**1**) With respect to the partners,

    (**a**) When the dissolution is not by the act, bankruptcy or death or a partner; or

    (**b**) When the dissolution is by such act, bankruptcy or death of a partner, in cases where section 34 so requires.

(**2**) With respect to persons not partners, as declared in section 35.

§34. Right of Partner to Contribution from Co-Partners after Dissolution. Where the dissolution is caused by the act, death or bankruptcy of a partner, each partner is liable to his co-partners for his share of any liability created by any partner acting for the partnership as if the partnership had not been dissolved unless

    (**a**) The dissolution being by act of any partner, the partner acting for the partnership had knowledge of the dissolution, or

    (**b**) The dissolution being by the death or bankruptcy of a partner, the partner acting for the partnership had knowledge or notice of the death or bankruptcy.

§35. Power of Partner to Bind Partnership to Third Persons after Dissolution.

(**1**) After dissolution a partner can bind the partnership except as provided in paragraph (3).

    (**a**) By any act appropriate for winding up partnership affairs or completing transactions unfinished at dissolution;

    (**b**) By any transaction which would bind the partnership if dissolution had not taken place, provided the other party to the transaction

        (**I**) Had extended credit to the partnership prior to dissolution and had no knowledge or notice of the dissolution; or

        (**II**) Though he had not so extended credit, had nevertheless known of the partnership prior to dissolution, and, having no knowledge or notice of dissolution, the fact of dissolution had not been advertised in a newspaper of general circulation in the place (or in each place if more than one) at which the partnership business was regularly carried on.

(**2**) The liability of a partner under paragraph (1b) shall be satisfied out of partnership assets alone when such partner had been prior to dissolution

    (**a**) Unknown as a partner to the person with whom the contract is made; and (**b**) So far unknown and inactive in partnership affairs that the business reputation of the partnership could not be said to have been in any degree due to his connection with it.

(**3**) The partnership is in no case bound by any act of a partner after dissolution

(**a**) Where the partnership is dissolved because it is unlawful to carry on the business, unless the act is appropriate for winding up partnership affairs; or

(**b**) Where the partner has become bankrupt; or

(**c**) Where the partner has no authority to wind up partnership affairs; except by a transaction with one who

(**I**) Had extended credit to the partnership prior to dissolution and had no knowledge or notice of his want of authority; or

(**II**) Had not extended credit to the partnership prior to dissolution, and, having no knowledge or notice of his want of authority, the fact of his want of authority has not been advertised in the manner provided for advertising the fact of dissolution in paragraph (1bII).

(**4**) Nothing in this section shall affect the liability under section 16 of any person who after dissolution represents himself or consents to another representing him as a partner in a partnership engaged in carrying on business.

§**36. Effect of Dissolution on Partner's Existing Liability.**

(**1**) The dissolution of the partnership does not of itself discharge the existing liability of any partner.

(**2**) A partner is discharged from any existing liability upon dissolution of the partnership by an agreement to that effect between himself, the partnership creditor and the person or partnership continuing the business; and such agreement may be inferred from the course of dealing between the creditor having knowledge of the dissolution and the person or partnership continuing the business.

(**3**) Where a person agrees to assume the existing obligations of a dissolved partnership, the partners whose obligations have been assumed shall be discharged from any liability to any creditor of the partnership who, knowing of the agreement, consents to a material alteration in the nature or time of payment of such obligations.

(**4**) The individual property of a deceased partner shall be liable for all obligations of the partnership incurred while he was a partner but subject to the prior payment of his separate debts.

§**37. Right to Wind Up.** Unless otherwise agreed the partners who have not wrongfully dissolved the partnership or the legal representative of the last surviving partner, not bankrupt, has the right to wind up the partnership affairs; provided, however, that any partner, his legal representative or his assignee, upon cause shown, may obtain winding up by the court.

§**38. Rights of Partners to Application of Partnership Property.**

(**1**) When dissolution is caused in any way, except in contravention of the partnership agreement, each partner, as against his co-partners and all persons claiming through them in respect of their interests in the partnership, unless otherwise agreed, may have the partnership property applied to discharge its liabilities, and the surplus applied to pay in cash the net amount owing to the respective partners. But if dissolution is caused by expulsion of a partner, bona fide under the partnership agreement and if the expelled partner is discharged from all partnership liabilities, either by payment or agreement under section 36(2), he shall receive in cash only the net amount due him from the partnership.

(**2**) When dissolution is caused in contravention of the partnership agreement the rights of the partners shall be as follows:

(**a**) Each partner who has not caused dissolution wrongfully shall have,

(**I**) All the rights specified in paragraph (1) of this section, and

(**II**) The right, as against each partner who has caused the dissolution wrongfully to damages for breach of the agreement.

(**b**) The partners who have not caused the dissolution wrongfully, if they all desire to continue the business in the same name, either by themselves or jointly with others, may do so, during the agreed term for the partnership and for that purpose may possess the partnership property, provided they secure the payment by bond approved by the court, or pay to any partner who has caused the dissolution wrongfully, the value of his interest in the partnership at the dissolution, less any damages recoverable under clause (2aII) of this section, and in like manner indemnify him against all present or future partnership liabilities.

(c) A partner who has caused the dissolution wrongfully shall have:

    (I) If the business is not continued under the provisions of paragraph (2b) all the rights of a partner under paragraph (1), subject to clause (2aII), of this section,

    (II) If the business is continued under paragraph (2b) of this section the right as against his co-partners and all claiming through them in respect of their interests in the partnership, to have the value of his interest in the partnership, less any damages caused to his co-partners by the dissolution, ascertained and paid to him in cash, or the payment secured by bond approved by the court, and to be released from all existing liabilities of the partnership; but in ascertaining the value of the partner's interest the value of the good-will of the business shall not be considered.

§39. Rights Where Partnership Is Dissolved for Fraud or Misrepresentation. Where a partnership contract is rescinded on the ground of the fraud or misrepresentation of one of the parties thereto, the party entitled to rescind is without prejudice to any other right, entitled,

    (a) To a lien on, or a right of retention of, the surplus of the partnership property after satisfying the partnership liabilities to third persons for any sum of money paid by him for the purchase of an interest in the partnership and for any capital or advances contributed by him; and

    (b) To stand, after all liabilities to third persons have been satisified, in the place of the creditors of the partnership for any payments made by him in respect of the partnership liabilities; and

    (c) To be indemnified by the person guilty of the fraud or making the representation against all debts and liabilities of the partnership.

§40. Rules for Distribution. In settling accounts between the partners after dissolution, the following rules shall be observed, subject to any agreement to the contrary:

    (a) The assets of the partnership are:

    (I) The partnership property,

    (II) The contributions of the partners necessary for the payment of all the liabilities specified in clause (b) of this paragraph.

(b) The liabilities of the partnership shall rank in order of payment, as follows:

    (I) Those owing to creditors other than partners,

    (II) Those owing to partners other than for capital and profits.

    (III) Those owing to partners in respect of capital,

    (IV) Those owing to partners in respect of profits.

(c) The assets shall be applied in order of their declaration in clause (a) of this paragraph to the satisfaction of the liabilities.

(d) The partners shall contribute, as provided by section 18(a) the amount necessary to satisfy the liabilities; but if any, but not all, of the partners are insolvent, or, not being subject to process, refuse to contribute, the other partners shall contribute their share of the liabilities, and, in the relative proportions in which they share the profits, the additional amount necessary to pay the liabilities.

(e) An assignee for the benefit of creditors or any person appointed by the court shall have the right to enforce the contributions specified in clause (d) of this paragraph.

(f) Any partner or his legal representative shall have the right to enforce the contributions specified in clause (d) of this paragraph, to the extent of the amount which he has paid in excess of his share of the liability.

(g) the individual property of a deceased partner shall be liable for the contributions specified in clause (d) of this paragraph.

(h) When partnership property and the individual properties of the partners are in possession of a court for distribution, partnership creditors shall have priority on partnership property and separate creditors on individual property, saving the rights of lien or secured creditors as heretofore.

(i) Where a partner has become bankrupt or his estate is insolvent the claims against his separate property shall rank in the following order:

    (I) Those owing to separate creditors,

(II) Those owing to partnership creditors,

(III) Those owing to partners by way of contribution.

§41. Liability of Persons Continuing the Business in Certain Cases.

(1) When any new partner is admitted into an existing partnership, or when any partner retires and assigns (or the representative of the deceased partner assigns) his rights in partnership property to two or more of the partners, or to one or more of the partners and one or more third persons, if the business is continued without liquidation of the partnership affairs, creditors of the first or dissolved partnership are also creditors of the partnership so continuing the business.

(2) When all but one partner retire and assign (or the representative of a deceased partner assigns) their rights in partnership property to the remaining partner, who continues the business without liquidation of partnership affairs, either alone or with others, creditors of the dissolved partnership are also creditors of the person or partnership so continuing the business.

(3) When any partner retires or dies and the business of the dissolved partnership is continued as set forth in paragraphs (1) and (2) of this section, with the consent of the retired partners or the representative of the deceased partner, but without any assignment of his right in partnership property, rights of creditors of the dissolved partnership and of the creditors of the person or partnership continuing the business shall be as if such assignment had been made.

(4) When all the partners or their representatives assign their rights in partnership property to one or more third persons who promise to pay the debts and who continue the business of the dissolved partnership, creditors of the dissolved partnership are also creditors of the person or partnership continuing the business.

(5) When any partner wrongfully causes a dissolution and the remaining partners continue the business under the provisions of section 38(2b), either alone or with others, and without liquidation of the partnership affairs, creditors of the dissolved partnership are also creditors of the person or partnership continuing the business.

(6) When a partner is expelled and the remaining partners continue the business either alone or with others, without liquidation of the partnership affairs, creditors of the dissolved partnership are also creditors of the person or partnership continuing the business.

(7) The liability of a third person becoming a partner in the partnership continuing the business, under this section, to the creditors of the dissolved partnership shall be satisfied out of partnership property only.

(8) When the business of a partnership after dissolution is continued under any conditions set forth in this section the creditors of the dissolved partnership, as against the separate creditors of the retiring or deceased partner or the representative of the deceased partner, have a prior right to any claim of the retired partner or the representative of the deceased partner against the person or partnership continuing the business, on account of the retired or deceased partner's interest in the dissolved partnership or an account of any consideration promised for such interest or for his right in partnership property.

(9) Nothing in this section shall be held to modify any right of creditors to set aside any assignment on the ground of fraud.

(10) The use by the person or partnership continuing the business of the partnership name, or the name of a deceased partner as part thereof, shall not of itself make the individual property of the deceased partner liable for any debts contracted by such person or partnership.

§42. Rights of Retiring or Estate of Deceased Partner When the Business Is Continued.
When any partner retires or dies, and the business is continued under any of the conditions set forth in section 41 (1, 2, 3, 5, 6), or section 38(2b) without any settlement of accounts as between him or his estate and the person or partnership continuing the business, unless otherwise agreed, he or his legal representative as against such persons or partnership may have the value of his interest at the date of dissolution ascertained, and shall receive as an ordinary creditor an amount equal to the value of his interest in the dissolved partnership with interest, or, at his option or at the option of his legal representative, in lieu of interest, the profits attributable to the use of his right in the property of the dissolved partnership; provided that the creditors of the dissolved partnership as against the separate creditors, or the representative of the retired or deceased partner, shall have priority on

any claim arising under this section, as provided by section 41(8) of this act.

§**43. Accrual of Actions.**   The right to an account of his interest shall accrue to any partner, or his legal representative, as against the winding up partners or the surviving partners or the person or partnership continuing the business, at the date of dissolution, in the absence of any agreement to the contrary.

Part VII   Miscellaneous Provisions

§**44. When Act Takes Effect.**   This act shall take effect on the . . . day of . . . one thousand nine hundred and. . . .

§**45. Legislation Repealed.**   All acts or parts of acts inconsistent with this act are hereby repealed.

Revised Model Business Corporation Act (1984) (Excerpts)

§1.02. Reservation of Power to Amend or Repeal. The [name of state legislature] has power to amend or repeal all or part of this Act at any time and all domestic and foreign corporations subject to this Act are governed by the amendment or repeal. . . .

§1.40. Act Definitions. In this Act:

(**1**) "Articles of incorporation" include amended and restated articles of incorporation and articles of merger.

(**2**) "Authorized shares" means the share of all classes a domestic or foreign corporation is authorized to issue. . . .

(**4**) "Corporation" or "domestic corporation" means a corporation for profit, which is not a foreign corporation, incorporated under or subject to the provisions of this Act. . . .

(**8**) "Employee" includes an officer but not a director. A director may accept duties that make him also an employee. . . .

(**10**) "Foreign corporation" means a corporation for profit incorporated under a law other than the law of this state. . . .

(**17**) "Principal office" means the office (in or out of this state) so designated in the annual report where the principal executive offices of a domestic or foreign corporation are located. . . .

(**21**) "Share" means the unit into which the proprietary interests in a corporation are divided.

(**22**) "Shareholder" means the person in whose name shares are registered in the records of a corporation or the beneficial owner of shares to the extent of the rights granted by a nominee certificate on file with a corporation. . . .

(**24**) "Subscriber" means a person who subscribes for shares in a corporation, whether before or after incorporation. . . .

§2.01. Incorporators. One or more persons may act as the incorporator or incorporators of a corporation by delivering articles of incorporation to the secretary of state for filing.

§2.02. Articles of Incorporation.

(**a**) The articles of incorporation must set forth:

(**1**) a corporate name for the corporation that satisfies the requirements of section 4.01;

(**2**) the number of shares the corporation is authorized to issue;

(**3**) the street address of the corporation's initial registered office and the name of its initial registered agent at that office; and

(**4**) the name and address of each incorporator. . . .

§2.03. Incorporation.

(**a**) Unless a delayed effective date is specified, the corporate existence begins when the articles of incorporation are filed.

(**b**) The secretary of state's filing of the articles of incorporation is conclusive proof that the incorporators satisfied all conditions precedent to incorporation except in a proceeding by the state to cancel or revoke the incorporation or involuntarily dissolve the corporation.

§2.04. Liability for Preincorporation Transactions. All persons purporting to act as or on behalf of a corporation, knowing there was no incorporation under this Act, are jointly and severally liable for all liabilities created while so acting.

§2.05. Organization of Corporation.

(**a**) After incorporation:

(**1**) if initial directors are named in the articles of incorporation, the initial directors shall hold an organizational meeting, at the call of a majority of the directors, to complete the organization of the corporation by appointing officers, adopting bylaws, and carrying on any other business brought before the meeting;

(**2**) if initial directors are not named in the articles, the incorporator or incorporators shall hold an organizational meeting at the call of a majority of the incorporators: . . .

§2.06. Bylaws.

(a) The incorporators or board of directors of a corporation shall adopt initial bylaws for the corporation.

(b) The bylaws of a corporation may contain any provision for managing the business and regulating the affairs of the corporation that is not inconsistent with law or the articles of incorporation. . . .

§3.01. Purposes.

(a) Every corporation incorporated under this Act has the purpose of engaging in any lawful business unless a more limited purpose is set forth in the articles of incorporation. . . .

§3.02. General Powers.   Unless its articles of incorporation provide otherwise, every corporation has perpetual duration and succession in its corporate name and has the same powers as an individual to do all things necessary or convenient to carry out its business and affairs, including without limitation power:

(1) to sue and be sued, complain and defend in its corporate name; . . .

(3) to make and amend bylaws, not inconsistent with its articles of incorporation or with the laws of this state, for managing the business and regulating the affairs of the corporation;

(4) to purchase, receive, lease, or otherwise acquire, and own, hold, improve, use, and otherwise deal with, real or personal property, or any legal or equitable interest in property, wherever located;

(5) to sell, convey, mortgage, pledge, lease, exchange, and otherwise dispose of all or any part of its property; . . .

(11) to elect directors and appoint officers, employees, and agents of the corporation, define their duties, fix their compensation, and lend them money and credit; . . .

(15) to make payments or donations, or do any other act, not inconsistent with law, that furthers the business and affairs of the corporation. . . .

§3.04. Ultra Vires.

(a) Except as provided in subsection (b), the validity of corporate action may not be challenged on the ground that the corporation lacks or lacked power to act.

(b) a corporation's power to act may be challenged:

(1) in a proceeding by a shareholder against the corporation to enjoin the act;

(2) in a proceeding by the corporation, directly, derivatively, or through a receiver, trustee, or other legal representative, against an incumbent or former director, officer, employee, or agent of the corporation; or

(3) in a proceeding by the Attorney General under section 14.30. . . .

§4.01. Corporate Name.

(a) A corporate name:

(1) must contain the word "corporation," "incorporated," "company," or "limited," or the abbreviation "corp.," "inc.," "co.," or "ltd.," or words or abbreviations of like import in another language; and

(2) may not contain language stating or implying that the corporation is organized for a purpose other than that permitted by section 3.01 and its articles of incorporation.

(b) Except as authorized by subsections (c) and (d), a corporate name must be distinguishable upon the records of the secretary of state from:

(1) the corporate name of a corporation incorporated or authorized to transact business in this state; . . .

§5.01. Registered Office and Registered Agent.   Each corporation must continuously maintain in this state:

(1) a registered office that may be the same as any of its places of business; . . .

§6.01. Authorized Shares.

(a) The articles of incorporation must prescribe the classes of shares and the number of shares of each class that the corporation is authorized to issue. If more than one class of shares is authorized, the articles of incorporation must prescribe a distinguishing designation for each class, and, prior to the issuance of shares of a class, the preferences, limitations, and relative rights of that class must be described in the articles of incorporation. All shares of a class must have preferences, limitations, and relative rights identical with those of other shares of the same class except to the extent otherwise permitted by section 6.02. . . .

§6.03. Issued and Outstanding Shares.

(a) A corporation may issue the number of shares of each class or series authorized by the articles of incorporation. Shares that are issued are outstanding shares until they are reacquired, redeemed, converted, or cancelled.

(**b**) The reacquisition, redemption, or conversion of outstanding shares is subject to the limitations of subsection (c) of this section and to section 6.40.

(**c**) At all times that shares of the corporation are outstanding, one or more shares that together have unlimited voting rights and one or more shares that together are entitled to receive the net assets of the corporation upon dissolution must be outstanding. . . .

§6.20. Subscription for Shares before Incorporation.

(**a**) A subscription for shares entered into before incorporation is irrevocable for six months unless the subscription agreement provides a longer or shorter period or all the subscribers agree to revocation. . . .

§6.21. Issuance of Shares.

(**a**) The powers granted in this section to the board of directors may be reserved to the shareholders by the articles of incorporation.

(**b**) The board of directors may authorize shares to be issued for consideration consisting of any tangible or intangible property or benefit to the corporation, including cash, promissory notes, services performed, contracts for services to be performed, or other securities of the corporation. . . .

§6.22. Liability of Shareholders.

(**a**) A purchaser from a corporation of its own shares is not liable to the corporation or its creditors with respect to the shares except to pay the consideration for which the shares were authorized to be issued (section 6.21) or specified in the subscription agreement (section 6.20).

(**b**) Unless otherwise provided in the articles of incorporation, a shareholder of a corporation is not personally liable for the acts or debts of the corporation except that he may become personally liable by reason of his own acts or conduct. . . .

§6.27. Restriction on Transfer of Shares and Other Securities.

(**a**) The articles of incorporation, bylaws, an agreement among shareholders, or an agreement between shareholders and the corporation may impose restrictions on the transfer or registration of transfer of shares of the corporation. A restriction does not affect shares issued before the restriction was adopted unless the holders of the shares are parties to the restriction agreement or voted in favor of the restriction.

(**b**) A restriction on the transfer or registration of transfer of shares is valid and enforceable against the holder or a transferee of the holder if the restriction is authorized by this section and its existence is noted conspicuously on the front or back of the certificate or is contained in the information statement required by section 6.26(b). Unless so noted, a restriction is not enforceable against a person without knowledge of the restriction. . . .

§6.30. Shareholders' Preemptive Rights.

(**a**) The shareholders of a corporation do not have a preemptive right to acquire the corporation's unissued shares except to the extent the articles of incorporation so provide. . . .

§6.31. Corporation's Acquisition of Its Own Shares.

(**a**) A corporation may acquire its own shares and shares so acquired constitute authorized but unissued shares.

(**b**) If the articles of incorporation prohibit the reissue of acquired shares, the number of authorized shares is reduced by the number of shares acquired, effective upon amendment of the articles of incorporation. . . .

§6.40. Distributions to Shareholders.

(**a**) A board of directors may authorize and the corporation may make distributions to its shareholders subject to restriction by the articles of incorporation and the limitation in subsection (c).

(**b**) If the board of directors does not fix the record date for determining shareholders entitled to a distribution (other than one involving a repurchase or reacquisition of shares), it is the date the board of directors authorizes the distribution.

(**c**) No distribution may be made if, after giving it effect:

(**1**) the corporation would not be able to pay its debts as they become due in the usual course of business; or

(**2**) the corporation's total assets would be less than the sum of its total liabilities plus (unless the articles of incorporation permit otherwise) the amount that would be needed, if the corporation were to be dissolved at the time of the distribution, to satisfy the preferential rights upon dissolution of shareholders whose preferential rights are superior to those receiving the distribution. . . .

(**f**) A corporation's indebtedness to a shareholder incurred by reason of a distribution made in accordance with this section is at parity with the corporation's indebtedness to its general, unsecured creditors except to the extent subordinated by agreement.

§7.01. Annual Meeting.

(a) A corporation shall hold a meeting of shareholders annually at a time stated in or fixed in accordance with the bylaws.

(b) Annual shareholders' meetings may be held in or out of this state at the place stated in or fixed in accordance with the bylaws. If no place is stated in or fixed in accordance with the bylaws, annual meetings shall be held at the corporation's principal office.

(c) The failure to hold an annual meeting at the time stated in or fixed in accordance with a corporation's bylaws does not affect the validity of any corporate action.

§7.02. Special Meeting.

(a) A corporation shall hold a special meeting of shareholders:

> (1) on call of its board of directors of the person or persons authorized to do so by the articles of incorporation or bylaws; or
>
> (2) if the holders of at least 10 percent of all the votes entitled to be cast on any issue proposed to be considered at the proposed special meeting sign, date, and deliver to the corporation's secretary one or more written demands for the meeting describing the purpose or purposes for which it is to be held. . . .

(d) Only business within the purpose or purposes described in the meeting notice required by section 7.05(c) may be conducted at a special shareholders' meeting.

§7.03. Court-Ordered Meeting.

(a) The [name or describe] court of the county where a corporation's principal office (or, if none in this state, its registered office) is located may summarily order a meeting to be held:

> (1) on application of any shareholder of the corporation entitled to participate in an annual meeting if an annual meeting was not held within the earlier of 6 months after the end of the corporation's fiscal year or 15 months after its last annual meeting; . . .

§7.04. Action without Meeting.

(a) Action required or permitted by this Act to be taken at a shareholders' meeting may be taken without a meeting if the action is taken by all the shareholders entitled to vote on the action. The action must be evidenced by one or more written consents describing the action taken, signed by all the shareholders entitled to vote on the action, and delivered to the corporation for inclusion in the minutes or filing with the corporate records. . . .

§7.05. Notice of Meeting.

(a) A corporation shall notify shareholders of the date, time, and place of each annual and special shareholders' meeting no fewer than 10 nor more than 60 days before the meeting date. Unless this Act or the articles of incorporation require otherwise, the corporation is required to give notice only to shareholders entitled to vote at the meeting.

(b) Unless this Act or the articles of incorporation require otherwise, notice of an annual meeting need not include a description of the purpose or purposes for which the meeting is called.

(c) Notice of a special meeting must include a description of the purpose or purposes for which the meeting is called. . . .

§7.06. Waiver of Notice.

(a) A shareholder may waive any notice required by this Act, the articles of incorporation, or bylaws before or after the date and time stated in the notice. The waiver must be in writing, be signed by the shareholder entitled to the notice, and be delivered to the corporation for inclusion in the minutes or filing with the corporate records.

(b) A shareholder's attendance at a meeting:

> (1) waives objection to lack of notice or defective notice of the meeting, unless the shareholder at the beginning of the meeting objects to holding the meeting or transacting business at the meeting;
>
> (2) waives objection to consideration of a particular matter at the meeting that is not within the purpose or purposes described in the meeting notice, unless the shareholder objects to considering the matter when it is presented. . . .

§7.20. Shareholders' List for Meeting. . . .

(b) The shareholders' list must be available for inspection by any shareholder, beginning two business days after notice of the meeting is given for which the list was prepared and continuing through the meeting, at the corporation's principal office or at a place identified in the meeting notice in the city where the meeting will be held. A shareholder, his agent, or attorney is entitled on written demand to inspect and, subject to the requirements of section 16.02(c), to copy the list, during regular business hours and at his expense, during the period it is available for inspection.

(c) The corporation shall make the shareholders' list available at the meeting, and any shareholder, his agent, or attorney is entitled to inspect the list at any time during the meeting or any adjournment. . . .

§7.22. **Proxies.**

(a) A shareholder may vote his shares in person or by proxy.

(b) A shareholder may appoint a proxy to vote or otherwise act for him by signing an appointment form, either personally or by his attorney-in-fact.

(c) An appointment of a proxy is effective when received by the secretary or other officer or agent authorized to tabulate votes. An appointment is valid for 11 months unless a longer period is expressly provided in the appointment form.

(d) An appointment of a proxy is revocable by the shareholder unless the appointment form conspicuously states that it is irrevocable and the appointment is coupled with an interest. . . .

§7.25. **Quorum and Voting Requirements for Voting Groups.**

(a) Shares entitled to vote as a separate voting group may take action on a matter at a meeting only if a quorum of those shares exists with respect to that matter. Unless the articles of incorporation or this Act provides otherwise, a majority of the votes entitled to be cast on the matter by the voting group constitutes a quorum of that voting group for action on that matter.

(b) Once a share is represented for any purpose at a meeting, it is deemed present for quorum purposes for the remainder of the meeting and for any adjournment of that meeting unless a new record date is or must be set for that adjourned meeting. . . .

§7.27. **Greater Quorum or Voting Requirements.**

(a) The articles of incorporation may provide for a greater quorum or voting requirement for shareholders (or voting groups of shareholders) than is provided for by this Act. . . .

§7.28. **Voting for Directors; Cumulative Voting.**

(a) Unless otherwise provided in the articles of incorporation, directors are elected by a plurality of the votes cast by the shares entitled to vote in the election at a meeting at which a quorum is present.

(b) Shareholders do not have a right to cumulate their votes for directors unless the articles of incorporation so provide. . . .

§7.30. **Voting Trusts.**

(a) One or more shareholders may create a voting trust, conferring on a trustee the right to vote or otherwise act for them, by signing an agreement setting out the provisions of the trust (which may include anything consistent with its purpose) and transferring their shares to the trustee. When a voting trust agreement is signed, the trustee shall prepare a list of the names and addresses of all owners of beneficial interests in the trust, together with the number and class of shares each transferred to the trust, and deliver copies of the list and agreement to the corporation's principal office. . . .

§8.01. **Requirement for and Duties of Board of Directors.**

(a) Except as provided in subsection (c), each corporation must have a board of directors.

(b) All corporate powers shall be exercised by or under the authority of, and the business and affairs of the corporation managed under the direction of, its board of directors, subject to any limitation set forth in the articles of incorporation.

(c) A corporation having 50 or fewer shareholders may dispense with or limit the authority of a board of directors by describing in its articles of incorporation who will perform some or all of the duties of a board of directors. . . .

§8.03. **Number and Election of Directors.**

(a) A board of directors must consist of one or more individuals, with the number specified in or fixed in accordance with the articles of incorporation or bylaws. . . .

(d) Directors are elected at the first annual shareholders' meeting and at each annual meeting thereafter unless their terms are staggered under section 8.06. . . .

§8.08. **Removal of Directors by Shareholders.**

(a) The shareholders may remove one or more directors with or without cause unless the articles of incorporation provide that directors may be removed only for cause. . . .

§8.10. **Vacancy on Board.**

(a) Unless the articles of incorporation provide otherwise, if a vacancy occurs on a board of directors, including a vacancy resulting from an increase in the number of directors:

(1) the shareholders may fill the vacancy;

(2) the board of directors may fill the vacancy; or

(3) if the directors remaining in office constitute fewer than a quorum of the board, they may fill the vacancy by the affirmative vote of a majority of all the directors remaining in office. . . .

§8.11. Compensation of Directors. Unless the articles of incorporation or bylaws provide otherwise, the board of directors may fix the compensation of directors.

§8.20. Meetings.

(a) The board of directors may hold regular or special meetings in or out of this state.

(b) Unless the articles of incorporation or bylaws provide otherwise, the board of directors may permit any or all directors to participate in a regular or special meeting by, or conduct the meeting through the use of, any means of communication by which all directors participating may simultaneously hear each other during the meeting. A director participating in a meeting by this means is deemed to be present in person at the meeting.

§8.21. Action without Meeting.

(a) Unless the articles of incorporation or bylaws provide otherwise, action required or permitted by this Act to be taken at a board of directors' meeting may be taken without a meeting if the action is taken by all members of the board. The action must be evidenced by one or more written consents describing the action taken, signed by each director, and included in the minutes or filed with the corporate records reflecting the action taken.

(b) Action taken under this section is effective when the last director signs the consent, unless the consent specifies a different effective date.

(c) A consent signed under this section has the effect of a meeting vote and may be described as such in any document. . . .

§8.23. Waiver of Notice.

(a) A director may waive any notice required by this Act, the articles of incorporation, or bylaws before or after the date and time stated in the notice. Except as provided by subsection (b), the waiver must be in writing, signed by the director entitled to the notice, and filed with the minutes or corporate records.

(b) A director's attendance at or participation in a meeting waives any required notice to him of the meeting unless the director at the beginning of the meeting (or promptly upon his arrival) objects to holding the meeting or transacting business at the meeting and does not thereafter vote for or assent to action taken at the meeting.

§8.24. Quorum and Voting.

(a) Unless the articles of incorporation or bylaws require a greater number, a quorum of a board of directors consists of:

(1) a majority of the fixed number of directors if the corporation has a fixed board size: . . .

§8.30. General Standards for Directors.

(a) A director shall discharge his duties as a director, including his duties as a member of a committee:

(1) in good faith;

(2) with the care an ordinarily prudent person in a like position would exercise under similar circumstances; and

(3) in a manner he reasonably believes to be in the best interests of the corporation.

(b) In discharging his duties a director is entitled to rely on information, opinions, reports, or statements, including financial statements and other financial data, if prepared or presented by:

(1) one or more officers or employees of the corporation whom the director reasonably believes to be reliable and competent in the matters presented;

(2) legal counsel, public accountants, or other persons as to matters the director reasonably believes are within the person's professional or expert competence; or

(3) a committee of the board of directors of which he is not a member if the director reasonably believes the committee merits confidence.

(c) A director is not acting in good faith if he has knowledge concerning the matter in question that makes reliance otherwise permitted by subsection (b) unwarranted.

(d) A director is not liable for any action taken as a director, or any failure to take any action, if he performed the duties of his office in compliance with this section.

§8.31. Director Conflict of Interest.

(a) A conflict of interest transaction is a transaction with the corporation in which a director of the corporation has a direct or indirect interest. A conflict of interest transaction is not voidable by the corporation solely because of the director's interest in the transaction if any one of the following is true:

(1) the material facts of the transaction and the director's interest were disclosed or known to the board of directors or a committee of the board of directors and the board of directors or committee authorized, approved, or ratified the transaction;

(2) the material facts of the transaction and the director's interest were disclosed or known to the shareholders entitled to vote and they authorized, approved, or ratified the transaction; or

(3) the transaction was fair to the corporation. . . .

§8.33. Liability for Unlawful Distributions.

(a) Unless he complies with the applicable standards of conduct described in section 8.30, a director who votes for or assents to a distribution made in violation of this Act or the articles of incorporation is personally liable to the corporation for the amount of the distribution that exceeds what could have been distributed without violating this Act or the articles of incorporation.

(b) A director held liable for an unlawful distribution under subsection (a) is entitled to contribution:

(1) from every other director who voted for or assented to the distribution without complying with the applicable standards of conduct described in section 8.30; and

(2) from each shareholder for the amount the shareholder accepted knowing the distribution was made in violation of this Act or the articles of incorporation.

§8.40. Required Officers.

(a) A corporation has the officers described in its bylaws or appointed by the board of directors in accordance with the bylaws. . . .

§8.41. Duties of Officers.
Each officer has the authority and shall perform the duties set forth in the bylaws or, to the extent consistent with the bylaws, the duties prescribed by the board of directors or by direction of an officer authorized by the board of directors to prescribe the duties of other officers.

§8.42. Standards of Conduct for Officers [*See Section 8.30. Same standards.*]

§8.43. Resignation and Removal of Officers.

(a) An officer may resign at any time by delivering notice to the corporation.

(b) A board of directors may remove any officer at any time with or without cause. . . .

§10.01. Authority to Amend Articles of Incorporation.

(a) A corporation may amend its articles of incorporation at any time. . . .

§10.03. Amendment by Board of Directors and Shareholders.

(a) A corporation's board of directors may propose one or more amendments to the articles of incorporation for submission to the shareholders.

(b) For the amendment to be adopted:

(1) the board of directors must recommend the amendment to the shareholders unless the board of directors determines that because of conflict of interest or other special circumstances it should make no recommendation and communicates the basis for its determination to the shareholders with the amendment; and

(2) the shareholders entitled to vote on the amendment must approve the amendment as provided in subsection (e). . . .

§10.20. Amendment of Bylaws by Board of Directors or Shareholders.

(a) A corporation's board of directors may amend or repeal the corporation's bylaws unless:

(1) the articles of incorporation or this Act reserve this power exclusively to the shareholders in whole or part; or

(2) the shareholders in amending or repealing a particular bylaw provide expressly that the board of directors may not amend or repeal that bylaw.

(b) A corporation's shareholders may amend or repeal the corporation's bylaws even though the bylaws may also be amended or repealed by its board of directors. . . .

§11.03. Action on Plan.

(a) After adopting a plan of merger or share exchange, the board of directors of each corporation party to the merger, and the board of directors of the corporation whose shares will be acquired in the share exchange, shall submit the plan of merger . . . for approval by its shareholders.

(b) For a plan of merger or share exchange to be approved:

(1) the board of directors must recommend the plan of merger or share exchange to the share-

holders, unless the board of directors determines that because of conflict of interest or other special circumstances it should make no recommendation and communicates the basis for its determination to the shareholders with the plan; and

(**2**) the shareholders entitled to vote must approve the plan. . . .

§11.04. Merger of Subsidiary.

(**a**) A parent corporation owning at least 90 percent of the outstanding shares of each class of a subsidiary corporation may merge the subsidiary into itself without approval of the shareholders of the parent or subsidiary. . . .

§12.01. Sale of Assets in Regular Course of Business and Mortgage of Assets.

(**a**) A corporation may, on the terms and conditions and for the consideration determined by the board of directors:

(**1**) sell, lease, exchange, or otherwise dispose of all, or substantially all, of its property in the usual and regular course of business; . . .

(**b**) Unless the articles of incorporation require it, approval by the shareholders of a transaction described in subsection (a) is not required.

§12.02. Sale of Assets Other than in Regular Course of Business.

(**a**) A corporation may sell, lease, exchange, or otherwise dispose of all, or substantially all, of its property (with or without the goodwill), otherwise than in the usual and regular course of business, on the terms and conditions and for the consideration determined by the corporation's board of directors, if the board of directors proposes and its shareholders approve the proposed transaction.

(**b**) For a transaction to be authorized:

(**1**) the board of directors must recommend the proposed transaction to the shareholders unless the board of directors determines that because of conflict of interest or other special circumstances it should make no recommendation and communicates the basis for its determination to the shareholders with the submission of the proposed transaction; and

(**2**) the shareholders entitled to vote must approve the transaction. . . .

§14.02. Dissolution by Board of Directors and Shareholders.

(**a**) A corporation's board of directors may propose dissolution for submission to the shareholders.

(**b**) For a proposal to dissolve to be adopted:

(**1**) the board of directors must recommend dissolution to the shareholders unless the board of directors determines that because of conflict of interest or other special circumstances it should make no recommendation and communicates the basis for its determination to the shareholders; and

(**2**) the shareholders entitled to vote must approve the proposal to dissolve as provided in subsection (e). . . .

§16.01. Corporate Records.

(**a**) A corporation shall keep as permanent records minutes of all meetings of its shareholders and board of directors, a record of all actions taken by the shareholders or board of directors without a meeting, and a record of all actions taken by a committee of the board of directors in place of the board of directors on behalf of the corporation. . . .

§16.02. Inspection of Records by Shareholders.

(**a**) A shareholder of a corporation is entitled to inspect and copy, during regular business hours at the corporation's principal office, any of the records of the corporation described in section 16.01(e) if he gives the corporation written notice of his demand at least five business days before the date on which he wishes to inspect and copy.

(**b**) a shareholder of a corporation is entitled to inspect and copy, during regular business hours at a reasonable location specified by the corporation, any of the following records of the corporation if the shareholder meets the requirements of subsection (c) and gives the corporation written notice of his demand at least five business days before the date on which he wishes to inspect and copy: . . .

§16.03. Scope of Inspection Right.

(**a**) A shareholder's agent or attorney has the same inspection and copying rights as the shareholder he represents.

(**b**) The right to copy records under section 16.02 includes, if reasonable, the right to receive copies made by photographic, xerographic, or other means.

(**c**) The corporation may impose a reasonable charge, covering the costs of labor and material, for copies of any documents provided to the shareholder. The charge may not exceed the estimated cost of production or reproduction of the records. . . .

The Constitution of the United States of America (Excerpts)

Preamble

We the People of the United States, in Order to form a more perfect Union, establish Justice, insure domestic Tranquility, provide for the common defence, promote the general Welfare, and secure the Blessings of Liberty to ourselves and our Posterity, do ordain and establish this Constitution for the United States of America. . . .

Article I
Section 8.

(1) The Congress shall have Power To lay and collect Taxes, Duties, Imposts and Excises, to pay the Debts and provide for the common Defence and general Welfare of the United States; but all Duties, Imposts and Excises shall be uniform throughout the United States;

(2) To borrow money on the credit of the United States;

(3) To regulate Commerce with foreign Nations, and among the several States, and with the Indian Tribes;

(4) To establish an uniform Rule of Naturalization, and uniform Laws on the subject of Bankruptcies throughout the United States;

(5) To coin Money, regulate the Value thereof, and of foreign Coin, and fix the Standard of Weights and Measures;

(6) To provide for the Punishment of counterfeiting the Securities and current Coin of the United States;

(7) To Establish Post Offices and Post Roads;

(8) To promote the Progress of Science and useful Arts, by securing for limited Times to Authors and Inventors the exclusive Right to their respective Writings and Discoveries;

(9) To constitute Tribunals inferior to the Supreme Court;

(10) To define and punish Piracies and Felonies committed on the high Seas, and Offenses against the Law of Nations;

(11) To declare War, grant Letters of Marque and Reprisal, and make Rules concerning Captures on Land and Water;

(12) To raise and support Armies, but no Appropriation of Money to that Use shall be for a longer Term than two Years;

(13) To provide and maintain a Navy;

(14) To make Rules for the Government and Regulation of the land and naval Forces;

(15) To provide for calling forth the Militia to execute the Laws of the Union, suppress Insurrections and repel Invasions;

(16) To provide for organizing, arming, and disciplining, the Militia, and for governing such Part of them as may be employed in the Service of the United States, reserving to the States respectively, the Appointment of the Officers, and the Authority of training the Militia according to the discipline prescribed by Congress;

(17) To exercise exclusive Legislation in all Cases whatsoever, over such District (not exceeding ten Miles square) as may, by Cession of particular States, and the Acceptance of Congress, become the Seat of the Government of the United States, and to exercise like Authority over all Places purchased by the Consent of the Legislature of the State in which the Same shall be, for the Erection of Forts, Magazines, Arsenals, dock-Yards, and other needful Buildings;—And

(18) To make all Laws which shall be necessary and proper for carrying into Execution the foregoing Powers, and all other Powers vested by this Constitution in the Government of the United States, or in any Department or Officer thereof.

Section 9.

(1) The Migration or Importation of Such Persons as any of the States now existing shall think proper

to admit, shall not be prohibited by the Congress prior to the Year one thousand eight hundred and eight, but a Tax or duty may be imposed on such Importation, not exceeding ten dollars for each Person.

(2) The privilege of the Writ of Habeas Corpus shall not be suspended, unless when in Cases of Rebellion or Invasion the public Safety may require it.

(3) No Bill of Attainder or *ex post facto* Law shall be passed.

(4) No Capitation, or other direct, Tax shall be laid, unless in Proportion to the Census or Enumeration herein before directed to be taken.

See also the Sixteenth Amendment.

(5) No Tax or Duty shall be laid on Articles exported from any State.

(6) No Preference shall be given by any Regulation of Commerce or Revenue to the Ports of one State over those of another; nor shall Vessels bound to, or from, one State be obliged to enter, clear, or pay Duties in another.

(7) No money shall be drawn from the Treasury, but in Consequence of Appropriations made by Law; and a regular Statement and Account of the Receipts and Expenditures of all public Money shall be published from time to time.

(8) No Title of Nobility shall be granted by the United States: And no Person holding any Office of Profit or Trust under them, shall, without the Consent of the Congress, accept of any present, Emolument, Office, or Title, or any kind whatever, from any King, Prince, or foreign State.

Section 10.

(1) No State shall enter into any Treaty, Alliance, or Confederation; grant Letters of Marque and Reprisal; coin Money; emit Bills of Credit; make any Thing but gold and silver Coin a Tender in Payment of Debts; pass any Bill of Attainder, *ex post facto* Law, or Law impairing the Obligation of Contracts, or grant any Title of Nobility.

(2) No State shall, without the Consent of the Congress, lay any Imposts or Duties on Imports or Exports, except what may be absolutely necessary for executing its inspection Laws: and the net Produce of all Duties and Imposts, laid by any State on Imports or Exports, shall be for the Use of the Treasury of the United States; and all such Laws shall be subject to the Revision and Control of the Congress.

(3) No State shall, without the Consent of Congress, lay any Duty of Tonnage, keep Troops, or Ships of War in time of Peace, enter into any Agreement or Compact with another State, or with a foreign Power, or engage in War, unless actually invaded, or in such imminent Danger as will not admit of delay. . . .

AMENDMENTS TO THE CONSTITUTION OF THE UNITED STATES

Amendment I [1791]

Congress shall make no law respecting an establishment of religion, or prohibiting the free exercise thereof; or abridging the freedom of speech, or of the press; or the right of the people peaceably to assemble, and to petition the Government for a redress of grievances.

Amendment IV [1791]

The right of the people to be secure in their persons, houses, papers, and effects, against unreasonable searches and seizures, shall not be violated, and no Warrants shall issue, but upon probable cause, supported by Oath or affirmation, and particularly describing the place to be searched, and the persons or things to be seized.

Amendment V [1791]

No person shall be held to answer for a capital, or otherwise infamous crime, unless on a presentment or indictment of a Grand Jury, except in cases arising in the land or naval forces, or in the Militia, when in actual service in time of War or public danger; nor shall any person be subject for the same offence to be twice put in jeopardy of life or limb, nor shall be compelled in any criminal case to be a witness against himself, nor be deprived of life, liberty, or property, without due process of law; nor shall private property be taken for public use, without just compensation.

Amendment VI [1791]

In all criminal prosecutions, the accused shall enjoy the right to a speedy and public trial, by an impartial jury of the State and district wherein the crime shall have been committed; which district shall have been previously ascertained by law, and to be informed of the nature and cause of the accusation; to be confronted with the witnesses against him; to have compulsory process for obtaining Witnesses in his favor, and to have the Assistance of Counsel for his defense. . . .

Amendment VIII [1791]

Excessive bail shall not be required, nor excessive fines imposed, nor cruel and unusual punishments inflicted. . . .

Amendment X [1791]

The powers not delegated to the United States by the Constitution, nor prohibited by it to the States, are reserved to the States respectively, or to the people. . . .

Amendment XIII [1865]

Section 1.   Neither slavery nor involuntary servitude, except as a punishment for crime whereof the party shall have been duly convicted, shall exist within the United States, or any place subject to their jurisdiction.

Section 2.   Congress shall have power to enforce this article by appropriate legislation.

Amendment XIV [1868]

Section 1.   All persons born or naturalized in the United States, and subject to the jurisdiction thereof, are citizens of the United States and of the State wherein they reside. No State shall make or enforce any law which shall abridge the privileges or immunities of citizens of the United States; nor shall any State deprive any person of life, liberty, or property, without due process of law; nor deny to any person within its jurisdiction the equal protection of the laws. . . .

Glossary

This glossary is designed to be not only a source of definitions but also a means of identifying the chapters in which a term is most fully defined and discussed. Toward this end, most definitions include an indication in parentheses of where this discussion will be found.

Another distinguishing feature of this glossary is its grouping of terms under the common word contained in each. For example, under "contract" appear "bilateral contract," "unilateral contract," "contract implied in fact," and all other key terms containing the word "contract." Among the other words treated in this fashion are damages, fraud, goods, lien, negligence, and warranty.

A glossary is not a dictionary. It cannot include every term introduced in the text. Space limitations dictate that a glossary include only those terms which appear in more than one chapter or which are critically important to comprehension.

In developing the definitions for this book, and therefore for the glossary, the authors of course consulted the standard sources: *Black's Law Dictionary,* 5th ed., West Publishing Co., 1979; *Ballentine's Law Dictionary,* 3d ed., Lawyers Co-op/Bancroft Whitney, 1969; several Restatements of the Law; and the various uniform acts.

In addition, the authors regularly looked to the *American Heritage Dictionary,* 2d ed., Houghton Mifflin, 1984; *Chambers Etymological English Dictionary,* new ed., Pyramid Books, 1966; *Cochran's Law Lexicon,* 5th ed., Anderson Publishing Company, 1977; S. Lee, *ABZs of Money and Finance,* Poseidon Press, 1988; *The Oxford Companion to Law,* Oxford University Press, 1980; *The Oxford English Dictionary,* Oxford University Press, 1971; *The Oxford Dictionary of English Etymology,* Oxford University Press, 1966; *Webster's New Collegiate Dictionary,* Merriam, 1980; and *Webster's New World Dictionary,* 2d college ed., Simon & Schuster, 1984.

Abandonment. See *Property.*

Abatement. Reduction.

Abrogate. To revoke or cancel.

Abstract of title. See *Title.*

Acceleration clause. A clause in a promissory note that permits the creditor to demand payment of the entire debt upon the debtor's failure to make scheduled payments or upon another material breach.

Accept. Under UCC Article 3, to promise to pay a draft.

Acceptance. (1) An offeree's manifestation of assent to an offer to form a contract. (2) Under UCC Article 2, the state which occurs when the buyer has possession of the goods and intends to own them or fails to reject them. (3) Under UCC Article 3 [UCC §3-410(1)], a signed notation on a draft that the drawee will honor it upon presentment for payment; a drawee's signed promise to honor a draft when it is presented in the future.

> **Means of acceptance.** The way in which the offeree accepts the offeror's proposal, including the mail, telegram, telephone, and the like; also referred to as the "medium of acceptance."

> **Revocation of acceptance.** Under UCC Article 2, an act by the buyer which voids an acceptance of goods.

Acceptor. A person who is designated to accept a draft.

Accommodation. Under UCC Article 2, the situation which arises when nonconforming goods are shipped to a buyer as a favor.

Accommodation parties. Sureties; persons who by cosigning an instrument agree to pay it if the maker or issuer does not.

Accord. An agreement to accept a substituted performance.

Accounting. A formal audit and report, ordered by a court, on the financial condition of a partnership; an equitable remedy compelling a party to account for profits which belong to another.

Acquittal. A formal discharge of a person charged with a crime.

Act. (1) A proposed law adopted by Congress or a state legislature. (2) Conduct; the term includes omissions, the failure to act when there is a duty to do so.

Action. A form of legal proceeding which takes place only in courts.

Actual malice. See *Malice*.

Actual notice. Direct notice, as by letter or a telephone call.

Addendum. An additional clause attached to an agreement.

Administrative agency. A division of the executive branch of government which is created by statute and granted defined powers to act.

Administrative law judge. An individual assigned to an administrative agency to make decisions in quasi-judicial proceedings.

Administrator. A personal representative appointed by a probate court to dispose of the estate of an intestate or a testator whose named executor has declined to serve. (Fem.: administratrix.)

Adverse action notice. Under the Women's Business Ownership Act of 1988, a written statement of the reasons for any denial of credit.

Adverse possession. The acquisition of legal title to real property of another by notorious, open, adverse and hostile possession of it for a period of time stipulated by state statute.

Affidavit. A written statement of fact made under oath.

Affirm. Uphold; the term used by appellate courts to indicate approval of a lower court's judgment.

After-acquired property. See *Property*.

Agent. Someone who represents another person, called a principal.

    General agent. An agent authorized to conduct a series of transactions over time.

    Insurance agent. A person authorized to sell insurance on behalf of an insurance company, the principal.

    Special agent. A person employed by a principal to conduct a single transaction or a limited series of transactions.

Agreement to discharge. A contract to terminate a prior, existing contract.

Answer. A response to a complaint which responds to each of the complaint's factual allegations and presents all legal defenses available to the defendant.

Antecedent debt. Past *consideration*.

Antenuptial agreement. A contract between two persons who are about to be married usually dealing with the disposition of property in the event of divorce or the death of one of the parties. See *Cohabitation agreement*.

Anticipatory breach. An act or statement before performance is due that clearly reveals an intent not to perform contractual duties.

Anticipatory repudiation. An anticipatory breach; under UCC Article 2, a party's unequivocal notice, either in words or by actions, that the party does not intend to perform when performance is due.

Appellant. A person appealing a final order of a lower court or administrative agency to a higher court.

Appellee. The party who defends a lower court's or administrative agency's final order in a higher court.

Appraisal. Under the MBCA, the right of minority shareholders to have the corporation purchase their shares at an appraised price.

Arbitration. The referral of a dispute to an impartial third party—an arbitrator—whose decision the parties have agreed will bind them.

Articles of incorporation. A document filed with the secretary of state that describes a corporation's organization, powers, and authority.

Articles of partnership. A written partnership agreement.

Assault. An act by a defendant which puts a plaintiff in fear of an imminent *battery*.

Assignee. The person to whom an assignment is made.

Assignment. A transfer of an existing contractual right from a party to a contract to a third party.

> **Assignment for the benefit of creditors.** An arrangement by which a debtor voluntarily assigns all of his or her assets to a trustee to manage for his or her creditors' benefit.

Assignor. A person making an assignment.

Assumption of risk. In tort law, the principle that a party who knowingly takes on a risk of injury, loss, or damage may not recover from the party who would ordinarily be responsible.

Attachment. The process by which a creditor gains a secured interest in property of a debtor.

Auction. A method of sale in which an auctioneer invites offers, called bids, from prospective buyers.

Authority. An agent's legal ability to act for another.

> **Apparent authority.** That power to bind the principal which an agent has simply because of his or her agency status.
>
> **Emergency authority.** That authority to handle an emergency for a principal which the law presumes an agent for an employee has.
>
> **Express authority.** The authority a principal specifically grants an agent.
>
> **Implied authority.** Implementation authority; that authority necessary to carry out the express authority the principal grants the agent.
>
> **Renunciation of authority.** The means by which an agent terminates a relationship with a principal.
>
> **Revocation of authority.** The means by which a principal ends an agency relationship.

Bailee. The person who receives property for the purpose of a bailment; a person who by a warehouse receipt, bill of lading, or other document of title acknowledges possession of goods and contracts to deliver them [UCC §7-102(1)(a)].

Bailment. The act of one party, the bailor, giving goods to another, the bailee, to hold in storage.

Bailor. A person who bails property.

Bank. "Any person engaged in the business of banking" [UCC §1-201(4)]; a business—virtually always a corporation—that takes money on deposit, cashes checks and drafts, makes loans, issues promissory notes, and performs similar functions.

> **Collecting bank.** A bank other than a payor bank that handles an item (for example, a check) for collection.
>
> **Depositary bank.** The bank where the check is deposited—that is, "cashed."
>
> **Intermediary bank.** A bank through which a check passes on its way from the depositary bank to the payor bank; "any bank to which an item is transferred in course of collection except the depositary or payor bank" [UCC §4-105(c)].
>
> **Payor bank.** The bank that is the drawee of a check.
>
> **Presenting bank.** The intermediary bank that presents the check to the payor bank.

Battery. An intentional, unauthorized contact with any part of another's body or anything attached to it or identified with it.

Bearer paper. Commercial paper payable to the person who has physical possession of it.

Beneficial interest. A trust beneficiary's right to income or principal under a trust.

Beneficiary. One who benefits from another's act; a person with a present or future beneficial interest in a trust.

> **Creditor beneficiary.** A third party beneficiary who benefits from a contract as a result of a party to the contract wishing to satisfy a debt or meet a duty to the beneficiary.
>
> **Intended beneficiary.** A third party beneficiary whom the parties to a contract intend to benefit.
>
> **Third party beneficiary.** A stranger to a contract who stands to benefit from it in some way.
>
> **Unintended beneficiary.** A third party who may benefit under a contract but whom the parties do not intend to benefit.

Bequest. A gift made by will.

Bill of lading. A document evidencing a carrier's receipt of goods for shipment and stating the terms of the transportation contract; if negotiable, a document of title.

Blank indorsement. See *Indorsement*.

Blue sky law. Refers to state laws concerning the issuance of new securities within that state.

Bona fide purchaser. A ''good faith'' purchaser; one who buys an item for value and without knowledge or notice of any defense; under UCC Article 8, a good faith purchaser of securities who takes them free of certain types of adverse claims.

Bond. A long-term debt security secured by particular assets of the issuer.

Breach. A violation of a duty.

> **Breach of contract.** A violation of a duty established solely by a contract; any failure to perform the terms of a contract without legal excuse.

Brief. A memorandum containing legal arguments.

Broker-dealer. Under the Securities Exchange Act of 1934, a person who deals in securities issued by others.

Bulk transfer. The sale of all or a major part of a merchant's inventory not in the ordinary course of the merchant's business [UCC §6-102(1)].

Burden of persuasion. The duty of a party to a lawsuit to prove its case. Upon the plaintiff's establishing a prima facie case of liability, the burden shifts to the defendant.

Burden of proof. A party's obligation to establish that the evidence in its favor is more convincing than the evidence that the other party offers.

Business judgment rule. Rule which immunizes directors and officers of corporations from liability when performing their duties in good faith and exercising due care.

Buy-out provision. A provision in articles of incorporation requiring a shareholder wishing to sell stock to offer it first to either the remaining shareholders proportionally or the corporation.

Bylaws. Rules for the internal governance of a corporation.

Cancellation. An act by which a party terminates a contract because of another party's breach.

Capacity. A person's ability to comprehend and understand contractual obligations.

Capital contribution. The amount of property or cash or both provided in exchange for a partnership interest or shares of stock in a corporation.

Carrier. The UCC's term for a *common carrier*.

Cause of action. A claim recognized by the courts as warranting relief, if proven.

Cease and desist order. An order by a judge directing a party to immediately stop doing an act or action.

CERCLA. The Comprehensive Environmental Response, Compensation and Liability Act. CERCLA applies to environmental waste.

Certificate of deposit (CD). A promissory note from a bank (the maker) to a customer (the payee).

Certificate of incorporation. A document issued by a secretary of state that signifies that a corporation has come into existence.

Certificate of limited partnership. A document filed with the secretary of state which brings a limited partnership into existence.

Certified check. A check accepted by a bank for later payment.

Chain of title. The history of ownership of a particular piece of property.

Chattel. Personal property.

> **Chattel mortgage.** A document by which a debtor gives a creditor a security interest in personal property; the common law device on which UCC Article 9's security agreement is based.

> **Chattel paper.** Combined promissory notes and security agreements, commonly used in retail consumer credit sales.

Check. A draft whose drawee is a bank.

> **Stale check.** A check presented for payment more than 6 months after the date on its face.

Circuit. The territorial jurisdiction of certain courts, usually appellate.

> **Circuit court.** (1) A court that hears cases drawn from a circuit. (2) In state systems, a proper name for either a trial court of general jurisdiction or a court of appeals. (3) In the federal system, an archaic term for a U.S. court of appeals.

Circumstantial evidence. Evidence based not on actual personal knowledge but on facts from which a conclusion may be drawn.

Citizens' suits. Suits brought by private persons to enforce an administrative agency's enabling act or brought against the agency to compel it to enforce its enabling act.

Civil law. All law which is not criminal.

Civil law legal system. The legal system based on Roman law that today predominates in continental Europe as well as Asian, African, and Latin American countries colonized by Spain, France, Portugal, and the Netherlands. The sources of law are codes, statutes, and regulations, but not judicial decisions.

Class action. A procedural device allowing one member of a class to litigate a claim in one action on behalf of numerous persons with common interests.

Clerk of court. A court's administrator, the person in charge of the filing of all documents.

Close corporation. See *Corporation*.

C.O.D. "Cash on delivery"; a delivery term requiring payment on delivery; usually before inspecting the goods.

Codicil. An addendum to an existing will.

Cohabiting. Living together, usually used in the sense of persons of different sexes living together in a sexual relationship without being married.

Cohabitation agreements. Contracts defining the property rights of *cohabiting* parties.

Collateral. Property designated as security for a loan; property which secures an obligation.

Collecting bank. See *Bank*.

Commerce clause. Article 1 §8(3) of the U.S. Constitution. It is the basis for federal regulation of activity between states or affecting interstate commerce.

Commercial impracticability. A term used in UCC Article 2 to describe a business situation in which radically changed circumstances cause one party to a contract a substantial and unjust loss.

Commercial paper. Short-term debt securities.

Commercially reasonable. As used in UCC Article 2, a term meaning that every facet of a sale—including the method, manner, time, place, and terms—must be appropriate.

Commingling. Mixing; the mixing of a principal's funds with an agent's.

Common carrier. A corporation licensed by the government to provide transportation services to the public.

Common law. (1) A body of judge-made law whose origins date to the fourteenth century in England. (2) What the law was on a particular point before it was superseded by statutes. (3) The process by which courts look to earlier judicial decisions for guidance in deciding cases before them. (Chapter 1)

Common stock. See *Stock*.

Compensatory damages. See *Damages*.

Complaint. A short, plain statement notifying the defendant of the plaintiff's cause of action and the relief demanded.

Composition agreement. A private agreement between a debtor's creditors for the repayment of the debtor's debt over time.

Condition. A provision in a contract, will, or deed which limits or modifies rights or duties.

> **Concurrent conditions.** In contracts, the normal situation, in which each party's obligation depends on the other's performance.
>
> **Condition precedent.** An event or circumstance which must occur or exist before either party must perform a contract.
>
> **Condition subsequent.** A condition of a contract which terminates contractual obligations if a specified event occurs.
>
> **Express condition.** A condition stated in words in a contract.
>
> **Presupposed conditions.** Expectations which are fundamental to a sales contract but which are not routine business concerns; events which the parties assume would not happen and whose occurrence voids the contract [UCC §2-615].

Conditional sales contract. See *Contract*.

Conduct. In torts, a particular action or omission which breaches the defendant's legal duty.

Conforming goods. Goods which meets a sales contract's specifications.

Confusion. A situation in which two or more owners' goods are so mixed together that it is not possible to separate them and restore them to their owners.

Conscious parallelism. An argument by an anti-trust plaintiff that, though an overt agreement among the defendants is unprovable, the circumstantial evidence of action by competitors in the same market is so closely parallel that it points to the likelihood of an agreement.

Consent. A factual defense to an intentional tort which negates the tortious character of an act on the grounds that the plaintiff agreed to submit to the act.

Consent decree or judgment. A judgment, which lacks precedential value, entered by the agreement of the parties and with the approval of the court, resolving an action brought by the government against an individual in business.

Consequential damages. See *Damages*.

Consideration. The legal value for which each party to a contract bargains.

Consignee. (1) Under UCC Article 2, a merchant receiving goods on consignment. (2) A person to whose order a bill of lading promises delivery.

Consignment. (1) Under UCC Article 2, the placing of goods with a merchant who has agreed to act as the seller's agent in selling them. (2) A contract to ship goods by common carrier.

Consignor. (1) A person who makes a consignment. (2) A bailor who contracts to have goods shipped by a common carrier.

Constitution. A written document establishing the relationship between a government and those it governs, and specifying the form the government will take.

Constructive notice. Legal notice; the presumption that a person has notice of what the public records or the legal notice column of a trade journal or newspaper contain.

Constructive trust. An equitable remedy imposed by a court on a constructive trustee requiring him or her to transfer to others property he or she wrongly acquired or holds.

Construe. To interpret.

Consumer. A natural person who engages in transactions involving money, property, or services primarily for personal, family, and household purposes.

Consumer goods. See *Goods*.

Contemporaneous traders. Persons who can show they bought or sold during the time of illegal trading activity by an insider.

Continuation statement. (1) An agreement between partners that the partnership business may continue after dissolution. (2) A renewal of a financing statement.

Contract. (n.) An agreement between two parties which creates legal rights and duties and which is enforceable in a court of law; a promise or a set of promises that a court will enforce. (v.) To agree on a set of promises a court will enforce.

Bilateral contract. An exchange of one party's promise for the other party's promise.

Conditional contract. A contract in which performance depends on an event or circumstance happening or not happening.

Conditional sales contract. A contract for the sale of goods in which the seller retains title but not possession until the buyer completes payment for the goods.

Destination contract. Under UCC Article 2, a contract for the sale of goods in which the seller's duty is to deliver conforming goods to a particular place.

Executed contract. A contract which the parties have fully performed.

Executory contract. A contract which the parties have not yet performed.

Express contract. A contract whose terms are actually stated, whether orally or in writing.

Formal contract. A contract that by law must be written in a particular form with certain characteristics in order to be enforceable.

Contract implied in fact. A contract which is not expressly stated, but whose existence a court implies from the facts, circumstances, and the parties' conduct.

Contract implied by law. An obligation imposed by a court to do justice between the parties, even though the parties have never exchanged, or intended to exchange, promises.

Informal contract. A contract that is not required by law to have a particular form.

Option contract. A contract which keeps open an offer to contract for a specified period.

Output contract. An agreement to sell all production of a specified item, if any, during a specified period to a particular buyer.

Requirements contract. An agreement to buy all goods of a specified type needed during a specified period from a particular seller.

Shipment contract. Under UCC Article 2, a contract which requires the seller to make a contract for shipment with a carrier and to deliver the goods to the carrier, at which point the risk of loss shifts to the buyer.

Unilateral contract. A contract in which the offeror has specified a particular action as the acceptance he or she wants.

Contributory negligence. See *Negligence.*

Control. In corporate law, the ability of a shareholder or group of shareholders to run a corporation.

Control premium. The additional value per share of that quantity of shares which gives the purchaser the power to control a corporation.

Controlled persons. Persons who work directly for a *controlling person*, including financial advisors, brokers, and the like.

Controlling person. Under the Securities Act of 1933, a person who can greatly influence decisions of a corporation, regardless of the amount of stock in the corporation he or she holds.

Conversion. A tortious act by which a defendant deals with the plaintiff's goods in a manner inconsistent with the plaintiff's ownership.

Convertible. Exchangeable for stock.

Conveyance. A transfer of title to property.

Copyright. The exclusive right accorded to persons (and their heirs) who create works, like books or films or works of art, to publish their works and to determine who else may publish them.

Corporation. A form of business which comes into existence when, upon an application by one or more persons, the secretary of state of a state issues a certificate of incorporation and whose owners' liability for its debts ordinarily is limited to the amount of their investment.

Close corporation. A small corporation, usually with less than fifty shareholders.

Foreign corporation. A corporation incorporated under laws of another state.

For-profit corporation. A private corporation generally engaged in a business.

Nonprofit corporation. A corporation not organized to make profits.

Privately held corporation. A corporation whose stock is not publicly traded.

Professional corporation. A corporation whose shareholders have joined together to offer legal, medical, architectural, or other professional services.

Public corporation. A corporation created by an act of Congress or of a state legislature.

Publicly traded corporation. A corporation whose stock or debt or both is bought and sold on a stock exchange.

Quasi-public or public service corporation. A private, for-profit corporation which receives privileges from the government in return for providing special services to the public; a public utility.

Subchapter S corporation. A corporation which has elected to be taxed as a partnership under the federal tax laws.

Cosurety. One of two or more persons who serve as sureties for the same debt to the same creditor.

Counterclaim. A cause of action a defendant has against the plaintiff, which is stated in the answer and arises out of the same facts that give rise to the complaint.

Counteroffer. See *Offer.*

Course of dealing. A pattern of prior dealings between the same parties; previous conduct between the parties which a court may regard as establishing a common basis of understanding for interpreting their writings and other conduct [UCC §1-205(1)].

Course of performance. The conduct of two contracting parties over past contractual relationships.

Court. A unit of the judicial system; a tribunal. (2) An individual judge.

Court of appeals. Intermediate appellate courts, except in New York and Maryland, where the term describes the supreme courts.

Covenant. A promise; a contract; a clause in a contract.

Implied covenant of good faith and fair dealing. The most liberal exception to the employment at will doctrine, which holds an employer has a duty of good faith to an employee and, as a corollary, a duty not to terminate an employee unjustly.

Restrictive covenant. A clause in a contract which directly restrains one party's ability to compete with the other.

Cover. Under the UCC, it is the buyer's right to purchase substitute goods upon the breach or anticipated breach by the seller.

Creditor beneficiary. See *Beneficiary*.

Crime. A breach of a statutorily defined duty to society punishable in an action brought by a government unit.

> **White collar crime.** Illegal acts in a business context committed by means of concealment or guile and usually without threat or force.

Criminal law. Law which defines the duties citizens owe to society and prescribes penalties for violations.

Cross-examination. Examination of a witness by counsel for the party opposed to the party that offers the witness's testimony as evidence.

Culpability. Blameworthiness.

Cumulative voting. Scheme devised to provide for minority representation on corporate boards of directors.

Cure. Under UCC Article 2, the seller's right to remedy a nonconforming tender of goods without liability for breaching the contract.

Customer. Under UCC Article 9, the drawer of a check.

Damage. The loss, harm, or hurt which results from an injury.

Damages. A monetary valuation, made by a court, of the effects of a party's injury.

> **Compensatory damages.** (1) A quantifiable amount of money which compensates for an injury. (2) In contract actions, damages measured by the difference between the contract price and the market price.

> **Consequential damages.** (1) Damages which arise from an injured party's special needs or unique position as an indirect, but foreseeable, consequence of the original injury. (2) Any losses under a sales contract that result from the buyer's situation if the seller had reason to know of it at the time they contracted and if the buyer could not reasonably prevent the loss by cover or other mitigating measures.

Mitigation of damages. The duty of a party injured by a breach of contract to minimize the damages suffered.

> **Nominal damages.** An insignificant amount, usually $1 or $10, awarded to a plaintiff who receives a judgment to vindicate a legal right, but is unable to prove any actual damages.

> **Punitive damages.** Damages awarded when a defendant's conduct is outrageous or particularly blameworthy. They are not awarded in contract actions.

> **Treble damages.** An award of three times the amount of the actual damages proved.

Debenture. An unsecured debt security.

Debt securities. Corporate borrowings in the form of bonds, debentures, or commercial paper.

Debtor in possession. Under bankruptcy law, a debtor allowed to retain operations of a business going through Chapter 11 bankruptcy proceedings.

Decedent. A dead person.

Declaratory judgment. See *Judgment*.

Deed. A document conveying title to real property.

> **Warranty deed.** A deed in which the grantor grants title and warrants the title is marketable.

> **Quitclaim deed.** A deed in which the grantor conveys whatever title he or she has, if any.

> **Deed of trust.** A security arrangement similar to a mortgage in which a borrower places property in trust for the benefit of the lender.

Defalcation. Embezzlement.

Default judgment. See *Judgment*.

Defendant. (1) A person against whom a legal case is brought in court. (2) Sometimes used to refer to the counsel for the party against whom a lawsuit is brought.

Defense. (1) A reason why the plaintiff should not recover from the defendant. (2) An excuse or justification available to someone who has committed a criminal act.

> **Personal defenses.** Under UCC Article 3, defenses which the maker or a previous holder of a negotiable instrument may not assert against a holder in due course.

> **Real defenses.** Under UCC Article 3, defenses which are valid against a holder in due course.

Deficiency judgment. See *Judgment*.

Defraud. To commit a fraud.

Delegate. (n.) A person assigned duties by another.

Delegation. An assignment of duties under a contract. (v., To delegate.)

Delegator. A person who delegates a duty.

Delivery. The actual transfer of possession of goods from one party to another. (2) In the context of a gift, the surrender of control and the placing of the property beyond recall. (3) In the context of negotiable instruments, a change of possession.

Depositary bank. See *Bank*.

Derivative action. An action brought on behalf of a corporation by shareholders to enforce a corporate right or to recover a corporate loss.

Descent and Distribution Statutes. See *Intestate Succession laws*.

Destination contract. See *Contract*.

Direct examination. In the context of a trial or a quasi-judicial administrative proceeding, the examination of a witness by counsel for the party offering the testimony as evidence.

Disaffirm. Void.

Discharge. (n.) A release from, or termination of, an obligation. (v.) To terminate or release from a contractual obligation.

> **Discharge in bankruptcy.** A discharge of contractual obligations granted by a federal bankruptcy court.

Disclaim. Under UCC Article 2, to revoke or to refuse to make a warranty as to goods under a sales contract.

Disclaimer. A denial of, or refusal to make, warranties.

Discount. As applied to negotiable instruments, a reduction from an instrument's face value.

Discovery. A process which permits a party to obtain information from the other party for the purpose of preparing for trial.

Dishonor. A refusal to pay or accept a negotiable instrument.

Dissolution. (1) The change in the relation of the partners caused by any partner ceasing to be associated in the carrying on of the business [UPC §29]. (2) A corporation's going out of business. (v., To dissolve).

Dividend. A portion of the corporation's earnings distributed pro rata among the shares outstanding in a class of stock.

> **Property dividend.** A distribution of corporate assets or of stock in another corporation to shareholders.

> **Stock dividend.** A distribution of additional shares of the corporation's own stock.

Document of title. A writing indicating ownership of goods; a bailment receipt addressed to or issued by either warehousemen or common carriers.

Dominion. Possession; control.

Donative intent. See *Intent*.

Donee. The recipient of a gift.

> **Donee beneficiary.** See *Beneficiary*.

Donor. The giver of a gift.

Draft. A three-party instrument in which the drawer draws an instrument which unconditionally orders the drawee to pay a sum to the payee.

Drawee. The party on a draft to whom the order to pay is directed, most often a bank.

Drawer. The party who issues or writes a draft to the payee.

Drawn. Written.

Due course. The ordinary course of events; not highlighted by unusual or extraordinary events.

Due diligence defense. A defense to an alleged SEC violation whereby a defendant claims to have made a reasonable investigation into the truth of a matter and reasonably believed, in good faith, that what was said was true.

Due process of law. The legal process which is due a person subject to a particular law or set of laws; fairness or justice; derived from U.S. Constitution Amendments V and XIV.

Duress. (1) Bodily harm or threats of bodily harm. (2) Improper pressure or coercion used by one party against another in the bargaining process.

Duty. A standard of care society imposes on reasonable persons in similar circumstances.

> **Nondelegable duty.** A duty for which the employer remains liable even if it turns work over to an independent contractor.

Easement. A right to cross another's property.

Embezzlement. The fraudulent appropriation of another's property by a person to whom such property has been entrusted or into whose hands it has lawfully come; a defalcation.

Eminent domain. The government's power to take private real property for public purposes in exchange for compensation to its owner.

Employee. Anyone who works for an *employer* other than an *independent contractor*.

> **Employee at will.** A person who is hired without an established term of employment and who is subject to discharge at any time with or without cause.

Employer. A person who employs others; a principal.

Employment at will. A contractual relationship whose subject matter is personal services that either party may terminate at any time with or without cause.

Enabling act. A statute delegating certain tasks to an administrative agency.

Encumbrance. Burdens on the ownership interest consisting of rights or interests in land which would diminish its value to the buyer.

Entity. Being.

Entrustment. Under UCC Article 2, giving possession—not title—of goods to a merchant who deals in goods of that kind.

Environmental impact statement. A study required under federal environmental laws to determine whether significant environmental damages may result from an action or nonaction involving the environment.

Equipment. Goods primarily used in business—including farming or a profession—which are neither inventory nor farm products [UCC §9-109(2)].

Equitable remedy. A court order, available only where money damages would not be a sufficient remedy, commanding a party to do or not to do something.

Equity of redemption. The mortgagor's statutory right to pay all of the principal, interest, and penalties due to date after default in order to reinstate the loan or to secure the return of the property.

Equity securities. Ownership interests in a corporation; stock; intangible personal property, ownership of which is usually represented by a *share certificate* or *stock certificate*.

Ethics. Standards of conduct or of moral judgment.

Error. In the context of an appeal, mistakes made by the trial court.

Estate. All of a decedent's property, both personal and real, which his or her heirs will inherit.

Estoppel. A situation in which one person leads another to do something the other would not have done and as a result of which the law will not permit the first party to subject the other to an injury by destroying his or her expectations.

Eviction. Dispossession of leased premises.

Evidence. Proof of any sort (e.g., demonstrations, documents, testimony) offered by a party to establish or disprove a contention of fact.

> **Extrinsic evidence.** In cases involving a written contract, evidence from outside the document relating to its interpretation, accuracy, or truthfulness.

Exclusionary rule. A principle derived from the Fourth Amendment to the Constitution that forbids the use of illegally or wrongfully obtained evidence in a criminal proceeding.

Exculpatory clause. (1) A contract clause which relieves a person of liability for nonwillful torts. (Chapter 9) (2) A clause in a written contract which disclaims the principal's liability for any of the agent's representations not stated in the written contract.

Execute. Sign; perform; fulfill the terms of a contract.

Executor. A decedent's personal representative, appointed by will. (Fem.: executrix.)

Existing goods. Goods which are in existence at the time a sales contract is made.

Express. Explicit; stated.

Extraordinary transactions. Transactions which are not in the ordinary course of business; transactions for which a corporation must receive shareholder approval.

Extrinsic evidence. See *Evidence*.

Farm products. Crops of livestock and the products of crops and livestock, as well as supplies used or produced in farming, so long as they are in the hands of the debtor engaging in farming operations [UCC §9-10].

Fee simple. The greatest interest one can own in real property; absolute ownership.

Felony. A more serious crime than a misdemeanor; a criminal act punishable either by more than 1 year in prison or by death.

Fiduciary. Characterized by trust.

Financing statement. A one-page summary of a security agreement which is placed on the public record.

Firm offer. See *Offer.*

Fixtures. Items of personal property which have become so attached to real property as to be considered part of it.

Floating lien. A lien which is released as to inventory being sold and attaches to inventory being acquired.

Forbearance. The giving up of something one otherwise has the legal right to do as consideration in a contract.

Foreclosure. The process by which a creditor may sell property to satisfy a debt.

Foreseeability. The ability to predict the consequences of conduct at the time the conduct occurs.

Forfeiture. The loss of a right as a penalty for nonperformance.

Forgery. Signing another's name to a document with the intent to defraud.

Forum. Place where a dispute may be resolved.

Franchise. A license to do business under a certain name and/or to market certain products.

Franchisee. A person holding a franchise.

Franchisor. An entity granting a franchise.

Fraud. (1) An intentional misrepresentation intended to deceive, whether by misstating or by concealing the truth. (2) A statement made with reckless disregard for whether it is true or not.

    Actual fraud. The knowing misrepresentation of facts or covering up of information.

    Constructive fraud. When applied to accountants, gross negligence; an extreme, flagrant, or reckless departure from standards of due care and competence.

    Fraud in the execution. With respect to a contract's formation, a deceptive act by which one party is intentionally misled concerning the basic nature of the contract; also called "real fraud."

    Fraud in the inducement. A party's knowing concealment or misrepresentation of facts with the intention of inducing another's assent.

Freeze out. (n.) The denial of the rights of a minority shareholder by the majority in violation of its fiduciary duty.

    Freeze-out merger. A merger designed to eliminate public ownership of a corporation by means of corporate processes and corporate assets.

Frustration of purpose. An extraordinary event or condition which so alters the nature of a party's performance that it becomes vitally different from what the parties originally expected.

Full warranty. See *Warranty.*

Fungible goods. See *Goods.*

Future advance. Money borrowed after the original security interest has attached that is covered by the original security agreement.

Future goods. See *Goods.*

Gap fillers. A nickname given to various provisions of UCC Article 2 that provide guidelines to courts for supplying terms omitted from contracts.

Gift. A voluntary transfer of ownership without consideration.

    Gifts inter vivos. Gifts made by one living person to another living person.

    Gifts causa mortis. Gifts made by donors who anticipate imminent death.

    Testamentary gifts. Gifts made by will.

Good faith. "Honesty in fact in the conduct or transaction concerned" [UCC §1-201(19)].

Goods. Anything that is movable at the time of identification to the sales contract, other than the money in which the price is to be paid and investment securities [UCC §2-501(1)].

    Consumer goods. Goods bought primarily for personal, family, or household purposes [UCC §9-109(1)].

    Fungible goods. Goods which are so similar as to be interchangeable.

    Future goods. Goods which are not both existing and identified to a sales contract.

    Nonconforming goods. Goods which do not meet a sales contract's specifications.

Grantee. A person receiving a deed.

Grantor. A person giving a deed.

Guarantor. A person who conditionally promises to pay a creditor if the principal debtor does not.

Holder. A person who possesses a negotiable instrument that is drawn, issued, or endorsed to him or his order or to bearer or in blank [UCC §1-201(20)].

> **Holder in due course.** A holder who is protected under UCC Article 3 from certain defenses which the obligor has against the original payee of an instrument.
>
> **Holder by due negotiation.** Under UCC Article 7, a transferee of a document of title who takes the instrument free from certain defenses of the bailor and prior holders.

Homicide. The killing of one human being by another.

Identification. The process of setting aside or otherwise distinguishing particular goods as applying to a particular contract; (v., identify.)

Illegality. A concept in contract law which permits a court to void a contract on the grounds that it conflicts with statutes or public policy.

Implied contract. See *Contract implied in fact*.

Implied covenant of good faith and fair dealing. See *Covenant*.

Implied warranty. See *Warranty*.

Impossibility. A condition which discharges performance of a contract.

Improvements. Alterations to real property, including erection, repair, alteration, or demolition.

Incidental expenses. As used in UCC Article 2, all commercially reasonable expenditures made as to goods after breach.

Incorporation. The act of forming a corporation.

Incorporator. An individual or agent who signs the articles of incorporation and files them with the secretary of state.

Indemnification. The legal right of a person or party to recover for losses or payments paid on behalf of another. This right is most commonly exercised in principal-agency and debtor-surety relationships.

Indemnify. To secure against damage or loss; to reimburse.

Independent contractor. Person engaged in a business distinct from that of his or her employer.

Indorse. To sign.

Indorsee. The person to whom an indorser indorses an instrument.

Indorsement. A signature, usually on the back of an instrument.

> **Blank indorsement.** An indorsement in which the party indorsing the instrument does not make the instrument payable to a specific person or party.
>
> **Nonrestrictive indorsement.** Blank and special indorsements which do not limit the indorsee's ability to negotiate the instrument.
>
> **Qualified indorsement.** An indorsement which indicates that the indorser assumes no liability under the usual indorsement contract.
>
> **Restrictive indorsement.** An indorsement which limits the indorsee's ability to negotiate the instrument in some manner.
>
> **Special indorsement.** An indorsement which names a specific person as the indorsee.
>
> **Unqualified indorsement.** An indorsement which does not disclaim liability under the indorser's contract.

Indorser. A person indorsing an instrument.

Infancy. The status of being a *minor*.

Informal contracts. See *Contract*.

Infringement. Violation. (v., to infringe.)

Injunction. An equitable remedy in which a court orders a party to do or not to do specified acts.

> **Permanent injunction.** An order compelling a party to act or not to act that is part of a final order disposing of a case.
>
> **Preliminary injunction.** An order, which normally expires upon final judgment, issued by a court upon a showing that a party will suffer immediate and irreparable injury or loss as a result of another party's action or inaction.

Injury. The invasion of a legal right.

Innocent misrepresentation. See *Misrepresentation*.

Insider. Generally, under the securities laws, a person with access to confidential corporate information; under SEC Rule 10b-5, an officer or director of a person holding 10 percent of the corporation's stock.

Insolvency. There are two types of insolvency under the bankruptcy laws:

> **Insolvency in the bankruptcy sense.** A debtor's total liabilities exceed his assets. This is the test used to determine if a preferential payment of fraudulent conveyance has occurred.

> **Insolvency in the equity sense.** The inability to pay debts as they come due. This is the test for actions of involuntary bankruptcy.

Inspection. Under UCC Article 2, the right to examine goods after delivery to determine whether they conform to the contract and to decide whether or not to accept them on that basis.

Insurable interest. A legal right or interest which may be protected by insurance.

Insurance agent. See *Agent*.

Insurance policy. The contract between an insurer and an insured.

Insured. A person whose life is covered by a life insurance policy; a person whose property is insured under an insurance policy.

Insurer. An insurance carrier or company.

Integrated agreement. A contract which incorporates both parties' expectations.

Integration clauses. Contractual clauses signifying that the writing is the final expression of the parties' agreement and that the document supersedes any earlier statements or documents.

Intended beneficiary. See *Beneficiary*.

Intent. The purpose or resolve to do a voluntary act or omission designed to bring about a consequence.

> **Donative intent.** The intent to make a gift.

> **Objective intent.** What a reasonable person would believe a party's outward manifestations to mean.

> **Subjective intent.** What the offeror was thinking at the moment he made the alleged offer.

> **Transferred intent.** The legal presumption that an actor intends the consequences of his or her acts even though they do not occur precisely as the actor anticipated.

Intentional misrepresentation. See *Misrepresentation*.

Intentional tort. See *Tort*.

Intermediary bank. See *Bank*.

Interstate commerce. A term used to describe that aspect of commerce which Congress may regulate under the U.S. Constitution's commerce clause.

Intestate. (adj.) The state of dying without leaving a valid will.

> **Intestate succession laws.** State statutes which define how the estate of a person who dies intestate will be distributed; also called descent and distribution statutes.

Inventory. Goods held for sale in the ordinary course of business [UCC §9-109(4)].

Investment securities. Under UCC Article 8, negotiable instruments issued by a corporation which evidence ownership interests or debt obligations.

Irrevocable offer. See *Offer*.

Issuance. The first delivery of the negotiable instrument to a holder [UCC §3-102(1)(a)].

Issue. (v.) To sell securities to their first holders; to deliver commercial paper to its first holder. (n.) A particular group of securities.

Issuer. An entity for whose benefit securities are issued.

Joint liability. See *Liability*.

Joint and several liability. See *Liability*.

Joint tenancy. See *Tenancy*.

Joint venture. A business organization which resembles a partnership except that it is not an ongoing association and its coventurers lack the apparent authority of partners.

Judgment. An order of a court which finally resolves a case.

> **Consent judgment.** See *Consent decree*.

> **Declaratory judgment.** A statutory remedy which permits a plaintiff to ask a court to define the parties' rights and duties under a contract or another statute.

> **Default judgment.** A final order in a civil case entering judgment for the plaintiff, issued by a court where a defendant fails to respond to a complaint.

Deficiency judgment. (1) A judgment for damages awarded when the proceeds of the sale of goods under a breached contract are less than the contract price. (2) A judgment for damages awarded when the proceeds of the sale of collateral are insufficient to satisfy the obligation the collateral secures.

Judicial sale. A court-ordered auction.

Jurisdiction. (1) A court system. (2) A court's authority within specific geographic boundaries. (3) A court's authority to hear a particular case; also called subject matter jurisdiction. (4) The power of a court in a judicial system to decide a case involving a particular defendant; also called in personam jurisdiction.

Jury. Persons from the court's geographic jurisdiction who collectively act as the trier of fact in civil or criminal cases.

Land contract. A contract to buy real property under which the seller finances part or all of the purchase price for a specific period.

Lapse. (v.) Fail; lose effect.

Latent defect. A hidden or not obvious flaw.

Lawyer. A person who has satisfied a state's educational and licensing prerequisites for the practice of law.

Leading object rule. Under the Statute of Frauds, if the primary reason for a surety agreeing to stand behind a debt is to benefit the surety, then the promise need not be in writing to be enforceable.

Lease. A contract by which a person owning property (the lessor) grants another (the lessee) the right to possess and use it for a specified period at a set price.

Lease-purchase agreement. A lease that permits the lessee to purchase the leased property at a specified price usually at the end of the leasehold.

Leasehold. A possessory interest in property which comes into existence when the owner grants possession to another for a time.

Legal cause. In tort law, what the law regards as the conduct causing an injury.

Legal remedy. Normally, damages.

Liability. The assignment of financial responsibility for the violation of a legal duty.

Joint and several liability. A phrase indicating that a plaintiff may recover damages from any one or all of those persons who may be liable for his or her injuries.

Joint liability. A phrase used to describe those limited cases in which the law permits one defendant to insist that the plaintiff join another as a defendant.

Strict liability. A legal doctrine that imposes responsibility for the consequences of activities involving abnormally dangerous activities or unreasonably dangerous products without reference to fault.

License. A temporary permission to use another's property for a limited purpose.

Lien. A creditor's claim on property for the satisfaction of a debt.

Artisan's lien. A possessory lien conferred by law on persons who repair or enhance the value of goods permitting them to retain them until the bailor pays for them.

Attachment lien. A lien against specific real property which serves as collateral in the event that an unsecured creditor wins a lawsuit against the debtor.

Execution lien. A notice, usually filed by the sheriff, that a particular piece of real property is to be sold at a public sale to settle an unpaid judgment.

Floating lien. A security interest in after-acquired goods.

Involuntary lien. A lien which arises under a statute that permits a creditor to assert a security interest in the debtor's property.

Judgment lien. A lien which results when a party awarded damages files the court's judgment against the losing party's real estate in the county in which the land is located.

Materialman's lien. A nonpossessory lien granted to a supplier whose goods are permanently incorporated into another's land or property.

Mechanic's lien. An involuntary, possessory security interest in property for the value of improvements.

Nonpossessory lien. A security interest in property which the lienholder does not possess.

Possessory liens. Liens which apply only so long as the bailee actually has the property.

Voluntary lien. A lien which the holder of a property interest grants another, usually in exchange for credit or services.

Life estate. A possessory interest in property measured by either the recipient's or another's lifetime.

Limitations on action. Statute of limitations under Article 2.

Limited partnership. A business form organized under a state statute which consists of one or more general partners and one or more limited partners.

Limited warranty. See *Warranty*.

Liquidate. To turn into cash.

Liquidated. (adj.) Unquestioned as to existence or amount.

Liquidated damages clause. A contract clause establishing an amount the parties agree will compensate for a material breach.

Litigants. The parties to litigation.

Litigation. Adversary proceedings before either a court or an administrative agency.

Living will. See *Will*.

Long-arm statute. See *Statute*.

Lost profits. A measure of damages; those profits which a seller would have made from a sale of goods plus his incidental expenses less the expenses saved as a result of the breach.

Majority. Adulthood.

Maker. An obligor who issues an instrument.

Malice. The intentional, unjustified commission of a wrongful act from which the law may infer the actor's intent to injure.

Actual malice. In the law of defamation, the state of mind indicated by making statements with knowledge that they are false or with reckless disregard of whether they are true or not.

Malpractice. A term used to describe negligence by a lawyer, accountant, doctor, or other professional.

Manifestation. An outward sign.

Marketable title. Ownership a reasonably prudent investor would accept.

Material. (adj.) Substantial; important.

Means of acceptance. See *Acceptance*.

Medium of acceptance. See *Acceptance*.

Merchant. "[A] person who deals in goods of the kind or otherwise by his occupation holds himself out as having knowledge or skill peculiar to the practices or goods involved in the transaction or to whom such knowledge or skill may be attributed by his employment of an agent or broker or other intermediary who by his occupation holds himself out as having such knowledge or skill" [UCC §2-104(1)].

Minor. A person under the age of eighteen.

Misdemeanors. Crimes with penalties of less than a year in jail.

Mislaid property. See *Property*.

Misrepresentation. A false or misleading statement or inference.

Innocent misrepresentation. A defense against the enforcement of a contract that arises from a party's material assertion which was not in accord with the facts and from the justifiable reliance of the other party on the assertion.

Intentional misrepresentation. In the law of fraud, a deliberate misstatement or a knowing concealment of the facts.

Mistake. As a criminal defense, a mistake insulates a defendant from liability if the defendant reasonably interpreted the facts of a situation in such a way that if the defendant had been correct, an act would not have been a crime.

Mitigation of damages. See *Damages*.

Model. A representation of goods to be sold.

Mortgage. An interest in land often given by a buyer as security for a loan; a security interest in real property which a debtor gives a creditor to secure an obligation; a voluntary security interest in real property.

Second mortgage. A mortgage subsequent to a first mortgage; a generic term referring to any mortgage after the first.

Purchase money mortgage. A mortgage taken by the seller of real property for part of the purchase price; normally a purchase money mortgage is a second mortgage.

Mortgagee. A party receiving a mortgage.

Mortgagor. A person giving a mortgage, usually in exchange for credit.

Motion. The means by which a party asks a court to act; a request that a court issue an order.

> **Motion for a directed verdict.** A request for an order that the jury find in favor of the moving party because the opposing party has offered no evidence to support a judgment in its favor.

> **Motion for summary judgment.** An order of the court which resolves the case without a full trial.

> **Motion to dismiss.** A request for an order disposing of a complaint in the defendant's favor for procedural reasons primarily related to venue, jurisdiction, the court's ability to decide the dispute as the plaintiff has presented it, and the plaintiff's failure to state a claim against the defendant which the law recognizes.

Motive. The thought behind an intent; the reason or moving cause of an act.

Mutual assent. Offer and acceptance.

Mutual mistake. A situation in which both parties to a contract are mistaken as to a material fact.

Necessaries. In the context of a minor's ability to contract, the necessities of life.

Negligence. A cause of action in tort involving primarily acts of carelessness; the name given to a class of torts which do not require proof of an intent; an act that a person exercising ordinary caution and prudence could have foreseen would produce an injury.

> **Comparative negligence.** An approach to liability in negligence actions which reduces the damages owed by the defendant by a percentage representing the degree of the plaintiff's fault.

> **Contributory negligence.** A defense to negligence actions alleging that the plaintiff's conduct led in some way to his or her injuries.

Negotiability. Under UCC Article 3, an instrument's capacity to be transferred in such a way as to make the transferee a holder.

Negotiable. Capable of being negotiated.

Negotiable instrument. Under the UCC, commercial paper, documents of title, and investment securities which meet requirements of specific form provide possible protected transfer rights in certain transferees.

Negotiate. To transfer a negotiable instrument in such a way that the transferee becomes a holder. (n., Negotiation.)

No-fault systems. A statutory approach to certain types of tort liability which eliminates most considerations of fault.

Nolo contendere. A plea of no contest entered in a criminal case; a plea which does not admit guilt but does not contest the charges.

Nominal damages. See *Damages*.

Nonconforming goods. See *Goods*.

Nonconforming uses. Uses of property that are not in accordance with the applicable zoning ordinance.

Nondelegable duty. See *Duty*.

Nondischargeable debts. In a bankruptcy proceeding, obligations of the bankrupt which may not be discharged under the bankruptcy code.

Nonperformance. Failure to sufficiently or substantially perform a contractual obligation or to perform when performance is due.

Nontrading partnership. See *Partnership*.

Note. A maker's unconditional promise to pay a certain sum on a fixed date; a promissory note.

Novation. An agreement between the parties to the original contract to substitute the delegate's performance for the delegator's; the exchange of a new party and a new contract for one of the original parties and the old contract.

Nuisance. A tort action to prevent the unreasonable interference by one party with the rights of others to use their property.

Objection. In the context of a trial or a quasi-judicial proceeding, a notification by a party of the court that the admission of evidence, an instruction to the jury, or the like is in error as a matter of law.

Objective intent. See *Intent*.

Objective test. The reasonable person standard; an evaluation of conduct by external standards.

Obligee. With respect to a promise, the party to whom the duty is owed.

Obligor. With respect to a promise, the person owing a duty.

Offer. The offeror's proposal stating what he or she is willing to do or not do in exchange for a specified action or promise by the offeree.

> **Counteroffer.** An offeree's response to an offer which simultaneously rejects the original offer and presents the offeror with a new offer.

> **Firm offer.** An offer made in writing and signed by a merchant indicating that the offer will be kept open for a stated time or, if no time is stated, for a reasonable time up to three months [UCC §2-205].

> **Irrevocable offer.** An offer which cannot be revoked.

Offeree. The party to a contract who accepts the offer.

Offeror. The party to a contract who makes the offer.

Opinion. A court's written or oral appraisal of the questions before it.

Option contract. See *Contract*.

Oral argument. A presentation to a court by lawyers in a format much like a debate.

Order. An action taken by a court.

Order of relief. The court order by the bankruptcy judge granting the debtor a discharge in bankruptcy.

Order paper. An instrument which is payable to the order of a named payee or the payee's transferee.

Ordinances. Laws adopted by the legislative branch of a municipal government.

Output contract. See *Contract*.

Par value. The value printed on a stock certificate.

Parol. Extrinsic; outside.

> **Parol evidence rule.** A rule of evidence to the effect that when contracting parties intend a confirmation or a written contract to be the final expression of their agreement, that writing cannot be contradicted by evidence of any prior agreement or of a contemporaneous oral agreement [UCC §2-202].

Partnership. A voluntary association of two or more persons to carry on a business for profit as coowners; also called a general partnership.

> **Apparent Partnership.** A legal presumption that a partnership exists when a person consents to a representation by another that a partnership exists between them.

Partnership at will. A partnership which has no set term or whose term has elapsed or whose particular undertaking specified in the partnership agreement has occurred.

Partnership agreement. A contract between partners stating the terms of their agreement to become partners.

Partnership by estoppel. An *apparent partnership*.

Nontrading partnership. A partnership which engages in a service-oriented business; any partnership which is not a trading partnership.

Trading partnership. A partnership which engages in commercial or merchandising businesses.

Patent. A right granted by the federal government to the exclusive exploitation of new processes, machines, manufactured goods, or new useful, and not obvious improvements to existing processes for a period of 17 years.

Payee. The obligee to whom an instrument is made payable.

Payor. One who pays or is to pay something, particularly a draft or note.

> **Payor bank.** See *Bank*.

Perfect tender rule. See *Tender*.

Perfection. The creation of a security interest effective against third parties by giving them actual or constructive notice of its existence (v., to perfect).

> **Temporary prefection.** An implied perfection for a limited period, usually a matter of days.

Performance. The fulfillment of a party's obligation under a contract.

> **Performance bond.** Suretyship contracts, usually involving construction projects.

> **Substantial performance.** Level of performance which discharges an obligation.

Perjury. Lying under oath.

Permanent injunction. See *Injunction*.

Personal defenses. See *Defenses*.

Personal representative. A person appointed by the probate court and charged with administering a decedent's estate; an administrator or an executor.

Personalty. Personal property.

Plaintiff. The person bringing an action in court; sometimes used to refer to the attorney for the litigant bringing suit.

Pleadings. Documents which notify the parties in the trial court of what the case is about. The pleadings consist only of the complaint, the answer, and the reply, if any.

Pledge. A security arrangement in which the debtor gives the creditor actual possession of the debtor's personal property to hold as security.

Poison pill. A type of shareholder rights agreement intended to ward off hostile takeovers which, upon some triggering event such as the acquisition by a tender offeror of a certain percentage of a corporation's common stock, entitles the remaining shareholders to receive additional shares of common stock (or other securities) at bargain prices.

Police powers. A state's ability, conferred upon it by its constitution, to protect the health, safety, morals, and general welfare of its citizens.

Polygraph. An electromechanical device, commonly called a "lie detector," designed to measure a subject's physiological responses to an operator's questions.

Power of attorney. A document by which a principal and an agent create an agency relationship.

Powers. A corporation's authority or right to act under the law, its articles of incorporation, and its bylaws.

> **Express powers.** Those powers granted to the corporation by the articles of incorporation.
>
> **Implied powers.** Those powers that are reasonably necessary to fulfill the corporation's objectives and that do not violate its express powers or the law.

Precedent. A court's holding on a question of law.

Preemption. The effect of a Congressional or judicial determination, based on the supremacy clause of the U.S. Constitution, that a state or local law or regulation is inconsistent with a federal law or regulation and therefore unconstitutional.

Preemptive right. A right granted by articles of incorporation to shareholders, permitting them to purchase a percentage of any new issues proportional to their holding in the company.

Preferred stock. See *Stock*.

Preliminary injunction. See *Injunction*.

Premium. Money to be paid by an insured to an insurer as the consideration for insurance.

Preponderance of the evidence. The plaintiff's burden of proof in most civil actions for damages; refers to the fact that the plaintiff's evidence only has to outweigh the defendant's.

Presenting bank. See *Bank*.

Presentment. A demand for payment or acceptance made upon the issuer, maker, acceptor, drawee, or other payor on behalf of the holder [UCC §3-504(1)].

Presupposed conditions. See *Condition*.

Price discrimination. An illegal action by a seller charging different prices to different non-retail buyers in the same market.

Price fixing. An illegal action by two or more parties to set prices for sale to third parties.

Prima facie case. As used in the context of a judicial proceeding, on the face of what the plaintiff has presented, the defendant is liable.

Principal. A person represented by an agent.

> **Disclosed principal.** A principal whose existence and identity are known to the third party with whom an agent deals.
>
> **Partially disclosed principal.** A principal whose existence but not identity is known to the third party with whom the agent deals.
>
> **Undisclosed principal.** A principal whose existence and identity are not disclosed to the third party with whom the agent deals.

Principal debtor. The person primarily liable on an agreement of debt.

Privilege. (1) A legal defense to an intentional tort which protects an individual's freedom of action in certain limited circumstances. (2) In the context of communications involving certain professionals, such as doctors and lawyers, an exemption by law from disclosure of their content in court.

Privity. The state of being in a direct contractual relationship.

Probate. The administration of a decedent's estate; the proving of the validity of a decedent's will.

> **Probate court.** A court which oversees the administration of all estates.

Procedural law. Law which defines how something is to be done.

Proceeding. A technical but very broad term which includes virtually every way in which courts or administrative agencies conduct their business.

Proceeds. Whatever the sale, exchange, collection, or other disposition of collateral generates [UCC §9-306(1)].

Product liability. A body of law that describes the responsibilities of sellers and manufacturers for goods they place in commerce.

Promissory estoppel. A means of enforcing a promise, unsupported by consideration, in which the promisor reasonably expects that his/her promise will cause action or forbearance by the promisee.

Promissory note. A writing containing the promise of one party to pay an amount to another.

Promoter. A person who develops a business idea for a corporation and takes the initial steps to organize and finance it.

Prompt shipment. A provision of Article 2 of the UCC whereby a seller receiving an order can cause a contract to result by either responding with a promise to ship or immediately shipping conforming goods.

Promulgate. Issue.

Property. A right to possess, use, and dispose of something, usually to the exclusion of other people.

  Abandonment. In regards to property, property in which ownership is intentionally given up.

  After-acquired property. In the context of UCC Article 9, property that does not exist or that the debtor has not acquired at the time the security agreement is executed.

  Community property. A form of multiple ownership of real and personal property between spouses.

  Intangible property. Items of personal property which do not have a real physical existence, such as stocks or patents.

  Lost property. Property which was accidentally and casually lost.

  Mislaid property. Property which is intentionally placed somewhere and then forgotten.

  Personal property. Anything that is not real property; things which are movable.

  Real property. Land and anything permanently attached to it.

  Tangible property. Items of personal property which have a real existence; property which can be touched.

  Unowned property. Property which is capable of being owned but is not owned.

Property insurance. Insurance which covers for loss of property. Generally covers for losses attributable to fire, vandalism, storm, and related damages.

Proximate cause. In tort law, the legal cause of an injury; a negligent act that as a direct and existing cause actively aids in producing an injury.

Proxy. A power of attorney often used to vote shares in a corporation.

  Proxy statement. A booklet describing candidates for election to the board of directors and all other matters to be dealt with at a shareholders' meeting.

Public policy. An extremely vague term referring either (1) to the principle that no member of society may act in a manner that threatens the common good or (2) to a specific statutory or constitutional expression. Most commonly, the phrase appears in the negative, as "a violation of public policy."

Public sale. Normally, an auction [UCC §2-706 Comment 4].

Puffing. An inflated sales pitch unrelated to the goods' characteristics.

Punitive damages. See *Damages*.

Purchase money mortgage. See *Mortgage*.

Purchase money security interest (PMSI). A security interest perfected on attachment in consumer goods for whose purchase specifically a creditor has lent money [UCC §9-107].

Quasi-contract. A contract imposed by law to prevent injustice, in the absence of an agreement. Sometimes called an implied-in-law contract.

Quid pro quo. What a party to an agreement receives in return for his or her act or promise.

Quitclaim deed. See *Deed*.

Quorum. The minimum number of persons defined by an organization's bylaws or a state's partnership or corporation laws who must be present in order to transact business.

Race-notice statute. In regards to real property recordings at the courthouse, the first to file a legal document in the courthouse, without notice of possible defects, prevails.

Ratification. (1) An indication by a person who formerly had the power to void contracts that he or she intends to be obligated under a contract made while under the disability. (2) An act by which a principal endorses an unauthorized action taken by an agent which otherwise would not have bound the principal.

Real defenses. See *Defenses*.

Realty. Real property.

Reasonable person. A judicial creation who always acts prudently and does the right thing; an expression of the conduct society demands.

Receiver. A party appointed to manage the affairs of an insolvent business, usually in order to preserve assets for liquidation and distribution to creditors.

Record. (n.) The documents, transcript, and other matters brought before a trial court or an administrative agency; the material reviewed by an appellate court and certified to the appellate court by a trial court or administrative agency.

> **Public record.** The public repository of data on land transactions, security interests, and the like, which is usually maintained in a courthouse. (v. To record.)

Recording. The filing of a document relating to a property interest with the state or county office that maintains the appropriate public record of such interests.

> **Recording statute.** A statute governing what can be placed on the public record, how it may be done, and what the effects of recording are.

Redemption. A statutory right permitting a mortgagor to redeem the property after a judicial sale by paying the amount of the sale price plus a statutory rate of interest.

Regional clearinghouse. An association organized by a group of banks in an area to exchange checks drawn on their establishment.

Register. To file a report describing an offering under the Securities Act of 1933.

Regulations. Administrative rules.

Regulatory statute. See *Statute*.

Rehabilitation. A process, usually under the supervision of a state regulatory agency, designed to restore an insurance company in financial difficulty to stability.

Rejection. (1) The offeree's notification to the offeror that he or she will not accept the offer; in effect, it terminates the offer. (2) A buyer's manifestation of an intent not to accept delivery of goods tendered under a sales contract; nonacceptance.

Release. A statement by one party to a contract which relieves another party of any further obligation to perform; discharge.

Relief. Remedy.

Remainder. The interest in a life estate which passes upon the death of the life tenant.

Remand. When used by a court, to send a matter back to a lower court or administrative agency.

Remedy. A resolution or correction of something which has caused injury, harm, loss, or damage.

Requirements contract. See *Contract*.

Res ipsa loquitur. A doctrine applied in negligence actions where the instrument causing an accident was under the control of the defendant or its employees but the actual conduct causing the injury cannot be shown.

Rescind. To void.

Recission. An equitable remedy which discharges the parties' contractual obligations.

> **Mutual rescission.** An agreement to discharge which rescinds the parties' contractual obligations.

Resolution. A statement authorizing an action adopted by a formal vote of a board of directors.

Respondeat superior. A Latin phrase meaning "let the master respond" that expresses the doctrine that an employer is responsible for the negligent acts its employees commit during the course of employment.

Restitution. An equitable remedy ordering the return of part or all of a party's consideration.

Restraint of trade. A business activity which violates the antitrust laws.

Restricted security. The sale of new securities which contain restrictions in the ability of the purchaser to offer them for resale.

Restrictive covenant. See *Covenant*.

Restrictive indorsement. See *Indorsement*.

Reverse. A term used by appellate courts when they reach a conclusion opposite to that of the trial court. A *reversal* may apply to part or all of the trial court's judgment.

Revocation. The offeror's withdrawal of an offer.

Revocation of acceptance. See *Acceptance*.

Revocation of authority. See *Authority*.

Risk of loss. Under Article 2, the allocation of potential loss between contracting parties to a sales contract if the goods should become lost, damaged, or destroyed before the buyer accepts the goods.

Rules. (1) In the context of court litigation, the *rules of civil procedure*. (2) In the context of administrative law, regulations of administrative agencies.

Rules of civil procedure. Rules adopted by a jurisdiction to govern the conduct of litigation in the trial courts. Some states use codes of procedure adopted by their legislatures.

Rules of construction. Rules of interpretation.

/S/. A sign indicating that the name following it appeared in handwriting in the original document.

Sale on approval. Under Article 2, a sales arrangement whereby the seller guarantees the buyer the right to return conforming goods delivered primarily for the buyer's use.

Sale on return. Under Article 2, a sales arrangement whereby the seller guarantees the buyer the right to return goods delivered primarily for resale.

Satisfaction. The fulfillment of the substituted performance required by an accord.

Scope of employment. An employee's activities which relate directly to the manner in which the employer conducts its business.

Second mortgage. See *Mortgage*.

Secretary of State. A state official who is normally in charge of maintaining records of corporations and of acts enacted by the legislature and signed by the governor.

Secured creditor. A person or party having a legal interest in the property of another to secure a promise of repayment of debt.

Secured party. A party which has a security interest.

Security. An instrument which is issued in bearer or registered form, and which is of a type commonly dealt in upon securities exchanges or markets or dealt in as a medium for investment. It is either one of a class or series or by its terms is divisible into a class or series of instruments, and evidences a share, participation, or other interest in property or in an enterprise or evidences an obligation of the issuer [UCC §8-102(1)(a)].

Security agreement. An agreement defined by UCC Article 9 which creates or provides for a security interest.

Security deposit. A sum required by a landlord to cover damages to the premises or losses resulting from a breach of the lease.

Security interest. A property interest by a creditor, called a lien, in the property of another.

Self-defense. A defense to intentional tort and criminal actions which arises when the defendant takes an action against the plaintiff to avoid a threatened harm at the plaintiff's hands; the use of force to protect one's self or one's property.

Servant. An archaic term for employees; employees who do not have agency powers.

Service of process. The procedure for the delivery to the defendant of the summons and the complaint.

Settlor. A person who establishes a trust.

Share. In the law of corporations, a unit of ownership.

> **Share certificate.** Evidence of ownership of equity securities; *stock certificate*.

Shareholder. The owner of a share, or ownership interest, in a corporation.

Shelter rule. Under UCC Article 3, when the transferor is a holder in due course, a transferee who does not qualify independently may secure the same protection as if he or she were a holder in due course. Articles 7 and 8 also have shelter rules.

Shipment contract. See *Contract*.

Signature. Any name, including a trade or assumed name, or any word or mark used instead of a handwritten signature [UCC §3-401(2)].

Sole proprietorship. Essentially an individual (the sole proprietor) in business alone. Sole proprietorships are not incorporated.

Special indorsement. See *Indorsement*.

Specific performance. An equitable remedy compelling a party to perform obligations under a contract; usually granted only in the cases involving the sale of real estate or of unique personal property.

Stale check. See *Check.*

Stare decisis. A Latin term meaning "to stand by decisions"; it refers to the way courts apply *precedent* to particular cases.

Stated value. Under the MBCA, a value placed on shares by a corporation's board of directors.

Status quo. The position a party was in before an event occurred.

Statute. An act adopted by the legislative branch and either not vetoed by the chief executive or passed over his veto; a law; (adj., statutory).

> **Long-arm statute.** A state statute that defines the jurisdiction of the state's courts over nonresident individuals and corporations.
>
> **Recording statute.** See *Recording.*
>
> **Regulatory statute.** A statute whose purpose is the protection of the public's health, safety, morals, or welfare.
>
> **Statute of Frauds.** A statute regulating when the parties must put their agreement in writing.
>
> **Statute of limitation.** A statute which defines the time during which an action can be brought to enforce an obligation.

Stock. Ownership shares in a corporation.

> **Common stock.** An equity security; shares in a corporation which typically have voting rights but have the lowest priority when the corporation makes distributions of earnings or in liquidation.
>
> **Preferred stock.** An equity security which has preference over common stock as to dividends or asset distributions upon dissolution of the company.
>
> **Stock certificate.** Evidence of ownership of equity securities; *share certificate.*
>
> **Stock dividend.** See *Dividend.*
>
> **Stock split.** The exchange by a corporation of one existing share for two or more new shares.
>
> **Treasury stock.** Issued shares which the corporation has reacquired but has not cancelled or destroyed.
>
> **Watered stock.** Stock for which the first purchaser paid less than its par value.

Stockholder. See *Shareholder.*

Stop payment order. An instruction to a bank, issued by a drawer or an interested party, not to pay a particular check.

Street name. The name of a brokerage recorded as the nominal owner of shares it purchased for the account of one of its clients.

Strict liability. See *Liability.*

Subjective intent. See *Intent.*

Subjective test. An evaluation of a party's conduct in light of what that party actually believed.

Sublet. The transfer of part or all of a tenant's possessory interests for a specified period.

Subrogation. The right of a party who has paid another party's debt to press claims that it has indemnified.

Subscriber. A person who contracts to purchase shares in a corporation before the corporation comes into existence.

Subscriptions. Written contracts to purchase shares.

Substantial performance. See *Performance.*

Substantive law. Law which prescribes what a person can or cannot do.

Supremacy clause. Article 6 §2 of the Constitution, which states the supremacy of federal over state laws in matters committed to the federal government under the U.S. Constitution.

Supreme court. Generally the highest appellate court in a jurisdiction.

Surety. A person who by cosigning an instrument agrees to pay it if the maker or issuer does not.

Suretyship. A contractual relationship that results from the surety's unconditional promise to be answerable to the creditor for the obligation of the principal debtor should he or she default.

Surprise rejection rule. Under Article 2, a seller who attempts to deliver nonconforming goods in reasonable anticipation that the buyer will accept the goods is given the opportunity to cure the delivery when the nonconforming goods are rejected.

Temporary perfection. See *Perfection.*

Temporary restraining order (TRO). An emergency order issued by a court, usually after a brief hearing, that prevents a party from taking an action until the court can hold a hearing on a *preliminary injunction*. See *Injunction*.

Tenancy. A right to hold property.

> **Tenancy in common.** A form of multiple ownership of property in which the interest may be unequal.

> **Tenancy by the entirety.** A form of multiple ownership applied to married couples in which neither spouse may convey an interest without the consent of the other.

> **Joint tenancy.** A form of multiple ownership in which the ownership interests are equal undivided interest which upon the death of a joint tenant pass to the surviving joint tenant or tenants.

> **Tenancy in partnership.** A partner's interest in the partnership's property.

> **Periodic tenancy.** A leasehold which runs from one period to another and is automatically renewed for the next period unless one party notifies the other of its termination.

> **Tenancy at sufferance.** A situation in which a leasehold has terminated but the tenant continues in possession.

> **Tenancy at will.** A leasehold for which the parties do not establish a termination date.

> **Tenancy for years.** Any leasehold with a set termination date.

Tenant. A person who has a right to use or occupy property.

Tender. (n.) An offer of delivery; the act of making goods available to the buyer. (v.) To be ready, willing, and able to perform; to offer to perform.

> **Perfect tender rule.** Under UCC Article 2, the right of a buyer in a sale of goods involving a single delivery to reject the entire shipment if the goods or any part of them fail to conform.

> **Tender offer.** An offer to acquire stock for a certain period at a stated price that is made either to an issuer or its shareholders, who may accept by delivering the stock to the offeror.

Termination. The actual ending of a partnership relation after the winding up.

Termination statement. A document placed on the public record stating that a party no longer claims a security interest under a financing statement which is referenced by file number [UCC §9-404].

Testamentary. (adj.) Having to do with a will.

Testate. (adj.) Having left a valid will.

Testator. A person who leaves a valid will.

Theft. The wrongful but nonviolent taking of another's property.

Third party. A person whose relationship to a contract is not that of being the offeror or the offeree.

Third party beneficiary. See *Beneficiary*.

Three-party instrument. An instrument which requires a drawer, a drawee, and a payee; drafts, checks, and trade acceptances.

Title. The right of ownership of property; a document evidencing ownership.

> **Abstract of title.** A condensed history of the title to real estate drawn from the appropriate county records.

Tort. A breach of a duty created by law which the wronged individual—not society—enforces by seeking compensation from the wrongdoer; (adj. tortious).

> **Intentional tort.** A tort involving an act that the defendant intended to commit, even though the defendant may not have intended the consequences.

Tortfeasor. A person who commits a tort.

Trade acceptance. A form of draft in which the seller is the drawer, the buyer is the drawee, and the bank holding the bill is the payee.

Trademark. An identifying word, name, or symbol used by a seller to distinguish his goods from those of another.

Trading partnership. See *Partnership*.

Transferee. A person receiving a transfer of an interest in property.

Transferor. A person transferring an interest in property.

Treasury stock. See *Stock*.

Treble damages. See *Damages*.

Trespass. Any wrongful entry onto real property; an intentional tort or a crime.

Trial courts. Courts in which trials are normally held; courts which hear witnesses, evaluate testimony, and make findings of fact.

Trier of fact. In the trial court, either the judge or the jury, whichever applies the law to the facts of the case.

Trust. A device established when the person who

creates the trust, the settlor, transfers title to property to a person or entity, the trustee, to hold, manage, and invest for the benefit of the trust's beneficiaries.

Trustee. A person who holds, manages, and invests property for the benefit of a trust's beneficiaries.

> **Trustee in bankruptcy.** A neutral person charged with handling a debtor's bankruptcy estate and with collecting the debtor's assets and identifying liabilities.

Two-party instruments. Instruments which require only a maker and a payee; promissory notes and certificates of deposit.

Ultra vires. A Latin phrase meaning "beyond the powers"; used to describe actions by a corporation which exceed its legal powers.

Unauthorized signature. Under Article 3, a signature supplied on a negotiable instrument by a person without authority. If a required signature, the signature will prevent further negotiation.

Unconscionable. An adjective describing a contract or a clause which is so one-sided, oppressive, or unfair that it shocks a court's conscience [UCC §2-302].

Underlying obligation. The transaction which gave rise to the issuance of a negotiable instrument.

Undue influence. The improper use of a position of trust or confidence one party has in relation to another.

Unilateral contract. See *Contract*.

Unilateral mistake. A mistake by one party to a contract as to a material fact.

Unintended beneficiary. See *Beneficiary*.

U.S. court of appeals. The intermediate federal appellate courts, commonly referred to as *circuit courts*.

U.S. district courts. The trial courts of general jurisdiction in the federal system.

Unliquidated. Not specific or agreed upon.

Unsecured debt. A debt in which the debtor has provided no property as collateral.

Usage of trade. "[Any] practice or method of dealing having such regularity of observance in a place, vocation or trade as to justify an expectation that it will be observed with respect to the transaction in question" [UCC §1-205(2)].

Usury. Charging a rate of interest on a loan in excess of what is decent or what the legislature has defined as a fair rate of return.

Value. For the purposes of UCC Article 9, any consideration sufficient to support a simple common law contract—including a binding commitment to extend credit, whether or not drawn—plus antecedent debt[UCC §1-201(44)].

Vehicles. Financing or investment options.

Venue. The actual geographical location of the court which hears the case.

Verdict. A jury's finding.

Vest. As to a person's rights under a contract, to become fixed and enforceable by a court.

Waiver. The intentional giving up of a known right or privilege.

Warehouse receipt. A document of title by which a warehouseman acknowledges receiving property for storage.

Warehouseman. A person engaged in the business of storing goods for hire [UCC §7-102(1)(h)].

Warrant. To guarantee or make an assurance.

Warrantor. A person making a warranty.

Warranty. A guarantee or an assurance or representation about a product.

> **Warranty deed.** See *Deed*.

> **Express warranty.** Affirmations of fact or guarantees by the seller which result from the parties' negotiations.

> **Full warranty.** Under the Magnuson-Moss Act, a warranty under which the seller agrees to repair or replace a defective product without charge within a reasonable time after purchase.

> **Implied warranty.** A warranty imposed by law.

> **Implied warranty of fitness for a particular purpose.** A guarantee imposed by law which arises when the buyer makes known to the seller the particular purpose for which the buyer is purchasing the goods and the seller represents that they are suitable for the purpose.

> **Implied warranty of merchantability.** (1) Under UCC Article 2, a guarantee made by a merchant

that a product is fit for the ordinary purposes for which it is sold. (2) As applied to the sale of used homes, an affirmation that the seller does not know of any serious latent defect which would impair its normal use.

Implied warranty of habitability. (1) A warranty made by home builders that a home is free from defects in design or workmanship which would impair its normal use. (2) A landlord's affirmation that the premises are suitable for habitation.

Limited warranty. Under the Magnuson-Moss Act, any warranty which falls short of a full warranty.

Warranty of performance. A guarantee which assures the buyer that the goods will meet certain standards of performance and which leads to legitimate expectations in the buyer as to how the goods should perform.

Warranty of title. A guarantee of the seller's legal right to transfer goods.

Waste. Conduct which lessens a property's value.

Watered stock. See *Stock*.

Whistleblower statutes. Statutes which protect employees for reporting their employers for engaging in illegal or unsafe activities.

White collar crime. See *Crime*.

Will. A document directing the disposition of a decedent's property upon death.

> **Living will.** A formal declaration sometimes included in a will by an individual stating that he or she wishes to "die naturally" rather than be kept alive by "heroic" or "artificial" means during a painful, terminal illness or while hopelessly comatose.

> **Will contest.** A challenge to a will's admission to probate.

Williams Act of 1968. A series of amendments to the Securities Exchange Act of 1934 designed to make corporate acquirers or raiders reveal their positions.

Winding up. The process of putting a partnership out of business.

Wood's rule. See *Employment at will*.

Writing. A document; a written contract.

Index